Frommer's

9th
Edition

Canada

Macmillan • USA

AUTHORS

Marilyn Wood: Chapters 11–16 (Ontario, Manitoba, and Saskatchewan)
Bill McRae: Introductory essays, Chapters 17 and 20 (Alberta and the Rockies, the Yukon, and the Northwest Territories)
Herbert Bailey Livesey: Chapters 8–10 (Québec)
Barbara Radcliffe Rogers and Stillman Rogers: Chapters 4–7 (Nova Scotia, New Brunswick, Prince Edward Island, and Newfoundland/Labrador)
Anistatia Miller and Jared Brown: Chapters 18–19 (British Columbia)

MACMILLAN TRAVEL

A Simon & Schuster Macmillan Company
1633 Broadway
New York, NY 10019

Find us online at **http://www.mcp.com/mgr/travel** or
on America Online at **Keyword: SuperLibrary.**

ISBN 0-02-860707-4
ISSN 1044-2251

Executive Editor: Lisa Renaud
Editors: Robin Michaelson, Erica Spaberg
Special thanks to Ron Boudreau, Reid Bramblett, and Ian Wilker
Production Editor: Matt Hannafin
Digital Cartography by Ortelius Design and John Decamillis
Design by Michele Laseau
Maps copyright © by Simon & Schuster, Inc.

SPECIAL SALES

Contents

9   The Laurentides & Estrie   263

by Herbert Bailey Livesey

10   Québec City & the Gaspé Peninsula   285

by Herbert Bailey Livesey

14   Southern & Midwestern Ontario   453

by Marilyn Wood

15   North to Ontario's Lakelands & Beyond   481

by Marilyn Wood

16   Manitoba & Saskatchewan   515

by Marilyn Wood

17   Alberta & the Rockies   556

by Bill McRae

18   Vancouver 629

by Anistatia R. Miller and Jared M. Brown

19   Victoria & the Best of British Columbia 672

by Anistatia R. Miller and Jared M. Brown

20 The Yukon & the Northwest Territories: The Great Northern Wilderness   740

by Bill McRae

List of Maps

AN INVITATION TO THE READER

In researching this book, we discovered many wonderful places—hotels, restaurants, shops, and more. We're sure you'll find others. Please tell us about them, so we can share the information with your fellow travelers in upcoming editions. If you were disappointed with a recommendation, we'd love to know that, too. Please write to:

Frommer's Canada
Macmillan Travel
1633 Broadway
New York, NY 10019

AN ADDITIONAL NOTE

Please be advised that travel information is subject to change at any time—and this is especially true of prices. We therefore suggest that you write or call ahead for confirmation when making your travel plans. The authors, editors, and publisher cannot be held responsible for the experiences of readers while traveling. Your safety is important to us, however, so we encourage you to stay alert and be aware of your surroundings. Keep a close eye on cameras, purses, and wallets, all favorite targets of thieves and pickpockets.

WHAT THE SYMBOLS MEAN

✪ Frommer's Favorites

Hotels, restaurants, attractions, and entertainment you should not miss.

Ⓢ Super-Special Values

Hotels and restaurants that offer great value for your money.

The following abbreviations are used for credit cards:

AE	American Express	EU	Eurocard
CB	Carte Blanche	JCB	Japan Credit Bank
DC	Diners Club	MC	MasterCard
DISC	Discover	V	Visa
ER	enRoute		

AN IMPORTANT NOTE ON PRICES

Unless stated otherwise, **the prices cited in this guide are given in Canadian dollars,** which is good news for U.S. travelers because the Canadian dollar is worth about 25% less than the American dollar, but buys nearly as much. As we go to press, $1 Canadian is worth about 75¢ U.S., which means that your $100-a-night hotel room will cost only U.S. $75, and your $6 breakfast costs only U.S. $4.50.

The Best of Canada

Planning a trip to such a vast and diverse country can present you with a bewildering array of choices. We've scoured all of Canada from sea to sea in search of the best places and experiences, and in this chapter we'll share our very personal and opinionated choices. We hope they'll give you some ideas and get you started.

1 The Best Travel Experiences

- **Marveling at Geologic Wonders in Gros Morne National Park** (Newfoundland): When the earth's land masses broke apart and shifted 500 million years ago, a piece of the earth's mantle, the very shell of the planet, was thrust upward to form tableland mountains of rock. Nearby, in the park's northern section, glaciers formed a long, deep fjord, whose access to the sea was later cut off by glacial debris. These natural phenomena created stunning rock walls that drop hundreds of feet into lakes. The best way to view the landscape is on a Tablelands Boat Tour (☎ 709/451-2101). See Chapter 7.
- **Watching the World Go By in a Québec City Cafe:** On a sunny Saturday in late June or September, sit outside at the Marie-Clarisse restaurant in the Quartier Petit Champlain. From here you can watch the goings-on in one of the oldest European communities in the New World. A folk singer may do a half-hour set, followed by a classical guitarist. See Chapter 10.
- **Houseboating on the Trent-Severn Waterway** (Ontario): The Trent-Severn Waterway will take you 240 miles via 44 locks from Trenton to Georgian Bay on Lake Huron. Enjoy drawing into the locks or being drawn up or let down by the lockmaster. You can cruise aboard a fully equipped houseboat that usually sleeps up to six; weekly rentals on the canal system in summer average $1,000. Call Big Rideau Boats (☎ 613/828-0138); or Houseboat Holidays (☎ 613/382-2842). See Chapter 13.
- **Seeing the Polar Bears in Churchill** (Manitoba): In October or November, travel by train or plane as far north to Churchill and the shores of Hudson Bay to view hundreds of magnificent polar bears, who migrate to the bay's icy shores and even lope into Churchill itself. In the evening, you can glimpse the famous Aurora Borealis (northern lights). Either take VIA Rail's Hudson Bay (☎ 800/561-3949) train, a two-night, one-day trip from

Winnipeg, or fly in on Canadian Airlines International (☎ 204/632-2811). See Chapter 16.

- **Horseback Riding in the Rockies:** Rent a cabin on a rural guest ranch, and get back in the saddle again. Spend a day fishing, then return to the lodge for a country dance or a barbecue. Ride a horse to a backcountry chalet in the rugged mountain wilderness. Forget the crowded park highways and commercialized resort towns and just relax. Brewster's Kananaskis Guest Ranch (☎ 403/762-5454) in Kananaskis Village near Banff, Alberta, offers a variety of guided horseback trips, ranging from $125 to $140 a day, including all food, lodging, and the horse you ride in on. See Chapter 17.

- **Taking the Inside Passage Ferry** (Vancouver): The 15-hour trip on the Inside Passage ferry takes you from Vancouver Island's Port Hardy on a cruise across open Pacific waters into an otherwise inaccessible series of straits and channels that stretch north to the Alaskan Panhandle's southern tip at Prince Rupert. Orcas swim past, bald eagles soar overhead, and rare white black-bears known as kermodei emerge from old-growth forests to fish for salmon along the rain-forested coast while you lounge on the deck and take it all in. Contact B.C. Ferries (☎ 604/386-3431 or 604/669-1211) about the MV *Queen of the North*. See Chapter 18.

- **Dog Sledding Through Baffin Island:** Spectacular fjords, knife-edged mountains draped with glaciers, and friendly craft-oriented Inuit villages make this rarely visited island—the world's fifth-largest—a great off-the-beaten-path destination. Arrange a dog-sled tour to the floe edge, where the protected harbor ice meets the open sea, and where seals, polar bears, and bow-head whales converge. A week-long dog-sledding trip with Northwind, an Iqaluit-based outfitter (☎ 819/979-0551), costs $1,600. See Chapter 20.

2 The Best Family Vacations

- **Cavendish** (Prince Edward Island): Beaches that seem to go on forever and attractive cottages with housekeeping facilities make Cavendish a family favorite. Prince Edward Island National Park offers nature programs for children, and the campgrounds offer well-spaced tent or trailer sites, with barbecue grills and playgrounds. See Chapter 6.

- **Club Tremblant** (Laurentian Mountains; ☎ 819/425-2731): This resort faces Mount Tremblant, eastern Canada's highest peak, with a ski village at the base and gondola and chairlifts to the top, summer and winter. Ten lakes and connecting rivers around the mountain offer boating, swimming, and windsurfing. There are indoor and outdoor pools, plus inviting biking and hiking trails. A day-care program for children ages 3 to 13 lets parents take a break. Most lodgings are one to three-bedroom suites. See Chapter 9.

- **Ottawa:** In this family-friendly city, families can watch soldiers strut their stuff, and red-coated Mounties polish their equestrian and musical skills. There's also canoeing or skating on the canal, plus a host of live museums to explore—the National Aviation Museum, the National Museum of Civilization, and the National Museum of Science and Technology. See Chapter 11.

- **The Muskoka Lakes** (Ontario): This region is filled with resorts that welcome families. Children can swim, canoe, bike, fish, and more. Since most resorts offer children's programs, parents can enjoy a rest as well. See Chapter 15.

- **Whistler/Blackcomb Ski Resort** (British Columbia): At this family retreat, your kids can join in organized year-round ski or snowboarding camps that meet on top of Blackcomb glacier, horseback riding tours, mountain-biking clinics, and in-line skating contests while you golf, paraglide, heli-ski, swim, kayak, shop, or just relax at one of the many cafes in Whistler Village. See Chapter 19.

- **Traveling the Klondike Gold Rush Route** (The Yukon): Follow the Klondike Gold Rush, traveling from Skagway, Alaska, up over White Pass, to the Yukon's capital, Whitehorse. Canoe through the once-daunting Miles Canyon on the mighty Yukon River. Drive to Dawson City, and visit the gold fields, walk the boardwalks of the old town center, and listen to recitations of Robert Service poetry. Pan for gold and attend an old-fashioned musical revue at the opera house. Inexpensive public campgrounds abound in the Yukon, making this one of the more affordable family vacations in western Canada. See Chapter 20.

3   The Best Nature & Wildlife Viewing

- **The Fundy Tides at Hopewell Cape Rocks** (Highway 114, near Moncton, New Brunswick): You'll best appreciate the powerful force of the Fundy tides by walking on the floor of the sea under these red sandstone formations during low tide. Once part of the nearby cliffs, they have been worn and carved by tidal action into magical caves and arches. See Chapter 5.

- **Caribou at Avalon Wilderness Reserve** (Newfoundland): On the peninsula south of St. John's lives one of Newfoundland's greatest natural treasures: a herd of 13,000 caribou, the most southerly herd of its size found anywhere. In winter, spring, and early summer, the best place to see them is along Route 10 between Trepassy and Pete's River. Later in summer the herd goes north into the Avalon Reserve, where spotting them takes a little more effort. Eco Adventure Tours (☎ 709/432-2659) can help you find them. See Chapter 7.

- **Iceberg Alley** (Strait of Belle Isle, Newfoundland): As you drive along the Viking Trail, north of Gros Morne National Park, you often can see Labrador across the strait and the channel through which the chill Labrador current enters the Gulf of St. Lawrence. With the current come icebergs, calved from the icecaps of Greenland and the high Arctic, and these giant white ice cubes drift along the shore well into July. See Chapter 7.

- **Whales at Baie-Ste-Catherine** (Québec): At Baie-Ste-Catherine, about two hours' drive northeast of Québec City, and along the northern shore to the resort area of La Malbaie, hundreds of resident beluga and minke whales are joined by several additional species of their migratory cousins, including humpbacks and blue whales. From mid-June to early October, the graceful giants can often be sighted from land, but whale-watching cruises depart from Baie-Ste-Catherine for closer looks. See Chapter 10.

- **Pelicans in Prince Albert National Park** (Saskatchewan): On Lavallee Lake roosts the second largest pelican colony in North America. Bison, moose, elk, caribou, black bear, and red fox also roam free in this million acres of wilderness. See Chapter 16.

- **Bison at Elk Island National Park** (east of Edmonton): Before homesteaders put the plow to the northern Canadian prairies, bison, elk, deer, moose, beaver, and dozens of other animals roamed across the land. This small and easily accessible national park preserves the original prairie lake ecosystem and large numbers of wildlife, including two different species of bison and a genetically pure herd of prairie elk. See Chapter 17.

- **Orcas Off Vancouver Island** (British Columbia): At Tofino and Ucluelet on Vancouver Island's west coast you can watch pods of feeding gray whales on their annual migration north. But it's on the east coast, at Alert Bay, where you'll find

the perfect on-shore spot for watching orcas as they glide through the Johnstone Strait in search of salmon, or perhaps even rubbing their tummies on the pebbly beaches at Robson Bight. See Chapter 19.
- **Musk Oxen on Banks Island** (Northwest Territory): This tundra-covered island is home to the world's largest population of musk oxen. Flights from Inuvik visit Aulavik National Park, established to protect the island's 10,000 musk ox; also watch for caribou, grizzly bear, and whales during the flight. Hike through delicate tundra and marshland, a mass of tiny blossoms in summer. Arctic Nature Tours (☎ 403/979-3300 or 800/661-0724) in Inuvik runs a day-long flight and excursion for $400. See Chapter 20.

4 The Best Views

- **The Harbor at Brigus South** (Newfoundland): South of St. John's, the coast is steep and rocky, deeply indented with long estuaries and bays. Villages cling to the shore, but none so dramatically as Brigus South. You'll drive into the village on an alarmingly steep road that seems to disappear in front of the car. Bright painted little fishing shacks can barely find a foothold around the tiny harbor, where boats bob in front of the sheer headwall and grass-covered island outcrops. See Chapter 7.
- **Terrace Dufferin in Québec City:** This classic boardwalk promenade with benches and green-and-white-roofed gazebos runs along the cusp of the bluff that rears up behind the original colonial settlement. At its back is the landmark Château Frontenac, and out front is the long silvery sweep of the mighty St. Lawrence, where ferries glide back and forth and cruise ships and Great Lakes freighters and tankers putt in at the port below. To the east is the trailing edge of the Adirondacks, and downriver can be seen the last of the Laurentian Mountains. See Chapter 10.
- **Niagara Falls:** This is still a wonder of nature despite its commercial exploitation. You can experience the falls from the decks of the Maid of the Mist, which takes you into the roaring maelstrom, or look down from the cockpit of a helicopter. The least scary view can be had from the Skylon Tower. See Chapter 13.
- **Agawa Canyon** (northern Ontario): To see the Northern Ontario wilderness that inspired the Group of Seven, take the Agawa Canyon Train Tour on a 114-mile trip from the Soo to Hearst through the Agawa Canyon, where you can spend a few hours exploring scenic waterfalls and vistas. The train snakes through a vista of deep ravines and lakes, hugging the hillsides and crossing gorges on skeletal trestle bridges. See Chapter 15.
- **Takakkawa Falls in Yoho National Park:** One of Canada's highest falls, Takakkawa Falls plunges more than 1,200 feet into a glacier-carved valley. Hike up to the base of the falls, hear the roar of crashing water, and stand in clouds of mist. See Chapter 17.
- **Moraine Lake in Banff National Park:** Ten snow-clad peaks towering more than 10,000 feet high rear up dramatically behind this tiny, eerily green lake. Rent a canoe and paddle to the mountains' base. See Chapter 17.
- **Vancouver as Seen from Mount Seymour:** This small ski area overlooks Vancouver, and on a clear day, the entire city and the coastal islands spread out below. You can see a similar view from Grouse Mountain, which is easily accessible by a tram. See Chapter 18.
- **The Ancient Trees of Kitilope** (British Columbia): An ancient river snakes through Kitilope, an 800-year-old Sitka spruce forest bordered on either side by

steep craggy mountains. Designated a United Nations World Heritage Site, Kitilope is considered sacred by the Haisla tribe that cares for it. Viewed from any angle, near or far, it is truly a spectacular place. See Chapter 19.

5 The Most Dramatic Driving Tours

- **Bras d'Or Lake Scenic Drive** (Cape Breton Island, Nova Scotia): Cape Breton Island is really a series of loosely connected islands surrounding the many-armed, 450-square-mile Bras d'Or Lake, an enormous saltwater lake that's home to the largest population of bald eagles in North America (250 pairs). The route circling the lake, marked by signs with an eagle logo, has plenty of overlooks, as well as boat tours, birding sites, and beaches. Attractive towns alternate with fine scenery along the narrow arms of the lake. See Chapter 4.
- **The Viking Trail** (Newfoundland): The Viking Trail follows the shore of the Great Northern Peninsula, over the shoulders of the mountains, near the waters of the fjords, and along the edge of the Strait of Belle Isle until it swings inland toward St. Anthony, not far from the Viking settlement at L'Anse aux Meadows. New vistas of sea and land unfold as low headlands alternate with sandy coves. See Chapter 7.
- **The Icefields Parkway** (Highway 93 through Banff and Jasper National Parks): This is one of the grandest and most beautiful mountain drives in the world. Driving along it is like a trip back to the Ice Ages. The Parkway climbs past glacier-notched peaks to the Columbia Icefields, a sprawling cap of snow, ice, and glacier at the very crest of the Rockies. See Chapter 17.
- **Highway 99** (British Columbia): The Sea to Sky Highway from Vancouver to Lillooet takes you from a dramatic seacoast past glaciers, pine forests, and a waterfall that cascades from a mountaintop and through Whistler's majestic glacial mountains. The next leg of the four-hour drive winds up a series of switchbacks to the thickly forested Cayoosh Creek valley and on to the craggy, arid mountains surrounding the Fraser River gold rush town of Lillooet. See Chapter 19.
- **The Dempster Highway** (from Dawson City to Inuvik): Canada's most northerly highway, the Dempster is a year-round gravel road across the top of the world. From Dawson City, the road winds over the Continental Divide three times, crosses the Arctic Circle, and fords the Peel and the Mackenzie River by ferry, before reaching Inuvik, a native community on the mighty Mackenzie River delta. See Chapter 20.

6 The Best Walks & Rambles

- **River Walk** (Fredericton, New Brunswick): Bordering 3 miles of the Saint John River as well as the capital's downtown area, the River Walk winds past the Anglican Christ Church Cathedral and the Waterloo row houses to the remains of an old Loyalist cemetery dating from 1783. Don't miss the row houses, Fredericton's prettiest stretch of houses. See Chapter 5.
- **Old Montréal:** Wander the streets, where some of what founder de Maisonneuve christened Ville-Marie in 1642 remains—both above and below the streets. Above ground, buildings have been restored into residences, stores, restaurants, and nightclubs. Horse-drawn carriages clop and creak along the cobblestone streets, past the heart of the district, the place Jacques-Cartier, lined on both sides with cafes. Below, a tunnel leads from the new Museum of Archaeology to the old Custom House. See Chapter 8.

- **Lake Superior Provincial Park** (Ontario): Follow any trail in this park to a rewarding vista. The 10-mile (16km) Peat Mountain Trail leads to a panoramic view close to 500 feet above the surrounding lakes and forests. The moderate Orphan Lake Trail offers views over the Orphan Lake and Lake Superior, plus a pebble beach and Baldhead River falls. The 16-mile (26km) Toawab trail takes you through the Agawa Valley to the 81-foot Agawa Falls. See Chapter 15.
- **Johnson Creek** (Banff National Park): Just 15 miles west of Banff, Johnson Creek cuts a deep, very narrow canyon through limestone cliffs. The trail winds through tunnels, passing waterfalls, edging by shaded rock faces and crosses the chasm on footbridges, before reaching a series of iridescent pools, formed by springs that bubble up through highly colored rock. See Chapter 17.
- **Plain of Six Glaciers** (Lake Louise): From Château Lake Louise, a lakeside trail rambles along the edge of emerald green Lake Louise, then climbs up to the base of Victoria Glacier. Here, at a rustic teahouse, you can order a cup of tea and a scone—each made over a wood burning stove—and gaze up at the rumpled face of the glacier. See Chapter 17.
- **West Coast Trail** (Vancouver Island): The first 4 miles (7km) of Vancouver Island's West Coast Trail are not too difficult. The trail takes you through an incredible rain forest edged by a sandy beach, roaring surf, and awe-inspiring views of migrating gray whales, basking sea lions, and soaring eagles. See Chapter 19.

7 The Best Biking Routes

- **Trinity Bay** (Newfoundland): Historic fishing villages, secluded coves, cool forests, and rocky headlands encircle Trinity Bay, on the Bonavista Peninsula. An abandoned railway line rounds the bay and its many deep coves. If you don't feel like bicycling the same route in reverse, you can hitch a boat ride in Trinity back to your starting point in Trinity East. See Chapter 7.
- **Old Port Route** (Montréal): The city has 148 miles of biking paths, and the Metro permits bicycles in the last car of its trains. One popular route is from the Old Port, west along the side of the Lachine Canal. A little under 7 miles one way, it's tranquil, vehicle-free, and flat most of the way. Bicycles can be rented at the Old Port. See Chapter 8.
- **Île d'Orléans** (Québec): You can enjoy a day or two of biking around this bucolic island 15 minutes downriver from Québec City. A main road runs around the island, never far from water's edge. You can stop at a pick-your-own orchard or strawberry field or in a tiny village with 18th- and 19th-century houses and churches. Two roads cut across the island at the southern end, and a third does the same a little beyond midpoint. Bikes can be rented on the island. See Chapter 10.
- **The Niagara Region:** This very flat area is ideal biking terrain. A bike path runs along the Niagara Parkway, which follows the Niagara River. You'll bike past fruit farms, vineyards, and gardens with picnicking spots. See Chapter 13.
- **Highways 1 and 93 Through Banff and Jasper National Parks:** This wide, well-maintained highway winds through some of the most dramatic mountain scenery in the world. Take the Bow River Parkway, between Banff and Lake Louise, and Highway 93A between Athabasca Falls and Jasper for slightly quieter peddling. Best of all, there are seven hostels, some rustic, some fancy, at some of the most beautiful sights along the route, so you don't have to weigh yourself down with camping gear. See Chapter 17.

- **Seawall** (Vancouver): Vancouver's Seawall surrounds the Stanley Park shoreline on the Burrard Inlet and English Bay. Built just above the high-tide mark, it offers nonstop breathtaking views, no hills, and no cars. See Chapter 18.

8 The Best Culinary Experiences

- **Seafood Fresh from the Atlantic:** Look especially for oysters from Malpeque Bay in Prince Edward Island, scallops from Digby in Nova Scotia, salmon from the pristine rivers of Newfoundland, and lobster from Sediac, New Brunswick. In early summer, try panfried capelin. See Chapters 4 through 7.
- **Fine Dining in Montréal:** Montréal boasts one of the hottest dining scenes in Canada. The current favorite is Toqué (☎ 514/499-2084); it's the kind of restaurant that raises the gastronomic expectations of an entire city. The silky greeting-to-tab performance of kitchen and waitstaff is a pleasure to observe, and the post-nouvelle presentations are both visually winning and completely filling. No restaurant in eastern Canada surpasses this contemporary French restaurant. See Chapter 8.
- **Smoked Meat in Montréal:** Somewhere between pastrami and corned beef, this deli delight appears to have had its origins in the immigrations of eastern Europeans during the late 19th century. Meat eaters are ravenous at the sight and aroma of it, and the place to inhale smoked meat is at Chez Schwartz on The Main (☎ 514/842-4813). Elegant, it is not; immensely satisfying, it is. See Chapter 8.
- **Ethnic Meals in Toronto:** If you explore the city's neighborhoods you'll find ethnic dining spots in Little Italy, Little Portugal, and Greektown. Order spaghettini with seafood, garlic, capers, white wine, and a touch of anchovies at Trattoria Giancarlo (☎ 416/533-9619), poached filet of cod at Chiado (☎ 416/538-1910), or dolmades at Ouzeri (☎ 416/778-0500)—each is situated at the heart of its ethnic neighborhood. See Chapter 12.
- **A Hearty Dinner of Seasonal Game:** You can feast on bison, caribou, or reindeer at Dreen's, Saskatchewan (☎ 709/753-2380). On the frequently changing menu you might find bison served with fresh chanterelles and portobello mushrooms, or reindeer chops served with wild mushroom sauce. Other local specialties are fresh pickerel and the local Saskatoon berries, sometime used to enhance a cut of pork loin. See Chapter 16.
- **Organic Dining in Calgary:** You'll walk through a quiet, tree-filled park on an island in the Bow River to reach the bustling River Cafe (☎ 403/261-7670). At the restaurant's center, an immense wood-fired oven and grill produces soft, chewy flatbreads and smoky grilled meats and vegetables, all organically grown and freshly harvested. On warm summer evenings, picnickers loll in the grassy shade, nibbling this and that from the cafe's picnic-like menu. See Chapter 17.
- **Hotel Dining in Lake Louise:** At its cozy dining room with a low ceiling in an old log lodge, the Post Hotel (☎ 403/522-3989) serves up the kind of sophisticated yet robust cuisine that perfectly fits the backdrop of glaciered peaks, deep forest, and glassy streams. Both the wine list and the cooking are French and hearty, with the chef focusing on the best of local ingredients—lamb, salmon, and Alberta beef. After a hungry day out on the trail, a meal here will top off a quintessential day in the Rockies. See Chapter 17.
- **Dim Sum in Vancouver's Chinatown:** Here you'll find more than a half-dozen dim sum parlors where you can try steamed or baked barbecue pork buns, dumplings filled with fresh prawns and vegetables, or steamed rice flour crepes filled with spicy beef. See Chapter 18.

- **Salmon Barbecues in British Columbia:** The annual salmon barbecues that take place in cities, towns, and villages throughout coastal British Columbia pay tribute to a tradition that dates back thousands of years. Nothing is quite as good as Pacific sockeye salmon, hot smoked over alderwood. See Chapter 19.

9　The Best Festivals & Special Events

- **The Highland Games** (Antigonish, Nova Scotia): This lavish display of Highland lore, art, strength, and skill has been held annually since 1863, usually on a weekend in mid-July. Pregames festivities the preceding week include concerts, youth competitions, clan gatherings, Celtic workshops, and ceilidhs (small, festive gatherings with traditional fiddle music). A 10,000-meter race, hammer throwing, broad-jumping, and "tossing the caber," pipe bands, highland dancing and other events go on continuously, culminating in a massed band, where hundreds of players create an unforgettable display of Scottish color and ceremony. See Chapter 4.
- **International Jazz Festival** (Montréal): Ten days every summer glorify America's truest art form with the immensely successful International Jazz Festival, in operation since 1979. Big stars always appear, but their concerts cost money. No problem. Hundreds of free concerts are held, most often in the streets and plazas of midtown. See Chapter 8.
- **Winter Carnival** (Québec City): Think Mardi Gras in New Orleans, without the nudity (well, maybe a little). Ice sculptures, parades, a canoe race across the frozen St. Lawrence, and an impressive castle of ice are among the principal features. The general jollity is fueled by a nasty drink called Caribou, whiskey sloshed with red wine. See Chapter 10.
- **Toronto International Film Festival:** Up there right behind Cannes, the film festival, now the second-largest in the world, shows more than 250 films for 10 days in early September. See Chapter 12.
- **Northern Trapper's Festival** (in The Pas, Manitoba): This festival celebrates the traditions of the frontier pioneers each February with world-championship dogsled races, ice fishing, beerfests, bannock bathing, moose calling, and more. See Chapter 16.
- **The Calgary Stampede:** In all of North America, there's nothing quite like the Calgary Stampede. Of course it's the world's largest rodeo, but it's also a series of concerts, an art show, open-air casino, carnival, street dance—you name it, it's undoubtedly going on somewhere. In July, all of Calgary is converted into a party and everyone's invited. See Chapter 17.
- **Stratford Theatre Festival** (Ontario): This summer-long festival of superb repertory theater, launched by Tyrone Guthrie in 1953, produces shows that frequently move successfully to Broadway and beyond. Productions, which run from May to October on three stages, range from classic to contemporary. Visitors can also participate in informal discussions with company members. See Chapter 14.
- **Symphony of Fire** (Vancouver): This four-night fireworks extravaganza takes place over English Bay in Vancouver. Three of the world's leading manufacturers are invited to compete against each other, setting their best displays to music. Then on the fourth night, all three countries launch their finales. Last year at least 250,000 people showed up each night. The best seats are at the "Bard on the Beach" Shakespeare festival across False Creek. See Chapter 18.
- **Kamloops Cattle Drive** (southern British Columbia): This rollicking seven-day trail ride draws about 1,000 people annually. A parade of wagons, horses, and cows sets off from a different location every August, driving the cattle along a

predetermined route through the High Country's sagebrush mesas to a triumphant finish (and huge party) in Kamloops. Beginners are welcome, and horses (even space on wagons) can be rented. See Chapter 19.

10 The Best Luxury Hotels & Resorts

- **Algonquin Hotel** (St. Andrews, NB; ☎ 506/529-8823 or 800/563-4299 in the U.S.): The Algonquin is one reason St. Andrews has survived and become the charming town it is today. Built by Canadian Pacific Railway at the Atlantic terminus of its transcontinental line, the hotel attracted wealthy city people who later built mansions of their own within sight of the grand hotel. Grand it still is, with modern amenities and all the grace of its age. Its white stucco timbered walls and distinctive red roof are widely recognized symbols of the Atlantic Provinces. See Chapter 5.
- **Hotel Vogue** (Montréal, PQ; ☎ 514/285-5555 or 800/465-6654): What was just an anonymous midrise office building has turned into the king of the hill of Montréal hotels. The Vogue targeted international executives on the go, and little was left to chance. Even standard rooms come with fax machines, four phones, computer ports, bathroom TVs, and whirlpool baths. Tins of caviar are tucked into the minibars. People with cell phones at the ready fill the lobby espresso bar and adjacent dining room. Even after two changes in management, the Vogue remains steady on its course. See Chapter 8.
- **Langdon Hall** (Cambridge, ON; ☎ 519/740-2100 or 800/268-1898): This quintessential English country house, built in 1902 for the granddaughter of John Jacob Astor, is now a small country house hotel where guests can enjoy 200 acres of lawns, gardens, and woodlands. Rooms feature the finest amenities, fabrics, and furnishings. Facilities include a full spa, plus a swimming pool, tennis court, croquet lawn, and exercise room. The light and airy dining room overlooking the lily pond offers fine continental cuisine. See Chapter 14.
- **Manitowaning Lodge and Tennis Resort** (Manitowaning, ON; ☎ 705/859-3136): This resort on Manitoulin is an idyllic island retreat. A lodge and cottages are set on 11 acres of beautiful gardens. The lodge, with its huge hand-hewn beams, a mask of the Spirit of Manitowaning, and images of the Native American protective spirit, provides a serene setting to restore the spirit. This unpretentious place delivers on the promise of luxurious peace and quiet. See Chapter 15.
- **Château Lake Louise** (Banff National Park, AB; ☎ 403/522-3511 or 800/441-1414): First of all, there's the view. Across a tiny gem-green lake rise massive cliffs shrouded in glacial ice. And then there's the hotel. Part hunting lodge, part European palace, the Chateau is its own community, with sumptuous boutiques, sports rental facilities, seven dining areas, two bars, magnificent lobby areas, and beautifully furnished guest rooms. See Chapter 17.
- **Hotel Macdonald** (Edmonton, AB; ☎ 403/424-5181 or 800/441-1414): When the Canadian Pacific bought and refurbished this landmark hotel in the 1980s, all the charming period details were preserved, while all the inner workings were modernized and brought up to snuff. The result is a regally elegant but friendly small hotel. From the kilted bellman to the gargoyles on the walls, this is a real class act. See Chapter 17.
- **Château Whistler** (Whistler, BC; ☎ 604/938-8000): Canadian-Pacific's Chateau Whistler has sterling service and excellent accommodations right next to the Blackcomb Mountain ski lift. The après-ski lounge has comfortable sitting with a great view of the lifts. Ski and bike valet service as well as storage, a full-service

spa and health club and Whistler's best buffet-style brunch top off the experience. See Chapter 19.

11   The Best Bed & Breakfasts

- **Murray Manor B&B** (Yarmouth, NS; ☎ 902/742-9625): Beautifully restored and decorated, this B&B has added every detail with the guests comfort and convenience in mind: large bright rooms, fine bed linens, fresh flowers, huge towels, extra pillows, ample reading lights, dressing gowns, and even a personal bath basket. See Chapter 4.
- **The Walker Estate** (St. Andrews, NB; ☎ 506/529-4210): From the moment you enter the foyer of this French château-style house, you are the pampered houseguest in a classy but very comfortable summer estate. Rooms are large, airy, bright, and beautifully decorated in a style that suits each room's size and architectural detail. Despite the house's grandeur, you'll feel comfortable with your feet curled under you on the parlor sofa as you enjoy afternoon tea with fresh scones or lemon bars. See Chapter 5.
- **Waterford Manor** (St. John's, NF; ☎ 709/754-4139): A Queen Anne mansion with three turrets and a wraparound porch where tea is served, this slightly-out-of-town beauty is furnished with carefully chosen antiques and tasteful Victorian decorative touches. The building's quirky architecture is used to its best advantage—guest rooms have parlors in turrets, giant windows overlooking the garden, alcoves, and interesting shapes. Breakfast is as elegant as the dining room it's served in. See Chapter 7.
- **Les Passants du Sans Soucy** (Montréal, PQ; ☎ 514/842-2634): The only B&B in Old Montréal has a lot more going for it than that enviable distinction. Indeed, it almost qualifies as a boutique hotel, but with much lower prices. Housed in a renovated 1723 building, it makes the most of its stone walls and exposed dark ceiling beams, using them to contain brass or wrought-iron beds and cushy sofas. A fireplace is the focal point of the common room. Breakfast includes café au lait and chocolate croissants. See Chapter 8.
- **Clifton Manor Inn** (Bayfield, ON; ☎ 519/565-2282): You'll find instant romance at this elegant house, built in 1895 for the reve of Bayfield. All the bathrooms have candles and bubble bath, and one has a deep tub for two. Four comfortable rooms are named after an artist or composer. All rooms have cozy touches like mohair throws, sheepskin rugs, wingback chairs, fresh flowers, and so on. Breakfast consists of egg dishes like omelets or crepes, plus fresh fruit often plucked from the very trees in the garden. See Chapter 14.
- **Beild House** (Collingwood, ON; ☎ 705/444-1522): On Friday nights, you can sit down to a splendid five-course dinner before retiring to the bed that belong to TRH Duke and Duchess of Windsor. A sumptuous breakfast will follow the next morning. In this handsome 1909 house are 17 rooms, seven with bath. See Chapter 15.
- **Nakiska Ranch** (Clearwater, BC; ☎ 604/674-3655): This B&B is set at the edge of the mountains along an alpine creek where moose and deer graze amid towering Douglas fir trees and lupine-filled alpine meadows. Guests can choose rooms in the main two-story log chalet or one of two separate, secluded two-story log cabins with full kitchens that look like they're straight from the pages of *Metropolitan Home*. Congenial Swiss service and a hearty breakfast await before you set out on a day hike or a Nordic ski run through nearby Wells Gray Provincial Park. See Chapter 19.

- **Pearson's Arctic Home Stay** (Baffin Island, NT; ☎ 819/979-6408): Staying at this lovely private home overlooking Frobisher Bay is like staying at a museum of Inuit arts and crafts. The innkeeper is the town's former mayor and currently the island's public coroner, so you also get a real insight into life and death on Baffin Island! See Chapter 20.

12 The Best Camping & Wilderness Lodges

- **Kouchibouguac National Park** (New Brunswick): These well-maintained campgrounds have well-spaced sites, cut grass, and spotless facilities. And are they popular. Although the number of campsites in the park is large, competition for sites is fierce in July and August, particularly on weekends. Get there early for the best chance of a site in this premier park. See Chapter 5.
- **Sir Sam's Inn** (Eagle Lake, ON; ☎ 705/754-2188): You'll have to search a bit for this remote stone and timber lodge built in 1917 in the woods above Eagle Lake for politician and militarist Sir Sam Hughes. You can either stay in the inn, or in new chalets or lakefront suites. At this friendly yet sophisticated place you can play tennis, swim, sail, windsurf, water-ski, canoe, or go mountain biking. See Chapter 15.
- **Arowhon Pines** (Algonquin Park, ON; ☎ 705/633-5661 in summer, 416/483-4393 in winter): Located 8 miles off the highway down a dirt road, this is one of the most entrancing places anywhere. Guests here enjoy peace, seclusion, and natural beauty, plus comfortable accommodations and fresh, good food. There are no TVs or telephones—just the call of the loons, the gentle lapping of the water, the croaking of the frogs, and the splash of canoe paddles cutting the smooth surface of the lake. See Chapter 15.
- **Tunnel Mountain** (Banff): If you find Banff too expensive and too crowded, these campgrounds—three within 3 miles of town— are a great antidote. There are showers and real toilets, and most sites have full hook-ups. And you'll pay just $^1/_{10}$ of what hotel dwellers are paying for equally good access to the Rockies. See Chapter 17.
- **Emerald Lake Lodge** (Yoho National Park): This historic log lodge (☎ 604/343-6321) sits on the edge of a glacial lake just below the rim of the Continental Divide. Rent a cabin that sleeps four and come here in the winter, when the snowbound lodge is a center for cross-country ski expeditions. See Chapter 17.
- **Bowron Lakes Provincial Park** (British Columbia): Every summer canoeists and kayakers set out to navigate the perfect 72-mile circle of six alpine lakes, with minimal portages in between. A 1949 Wells Grey map listed the Bowron Area as "uncharted mountains"; there are no roads or other signs of civilization beyond the launch point, except some well-placed cabins, campsites, and shelters set up and maintained by the province for the public. It's a seven-day trip, but the memories will last a lifetime. See Chapter 19.
- **Wells Grey Back Country Chalets** (British Columbia): Since these chalets aren't accessible by car, guests have to hike, ski, or travel by horse to these three fully equipped log chalets built inside one of the province's largest and most spectacular parks. True adventurers can opt for packages that include chalet hopping, hiking deeper into the wilderness each day. See Chapter 19.

2 Getting to Know Canada

The sheer amount of elbow space in Canada makes you dizzy. Measuring 3.8 million square miles (200,000 more than the United States), this colossal expanse contains only 25 1/2 million people—barely three million more than California. Most of the population is clustered in a relatively narrow southern belt that boasts all the nation's large cities and nearly all its industries. The silent north of the Yukon and Northwest Territories—where 51,000 people dot 1 1/2 million square miles—remains a frontier, a mysterious vastness stretching to the Arctic shores, embracing thousands of lakes no one has ever charted, counted, or named. It's impossible to easily categorize this land or its people—just when you think you know Canada, you discover another place, another temperament, another hidden side.

1 Canada Today

by Bill McRae

Canada has always been a loosely linked country, a confederation of provinces, not a union of states. Canadians are also quick to tell you that theirs is a "cultural mosaic" of people, not a "melting pot." These factors account in great part for two of Canada's most striking characteristics: its cultural vitality, and its habits of mistrust and contention. While Canada has weathered many storms in the past, recent events indicate that the country will continue to face extremely divisive social and cultural challenges, some with the potential to alter its political cohesion and economic power.

The ongoing debate on the "Québec Question" serves to divide the majority of both English-speaking and French-speaking Canadians. Twenty-five years after the heyday of the Québec separatist movement, many Canadians cynically evaluated the current independence movement as simply an employment program for regional politicians. But then Québec again faced a referendum in October 1995, asking whether the French-speaking province should separate from the rest of Canada, and suddenly Canada teetered on the brink of splitting apart. The vote went in favor of the prounity camp by a razor-thin margin, but the issue was hardly resolved: In all likelihood it lives to be reborn as another referendum.

Meanwhile, as public officials debate separatism, Québec's younger generation is voting with its feet. Many of Québec's brightest and best are heading west, particularly to more prosperous British Columbia and Alberta. However, these western provinces—no lovers of Ottawa—themselves dream of loosening the federal laws that bind them to eastern Canada.

In 1999, the huge Northern Territories will be divided into two smaller territories. The eastern half, which takes in Baffin Island, the land around Hudson's Bay and most of the Arctic islands, will be called Nunavut, and will essentially function as an Inuit homeland. (As for what becomes of the rest of the Northwest Territories, no one seems to have thought much about that; there's not even a name yet for the new territory.)

Nunavut lacks adequate resource development or industry to become self-sufficient, and billions of Canadian tax dollars will still flow into Nunavut from Ottawa. At the same time, all non-Inuit owned business will be forced to leave Nunavut or become at least partly owned by Inuits, and federal government agencies will come under Inuit control. While the territory of Nunavut will give its native people more control over their lands and government, it also looks like a recipe for short-term social and economic destabilization.

The success of the Nunavut negotiations has emboldened other native groups to settle their own land claims with the Canadian government. While many of the land claims in northern Canada can be settled by transferring government land and money to native groups, the claims in southern Canada are more complex. Some tribes assert a prior claim to land that is currently owned by non-Indians; in other areas, native groups refuse to abide by environmental laws that seek to protect endangered runs of salmon. The situation in a number of communities has moved on beyond protests and threats to armed encounters and road barricades. The path seems set for more and increasingly hostile confrontations between official Canada and its native peoples.

Elements of the Canadian economy are still adapting to the landmark Free Trade Agreement concluded with the United States in 1989. While free trade hasn't done much to revive the smokestack industries that once were the engines of eastern Canada, the agreement, combined with the weak dollar, has actually been good for much of Canada's huge agricultural heartland. However, the globalization of trade is transforming the Canadian economy in ways that produce confusion and hostility in the average citizen. Many Canadians are deeply ambivalent about being so closely linked to their powerful southern neighbor, and the trade agreement (and U.S. culture in general) often gets the blame for everything that's going wrong with Canada.

Public interest in protecting the environment runs high, and this is reflected in public policy. Recycling is commonplace and communities across the country have made great strides in balancing economic interests with environmental goals. On Vancouver Island, for example, environmentalists and timber companies agreed in 1995 on forestry standards that satisfy both parties.

Canada is challenged internally on many fronts. Social and economic forces are working to fragment a cohesive sense of national identity. Whether the long-standing cultural and political institutions that have guided the country successfully for so many years will survive is a question that will be answered in the very near future.

2 History 101

The Vikings landed in Canada more than 1,000 years ago, but the French were the first Europeans to get a toehold in the country. In 1608 Samuel de Champlain established a settlement on the cliffs overlooking the St. Lawrence River—today's

Dateline

■ **1608** Samuel de Champlain founds the settlement of Kebec—today's Québec City.

continues

Canada

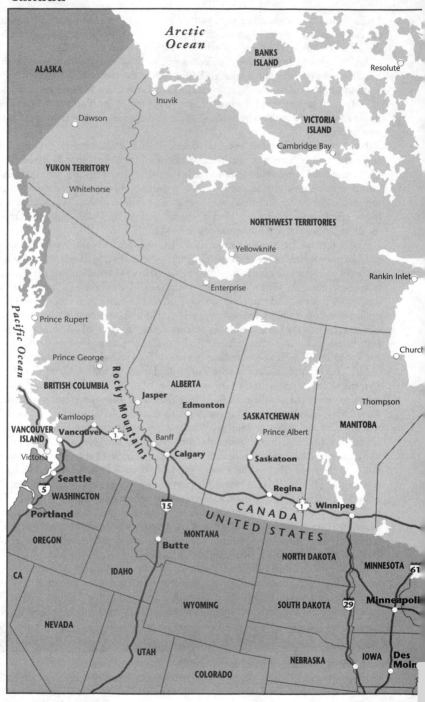

- **1642** French colony of Ville-Marie established, later renamed Montréal.
- **1759** British defeat French at the Plains of Abraham. Fall of Québec City.
- **1763** All of "New France" (Canada) ceded to the British.
- **1775** American Revolutionary forces capture Montréal, but are repulsed at Québec City.
- **1813** Americans blow up Fort York (Toronto) in the War of 1812.
- **1841** Act of Union creates the United Provinces of Canada.
- **1855** Ottawa becomes Canada's capital.
- **1869** The Hudson's Bay Company sells Rupert's Land to Canada. It becomes the Province of Alberta.
- **1873** Creation of the Northwest Mounted Police (the Mounties).
- **1875** West Coast community of Gastown incorporated as the city of Vancouver. The Northwest Mounted Police builds the log fort that developed into the city of Calgary.
- **1885** Rebellion of the Metis under Louis Riel in western Saskatchewan.
- **1887** The Transcontinental Railroad reaches Vancouver, connecting Canada from ocean to ocean.
- **1896** The Klondike gold rush brings 100,000 people swarming into the Yukon.
- **1914** Canada enters World War I alongside Britain. Some 60,000 Canadians die in combat.
- **1920** The Northwest Territories separated from the Yukon.

continues

Québec City. This was exactly a year after the Virginia Company founded Jamestown. Hundreds of miles of unexplored wilderness lay between the embryo colonies, but they were inexorably set on a collision course.

The early stages of the struggle for the new continent were explorations, and there the French outdid the English. Their fur traders, navigators, soldiers, and missionaries opened up not only Canada but most of the United States. At least 35 of the 50 United States were either discovered, mapped, or settled by the French.

Gradually they staked out an immense colonial empire that, in patches and minus recognized borders, stretched from Hudson Bay in the Arctic to the Gulf of Mexico. Christened New France, it was run on an ancient seigniorial system, whereby settlers were granted land by the Crown in return for military service.

The military obligation was essential, for the colony knew hardly a moment of peace during its existence. New France blocked the path of western expansion by England's seaboard colonies with a string of forts that lined the Ohio-Mississippi Valley. The Anglo-Americans were determined to break through, and so the frontier clashes crackled and flared, with the native tribes participating ferociously. These miniature wars were nightmares of savagery, waged with knives and tomahawks as much as with muskets and cannon, characterized by raids and counterraids, burning villages, and massacred women and children. According to some historians, the English introduced scalping to America by offering a cash bounty for each French scalp the native braves brought in!

The French retaliated in kind. They converted the Abenaki tribe to Christianity and encouraged them to raid deep into New England territory where, in 1704, they totally destroyed the town of Deerfield, Massachusetts. The Americans answered with a punitive blitz expedition by the famous green-clad Roger's Rangers, who wiped out the main Abenaki village and slaughtered half its population.

By far the most dreaded of the tribes was the Iroquois, who played the same role in the Canadian east as the Sioux (another French label) played in the American west. Astute politicians, the Iroquois learned to play the English against the French and vice versa, lending their scalping knives now to one side, then to the other. It took more than a century before they finally succumbed to the whites' small-pox, firewater, and gunpowder—in that order.

THE FALL OF QUÉBEC   There were only about 65,000 French settlers in the colony, but they more than held their own against the million Anglo-Americans, first and foremost because they were natural forest fighters—one Canadian trapper could stalemate six redcoats in the woods. Mainly, however, it was because they made friends with the local tribes whenever possible. Thus the majority of tribes sided with the French and made the English pay a terrible price for their blindness.

Even before French and English interests in the New World came to the point of armed struggle in the Seven Years' War, the British had largely taken control of Acadia, though its lush forests and farm-lands were dotted with French settlements. The governors knew there would be war, and, suspicious of Acadia's French-speaking inhabitants, they decided on a bold and ruthless plan: All Acadians who would not openly pledge allegiance to the British sovereign must be deported from the land. The deportation order came in 1755, and French-speaking families throughout the province were forcibly moved from their homes, many resettling in the French territory of Louisiana, where their Cajun language and culture are still alive today. To replace the Acadians, shiploads of Scottish and Irish settlers arrived from the British Isles, and the province soon acquired the name Nova Scotia—the New Scotland.

When the final round of fighting began in 1754, it opened with a series of shattering English debacles. The French had a brilliant commander, the marquis de Montcalm, exactly the kind of unorthodox tactician needed for the fluid semiguerrilla warfare of the American wilderness.

- **1930** Depression and mass unemployment hit Canada.
- **1939** Canada enters World War II with Britain.
- **1947** Huge oil deposits discovered at Leduc, southwest of Edmonton. Start of the Alberta oil boom.
- **1959** Opening of St. Lawrence Seaway turns Toronto into a major seaport.
- **1967** Montréal hosts World Expo.
- **1968** Parti Québécois founded by René Lévesque. Beginning of separatist movement.
- **1970** Kidnap-murder of Cabinet Minister Pierre Laporte. War Measures Act imposed on Québec Province.
- **1976** Montréal becomes site of Olympic Games.
- **1988** Calgary hosts the Winter Olympics.
- **1989** Canada-U.S. Free Trade Agreement eliminates all tariffs on goods of national origin moving between the two countries.
- **1993** Conservative party is swept out of power in elections.

Britain's proud General Braddock rode into a French-Indian ambush that killed him and scattered his army. Montcalm led an expedition against Fort Oswego that wiped out the stronghold and turned Lake Ontario into a French waterway. The following summer he repeated the feat with Fort William Henry, at the head of Lake George, which fell amid ghastly scenes of massacre, later immortalized by James Fenimore Cooper in *The Last of the Mohicans*. Middle New York now lay wide open to raids, and England's hold on America seemed to be slipping.

Then, like a cornered boxer bouncing from the ropes, the British came back with a devastating right-left-right that not only saved their colonies but also won them the entire continent.

The first punches were against Fort Duquesne, in Pennsylvania, and against the Fortress of Louisbourg, on Cape Breton, both of which they took after bloody sieges. Then, where least expected, came the ultimate haymaker, aimed straight at the enemy's solar plexus—Québec.

In June 1759 a British fleet nosed its way from the Atlantic Ocean down the St. Lawrence River. In charge of the troops on board was the youngest general in the army, 32-year-old James Wolfe, whose military record was remarkable and whose behavior was so eccentric that he had the reputation of being "mad as a march hare."

The struggle for Québec dragged on until September, when Wolfe, near desperation, played his final card. He couldn't storm those gallantly defended fortress walls, although the British guns had shelled the town to rubble. Wolfe therefore loaded 5,000 men into boats and rowed upriver to a cove behind the city. Then they silently climbed the towering cliff face in the darkness, and when morning came Wolfe had his army squarely astride Montcalm's supply lines. Now the French had to come out of their stronghold and fight in the open.

The British formed their famous "thin red line" across the bush-studded Plains of Abraham, just west of the city. Montcalm advanced upon them with five regiments, all in step, and in the next quarter of an hour the fate of Canada was decided. The redcoats stood like statues as the French drew closer—100 yards, 60 yards, 40 yards. Then a command rang out, and—in such perfect unison that it sounded like a single thunderclap—the English muskets crashed. The redcoats advanced four measured paces, halted, fired, advanced another four paces with robot precision—halted, fired again. Then it was all over.

The plain was covered with the fallen French. Montcalm lay mortally wounded, and the rest of his troops were fleeing helter-skelter. Among the British casualties was Wolfe himself. With two bullets through his body, he lived just long enough to hear that he had won. Montcalm died a few hours after him.

Today, overlooking the boardwalk of Québec, you'll find a unique memorial to both these men—a statue commemorating both victor and vanquished of the same battle!

THE U.S. INVASION   The capture of Québec determined the war and left Britain ruler of all North America down to the Mexican border. Yet, oddly enough, this victory generated Britain's worst defeat. For if the French had held Canada, the British government would certainly have been more careful in its treatment of the American colonists.

As it was, the British felt cocksure and decided to make the colonists themselves pay for the outrageous costs of the French and Indian Wars. Hence the taxes slapped on all imports—especially tea—infuriated the colonists to the point of open rebellion against the Crown.

But if the British misjudged the temper of the colonists, the Americans were equally wrong about the mood of the Canadians. Washington felt sure that the French in the north would join the American Revolution, or at least not resist an invasion of American soldiers. He was terribly mistaken on both counts.

The French had little love for either of the English-speaking antagonists. But they were staunch Royalists and devout Catholics, with no sympathy for the "godless" republicans from the south. Only a handful changed sides, and most French Canadians fought grimly shoulder to shoulder with their erstwhile enemies.

Thirty-eight years later, in the War of 1812, another U.S. army marched up the banks of the Richelieu River where it flows from Lake Champlain to the St. Lawrence. And once again the French Canadians stuck by the British and flung back the invaders. The war ended in a draw, but with surprisingly happy results. Britain and the young United States agreed to demilitarize the Great Lakes and to extend their mutual border along the 49th parallel to the Rockies.

LOYALISTS & IMMIGRANTS   One of the side effects of the American Revolution was an influx of English-speaking newcomers for Canada. About 50,000 Americans who had remained faithful to King George, the United Empire Loyalists, migrated to Canada because they were given rough treatment in the United States. They settled mostly in Nova Scotia and began to populate the almost empty shores of what is now New Brunswick.

After the Napoleonic Wars, a regular tide of immigrants came from England, which was going through the early and cruelest stages of the Industrial Revolution. They were fleeing from the new and hideously bleak factory towns, from workhouses, starvation wages, and impoverished Scottish farms. Even the unknown perils of the New World seemed preferable to these blessings of the Dickens era.

By 1850 more than half a million immigrants had arrived, pushing Canada's population above two million. And now the population centers began to shift westward, away from the old seaboard colonies in the east, opening up the territories eventually called Ontario, Manitoba, and Saskatchewan.

With increased population came the demand for confederation, largely because the various colony borders hampered trade. Britain complied rather promptly. In 1867 the British Parliament passed an act creating a federal union out of the colonies of Upper and Lower Canada, Nova Scotia, and New Brunswick. British Columbia hesitated over whether to remain separate, join the United States, or merge with Canada, but finally voted itself in. Remote Newfoundland hesitated longest of all. It remained a distinct colony until 1949, when it became Canada's 10th province.

THE REBELLION OF THE METIS   Geographically, Canada stretched from the Atlantic to the Pacific Ocean, but in reality most of the immense region in between lay beyond the rule of Ottawa, the nation's capital. The endless prairies and forest lands of the West and Northwest were inhabited by about 40,000 people, more than half of them nomadic tribes pushed there by the waves of white settlers from the east. They lived by hunting, fishing, and trapping, depending largely on buffalo for food, clothing, and shelter. As the once enormous herds began to dwindle, life grew increasingly hard for the nomads. Adding to their troubles were whisky traders peddling poisonous rotgut for furs, and packs of outlaws who took what they wanted at gunpoint.

Ordinary law officers were nearly useless in this environment. In 1873 the federal government therefore created a quite extraordinary force: the Northwest Mounted Police, now called the Royal Canadian Mounted Police (and now rarely mounted). The scarlet-coated Mounties earned a legendary reputation for toughness, fairness, and the ability to hunt down wrongdoers. And unlike their American counterparts, they usually brought in prisoners alive.

But even the Mounties couldn't handle the desperate uprising that shook western Saskatchewan in 1885. As the railroad relentlessly pushed across the prairies and the buffalo vanished, the people known as Metis felt they had to fight for their existence. The Metis, offspring of French trappers and native women, were superb hunters and trackers. The westward expansion had driven them from Manitoba to the banks of the Saskatchewan River, where some 6,000 of them now made their last stand against iron rails and wooden farmhouses. They had a charismatic leader in Louis Riel, a man educated enough to teach school and mad enough to think that God wanted him to found a new religion.

With Riel's rebels rose their natural allies, the Plains tribes, under chiefs Poundmaker and Big Bear. Together they were a formidable force. The Metis attacked the Mounted Police at Duck Lake, cut the telegraph wires, and proclaimed an independent republic. Their allies stormed the town of Battleford, then captured and burned Fort Pitt.

The alarmed administration in Ottawa sent an army marching westward under General Middleton, equipped with artillery and Gatling machine guns. The Metis checked them briefly at Fish Creek, but had to fall back on their main village of Batoche. There the last battle of the west took place—long lines of redcoats charging with fixed bayonets, the Metis fighting from house to house, from rifle pits and crude trenches, so short of ammunition that they had to shoot lead buttons instead of bullets.

Batoche fell (you can still see the bullet marks on the houses there) and the rebellion was completely crushed shortly afterward. Louis Riel was tried for treason and murder. Although any court today probably would have found him insane, the Canadian authorities hanged him.

RAILROADS, WHEAT & WAR   The reason that the army was able to crush Riel's rebellion so quickly was also the reason for its outbreak: the Canadian Pacific Railway. The railroad was more than a marvel of engineering—it formed a steel band holding the country together, enabling Canada to live up to its motto, *A Mari Usque ad Mare* ("From Sea to Sea").

Although the free-roaming prairie people hated the iron horse, railroads were vital to Canada's survival as a nation. They had to be pushed through, against all opposition, if the isolated provinces were not to drift into the orbit of the United States and the Dominion cease to exist. As one journalist of the time put it: "The whistle of a locomotive is the true cradle song and anthem of our country."

As the country's transportation system developed, the central provinces emerged as one of the world's biggest breadbaskets. In one decade wheat production zoomed from 56 million bushels to more than 200 million, which put Canada on a par with the United States and Russia as a granary.

And despite the bitterness engendered by the execution of Riel, in the following year Canada elected its first prime minister of French heritage. Sir Wilfrid Laurier had one foot in each ethnic camp and he proved to be a superlative leader—according to some, the best his country ever produced. His term of office, from 1896 to 1911, was a period in which Canada flexed its muscles like a young giant and looked forward to unlimited growth and a century of peaceful prosperity—just like an equally optimistic American neighbor to the south.

With the onset of World War I, the Dominion went to war allied with Britain and likewise tried to fight it on a volunteer basis. It didn't work. The tall, healthy Canadians, together with the Australians, formed the shock troops of the British Empire and earned that honor with torrents of blood. The entire Western Front in France was littered with Canadian bones. The flow of volunteers became a trickle, and in 1917 the Dominion was forced to introduce conscription. The measure ran into violent opposition from the French-speaking minority, who saw conscription as a device to thin out their numbers.

The draft law went through, but it strained the nation's unity almost to the breaking point. The results were ghastly. More than 60,000 Canadians fell in battle, a terrible bloodletting for a country of ¼ million inhabitants. (In World War II, by contrast, Canada lost 40,000 from a population of 11½ million.)

TOWARD WORLD POWER   Between the wars the fortunes of Canada more or less reflected those of the United States, except that Canada was never foolish enough to join the "noble experiment" of Prohibition. Some of its citizens, in fact, waxed rich on the lucrative bootlegging trade across the border.

But the Depression, coupled with disastrous droughts in the western provinces, hit all the harder in Canada. There was no equivalent of Roosevelt's New Deal in the Dominion. The country staggered along from one financial crisis to the next until the outbreak of World War II totally transformed the situation. The war provided the boost Canada needed to join the ranks of the major industrial nations. And the surge of postwar immigration provided the numbers required to work the newly developed industries. From 1941 to 1974 Canada doubled in population and increased its gross national product (GNP) nearly tenfold.

With the discovery of huge uranium deposits in Ontario and Saskatchewan, Canada was in the position to add nuclear energy to its power resources. And the opening of the St. Lawrence Seaway turned Toronto—which lies more than 1,000 miles from the nearest ocean—into a major seaport.

All these achievements propelled Canada into its present position: a powerhouse of manufacturing and trading, with a standard of living to match that of the United States. But, simultaneously, old and never-banished ghosts were raising their heads again.

TROUBLE IN QUÉBEC   As an ethnic enclave the French Canadians had won their battle for survival with flying colors. From their original 65,000 settlers they had grown to more than six million, and had done so without receiving reinforcements from overseas.

The French Canadians had preserved and increased their presence by means of large families, rigid cultural cohesion, and the unifying influence of their Catholic faith. But they had fallen far behind the English-speaking majority economically and politically. Few of them held top positions in industry or finance, and they enjoyed relatively little say in national matters.

What rankled most with them was that Canada never recognized French as a second national language. In other words, the French were expected to be bilingual if they wanted good careers, but the English-speakers got along nicely with just their own tongue. On a general cultural basis, too, the country overwhelmingly reflected Anglo-Saxon attitudes rather than an Anglo-French mixture.

By the early 1960s this discontent led to a dramatic radicalization of Québécois politics. A new separatist movement arose that regarded Québec not as simply one of 10 provinces but as *l'etat du Québec,* a distinct state and people that might, if it chose, break away from the country. The most extreme faction of the movement, the Front de Liberation du Québec (FLQ), was frankly revolutionary and terrorist. It backed its demands with bombs, arson, and murder, culminating in the kidnap-killing of Cabinet Minister Pierre Laporte in October 1970.

The Ottawa government, under Prime Minister Pierre Trudeau, imposed the War Measures Act and moved 10,000 troops into the province. The police used their exceptional powers under the act to break up civil disorders, arrested hundreds of suspects, and caught the murderers of Laporte. And in the provincial elections of 1973, the separatists were badly defeated, winning only six seats from a total of 110.

The crisis calmed down. In some ways its effects were beneficial. The federal government redoubled its efforts to remove the worst grievances of the French Canadians. Federal funds flowed to French schools outside Québec (nearly half the schoolchildren of New Brunswick, for example, are French-speaking). French Canadians were appointed to senior positions. Most important, all provinces were asked to make French an official language, which entailed making signs, government forms, transportation schedules, and other printed matter bilingual. Civil servants had to bone up on French to pass their examinations and the business world began to stipulate bilingualism for men and women aiming at executive positions. All these measures, it should be noted, were already afoot before the turmoil began, but there is no doubt that bloodshed helped to accelerate them.

UNION OR SEPARATION?   Ever since this violent crisis, Canadian politicians of all hues have been trying to patch up some sort of compromise that would enable their country to remain united. They appeared close to success when they formulated the so-called Meech Lake Accord in the 1980s—only to see it destroyed by a whole series of opposition moves stemming not only from French Canadians but also from Native Canadian groups. The separatist Parti Québécois rallied its forces and staged a political comeback. The rift between Québec's French and English speakers is today wider than ever.

Québec's premier set up a commission to study ways to change the province's constitutional relationship with the federal government in Ottawa. This, in turn, aroused the ire of other provinces, which failed to see why Québec should be granted a "special"—meaning privileged—position within Canada. So the proposals, memorandums, and referendums go on and on; each one vetoed by the other camp and none coming closer to a solution.

By now most Canadians are heartily tired of the debate, though nobody seems to have a clear idea how to end it. Some say that secession is the only way out; others favor the Swiss formula of biculturalism and bilingualism. For Québec the breakaway advocated by Francophone hotheads could spell economic disaster. Most of Canada's industrial and financial power is located in the English-speaking provinces. An independent Québec would be a poor country. But all of Canada would be poorer by losing the special flavor and rich cultural heritage imparted by the presence of "La Belle Province."

3 The People

Canada's people are even more diverse than its scenery. In the eastern province of Québec live six million French Canadians, whose motto *Je me souviens*—"I remember"—has kept them "more French than France" through two centuries of Anglo domination. They have transformed Canada into a bilingual country where everything official—including parking tickets and airline passes—comes in two tongues.

The English-speaking majority of the populace is a mosaic rather than a block. Two massive waves of immigration—one before 1914, the other between 1945 and 1972—poured 6^1/$_2$ million assorted Europeans and Americans into the country, providing muscles and skills as well as a kaleidoscope of cultures. Thus Nova Scotia is as Scottish as haggis and kilts, Vancouver has a Germanic core alongside a Chinatown, the plains of Manitoba are sprinkled with the onion-shaped domes of Ukrainian churches, and Ontario offers Italian street markets and a Shakespeare festival at—yes, Stratford, Ontario.

You can attend a Native Canadian tribal assembly, a Chinese New Year dragon parade, an Inuit spring celebration, a German Bierfest, a Highland gathering, or a Slavic folk dance. There are group settlements on the prairies where the working parlance is Danish or Czech or Hungarian, and entire villages that speak Icelandic. For Canada has not been a "melting pot" in the American sense, but rather has sought "unity through diversity" as a national ideal.

NATIVE CANADIANS   There are actually more Native Canadians living in Canada today than existed at the time of the first white settlements. Anthropologists have estimated that the original population was about 200,000. The native population began to decline with the arrival of the Europeans. By the early 20th century it was down to almost half, and common belief labeled the native peoples a dying race. At the last census, however, the total number had reached 282,000.

Ethnically Canada's native peoples are the same as some tribes in the United States. Some tribes, such as the Cree, Sioux, and Blackfoot, are found on both sides of the border. In Canada they belong to 10 distinct linguistic groups, subdivided into widely differing local dialects. Their customs, religion, and methods of hunting and warfare were very similar to those of tribes near the border in the United States. The treatment they received, however, was rather different.

In the 1870s—before most white settlers reached the West—the Canadian government began to negotiate a series of treaties with the prairie tribes. By the end of the decade most of the western tribes had agreed to treaties in which they surrendered their lands in return for guaranteed reservations, small cash payments for each individual member, supplies of seeds and tools, and assistance in changing over to farming for a livelihood. By and large, with a few inglorious exceptions, those treaties were kept.

The Canadian government wielded much greater control over the white settlers than its counterpart in Washington. It was thus able to prevent the continual incursions by gold prospectors, buffalo hunters, railroad companies, and squatters that sparked most of the Indian wars south of the border. The Mounties, as distinct from the U.S. Cavalry, actually protected native tribes. As the Blackfoot chief Crowfoot said: "The police have shielded us from bad men as the feathers of birds protect them from the winter frosts. If the police had not come, very few of us would have been left today."

The decline of the native population was due mainly to sickness brought in by the whites. In addition, tens of thousands of erstwhile nomadic hunters simply couldn't bear a life tied to one patch of soil; they died from sheer discouragement, unwilling to continue an existence that appeared joyless and stale.

Today the country has 574 separate Native Canadian communities, known as "bands." A few—a very few—of them still roam the northern regions. The others share 2,110 reserves, although less than two-thirds actually live on reservations. Today they are successful farmers, nurses, builders, secretaries, doctors, teachers, clergy, salespeople, and industrial workers, both on and off the reserves. In 1973 the government accepted a proposal by the National Indian Brotherhood by which increasing numbers of bands now manage their own schools. Instead of trying to erase their past, the new school curricula include history and native-language courses for children who have almost forgotten their native tongues.

This is only fair, since the very name *Canada* derives from the Huron word for settlement, *kanata*.

INUIT   *Inuit* means "people," and that is what the Canadian Eskimos call themselves. So remote was their native habitat, so completely isolated from the rest of the world, that they were unaware that any people except themselves existed.

The Eskimos are a unique people, the Canadian branch even more so than the others. There are only around 80,000 Eskimos in the entire world, forming part of four nations: Russia, the United States, Canada, and Denmark (in Greenland, which is a Danish possession). This makes the Eskimos the only natives of the same ethnic group to live in both Asia and America.

Some 22,000 Inuit live in Canada today, and we have no idea how many there might have been originally. They inhabited the far north, the very last portion of the country to be explored, much later than the other Arctic lands of the globe. While their cousins elsewhere were trading with the white settlers, the Inuit initially had limited contact with Europeans.

The Inuit were traditionally coastal people who lived by fishing and by hunting seals, whales, and polar bears. These animals supplied their food, clothing, light, and heat (in the form of blubber-fueled lamps and stoves), and were used to their last shred of skin. The Inuit's earliest contact, therefore, was with whalers, frequently with tragic results. The Inuit were gentle people, intensely hospitable and so averse to violence that their language had no term for war.

When the first British and American whaling ships touched Baffin Bay in the 1820s, they found that the Inuit had no conception of private property, of food and clothing that was not shared with whoever needed it. The Inuit marveled at the white sailors' wooden whaleboats, firearms, iron tools, and glass bottles—none of which they had ever seen. They had no idea of the dangers associated with these wonders.

Murder and rape were the least of them. Liquor was far more destructive, but worst of all were the diseases the whalers introduced. For all its harshness, the Arctic was a healthy region, free of bacteria. The Inuit might starve and freeze to death, but they rarely succumbed to illness. As a result their bodies had no resistance to the measles, smallpox, and tuberculosis that the whites brought in along with their rum and gadgetry.

The Inuit—particularly their children—died like flies. The only doctors available to them were a handful of missionaries, usually with very limited medical supplies. Today's Inuit, therefore, are a race of survivors, the strain that somehow battled through a century that killed uncounted numbers of their kind.

It was not until the 1950s that the Canadian government took serious steps to assure the Inuit their rightful place in their Arctic homeland. As air transportation and radio communications broke down the isolation of the far north, the government introduced improved educational, health, and welfare services. The Inuit are now full citizens in every respect—not in name only—electing members of the Territorial Council of the Northwest Territories and running their own communities.

They have ceased to be nomads and have moved into permanent settlements. But unlike the prairie tribes, the Inuit are still basically hunters, although nowadays they use rifles instead of the traditional harpoons. But don't compare their hunting with weekend activity. The Inuit hunt in order to eat, and no one is more ecologically conscious than they are. Everything in their prey is used—a walrus represents a miniature supermarket to an Inuit—and they kill nothing for pleasure and not one animal more than is absolutely necessary.

The Inuit Tapirisat (Inuit Brotherhood) is their nonpolitical organization dedicated to preserving the Inuktetut language and culture and to helping them achieve full participation in Canada's society. This would include legal rights to some of the enormous lands the Inuit once roamed and used, but without establishing fixed borders for their domain. Some of these areas have been found to contain valuable deposits of oil, natural gas, and minerals, which makes the question of ownership more than merely academic.

If you want a glimpse of the Inuit soul, look at their art, which you'll find in stores all over Canada. Their artistry shouldn't surprise you: The Inuit are perhaps the greatest needle (fish bone) experts in the world, and their completely waterproof sealskin kayak canoe is possibly the best-designed vehicle in marine history.

But Inuit carvings of people and animals have a quality all their own. They are imbued with a sense of movement, a feeling for anatomy, almost a smell. Their expressions are so hauntingly lifelike, yet so curiously abstract, that they give you an eerie notion of having seen them before in some strange dream.

4 Wilderness & Wonder: Canada's National & Provincial Parks

by Bill McRae

THE NATIONAL PARKS

Canada is in the process of creating several new national parks in the Far North. Recently accorded agreements with the region's native peoples call for the development of parks on part of the land that was once administered by the federal government. Additionally, Parks Canada operates hundreds of Historic Parks across the country, which feature historic buildings or sites (often with summer programs and activities). But these exceptions aside, we've listed below the national parks, offering a quick rundown on the defining characteristics of each.

Kejimkujik National Park (Nova Scotia): There are two parts to the park. The first is a wilderness of rolling hills and lakes in the heart of Nova Scotia. The park's other section preserves a stretch of wild and undeveloped southern coastline flanked by steep cliffs. This section of the park protects the rare shorebird, the piping plover, and marine animals.

Cape Breton Highlands National Park (Nova Scotia): This far-flung coastal wilderness, similar in terrain and grandeur to the Scottish Highlands, appealed to hearty Scots who founded small settlements among the mountains. The Cabot Trail highway rings the park, with tremendous views down from pink granite coastal cliffs.

Fundy National Park (New Brunswick): Covered bridges, the world's highest tides, and plenty of hiking trails characterize this small coastal park on the southern New Brunswick coast.

Kouchibouguac National Park (New Brunswick): A small, low-key park located on the Acadian Coast, Kouchibouguac features beaches, bike paths, and hikes to salt marshes and offshore dunes. Swimmers will enjoy the park's pleasant lagoon waters, known as the warmest north of the Carolinas.

Prince Edward Island National Park (Prince Edward Island): This park combines a popular stretch of sandy beach on the Gulf of St. Lawrence, and Green Gables House, a Victorian estate that served as the setting for the popular children's tale *Anne of Green Gables*.

Gros Morne National Park (Newfoundland): A spectacular preserve with glacier-carved mountains and fjords, Gros Morne stretches along the west coast of Newfoundland. Hiking trails lead to Western Brook Pond, which is in fact a freshwater fjord lined by cliffs towering 2,000 feet high.

Terra Nova National Park (Newfoundland): A scenic spot on the Labrador Sea, Terra Nova is covered with dense coniferous forests that provide backcountry adventure. Sea kayakers come here to probe the multitudes of tiny inlets and coves found along the headlands.

La Mauricie National Park (Québec): A maze of lakes, rivers, and deep forest, La Mauricie is popular with canoe-campers who paddle through the extensive natural water system much as did the early Indians and French trappers. In winter, 50 miles of cross-country ski trails are groomed, with warming huts every three miles.

Mingan Archipelago National Park (Québec): A string of 47 limestone islands along the northern shores of the Gulf of St. Lawrence, Mingan is uninhabited except by sea birds and marine mammals.

Forillon National Park (Québec): Located at the end of the Gaspé Peninsula, this park is famous for its 600-foot-high limestone cliffs that drop into the Gulf of St. Lawrence. Hiking trails lead to dizzying overlooks; watch for whales in summer months.

St. Lawrence Islands National Park (Ontario): Canada's smallest national park, these 23 islands in the St. Lawrence River are part of the larger Thousand Islands area. The tiny, flower-covered islands in the park are mostly undeveloped, and offer free campsites to those with boats.

Pukaskwa National Park (Ontario): Ontario's largest national park, Pukaskwa is located in the boreal forests on the north shore of Lake Superior. Preserved as a wilderness, it can be accessed by boat only.

Bruce Peninsula National Park (Ontario): The rugged, 50-mile Bruce Peninsula juts into Lake Huron, and is popular with long-distance hikers on the Bruce Trail. From a point near the park's headquarters at Tobermory, ferries leave for Manitoulin Island.

Georgian Bay Islands National Park (Ontario): A collection of 50 islands in Lake Huron's Georgian Bay, this park is popular with boaters, who are able to access the more remote islands. Water taxis are available to Beausoleil Island, the park headquarters.

Point Pelee National Park (Ontario): Point Pelee is famous for its bird-watching (this peninsula of sand in Lake Erie is at the junction of two migratory flyways) and for the fall gathering of monarch butterflies, which flock here before their annual migration.

Riding Mountain National Park (Manitoba): Manitoba's only national park, Riding Mountain is a habitat crossroads where prairie, boreal forest, and deciduous life zones intersect. Wolf, moose, bison, and elk are found here in great numbers. The park is popular with summertime campers, who fish and boat in the park's many lakes.

Grasslands National Park (Saskatchewan): The first national park to preserve the native prairie ecosystem, this park in southern Saskatchewan protects the only remaining black-tailed prairie dog colony in Canada. Other wildlife includes coyotes, deer, pronghorn, and many bird species.

Prince Albert National Park (Saskatchewan): Located where the southern prairies give way to the lake country, this national park is the nesting ground for one of Canada's largest colonies of white pelicans; moose, wolf, caribou, and bison also live here. The early environmentalist and author Grey Owl lived here in the 1930s; his cabin still stands on Ajawaan Lake.

Waterton Lakes National Park (Alberta): Joined with Montana's Glacier National Park, this international peace park is famed for its beautiful lakes glimmering in glacial basins between finlike mountain ranges. The most popular activity is the boat ride from the Canadian to the U.S. sides of the park.

Banff National Park (Alberta): The most popular tourist destination in all of Canada, Banff Park is extremely beautiful and often very crowded. The views onto towering, cliff-sided mountains are unforgettable; easy hiking trails to lakes and alpine meadows make this a popular park for families. Banff Townsite and Lake Louise Village provide world-class accommodations and boutiques.

Jasper National Park (Alberta): The largest park in the Canadian Rockies, Jasper sits astride the central crest of the continent. The Columbia Icefields, natural hot springs, shimmering glacial lakes, soaring mountain peaks, and superb long-distance hiking trails make this one of the gems of the Canadian Park system.

Yoho National Park (British Columbia): Yoho means "awe" in Cree and the park's many lakes, towering peaks and mighty waterfalls (Takakkawa Falls drops 1,200 feet) certainly provoke it. The Kicking Horse River is one of the best white-water rivers in the Rockies, and glacier-fed Emerald and O'Hara lakes are famed beauty spots.

Glacier National Park (British Columbia): Heavy snowfalls maintain more than 400 glaciers and snowfields in this park located at the crest of the rugged Columbia Mountains; more than 14% of the park's landscape is covered in permanent ice.

Kootenay National Park (British Columbia): A collection of natural marvels on the western slopes of the Rockies's Main Range, Kootenay is noted for its rugged lime-stone canyons, Radium Hot Springs resort, and highly colored mineral springs.

Elk Island National Park (Alberta): A major preserve of the wildlife that once roamed the northern prairies, Elk Island is located just east of Edmonton. Moose, two species of bison, a large number of elk, beaver, and other species are all easily viewed from hiking trails.

Wood Buffalo National Park (Alberta/Northwest Territory): The largest national park in the world, Wood Buffalo protects many animal species, including the once-feared-extinct wood buffalo and the whooping crane. The park also preserves unique ecosystems, like the Peace-Athabasca river delta and a natural salt plain.

Pacific Rim National Park (British Columbia): The only national park on Vancouver Island, Pacific Rim is comprised of three different units: Long Beach; Broken Group Islands, an archipelago of more than 100 islets in Barcley Sound; and the West Coast Trail, a long distance trail that skirts the rugged coastline.

Gwaii Haanas National Park (British Columbia): Located on the southern end of the Queen Charlotte Archipelago, Gwaii Haanas is jointly administered by Parks Canada and the Haida Nation. The 138-island park is filled with ancient village and totem sites sacred to the Haida.

Mount Revelstoke National Park (British Columbia): Roads lead to the top of Mt. Revelstoke, a peak in the Selkirk Mountains. Hiking trails lead into inland rain forests and alpine meadows.

Kluane National Park (Yukon): Canada's highest peaks and largest non-polar ice caps are found in this rugged park on the Gulf of Alaska. Long-distance trails lead to enormous valley glaciers; the park's mighty rivers are popular with white-water rafters.

Nahanni National Park (Northwest Territories): Known throughout the world for its superlative rafting and canoeing, Nahanni is also famous for massive Virginia Falls, twice as high as Niagara.

Ivvavik National Park (Yukon): Fronting onto the Arctic Ocean, and accessible only by small aircraft, Ivvavik was formed to protect the porcupine caribou herd. Approximately 10 percent of the world's caribou live here.

Vuntut National Park (Yukon): Located just south of Ivvavik National Park, Vuntut is a habitat preserve for caribou, grizzly bear, and other Arctic animals. The park was the hunting grounds for the native Gwitchin, who called the area Old Crow Flats.

Aulavik National Park (Northwest Territories): Banks Island is home to the largest musk oxen herds in the world, and this Arctic island park is designed to preserve their fragile tundra habitat.

Ellesmere Island National Park (Northwest Territories): The most northerly and second largest of Canada's national parks, this remote and rugged wilderness of tundra, glacier, and mountains is literally at the top of the world.

Auyuittuq National Park (Northwest Territories): Auyuittaq means "the land that never melts," and much of this precipitously rugged, fjord-bit park on Baffin Island is covered with a permanent ice cap. A long-distance fjord-to-fjord hiking trail leads across the park, accessing some of the world's longest rock faces, popular with climbers.

THE BEST OF THE PROVINCIAL PARKS

Canada has hundreds of provincial parks (British Columbia alone has 330), many of them simply campgrounds or public beaches in popular recreation areas. Others contain sites of great scenic or historical interest and definitely deserve a detour. Below are some that we consider outstanding.

Mont Orford (Québec): Always popular with family camping groups, this mountainous park is ablaze with autumn color each year. The hiking paths through hardwood forest that are so popular in summer become cross-country ski trails when the snow falls.

Algonquin Provincial Park (Ontario): A wilderness of lakes and deep forest, Algonquin is perfect for extended canoe-camping trips, with nearly 1,000 miles of charted routes.

Dinosaur Provincial Park (Alberta): The Badlands of Alberta are filled with Cretaceous-era dinosaur bone fossils, and this park protects one of the richest quarry areas. Visitors can tour, or join, a dig, and watch fossils being prepared at the visitors center.

Head-Smashed-In Buffalo Jump (Alberta): The Plains Indians once stampeded bison off cliffs as part of their yearly food gathering cycle. This interpretive center preserves one of these cliffs, and relates the natural and human history of the area.

Mt. Robson (British Columbia): The highest peak in the Canadian Rockies, Mt. Robson towers above glacial lakes and roaring rivers just west of Jasper National Park.

Strathcona (British Columbia): Strathcona is the largest wilderness park on Vancouver Island, with lots of skiing and hiking. The high point, though, is the two-day hiking trail into Dalla Falls; at more than 1,440 feet, they're the highest in North America.

Planning a Trip to Canada 3

Reading this chapter before you set out can save you money, time, and headaches. Here's where you'll find travel know-how, such as when to visit, what documents you'll need, and where to get more information. These basics can make the difference between a smooth ride and a bumpy one.

1 Visitor Information & Entry Requirements

VISITOR INFORMATION   The various provincial offices, listed below, dispense visitor information. Canadian consulates do *not* handle such information.

- Alberta Economic Development and Tourism, Commerce Place, 10155 102 St., Edmonton, AB, T5J 4L6 (☎ 800/661-8888).
- Tourism British Columbia, Parliament Building, Victoria, BC, V8V 1X4 (☎ 604/387-1642 or 800/663-6000).
- Travel Manitoba, 155 Carlton St., Winnipeg, MB, RC3 3H8 (☎ 800/665-0040).
- Tourism New Brunswick, P.O. Box 12345, Fredericton, NB, E3B 5C3 (☎ 800/561-0123).
- Newfoundland and Labrador, Dept. of Tourism, Culture and Recreation, P.O. Box 8700, St. John's, NF, A1B 4J6 (☎ 709/729-2806 or 800/563-6353).
- Nova Scotia Dept. of Tourism, P.O. Box 130, Halifax, NS, B3J 2M7 (☎ 800/565-0000).
- Northwest Territories Economic Development and Tourism, P.O. Box 1320, Yellowknife, NWT, X1A 2L9 (☎ 800/661-0788).
- Ontario Travel, Queen's Park, Toronto, ON, M7A 2E5 (☎ 800/668-2746).
- Prince Edward Island, Tourism P.E.I., West Royalty Industrial Park, Charlottetown, PEI, C1E 1B0 (☎ 800/463-4734).
- Tourisme Québec, C.P. 979, Montréal, PQ, H3C 2W3 (☎ 800/363-7777).
- Tourism Saskatchewan, 500-1900 Albert St., Regina, SK, S4P 4L9 (☎ 800/667-7191).
- Tourism Yukon, P.O. Box 2703, Whitehorse, YK, Y1A 2C6 (☎ 403/667-5340).

For general information about Canada's national parks, contact **Canadian Heritage**, Publications Unit, Room 10H2, Hull, Québec, K1A 0M5 (☎ 819/994-6625; fax 819/953-8770).

ENTRY REQUIREMENTS U.S. citizens or permanent U.S. residents, or British, Australian, New Zealand, or Irish nationals, require neither passports nor visas. You should, however, carry some identifying papers such as a passport or birth, baptismal, or voter's certificate to show your citizenship. Permanent U.S. residents who are not U.S. citizens must have their Alien Registration Cards.

Customs regulations are very generous in most respects, but get pretty complicated when it comes to firearms, plants, meats, and pet animals. Fishing tackle poses no problems, but the bearer must possess a nonresident license for the province or territory where he or she plans to use it. You can bring in free of duty up to 50 cigars, 200 cigarettes, and two pounds of tobacco, providing you're over 16 years of age. You are also allowed 40 ounces of liquor or wine.

One important point for teen travelers: Any person under 19 years of age requires a letter from a parent or guardian granting him or her permission to travel to Canada. The letter must state the traveler's name and duration of the trip. It is therefore essential that teenagers carry proof of identity; otherwise their letter is useless at the border.

For more detailed information concerning Customs regulations, write to: Customs and Excise, Connaught Building, Sussex Drive, Ottawa, ON, K1A 0L5.

2 Money

Canadians use dollars and cents, but with a very pleasing balance: The Canadian dollar is worth around 75¢ in U.S. money, give or take a couple of points' daily variation. So your American money gets you 25% or 26% more the moment you exchange it for local currency. And since the price of many goods is roughly on a par with the United States, the difference is real, not imaginary. (Before you get too excited, however, remember that sales taxes are astronomical.) You can bring in or take out any amount of money, but if you are importing or exporting sums of $5,000 or more, you must file a report of the transaction with U.S. Customs. Most tourist establishments in Canada will take U.S. cash, but for the best rate you should change your funds into Canadian currency.

If you do spend American money at Canadian establishments, you should understand how the conversion is done. Often there will be a sign by the cash register that reads "U.S. Currency 20%." This 20% is the "premium," and it means that for every U.S. greenback you hand over, the cashier will see it as $1.20 in Canadian dollars. Thus, for a $8 tab, you need pay only $6.40 in U.S. bills.

When you cash U.S. traveler's checks at a bank, most banks will charge you a $2 fee per transaction (not per check). Hotels, restaurants, and shops don't charge fees as a rule, but their exchange rate may be somewhat lower than the current figure.

The best rate of exchange is usually through use of an ATM with a bank card. Not only is it convenient not to have to carry cash and checks, but you will get the best commercial rate. It's always wise to bring in sufficient Canadian cash to pay for an initial cab or bus and a meal.

A final word: Canada has no $1 bills. The lowest paper denomination is $2. Single bucks come in brass coins bearing the picture of a loon—hence their nickname "loonies."

The Canadian Dollar & the U.S. Dollar

Unless stated otherwise, **the prices cited in this guide are given in Canadian dollars,** which is good news for U.S. travelers because the Canadian dollar is worth 25% less than the American dollar, but buys nearly as much. As we go to press, $1 Canadian is worth 75¢ U.S., which means that your $100-a-night hotel room will cost only U.S. $75, and your $6 breakfast costs only U.S. $4.50.

Here's a quick table of equivalents:

Canadian $	U.S. $
1	0.75
5	3.75
10	7.50
20	15.00
50	37.50
80	60.00
100	75.00

3 When to Go

THE CLIMATE   In southern and central Canada the weather is the same as in the northern United States. As you head north the climate becomes arctic, meaning long and extremely cold winters, brief and surprisingly warm summers (with lots of flies), and magical springs.

As a general rule, spring runs from mid-March to mid-May, summer from mid-May to mid-September, fall from mid-September to mid-November, and winter from mid-November to mid-March. Pick the season best suited to your tastes and temperament, and remember that your car should be winterized through March and that snow sometimes falls as late as April (in 1995 a foot of snow blanketed Prince Edward Island in May). September and October bring autumn foliage and great opportunities for photographers.

Evenings tend to be cool everywhere, particularly on or near water. In late spring and early summer you'll need a supply of insect repellent if you're planning bush travel or camping.

With the huge size of some provinces and territories, you naturally get considerable climate variations inside their borders. Québec, for instance, sprawls all the way from the temperate south to the Arctic, and the weather varies accordingly. British Columbia shows the slightest changes: It rarely goes above the 70s in summer or drops below the 30s in winter.

HOLIDAYS   National holidays are celebrated throughout the country, meaning that all government facilities close down, as well as banks, but some department stores and a scattering of smaller shops stay open. If the holiday falls on a weekend the following Monday is observed.

Canadian holidays include New Year's Day, Good Friday, Easter Monday, Victoria Day (in mid- to late May), Canada Day (July 1), Labor Day, Thanksgiving (in mid-October), Remembrance Day (November 11), Christmas Day, and Boxing Day (December 26). In addition, you may run into provincial holidays.

4 The Outdoor Adventure Planner

by Bill McRae

SPORTS A TO Z

BIKE TOURING   Most of Canada's highways are wide and well maintained, and thus well suited for long-distance bicycle touring. Most resort areas have ample supplies of rental bikes, so you don't have to worry about transporting your own (it's a good idea to call ahead and reserve a bike, though). You'll need to be in good shape to embark on a long bike trip, and able to deal with minor bike repair.

While most hiking trails are closed to mountain bikes, other trails are developed specifically for backcountry biking. Ask at national park and national forest information centers for a map of mountain bike trails.

Probably the most rewarding biking anywhere is in Banff and Jasper national parks. The Icefields Parkway, which runs between the parks, is an eye-popping route past soaring peaks and glaciers, and is wide and well graded.

CANOEING & KAYAKING   Much of Canada was first explored by canoe, as low-lying lakes and slow rivers form vast waterway systems across the central and northern parts of the country. Canoes are still excellent for exploring the backcountry. Several-day canoe-camping trips through wilderness waterways make popular summer and early fall expeditions for small groups; you'll see lots of wildlife (especially mosquitoes) and keep as gentle a pace as you like. Generally speaking, the longer the trip, the more experience you should have with a canoe and with wilderness conditions (dealing with weather, wildlife, and chance of injury). Lake-filled Manitoba is a good place to plan a canoe trip.

DOG-SLED TRIPS   Just imagine taking a traditional dog sled out into the Arctic ice floes and snowy tundra. Outfitters in the north run several-day trips to see the aurora borealis in early spring, and in late spring offer trips out to the floe edge where wildlife viewing is best: This is your best chance to see a polar bear. You'll get a turn at driving the dog team and will sleep in comfort in special room-sized tents heated with small stoves (no igloos!). Outfitters will usually provide all the gear necessary for the weather, though you should be prepared to get a little cold. Outfitters on Baffin Island provide dog-sled trips ranging from part-day to a week out on the tundra amid dramatic mountain and fjord scenery; February through May are the best months.

HIKING   Almost every national and provincial park in Canada is webbed with hiking trails, ranging from easy, interpretive nature hikes to long-distance trails into the backcountry. Late summer and early fall is a good time to plan a walking holiday, since spring comes late to much of Canada—trails in the high country may be snowbound until July.

Most parks have developed free hiking and trail information, as well as information on accessible trails for people with mobility concerns. Before setting out, be sure to request this information and buy a good map. If you're taking a long trip, make sure to evaluate your fitness and equipment before you leave; once in the backcountry, there's no way out except on foot, so make sure that your boots fit and that you understand the risks you are undertaking.

Although there are great trails and magnificent scenery across Canada, for many people the Canadian Rockies, with their abundance of parks and developed trail systems, provide the country's finest hiking.

FISHING   Angling is another sport enjoyed across the entire country. The famed salmon fisheries along both the Atlantic and Pacific coasts face highly restricted catch limits in most areas, and outright bans on fishing in others. However, not all species of salmon on all rivers are threatened, and rules governing fishing change quickly, so check locally with fishing outfitters to find out if a season will open while you are visiting. Other species are not so heavily restricted and probably make a better focus for a fishing-oriented vacation. Trout are found throughout Canada, some reaching great size in the thousands of lakes in the north country; northern pike and walleye are also wary fish that grow to massive size in the north. The Arctic char, a cousin of the salmon, is an anadromous fish that runs in the mighty rivers that feed into the Arctic Ocean; char fishing is often combined with other backcountry adventures by Arctic outfitters.

Fishing in Canada is regulated either by local government or by tribes, and appropriate licenses are necessary. Angling for some fish is regulated by season; in some areas, catch-and-release fishing is enforced. Be sure to check with local authorities before casting your line.

Perhaps Canada's most famous fishing hole is Great Slave Lake. This deep and massive lake is home to enormous lake trout and northern pike; the latter can reach lengths over six feet. You'll want to plan a trip with an outfitter, as weather conditions change rapidly up here, and maneuvering small craft can be very dangerous.

HORSEBACK RIDING   Holidays on horseback have a long pedigree in western Canada. Most outfitters and guest ranches offer a variety of riding options. Easiest are short rides that take a morning or afternoon; on these, you'll be given an easy-going horse and sufficient instruction to make you feel comfortable no matter what your previous riding ability. Longer pack trips take riders off into the backcountry on a several-day guided expedition, with lodging either in tents or at rustic camps. These trips are best for those who don't mind "roughing it": You'll probably go a day or two without showers or flush toilets, and you'll end up saddle sore and sunburned. While these trips are generally open to riders with varying degrees of experience, it's a good idea to spend some time on horseback before heading out: You get very sore if you haven't been in a saddle for a while. The Canadian Rockies in Alberta are filled with guest ranches that offer a wide range of horseback activities.

SEA KAYAKING   Though it may seem like a newer sport, sea kayaking is in fact a very ancient activity: The Inuit have used hide-covered kayaks for centuries. New lightweight kayaks make it possible to transport these crafts to remote areas and to explore previously inaccessible areas along sheltered coastlines; kayaks are especially good for wildlife viewing. Most coastal towns in British Columbia will have both kayak rentals and instruction, as well as guided trips. Handling a kayak isn't as easy as it looks, and you'll want to have plenty of experience in sheltered coves before heading out onto the surf. Be sure to know the tide schedule and weather forecast before setting out, as well as what the coastal rock formations are. You'll need to be comfortable on the water and ready to get wet, as well as a strong swimmer. One of the best places in the world to practice sea kayaking is in the sheltered bays, islands, and inlets along the coast of British Columbia.

SKIING   It's no wonder that Canada, a mountainous country with heavy snowfall, is one of the world's top ski destinations. If you've never skied before, then you've got a basic choice between the speed and thrills of downhill skiing, or the quieter, more Zen-like pleasure of cross-country skiing. Both sports are open to all ages, though downhill skiing is less forgiving of older bones and joints, and carries a higher price tag: A day on the slopes, with rental gear and lift ticket, can easily top $80.

For **downhill skiing,** the Canadian Rockies are the primary destination. The 1988 Winter Olympics were held at Nakiska, just outside of Banff National Park, and the park itself is home to three other ski areas, including Lake Louise, the country's largest. If you're just learning to ski, or are skiing with the family, then the easier slopes at Mystic Ridge and Norquay are made to order. At all these ski areas, instruction, rentals, and day-care are available, and world-class lodging is available at Banff and Lake Louise. The slopes are usually open from November through May.

The dry, heavy snows of eastern Canada make this the best destination for a **cross-country skiing** vacation. The Laurentians, north of Québec, are a range of low mountains with many ski trails and small resort towns with rural French-Canadian charm. The best skiing is from January through March.

WHITE-WATER RAFTING   Charging down a mountain river in a rubber raft is one of the most popular adventures for many people visiting Canada's western mountains. Trips range from day-long excursions that demand little of a participant other than sitting tight to long-distance trips through remote backcountry where all members of the crew are expected to hoist a paddle through the rapids. Risk doesn't correspond to length of trip: Individual rapids and water conditions can make even a short trip a real adventure. On long trips, you'll be camping in tents and spending evenings by a campfire. Even on short trips, plan on getting wet; it's not unusual to get thrown out of a raft, so you should be comfortable in water and a good swimmer if you're floating an adventurous river (outfitters will always provide lifejackets).

Jasper National Park is a major center for short yet thrilling white-water trips. For a week-long white-water adventure in a wilderness setting, contact an outfitter about trips through Nahanni National Park.

SHOULD YOU USE AN OUTFITTER OR PLAN YOUR OWN TRIP?

A basic consideration for most people who embark on an adventure vacation is time versus money. If you have time on your hands and have basic skills in dealing with sports and the outdoors, then planning your own trip can be fun and satisfying. On the other hand, making one phone call and writing one check makes a lot more sense if you don't have a lot of time and lack the background to safely get you where you want to go.

Getting There & Equipment Transportation   In general, the more remote the destination, the more you should consider an outfitter. In many parts of Canada, simply getting to the area where your trip begins can require a great deal of planning. Frequently outfitters will have their own airplanes or boats, or work in conjunction with someone who does. These transportation costs are usually included in the price of an excursion, and are usually cheaper than the same flight or boat trip on a chartered basis.

The same rule applies to equipment rental. Getting your raft or canoe to an out-of-the-way lake can be an adventure in itself. But hire an outfitter and they'll take care of the hassle.

Another option is to use an outfitter to "package" your trip. Some outfitters offer their services to organize air charters and provide equipment for a fee, but leave you to mastermind the trip.

Safety   Much of Canada is very remote and given to extremes in weather. What might be considered a casual camping trip or boating excursion in more populated or temperate areas can become life-threatening in the Canadian backcountry—which often starts right at the edge of town. Almost all outfitters are certified as first-aid providers, and most will carry two-way radios in case there's a need to call for help. Local outfitters also know the particular hazards of the areas where they lead trips.

In some areas, like the Arctic, where hazards range from freakish weather, ice floe movements, and polar bears, outfitters are nearly mandatory.

Other People Most outfitters will only lead groups out on excursions after signing up a minimum number of participants. While this is usually a financial consideration for the outfitter, for the participants this can be both good and bad news. Traveling with the right people can add to the trip's enjoyment, but the wrong traveling companions can lead to exasperation and disappointment. If you're sensitive to other peoples' idiosyncrasies, ask the potential outfitter specific questions regarding who else is going on the trip.

HOW TO SELECT AN OUTFITTER

An outfitter will be responsible for your safety and your enjoyment of the trip, so make certain that you choose one wisely.

All outfitters should be licensed or accredited by the province, and be happy to provide you with proof. This means that they are bonded, carry the necessary insurance, and have money and organizational wherewithal to register with the province. This rules out fly-by-night operations and college students who've decided to set up business for the summer. If you're just starting to plan an excursion, ask the provincial tourist authority for its complete list of licensed outfitters.

Often a number of outfitters offer similar trips. When you've narrowed down your choice, call and talk to the outfitters in question. Ask questions, and try to get a sense of who these people are; you'll be spending a lot of time with them, so make sure you feel comfortable. If you have special interests, like bird or wildlife watching, be sure to mention those interests to your potential outfitter. If you establish that both you and your outfitter share an interest in Native American lore, for instance, then the chances are good that you'll have other things in common. A good outfitter will also take your interests into account when planning a trip.

If there's a wide disparity in prices between outfitters for the same trip, find out what makes the difference. Some companies economize on food. If you don't mind having cold cuts for each meal of your week-long canoe expedition, then perhaps the least expensive outfitter is okay. However, if you prefer a cooked meal, or alcoholic beverages, or choice of entrees, then be prepared to pay more. On a long trip, it might be worth it to you.

Ask how many years an outfitter has been in business, and how long your particular escort has guided this trip. While a start-up outfitting service can be perfectly fine, you should know what level of experience you are buying. If you have questions, especially for longer or more dangerous trips, ask for referrals.

OUTFITTERS & ADVENTURE TRAVEL OPERATORS

All outfitters should be licensed by the province, and local tourist offices can provide listings of outfitters who operate in the areas you intend to visit. Most outfitters offer trips in a specific geographic areas only, though some larger outfitters package trips across the country. In the chapters that follow, we'll recommend lots of local operators and tell you about the outings they run. We've found a few, though, that operate in more than one region of Canada.

Whitewolf Adventure Expeditions, 1355 Citadel Dr. no. 41, Port Coquitlam, BC, V3C 5X6 (☎ 800/661-6659), offers canoe and white-water trips in rivers across northern and western Canada.

Canusa Cycle Tours, P.O. Box 45, Okotoks, AB, T0L 1T0 (☎ 403/560-5859), offers guided cycle tours along some of Canada's most scenic highways.

Canada North Outfitting, P.O. Box 3100, 87 Mills St., Almonte, ON, K0A 1A0 (☎ 613/256-4057; fax 613/256-4512), offers fishing and hiking trips in several locations in the Arctic, including Ellesmere National Park.

WHAT TO PACK

Be sure that it's clearly established between you and your outfitter what you are responsible for bringing along. If you need to bring a sleeping bag, find out what weight of bag is suggested for the conditions you'll encounter. If you have any special dietary requirements, bring them along.

While it's fun and relatively easy to amass the equipment for a backcountry expedition, none of the equipment will do you any good unless you know how to use it. Even though compasses aren't particularly accurate in the north, bring one along and know how to use it. If you're trekking on your own, bring along a first aid kit.

For all summer trips in Canada, make sure to bring along insect repellent, as mosquitoes are particularly numerous and hungry in the north. If you know you're heading into particularly bad mosquito country, consider buying specialized hats with mosquito netting attached. Sunglasses are a must, even above the Arctic Circle. The further north you go in summer, the longer the sun stays up; the low angle of the sun can be particularly annoying. In winter, the glare off snow can cause sun blindness. For the same reasons, sunscreen is a surprising necessity.

Summer weather is very changeable in Canada. If you're planning outdoor activities, be sure to bring along wet weather gear even in high summer. The more exposure you'll have to the elements, the more you should consider bringing along high-end Gortex and artificial fleece outerwear. The proper gear can make the difference between a miserable time and a satisfying adventure.

If you're traveling in Canada in winter, you'll want to have the best winter-weight coat, gloves, and boots that you can afford. A coat with a hood is especially important, as Arctic winds can blow for days at a time.

5 Getting There

BY PLANE   Canada is served by almost all the international air carriers. The major international airports in the east are in Halifax, Toronto, and Montréal; in the west they're in Winnipeg, Edmonton, Calgary, and Vancouver.

Air Canada (☎ 800/776-3000) has by far the most flights between the United States and Canada (including 18 daily from New York to Toronto), but most major U.S. and Canadian carriers fly daily between major cities in Canada and the United States as well, including **America West** (☎ 800/292-9378), **American Airlines** (☎ 800/433-7300), **Canadian Airlines International** (☎ 800/426-7000), **Delta** (☎ 800/221-1212), **Northwest** (☎ 800/447-4747), **USAir** (☎ 800/ 428-4322), and **United** (☎ 800/241-6522).

If you're looking for the cheapest fare possible, you have a few options, including charter flights. Try calling the **Council on International Educational Exchange (Council Charters)**, 205 E. 42nd St., New York, NY 10017 (☎ 800/223-7402). **Travel Avenue,** 10 S. Riverside Plaza, Suite 1404, Chicago IL 60606 (☎ 312/ 876-1116 or 800/333-3335), is a reputable rebator that often offers remarkable bargains.

BY CAR   Hopping across the border by car is no problem, since the U.S. highway system leads directly into Canada at 13 points. Once across the border you can link up with the Trans-Canada Highway, which runs from St. John's, Newfoundland, to Victoria, British Columbia—a total distance of 5,000 miles.

BY TRAIN   Amtrak serves the East Coast with four main routes into Canada. The *Adirondack,* which starts at Penn Station, New York, is a day train that travels daily via Albany and upstate New York to Montréal. The *Montrealer* travels nightly from New York's Pennsylvania Station through Vermont to Montréal. Round-trip coach fares range from $90 to $292. The *Maple Leaf* links New York City and Toronto via Albany, Buffalo, and Niagara Falls, departing daily from Penn Station. Round-trip coach fares range from $122 to $186. From Chicago, the *International* carries passengers to Toronto via Port Huron, Michigan, for a round-trip coach fare ranging from $102 to $186.

From Buffalo's Exchange Street Station you can make the trip to Toronto on the Toronto/Hamilton/Buffalo Railway (THB), which is a two-car Budd train. In Toronto you can make connections to Montréal, Ottawa, and so on.

Connecting services are available from other major cities along the border in addition to these direct routes. Call **Amtrak** (☎ 800/USA-RAIL or 800/872-7245) for further information and fares. Remember that the prices do not include meals; you can buy meals on the train or carry your own food.

BY FERRY   Ocean ferries operate from Maine to Nova Scotia and New Brunswick and from Seattle to Victoria and Vancouver, British Columbia. For details, see the relevant chapters.

6 Package Tours & Escorted Tours

Tour packages divide into two main categories: tours that take care of all the details from transportation to putting your luggage into your hotel room, and tours that simply give you a package price on the big ticket items and leave you free to find your own way. Independent tours give you much more flexibility, but require more effort on your part. Those who prefer not to drive and don't relish the notion of getting from train or bus stations to hotels on their own might prefer an escorted tour. But if you're the kind of traveler who doesn't like to be herded around in a group and wants to be able to linger at various sights at your leisure, a bus tour will drive you to distraction. The samples below will give you an idea of your choices.

INDEPENDENT PACKAGES   Air Canada has a "Go As You Please Self-Drive" package to Newfoundland in combination with Brian Moore International Tours. This includes round-trip airfare to St. John's from a dozen U.S. departure cities, use of a rental car for three days, plus accommodation vouchers for three nights in either hotels or inns. Prices vary according to the accommodation you choose. Similar packages are offered for other provinces as well. Contact **Brian Moore International Tours,** 116 Main St., Medway, MA 02053 (☎ 508/533-4426).

Air Canada also offers an array of package deals specially tailored to trim the costs of your vacation jaunts. Collectively these packages come under the title "Air Canada's Canada." This term covers a whole series of travel bargains that range from city packages to fly-drive tours, escorted tours, motorhome travel, ski holidays, and Arctic adventures. For detailed information, pick up the brochure from an Air Canada office, or have it sent to you by calling ☎ 800/776-3000.

Canadian Airlines International operates an array of package tours in conjunction with Canadian Holidays, including a number of fly/rail packages. Contact **Canadian Holidays,** 3507 Frontage Rd., Suite 100, Tampa, FL 33607 (☎ 800/237-0190).

FULLY ESCORTED TOURS   Collette Tours offers a wide variety of trips by bus, including several in the Rockies and several in the Atlantic Provinces. A 10-day tour of Newfoundland includes the seldom-visited northern peninsula and the Viking site at L'Anse aux Meadows, as well as a visit to Labrador. Shorter trips explore the Toronto-Niagara area and some combine Québec with New England or the Yukon with Alaska. An escorted train tour goes from Vancouver to Banff aboard the *Rocky Mountaineer.* Ask for its "USA and Canada" brochure by contacting **Collette Tours,** 162 Middle St., Pawtucket, RI 02860 (☎ 800/248-8991).

7 Getting Around

Canada is a land of immense distances, which means that transportation from point A to point B forms a prime item in your travel budget as well as your timetable. Here are some sample distances (in miles) between major cities: Montréal to Vancouver, 3,041; Vancouver to Halifax, 3,897; Toronto to Victoria, 2,911; Winnipeg to St. John's, 3,159; Calgary to Montréal, 2,299; St. John's to Vancouver, 4,723; Ottawa to Victoria, 2,979.

BY PLANE   Canada has two major transcontinental airlines: **Air Canada** (☎ 800/ 776-3000) and **Canadian Airlines** (☎ 800/426-7000). Together with their regional partner companies, they handle most of the country's air transportation. There are also numerous small local outfits, but these will concern us only when we get into their particular territories.

Within Canada, Air Canada operates daily service between 18 major cities, and its schedules dovetail with a string of allied connector carriers such as Air Nova, Air Ontario, Northwest Territorial Airways, etc., to serve scores of smaller Canadian towns. Fares vary widely with day of the week and the availability of seats.

BY CAR   Canada has scores of rental-car companies, including **Hertz** (☎ 800/ 654-3131), **Avis** (☎ 800/331-1212), **Dollar** (☎ 800/800-4000), **Thrifty** (☎ 800/ 367-2277), and **Budget** (☎ 800/527-0700). Nevertheless, rental vehicles tend to get very tight during the tourist season, from around mid-May through the summer months. It's a good idea to reserve a car as soon as you decide on your vacation.

The biggest and most thoroughly Canadian car-rental outfit is **Tilden Interrent,** with 400 locations coast to coast and affiliates in the United States and throughout the world. To book a Tilden car or get additional information while in the United States, contact **National Car Rental** (☎ 800/CAR-RENT). In Canada, contact the local stations listed in this book or Tilden Interrent headquarters at 250 Bloor St. East, Suite 1300, Toronto, ON, M4W 1E6 (☎ 800/387-4747).

Tilden rentals offer a Roadside Assistance Program. In case of an accident, break-down, dead battery, flat tire, dry gas tank, getting stuck, or locking yourself out of your car you can call a 24-hour number (☎ 800/268-9711) and get an immediate response for roadside help anywhere in Canada.

Members of the **American Automobile Association (AAA)** should remember to take their membership cards since privileges are extended to them in Canada.

Gasoline   As in the United States, the trend in Canada is toward self-service gas stations. In some areas, in fact, you may have difficulty finding the other kind. And although Canada—specifically Alberta—is a major oil producer, gasoline is not particularly cheap. Gas sells by the liter, and pumps at around 55¢ to 60¢ per liter ($2.20 to $2.40 per gallon); prices vary slightly from region to region. Filling the tank of a medium-sized car will cost you roughly $19.

Driving Rules   Wearing seat belts is compulsory (and enforced) in all provinces, for all passengers. Throughout the country, pedestrians have the right-of-way and cross-walks are sacrosanct. The speed limit on the autoroutes (limited-access highways) is

---

The Rocky Mountaineer: One of the World's Great Train Trips

It's billed as "The Most Spectacular Train Trip in the World," and it may very well be. Operated by the privately owned Great Canadian Railtour Company, this sleek blue-and-white train winds past foaming waterfalls, ancient glaciers, towering snowcapped peaks, and roaring mountain streams. *The Rocky Mountaineer* gives you the option of traveling either east from Vancouver, west from Jasper or Calgary, or taking a round-trip. The journey entails two days on the train, one night in a hotel, and lets you see the Rocky Mountains as you never would behind the wheel of a car.

The train operates from late May into October, entirely in daylight hours. For information and bookings contact the **Great Canadian Railtour Company,** Suite 104, 340 Brooksbank Ave., North Vancouver, BC, V7J 2C1 (☎ 800/665-7245).

---

100 kilometers per hour (62 m.p.h.). Right turns cannot be made at red lights unless a sign or green arrow makes an exception.

BY TRAIN   Most of Canada's passenger rail traffic is carried by the government-owned **VIA Rail.** You can traverse the continent very comfortably in sleeping cars, parlor coaches, bedrooms, and roomettes. Virtually all of Canada's major cities are connected by rail, though service is less frequent than it used to be. Some luxury trains, like *The Canadian,* boast dome cars with panoramic picture windows, hot showers, and elegant dining cars.

You can also purchase a Canrailpass that gives you 12 days of unlimited travel throughout the VIA national network, providing you do this within 30 days. A Canrailpass costs $572 in high season, $352 in low season. Seniors aged 60 and over and students receive a 10% discount on all fares. Fares for children up to 11 are half the applicable adult rate.

For information about services, times, and fares call VIA Rail (☎ 800/561-3949).

FAST FACTS: Canada

American Express   We'll give you the locations of American Express offices in the city chapters that follow. To report lost or stolen traveler's checks, call 800/221-7282.

Car Rentals   See "Getting Around," earlier in this chapter.

Climate   See "When to Go," earlier in this chapter.

Currency   See "Money," earlier in this chapter.

Customs   See "Visitor Information and Entry Requirements," earlier in this chapter.

Documents Required   See "Visitor Information and Entry Requirements," earlier in this chapter.

Driving Rules   See "Getting Around," earlier in this chapter.

Electricity   Canada uses the same electrical current as does the United States, 110-115 volts, 60 cycles.

Embassies and Consulates   All embassies are in Ottawa, the national capital; the U.S. embassy is at 100 Wellington St., Ottawa (☎ 613/238-4470).

You'll find U.S. consulates in the following locations: Nova Scotia—Cogswell Tower, Suite 910, Scotia Square, Halifax, NS, B3J 3K1 (☎ 902/429-2480); Québec—2 Place Terrasse-Dufferin (P.O. Box 939), Québec City, PQ, G1R 4T9 (☎ 418/692-2095) and Complexe Desjardins, South Tower, Ground Floor, Montréal, PQ, H5B, 1E5 (☎ 514/398-9695); Ontario—360 University Ave., Toronto, ON, M5G 1S4 (☎ 416/595-1700); Alberta—Room 1050, 615 Macleod Trail SE, Calgary, AB, T2G 4T8 (☎ 403/266-8962); British Columbia—1095 W. Pender St., Vancouver, BC, V6E 2Y4 (☎ 604/685-4311).

There's also a British consulate general at 777 Bay St., Toronto (☎ 416/593-1267), and an Australian consulate general at 175 Bloor St. East, Toronto (☎ 416/323-1155).

Emergencies   In life-threatening situations, call 911.

Holidays   See "When to Go," earlier in this chapter.

Liquor Laws   Beer and wine are sold in supermarkets and most grocery stores; spirits are sold only in government liquor stores. The minimum drinking age is 19.

Mail   At the time of writing, it costs 42¢ to send a first-class letter or postcard within Canada, and 48¢ to send a first-class letter or postcard from Canada to the United States. First-class airmail service to other countries costs 84¢ for the first 10 grams (about ¹/₂ oz.). Rates are expected to go up.

Taxes   In January 1991 the Canadian government imposed the goods and service tax (GST), a 7% federal tax on virtually all goods and services. Some hotels and shops include the GST in their prices, others add it on separately. When included, the tax accounts for the odd hotel rates, such as $66.04 a day, that you might find on your final bill. The GST is also the reason you pay 50¢ for a newspaper at a vending machine, but 54¢ over a shop counter: The machines haven't been geared for the new price.

Thanks to a government provision designed to encourage tourism, you can reclaim the GST portion of your hotel bills and the price of goods you've purchased in Canada—in due course. The minimum GST rebate is $7 (the tax on $100) and the claim must be filed within a year of purchase. You must submit all your original receipts (which will be returned) together with an application form. Receipts from several trips within the same year may be submitted together. Claims of less than $500 can be made at certain designated duty-free shops at international airports and border crossings. Or you can mail the forms to Revenue Canada, Customs and Excise, Visitors' Rebate Program, Ottawa, ON, K1A 1J5. You can get the forms in some of the larger hotels, in some duty-free shops, or by phoning 613/991-3346 outside Canada, or 800/66-VISIT in Canada.

The rebate does not apply to car rentals or restaurant meals. And the GST is not levied on airline tickets to Canada purchased in the United States.

Time   Six time zones are observed in Canada. In the winter, when it's 7:30pm Newfoundland standard time, it's 6pm Atlantic standard time (in Labrador, Prince Edward Island, New Brunswick, and Nova Scotia); 5pm eastern standard time (in Québec and most of Ontario); 4pm central standard time (in western Ontario, Manitoba, and most of Saskatchewan); 3pm mountain standard time (in northwestern Saskatchewan, Alberta, eastern British Columbia, and the Northwest Territories); and 2pm Pacific standard time (in the Yukon and most of British Columbia). Each year, on the first Sunday in April, daylight saving time comes into effect in most of Canada and clocks are advanced by one hour. On the last Sunday in October, Canada reverts to standard time. During these summer months, all of Saskatchewan observes the same time zone as Alberta.

Nova Scotia 4

by Barbara Radcliffe Rogers and Stillman Rogers

Barbara and Stillman Rogers began their explorations of the
Atlantic Provinces on their honeymoon and have summered
there for many years. They have written travel guides to
New Hampshire, Vermont, Portugal, the Galápagos Islands,
African safaris, and boat travel in Europe.

Contrary to what you may have pictured, Nova Scotia is more than
a chain of seaside towns. If you venture through its interior, miles
of road wind past hay bales and meadows of gentle grazing cows. In
other places the road is bordered by forests and ponds that beg to be
explored by canoe. The dramatic mountain scenery of Cape Breton's
highlands and the lush, fertile fields lining the Fundy shores are, to
our minds, as memorable as the rugged coastline.

But it's those picture-perfect old fishing towns that take center
stage on postcards and provide the popular image of this land. And
its life does revolve around the sea. Its beaches may not be as deserted
as the magnificent stretches of Kouchibouguak in New Brunswick,
but they're still quiet and picturesque.

1 Exploring Nova Scotia

Unfortunately, you probably don't have a month to search out Nova
Scotia's delightful back corners. If you have a week, we suggest you
choose one end of the province or the other, and add on a stop in
Halifax. Come back for another week to see the rest. Which side to
choose? If seaside villages, history, and fine dining every evening are
your priorities, go west. If mountain-meets-sea scenery, Celtic culture, slightly more authentic and rough-hewn villages, and a complete French colonial fortress town appeal to you—or if you are on
your way to Newfoundland via ferry—go east.

Assuming that most visitors coming by land will cross from New
Brunswick on the Trans-Canada Highway, this chapter is arranged
to start at Amherst, coming south to Halifax, and then touring the
peninsula on the driving routes mapped out by the provincial tourist authorities. Then it's off to Cape Breton Island, Nova Scotia's
most exciting tourist destination.

VISITOR INFORMATION   For information about Nova Scotia, call
☎ 800/565-0000. In Halifax or Dartmouth, call 902/425-5781.

For information before you go, write to **Nova Scotia Tourism,**
P.O. Box 130, Halifax, NS, B3J 2M7. Request the free, 300-page
Nova Scotia: The Doers and Dreamers Complete Guide, which contains driving information, accommodations and campground listings, and descriptions of the province's many scenic trails, parks,
historic sites, festivals, and museums.

When you get to Nova Scotia, any travel bureau or information center operated by the provincial authorities will help you find a room through the **Check-In** system. On Cape Breton look for the "**Cape Breton Bed & Breakfast**" list.

GETTING THERE   By Plane   Halifax is the air hub of the Atlantic Provinces. (The Atlantic Provinces—also called the Maritime Provinces—include New Brunswick, Nova Scotia, Prince Edward Island, and sometimes Newfoundland.) **Air Nova,** the commuter partner of Air Canada, provides direct service from New York (Newark Airport) and Boston. The airline (☎ 800/776-3000 in the U.S., 800/565-3940 in Maritime Provinces) also serves Sydney and Yarmouth, plus 13 other Atlantic Provinces destinations. Halifax, Sydney, and Yarmouth are also served by **Air Atlantic,** the commuter partner of Canadian Airlines International (☎ 902/427-5500, 800/426-7000 in the U.S., 800/665-1177 in Maritime Provinces, and 709/576-0274 in Newfoundland).

By Car & Ferry   Coming overland by car, you enter Nova Scotia from New Brunswick, probably along the Trans-Canada Highway at Amherst. Several ferry connections shorten the overland route: from New Brunswick (Saint John) to Digby, Nova Scotia; and from Maine (Bar Harbor and Portland) to Yarmouth, Nova Scotia. Ferries also connect Prince Edward Island (Wood Islands) to Caribou, Nova Scotia, and Newfoundland (Port aux Basques and Argentia) to North Sydney, Nova Scotia.

Portland/Yarmouth: From Portland, Maine, Prince of Fundy Cruises operates the MS *Scotia Prince* to Yarmouth, saving 858 miles of driving from May through October. The ship departs Portland at 9pm on alternate days, arriving in Yarmouth at breakfast time after an 11-hour cruise. Departure from Yarmouth is at 10am, arriving in Portland around 8pm. Reservations are necessary; confirm sailing dates with the company. One-way fares are $77 in season ($57 off-season) for adults, half price for children ages 5 to 14 accompanied by an adult, without cabin. Vehicle fare in high summer is $98 one way per car, $80 from mid-May to late June and early September to late October. Campers/trailers over seven feet cost $8 per foot, or $12 per foot in high season; bicycles are charged $7 ($10 in high season). Cabins on the night trip from Portland cost from $20 to $95 depending on season and number of berths, suites are $125 to $165. Note that all these prices are in U.S. dollars and credit cards are accepted for fares. Ask about money-saving package deals. Contact **Prince of Fundy Cruises,** International Terminal, Portland, ME 04101 (☎ 207/775-5616, 902/742-6460 in Yarmouth, or 800/341-7540, 800/482-0955 in Maine; call collect from elsewhere in Maritime Provinces).

Bar Harbor/Yarmouth: Between Bar Harbor, Maine, and Yarmouth, Nova Scotia, Marine Atlantic's MV *Bluenose* operates the six-hour run year-round. In high season from late June to mid-September, daily departures leave from Bar Harbor in the morning, from Yarmouth in the late afternoon. Fares are $41.50 per adult, $51 per car, and $22.10 per child 5 to 12. Off-season, there are only a few departures in either direction each week, and fares drop to $28 per adult, $47 per car, and $11.05 for children. Day cabins are available. Fares are payable in U.S. dollars in Bar Harbor, in Canadian dollars in Yarmouth. For reservations, contact **Marine Atlantic Reservations Bureau,** P.O. Box 250, North Sydney, NS, B2A 3M3 (☎ 800/341-7981 in the U.S., or call Bar Harbor at ☎ 207/288-3395).

By Train   Halifax has limited rail service, but is served by several weekly trains originating in Québec and stopping to pick up passengers in New Brunswick. For specific schedule and fare information, call **VIA Rail** (☎ 800/561-3949 in the U.S.).

Eastern Canada

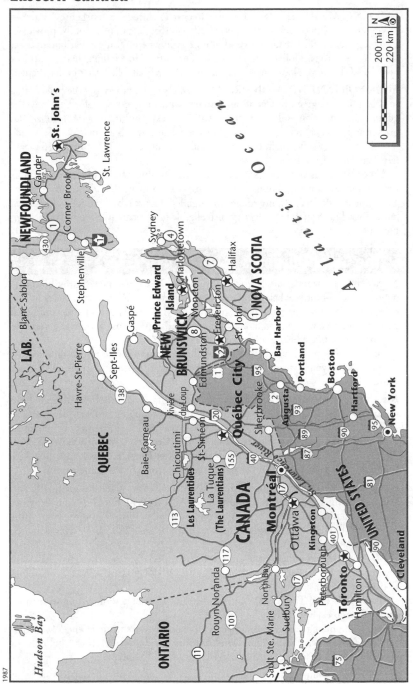

NEWFOUNDLAND
St. John's
Gander
Corner Brook
St. Lawrence
(1)
(430)
Stephenville
LAB.
Blanc-Sablon
Sydney
Prince Edward Island
(4)
Charlottetown
NOVA SCOTIA
Halifax
(7)
(1)
Moncton
NEW BRUNSWICK
Fredericton
(8)
St. John
Bar Harbor
Edmundston
(1) (2)
(1)
Québec City
(1)
(95)
Portland
Boston
Gaspé
QUEBEC
Havre-St-Pierre
Sept-Iles
(138)
Rivière-du-Loup
(20)
Sherbrooke
(2)
Augusta
Hartford
(93)
New York
(95)
Baie-Comeau
Chicoutimi
St-Siméon
(155)
(40)
(89)
(90)
(87)
Les Laurentides
La Tuque
(The Laurentians)
Montréal
(17)
St. Lawrence River
(81)
CANADA
Ottawa
Kingston
UNITED STATES
(113)
(117)
North Bay
(17)
Peterborough
(401)
(90)
Cleveland
Rouyn-Noranda
Sudbury
Toronto
Hamilton
ONTARIO
(101)
Sault Ste. Marie
(11)
(75)

Hudson Bay

Atlantic Ocean

N

200 mi
220 km
0

1987

GETTING AROUND   Nova Scotia is best explored on its scenic "trails"—driving routes mapped out by the tourism officials that take in many of the province's scenic highlights. The roads are good almost everywhere. You can easily rent a car from Budget, Avis, Dollar, Thrifty, or Tilden offices in Halifax, Dartmouth, or Sydney. We'll give you locations in the relevant sections that follow later in this chapter.

AN IMPORTANT NOTE ON PRICES   Unless stated otherwise, **the prices cited in this guide are given in Canadian dollars,** which is good news for U.S. travelers because the Canadian dollar is worth about 25% less than the American dollar, but buys nearly as much. As we go to press, $1 Canadian is worth about 75¢ U.S., which means that your $100-a-night hotel room will cost only U.S. $75, and your $6 breakfast costs only U.S. $4.50.

Almost all goods and services in Nova Scotia are subject to an 11% provincial tax (which applies to your accommodations, too—even in B&Bs) and a 7% national government tax (GST). Nonresidents are eligible for a tax rebate on goods purchased but not used in the province; they are also eligible for a rebate (GST only) on accommodations, except for camping fees.

2 The Great Outdoors

Nova Scotia is a wonderful place to enjoy nature. Miles of sea coast offer bountiful opportunities for bird-, whale-, and seal-watching. You'll find plenty of places to lean back and enjoy your surroundings. The province has created small picnic and beach parks by the side of the road along its designated trails, most with ocean views or overlooks onto marshes and other natural features.

Find your favorite activity below, and we'll point you to the best places in the province to pursue your interest or give you the general information you need to get started.

BIKING   The province's terrain is great for biking. The hills are challenging but not overly steep. Roads are in excellent condition, although narrow at places.

While it's easy to plan your own tour, at least two cycling clubs offer ongoing tours throughout the province. Contact the **Pictou County Cycling Club** (☎ 902/755-2704 or 902/752-8904), or the **Velo Halifax Bicycle Club,** P.O. Box 125, Dartmouth, NS, B2Y 3Y2 (no permanent phone), for tour dates and details.

BIRDING   Since the province is on the Atlantic flyway, you'll see many different species during spring and fall migrations. An excellent booklet from Seawind Landing Country Inn (see Marine Drive section below) lists 298 birds seen in the province. North America's largest bald eagle population—250 pairs—lives along the shore of Bras d'Or Lake.

Many whale cruises also focus on sea birds, especially around Digby Neck. On the 2¹/₂-hour **Bird Island Tour** at Big Bras d'Or (☎ 902/674-2384), you'll view puffins and more.

MacLeod's Bird Tours (☎ 902/852-5209) will arrange tours fitting your interests or focus on specific birds.

You'll find hiking guides to Brier Island, a major flyway site, in *Hiking Nova Scotia* and in *Coastal Nova Scotia Outdoor Adventure Guide* (see "Hiking," below); the latter includes a kayak tour of the Bird Islands off of Tangier.

CAMPING   Campgrounds in both national parks and 22 provincial parks are large, well maintained, and generally well spaced. Most have RV hook-ups, and many have shower facilities. There are also private campgrounds throughout the province.

Nova Scotia, Cape Breton Island & Prince Edward Island

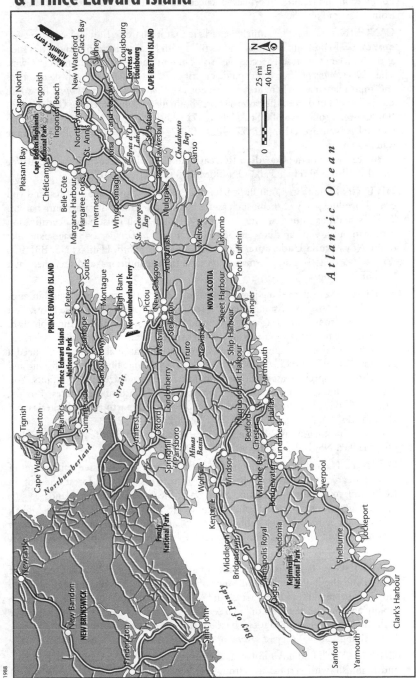

1988

For location and facilities information, check the *Doers and Dreamers Guide* available from Tourism Nova Scotia.

CANOEING   There's so much water here that it's hard to find a place where you *can't* canoe. Kejimkujik National Park is filled with lakes and streams, and rivers such as the St. Mary's are readily accessible. You can rent good equipment in most towns. The *Canoe Routes of Nova Scotia* guide describes 70 canoeing areas with sketch maps and topo references. There are also versions of *Coastal Paddling Routes* for south shore–Bay of Fundy and the eastern shore. Both are available from the **Government Bookstore,** 1700 Granville St., Halifax (☎ 902/424-7580), and the latter from **Coastal Adventures,** Tangier (☎ 902/772-2774). The bookstore also has canoe waterway maps.

You can write to the **Canadian Recreational Canoeing Association,** 1029 Hyde Park Rd., Box 500, Hyde Park, ON N0M 1Z0 (☎ 519/472-0768).

DIVING   More than 3,000 ships have wrecked off the province's shores, and you can still explore many of them, such as the 366-foot destroyer in Lunenburg harbor. The best months to dive are June through October. You must have a certification card; without it you can't buy air. Send for *Passport to Diving,* a 48-page pamphlet of the **Nova Scotia Underwater Council,** Box 3010 South, Halifax, NS, B3J 3G6 (☎ 902/425-5450). For information on local tides, conditions, and site, check at a local diving shop.

FISHING   Saltwater fishing is available from party and charter boats found in most harbors of any size. No fishing license is required for fishing from these boats. You can also fish from many piers and jetties, and from the shore. Bluefin tuna, bluefish, and shark are the most popular fish, and there's mackerel, cod, and other varieties.

Freshwater fishing requires a license, and within national parks, you'll need a National Parks Fishing License. Many rivers and streams are limited to fly fishing and may also have special seasons, licensing requirements, and size and bag limits. You can obtain the regulations from the **Department of Natural Resources,** Box 68, Truro, NS, B2N 5B8; for salmon fishing, contact the **Department of Fisheries and Oceans,** Box 550, Halifax, NS, B3J 2S7 (☎ 902/426-5952).

General information is available from the **Nova Scotia Wildlife Association,** Box 654, Halifax, NS, B3J 2T3 (☎ 902/423-6793).

HIKING   National parks and most provincial parks have extensive trail systems of varying degrees of difficulty, which range from treks through forest and bog in Kejimkujik to the more mountainous terrain of the Cape Breton Highlands.

For suggestions from easy walks to more arduous treks, refer to Joan Light's *Hiking Nova Scotia* (Nimbus Publishing, 1995) and her *Coastal Nova Scotia Outdoor Adventure Guide* (Nimbus Publishing, 1993). For hikes in Cape Breton, look at *Explore Cape Breton,* by Pat O'Neil (Nimbus Publishing, 1994).

KAYAKING   The hundreds of miles of seacoast along the Atlantic, the Bay of Fundy, and the Northumberland Strait offer great opportunities for sea kayaking. However, strong tides and heavy seas can be challenging. These conditions can change rapidly and unexpectedly, so only go sea kayaking after consulting experts familiar with the area you intend to use. The *Coastal Nova Scotia Outdoor Adventure Guide* (see "Hiking," above) suggest several options; also refer to "Canoeing," above.

SKIING   You'll find **downhill** areas at Windsor, Wentworth, Antigonish, East Bay, and Ingonish, with vertical rises from 465 feet (Keppoch Mountain, Antigonish) to 1,000 feet (Keltic Cape Smokey, Ingonish). The ski areas usually operate from mid-December to April. Contact the Nova Scotia Ski Area Association, c/o Ski Martock, RR 3, Windsor, NS, B0N 2T0 (☎ 902/798-9501).

Kejimkujik National Park has 26 miles (43km) of trails used for **cross-country skiing** during the winter, and Cape Breton Highlands National Park offers 60 miles (100km) of trails. Some trails have shelters. Also on Cape Breton, Fortress Louisbourg has 14 miles (23km) of marked trails. In the Digby area, Upper Clements Wildlife Park has 6 miles (10km) of trails. For information on other places to cross-country ski, write to Administrator, Nordic Skiing, Box 3010 South, Halifax, NS, B3J 3G6.

Many country inns and B&Bs have their own cross-country trails or maps of trails near their properties. The Whitman Inn at Caledonia (listed in the Kejimkujik section) will make arrangements for you, and the Milford House up the road has two winterized cabins to accommodate skiers.

SNOWMOBILING   The province's sparsely settled interior and its logging industry set the stage for plentiful snowmobiling. Approximately 1,500 miles (2,500km) of trails cut through the Cape Breton Highlands and the Cobequid mountains. Clubs throughout the province operate hundreds of miles of other trails. For trail and other information, contact the **Snowmobile Association of Nova Scotia,** Box 3010, Halifax, NS, B3J 3G6 (☎ 902/425-5450).

WHALE- & SEAL-WATCHING   At any point along the province's coast, you're never more than an hour or so away from a boat that will take you on a whale watch. You'll find the greatest concentration of whales, including humpback, Minke, and pilot whales, in the Bay of Fundy along the Evangeline Trail, because the bay is a massive nursery for plankton, a whale's favorite food. The plankton also attract fish, which in turn attract seals. Along Digby Neck, which stretches into the Bay of Fundy creating St. Mary's Bay, no fewer than six whale-watching cruises operate.

3 Driving from Amherst to Halifax

AMHERST: YOUR STARTING POINT

Coming from New Brunswick, the first town you reach across the Nova Scotia border is Amherst. There's a provincial tourism office here that's well stocked with information.

If you'd like to stop for the night in Amherst, it's no problem. Just after passing the tourist office, look for the LaPlanche Street exit, and it will lead you to a string of basic roadside motels.

From Amherst, you have a couple of choices of how to explore the province.

The **Sunrise Trail,** one of eight driving routes designated by Nova Scotia's Department of Tourism, starts in Amherst and stretches along the northern coast all the way to the Canso Causeway, entrance to Cape Breton Island. To follow it, take Highway 6 to the coast and proceed east; you'll meander along past inlets, beaches, and villages along the way. We'll discuss the eastern portion of this drive in Section 8, later in this chapter.

But if you're just interested in getting to Halifax as fast as possible, head southeast along Highway 104 instead. That will get you to Truro, where you'll pick up Highway 102 bound for Halifax.

TRURO

Here you'll find 1,000-acre **Victoria Park,** one of the Atlantic Provinces' loveliest parks. A deep gorge cuts through the park and a clear stream falls dramatically among the rocks. It's an easy walk from the parking area along the stream, through the gorge to **Howe Falls**. A substantial part of this gravel path is wheelchair accessible. Board-walks and wooden stairs provide access to the top of the falls area and to trails else-where in the park. You can picnic at tables along the stream.

Truro is also known for the **tidal bore**—a rushing current that can develop into a wall of water several feet high—that rushes up the Salmon River from the Bay of Fundy via Cobequid Bay. Usually, the days of the full moon in August or later in autumn bring the bore in like a torrent. To see it, consult the tide table, available everywhere, or call Dial-a-Tide (☎ 902/426-5494), and plan to be at **Tidal Bore Park** at least 10 minutes before high tide. This twice-daily event is floodlit at night. The park is located at the riverbank on the Palliser Restaurant grounds (see below).

WHERE TO STAY & DINE

The **Best Western Glengarry,** at 150 Willow St. (☎ 902/893-4311 or 800/567-4276; fax 902/893-1759), is part of the Truro Trade and Convention Centre and charges $75 to $95 for a double. Take Exit 13 off Highway 102.

The Palliser Hotel. Tidal Bore Road, Truro, NS, B2N 5G6. ☎ **902/893-8951.** 40 rms. TV. $47 double. Rates include buffet breakfast. 15% discount on dinner in the dining room. Extra person $4. AE, DC, ER, MC, V. Take Exit 14 from Highway 102.

At the Palliser, with any luck, you won't even have to leave your room to see the tidal bore. The marshy estuary of the Salmon River is all around you. Most units have baths and showers; some have showers only.

The Palliser Restaurant is well known locally; its windows overlook the Salmon River and tidal bore. The food is solid and tasty rather than exotic, with dishes running from $6 to $17.

SHUBENACADIE PROVINCIAL WILDLIFE PARK & TIDAL BORE

Set in natural woodland, the park gives visitors a close look at the animals and birds that inhabit this province, along with a few imported species. Roaming in large enclosures are ducks, swans, reindeer, moose, cougar, Sable Island horses, and more. Most of the birds aren't restrained at all.

At the park entrance, the **Creighton Forest Environment Centre** teaches about the forests, wildlife, and forestry management. A 25-acre picnic area with shelters and a playground is adjacent to the wildlife display area.

At the town of Shubenacadie, follow signs for Route 2 north to the park (☎ 902/758-2040, fax 902/758-7011), which is 24 miles (38km) south of Truro and 40 miles (65km) north of Halifax. Take Exit 10 off Highway 102. Admission is $2 for adults, $1 for children ages 12 to 17, and $5 for families. Park hours are 9am to 7pm daily from May 15 to October 15.

On Route 215, also north of Shubenacadie, you can make a stop for a memorable adventure: ✪ **rafting the tidal bore** on a Zodiac. To do this, call **Shubenacadie Tidal Bore Park** (☎ 902/758-2177, ext. 4032, or within the province 800/565-RAFT); this is a private park that's also the best place to view this twice-daily phenomenon. The park, which you can visit for $2 ($1.50 for children and seniors), is 7 miles (10km) north of Exit 10 on the Trans-Canada Highway. A wooden plat-form overhanging the river and steps down the steep bank provide safe access close to the water. Someone there will explain the forces that create this onrush of water; waves can be 10 feet high. Those not taking the boat trip can watch the Zodiac cavorting in the bore. The two-hour trip costs $45 ($35 for children under 12).

4 Halifax

Above all, Halifax is a friendly city without pretensions. The historic waterfront and downtown area are not just for tourists; they're a favorite venue for Haligonians as well. Travelers who venture into the restaurants, cafes, and lively pubs of Spring Garden Road quickly feel at home.

You'll see pictures of the queen of England everywhere—Halifax is unabashedly Anglophile. Most of Nova Scotia was settled by French, Irish, and Scots, but this town was to be Britain's commercial center and naval stronghold in the New World, and settlers were recruited from England rather than from other British lands.

They picked a superb location for the city, on a hilly peninsula surrounded by one of the world's great natural harbors. Fortresses crowned the hills; a few survive, and the pastures that once surrounded them have been turned into parks, making Halifax one of the greenest cities you'll visit.

Although this city shoulders the responsibilities of a regional and provincial capital, a major seaport and airline hub, and a business and communications center, it's surprisingly compact. With a population of more than 114,000, Halifax has all the vibrant activity and cultural opportunities of a much larger city, but none of the crowding and sprawl.

Keep in mind that while exploring Halifax, you'll be walking up and down its hillside a lot, and the sun will play hide-and-seek with the fog.

ESSENTIALS

VISITOR INFORMATION   The well-stocked **Nova Scotia Tourist Information Centre** (☎ 902/424-4247) is on the waterfront in the Red Building, Historic Properties, open daily from 8:30am to 7pm June to mid-September, to 4:30pm weekdays the rest of the year. The province also maintains information offices at the Halifax

The Great Explosion of 1917

Everything in Halifax was affected, in one manner or another, by the Great Halifax Explosion of December 6, 1917, the world's most powerful human-made explosion until the bombing of Hiroshima. A French munitions ship, the *Mont Blanc*, laden with eight million pounds of TNT and fuel, collided with another ship, the *Imo*, and exploded. Two thousand Haligonians were killed outright or later died from the blast, and about 9,000 others were injured. The explosion and the fires that immediately followed flattened half the city, and the rest was in havoc. Damage ran to the tens of millions of dollars, even at 1917 prices. The blast was so strong it shattered windows in Truro, 60 miles away, and rattled dishes in Cape Breton and Prince Edward Island. For a look at Halifax during and after the catastrophe, visit the Maritime Museum (see "Attractions") and request a copy of the free leaflet that will guide you to various sites connected with the explosion. The displays and recorded eyewitness accounts in the museum are particularly poignant for me. My father was a young sailor on board the closest naval vessel in the North Atlantic at the time, and his ship was sent immediately to help the stricken city; I grew up with his stories of Halifax in that December.

—*Barbara Radcliffe Rogers*

International Airport (☎ 902/873-1223) and along Route 102 at the airport interchange (☎ 902/873-3608).

Tourism Halifax, in the Old City Hall, on Duke Street at Barrington (☎ 902/421-8736; fax 902/421-6897), is open daily in summer, usually from 8:30am to 6pm (to 8pm on Thursday and Friday), from 9am to 4:30pm weekdays only during the rest of the year. Check the bulletin board for current goings-on about town.

GETTING THERE   Entering the province from New Brunswick, take Highway 104 to Truro; from there, Highway 102 leads to Halifax. If you arrived in Nova Scotia at the Yarmouth ferry landing, take Highway 103 east.

Halifax International Airport is approximately 25 miles (40km) north of the city on Highway 102. A regular cab from the airport to downtown costs about $32 plus tip, a "share a cab" around $18. The **Aerocoach City Shuttle** (☎ 902/468-1258) makes more than a dozen trips daily between the airport and downtown hotels; the fare is $11 one-way, $18 round-trip (children under 10 accompanied by an adult ride free).

Trains run six days a week between Montréal and Halifax. The train station is at 1161 Hollis St. (☎ 902/494-7900 or 800/872-7245 in the U.S.). The information/ticket window is open daily from 9am to 5:30pm.

GETTING AROUND   The best way to see Halifax is on foot. Streets parallel to the harbor are relatively flat; perpendicular streets are steep. In inclement weather, take advantage of the "pedways" (covered pedestrian walkways) linking downtown stores, hotels, and office buildings (the *Visitor Guide* has a map of them); you can work your way indoors all the way from the waterfront to Citadel Hill.

Local buses cost $1.15 per trip for adults, 65¢ for seniors or children 5 to 12; if you need a transfer, ask for it when you board. Bus fares include transfers for the ferries to Dartmouth, so be sure to ask. For routes and timetables, call ☎ 902/421-6600.

Car-rental agencies based in Halifax include **Budget, Avis, Dollar,** and **Thrifty,** all of which have locations at the airport and elsewhere in the city. Reserve your rental car well in advance during the busy summer months.

If you need a taxi, call **Aero Cab** (☎ 902/445-3333) or **Yellow Cab** (☎ 902/422-1551).

EXPLORING THE CITY

Any visit to Halifax should begin at the lively and historic **waterfront,** as much a focal point of today's social and commercial activity as it was in the mid-1700s. In good weather cafes fill the area, and the old mercantile buildings are now arcades of stylish shops.

At the landing is the striking bronze statue of *The Sailor,* a monument to all Canadian seamen. Their vessels are represented around the base. Nearby, the HMS *Halcyon,* a ship-shaped playground, allows young sailors to exercise their imagination.

The second major place to start exploring is the **Grand Parade,** originally the drilling ground for Halifax's militia and now a centrally located square and park at George and Argyle streets. Here office workers and tourists mingle to eat lunch outside. **Free concerts** are given here in summer from noon to 1pm, usually on Wednesday, Thursday, and Friday. Popular restaurants line the streets surrounding the Grand Parade.

For an afternoon break and an example of Halifax hospitality, stop for **tea with the mayor,** in the Old City Hall at the end of the Grand Parade. It's free and held every weekday in July and August—at tea time, of course (3:30 to 4:30pm).

Halifax

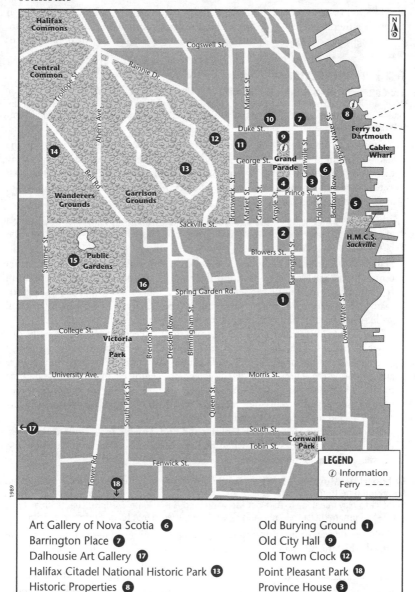

Art Gallery of Nova Scotia **6**
Barrington Place **7**
Dalhousie Art Gallery **17**
Halifax Citadel National Historic Park **13**
Historic Properties **8**
Maritime Museum of the Atlantic **5**
Metro Centre **11**
Neptune Theatre **2**
Nova Scotia Museum of Natural History **14**

Old Burying Ground **1**
Old City Hall **9**
Old Town Clock **12**
Point Pleasant Park **18**
Province House **3**
Public Gardens **15**
Restaurant Area **16**
St. Paul's Church **4**
Scotia Square **10**

While you're there, you can tour the building, constructed in 1890. Use the Grand Parade rather than the Argyle Street entrance. For information, call 902/421-6448. The flagpole, by the way, is the world's largest wooden flagpole made of one piece of timber.

THE TOP ATTRACTIONS

Art Gallery of Nova Scotia. 1741 Hollis St. (at Cheapside). ☎ **902/424-7542.** Admission $2.50 adults, $1.25 seniors and students, $5.50 family; children under 12 free. Free on Tues. June–Aug Tues–Wed and Fri–Sat 10am–5:30pm, Thurs 10am–9pm, Sun noon–5:30pm; Sept–May Tues–Fri 10am–5pm, Sat–Sun noon–5pm.

As much folk museum as art gallery, the Art Gallery of Nova Scotia is housed in the stately Dominion Building (1868). The four levels of gallery space primarily display the works of Maritime Provinces artists, among them Maud Lewis (1903–70), known as the mother of Nova Scotian folk art. Other exhibits feature Canadian, European, and British paintings, and Inuit art.

The Citadel. Citadel Hill. ☎ **902/426-5080.** Mid-June–Labor Day admission $2 adults, $1 children 5–16, $5 family; free for seniors and children; free rest of year. Mid-June to Labor Day daily 9am–6pm; rest of year daily 10am–5pm.

Halifax was founded as a military and naval defense point as well as a commercial center. In 1825, a long-lasting and formidable masonry fort, the Citadel, was begun. It was not completed until 1856, and its construction ran to twice the original estimate—pretty expensive for a structure that was rendered obsolete by 1870 (by then, artillery had become powerful enough to damage even these thick walls).

The Citadel is Canada's most visited historic site. Peer down into the wells, one of which could hold almost 19,000 gallons of water, and marvel at the seemingly impregnable powder magazines. A guide will take you around for free if you inquire at the information center, on the left as you enter. Slightly before noon is a good time to visit, when soldiers in period uniforms prepare for the firing of the noonday cannon, an everyday occurrence here since the mid-19th century. The panoramic views of the city and harbor are outstanding.

Before you leave Citadel Hill, look for the **Old Town Clock**, built at the direction of Queen Victoria's father when he was stationed here with the British army. He was a stickler for punctuality.

✪ **Maritime Museum of the Atlantic.** 1675 Lower Water St. ☎ **902/424-7490.** Admission June to mid-Oct $3 adults, 50¢ children 5–16, $6.50 family; free Tues 5:30–8pm. Mid-Oct to May free. June to mid-Oct Mon and Wed–Sat 9:30am–5:30pm, Tues 9:30am–8pm, Sun 1–5:30pm; mid-Oct to May Tues 9:30am–8pm, Wed–Sat 9:30am–5pm, Sun 1–5pm.

Right on the waterfront, this impressive museum combines a modern new structure and the historic William Robertson and Son ship outfitters building. Outside the entrance, note the plaque to native son Samuel Cunard (1787–1865), founder of the Cunard Steam-Ship Company. Inside, visit Robertson's store (left of the entrance), which for more than a century sold marine hardware, from fishhooks to harpoons to canvas for making sails. In the new wing are artifacts from the *Titanic* and Queen Victoria's barge, donated by Queen Elizabeth in 1959. The upper level "Age of Steam" exhibit is an outstanding collection of ship models and exhibits on Samuel Cunard and his shipping line.

Allow a couple of hours to tour the museum, before continuing to the dock where the **CSS *Acadia*** is moored; admission to the ship is included in your museum ticket. Built in 1913 in England, the ship always worked in Canadian waters, charting the coasts of Nova Scotia, Newfoundland, and Labrador until it retired in 1969.

HMCS Sackville. Behind the Maritime Museum of the Atlantic. ☎ **902/429-5600.** Admission free. Mon–Sat 10am–5pm, Sun noon–5pm. Closed Oct–May.

Built in 1941, the HMCS *Sackville* has been restored to its World War II configuration as a memorial to Canadians who served in the navy during that war. A 15-minute audiovisual presentation, *Battle of the Atlantic,* is shown on the hour and the half hour in the visitor center. Recorded audio descriptions aboard the ship describe the function of each part of the ship and bring it to life.

St Paul's Church. On the Grand Parade between Barrington and Argyle streets. ☎ **902/429-2240.** Daily 9am–4:30pm; Sun services 8:30 and 10:30am.

Forming one end of the Grand Parade, St. Paul's was the first Anglican cathedral established outside of England and is Canada's oldest Protestant place of worship. Part of the building, which dates from 1750, was fabricated in Boston, then a British colony, and erected in Halifax with the help of a royal endowment from King George II. A classic white Georgian building, St. Paul's has fine stained-glass windows. A piece of flying debris from the explosion of 1917 is lodged in the wall over the doors to the nave.

MORE ATTRACTIONS

The **Dalhousie Art Gallery,** on the university campus at 6101 University Ave. (☎ 902/494-2403), offers changing exhibits of historical and contemporary art, often with a regional theme; admission is free. And located west of the Citadel, the **Nova Scotia Museum of Natural History,** 1747 Summer St. (☎ 902/424-7353), has an archaeology gallery and Micmac collection. Admission is $3 for adults, 50¢ children 5 to 16, $6.50 family, free Wednesdays from 5:30 to 8pm.

The seat of the Nova Scotia Legislative Assembly, **Province House,** on Hollis Street near Prince Street (☎ 902/424-4661), is a handsome Georgian mansion of weathered stone that was finished in 1819; the assembly has occupied it ever since. Guided tours are free; you'll see the Legislative Assembly chamber and the Red Chamber, a sumptuous room with fine oil paintings. In July and August it's open Monday to Friday from 9am to 5pm, weekends and holidays 10am to 4pm; the rest of the year Monday to Friday 9am to 4pm.

The new home of the **Nova Scotia Sports Hall of Fame,** Suite 101, 1645 Granville St. (☎ 902/421-1266), opened downtown in fall 1995. It features all sports (and, unlike many sports museums, it doesn't slight women athletes). The large, bright exhibit spaces are great for kids—for any sports fan, in fact. Admission is $2.

The **Old Burying Ground** at Barrington Street and Spring Garden Road is the final resting place for Halifax's first citizens. It opened when the city was founded in 1749 and was in use until 1844. Only 10% of the more than 12,000 graves are marked; many stones are from the 1700s. No rubbings are allowed in the cemetery, which is open 9:30am to 5:30pm daily.

CRUISES & TOURS

The cheapest excursion in town is the **Halifax-Dartmouth ferry,** which costs only $1.10 one way (80¢ for kids 5 to 12), or round-trip if you don't get off in Dartmouth. The ferry leaves from the foot of George Street, off Water Street, in Historic Properties, and has been making the crossing since 1752. Bus travel includes transfer to the ferries. Take the trip across to see the harbor or to have lunch or dinner at **MacAskill's Restaurant,** visit the shops and food courts of Alderny Market inside the Dartmouth terminal, or walk in the harborside park. The compact blue-and-white boats operate from about 6:30am to 11:30pm Monday through Saturday, and from the first weekend in June to the last weekend in September on Sunday from noon to 5:30pm; but if you're going over at night, check the time for the last return trip, usually at midnight.

To explore the harbor of one of the world's great ports, board the ✪ *Bluenose II,* a replica of Canada's trophy-winning two-masted fishing schooner. It's moored at Privateers' Wharf, and when in Halifax, tours are conducted Tuesday through Sunday. Half the space on the three daily sailings may be reserved in advance; the rest is first-come, first-served, and spaces get snapped up quickly. Pick up tickets at Privateers' Wharf. The cost for the two-hour cruise is $14 for adults, $7 for seniors and children 12 and under (☎ 902/422-2678 in July and August, 902/424-5000 year-round).

Several other harbor tours and fishing trips depart regularly from Cable Wharf, within walking distance of Privateers' Wharf. For information, contact **Murphy's on the Water** at Cable Wharf (☎ 902/420-1015).

Metro-Ped has compiled a list of existing bicycle, walking, and jogging paths in the Halifax-Dartmouth area. Maps and routes are provided. Contact Metro-Ped at ☎ 902/420-3474; fax 902/424-5334.

The guided tours provided by **Alexander Keith's Brewery wagon tours** are free. You can reserve rides through the waterfront information office or in City Hall. The open horse-drawn wagons, fitted with comfortable seats, hold 10 people. The narrated tours take you all over, including the navy area, the 1917 explosion site, and the yacht harbor.

For a knowledgeable walking-tour guide, contact **DTours** (☎ 902/429-6415), which offers 90-minute strolls for about $3 per person, from June to October, other months by appointment.

The **Velo Halifax Bicycle Club** conducts frequent bicycle tours throughout the Nova Scotia peninsula, from short evening rides to day rides or even week-long camping rides. For tour dates and details, write P.O. Box 125, Dartmouth, NS, B2Y 3Y2.

PARKS & GARDENS

In the beautiful ✪ **Public Gardens,** ducks and swans cruise across the glassy surfaces of ponds, fountains play in the breeze, and the sweet fragrance of flowers greets you. The 18-acre formal English gardens have been soothing the souls of Haligonians since Queen Victoria's reign; in the center a painted bandstand is so resplendent that you can almost hear "Hail Britannia" as you pass. Watch for a summer schedule of free band concerts. Discreet bronze markers note plantings in memory of people and events—a local teacher who served in the Boer War, the 1937 Coronation, a royal visit. It's a living history of Halifax: the most recent planting commemorates the 1995 G-7 meeting. The gardens, bounded by Sackville Street, South Park, Spring Garden Road, and Summer Street, are open daily from 8am to sunset.

Point Pleasant Park, at the southern tip of Halifax peninsula, is a 186-acre forest laced with 10 miles of walking trails and dotted with picnic spots and views. Park your car in the lot near the end of Young Avenue, the southern extension of South Park Street. No cars are allowed past here, so you must proceed on foot. Established in 1866, Point Pleasant Park has an old martello tower, one of the cylindrical defense towers erected throughout the British Isles and eastern Canada in the 19th century.

SHOPPING

Historic Properties, on the waterfront, is filled with stores and boutiques. The **Harbour Swan** is a pleasant, all-purpose gift shop. Nearby, in the Sheraton Hotel, the **Houston North Gallery,** 1919 Upper Water St., specializes in Inuit art and Nova

Scotia folk art. The shop of the **Art Gallery of Nova Scotia,** downtown at 1741 Hollis St., also sells local folk art.

Scotia Square, a tremendous indoor mall bounded by Barrington, Duke, Market, and Cogswell streets, has more than 100 shops and services on two levels. Right across the street is **Barrington Place,** at 1903 Barrington St., with a number of fashionable boutiques, and **Micmac Heritage Gallery,** on the ground (Granville) level, selling quality native crafts.

The smaller (and less confusing) **Maritime Centre,** at 1505 Barrington at the corner of Spring Garden Road, has two levels of shops and a food court. At 5657 Spring Garden Rd. and Dresden Row, half a block from the Public Gardens, the upscale **Park Lane** has three floors filled with boutiques, an eight-screen cinema, and a food court.

The blocks along Spring Garden Road between Queen Street and Park Street are a pleasant stretch of varied and interesting shops.

WHERE TO STAY
VERY EXPENSIVE
✪ **Chateau Halifax.** 1990 Barrington St., Halifax, NS, B3J 1P2. ☎ **902/425-6700,** 800/ 441-1414. Fax 902/425-6214. 300 rms. AC MINIBAR TV TEL. $125–$160 double. Extra person $15. Off-season rates lower. AE, ER, JCB, MC, V. Adjacent parking and connected garage, $10 a day with hotel voucher.

This hotel is a mere block from the waterfront. Largely renovated for the 1995 G-7 Economic Summit (President Clinton stayed here), it is up to Canadian Pacific's usual high standards. The large and comfortable rooms have armchairs, reading lights, and well-appointed bathrooms. Few big hotels manage to combine personal warmth with formal professionalism, but this one does. It's well staffed, and the personnel couldn't be nicer or more helpful.

A coffee shop serves light meals and is handy because of its hours; however, the service was a bit surly and too much like a lunch wagon in the morning.

Facilities: The hotel has a large indoor heated pool with a big whirlpool, an exercise room, and saunas in the dressing rooms.

Prince George Hotel. 1725 Market St., Halifax, NS, B3J 3N9. ☎ **902/425-1986,** 800/ 565-1567. Fax 902/429-6048. 205 rms, 9 suites. A/C MINIBAR TV TEL. $160–$170 double; from $190 suite. Extra person $15. Children under 18 stay free with parents. Weekend rates and honeymoon packages available. AE, CB, DC, DISC, ER, MC, V. Underground parking $6 a day.

Set high up on the hill, one block from the Citadel and Clock Tower, the Prince George is centrally located if you want to walk to nearby shopping, restaurants, and nightlife. An underground passage connects the hotel to the Metro Centre and World Trade Centre. Comfortable, tastefully decorated rooms come with a hair dryer, tea and coffeemaker, and windows that open; most look out over the city and the harbor. Add to that a friendly staff. There are also nonsmoking floors and a concierge floor.

The Terrace Room serves breakfast only, and there's also a quick, inexpensive breakfast wagon in the lobby.

Services: The hotel offers automated message service, complimentary weekday newspaper, in-room movies, same-day valet, babysitting.

Facilities: Indoor pool.

EXPENSIVE
Cambridge Suites. 1583 Brunswick St., Halifax, NS, B3J 3P5. ☎ **902/420-0555** or 800/ 565-1263. Fax 902/420-9379. 200 rms. A/C MINIBAR TV TEL. From $110 one-bedroom suite.

Rates include continental breakfast. Children under 18 stay free with parents. Monthly, weekly, and off-season rates available. AE, DC, ER, MC, V. Indoor parking $6 a day.

Across the street from the Citadel, Cambridge Suites provides a comfortable home away from home for vacationing families and business travelers. Each unit has two telephones, hair dryer, and a dining/living area, with a microwave, refrigerator, dishes, and cutlery. There are nonsmoking rooms available.

Facilities: The rooftop fitness center has a whirlpool, sauna, free weights, and exercise bikes. There's also a sundeck, a terrace barbecue, laundry facilities, and a licensed dining room.

✪ Halliburton House Inn. 5184 Morris St., Halifax, NS, B3J 1B3. ☎ **902/420-0658.** Fax 902/423-2324. 25 rms, 3 suites. A/C MINIBAR TV TEL. $110–$125 double; from $160 suite. Rates include continental breakfast. Extra person $15. Children under 18 stay free with parents. Honeymoon package available. Senior discounts. AE, DC, ER, MC, V. Limited free parking.

This exquisite small inn feels like a country estate though it's right downtown. The 1809 inn, which includes two adjacent buildings, is impeccably restored and furnished, and maintained with attention to detail. Each room is different: some are particularly large, others have balconies, fireplaces, or minibars. Smoking is permitted.

MODERATE

The Inn on the Lake. P.O. Box 29, Waverley, NS, B0N 2S0. ☎ **902/861-3480.** Fax 902/861-4883. 31 rms, 4 suites. A/C TV TEL. $79–$89 double; from $185 suite. Extra person $10. Children under 16 stay free. AE, DC, ER, MC, V. Free on-site parking. Go south on Route 102 from the airport to Exit 5 (*not* 5A).

Only 10 miles from the airport, and set on five acres of parklike grounds on Lake Thomas, this inn seems like a small country resort. The rooms are large and comfortable; suites, like room 357, have a Jacuzzi, balcony with a lake view, and coffeemaker. Standard rooms, on the first and second (nonsmoking) floors, have quality contemporary furnishings, balconies, and tub/showers. The dining room prepares fresh seafood in innovative ways. There's also a bar, tennis courts, shuffleboard, volleyball, pool and water sports, and a free airport shuttle.

Sterns Mansion. 17 Tulip St., Dartmouth, NS, B3A 2S5. ☎ **902/465-7414.** Fax 902/466-8832. 5 rms. TV. $75 double; $110 double with Jacuzzi. Rates include breakfast. Honeymoon and golf packages available. MC, V.

In a quiet, residential area of Dartmouth, a 10-minute walk from the ferry to Halifax and 20 minutes from the airport, this bed-and-breakfast is as romantic a place as you're likely to find. Victorian antiques and eclectic collectibles fill the rooms. Two rooms feature pool-size Jacuzzis with candles and dimmer switches to set the mood. Guests enjoy musical instruments, games, books, and a VCR in the living room, as well as a back patio and barbecue. The four-course breakfast starts off with a wake-up beverage served in your room. In the evening tea and cakes are served downstairs. No smoking.

The Waverley Inn. 1266 Barrington St. (between Morris and South streets), Halifax, NS, B3J 1Y5. ☎ **902/423-9346,** or 800/565-9346 in the Maritime Provinces. Fax 902/425-0167. 32 rms. A/C TV TEL. $72–$97 double; $97–$115 deluxe room. Extra person $10. Rates include continental breakfast and snacks. MC, V. Free parking behind the house; lot entrance on Morris Street.

The Waverly, built in 1866, became an inn 10 years later, welcoming notables such as Oscar Wilde (who stayed in room no. 124) and P. T. Barnum. It's only six blocks from Halifax's center. Although the guest and public rooms are decorated with fine oak and mahogany antiques, the hallway's original woodwork is marred by pink paint. The inn does not have the fine touch of the nearby Halliburton, but it's less expensive (rooms on the third floor are particularly good buys). Each room is furnished differently—one has a Chinese wedding bed—and baths have either a tub or a shower. Guests may sit out on the second-floor deck, and swim at the YWCA across the street.

INEXPENSIVE

Heritage House Hostel. 1253 Barrington St., Halifax, NS, B3J 1Y3. ☎ and fax **902/ 422-3863.** 12 rms (6 with private bath, 3 with shared baths). $13.75 IHA members, $16.75 Canadian nonmembers, $17.75 international nonmembers; $30 private room; $40 family room. V.

Opposite the Waverley Inn, Halifax's downtown hostel opened in 1992. The new manager plans to upgrade the facilities and restore the historic building. Most accommodations are dormitory style with two to six beds per room; in addition, there are two private rooms and two family rooms. There's a common room with books and magazines, a laundry, a modest kitchen, a dining room, lockers, a pay phone, and a bulletin board. No smoking.

WHERE TO DINE

Locals, not just tourists, fill restaurants along the busy waterfront. Menus here are posted, which makes predinner shopping a local pastime. "Taste of Nova Scotia" signs in restaurant windows generally mean good dining experiences; members, listed in a free guidebook available at the Tourist Information Center, are known for quality food emphasizing Nova Scotia produce and recipes.

EXPENSIVE

Halliburton House. In the Halliburton House Inn, 5184 Morris St. ☎ **902/420-0658.** Reservations recommended. Main courses $16–$28. AE, DC, ER, MC, V. Daily 5:30–9pm. WILD GAME.

Specializing in game, including pheasant and buffalo, in addition to more traditional fare, Halliburton House serves such stylish dishes as grilled medallions of Arctic musk ox with bourbon cream. The menu changes seasonally and emphasizes fresh ingredients. For a romantic evening, reserve the small private dining room at no extra charge. In warm weather meals are served in the pleasant tree- and flower-filled garden in the rear.

Ryan Duffy's. 5640 Spring Garden Rd. ☎ **902/421-1116.** Reservations recommended. Main courses $13–$23. AE, MC, V. Mon–Sat 11:30am–3pm; Mon–Wed 5–11pm, Thurs–Sat 5pm–midnight, Sun 5–10pm. STEAK/SEAFOOD.

Known primarily for its steaks, cooked over wood charcoal with a blend of spices, Duffy's charges by the ounce at rates displayed on a chalkboard at the front desk. Lunch is served in casual Duffy's Bar and Grill. The bar stays open until 2am nightly except Sunday, when its hours are 5 to 11pm. Duffy's Speakeasy is a sports bar with four pool tables, big-screen TV, dartboards, and a dance floor.

✿ Upper Deck Restaurant. Third floor of the Privateer's Warehouse, on the waterfront, Historic Properties. ☎ **902/422-1501.** Reservations recommended. Main courses $13–$27. AE, DC, ER, MC, V. Daily 5:30–10pm. SEAFOOD/REGIONAL.

Privateer's Warehouse features eateries on three levels, in three styles. The Upper Deck is the top-of-the-line venue, excelling in food and service. The varied menu emphasizes seafood with specialties such as Cajun shrimp and Atlantic seafood stew. Tired of seafood? Try chicken and artichoke hearts over angel-hair pasta with sun-dried tomatoes. The dining room's exposed stone walls and woodwork, combined with fine ship models and well-spaced tables, create a romantic experience. You can try three tempting desserts with the dessert sampler for two. The wine list is substantial.

Down one level, the **Middle Deck restaurant** (☎ 902/425-1500) offers pasta at lower prices; on ground level, the noisier **Lower Deck** (☎ 902/422-1289) is a pub filled with lively Maritime music.

MODERATE

Salty's on the Waterfront. 1869 Lower Water St. ☎ **902/423-6818.** Reservations recommended for upstairs dining room. Main courses $13–$23. AE, DC, ER, MC, V. Mon–Fri 11:30am–2:30pm; daily 5–10pm; bar daily 11:30am–1am. SEAFOOD/CANADIAN.

Right on the water at Historic Properties, Salty's overlooks the harbor and the historic ships berthed there. The dinner menu features pastas and fresh Atlantic seafood served in imaginative and interesting ways. Lunch, served in the restaurant and in the first-floor Salty Dog Bar and Grill, is lighter, with choices like fish-and-chips or poached salmon. The Bar and Grill, popular for its view, outdoor patio, and weekend entertainment (8pm to midnight Friday and Saturday), serves the lunch menu all day, until 10pm.

☯ **Sweet Basil Bistro.** In Historic Properties, 1866 Upper Water St. ☎ **902/425-2133.** Main courses $8–$14.95. AE, DC, ER, MC, V. Daily 11am–11pm; shorter hours in winter. Early bird specials served 4:30–6pm. NOUVELLE.

This restaurant has the flavor of an Italian trattoria, but its dishes have greater flair than that description implies. Combinations and seasonings are well tuned—as in squash ravioli served with hazelnuts in a light Parmesan sauce—and daily specials may feature a Maritime version of bouillabaisse. While it's hard to leave room for dessert, you really should meet King Olaf, a concoction with a chocolate nut base topped by velvety rich dark chocolate mousse. Upbeat decor, good lighting, a nice wine list, and a personable staff make for relaxed dining in the old waterfront building with fieldstone walls.

INEXPENSIVE

Trendy cafes, lounges, and restaurants line Market, Grafton, and Argyle streets between George and Blowers streets. Most run daily lunch specials announced on convenient outside bulletin boards.

The area bounded by Granville, Argyle, and Blowers streets is a funky, "New Age" neighborhood with some interesting choices. **Gourmet Your Way,** at 5237 Blowers St. (☎ 902/422-6021), has takeout pastas with a variety of sauces for about $4. The flavor of Vietnam is represented at the **Cafe Cap St. Jacques,** 5190 Blowers St. (☎ 902/422-9131), open Monday through Saturday. Lunch combos and entrees cost $6 to $8, dinner from $8 to $15.

A perfect place to settle in for a relaxing break or on a rainy day is the **Trident Booksellers and Cafe,** at 1570 Argyle St. (☎ 902/423-7100), a bookstore (selling secondhand books and remainders) and adjoining cafe. The menu is short and inexpensive: muffins, pastries, and a wide choice of hot and iced teas and coffees.

☯ **Il Mercato.** 5475 Spring Garden Rd. ☎ **902/422-2866.** Main courses $5–$11. Mon–Sat 11am–11pm. NORTHERN ITALIAN.

Light-colored Tuscan sponged walls, big rustic terra-cotta tiles on the floor, and a fountain in the middle of the room instantly transport you to northern Italy. You'll find top quality at low prices here. Pasta dishes are $9, an oven full of focaccias and pizzas range from $6.50 to $8, and grilled entrees are $10 to $11. The focaccia is as good as any we've had in Italy; it's crispy and crunchy and the flavors perfectly blended.

Peddler's Pub. Granville Street. ☎ **902/423-5033.** Menu items $1–$5. MC, V. Mon–Sat 11am–midnight, Sun noon–10pm. LIGHT FARE.

Located on the Barrington Place pedestrian mall, this is a local favorite for a glass of beer and a light meal—say, chicken wings and the steak special, both under $4. On a warm, sunny day, you can sit outside and watch the world go by. Since 1980, a local group called Ken and Alex and the Swell Guys has been performing here on Saturdays from 3 to 6pm.

Satisfaction Feast. 1581 Grafton St. (between Sackville and Blowers). ☎ **902/422-3540.** Main courses $8–$11. AE, MC, V. Mon–Sat 7–11am; brunch Sun 10:30am–2:30pm; Mon–Sat 11:30am–4pm; daily 4–10pm (to 9pm Mon–Thurs in winter). VEGETARIAN.

Located in a plain wood-frame house, this bright and airy vegetarian restaurant offers a casual self-service breakfast. The lunch and dinner menus include a Thai plate, lasagne Romano, burritos, and tofu burgers. Desserts include blueberry grunt, a Nova Scotia favorite. All items are available for takeout; fresh bread, muffins, and cookies are on sale beside the cashier.

HALIFAX AFTER DARK

THE PERFORMING ARTS The modern **Metro Centre,** downtown at 5284 Duke St., draws crowds for concerts and sports events. It's easy walking distance from major downtown hotels. The box office is open Monday to Friday from 11am to 5pm (☎ 902/451-1221 to place orders, 902/451-1202 for recorded event information).

The small and unprepossessing **Neptune Theatre,** 5216 Sackville St., at Argyle (☎ 902/429-7070), offers some of the city's liveliest drama and comedy. The season runs from October to May. Tickets are $17 to $26, with a discount for students and senior citizens Sunday through Thursday. The box office is open Monday through Saturday from 10am to 6pm, later on performance days.

The **Grafton St. Dinner Theatre,** 1741 Grafton St. (☎ 902/425-1961), offers musical comedies with themes ranging from murder mysteries to a 1945 Victory party. Performances run Tuesday through Sunday, and the three-course meal costs about $30.

The **Historic Feast Co.** (☎ 902/420-1840) at Historic Properties has lively dinner shows with historic themes focused on the 1840s. The cost is about $30 per person.

THE CLUB & MUSIC SCENE The **Misty Moon Cabaret,** at 1595 Barrington St. (☎ 902/423-8223), and the **Palace Cabaret,** 1721 Brunswick St. (☎ 902/429-5959), throb with the beat of live bands nightly. The action doesn't heat up until after 10pm, but continues until 3:30am. The cover charge varies with the act but is usually is $2 to $12 at the Misty Moon, open Wednesday to Sunday, and $3 to $5 at the Palace, open nightly.

In Historic Properties, the **Lower Deck Pub,** in Privateers' Warehouse at street level (☎ 902/425-1501), is the best place to hear live folk songs from the Maritime Provinces. Local bands play Monday through Saturday, and the music starts at 9:30pm. Expect to pay $2 to $3 admission Wednesday through Saturday.

For live jazz, head for the **Birmingham Grill,** 5657 Spring Garden Rd. (☎ 902/420-9622), any night of the week. The outdoor patio is popular in summer.

Most Halifax bars have small dance floors. The **Harbourfront Bar,** at the Sheraton, 1919 Upper Water St. (☎ 902/421-1700), has a popular dance floor nightly at 9pm. The location, overlooking the water, is part of the appeal; there's a deck and live local entertainment in summer.

Guppy's, in the Prince George Hotel, on the corner of Grafton and George streets (☎ 902/425-1986), spins discs from the fifties to the nineties and appeals to all ages. The staff even gets into the act here, performing their own dance number around midnight.

THE BAR SCENE   Generally called lounges or beverage rooms, bars abound in Halifax; they're all busy weeknights, but packed on Thursday, Friday, and Saturday evenings.

Located in a historic stone house, the **☉ Granite Brewery,** 1222 Barrington St. (☎ 902/423-5660), eastern Canada's first brewpub, produces and sells its unpasteurized and unfiltered product on premises. Try its "Best Bitter," made with an 80-year-old strain of English yeast, or the "Peculiar," an old-style dark English ale with a sweeter taste. You can dine here, too, on terrific, inexpensive fare.

AN EXCURSION TO PEGGY'S COVE

A boulder-strewn and rockbound setting and a studied effort to keep everything in postcard arrangement has made Peggy's Cove leitmotiv of Nova Scotia. If you want to meet every other tourist in the province, join the tour buses in this mass migration 27 miles (43km) due west of Halifax on Highway 333. We suggest going before 8am or during the off-season, and maybe if you've only got time for a short excursion from Halifax. Otherwise, buy a picture postcard and save your film for the real fishing villages elsewhere along the shore. The buoys and lobster traps might not be arranged as artfully (they may actually be in the water trapping lobsters!), but you'll see a real place, not a stage set.

5 The Lighthouse Route from Halifax to Yarmouth

The Lighthouse Route follows the southwestern coast along Highway 103 from Halifax to Yarmouth, passing through or near dozens of coastal villages and several interesting small cities.

You can stop at Peggy's Cove on your way from Halifax via Route 33 (see above), or leave Halifax by Highway 103 heading west and south. Your first stop will be the charming town of Chester. If you're pressed for time, you can follow the Lighthouse Route only as far as Lunenberg, only 70 miles from Halifax, and return in the fast lane on Highway 103.

CHESTER

Take Route 3 to reach Chester, a New England–style village by the sea, 42 miles (70km) southwest of Halifax. In the mid-1800s it became a summer vacation retreat, with fine homes and several hotels.

In mid-August the town comes alive for **Chester Race Week,** the largest keelboat sailing regatta in eastern Canada. It's a good time to enjoy the colorful harbor.

The **Chester Visitor Information Center,** on Highway 3, is in an old railroad station on a hillside to the left as you enter town. It's open from 9am until 6pm daily, June through September (☎ 902/275-4616). You'll find a collection of restaurant menus here and a photo album of local lodgings, including pictures of rooms. The friendly staff will provide a map of Chester with a suggested walking tour, as well as the ferry schedule for Big Tancook Island.

EXPLORING THE TOWN & BIG TANCOOK ISLAND

Drive into town and follow King Street to the shore, then turn right on South Street. You'll come to a pretty gazebo, the Chester Yacht Club, and a statue of a soldier in a kilt, which honors the town's World War I heroes and the area's Scottish heritage.

After you've walked around town and looked in the galleries and shops, take a ferry ride out to Big Tancook Island in Mahone Bay. The passengers-only ferry makes four round-trips Monday through Thursday, more on weekends and holidays. The charge for the 4.8-mile (8km) trip is $1. Tancook has nice picnic areas and walking.

If you're in town in the evening in July or August, you might take in a play or musical event at the **Chester Playhouse,** 22 Pleasant St. (☎ 902/275-3933 or 800/363-7529); tickets cost about $15, less for students and seniors. They also perform December through February.

For an offbeat adventure, hook up with **S&J Shark Fishing Charters** (☎ 902/275-5551). They fish from a 22-foot Boston Whaler and do sightseeing and shark and mackerel fishing from Chester daily. **South Shore Charters,** RR 1, Chester, NS, B0J 1J0 (☎ 902/275-2338), does harbor and starlight cruises, or picnics aboard a 32-foot sloop.

A short excursion from Chester takes you about 20 miles (32km) north along Highway 12 to the **Ross Farm Museum** (☎ 902/689-2210). This "living museum" transports you back to a working farm in 19th-century Nova Scotia. Children love to see the farm animals and ride in a horse-drawn wagon or sleigh. Admission is $4.25 adults, 75¢ children 5 to 16, $9.75 for families. It's open June to mid-October daily from 9:30am to 5:30pm (otherwise, call for schedule).

WHERE TO STAY

Mecklenburgh Inn. 78 Queen St., Chester, NS, B0J 1J0. ☎ **902/275-4638.** 4 rms (all share two baths). $59–$63 double, $79 triple. Rates include full breakfast. V. Closed late Oct–May.

Upbeat and casual, this little 1890 inn with wood floors, pine furnishings, and a garden is the kind of place where you can settle in for a while.

We prefer the two front units, Winter's and Mrs. Finney's Hat, because of their access to the large second-floor porch. Comfortable and light, all rooms are furnished with antiques, including some fine Victorian beds, which have firm mattresses and quilts. Tartan robes are placed in the rooms for guests' use, a nice touch when baths are shared.

Guests can use the living room, with TV and VCR, or lounge on the balcony. Fine breakfasts are served around a big dining room table (originally a cutting table in a milliner's shop). The inn is a block or so from the Chester Theater, and a few blocks from the Tancook Island ferry dock.

WHERE TO DINE

At lunchtime you'll have to go far to beat ⑤ **Julien's Bakery,** on Queen Street. Their sandwiches, on their own breads, are the best in the Canadian Provinces. But you can't stop there, because the pastries are unforgettable. If you want to wet your whistle, the **Fo'c'sle Tavern** at 42 Queen St. has beer and inexpensive pub food.

Campbell House. Lacey Mines Road, RR 3, Chester Basin ☎ **902/275-5655.** Main courses $15–$20, lunches $5–$10. MC, V. Tues–Sun noon–3pm and 5–9pm. Just off Exit 9 from Highway 103, take the first left; or take Highway 3 from Chester to Highway 12, then head north on Highway 12 (over Route 103) to Lacey Mines Road. ECLECTIC.

The road winds up a hill to this white house with windows all around overlooking the gardens. While the atmosphere in the understated and relaxed dining room is traditional, the menu is fascinating: breast of chicken in a pumpkin-seed crust, roast duck in a black rum and pecan glaze, or halibut with garlic and leeks baked in puff pastry.

Chester Golf Club. Golf Club Road. ☎ **902/275-4543.** Lunch $2.50–$5, dinner $5–$8.50. V. Daily 8am–9 or 10pm during the season, depending on the weather. Follow Water Street out of town past the ferry landing, keeping to the shore until you get to Golf Club Road on the right. SANDWICHES/SEAFOOD.

This is definitely not a fancy place. But a local woman tipped us off that the fish and chips (for $4.95) were the best in town. You can get a club sandwich and fries for the same price. You can't go wrong.

MAHONE BAY

Mahone Bay is 15 miles (24km) southwest of Chester, and as you enter from the east on Highway 3, you'll see three church steeples reflected in the waters of the bay. The town is just beautiful. People come here for lunch and an afternoon of browsing along its waterfront Main Street.

The **Visitor Information Centre** is on your right as you enter town. It's open May through October from 10am to 5pm (9am to 7:30pm in midsummer).

The **Settlers Museum,** on Main Street near the center of town, houses antiques and an outstanding collection of ceramics. Out of the town's wooden boat-building heritage has sprung Atlantic Provinces' only **Wooden Boat Festival,** held annually the last week in July. Of the many antique and craft shops, don't overlook **Wholly Mackerel,** at 668 Main St. (☎ 902/624-1288), a craft shop specializing in Nova Scotia folk art, twig furniture, local fine art, whirly gigs and much more. Also on Main Street, **The Teaser** carries a large selection of handmade clothing and crafts, plus Nova Scotia tartans.

Those who'd rather be on the water should stop by **Mahone Bay Adventures** at 618 Main St. (☎ 902/624-6632), for kayak and canoe rentals, outfitting, lessons, and tours. Kayaks are $15 for two hours, $40 per day; canoes are $15 for four hours, $30 per day. **Discovery Charters** (☎ 902/542-7988) conducts full, part-day, or overnight sails, and will even prepare your picnic. The **Oakland Centre for Outdoor Education,** 189 Hirtle Cove Rd., RR no. 2 (☎ 902/624-8864), has morning, afternoon, and evening sailing lessons and does half- and full-day sailing cruises. **Sunnybrook Riding and Sailing,** 340 Herman's Island Rd., RR no. 1 (☎ 902/634-3735), lets you custom design your trip on their 37-foot Contessa sailing yacht. They also have a large outdoor horse riding arena with lessons available.

Mahone Bay is also home to Ronald Redden, an outstanding **wood sculptor** who specializes in carving great blue, northern right, sperm, humpback, and fin whales. Using a scale of 1:32, he creates groups and single whales so beautiful that they were used as the artistic centerpiece of the 1995 G-7 Economic Conference. You can meet him at the Sou'wester, where he doubles as innkeeper.

WHERE TO STAY

Sou'wester Inn. 788 Main St., Mahone Bay, NS, B0J 2E0. ☎ **902/624-9296.** 4 rms. $75 double. Extra person $15. Rates include full breakfast and evening tea. MC, V.

Formerly the home of a local shipbuilder, this stately Victorian overlooks the bay. Airy, carpeted rooms feature antiques mixed with newer furnishings in a comfortable blend. Room no. 4 has a wonderful bed, no. 3 a sofa that converts to a bed for older children. Over your full breakfast and evening tea, or a leisurely chat on the veranda overlooking the bay, the congenial hosts will help you plan your itinerary or shore hikes. No smoking or small children, please.

WHERE TO DINE

The Innlet Cafe. Edgewater Street, RR no. 2. ☎ **902/624-6363.** Main courses $6.35–$15. MC, V. Daily 11:30am–9pm. Closed Dec 24–25 and Jan 1. SEAFOOD/GRILL.

On the edge of town, the Innlet's terrace looks across the bay to the fine buildings on the opposite shore. The menu offers a wide choice of fish and shellfish, plus choices for carnivores. The seafood skibbereen is the chef's own special casserole of scallops, shrimps and mussels in a cream sauce with Irish cream.

Mimi's Ocean Grill. 664 Main St. ☎ **902/624-1349.** Reservations recommended at dinner. Main courses $9–$15. MC, V. ECLECTIC.

The casual, modern, slightly offbeat cafe atmosphere sets the stage for Mimi's innovative cuisine. Pecan chicken is paired with rhubarb chutney, mussels are served in a pesto cream, and fresh-made lamb sausage with rosemary and garlic is served over a lentil salad. If you're not feeling exotic, have knackwurst and sauerkraut or crab cakes.

Tingle Bridge Tea House. Route 3, ³/₄ mile west of Mahone Bay. ☎ **902/624-9770.** Reservations recommended. Cream teas $4.75–$6.25, lunch $5–$8. MC, V. May–Nov Wed–Sun noon–6pm.

Overlooking the quiet bay from well-kept gardens, this tea room offers unlimited tea refills, hot scones with strawberry compote, cheesecake, and shortcake all afternoon, as well as lunches of mussels, fish chowder, or creamed chicken on a homemade biscuit.

LUNENBURG

Continuing along Highway 3, a few minutes' drive will bring you into Lunenburg, 69 miles (111km) from Halifax and the center of Nova Scotia's fishing industry. The town was settled in 1753, and many of its first inhabitants were Germans, so it's not surprising that Lunenburg is known for locally produced sausages. Nova Scotians stock up when they visit here.

The **Lunenburg Tourist Bureau** (☎ 902/634-8100), in a lighthouse at the top of Blockhouse Hill Road, books rooms, answers questions, and supplies a town map and walking tour brochure that showcases its splendid architecture. The bureau is open from 9am to 9pm daily in high summer; there's a lookout deck in the top of the lighthouse. To get there, follow Lincoln Street up the hill.

EXPLORING THE TOWN

If you love ships, Lunenburg is for you, with its waterfront looming at the end of every street. In August the **Lunenburg Folk Harbour Festival** features Maritime Provinces music, and the **Nova Scotia Fisheries Exhibition and Fishermen's Reunion** has contests of traditional skills like scallop shucking and fish filleting.

East of the Fisheries Museum of the Atlantic, along the waterfront, scallop draggers tie up and unload. Farther east, at the end of Montague Street, are the **Scotia Trawler Shipyards,** where fishing vessels are winched into dry dock for hull maintenance. The original *Bluenose* and *Bluenose II* were built here, as was the *Bounty* for the movie *Mutiny on the Bounty.* When in Lunenburg keep an eye out for the *Bluenose II,* for it is often docked right next to the Museum area.

Walk or drive through the older part of town, up on the hill. Right by the Town Hall at Duke and Cumberland Streets is Canada's second-oldest church, **St. John's Anglican Church,** a lovely old clapboard building painted white with dramatic black trim; its oak frame was brought here from Boston. **St. Andrew's Presbyterian Church,** a block away at King and Townsend, has a 5¹/₂-foot copper codfish weather-vane atop its spire.

A mid-July **Crafts Festival** attracts more than 25,000 visitors. A fine place to see folk and Inuit art is the **Houston North Gallery,** at 110 Montague St. (☎ 902/ 634-8869).

Eric Croft conducts **Lunenburg Town Walking Tours** (☎ 902/634-3848 or 902/527-8555 for reservations) with commentary on history, architecture, the *Bluenose,* superstitions, and myriad other subjects. Tours cost $6 or $10 with a traditional Mug-Up at the end.

From the wharf, **Discover Lunenburg By Sail** has 1¹/₂-hour sailing tours on board their 48-foot classic wooden ketch *Eastern Star* in July and August at 10:30am, 12:30, 2:30, and 4:30pm, and at sunset. Rates are $15.50 for adults, $12 for seniors, $9.50 for children under 18. Sunset cruises are slightly higher, and a family rate is available.

✪ **Fisheries Museum of the Atlantic.** On the waterfront. ☎ **902/634-4794.** Admission $4.50 adults, 50¢ children over 5, family ticket available; rates likely to change. June to mid-Oct daily 9:30am–5:30pm, mid-Oct to May Mon–Fri 8:30–4:30pm.

The Fisheries Museum is comprised of a large red wharfside building, the wharf itself, and the two vessels tied up there: the salt-bank schooner *Theresa E. Connor* and the trawler *Cape Sable,* both open for touring. At the end of the wharf is the wheelhouse and Captain's cabin of the side-trawler *Cape North* and alongside is the *Royal Wave,* a Digby scallop dragger. Three floors of outstanding exhibits explain Lunenburg's and Nova Scotia's life as the haven of fisherfolk, including one on the legendary *Bluenose* and its captain, Angus Walters. There is also an aquarium, a theater, a demonstration room, and a working dory shop.

WHERE TO STAY

Bluenose Lodge. 10 Falkland St., Lunenburg, NS, B0J 2C0. ☎ **902/634-8851** or 800/ 565-8851. 9 rms. $65–$70 double. Rates include breakfast. Extra person $15. Packages available. Nov–Mar, by reservation. AE, DISC, MC, V. On-site and street parking. Look for the towering Victorian house with blue-gray trim.

This old Lunenburg mansion, set in a big yard surrounded by trees, has rooms of varying sizes and decor; all have private baths (shower, no tub). Smoking is allowed only in the sitting area on each floor. The new Carriage House is good for couples traveling together; the elegant Ashlea House, a formal Victorian, is only four houses away.

Breakfast and dinner are served in the inn's dining room, Solomon Gundy's; dinner features seafood entrees priced from $15 to $26.

Compass Rose Inn. 15 King St., Lunenburg, NS, B0J 2C0. ☎ **902/634-8509** or 800/ 565-8509. 4 rms. $65–75 double. Packages available. AE, ER, MC, V.

The Compass Rose Inn, in a restored 1825 Georgian home, has wonderful ambience, decor, cuisine, and location (downtown, a block above the harbor). The interior reflects its period, with comfortable antiques and beds covered with quilts.

The owners operate another bed-and-breakfast, the Lion Inn (ca. 1835), a few blocks away.

Dining/Entertainment: The licensed dining room, open to the public from 5 to 9pm, features entrees such as finnan haddie or scallops in a Pernod and tarragon sauce. The Compass Rose also has a guest lounge, an outdoor garden patio, and a gift shop.

Kaulbach House Historic Inn. 75 Pelham St., Lunenburg, NS, B0J 2C0. ☎ **902/634-8818** or 800/568-8818. 8 rms (6 with bath). TV. $50–$80 double. Rates include full breakfast. Packages available. AE, MC, V. Closed two weeks at Christmas. Open Nov–Apr by advance reservation only.

This striking house (ca. 1880) with mansard roof and dormer and bay windows has been lovingly restored. Six rooms have private bath with a shower (no tub); two others share a bath with a claw-foot tub. In the Tower Room (no. 6), two sitting areas overlook the harbor.

The three-course breakfast is served family style, and dinner is served to guests only in the fully licensed dining room. Guests can sip sherry in the Victorian parlor. No smoking, small children, or pets, please.

The Lunenburg Inn. 26 Dufferin St., Lunenberg, NS, B0J 2C0. ☎ **902/634-3963** or 800/565-3963. 7 rms, 2 suites. $65–$90 double. Rates include breakfast. Packages available. AE, DISC, MC, V. Limited parking.

All rooms in this richly appointed 1893 inn have private baths, and the third-floor suite has a Jacuzzi. Smoking is only allowed in the sitting rooms, or upstairs balcony. Don't park by the old train station—it's the police station and they ticket. You can easily walk to town from here.

Topmast Motel. 76 Masons Beach Rd., Lunenburg, NS, B0J 2C0. ☎ **902/634-4661.** Fax 902/634-8660. 16 rms. TV TEL. $55–$65 double; $70–$80 housekeeping unit. Extra person $5. Children under 5 stay free. AE, DISC, MC, V.

All units at the Topmast Motel have balconies; all but one overlook the harbor. Guests are encouraged to use the barbecue and picnic tables. A VCR and videos are available for rent and a golf course and tennis court are within walking distance. Nonsmoking rooms are available.

WHERE TO DINE

Even if you're not a guest at the **Bluenose Lodge** or the **Compass Rose Inn,** you can still have a meal there (see above). In the morning or mid-afternoon you might want to try out the **Piping Hot Bakery** on Lincoln Street.

The Old Fish Factory. 68 Bluenose Dr. ☎ **902/634-3333** or 800/533-9336. Main courses $14–$17. AE, DISC, ER, MC, V. Daily 11am–9pm. Closed mid-Oct to mid-May.

On the second floor over the Fisheries Museum, this restaurant not surprisingly has seafood (nicely prepared and seldom deep fried) as its specialty, but also serves pasta, chicken, and steaks. Casual, comfortable, and affordable, it's right in the center of activity.

A SHORT DETOUR TO BLUE ROCKS

To see a small fishing village that we like better than Peggy's Cove, take a short ride out Pelham Street from Lunenburg to **Blue Rocks,** which hasn't been gussied up for tourists. Dory-filled Blue Rocks harbor lies right along the road, with fisherman's shacks along the shore. Take Herring Rock Road to its end as it passes several more colorful mini-harbors along the way. At the end is yet another harbor, protected by a grass-covered rock island. Here is based **Lunenburg Whale Watching Tours** (☎ 902/527-7175). Sailings to see whales, seals, puffins, and other sea birds are at 9 and 11am and 2pm.

On the way, only five minutes from the center of Lunenburg, you'll see the **Blue Rocks Road B&B,** RR no. 1, Garden Lots, Lunenburg (☎ 902/634-3426). It has three cozy and comfortable rooms with firm beds and homemade quilts with $55 to $65 double rates. A full breakfast is served.

If you want see Lunenburg and Blue Rocks on a bike, see Al Heubach at **Lunenburg Bicycle Barn,** located at the B&B (☎ 902/634-3426). Along with repairs, he rents bicycles at $8 a half day, $15 per day, $90 per week. Route maps and great advice come along with the bikes.

SHELBURNE

"A Loyalist Town," like many others along the South Shore, Shelburne was settled by families loyal to the Crown who opposed the American Revolution. By 1783 upward of 10,000 people had flocked to Shelburne, then called Port Roseway. They put their wealth and skills as tradespeople, merchants, and ship builders to work here on the banks of one of the world's finest natural harbors. By 1790 Shelburne was North America's third-largest city—bigger even than Montréal and Québec. But the boom was short lived, because the land surrounding the busy port could not sustain its population. By the 1820s only 300 people were left.

A dozen old Loyalist houses still stand in Shelburne, now home to about 2,200 people. The **information center** at the foot of King Street, beside the water (☎ 902/875-4547), open from 9am to 9pm from mid-May to mid-October, will provide you with a walking tour map.

WALKING BACK IN TIME

Your first stop should be the **Shelburne Historic Complex,** made up of the Shelburne County Museum, the Ross-Thomson House, the Dory Shop, and Tottie's Crafts, all on or just off Dock Street. The **Shelburne County Museum,** at the corner of Dock Street and Maiden Lane (☎ 902/875-3219), displays artifacts detailing the area's Micmac history and the turbulent end of the 18th century. The museum also has an excellent genealogical reference center, with records of Loyalists who passed through from all along the American eastern seaboard. It's open mid-May through October from 9:30am to 5:30pm daily, in winter Tuesday through Saturday.

The **Ross-Thomson House** on Charlotte Lane was built as a store by Loyalists George and Robert Ross. It thrived during the town's boomtime in the late 1700s and continued in operation until the 1880s. The store has been restored with its long counter, stacks of hides, and barrels of provisions. Open daily June to mid-October from 9:30am to 5:30pm.

The **John C. Williams Dory Shop** is a living museum where wooden dories used by North American fishermen for the past two centuries are built. Open June to mid-September daily from 9:30am to 5:30pm.

Across the street from the Cooper's Inn is a brand new "17th-century" building erected for the movie *The Scarlet Letter*. Looking suspiciously like the House of Seven Gables in Salem, Massachusetts, it houses a **working cooper,** who still makes barrels the old-fashioned way, by fashioning staves from blocks of wood.

WHERE TO STAY

Cape Cod Colony Motel. 234 Water St., Shelburne, NS, B0T 1W0. ☎ **902/875-3411.** Fax 902/875-1159. 23 rms. A/C TV TEL. $49 double. Extra person $8. Children under 10 free. AE, DC, DISC, ER, MC, V.

Shelburne's motels are west of the town center on Highway 3, and the Cape Cod Colony Motel is one of the most handsome. It has fully equipped rooms and well-tended grounds with tables, umbrellas, and a swing. Guests are provided with complimentary coffee. The dining room is open from 7am to 10pm daily.

✪ **Cooper's Inn.** 36 Dock St. (at Mason Street), Shelburne, NS, B0T 1W0. ☎ **902/875-4656.**
7 rms. $55–$75 double. Rates include full breakfast. AE, DC, ER, MC, V. Closed Nov–Mar.

This is a fine choice if you want a historic bed-and-breakfast. Originally built as a log house in New England, then disassembled and erected here in 1785. It offers beautifully furnished rooms decorated with antiques. The bright blue and white Thomas Crowell room on the second floor has a big bay window sitting area that looks out over the harbor.

Dining/Entertainment: The rear dining room is actually in the small original log cabin, now swallowed up inside the large square hip-roofed colonial. Breakfast features fruit and homemade breads and muffins. Dinner, served nightly from 5:30 to 8:30pm, is prepared with fresh ingredients, artistically presented and served by candlelight. The scallops were some of the largest, most tender and delicious we've ever enjoyed, served in pine nut butter—a perfect combination. Even if you don't have room for it, order dessert—the aesthetic presentation will do your soul good. Dinner entrees range from $10 to $20.

WHERE TO DINE
Claudia's Diner. 149 Water St. ☎ **902/875-3110.** Most items $2–$11; dinners $8–$15. V.
May–Sept Mon–Wed and Fri 7am–9pm, Thurs 7am–7pm, Sat 9am–2pm, Sun noon–9pm.
Oct–Apr Mon–Fri 9am–9pm, Sat 9am–2pm, Sun noon–7pm. LIGHT FARE.

Claudia's has Nova Scotia home cooking and no pretensions. Short orders include hamburgers, fish chowder, lobster sandwiches, pork chops, and liver and onions.

HEADING WEST EN ROUTE TO YARMOUTH

On your way to Yarmouth you can continue your historic explorations at Barrington, west of Shelburne on Highway 103. The **Barrington Woolen Mill,** in operation from 1884 to 1962, displays much of its original machinery. The staff demonstrates spinning. It's free and open mid-June to the end of September Monday to Saturday from 9:30am to 5:30pm, Sunday 1 to 5:30pm. A picnic area is beside the river. Within 500 feet are the 1765 **Old Meeting House,** the **Western Nova Scotia Military Museum,** a replica of Seal Island Light and the **Cape Sable Historical Society Center.**

If you get hungry, stop at the **Old School House Restaurant,** at Barrington Passage (☎ 902/637-3770), open Monday through Saturday from 11am to 8pm, Sunday noon to 8pm. The schoolhouse has been so renovated that you'll barely recognize it, but the meals are well priced and filling.

YARMOUTH

Many visitors first see Nova Scotia from the ferry as it arrives in Yarmouth from Bar Harbor and Portland, Maine. The traveler who simply arrives and follows the signs to Route 101 might easily dismiss Yarmouth as dull. But that would be a mistake. It's worth spending some time here for the architecture alone. The sea captains who settled here brought home new ideas and styles from their voyages, and Yarmouth became a cosmopolitan city whose architecture and landscaping reflected many foreign influences. The hedges that replace fences around many houses have their origins in English Victorian gardens.

For information, drop by the huge, modern **Provincial Visitor Information Center,** at 342 Main St., perched above the ferry docks—you can't miss it as you come off the boat. For more detailed local information, check with the **Yarmouth County Tourist Association,** P.O. Box 477, Yarmouth, NS, B5A 1G2 (☎ 902/742-5355; fax 902/742-6644).

EXPLORING YARMOUTH

Available at the county information office are an architectural walking tour brochure, with commentary on more than 26 buildings, and a walking tour of gardens and parks put out by the Garden Club.

Off Main Street between the ferry terminal and Frost Park, the **Yarmouth County Museum,** 22 Collins St. (☎ 902/742-5539), exhibits ship models and paintings, authentic period rooms, and artifacts illuminating local arts and industries. It also has an active archive of genealogical materials and historical documents. Admission is $2 adults, 50¢ students, 25¢ for children, with a family maximum of $4; for the archives it's $3. From June to mid-October hours are Monday to Saturday 9am to 5pm, Sunday 1 to 5pm; from mid-October to May it's Tuesday to Sunday 2 to 5pm.

In the downtown shopping district, the **Firefighters Museum of Nova Scotia,** 451 Main St. (☎ 902/742-5525), shows how firefighters have battled blazes from 1819 to the present. It's heaven for anyone who has ever loved the big red machines. Admission is $1 adults, $2 for families. Open July and August Monday to Saturday from 9am to 9pm, Sundays 10am to 5pm; in June and September hours are Monday to Saturday 9am to 5pm; October through May it's Monday to Friday 10am to noon and 2 to 4pm.

Just outside of town on Route 1, **The Sign of the Whale** craft shop, run by potters Frances and Michael Morris, displays and sells fine Nova Scotia artwork and crafts.

WHERE TO STAY

The many lodgings in town fill up fast, particularly in summer, so reserve as early as possible. A few Yarmouth hostelries are within a block of the ferry docks. If you can't find a spot in town, try the **El Rancho Motel** (☎ 902/742-2408 or 800/565-2408), on Route 1 just outside of town overlooking Lake Milo at the beginning of the Evangeline Trail, or the **Coastal Inn Voyager** (☎ 902/742-7157 or 800/565-5026), near the Sign of the Whale Craft Shop, also on Route 1. Both are within a 10-minute drive from the ferry.

Best Western Mermaid Motel. 545 Main St., Yarmouth, NS, B5A 1S6. ☎ **902/742-7821** or 800/528-1234. Fax 902/742-2966. 45 rms. A/C TV TEL. $89–$96 double or triple. AE, ER, MC, V.

On the north end of Main Street, which becomes the road to Digby, the Best Western is a five-minute drive from the ferry landing. Five rooms in the two-story motel, which accepts pets, have kitchenettes. You'll also find a heated swimming pool, laundry facilities, and a gift shop. Captain Kelley's restaurant is five doors away.

The same management operates the less expensive Capri Motel nearby (☎ 902/742-7168; fax 902/742-2966).

✪ **Murray Manor B&B.** 225 Main St., Yarmouth, NS, B5A 1C6. ☎ **902/742-9625.** 3 rms (with shared bath). $55 double. Rates include full breakfast. V.

Consummate hosts George and Joan Semple not only have beautifully restored and decorated their home, but they have added every detail with their guests' comfort and convenience in mind. The large and light rooms have what are sometimes called prayer windows, set low under the eaves (you have to kneel to look out). Rooms feature white cutwork and filet crochet bed linens, fresh flowers, huge towels, extra pillows, ample reading lights, dressing gowns, and even a personal bath mat for the shared bath. Murray Manor is centrally located, just up the hill from the ferry landing (you can walk, or they will meet you), and at the very edge of the shopping district, but the dense hedge surrounding the landscaped yard gives the Gothic cottage-style house the feeling of a secluded country home. Joan serves afternoon tea in the garden or parlor from 3 to 4pm for $5 per couple.

Victorian Vogue Bed & Breakfast. 109 Brunswick St., Yarmouth, NS, B5A 2H2. ☎ **902/742-6398.** 6 rms (with shared baths). $45–$60 double. Rates include breakfast. Extra person $10. MC, V. Turn left on Main Street after leaving the ferry terminal, then right on Parade Street, and left on Brunswick.

An 1872 Queen Anne Revival, the house features five fireplaces, a three-story turret, stained-glass windows, and an abundance of oak and birch throughout. The rooms share two baths, though one room has its own sink and toilet.

The breakfast menu includes oatcakes, muffins, brown bread, maple-apple upside-down pancake, and orange rings. The Dessert Parlor is open Tuesday through Sunday from 1 to 4pm during July and August.

WHERE TO DINE

Captain Kelley's Restaurant. 577 Main St. ☎ **902/742-9191.** Reservations recommended. Main courses $5–$14. AE, ER, MC, V. Daily 4–8pm. SEAFOOD.

Located in a big, white sea captain's house, a 20-minute walk from the ferry docks, this popular dining place has a half-modern, half-old-time decor. The menu includes Nova Scotia lobster, prepared most any way you like it, and clam, scallop, or haddock dinners. The short yet good wine list can get expensive. Captain Kelley's Sports Pub, in the same house, is open from 11am to 1am daily.

The Five Corners. Main Street, at the Golden Horse. ☎ **902/742-6061.** Reservations recommended. Main courses $10–$19 (for the seafood platter). AE, MC, V. Daily 8am–10pm. CANADIAN.

From the outside, the Five Corners appears quite ordinary, but inside it's very pleasant, with lots of windows. Seat yourself at a table or one of the booths for scallops served in a cream sauce with mushrooms and garlic, or traditional rapure pie (pronounce it "rappie"), an Acadian favorite made of grated potato filled with clams, rabbit, or chicken. If you are staying at Murray Manor, ask your hosts for a free dessert coupon.

6 The Evangeline Trail, Kejimkujik National Park & Annapolis Valley

The Evangeline Trail, named for the heroine of Longfellow's romantic poem about the deportation, leads you through the original land of the Acadians, who were forced from their homes in 1755 by British authorities who feared that these French-speaking settlers would turn on them in their escalating struggle with the French. After the hostilities ended, many Acadians returned to Nova Scotia where their ancestors had first settled in the rich Annapolis Valley; they took their place beside Scottish and Irish settlers to cultivate their farms and fishing grounds in peace. Tidy French towns and villages, each with its church of wood or stone, line Highway 1, alternating with stately towns built in British colonial style.

EN ROUTE TO DIGBY

About halfway between Yarmouth and Church Point, a marked road to the left at Mavilette points you to **Mavilette Beach,** a beautiful and unpopulated sandy place to bask in the sun, just a short distance from Route 1. The **Cape View Motel** (P.O. Box 9, Salmon River, NS, B0W 2Y0; ☎ 902/645-2258), is a two-minute walk from the sand.

Further along the Evangeline Trail at Church Point and St. Bernard you'll pass two churches of note, both built by volunteer labor. Striking **St. Mary's Church,** at Church Point, is North America's largest and tallest wooden church. The spire extends 185 feet (56.3km) and has ballast (40 tons' worth) in the base to steady it from the buffeting winds of St. Mary's Bay. A bilingual guide gives tours of the church from June to mid-October; a museum holds vestments, photos, and other items (☎ 902/769-2832). From June through September on Saturdays at 8pm (July and August Tuesday through Saturday), the Université Sainte-Anne's **Theatre Marc Lescarbot** presents a musical adaptation of *Evangeline,* performed in Acadian French, with an English synopsis supplied (☎ 902/769-2114).

Further down the road, the granite **St. Bernard Church,** in the village of the same name on Highway 1, exemplifies the unity and self-sacrifice of the Acadian people who built it, adding one course of stone blocks per year from 1910 to 1942. The stone, hauled by an ox team from the railroad siding, was cut and dressed with hand tools. Both churches are open for visitors; if not, ask at the rectories next door.

WHERE TO STAY

Bayshore Bed & Breakfast. Highway 1, Saulnierville, NS, B0W 2Z0. ☎ **902/769-3671.** 3 rms (1 with bath). $35–$40 double; $50 suite. Rates include full breakfast. No credit cards. Open July–Aug; off-season by advance reservation only.

The circa-1830 Cape Cod–style cottage overlooks St. Mary's Bay. The small family suite has two rooms and a private bath with shower; the other rooms share a bath with shower. Guests can use the TV room and VCR. Rooms come with "a full break-fast—your call." An 18-hole golf course is a mile away, and a lake for swimming is a 10-minute drive.

WHERE TO DINE

Cape View Restaurant. On Mavilette Beach Road ☎ **902/645-2519.** Most items $5–$10. MC, V. Daily 7am–9:30pm. Closed Nov–Apr. FAST FOOD/ACADIAN.

Sitting on a hillside overlooking the beautiful beach and Cape St. Mary, Cape View serves traditional breakfast (try the fish cakes) and Acadian specialties, including rapure pie, for lunch and dinner. They also have fried clams, fried chicken, and sea-food combo plates, all at reasonable prices.

DIGBY

After Yarmouth, the first town of size along the Evangeline Trail is Digby, famous for its scallops gathered from the Bay of Fundy and for "Digby chicken" (locally cured smoked herring). Digby is probably best known as the Nova Scotia terminus of Marine Atlantic's MV *Princess of Acadia,* a car-ferryboat connecting the town with Saint John, New Brunswick, across the Bay of Fundy. The three-hour crossing (slightly shorter in summer) saves miles and hours of travel. For details on ferry cross-ings, see the section on Saint John in Chapter 5.

The **Evangeline Trail Visitor Information office,** in town by the water, is open daily from 9am to 5pm in early June, from 9am to 8:30pm daily for the summer (☎ 902/245-5714). The **Nova Scotia Information Centre** is on the shore road to the ferry, opposite the Annapolis Basin, open daily from mid-May to mid-October.

WHALE & SEABIRD WATCHING FROM DIGBY NECK

From Digby, a long narrow spit of land—Digby Neck—extends southwestward into the Bay of Fundy; St. Mary's Bay lies between it and the shore. Only Route 217 traverses Digby Neck (also known as "the neck"), so you can't get lost. The Bay of Fundy environment is unusually favorable for sea life and birds, making the neck and Brier Island an important stopover for birders.

Six **whale- and seabird-watching cruises** use the scenic Digby Neck as a base. Before you venture out, however, make reservations. **Bay to Bay Adventures** (☎ 902/834-2618) meets passengers for transports to its dock at East Ferry at its Little Bay office. The four-hour trips leave at 8:30am, 12:30, and 4:30pm. **Petite Passage Whale Watch** (☎ 902/834-2226) has cruises at 8:35am and 12:35pm from East Ferry; get tickets ($33 for adults, children under 12 half fare), at the East Ferry General Store. It takes 45 minutes from Digby to the first ferry. Across from East Ferry at Tiverton, via the short ferry ride, **Pirate's Cove Whale and Seabird Cruises** (☎ 902/839-2242) runs cruises aboard the 34-foot MV *Todd*. The three-hour cruises, requiring reservations, cost $33; family rates are available. They sail at 8am, 1pm, and if the conditions are right, they have a 5:30 sunset cruise.

At the neck's far end, another small ferry runs to Westport, on Brier Island, where there are three more cruising companies. Please note that the East Ferry to Long Island leaves hourly *on the half hour*, while the ferry from Long Island to Brier Island leaves hourly *on the hour*. Thus, if you want to catch the next Brier Island ferry, you must go directly from Tiverton to the ferry without stopping. **Mariner Cruises** (☎ 902/839-2346) has three daily cruises from June through October. If you want to be under sail, try **Timberwind Cruises** (☎ 902/839-2683), which operates the 35-foot *Timberwind No. 1* from Westport at 9am, 1, and 5pm daily. With a $30 per person fare, they'll do a fishing or sightseeing trip if you want. **Brier Island Whale and Seabird Cruises** (☎ 902/839-2995) runs research and educational cruises on 52-foot and 45-foot vessels. Reservations are necessary. Naturalists accompany all the cruises.

WHERE TO STAY & DINE

Several motels and restaurants are in Digby, but many others are scattered in the outskirts, especially in the resort hamlet of Smith's Cove, a few miles east along Highway 1.

The **Admiral Digby Inn**, on Shore Road (☎ 902/245-2531), is three miles from Digby and a half mile from the Marine Atlantic ferry dock; it's the closest hostelry to the boats. The motel-style inn has private baths, an indoor heated swimming pool, and a licensed dining room.

If you're hungry in Digby, **The Captain's Cabin** at 2 Birch St. (☎ 902/245-5133) has good food at reasonable prices, and takes you back to the 1950s. Open 10am to 10pm daily (but closed November through April), it serves seafood lasagne, scallops, fish or clams and chips, and sandwiches.

Another option is the **Red Raven Pub**, at 100 Water St. (☎ 902/245-5533), which serves filling, no-frills food and has a children's menu. Most items are under $10. Open Sunday to Monday 11am to 9pm, Tuesday through Saturday 11am to 2am. Weekend brunch is 10am to 2pm.

KEJIMKUJIK NATIONAL PARK

The park is reached via Route 8, called the Kejimkujik Drive. It runs from Annapolis Royal on the Bay of Fundy to Liverpool on the Atlantic coast, passing through historic towns and sites as it crosses the province's center. **Queens County Tourism**, in Liverpool (☎ 902/354-5741), has a good pamphlet on the drive and its attractions.

SEEING THE PARK'S HIGHLIGHTS: CANOEING, WILDLIFE WATCHING, HIKING & MORE

The park's freshwater lakes and streams support and sustain a variety of wild land and aquatic life.

The park has 329 **camping sites,** both for tenting and RVs. The tenting sites in particular are well spaced and private. Camping rates are $10.50. Primitive camping sites are also available. A public swimming area, at Merrymakedge within the park, has a picnic area. For more information contact the Superintendent, Kejimkujik National Park, Box 36A, Maitland Bridge, NS, B0T 1N0 (☎ 902/682-2772).

At the **visitors center** near the park entrance, you can get four excellent booklets about the park's animal, aquatic, and plant life, plus a map of hiking trails.

You can fish or canoe on two rivers and more than 15 lakes. A grading system identifies routes that can be enjoyed by inexperienced as well as more experienced canoeists. Canoes can be rented at **Pabek Recreation** in Caledonia (☎ 902/682-2817), or at **Jake's Landing** within the park. You'll get the canoe, paddles, PFDs (personal flotation devices), bailer, and whistles for $3 per hour and $16 per day; shuttle service is available for a variable fee.

The park also offers miles of hiking trails and roads for biking. **Hikes** range from less than an hour to extended hikes into more remote areas. A popular route is the 3.7-mile (6km) Hemlocks and Hardwoods walk that starts to your right just past the visitors center; it takes you through a 300-year-old grove of hemlock and offers views of Big Dam Lake. Bicyclists can go on paved and gravel roads, but not the gravel walking paths. You can rent **bicycles** at Jake's Landing.

In 1988 the park acquired a 14-square-mile parcel of land on the Port Mouton peninsula coast. This day-use area abounds in **wildlife.** The endangered piping plo-ver nests in a protected area, and in autumn and spring, many waterfowl stop here on their migration. Three- and eight-kilometer hiking trails cross bogs, boulders, and glacier-scraped bedrock and pass through forests of white and black spruce, balsam, and alder. To reach the longer trail, take Exit 21 off Route 103 and go past South-west Port Mouton. The shorter trail is past Port Joli. For information on the park's **Seaside Adjunct,** write or call the Senior Park Warden, 19 Fort Point Rd., Liverpool, NS, B0T 1K0 (☎ 902/354-2880).

OUTSIDE THE PARK

Along Route 8, look for Pocket Wilderness parks, small reserves with picnic facili-ties and trails; one even has swimming.

Settled as a farming town in 1820, **Caledonia** experienced a short-lived gold rush in the 1880s, still celebrated every year the first full weekend in July during Gold Rush Days with a gold mine trail tour and traditional entertainment.

Loon Lake Outfitters, Maitland Bridge, RR no. 2, Caledonia (☎ 902/242-2220), rents canoes or bicycles from mid-April through mid-November. Canoe rentals are $15 per day or $75 per week; you can also rent tents, stoves, and canoe packs. They offer completely outfitted trips including gear and food for $35 a person per calen-dar day, $23 per child—a great deal. General and topographical maps are available and they can outfit backpackers as well.

Nearby is the **McGowan Lake Fish Hatchery,** which raises half a million speck-led trout for release every year. You can tour the fish hatchery facilities or walk a nature trail. Fine native basketwork is found at **Bodaladamooge Trading Post** ("little people" in Micmac), a gift and craft store operated by Micmac people. Split ash handmade baskets cost $30 to $40. You'll also find quillwork and sweetgrass and birch bark baskets and boxes.

WHERE TO STAY & DINE JUST OUTSIDE THE PARK

Milford House. P.O. Box 521, Annapolis Royal, NS, B0S 1A0. ☎ **902/532-2617** or 902/532-7360 off season. $151 double for category 1 cabins (seventh day free with weekly rental), each additional person $58; $139 double category 2 cabins. Rates are modified American plan (MAP). Discounts for more extended stays. Closed mid-Sept to mid-June (except 2 cottages available off-season).

Before getting to the park entrance, you'll reach **Milford House,** one of the few remaining old sporting hotels. It's right along Route 8 in South Milford, only 14 miles (21km) from Annapolis Royal. Scattered along the lakeshore are 27 cottages, each with a stocked fireplace, refrigerator, and either tub or shower. The number of bedrooms varies in each unit, reaching as high as five. Our favorite is the Colonel, which offers privacy and instant water access. The cottages are comfortable and rustic, but the beds are on the soft side, and deferred maintenance makes the cabins more rustic than they should be. But the point of this place is getting back to nature. The lake connects to several others, allowing extended canoe trips; guests can rent canoes. The main lodge houses the office, guest lounges, library, and dining room, which serves homemade meals for guests. But even with meals, we think the buildings' condition makes this a bit overpriced.

The Whitman Inn. RR no. 2, Caledonia, NS, B0T 1B0. ☎ **902/682-2226.** Fax 902/682-3171. 10 rms. $55–$60 double; $110 apt. Special packages and extended-stay rates available.

Located on Route 8 just south of the park entrance, the Whitman Inn offers the flexibility to explore the north and south shores and the interior of this part of Nova Scotia. This large yellow 1900 country farm house has an indoor pool, Jacuzzi, and sauna. The well-cared-for and comfortable rooms are nicely furnished in country antiques. During summer, canoe and bicycle rentals can be arranged; in winter, cross-country skiing and snowshoeing. Also offered are special programs, such as photography workshops, nature painting workshops, and canoe clinics.

With an advance reservation, you can eat in the bright airy dining room Tuesday through Saturday. The interesting menu changes frequently, with dinner running $18.

ANNAPOLIS ROYAL

Samuel de Champlain built his original *habitation* not far from the modern town of Annapolis Royal. The fortified enclosure put up by the earliest French settlers had long since passed into ruin by the time a modern reconstruction effort was begun. The replica is now Port Royal National Historic Site.

The town changed locations over the years as the French and English battled for control of the narrow mouth of the Annapolis River, where it empties into the Annapolis Basin. In 1710 the English won decisively, setting up a garrison at the French town of Port Royal and changing its name (to honor Queen Anne) to Annapolis Royal. Until the Acadians were deported, Annapolis Royal was an English enclave in a region of French-speaking people.

Request the brochure with a walking tour and scenic drives from the **Annapolis Royal and Area Information Centre,** in the Annapolis Tidal Power Project on Route 1 (☎ 902/532-5454), open daily from mid-May to mid-October from 9am to 7pm.

EXPLORING THE TOWN

The Historic Restoration Society of Annapolis County owns and maintains five historic structures on lower St. George Street; three are open to the public. The **O'Dell Inn Museum** (ca. 1869) is a restored Victorian stagecoach inn with 15 rooms depicting aspects of life a century ago: a Victorian kitchen, a mourning room with coffin plaques and memorial pictures, and Maritime Provinces shipping memorabilia and models. The **Robertson-McNamara House Museum of Childhood** (ca. 1785) has clothing, games, books, and other childhood toys through the centuries, plus a display about the Foster Midgets, known as The Fairy Sisters (rivals of P. T. Barnum's Gen. Tom Thumb). It's open free to the public in summer only, daily from 9:30am to 5pm. The **Sinclair Inn,** dating from 1710, is one of Canada's oldest buildings. Acquired in 1995, it may be open for limited viewing in 1996.

Other historic buildings include the **Adams-Ritchie House,** now housing Leo's Café and Restaurant, and the **Farmers Hotel** (ca. 1710). More stunning Victorian houses line the residential streets.

On a 10-acre tract in the middle of town are the tranquil ✪ **Annapolis Royal Historic Gardens**, at 441 St. George St. (☎ 902/532-7018). The region's botanical history is displayed here, from the Acadian Garden, just like those the first settlers tilled, to a 1740 colonial style Governor's Garden and a Victorian Garden. The rose garden contains a maze made up of 2,000 bushes. There's a small charge for the gardens, open daily from 9am to dusk from May through October.

✪ **Fort Anne National Historic Site.** Entrance on St. George Street. ☎ 902/532-2321. Admission $2.75 adults, $1.75 seniors, $1 child 6–16. Mid-May to mid-Oct daily 9am–5pm; rest of the year by chance or appointment. Closed holidays.

In the center of Annapolis Royal, Fort Anne, built by the French in the early 1700s, was never actually completed. But it still saw a lot of action in the fierce sieges and battles that raged around here. Today costumed guides interpret artifacts discovered on site and the turbulent history of the town and fort. You can explore the powder magazines and the largely rebuilt officers' quarters buildings. A twice weekly candlelight tour of the adjacent Garrison Cemetery focuses on the old headstones' artwork.

ATTRACTIONS NEAR ANNAPOLIS ROYALE

Nova Scotia's theme/amusement park, **Upper Clements Park** (☎ 902/532-7557, or 800/565-PARK in Atlantic Canada), is located in Clementsport, only 4 miles (6km) from Annapolis Royal. From Upper Clements Park, a tunnel leads to a **provincial wildlife park,** where you might spot moose, Sable Island ponies, and bald eagle. Theme park aside, the Annapolis Valley is replete with farms and forests and views across the Annapolis Basin and River.

✪ **Port Royal Habitation National Historic Site.** Four miles past Granville Ferry. ☎ 902/532-2898. Admission $2.50 adults, $2 seniors, $1.25 child 6–16. Daily 9am–6pm. Closed Nov–Apr.

The Port Royal Habitation, a fur-trading post established by Sieur de Omns and designed by Champlain, was the first permanent settlement (1605) by Europeans north of St. Augustine, Florida. A British raiding party burned it in 1613, and several hundred years later, archeological digs unearthed some of the foundations. Reconstructed in 1938 and 1939, this simple and rustic place is a step back into another century. As you walk through the bunkrooms, chapel, kitchens, storerooms, and the governor's lodgings, costumed interpreters help you better understand life here in the early 17th century, thousands of sea miles from France, with unknown people and perils all around. Not surprisingly, the "Habitants" founded the "Order of Good Cheer," a fraternal body dedicated to making each evening's meal a happy and memorable banquet, dispelling gloom, fear, and loneliness.

WHERE TO STAY

At least half a dozen elegant Victorian houses have been converted to receive guests in this historic and exceptionally pretty town. The Garrison House Inn also has a fine dining room. You'll spot several inns along St. George Street, also known as Highway 8, the road into town from Digby.

Bread & Roses Country Inn. 82 Victoria St., Annapolis Royal, NS, B0S 1A0. ☎ 902/532-5727. 9 rms. $70–$85 double; $95 suite. Extra person $10. Rates include breakfast. Extended-stay discount. MC, V.

Topped by a slate roof, this red-brick Queen Anne revival mansion with a circular driveway and vine-covered porch is filled with fine woodwork, tile fireplaces, and Inuit and contemporary Canadian art. The rooms are furnished with many pieces from the 1880s, when the house was built. Ancestral photographs add to the historic ambience. Breakfasts are plentiful, and complimentary tea and cakes are served in the parlor in the evening. No children under 12, smoking, or pets are allowed.

Garrison House Inn. 350 St. George St., Annapolis Royal, NS, B0S 1A0. ☎ 902/532-5750. Fax 902/532-5501. 5 rms, 1 suite. $53–$72 double. Extra person $10. Honeymoon package available. AE, MC, V. Street parking. Open only June–Oct; possibly weekends the rest of the year.

Surrounded by a white picket fence, the Garrison House Inn sits directly across from Fort Anne in the town center. Built as an inn in 1854, it still serves meals to guests and the public. Bouquets of lupine, peonies, and Johnny-jump-ups fill the parlors, and the country-style bedrooms have comfortable beds, good lighting, and are quiet. Room 7, the "crow's nest," at the back of the house, is the perfect place to get away from the world. Children are welcome.

Dining/Entertainment: Even if you don't stay here, come for a meal in the inn's dining room; lunch costs from $5 to $10, dinner $20 to $25, and afternoon tea $4. For dinner, choose from 10 healthful main dishes, such as fresh pasta with Thai chicken and Acadian jambalaya. Breakfast is available but not included in room rates, and the private bar is just for guests.

☯ Queen Anne Inn/The Hillsdale House. 494 Upper St. George St. (near the Gardens on Route 8), Annapolis Royal, NS, B0S 1A0. ☎ 902/532-7850. 10 rms. $50–$90 double. Extra person $10. Rates include full breakfast. MC, V.

This 22-room house, built in 1865 in the Second Empire style, is among the most delightful extravagances of Victorian architecture. And it's as elegant on the inside as it is on the outside. Three parlors with high ceilings are filled with antiques. Most rooms are large, with full bath; some have only a shower, such as romantic room 4. Fresh flowers often greet you when you enter the room. No smoking.

A companion inn, the **Hillsdale House** (1849), on a 15-acre estate, has been renovated and reopened across the street by the same owners. The rates there are slightly lower, most from $60 to $75. You can easily walk to the town center from here.

A Place to Stay in Nearby Granville Ferry

Just to the north, less than a mile away across the Annapolis River, lies the village of Granville Ferry. You pass through here on the way to Port Royal National Historic Site, 4 miles away, and you might prefer making it your headquarters.

Nightengale's Landing. P.O. Box 30, Granville Ferry, NS, B0S 1K0. ☎ 902/532-7615. 2 rms (shared bath), 1 suite (with bath). $45–$50 double; $60 suite. Extra person $10. Rates include full breakfast. V. Closed Nov–Apr, except by reservation.

Set on four acres in the village, this 1870 Victorian gingerbread house boasts views of the water from the front bedrooms, sitting area, dining room and verandah. The inn has been carefully restored and furnished with antiques, but the feeling here is informal. Tea is served in the afternoon or evening. A folk art shop on the premises features the work of the owner, and other artisans' studios are a short walk away. No smoking or pets, please.

WHERE TO DINE

Leo's. 222 St. George St. ☎ **902/532-7424.** Breakfast $1–$3; lunch $3–$6; dinner main courses $7–$10. MC, V. Summer daily 9–11am, 11:30am–3pm, and 5:30–9pm; rest of the year daily 9am–5pm. LIGHT FARE.

Located in eastern Canada's oldest building (1712), Leo's is good for a quick breakfast or lunch, or a more leisurely dinner. The coffee's good, and there's a good tea list. You can't beat the hefty sandwiches, with a good choice of ingredients between slabs of 12-grain bread, or two hearty soups prepared daily. The dinner menu changes often, but keeps Leo's Famous Linguine, tossed with scallops, tomatoes, and green onions in a saffron cream sauce. Special diets and children's tastes can be accommodated. The country cafe is downstairs; the dining room and a deck are upstairs.

Newman's. 218 St. George St. ☎ **902/532-5502.** Reservations recommended. Main courses $12–$25; specials $16–$22. V. July–Aug daily 11:30am–9pm; June and Sept Tues–Sun 11:30am–9pm; May and Oct Tues–Fri 11:30am–2:30pm and 5:30–8:30pm, Sat 11:30am–8:30pm, Sun noon–8:30pm. SEAFOOD.

Newman's menu changes daily to assure the freshest products. Consider homemade baguettes and pâté, Greek salad, homemade lamb sausage with pine nuts, charcoal-broiled gravlax, Nova Scotia mutton chops, local black bear braised in red wine, cornmeal johnnycakes, or a serving of strawberry, blueberry, or peach shortcake big enough to feed a family of four. They serve select wines, but the house wines are quite drinkable and laudably inexpensive.

WOLFVILLE

In Willow Park, the **tourist office** is fronted by a fountain (you'll spot it easily as you drive along elm-lined Main Street), open from 9am to 7pm daily from late June to Labor Day; otherwise, 9am to 5pm daily. Ask for the self-guided walking tour brochure and about the tidal bore.

One of the first Georgian houses built in Wolfville, the **Randall House** (1808), 171 Main St. (☎ 902/542-9775), is furnished primarily with the late 19th- and early 20th-century belongings of the descendants of New Englanders who settled this district. It is now open to the public free from mid-June to mid-September, Monday to Saturday from 10am to 5pm, and Sunday 2 to 5pm.

The **Acadia University Art Gallery,** in the Beveridge Arts Centre, at the corner of Main Street and Highland Avenue (☎ 902/542-2201, ext. 373), showcases contemporary local, national, and international art in a variety of media year-round. Summer hours are daily noon to 5pm.

Favorite local pastimes in Wolfville include the simple pleasures of watching the tides and the birds. To see tides right in town, pick up the **walking trail** across the road from the Blomidon Inn and follow it to the water's edge (the highest tides are in the Minas Basin, however, and the best place to see the tidal bore is along the Meander River near Windsor).

For some unique bird-watching, make your way downtown to the **Robie Tufts Nature Centre,** built around an old chimney that once was part of a milk factory.

Just before dusk, the chimney beside the liquor store on Front Street attracts a swarm of **chimney swifts** (and a flock of human onlookers).

If you want to explore the surrounding area but don't want to drive, call **Kan-Active Tours** (☎ 800/933-8687) for their five-hour "Micmac Legends/Acadian History/Mighty Tides" tour that includes Grand Pre, the cliffs at Blomidon, the Look-off, artists studios, fruit farms, and a picnic at Halls Harbour if you want. Customized tours for groups of four or more are available.

The **Eastern Kayak Group** (☎ 902/542-9158) provides rentals, instruction, and guided outings for beginners and intermediates. Rentals include personal flotation devices (PFDs), kayak, spray skirt, paddle, tether, and transport to the launch site, and cost $20 per day for a single, $28 for a double. Groups equally divide the approximate $100 guide fee.

THE ATLANTIC THEATRE FESTIVAL

The new ✪ **Atlantic Theatre Festival** has risen immediately to the ranks of Canada's finest theater companies. Committed to developing theatrical talent throughout eastern Canada, it stages performances of three major works every summer at its Wolfville theater, also occasionally performing in Chester, Antigonish, and Annapolis Royal. Plays by Shakespeare, Chekhov, and Feydeau were performed for the 1995 season. Make reservations well in advance, because the theater's popularity fills its seats and area inns. Contact the Theatre Festival at 356 Main St. (P.O. Box 1441), Wolfville, NS, B0P 1X0 (☎ 902/542-4242 or 800/337-6661). Performances are held Tuesdays through Sundays from mid-June to early September. Tickets are $20 to $28, and a three-play series is $54 to $87 (prices inclusive of senior/student discounts), depending on day and section.

WHERE TO STAY

Blomidon Inn. 127 Main St., Wolfville, NS, B0P 1X0. ☎ **902/542-2291.** Fax 902/542-7461. 26 rms, 5 suites. May–Oct $79–$129 double; Nov–Apr $59–$99 double; $129 double suite. Extra person $12. Rates include continental breakfast and afternoon tea. AE, ER, MC, V.

The shipping magnate who built the Blomidon Inn in 1877 lavishly used his ship's cargoes of exotic woods from the tropics to construct this fine old building, with rich wood paneling, carved details, and fine fireplaces with overmantels. However, staying here is a mixed experience. While the rooms are nicely decorated with good furniture and firm beds, the tiny bathrooms only have showers, and slack maintenance permits dripping air conditioners, worn carpets, and badly abused woodwork in the dining room. The staff was friendly, but during our stay, no host was present so the inn lacked the warmth and friendliness you'd expect. That said, it is still a fine inn, whose reputation simply exceeds it.

Ⓢ **Gingerbread House Inn.** 8 Robie Tufts Dr., Wolfville, NS, B0P 1X0. ☎ **902/542-1458.** 2 rms, 3 suites. $59–$79 double; $125 Garden House Suite. Extra person $15. Rates include full breakfast. V.

This small inn has so much Victorian architectural detail that you would swear it was built at that period's height. But it started as a barn 12 years ago and has grown into an elegant contemporary inn. The most inexpensive room has its own tree-shaded terrace, while the most expensive, the Garden House Suite, has a huge in-floor whirlpool, an enormous living room with a 50-inch TV, a Franklin stove, a king-sized bed, and balcony sleeping alcove. This is the ultimate honeymoon suite. Each room, with fine contemporary furnishings and outstanding decorative details, has a private outside entrance and private bath. This place is a fantasy built by owners who are obviously having fun. But it's real and probably the best buy in town. Please, no smoking, no pets, no small children.

✪ **Victoria's Historic Inn.** 416 Main St., Wolfville, NS, B0P 1X0. ☎ **902/542-5744** or 800/556-5744. Fax 902/542-7794. 8 rms, 1 two-bedroom suite, 6 new units in the converted coachman's house. TV TEL. $65–$118 double; $118 suite. Extra person $10. Packages available. DISC, MC, V.

This gem of an inn, with beautiful architectural detail and furnishings, is impeccably cared for and wonderfully inviting. The elegant Victorian house, with wicker chairs on the porch and attractive grounds, was built for a prosperous apple merchant in 1893. The most elegant of the distinctively decorated rooms are on the second floor. Some rooms have air-conditioning, and VCRs are available for use. If you want complete privacy (and your own entrance), ask for the Hunt Room in the coach house, with an iron four-poster bed. Rates depend on room size and whether or not the bath has a Jacuzzi. No smoking or pets allowed.

Dining/Entertainment: Make a reservation early for dinner; a Québec chef prepares fine French cuisine, including seafood coquilles and breast of chicken stuffed with spinach, or a three-course dinner for $23. The dining room, open May to October, serves Tuesday through Sunday, from 5:30 to 8:30pm (daily during summer). A full breakfast is $3.75.

In Nearby Port Williams

Planters' Barracks Country Inn. 1468 Starr's Point Rd., RR no. 1, Port Williams, NS, B0P 1T0. ☎ **902/542-7879** or 800/661-7879 for reservations. Fax 902/542-4442. 9 rms. $69–$109 double. Rates include full country breakfast. AE, MC, V. Closed mid-Dec to mid-Jan. Pick up Route 358 (to Port Williams) 2 miles west of Wolfville and watch for signs for the inn; turn right onto Starr's Point Road at the flashing light and drive another 2 miles.

The inn is in one of Kings County's oldest buildings, now a National Heritage property. The early Georgian buildings (1778) started as Fort Hughes, built by the British to oversee resettlement of farmland evacuated by Acadians in 1755.

Six guest rooms are in the main house, three in what once was used as a customs house. The large bedrooms come with robes, hair dryers, old-fashioned tubs, and are carpeted for noise control, but public rooms retain their wide-board floors. The main house breakfast room is in the old kitchen with a large fireplace, plus guests can use a small kitchen. Guests enjoy tennis courts, complimentary mountain bikes, and a backyard barbecue set in a lovely garden. The beautiful and well-kept Planters' Barracks is a rare chance to stay in a Heritage Property. The efficient service is somewhat cool and impersonal, which heightens the sense that you are staying in a museum rather than a warm and inviting country inn—you expect more hospitality.

Dining/Entertainment: The inn is licensed for guests, and dinner can be arranged with 24 hours' notice. The Acacia Croft Tearoom, in the old Customs House, is open daily from noon to 5pm from mid-March to mid-December for lunch and for afternoon tea from 2 to 5pm with delicious scones and cream with strawberry jam. You can enjoy a Ploughman's lunch for $7.95 on the patio.

WHERE TO DINE

Two good options exist for breakfast, lunch or a snack. The **Coffee Merchant,** 334 Main St. (☎ 902/542-4315), open weekdays 7am to 11pm, from 8am on weekends, sells coffee, muffins, cheesecake, ice cream, sandwiches, bagels, and teas for $1 to $6. On Front Street, which parallels Main Street, **The Kitchen Door** has takeout service and is a good place to pick up a picnic.

✪ Chez la Vigne. 17 Front St. ☎ **902/542-5077.** Reservations recommended. Main courses $15–$20. AE, ER, MC, V. Tues–Sun 11am–midnight. Closes at 9pm in the winter. FRENCH.

We rate this as one of the best restaurants in Nova Scotia—and in all of the Atlantic Provinces. Chef Alex Clavel serves outstanding food in a quiet atmosphere, with soft music and lighting. The lunch menu, which includes salads, pasta dishes, omelets, and vegetarian crepes, is served all day long. The ragu of seafood with Cajun spicing and cumin in a light cream sauce includes sliced large scallops, small shrimp, mussels, and a flaky fish blended into a mouth-watering mélange. For dessert, if there is room, order the homemade sorbets, a scoop each of lemon, black currant, and raspberry.

If you're not going to the theater, reserve for 8 to 8:30pm, when the pace is more relaxed. If you do go to theater, come back afterward for dessert or a light dinner from a special menu. There's an extensive list of premium wines; the reasonably priced house wine is good.

GRAND PRÉ NATIONAL HISTORIC SITE

Acadian history's saddest times began at Grand Pré, the center of Acadian settlement in the early 1700s. Grand Pré National Historic Park is a memorial garden dedicated to the Acadians who suffered through the deportation, to those who returned, and to those who remained in the province. The memorial stone church, built in 1922 in French style on the church site where the deportation order was read, holds exhibits detailing Acadian history. You'll read sad letters of petition written to Massachusetts officials by impoverished Acadians asking for assistance. A small park and gardens surround the church, and in front of it is a statue of Longfellow's tragic heroine, Evangeline.

To get there, take Exit 10 off Highway 101. If you're driving from Wolfville, it's easy to miss the turnoff—turn at the sign for Evangeline Beach and if you see a sign for Windsor, you've gone too far. Parking is to your right just after the railroad tracks. The site is open from mid-May to mid-October from 9am to 6pm daily. Admission is free.

7 Marine Drive

Marine Drive includes all the jagged southeast coast from Canso to Halifax, a stretch that's perhaps the province's least visited and most underrated area. Here you'll find beaches, waterfront villages, coves, harbors, lush farmland, and wildlife. The route changes its number frequently, starting as Route 344 at Canso, becoming Route 16 at Boylston, Route 316 beyond Queensport, Route 211 from Isaacs Harbor North to Stillwater, and Route 7 from there to Halifax. However, it always closely follows the coast, meandering along inlets, peninsulas, and harbors. Driving is slow and circuitous.

CANSO & ENVIRONS

The road along the Straits of Canso skirts one of the world's deepest and most impressive harbors, looking across to the island of Cape Breton, following along cliffs, and passing several deep-water docks.

Port Shoreham Beach Provincial Park, as the road curves around Chedabucto Bay, is a great place for a picnic and swim—the sandy horseshoe beach stretches as far as you can see and there's hardly ever anyone there. Changing rooms and restrooms are available.

WHERE TO STAY & DINE

Seawind Landing Country Inn. RR no. 2, Charlos Cove, NS, BOH 1T0. ☎ 800/563-4667. 12 rms. $70–$85 double. Rates include breakfast. MC, V.

If you owned land on a point surrounded by sea, with small islands facing it across a narrow channel, you'd build this kind of house. Large casement windows overlook the water, and the views make even small guest rooms seem big as the whole outdoors. Hand-pieced quilts and small decorative touches make each room unique, but the overriding atmosphere is of the sea and the natural world that borders it.

Boat trips to islands where eiderducks nest and seals sun on the rocks, outings to clam flats where guests can dig their own supper, and guided trail walks through the nearby glacial barrens are a sampling of activities the hosts have lined up. On hikes, birders can see bald eagles, osprey and a flock of Hudsonian curlew. Beautifully prepared dinners for guests are $14.50 to $16.50.

DRIVING ON TO SHERBROOKE

Follow Route 316 to Isaacs Harbor where you follow signs to the ferry. Part of the highway system, this cable ferry (50¢) takes you across the channel west of Isaacs Harbor and saves miles of driving around the long Country Harbour estuary.

Just beyond Stillwater, where the Drive picks up Route 7, is **Sherbrooke,** a small community that boasts the major attraction along Marine Drive: **Sherbrooke Village** (☎ 902/522-2400), which lies less than a mile off Highway 7 (signs clearly point the way). Unlike other "living museums," this is the genuine article. An entire section of town has been preserved as it was in the 1800s, and people still live and work in many of its 80 restored buildings, and you can visit about 20 of these—churches, a jail, craft workshops, the schoolhouse, and more. Costumed guides interpret daily from 9:30am to 5:30pm from mid-May to mid-October. Admission is $4.

Sherbrooke lies on the St. Mary's River, one of Nova Scotia's best salmon rivers. At the **Sherbrooke Tourist Center,** you can **rent bikes** for $5 a hour or $25 per day (they have children's bikes, a child bike trailer, helmets, and water bottles) or **canoes and kayaks** at $6 per hour or $35 per day. For tour maps and advice, contact them at Camtech, Sherbrooke Tourist Center (☎ 902/522-2192; fax 902/522-2435). Ask about Riverview Nature Tours. Across the street, a nice little takeout place has good ice cream.

WHERE TO DINE

Bright House. Main Street, Sherbrooke. ☎ 902/522-2691. Reservations recommended. Lunch items $6–$8; main courses $10–$15.50. MC, V. June and Sept–Oct daily noon–8pm; July–Aug daily 11:30am–9pm. Closed Nov–May. COUNTRY DINING/SEAFOOD.

Restored in the spirit of Sherbrooke Village, Bright House (1850) is characterized by its wood floors, hanging plants, hooked rugs, and friendly service. The limited lunch menu features minced beef pie, chicken potpie, home-baked beans, Ploughman's plate, and the quiche of the day. Dinner choices include seafood chowder, fresh fish, farmed salmon, mussels, roast beef and Yorkshire pudding, or steak-and-kidney pie. The on-premises bakery makes breads and pastries, and it has a full license.

CONTINUING WEST

Near Spry Bay, farther west on Route 7, **Taylor's Head Beach Park** is another handy and attractive small beach and picnic park on a long peninsula.

A short distance beyond, the small town of **Tangier** is the jumping-off point for **Coastal Adventures** (☎ and fax 902/772-2774). Several of their dozen kayak outings explore the coast along the Marine Drive. They offer all-women tours, pedal and paddle tours, and even a land-based nature tour during which you spend your evenings in a B&B.

WHERE TO STAY & DINE

Liscombe Lodge. Liscomb Mills, NS, B0J 2A0. ☎ **902/779-2307,** 800/341-6096 in the U.S., or 800/565-0000 in Canada. Fax 902/779-2700. 30 rms, 15 chalets, 5 cottages (including 5 suites). TV TEL. $105 double; $260 cottage/suite. Extra person $10. Children 17 and under stay free in parents' room. Packages and optional meal plan, with breakfast and dinner, available. AE, DC, ER, MC, V.

The chalets in this seaside complex have fireplaces and porches; cottages are more elaborate, with verandas and four bedrooms each, plus a common living room with a fireplace. The guest lodge contains superior rooms, each with a balcony overlooking the marina.

Dining/Entertainment: The main lodge's dining room is open to guests and passersby from noon to 2:30pm and 5:30 to 9pm. The smoked fish is prepared in the resort's own smokehouse, and the salmon is cooked in an outdoor pit, an old Micmac method.

Facilities: An enclosed swimming pool, fitness center, nature trails, tennis, biking, boating, and fishing, including deep-sea charters, keep guests busy.

Marquis of Dufferin Seaside Inn. RR no. 1, Port Dufferin, B0J 2R0. ☎ **902/654-2696** and 800/561-2696. 12 rms. TV. $70 double. Extra person $10. Children under 2 free. Packages available. MC, V. Closed mid-Oct to May.

Rooms in this small, family run motel on Highway 7 all have balconies overlooking the broad cove and harbor. The clean and comfortable rooms are reminiscent of the 1950s. A rowboat, canoes, bikes, and maps for hiking are available. The dining room features simple but well-prepared fresh seafood and local products, serving dinner only from 6 to 8pm. Reservations are suggested.

As we write, new young German owners have just taken over—and the previous owners removed most of the better furnishings. There are plans to improve the inn, so expect substantial style and decor changes.

8 The Sunrise Trail from Pictou to Antigonish

Following the sheltered coast of the Northumberland Strait, the Sunrise Trail stretches east from Amherst (see Section 3 of this chapter) to the Canso Causeway, the entry point to Cape Breton Island. In this region, the skirl of bagpipes is never far away.

PICTOU

Once a Micmac town, Pictou (that's "*Pick*-toe") was chosen as home by a band of settlers from Philadelphia in 1767. They were joined in 1773 by the first shipload of immigrants to arrive from the Scottish Highlands aboard the *Hector.* Many more were to arrive in succeeding years.

The **Nova Scotia Tourist Office,** at the junction of Route 6 and Highway 106, just to the left off the traffic circle into Pictou, is open daily from 8am to 8pm mid-May to mid-Oct. If you are traveling on I-104, you'll pass a tourist information cabin about 18^1/2 miles (30km) south of town. It's open from 8am to 8pm daily in summer.

EXPLORING THE TOWN

Follow the signs for Braeside, and you'll soon come upon the **Northumberland Fisheries Museum,** in the gabled former Canadian National Railway station (1904), which holds fishing industry artifacts, including an authentically furnished original fisherman's bunkhouse. Be sure to see the *Silver Bullet,* a locally built lobster boat and three-time winner in Pictou's Lobster Carnival races, held in early July since 1934. Open only in summer, daily from 9:30am to 5:30pm Monday through Saturday, and from 1:30pm on Sunday; admission is free.

The **Hector Festival,** held for five days in mid-August, pays tribute to the area's Scottish heritage.

The nine-hole **Pictou Golf and Country Club** (☎ 902/485-4435), on the shore just inside town on Beeches Road, is on the water and open to the public. Club rental is $6; the greens fee is $14 weekdays, $16 weekends and holidays, 8am to 10pm.

The **Pictou County Cycling Club's** season runs from May through October. All tours have designated lead and sweep riders and they welcome anyone to join them. Call ☎ 902/755-2704 or 752-8904 for information.

✪ **Hector Heritage Quay.** 29-33 Caladh Ave., Pictou, NS, B0K 1H0, on the waterfront. ☎ 902/485-8028. Admission $4 adults, $3.25 seniors and ages 13–18, 75¢ children 6–12; children under 6 free; $10.50 families. June Mon–Fri 9am–5pm, July–Sept daily Mon–Sat 9am–5pm, Sun noon–5pm.

The *Hector* brought the first Scots to Nova Scotia in 1773 after a 10-week voyage that got them to Pictou too late to plant and harvest crops before winter set in. Their story is told here, where a full-size replica of the ship is now being reconstructed. You can visit the carpentry shop and blacksmith shop to watch these craftsmen at work. After viewing the exhibit, you'll feel you were on board the ship during the grueling voyage. Notice particularly the bluntness of the *Hector's* bow—it must have sailed like a bathtub!

McCulloch House & Hector National Exhibit Centre and Archive. Old Halliburton Road. ☎ 902/485-4563. McCulloch, June to mid-Oct Mon–Sat 9:30am–5:30pm, Sun 1–5:30pm. Exhibit Centre and Archive, June to mid-Oct Mon–Sat 9:30am–6:30pm, Sun 1:30–5:30pm; mid-Oct to May Mon–Fri 9am–5pm.

These three attractions are on six landscaped acres with fine flower gardens. Thomas McCulloch, a Presbyterian minister, educator, and naturalist friend of John J. Audubon, built the house in 1806. McCullough was not a rich man and Pictou was never a wealthy place, so it's not grand, but it's a monument to the people who came to Canada's wild backwoods and brought a bit of civilization with them. The McCulloch House, with its original furniture and artifacts from the town's early history, also displays some of Reverend McCulloch's ornithology collection, proclaimed by Audubon to be one of North America's finest.

WHERE TO STAY

The Braeside Inn. 126 Front St., Pictou, NS, B0K 1H0. ☎ 902/485-5046 or 800/565-0000. Fax 902/485-1701. 21 rms. TV TEL. $55–$95 double. AE, MC, V. From the end of Water Street make a short right onto Coleraine Street, then a left onto Front Street.

Recent refurbishing and excellent maintenance have retained the Braeside's genteel period character (circa 1938) while providing the comforts of a contemporary lodging. The inn is also warm and charming, the result of owners/hosts who enjoy interacting with their guests. The carpeted rooms are nicely furnished. The guest lounge, with wing chairs, is a great place to while away the time with a book.

Dining/Entertainment: Known as the best place in town for fine dining, the restaurant is casual yet quite elegant, with hardwood floors, botanical prints, and upholstered cameo-back chairs. It overlooks the harbor, as does the cafe. The menu includes filet mignon, salmon, lamb, lobster, and scallop pasta, priced from $14 to $23.50.

$ Consulate Inn. 115 Water St., Pictou, NS, B0K 1H0. ☎ **902/485-4554.** 3 rms, 2 house-keeping units, 1 deluxe cottage, 1 deluxe suite. TV. $50–$90 double, $85–$115 housekeeping unit, suite, or cottage. Extra person $10. Rates include continental breakfast. AE, MC, V.

Housed in a stately stone building that was the U.S. consulate in 1865, the inn has three large rooms upstairs in the main building and a large second-floor sitting room where you can picture yourself at an 1860s Consul's Ball. The Harborview Room has a deep tub, whirlpool, and a deck where you can relax and see the harbor. The third-floor Penthouse Suite, which only costs $65 for two, has a separate living room, a minikitchen, a harbor view, and sleeps five. Next door, in a new cottage, is a suite with multiple bedrooms, a living room, bubble tubs, kitchen, a wraparound balcony, and barbecue, surely one of the best buys around. The inn is not suitable for small children.

Pictou Lodge Resort. P.O. Box 1539, Pictou, NS, B0K 1H0. ☎ **902/485-4322** or 800/495-6343. Fax 902/485-4945. 65 rms and suites. TV TEL. $69–$99 double; from $99 suite. Extra person, crib, or cot $10. Senior discount. DISC, MC, V. May to mid-Oct.

Built in the 1920s as a getaway for Canadian Pacific Railway executives, this log cabin retreat by the sea has cabins that look a bit dowdy but are in good repair and have many attractive features. The resort occupies a secluded, serene spot on the ocean, 2¹/₂ miles (4km) from the Prince Edward Island (PEI) Ferry. Most of the three-bedroom log cottages have stone fireplaces (with wood provided), fully equipped kitchens, living rooms, and screened-in porches overlooking the ocean or lake. Rooms in new motel-style units have coordinated furnishings, good beds, carpeting, and tub/showers.

Dining/Entertainment: The main lodge, a massive log building in the Adirondack tradition, houses the rustic but elegant dining room; its wraparound porch has an unobstructed view of the sea. Lunch and dinner are served; dinner entrees, from $13 to $24, include scallops flambé in Pernod and beef roulade.

Services: Laundry and business services.

Facilities: Guests can use a canoe, rowboat, and pedal boats on the pond, or play badminton and horseshoes; a nine-hole golf course is only 4 miles away. Recently added facilities include places to barbecue and picnic, a recreation building, and a children's play area, with a pool planned for 1996. The lodge also has games and a library.

Walker Inn. 34 Coleraine St., Pictou, NS, B0K 1H0. ☎ **902/485-1433.** 10 rms. TV. $66–$79 double. Extra person $10. Rates include continental buffet breakfast. AE, MC, V. On-street parking and lot one block away.

As was common in 1865 when this house was built, commercial rooms are on the ground level, elegant living quarters on the upper floors. Today, the recently renovated house has been converted into a fine small inn only a few minutes' walk from the town's main attractions. A young, enthusiastic Swiss couple runs it. Rooms, some overlooking the main street, others a side street, are quiet, comfortable, and beautifully furnished. Room no. 5, with a view of the town center, features a 200-year-old four-poster bed. On the third floor, room no. 10 feels like a private suite with a harbor view. All rooms have baths with showers and are well lit. Guests can reserve for a stylish three-course dinner that costs approximately $20; the inn is fully licensed.

WHERE TO DINE

Fougere's. Ferry Road (off Shore Road, to your left just before the turnoff for the Caribou ferry). ☎ **902/485-6984.** Reservations recommended. Main courses $13–$22. MC, V. Mon–Sat 5–10pm, Sun 4–9pm. SEAFOOD.

Known for its seafood, not to mention "the best French onion soup this side of Montréal," this place also features roast beef, leg of lamb, pork chops, and a roast turkey dinner. Ben cuts his own beef and is so proud of his kitchen that he invites guests to tour it.

Stone House Cafe. 13 Water St. ☎ **902/485-6885.** Reservations not needed. Main courses $6–$20 (most items $7–$11). MC, V. Mon–Thurs 11am–midnight, Fri–Sat 11am–2am, Sun noon–midnight. PUB.

Start with the seafood chowder (chock-full of lobster!), and then try a German specialty or seafood, fried or otherwise. If you're not that hungry, the menu is full of snack choices, including pizza. On Sundays, don't miss the Black Forest cake, made on the premises. It's dark inside, but you can sit on the popular enclosed deck overlooking the harbor.

ANTIGONISH

Halfway between Halifax and Sydney, Antigonish (pronounced "An-ti-ga-*nish*") is best known for its annual **Highland Games,** held early to mid-July and attended by devotees of Scottish sports, pipe bands, and dances.

The **Nova Scotia Tourist Office,** at 56 West St. (take Exit 32, off Highway 104; ☎ 902/863-4921 or 800/565-0000), is open July and August from 8am to 8pm in summer, and 8am to 5pm in June and September.

Festival Antigonish, a summer-long extravaganza of professional theater, including drama, musicals, and revues and children's theater, is held at the Bauer Theatre on the university campus in July and August. Call ☎ 902/867-3954 or 800/563-7529 for their schedule.

WHERE TO STAY

During the Highland Games and graduation week in mid-May (the town is home to St. Francis Xavier University), inns and motels fill up quickly, so make reservations well in advance. If they're full, get a reservation outside Antigonish; Pictou's abundant good lodgings are not too far away.

Ⓢ **Old Manse Inn.** 5 Tigo Park, Antigonish, NS, B2G 1M7. ☎ **902/863-5696** or 902/863-5259 off-season. 5 rms (3 with bath), 1 apt. $40–$50 double; $80 two-bedroom suite. Extra person $10, child $8. Weekly rates available. Rates include full breakfast. No credit cards. Closed Labor Day–June. From Highway 104, take Exit 32 into town; turn left at the William Alexander Henry Government Building onto Hawthorne Street; take the second left, onto Tigo Park, and the Old Manse is on your immediate left.

A renovated 1874 Victorian house with a lot of character, the Old Manse Inn sits up on a hill just a five-minute walk from the downtown district. Three downstairs bedrooms have private baths, while the two bedrooms upstairs share a large full bath. The two-story apartment, great for families, has a private entrance, two upstairs bedrooms, a large kitchen, and a TV. Breakfast includes fresh farm eggs, bacon, and homemade jam and muffins. Guests enjoy the porch, picnic table, and well-tended yard, and can canoe in a secluded estuary or fish in the private trout pond.

Wandlyn Inn. 158 Main St., Antigonish, NS, B2G 2B7. ☎ **902/863-4001** or 800/561-0000. Fax 902/863-2672. 34 rms. A/C TV TEL. $60–$80 double. Children under 18 stay free in parents' room. Senior discounts, Wandlyn Pass Program, and special rates available. AE, DC, ER, MC, V.

The downtown Wandlyn Inn is a friendly, modern place in the Scottish tradition. Each nicely appointed room also comes with a sofa bed. Guests may enjoy the quiet library lounge and free use of the university's health facilities, including a pool and weight room.

The Highland Games

Antigonish's lavish display of Highland lore, art, strength, and skill—the **Highland Games**—has been held annually since 1863, usually Friday through Sunday in mid-July. Lead-up events begin as early as the preceding Saturday, with concerts, youth competitions, clan gatherings, Celtic workshops, ceilidhs, and a host of other pregames festivities. For the admission price (about $7 per day, or a pass for all events for $25), you can enter and leave Columbus Field as often as you please throughout the day.

At one end of the field are the Highland dancers, at the other brawny athletes running a 10,000-meter race, throwing the hammer, broad-jumping, and "tossing the caber," while pipe bands march and skirl in between. The caber, a peeled log about 26 feet long and six inches in diameter, is lifted and tossed end-over-end by any who can handle it, a feat requiring immense strength and skill. Highlights include the dance and pipe band competitions.

For sheer emotional thrill, the bands alone are worth scheduling your Nova Scotia visit around the Highland Games. After competing all day for points in playing, marching, uniforms, and bearing, the bands come together, hundreds of players forming an unforgettable display of Scottish color and ceremony. The tremendous presence of that night will come back to you wherever you hear a pipe's skirl. For more information, tickets, or entry forms, contact the secretary at **Antigonish Highland Society,** 274 Main St., Antigonish, NS, B2G 2C4 (☎ 902/863-4275). It's located in Room 206 of the Town Hall.

WHERE TO DINE

✪ **Sunshine Cafe.** 332 Main St. ☎ **902/863-5851.** Lunch $3.75–$5.95; Main courses $13–$14. MC, V. Mon–Fri 7am–9pm, Sat 8am–9pm, Sun 11am–9pm. ECLECTIC/NOUVELLE.

Trained in French classical cuisine, chef/owner Mark Gabrieau has created a vibrant health-conscious cuisine, using fresh local produce, cheeses, meats, and seafood, including succulent farm-grown scallops when available. Fresh-baked croissants are our favorite breakfast. The dinner menu not only offers a broad selection of salads, innovative appetizers, and pastas, but also offers original entrees such as salmon with a lime, ginger, and pistachio vinaigrette. Don't even think about leaving without a piece of "bumbleberry" pie, created from four different locally grown berries. An extraordinary wall mural by local artist Kate Brown dominates the informal, bright, and upbeat dining room.

9 Cape Breton Island

The wild and beautiful eastern end of Nova Scotia is actually several islands surrounding the many-armed, 450-square-mile saltwater Bras d'Or Lake (meaning "Golden Arm" and pronounced "Brah-*door*"), home to North America's largest population of bald eagles. Cape Breton's mountainous landscape kept it from being heavily settled, yet it was precisely this remoteness that appealed to a handful of hardy Scots settlers who founded small towns back in the mountains.

Cape Breton is a land of rugged highlands, dramatic mountains and valleys, rocky coasts, tranquil lakes—and hospitality. Except for Sydney and Glace Bay, twin industrial centers in the northeast, Cape Breton is a small-town destination; many are nothing more than a dozen houses, a general store, and a post office.

North Sydney, a suburb of Nova Scotia's second-largest city, is the departure point for ferries to Newfoundland. The Fortress of Louisbourg, south of Sydney, is Cape Breton's most impressive and exciting historical site.

The best way to see Cape Breton (and one of the world's great drives) is to take the Cabot Trail through the northern tip of the island in Cape Breton Highlands National Park.

The route we've mapped out starts at Canso Causeway, the only road to Cape Breton from the mainland, and heads north to the national park. From the park, you'll drive south to North Sydney and Louisbourg, and then west to the shores of Bras d'Or before returning to Canso Causeway.

Cape Breton's unique **bed-and-breakfast program** lets visitors find cape residents who have spare rooms to rent. You'll frequently see the distinctive "Cape Breton Bed and Breakfast" sign along the road. A house may have one, or several, rooms for rent, but the cost, including breakfast, will always be about $35 for one, $40 for two. Any tourist bureau on the island has a list, or call ☎ 902/539-9876.

OVER THE CANSO CAUSEWAY

Opened in 1955, the Canso Causeway, the world's deepest causeway at 217 feet deep, connects Cape Breton with the mainland. The bridge leads to Port Hastings, where the **tourist bureau** (☎ 902/625-9991) is open daily from 9am to 7pm (to 9pm in July and August). A cluster of motels greets you at the Port Hastings side of the causeway and in nearby Port Hawkesbury.

CHOOSING A ROUTE

Visitors debate the pros and cons of how to drive around the island, but, truth is, it really doesn't matter which way you choose. The roads are excellent and safe, and the scenery is gorgeous whichever way you go.

If you want to get to North Sydney for the Newfoundland ferry, take Route 105 up the island's center along the west side of Patrick's Channel.

If you're going to the national park, take scenic Route 19, the **Ceilidh Trail,** along the western shore to Margaree Harbour, where you will pick up the **Cabot Trail.**

If you can't wait to get to Louisbourg, go to Port Hawkesbury, and then take Route 104 and follow the Bras d'Or Lake Scenic Drive along the eastern shore of Bras d'Or Lake (and Route 4) to Sydney. Take the Sydney circumferential highway (Route 125) east to Exit 8 and follow Route 22 to Louisbourg.

If you have a few days to explore Cape Breton Island—and we hope you do—take the western, or clockwise, route starting with Route 19. The park entry here is dramatic; and you'll come to the information center at the Cheticamp gateway, which is much larger than the one at Ingonish and provides a more extensive orientation to the park.

While you can drive up and around Cape Breton Highlands National Park in one long day (if you start early), we suggest taking more time to explore the park. Also, we suggest spending a full day at the Louisbourg National Historic Site.

MABOU

The peaceful village of Mabou (pronounced "*Mah*-boo"), on Route 19 north of Canso, makes a fine base for exploring this area. You might get a chance to go to a ceilidh for some authentic Scottish music and dance.

EXPLORING THE AREA

In west Mabou, less than a mile out of town, **square dances** are held every Saturday night year-round; in summer there's one almost every night in some nearby town. A local fiddler plays, and people of all ages are welcome to these nonalcoholic events.

Drive out Mabou Harbour Road to Mabou Coal Mines Road and follow it about 3.7 miles (6km) to the wharf. You can ride out to the lighthouse at Mabou Harbour (watch for bald eagles), where you'll find a hiking trail. **Port Hood Beach,** just south of town, is one of the island's nicest—sandy, scenic, and uncrowded.

On Route 19, the surprisingly touching **Mother of Sorrows Pioneer Chapel and Shrine** honors the area's pioneer settlers; it's open in July and August from 10am to 4pm.

Scotch drinkers will enjoy the **Glenora Distillery,** on Route 19, 5.6 miles (9km) north of Mabou (☎ 902/258-2662), North America's only single-malt whisky distillery. Set on 200 acres, the black-and-white complex with a distinctive cupola and a seven-foot holding tank in front has tours that include the Mash House and Still House, where the distillation process takes place. You can sample "Cape Breton Silver," which one visitor called "the best damned moonshine I ever had." Admission is $2 and it's open daily 11am to 4pm. Their dining room serves three meals daily; don't miss the cranachan, a dessert of cream and rum-flavored fruit. They also operate an inn and often host traditional local performances.

WHERE TO STAY

⑤ Clayton Farm B&B. Route 19, Mabou, NS, B0E 1X0. ☎ **902/945-2719.** 3 rms (with shared bath). $55–$60 double. Extra person $25. Rates include full breakfast. No credit cards.

This 195-acre working farm, surrounded by water on three sides, stands about ¹/₂ mile (1km) south of town on Route 19; look for the sign and the big red barn. The farm has been in the Smith family since 1835, and offers stunning views. The large upstairs guest rooms, with wrought-iron beds and a fan, share a huge cheery bath. For breakfast, expect Acadian pancakes with maple syrup and local sausage. You can sit on the porch, walk down the lane behind the house, swing under the canopy of linden trees, or find the swimming hole in the river. In summer, a nightly square dance is just down the road.

◯ Duncreigan Inn. Route 19, Mabou, NS, B0E 1X0. ☎ **902/945-2207.** 3 rms, 1 suite with whirlpool. TV. $70–$80 double; $80 suite. Extra adult $10, child $5. MC, V.

The perfectly situated Duncreigan Inn looks across the harbor to the white spire of St. Mary's Church. The newly built inn is elegant, architecturally appealing, and beautifully decorated with antiques, and the owner is just as charming as the surroundings. The view from room no. 3, a large suite with a Jacuzzi, is beautiful by day and dramatic by night. In-room telephone or VCR is available, as is a canoe and two mountain bikes, and infinite suggestions for places to explore.

Dining/Entertainment: The licensed dining room, open Tuesday through Sunday from 5:30 to 8:30pm mid-June to mid-October, is one of province's best, with a daily changing menu that includes seafood and Cape Breton lamb and beef. Dishes are all prepared with flair and presented with style. The four-course dinner is $29, or you may order à la carte; some guests come by just for the Maritime Antipasto Plate, soup, and dessert. Reservations are suggested, since the popular place fills up fast.

Haus Treuburg Guest House. Route 19, Port Hood, NS, B0E 2W0. ☎ **902/787-2116.** Fax 902/787-3216. 3 rms, 3 cottages. TV TEL. $65–$85 double. Extra person $5. Cottages $85 daily, $450 weekly. Rates include full breakfast. MC, V. Closed mid-Oct to mid-May. From Mabou, take the second exit for Port Hood and follow Main Road; it's on the left after the co-op food store.

Haus Treuburg sits in farmland along the Northumberland Strait; Port Hood has sandy beaches and some of eastern Canada's warmest waters. The comfortable rooms are furnished with country antiques. The popular cottages overlook the ocean and come with a large sitting room, a kitchen, a separate bedroom, a large, full bath, and a deck with barbecue.

Dining/Entertainment: The inn serves a wonderful full German breakfast, and in the evening offers a five-course fixed-price dinner daily, by reservation only, for $29 (inn guests may eat à la carte). The cuisine is a mix of German, Italian, and French, and the menu changes daily. You might find homemade French baguettes, gravlax, salmon, or halibut steak, followed by apple strudel or cognac sorbet. Lighter fare is served in the bar/lounge.

WHERE TO DINE

Mull Cafe. Route 19. ☎ **902/945-2244.** Lunch items $3.50–$10; dinner courses $9–$15. MC, V. Daily 11am–9pm. LIGHT FARE/DELI FOOD.

If you're on your way to the Cabot Trail, you can get takeout from the deli or eat in at this popular local cafe. Try the veggie fritters or a daily stir-fry at lunch. Dinners are good and filling, and the desserts, such as brownie pudding pie and strawberry daiquiri cream puffs, are tempting. It's licensed.

CHÉTICAMP

The "Hooked-Rug Capital of the World," the gateway to Cape Breton Highlands National Park, and the center of Acadian life on the island's north shore, Chéticamp is a pleasant French-speaking fishing town famous for its folk art and handicrafts shops.

WHAT TO SEE & DO: CRAFTS, FOLK ART & MORE

There are numerous craft stores in Chéticamp, most notably **Flora's,** just south of town, which has inexpensive merchandise and an adjacent ice-cream parlor. **Whale-watching excursions** leave from the dock in the center of town.

If you only have time for one stop in Chéticamp, make it the **Bill Roach Folk Art/ Sunset Art Gallery,** on Route 19 about a mile north of town (☎ 902/224-2119). The gallery displays the work of local Acadian artist Bill Roach, whose whimsical pine and cedar carvings capture the character of fish, birds, roosters, cats, mice, sea gulls, and even six-foot giraffes. Prices range from $50 to $3,000, and he'll mail the work home to you. The studio also sells the work of a few other local artists, as well as handmade quilts at good prices. Open May to October daily 9am to 6pm, otherwise by appointment.

In town at 774 Main St., **Musée Acadien and Craft Co-Op Artisanale** (☎ 902/ 224-2170) is open mid-May to mid-October daily from 7am to 9pm. Downstairs, the two-room Acadian Museum houses a small collection of artifacts from Acadian traditional life; there's often a guide to show you around. Upstairs, in the Handcrafts Cooperative, hooked rugs and other craft items are on sale, as well as local music.

Just north of town on Route 19 to the right is the red, white, and blue **Les Trois Pignons** ("The Three Gables"), a combination **information center,** gallery, and museum (☎ 902/224-2642). The museum houses an eclectic collection from Canada, the United States, and Europe of everything from bottles to dolls. Of particular note are 20 historical tapestries by local artist Elizabeth LeFort, whose work has hung in the White House, Buckingham Palace, and the Vatican. She dyes her own wools, and some of her creations use more than 500 colors. Admission is $2.50 adult, children under 12 free. Open July and August daily from 9am to 6pm, the rest of the year Monday to Friday from 9am to 5pm.

WHERE TO STAY

Laurie's Motor Inn & Dining Room. Route 19, Chéticamp, NS, B0E 1H0. ☎ **902/ 224-2400.** Fax 902/224-2069. 48 rms, 6 suites. TV TEL. July–Sept $85–$125 double, $95–$125 suite; mid-Oct to mid-June $70–$85 double. Extra person $10. Children under 12 free. MC, V.

One of the region's largest motels, Laurie's offers large rooms downstairs in the Highlander section, each with a sitting area and an enormous bath; upstairs rooms are smaller but have balconies overlooking the Highlands. The honeymoon suite has a Jacuzzi for two and private patio.

The motel features a lounge with occasional Acadian entertainment for guests, Laundromat, VCR and bicycle rentals, and a bilingual staff who will also arrange whale and nature cruises. The licensed on-premises restaurant specializes in seafood and Acadian dishes.

WHERE TO DINE

Le Chaloupe. Whale-Watching Tour Wharf, Main Street. ☎ **902/224-3710.** Main courses $8–$13. AE, MC, V. Daily 11:30am–9pm. HOME COOKING.

In the town center, this is a pleasant spot simply to sit, sip something, and look out over the water. If you're hungry, they've got sandwiches, mussels, and good spicy chili, as well as ham, fish, and chicken dinners with mashed potatoes or fries, vegetables, coleslaw, and bread. It's a light, airy, and clean place, with seating on the deck, inside, and upstairs.

Restaurant Acadien. 774 Main St. ☎ **902/224-3207.** Reservations not needed. Dinner items $6–$12. AE, MC, V. Mid-May–mid-Oct daily 11am–9pm; mid-Oct–mid-May daily 9am–7pm. ACADIAN/HOME COOKING.

This small cafe specializes in Acadian dishes, with a fairly extensive menu of light lunches, suppers, and snacks. The dinner menu features codfish cakes, fresh breaded scallops, other fish and shellfish dishes, and turkey or pork chop entrées. It's real home cooking, a bit heavy on sugar. The cafe is licensed to serve beer and wine.

CAPE BRETON HIGHLANDS NATIONAL PARK

This is one of Canada's most spectacular parks, a place of mountains, forests, and cliffs that fall away into the sea.

Access to the park is via the **Cabot Trail**, which begins at Baddeck, heads to Chéticamp, and then in a few miles enters the national park to wind above the sea through the dramatic scenery of the Highlands. If you're following Route 19 you'll pick up the Cabot Trail at Chéticamp. The drive, which measures almost 70 miles (113km) from Chéticamp to Ingonish, was created along with the park in 1936. En route, in the Grand Anse Valley, you'll pass one of the largest and oldest uncut stands of hardwood timber in the Atlantic Provinces.

The drive can be done in a day, or even half a day, but to hike its trails and savor your surroundings, allow two days or more. Camping areas, picnic sites, and scenic lookouts are spaced at good intervals along the trail. If you plan to make any stops in the park, including stopping at lookouts or using a picnic area, you'll have to pay a user's fee of $6 a day, or $18 for four days, per car. If you stop your car without paying, you can't look.

Lookout points are well marked and usually have descriptive signs. You'll also see many hiking trails; a booklet describing all the trails, giving lengths and hiking times, is available at park offices. Ask for it, and any other information, at the **Information Centre** at the park's Chéticamp gateway, where you will find a good bookstore along with exhibits, picnic tables, and a play area for kids. In summer it's open from 8am to 8pm daily. Several hiking trails begin from here.

The highway wanders outside the national park boundaries at several points, including Pleasant Bay, Cape North, and South Harbour. At these points you can buy gasoline and food, or even find lodging for the night.

DRIVING THROUGH THE PARK TO DINGWALL

The first "inhabited area" in the Highlands you'll come upon is the small community of Pleasant Bay, nestled between MacKenzie Mountain and North Mountain. You can take a 2¹/₂-hour whale- and seabird-watching tour with **Pleasant Bay Whale and Seal Tours** (☎ 902/224-1315), offered from July to mid-September three times daily (the charge for adults is $24, $10 for children 6 to 15). There's also **Highland Coastal Tours and Charters** (☎ 902/224-1825), also running three tours daily from mid-June to mid-September, with prices of $20 for adults, $10 for children 6 to 15.

If you're ready for a break from driving, or if nightfall is about to overtake you, Pleasant Bay offers the **Salty Mariners Resort and Motels** (☎ 902/224-1400), set on 20 acres of oceanfront property, and the **Black Whale** seafood restaurant, a rustic place that does little to disturb the forest scenery (open from June to mid-October).

From here, the Cabot Trail climbs North Mountain, 1,460 feet (445m). Even if you're not a hiker, take time to stop at the **Lone Sheiling** (watch for the sign). This replica of a Scottish sheep crofter's thatched hut is set amid 300-year-old maple trees just off the highway. The half-mile trail to the hut is an easy 10-minute walk. The hut, by the way, was built to provide a visual, cultural "link" between life in the Scottish Highlands and that in the Cape Breton Highlands of "New Scotland."

Continuing along the Cabot Trail, before the turnoff to Beulach Ban Falls, just when you think you've seen about as many lupines as a person can see, you'll come upon an entire mountainside of purple ones, in bloom early in the summer. This stunning sight makes the drive worthwhile even if the lovely Aspy River Valley is shrouded in fog.

DINGWALL

Ideally located for those who plan to take two or three (or more) days to explore and enjoy Cape Breton Highlands National Park, Dingwall is a place to enjoy nature. Walk along the sandy beaches of Aspy Bay, or in the old gypsum quarry, with its interesting rock formations and pools. Go birding and try to spot bald eagles, merlin falcons, great blue herons, seabirds, and swallows.

Aspy Bay Tours in Dingwall (☎ 902/383-2847) offers three-hour whale-watching and seabird tours, and **Capt. Dennis Cox** in nearby Bay St. Lawrence (☎ 902/383-2981) has a 2¹/₂-hour tour.

Where to Stay & Dine
The Markland. P.O. Box 62, Dingwall, NS, B0C 1G0. ☎ **902/383-2246** or 800/872-6084. Fax 902/383-2092. E-mail Markland@fox.nstn.ca. 12 rms, 8 cabins. TV TEL. $86–$129 double; $145–$189 cabins. Rates include buffet breakfast. Extra person $12. Children under 12 free with parents (meals not included). Packages available. AE, ER, MC, V.

The sound of waves pervades the Markland, which offers simple and understated accommodations. Each pine-paneled room has high ceilings, a fan, a sitting area, and a picture window overlooking the water. The one- and two-bedroom cabins have cathedral ceilings, full kitchens with microwaves and stoves, and cassette players. Cabin 8 sits in the woods overlooking the ocean, and cabin 1 is tucked into the woods by itself—both very romantic. It's a great place for stargazing (no other lights interfere).

Dining/Entertainment: At dinner, entrées run $17 to $19, and include steamed mussels, rack of lamb, and beef medallions with cognac peppercorn sauce. Lunch items cost a reasonable $5 to $8, and there's a breakfast buffet.

Facilities: You may relax in the lawn chairs or gazebo, use the barbecue, swim in the outdoor pool, play lawn games, or enjoy a complimentary canoe or bicycle.

⑨ **Oakwood Manor B&B.** North Side Road, Cape North, NS, B0C 1G0. ☎ and fax **902/ 383-2317.** 4 rms (with sinks but no private bath). $43 double. Extra person $7. Rates include full breakfast. V. Closed Nov–Apr. Turn off the Cabot Trail at Cape North onto the road to Bay St. Lawrence for 1 mile (1¹/₂km), then turn left onto North Side Road for ³/₄ mile (1.1km) to Oakwood Manor.

In the same family since it was built in 1930, Oakwood Manor, located down a short country road that opens onto pastures with grazing cattle and a series of weathered barns, is a place for a relaxed and comfortable farm stay. Its walls, ceilings, floors, and even doors are made from oak harvested on the property. Guests are free to walk in the orchard and visit the gardens.

Driving on to the Ingonishes

Stop by **Neil's Harbour,** a fishing village with a distinctive Newfoundland flavor and heritage, with houses built close to the water. South of Neil's Harbour, **Lakie's Head Lookout,** in the park, is a particularly scenic spot, with a natural play of rocks, sea, wind-sculpted trees, and wildflowers.

If you have at least half an hour for a side trip, turn off the Cabot Trail to **Mary Ann Falls** and drive 4 miles (6¹/₂ km) along a dirt road to this moderately sized waterfall that spills into a secluded swimming hole. This drive takes about 12 minutes, and there's a nice picnic area here.

A popular hike in this part of the park is along the trail to the top of **Broad Cove Mountain.** On Tuesdays in summer, the Broad Cove campground (173 tent sites, 83 RV sites) is the site of interpretive evening programs and Scottish concerts.

The Ingonishes

At the southeastern entrance to Cape Breton Highlands National Park, strung along 8 miles (13km) of the Cabot Trail, are the villages of **Ingonish, Ingonish Centre,** and **Ingonish Beach.** Most of the national park recreational facilities—golf, tennis, hiking trails, boating, and sailing, and the fine sandy beaches in both Ingonish and Ingonish Beach—are in this area, as are the park's administrative headquarters and a small **information center** where maps are available.

Where to Stay & Dine

Ingonish Chalets. P.O. Box 196, Ingonish Beach, NS, B0C 1L0. ☎ **902/285-2008.** 3 chalets, 5 suites. TV. $75 motel double, $120 chalet. Special rates off season. AE, MC, V.

These pine log housekeeping chalets have full baths and woodstoves. They are so comfortable and cozy that you might want to return in winter, when the woods and fields surrounding them are deep in snow and criss-crossed by ski trails. Motel units also have light housekeeping facilities and all have gas barbecues. Access to one of the loveliest beaches on the island's eastern shore, hiking trails, and a play area make it a good choice for a several-day stay. In winter, downhill skiing is close by.

Keltic Lodge. Middle Head Peninsula, Ingonish Beach, NS, B0C 1L0. ☎ **902/285-2880** or 800/565-0444. Fax 902/285-2859. 72 rms, 26 cottages. TV TEL. $247–$262 double (MAP). Extra person $76. Children 4–17 half price on room and meals. Packages available. AE, DISC, ER, MC, V. Closed mid-Oct to Dec; Apr–May.

The Keltic Lodge, a resort run by the Nova Scotia government and located at the end of a birch-lined drive on a vast estate, is breathtaking. The views go on forever. Guest rooms are in the baronial Main Lodge, the modern White Birch Inn, and in two- and four-bedroom cottages; rates vary with accommodations.

Dining/Entertainment: The Purple Thistle dining room is open to the public, and there's also the more casual Atlantic Restaurant.

Facilities: The lodge offers a large pool, a freshwater lake, a mile-long beach, three tennis courts, and a 7-mile-long, 18-hole golf course (with resident moose and deer!), and nearby skiing in the winter. Be prepared to walk the golf course; carts aren't allowed in the national park.

SOUTH TO BADDECK

The Cabot Trail heads southwest from the Ingonishes to rejoin the Trans-Canada Highway at South Gut St. Ann's. Along the way, you'll pass Wreck Cove and the **Wreck Cove General Store** (☎ 902/929-2929). At this good rest spot, you can buy a fresh lobster sandwich on homemade bread. The store also carries camping and other supplies; ask for Mike and he'll tell you about the best local fishing spots. A covered picnic area with a barbecue pit is available from 7am to 9pm daily, June through September, or go south to the **Plaster Picnic Park** down the road about 8 miles (12¹⁄₂km) on the left. Wreck Cove is a little over an hour away from Baddeck.

Before meeting the highway, the Cabot Trail passes by the tiny hamlet of St. Ann's (marked as Goose Cove on some maps) where you'll see the **Gaelic College of Celtic Folk Arts,** founded in 1938 (☎ 902/295-3411). Set on a 350-acre campus, it offers summer courses in the Gaelic language and music, bagpipe and drum, Scottish country dancing, Cape Breton step dancing, and kilt making and weaving. In early August the **Gaelic Mod,** a merry festival with dance competitions, is held. The college shop sells kilts, quilts, Nova Scotia songbooks, and music. In the same building a small museum exhibits Scottish clans, life, dress, and music, as well as a statue of the "Cape Breton Giant," Angus MacAskell, who was seven feet, nine inches tall and weighed 425 pounds. Admission is $2 (children under 12 free). Open 8:30am to 5pm daily July and August, and Monday to Friday only from mid-May to June and September to mid-October (closed the rest of the year).

When you reach the Trans-Canada Highway (Highway 105), you can go left (east) to Bras d'Or Lake, North Sydney, and Louisbourg, or right (west) to Baddeck and back to the Canso Causeway. Both routes are outlined below, beginning with Baddeck.

WHERE TO DINE

Lobster Galley. South Gut St. Ann's, at the intersection of the Trans-Canada Highway 105 and the Cabot Trail (Exit 11). ☎ **902/295-3100.** Reservations not needed. Main courses $7–$23; daily fish special $16. AE, MC, V. May–June and Sept–Oct daily 11am–9pm; July–Aug daily 10am–10pm. SEAFOOD.

Near the Gaelic College, the Lobster Galley is a good place for lunch or dinner. Its forte is fresh lobster from its own pound, with a near one-pounder starting at $17 and up. The menu also features St. Ann's Bay mussels, deep-fried bay scallops, pasta primavera, poached or grilled Atlantic salmon, chicken and vegetable stir-fry, and vegetarian lentil casserole. And save room for the popular German apple cake or bumbleberry tart with English cream.

BADDECK

Baddeck (pronounced "Bah-*deck*") is one of Cape Breton's most delightful old resort towns, famed for its tranquil beauty and fine views of St. Patrick's Channel, part of

Bras d'Or Lake. Many visitors use it as a base for exploring the island, given its strategic location at the island's center.

But Baddeck has an even greater claim to fame: Inventor Alexander Graham Bell spent his summers here, and now the **Alexander Graham Bell National Historic Site,** on Chebucto Street (☎ 902/295-2069), celebrates his life and work, particularly experiments with the *Silver Dart,* an early airplane, and the HD-4, an early type of hydrofoil boat, the original hull of which is displayed. The free site is open daily from 9am to 9pm from July through September, 9am to 5pm daily the rest of the year.

WHERE TO STAY

Auberge Gisele. 387 Shore Rd., Baddeck, NS, B0E 1B0. ☎ **902/295-2849.** Fax 902/295-2033. 60 rms, 3 suites, 3 housekeeping units. TV TEL. July–Sept $95 double, $150 housekeeping unit, from $150 suite; mid-May–June and Oct $85 double, $125 housekeeping unit, $125 suite. Extra person $8. Children under 10 free. Honeymoon packages available. AE, ER, MC, V. Closed Nov–early May.

A bright new complex of 46 rooms and the newly refurbished original inn overlook Bras d'Or Lake. Nonsmoking rooms are available. The suites have kitchenettes and fireplaces.

Dining/Entertainment: The well-known restaurant, with a summer patio, serves breakfast and dinner, with dishes like filet of halibut with almonds or rack of lamb with herbs, priced from $15 to $35. There's a licensed lounge with a fireplace and dance floor.

Facilities: Whirlpool, sauna, and solarium.

Duffus House. 2878 Water St., Baddeck, NS, B0E 1B0. ☎ **902/295-2172.** Fax 902/752-7737 or 902/928-2878 off-season. 9 rms (3 with bath), 1 suite. $65–$90 double, $100–$115 suite. Extra person $10. Rates include breakfast. No children under 6. V. Closed mid-Oct to mid-June. Street parking.

Duffus House, at the water's edge and with its own private dock, is actually two 19th-century houses, side by side. Between them, they offer nine guest rooms and one suite with a private sitting room that opens onto a patio. Most rooms have sinks. Guests enjoy four sitting rooms, a library, garden and large pond out back, plus a home-baked breakfast in the country kitchen. The Baddeck boardwalk and the center of town are within walking distance. No smoking.

Inverary Inn Resort. Shore Road, Baddeck, NS, B0E 1B0. ☎ **902/295-3500** or 800/565-5660. Fax 902/295-3527. 137 rms, 3 efficiency apts. TV TEL. May to mid-Oct $91–$130 double. Extra person $8. Lower off-season rates available. AE, MC, V.

The inn, a collection of tidy dark-colored buildings with white trim, has the easy feeling of a family resort, set well back from the road on spacious grounds. Rooms are spread out: in the main lodge, in 10 cottages, including three efficiency apartments, and in a motel-type building. In some rooms, the decor is country style, and in others it's modern. Family rooms are available.

Dining/Entertainment: The air-conditioned dining room is open to the public as well as inn guests for breakfast and dinner. The five-entrée dinner menu is prepared with some flair; it's certainly not "plain old resort food." The Fish House on the lakeside offers lunch and dinner in a less formal atmosphere.

Facilities: Private beach, indoor and outdoor pool, children's playground, complimentary boat cruises and bicycles, canoes, paddle boats, tennis courts, hot tub, sauna. Cross-country skiing, snowshoeing, and tobogganing in winter. Fishing trips, tours, and sleigh rides can be arranged.

WHERE TO DINE

✪ **Bell Buoy.** Chebucto Street. ☎ **902/295-2581.** Main courses $9–$20; three-course dinner $28. AE, DC, DISC, ER, MC, V. Daily 11am–10pm. Closed Nov–May. SEAFOOD.

Overlooking the pier and St. Patrick's Channel, this pleasant licensed dining room features prompt, attentive service. At lunch, choose from sandwiches (clubs to seafood melts), a vegetable basket, stuffed filet of sole, Caesar salad, a cold lobster plate, burgers, or eggs Benedict. At dinner, go light with the Bluenose chowder and a lobster sandwich, or have steamed mussels or marinated herring for starters, followed by a fish or seafood dinner. There's a children's menu.

Herring Choker Deli. Highway 105. ☎ **902/295-1440.** Most items $3–$7. MC, V. Daily 8am–8pm. Closed Oct–June. DELI.

Six miles west of Baddeck before the turnoff for the Cabot Trail, this deli and its companion bakery join forces to serve sandwiches on freshly baked bread with fillings such as smoked fish and meat, and Canadian cheeses. Soup and a sandwich eaten inside, on the deck, or takeout, runs about $6. A "herring choker," by the way, is a fisherman.

THE SYDNEY AREA

The only city on Cape Breton Island, Sydney is Nova Scotia's third-largest city and a steel manufacturing center. British and Loyalist settlers founded it in 1785, and a rich variety of immigrants—including Irish, Scottish, French, Spanish, Portuguese, Ukrainian, Lebanese, Polish, and others—have come since then. In March 1909, Adm. Robert Peary departed from here on his expedition to the North Pole, and he returned here as well. And in May 1915, the survivors of the torpedoed *Lusitania* landed in Sydney.

North Sydney, 15 miles from Sydney, is the point from which Newfoundland-bound ferries depart for Port aux Basques and Argentia. Budget has a car-rental office at Sydney Airport and 501 Esplanade.

The town of **Louisbourg** has recently been spruced up and now offers shops, a few B&Bs, and an RV park along the waterfront, only a block off the main street. Restaurants are too new here for us to make reliable suggestions, but the tourist kiosk at the Fortress Visitor Centre has menus you can peruse. The **Savoy,** a 1928 Victorian-style theater on Lower Union Street in Glace Bay (☎ 902/849-1999), often has live performances by well-known Nova Scotia singers or fiddlers.

About 22 miles (35km) northeast of Louisbourg is the **Miners' Museum,** 42 Birkley St., off South Street, in Glace Bay (☎ 902/849-4522). For an inside look at what shaped industrial Cape Breton, take a 20-minute guide tour of the coal mine. Retired miners, who are full of fascinating stories, conduct the tours. It's damp and cool down below (it's 50°F underground), and the subterranean tour is not for those with bad backs or claustrophobia. Protective clothing is provided, but you should wear sturdy, comfortable shoes and bring a sweater. In the reconstructed Miner's Village, you'll find miners' homes from 1850 and 1900, a small company store, and a restaurant serving home-cooked meals at reasonable prices, from 9am to 10pm mid-June through September.

FORTRESS OF LOUISBOURG NATIONAL HISTORIC SITE

It is said that so much money was spent on the construction of the Fortress of Louisbourg that the King of France commented that he fully expected to see its walls rising above the horizon. It was begun shortly after the Treaty of Utrecht (1713) took away the French bases in Newfoundland; Cape Breton then became France's major center for cod fishing in the Grand Banks. A prosperous commercial town grew within this massive fortified enclosure. While the fortifications looked impregnable and daunting, bad positioning virtually assured its capture when the English laid siege in 1745, and it fell in less than two months. Eventually the great fortifications were blown up and the French town abandoned.

The government began large-scale restoration of the town and fort in the 1960s. Today visitors find themselves in a prosperous 18th-century French base. In summer, people in period dress fill the streets, houses, kitchen gardens, workshops, and store-rooms. Costumed vendors sell bread freshly baked in the old ovens. Chickens and geese wander the pathways, and the inns and taverns serve meals and refreshments of the kind popular when Louisbourg flourished. You'll be challenged by the guards as you enter, since the fort is always at war, but they'll let you pass.

When you arrive at the fortress, park at the Visitor's Centre, buy your tickets, and board the free bus, which will take you the mile or two to the site. Allow at least three or four hours there, opening doors, exploring buildings and buttonholing guards in the "Bastion du Roi" (the central part of the fortress) with questions about where the soldiers slept, what they ate, why they couldn't marry, and what caused them to be tossed in the guardhouse.

To get the most out of your visit come early in the day or right after lunch; wear shoes that will be comfortable on rough, cobbled streets; and bring a sweater and a waterproof jacket, since fog and drizzle can sweep in unexpectedly.

If it's a clear day, take a short detour to view the fortress from across the harbor at Lighthouse Point; the road will be to the left before you reach the center of the modern town of Louisbourg. This is one of the best places to photograph the fortress and grasp its size.

Admission to the fortress (☎ 902/733-2280) costs $6.50 for adults, $3.50 children over 5, $16 family pass covering two adults and their children. Open June daily from 9:30am to 5pm; July to August daily 9am to 6pm; after September 1, times revert to June hours (limited access during off-season). A sign on Highway 22 well north of Louisbourg has current closing times posted.

WHERE TO STAY

Cranberry Cove Inn. 17 Wolfe St., Louisbourg, NS, B0A 1M0. ☎ **902/733-2171.** 4 rms, 3 suites. TV TEL. $75–$85 double; $105–$115 suites. AE, MC, V.

Completely restored and carefully renovated to add full bathrooms to each guest room (six even have Jacuzzis), the inn opened in 1995, retaining much of its Victorian character. Each room conveys a different mood. Mixed antique and modern furnishings are well coordinated and stylish. About a half mile from the fortress visitors center and even closer to the town center, the inn is the area's best located lodging. The dining room serves both inn guests and the public, by reservation only, with reasonably priced entrées. While it lacks the museum quality of Gowrie House, its atmosphere is more relaxed.

Gowrie House Country Inn. 139 Shore Rd., Sydney Mines, NS, B1V 1A6. ☎ **902/544-1050.** 11 rms (5 with private bath). $65–$85 double; $115–$125 Garden House suite. Extra person $15. Rates include full breakfast. MC, V. Closed Nov–Mar.

The house, built between 1820 and 1830, is set on five acres of grounds with outstanding gardens and towering trees; it's a five-minute drive from the Newfoundland ferries, and 45 minutes from the Miner's Museum and Fortress of Louisbourg. The four guest rooms in the gray-shingled main house are decorated with an impressive mix of antiques and other collectibles, and share two full baths. The four suites, in the Garden House, have rich wall coverings, working fireplaces, TV, and private bath; one is decorated solely with pre-1870 Cape Breton furniture.

Dining/Entertainment: The inn's dining room serves a four-course dinner nightly June through September for $35, which includes a minicarafe of wine. Reserve ahead for the one seating at 7:30pm. The dining room is strangely hushed; when we were there guests didn't relax until the presentation of dessert, the most memorable part of the meal (although there may not be enough of each selection to offer a choice to the last people served).

HEADING BACK TO THE MAINLAND

From the Sydney area and Louisbourg, two routes lead back to the Canso Causeway and the mainland, one through Iona and the other through St. Peters.

VIA HIGHWAY 223 THROUGH IONA   Highway 223 follows the eastern shore of St. Andrew's Channel to Grand Narrows, where a bridge crosses the Barra Strait to the village of **Iona,** home of the 43-acre, open-air **Nova Scotia Highland Village Museum**, just south of the bridge (☎ 902/725-2272). Ten historic buildings on a hillside overlooking the Barra Strait depict the life of Scottish settlers in the region over a 180-year period. Starting with a Scottish "Blackhouse," the exhibit has an 1800 log cabin, frame houses from 1830 through 1900, a school, forge, general store, a farm with Highland cattle, and much more. It's open Monday to Saturday from 9am to 5pm, Sunday 10am to 6pm, mid-June to mid-Sept. Admission for adults is $4, seniors $3.50, family $8. **Highland Village Day** is celebrated here the first Saturday in August and ceilidh (lively gatherings with folk music), codfish dinners, and other entertainment take place through the season.

From June through September, you can stay at the **Highland Heights Inn** just south of the Barra Straits Bridge and next to the museum (☎ 902/725-2360; fax 902/725-2800). Overlooking the Bras d'Or lakes, it offers 26 motel-style rooms (all with bath), meals (including a picnic lunch), bicycles, a walking map, a great view, and Cape Breton hospitality. Rates are $70 for a double, $8 for an extra person. The licensed dining room, open from 7am to 9pm, features country cooking, seafood specialties, and homemade breads and pastries. The Canso Causeway is 50 minutes away.

VIA HIGHWAY 4 THROUGH ST. PETERS   The other route west from North Sydney is Highway 4, the Bras d'Or Lake Scenic Drive, south and west to St. Peters, a historic hamlet on St. Peters Bay. The beauty of the little town is best appreciated from across the bay at Battery Park. Entering St. Peters, take the road to the left immediately before the canal (dug in 1854). Along with a great view you'll find picnic tables and signs describing the history of the town. If you'd like to stay in town, try the **Inn on the Canal,** P.O. Box 9, St. Peters, NS, B0E 3B0 (☎ 902/535-2200). This big log lodge, beside the bridge, only ¹/₃ mile (¹/₂ km) east of town, is comfortable, and its licensed dining room serves home-style meals.

From St. Peters, Highway 4 goes east to Port Hawkesbury and Port Hastings, where it joins the Trans-Canada (Highway 105) to cross the Canso Causeway back to the mainland.

New Brunswick 5

by Barbara Radcliffe Rogers and Stillman Rogers

New Brunswick deserves more than the passing glance it gets from many visitors intent on reaching other Atlantic Provinces. It boasts charming villages and vibrant small cities, a majestic river, exceptional wildlife, good hiking areas, several national parks, and 1,400 miles of scenic coastline—including miles of warm beaches. And New Brunswick is rich in heritage inns that rival any in Canada for accommodations and cuisine.

New Brunswick was founded by two groups of refugees—British fleeing from the Americans and French fleeing from the British—who have lived together peacefully since they settled here. Some of Canada's oldest cities and towns were begun by Loyalists escaping the American Revolution, while the French towns and villages dotting New Brunswick's northern shores are populated by descendants of the Acadians who were driven from Nova Scotia. This dual heritage remains strong: New Brunswick is Canada's only officially bilingual province, and French-speakers make up almost 38% of its population. You'll see the Stella Maris flag flown often, but here it's a symbol of heritage, not a separatist statement. This province's success in nourishing its diversity is an encouraging example.

1 Exploring New Brunswick

New Brunswick's shape makes it easy to see in a circular route or in a series of small loops. Whether you enter from Maine through St. Stephen or the Fundy Isles, from Nova Scotia via the Digby–Saint John ferry, or overland through Amherst, you'll be close to a point in this circle.

We begin this chapter at the Maine border with the Quoddy Loop and continue east to Saint John. From there you have two choices: going northwest to Fredericton and taking Route 8 along the wild Miramichi Valley to the Acadian Peninsula; or heading northeast to Moncton and up Route 11 to the Acadian Peninsula. Whichever route you choose, you can return by the other. If you don't have time to go all the way to the northern part of the province, you can cut quickly from Fredericton to Moncton via Route 2 (the Trans-Canada highway) and Route 112.

Remember: This province and all the other Atlantic Provinces (except Newfoundland and Labrador) operate on Atlantic time, one hour ahead of Eastern time. Set your watch ahead one hour as you cross the border, summer or winter.

VISITOR INFORMATION   To learn more, call ☎ 800/561-0123 from Canada or the continental United States. When you're traveling, provincial information centers at major entry points will assist you in finding accommodations during the summer through the "Dial-a-Night" hotel reservations service, available free at any bureau. For printed information, contact **Tourism New Brunswick,** P.O. Box 12345, Fredericton, NB, E3B 5C3.

GETTING THERE   New Brunswick, the "gateway to Atlantic Canada," links the rest of Canada to Prince Edward Island, Nova Scotia, Newfoundland, and Labrador.

By Plane   Within New Brunswick and the other Atlantic Provinces and from Boston and Newark airports, the local carrier is **Air Nova,** the commuter partner of Air Canada (☎ 800/776-3000 in the U.S. or 800/565-3940 in Maritime Provinces, 800/563-5151 in Newfoundland), with stops in Fredericton, Saint John, Moncton, Bathurst, and St. Leonard. **Air Atlantic,** the commuter partner of Canadian Airlines International (☎ 800/426-7000 in the U.S. or 800/665-1177 in Canada), flies to Fredericton, Saint John, Moncton, Charlo, and Chatham.

By Car   Entering from Maine via St. Stephen, take I-95 to Maine 9 to Calais, Maine, and over the St. Croix River into St. Stephen.

From Maine, you could also come via U.S. 1 to Me. 189 into Lubec. Cross from Lubec to Campobello Island; then take the ferry to Deer Island and the free government ferry from Deer Island to Letete, on the mainland. It's scenic and historic—you'll want to take time to explore Campobello—yet subject to possible delays by weather and ferry lines.

Those headed straight for the capital, Fredericton, may want to take I-95 to Me. 6 to Vanceboro—on the New Brunswick side it's St. Croix (and nearby McAdam). This varies the route and allows you to make a circle, returning via the shores of the Bay of Fundy.

From Québec City and the south shore of the St. Lawrence, the Trans-Canada Highway (105) crosses the wilds of Québec to the St. John River Valley, and thence to Fredericton. If you've just come all the way around Québec's Gaspé Peninsula, cross via the bridge at Pointe-à-la-Croix to Campbellton and take Highway 11.

By Train   **VIA Rail Canada** connects Rivière-du-Loup, Québec, with Amherst, Nova Scotia, running daily through the New Brunswick towns of Matapédia, Campbellton, Bathurst, Newcastle, Moncton, and Sackville. It originates in Montréal. Sleeping cars are included since the trip from Rivière-du-Loup to Moncton takes about 10¹/₂ hours.

For more specific information, call VIA Rail at ☎ 800/561-3949 in the U.S., 800/561-3952 in the Maritime Provinces, or 800/361-5390 in Québec between 6am and midnight.

GETTING AROUND   You can rent a car at the airport in Saint John, Fredericton, or Moncton, where all the major companies have desks; you should reserve in advance. **Tilden Car Rentals** can be reached in Saint John (☎ 506/696-3340), Fredericton (☎ 506/446-4105), Moncton (☎ 506/382-6104), or the United States through National Car Rental (☎ 800/328-4567). Avis, Budget, and Hertz can all be reached via their U.S. toll-free numbers.

Within New Brunswick, trains connect Moncton and Saint John on Monday, Thursday, and Saturday in less than two hours.

New Brunswick & the Gaspé PeniNsula

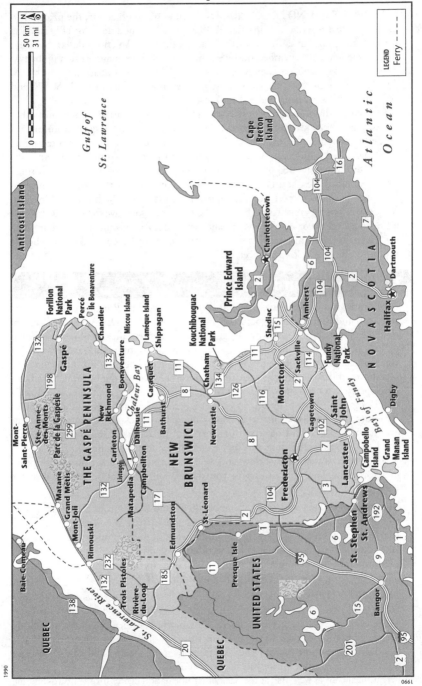

N

50 km
31 mi

0

Gulf of
St. Lawrence

Anticosti Island

Atlantic
Ocean

Cape
Breton
Island

Prince Edward
Island

16

104

104

7

104

6

104

2

Charlottetown

Shediac

15

Amherst

N O V A   S C O T I A

Halifax

Dartmouth

2

11

Kouchibouguac
National
Park

Sackville

114

Fundy
National
Park

Digby

Forillon
National
Park

Percé

île Bonaventure

Chandler

Miscou Island

Lamèque Island

Shippagan

Bonaventure

132

Gaspé

198

Ste-Anne-
des-Monts

Parc de la Gaspésie

New
Richmond

299

132

THE GASPÉ PENINSULA

Carleton

Chaleur Bay

Dalhousie

Caraquet

Chatham

11

134

8

126

Moncton

2

116

Cagetown

102

Saint
John

Bathurst

11

Newcastle

8

Campbellton

Matapedia

NEW
BRUNSWICK

17

St-Léonard

104

Fredericton

7

Lancaster

Campobello
Island

Grand
Manan
Island

Bay of Fundy

Mont-
Saint-Pierre

Matane

Grand Métis

Mont-Joli

Rimouski

132

232

Trois Pistoles

138

Rivière-
du-Loup

185

Edmundston

20

QUEBEC

St. Lawrence River

QUEBEC

Baie-Comeau

2

1

Presque Isle

11

UNITED STATES

95

6

3

6

15

201

95

Bangor

9

192

St. Stephen

St. Andrews

2

1

Litugoj

1990

0661

AN IMPORTANT NOTE ON PRICES   Unless stated otherwise, **the prices cited in this guide are given in Canadian dollars,** which is good news for U.S. travelers because the Canadian dollar is worth 25% less than the American dollar, but buys nearly as much. Do remember, however, that most of this savings is eaten up by two sales taxes of 11% and 7% respectively. As we go to press, $1 Canadian is worth U.S. 75¢, which means that your $100-a-night hotel room will cost only U.S. $75 and your $6 breakfast costs only U.S. $4.50 (plus taxes).

One costly detail is the 11% sales tax added to all restaurant, hotel, and other prices, plus 7% goods and services tax (GST). **The rates we've quoted do not include tax unless stated otherwise.** Very few items are exempt, and posted prices never include the sales tax. Avoid being unpleasantly surprised by figuring an additional 18% into the stated price. Exceptions include some clothing, footwear, small B&Bs, camping fees, and takeout food orders. You can get the tax back on some purchases but not on most travel expenses. If you leave via the border at Houlton, Maine, you can get an instant rebate on the GST, but you have to apply by mail for a Provincial rebate or if you leave by another route. Any visitor information office can give you the forms and instructions, but you must have over $100 in eligible purchases. Be sure to keep all receipts.

2 The Great Outdoors

New Brunswick has recently begun a unique Day Adventure Program called "Adventures Left and Right." Throughout the province, the staff of Day Adventure Centers (found in the lobbies of major hotels, in some information offices, and in the national parks) can give you details and make reservations for exciting outdoor activities. Or you can request a copy of the catalog of adventures by calling 800/561-1112 and then making reservations directly with the operators. Many of the options have been developed just for this program and include activities for all ages, interests, and abilities. Prices range from $10 to $175—most are under $50 and a substantial number are under $30. The list is long: boat trips, fishing, horseback riding, canoe and kayak excursions, garden and nature tours, cycling, whale watching, walking tours, children's programs, hunting, birding, even diving and an air tour.

Find your favorite activity below, and we'll point you to the best places in the province to pursue your interest or give you the general information you need to get started.

BIKING   The Fundy Islands—Campobello, Grand Manan, and Deer Island—are favorites of cyclists. You can rent bikes on Grand Manan; if you're going to Deer Island, you can rent at the Granite Town Hotel in St. George and their shuttle will take you and the bike to the ferry landing for the island.

Mountain bikers can get a free map and guide to trails in the Fundy area by calling the **King's County Tourism Association** at ☎ 506/432-6116.

BIRDING   The marshlands near Sackville and the area between there and the Nova Scotia border are filled with prime birding sites. Begin in Sackville's Waterfowl Park, where 160 species have been recorded. Tintamarre National Wildlife Area, Eddy Marsh, Fort Beausejour, and Cape Tormentine all offer good birding. Dorchester Cape, at the end of the Bay of Fundy, is visited by more than 50,000 sandpipers *daily* during their migration in late July and early August. Look here for bald eagles and peregrine falcons as well. Ask at the Sackville Information center for the "Bird-Finding Guide."

Machias Seal Island, near Grand Manan, is a sanctuary for puffins, arctic terns, and razorbill auks. Look for loons at Wolfe Lake in Fundy National Park and chimney swifts (3,000 of them) on the University of New Brunswick campus in Fredericton. That city's Odell Park is a good place to find songbirds, including the scarlet tanager. To see a sea stack covered in cormorants, stop at Pokeshaw Provincial Park near Caraquet on the Acadian Peninsula.

CANOEING New Brunswick has 2,200 miles of inland waterways, plus lakes and protected bays, so the canoeist can find everything from glass-smooth waters to rapids of all classes. Some of the most scenic parts of the Miramichi River offer easy canoeing and one of the Day Adventure Programs will take you on a guided nature tour of this unspoiled area with **Clearwater Hollow Expeditions** (☎ 800/563-8724). **Loon Bay Lodge,** near St. Stephen, offers white-water canoeing on the St. Croix River (☎ 506/466-1240). Both rent canoes and offer put-in shuttle service.

CROSS-COUNTRY SKIING Fundy and Kouchibouguac national parks and the Upper Saint John River offer some of the finest trails in the northeast. And others are found throughout the province—in fact, more than 2,400 miles (4,000km) of groomed trails await you. Several inns have trails leading literally from their back doors, including the **Cornish Corner Inn** in Stanley (☎ 506/367-2239) and the **Habitant Motel** in Richibucto, near Kouchibouguac National Park (☎ 506/523-4421).

DIVING The sea bottom surrounding Grand Manan is scattered with shipwrecks, making it a popular place for divers. Two shipwrecks and marine habitats are the focus of dives offered in the Day Adventures program, with **Club des Oursins** in Anse Bleue, near Caraquet on the Acadian Peninsula (☎ 506/732-5238); **Seascape Divers** has rental equipment and a diving center in Shediac (☎ 506/858-5663).

FISHING The Miramichi is a fishing legend—all the greats have fished there and many own camps near its waters. **Clearwater Hollow** (☎ 800/563-8724) is the headquarters for guides, camps, and other facilities for those wishing to test its waters (and themselves). **The Ponds** (☎ 506/369-2612), a lodge with cabins on the banks of the river, has been home to Miramichi fishing enthusiasts since 1925. Ask for a copy of "Fish New Brunswick" from P.O. Box 20211, Fredericton, NB, E3B 2A2, for regulations and for the other rivers and lakes.

HIKING Fundy National Park has a circuit of 30 miles (50km) of linked trails taking hikers through all the park's ecosystems, alongside brooks, lakes, rivers, and the Bay of Fundy's shore, past waterfalls and through forests—three to five days in all, with wilderness campsites along the way. One of the most interesting of the day adventures is a hike alongside pristine Big Salmon River, through a wilderness uncut by roads (☎ 800/56-FUNDY or 506/833-2534). They arrange longer hiking tours in the region as well. An excellent book is *A Hiking Guide to New Brunswick* by Marianne Eiselt and H. A. Eiselt, available in bookstores throughout the province.

KAYAKING The rocky shore of Grand Manan is best explored from the sea, and the area is popular with kayakers; Passamaquoddy Bay's numerous wooded islands are also best explored by water. **Outdoor Adventure Company** (☎ 800/365-3855 or 506/755-2007) in St. George (near St. Stephen) does guided kayak tours suitable for the experienced or the beginner. The Saint John River and its tributaries near Gagetown are often called the "Everglades of the North" for their abundance of waterways.

ROCK COLLECTING Geologists come to Grand Manan to see the effects of an undersea volcano that erupted some 16 million years ago, thrusting up newer rock into the much older sedimentary layer. It's not uncommon to find amethyst and agate here. The beaches at St. Andrews, on the nearby mainland, are strewn with a wide variety of rock types—from flint (which arrived as ballast) to granite, quartz, jasper, agate, and peridotite.

SHELLFISHING   Clams, mussels, and periwinkles may be dug or gathered along the shore, in most places without a license or limit. In parks, check with rangers; in other places, check with town offices for permission and to be sure the waters are safe from red tide or other problems.

WHALE WATCHING   More kinds of whales can be found more often in the Bay of Fundy than anywhere else on earth, and whale-watch expeditions are abundant from Grand Manan and St. Andrews. In the latter, go to the kiosk at Market Wharf or reserve through the Day Adventures desk at the Algonquin Hotel (not just for hotel guests). **Cline Marine** (☎ 506/529-4188) picks up passengers for whale watching on Deer Island and Campobello, as well as St. Andrews. **Fundy Tide Runners** (☎ 506/529-4481) uses diesel-powered Zodiac Hurricanes, cruising at 30 to 35 m.p.h.

3 Campobello Island & St. Stephen

CAMPOBELLO ISLAND

Campobello is part of Canada, though the only access road to the island comes from Lubec, Maine. Franklin Roosevelt's father bought land here in 1883, when many important people were building summer "cottages" at Bar Harbor and Passamaquoddy Bay. Young Franklin came here long before he was president and spent many a summer rowing, paddling, and sailing on the waters and hiking through the woods. It was here, in 1921, that he was stricken with polio. When he left the island that September, he had no way of knowing that the few more times he'd see the cottage would be brief weekend visits—as president of the United States. In 1960, the movie *Sunrise at Campobello,* starring Greer Garson and Ralph Bellamy as Eleanor and Franklin Roosevelt, was filmed here.

The **visitor information center,** just over the bridge to your right, is open daily from 9am to 7pm, May to mid-October (☎ 506/752-7043).

EXPLORING THE ISLAND

Campobello Island is only 3 miles wide and 10 miles long, and it's a pleasure to drive it, bike it, or walk it.

At **Herring Cove Provincial Park,** you'll find a camping area, a nine-hole golf course, and a mile-long beach with unsupervised swimming; inside the park is also a seafood restaurant. At **Friar's Head,** you can park and walk up the hill to the observation deck, which has interesting descriptions of the sights you're seeing, including "the Bay of Fundy, known for its bad temper and bountiful seafood harvest." Walk out to the bog, filled with birds singing and low-growing vegetation.

You can also drive to the end of the island to admire the **East Quoddy Head Lighthouse,** eastern Canada's most photographed lighthouse; you can walk (well, scramble) out to it at low tide.

Whales are not an uncommon sight in the waters. To go on a **whale-watch** trip from Campobello, contact Cline Marine at ☎ 506/529-4188; the boat leaves Head Harbour at 10am and 3pm daily in July and August and the price is $30 for adults and $15 for children, taxes included.

✪ **Roosevelt Campobello International Park.** Route 774. ☎ **506/752-2922.** Free admission. Daily 10am–6pm; last cottage tour at 4:45pm. Closed mid-Oct to late May.

Step back in time and take a fascinating look at how a well-to-do powerful family spent its summers at the turn of the century, with long, leisurely days filled by sports, games, and family activities. The Roosevelt Cottage is now part of a 2,800-acre nature preserve administered jointly by the Canadian and American parks services. The 34-room Roosevelt Cottage bears no resemblance to Newport-style summer homes. It's a rustic, comfortable seaside home, and seeing where the Roosevelts went to relax makes these larger-than-life historical figures seem more real and human. See the 15-minute film *Beloved Island* in the visitor center before you go and take time to stroll in the beautifully kept gardens. Ask for a map of the 8¹/₂ miles of walking trails in the park.

WHERE TO STAY & DINE

Friar's Bay Motor Lodge & Restaurant. Route 774, Welshpool, Campobello, NB, E0G 3H0. ☎ 506/752-2056. 10 rms. TV. $33–$40 double. V.

On the beach side of the road, not far from the international park, this motel is within easy walking distance of the beach. The efficiency units are convenient for long stays, since there are few dining options on the island. The restaurant serves traditional home cooking (main courses $6 to $19.50) in a rustic dining room overlooking gull-topped posts and fishing weirs. A country breakfast costs about $5.

Owen House. Route 774, Welshpool, Campobello, NB, E0G 3H0. ☎ **506/752-2977.** 8 rms (4 with bath), 1 suite. $55 double without bath, $65 double with bath. Extra person $15. Rates include full breakfast. V. Closed Nov–May.

This retreat overlooking the bay is popular with artists, photographers, and bicyclists. The house provides inviting nooks for guests, like a glassed-in porch with ship models, a sitting room made cozy by a nightly fire in the hearth, and a beautiful dining room. A breakfast of limitless pancakes, sausage, juice, and coffee is served family style at 8:30am. The old-fashioned rooms have white curtains and double beds. The four second-floor rooms have baths (room no. 1 overlooks the water), and the smaller four on the third floor share a bath with a shower. The two-room suite is ideal for families.

ST. STEPHEN

Residents of Maine and New Brunswick, while the best of friends, cling to memories of their ancestors' fervent support for, respectively, George Washington and George III. "Loyalist" and "Revolutionary" towns preserve this good-natured rivalry.

But things are different in St. Stephen (pop. 5,100) and its neighbor, Calais, Maine (pronounced "callous"). Cheek-by-jowl on the St. Croix River, the two towns ignored the affinities of *both* sides during the War of 1812. St. Stephen even supplied powder-poor Calais with gunpowder for its Fourth of July celebrations. By the time the war came, families in the towns were so closely intermarried that no one wanted to take the time to sort out who should be loyal to whom.

They still celebrate their philosophy with an **International Festival** in the first week of August. The two bridges over the river between the towns are thronged with merrymakers moving back and forth—under the watchful but benevolent eyes of customs officials, of course—and Canadian and American flags fly everywhere.

A New Brunswick **visitor information center** (☎ 506/466-7390) is on King Street (Route 1), half a mile from Customs, with a money-exchange counter, a gift shop selling provincial arts and crafts, and a picnic area. Hours from May to August are daily from 8am to 9pm and from September to mid-October daily from 9am to 7pm.

A Chocoholic's Fantasy

Loyalists of a different sort also flock to St. Stephen during the International Festival, these to attend the chocolate fantasy dinner, the "choctail" hour, or the great chocolate-chip-cookie-decorating affair, all part of the annual **Chocolate Fest.**

St. Stephen is home to **Ganong Chocolatier,** 73 Milltown Blvd. (☎ 506/465-5611), which invented the chocolate bar in 1910. Tired of finding sticky bits of melted chocolate in his pockets, a fisherman tried wrapping the chocolate in foil, and the idea caught on. Founded in 1873 and Canada's oldest candy company, Ganong was Canada's first to make lollipops, in 1895, and first to sell heart-shaped boxes of chocolates on Valentine's Day, in 1932. Factory tours are given only during Chocolate Fest, and only by advance reservation. The store sells more than 80 kinds of chocolates; the best bargain are the double-dipped chocolates, seconds that had to be redipped because of imperfect first coatings. Ganong is open Monday to Friday from 9am to 8pm, Saturday from 9am to 5pm, and Sunday from 11am to 5pm.

A MUST-SEE FOR SERIOUS GARDENERS

Garden and herb enthusiasts should leave town on Prince William Street, past the Victorian **Christ Church,** one of the province's oldest, and head to **Crocker Hill Studios** (☎ 506/466-4251). These herb gardens overlooking the river are a joy to stroll in and are among Canada's 20 best gardens. With a reservation, you can have a guided tour and a sample of some herbal delicacy. The gardens and small shop, where the bird paintings of artist Steve Smith are sold, are open June to September, daily from 10am to 5pm. The gardens are a prime spot for birds, with humming-birds visiting the blossoms, osprey fishing in the river, and a pair of eagles appearing at least once each day.

WHERE TO STAY

Blair House. 38 Prince William St., St. Stephen, NB, E3L 2W9. ☎ **506/466-2233.** Fax 506/466-2233. 3 rms. $46–$53 double; $61–$77 family room. Extra person $10. Rates include full English breakfast. MC, V (traveler's checks and U.S. dollars also accepted). Go east from King Street onto Prince William.

Set back from the street with an English garden in front, Blair House offers a relaxed, freewheeling ambience behind an elegant mid-19th-century facade. Each room has a bath and ceiling fan; the two with a double bed are the roomiest. English and veg-etarian breakfasts are served. Look forward to tea and cookies on arrival and a snack in the evening.

4 Grand Manan Island: A Paradise for Bird-Watching

There's something particularly relaxing about an island, for you can leave the cares of the world behind on the mainland. (You'll leave behind such details as street addresses on the mainland, too.) On Grand Manan they all seem to be washed away in the Fundy tides. Anchored far out in Fundy's waters like a mammoth aircraft carrier, this island is visited daily by about 250 kinds of feathered "aircraft." John James Audubon first discovered the exceptional variety of bird life here in 1831, and ornithologists have been coming to see puffins, arctic terns, and an occasional bald eagle ever since.

Another draw for scientists is Grand Manan's geology, split fantastically between six-billion-year-old formations and much younger volcanic deposits. But most people come just to relax or take walks through the wildflowers dotting the rocky countryside or along the rugged cove-indented shores.

ESSENTIALS

VISITOR INFORMATION   There's no official visitor information office on the island, but you can get information in St. Andrews or at Black's Harbour before you board the ferry or ask at island hotels. Write to the **Grand Manan Tourism Association,** P.O. Box 193, North Head, NB, E0G 2M0, ahead of time.

GETTING THERE   Two ferries (the new and the old *Grand Manan*) from Blacks Harbour depart six times daily in each direction Monday to Friday from June 30 to Labor Day (five times on Saturday and Sunday and three times daily off-season) at about two-hour intervals. In the busy summer the line of cars waiting to board the ferry can be so long that some people have to wait for the next sailing. Allow lots of time to get there and return and enough time to spend on the island. Put your car in the waiting line as soon as you arrive or leave it in Blacks Harbour and just sail over as a passenger and see it on foot or by bicycle. The trip is $1^1/_2$ hours each way.

You can go for the day, taking the first morning ferry and returning by the last, but it's a lot of sailing for a short time on the island. Round-trip fares are $24.60 per car, $8.20 per adult (including driver), $4.10 per child 5 to 12, and $2.80 per bike, paid on the return voyage. For information, call **Coastal Transport Ltd.** on Grand Manan at ☎ 506/662-3724; in Saint John, call ☎ 506/636-3922. No reservations are accepted.

EXPLORING THE ISLAND

Grand Manan is about 15 miles (24km) long by 5 miles (8km) wide, and exploring is the thing to do here—on foot, by bicycle, or by kayak.

The **Red Trail** to the **Hole-in-the-Wall** rock formation starts at the Marathon Inn and takes you to **Whale Cove,** where novelist Willa Cather spent her summers. Another walk takes you to **Swallowtail Light,** a picturesque lighthouse of the sort that appears in tourist brochures, towering above the rugged seashore.

Anywhere you see **fishing boats,** you can ask about going out in the morning on a herring boat. Smoked mackerel, herring, and salmon are among the finest delicacies produced by this seafood-rich island. Smokehouses start up in late July and continue into fall and winter. From mid-June to September you can buy the smoked product on Saturday mornings at the **Farmers' Market** in North Head, along with produce, preserves, and island crafts.

In Grand Harbour, the **Grand Manan Museum** (☎ 506/662-3524) has a collection of the many varieties of birds that visit the island, plus displays explaining the island's unique geology and Loyalist past. It's open mid-June through September, Monday to Saturday from 10:30am to 4:30pm and Sunday from 2 to 5pm.

Try not to leave Grand Manan without getting a glimpse of the **puffins,** the big-beaked island mascots. In the clear Fundy waters they dip beneath the surface and swim swiftly like seals to catch their small prey. A puffin's wings are as effective deep in the water as they are high in the air. On Monday to Saturday in late June through early August, **Seawatch Tours** (☎ 506/662-8552) runs a charter-boat service from Seal Cove Wharf to Machias Seal Island. At the bird sanctuary there, only a limited number of visitors can observe the birds from enclosed blinds, so reservations are essential. In addition to the puffins, you're likely to see nesting razor-billed auks and

Arctic terns, as well as a number of other species on the way to the island and back. Seawatch also runs **whale-watching** trips in August and September.

To explore Hole-in-the-Wall Rock and other coastal formations by kayak, you can join a guided sea-going adventure—from a short sunset paddle to a multiday trip— with **Adventure High Sea Kayaking** in North Head (☎ 506/662-3563).

Ocean Search (☎ 506/662-8488) offers a full day at sea with a marine biologist on board, a hot lunch, and plenty of tea, coffee, and juice.

WHERE TO STAY & DINE

It's wise to have a reservation before you arrive, since rooms are limited, especially in summer. In addition to the two places below, we've heard good reports on the following: **Shore Crest Lodge,** at North Head (☎ 506/662-3216); **McLaughlin's Wharf Inn,** at Seal Cove (☎ 506/662-8760); and **Aristotle's Lantern,** at North Head (☎ 506/662-3788), whose owners are known for their sense of humor and their afternoon teas. It's also a good idea to reserve a table for dinner as early in the day as possible.

Camping is available at **Anchorage Provincial Park** (☎ 506/662-3215), which has a beach, along with campsites and hook-ups. It is located between Grand Harbour and Seal Cove.

Compass Rose. North Head, Grand Manan, NB, E0G 2M0. ☎ **506/662-8570** or 514/ 458-2607 off-season. 9 rms (none with bath). $58 double. Rates include breakfast. MC, V. Closed Nov–Apr.

A short walk from the wharf, these two old houses have rooms simply furnished with pine. Guests get to know one another around Franklin stoves in the sitting rooms.

The dining room offers three meals Monday to Saturday, but Saturday dinner is by reservation only. The menus feature traditional local dishes and seafood used in nontraditional ways (say, in seafood lasagne); dishes are $9 to $15. Afternoon tea is served from 3 to 4pm.

Marathon Inn. North Head, Grand Manan, NB, E0G 2M0. ☎ **506/662-8144.** 28 rms (some with shared bath). TV TEL. $49–$89 double. MC, V.

With good swimming spots nearby and its own tennis courts, Marathon Inn has become a center for active sports on the island. Trails begin at its door, and the owners will help you arrange outings.

5 St. Andrews

The Loyalists who founded St. Andrews may have brought with them Canada's first prefab houses. During the American Revolution these families had already moved north to the safe harbor of British-controlled Fort George (later Castine, Maine). Having built homes there, they weren't pleased when the new British-American boundary was set at St. Croix River (at St. Stephen) and not the Penobscot (at Bucksport, Maine). They took their houses apart, loaded the timber onto ships, and sailed the entire town northward to another perfectly situated location, St. Andrews.

They weren't disturbed again, even during the War of 1812. Prosperity came after the war with the shipbuilding trade, but as the century wore on and iron ships replaced wooden ones, St. Andrews began to stagnate. Just in time it was "discovered" by the railroads.

The Canadian Pacific Railway Company owned the line from Québec to the southern New Brunswick coast, and the company put up a grand hotel in St. Andrews. Company directors and managers built sumptuous summer "cottages" in the vicinity, and today St. Andrews tells its history through its houses: At least two of those brought from Castine are still standing, along with many more from that era and those raised by magnates in the 19th-century lumber and shipbuilding boom. These and the sumptuous, continually modernized Algonquin Hotel lend St. Andrews an air of quiet opulence and gentility rare along the coast.

Today the town remains a summer visitors' haven, but it's beautiful in September and October as well.

ESSENTIALS

VISITOR INFORMATION   The **St. Andrews Tourist Bureau** is on Highway 1, outside of town (☎ 506/466-4858); a **Welcome Centre** is at 46 Reed Ave., at Harriet Street (☎ 506/529-3000). It's open daily from 9am to 6pm in May and September, to 8pm in July and August. The rest of the year, contact the chamber of commerce, in the same building (☎ 506/529-3555 or 800/563-7397), or write P.O. Box 89, St. Andrews, NB, E0G 2X0.

GETTING THERE   Drive east from St. Stephen on Highway 1 and turn south on Highway 127.

A shuttle service carries guests between the Algonquin Hotel and the Saint John airport. Call the hotel at ☎ 506/529-8823, ext. 174, or call 506/529-3101.

EXPLORING THE BAY

Passamaquoddy Bay is a world of its own: Sandbars interrupt the waters here and there, evergreen-cloaked islets seem to float on the high tide, and wisps of morning mist hover off the shore. The sunset turns it every color in turn. The frequent fogs hide it altogether and bring a damp chill over a hot summer day. Like the Bay of Fundy, Passamaquoddy Bay is subject to the world's highest tides. The steep shoreline, the narrow channels, and the orientation of Fundy all contribute to the twice-daily rushing in and out of immense volumes of water.

You can explore the waters around St. Andrews on several kinds of craft, from kayak to sailboat. Most of these boats have representatives at the Adventure Center at Market Wharf in the center of town, or you can reserve them through the Day Adventures desk in the lobby of the Algonquin. **Fundy Tide Runners** (☎ 506/529-4481) explores bird and marine life among the islands on a Zodiac—an exciting means of travel at high speed, but capable of slipping in close to land for wildlife watching. **Prince Yacht Charters** (☎ 506/529-4185) sails on a three-hour bay cruise around the island where Champlain wintered in 1604; you can help with the sails if you wish or just enjoy the ride. **Quoddy Link Marine,** at the town wharf (☎ 506/529-2600) runs a passenger ferry service to Campobello on a sleek new cruiser-style craft designed especially to accommodate passengers; they also do scenic, nature, sunset, and aquaculture tours. **Cline Marine** offers five-hour whale watches leaving at 8:30am and 2pm daily (☎ 506/529-4188). **Seascape Kayak Tours** offers instruction, equipment, and guided trips (☎ 506/529-4866).

The swimming beach at **Katy's Cove,** opening onto Passamaquoddy Bay but protected from the cold tides, has a bath house, a snack bar, and facilities for wheelchairs. From there, the old railway bed provides a level walking path paralleling the shore, bordered by ferns and wildflowers.

OTHER THINGS TO SEE & DO

The **Algonquin Golf Club's** 9- and 18-hole courses (☎ 506/529-3062) are open to the public, and you can rent clubs and carts. Greens fees for the 18-hole course are $34 weekdays and $36 weekends, $25 off season, tax included.

Possibly the most enjoyable experience is simply strolling through the historic streets admiring the perfectly kept old homes and their architecture. The town has a little of everything, and the buildings blend so harmoniously it's hard to believe they span more than two centuries. Pick up a copy of *A Guide to Historic St. Andrews,* free at the information office, and follow its map of the streets. In it you'll find addresses of the nine homes designed by long-time summer resident Edward S. Maxwell, the two buildings with surviving portions brought from Castine (one is at 75 Montague St.), and the town's architectural prize, the **Greenock Church** (1824), also on Montague Street. Look inside at the hand-carved pulpit of bird's-eye maple and mahogany.

If you're traveling with children, check out the free public **Creative Playground** at 168 Frederick St. Built in five days in a volunteer community effort, it's one of the finest playgrounds we've seen anywhere, with activities, structures, and engaging architecture that delights adults as well.

Another children's favorite is the "Please Touch" aquarium, inhabited by starfish, sea cucumbers, lobsters, and sea potatoes, at the **Huntsman Aquarium Museum,** Brandy Cove Road (☎ 506/529-1202 or 506/529-1200). Admission is $3.50 adults, $2.50 children, $3 seniors, $10 maximum family rate. Hours are May to June and September to October daily 10am to 4:30pm; July and August daily 10am to 6pm. The seals are fed at 11am and 4pm.

St. Andrews Blockhouse National Historic Site. Northwest end of Water Street. No phone. Free admission. June and early Sept daily 9am–5pm; July–Aug daily 9am–8pm.

The sole surviving wood fortress of the 12 built on the New Brunswick coast at the outbreak of the War of 1812, the blockhouse reopened in 1995 following restoration after damage by fire. Generations of children have had their pictures taken astride its cannons overlooking the harbor. Centennial Park is across the street.

Ministers Island Historic Site. On Ministers Island. ☎ **506/529-5081.** Ministers Island is reached at low tide only, via Bar Road. It's important to read the tide sign at the entrance to the road, since at high tide the road is under 8 feet of water. It's not a nice way to learn about the famous Fundy tides.

Sir William Van Horne was, more than any other person, responsible for the St. Andrews of today. As president of Canadian Pacific Railways, he was the driving force behind the line's extension to St. Andrews and the building of the Algonquin. These two factors made the town a mecca for wealthy families, who in turn built the "cottages" and took an interest in restoring and preserving the many buildings from earlier days. His own somewhat eccentric summer home, including the tremendous livestock barn, are open to visitors on two-hour tours, which are offered during low tide from June until mid-October.

SHOPPING

Head for Water Street, where nearly all the shops are located in restored or nicely replicated buildings; shops selling English goods, fine crafts, clothing, and gifts stand beside everyday hardware and grocery stores.

Cottage Craft Ltd. on Market Wharf (☎ 506/529-3190), founded in 1915, represents 140 local knitters. It features yarns, handwoven tweeds, and handmade cardigans and pullovers, including the Fundy fisherman sweater.

On Water Street, Tom and Ellen Smith operate a classy **pottery studio,** 170 Water St. (☎ 506/529-8823), where they demonstrate and explain the unique firing process of Raku ware. Along with their own pottery, they carry the work of noted

Canadian craftspeople. It's open daily from 9am to 9pm; ask here for a map of the other craft studios in town.

WHERE TO STAY & DINE

Camping couldn't be more convenient than in **Passamaquoddy Park,** on the point at the far end of Water Street. Operated by the Kiwanis Club, it's well maintained, with 135 sites for tents and trailers. They accept reservations; write to them at P.O. Box 116, St. Andrews, NB, E0G 2X0 (☎ 506/529-3439).

❂ **The Algonquin Hotel.** 184 Adolphus St., St. Andrews by the Sea, St. Andrews, NB, E0G 2X0. ☎ **506/529-8823** or 800/563-4299 in the U.S. Fax 506/529-4194. 250 rms and suites. MINIBAR TV TEL. $156–$191 double; $168–$542 suite. Children 18 and under stay free in parents' room. MAP (breakfast and dinner) available for about $41 per person per day. Packages available. AE, CB, DC, DISC, ER, MC, V. Limousine transport from the Saint John airport, 70 miles (113km) away, by prior arrangement with the hotel, $35 per person, three or more/ $50 for two or fewer people.

The splendid Algonquin, with its dark-timbered white stucco and red-tile roof, is set in its own park and is the town's showplace. The rooms and suites are modern and comfortable. A new wing contains 45 rooms and 9 three-room suites; all have two queen-size beds and air-conditioning and some have kitchenettes. CP Hotels operates the hotel, offering four-star food, service, and personal attention.

Dining/Entertainment: Dinner is an event in the glassed-in Van Horne Veranda, overlooking the front gardens. There's also a pleasant coffee shop; the Dock Side Pub, with live bands, and the Library Bar, with piano music. A bagpiper parades up and down the front lawn at tea time.

Services: Kids have their own check-in and get a sand pail full of goodies, as well as a lot of special attention.

Facilities: 18-hole oceanside golf course and a 9-hole woodland course, an outdoor heated pool, tennis courts, biking, shuffleboard, aerobics, lawn croquet, a rooftop garden, and a health club.

Ⓢ **Picket Fence Motel.** 102 Reed Ave., St. Andrews, NB, E0G 2X0. ☎ **506/529-8985.** Spring and fall $45–$55 double; July–Aug $55–$65 double; $65 housekeeping units. Extra person $5. AE, CB, DISC, MC, V. Closed Nov–Apr.

This tidy motel, set in well-kept lawns, is opposite the Algonquin golf course. Rooms with one double bed have bathtubs and showers, those with two double beds have showers only. The rooms are functional but attractive. Housekeeping units have a two-burner stove, refrigerator, and sink. In a town where things tend to be overpriced, this motel is a nice change.

Ⓢ **Salty Towers.** 340 Water St., St. Andrews, NB, E0G 2X0. ☎ **506/529-4585.** 12 rooms. $33 double with shared bath, $45 double with bath. MC, V.

In a town that's preserved and tidy beyond belief, the quirky, casual attitude of Salty Towers comes like a refreshing breeze off Passamaquoddy Bay. It's "in the process" and certainly not for everyone. Salty Towers is caught somewhere between an 1890s home, a 1940s seaside boarding house, and a 1960s commune. It's owned by a warm, witty, and outgoing artist who has all the right visions for it. New treasures are unearthed from its attic almost daily, and the historic paintings in the parlor are on loan from a museum. Guests make their own breakfast in the kitchen. If you like things offbeat and casual, you'll be right at home on its big front veranda.

Seaside Beach Resort. 339 Water St., St. Andrews, NB, E0G 2X0. ☎ **506/529-3846.** 24 apts and cottages. $55–$75 double. Extra person $5. MC, V. Closed Nov–Apr.

Only blocks from the heart of downtown, these modest waterfront units, all with kitchens, include six two-bedroom apartments overlooking the harbor. Guests may use the barbecues, picnic tables, sundecks, and rowboats. Pets are welcome. The friendly hosts are part of the reason families return season after season.

Treadwell Inn. 129 Water St., St. Andrews, NB, E0G 2X0. ☎ **506/529-1011.** 4 rms, 1 suite. $75–$95 double; $125 suite. MC, V.

Down comforters wrapped in Battenburg lace, antique furnishings, freshly restored rooms in an 1820s house right in the center of town, sea views—the combination is hard to resist. In summer, guests breakfast outdoors overlooking the wharves as they enjoy fresh-baked croissants. Room no. 3 overlooks busy Water Street—a little noisy in the daytime but perfect for people-watching. No smoking.

✪ **The Walker Estate.** 109 Reed Ave., St. Andrews, NB, E0G 2X0. ☎ **506/529-4210.** Fax 506/529-4311. 5 rms. $85–$110 double; $145 Bridal Suite. MC, V.

Elegant but comfortable, the Walker Estate is favorite of the showcase B&Bs in town. Built in 1912 for the family who owned Hiram Walker Distilleries, the French château–style house has been perfectly restored and renovated. The guest rooms are architecturally interesting, large, airy, and beautifully appointed without any fussiness. We like room no. 2, with a queen-size bed, baroque mirror, and huge bath with a claw-foot tub. The velour wing chairs are just right for relaxing and enjoying the room's fine view.

Dining/Entertainment: Breakfast, served in the formal dining room or, in summer, on the terrace overlooking the extensive grounds (and often a deer herd that includes a rare albino), includes homemade breads. With prior reservations, guests can enjoy a fixed-price dinner here as well for $34, with entrées that may include grilled salmon with mustard sauce. Arriving guests are served tea and fresh scones or lemon bars in the huge parlor.

WHERE TO DINE

The best fish and chips in town are served up at the **Chef's Cafe,** a retro-style spot on Water Street. For lobster, locals go to the **Lighthouse Restaurant** and the bar of choice is the crowded back room of **L'Europe** (both below). For breakfast (great scones) or sandwiches on fresh-baked bread, try **The Dory,** 252 Water St. (☎ 506/ 529-8288); the coffee is anemic, but there's a wide choice of good teas by the pot.

The Gables. 143 Water St. ☎ **506/529-3440.** Reservations not needed. Main courses $5–$22 (most $14–$16). MC, V. Daily 11am–11pm. SEAFOOD/LIGHT FARE.

This casual place, in an 1870s seaside shanty, serves generous portions of fresh food: bruschetta, lobster rolls, pasta, steamers, creamy chowder, salads, and seafood platters, which are offered deep-fried, pan-fried, or grilled. There's a children's menu, too. In summer, you can eat on the deck, encircled by a picket fence and trees. It's popular, so expect slow service.

L'Europe. 48 King St. ☎ **506/529-3818.** Reservations recommended. Main courses $16–$33. V. Tues–Sun 6pm–midnight. Closed Oct–Apr. CONTINENTAL.

A solidly Germanic air prevails at the chef-owned L'Europe. Tables in the three small dining areas are covered in pink and white linen, with candles and flowers. All meals come with homemade pâté, Black Forest farmer bread, a salad, vegetables, and rice or potatoes. Thirty main courses, among them whole trout fried in butter with almonds, Cornish hen, duck à l'orange, and jumbo shrimp, are supplemented by daily specials at about $17, or you can make a meal of two of the generous appetizers. The restaurant is best known for its rack of lamb with juniper berries and mint sauce.

Lighthouse Restaurant. Patrick Street. ☎ **506/529-3082.** Reservations recommended. Main courses $10–$23.50, MC, V. Daily 11:30am–2pm and 5–9pm. SEAFOOD.

Lobster's the specialty here—boiled while you wait and served with potato salad at lunch and a baked potato at dinner. Whatever's fresh off the boat shows up on the menu. You'll also find steamed clams, lobster bisque, and a fisherman's plate with scallops, jumbo shrimp, and filet of haddock. There's a children's menu. The dining room, with blue cafe-style curtains, overlooks the bay and every table has a view of Navy Island, Deer Island, and the cottages of St. Andrews.

6 Saint John

Every time we go to Saint John, we find something in the process of being restored—the Imperial Theater, the elegant iron bandstand in King Square, a street, an entire neighborhood. The city has a rich history and its residents love to show it off. It's one place where we suggest you take a guided walking tour, because the city has so many wonderful little stories to tell—maybe you'll learn the reason behind the ugly faces on the building at 111 Prince William Street.

The English were well established here by 1783, when thousands of Loyalists fled here from the new United States seeking the protection of the Crown. They had been among the colonial leaders of New England, hardworking and industrious, and they soon turned their new city into a great shipbuilding port. As iron ships began replacing wooden ones, Saint John's builders switched to iron. Ships sailing in and out of the harbor are a common sight, although people still line the shore to watch as the *QE II* comes in.

The terrain of the city gives it grandeur as it rises abruptly from the harbor. The main business street goes uphill at a noticeable pitch, and rows of fine buildings look out over one another's roofs toward the water. The waterfront has recently been renewed, and a convention center was built with all the accoutrements: a luxury hotel, shopping concourses, restaurants, and office towers. These are all connected by covered walkways that also extend to the City Market, to the enormous pool in the city's sports complex, and to the Hilton, right on the water's edge. Enclosed access is particularly welcome on windy or foggy days, of which the city has a fair share. Saint John is even cool on sunny days, when Fredericton and Moncton are sweltering. It's a Loyalist city right down to its British weather.

ESSENTIALS

VISITOR INFORMATION   Saint John has four **municipal visitor information centers.** Three of them are at Reversing Falls Bridge on Route 100 (☎ 506/658-2937); in the Little Red Schoolhouse, Market Slip near Market Square Complex (☎ 506/658-2855); and on Highway 1, on the west side of the city (☎ 506/658-2940). These three are open from mid-May to mid-October, daily from 9am to 6pm with extended hours in July and August. The **Visitor and Convention Bureau,** on the 11th floor at City Hall (P.O. Box 1971), Saint John, NB, E2L 4L1 (☎ 506/658-2990), is open all year on weekdays from 8:30am to 4:30pm. They'll supply you with city maps and tide tables so you won't miss the Reversing Falls Rapids.

GETTING THERE   Driving from Calais, Maine, or St. Stephen, New Brunswick, take Highway 1 east.

The **Marine Atlantic ferry** from Digby, Nova Scotia, arrives on the west side of town three times daily.

Air Nova serves Saint John from U.S. cities via Halifax and from some Canadian cities directly.

PARKING   Parking can be found underneath Market Square and at the waterfront, and free parking is provided for RVs at the foot of Water Street; ask at the information center for a parking map.

SPECIAL EVENTS   During the city's **Loyalist Days,** held the third week of July, everybody dresses up in colonial costumes for a reenactment of the 1784 Loyalists' landing. Special programs and concerts, parades, and pageants fill the festival week.

For 10 days in mid-August Saint John hosts the **Festival by the Sea.** The performing arts of a different culture are highlighted every day, from Nova Scotia Highland dancers to Ukrainian dancers from Manitoba, on the outdoor stage at Market Slip.

SEEING THE SIGHTS

Begin your explorations of the city at its historic heart, at Market Slip, where King Street ends at the water, and the Little Red Schoolhouse provides maps and advice to visitors. Next door is **Barbour's General Store** (☎ 506/658-2939), which will transport you back to cracker barrel days. Salt cod to spats and whisky to molasses, the museum is fully stocked. While you can't buy the herbal remedies, you can get a free snack of dulse, New Brunswick's popular edible seaweed. Open daily in season.

To get to know the city, take a self-guided walking tour along Saint John's **Loyalist Trail,** filled with historical landmarks. The visitor information centers can supply you with a map and brochure.

Highlights of the walk include the old **County Courthouse,** with its unsupported spiral staircase of 49 steps, each a single piece of stone; **Trinity Church,** built in 1880 to replace one destroyed by Saint John's Great Fire of 1877 (the British royal arms over the west door was saved from the original church); **St. John's Stone Church,** on Carleton Street at the end of Wellington Row, the city's oldest church building (1825), made completely from stone brought as ballast in ships from England, with a 12-story steeple crowned with a six-foot-long salmon in gold leaf; and the **Loyalist Burial Ground,** east of King's Square, with tombstones dating from 1784.

Farther along, at the southern end of Prince William Street at St. Patrick's Square, are the city's distinctive Trinity Lamps, better known as the **"Three Sisters."** Visible from as far as 5 miles away, they once guided ships safely into the harbor.

To see some of the city's finest homes (some now posh apartments), wander around Queen Square and along Germain Street. The striking painted teak doors are part of the city's Irish tradition.

Many of the Saint John's historic sights are in the few blocks uphill from Market Square to King Square (notice the Union Jack layout of the walkways) and the adjacent streets to the east—Prince William, Princess, Canterbury, Germaine, and Charlotte. Here also are most of the shops and restaurants. For New Brunswick fine arts or crafts, look into **Handworks,** at 116 Prince William St., in the old City Hall. Check also **Ring Gallery of Art** up the street at no. 97, and **Wilson Studio,** at no. 110, which has framed sepia prints of historic local photographs. At no. 114, browse in **The Great New Brunswick Book Store,** boasting the world's largest collection of books, new and used, on the province.

The five galleries of the **Aitken Bicentennial Exhibition Centre (ABEC),** 20 Hazen Ave. (☎ 506/633-4870), present changing exhibitions of art, science, photography, crafts, and historical memorabilia, plus live performances, workshops, and lectures. Sciencescape is a hands-on exploration gallery for children. Admission is free. Open in summer daily 10am to 5pm; fall/winter Tuesday to Sunday 11:30am to 4:30pm.

Rain or shine, kids and adults can relax at Saint John's indoor playground, the **Canada Games Aquatic Centre,** 50 Union St. (☎ 506/658-4715). Admission for swimming or an exercise class is $4.50 adults, $3.75 students over 18 and children under 18; the family rate for four is $13.50. Use of the fitness center facilities is $7. Hours and programs vary; call ahead. Lifeguards watch over the eight-lane Olympic-size pool, the leisure pools, and the tot pool. Two water slides, a Tarzan rope, whirl-pools, saunas, and two weight and exercise rooms complete the center.

Moosehead Breweries Limited, 89 Main St., West Saint John (☎ 506/635-7000), produces every bottle of Moosehead beer sold in the world. Tours of the brewing and bottling process are offered twice daily on weekdays in season and last about an hour; sign up for one at the Moosehead Country Store, 49 Main St., which also sells souvenir items with the Moosehead logo. You can sample a bit of the product (on the house) at the end of the tour.

Loyalist House. 120 Union St. ☎ **506/652-3590.** Admission $2 adults, 25¢ children. July–Aug Mon–Sat 10am–5pm, Sun 1–5pm; Sept–June Mon–Fri 10am–5pm.

This is Saint John's oldest unchanged building, dating from 1817, and typical of the homes of United Empire Loyalists. A locally prominent well-to-do Loyalist family had the house built in Georgian style and furnished with the elegant pieces of the time. Guides from the New Brunswick Historical Society interpret the house's history and importance as home to five generations.

Carleton Martello Tower. ☎ **506/636-4011** for information. Free admission. May–Oct daily 9am–5pm. Follow Lancaster Avenue to the left from Bridge Road at Reversing Falls.

Massive cylindrical stone defense fortifications like this one were built throughout England and Ireland in the early years of the 19th century and were called Martello towers. Over a dozen were also built in North America. Guides are available to discuss the exhibits, which cover the tower's history right through its use as a command post for World War II harbor defenses.

Cherry Brook Zoo. Sandy Point Road in Rockwood Park. ☎ **506/634-1440.** Admission $3.25 adults, $2.25 seniors and students, $1.40 preschoolers; children 2 and younger free. Daily 10am–dusk all year. Served by Saint John Transit buses June–Sept and weekends.

The only exotic animal zoo in the Atlantic Provinces, Cherry Brook has more than 100 animals, many of them endangered species. Their breeding program with the brown lemur, golden lion tamarins, and black wildebeest help to ensure the survival of those species.

New Brunswick Museum. 277 Douglas Ave. (between downtown and Reversing Falls). ☎ **506/643-2349.** Admission $2 adults, $1 students, children under 4 free, family pass $5. Museum daily 10am–5pm (Discovery Centre closed noon–1pm); library and archives daily 1–5pm or by appointment.

Paintings and displays of sailing vessels chart Saint John's long maritime past, while colonial uniforms and weapons, furniture, and other artifacts illustrate the New Brunswick of two centuries ago. Natural history collections are there, too. Be sure to see the original copy of Saint John native Clement Moore's beloved poem "'Twas the Night Before Christmas." An "annex" housing additional displays will open in Market Square in 1996.

REVERSING FALLS RAPIDS & OTHER PARKS

✪ **Reversing Falls Rapids,** under Highway 100, at the bridge over the Saint John River, is Saint John's best-known attraction. Don't expect to see a waterfall leaping backward up the rocks, but what you will see is equally fascinating. At a viewing point above the falls is an **information center,** with a 20-minute film ($1.25) explaining the nature of the Bay of Fundy tides. When tide recedes, the Saint John River empties into the Bay of Fundy, flowing over a stone barrier under the bridge. With the rising tide the flow of water reverses, and soon the water level below the bridge is higher than the river and a swift current flows over the stone barrier and back up the Saint John River.

High tide comes twice a day, and tide tables are available everywhere. Watch from the little grassy park nearby, or, for the best view of the phenomenon, from Riverside Falls View Park, across the bridge.

Due north of downtown, **Rockwood Park,** Mount Pleasant Avenue (☎ 506/658-2829), is a much-loved and much-used 2,000 acres filled with activities: lakes for swimming, boating (even bumper boats), fishing, and ice skating; an enclosed picnic area; hayrides in summer; a children's petting farm; and a playground. Camping facilities for tents ($13) and trailers ($15) are separate, the hilltop tent sites commanding a fine view over the water. Improve your golf swing at Atlantic Canada's only aquatic driving range, using floating golf balls; an 18-hole municipal course is located here as well. Its trails are groomed for cross-country skiing in winter.

Irving Nature Park, off Sand Cove Road (☎ 506/634-7135), is 450 acres on a point jutting into the Bay of Fundy; it's only minutes from downtown but seems far removed from civilization. A well-maintained mile-long dirt road loops around it, hugging the shore and passing a number of covered picnic areas and parking spots. Follow one—or all—of the four interconnected hiking trails (from .8 to 4 miles), or sit on a split-log bench and soak in the tranquillity. You're likely to see birds (more than 200 species have been sighted), as well as seals and deer. Maps are available at the entrance. Admission is free. The park is open daily from dawn to dusk; hikers are welcome year-round, but vehicles are permitted from June to November only. From Saint John, take Highway 1 West to Exit 107A; go over the overpass, through the flashing light to the top of the hill; turn right onto Sand Cove Road and drive 2 miles (3km).

ORGANIZED TOURS

Free 90-minute **walking tours** leave Barbour's General Store (above) at 10am and 2pm in July and August. More offbeat **ghost walks** in Rockwood Park are offered occasionally by the Interpretation Center (☎ 506/658-2829). **Horse-drawn carriage** rides begin from Market Square; no reservations are necessary, but they're very busy on days when a cruise ship is in.

For **nature and historical cruises** on the Saint John River and Grand Bay to the old riverboat landing, book with NorthEast Yacht Charters (☎ 506/652-4220). The three-hour cruises aboard MV *Shamrock III* leave daily at 10am, June to mid-October. The rate is $30 for adults and $10 for children, including a box lunch. They can pick you up at your hotel.

WHERE TO STAY

If you want only basic accommodation for one night, look on Route 100 (Fairville Boulevard) where the motels are clustered. **Comfort Inn by Journey's End,** at 1155 Fairville Blvd. (☎ 800/688-4200) and **Country Inn and Suites,** at no. 1011 (☎ 800/456-4000) are both reliable. (**Aquarius** is a nearby pub offering inexpensive food.)

If you're arriving between mid-May and mid-October without a reservation, ask at the Information Center about the ⑤ **Saint John Hilton**'s "Special Rate of the

Day," an unbelievable deal on the city's premier property, but available only through the information office.

The **Delta Brunswick,** 39 King St. (☎ 506/648-1981, 800/877-1133 in the U.S., or 800/268-1133 in Canada), is located in Brunswick Square, a large King Street atrium shopping complex. It's the largest hotel in town and your best chance for a room if the city is full. Facilities include an indoor pool, a whirlpool bath, saunas, an exercise room, and a children's playroom and outdoor playground. Rates are $75 to $125 for a double.

⑤ Dufferin Inn & San Martello Dining Room. 357 Dufferin Row, Saint John, NB, E2M 2J7. **☎ 506/635-5968.** Fax 506/674-2396. 6 rms. $55–$75 double. Extra person $10. Weekend packages available. Children under 10 free. Rates include full breakfast. MC, V.

If you're taking an early ferry to Digby, consider this well-appointed inn four blocks from the ferry landing. The house, which once belonged to a premier and chief justice of New Brunswick, has a leaded-glass front door and a paneled dining room, where a full breakfast is served every morning, even to those leaving on the early ferry. The house is decorated with European oak furniture (much of it made from one enormous tree), old-fashioned lights, and overstuffed chairs. The library/bar is a showplace.

Dining/Entertainment: The licensed dining room features seasonal menus of fresh Canadian ingredients, prepared with European flair. Expect such dishes as cream of cheese soup with fiddleheads, escargot quiche, or a duet of scallops and clams in Chablis. Main courses run $18 to $27. Lunch is served in summer only on Tuesday to Sunday, dinner year-round Tuesday to Sunday, by reservation only.

✪ Inn on the Cove. 1371 Sand Cove Rd., Saint John, NB, E2M 4X7. **☎ 506/672-7799.** Fax 506/635-5455. 5 rms. $70–$115 double. Discounts for longer stays; two-night Romance Package available. Rates include full breakfast. MC, V. From Saint John, take Route 1 West to Exit 107A; turn right at exit and go to the top of Bleury Street to the flashing light; turn right onto Sand Cove Road and drive 1 mile (2km) to the inn. The Irving Nature Park is ¹/₂ mile (1km) farther.

This bed-and-breakfast overlooks the water, with views out to Partridge Island. The four-level house (you enter on the second level) was built in 1910 by Alexander Graham Bell's gardener. The five rooms are tastefully decorated—one has a working gas fireplace and a picture window; another, with its own Jacuzzi overlooking the bay, is one of the most romantic rooms in the province. Arrangements can be made through the inn for a qualified naturalist and guide to show you the shore or nearby Irving Nature Park. The Maritime Television Cooking Show *Tide's Table* is produced and hosted by the owners and filmed at the inn. The dining room is open to guests and the public, with reservations at least a day in advance; it's closed Sunday and Monday. No smoking and no children allowed.

✪ Mahogany Manor. 220 Germain St., Saint John, NB, E2L 2G4. **☎ 506/636-8000.** 3 rms. $60–$65 double. Rates include taxes. MC.

A gracious Victorian bed-and-breakfast, gleaming after restoration, Mahogany Manor is on a quiet tree-lined street, within a few blocks of the center of town. The bright, tastefully decorated rooms (no-smoking) are furnished in antiques. Guests eat breakfast in the kitchen overlooking the garden; a full breakfast with home-baked muffins or breads is served. The first-floor room is wheelchair accessible. Gregarious hosts with a sense of humor set the tone for a relaxed, sociable stay.

✪ Parkerhouse Inn. 71 Sydney St., Saint John, NB, E2L 2L5. **☎ 506/652-5054.** Fax 506/636-8076. 9 rms. TV TEL. $65, $79, or $95, depending on room size. Rates include breakfast. AE, MC, V. Free parking.

Popular with honeymooners and business travelers, the Parkerhouse Inn, a striking 1890 house with a romantic history, is adjacent to the Imperial Theatre and a block from King's Square. Its rooms are furnished with period antiques, cloud-soft bedcovers, and plush linens, and they have large private baths with color-coordinated bathrobes. Fine woodwork enhances the public areas.

A licensed dining room serves breakfast and dinner (5 to 9:30pm). A morning paper comes with breakfast.

✪ Saint John Hilton. One Market Square, Saint John, NB, E2L 4Z6. ☎ **506/693-8484,** 800/445-8667 in the U.S., or 800/561-8282 in Canada. Fax 506/657-6610. 186 rms, 11 suites. A/C MINIBAR TV TEL. Summer $89 double; rest of the year $120 double. From $150 suite. Extra person $12. Weekend rates and packages available. Children under 18 stay free in parents' room; children under 12 eat free. AE, DC, DISC, ER, MC, V. Parking $8.50 a day; free on summer weekends with package rates.

The only hotel on the water, the Hilton has the best location in town and an impressively friendly staff. You can watch boats come and go from the harbor-view rooms and walk to many attractions and restaurants. The rooms are large and newly decorated with furniture made from New Brunswick pine. Baths feature local marble and have hair dryers and lots of counter space. The hotel is connected to Market Square and the Trade and Convention Centre via an enclosed walkway.

Dining/Entertainment: The Brigantine Lounge overlooking the harbor has a pool table, a games area, a big-screen TV, and piano music from 5 to 9pm Monday through Saturday.

Facilities: Small indoor pool, Jacuzzi under a large skylight, saunas, an exercise room, and seven nonsmoking floors.

NEARBY PLACES TO STAY

St. Martins Country Inn. Highway 11, St. Martins, NB, E0G 2Z0. ☎ **506/833-4534.** Fax 506/833-4725. 10 rms, 3 suites. TEL. $70–$95 double; $125 suite. Extra person $15. Packages available. MC, V. Head due east of Saint John 35 miles (60km) on Highway 111 past the Saint John airport.

This restored Queen Anne mansion sits on its hillside like a dowager empress, commanding 100 acres of land overlooking the Bay of Fundy, where its builder launched many of the 500 ships sent to sea from this town between 1805 and 1880. It was built in 1859 by the sea captain son of a Loyalist who received the land by King's grant in 1786. The inn has eight working fireplaces, three dining rooms, two graceful drawing rooms, and romantic guest rooms with floral bedspreads, rugs, and wallpaper (five units have fireplaces, and a couple have whirlpool baths). There's a small pond in front of the house and hiking trails behind it.

The inn's dining room serves three meals a day. Lunch features a traditional Maritime dish daily (most items $5 to $10; dinner main courses are $17 to $22).

Shadow Lawn. 3180 Rothesay Rd., Rothesay, NB, E2E 5A3. ☎ **506/847-7539** or 800/561-1466. Fax 506/849-9238. 7 rms, 4 suites. TV TEL. May 15–Oct 15 $69–$125 double; Oct 16–May 14 $59–$115 double. Extra person $15. MC, V.

Eight miles northeast of Saint John, in the affluent town of Rothesay, the Shadow Lawn Inn (1871) is an elegant mansion, built as a summer home. Each of the large rooms is unique, with an antique bed, high ceilings, hardwood floors, and a private bath. Room no. 4 has a canopied bed and a bath with a claw-foot tub. Rooms nos. 8 to 11 have refrigerators and coffeepots.

The two elegant front dining rooms are in the original house; the back one is in a 1993 addition. Table settings, with baroque flatware and fine stemware, are impressive; you'll want to dress for dinner, served daily from 6 to 8pm (you might want to reserve a table when you reserve your room). Entrées ($14 to $20) include Grand Marnier and shrimp baked in ginger and cream sauce in a puff pastry.

WHERE TO DINE

The most hallowed of Saint John lunch traditions, the **City Market,** at 47 Charlotte St. off the corner of King's Square, is a historic site (it opened in 1876) and a stop on the Loyalist Trail. Among the highlights are **Vern's Bakery** for the famous cheese bread and for sweets, **Lord's Lobster** for fish and chowder (they'll pack lobster and salmon for you to take on your flight or drive home), and **Slocum and Ferris** for picnic baskets extraordinaire. There's a solarium where you can sit and enjoy the lunch you've gathered. Open Monday to Saturday.

✪ **Billy's Seafood Company Fish Market & Oyster Bar.** 49–51 Charlotte St. ☎ 506/672-3474. Reservations accepted. Main courses $5–$17. Mon–Thurs 11am–10pm, Fri–Sat 11am–11pm, Sun 11am–9pm. SEAFOOD.

One of our tests of a restaurant is how the chef prepares salmon; if it's cooked a minute too long or the flavor is drowned by too assertive a sauce or marinade, the restaurant fails. Billy's not only passed—it served one of the two best plates of salmon we enjoyed in a whole summer of Maritime Provinces travels. The lobster roll is just as outstanding, filled with chunks of firm meat instead of the shreds that most places use. Be sure to look at the display of seafood, artfully arranged in the glass case.

Grannan's Seafood Restaurant & Oyster Bar. Market Square. ☎ 506/634-1555. Reservations recommended for dinner. Main courses $5–$30. AE, ER, MC, V. Mon–Sat 11:30am–midnight, Sun 11:30am–10pm. SEAFOOD.

Relaxed and crowded, Grannan's serves up big portions at moderate prices. The Captain's Platter has been called the "Cadillac of all meals"—but you can also get good prime rib. Light fare at lunch includes sandwiches and salads, and in summer patio dining features barbecue.

Incredible Edibles Cafe. 42 Princess St. ☎ 506/633-7554. Reservations recommended. Main courses $9–$23. AE, DC, MC, V. Mon–Sat 11am–10:30pm. INTERNATIONAL.

Best known for its cheesecake (the perfect pick-me-up with a cup of aromatic espresso in the afternoon), Incredible serves lunch-time salads, pasta dishes, house pizza, and pita sandwiches filled with lobster or spicy stir-fry. The evening menu offers chicken paprikash with spaetzle, grilled salmon, and linguine with clam sauce. The outdoor patio can get chilly, so bring a sweater.

✪ **Turn of the Tide.** In the Hilton Hotel, 1 Market Square. ☎ 506/693-8484. Reservations recommended. Main courses $19–$26. AE, DC, DISC, ER, MC, V. Breakfast and lunch daily plus Mon–Sat 5:30–9:30pm. MARITIME/NOUVELLE.

Turn of the Tide sits on the water and evokes the feel of a dining room on a small luxury ship, with rich wood paneling and fine furnishings. Expect game dishes—like pheasant in wine sauce with raspberries or venison medallions with feta cheese—as well as abundant seafood choices. A cold platter of Maritime Provinces seafood is served with a creamy lemon-garlic dressing, and this is one of the rare places that serves a real mixed grill, adding seafood to the usual choices.

SAINT JOHN AFTER DARK

The **Imperial Theatre** (1913) reopened in 1994 as a center for performing arts. In its heyday, it hosted Ethel Barrymore, Harry Houdini, Edgar Bergen, and John Philip Sousa. The intricate interior plasterwork has been reproduced, and the original chandelier refurbished and rehung. All the seats offer unobstructed views. **Symphony New**

Brunswick presents its concerts here (☎ 506/634-8379), as do a variety of performers. Check at the information office to see what's on.

For live folk music, try **O'Leary's**, 46 Princess St. (☎ 506/634-7135), Thursday to Saturday. There's no cover; go early to get a seat. Bands are on stage at the boardwalk, in front of Market Square, all summer long.

THE FERRY TO DIGBY, NOVA SCOTIA

Marine Atlantic's MV *Princess of Acadia* plies the Bay of Fundy between Saint John, New Brunswick, and Digby, Nova Scotia, year-round, making the crossing in approximately 2³/₄ hours. In the peak summer period from mid-June through September, the ship carries its load of 159 cars and 650 passengers three times a day (two times on Sunday) in each direction. Crossings are less frequent the rest of the year. Summer fares for adults are $20 one-way; seniors, $15; and children 5 to 12, $10. Charge for a car is $45. You should have reservations: In Saint John, call ☎ 506/636-4048; in Digby, 902/245-2116; in the United States, 800/341-7981.

DRIVING ON TO FREDERICTON

Two roads lead from Saint John to Fredericton. Highway 7 is fast but not memorable, while Highway 102 north follows the sinuous banks of the Saint John River north through a valley of patchwork fields, heavily laden apple trees, and hamlets where church suppers and quilting bees still take place.

If you're planning to visit Gagetown, consider a third alternative that provides a pure New Brunswick experience involving back roads and three short ferry crossings, all free: Take Route 1 east from Saint John to Rothesay (you'll already be there if you're staying at Shadow Lawn Inn). From Rothesay go to Gondola Point via Highway 100 west to Highway 119 and follow the signs. Take the ferry across Kennebecasis Bay. Then drive along Route 845 east to Kingston, where you'll take Route 850 to get the second ferry, across Belleisle Bay. From here, take Route 124W to the third and final ferry, to Evandale and Route 102 north.

The ferries make the short trips back and forth all day, and the longest wait you can expect is about 10 minutes. This is a delightful way to travel.

GAGETOWN

Time seems to have bypassed Gagetown, nestled on the bank of Gagetown Creek, along Route 102. The creek feeds into the Saint John River, and Route 102 leads on to Fredericton, but we suggest you linger here a while. A walk down Front Street will reward you with fine examples of the 19th-century architecture of a small prosperous town.

Gagetown is a village of artists and craftspeople. You can see their handiwork at the outstanding **Acacia Gallery of Canadian Art** (☎ 506/488-2591), on Front Street beside the Steamers Stop Inn, and at the **Loomscrofters** shop (☎ 506/488-2400), housed in an old trading post (1761) beside the river and selling handwoven tartans and afghans made to order.

Where to Stay & Dine

Steamers Stop Inn. Front Street, Village of Gagetown, NB, E0G 1V0. ☎ **506/488-2903.** Fax 506/488-1116. 7 rms. $55–$65 double. Rates include continental breakfast. Extra person $15. Packages available. MC, V. Closed Oct–Apr and weekdays in May and Sept.

This is the valley's most delightful small hotel. From the broad veranda facing the Gagetown Creek to the cluster of five intimate dining rooms and the Victorian decor in the sitting room and guest rooms, the inn recalls the atmosphere of the days when it was a stop for well-heeled passengers aboard the river boats. The rooms, five of which overlook the river, have floral wallpaper and antique furnishings. Along with the Body Shop bath amenities, notice the original works of art in the brand new baths—and ask to hear their story. There are horseshoes, canoes, kayaks, and a dock for guests. Reserve ahead, since the inn is popular.

Dining/Entertainment: The country cooking here is a treat. Reserve ahead for lunch, daily from noon to 4pm, or dinner, from 8 to 9pm, weekends only in May and September. On Sunday, stop for the all-you-can-eat brunch buffet from 11am to 3:30pm. Lunches are $4 to $10, dinners $15 to $23. Look for homey favorites—chicken and dumplings or hot gingerbread, for example—as well as classic dishes. Their list includes 30 wines ($15 to $22) and imported beers.

7 Fredericton

"Fredericton is the unmarred and unscratched relic, the perfect museum piece, and with that final rarity in our time, a complete unconsciousness of itself, for it has never been discovered, extolled, or exploited by the traveller." Bruce Hutchinson wrote those words in 1946, in *The Unknown Dominion,* and they're just as true today. The city's easy grace and refinement seem to be in the air itself: Strangers ask if you need directions; drivers stop for pedestrians even when their light is green. A woman can travel alone here comfortably. Yet for all its charms it draws relatively few tourists.

There's no shortage of things to do, and certainly no lack of historic interest, for New Brunswick's capital is older than the province itself. Three hundred years ago the Saint John River was prime fishing territory and settlements dotted its shores. By the end of the 1600s the French had built a fort here and a civilian town soon followed. The British took control in the mid-1700s, but it was really the Loyalists fleeing the American Revolution who shaped the city.

Today Fredericton is a genteel, easygoing place with a village green overlooking the river and a river walk along its banks. The province's most famous native son, Lord Beaverbrook, had an enduring affection for the city and made several generous gifts, including its outstanding fine arts gallery and playhouse.

ESSENTIALS

VISITOR INFORMATION   The main source of maps and information is the **Fredericton City Hall,** at 397 Queen St. (at York Street), by the river (☎ 506/452-9616). It can provide the excellent *Fredericton Visitor Guide,* which has a good self-guided walking tour, as well as a free **"Tourist Parking Pass,"** allowing out-of-province visitors to park free at meters and in town lots. (Parking is always free on Saturday and Sunday.) In mid-May to August, the office is open daily from 8am to 8pm; in September, daily from 8am to 4:30pm; and the rest of the year, Monday to Friday from 8am to 4:30pm. Or write ahead to the City Hall Visitors' Information Centre, 397 Queen St. (P.O. Box 130), Fredericton, NB, E3B 4Y7.

Another **information center** is on the Trans-Canada Highway near the Hanwell Road exit, no. 289 (☎ 506/458-8331 or 506/458-8332), open daily during the summer tourist season from 9am to 5pm (8am to 8pm from July to mid-August).

GETTING THERE   From Saint John, take Highway 7, or the more scenic Highway 102 north. From Gagetown, follow Highway 102 north. **Air Nova** has direct flights from Boston, or you can fly here from Halifax or other Maritime Provinces cities. (If you arrive from outside Canada, be warned that the only rude immigration officers we've ever encountered in Canada are stationed here, guarding the gate like pit bulls. Don't blame the city, however, since its residents are among the friend-liest and most helpful a stranger could find anywhere.)

SEEING THE SIGHTS

The starting point for any Fredericton tour should be **Officers' Square,** on Queen Street between Carleton and Regent. Today a fine downtown park, it was once the city's military parade ground, and Tuesday to Saturday during July and August, the changing of the guard is reenacted here at 11am and 7pm. Quarters for officers of the British garrison, built between 1839 and 1851, flank the square's western side and now house the **York-Sunbury Historical Society Museum** (see below).

From here, walk to old **City Hall** (1876), at Queen Street and Phoenix Square. In the Council Chamber, where the mayor and city council members meet, hang 27 wool tapestries tracing the history of Fredericton, and someone is usually on hand to show them to you.

The changing exhibits on the ground floor of the French Revival–style **Fredericton National Exhibition Centre** 503 Queen St. (at Carleton; ☎ 506/453-3747), might be anything from a collection of Japanese kites to a display of the latest in computer technology. Hands-on exhibits are nearly always featured. On the second floor is the New Brunswick Sports Hall of Fame. Admission is free. Open May to Labor Day Saturday to Thursday 10am to 5pm, Friday 10am to 9pm; the rest of the year Tuesday to Friday noon to 4:30pm, Saturday 10am to 5pm, Sunday 1 to 5pm.

A favorite activity here is strolling along the **River Walk,** which you can pick up anywhere downtown. It traces the river for about 3 miles, from the Sheraton hotel, alongside downtown and the Green (note the abutment marking the flood water lines), past the **Waterloo row houses** (Fredericton's prettiest stretch of houses), to the remains of an old Loyalist cemetery, with a marker and a couple of tombstones dating from 1783 (it's just beyond Morell Park; follow the road beside the baseball field). If you choose to walk only part way, try not to miss the row houses.

At the intersection of Brunswick and Church streets, you'll see the Anglican **Christ Church Cathedral** (☎ 506/450-8500), built between 1845 and 1853. It's undergoing major renovation outside, but its fine interior is undisturbed. From mid-June to Labor Day, free tours of the church are given Monday to Friday from 9am to 8pm, Saturday from 10am to 5pm, and Sunday from 1 to 5pm.

The Old Burial Ground, bounded by Brunswick, George, Regent, and Sunbury streets, was in use from 1787 to 1878 and contains the graves of Loyalists' families, British settlers and soldiers, and the founders of Fredericton. At the corner of King and Carleton you can't miss the imposing white **Wilmot United Church** (1852; ☎ 506/458-1066), the last of the several large wooden churches that marked Fredericton in the 19th century. The interior is decorated in hand-carved native woods; guided tours are given weekdays.

To explore the Saint John River, you can rent a canoe or kayak at the **Small Craft Aquatic Centre** (☎ 506/458-5513), downtown on the river (walk to it or take the Victoria Health Centre driveway off Queen Street); they offer short courses in canoeing, kayaking, and rowing, as well as three-day river ecology tours for adults, teens, and families.

York-Sunbury Historical Society Museum. West side of Officers' Square. ☎ **506/455-6041.** Admission $1 adults, 50¢ seniors and students, $2.50 family pass; children under 6 free. May–early Sept Mon–Sat 10am–6pm; July–Aug until 9pm on Mon and Fri and Sun noon–6pm; autumn Mon–Fri 9am–5pm, Sat noon–4pm; winter Mon, Wed, and Fri 11am–3pm or by appointment.

Housed in the old officers' quarters of the British regiments, the museum is filled with exhibits depicting local military and civilian history from the native period to the Loyalists to the pioneers to the recent past. On the third floor, is—are you ready?—

Fredericton

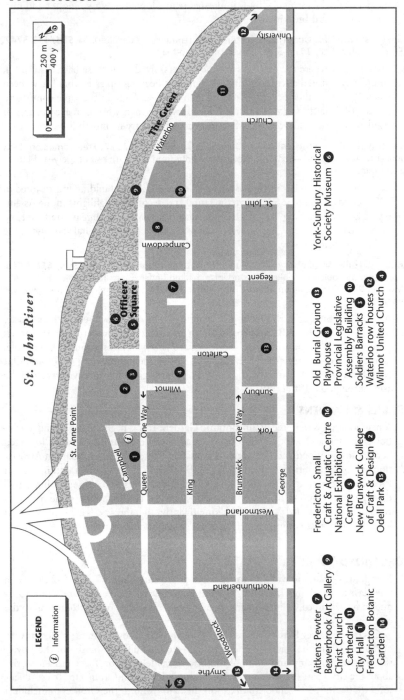

LEGEND
ⓘ Information

St. John River

St. Anne Point

The Green

Officers' Square

Aitkens Pewter ⑦
Beaverbrook Art Gallery ⑨
Christ Church
Cathedral ⑪
City Hall ①
Fredericton Botanic
Garden ⑭

Fredericton Small
Craft & Aquatic Centre ⑯
National Exhibition
Centre ⑤
New Brunswick College
of Craft & Design ②
Odell Park ⑮

Old Burial Ground ⑬
Playhouse ⑧
Provincial Legislative
Assembly Building ⑩
Soldiers Barracks ③
Waterloo row houses ⑫
Wilmot United Church ④

York-Sunbury Historical
Society Museum ⑥

250 m
400 y

a taxidermically preserved 42-pound frog. Fredericton's legendary Coleman frog was the pet of Fred Coleman, a local innkeeper who adopted it as a youngster and nurtured it to record-breaking size.

Soldiers' Barracks. Queen and Carleton streets (entrance off Carleton). ☎ **506/453-3747.** Free admission. Daily 10am–6pm. Closed Labor Day–May.

For a look at where the soldiers (not the officers) lived, visit these barracks (1827), completely restored a few years ago. A room has been set up as it would have been when 19 infantrymen occupied it more than 100 years ago. In the same compound stands the Guard House (1828), the lockup where men who disobeyed orders or regulations were held. It's now a free museum of military memorabilia.

Legislative Assembly Building. Queen St. ☎ **506/453-2527.** Free admission. Early June–late Aug daily 9am–8pm (tours every half hour from 9:15am); rest of the year Mon–Fri 9am–4pm.

The seat of government in New Brunswick since 1882, this building was restored in 1988. Guides will point out the architectural and decorative highlights in the Assembly Chamber, including Waterford crystal chandeliers and two large portraits of King George III and Queen Charlotte. Be sure to see the handsome spiral staircase at the end of the main hallway.

Beaverbrook Art Gallery. 703 Queen St. (at Saint John Street). ☎ **506/458-8545.** Admission $3 adults, $2 seniors, $1 students; children under 6 free; family rate $6. July–Aug Mon–Fri 9am–6pm, Sat–Sun 10am–5pm; winter Tues–Fri 9am–5pm, Sat 10am–5pm, Sun noon–5pm.

Across from the Legislative Assembly Building is the center of Fredericton's artistic life, a gift from Lord Beaverbrook. Don't miss this fine modern gallery and its impressive collection of British paintings (Reynolds, Gainsborough, Constable, Turner, and other greats) and Salvador Dalí's monumental *Santiago El Grande.* One wing features period rooms, with displays of paintings and decorative arts from the 14th through the 19th centuries.

PARKS & GARDENS

A new addition is the **Fredricton Botanic Garden.** It was begun in 1992, and a wild-flower garden and walking trails have already been established. A well-illustrated booklet to the Woodland Fern Trail is available. Write the Botanic Garden Association at Box 57, Station A, Fredericton, NB, E3B 4Y2. The garden entrance is on Prospect Street, next to the ball park. **Odell Park** offers a mile-long walking trail through an arboretum of New Brunswick's native trees, including some over 400 years old. An additional 7 miles of walking trails through the woods are kept groomed in winter for cross-country skiers. The park's entrance is at the end of Rookwood Street.

ORGANIZED TOURS

Free guided **dramatic walking tours** begin at the City Hall (☎ 506/452-9616) on weekdays at 10am and 2, 4, and 7pm and weekends at 10am and 4 and 7pm. Conducted by costumed Calithumpians, they're great fun and a good introduction to the city.

    Checker Charter River Cruises (☎ 506/451-0051) shows visitors a different view of the city, from the water. In the two-hour cruise you'll see the site of the Loyalists' first winter camp and some of the fine riverside mansions, as you hear stories about the city's past ($15 adults, $7.50 children). Five-hour Oromocto River Adventures ($50 adult, $25 schoolchildren) on the Saint John to the Oromocto include a barbecue and kite flying from the upper deck. Other options include houseboat rental on the river, a cruise to Gagetown, and an airborne tour of the river from a Cessna. They also **rent bicycles** for $5 per hour or $25 per day. They're open every day at the kiosk at the Regent Street wharf near the lighthouse from June 1 to October 15.

SHOPPING

Table for Two, 440 King St., in King's Place (☎ 506/455-1401), focuses on New Brunswick crafts, as well as kitchenware; also in King's Place, a **Hat Museum** offers a retrospective of the past century's fashions in headwear, with more than 50 hats and a **Boutique Chapeau.** Opposite the Cathedral at 103 Church St., the **New Brunswick Crafts Council** (☎ 506/450-8989) offers high-quality weaving, pottery, glassware, smocking, wood inlay, and work in other media. In late November each year they hold a craft festival.

WHERE TO STAY

Carriage House Bed & Breakfast. 230 University Ave., Fredericton, NB, E3B 4H7. ☎ **506/452-9924** or 800/267-6068. Fax 506/458-0799. 10 rms (5 with bath). TEL. $60 double without bath, $75 double with bath. Extra person 12 and older $15; children under 12 $5. Rates include breakfast. MC, V.

At this lovely turn-of-the-century home, the outgoing owners have created a quiet nonsmoking retreat only a five-minute walk from downtown. The large porches look out over the tree-shaded lawn and one of the city's most elegant streets. All rooms, some large, some small, are furnished with antiques, as are the common areas. A full home-cooked breakfast with their own maple syrup is served in the solarium.

Lord Beaverbrook Hotel. 659 Queen St., Fredericton, NB, E3B 5A6. ☎ **506/455-3371** or 800/561-7666 in Canada and New England. Fax 506/455-1441. 153 rms, 10 suites. A/C TV TEL. $89–119 double ($67.50 weekends); $150 suite. Weekend specials and packages available. AE, DC, DISC, ER, MC, V. Free parking.

A comfortable, British sort of hotel, the Lord Beaverbrook is the most conveniently located of all the city's lodgings, on the main street, next door to the Beaverbrook Art Gallery, across from the Playhouse and the Legislative Assembly Building, and very near the SMT bus station. Despite frayed upholstery and postage stamp–size towels, the rooms are large and have some unexpected amenities, like computer jacks; those on the executive floor have hair dryers and pants presses. Five new rooms are fully wheelchair accessible.

Dining/Entertainment: Gentility reigns in the Terrace Dining Room, overlooking the river. There are few surprises on the menu, but you get a good variety of well-prepared old favorites—roast beef, lamb chops, poached salmon. Prices are quite reasonable. The more formal Governor's Room serves dinner only, with nouvelle cuisine ($19 to $26). The casual River Room Lounge has entertainment nightly.

Services: An airport shuttle service is a bargain at $6.

Facilities: A large indoor pool and a kiddie pool; a Jacuzzi; a sauna; a games room; nonsmoking floors.

Sheraton Inn. 225 Woodstock Rd., Fredericton, NB, E3B 2H8. ☎ **506/457-7000** or 800/325-3535. Fax 506/457-4000. 208 rms, 15 suites. A/C MINIBAR TV TEL. Sun–Thurs $122 double, Fri–Sat $79 double; from $145 suite. Extra person $10. Children under 17 stay free with parents. Packages available. AE, CB, DC, ER, MC, V. Free parking.

This hotel is set on a wide bend in the river, and its focal point is the riverside pool and poolside cafe/bar and grill open 11am to midnight daily in summer, weather permitting. The rooms, some of which offer a fine river view, are large, modern, and attractive. They have good reading lights, coffeemakers, and irons and ironing boards.

It's a pleasant 10-minute walk along the riverside park to the historic center of town. Facilities include indoor and outdoor pools, a Jacuzzi, a sauna, and a small but well-equipped exercise room.

Town & Country Motel. 967 Woodstock Rd. (RR 3), Fredericton, NB, E3B 4X4. ☎ **506/ 454-4223.** 17 units, 11 with kitchenette. A/C TV TEL. June–Sept $63–$71 double; Oct–May $46–$49 double. Extra person $10. MC, V.

"People shouldn't have to sleep on sheets dried in a machine," the owner of this tidy motel on the banks of the Saint John River told us as we walked past the long line of linens billowing in the summer breeze. It's an example of how they take care of guests, even after 30 years of ownership. Each of the units has one or two double beds with good mattresses, and the rooms with kitchenettes are supplied with dishes and utensils. Rooms 12, 13, and 14 have great river views. In 25 years, the Delmases haven't lost their enthusiasm for welcoming guests or keeping the property neat and clean. There's a lot to be said for that.

WHERE TO DINE

Frederictonians love good food, local friends assure us, but they eat it at home. Restaurants, they add, don't reflect the city's real culinary mood. Not much consolation for the traveler. But while there may be no great restaurants, there are a number at which you'll be well fed for reasonable prices. For lobster, try the **Lobster Hut** on Regent Street at Route 7 (☎ 506/455-4413). German and European specialties are found at **Schade's** on Queen Street (☎ 506/450-3340), and **Dimitri's** on Piper's Lane (☎ 506/452-8882) has really good Greek food. Buy picnic fixings or hearty German sausages for breakfast on Saturdays from 7am to 1pm, at the **Boyce Farmers' Market,** on George Street between Regent and St. John. More than 100 stalls indoors and outdoors sell fresh fruits and vegetables and all sorts of homemade edible goodies and craft items. On other days go to **J, M & T Deli,** on Regent Street just off Queen (☎ 506/458-9068).

The Barn. 540 Queen St. ☎ **506/455-2742.** Reservations not needed. Main courses $4–$12. AE, DC, ER, MC, V. Daily 11am–11pm. CANADIAN/FRENCH.

Ask strangers where to eat in Fredericton and they're likely to send you here, but they'll call it the BarBQ Barn. Well-worn wooden booths, a menu filled with dishes from chicken Creole to frogs' legs, and a wide variety of wines priced from $15 to $20 a bottle and available by the glass, explain its local popularity. Look here for regional dishes with a French accent—like tourtièrre (pork pie) and pâté maison.

Cafe du Monde. 610 Queen St. ☎ **506/457-5534.** Reservations recommended at dinner. Main courses $7.25–$12. AE, DC, ER, MC, V. Mon–Thurs 7:30am–11pm, Fri 7:30am–midnight, Sat 9am–midnight, Sun 11am–midnight.

For our money, the up-and-comer is Cafe du Monde. Stylishly European in its decor and eclectic in its menu, this is a real cafe—a place for an espresso or pot of tea, a lunch sandwich, and interesting dinner dishes, plus a place to meet friends for a glass of wine. Don't miss the shrimp and fennel over homemade fettucine. Tea drinkers will appreciate their selection of china pots; you pick the size you want.

The Diplomat. 253 Woodstock Rd. ☎ **506/454-2400.** Reservations accepted. Main courses $7–$17. AE, CB, ER, MC, V. Daily 24 hours. Closed Christmas. CHINESE/CANADIAN.

Not only is it open 24 hours, but The Diplomat's always busy. It's bright, lively, nicely furnished, and casual. Along with the classic Chinese dishes from the menu, a Chinese buffet is served every day at lunch and dinner for $7.95 weekday lunch, $8.95 weekends, $11.95 Monday to Thursday dinner, and $13.95 Friday to Sunday dinner. The dinner buffet includes dessert. However incongruous it may seem, this place is best known for its dessert pastries, baked in-house, along with all its breads. Canadian fare includes fish and chips, Fundy scallops broiled in lemon butter with dill sauce, and baby back ribs. A children's menu offers three selections at $3.95.

FREDERICTON AFTER DARK

You may want to attend a play at the **Playhouse,** Queen Street, a gift of Lord Beaverbrook. Call ☎ 506/458-8344 for the latest information on works staged by Theatre New Brunswick, the resident company. The season runs from October to mid-May and a production in August. Officers' Square is the site of free summer **band concerts** on Tuesday and Thursday at 7:30pm. Pipe, marching, and military bands from the city and the region provide the music; you provide your own blanket, cushion, or chair. Lord Beaverbrook's statue overlooks in benign approval. Here in the daytime, the **Calithumpians** present humorous historical theater, free at 12:15pm on weekdays and 2pm on weekends (☎ 506/452-9616 for information on schedules for both).

Maritime Provinces music is performed in the summer on the deck of the Lighthouse, just off Officers' Square, or you can hear it with a stout in hand at **Dolan's** on Piper's Lane (open Thursday to Saturday from 9:30pm to 1:30am without a cover charge). On St. Patrick's Day, this is the place to be, if you can get a seat—or a place to stand.

SIDE TRIPS WEST OF FREDERICTON

Route 2, the Trans-Canada Highway, follows the Saint John River westward and leads to three attractions within a short distance of one another, one historical and two recreational. Each of these is close enough (15 to 20 miles from Fredericton) to be enjoyed as a day trip out of the city.

✪ **King's Landing Historical Settlement.** Exit 259 off the Trans-Canada Highway (Highway 2 west). ☎ **506/363-5090** or 506/363-5805 for recorded information. Admission $8 adults, $6.50 seniors, $6 students over 18, $4.50 youths 6–18, $20 family pass. July–Aug daily 10am–6pm; June and Sept–Oct daily 10am–5pm. Closed Canadian Thanksgiving (second Mon in Oct).

King's Landing, on the bank of the Saint John River, is 21 miles (34km) and at least 150 years from Fredericton. The authentic re-creation brings to life the New Brunswick of 1790 to 1900, in 10 historic houses and 9 other buildings relocated here and saved from destruction by the flooding of the Mactaquac hydro project. The aroma of freshly baked bread mixes with the smell of horses and livestock, and the sound of the blacksmith's hammer alternates with that of the church bell. More than 100 "early settler" docents chat about their lives.

You could easily spend a day exploring its 300 acres, but if you haven't that much time, look for the Hagerman House (with furniture by Victorian cabinetmaker John Warren Moore), the Ingraham House with its fine New Brunswick furniture, the Morehouse House (where you'll see a clock Benedict Arnold left behind), the Victorian Perley House, and the sawmill and gristmill. The Ross Sash and Door Factory, in process, will demonstrate the work and times of a turn-of-the-century manufacturing plant.

If all this makes you tired, hitch a ride in an oxcart, or relax at the King's Head Inn, which served up grub and grog to hardy travelers along the Saint John River a century or more ago. Today it serves lemonade, chicken pie, and corn chowder, along with other traditional dishes. Lunch prices are $8 to $13 and dinner is $13 to $19.

Children may become "Visiting Cousins," living for five days in period costume, attending school, making butter or candles, and eating Loyalist-style meals with their "families."

Woolastook Park. Off the Trans-Canada Highway ☎ **506/363-5410.** Wildlife park $5.50 adults, $4 children 6–15, family pass $17. Miniature golf $4.75 adults, $3.25 age 15 and under. July–Aug daily 9am–9pm; mid-May to June and Sept daily 9am–5pm.

Along with its amusement park aspects, Woolastook provides a living lesson in Canadian fauna, with enclosures for deer, caribou, moose, seals, cougars, coyotes, raccoons, skunks, and muskrats lined along a trail. A nursery cares for orphaned baby animals—fawns, bear cubs, fox pups, and others. For a different type of wild life, the park has four water slides and a deluxe minigolf course. A campground of 200 campsites, a canteen, a licensed restaurant, and a gift shop complete the complex, which, like neighboring Mactaquac, is crowded in summer.

8 Fundy National Park & Hopewell Cape

Traveling east toward Moncton from Fredericton or Saint John, the Trans-Canada Highway meets Highway 114, the road to Fundy National Park. While you can drive through the park as a detour between two cities, you should plan to stay over if you plan to do any hiking on its trails. In addition, Hopewell's famous rocks are visible only at low tide, so your travel plans need to consider the tide schedule, available at any tourist information center. Alma is the service center for the park, with shops, lodging, and other facilities. Cape Enrage is a long point extending into the bay, north of Alma.

FUNDY NATIONAL PARK

The park harbors forests and bogs resembling those found in Newfoundland, and the Fundy tides are truly unique. At low tide the park offers good beachcombing and an abundance of little marine creatures to study. The park has 60 miles (104km) of hiking trails, including the Caribou Plain Trail, a ¹/₂-km wheelchair-accessible boardwalk. Fundy Park also has a number of "auto trails," one-lane dirt roads kept in good condition.

Civilized amusements compete with the call of the wild: a heated saltwater pool, tennis courts, a lawn-bowling green, and a nine-hole golf course. To drive into the park you'll have to buy a one-day permit ($6) or four-day permit ($18), entitling you to drive around, swim, picnic, and hike; other activities require an extra fee. The permit is for the car, no matter how many passengers.

For information on the park, write to P.O. Box 40, Alma, NB, E0A 1B0 (☎ 506/887-6000). The park is open year-round.

CAMPING   Four campgrounds provide a variety of locations as well as a variety of services, from full hook-ups to wilderness sites. Reservations are not accepted, so it's a good idea to get to the campground early in the day.

TIDE WATCHING   Although no bore comes rushing through as a wall of water, the Fundy tides are still dramatic here, as they rise as much as 40 feet (13 meters) twice a day. **Alma Beach** has a platform with a boardwalk and a tide-measuring pole. At **Herring Cove** you can explore tidal pools when the water is its lowest, as well as a sea cave.

HIKING TRAILS   Thirty miles (50km) of the park's trails are linked into **The Fundy Circuit**, an excursion of three to five days through the various park ecosystems, with wilderness campsites along the way. **Dickson Falls,** a cascade, can be reached by an easy 30-minute walk along a boardwalk. **Third Vault Falls,** the park's highest at over 50 feet (16 meters), is a more difficult hike into a steep valley, 2 miles (3.7km) each way. An easy 15-minute walk to **Shiphaven** rewards with a splendid estuary view.

BOATING   At Bennett Lake you can rent canoes, rowboats, and sailboats, from $3 to $5 an hour.

SKIING   Thirty miles (50km) of trails are groomed for skiers in winter, and the **Fundy loppet** in February is a family cross-country event. The park is open for winter camping, and some of the accommodations in Alma stay open year-round.

WHERE TO STAY & DINE

Fundy Park Chalets. Fundy National Park, P.O. Box 72, Alma, NB, E0A 1B0. ☎ **506/ 887-2808.** 29 cabins. TV. Mid-June to Labor Day $65 one to four people; May to mid-June and early Sept to mid-Oct Sun–Thurs $50 one to four people, Fri–Sat $65. Extra person $3; crib or cot rental $2. No credit cards. Closed Oct to mid-May.

Near the park's headquarters and the Alma entrance, the chalets are clustered in a wooded area. Each has a fully equipped kitchenette, a bath with shower, a black-and-white TV, and a bed/living room with two double beds (a full curtain can be used for privacy). Management provides sheets, blankets, and towels and welcomes pets on a leash. A pro shop is a few minutes' walk away, and there's a large children's playground across the road, with a golf course and a heated saltwater pool nearby. You can buy groceries in Alma or eat in the Seawinds Dining Room across the road. Off-season, write or call for reservations. They accept personal checks and traveler's checks.

THE HOPEWELL CAPE ROCKS

Follow Route 114 out of the park toward Moncton and watch for signs for the rocks (☎ 506/734-2026), perhaps the best place to appreciate the powerful force of the Fundy tides. The red sandstone formations, some topped by trees, were once part of the nearby cliffs. Tidal action has eroded and sculpted them into shapes with caves and arches. The rocks are known as "flowerpots" because at high tide all you see is the tops of the formations, crowned by the vegetation they support. During low tide you can descend the many flights of steps to get a closer look at nature's ongoing sculpting. Keep your eye on your watch and ascend when the "giant clock" advises or you'll find yourself in deep and dangerous trouble. Park interpreters are on hand in summer to answer questions. Admission is $3.50 per vehicle. The rocks are open daily from 8am to 9pm; closed from November to April.

CAPE ENRAGE INTERPRETIVE CENTER

The Interpretive Center, Cape Enrage, Albert County, NB (☎ 506/887-2273; off-season, Site 5-5, RR 1, Moncton, NB, E1C 8J5, ☎ 506/856-6081), is available free; nominal fees are charged for programs, tours, escorted hikes, and overnight trips. Offered here are sea canoeing, rappelling, and wilderness hikes to explore caves, underground lakes, and waterfalls.

9 Moncton & the Shediac Peninsula

Acadians and English mix with Irish and German descendants in this crossroads region that forms the isthmus by which Nova Scotia attaches tenuously to the rest of Canada. Moncton is the big, bright city, Shediac the summer playground, and Sackville the little gem most travelers miss entirely.

MONCTON

To New Brunswickers, Moncton is the brash young town on the Atlantic coast, lacking Saint John's sense of history or Fredericton's gentility but with business savvy and eyes on the future. Coming into the city, you'll see the Telephone Tower (not one of their better ideas) poking an impertinent finger into the sky. For travelers, the tower usually marks the route to somewhere else—to Maine, Nova Scotia, or Cape Tormentine and the ferry to Prince Edward Island. The city sits like a great junction box connecting all these routes, and too few people who pass stop to explore it.

Moncton is 30% Francophone and home to the sprawling campus of the French-language Université de Moncton, north of the town center. Its interest to travelers lies in the Acadian Museum on the campus (see "Seeing the Sights," below) and a **hostel** open May to August with lodging for about $20 a night (☎ 506/858-4008).

ESSENTIALS

VISITOR INFORMATION　　The **Public Relations and Tourism Office** at City Hall, 774 Main St. (☎ 506/853-3590), will answer questions and hand out free visitor guides and maps Monday to Friday from 8am to 5pm year-round. In addition, from mid-May to Labor Day two tourist information centers are in operation, one on Main Street (the address varies from year to year, but it's easy to find) and the other at Magnetic Hill on Highway 2 (the Trans-Canada) at the intersection with Highway 126.

GETTING THERE　　From Saint John, take Highway 1 to Sussex and pick up the Trans-Canada Highway (Highway 2); the slow, scenic route follows Highway 2 to Penobsquis, picks up Route 114 through Fundy Park and up the coast past Hopewell Rocks and then into Moncton.

From Fredericton, the prettiest route is along the Trans-Canada Highway all the way; the quickest way is via Coles Island and Route 112, through mostly wooded, scantly populated areas; no trucks are allowed on this route.

PARKING　　This can be tough in downtown Moncton. No parking is allowed on Main Street, but some meters and two-hour zones are on side streets. A multilevel garage and a large surface lot, run by the city, are just off Main Street, and most merchants validate tickets. Guests of the Hotel Beausejour have free downtown parking.

SEEING THE SIGHTS

Depending on when you see the city, it's either bounded by water or by a great gully of mud. Into that gully twice a day rushes the **tidal bore,** a volume of water pushed on by the world's highest tides and compressed into a very narrow space. While the bore is far less dramatic than it used to be, having been altered by the construction of a causeway, the sudden rise is still worth seeing. A good viewpoint is **Bore View Park,** where a large sign gives the time of the next inrush. Even if you miss watching the water rise, you can't help noticing the difference between the high and low levels of the water that bounds the southern side.

Moncton's other famous landmark is **Magnetic Hill,** northeast of the city near the Trans-Canada Highway. Here's the drill: As you approach the hill, signs will instruct you to drive down the slope. At the bottom, cross to the left side of the roadway and stop your car by the white post. Put it in neutral, let off the brakes, and voilà—back you go up the gentle slope to the top where you started. There is, of course, nothing magnetic about it. Your car would do the same thing if it were made entirely of plastic. It's all an illusion, as you can see if you drive or walk to the top of the hill past the white post, near the turnaround area for cars with trailers. Whether it's worth $2 per car to try it is debatable, but if your kids are old enough to know that water and wheeled vehicles run downhill, it'll be worth it to watch their faces when your car goes the "wrong way."

The **Capitol Theatre,** 811 Main St. (☎ 506/856-4377), after a $3.5-million restoration, is Moncton's cultural center. The luxurious 875-seat theater, complete with box seats, first opened in 1922 and now hosts Canadian and international artists, including the New Brunswick Symphony and Les Grands Ballets Canadiens.

The city's 450-acre **Centennial Park** has lawn bowling, tennis courts, paddleboat and canoe rentals, an English garden, a bowling green, a large playground, and a beach. The 2¹/₂-mile dirt road around the park, part of which is lighted at night, is popular with walkers, joggers, and cross-country skiers. Sleigh rides and ice skating keep the park busy in winter. Look for the locomotive, airplane, and tank mounted at the entrance.

Head north on Archibald Street to reach the **Musée Acadien,** in the Clement Cormier Building, Université de Moncton (☎ 506/858-4088). New Brunswick absorbed large numbers of the Acadian settlers driven from Nova Scotia, and this collection provides a visual history of the daily life of this displaced people. Admission is free. Open in summer Monday to Friday 10am to 5pm, Saturday and Sunday 1 to 5pm; rest of the year Tuesday to Friday 1 to 4:30pm, Saturday and Sunday 1 to 4pm.

Visit the local **Farmers' Market,** 132 Robinson St. (☎ 506/383-1749), on Saturday morning from 7am to 1pm (and in August on Wednesday from noon to 4pm). Throughout the year you'll find European, Canadian, and Mexican cooked foods, shish kebab, sausage, homemade breads and pastries, and a large selection of crafts in addition to fresh meats and produce. The market is down the hill from Main Street.

There's a large indoor amusement park out at the **Crystal Palace.** Parents ride free with children on certain rides. You buy a book of tickets and "spend" them as you go; each ride is one to three tickets. In the same vein, **Magic Mountain Water Park** at the Magnetic Hill exit of the Trans-Canada Highway, has a 40-m.p.h. water slide, along with a replica of a Mississippi paddlewheeler, and is open early June to the last half of August daily from 10am to 6pm; late June to mid-August, daily from 10am to 8pm. Nearby, **Magnetic Hill Zoo** (☎ 506/384-9381), open daily from mid-May to October, has about 100 species of native and exotic animals and a petting zoo. A train for unlimited rides throughout the park costs $4; admission is $3.75 adults, $2.75 seniors and youths 12 to 17, $2.25 children 6 to 11.

Moncton Museum/Free Meeting House. 20 Mountain Rd. (near the corner of Belleview). ☎ 506/853-3003. Free admission. Summer daily 10am–5pm; winter Tues–Fri and Sun 1–5pm, Sat 10am–5pm.

You'll be into the realm of Old Moncton even before you enter the museum: The entry was once part of the facade of Moncton's old City Hall. When it was razed, its front was preserved and re-erected as part of the facade of the modern museum. Inside you'll find a permanent exhibit on the history of Moncton (upstairs), as well as changing exhibits, often imported from Montréal's Museum of Fine Arts. Ask to see Moncton's Free Meeting House (next door), the oldest building in the city, built in 1821 and restored in 1990. Over the years it has been used by a dozen congregations, Protestant, Catholic, and Jewish among them.

Thomas Williams Heritage House. 103 Park St. (at the corner of Highfield). ☎ 506/857-0590. Free admission. May and Sept to mid-Oct, Mon, Wed, and Fri 10am–3pm; June Tues–Sat 9am–5pm, Sun 1–5pm; July–Aug Mon–Sat 9am–5pm, Sun 1–5pm; tea room hours are slightly shorter.

Built in 1883, this elegant 12-room Second Empire–style home was in the Williams family for 100 years before it was painstakingly restored and opened to the public. Many of the furnishings belonged to the family. In summer, drop by the Verandah Tea Room here for muffins, ice cream, tea, coffee, ice tea, or lemonade.

WHERE TO STAY

Bonaccord House. 250 Bonaccord St. (at Mountain Road), Moncton, NB, E1C 5M6. ☎ **506/ 388-1535.** Fax 506/853-7191. 4 rms (2 with bath), 1 suite. $45–$56 double; from $53 suite. Rates include full breakfast. Extra person $8. V.

Special touches fill this bed-and-breakfast: premium toiletries, fresh flowers, chilled spring water, turndown service with chocolates on the pillow, and a separate telephone line and fax for guests. The four rooms, all with two beds, most a queen size and single, share three baths (two of which can be designated private for an additional $8 charge). There's also a family suite with a queen-size bed, two twin beds, a couch, and a full bath. The house, built around 1889, is a 10-minute walk from downtown Moncton. No smoking or pets or shoes are allowed indoors.

✪ **Hotel Beausejour.** 50 Main St., Moncton, NB, E1C 1E6. ☎ **506/854-4344**, 800/ 828-7447 in the U.S., or 800/268-9411 in Canada. Fax 506/854-4344. 301 rms, 13 suites. A/C TV TEL. $112 double. Rates drop 15% to 20% in summer and on weekends the rest of the year. AE, DC, ER, MC, V. Free parking.

Business travelers gravitate to the downtown Beausejour, which is near restaurants and the Capitol Theatre. The rooms are modern and spacious (ask for one with a city view). Those on the business-class floor are particularly comfortable, but the reason so many repeat travelers choose this level is for the relaxed breakfast in the parlorlike lounge, presided over by an energetic woman who will share the skinny on what's happening in town and the latest on the local restaurants. The rooftop pool has a lifeguard and sundeck. The hotel also offers 24-hour room service, dry cleaning, in-room movies, and nonsmoking wings.

✪ **Hotel Canadiana.** 46 Archibald St. (at Queen), Moncton, NB, E1C 5H9. ☎ **506/ 382-1054.** 14 rms, 2 suites. TV. $80–$90 double; from $85 suite. Extra person $10. Special family rates for children. MC, V.

A fine Moncton mansion (1887), a short stroll from Main Street, has been lovingly converted to an inn with hardwood floors, Victorian parlors (among six public rooms), graceful verandas, and a dining room with a mural painted by a guest more than 20 years ago. Each room is unique, homey, and blessedly quiet, and all the windows open. With cheerful hosts, the Canadiana is a comfortable and friendly place to stay. A full breakfast is available in the dining room (an additional charge), and they'll provide overnight laundry service for $3. If you don't feel like eating out, gather picnic fixings and eat on the inside or outside porch.

WHERE TO DINE

Get a breakfast of pancakes or eggs for $3 at the counter inside the **Farmers' Market,** Saturday from 7am to noon, or stop any day at **Joe Moka's** at 187 Robinson St., an espresso bar serving breakfast and light lunches.

✪ **L'Auberge.** In the Hotel Beausejour, 750 Main St. ☎ **506/854-4344.** Reservations recommended. Main courses $10–$18. AE, DC, DISC, ER, MC, V. Daily 7am–10:30pm. ECLECTIC.

Less expensive and more casual than The Windjammer but with the same chef, L'Auberge might not have such an ambitious menu, but the quality of the food is just as good. Nightly specials may include seared caribou, mussels steamed in wine and fennel, or shrimp and scallops in a sauté with wild mushrooms. The wines, while well chosen (including several fine selections from South Africa), are a little pricey, with the least expensive at $23.

⑤ Pastalli's Pasta House. Main St. ☎ **506/383-1050.** Reservations accepted. Main courses $9–$11, pastas $6–$8. AE, CB, DC, ER, MC, V. Mon–Thurs 11am–11pm, Fri–Sat 11am–midnight, Sun 4–11pm. ITALIAN.

This place features a crisp Euro-decor of etched-glass panels and deep-green walls, with candlelight, fresh flowers, and carpeting; the casual atmosphere is maintained by an open grill where patrons toast their own garlic bread with a variety of herbed butters and unlimited supply of thick-cut bread. Pasta choices include ravioli with fiddleheads, fettucine with olives, tomato, and béchamel, and vegetable lasagne; a pasta sampler offers a bit of each. Ten wines are priced from $10 to $18, with house wine at $12.95 a liter.

Tivoli Bakery. Landing at the Bend, Main Street. ☎ **506/862-0011.** Lunch $3–$5. No credit cards. Tues–Sat 9am–10pm, Sun 10am–7pm. LIGHT FARE.

At this cafe-bakery, serving breads, pastries, sandwiches, soups, salads, and ice cream, the pastries are so good that they supply the city's best restaurants. A good place to buy bread for a picnic or let them make up sandwiches for you. The croissants (99¢) are worth traveling for.

The Windjammer. In the Hotel Beausejour, 750 Main St. ☎ **506/854-4344.** Reservations recommended. Main courses $17–$26 (most under $20). AE, DC, DISC, ER, MC, V. ECLECTIC.

The flagship of Moncton dining, The Windjammer serves dinner only in an intimate and richly paneled room reminiscent of shipboard dining on an elegant 19th-century liner. The setting and the quality of the menu, which features sautéed breast of guinea fowl, tiger shrimp, or tournedos of caribou with shallots and shiitake and oyster mushrooms, make this an outstanding experience. A four-course fixed-price menu is reduced in price for those arriving between 5:30 and 6:30pm.

SHEDIAC

A beach town welcoming half a million visitors each year, Shediac has a good share of New Brunswick's balmy Northumberland Strait beaches. Special conditions—a confluence of the Gulf of St. Lawrence, the Gulf stream, low sandbars, and shallow waters—allow the sun to warm up the chilly waters of the strait to bath temperature.

   Parlee Beach, east of Shediac, is the most popular (and the most crowded during high season), but other beaches north and east of Shediac are almost as warm and less populated. On your beach search, get off Highway 15 at Exit 31B and wander the shorefront roads: 133, 134, 950, and 530.

   We have trouble understanding why Shediac is so highly touted as a destination. Even though it has beaches, it's not particularly attractive, and although the town has put tasteful markers on its historic houses (of which there are many, mostly of the Victorian era), the whole of rue Main has a boardwalk aspect, with gull-shaped wire frames strung with Christmas-tree lights atop the buildings. At night it's cute; by daylight it's tacky and adds to the general unkempt appearance of the downtown area.

   Shediac's **Information Center** is on your right as you drive into town from Moncton. You can't miss the 35-foot-long, 55-ton lobster in front of it, a real work of art (and it's not bright red). The center is open June to September, daily from 9am to 9pm. For an extensive list of **cottage rentals** and another of inns, hotels, and restaurants, write the Town of Shediac, C.P./P.O. Box 969, Shediac, NB, E0A 3G0 (☎ 506/532-6156).

From May to October, **5 D Tours Ecotourism** offers a variety of boat tours, including a visit to a fish processing and smoking plant in Cap-Pele, a shipyard for fishing boats and a nature walk ($25 adults, $15 children 6-14), and nature cruises on the St. Louis River and Kouchibouguac National Park. Call ☎ 506/576-1994 or 800/716-TOUR (fax 506/576-6660) or write Paul Germain, P.O. Box 475, RR no. 1, Cocagne, NB, E0A 1K0. The tours begin from the Giant Lobster, several times a day, by reservation. **Seascape Divers,** at 705 E. Main St. (☎ 506/858-5663), offers diving excursions.

WHERE TO STAY

Camping is available at **Parlee Beach Provincial Park**, P.O. Box 1537, Shediac, NB, E0A 3G0 (☎ 506/532-1500).

Auberge Belcourt Inn. 112 rue Main (C.P. 631), Shediac, NB, E0A 3G0. ☎ **506/532-6098.** 7 rms (5 with bath). $60–$75 double. Extra person $10. Rates include breakfast. AE, DC, ER, MC, V.

The Auberge Belcourt is an inviting inn with well-lit rooms that have ceiling fans and handmade quilts; many feature brass beds. Be sure to reserve ahead.

Chez Françoise. 93 rue Main (C.P./P.O. Box 715), Shediac, NB, E0A 3G0. ☎ **506/532-4233.** 19 rms (10 with bath). $50–$70 double. Extra person $10. Packages available. Rates include continental breakfast. AE, ER, MC, V. Closed Jan–Apr.

A country inn popular with French-speaking travelers, Chez Françoise is a late 19th-century house, surrounded by elms. It has an elaborate leaded-glass entry, five fireplaces, heavy wooden doors, and simply appointed rooms. Another 10 rooms are available across the street.

Three attractive dining rooms are decorated with fresh flowers and hanging plants. The menu features milk-fed veal, seafood brochette, and other dishes prepared with French flair, as well as daily specials. Main courses run $16 to $25. Dinner is served from 5 to 10pm, Sunday brunch from 11am to 3pm.

WHERE TO DINE

Seafood and Acadian and French cuisines are featured in local restaurants, and in the middle of July the town hosts an annual **Lobster Festival**, when the crustaceans of New Brunswick's waters are offered in greater quantity and at lower prices than normal. Eating seafood is what Shediac is all about.

Ⓢ **Aboiteau Fisheries.** On the pier, Cape Pele. ☎ **506/577-2950.** Reservations not accepted. Full dinners $5–$12; lobster dinners $14–$22. MC, V. SEAFOOD.

Our search for lobster-in-the-rough ended here, at a window in the back of the fisheries plant. Giant servings of clams, scallops, fish and chips, and huge bowls of chowder are served on plastic plates, which you carry to a picnic table under the plastic enclosure. The best buy in lobster is to go to the fish market in the same building and buy your live lobster, then bring it to the window; they'll cook it for you and give you a plate, napkins, forks, and butter free. It makes perfect sense—for the consumer, at least—since you are getting the market, not restaurant, price.

Fisherman's Paradise. Main Street. ☎ **506/532-6811.** Reservations not needed. Main courses $9–$27. AE, DC, ER, MC, V. Mid-Apr to mid-Sept daily 11:30am–11pm. SEAFOOD.

Fisherman's Paradise is on the eastern outskirts of town, not far from the intersection with Highway 15 (Exit 37). The dining room, with ship replicas and nautical touches, sets the mood for their Fisherman's Paradise special: half a lobster, fried clams, scallops, stuffed shrimp, and several kinds of fish, for $27. There's seafood chowder, a full range of lobster dishes, fried and nonfried seafood, plus chicken, steaks, and sandwiches fill out the list. There's a full bar and a limited wine list.

Fred's Restaurant. Route 15, Cape Pele. ☎ **506/577-4269.** Reservations not needed. Main courses $9–$18. MC, V. Sun–Wed 7:30am–9pm, Thurs–Fri 7:30am–10pm, Sat 7:30am–11pm. SEAFOOD.

We heard about Fred's in Moncton, when friends told us we'd find the area's best fried clams here. We did. They forgot to mention that the lobster rolls are huge fat sandwiches fairly bursting from between thick slices of bread.

Paturel Shore House. Cape Bimet Road, Route 133. ☎ **506/532-4774.** Reservations recommended, especially on summer weekends. Main courses $7–$26. AE, ER, MC, V. Daily 4–10pm. Closed Oct–Apr. From Route 133, about 3 miles east of Shediac, turn left onto Cape Bimet Road; Paturel Shore House is on your left at the water's edge. SEAFOOD.

The Paturel Shore House is a quintessential seafood restaurant in a simple white house on the shore, next to a fish-packing plant. Arrive with a good appetite and start with the hearty lobster stew, a meal in itself. Or skip the preliminaries and go for the mammoth seafood platter.

SACKVILLE

From Moncton, you can either follow the Trans-Canada Highway (Highway 2) all the way or take the more scenic route through farmland and small French communities—Highway 2 to St. Joseph to Route 106 east, which is only 15 minutes longer. Just before you arrive in Sackville you'll pass signs for historic Fort Beausejour. The Sackville **Information Center,** on East Main Street, is open June to October (☎ 506/364-0431 or 506/364-0400 November to May), staffed by enthusiastic students from adjoining Mount Albion College.

EXPLORING THE AREA

Sackville is a small community, easy to walk around, with some interesting shops, including that of the only manufacturer of handmade horse collars in North America. **Sackville Harness Shop** is at 50 West Main St., just at the top of the hill. **Struts Center,** in Willow Place, off West Main Street (☎ 506/536-1211), is an art gallery exhibiting and selling the work of the numerous artists, some of national note, who live and work in the area. At Albion College, whose red sandstone buildings you see atop the hill, you can visit the **Owens Art Gallery,** the first art museum in Eastern Canada, established in 1894. It's rich in works by European and North American artists.

Beside the Anglican Church in the center of town, a trail leads into the **Sackville Waterfowl Park.** Fifty-five acres, spanned by more than a mile of boardwalk and trails though the marsh habitat, are set aside for birds and their enthusiasts. Nine species of duck breed there, and 150 other bird varieties have been recorded. Another trail enters opposite the information center on East Main Street, where you can park your car. The park is open daily from 5am until half an hour after sunset. Birders should ask at the information center for the booklet on birding sites in the area, among the best in the Atlantic provinces, and about the guided bird walks in the park.

Down the road from Sackville, near the hamlet of Aulac and almost at the Nova Scotia border, Fort Beausejour (1751–55), in the **Fort Beausejour National Historic Park** (☎ 506/536-0720), commands the sprawling Tantramar marshes and the head of the Bay of Fundy. The French built it, but New England militia forces, under British command, captured the fort in June 1755, and their leader, young Colonel Monckton, renamed it Fort Cumberland. Visit the impressive earthworks and explore its underground passages; park staff will tell you about the fort and its history. Indoor and outdoor picnic facilities are available, all with a view. A visitor center and a gift shop are on site. Admission is $2.25 for adults, $1.75 for seniors, and $1.25 for children. The park's open daily from 9am to 5pm (closed late October to May).

WHERE TO STAY & DINE

Savoy Arms Bed & Breakfast. 55 Bridge St., Sackville, NB, E0A 3C0. ☎ **506/536-0790.** 3 rms. $55 double. Rates include tax and full breakfast.

Gilbert and Sullivan fans will love the subtle double entendres of the room names and decor at this fine home. Guests' comfort comes first, with a big library/lounge for their use, filled with travel books, and an adjoining terrace where they can eat breakfast on nice days. We especially liked the Iolanthe Room, in the rich green of peers' robes.

Marshlands Inn. 59 Bridge St., Sackville, NB, E0A 3C0. ☎ **506/536-0170.** Fax 506/536-0721. 21 rms. TV TEL. $55–$95 double. AE, DC, ER, MC, V.

The molded ceilings, beveled glass windows, an original William Morris frieze, and fine woodworking of this Victorian inn have just been refurbished and redecorated with a fine hand. There are elegant touches, like double-carpeted stairs, claw-foot bathtubs, antique furnishings, a grandfather's clock, and original works by local artists. You can stay in the same room where Elizabeth II kicked off her shoes during a stop for "tea" on her 1984 tour. (The tea was actually a big cold gin and tonic, but the press thought gin didn't sound royal enough.) It's a lovely big room with a mammoth four-poster bed and windows on three sides overlooking the marshes; the sweet scent of marsh grass blows in on the summer breeze.

Dining/Entertainment: Along with the inn, the dining room has been updated, with a new chef, though they've kept those old traditional dishes everyone asks for—snow pudding, codcakes, and foxberries. The breast of duck is now served with blueberry sauce and the salmon roulade is stuffed with spinach and mushrooms. Main courses range from $12 to $25, most between $12 and $16, with vegetarian main courses at $8.

10 Kouchibouguac National Park

If you've avoided this park because you didn't know how to pronounce it so you could ask directions to get there, say "COO-she-boo-quack." Best known for its beaches—stretching along the Northumberland Straits as far as you can see—the park has a lot more to attract visitors. Even if you don't want to swim or sunbathe, walk the boardwalk out to **Kelly's Beach;** the 10-minute walk takes you across tidal pools, inlets, and dunes to a true barrier island that protects the fragile ecosystem between it and the mainland. Hiking trails interlace the park and the rivers are perfect for canoeing. The variety of ecosystems includes beach, lagoon, barrier island, marsh, bog, and river banks. As in other national parks, you must pay a car fee of $6 per day or $18 for a four-day pass.

NATURE TRAILS Ten nature trails, ranging in length from 1/4 mile to more than 8 miles, explore the park's varied habitats. The **Osprey Trail,** as might be expected, often yields views of these birds diving in the lagoons for fish. The **Bog Trail,** which takes about 45 minutes, leads across the bog on a boardwalk to an observation deck.

CANOEING One of the most popular sports in the park, canoeing provides access to eight class 1 (flat-water) rivers. Canoe and boat rentals are available at the rental center (call 506/876-2443 or ask the park warden). The **Voyageur Marine Adventure** provides tours on board the 10-passenger canoe to see seals at close range, as well as view common terns and piping plover. Tours last three hours, go out four times a week, and cost $25 ($15 for under 12). For reservations, call 506/876-2443.

BEACHES   At Kelly's Beach, lifeguards are on duty; other beaches—by far the less crowded ones—have no lifeguards but lots more elbow room.

CAMPING   One of the finest and best maintained campgrounds we've ever seen is Kouchibouguac's. The sites are well spaced, the grass cut, and the facilities spotless. Though the number of campsites is large and growing, the number of campers who vie for them in July and August—particularly on weekends—is even larger, and growing even faster. Get there early for the best chance of a site and have a back-up plan in case you don't get one. Camping fees drop off-season, ranging from $10 to $14.

11 The Acadian Peninsula

Bounded by the Gulf of St. Lawrence and the Baie de Chaleur, the peninsula is a world of its own, French, but as far removed from Québec, just across the bay, as it is from Paris. It's bilingual, but with the rich accents of a 1940s movie. The feeling is one of having stepped back a few decades into a French outpost; you half expect to see Humphrey Bogart at the next table in the Hotel Paulin.

Acadians have lived here since 1755, when their ancestors were forced from their Nova Scotia settlements and moved here to fish, farm, and harvest the peat and peat moss that lie in deep layers along the shore.

The Acadian peninsula stretches from Neguac, on the east coast, around to Bathurst, on the northern coast. Depending on where you're coming from, you can get there by taking Highway 11 north from Shediac, Highway 126 north from Moncton, or Highway 8 along the Miramichi Valley from Fredericton. If you're entering the province from the Gaspé, you'll approach the peninsula from Campbellton, via Highway 11.

CARAQUET

The center for Acadian culture in New Brunswick, Caraquet is 97% French-speaking. Founded in 1758, it hosts an annual **Acadian Festival** in August, highlighted by the **Blessing of the Fleet,** and has three Acadian-related attractions.

In Caraquet, Highway 11 becomes boulevard St-Pierre, and the hostelries and major points of interest are spread along the west end of it, where you'll also find the **information center,** open daily from 10am to 8pm in summer. Caraquet was once the longest village in the world, measuring nearly 14 miles, stretched along boulevard St-Pierre; it's now a town and only 5 miles long.

SEEING THE SIGHTS

The beaches are a big draw here, but Caraquet is also home to one of New Brunswick's largest commercial fishing fleets, so the **wharves** are a busy, colorful place to get a sense of local life. If you savor more serene spots, visit the tiny **Chapel of Sainte-Anne-du-Bocage,** west of Caraquet on Route 11, founded in memory of the Acadian settlers. At this small wooden chapel, with only six short pews, is **"the Source,"** a water fountain locally popular for a drink at sunset. Open daily from 9am to 9pm.

West of Caraquet along the northern coast of the Acadian peninsula on Highway 11, you'll come to **Grande-Anse,** with its huge stone church, and an **information center,** with a children's playground beside it. The **Musée des Papes** (Popes

Museum), housed in a big modern building on the highway, chronicles the history of Roman Catholicism, a central part of Acadian life, and displays a large model of St. Peter's Basilica in Rome. It's open from June to September.

Just down the road, **Pokeshaw Provincial Park** is open daily from 9am to 9pm; from the lookout here you can see a drum-shaped sea stack, a huge rock island that was once part of the cliffs on which you stand. It's covered with **cormorants.** Go to the far left end of the rail fence for a view of the next point, also alive with cormorants, where the sea has worn a round hole through the rock. Across the bay is Québec's Gaspé Peninsula. Come here at sunset if you can.

Village Historique Acadien. Six miles (10km) west of Caraquet. ☎ **506/727-3467.** Admission June–early Sept, $7.50 adults, $4.25 children, $15 family (less than half price early Sept–early Oct). June–early Sept daily 10am–6pm; early Sept–early Oct daily 10am–5pm. Closed mid-Oct–May.

The Historic Acadian Village, a living museum of 42 buildings, is a 15-minute drive west of Caraquet. Here interpreters in period costumes work at the trades, do the daily chores, and play the games that made up the fabric of town and home life in Acadia between 1780 and 1890. Kids can become part of the "family" for the day, joining in the village life in costume; the $15 fee includes lunch. English speakers are introduced as a "cousin from the States." Their restaurant serves Acadian dishes and, during July, offers a dinner theater with song and dance (both with audience participation) for $35. Even if you don't speak French, it's fun and you'll catch the drift. Reserve for the children's program or dinner theater through the museum or the Day Adventures program.

Musée Acadien. 15 bd. St-Pierre Ouest. ☎ **506/727-1713.** Admission $3 adults, $2 seniors, $1 students; children free. Sun–Fri noon–5pm, Sat 10am–5pm. Closed Oct–May.

If you don't have time to drive out to the Acadian Village, you can still get a good sense of Acadian life by visiting this museum. Its two floors of exhibits interpret the daily lives of Acadians from the late 1700s to the early 1900s, through items from clothing to fishing equipment and religious artifacts. Notice the 1926 bicycle with wooden wheels. An interactive computer helps bring the exhibits to life.

WHERE TO STAY

There's also the **Auberge de Jeunesse** (Youth Hostel), at 577 bd. St-Pierre Ouest (☎ 506/727-2345), offering 15 beds in summer for $12 adults, $7 children 12 to 18; younger children stay free. It has picnic tables, a bright kitchen, one room with 10 bunk beds and another with 5, two showers, and one toilet.

✪ Hotel Paulin. 143 bd. St-Pierre Ouest, Caraquet, NB, E0B 1K0. ☎ **506/727-9981.** 9 rms (2 with bath). $51–$55 double without bath, $65 double with bath. MC, V. Closed Nov–May.

The owner, the third generation of the family that built it, has updated the hotel without losing its old-fashioned charm. He's created a finely tuned balance between the square mansard-roofed building, its interior original under a coat of fresh paint, and its modern amenities: sparkling new baths and stylish but appropriate furnishings. In less talented hands it could easily have been dowdy or worse yet, cute.

All the rooms are on the second floor; some share baths, but most have sinks. The lobby parlor is a comfortable place to relax with a glass of wine. The hotel sits above low bluffs, and it's a short walk through the back yard to a small cove beach. Walk down after sunset, when the Gaspé is silhouetted across the water and the lights on both shores have begun to twinkle on.

Dining/Entertainment: The dining room, with only eight tables, draws locals and visitors alike. Hotelier/chef Gerard Paulin claims it's just simple cooking, but his cuisine is an Acadian version of nouvelle with the emphasis on substance, not sauces. He offers a nice selection of dishes (including succulent local mussels and scallops) and a reasonably priced wine list. Entrees run $8 to $14. Breakfast is served daily from 7:30 to 10am, dinner from 5:30 to 10pm. They'll pack a picnic basket for your lunch.

🅂 **Maison Touristique Dugas.** 683 bd. St-Pierre Ouest, Caraquet, NB, E1W 1A1. ☎ **506/ 727-3195.** 11 rms (none with bath), 2 suites, 5 cabins, RV or tent camping. Main house $29 double; suite $40–$50 double. Cabin $40–$50 double. Camping $6–$8 tent; $10–$16 camper. Breakfast about $2–$5. MC, V.

The Maison Touristique Dugas offers something for every vacation style. In the main house the guest rooms share a small sun room and lounge. Two suites with a large kitchen and living room are in another building, and there are five rustic cabins, with kitchen. You're also welcome to camp, in a tent or an RV. The well-tended grounds are filled with clover, lupine, and pansy beds, and it has picnic tables and a private beach at the end of a dirt road through woods sprinkled with wild roses.

SHIPPAGAN & LAMÉQUE & MISCOU ISLANDS

For a pleasant excursion out of Caraquet, explore the fishing communities and beaches on the islands of Laméque and Miscou, at the tip of the peninsula, and the upbeat town of Shippagan.

WHAT TO SEE & DO

Your first stop should be **Shippagan's colorful waterfront,** where from early May boats unload their catch of crabs every day. (It's a tough but profitable line of work: They can make $350,000 to $800,000 in a single six- or eight-week season.) **The Blessing of the Fleet** takes place here on the third Sunday of July.

From Shippagan, take Route 113 to the islands of **Laméque and Miscou,** where you'll find birds, bogs, and beaches. You won't find many places to eat, so bring a picnic lunch. In mid-July, Laméque hosts a major **International Festival of Baroque Music,** with artists from all over the world. For a schedule and tickets, write to C.P. 644, Laméque, NB, E0B 1V0 (☎ 506/344-2296). Drive to **Pigeon Cove,** on the eastern side, to the small fishing harbor filled with brightly painted boats, and to see the old **capstans,** which hauled boats ashore. (They're straight ahead, past the blue fence, where the road makes an elbow turn to the left.) Near the harbor, notice the peat being harvested.

Sadly, a bridge is replacing the delightful little red cable ferry that has long carried cars free to **Miscou Island**—island residents are not pleased at the disruption it'll bring to their way of life. The island is flat and perfect for bicycling. An interpretive **boardwalk trail** leads across one of the bogs, a good place to observe birds as well as learn about the life of a bog. The entire island is a stopover on the **bird migration route;** more than 250 breeding and migratory species have been reported. To get a bird's-eye view of the bogs and the 360 lakes that lie in them, climb to the top of **Miscou Lighthouse** (1856), oldest on the peninsula. Beyond the light, walk to the point, along a beach that gives way to a multicolored shingle, made up of stones washed from quite far away. We found a large piece of well-worn coral there.

Camping Shippagan, 4 miles west of town, has 80 tent and trailer sites as well as a beach, playground, and boat ramp. Rates are $15 a day with electricity, $11 without.

Aquarium & Marine Center. Route 113, Shippagan. ☎ **506/336-3013.** Admission $5.35 adults, $2.15 ages 6–18, family $10.70. MC, V. Daily 10am–6pm. Closed Oct–Apr.

Everything to do with the sea, from the entire wheelhouse of a state-of-the-art fishing boat to huge tanks of native fishes, is displayed and interpreted in a lively modern setting. The aquarium is exciting even for those who care little about fish unless they're grilled on a plate. Be sure to look for the rock gunnel, tiny fish that live in cast-off shells. At 11am and 4pm, the seals are fed, a great show for all ages, as they impatiently slap the water, demanding another fish.

WHERE TO DINE

Jardin de la Mer. Pavillon Aquatuque (next to Aquarium), Shippagan. ☎ **506/336-8454.** Reservations accepted. Main courses $11–$23; pastas $8–$14; table d'hôte lunches $6–$7; children's menu $5–$6. MC, V. July–Aug daily 9am–10pm; May–June and Sept–Dec daily 9am–9pm. Closed Jan–Apr.

Overlooking the marina, where there's often music in summer, this bright modern restaurant is surrounded by glass to make the best of its fine view. Champagne mussels, garlic shrimp, snow crab, and other seafood highlight the menu, although rack of lamb with garlic is popular. For a feast, order the $36.95 "Sea in Your Plate," with lobster, crab, shrimp, scallops, and mussels. If you do, you should probably skip the chowder.

ALONG THE NORTH COAST

Bathurst is an industrial town of 16,000, many of whom make their living at the city's large pulp-paper mill. In recent years other industries have moved nearby, and when important strikes of minerals and metals were discovered in the region, the result was a mining boom. When anything booms, can museums be far behind? No, and 1995 saw the opening of **Mining World,** on Route 134 in Petite-Rocher (☎ 506/783-0824), with an elevator that simulates a descent to 2,800 feet below the surface. It's open daily from 10am to 6pm.

Those who prefer fresh air will enjoy the free **Youngall Beach Park,** on Youngall Drive, off Route 134, 3 miles (5km) north of Bathurst. Across the bay, **Daley Point Reserve** has five walking trails and an observation deck overlooking the bay and salt marshes. Thousands of Canada geese pass through in the fall, and the park is one of only four salt marshes in the world where you can see the rare Maritime Provinces ringlet butterfly. To get there from Caraquet, leave Route 11 in Janeville and follow the shore road (Promenade Carron). From Bathurst, turn left onto Promenade Carron from Bridge Street (you'll see signs).

WHERE TO STAY

Auberge d'Anjou. 587 rue Principal, Petit-Rocher, NB, E0B 2E0. ☎ **506/783-0587.** Fax 506/783-5587. 14 rms, 2 suites. TV. $55 double, $80 suite. Rates include breakfast. AE, ER, MC, V.

Six airy, stylishly decorated rooms are in the main house, built just after the turn of the century, and 10 (some with shared bath) in the recently renovated former convent next door. We especially liked the bridal suite, with its Victorian bathtub and demure dressing screen. The Frenette suite is ideal for families, with two baths.

Guests in the main house have a full breakfast, those in the convent have a continental. A new chef will offer Acadian specialties as well as local seafood. It's open for dinner daily mid-June to September, Saturday only in spring and fall; lunch is served Monday to Friday year-round.

WHERE TO DINE

La Fine Grobe-sur-Mer. Route 134, Nigadoo. ☎ **506/783-3138.** Daily 11:30am–10pm. Main courses $15–$36. AE, CB, DC, MC, V. Take Exit 321 off Route 11 and turn left in Nigadoo, then right immediately after the Nigadoo River bridge.

The owner/chef gathers herbs from the garden and bakes bread in a clay oven behind the restaurant. The wine list is long, the coffee good, and no one hurries you after dinner. They have a six-room B&B, with private and shared baths at $35 to $45 double.

ONWARD TO THE GASPE

Highway 11 skirts the shore of the Baie de Chaleur to Dalhousie and Campbellton. Past Campbellton is Matapédia, Québec, on the road across the Gaspé to Mont-Joli. A much more scenic route, however, is around the tip of the Gaspé, and you can reach that road much more quickly by taking the bridge from Campbellton to Pointe-à-la-Croix or the ferry at Dalhousie (for $15). For full information on the Gaspé Peninsula, see Chapter 10.

WHERE TO STAY   Should you wish to stay the night in Campbellton, there's a **Journey's End** at 3 Sugarloaf St. W., Campbellton, NB, E3N 3G9 (☎ 506/753-4121 or 800/668-4200). Take Exit 415 off Highway 11 and pass the Sugarloaf Mall; the motel is on the right. Rates are about $63 double. Another good choice is **Aylesford Inn B&B,** 8 McMillan Ave., Cambellton NB, E3N 1E9 (☎ 506/759-7672). Rates are $50 to $60 double, $100 for the suite.

6 Prince Edward Island

by Barbara Radcliffe Rogers and Stillman Rogers

The images of Prince Edward Island that linger longest in our memories are in full color. We remember its vivid green crops bursting forth from a brick-red soil, its roadsides white with Queen Anne's lace or pink with thyme blossoms, and its dark green fir trees, framing an intensely blue sea—features that make this a land of colorful but simple beauty.

None of this came about by accident: Prince Edward Island (usually referred to simply as P.E.I.) is carefully preserved by people proud of their land and their traditions. Their lives are centered around the red soil and blue water. Tidy farms along its country roads grow potatoes (the island's principal crop), broccoli, tomatoes, strawberries, and grains, or raise dairy cattle. The waters just offshore teem with lobsters, clams, scallops, and world-famous Malpeque Bay oysters. And island streams and lakes yield trout and salmon. Never fear: You'll eat well here.

While harvesting the island's natural wealth is the prime industry on Prince Edward Island, tourism is a close second. And the two fit together very nicely: A number of island farmers supplement their incomes by renting rooms to visitors. Most people who come to the island are looking for a week or two of peace and quiet, simple living, pastoral scenery, and warm beaches—they're rarely disappointed.

1 Exploring Prince Edward Island

The Department of Tourism has mapped out three scenic drives, which roughly correspond to the three counties that constitute the island. **Lady Slipper Drive** (180 miles, 288km) circles the sparsely populated and unspoiled western reaches of the island. **Blue Heron Drive** (120 miles, 190km) circles the central portion of the island, through Charlottetown, past Summerside, and along the northern beach route. **King's Byway Drive** (234 miles, 375km) connects the other two, winding along the sinuous coasts of the eastern portion. No matter where you go in Prince Edward Island, you'll never be more than 10 miles (16km) from the water.

VISITOR INFORMATION   For information about Prince Edward Island and the free 152-page Visitors Guide, call ☎ 800/463-4PEI (☎ 902/629-2380 outside North America), or write to Visitor Services, West Royalty Industrial Park, Charlottetown, PEI, C1E 1B0.

Prince Edward Island

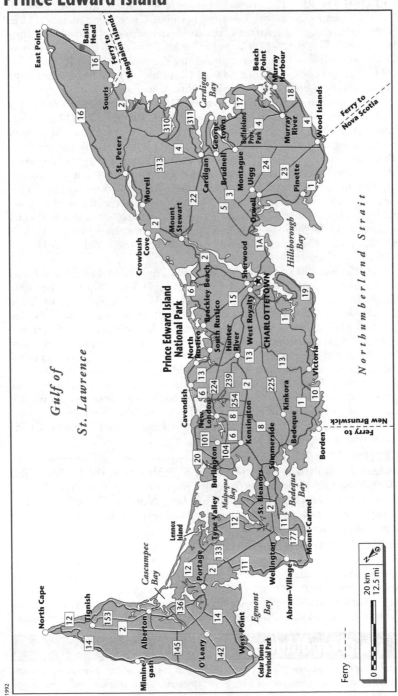

1992

GETTING THERE   The commuter partner of Air Canada, **Air Nova** (☎ 800/776-3000 in the U.S., 800/565-3940 in Maritime Canada, or 800/563-5151 in Newfoundland), and **Air Atlantic**, the commuter partner of Canadian Airlines International (☎ 800/426-7000 in the U.S. or 800/665-1177 in Canada), both serve Charlottetown from other points in the Atlantic Provinces.

Most people come to Prince Edward Island by car-ferry from either Cape Tormentine, New Brunswick, or Caribou, Nova Scotia.

From Cape Tormentine, New Brunswick, **Marine Atlantic** (121 Eden St., Bar Harbor, Maine) operates huge car-ferries to Borden, Prince Edward Island. Boats leave every hour on the half hour in summer between 6:30am and 11:30pm, with extra morning sailings at 12:30am and 1:30am. Extra sailings are added at peak times during busy midday hours. The ferry works quite efficiently. You pay nothing to get onto the island—just drive down the wharf and onto the boat—but pay a round-trip fare on your return. Prices are $7.75 for adults, $5.75 for seniors, $4 for children 5 to 12, and $18.75 for a car. You can't make reservations—and none are necessary—but if you want to know how they're running, listen to a local radio station or call ☎ 506/538-7654 in Cape Tormentine, New Brunswick; 902/855-2030 in Borden, Prince Edward Island; or 800/341-7981 in the U.S. The trip takes about 45 minutes.

From Caribou, Nova Scotia, to Wood Islands, Prince Edward Island, four ferries are operated by **Northumberland Ferries Ltd.,** 94 Water St., P.O. Box 634, Charlottetown, PEI, C1A 7L3 (☎ 902/566-3838 or 800/565-0201 in Prince Edward Island and Nova Scotia; fax 902/566-1550). Service is seasonal, from May 1 to December 20, and the sailing schedule varies, depending on time of year, but generally begins at 6am and runs to about 9pm. Sailings are approximately every 50 minutes, and crossing time is one hour and 15 minutes. A cafeteria is on board the boat. Rates, paid only when exiting Prince Edward Island (if you stay you've beat the system), are $9 per adult, $6.50 senior, $4.25 children 5 to 12, and $28.50 per car. Call or write for a printed schedule. They don't take reservations and the fare can be paid with cash, a credit card (AE, MC, V), or traveler's check.

Finally, there is car-ferry service between Souris, Prince Edward Island, and Grindstone, Magdalen Islands, Québec.

GETTING AROUND   Charlottetown has several car-rental offices, among them **Budget**, 215 University Ave. (☎ 902/892-8333); **Hertz,** 47A St. Peter's Rd. (☎ 902/566-5566); **Tilden,** Charlottetown Airport or 21 St. Peter's Rd. (☎ 902/894-8311); and **Discount Car Rental,** 640 University Ave. (☎ 902/566-3213). While Discount doesn't have a booth at the arrival terminal, they're just outside the airport and provide free transport.

AN IMPORTANT NOTE ON PRICES   Unless stated otherwise, **the prices cited in this guide are given in Canadian dollars,** which is good news for U.S. travelers, because the Canadian dollar is worth 25% less than the American dollar, but buys nearly as much. As we go to press, $1 Canadian is worth about 75¢ U.S., which means that your $100-a-night hotel room will cost only U.S. $75, and your $6 breakfast costs only U.S. $4.50. Remember to add on taxes, though, which are substantial.

2 The Great Outdoors

Find your favorite activity below, and we'll point you to the best places in the province to pursue your interest or give you the general information you need to get started.

BIKING   Country roads abound on Prince Edward Island, but the Confederation Trail (see "Walking," below) provides the best path for biking. Bring your own bike on the ferry or rent one in Charlottetown from **Smooth Cycle** (☎ 902/566-5530). For information on day cycling tours, call **Sport PEI** at 902/368-4110. **MacQueen's,** 430 Queen St., Charlottetown (☎ 800/969-2822; fax 902/894-4547), offers custom bicycle tours of the island. Prices include bicycle, accommodation arrangements, bike route cards and maps, luggage transfer, and emergency road repair service. Rental rates are $20 per day; $80 per week. Five- and seven-night tours with inn lodging, breakfast, luggage transfer, and emergency repair service are $649 and $829.

CLAM DIGGING   The red-sand beaches at Prince Edward Island National Park in Cavendish are well-known spots for clam digging. And Pinette, on the Kings Byway, east of Charlottetown, is perhaps even better known for its clams. Wherever you choose to go, don't forget to bring along your own trowel or hoe. A tip for cooking plump and sandless clams: Before you steam them, soak them for several hours in a bucket of water into which you have sprinkled some cornmeal.

CROSS-COUNTRY SKIING   Although cross-country skiing has been popular on the island for some time, it has been given a great boost with the development of the Confederation Trail (see "Walking," below), a path that makes it possible to ski from one end of the island to the other. The **Brookville Nordic Ski Centre,** which has hosted the Canada Winter Games, offers world-class cross-country trails. And **Mill River Provincial Park** also has lighted trails for night skiing.

FISHING   Most deep-sea fishing trips leave from the Rustico Bay area; they are listed in Section 4 of this chapter.

You must have a nonresident fishing license to fish in the lakes and streams of Prince Edward Island. Families may fish for trout on a single license for two weeks from the date of issue, but each person must purchase a separate salmon license. For specifics, contact any Visitor Information Centre or the **Department of Environmental Resources,** P.O. Box 2000, Charlottetown, PEI, C1A 7N8 (☎ 902/368-4683).

GOLF   Eleven courses, of varying difficulty, are open to the public across the island. The two best are the **Links at Crowbush Cove** (☎ 902/652-2356), near Prince Edward Island National Park, and the 18-hole championship **Brudnell River Provincial Golf Course** near Mantaque (☎ 902/652-2342).

SEA KAYAKING   Several places along the shore rent kayaks; tours of two days or longer are outfitted by **Outside Expeditions in Charlottetown** (☎ 902/892-5425). Some of their trips offer lodgings in country inns along the way, others camp on the shore. See the Charlottetown section of this chapter for more information.

SEAL WATCHING   Harbor seals spend their summers in the wide river estuaries of Prince Edward Island, especially those of the Brudenell and Murray Rivers on the eastern shore. Seal-watching expeditions go out of Murray River and Montague. In the winter, seals live on the ice floes and **Atlantic Marine Adventure Tours** (☎ 506/459-7325) can arrange for you to see baby harp seals just after they are born, in late February.

WALKING   Through the work of several agencies, private groups, and CN Rail, **The Confederation Trail,** following the track of a now-defunct railroad bed, is well on its way to completion. When finished, this smooth-surfaced trail for walkers, cyclists, skiers, and snowmobilers will extend the entire length of the island, with branches to several other areas. Because the original railroad builders were paid by the mile, with no limit on the number of miles they covered, they apparently went to great lengths to avoid hills and other obstructions: The result is a surprisingly level route that winds in a most un-railroadlike manner and is just perfect for its present use. For trail updates, call ☎ 800/463-4PEI.

3 Charlottetown

The capital of Prince Edward Island is a lovely old town of 33,000, with fine colonial and Victorian buildings and the new, ultramodern Confederation Centre of the Arts. *Confederation* is a term much bandied about in Charlottetown, for it was here, in Prince Edward Island's Province House, that the first discussions on the subject of Canada's confederation were held in 1864. At first it seems odd that the island province did not join the confederation until 1873, but the delay was entirely reasonable. Islanders had nothing against joining—they just wanted the details to be worked out first, especially communications between Prince Edward Island and the rest of Canada. No doubt the easy access to the island today is the result of that prudence a century ago. Today, in the summer months, islanders dressed up as Fathers and Mothers of Confederation present short theatrical programs outdoors at Peake's Wharfe throughout the day—a lively, visual way to learn about the beginnings of Canada.

ESSENTIALS

VISITOR INFORMATION   The **Provincial Tourism Information Centre** (scheduled to move during 1996) is on University Avenue at Summer Street (which is also Highway 1, the Trans-Canada Highway), P.O. Box 940E, Charlottetown, PEI, C1A 7M5. If you come into town from the Borden ferry dock, you'll pass it on your right, in a shopping center. If you arrive after hours during July and August, call ☎ 902/368-4444 for help, 24 hours a day.

For local information in Charlottetown, go to the **tourist bureau** at City Hall on Queen Street (☎ 902/566-5548).

GETTING THERE   See Section 1 of this chapter. If you're arriving by plane, the Charlottetown Airport is 5 miles (8km) from the center of the city. Allow 15 to 20 minutes' travel time and $7 per person for the taxi ride downtown.

GETTING AROUND   It's virtually impossible to get lost for long in Charlottetown's small downtown section. Use the Confederation Centre of the Arts, bordered by Queen, Grafton, Prince, and Richmond streets, as your point of reference. Most of the city's attractions and hotels are within easy walking distance of the center.

Taxi stands located on lower University Avenue are **City Cab** (☎ 902/892-6567) and **Ed's Taxi** (☎ 902/892-6561).

Car rental agencies based in Charlottetown include **Budget, Tilden, Hertz,** and **Discount Car Rental.** All except Discount have booths at the airport, but they also provide free transport to their office just outside the airport.

Downtown parking is scarce. Metered spaces (if you can find them) cost 25¢ for 30 minutes but are free weekdays after 6pm and on weekends. The Pownal Parkade, on Pownal Street between Grafton and Richmond, charges 60¢ an hour, up to a maximum of $4 a day, from 6:30am to midnight (☎ 902/368-3653).

SPECIAL EVENTS   The annual **Charlottetown Festival** is held at The Confederation Centre for the Arts from late June to mid-September. Guest performers, special shows, and a list of musical performances are highlights, and a lively musical

Charlottetown

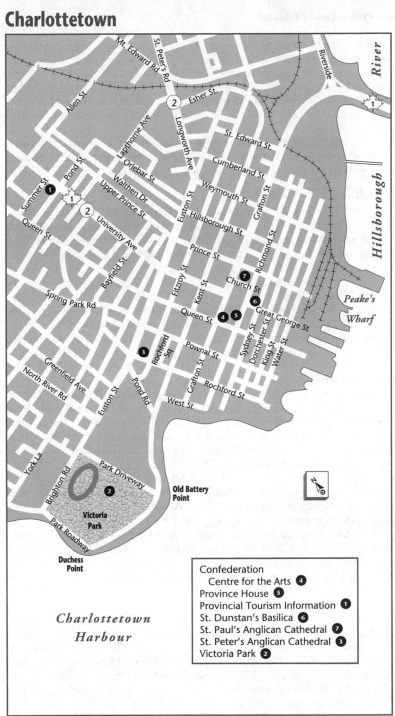

Confederation
  Centre for the Arts ④
Province House ⑤
Provincial Tourism Information ①
St. Dunstan's Basilica ⑥
St. Paul's Anglican Cathedral ⑦
St. Peter's Anglican Cathedral ③
Victoria Park ②

based on Prince Edward Island's own *Anne of Green Gables* is always part of the showbill. Schedules and tickets are at the box office near the corner of Queen and Grafton streets. For reservations, call ☎ 902/566-1267 or 800/565-0278 in North America year-round; fax 902/566-4648. Tickets can be purchased at the box office from 9am to 9pm Monday through Saturday from late June through mid-September. Prices range from $16.50 to $30. The children's theater has several productions as well.

In July and August, you can catch **"Spirit of a Nation,"** a rousing and inspiring outdoor production in music and dance at the center, featuring an ethnic and geographic mix of talented young Canadians. The program is free.

EXPLORING THE TOWN

The people you see walking the streets of Charlottetown and nodding or tipping their hats to you in period dress are students with unusual summer work, portraying the fathers (and a couple of mothers) of the confederacy. Not only are they in costume, they're also in character. Ask them who they are and learn some Canadian history.

You can learn about the domestic life of the late 19th century in the 11 furnished rooms of **Beaconsfield,** at 2 Kent St. (☎ 902/892-9127), a Victorian mansion designed by William Harris for a prominent shipbuilder. Island Tree Bookstore and Gift Shop in back of the house sells books about the island; you can have tea and scones on the veranda in the afternoon. Admission is $2.50 adults, children under 12 admitted free. Open in summer Tuesday to Sunday from 10am to 5pm, Tuesday to Friday and Sunday 1 to 5pm the rest of the year; closed mid-December to mid-January.

Start your explorations in the area near the Confederation Centre (see below). There are three historic churches worth a visit nearby. **St. Paul's Anglican Cathedral,** on Church Street (☎ 902/892-1691), was built in 1777 of local red sandstone, and is the oldest Protestant church on the island. Open Monday to Friday 10am to 4pm in July and August. **St. Peter's Anglican Cathedral,** on the corner of Rochford and Fitzroy streets (☎ 902/566-2102), was founded in 1869, and is perhaps Canada's smallest cathedral. Its All Souls' Chapel was a collaborative effort of the Harris brothers: William, the architect, and Robert, the artist, who created 18 paintings that hang inside. Evensong is held daily at 5pm and there are special concerts in summer. Open daily 9am to 5:30pm, the cathedral often has a tour guide on hand who will show you around for free. **St. Dunstan's Basilica,** at the corner of Great George and Richmond streets (☎ 902/894-3486), is a Gothic-style Roman Catholic church with 250-foot-high twin spires and an elaborate interior, including a nave and alter with handsome Italian carved work and a medallion stained-glass window. It is open Monday to Friday from 8am to 4pm, and Saturday and Sunday from 9am to 5pm.

Richmond Street is the place to shop, with three gift shops in the block opposite Confederation Centre: **Island Crafts Shop,** 156 Richmond St. (☎ 902/892-5152); **Confederation Gift Shop** at 145 Richmond Street (☎ 902/628-6149), for quality handicrafts and island books; and the **Anne of Green Gables Store,** 110 Queen St. (☎ 902/368-2663), for well-heeled Anne fans. This shop sells first editions of L. M. Montgomery's books, books by and about the author, and *Your Guide to Finding Anne.* A number of shops are clustered in Peake's Wharf, at the water between Queen and George streets.

Popular **Victoria Park** on Old Battery Point, overlooking the harbor, has walking trails, a boardwalk, an outdoor pool, and a large children's playground. The striking white mansion in it is Government House, since 1835 the residence of the island's lieutenant governor. It's not open to visitors, but you can stroll through the grounds and garden. To get there, follow Kent or Euston streets west.

Confederation Centre for the Arts. Queen and Grafton streets. ☎ **902/628-1864** (box office for theatrical events, 902/566-1267 or 800/565-0278). Art gallery and museum admission $3 adults, $2 seniors and children 16 and under, $5 families. Mainstage theater tickets $16–$32; Mackenzie theater tickets $20; choral music concerts $8–$12. July–Sept daily 10am–8pm; Oct–June Tues–Sun 10am–5pm.

Built in 1964 and the impetus for the city's downtown revitalization, the Confederation Centre of the Arts houses a library, three theaters (see "Special Events," above), an art gallery, a museum, a restaurant, and a gift shop. The art gallery, on the second level, has more than 15,000 notable works by Canadian artists of the past and present, including many paintings by Robert Harris, one of Canada's most renowned painters from the turn of the century (his equally talented brother, William, designed Province House; see below). Be sure to see the scrapbook of Lucy Maud Montgomery and her tidy 716-page manuscript for *Anne of Green Gables*, handwritten on both sides.

Three theaters are the venues for performances of The Charlottetown Festival during the summer (see "Special Events," above). Throughout the rest of the year, many other programs and concerts are offered covering everything from lively fiddle music and storytelling to Broadway shows and chorale music.

Province House National Historic Site. 165 Richmond St. ☎ **902/566-7626.** Free admission, but donation requested. July–Aug daily 9am–8pm; Sept–June Mon–Fri 9am–5pm.

Next door to Confederation Centre is the "Birthplace of Canada," a three-story sandstone structure built (1843–47) as the colonial legislative building. Along with a market, office, and post office buildings, it formed Queen's Square Gardens. The other buildings were torn down in 1963 to make way for Confederation Centre, but by visiting the exhibit on Province House's second floor you can see what it must have been like when the 26 delegates walked up Great George Street to discuss the idea of a union. Province House is still the seat of Prince Edward Island's legislature, but visitors are welcome. A 15-minute film about the building and what went on inside it is shown continuously throughout the day.

On the ground floor are two realistically restored offices, those of the commissioner of Crown lands and the lieutenant governor. The second floor has the restored 1864 Confederation Chamber and the active legislative chamber. When the House is in session you'll get to see the speaker in ceremonial black robes and formally clad pages, as well as the attending members.

GUIDED TOURS & CRUISES

The city of Charlottetown sponsors **free walking tours** from 10am to 5pm daily in July and August. Tours begin on the corner of Queen and Kent streets and last an hour. For details, call 902/566-5548.

Charlottetown Harbour Cruises (☎ 902/368-2628) runs daily, hour-long ferryboat tours of the harbor from the Prince Street Wharf, at 3pm (tickets are $8 for adults; $5 for children under 12). A 90-minute 6pm cruise includes a shared pot of freshly steamed mussels and costs $16 a person.

To cruise from Charlottetown under sail, book on board the *Mercy Coles,* a typical salt banker—a two-masted schooner used for fishing throughout the 19th century. They sail from Peake's Wharf, right behind The Prince Edward Hotel, at 10am, 2, and 6pm daily in the summer.

WHERE TO STAY

EXPENSIVE

○ **Prince Edward Hotel.** 18 Queen St., Charlottetown, PEI, C1A 8B9. ☎ **902/566-2222,** 800/828-7447 in the U.S., or 800/268-9411 in the Atlantic Provinces. Fax 904/566-1745. 211 rms, 34 suites. A/C MINIBAR TV TEL. Mid-June to mid-Oct $135–$175 double, $250 suite; mid-Oct to mid-June $106–$133 double, $190 suite. Extra person $15. Children under 16 stay free in parents' room. Special rates and packages. AE, DC, DISC, ER, MC, V. Parking $5.

The largest Charlottetown hostelry is the downtown Prince Edward Hotel, right on the water overlooking the harbor. It has everything you expect in a modern luxury hotel: stylish opulence, nonsmoking rooms, in-room movies, room service, same-day dry cleaning and laundry, an outdoor patio for barbecues, a large indoor swimming pool, Jacuzzi, sauna, fitness center, masseuse, shops, two dining rooms, and a lounge. Add to that a waterfront park and marina and, in summer, a popular cabaret. Harbor cruises are available within a stone's throw of the hotel.

MODERATE

Best Western Maclauchlan's Motor Inn. 238 Grafton St., Charlottetown, PEI, C1A 1L5. ☎ **902/892-2461,** 800/528-1234 in North America, or 800/463-2378 in Canada. Fax 902/566-2979. 143 rms, 25 suites. A/C TV TEL. $97–$121 double; from $114 housekeeping unit; from $123 suite. AE, CB, DC, DISC, ER, MC, V. Free parking.

Rooms at the Best Western, in the main building or in the annex, are comfortable and attractively decorated. Recent major renovations have made the facility fully accessible to the disabled, and nonsmoking rooms are available. There's an indoor pool and a sauna, and The Marina restaurant serves breakfast, lunch and dinner with dinner entrées from $6 to $16.

Dundee Arms Inn. 200 Pownal St. (at Fitzroy), Charlottetown, PEI, C1A 3W8. ☎ **902/892-2496.** Fax 902/368-8532. 6 inn rms, 10 motel rms, 2 suites. TV TEL. Mid-June to mid-Oct $98 double motel rm, $110 double inn rm, $135 suite; off-season $80 double motel rm, $100 double inn rm, $110 suite. Extra adult $15. Rates include continental breakfast. Packages and senior discounts available. No children under 12 allowed in the inn; children under 12 stay free in motel section. AE, MC, V. Free parking.

This Queen Anne Revival–style mansion, built in 1903, is evocative of another era, with rooms that are filled with period decor and old-fashioned charm. But they also have such modern conveniences as private baths and air-conditioning. The Dundee has motel-style rooms with no air-conditioning next to the original inn, all with two double beds and bath-shower combinations. The pine-paneled Hearth and Cricket Pub has a huge fireplace, and there's also the colonial-style Griffon Room, which serves meals with an emphasis on seafood.

Edwardian. 50 Mount Edward Rd. (at Confederation Street), Charlottetown, PEI, C1A 5S3. ☎ and fax **902/368-1905.** 4 rms. $95–$105 double. Rates include continental breakfast. Extra person $15. MC, V. Free parking.

The Edwardian is part of the 1850s country estate of William Henry Pope, a Father of Confederation. The house is a five-minute drive or 20-minute walk from downtown Charlottetown, across from Ardgowan National Historic Site (Mount Edward Road is one block east of University Avenue). Three of the guest rooms have queen-size beds, and one has a four-poster hand-carved double bed; all have private baths. The Loft room, overlooking the garden, has a sitting area, a stained-glass window, a kitchenette, and a bath with a claw-foot tub. All rooms come with that ultimate luxury, a down duvet. Guests have use of the living room and sun porch. No smoking.

The Elmwood. 121 North River Rd. (opposite Green Street), P.O. Box 3128, Charlottetown, PEI, C1A 7N8. ☎ **902/368-3310.** 1 rm, 2 suites. A/C TEL. May–Sept $90 double, $135 suite;

Nov–Apr $70 double, $95 suite. Extra person $15. Rates include continental breakfast. CB, DC, ER, MC, V. Free parking.

The Elmwood, built in 1889 by Charlottetown's famous architect William Harris, sits at the end of a 300-foot elm-lined drive. It's a 15- to 20-minute walk from town, and Victoria Park and a swimming pool are just down the street. Today it is a memorable home away from home, with three guest units, each with a queen-size bed and full bath. Guests use a private entrance and share a sitting room with fireplace, balcony, refrigerator, books, and games. The two suites have fireplaces and one has a kitchen. The third unit, the Victorian Room, features a bed alcove, wingback chairs, and an old-fashioned tub and shower. The owner made the quilts on all the beds. No smoking.

WHERE TO DINE

The ambience of Charlottetown's restaurants is largely influenced by whether the provincial legislature is in session. When it is, legislators tend to gather in expanding groups and treat an entire restaurant like one giant cocktail party, wandering from table to table and in general dominating the atmosphere. Apart from that, the quality of dining in the city is quite good, with at least two really outstanding restaurants.

MODERATE

✪ The Lord Selkirk. In the Prince Edward Hotel, 18 Queen St. ☎ **902/566-2222.** Reservations recommended. Main courses $14–$23. AE, CB, ER, JCB, MC, V. NOUVELLE CANADIAN.

The elegant Lord Selkirk Restaurant has been completely rebuilt and has live piano music in the evening. Among the outstanding choices are salmon, scallops, and oysters marinated in lime soya sauce with garlic and ginger; chicken breast with Thai curry sauce and a skewer of exotic fruit; and whole-wheat spaghettini in a tomato coulis with pesto and lobster. There is also a nice lunch menu (two pounds of island blue mussels with French bread for $9). The wine list is one of the best in the Atlantic Provinces.

Off Broadway Cafe. 125 Sydney St. ☎ **902/566-4620.** Reservations recommended. Main courses $7–$23. AE, DC, ER, MC, V. Mon–Sat 11:30am–2pm; Sun–Thurs 5–10pm, Fri–Sat 5–11pm. INTERNATIONAL.

The Off Broadway Cafe is small, quiet, and tucked away from the bustle of downtown Charlottetown. The inviting decor includes a beamed wood ceiling, brick walls, and pine booths. The menu tempts with such dishes as crepes (Florentine or beef Stroganoff), cheese and broccoli pie, and seafood linguine, all served with Caesar salad. Desserts are their specialty; wine is available by the glass or the bottle.

✪ Sirenella. 83 Water St. ☎ **902/628-2271.** Reservations recommended. Main courses $13–$19 (most under $15, pastas $8–$14). AE, MC, V. Mon–Fri 11:30am–2pm; daily 5–10pm. ITALIAN.

We learned of this restaurant from the chef at another of the island's top choices, and weren't disappointed. The dining room is small and intimate, with linens, fresh flowers, and comfortable chairs. But you won't even notice your surroundings when the food arrives—tender juicy mussels with a hint of fennel in a very delicate tomato and cream sauce, or chicken breast sautéed in Galliano with leeks and cranberries. We also loved spinach gnocchi in a light gorgonzola sauce, and a fine-textured cassata with a chocolate glaze and swirls of mascarpone. Everything we tasted was excellent, including the vegetables (which were cooked to perfection). The house wine, at $16.50 a liter, is also quite acceptable.

INEXPENSIVE

Cedar's Eatery. 81 University (between Fitzroy and Kent). ☎ **902/892-7377.** Reservations not needed. Lunch specials $4; dinner specials (served Mon–Wed) $5; main courses $6–$13. MC, V. Mon–Thurs 11am–midnight, Fri–Sat 11am–1am, Sun 4–10:30pm. LEBANESE/CANADIAN.

Cedar's serves hearty portions at low prices. It's an unassuming seat-yourself place, with rustic atmosphere and wooden tables and booths, but it is popular among locals for its cooking. Filling soup-and-sandwich specials are offered at lunch. Lebanese favorites include kibbe, falafel, hummus, stuffed vine leaves, kebab, tabbouleh, shwarma, or "shish taouk" (boneless chicken on two skewers), all served with Greek salad and Lebanese-style rice. And no one looks at you funny if you just order dessert.

ICE CREAM & PICNIC SUPPLIES

At **Cow's Ice Cream** (☎ 902/992-6969), opposite Confederation Centre at 150 Queen St. at the corner of Grafton, you can choose among such flavors as chocolate mud, bubblegum, grapenut, Oreo cookie, peppermint, heifermint, and many others served in waffle cones (dipped in chocolate, if you like). Don't be daunted by the lines, they move quickly. Cow's, housed in an 1810 pharmacy with a beautiful tin ceiling and woodwork, also sells clothing and other merchandise with cow motifs.

For munchies to take with you on a walk or hike, visit the **Root Cellar,** 34 Queen St. (☎ 902/892-6227). They have trail mix, raisins, nuts, baked goods, fresh fruit and a large selection of cheeses. The store is open Monday to Thursday 9am to 5:30pm, Friday to 6pm, and Saturday to 5pm.

CHARLOTTETOWN AFTER DARK

For pub food in a lively setting that attracts a young crowd, go to **the Anchor and Oar House** on Peake's Wharfe, where you can sit inside or out; for a more traditional English-style pub and an older crowd, try **The Merchantman Pub** (☎ 902/892-9150), opposite the Prince Edward Hotel.

To hear Irish music, head to the **Olde Dublin Pub,** at 131 Sydney St. (☎ 902/892-9661), and climb to the second floor; on certain nights, there may be a cover charge.

For a trendier style and occasional live music, try **Myron's,** 151 Kent St. (☎ 902/892-4375), with a modern interior and sleek counters. **Tradewinds,** at 189 Kent (☎ 902/894-4291), is a DJ/rock bar with inexpensive food. It's a party place, with popular theme nights and food and drink specials. Between Tradewinds and Myron's, at 187½ Kent St., there's **Doc's,** where professionals meet after work for a drink (☎ 902/566-1069).

4 Blue Heron Drive

Along the southern parts of the Blue Heron Drive between Charlottetown and Summerside lie several provincial parks with beaches, campgrounds, and picnic areas. Here also, 31 miles (50km) from Charlottetown, is the turnoff for **Borden,** the departure point for car ferries to Cape Tormentine, New Brunswick.

Near the ferry landing, on Highway 1, you'll see the sign for **Tea Cups and Roses** (☎ 902/658-2463). Open in summer only, this mother-daughter operation serves an all-you-can-eat (and drink) afternoon tea, with a bottomless basket of scones served with preserves and clotted cream; you can also get desserts made from scratch.

Near the intersection of Highway 1 and Route 10 is one of the most charming towns on the island, the seaside community of Victoria.

VICTORIA

The Trans-Canada Highway bypasses Victoria, and so has time. On an island where everything seems small, slow-moving, and tranquil, this tiny 19th-century seaport is even more so. Take Route 116 off Highway 1 to get there.

The focal point of the town, the **Victoria Playhouse** (1918), at Howard and Main streets, has a busy summer season, with a repertory theater and concerts. Ticket prices are a reasonable $14 for adults, $12 for seniors and students, and $6 for children under 12 (☎ 902/658-2025); you can get tickets in Charlottetown at Confederation Centre Ticketworks (☎ 800/565-0278).

At the **Studio Gallery** (☎ 902/658-2733), across from the Victoria Playhouse, you may see artist-in-residence Doreen Foster at work on one of her etchings. The gallery, open Tuesday to Sunday from 10am to 5pm or by appointment also shows the work of other artists, notably stained glass and glass sculptures.

Walk down by the wharf and gaze out to sea. It's hard to imagine three busy wharves here 100 years ago, bustling with fishing and trade activities.

WHERE TO STAY

The Orient Hotel. Main Street, Victoria, PEI, C1A 7K4. ☎ **902/658-2503.** 4 rms, 2 suites. Mid-June to mid-Sept $70–$80 double; $95 suite; rates $10 less May to mid-June and mid-Sept to Oct; even lower rates off-season. Extra person $10. Weekly rates available. AE, ER, MC, V.

At the turn of the century, the Orient Hotel welcomed sea captains, schoolteachers, traveling salesmen, bankers, and vaudeville troupes. The clientele has changed, but the old-fashioned ambience remains. Despite its name, this looks like a place right out of Dodge City. Rooms are comfortable, with private baths; room no. 7 has a nice view of the river and fields (the bath has shower only), and room no. 8 in the front of the house has a queen-size bed and full bath.

Mrs. Profitt's Tea Room, in the original lobby of the hotel, serves a full breakfast to guests and is open to the public for lunch and dinner in July and August, Tuesday through Sunday from noon to 8pm (dinner by request only, off-season).

WHERE TO DINE

Landmark Cafe. Main Street. ☎ **902/658-2286.** Reservations accepted. Most items $8–$13. MC, V. May–Oct daily 10am–11pm. LIGHT FARE.

A popular place before or after the theater, the Landmark Cafe serves hot Gouda with crackers, cream cheese quiche, meat pies, salads, and praline cheesecake. For main dinner courses expect lasagne, steamed salmon, and stuffed grape leaves. The owners know a lot about Victoria and love sharing it. The crafts shop sells local art and music, maritime items, books, T-shirts, and other gift items.

SUMMERSIDE

Spread leisurely along the southern shore of Prince Edward Island, 44 miles (71 km) west of Charlottetown and close to the ferry landing (and soon, the bridge) from New Brunswick, Summerside is everything its name implies. It's made for lazy summer days, with plenty of places to stop for ice cream and a wharf filled with music.

The province's second-largest city and the commercial center for western Prince Edward Island, Summerside takes its name from its location on the "summer side of the island," to which Charlottetown residents used to move for the season.

ESSENTIALS

VISITOR INFORMATION   The **Lady Slipper Drive Visitor Centre** is located 1 mile (2km) east of Summerside, on Route 11 in Wilmot (☎ 902/888-8364). It's open from 9am to 9pm in July and August, and from 9am to 6pm in June and

September. Either here or at one of the hotels in Summerside, request the excellent pamphlet "Of Merchant, Fox, and Sail: A Walking Tour of Summerside." It gives the best possible orientation to the town.

SPECIAL EVENTS   Summerside is famous for its annual **Lobster Carnival,** which occupies everyone in town for a week in mid-July. Lobster feasts are held nightly in the civic stadium, while baseball games, fiddling contests, and other good-time events fill the days and nights.

EXPLORING THE TOWN

Using the walking tour pamphlet as your guide, walk or drive around Summerside. The walk takes about an hour and passes many of the beautiful homes here. If you're pressed for time, take Granville Street to Church Street, then to Summer Street, and back to Granville via Water Street.

Spinnakers' Landing is right in the heart of town. A boardwalk with harbor-front shops and a lively schedule of entertainment, it's the focal point for any festival, such as the Strawberry Social in July or the occasional arrival of tall ships. At noon, a town crier in period costume announces the day's happenings. Bring the kids between 4:30 and 5pm daily in the summer for a pirate-themed look at Summerside's colorful past, complete with a treasure map ($7 adults, $5 children). **The College of Piping** presents bagpipe performances here, and you can take a variety of cruises from the landing's dock. The Historical Cruise leaves twice a day for $12 ($10 seniors, $6 children), a fishing tour gives everyone a chance to hand-jig for bay fish ($15 adult, $13 senior, $6 children), and a sunset mussel cruise for $15 features beer, wine and mussels. These run from mid-June until mid-September (☎ 902/436-6692 in the summer, 902/436-2246 in the winter).

The **International Fox Museum,** in the Holman Homestead, at Fitzroy Street between Central and Summer streets, explains the history of the fox-farming industry, which began on the island in 1894 and was concentrated in the Summerside area. (In its heyday, between 1915 and 1920, a pair of silver foxes sold for as much as $35,000.) The museum is open May through September from 9am to 6pm (☎ 902/436-2400). For one day in early December, the museum is returned to the home it once was, and is furnished and decorated for the holidays of the 1860s. Singers entertain at a tea, where such typical refreshments as chocolate-covered dates and mulled cider are served.

WHERE TO STAY

Prices in Summerside tend to be well below those of Charlottetown and the northern beach communities, which are only a short drive away.

Loyalist Country Inn. 195 Harbour Dr., Summerside, PEI, C1N 5R1. ☎ **902/436-3333** or 800/361-2668. Fax 902/436-4304. 50 rms. TV TEL. June–Sept $103–$115 double, from $115 housekeeping unit, $155 suite. Rates $10 less off-season. Golf and other packages available. AE, ER, MC, V.

Looking every inch the historic Victorian hotel, the inn faces the marina and Spinnaker's Landing shopping and dining complex. This stylish property is thoroughly new inside, with an atrium lobby of Mexican tiles and a sparkling chandelier. Guest rooms are tastefully decorated with cherry furniture and quilted bedspreads. Most have two double beds, though you'll find some with king-size beds, a Jacuzzi, minibar, or housekeeping facilities. Twenty units are nonsmoking. Guests enjoy the indoor pool, sauna, fitness room, tennis court, garden, and handicrafts shop.

Dining/Entertainment: The dining room serves three meals a day, with a focus on healthful eating; we especially appreciated the care they take with vegetables, which are never overcooked. For lighter fare, including crepes, the tavern, with a mural depicting Summerside, is open Monday to Saturday from 11am to midnight, with entertainment and an occasional sing-along on Friday and Saturday nights.

Quality Inn—Garden of the Gulf. 618 Water St. East, P.O. Box 1627, Summerside, PEI, C1N 2V5. ☎ **902/436-2295** or 800/228-5151. Fax 902/436-6277. 85 rooms. TV TEL. $83 double. Lower rates Nov–May. Extra person $7. Children under 18 stay free. AE, DC, ER, MC, V.

This large vacation complex, less than a mile from the center of town, focuses on outdoor activities. The rooms have one or two double beds (some have king-size beds); Jacuzzi rooms and nonsmoking rooms are available. A heated outdoor pool, a new indoor pool, a beach down on the bay, shuffleboard, and even a nine-hole golf course keep guests busy. There is a coffee shop for breakfast and the Moby Dick poolside lounge during the summer.

Silver Fox Inn. 61 Granville St., Summerside, PEI, C1N 2Z3. ☎ **902/436-4033** or 800/ 436-4033. 6 rms. $65–$80 double. Rates include continental breakfast. Extra adult $10, child $5. No children under 10. AE, MC, V.

The Silver Fox Inn retains all of the distinctive qualities of a vintage (1892) home, while providing the modern comforts its guests expect. Upstairs, each double room has a private bath, while the first floor features a sitting room with a fireplace and breakfast area. The hosts are knowledgeable about the area and are happy to help you organize your days. Nonsmoking.

⑤ **Sunny Isle Motel.** 720 Water St., Summerside, PEI, C1N 4J1. ☎ **902/436-5665.** 21 rms. TV. $39 double with one bed; $43 double with two beds. MC, V.

The Sunny Isle Motel is on the highway just 2 miles from the center of town, surrounded by fine lawns with plots of flowers. Each room has a radio, color TV with cable, and tub-shower bathroom; room numbers 8 to 22 are quieter and have a view of the lawn and trees. Picnic tables are provided.

WHERE TO DINE

○ **Fox Tea Room.** In the Holman Homestead/Fox Museum, 286 Fitzroy St., Summerside. ☎ **902/436-6707.** Reservations recommended. Main lunch courses $6–$7.50; table d'hôte dinners $23–$25. MC, V. Tues–Wed 11am–5pm, Thurs–Sat 11am–10pm, Sun 5–9pm.

Mushroom lovers take note: Stuffed mushroom caps will always be on the menu, and although the stuffings change at a whim, they're always delicious. The house Dijon salad dressing on the giant salad that comes with luncheon sandwiches is so good you'll be tempted to eat it with a spoon. The table d'hôte dinner menu has a choice of main courses—steak in a rich peppery sauce or chicken marinated in honey and thyme on our last visit—and may begin with smoked salmon or prosciutto with melon. The portions are generous, breads are baked in house, and the cheesecakes are so tasty other restaurants in town have asked the chef to cater theirs. A shaded patio is open until 6pm each day; the restaurant is licensed.

CAVENDISH & ENVIRONS

When you enter Cavendish, you are literally driving into a storybook setting, for here is the home that inspired Green Gables (now managed by the Canadian Parks Service), the Haunted Wood, and Lover's Lane, all described in Lucy Maud Montgomery's books.

Although it is less than 25 miles (40km) from Charlottetown or Summerside, it has an altogether different flavor from either. Cavendish itself is a bustling tourist town, with its share of shops, fast-food eateries, and vacation cottages. Most residents find the jumble of made-for-tourists places just as out of place on their main street as you will, and they have done something about it. Sign ordinances, visual barriers, and other efforts will go into place over the next few years, and a total freeze on new development is already in place. Travel a couple of miles in either direction from the town, and once again you're in "The Land of Anne," a serene landscape blessedly free of honky-tonk.

ESSENTIALS

VISITOR INFORMATION   The **Cavendish Visitor Centre** is open daily from 9am to 10pm in July and August, and 9am to 6pm June and September to early October (☎ 902/368-4444). It has exhibits of local crafts and others devoted to Lucy Maud Montgomery, along with books and an audiovisual presentation about her. If you're shopping for gifts, they're here too, though the area has some good gift shops.

GETTING THERE   From Summerside, pick up Highway 1A, and at Travellers Rest, take the Blue Heron Drive (Highways 2 and 6) to Cavendish on the North Shore. If you are traveling from Charlottetown, follow Highway 2 to Hunter River, and pick up Route 13 to Cavendish.

GETTING AROUND   All the attractions are within about 6 miles (10km) of each other, so you can walk or bike among them or simply hop the **Cavendish Trolley,** which stops at the Visitor Centre. It makes its rounds of the area's attractions from 9am to 9pm in peak summer season. A full tour costs about $3.50, a partial tour $2.

   Rent A Bike (☎ 902/566-2295) is located in the Cavendish Petro Canada station at the junction of Routes 6 and 13 in Cavendish. Bike rentals are $5 an hour and $17 a day for adults, about $1 less for kids. It's open daily 8am to 8pm in May, June, September, and October, and 7am to midnight in July and August.

EXPLORING CAVENDISH

Those who have come to Cavendish to do a bit of reminiscing over the books they loved as a child will be pleased to learn of the **new walking path between all the "Anne" sites** in Cavendish. It begins at the peaceful site of Lucy Maud's Cavendish home, marked by a sign just east of the United Church on Route 6. The house is gone, but there is an old well, and the gardens have been restored. You can leave your car there. Along the path are some of the places mentioned in the books. The Parks and People Association has printed a map of the trail, which you can get at any information center.

   Those not enthralled by the Anne mystique will find plenty to do in the Cavendish/ Rustico Bay area. **Deep-sea fishing** trips are enjoyable for the whole family. Several leave from North Rustico: **The Doucette brothers** each have boats (☎ 902/ 963-2465 and 902/963-2666, respectively) as does **Aiden Dioron** (☎ 902/ 963-2442). **Gauthier's** (☎ 902/963-2295) leaves from Rusticoville. Prices for all trips are $15 for adults, $10 for children.

   Sea-kayaking trips are another way to get away from the crowd, and **Outside Expeditions,** Charlottetown (☎ 902/892-5425) operates a five-day trip exploring the north coast and its waters, camping along the way. (See "The Great Outdoors," above, for other sea-kayaking trips).

   In Brackley Beach, on Route 15 a mile from the national park gate, **The Dunes studio and gallery** represents 40 artists (☎ 902/672-2586). Stop by to see the exquisite pottery of Dunes owner and designer Peter Jansons (you may recognize his work from shops in Charlottetown), and the view of Brackley Bay from the upper gallery. The shop sells candleholders, lamp bases, glasses, bowls, and vases, as well as cassettes and books about the island.

SOUTH RUSTICO

Continuing west along Highway 6, you'll come to South Rustico, a bilingual pocket of Prince Edward Island and proof that small is beautiful. It's little more than a cluster of houses, a church, a museum, an inviting bed-and-breakfast, and a gift shop.

The **Farmer's Bank of Rustico** (1864), in South Rustico, the oldest bank building in Prince Edward Island, is now a museum. Built of island sandstone with walls that are three feet thick, it printed its own currency until 1894. Farm artifacts, belongings of founder, Georges Belcourt from Québec, and some bank items are displayed. Open Monday through Saturday from 9:30am to 5pm and on Sunday from 11:30am to 4pm. A guide will show you around. Adults pay $2 to enter; children under 12 are free (☎ 902/963-2505).

At the corner of Highway 6 and Highway 243 stands the **Old Forge Pottery,** a studio and shop showcasing and selling the graceful, functional, and affordable pottery of owner-potters Carol and Ken Downe. Along with the stoneware and porcelain, the work of other island craftspeople is also for sale—weaving, iron, and woodworking. It's open late May to late September (☎ 902/963-2878).

Green Gables House. Route 6 (1 mile west of Cavendish). ☎ **902/672-2211.** Mid-June to Labor Day daily 9am–8pm; May–early June and Sept–Oct daily 9am–5pm.

Green Gables House is a re-creation of the fictional farmhouse where orphan Anne Shirley was taken in by Matthew and Marilla Cuthbert, and it has been lovingly built with many of the details from Montgomery's books. Anne's room is upstairs on the left; downstairs are photographs of the author at age 6, 21, 33, and 60. A 10-minute history of Green Gables, given in the front yard every half hour from 10am to 4pm from July to mid-August, will enhance your tour of the house. To avoid the crowds, go before 11am or after 3pm. The house, a small tea room, large gift shop, picnic area, and recreational facilities nearby are all part of the national park.

EXPLORING WEST OF CAVENDISH

The drive along Highway 6 passes many of the tourist attractions and amusement parks on the island. **Rainbow Valley** (☎ 902/963-2221 in summer or 902/836-3610 off-season) is a large amusement area just outside Cavendish on Route 6, a quarter mile from Green Gables House. The 37-acre park, with its landscaped grounds and castle turrets peeking over trees, has been an area fixture since the parents of children who now enjoy it came here as children themselves. Three island-dotted lakes and a variety of boats, six water slides, exhibits and displays, live animals, and shows are all included in the price of admission: $8.50 for adults, $7.50 for seniors, $7 for children; preschoolers free. It's open June to Labor Day (sometimes later) Monday through Saturday from 9am to 7pm and on Sunday from 1 to 7pm.

The **Lucy Maud Montgomery Birthplace** is at the intersection of Routes 6, 20, and 8, in New London, 7 miles west of Cavendish (☎ 902/886-2099). The author was born in 1874 in this unassuming house where today you can see her scrapbook and wedding dress. Open 9am to 5pm from May 23 through June and September to mid-October, 9am to 7pm from July through August. Admission is $1 for adults, 50¢ for children.

Right across the road, **Memories** gift shop (☎ 902/886-2020) is filled with many items for children; upstairs are handmade quilts, rugs, and afghans. **Memory Lane Antiques and Crafts,** housed in an old school (1832) on Route 234, 6¹/₂ miles from New London and 1¹/₂ miles from Route 20. Here you'll find outstanding gift items and sweaters at good prices.

Woodleigh, a unique park, is filled with detailed scale model replicas of some of Great Britain's most famous landmarks, including the Tower of London, York Minster Cathedral, Robert Burns's cottage, Shakespeare's birthplace, Anne Hathaway's cottage, and Dunvegan Castle. It was the dream of Lt. Col. E. W. Johnstone, who created the amazing models, some of which are large enough to enter. Woodleigh is on Route 234 in Burlington (P.O. Box 59, Kensington, ☎ 902/ 836-3401). Admission is $6.25 for adults, $5.75 for seniors, $3.50 for children 6 to 15; younger children are admitted for free. The park is open from 9am to 8pm July to August; 9am to 5pm late May to June and September to mid-October.

Anne of Green Gables Museum stands located at Silver Bush on Route 20 near Park Corner and the intersection with Route 6 (☎ 902/886-2003 or 800/665-2663; 902/436-7329 September to June), a location rich in Anne lore. Built in 1872 by the husband of Lucy Maud Montgomery's aunt, it was home to Montgomery as a girl and the time she spent here provided her with material for her later stories. (The house is still in the family, and the museum is run by her great-great-nephew.) Maud was married here on July 5, 1911; if you wish, you can be married here, too, as long as you reserve at least a year in advance (the house is especially popular with couples from Japan). The Lake of Shining Waters, which Montgomery wrote about, is across the road. To see it as Anne did, take Matthew's Wagon Ride in a horse-drawn wagon around the museum, or in a special picnic tour. Make reservations with the museum. A tearoom and excellent gift shop are on the grounds. Admission is $2.50 for adults, 75¢ for children under 16. Open daily 9am to 6pm in June and September to October; 9am to 8pm in July and August. Tea and craft shops close at the end of September.

WHERE TO STAY IN CAVENDISH

Kindred Spirits Country Inn & Cottages. Memory Lane (on Route 6 just west of the Cavendish intersection), Cavendish, PEI, C0A 1N0. ☎ and fax **902/963-2434.** 10 rms, 5 suites, 13 cottages. TV. Inn rooms (including continental breakfast buffet) $65–$100 double, $105–$140 suite; extra person $10. Housekeeping cottages $70–$150, extra person $5. Off-season rates available. MC, V.

On six acres next to the Anne of Green Gables House, the inn is removed from the hubbub next door by a golf course and tree barrier. Along with friendly hospitality, you'll find nicely furnished inn rooms with private baths, toiletries, and hair dryers; suites with living rooms and hardwood floors; and one- and two-bedroom house-keeping cottages. There's a large, heated outdoor swimming pool, and a large whirl-pool. Definitely family oriented, it provides movies, books, toys, special activities, and a playground for kids. Adults get attention, too, however: Afternoon tea and lemonade are served in front of the fireplace daily.

Shining Waters Country Inn. Route 13, Cavendish, PEI, C0A 1N0. ☎ **902/963-2251.** Fax 902/963-2251. 10 rms, 20 housekeeping cottages. TV. Inn rms (including full breakfast buffet) $55–$64 double; two-bedroom housekeeping cottages $86–$94. Weekly rates available. MC, V. Closed mid-Oct to mid-May.

Located near the national park entrance, this inn was once the real home of Rachel McNeel and the fictional home of Rachel Lynn in *Anne of Green Gables.* It offers guests an airy breakfast room overlooking the Gulf of St. Lawrence and a large sitting room and library with a stone fireplace. The 10 newer pine-paneled cottages are built around a small children's playground, an outdoor pool, and two indoor whirlpools. Only adults may stay in the inn; families are welcome in the cottages, which sleep two to six people. Basketball, shuffleboard, and Ping-Pong are available. This property's age was beginning to show, but new owners are restoring its sparkle.

✪ **Sundance Cottages.** McCubry Lane, just off Route 6, Cavendish (RR no. 1, Hunter River, PEI, C0A 1N0). ☎ **902/963-2149** in summer or 902/566-1256 in winter. 10 cottages. TV. July 15–Aug 19 $120–$170 double, early July and late Aug $110–$155, $60–$105 before June 24 and after Sept 4. Extra person $6. MC, V.

If you owned your own cottage and hired a decorator to fix it up, this is what you'd want it to look like: crisp and stylish, bright, and enormously comfortable. These are the nicest cottages we've seen, bar none. One and two bedrooms with tub and shower (some with whirlpool tub), each has a fully equipped kitchen with a microwave, a barbecue grill, and a wide sundeck. The property is surrounded by mowed lawns and has a heated pool. There's also a small gym. The genial people who own it know every inch of the area and can help you plan your travels.

WHERE TO STAY IN THE RUSTICO BAY AREA

Barachois Inn. Route 243, South Rustico (mailing address: P.O. Box 1022, Charlottetown, PEI, C1A 7M4). ☎ **902/963-2194.** 2 rms, 2 suites. $100 double or suite. Extra person $18. Rates include full breakfast. No credit cards. Closed Nov–Mar.

With a cedar-shingled mansard roof and rockers on the porch, this inn has a country flavor. A collection of contemporary art is on display throughout the house and each room is individually decorated. The setting is first class; the inn is not suitable for very young children.

Shaw's Hotel. Brackley Beach, PEI, C1E 1Z3. ☎ **902/672-3000.** Fax 902/672-3000. 18 rms (15 with bath), 20 cottages (all with bath). $175–$225 double; $185–$245 cottage unit. Rates include breakfast and dinner. AE, MC, V. Closed mid-Oct to mid-May. From the airport follow Route 15 and look for the signs for Brackley Beach.

This immaculately kept and gracious Victorian resort hotel with cottages is tucked away down a long drive, five minutes from the beach. It looks just as it did when it was built in 1860 by the great-grandfather of the present innkeeper. Public rooms and guest rooms have been modernized for comfort, but their charm remains. The cottages don't have housekeeping facilities, but guests can dine in the hotel dining room, which is licensed, and a MAP (modified American plan) is available. The staff is young and congenial, and the Sunday supper buffet is an island event. Kids love the hayrides held just for them.

WHERE TO DINE NEAR CAVENDISH

Enjoy good home cooking, even if it's only coffee and rhubarb crisp or a lemon square, at the **tearoom at Anne of Green Gables at Silver Bush.** There is also a **tearoom at Green Gables House.** The boardwalk in Cavendish is chockablock with eateries (shops, too), including a branch of Charlottetown's famous **Cow's,** for ice cream.

Dunes Cafe. Route 15, just south of the national park gate. ☎ **902/672-2586.** Reservations recommended for dinner. Lunch items $3.50–$10; main courses $6–$17. AE, MC, V. Summer only. Hours vary, so call ahead. SEAFOOD/LOCAL.

Part of the Dunes complex, this cafe, with a gallery and shop, has a lively air, especially on nights when there's live jazz. At lunch, light fare includes soup of the day with beer and cheddar bread, pasta of the day, and grilled lambburger. For dinner, you might try island mussels steamed in ginger-sesame broth with scallions, tomatoes, and steamed greens or pan-seared sea scallops with spinach and roasted sweet potatoes. The plates you dine on are made right here. Even the bathrooms are memorable. No smoking is allowed.

Fisherman's Wharf. On the harbor in North Rustico. ☎ **902/963-2669.** Reservations not needed. Lobster (or steak) supper $22; "seafood extravaganza" $56 for two; most items

Lobster Suppers

Prince Edward Island is famous for its lobster suppers, not so much because of what is eaten at these events—lots of places throughout the Atlantic Provinces and New England serve lobster—but because of *how* it's eaten. The suppers began as local church fundraisers to which members of the congregation brought a covered dish to share and the church provided the lobsters. Everyone would pay a nominal amount, the church would make some money for charitable causes, and all would go home well-fed.

Things have changed a bit from this original setup (such as your presence), but not much. Some of the proceeds from these dinners still go to fund charitable work in the surrounding communities. And diners still eat their lobster supper in the church hall or basement. Each meal consists of a lobster and other fixings such as potato salad, tossed salad, rolls, corn on the cob, steamed clams, vegetables, coleslaw, french fries or baked potato, and dessert. For those who don't like lobster, roast beef (hot or cold) is often served. The atmosphere is simple but very convivial, and the food is plentiful and good. Prices these days run about $25 for the entire evening.

St. Ann's Church Lobster Suppers (☎ 902/964-2385), at St. Ann's on Route 224 between Hunter River and Stanley Bridge, originated lobster suppers in Prince Edward Island and is very popular and crowded during July and August. It has the advantage of being licensed (cocktails, wine, and beer are served), and for those who don't want lobster, steak, scallops, sole, or pork chops are also served (priced from $14 to $19). There's a children's menu, and live entertainment. Dinners are served from 11:30am to 2pm and 4 to 9pm from the last Monday in May to the first Saturday in October. No suppers are served on Sunday.

New Glasgow Lobster Suppers (☎ 902/964-2870) serves in the town recreation center of New Glasgow, on Route 224, from early June to mid-October; July and August are the busiest months. Tour buses abound, so go early. The lobster dinner with steamed mussels and chowder is $21 to $30, depending on the size of the lobster; other meals are priced from $12 to $16, and children's meals range from $3.50 to $10. Dinner is served daily from 4 to 8:30pm. Don't expect the kind of service you will get at St. Anne's; it's a hurried, herd-'em-in-and-out attitude.

You can also dine at the famed **Fisherman's Wharf** (☎ 902/963-2669), on the harbor in North Rustico (see above). They offer a lobster (or steak) supper for $22, or the "seafood extravaganza"—$56 will get two people an enormous meal including chowder, scallops, shrimp, clams, an array of fish, and, of course, lobster, all washed down with a bottle of Fisherman's Wharf wine. Lobster supper is served daily from 4 to 9pm.

$3–$23. AE, DC, MC, V. Mid-May to June and Sept to mid-Oct daily 11am–9pm; July–Aug daily 8am–10pm; lobster supper served 4–9pm only. SEAFOOD.

Living under strictly controlled conditions and segregated according to weight are 20,000 pounds of crawling lobster. Fisherman's Wharf does everything in a big way, from all those lobsters to gallons of chowder to seating for 400 to a 50-foot salad and dessert bar. And it's all part of their famed lobster supper. If this is too overwhelming, you can retreat to the smaller dining room, where there's a full menu, from sandwiches to the "seafood extravaganza," which includes chowder, lobsters, scallops, shrimp, clams, and an array of fish, a bottle of wine with the Fisherman's Wharf label, and finally, dessert and coffee. There's also a children's menu.

Prince Edward Island Preserve Co. RR no. 2, New Glasgow. ☎ **902/964-2524.** Breakfast and lunch items $1–$7; main courses $8.50–$14. AE, DC, MC, V. July–Aug daily 8am–5pm and 5:30–9:30pm; June and Sept daily 9am–5pm. LIGHT FARE.

If you're in the mood for something light, or a food gift item, stop here and pray there are no more than two tour buses when you arrive. Founded by Bruce MacNaughton (he's the one in the kilt), this place makes more than 20 kinds of preserves and lines them up for you to taste. For more in-depth food sampling, try the Preserve Co.'s cafe, overlooking the gentle River Clyde. Here the light fare includes homemade breakfast foods, sandwiches, soups, and salads, or more substantial items like cold lemon chicken with rice salad or a smoked fish plate. After 5pm in summer only, the menu expands to include poached salmon, mussels Provençale, and lemon-and-thyme chicken. Lobster is available, but only in the pasta. It's licensed.

5 Prince Edward Island National Park

The spectacular sand dunes and beaches of **Prince Edward Island National Park** stretch for 25 miles (40km) along the north shore of the island. The shallow waters of the Gulf of St. Lawrence are warmer than the waters that lap at the shores of the beaches at Brackley, Stanhope, and Cavendish farther south, making Prince Edward Island National Park a good spot for children to play in the gentle waves.

Other park activities include hiking along one of six easy trails, biking along Gulf Shore Parkway, picnicking, or attending one of the many interpretive events offered daily during the summer. In winter, the park offers cross-country skiing, snowshoeing, and ice skating. **Green Gables House,** on Route 6 in Cavendish (see separate listing above), and **Stanhope Cape Lighthouse,** the site of a disaster at sea, are also in the park.

Camping is available at several locations, with fees from about $9 to $19. Sites are fairly open and well spaced, with room for both tents and trailers. No reservations are accepted at this popular park, but you can get a number and appear at a specified time each day until a site is available.

To use the park, you must pay a national park motor entry fee of $4 per adult, $6 for a family; $18 for four days and $30 for the entire summer season. For more information, contact the **Cavendish Information Centre** or the **Department of Canadian Heritage** at 2 Palmer's Lane, Charlottetown, PEI, C1A 5V6, (☎ 902/963-2391 in summer, otherwise 902/566-7050).

✪ **The Links at Crowbush Cove** (☎ 902/652-2356), near the eastern edge of the park, a mile off Route 2, opened in 1993 and is considered one of Canada's top golf courses. Set among the north shore dunes, the course is challenging and offers panoramic views, including eight holes surrounded by dunes.

WHERE TO STAY & DINE IN THE PARK

✪ **Dalvay-by-the-Sea.** P.O. Box 8, Little York, PEI, C0A 1P0. ☎ **902/672-2048.** ☎ and fax in winter 902/672-3315. 26 rms, 1 cottage. $170–$270 double (including breakfast and four-course dinner). Extra adult $60, child 4–12 $50, child 1–3 $20. $240 cottage (add $80 for a third person). Two-night minimum in summer. AE, ER, MC, V. Take Highway 6 to Route 25, the national park exit.

No expense was spared when, in 1895, Alexander MacDonald, a partner of John D. Rockefeller, built this graceful mansion on the north shore of Prince Edward Island.

Rooms in this genteel hotel all have private baths and some have ocean views—all are quiet. The mansion, a stone's throw from Dalvay Beach, has a tranquil and grand air, good food, a commanding stone fireplace in the lobby, and lovely grounds. Demand is great, so reserve far in advance. It's inside the national park, but permit fees are waived for Dalvay guests.

Dining/Entertainment: If you can't stay the night, at least dine here; it's one of the four or five best restaurants on the island. One of our favorite entrées—Cajun spiced salmon with tomato coriander salsa and roasted seaweed—gives you an idea of what its innovative chefs regularly offer. You'll pay $16 to $25 for main courses at dinner. The dining room is open from 8 to 9:30am for breakfast, from noon to 2pm for lunch, and from 6 to 9pm for dinner. Reservations are recommended.

Facilities: Two tennis courts, a croquet green, a children's playground, a driving range, table tennis, canoeing, boating, and mountain bike rentals.

6   Western Prince Edward Island & Lady Slipper Drive

Like most of Prince Edward Island, the western region, encircled by Lady Slipper Drive, is agricultural. The farms are meticulously cared for, with neat, brightly colored farmhouses. You'll pass field after field of potatoes, this region's primary crop.

Western Prince Edward Island is an area where Acadian culture is still entrenched. Of the 15,000 Acadians who live on Prince Edward Island today, about 6,000 still speak French as their first language, and most of these live in the western counties.

ALONG LADY SLIPPER DRIVE

Following Route 11 from Summerside, Lady Slipper Drive is never far from the shore. While the entire drive can be covered in a day, give it two days so you can savor the land and its attractions, and stay in one of the island's most unique lodgings.

Cedar Dunes Provincial Park, at the southwestern tip of Prince Edward Island, has a supervised beach on the ocean, camping areas overlooking the sea, and the tallest operating lighthouse in the province. You can climb to the lantern deck at the top of this unique black-and-white striped square lighthouse for the fine panoramic view and to learn more about how a lighthouse works. Admission is $2 per adult, $1.65 for seniors, $1.25 for children. You can also spend a night there (see below).

Only the persistent wind, flocks of gulls, and a few playful seals greet those who stand on the cliffs at the end of the road. You'll receive a ribbon of recognition for having made it to **North Cape,** at the northern-most point of Lady Slipper Drive; then, if and when you get to East Point, just show your ribbon and you'll get a certificate proclaiming that you've traveled Prince Edward Island from tip to tip.

WHERE TO STAY & DINE

✪ **West Point Lighthouse.** Route 14 (RR no. 2), O'Leary, West Point, PEI, C0B 1V0. ☎ **902/ 859-3605,** 800/764-6854, or 902/859-3117 off-season. Fax 902/859-3117. 7 rms, 1 tower rm, 1 suite. Mid-May to mid-June and Sept $60 inland rm; $70 seaside rms and rms with two double beds; $100 tower and keepers suites. Extra person $5. Rooms in each category $10 more mid-June–Sept. AE, MC, V. Closed mid-Sept–mid-May. Follow the beacon or take Route 14 through the entrance to Cedar Dunes Provincial Park at the southwestern tip of the island.

You can actually spend the night in an operating lighthouse if you book the Tower Room, the only guest room in the original 1875 structure. With a view overlooking the beach and park, it takes up the entire second floor of the lighthouse and has a whirlpool bath. The Keeper's Quarters suite, located in the adjoining Keeper's House, is large and also has a sea view, whirlpool, and living room. All the rooms are furnished with antiques from Prince Edward Island and have private baths. Non-smoking units are available.

The popular dining room serves three home-style meals a day at reasonable prices. Nature trails and hints of buried treasure are added attractions, as are a large craft and gift shop. Hotel and restaurant guests can climb to the top of the lighthouse free of charge.

EXPLORING THE TYNE VALLEY

One of the most scenic parts of the province is the Tyne Valley west of Malpeque Bay—the body of water that almost separates Prince Edward Island into two islands. It is home to one of the island's finest restaurants and is the center of Micmac culture in the province.

Tyne Valley Studio, on Route 12 (☎ 902/831-2950), is open June to September daily 9:30am to 5pm; May and October by appointment or chance. In this delightful studio, owned by talented designer Lesley Dubey, striking sweaters are produced using local wool yarn. The designs are original, and the most popular is the Fair-Isle Lobster pattern. The sweaters may be ordered year-round from the studio, which also sells local handicrafts and memorable honey cream.

Just after Route 2 crosses Grand River, turn right onto Route 124 (which becomes Route 177) and head for Mont-Carmel at the southern tip of Prince County to find a glimpse of early Acadian culture. **Le Village Pionnier Acadien** is a faithful reproduction of an early 19th-century Acadian settlement that has a school, store, church, and all the other necessities of civilized town life. Admission is $2 for adults, 50¢ for children; preschoolers are admitted for free. Hours are mid-June to mid-September daily 9:30am to 7pm. Call ☎ 902/854-2227 for more information.

There are modern amenities here, too: **L'Etoile de Mer** restaurant, which serves traditional Acadian cuisine; the 20-unit Motel du Village ($45 single, $49 double); and the new L'Auberge du Village, with 30 guest rooms, many of which look out to sea ($64 single, $74 double); rates drop off-season. Bicycle rental is available.

Just north of the town of Tyne Valley is **Green Park Provincial Historic Park,** where you can visit the home of 19th-century shipbuilding magnate James Yeo Jr. Furnished with period pieces, the house was built in 1865, and you can wander as you like through its three floors, even clambering up to the cupola for the panoramic view. Look for the green glass "lusters" on the mantelpiece in one room, the old foot bath, the marble occasional tables, the four-poster beds, and the kitchen gadgets. The park also has a modern exhibition area with displays outlining the history of shipbuilding in Prince Edward Island, and a re-created 19th-century shipyard down by the water. It's all in Green Park Provincial Park, which offers areas for camping, picnicking, hiking, and swimming in Malpeque Bay. Call ☎ 902/831-2206 for the museum, 902/831-2370 for the park; off-season 902/859-8790. Admission to the house is $2.50 per person, $1.25 for seniors; children under 12 free. The park itself is free; there is a charge for camping. It's open from late June to Labor Day.

The **Micmac Nation,** part of the enormous group that once inhabited much of Maritime Canada, lives on a reserve on **Lennox Island** in Malpeque Bay, connected to the mainland by a causeway. To get there, follow Route 163, off Route 12. A small **museum** that outlines the history of the tribe is located across the street from the church. Micmac artifacts and paintings are displayed in the office/recreation building Monday to Friday from 8am to 4pm. Nearby there is a craft shop devoted to the promotion of North Native Canadian craftwork that carries pottery, beadwork, wood carving, leather items, sweet grass baskets, and many other items and museum-quality pieces. The crafts represent many tribes in North America. Ring the bell at the yellow house if the shop is closed. Open July to August from 10am to 7pm; the rest of the year by appointment (☎ 902/831-2653).

7 Eastern Prince Edward Island & King's Byway Drive

If western Prince Edward Island is traditionally Acadian French, the island's eastern reaches are still predominantly peopled by the descendants of early Scottish settlers, as a quick look at place names on the map will show. Farming and fishing are the prime occupations here, with tourism adding a healthy boost to the local economy.

King's Byway Drive begins in Charlottetown, wandering east and north along the coast past numerous beaches and provincial parks. On the route is the terminal for the Woods Islands ferry, by which many visitors arrive from Nova Scotia.

WHERE TO STAY ALONG THE SOUTHERN KING'S BYWAY

Dunvegan Farm Tourist Home & Motel. Route 24 (RR no. 2), Uigg, PEI, C0A 2E0. ☎ **902/651-2833.** 3 farmhouse rms (none with bath), 5 housekeeping motel units. Farmhouse rooms $30–$35 double; extra person $5. Motel rooms $50–$60 double; extra person $6. Weekly rates available. Breakfast $3 extra, $2 for children under 10. V.

Two miles off Route 1 in Uigg (pronounced "*You*-ig"), the Dunvegan Farm, owned by the same family since 1829, is set on 170 acres and provides a central location for exploring Kings County, the MacPhail Memorial, and historic Orwell Village. A red-and-white barn and assorted cats, a dog, flowers, and playground equipment are part of the scene. The farmhouse, built in 1906, has three guest rooms sharing one full bath; one room has a half bath. The motel units on the property have large rooms and full housekeeping facilities.

McLeod's Farm Home & Cottages. Route 24, Vernon Bridge P.O., Uigg, PEI, C0A 2E0. ☎ **902/651-2303** or 800/661-2303. $40 light housekeeping room, $60–$75 two-bedroom housekeeping cottage. Extra person $6. From Route 1 take Route 3 from Cherry Valley, then head right onto Route 24; or take Route 210 from Orwell and make a left on Route 24.

This is a real farm experience, a farmhouse set among the rolling lush green fields of inland Prince Edward Island—complete with kittens and Newfoundland dog.

Meadow Lodge Motel. On the Trans-Canada Hwy., P.O. Belle River, Wood Islands, PEI, C0A 1B0. ☎ **800/461-2022.** 19 rms. TV. $49–$71 double. Extra person $5. Rates lower off-season. MC, V. Closed mid-Oct to early May.

Only a mile from the ferry dock and the beaches, these motel units are grouped in a U shape around a grassy lawn. One is nonsmoking; one has a kitchen. The motel's restaurant, Pier 9, is down by the ferry terminal; it's open conveniently early, from 5:30am to 8:30pm daily in the summer.

WHERE TO DINE ALONG THE SOUTHERN KING'S BYWAY

Sir Andrew MacPhail Homestead. Route 209, Orwell. ☎ **902/651-2789.** Reservations required. Full dinner $10–$13, lunch main courses $3–$5.50. Tues–Sun 11:30am–2:30pm, Wed–Sun 5–8pm. Closed Oct–early June. SCOTTISH.

The unpretentious childhood home of a great Canadian is a charming place to enjoy cuisine of Scotland. The dining room is set with linen tablecloths and lit in the evening by oil lamps; the food is simple but delicious. You can choose from haggis served with crackers made right there, a ploughman's lunch, bannocks, or fish and beans (the beans are grown in the fields outside the farmhouse window). The menu always features a roast (often lamb), a chicken dish, and a vegetarian entrée. You can end with a fruit trifle or "sudden pudding." They serve beer and wine.

MURRAY RIVER & MURRAY HARBOUR

Set along the wide mouth of the Murray River, these twin towns offer quiet diversions and some nice craft shops. In Murray River, the **Old General Store** (☎ 902/962-2459) has three rooms filled with unabashedly romantic Victoriana, such as old-fashioned cotton nightgowns, aprons, embroidered cushions, and quilts. **Harbour Crafts** on Main Street (☎ 902/962-3666) carries an assortment of local crafts.

At **Beach Point** a small beach is quite close to the working lobster wharves and a lighthouse. **Seal cruises** are operated from Murray River by Gary's Boat Tours (RR no. 1, Murray River; ☎ 902/962-2494), leaving daily at 10am, and 1 and 3:30pm. Evening cruises operate by appointment only. During the 14-mile cruise, you will probably see Arctic terns, herons, cormorants, and an assortment of other birds in addition to harbor seals.

Not far from Murray River, your kids may want to detour to **King's Castle Provincial Park** (☎ 902/962-2401), an outdoor amusement area for children and their parents established and operated by the provincial government. Statues of fairy-tale characters people the wooded grounds; picnic tables and a nearby beach add to the park's appeal. Entrance to the park is free. It's open 9am to 9pm from late May to mid-September.

North of Murray River, King's Byway Drive follows Route 17 north and east, although many people turn left onto Route 4 instead, to visit **Buffaloland** (☎ 902/652-2356) and its small herd of American bison. Open year-round; admission is free.

Just a short drive north and you're at **The Harvey Moore Wildlife Management Area** (☎ 902/838-4834), only a few miles from Montague. One of Canada's leading naturalists, Harvey Moore, founded the sanctuary years ago as a haven for migrating waterfowl—Canada geese, black and wood duck, and other species. In early June, the Canada geese will be there with their tiny goslings. Free pamphlets will guide you on a nature trail through the sanctuary and its two ponds. The ponds are open for trout fishing, one in July, the other in August for a small fee. The sanctuary is still owned and managed by Harvey Moore's family. It's open free to the public from June to mid-September.

COTTAGES IN MURRAY HARBOUR

🟲 **Forest & Stream Cottages.** Off Route 18, Murray Harbour, PEI C0A 1V0. ☎ **902/962-3537.** 5 cottages. TV. $50–$55 double. MC, V. Closed Nov–Apr.

Set in light woods overlooking one end of a long, narrow lake, these cottages are ideal for those who love peaceful surroundings. One- and two-bedroom cottages are fully insulated, all electric, and have equipped kitchenettes. Each also has a picnic table and grill. Verandas are enclosed by screens. Use their boat to row in the lake or hike and watch birds on the nicely kept trails through their 20-acre property.

MONTAGUE

Montague, a country town with a bakery, an ice-cream kiosk, and well-tended homes, is also the commercial center for the eastern coast of Prince Edward Island. A **walking path** leads from Montague along the river to **Georgetown** on the point, following the old CN rail line.

Cruise Manada (☎ 902/838-3444), has departures from Montague Marina on Route 4 and from the Rodd Brudnell Resort Marina on Route 3. Seal-watching cruises pass a colony of harbor seals and often include pilot whale and porpoise sightings. The MV *Manada II* and *Manada III* ply the Montague and Brudenell rivers past historic homes and sites, and visit a mussel farm. Complimentary iced tea and lemonade are served. This unique cruise lasts two hours and 15 minutes and costs $12.50 for adults and $6.50 for children under 12. Ask about the champagne and mussels or Lobster Boil cruises. Adult tickets are $13.50, seniors $12, children under 12 $7, with special rates for the 10am cruise and for buffet and luncheon options.

Golfers will enjoy the new 18-hole, par-72 **Brudenell River Provincial Golf Course,** rated one of Canada's best, just north of Montague, off Route 3 to Georgetown. It has a pro shop, two practice greens, and a driving range (☎ 902/652-2342).

WHERE TO STAY

Lane's Cottages. 33 Brook St. (P.O. Box 548), Montague, PEI, C0A 1R0. ☎ **902/838-2433.** 18 cottages. $39 double; $49–$65 double with housekeeping facilities. Extra person $9. Weekly rates and packages available. MC, V.

If you'd like to have a little cottage all to yourself, just follow the signs in Montague down Brook Street, only a five-minute drive, to a quiet, bucolic hideaway. Each cottage has a shower, good views of the water and the forest, and 14 have housekeeping facilities. There's a playground, picnic tables overlooking the water, a gazebo on the river bank, minigolf, and a Laundromat.

Rodd Brudenell River Resort. Route 3 (P.O. Box 67), Cardigan, PEI C1A 7K7. ☎ **902/652-2332** or 800/565-RODD. Fax 902/652-2886. 103 units. A/C TEL. $119–$129 double; $149–$169 suite; $89–$106 chalet. Extra person $10. Children under 16 stay free. Senior discount. Reduced rates before July 1, after Sept 15. AE, ER, MC, V.

Beautiful, modern rooms with balconies overlook the Brudenell River from well-kept lawns that roll into a golf course. Two pools, activities, kids' pool, canoes, windsurfing, and lighted tennis courts—the works to assure a carefree family vacation.

En Route to Souris

North of Brundenell Resort, **King's Byway** follows the sinuous coastline past beaches and through fishing areas up to **Souris** (pronounced "*Soo*-ree"). Or you can travel along Highway 4 and then Highway 2 to get to Souris.

✪ **The Inn at Bay Fortune.** Route 310 (R.R. 4, near Highway 2), Souris, PEI, C0A 2B0. ☎ **902/687-3745** summer or 203/633-4930 off-season. Fax 902/687-3540. 11 rms. TEL. Summer $115–$165 double, off-season $85–$135 double. Extra person $25. AE, MC, V. Closed late Oct to mid-May.

The inn is gracious and historic, and its architecture is unique. Built in 1910 by Broadway playwright Elmer Harris (*Johnny Belinda*), it was the former summer home of the late actress Colleen Dewhurst. Now an elegant country inn after massive restoration, it has two rooms in the main house, seven around a courtyard, and two in what once was a water tower. The rooms have wood floors, radios, cassette players, cards and cribbage games, and full tiled baths with hair dryers. Guests share a library/TV room in the top of the tower, overlooking the bay. Bicycles and a canoe are available for rent.

Dining/Entertainment: The inn's well-known dining room serves nouvelle cuisine, offering such entrées as scallops in a coulis of carrot and ginger, and chicken stuffed with spiced prunes, molasses, and rum. There is also a tasting menu. Dinner will cost $30 to $35, without wine, tax, or tip. It's licensed and reservations are recommended.

SOURIS

The name is French for "mice," and the animals used to be a problem back when the French lived in these parts. The only staffed lighthouse left on the island is in Souris.

If you follow Highway 16 east from Souris to Bothwell and turn right onto the dirt road just before the Esso station, you'll soon come to the beautiful **Singing Sands Beach,** almost too good to be true. Along the way you'll pass the entrance to **Red Point Provincial Park,** in the town of the same name, where there is also a beach.

WHERE TO STAY & DINE

✪ **Matthew House Inn.** 15 Breakwater St. (P.O. Box 151), Souris, PEI, C0A 2B0. ☎ **902/ 687-3461.** 8 rms. TEL. $85–$140 double. Extra person $25. Rates include full breakfast. Romance, bird-watching, and lobster-fishing packages available. AE, DC, ER, MC, V.

One of the most memorable bed-and-breakfasts on Prince Edward Island, the Matthew House Inn looks across its tree-shaded lawn directly onto the harbor, only a short walk from the ferry to the Magdalen Islands. Painstakingly restored to its 19th-century grandeur, it has won an award for architectural preservation. There is a parlor, a library with books for travelers to swap, four working fireplaces, and, out in the restored barn, a hot tub.

Dining/Entertainment: The inn now serves dinner by reservation featuring fresh seafood with a Mediterranean and northern Italian influence. Gourmet box lunches for a beach outing are $18 for two, and a five-course dinner with wine is $25.

Facilities: Mountain bikes and fishing equipment are loaned to guests free; in the barn is an antique shop and a gift shop with Micmac baskets, jewelry, and rugs. A deserted, windswept beach is minutes away.

❸ **Needles & Haystacks.** Albion Cross (RR no. 2), St. Peter's Bay, PEI, C0A 2A0. ☎ **902/ 583-2928** or 800/563-2928. 4 rms (with shared baths). $45 double. MC, V.

Large country breakfasts, rooms decorated with stunning quilts, and the wealth of information you'll learn from the genial host—these things set this small B&B apart. A sundeck with a hot tub, the use of bikes or cross-country skis, and easy access to a major trail system that the host has been instrumental in establishing are a few more.

7

Newfoundland & Labrador

by Barbara Radcliffe Rogers
and Stillman Rogers

"The Rock," as Newfoundlanders fondly call their island home, is as much a metaphor as a physical description of the land. A rock it surely is, its exposed face showing all along its shore and nearly everywhere else. And this rock has a three-month growing season, open ocean exposure, steady winds, and almost no soil to cover it. So Newfoundland is the quintessential hard place as well—a hard place to eke out a living, to raise crops, to keep warm, to survive. Labrador, with its months of frozen winter and vast areas of nearly impenetrable wilderness, is even harder.

But nature endowed this land, for all its hardships, with extraordinary beauty and majesty. The landscape stretches like a vast green carpet before you until it reaches the sea. In places the rock drops straight to the water in dramatic cliffs; in others it is worn into deep fjords that reach like long fingers into the mountains.

While Newfoundland was the first place in North America to be explored and settled (the Pilgrims stopped at an already thriving community here to reprovision on their way to Plymouth), only the hardiest stayed or survived. Lord Baltimore founded a colony, but finding it too cold, moved on to Maryland and immortality. Others came and went; the tough and gritty folk stayed, and their descendants still call it home. Around the rock's watery rim cling villages that began as fishing settlements and remained so until just a few years ago when the fish gave out to intensive overuse by the Japanese and Russian megaships. These towns now struggle to survive. Tourism is a relatively new industry (many people knew nothing of the province before *The Shipping News,* the wonderfully evocative Pulitzer Prize–winning novel by E. Annie Proulx). People still greet travelers with interest and genuine hospitality. You will be a guest, not a customer.

Newfoundland is not for everyone. It's for the traveler with a sense of adventure, who doesn't demand the trappings of city life or decorator magazine B&Bs, who likes to get to know local people, or who thrills at sailing around an iceberg or having a whale so close he or she can notice its bad breath. And the history buff will be drawn, too, to see the settlement the Vikings called Vinland or to stand on the grass runway where Amelia Earhart began her transatlantic solo and see the exact same view she saw, unchanged by time.

Newfoundland & Labrador

300 km
186 mi

Cape Chidley

Ungava Bay

QUEBEC

Hebron

Atlantic Ocean

Nain

Davis Inlet

Hopedale

Lobstick Lake

LABRADOR

Makkovik

502

Michikamau Lake

Rigolet

Lake Melville

Cartwright

Esker

501

Labrador City

500

520

Happy Valley–Goose Bay

Churchill River

500

Mud Lake

Wabush

Mealy Mountains

510

389

Kenamu River

Battle Harbour

Pinware

Red Bay

L'Anse-Amour

L'Anse-au-Loup

Blanc Sablon

St. Anthony

Sept-Îles

Harrington Harbour

St. Barbe

430

Englee

Gros Morne National Park

Baie Verte

Terra Nova National Park

Anticosti Island

Twillingate

Lewisporte

330

Corner Brook

1

Gander

Deer Lake

Bonavista

Stephenville

Grand Falls

235

230

NEWFOUNDLAND

80

St. John's

360

70

480

Gulf of St. Lawrence

210

Channel-Port aux Basques

Grand Bank

Argentia

100

10

NEW BRUNSWICK

St-Pierre

90

Prince Edward Island

Havre-Aubert

Summerside

Charlottetown

Fredericton

Moncton

North Sydney

Saint John

Atlantic Ocean

NOVA SCOTIA

Halifax

Yarmouth

1994

LEGEND

Ferry - - - -

If thousands of puffins, moose at close range, and entire herds of caribou aren't enough of a draw, consider the spectacular scenery. The Appalachian mountains drop abruptly into the sea, and there are many dramatic fjords and sea cliffs. Waterfalls drop hundreds of feet from sheer cliffs, and for quieter beauty, add little fishing villages set in coves surrounded by steep headlands. Land meets sea so suddenly that the Flat Earth Society has certified a spot here as one of the four corners of the earth. Yes, you can travel to the ends of the earth in Newfoundland.

A LITTLE BACKGROUND   Newfoundland remained a separate British colony, related to Canada by friendship and proximity only, until 1949, when 51% voted for union with Canada. (Newfoundland and Labrador comprise a single province.)

Remote from the mainlands of Europe and North America, Newfoundland developed a lively and colorful language of its own. Newfoundlander talk was—and still is—salted with charming idioms. This language has its own dictionary, some 700 pages thick, and browsing through it is a fascinating look into a way of life. As you travel, it may puzzle you to hear that the road you want is just at the bottom of the mish (hill) or that someone is "all mops and brooms" (having a bad hair day). It's contagious, so if your own speech goes all asquish, you'll know why.

Newfoundland and Labrador also have a special place in the hearts of dog fanciers everywhere. Newfoundland is famous for that wonderful big, black, shaggy animal, the Newfoundland dog, here since the Beothuks inhabited the land. Newfies have rescued drowning shipwreck survivors and pulled 100-pound sleighs through the snow, helped in both places by their strong necks and webbed feet. A Newfoundland accompanied Lewis and Clark's 1804 expedition. Other proud owners have included George Washington, Lord Byron, and Queen Victoria. And Labrador, of course, has given us the Labrador retriever, also a strong swimmer and bred as a bird dog. Their sweet, affectionate nature has made them one of the most popular breeds in the world.

1 Exploring Newfoundland & Labrador

Most of what you'll want to see in Newfoundland lies close to its east and west coasts; points of interest are more scattered in the interior. While travelers arriving by car via ferry must drive across this long and often monotonous center, those arriving by air can explore one side, then fly to the other, rent another car, leaving the province directly from the second airport. You might consider visiting the coasts in separate trips.

Only the Trans-Canada Highway (TC1) crosses the island. Most other locations are close to the Trans-Canada Highway until you reach the Avalon Peninsula in the southeast, where roads form circles around the shore. Labrador roads are even more limited; some of its sections are not connected at all.

VISITOR INFORMATION   For a provincial map and a free guide to Newfoundland and Labrador, contact the **Department of Tourism, Culture, and Recreation,** P.O. Box 8730, St. John's, NF, A1B 4K2 (☎ 709/729-2830 or 800/563-6353). For specific Labrador information, contact **Destination Labrador,** 118 Humphrey Rd., Bruno Plaza, Labrador City, NF, A2V 2J8 (☎ 709/944-7788 or 800/ 563-6353); request the booklet *Labrador: Awaken Your Heart and Soul.*

TIME & WEATHER   Newfoundland and Labrador are on "Newfoundland time," which is a half hour *ahead* of Atlantic time. Temperatures along the east coast are moderate year-round due to the warm Gulf Stream currents—but when this flow meets the chilly Arctic Stream coming from the north, the result is fog. In summer, day temperatures can be quite warm, and the sun very bright. Yet nights tend to be chilly, even in summer. Winters are more severe inland, in the west, and in Labrador, so bring your parkas (or buy one of the locally favored cassocks or Grenfell coats).

GETTING TO NEWFOUNDLAND You can get to Newfoundland year-round either by air or by ferry. Ferries connect Newfoundland to Labrador from June through November.

By Plane In most cases, a visitor will have to change planes in Montréal, Toronto, or Halifax before continuing to Newfoundland. The major carriers serving Newfoundland from the Maritime Provinces are **Air Nova,** the commuter partner of Air Canada (☎ 800/776-3000 in the U.S., 800/565-3940 in the Maritime Provinces, or 800/563-5151 in Newfoundland), and **Air Atlantic,** the commuter partner of Canadian Airlines International (☎ 800/426-7000 in the U.S., 800/ 665-1177 in Canada). Both fly into St. John's, Deer Lake/Corner Brook, Gander; Air Nova also flies to St. Anthony, while Air Atlantic also flies into Stephenville.

By Ferry On the map, the Trans-Canada Highway reaches across the sea from North Sydney, Nova Scotia, to Port aux Basques, Newfoundland. The ferry across the Cabot Strait is legally part of the highway, under the terms of the 1949 agreement joining Newfoundland to Canada. In fact, the ferry operation is so big that it *is* almost like a highway across the water.

Ferries to **Port aux Basques** on the west coast (a five-hour trip) and **Argentia** in the east (14 hours) leave from North Sydney, Nova Scotia. Marine Atlantic's mammoth ferries depart North Sydney daily year-round, several times a day in summer. Between North Sydney and Argentia, ferries operate only a few times a week from mid-June through September. Fares to Port aux Basques are about $18 adult, $14 senior, $9 ages 5 to 12, and $55 one way for a car. Dormitory sleepers cost $12.

Travel to Argentia costs more, especially if you rent a cabin for the overnight voyage; a reclining seat is much less expensive. Fares are about $49 adult, $37 per senior, $25 ages 5 to 12; cars cost about $107; cabins cost $100 to $125; a "Daynighter" reclining chair, $12. For a couple, with a car and a normal, two-berth cabin, plus dinner and breakfast in the ship's cafeteria, the total cost exceeds $300, one way. Cabin and car space on the North Sydney–Argentia run is always heavily booked well in advance.

Marine Atlantic recommends that all passengers on either Newfoundland ferry make advance reservations, which you must arrive one hour before departure to claim. In summer, the reservation lines are often busy. Call ☎ 800/341-7981 in the U.S.; 902/564-7480 in North Sydney; 709/772-7701 in St. John's; 709/227-2413 in Argentia; or 709/695-7081 in Port aux Basques. If you get reservations and later decide not to use them, call and cancel. Think of all those people waiting in line.

If you don't have a reservation, try to arrive the night before the day you want to sail; get your tickets, get a waiting-line number, and park your car in line. You can sleep in your car, using the facilities in the terminal waiting room (open 24 hours a day). If you can't get there the night before, get to the docks by 5 or 6am on sailing day. If you're in line the night before, you will almost always get on the first boat in the morning; if that fails you'll have priority on the second boat of the day.

There are only two sailings to Argentia a week, on Tuesday and Friday, and they take only 20 names on the waiting list for cabins. If yours isn't one of those, you can book a reclining chair in a quiet area of the boat for the 14-hour voyage. The boat leaves at 8am, and cars begin to line up after midnight. Even with reservations, arrive at the dock at least one hour before sailing time or you'll lose the reservations.

Note: Government regulation and Marine Atlantic requires that all vehicle fuel tanks be no more than three-quarters full.

Once you've attended to all these prepassage details, you'll find the trip itself very enjoyable; ferries have restaurants, lounges with entertainment, children's play rooms, and movies.

After your arrival, you can get to Port aux Basques by bus; **CN Roadcruisers** provides bus service along the Trans-Canada Highway to St. John's, with stops along the way (☎ 709/737-5912). Wheelchair-accessible buses are available, but reservations must be made 48 hours ahead.

From the ferry terminal in Argentia, a van link to St. John's on **Newhooks Transportation Ltd.** (☎ 709/227-2552) and **G & J Transportation** (☎ 709/682-6245) costs about $15. If no van is running, you can stay over until the next day or get to St. John's by taxi. Find others to share the cost, then call **Bugden's Taxi** in St. John's (☎ 709/726-4400).

GETTING TO LABRADOR   By Plane   Goose Bay, Churchill Falls, and Wabush have airports served by daily flights from outside Labrador, most originating in Newfoundland.

Labrador Airways Limited (☎ 709/896-3387 or 800/563-3042 in Newfoundland) has scheduled air service from St. Anthony to and from the Labrador coast and Goose Bay. The company also offers charter air service using float, ski, and wheel aircraft (☎ 709/896-3658).

Air Nova (☎ 800/776-3000 in the U.S., 800/565-9513 in the Maritime Provinces, or 800/563-5151 in Newfoundland) and **Air Atlantic** (☎ 800/426-7000 in the U.S., 800/565-1800 in the Maritime Provinces, or 709/576-0274 in Newfoundland) both fly into Goose Bay and Wabush. Air Atlantic also has flights to Churchill Falls, and Air Nova flies into Blanc Sablon, Québec, where you can rent a car and drive the short distance into Labrador to L'Anse au Clair and beyond.

By Ferry   Marine Atlantic operates a biweekly ferry service from Lewisporte, Newfoundland, to Goose Bay, Labrador, either nonstop or via Cartwright, Labrador, from mid-June to Labor Day. The nonstop trip to Goose Bay takes about 35 hours, and the fare is $89 adult, $67 seniors, and $45 children 5 to 12 years old; a car costs $145. For more information and reservations, contact the Marine Atlantic Reservations Bureau (☎ 902/794-5700; in the U.S., 800/341-7982; in Newfoundland, 709/695-7081).

The **Strait of Belle Isle ferry** crosses from St. Barbe, near the northern tip of Newfoundland, to Blanc Sablon, Québec, 3 miles (5km) from L'Anse au Clair, in the Labrador Straits (☎ 709/931-2309 in Labrador; 418/481-2056 in Québec).

By Car   A paved road, Route 510, runs from Blanc Sablon, Québec, to Red Bay, in the Labrador Straits. Route 389, a combination paved and gravel road, connects Baie Comeau, Québec, to Labrador City, in Labrador West; the road is open year-round.

By Train   Rail service is provided between Sept-Isles, Québec, and Labrador City by the Québec, North Shore, and Labrador Railway (☎ 418/968-7805 in Québec; 709/944-8205 in Newfoundland or Labrador).

GETTING AROUND   While buses do run between the major towns, you'll need a car to travel into the countryside. Rental agencies can be found in St. John's, Corner Brook, Deer Lake, and at the airport in St. Anthony. In Labrador, you can rent a car in Labrador City and Goose Bay, as well as in Blanc Sablon, Québec, a few miles from L'Anse au Clair in Labrador.

Reserve your car from: **Avis** (☎ 800/879-2847); **Budget** (☎ 800/268-8900); **Hertz** (☎ 800/263-0600); **Thrifty** (☎ 800/367-2277); and **Tilden** (☎ 800/387-4747); these numbers also work within Canada.

In Newfoundland and Labrador, you must buckle seat belts in both front and back seats. Always be on the lookout for moose crossing the road; most accidents with these bulky animals occur during the summer months at night. If there's fog, drive with your low beams on.

Newfoundland has no passenger train service.

AN IMPORTANT NOTE ON PRICES & TAXES   Unless stated otherwise, **the prices cited in this guide are given in Canadian dollars,** which is good news for U.S. travelers because the Canadian dollar is worth 25% less than the American dollar, but buys nearly as much. As we go to press, $1 Canadian is worth 75¢ U.S., which means that your $100-a-night hotel room will cost only U.S. $75, and your $6 breakfast costs only U.S. $4.50.

The bad news is that the combined 7% goods and services tax (GST) and 12% provincial sales tax (PST) in the province eat up most of the savings. To make it worse, the taxes compound, so that the second tax it computed on the base price after the first tax has been added.

Rooms, meals, and almost everything else are subject to a 12% PST, plus an additional federal 7% GST. Both are refundable to visitors, although not for the expenditures most travelers make. Hotel rooms, meals, car rental, and gasoline do not qualify for PST rebates; meals, liquor, campground fees, and gasoline do not qualify for GST rebate. Note that in Newfoundland you will not be charged PST on handicrafts or books, nor on lodging in small B&Bs.

Rebates require purchases of $100 or more and the submission of original receipts and an official claim form. File for the GST rebate first, because all receipts will be returned to you. Then file for the provincial rebate; these receipts will not be returned to you.

For the GST rebate, mail the form to **Revenue Canada,** Customs and Excise, Visitors' Rebate Program, Ottawa, ON, K1A 1J5 (☎ 613/991-3346 outside Canada, or 800/66-VISIT in Canada for more information).

For the provincial tax rebate submit receipts and forms to the **Tax Administration Branch,** Office of the Comptroller General, Department of Finance, P.O. Box 8720, St. John's, NF, A1B 4K1 (☎ 709/729-3831).

2 The Great Outdoors

All this land, with so few people, makes the province perfect for outdoor adventures. Trout and salmon fill glacial lakes and streams; moose, caribou, and smaller animals roam freely over the vast forests and bogs; seabirds cluster on islands; and whales frolic along the rugged coasts.

Find your favorite activity below, and we'll point you to the best places to pursue your interest or give you the general information you need to get started.

BIKING   Hilly terrain and narrow roads make biking a challenge here. Many cyclists prefer to stay in public accommodations rather than carry the added weight of bedding on the hilly island routes. The scenery is spectacular, especially along the coastal routes of the Avalon. You can rent bikes from **Avalon Bicycle Tours** in St. John's (☎ 709/576-1951). **Burin Peninsula Bicycle Tours** offers multiday packages, including rentals (☎ 709/873-3330).

BIRDING   Few places provide the concentration of seabird nesting sites that Newfoundland does, with more than 12 world-class sites and 5¹/₂ million breeding pairs. One of the world's major gannetries is on the Avalon Peninsula at Cape St. Mary's. Baccalieu Island hosts more than three million nesting pairs of Leach's storm petrels and one of only three breeding sites for northern fulmar as well as a major puffin colony. The continent's largest concentration of puffins is on an island off Bay Bulls in Witless Bay, reached on a half-day trip out of St. John's. Off Cartwright, Labrador, is North America's largest razorbill colony. Local boat tours take visitors to all of these, except Cape St. Mary's, which you can see from land.

CAMPING   Provincial park campgrounds provide well-spaced sites and nicely maintained facilities in all parts of the province. Most cost $8 a night per site; some are free, such as the lovely seaside sites at Chance Cove, south of St. John's. Gros Morne and Terra Nova National Parks have campgrounds and backcountry sites; those at Terra Nova are reached by boat.

CANOEING   Lakes and rivers abound here. Novices can easily paddle along Grand Codroy River in Grand Codroy Provincial Park, just a short drive from Port aux Basques, while experts can take on 250 miles (400km) of major rivers in northern Labrador. Terra Nova National Park has both rivers and lakes (and canoe rentals); Gros Morne's Trout River Pond is perhaps the province's most scenic place for stillwater excursions.

CLIMBING   You'll find the best mountain climbing in Gros Morne National Park, where hikes of various lengths reach the summit of Gros Morne itself and overlooks above the fjords and sea. Serious, experienced climbers should head to northern Labrador's Torngat Mountains; these barren peaks reach 5,423 feet (1,652 meters). Supplies have to be brought in by boat or air to a primitive landing strip, then carried overland.

DIVING   North Atlantic waters are clear and cool, with visibility of 100 to 150 feet (30 to 45 meters). Marine life is rich in the deep fjords of Labrador and in the Bay d'Espoir along Newfoundland's southern coast. The most popular diving area is off Cape Race, where many of the island's 20,000 shipwreck sites are found. Vessels sunk by a German U-Boat are favorite dive sites off Bell Isle, near St. John's. **Oceanus Adventures** (☎ 709/738-0007) offers dive vacations, and can guide divers with physical impairments.

FISHING   The largest land-locked salmon ever recorded—a whopping 22-pound ouananiche—was caught in Labrador. Brookies of seven or eight pounds are almost commonplace in Newfoundland. Lake trout grow to 40 pounds, and more than 20,000 Atlantic salmon run more than 200 rivers.

Labrador has more than 50 fishing outfitters, Newfoundland close to 70, or you can simply buy a license ($5 for trout) and fish. Send for the current year's *Newfoundland and Labrador Hunting and Fishing Guide,* available free from the Tourism Branch of the Department of Development, P.O. Box 8700, St. John's, NF, A1C 5R8 (☎ 709/576-2830, or 800/563-6353 in Newfoundland). You will usually find the brochure at tourism information offices.

HIKING   Trails and paths wind along clifftops over the sea, on boardwalks over bogs, around lakes and ponds, through parks, between towns. Nearly every town has at least one hiking route; St. John's has several, the most spectacular of which circles the points below Castle Hill. In Gros Morne, one quite level path leads to the park's most outstanding scenic feature, the fjord at Western Brook Pond. The Avalon is a particularly good place to hike, since nearly every trail has a view of the sea. Get a

Newfoundland

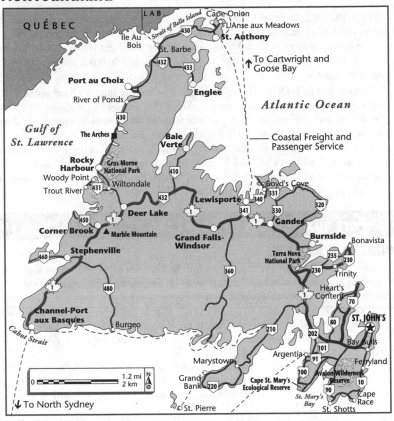

copy of *Trails of the Avalon*, by Peter Gard and Bridget Neame, for maps and directions to Avalon hikes.

KAYAKING   One of the province's fastest growing sports, kayaking is the best way to see the sea caves and fascinating rock formations along the coast. You can also get close to icebergs and seals and explore abandoned fishing villages. A thorough guide to prime kayaking spots, *Canyons, Coves, and Coastal Waters*, is available from Eastern Edge Outfitters, Box 17, Site 14, RR no. 2, Paradise, NL, A1L 1C2 for $21.95, plus $6 shipping to the U.S., $2.50 in Canada. They also offer package trips, including one to the seldom-visited remote south coast.

SKIING   Marble Mountain, just outside of Corner Brook, is a fast-growing alpine ski center, mainly because of its reliably high snowfall and its challenging terrain. The snowfall is the highest (an average of 16 feet) of any ski area in eastern North America. Kids and beginners ski free on the T-bar lifts.

Cross-country skiers will find groomed trails in both national parks and can ski on walking trails or logging roads. In Labrador, where you can ski nearly everywhere, a world-class center is at the Meniheck Nordic Ski Club, where the Canadian teams train on their 25 miles of groomed trails. Backcountry ski trips with guides are available in the Gross Morne, Long Range, and Blow Me Down mountains, with **Gros Morne Adventure Guides** (☎ 709/686-2241) and **New Found Adventures** (☎ 709/789-2809).

STARGAZING　In remote areas (most of the province), far from city lights, the stars are clearly visible right to the horizon and constellations are easy to spot. Watch for meteor showers in mid-August and for the northern lights in the fall and winter. Ask at national and provincial parks for the handy brochure identifying the constellations.

WHALE WATCHING　If you're traveling in June or July, it's hard *not* to watch whales. As soon as the capelin return, the whales are right with them, 20 species breaching and spouting in coves and wherever the water is deep enough for them, often right along the shore. Look for whales from Fishing Point in St. Anthony, at the tip of the Northern Peninsula, off St. Vincent's in the Southern Avalon, along the Viking Trail north of Gros Morne, or in dozens of other spots. Some of the best places for a whale-watching cruise are Witless Bay (near St. John's), L'Anse aux Meadows, Trinity, and Twillingate (north of Gander).

3 Port aux Basques to Deer Lake

PORT AUX BASQUES

As you cruise into Port aux Basques aboard the ferry, your first impression is of rocks. Treeless hills are covered by a thick carpet of brilliant green grass, ferns, and moss. No large plants or tall buildings obscure anything in the town. It's stark, but not barren.

Port aux Basques, named in honor of early Basque fishermen-explorers thought to have set foot on these shores even before the Vikings, is the major ferry and railroad freight terminus. It's a hometown of the old sort, where everyone knows everyone else, and close-knit community spirit prevails.

Information, including festivals and crafts directories, is available at the **Port aux Basques Information Centre,** a couple of miles out of town on the Trans-Canada Highway. The center is open from mid-May until the end of October (☎ 709/695-2262).

Accommodations are available in Port aux Basques at **Heritage Home,** a B&B next to the ferry terminal at 11 Caribou Rd. (☎ 709/695-3240); or at **St. Christopher's Hotel,** 1 mile (2km) away on Caribou Road (☎ 709/695-7034; fax 709/695-9841). **J. T. Chessman Provincial Park,** 8 miles (15km) north on the Trans-Canada Highway, has 101 campsites, three of which are wheelchair accessible, as well as one of the province's best swimming beaches, located inside a protected bay.

Setting out on the road north, a wild landscape rolls out before you as you drive: volcanic cones, blankets of mist and fog, copses of evergreen trees, rushing streams. Near the shore, sea chimneys jut upward from the chilly waters.

CORNER BROOK

Corner Brook, Newfoundland's second largest city, with a population of 30,000, is the first stopping point for many visitors who arrive via ferry. It rises in layers along the steep banks of the Humber Arm onto the slopes of the Blow Me Down Mountains.

For information, visit the helpful **Tourist Chalet** (☎ 709/639-9792) just off the Trans-Canada Highway on West Valley Road, opposite the Journey's End; it also sells crafts and gift items. Open daily from 9am to 8pm.

In summer, head out on the **Humber River** aboard a small motor cruiser. The river is home to a variety of wildlife, although it doesn't offer the stunning scenery of Gros Morne. Cruises cost $20 for adults, $15 for children 12 to 18 and $10 under 12. Boats leave from Steady Brook, 3 miles (5km) east of Corner Brook. Call ☎ 709/639-1538 for information.

SKIING AT MARBLE MOUNTAIN

Only 5 miles (8km) east of the center of Corner Brook is Marble Mountain, whose 26 ski trails on a 1,600-foot vertical drop (and one look at the mountain tells you just how vertical it is!) are reached by two quad lifts and a double. Trails range from easy to double diamond. Snowfall exceeds 200 inches a year, more than any other place in eastern North America, giving it one of the longest ski seasons east of the Rockies.

Shuttle buses carry skiers from their hotels in Corner Brook. A brand new multi-level base lodge provides all the bottom-of-the-mountain facilities. Prices are reasonable, and beginners, using the two T-bars, ski free. The resort is an outstanding value for families. For a brochure with information on money-saving packages and perks such as free lift tickets with car rentals, write P.O. Box 394, Corner Brook, NF, or call ☎ 709/639-8531.

WHERE TO STAY

Glynmill Inn. 1 Cobb Lane, Corner Brook, NF, A2H 6E6. ☎ **709/634-5181**, or 800/563-4400 in Canada. Fax 709/634-5106. 81 rms, 9 suites. TV TEL. $61–$90 double; from $95 suite. Weekend rates and senior discounts available. AE, DC, ER, MC, V.

Although the Glynmill is in the town center, it feels like a vintage resort hotel, complete with an accommodating staff and wooded, parklike grounds. New owners have extensively renovated the place, making rooms larger, creating comfortable suites, and upgrading the decor and furnishings in rooms and public areas. Reserve early for the poshest suites on the first floor; the Tudor Suite with its whirlpool tub is particularly popular with newlyweds. With competitive rates and an atmosphere chain hotels can't hope to match, this is clearly the top choice in town.

Dining/Entertainment: Partridgeberry tarts, a delicious local specialty, are baked daily for the Carriage Room, just off the hotel lobby. Frequented by local residents for special occasions, the restaurant serves three meals a day, with dinner entrées from $10.95 to $19.50. The Wine Cellar, downstairs, is a steakhouse known for its charbroiled beef and other meats, served in the intimate atmosphere of a circular stone-walled room.

Mamateek Inn. 64 Maple Valley Rd., Corner Brook, NF, A2H 6G7. ☎ **709/639-8901** or 800/563-8600. Fax 709/639-7567. 55 rms. A/C TV TEL. $83–88 double. Extra person $7. Children under 18 stay free in parents' room. AE, DC, ER, MC, V.

This Best Western property is opposite the Tourist Chalet just off the Masset Street exit of the Trans-Canada Highway. Rooms are quiet and have good area lighting. Some rooms have a desk and recliner, others a sofa bed and coffee table. Deluxe rooms have minibars. The hotel allows pets. The dining room overlooks the city and serves a pretty standard steak-and-seafood menu priced from $12.25 to $23.25.

WHERE TO DINE

✪ Thirteen West. 13 West St. ☎ **709/634-1300.** Reservations recommended on weekends. Main courses $13–$19.50. AE, ER, MC, V. Mon–Fri 11:30am–2:30pm and 5:30–9:30pm, Sat 5:30–10:30pm, Sun 5:30–9:30pm. ECLECTIC.

The innovative menu here is a great relief from standard western Newfoundland fare, which, although good, does begin to look the same after a while. No matter how warm the day, don't pass up the seafood chowder, made of fresh and smoked fish and shellfish in a rich, creamy base. The generous portion plus an order of the giant serving of bruschetta (topped with sautéed tomatoes, herbs, and provolone) makes a satisfying meal. Other menu highlights are a spicy Cajun crab soup and rack of lamb with roasted red peppers and Kalamata olives. The crusty Italian bread and the pastas are made in-house. Wine is available by the glass, but we think a bottle is the better buy.

DEER LAKE

Northeast of Corner Brook, the Trans-Canada Highway skirts Deer Lake on its way to the town of the same name, set at the turnoff for Highway 430. Also designated the Viking Trail, Highway 430 leads to Gros Morne National Park and the Great Northern Peninsula.

In 1991 a small airport opened here, with flights arriving from Halifax on **Air Nova** (flight time is 1 1/2 hours); rental cars are available at the airport.

The **Tourist Information Chalet,** on the Trans-Canada Highway, is open daily in the summer from 9am to 9pm, and May and September from 10am to 5pm (☎ 709/635-2202).

Just west of it is **Valley Crafts** (☎ 709/635-5633), open in summer 9am to 9pm, selling hand-knit sweaters, moose hide slippers, Grenfell jackets, and woodcarvings. The small, free **Humber Valley Heritage Center,** dedicated to depicting life here in the valley, is on the lower level and open the same hours.

North of town on Route 430 is **Granny Tucker's,** a re-creation of an old general store. Farm tools, clothing, kitchen utensils, kerosene flat irons, a three-legged bedroom stove, sausage press, tobacco cutter, gum boots—just what you'd expect to find in an old store in a small Newfoundland community. Admission is $2.50 for adults; $1 for children 10 and older; children under 10 free (☎ 709/635-7088). An ice-cream parlor and tearoom serve old-fashioned goodies.

WHERE TO STAY

Deer Lake Motel. P.O. Box 820, Deer Lake, NF, A0K 2E0. ☎ **709/635-2108,** or 800/ 563-2144 in Newfoundland. Fax 709/635-3842. 56 rms and suites. TV TEL. $69 double. AE, DC, ER, MC, V.

An oasis of city-style services in a small town, the Deer Lake Motel has a car-rental agency, a small shop, and a food take-out service for those just passing through town. The modern motel units have fans, coffeemakers, room service, in-room movies, and some have hair dryers. Nonsmoking rooms are available. The licensed Cormack Dining Room serves plain, substantial dinner entrées from $9 to $20.

4 Gros Morne National Park & the Viking Trail

At Deer Lake, you can take the Viking Trail—Highway 430—to Gros Morne National Park and the Great Northern Peninsula. It's known as the Viking Trail because the road stretches all the way to L'Anse aux Meadows National Historic Site, where the Vikings established the first European settlement in North America, about 1,000 years ago. It's 284 miles (443 km) from Deer Lake to the tip of the peninsula at St. Anthony (pop. 4,000).

No matter how much you've read about Gros Morne National Park's scenery, you'll still be surprised when you see it. And you won't be disappointed. Few travelers venture this far, and even fewer continue along the Viking Trail to its end at the tip of the Northern Peninsula. Those who do never forget it.

The park is blessedly uncrowded, but despite that fact, you should still make room reservations in advance, since facilities close to the park are somewhat limited. There are no accommodations on park land, but the few towns scattered within the park offer lodging.

THE SOUTHERN SECTION OF THE PARK

Eons ago, glaciers gouged and ground the Long Range Mountains at the Appalachian's northernmost end, leaving fjords and lakes that reach like long fingers among the mountains. Sheets of ice scraped the mountaintops clean, leaving rock faces and summits, where the only growth to this day is the tightly tangled evergreen scrub called tuckamore. (Hikers who've tried to shortcut through the tuckamore say it's practically impenetrable.)

The long East Arm of Bonne Bay cuts the park almost in two. Although the southern part is smaller, it contains some of the park's finest scenery, plus its outstanding geological phenomenon, the Tablelands, which gained the park its designation as a UNESCO World Heritage Site.

At Wiltondale on Highway 430, watch for the park sign that points to this section via Highway 431, which goes west to the small fishing villages of Glenburnie, Woody Point, and Trout River. Woody Point sits along the steep bank of the narrow South Arm, and the road there offers a constantly changing series of views of mountainsides rising sharply out of the water.

On the way to Trout River, the road travels along the **Tablelands,** a lunar landscape where nothing grows. This reddish crumbling rock mass is a piece of the earth's mantle, thrust up 500 million years ago as the continents of Europe and North America drifted closer together. It's the only place where geologists can study this segment of the earth, which elsewhere lies a mile beneath the surface.

The exhibit at the Tablelands Lookout describes the process that created it, but to really understand, you should take the ✪ **Tablelands Boat Tour,** an excursion into the sealed-off fjord at Trout River. During the cruise on Trout River Pond, between this stark upthrust and the sheer gray walls of the facing mountain, you can inspect closely some fascinating geological evidence that conclusively proves the theory of plate tectonics. If geology leaves you stone cold, you'll enjoy the magnificent scenery. As you come into Trout River, turn left to the Tablelands Boat Tour offices (☎ 709/451-2101). Tours operate daily June 15 to September 15 at 9:30am and 1 and 4pm and cost $25. The boat is wheelchair accessible.

Near the boat dock is the road to **Trout River Campground,** with nicely maintained, well-spaced sites in low woods and clearings. In mid-July plenty of campsites are empty; the daily fee is $7.25. The little fishing village sits at the mouth of the Trout River, clustered around a harbor and enclosed by two rocky headlands.

WHERE TO STAY IN WOODY POINT

Victorian Manor. Main Street, Woody Point, NF, A0K 1P0. ☎ **709/453-2485.** 3 rms (1 with private bath), 3 efficiency units, 1 guest house with whirlpool. $40–$70 double rm; $55 or $70 one- and two-bedroom efficiency units; $85 guest house. Rates include continental breakfast. MC, V.

Built in the 1920s, the house belonged to the innkeeper's great-grandfather. The room with private bath has a queen bed; the other rooms share a full bath. Rooms are nonsmoking. The efficiency units have full kitchens, cable TV, and telephone service, and the guest house has its own whirlpool.

WHERE TO DINE IN TROUT RIVER

Seaside Restaurant. Trout River. ☎ **709/451-3461.** Main courses $7.95–$15.95. MC, V. Daily noon–10pm. SEAFOOD.

In July, when the capelin return, you can join the gulls and the whales here for a lunch of these smelt-sized fish. It's easy to follow the location of the schools by watching the swooping white birds and by the spouts and flukes, all visible through the giant windows overlooking the beach. The seafood, which makes up most of the Seaside's menu, is equal to the view. Skip the overcooked vegetables and tuck into the generous portions of impeccably fresh fish. While the service is painfully slow and the famous berry pies a bit heavy, the fish can't get much better than this, nor can the view.

THE NORTHERN SECTION OF THE PARK

The ferry from Woody Point connecting the two parts of the park has not operated for several years, although there are rumblings that it may begin again. Even so, the local boat operator still includes it in a brochure schedule, which creates a lot of confusion for those who appear at the dock, only to discover that they must return to Wiltondale and approach the northern section via Highway 430. But the scenery on the drive back is just as beautiful.

On the way you will pass the **Gros Morne Visitor's Centre,** on Highway 430 just before Rocky Harbour. The 17-minute film entitled *A Wonderful Fine Coast* introduces the park's geology, flora, and fauna, and is well worth seeing. During the summer, park naturalists lead interpretive walks, give evening lectures with slides, and organize campfires. Check the monthly activities schedule at the visitors center (☎ 709/458-2066), open daily from 9am to 10pm late June to early August, and 9am to 4pm daily the rest of the year. If you have not paid the $4.25 daily permit fee, you can do it here.

Hiking trails abound throughout the park, and a publication called *Tuckamore,* available at the visitors center, lists them. A short, easy, but rewarding hike takes you to Southeast Brook Falls, which you can glimpse from the main road.

But the best trail by far is the 1 1/2-mile (3km) walk in to ✪ **Western Brook Pond.** The hour walk, mostly on boardwalks across peatbogs filled with wildflowers, with better and better views of the steep cliffs ahead, takes you to a low rise. Before you a deep blue lake disappears between the 2,000-foot (650-meter) walls of a land-locked fjord. The lake is one of the world's purest, so deep that its temperature stays just barely above freezing year-round. While the view from here is simply breathtaking, it gets better still—you can travel inside the narrow fjord by boat.

The vessels *Western Brook I* and *Western Brook II* travel the length of the narrow 10-mile (16km) freshwater fjord, past hanging valleys and long ribbonlike waterfalls to its spectacular terminus. Bring a wide-angle lens, plenty of film, and a sweater (even on a hot day it will be cool in the shade of these giant cliffs). Several trips a day are planned, weather permitting, from late May to early October; they go in rain but not in foggy conditions. Note that the regular schedule will be suspended to accommodate bus tours, so it is imperative to make reservations as far ahead as possible. Hikers may disembark at the end of the lake and be retrieved by a later tour, but be certain to make firm arrangements and double-check them with the skipper. For reservations and information, call the **Ocean View Motel** in Rocky Harbour (☎ 709/458-2730). Fares are $23 for adults, $6 for children 8 to 16. Allow an hour to walk to the boat.

Close to the park's northern border, another boat trip will interest seal enthusiasts. **Seal Island Boat Tours** (☎ 709/243-2376 or 2278) leave at 10am and 1, 4, and 7pm; the trip costs $20 for adults and $10 for children. Look for their sign by the bridge in St. Pauls.

WHERE TO STAY

Gros Morne Cabins. P.O. Box 151, Rocky Harbour, NF, A0K 4N0. ☎ **709/458-2020,** 709/458-2039, or 709/458-2525 for off-season reservations. Fax 709/458-2882. 22 cabins. TV.

$55 one-bedroom cabin; $75 two-bedroom cabin; $99 honeymoon cabin with Jacuzzi, champagne, and flowers. Children stay free. Extra person $5. Special rates available off-season. AE, MC, V.

Gros Morne Cabins, next door to Endicott's store, provide roomy and comfortable lodging in carpeted bedrooms with full kitchens and baths and ocean views. The impeccably kept log cabins are close together, surrounded by a lawn with picnic tables, a playground, and a barbecue. Two cabins are available for travelers with disabilities. Pay at Endicott's Store, which is open daily from 9am to 11pm (call if you'll arrive later and they'll leave the key for you). Pets are welcome. There's a laundry on the premises.

Ocean View Motel. P.O. Box 129, Rocky Harbour, NF, A0K 4N0. ☎ **709/458-2730.** Fax 709/458-2841. 37 rms. TV. $59 double; $5 extra for rooms in front. Extra person $5. AE, ER, MC, V.

Rooms in this two-story motel are modern but dimly lit. Tour groups can make the motel seem overrun, yet it's clean, centrally located, and accepts your pets. The constantly busy Ocean Room dining room serves three meals a day, from 7am to 9:30pm. The food's good, and the service friendly but sometimes slow.

Sugar Hill Inn. P.O. Box 100, Norris Point, NF, A0K 3V0. ☎ **709/458-2147.** Fax 709/458-2147. 4 rms. TV. $76–$96 double. Extra person $10. Packages available. Senior discount. AE, MC, V. Closed mid-Oct to mid-Jan; call ahead.

On a hill above the road as you drive into Norris Point, about 4 miles from the Gros Morne Visitor's Centre, the two-story, green-shingled Sugar Hill Inn is a showplace of pine, cedar, birch, and oak. Each guest room has a queen-size bed, feather-light duvet, and private bath: nos. 1, 2, and 4 are large with private entrances; no. 3 has a skylight. Guests may use the hot tub and adjacent sauna free of charge.

If you book dinner in the licensed dining room, expect to linger two or three hours over a four- to six-course meal, accompanied by fine wine. Breakfast costs $6 to $8; dinner, $25 to $35.

Camping

North of the national park, **River of Ponds Provincial Park** has wooded campsites (with outhouses, no showers) from June through early September. **Juniper Campground,** on Pond Road in Rocky Harbour (☎ 709/458-2917), has 54 campsites with hot showers and flush toilets and dumping station. Rates are $11 a day (semihookup) or $9 (no hookup). It's open from late May to mid-September.

WHERE TO DINE

Fisherman's Landing. Highway 430, Rocky Harbor. ☎ **709/458-2060.** Main courses $10–$15. MC, V. Summer daily 6am–11pm; shorter hours rest of year. SEAFOOD/GRILL.

The service is just as friendly and more energetic at this new informal restaurant next door to the Ocean View, where early birds can have breakfast for $2.99 before 7am. Whenever you arrive, ask for their homemade bread. Seafood is properly cooked, with alternatives to fried fish. It's one of the rare places you'll see bakeapples (cloudberries) on the menu: They serve them as a cheesecake topping.

Picnic Supplies

Across the road from Endicott's store, in Rocky Harbor, **Pizza Plus** (☎ 709/458-2577) has good pizzas for takeout only. You can also get home-baked goods, including bread, pies, and muffins. North of Rocky Harbor on Highway 430 in Sally's Cove, **Aunt Polly** operates a bakery open daily from 8am to midnight. You can sit at two little tables or carry away a dozen tender scones to eat on the way.

HEADING NORTH ALONG THE VIKING TRAIL

The scenery doesn't get any more dramatic than Gros Morne, but as the Viking Trail continues north up the western shore of the Great Northern Peninsula, new vistas of sea and land unfold, as low headlands alternate with sandy coves. Whales dive and spout, and as you move north, icebergs drift just offshore. They seem to pose, hesitating behind a lighthouse or just off a point capped by a weathered fishing shack.

The road (Highway 430) is fairly straight and in excellent condition, with sparse traffic. Moose are a common sight. Services, while widely spaced, are available, but we suggest bringing a picnic lunch to enjoy at some scenic spot overlooking the sea. It's 223 miles (372km) from Rocky Harbor to the tip of the peninsula at St. Anthony, and even though you'll return by the same road, the scenery, nature, and the little fishing villages untouched by tourism keep it interesting. Along the way are two major historic sites. If the joys of traveling aren't enough to lure you, the goal of reaching Lief Erikson's Vineland at L'Anse aux Meadows should.

Not far north of the park boundary, **The Arches,** a small provincial park just off the road, features a striking rock formation. Two arches have been cut under a huge outcrop of dolomite, which stands free in the edge of the sea, looking like a giant gnarled turtle. It's picture perfect on a clear day with bright blue sea visible through the white arches; it's also beautiful when angry waves beat at the rocks. In summer look for tiny wild iris growing along the shore. **River of Ponds Provincial Park** has picnic and swimming areas. It's one of the province's premier fishing areas, and trout here grow to more than three pounds. At **Port aux Choix** (pronounced "port-a-*shwaw*"), an archaeological site provides evidence of the southernmost Eskimo habitation in North America. Three ancient cemeteries have been excavated. The tools, implements, and skeletons that have been unearthed reveal hitherto unknown aspects of the lives of the Maritime Archaic people, who lived here more than 4,000 years ago; later remains from the Dorset and Groswater Paleo Eskimo cultures have also been found. The **Visitor Reception Center** (☎ 709/861-3522 summer, 709/623-2608 winter), with a small, very informative museum, is open daily from 9am to 6pm mid-June to Labor Day. Museum admission is $1 adults, 50¢ children. You can tour the sites a short distance away at **Philip's Garden,** overlooking the sea. For overnight lodgings in Port aux Choix, look to the clean and comfortable **Sea Echo Motel** (☎ 709/861-3777).

At St. Barbe a ferry (☎ 709/722-4000) makes two round trips daily, May through December, across the Strait of Belle Isle to **eastern Labrador.** This is the best way to reach this coastal area, since no roads connect eastern Labrador to the western part of Labrador. The ferry timing allows you to go over and back on the same day, with about five hours there, or you can make it an overnight trip. See the section on Labrador later in this chapter for details.

You can often see Labrador across the strait; through this channel the chilly Labrador current enters the Gulf of St. Lawrence. With the current come icebergs, which originate in the icecaps of Greenland and the high Arctic, and you can see these white giants well into July. At **Eddies Cove** the Viking Trail turns inland to cross a wild and barren area before reaching the peninsula's farthest tip, where the only thing farther north is Greenland.

EXPLORING L'ANSE AUX MEADOWS & ST. ANTHONY

Most travelers to this remote and beautiful area come to see the Viking settlement at L'Anse aux Meadows, but they'll find more. The western coast is dramatic, with massive headlands, rocky islands, sea caves, tiny coves, and harbors that cut deep into the land. Whales and icebergs abound: In late June or July you will see both regularly, but neither ever becomes a ho-hum sight. St. Anthony, the peninsula's largest town, overlooks a well-protected harbor that was the last provisioning point for Labrador-bound fishing vessels. You can follow any of the few roads to where it ends at the sea and be assured of a breathtaking view or a quiet little cove.

The best way to explore this area is from the sea, as the Vikings approached it more than 1,000 years ago. ✪ *The Viking Saga* is an authentic replica of a vessel called a *knaar*, a working ship used to carry cargo, like those that brought the first Norse settlers to L'Anse aux Meadows. Its owners traveled to Roskilde, Denmark, where a complete vessel of this type had been recovered from the fjord where it sank; they studied its construction to replicate it exactly, also adding the safety features and engine required by the Canadian Coast Guard for passenger boats. While those same regulations prohibit carrying passengers under sail, they demonstrate the sail's use before each cruise.

The trip includes a visit to a shipwreck, a sea view of the Viking settlement, and close-up views of whales and icebergs as the ship cruises among scenic and historic islands. The crew explains the special features of the boat's construction, including blocks with no moving parts, real Manila ropes, and a finish of linseed oil. No recorded, canned spiel here—the crew explains the wildlife, the history, and seamanship during the trip. To reserve a space on one of three daily trips, contact Viking Boat Tours, P.O. Box 45, St. Lunaire, NF, A0K 2X0 (☎ 709/623-2100; fax 709/623-2098). The price is $25 for adults, $12.50 ages 5 to 12.

To see whales and icebergs from dry land, drive to the far end of St. Anthony, out Fishing Point to the lighthouse, which began operation in 1889 with a single kerosene lamp. Wooden viewing platforms (one is wheelchair accessible) overlook the open Atlantic and the harbor, and trails circle the high cliffs of the point. Or, you can spot your bergs and whales as you dine at the Lighthouse Cafe.

✪ **L'Anse aux Meadows National Historic Site.** Route 436, L'Anse aux Meadows. ☎ **709/623-2608.** Admission $2.25. Daily 9am–8pm.

Guided by the verses of the 13th-century *Greenlanders' Saga*, Norwegian explorers in 1960 made one of the most exciting archaeological discoveries of modern times when they unearthed unmistakable evidence of a Viking settlement at L'Anse aux Meadows. Dating from AD 1000, it is the only known Viking settlement in North America, thought to be that of Leif Erikson. It's now designated a UNESCO World Heritage Site, with an exceptionally well designed visitors' center that explains the settlement and its history, as well as the life the Vikings led there. A walkway leads to the site itself, about a seven-minute walk away. You can clearly see the lines of the foundations. Several buildings have been reconstructed adjacent to the original site, showing how the sod homes and workshops were constructed from the abundant peat. Inside the dwelling is a smoky fire; you get an idea of just what life must have been like during the long winters on the windswept bare point.

Grenfell House & Dockhouse Museums. St Anthony. ☎ **709/454-3333.** Admission $2 adults, $1 seniors and children. Daily 10am–8pm. Closed mid-Sept to mid-May.

In 1894, Wilfred Grenfell, concerned that the Labrador fishing settlements lacked medical care, established the Grenfell Medical Mission. Headquartered in St. Anthony, the mission built nursing stations, hospitals, and orphanages in remote settlements. To finance the project, the Grenfells founded Grenfell Crafts, which employed local people to make weather-impenetrable parkas from a specially designed material, decorating them with embroidery. The company's profits paid for the medical stations. Today you can visit the Grenfells' home and a museum in the restored dockhouse, where artifacts and displays demonstrate life and work in a turn-of-the-century shipping and fisheries center. You can buy the handmade coats and jackets, as well as snowsuits, sweaters, mittens, and other apparel, at prices starting at $70 (without the provincial sales tax, from which local handicrafts are exempt). The shop is open Monday to Friday 9am to 9pm, Saturday 9am to 6pm and Sunday 1 to 6pm.

WHERE TO STAY

✪ **Tickle Inn.** RR no. 1, Cape Onion, NF, A0K 4J0. ☎ **709/452-4321** (June–Sept) or 709/739-5503 (Oct–May). 4 rms (2 shared baths). $50–$55 double. Extra person $10. Rates include continental breakfast. MC, V. Closed Oct–May.

The inn's setting could hardly be better: at the end of its road, caught in a cove between two headwalls, overlooking water and rock where whales cavort among the icebergs. (It's a 40-minute drive from St. Anthony or L'Anse aux Meadows.) The historic property is a graceful blend of an old island home (in the fourth generation of the same family) and gentle renovations that make it work as a B&B. The rooms are stylishly decorated without being fussy and come with amenities such as bathrobes. It's worth the long drive north just to stay here, hike, watch icebergs and whales, enjoy wildflowers, or just relax. Besides, where else can you have a chunk of 10,000-year-old glacier fizzing in your ice water at dinner?

Dining/Entertainment: Five-course dinners are served to guests by reservation, and they're well worth reserving. Dishes, prepared with skill and imagination, feature local ingredients: salmon, Atlantic char, fresh wild herbs, partridgeberries, and wild blueberries.

WHERE TO DINE

The Lightkeepers' Cafe. Fishing Point, St. Anthony. ☎ **709/454-4900.** Reservations recommended for dinner. Main courses $7–$17. V. June–Sept 8am–9pm. SEAFOOD.

The small dining room, with lots of windows, doesn't depend on its view to attract customers. Best known for the seafood chowder, the cafe serves Newfoundland favorites such as cod with scrunchions, but also some new takes on the local product, such as seafood linguine. A few nonfish dishes are offered. At the height of summer, they open at 7am for those who want to watch the sunrise during breakfast. You couldn't find a better spot to do it, or better muffins.

5 Central Newfoundland

From Deer Lake, the Trans-Canada Highway weaves its way through the glacial lakes and rivers that fill the Newfoundland interior. On your way to Newfoundland's east coast, you'll pass through Grand Falls-Windsor, Gander, and Terra Nova National Park. You'll also learn more about Beothuk history and culture.

GANDER

Gander is one of the world's great outposts. Before the 1930s it was only known as remote rail milepost 213. Then the British Air Ministry (remember that Newfoundland was not part of Canada then) chose to locate a new air base here, since it was the closest fog-free spot to England. Little did those early planners realize how essential that airfield would become during World War II, when it provided the supply link and final refueling point for nearly all Europe-bound military flights. A town sprang up beside the main runway, the sound of aircraft engines always in the air. The airlink from Gander was vital to the Allied victory, and in the postwar aviation boom that followed, Gander remained the primary stopping point on the way to

Europe. Gander survived the war but not the Boeing 707, which made such refueling stops en route to Europe unnecessary, and Gander redundant.

DISCOVERING GANDER'S AVIATION PAST

The traveler nostalgic for the 1940s or thrilled by aviation history will enjoy some of Gander's offbeat attractions. For full effect, we suggest arriving by air. Begin your explorations as you leave the airport, taking Garret and Circular roads, both to the right. Follow any of the paved streets running through the low birch woods on your left, and you'll find the ghost town of **the original Gander.** In summer vegetation covers most of the foundations, but even then you have an idea of how large the wartime town was. When you leave this slightly spooky place, you can almost picture the wide grassy area alongside the main runway (which was many times its present width) filled wing-tip to wing-tip with parked aircraft.

The town moved after the war, needing room to grow. The Gander of today was built less than 50 years ago, along streets named for pioneers of flight: Corrigan Street, Lindbergh Road, Earhart Street, Markham Place, Rickenbacker Road, and, more recently, Yeager Street. Look for **vintage aircraft**—a Voodoo CF101, for one—as you drive through town. A new **Aviation Museum** is under construction near the Trans-Canada Highway, just west of the **Visitors Center** (☎ 709/256-7110). The first week of August is devoted to a **Festival of Flight,** with a variety of aviation-related events and plenty of old aircraft.

The **Silent Witness Memorial,** 4 miles east of Gander on the Trans-Canada Highway near the airport, is dedicated to the 258 members of the 101st Airborne Division, the "Screaming Eagles," who died at that site in a December 1985 plane crash, as they returned from peacekeeping work in the Sinai Peninsula.

WHERE TO STAY & DINE

Gander has a number of hotels and motels, most of them lined up along the Trans-Canada Highway. These include a **Holiday Inn** (☎ 709/256-3981 or 800/ HOLIDAY).

Cape Cod Inn Bed & Breakfast. 66 Bennett Dr., Gander, NF, A1V 1M9. ☎ **709/651-2269.** 4 rms. TV. $40–$55 double. MC, V.

In a residential neighborhood, this modern home offers spotless, lushly decorated and fully carpeted rooms with private baths. You won't be able to tear your kids away from the playhouse in the backyard.

Hotel Gander. 100 Trans-Canada Hwy., Gander, NF, A1V 1P5. ☎ **709/256-3931.** Fax 709/ 651-2641. 148 rms, 5 suites. TV TEL. $66–$93 double. Children under 18 stay free in parents' room; children under 12 eat free in the restaurant. 20% discount for seniors. AE, DC, ER, MC, V.

Many repeat travelers—pilots, businesspeople, flight crews—choose this hotel, whose lobby is decorated with aviation-related photos of Gander. The modern rooms have good reading lights, in-room movies, and a desk and table; some have air-conditioning. Guests enjoy its small indoor pool and exercise area. The staff can arrange babysitting.

Sinbad's Motel. Bennet Drive, Gander, NF, A1V 1W8. ☎ **709/651-2678** or 800/563-4900. 61 rms, 57 efficiencies. A/C TEL TV. $67–$79 double. Seniors $60. Children under 18 stay free in parents' rooms; children under 12 eat free. AE, ER, MC, V.

This attractive modern hotel has well-decorated, well-lit rooms. Spacious efficiencies have dining and sitting areas, plus modern kitchens. Pets are welcome.

The dining room is the best in town. Entrées, which cost $9 to $17, include Jamaican pork chops, several cod dishes, and pasta (not common in Newfoundland). The chef cooks salmon to the exact second. It's open 7am to 2pm and 5 to 9pm daily.

DISCOVERING A LOST CULTURE NEAR GANDER

The Beothuk people (pronounced "Bee-*aw*-thuk") inhabited this region and much of Newfoundland's interior when the first European settlers came in the 1600s. These hunters constructed teepee-shaped homes called "mamateeks," built on stone foundations. From their inland winter villages they could hunt caribou, and in spring they migrated to the coast, where they lived on seals and salmon. Early contacts with the Europeans were friendly, but as the island continued to be settled by outsiders, the Beothuks were gradually squeezed out of their customary fishing places. Hostilities with the newcomers, combined with diseases—primarily tuberculosis—reduced the Beothuk to a few scattered bands and by 1829 to extinction.

In 1981 a major discover was made at Boyd's Cove, on the coast north of Gander, that shed new light on the Beothuk. Excavations yielded artifacts as well as stone mamateek foundations and information about the daily life of the Beothuk. The **Boyd's Cove Beothuk Visitor Center, Interpretive Trail, and Site** at Boyd's Cove has an exhibition hall and theater to interpret the artifacts found there. A raised walkway will surround 11 house pits that date from 1650 to 1720. A trail from the center to the site will go through the mixed forest, beaches, and meadows where the Beothuk spent their summers. For more information, contact the Provincial Department of Tourism, Culture, and Recreation (☎ 709/729-2830 or 800/563-6353). To get to Boyd's Cove, take Route 330 north from Gander; go left on Route 331, and then right onto Route 340.

You'll also find more on Beothuk history and culture at the **Mary March Regional Museum** (☎ 709/489-7331), on Cromer Avenue and St. Catherine Street, just off the Trans-Canada Highway in Grand Falls–Windsor, an hour west of Gander. Mary March, one of the last living Beothuks, has become a symbol of the fate of her people. The museum screens *Lost Race,* a 12-minute film about the Beothuks. Admission is free; open weekdays 9am to noon and 1 to 5pm, weekends 2 to 5pm, closed holidays. Behind the museum is **Beothuk Village** (☎ 709/489-3559), with replicas of the Beothuk dwellings and depictions of their lifestyle. Admission is $2. The village is open late May to early September.

TERRA NOVA NATIONAL PARK

Some 46 miles (74km) east of Gander, the Trans-Canada Highway runs right through the middle of **Terra Nova National Park** (☎ 709/533-2801). You'll drive conveniently close to the beaches, boat ramp, camping areas, trailheads, and moose, so keep an eye out, especially early and late in the day. The park's natural beauty, with jutting headlands and deeply indented bays and coves, is not nearly as dramatic as Gros Morne. If splendid scenery is your goal, you won't find it here, where headlands are lower and the shore more gentle. More highly developed for tourism, it is the kind of park that's suited for a family vacation.

Twin Rivers Golf Course (☎ 709/543-2626) located at the park's southern end, is considered to be one of the Atlantic Provinces' best courses. Eighteen-hole rates are $27 to $34.

Along with providing transportation, the MV *Northern Fulmar* takes passengers on cruises to view the coastal scenery and discover marine life. Their **Ocean Watch Expedition** (☎ 709/533-6024) lets you take part in whatever research project is underway. Sunset cruises travel along the coast to outports, stopping to see bald eagles on the way.

If you are interested in native cultures, ask if the **Burnside Project** is open. Accessible via Route 310 at the park's northern end, the excavations at Burnside have yielded evidence of an early Paleo-Eskimo site, rare in Newfoundland. More than 2,000 artifacts have been discovered, representing three different periods. The site, 6 miles (10km) north of Burnside, is open weekdays in summer from 9am to 5pm, but only while the dig is in progress, so check first.

CAMPING & ACCOMMODATIONS

The park's developed campground at Newman Sound has 387 sites, showers, laundry facilities, and a store. There are also backcountry campsites, accessible by hiking trails or campers can be dropped off by a scheduled ferry service. Two are in abandoned outports, once-thriving villages with access only from the sea. (You can also visit these towns by ferry or hike to them on the Outport Trail from the Newman Sound Campground.) Other backcountry sites, preferred by canoeists, are set around Dunphy's Pond.

Terra Nova Park Lodge. Port Blanford, NF, A0C 2G0. ☎ **709/543-2535** for reservations or 709/543-2525 for information. 79 rms. A/C TV TEL. $80 double; $85 efficiency; $100 suite; $145 efficiency suite. AE, DISC, MC, V.

This new, full-service resort appeals to golfers, since the Twin Rivers Golf Course begins at the back door. Golf packages and events are available; there's also a pro shop. Rooms are spacious and well furnished, and all have extra beds for families. Efficiencies, priced only $5 more, are well-equipped and thoroughly modern. Several rooms are wheelchair accessible.

Dining/Entertainment: Mulligan's Pub serves light meals and snacks and there is a snack bar next to the pool. A more formal dining room overlooks the golf course and water, serving lunches (the steamed mussels appetizer is enough for a meal) and dinners.

Facilities: Exercise room, Jacuzzi, heated outdoor pool, game room, ski trails, ski shop in winter, pro shop in summer.

6 The Bonavista Peninsula

Heading south from Terra Nova National Park on the Trans-Canada Highway you'll soon come to Route 230, which leads to the Bonavista Peninsula; the colorful Discovery Trail, which threads through its harbors and fishing villages; and the historic town of Trinity.

TRINITY

In a beautiful setting overlooking the bay, Trinity boomed as a center for trade and commerce until the early 1900s and the advent of the railroad. Trinity Roman Catholic Church, Newfoundland's oldest standing church, was built here in 1833. Picturesque St. Paul's Church, built in 1892, is perhaps the finest wooden church in the province. Today the museums and restoration properties mix easily with the life of the town. Trinity is also a center for outdoor activities, including sea kayaking and walking.

The early 19th-century **Tibbs House** is the Trinity Interpretation Center, where you can learn more about the town's history. Pick up the *Welcome to Trinity Bight* booklet.

The **Hiscock House** honors an "ordinary" hardworking woman, Emma Hiscock, who provided for her six children after her 39-year-old husband drowned in 1893. The house, restored to 1910, is filled with everyday family items. Note the interesting way the pictures are hung. Guides will show you around daily from 10am to 5:30pm from June to the second Monday in October (☎ 709/464-2042 summers). You may also visit the **Green Family Forge,** which operated here for 200 years until 1955; and the reconstructed **Ryan Building,** which served this community from the late 16th century to 1952 as a counting house, warehouse, and general store. These are open the same hours as Hiscock House. **Trinity Folk Art** sells high-quality handicrafts, including Inuit art.

In summer, an unusual drama is enacted daily at 2pm, as a cast of actors portray events in village history in the **Trinity Pageant.** The audience moves about town with the players to scenes that provide the stage sets—the fish flakes of Harvey's Cove, a lonely rock by the sea, ruins of a once-fine home. Admission is by donation (they hope for $5) and there are no reservations; just follow along for a rare look at an interesting town.

For a chance to watch whales up close, reserve a space with **Atlantic Adventures Natural History Tours** (☎ 709/464-3738), or go to the wharf where you will see their 46-foot motorsailer. Tours include exploring deserted outports, looking for fossils, and watching for seals, eagles, and arctic birds.

In nearby Trinity East, visit **Trinity Loop Fun Park and Railway Village,** a well-done amusement park for families. A miniature train ride follows a historic loop, which early trains descended from the hills to the shore village. A small free museum, paddleboats, kayaks, canoes, bumper boats, miniature golf, weekend entertainment, animals, pony rides, and the **Conductor's Choice Diner,** in a railway car, make this a popular place with kids and adults. The park is open daily from 10am to 7pm, the museum noon to 7pm, the diner 10am to midnight (☎ 709/464-2171). Park admission is $2.50 for adults, $2 seniors and children under 12.

WHERE TO STAY

✪ **Campbell House.** Trinity (mailing address: 24 Circular Rd., St. John's, NF, A1C 2Z1). ☎ **709/464-3377** or 709/753-8945 off-season in St. John's. 4 rms. TEL. $75 double. Extra person $10. MC, V. Closed mid-Oct to late May.

Filled with little luxuries such as bathrobes and down duvets, Campbell House is designed to pamper guests. All rooms overlook the sea and have doors that lock. One room has a queen-size bed; another, a double bed and a day bed. Breakfasts include homemade breads and jams, and brewed decaf, if you please. Owner Tineke Gow is an enthusiastic walker and provides guests with hiking maps and advice about the many local trails. Mountain bikes are available for rent. A flagstone patio with a picnic table overlooks the garden, which has been authentically restored as an 1840 outport garden. A neat two-bedroom housekeeping unit down the hill has its own porch overlooking the fishing wharves. No smoking, pets, or children younger than seven.

✪ **Peace Cove Inn.** Trinity East, NF, A0C 2H0. ☎ **709/454-3738** or 709/464-3419 (off-season 709/781-2255 in St. John's). 5 rms. $43–$52 double. Rates include continental breakfast. Extra person $10. V. Closed mid-Oct to late May.

The spirits of former owners, Aunt Lizzie and Skipper Dick, seem to linger in this cozy turn-of-the-century house, where a mournful foghorn in the bay lulls guests to sleep at night. Two of the functional bedrooms have half baths, and one has a full bath and private entrance. Meals are country cooking served family style; a full breakfast costs $3.50, lunch $7.50, and dinner $15 for three courses. No smoking.

WHERE TO DINE

The area's best meals (and value) are the **community suppers,** served on Labor Day and July 15, and any other time there's a community cause that needs money. These all-you-can-eat meals, which include scrumptious desserts, only cost $6. If you can't find one of those, try **Riverside Lodge** in Trouty (☎ 709/464-3780) for home-cooked meals served at one sitting each evening at 7pm. **Coopers,** on Route 230, is open until 11pm and is a good place to try the local favorite: fried cod tongues ($7.95). On the wharf is **The Dock Marina Restaurant,** where you buy your steak by weight and cook it to your own taste on their outdoor grill, or order seafood, most of which is not deep fried.

7 Northern Avalon

From the southern end of the Bonavista Peninsula, the Trans-Canada Highway drops southward to the Avalon Peninsula. This roughly H-shaped body, tethered by a mountainous isthmus, is a fragment of the African plate left behind as a result of continental drift 200 billion years ago. The highway runs along the crown of the narrow isthmus, which is nearly always bathed in fog (while Gander, 120 miles away, remains virtually fogless year-round). When the dense misty clouds rushing over the roadway interfere with visibility, use low beams and watch the highway lines.

Once off the isthmus and into Avalon, you have several choices. You can continue to St. John's and tour the peninsula in day trips from a base there; you can visit the northern arm of the H on your way to St. John's; or, if you are leaving the province immediately via the ferry to Nova Scotia, you can drive directly to the landing at Argentia by leaving the Trans-Canada at Route 202.

THE BACCALIEU TRAIL

North of the Trans-Canada Highway, a long, narrow peninsula separates Trinity and Conception Bays. Route 80, which clings to its western shore, and Route 70, along the eastern side, combine to form The Baccalieu Trail. You'll drive through some unusually named towns: Heart's Delight, Heart's Desire, and Heart's Content. In the latter is **TransAtlantic Cable Station,** the terminus of the first telegraph cable connecting Europe and North America. The station is now a museum that shows the challenge of laying 2,000 miles of cable at the bottom of the sea. In the Operations Room guides demonstrate how the messages, which all arrived in Morse Code, were relayed to their destinations. You can see the end of the cable as it connected inside the building, and across the road you can see it disappearing into the sea. The museum, which is free, is open 9am to 5:30pm daily in the summer.

Route 80 continues to the peninsula's northern tip, and birders will want to follow it to Bay de Verde. On a **Baccalieu Island Boat Tour** (☎ 709/587-2595) you'll see most of the 11 species of seabirds that nest there. Known for the world's largest colony of Leach's storm petrels, the island is also home to a major puffin colony and the northern fulmar.

HARBOUR GRACE: A SLICE OF AVIATION HISTORY

Aviation buffs should take Route 74 across to Harbour Grace on the eastern shore. At the south end of town, not far from **Visitors Information** (☎ 709/596-5561), follow the sign uphill to the **Harbour Grace Airstrip.** When the pavement ends, so do the signs, but you should take two right turns, cross the bottom of the runway, and follow the road to the top. You can stand on the spot where, on May 20, 1932, Amelia Earhart took off for her solo transatlantic flight. There's no visitor's center, no hoopla—just a weathered stone monument listing her flight and 19 other pioneer flights that challenged the Atlantic from here. Standing at the top—it slopes downhill to give the planes added lift—you see exactly what she saw on that May morning: a grassy field, the tree-covered hill ahead, and open sky.

To learn more about these daredevil pilots, visit the free **Conception Bay Museum** near the harbor on Water Street (☎ 709/596-1309), which contains a logbook with signatures and flight plans, and photographs of the planes and pilots, including *The Pride of Detroit, Winnie Mae,* and *Southern Cross.* Displays on the pirate Peter Easton, whose fort stood on this spot, and other local history fill the rest of the museum. Ask for the free booklet "Dirt Strip to Glory," as well as one on the SS *Kyle,* the last of the coal- and wood-burning coastal steamers, which you can see in its final rusting place, run aground in the harbor. Also ask for the walking tour to the considerable number of historic buildings in town.

WHERE TO STAY & DINE

Ⓢ **Garrison House.** Water Street, Harbour Grace, NF, A0A 2M0. ☎ **709/596-3658.** 3 rms. $55–$59 double. Rates include breakfast. MC, V.

Directly across the street from the museum, Garrison House is a painstakingly restored 19th-century home with wide board floors and period antiques in both guest and public rooms. Duvets, firm mattresses, and in-room baths with big Victorian tubs add comfort and an air of gentility far beyond its modest rates.

Four-course dinners (bring your own wine) are served for $18 by reservation, many of their ingredients coming from the restored kitchen garden which two of the rooms overlook.

BRIGUS

Instead of the square, almost flat-roofed buildings typical of Newfoundland, the Brigus houses, with steeply pitched roofs, resemble those in a New England village. Even more unusual is the bungalow style of **Hawthorne Cottage,** home of the Arctic explorer Capt. Robert A. Bartlett. Associated with Admiral Robert E. Peary in the 1898, 1905, and 1908 expeditions, Bartlet made 16 other arctic voyages. His home is a museum (☎ 709/753-9262), open June to Labor Day from 10am to 6pm, with an admission of $2.50. There's also the small stone **Brigus Museum** (☎ 709/528-3298); admission is $1.

You can drive out "The Walk" to the large stone outcrop that separates the town from its rock-enclosed deep-water harbor. In 1860, Abram Bartlett had a Cornish coal miner blast a tunnel through the rock so his ships could get to town. You can walk through the tunnel for a good view of the harbor. Continue around the harbor on South Side Road to see the town and its dramatic setting above the water. You'll see why Brigus is often compared to a Norwegian fishing village.

On North Street, **Village Crafts** sells handmade items, including fine sweaters and thick warm mittens and gloves at prices you won't see elsewhere. Across the street, the **North Street Cafe** serves soups, meat pie, and sandwiches at lunch, scones for tea. Or enjoy a picnic and stroll through **Wilcox Gardens,** a park with formal flower beds along the stone-banked river. From Brigus it's a short drive to St. John's, either via the Trans-Canada Highway or the more scenic coastal route through Holyrood.

As the Trans-Canada Highway turns northeast toward St. John's, it passes the entrance to **Butter Pot Provincial Park,** one of the province's most-used (and crowded) parks. Hiking trails lead through low forests of spruce, balsam fir, and white birch, through fields of wildflowers, and over rocky barrens to lookouts with views of the bay. The park also has more than 140 campsites, playgrounds, two swimming areas, trout ponds, and even a wooded 18-hole minigolf course set with a Newfoundland theme.

8 St. John's

In 1997, St. John's will celebrate the 500th anniversary of its European discovery by John Cabot, who is said to have sailed into the harbor on St. John's Day in 1497. Events are scheduled to begin on New Years Day and last until the final bell rings out the year. It's been a busy 500 years, or at least 469 of them, since the beginning of the first settlement in 1528. This remote summer fishing station grew into a thriving seaport, the hub of shipping across the Atlantic. St. John's is also the closest port—and point—to Europe, making it instrumental in the development of communications and aviation. Marconi received the first transatlantic wireless message in the Cabot Tower on Signal Hill, and the race to fly the Atlantic in 1919 began here. Lindbergh's last landmark on his solo flight in 1927 was Cabot Tower. During World War II the city served as a strategic and supply point, and the only enemy attack on the North American continent was made by German submarines in 1942 on Bell Island, just west of the city.

Today's lively city, its brightly painted wood buildings creating a patchwork of color along the steep streets, overlooks the harbor, where ships constantly load and unload, flying flags from all over the world. This provincial capital—hearty, hospitable, and genuine—is a jolly, lovable, overgrown seaport.

ESSENTIALS

VISITOR INFORMATION   Contact the **St. John's Economic Development and Tourism Division,** in City Hall on Gower Street (P.O. Box 908), St. John's, NF, A1C 5M2 (☎ 709/576-8106; fax 709/576-8246), open from 9am until 4:30pm weekdays. Or visit their desk at the airport or their distinctive railway car on Harbor Drive, open June through Labor Day.

GETTING THERE   Continue traveling east along the Trans-Canada Highway through the Avalon Peninsula. When you get to St. John's, you will have reached the Trans-Canada's beginning, not its end. At the City Hall, you will see a milestone and sign marking the start of the world's longest national artery. From Mile 0 it extends, over land and sea, to Victoria, B.C., 4,976 miles (7,775km) away.

Travelers arriving by air will find a small, tidy, and very user-friendly airport, with every service near the arrival gate. Car rentals and visitor information are directly in front of arriving passengers. Downtown is only 6 miles (10km) away. There's no bus, but Bugden's taxis have been meeting planes there since the first passenger flight arrived in 1942.

GETTING AROUND   **Metrobus** connects major hotels with downtown and the malls on the edge of the city, passing many of the places visitors want to go. Look for route signs or call ☎ 709/722-9400 for a schedule. Except for downtown St. John's, it's good to have a car for sightseeing.

If you are carless, contact **Bugden's Taxi,** 266 Blackmarsh Rd. (☎ 709/726-4400), and they'll arrange a cab tour for up to five people. Along Marine Drive to Torbay and back costs $40; to Cape Spear and Petty Harbour, $75.

EXPLORING THE TOWN

St. John's grew up around its harbor, so a walk along **Harbour Drive,** lined by ships, is a good way to start exploring.

Water Street, a block north of Harbour Drive, is called the oldest main street on the continent, because it served as a pathway for the earliest explorers and later for the settlers. Between Water and Duckworth streets, the next two streets away from the waterfront, the **War Memorial** stands on the spot where, in 1583, Sir Humphrey Gilbert proclaimed Newfoundland a territory under the British Crown. Many consider this event the beginning of the British Empire.

Duckworth and Water are the main shopping streets; many restaurants are located there as well. Behind the imposing granite **Court House,** which lies between the two, **Church Hill** rises steeply, bordered by fine wooden Victorian row houses, which climb in stairstep formation. The major churches are stationed at various points on the hill, which is topped by the Roman Catholic **Basilica of St. John the Baptist.** Its twin towers have served as a landmark for mariners since its construction in 1841.

As you walk through these old neighborhoods, you will see block after block of wood town homes, many excellent examples of the Victorian style and painted in bright colors. **Gower Street** has a particularly fine collection.

Cathedral of St. John the Baptist. 68 Queen's Rd. ☎ **709/726-5677.** Free tours late May to mid-Oct 10:30am–4:30pm.

Begun in 1843 and finished in 1885 under the supervision of Sir Gilbert Scott, this Anglican cathedral was gutted by fire in 1892, but restoration work done in 1905 gave it the look it has today. The Gothic nave, carved pews, Scottish sandstone, rough-hewn Newfoundland stone, and the 36 stained-glass windows (particularly the Kempe windows made in London), as well as its architecture, make it an internationally important example of Gothic revival style. Volunteer guides are available, but you should call first.

Commissariat House. King's Bridge Road. ☎ **709/729-6730.** Free admission. June to mid-Oct daily 10am–5:30pm.

This beautiful Georgian structure depicts what life was like when Newfoundland was a vital link in the defense chain of the young British Empire. The house, restored to its 1830 appearance, is now filled with beautiful Brussels carpets, English china, silver, lace, and fine paintings, as would have befitted the assistant commissary general.

Newfoundland Museum. 285 Duckworth St. ☎ **709/729-2329.** Free admission. July–Aug daily 9am–4:30pm; other months Mon–Fri 9am–5pm, Sat–Sun 9am–4:30pm.

The permanent exhibits, on the second and third floors, focus on the native peoples of Newfoundland and on 19th-century daily life. They include rural furnishings, toys, a schoolroom, cooperage, fishery stage, grocery, and stoves manufactured in St. John's. Exhibits are devoted to the Inuits, who have been on the Labrador coast since 1400, Dorset, Naskapi, and Montagnais Indians, and most poignantly, the Beothuks, called the "Red Indians" because they covered their bodies in red ocher. Guides are available at 11am and 2pm.

✪ **Signal Hill.** At the entrance to St. John's Harbour. ☎ **709/772-5367.** Small fees for special events. Mid-June to Labor Day daily 8:30am–9pm; rest of year daily 8:30am–4:30pm; grounds open year-round. City buses don't run to Signal Hill, but you can walk, take a taxi, or drive by following Duckworth Street east to Signal Hill Road.

The view from the hill at Signal National Historic Park (when it's not socked in by fog) is magnificent, and the breezes are cool even on the hottest summer day. Midway up the slope is the park's Visitor Centre, with exhibits explaining the history and importance of Signal Hill and the harbor and town it protected.

Beyond is the **Queen's Battery,** established by the British in 1796 and enlarged during the War of 1812. Originally an elaborate complex of barracks, blockhouses, and furnaces, all that remains are stabilized ruins. Six replacement 32-pounder guns represent those of the battery's 1860s period.

Across the mouth of the harbor from Queen's Battery you can see **Fort Amherst,** with a lighthouse on the point, built in 1813. Together with a chain that stretched across the Narrows, the two defenses were very effective in closing the harbor of St. John's to enemy attack until larger guns and ironclad vessels made them obsolete. Cape Spear, the most easterly point in North America.

Atop Signal Hill, **Cabot Tower** was begun in 1897 to commemorate Queen Victoria's jubilee, and the 400th anniversary of John Cabot's landing in 1497. It served as a lookout and signal tower until 1958, and here Guglielmo Marconi received the first transatlantic wireless broadcast from England, in 1901. It was Morse code for the letter *S,* and those three short dots made history. Cabot Tower maintains communications with the world through an amateur radio station on its second floor (open during the summer months). The observation deck above offers panoramic views. From here you can look down on a hiking path that skirts the tops of the sea cliffs. The path begins at the intersection of Duckworth Street and Signal Hill Road and ends at the Quidi Vidi Battery. It has some steep, rugged stretches, but offers fine views, often of icebergs.

In summer, the **Signal Hill Tattoo** reenacts military exercises from the 1800s. It's a great pageant, performed at 3 and 7pm on Wednesday, Thursday, Saturday, and Sunday from mid-July to mid-August, weather permitting. Since special activities may involve the Tattoo, call for exact times.

SHOPPING

Shopping (apart from the unremarkable malls outside of town) is mainly confined to the streets that closely parallel the harbor: Water and Duckworth. Water Street has an interesting assortment, from the floral elegance of **The Olde Victorian Shoppe** (☎ 709/754-5559), whose painted doors are easy to spot at no. 100, to the funky jumble of **The London** (☎ 709/579-7355), whose window at no. 179 is filled with everything from brass portholes to antique china. Next door, the **Newfoundland Weavery,** 177 Water St. (☎ 709/753-0496), sells crafts, including hand-knit sweaters, hooked mats, jams, and tote bags in the shape and colors of rainbow trout. If you're taken with alternately rollicking and haunting Newfoundland music, **Fred's** music store, 198 Duckworth St. (☎ 709/753-9191), sells CDs and tapes, and offers mail order. For outstanding art and handicrafts, follow Duckworth Street to the **Devon House Craft Center** (☎ 709/753-2749), at no. 59, opposite the Hotel Newfoundland, where you'll find glassware, intricate wood inlay, leather applique, caribou antler jewelry, and hand-knit mittens and sweaters.

PARKS & NATURE AREAS

In the city's northwest section, **Pippy Park** has an 18-hole golf course, swimming, walking trails (which are popular ski trails in the winter), ponds that become winter skating rinks, and a campground. On the shore of Long Pond, reached via Nagel's Place, is North America's only public **Fluvarium** (☎ 709/754-FISH), providing a close-up view of the insects, plants, and fish that live in the water. In winter, you can observe life under the ice. Open year-round; its extended summer hours are 9am to 5pm daily, with hourly guided tours.

Adjacent to the park is the Memorial University **Botanical Garden,** with plantings that include extensive native plant collections, as well as display beds. Naturalist-led walks are available (☎ 709/737-8590 for a schedule).

Take Highway 10 west (Waterford Bridge Road) from downtown to reach **Bowring Park,** the city's other favorite green spot, a few miles from the center. Tennis courts, ponds, well-kept gardens, and shaded walking and cycling paths fill the area between two merging streams. Look for the statues of *The Fighting Newfoundlander, Peter Pan* (a copy of the one in London's Kensington Park), and *The Caribou.*

QUIDI VIDI LAKE & BATTERY

Pronounced "Kitty Vitty," this area includes a lake to the east of town, a tiny village, and **The Battery,** which protected its harbor's narrow entrance channel, known as "The Gut." The battery was constructed in 1762 by the French troops who held St. John's for a short period that year. Within three months it was in British hands. The British reinforced it against American privateers during the Revolution, and again in 1812. Totally reconstructed in 1967 during Canada's centennial, the battery's little building houses a small, free museum, open daily from 10am to 5:30pm mid-June to mid-October (☎ 709/576-2460).

Take time to visit the little harbor village of **Quidi Vidi,** enclosed by steep rock cliffs, as photogenic a fishing village as you will find. **Mallard Cottage,** at 2 Barrows Rd., now an antique shop, is thought to be the oldest cottage in St. John's.

You may see scullers practicing on Quidi Vidi Lake for the **St. John's Regatta,** a popular all-day racing event held here (as it has been since 1826) the first Wednesday in August. You can walk around the lake on a level and well maintained path. We prefer **Rennie's River Walk,** a trail along the river connecting the lake to Long Pond, at the Fluvarium.

To get to Quidi Vidi, follow Signal Hill Road to Quidi Vidi Road; turn right onto Forest Road. To go to the Battery, bear right and uphill; to the harbor, bear left and downhill.

ORGANIZED TOURS & CRUISES

McCarthy's Party, Topsail, Conception Bay (☎ 709/781-2244; fax 709/781-2233), offers a 2¹/₂-hour tour of St. John's and environs for $25. Consider this outstanding family-run show on wheels as entertainment along with travel.

Bird Island Charters and Humpback Whale Tours, 150 Old Topsail Rd. (☎ 709/753-4850), runs boat excursions to the bird nesting islands in Witless Bay. The whales are usually in these waters from early July to early August, and the boats get quite close to them. The tour goes to the largest puffin colony on the east coast of North America—in fact, one of the world's largest puffin sanctuaries—where you can watch these little cartoon-like birds swoop, skim, and dive for fish to feed their hungry offspring. A shuttle bus ($10 extra) will pick up at hotels in St. John's for the ride to the dock in Bay Bulls, 19 miles (30km) to the south; the tour, which costs from $28 to $35, has daily departures at 9:30 and 11am, and 2, 5, and 6:30pm.

Wildland Tours, 124 Water St. (☎ 709/722-3335), takes more adventurous visitors on day trips to see the bird islands and whales of Witless Bay, then continues on to the caribou herds of the southern Avalon Peninsula. Another excursion travels along the rugged coast to Cape St. Mary's to see gannets covering a sea stack less than 30 feet from the trail.

At Pier no. 7, you'll find **sailing tours,** which leave on a regular schedule throughout the summer. **Adventure Tours of Newfoundland** (☎ 709/726-5000 or 800/77-WHALE) has been taking passengers aboard the schooner *Scademia* for nearly 20 years. The cost for a two-hour sail along the harbor, through the Narrows and to Cape Spear, is $20. **J&B Schooner Tours** (☎ 709/682-6585) offers five cruises daily; evening and sunset cruises are shorter. Monday is half price for seniors.

WHERE TO STAY
VERY EXPENSIVE
○ **Hotel Newfoundland.** Cavendish Square (P.O. Box 5637), St. John's, NF, A1C 5W8. ☎ **709/726-4980,** 800/268-9411 in Canada, or 800/828-7447 in the U.S. Fax 709/726-2025. 288 rms, 14 suites. A/C TV TEL. $170 double; from $200 suite. AE, CB, DC, DISC, ER, MC, V. Free parking.

When people in St. John's say "the hotel," they mean the Hotel Newfoundland, a CP Hotels property. This posh modern hotel, completely rebuilt in 1982, features splendid views over the harbor from most of its rooms. Room numbers 200, 300, etc., have the best views, encompassing the harbor, Narrows, and city. Many rooms are nonsmoking, and several are wheelchair accessible. Each of the unique minisuites has a round window in the bedroom, which is separated from the large sitting area by a screen. The standard rooms are nicely decorated, with a well-lit desk and upholstered chairs. The hotel has nice details, such as huge thick towels and good lighting, but also a few glitches, including noisy plumbing, insufficient hot water in the morning, and poor soundproofing between guest rooms and hallways. But these are small quibbles with what is unquestionably the premier property in town.

Dining/Entertainment: A waterfall, the highlight of the atrium lobby, is also the centerpiece for the Court Garden, an informal dining room that serves a buffet breakfast, complete with fish and brewis. The hotel's upscale restaurant, the Cabot Club, is elegant in every detail. The frequently changing menu includes well-prepared dishes.

Facilities: Indoor swimming pool, sauna, whirlpool, and squash courts, shops.

MODERATE TO EXPENSIVE
Compton House. 26 Waterford Bridge Rd., St, John's, NF, A1E 1C6. ☎ **709/739-5789.** 8 rms and suites. TV TEL. $69–$99 double; $138–$159 suite. Extra person $15. Rates include breakfast. AE, MC, V.

Although this home was built in 1919 by a wealthy local business tycoon, it is so starched and carpeted that it has the feel of a brand-new home. That is not a criticism—it's just that the home is so beautifully kept that it's easy to forget its age. Nor is it overfurnished or -decorated; the public and guest rooms feel spacious. The large rooms have new furnishings, several have working fireplaces, and five suites have whirlpool baths. Guests can choose either a buffet or full cooked breakfast.

○ **Kincora Hospitality Home.** 36 King's Bridge Rd. (at Empire Avenue), St. John's, NF, A1C 3K6. ☎ **709/576-7415.** 5 rms. TV. $70 double. Extra person $10. Rates include breakfast. No credit cards.

In this showpiece bed-and-breakfast, antiques and plush carpets are the norm, with historic and often dramatic beds the centerpiece of each room. Room no. 3 has a sturdy half-tester with lace hangings, room no. 4 a brass bed from an English castle. Fireplaces and goose down duvets make rooms particularly inviting in winter. The owner loves to cook and serves a full hot breakfast on fine china in a formal dining room.

Quality Hotel by Journey's End. 2 Hill O'Chips, St. John's, NF, A1C 6B1. ☎ **709/754-7788** or 800/668-4200. Fax 709/754-5209. 162 rms. A/C TV TEL. $95–$105 double. Extra person $4. Senior and weekend specials. AE, DC, ER, MC, V. Free parking.

Overlooking the harbor, the Quality Inn is the only downtown option other than staying in a B&B if you can't afford the high price of the Hotel Newfoundland. It has modern cookie-cutter decor, windows that open, and two double beds or a queen-size with a sofa bed in each room. Request a room with a harbor view. Guests get complimentary newspapers and coffee, in-room movies, and can make local calls free. Two floors are nonsmoking.

The Roses. 9 Military Rd., St. John's, NF, A1C 2C3. ☎ **709/726-3336.** 4 rms. TV TEL. $69 double. Rates includes tax and breakfast. AE, MC, V.

Patrick's pancakes, served in a bright and airy breakfast room on the third floor of this restored Victorian townhouse, are enough reason to stay here. Breakfast table conversation is another, as the engaging hosts (she is Phyllis Morrissey, a well-known Newfoundland singer) make guests feel at home. Rooms vary in decor and elegance, but all have private baths (one of which is in the room), mixed antiques, and a slightly eccentric decor. This is not a decorated-to-death B&B, but a very livable one. Room no. 2 has a working fireplace and a bay window, room no. 1 a large fireplace. The Roses is not suited to guests who have trouble climbing stairs, since breakfast is served at the very top; you certainly work up an appetite getting there. Location is a plus, with downtown, waterfront, and restaurants all within a short walk.

Traveller's Inn. 199 Kenmount Rd., St. John's, NF, A1B 3P9. ☎ **709/722-5540** or 800/528-1234. Fax 709/722-1025. 88 rms. TV TEL. $64–$87 double. Extra person $7. Children under 18 free with parents. Weekend rates and packages available. AE, CB, DC, DISC, ER, MC, V.

Renovated in 1992, the family owned and operated Traveller's Inn, a Best Western property, is outside the town center but has convenient access to the TC1 highway. It offers both motel-style and corridor-accessed rooms with full baths. Those in the back section are particularly quiet, with views of a hillside. Baths are on the small side except in the twin rooms, but they have good counter space. Outdoors is a pool and picnic area. The restaurant serves an inexpensive breakfast buffet daily.

✪ **Waterford Manor.** 185 Waterford Bridge Rd., St. John's, NF, A1E 1C7. ☎ **709/754-4139.** Fax 709/754-4155. TV TEL. $60–$145 double. Rates include breakfast. MC, V.

With three turrets, a wraparound porch and a perfectly kept paneled foyer, this Queen Anne mansion makes a fine first impression. Rooms are beautifully furnished, with carefully chosen antiques and just the right decorative touches to fit its Victorian air. There's also the thoughtful modern touch, such as VCRs. Owner Trish Balrudin has made the most of quirky architectural details—our favorite room, on the third floor, runs along one side of the house, with the double Jacuzzi at one end and the parlor in the front turret. Breakfast is served in the elegant dining room, but you should have breakfast in your room at least once. This B&B is not located within walking distance of downtown.

INEXPENSIVE

⑤ **The Tides Inn.** 407 Windgap Rd. (on the Marine Drive), Flatrock, NF, A1k 1C4. ☎ **709/437-1456.** 2 rms. $50 double.

Whales swim almost under the windows of these two beautifully appointed guest rooms. The inn overlooks a wide cove whose low ledges rise in layers on one side and almost straight up on the other. From the window of your room, you can watch icebergs, or ships on their way to Europe. The hearty breakfasts have touches hard to find in Newfoundland, such as brewed decaf coffee at breakfast. While the inn is 15 minutes from the airport and only a little longer to downtown St. John's, it is an appealing place to stay, given its incomparable views and the peace and quiet of a small village. Tea is served on the glass-enclosed front porch to guests and the public.

WHERE TO DINE
EXPENSIVE

✪ **The Cellar.** Baird's Cove. ☎ **709/579-8900.** Reservations recommended on weekends. Main courses $14–$25. AE, MC, V. Mon–Thurs 11:30am–2:30pm and 5:30–9:30pm, Fri–Sat 5:30–10:30pm, Sun 5:50–9:30pm. ECLECTIC.

Dark and intimate, this is the place for a candlelit supper for two. With quite possibly the most innovative menu in the province, although its ingredients aren't as exotic at those at Stone House, The Cellar gets consistent raves. Fillets of steelhead trout are charcoal grilled before being served with fresh ginger and pear butter; the pepper shrimp is spicy in a beer and butter sauce. Even something as simple as sautéed chicken breast gets a new twist with tarragon and green peppercorns. Pastas and breads are made in-house. If you're going to Corner Brook, in western Newfoundland, look for their sister restaurant, Thirteen West (see page 175).

✪ **Stone House.** 8 Kennas Hill. ☎ **709/753-2380.** Reservations recommended. Main courses $18–$28. AE, DC, DISC, ER, MC, V. Mon–Fri 11:30am–2:30pm; Sun–Thurs 5–10pm, Fri–Sat 5–11pm. SEAFOOD/GAME.

The elegant Stone House, built in 1834, has three-foot-thick walls, wide-board floors, and four dining rooms that retain the sense of dining in a fine old home. The menu features Newfoundland cuisine, highlighting the province's fresh produce, seafood, and game. Appetizers of gravlax (their specialty, and served in generous portions), cod tongues, or steamed mussels vie for your attention with more exotic escargot in strawberry coulis or wild game bourguignonne. Entrées offer even more choices you'll rarely see on a menu: pheasant breast with pecan and red currant dressings (a tad dry, but a delectable flavor blend), partridge, pheasant, caribou, wild boar, and moose. The wine cellar is well stocked.

MODERATE

Le Petit Paris. 73 Duckworth St. ☎ **709/579-8024.** Reservations accepted. Main courses $13–$18. AE, ER, MC, V. Sun–Thurs 11:30am–10pm, Fri–Sat 11:30am–11pm. Closed Mon–Thurs 2:30–5:30pm in winter. FRENCH.

Without being cute, Le Petit Paris has achieved a genuine French cafe atmosphere, using old wrought-iron work as room dividers and an outside terrace with a limited view over the Narrows. Parisian favorites, such as coquille St-Jacques and grilled lamb tenderloin, share the menu with local seafood prepared in original ways. Cod, for example, is marinated, wrapped in phyllo, and served with saffron sauce or prepared with green peppercorns. However it is prepared, the fish is cooked perfectly.

Stella's. 183 Duckworth St. ☎ **709/753-9625.** Reservations accepted for dinner until 7pm; if coming later, call 15 minutes before arrival to hold table if available. Main courses $10–$14. MC, V. Tues–Fri noon–3pm; Wed 6–9pm, Thurs–Fri 6–10pm, Sat noon–10pm. VEGETARIAN/SEAFOOD.

Upbeat, small, and always crowded, Stella's serves tasty vegetarian and seafood dishes, and specializes in nondairy main courses and desserts. Favorites on the dinner menu are basil pesto fettuccine, a black bean chicken burrito, and spanakopita. Desserts (which are the first thing locals will describe when you ask about Stella's) include cheesecake, pies, and chocolate cake. If you can't get a table, they do offer takeout.

Zachary's. 71 Duckworth St. ☎ **709/579-8050.** Reservations accepted. Main courses $8–$17. AE, ER, MC, V. Daily 8am–10pm. NEWFOUNDLAND.

This casual place with booths and tables offers cheerful service and mixed fare ranging from fried fish to stir-fry to pasta. The extensive breakfast menu features local favorites such as baked beans with bologna, fish and brewis, fish cakes, salmon and eggs, and toutons. Newfoundlanders enjoy these tasty fried dough cakes with molasses, but you can get jam or syrup instead.

INEXPENSIVE

Pubs (see "St. John's After Dark") also serve light, usually inexpensive dishes. Look for these anywhere in the downtown area, or try **The Ship Inn,** 265 Duckworth St. (☎ 709/753-3870). A second home to writers, musicians, actors, students, and artists of all ages, this congenial pub serves sandwiches, meat pies, and salads at lunchtime, when the place fills with a business crowd. Beer is the specialty here: Guinness, Harp, and Smithwick's on tap for about $5 a pint (half pints available).

For picnic supplies, try **Mary Jane's,** in a large, two-story building at 377 Duckworth St. (☎ 709/753-8466), open weekdays 11am to 3pm, where you can get all manner of healthy foods. There's a bakery and in-store snack bar, serving veggie pâté, hummus, sandwiches, and salads.

ST. JOHN'S AFTER DARK

Music is St. John's heartbeat. You'll hear it pouring from pubs, sung on the street, and played in shops and restaurants. Along with the latest tunes, you're likely to hear the lusty local sea songs, lively fiddle tunes, or the plaintive chords of a Celtic ballad.

For a small city, St. John's has a thriving nightlife; George Street, once the center of the mercantile district, has more pubs per square foot than any other Canadian city. It rivals Dublin. Bars and clubs get "blocked" (that's Newfoundland for crowded) early. Listen to Irish music at **Erin's Pub,** 184 Water St. (☎ 709/ 722-1916); blues every Thursday at **Lottie's Place,** 3 George St. (☎ 709/745-3020); or mainstream dance music at **Junctions,** 208 Water St. (☎ 709/579-2557). Cover at bars to listen to music is no more than $3. To find out what's happening where, pick up the free newspaper *Signal,* which lists all the pubs and their music schedule for the current week.

To get "screeched in"—that is to have your first drink of the local rum, which would make a cast-iron pot screech—go to **Trapper John's** on George Street (☎ 709/579-9630). Two of the city's most popular bars are **Nautical Nellies** (and the small and quieter Nelly's Belly, downstairs), 201 Water St. (☎ 709/726-0460), where popcorn is served free after 4pm; and, at the university, the **Breezeway Bar,** in the Thompson Student Centre (☎ 709/737-7464). Run by the student union, it's a nonprofit bar (beer and mixed drinks run a mere $2). There's taped music and a dance floor. A good place to meet students and young professionals, it gets crowded on Thursday and Friday nights.

SIDE TRIPS FROM ST. JOHN'S

No visitor should leave St. John's without taking a ride along **Marine Drive,** north of the city. Past Logy Bay to Outer Cove and Torbay is some of the area's finest scenery, composed of soaring headlands that jut out to enclose deep coves. The shape and color of rock formations provide their names and those of towns. At Flat Rock (enclosed by Red Head), the shore lies in a series of ledges that seem designed especially for picnics. Or you can stop instead at the tea room of The Tide's Inn, overlooking a cove where whales cavort in the summer.

Marine Drive goes to Pouch (pronounced "Pooch") Cove, where the paved road ends, but a rough road of dirt and crushed stone climbs into the hills, past more dramatic views, to the lighthouse at Cape St. Francis.

Seven miles (11km) south and east of downtown St. John's is **Cape Spear National Historic Site** (☎ 709/772-5367). The lighthouse (1836), perched on a rocky cliff, is at North America's most easterly point. A World War II gun battery has underground passages that connect two gun sites with magazines and equipment rooms. At the Visitor Reception Centre, you can learn about Cape Spear. Guides are on hand in the lighthouse from mid-June to early September. In late summer and fall the area is covered with blueberries; hiking trails lead to sea views at every turn.

9   The Southern Shore of Avalon & Cape St. Mary's

Known as the Irish Heart of Newfoundland, the area south of St. John's and across St. Mary's Bay is ringed in ragged rocky coast, with towering cliffs, tiny coves, and wild seas. While you can explore the area on day trips from St. John's, we don't think you should rush through the little coastal villages or past the endless views. We suggest a longer trip—at least two days; you can enjoy the warm hospitality of some modest lodgings along the way. Listen to a tape by *The Irish Descendants,* take some scenic coastal and nature walks described in *Trails of the Avalon* (sold in book shops and visitor centers), and take time to smell the sea air. Bring a waterproof jacket. It's no wonder the Irish settlers felt at home here.

From St. John's, head south on Route 10 toward Bay Bulls, home of **Bird Island Charters and Humpback Whale Tours** (see St. John's Tours). Or you can reach the Witless Bay Ecological Reserve from Bauline East, only a 10-minute boat ride from the islands where more than two million birds nest: puffins (the largest colony on the east coast), murres, storm petrels, kittiwakes, and others. **Codjigger Boat Tours** (☎ 709/334-2636 or 709/334-2155) leave the wharf seven times a day for the islands. Because the distance is shorter, their tours cost $15, substantially less than those leaving from Bay Bulls.

The road travels above the shore, which is quite steep in places, but you can nearly always see the water. **La Manche Provincial Park** lies between the road and the sea, with hiking trails leading to an abandoned outport fishing village and to a waterfall. The campground (☎ 800/563-NFLD), in the woods beside a pond, has 69 well-spaced sites and is open June to Labor Day. The camping fee is $8 a night.

South of La Manche, follow signs on a short detour to **Brigus South,** where you'll find one of the province's most rockbound harbors (and that's saying a lot). It's also one of the most picturesque, with high rock cliffs, tiny fishing shacks, and boats; a cemetery of white crosses rises on the opposite slope.

FERRYLAND & THE COLONY OF AVALON ARCHAEOLOGY PROJECT

As the road drops into Ferryland, look for a large white building on the left, almost opposite the Downs Inn. This is the museum and Visitor Centre for the **Colony of Avalon Archaeology Project** (☎ 709/432-2767 in summer; 709/432-2820 year-round). This project has uncovered the remains of one of the earliest English settlements, established in 1621 under the proprietorship of George Calvert. But Calvert and his family didn't like the Newfoundland winters and quickly moved on to Maryland, where he became the first Lord Baltimore. Remains of his buildings are being unearthed beside the harbor. You can observe the process and visit the field laboratory where the artifacts are sorted, on weekdays from 8am to 4:30pm and Saturdays until noon. The museum is open 9am to 8pm daily in the summer, shorter hours after Labor Day.

Adian Costello will take you on an interpretive tour of the site, as well as a horse and buggy ride (or sleigh in the winter) along the abandoned railway bed overlooking the town and bay. As you travel, the history of the town unfolds along with its scenery. The tour costs $20 for adults, $10 for children. His **Southern Shore Eco Adventures** (☎ 709/432-2659) also includes walking trips to the abandoned town in the La Manche park and nature explorations throughout Avalon.

Ferryland is a gritty little town, with a real sense of its past. It's not painted cute for visitors; instead, the town retains the feeling of what it's like to live in a fishing port. The stone church is being restored (for a look inside ask Junior O'Brien at the Downs Inn, the former convent next door). To learn more about the lives of local fishermen, go to the **Ferryland Museum** (☎ 709/432-2711), on the other side of the church; ask why the mountain behind Ferryland is called The Gaze, and stop by the shop, **Shoreline Crafts.** The three statues next to the church came from a shipwreck, pieces of which remain on the beach below.

WHERE TO STAY & DINE

⑤ **The Downs Inn.** Route 10, Ferryland, NF, A0A 2H0. ☎ **709/432-2808** or 709/432-2163. 4 rms. $45 double. Rates include full breakfast.

The owners of The Downs Inn decided to keep their place as authentic to its past as possible, so the inn retains the air of the former convent that it was, once home to 15 nuns. That's not to say the inn is austere: The spacious rooms have comfortable beds and homey furnishings. Each room has a sink—they share baths—and all the fireplaces work. The nuns' parlor is a tea room, well stocked with travel information; the O'Briens can advise you as well.

Dining/Entertainment: The dining room serves generous portions of well-prepared local foods; dinner is $14 and lunch $5 or $7 for lunch (bring your own wine). You'll feel like you're visiting old friends for dinner. If you're lucky, hearty moose stew will be your first course, and Patricia O'Brien's homemade pickles would win a blue ribbon at any fair.

EN ROUTE TO CAPE RACE & ST. SHOTTS

As you continue south on Route 10, you pass through a string of fishing villages, each set in a cove with a protected harbor. Detour long enough to drive to the dockside of some. We like Aquaforte, for its fine views of little fishing shacks set on wooden piers, boats moored below them. Renew is not much larger now than it was in 1620, when the *Mayflower* stopped here to reprovision on its way to Plymouth, Massachusetts. You can pick up supplies at J&D Convenience Store, and then picnic at the lovely Chance Cove Provincial Park. On the site of an abandoned fishing settlement, the 25 campsites are open, close to the sea, never crowded, and free. You can watch gray and harbor seals at almost any time of year as you walk along the pebble beach. During spring and fall, the campground is a migratory stop on the Atlantic flyway. You can sign up for a bird and seal watching boat trip at the campground, or you can reserve a space through Southern Shore Eco Adventures (see Ferryland, above).

Cape Race, reached via a dirt road from Portugal Cove, is not far past the park. Cape Race Lighthouse, built in 1856 at the main transatlantic navigation point where ships bound for North American ports changed direction, overlooks an area grimly known as the graveyard of the Atlantic. From here and Chance Cove—and from Ferryland, as well—you can look out over waters literally strewn with sunken ships. Off these rocks some of history's most famous sea disasters occurred—the *City of Philadelphia* and the *Anglo Saxon* were lost, and, not much farther out, the *Titanic* met the fatal iceberg. Many ships lie in water about 20 fathoms deep, 2 to 5 miles (4 to 8km) offshore; **Chance Cove Ventures** (☎ 709/363-2257), will take you on a three-hour dive for $30.

Finding the Avalon Caribou Herd

The Avalon Wilderness Reserve comprises most of the center of southern Avalon. In the reserve lives one of Newfoundland's greatest natural treasures: the 13,000 caribou in the most southerly herd of its size found anywhere. In the winter, spring, and early part of summer, the best place to see the caribou is along Route 10 between Trepassy and Pete's River. If they are not right along the highway, take the road to St. Shotts and turn left following the sign to Cape Pine. It is often foggy along here, so be careful. Later in the summer, the caribou make their way north into the Avalon Reserve, and spotting them takes a little more effort. Ask locals where the herd has been seen recently. If they are not easy to find, we suggest joining an Eco Adventure Tour (see Ferryland, above), since the guide always knows where to find caribou.

At nearby **Mistaken Point Ecological Reserve** you can see fossils of the oldest multicelled marine life found in North America and the world's only deep-water fossils of their age—more than 620 million years old. Your chances of finding these greatly increase with a knowledgeable local guide (see Eco Adventures in Ferryland, above). No collecting is allowed.

Past Trepassey, a town struggling to survive the loss of the fisheries that supported this entire area, another cape reaches the southernmost point of the Avalon Peninsula. An unnumbered road leads to the lonely village of St. Shotts. There is no harbor here; the waters are so exposed that fishing boats had to be pulled onto the shore at night. On the way, you can take a further detour by dirt road to see lonely **Cape Pine Lighthouse.**

Route 10 swings north at Pete's River, and becomes Route 90, following a ridge between St. Mary's Bay and Holyrood Pond, a long saltwater lake. As you pass St. Vincent's, watch for whales, which often swim quite close to land in the deep offshore waters. From St. Catherine's, farther north, you can continue on Route 90, past Salmonier Nature Park, or turn west on Route 91 to explore Cape St. Mary's.

WHERE TO STAY & DINE ON THE SOUTHERN SHORE

The **Trepassy Motel and Restaurant,** on Route 10 (☎ 709/432-2808 or 709/432-2163), was completely renovated with all new beds in 1991. The 13-room is very comfortable and clean, with laundry facilities and complimentary coffee. Doubles are $59. The adjoining dining room, which overlooks the town and the bay (often through fog), is a local favorite for fresh seafood (a shrimp or scallop dinner is only $7.95) and roast beef dinners ($8.95). Burgers and sandwiches are served as well, and a children's menu offers eight complete dinners at $2.99. Full breakfast is about $5.

SALMONIER NATURE PARK

On the way back to St. John's on Route 90, **Salmonier Nature Park** (☎ 709/729-6974) is designed to give visitors a look at the province's wildlife—both flora and fauna—that they might miss seeing in the wild. Open noon to 8pm daily year-round, the park has moose, snowy owls, beavers, red foxes, caribou, bald eagles, the rare peregrine falcon, spruce grouse, ducks and geese, otters, and hare, all living in natural mini-environments. Roomy enclosures keep the animals and some of the birds from roaming outside the park. Visitors circulate among the enclosures on a self-guided 1-mile (2km) boardwalk and wood-chip nature trail through the forest and bog. You'll need between one and two hours to watch the moose doze or the beavers slap the pond with their broad tails.

CAPE ST. MARY'S

Another natural attraction awaits travelers who opt to turn west at St. Catherine's and head toward Cape St. Mary's. Instead of turning south on Route 92, continue on Route 91, along a little over 2 miles (4km) of unpaved road to The Cataracts, a small provincial park set around a deep gorge and waterfall. The road crosses the gorge, and a series of very steep stairs and bridges give views of it from all angles.

Cape St. Mary's is dear to the hearts of Newfoundlanders, in part because of a well-loved yet haunting homeland song, "Let Me Fish off Cape St. Mary's." The song speaks not only of the land, but of the tough breed of people who settled here, and their plight as the fisheries that support them have closed. The fisheries are the lifeblood of Newfoundland and Labrador since the first settlers arrived, and their closing has affected almost every aspect of life here. No place in the province is so far inland that it has not been touched by the fisheries. This Irish area, with green, fogswept pastures filled with sheep, is reminiscent of the country their ancestors left. The language and customs are richly Celtic, as is the hospitality. The scenery, especially along the western shore, is superb.

The big draw is the ✪ **Cape St. Mary's Ecological Reserve** and its sea birds. Every year, millions of sea birds return to land to breed, and more than 26,000 pairs come to Cape St. Mary's. The cliffs that rise more than 300 feet almost straight from the sea provide ideal nesting grounds, and a giant sea stack—a vertical island of rock only a few feet from the cliffs—has become the favored spot for gannets, forming the fourth (some say second) largest ganetry in North America. In May, June, and July, the cliffs are solid white with birds. You can view them at close range from a trail just opposite the sea stack. The sea stack is about a half-mile walk along the rim of the cliffs; the trail begins at the lighthouse and Visitors Center, which is open in the summer. It's worth going to the lighthouse for the views, even if you don't care a squawk about birds.

WHERE TO STAY & DINE

🅢 **Atlantica Inn & Restaurant.** Route 100. St. Bride's, NF A0B 2Z0. ☎ **709/337-2860** or 709/337-2861. 5 rms. TV TEL. $35–$40 double. AE, MC, V.

Three of the spotless motel rooms here have two double beds, and the other two have one double bed each. They are functional, with no frills, but quite comfortable. The adjoining restaurant is cheerful and the kitchen is open from 7am to 8pm, but, "We never turn anybody away hungry." You'll like Elizabeth, the owner, and her dry sense of humor, as well as her cooking. Dinners range from liver and onions ($6) to a seafood platter/steak combo ($16); sandwiches cost $2 to $5. The food's good, the price right, and it's the only act in town.

🅢 **Bird Island Resort.** Route 100, St. Bride's, NF, A0B 2Z0. ☎ **709/337-2450.** 20 units. TV TEL. $49 double, $54 efficiency, $85 suite. Children under 16 stay free. AE, ER, MC, V.

This newly built miniresort overlooks the sea and is close to the Ecological Reserve, with bright, modern, roomy units, and there's a kitchen for guests who don't have kitchens. Facilities include laundry, playground, barbecue pit, miniature golf, and a fitness room, plus the staff is accommodating. There's an adjacent convenience store, but no restaurant.

CONTINUING THE DRIVE ALONG THE WEST COAST

Return north up the west coast, where the road alternately climbs over tall, cliff-edged headlands and drops into beach-lined coves where little villages cluster. Pause at **Point La Haye,** a beach where early Basque fishermen dried their catch.

Placentia, founded as a colony in 1662, is a small town today, but was once the French capital of the province. **Castle Hill National Historic Park** represents this era in the stabilized ruins of the French fort that overlooks the town and harbor far below. From here, regular attacks were mounted against British forts in St. John's, but then a treaty gave Newfoundland to the British and Cape Breton Island to the French. From Castle Hill, it is a short distance to Argentia, terminus for Marine Atlantic's car-ferry to North Sydney, Nova Scotia. (See "Getting to Newfoundland," earlier in this chapter, for details about ferries.)

10 Labrador

Labrador may be sparsely settled, but it has been inhabited for thousands of years. The Innu (Indian) culture in Labrador goes back 8,000 years, and the Inuit (Eskimo) culture, 4,000 years.

The Vikings sighted Labrador in A.D. 986, but did not come ashore until 1010. Traces of the Vikings remain in the shape of "fairy holes," deep, cylindrical holes in the rocks, angled away from the sea, where they were thought to have moored their boats.

The 16th century brought the Basque whalers, as many as 2,000 of them in 20 galleons, and they returned to Europe with 20,000 barrels of whale oil. It has been said that the whale oil of Newfoundland and Labrador was as valuable to the Europeans as the gold of South America. Vestiges of a whaling station remain on Saddle Island, off the coast of Red Bay on the Labrador Straits. Next came the British and French fishermen, fur traders, and merchants, first summering then settling in Labrador in the 1700s. Many of the Europeans married Innu and Inuit women, but conflicts between Inuit whalers and the European settlers along the south coast prompted the Inuit communities to move to the far north, where they remain today.

Only 30,345 people live in Labrador: 13,000 in western Labrador, 8,000 in Happy Valley–Goose Bay, and the remaining people along the coast. Approximately four-fifths of those born here remain here, with strong ties to family and neighbors. These close-knit communities welcome visitors warmly.

Many visitors come here for the sport fishing of brook trout, Atlantic salmon, arctic char, ouananiche, lake trout, white fish, and northern pike. Others come for wilderness adventure, hiking, and camping under the undulating northern lights; still others simply curious about a remote part of the world want to meet the warm people who call it home.

The world's largest barren-ground caribou herd roams across Labrador and the fantastically old Laurentian Shield, which has apparently remained unchanged since long before any hooves set foot on this planet. It's possible that Labrador is the only such spot in the world, and that alone might make it worth a visit: to see what the world was like when life began.

For most visitors to the "Big Land," there are three major destinations: **Labrador West,** including Labrador City and Wabush, reached by train from Sept-Iles, Québec (pronounced "Set-*teel*") and by Highway 389, also from Québec; the **Labrador Straits,** with tiny fishing villages and the rushing Pinware River, reached by plane or ferry; and **Central Labrador,** the commercial and industrial hub.

The most scenic route to Labrador—and the only way to visit some of its outposts—is by the coastal ferry along "Iceberg Alley," named for the giant chunks of arctic ice that float past in spring and summer on the strong Labrador Current. This Marine Atlantic ferry, which carries cabin as well as day passengers, is the only means of transportation along the Atlantic coast of Labrador. It takes two weeks to make the entire round-trip from Red Bay to Nain, or 16 days if you start and return at Lewisporte in Newfoundland.

Details on obtaining advance planning information, getting there, and getting around are found at the beginning of this chapter.

ESCORTED TOURS & SPECIAL-INTEREST/ADVENTURE TOURS   Close to 50 fishing camps, operated by 26 outfitters, are scattered throughout Labrador, and Destination Labrador can supply a list (see "Exploring Newfoundland and Labrador," at the beginning of this chapter).

Labrador Scenic Ltd. (☎ 709/497-8326) offers week-long snowmobile tours into the wilderness, as well as summer tours and flights over the interior. **Tasiujatsoak Wilderness Camp** (☎ 613/238-8181; fax 613/234-1991), arranges seal-watching, canoeing, hiking, and camping trips accompanied by Inuit guides in Northern Labrador.

THE LABRADOR STRAITS

From St. Barbe, Newfoundland, the ferry's two trips a day are timed so visitors can spend a few hours and return on the same day, with time for a quick drive up to **Red Bay** and back. We think it's better to plan an overnight stay; then you'll have a chance to meet the people, who are among the most compelling reasons to visit. There's only one road through the area, linking eight outpost villages from L'Anse au Clair to Red Bay. It's a mere 50 miles (80km) long, so you can get to know the straits well in a couple of days.

The terrain is rugged, and the colors muted except for a vibrant stretch of green along the Pinware River. The few small houses are clustered close together; during the winter it's nice to have neighbors so nearby. Homes are often brightened up with "yard art"—replicas of windmills, wells, and churches.

In summer, some 2,000 icebergs float by the coast and whales breach and spout offshore. The landscape is covered with cotton grass, clover, partridgeberries, bakeapples, fireweed, buttercups, and bog laurel. The fog rolls in easily and stays a while or just as easily rolls out again. The capelin roll, too. The tiny migrating fish crash-land on the shore by the thousands during a week in late June or early July. Local residents crowd the beach to scoop up the fish and take them home to cook for supper.

The **Visitor Information Center** in the small, restored **St. Andrews Church** in L'Anse au Clair, the first town from the ferry, is open from June to August (☎ 709/931-2013). Note the quilt that is the size and shape of the church's original stained-glass window. The tourist association has developed several footpaths and trails in the area, so be sure to ask about them; also ask about the "fairy holes."

If you come in mid-August, attend the annual **Bakeapple Festival,** celebrating the berry that stars in the desserts of Newfoundland and Labrador.

EXPLORING THE LABRADOR STRAITS

Drive the "slow road" that connects the villages of the Labrador Straits. Traveling west to east, here is some of what you'll find along the way.

In L'Anse au Clair, **Moore's Handicrafts,** 8 Country Rd., just off Route 510 (☎ 709/931-2022), sells handmade summer and winter coats, traditional cassocks, moccasins, knitted items, handmade jewelry, and other crafts, as well as homemade jams. They also do traditional embroidery on Labrador cassocks and coats, and if you stop on the way north and choose your design, they finish it by the time you return to the ferry— even the same day. Prices are very reasonable. It's open daily, often until late.

Just outside L'Anse Amour (pop. 25), 12 miles (19km) from L'Anse au Clair, stop at the **Labrador Straits Museum** (☎ 313/271-1620). Two exhibit rooms focus mainly on the role of women in the history of the Labrador coast. Here also are photographs of the pilots who flew the first nonstop east to west transatlantic flight; they flew off course in April 1928 and landed on Greely Island, off the Labrador/Québec coast.

The **Point Amour Lighthouse** (1857), at the western entrance to the Strait of Belle Isle, is the tallest lighthouse in the Atlantic Provinces and the second tallest in all Canada. The walls of the slightly tapered, circular tower are $6^1/_2$ feet thick at the base. You'll have to climb 122 steps for the view. The dioptric lens was imported from Europe at a cost of $10,000, quite a sum for its day. The lighthouse, which kept watch for submarines during World War II, is still in use and has a lightkeeper. Under restoration, it will soon have interpretation center, but until then, the lighthouse keeper explains its history. It's open to the public June to mid-October from 8am to 5pm (☎ 709/927-5826). The lighthouse is a 2-mile drive from the main road.

In L'Anse au Loup ("Wolf's Cove"), 9 miles (14km) from L'Anse au Clair, a modest little cafe, **Beryl's Place,** overlooks the water. After you pass West St. Modeste, the road follows the scenic Pinware River, where the trees become noticeably taller. Along this stretch of road, you'll see glacial "erratics," boulders deposited by the melting ice cap. **Pinware Provincial Park,** 27 miles (43km) from L'Anse au Clair, has a beach, picnic area, and campsites. The 50-mile long Pinware River is known for salmon fishing.

The highway ends in **Red Bay.** In addition to the **Visitor Centre** (☎ 709/920-2197), the town has a restaurant, cabins, a craft shop, and an Interpretation Centre for **Saddle Island,** the scene of Basque whaling stations from the 16th century. Free transportation to archaeological sites on the island is available in summer Monday through Saturday from 9am to 4pm. Be sure to see the exhibits that tell the story of the Basque, North America's first whalers who arrived as early as the 11th century. There's also a model of a cooperage and the tryworks, where blubber was made into oil. You can see Saddle Island from the observation level on the third floor.

In the Red Bay area, you're likely to see "komatiks"—long, low wooden sleds used for transportation in winter. In the late 19th century and early 20th century, the komatiks were pulled by teams of huskies and were used to carry the mail. Today they are used to transport people (behind dogsleds or snowmobiles), on caribou hunts, and for hauling wood, cargo, and supplies.

WHERE TO STAY ALONG THE ROUTE

L'Anse Amour calls itself "the smallest community with the most to offer," and one of its best offerings is the **Davis Hospitality Home** (☎ 709/927-5690), which has three rooms sharing two baths. It overlooks the rocks, water, and beach. The hosts have lived here for 40 years, so they can tell you all about the place. A double bed is one room, a three-quarter bed in another. A light breakfast is included in the room rate; full breakfast and seafood supper are available on request, at an extra charge. A double is $36. From here, you can walk along a footpath to Point Amour Lighthouse.

Beachside Hospitality Home. 9 Lodge Rd., L'Anse au Clair, Labrador, A0K 3K0. ☎ **709/ 931-2662.** 6 rms (with shared bath). $38 double. Extra person $5. V.

A stay here is your best opportunity to meet a local family and learn firsthand about life in this region of Labrador. Yet there is privacy as well. Three bedrooms have a separate entrance and share two full baths. There is a whirlpool bath and guests have access to a telephone. Delicious home-cooked meals are available by arrangement or you can cook in the kitchen or outdoors on the grill. To get here, follow the red, white, and blue signs.

Northern Light Inn. L'Anse au Clair, Labrador, A0K 3K0. ☎ **709/931-2332.** Fax 709/931-2708. 28 rms, 1 suite, 5 housekeeping units. TV TEL. $65–$85 double. AE, DC, ER, MC, V.

The largest accommodation in the area, here since 1974, the Northern Light Inn is well set up for guests, with comfortable, well-maintained rooms, a gift shop, a friendly staff, and good home cooking.

The coffee shop, open from 8am to 11pm, serves strong coffee, soups, sandwiches, baskets of scallops, fried chicken, and pizza, from $2 to $9. In the adjacent Basque Dining Room, seafood is the specialty, with prices ranging from $2 to $5 for appetizers and $11 to $14 for main courses. The coffee shop doubles as a lounge.

WHERE TO DINE
Sea-View Restaurant. 35 Main St., Forteau. ☎ **709/931-2840.** Most items $2–$13. AE, MC. Summer daily 9am–11:30pm; rest of year Mon–Sat 9am–11:30pm, Sun noon–10pm. HOME COOKING.

This family style restaurant in Forteau, 8 miles from L'Anse au Clair, offers eat-in or takeout meals. Seafood dishes are the specialty; the $13 seafood basket is particularly popular. The fully licensed dining room is decorated with photographs of local scenes. There's an adjacent grocery store and bakery where you can buy homemade bread, peanut butter cookies, and much more. Across the road, the same management has four motel rooms, with television and telephone jack; two are efficiency units ($55 single, $65 double). It's 12 miles (19km) from Blanc Sablon.

LABRADOR WEST
The most affluent and industrialized part of Labrador, Labrador West lies on the Québec border and is home to the twin towns of **Wabush** and **Labrador City,** 4 miles (7km) apart. The two share many attractions, activities, and services. This region offers top-notch cross-country skiing and has hosted two World Cup events. Labrador West is also home to the largest open-pit iron ore mine in North America, which produces almost half of Canada's iron ore. For indoor activities, go to the **Labrador West Arts and Culture Centre,** which draws performers from throughout North America.

Labrador City or Wabush makes a good base for hiking, canoeing, and birding trips. Ask directions to **Crystal Falls,** where a half-mile hike takes you to the falls and a view over the city. You can also play 18 holes at the **Tamarack Golf Course,** or go windsurfing, scuba diving, or sailing on one of the many surrounding lakes. And, in the winter, go ski cross-country at **Meniheck Nordic Ski Club** (☎ 709/944-6339), a complete ski center with 40km of groomed trails in all skill levels.

The annual **Labrador 400 Sled Dog Race,** held here in March, draws about 25 teams from Canada and the United States, who match skills on 400 miles of challenging terrain.

Labrador City is the terminus of the **Québec North Shore and Labrador Railway (the QNS&L),** which departs from Sept-Iles, Québec, and is the only passenger train service in the entire province of Newfoundland and Labrador. The 8- to 10-hour trip covers 260 miles, across 19 bridges, 11 tunnels, along riverbanks, through forests, and past rapids, mountains, and waterfalls, and finally through subarctic vegetation. In summer a highlight is the vintage dome car (1958) with sofa seats that was once part of the Wabash Cannonball (☎ 418/968-7805 in Québec; 709/944-8205 in Newfoundland and Labrador).

CENTRAL LABRADOR

From the North West River and Mud Lake to the Mealy Mountains, a visit to the interior of Labrador is filled with vivid images of water and spruce forests that seem to go on forever. Many believe that Lake Melville is "Markland, the land of forests" in the Viking sagas.

Outdoor activities include berry-picking from August to the first snowfall of November, excellent sportfishing, canoeing the **Churchill River,** kayaking the rapid-filled **Kenamou River,** and snowmobiling.

The Montagnais band of Innu live near Happy Valley–Goose Bay, in Sheshatshit, along with the descendants of English, French, and Scottish settlers. *Them Days* quarterly magazine, which chronicles the stories and memories of Labrador's people, published in Happy Valley–Goose Bay, is sold everywhere.

To take a little bit of Labrador home with you, stop by **Labrador Crafts and Supplies,** 367 Hamilton River Rd., in Happy Valley–Goose Bay. The largest craft store in Labrador, it sells Innu tea dolls, grasswork, soapstone carvings, Labradorite jewelry, hooked rugs, and parkas.

WHERE TO STAY & DINE

Convenient to the airport and TransLab Highway, and marine dock, the full-service **Labrador Inn** (☎ 709/896-3351 or 800/563-2763) provides comfort and hospitality. The well-kept modern building has 74 rooms; doubles are $64 to $110. Its restaurant serves traditional Canadian cuisine with some local dishes, including game meats and, of course, seafood.

THE NORTH COAST

Take the Marine Atlantic coastal ferry northward to enjoy the remote beauty of Labrador's North Coast, its magnificent fjords, and Innu and Inuit culture and crafts. The ferry calls on small communities here as far north as Nain.

Beginning in 1771, Moravian missionaries arrived, bringing with them prefabricated buildings from Germany, some of which are still standing. The **Hopedale Mission** (1782) is the oldest wooden-frame building east of Québec and a National Historic Site. **Piulimatsivik-Nain Museum,** in Nain, displays a fine collection of Moravian mission and Inuit artifacts, housed in one of the mission buildings. The free museum is open by appointment year-round (☎ 709/922-2842).

The Inuit live along the North Coast, in Makkovik, Rigolet, Hopedale, and Nain, while the Naskapi band of Innu are in Davis Inlet and in central Labrador, in Sheshatshit. They continue to fish, hunt, and carry on many aspects of their traditional culture.

Skilled outdoor enthusiasts love the North Coast for hiking, sea kayaking, camping, climbing in the Torngat Mountains, skiing, ice climbing, snowmobiling, and dog sledding.

WHERE TO STAY & DINE

In Nain, there's the **Atsanik Lodge** (☎ 709/922-2101). It's a small hotel (nine rooms), but then again, Nain isn't very big either. Doubles are $84 for a clean and comfortable room. The dining room serves traditional fare, with many seafood dishes.

8 Montréal

by Herbert Bailey Livesey

Herbert Livesey has written about travel and food
for many magazines, including *Travel and Leisure,*
Food and Wine, and *Playboy,* and is the author
or co-author of several guidebooks, including
Frommer's Walking Tours: Spain's Favorite Cities.

The distinct cultures that inhabit Canada have been called the "Twin
Solitudes." One, English and Calvinist in origin, is portrayed as staid,
smug, and work-obsessed. The other, French and Catholic, is more
creative and lighthearted—inclined to see pleasure as the purpose of
labor, or so goes the stereotype. These two peoples live side by side
throughout Québec and the nine provinces of English Canada, but
the blending occurs in a particularly intense fashion in Québec
province's largest city, Montréal. French speakers, known as
Francophones, constitute 66% of the city's population, while most
of the rest of its residents speak English. While both groups are
decidedly North American, they are about as much alike as François
Mitterand and Margaret Thatcher.

There is an impression, buttressed by a recent rash of *Vente* ("For
Sale") signs, that Montréal is in the midst of a steep decline. American expatriates I know report that a bleak mood prevails, brought
about, they believe, by a lingering recession and uncertainty over the
future. There is a large measure of truth in this observation. After all,
it is possible that Québec may choose to fling itself into independence, an event that could lead to Anglo flight and a loss of federal
subsidies—even outright civil war.

But to many American city dwellers, Montréal might well seem
an urban paradise. The subway system, the Metro, is modern and
swift. Streets are clean and safe. There were only 52 homicides in
Montréal in 1994, compared to the hundreds of murders that occur
annually in every American city of comparable size. Montréal's best
restaurants are the equal of their south-of-the-border compatriots in
almost every way, yet they are as much as 30% or 40% cheaper. And,
the government gives visitors back most of the taxes they collect.

Yet the defining dialectic of Canadian life is language, the thorny
issue that might yet tear the country apart. It manifests itself in the
assumption of many Québécois that a separate state is the only way
to maintain their culture in the face of the Anglophone ocean that
surrounds them. The role of Québec within the Canadian federation
is the most debated and volatile issue in Canadian politics. People
talk about separation in Québec as often as those elsewhere discuss
the weather. In bars and around kitchen tables, the same questions
continue to be voiced, with numbing regularity. Would a politically

independent Québec continue to share a common currency, a common central bank, and a tariff-free relationship with the rest of Canada? Would the Canadian-U.S. Free Trade agreement be extended to an independent Québec? Would the Atlantic Provinces, cut off from the rest of Canada, apply to the United States for statehood?

There are reasons for the intransigence of the Québécois that go back two centuries. After "The Conquest" (as French speakers often call it), the English made a few concessions to French-Canadian pride, including allowing them a Gallic version of jurisprudence. But a kind of linguistic racism prevailed, with wealthy Scottish and English bankers and merchants ensuring that French-Canadians were repeatedly denied access to the upper echelons of business and government. Intentionally or thoughtlessly, Anglophones lowered an opaque ceiling on Francophone advancement.

Resentment over this treatment festered for years, and in the 1960s, the Québécois began to assert their pride in their French roots and culture. This fueled a burgeoning nationalism, unfortunately punctuated by a series of violent extremist acts. By 1976, mainstream sentiments of the French-speaking majority in the province resulted in the election of the separatist Parti Québécois. Its leader, René Lévesque, promoted a referendum on sovereignty in 1980, but the measure was defeated.

Federalists later attempted to assuage the Québécois sensitivities with formal recognition of the province as a "distinct society." Those efforts failed, leading with glacial certainty to the sovereignty referendum of October 30, 1995. That vote went in favor of the pro-unity camp, but the issue was hardly resolved. The thread-thin margin of barely 1% ensured only that heated debate, ideological posturing, and extended negotiations will continue for years to come.

None of this fractious history should deter visitors, however. The Québécois are gracious hosts. While Montréal may be the largest French-speaking city outside Paris, most Montréalers grow up speaking both French and English and thus switch effortlessly from one to the other as the situation dictates. Telephone operators go from French to English the instant they hear an English word from the other party, as do most store clerks, waitstaff, and hotel staff. This is less true in country villages and in Québec City, but there is virtually no problem that can't be solved with a few French words, some expressive gestures, and a little goodwill.

AN IMPORTANT NOTE ON PRICES   Unless stated otherwise, **the prices cited in this guide are given in Canadian dollars,** which is good news for U.S. travelers because the Canadian dollar is worth 25% less than the American dollar but buys nearly as much. As we go to press, $1 Canadian is worth U.S. 75¢, which means that your $100 a night hotel room will cost only U.S. $75, and your $6 breakfast costs only U.S. $4.50. Remember, though, that taxes in Canada are substantial.

1 Orientation

ARRIVING

BY PLANE   Montréal's two international airports, Dorval and Mirabel, are served by most of the world's major airlines. All the major car-rental agencies have desks at the airports.

By far the greatest number of visitors fly into Dorval from other parts of North America on **Air Canada** (☎ 800/776-3000), **American Airlines** (☎ 800/433-7300), **Canadian Airlines International** (☎ 800/426-7000), **Continental** (☎ 800/525-0280), or **Delta** (☎ 800/241-4141). In the United States, Air Canada flies out of New York (Newark and LaGuardia), Miami, Tampa, Chicago, Los Angeles, and San Francisco. Other carriers that serve Montréal include **United Airlines** (☎ 800/241-6522), **USAir** (☎ 800/428-4322), **Air France** (☎ 800/237-2747), and **British Airways** (☎ 800/247-9297). Regional airlines, such as **Air Atlantic, American Eagle,** and **Inter-Canadian,** also serve the city. From Dorval it takes about 30 minutes to get downtown.

Travelers arriving from Europe and other countries outside North America arrive at Mirabel. The ride downtown from Mirabel takes about 45 minutes.

BY CAR   Interstate 87 runs due north from New York City to link up with Canada's Autoroute 15, and the entire 400-mile journey is on expressways.

From Boston, I-93 north joins I-89 just south of Concord, New Hampshire. At White River Junction you can continue north on I-89 to Lake Champlain, crossing the lake by roads and bridges to join I-87 and Canada Autoroute 15, or you can pick up I-91 at White River Junction to go due north toward Sherbrooke, Québec. At the border I-91 becomes Canada Route 55, and joins Route 10 through Estrie to Montréal.

The Trans-Canada Highway runs right through the city, connecting both ends of the country.

The distance from Boston to Montréal is approximately 320 miles, from Toronto, 335 miles (540km), and from Ottawa, 120 miles (190km). Once you're in Montréal, Québec City is an easy three-hour drive away.

See also "Driving Rules," in Section 2, "Getting Around," later in this chapter.

BY TRAIN   For VIA Rail information from the United States, call 800/561-3949. Montréal is a major terminus on Canada's VIA Rail network, with its station at 935 rue de la Gauchetière ouest (☎ 514/871-1331). The city is served by comfortable VIA Rail trains—some equipped with dining cars, sleeping cars, and cellular telephones—from other cities in Canada. There is scheduled service to and from Québec City via Trois-Rivières, and to and from Ottawa, Toronto, Winnipeg, and points west.

Amtrak (☎ 800/872-7245) runs one train daily to Montréal from Washington, New York, and intermediate stops. The *Adirondack* takes about 10-plus hours, if all goes well, but delays aren't unusual. Passengers from Chicago can get to Montréal most directly by taking Amtrak to Toronto, then switching to VIA Rail.

Seniors 62 and older are eligible for a 15% discount on some Amtrak trains on the U.S. segment of the trip. VIA Rail also has senior discounts.

Don't forget to bring along proof of citizenship (a passport or birth certificate) for passing through Customs.

BY BUS   Montréal's main bus terminal is the **Terminus Voyageur,** 505 bd. de Maisonneuve est (☎ 514/842-2281). The **Voyageur** company operates buses between here and all parts of Québec, with frequent runs through the Eastern Townships to Sherbrooke, to the various villages in the Laurentides, and to Québec City. Morning, noon, early afternoon, and midnight buses cover the distance between Toronto and Montréal in about seven hours.

From Boston or New York there is daily bus service to Montréal on **Greyhound/ Trailways** (☎ 800/231-2222). The trip from Boston takes about eight hours; from New York City, with five buses daily, it takes nine hours.

VISITOR INFORMATION

Québec tourism authorities produce volumes of detailed and highly useful publications, and they're easy to obtain by mail, phone, or in person. To contact **Tourisme**

Québec, write C.P. 979, Montréal, PQ, H3C 2W3 or call ☎ 800/363-7777, operator 806 (within the Montréal area, call ☎ 514/873-2015).

The main information center for visitors in Montréal is the large and efficiently organized **Infotouriste,** at 1001 rue du Square-Dorchester, between rues Peel and Metcalfe in the downtown hotel and business district. The office is open from June to early September, from 8:30am to 7:30pm; early September to May from 9am to 6pm. Its bilingual staff can help with questions about the entire province, as well as Montréal.

The city has its own **information bureau** at 174 rue Notre-Dame (☎ 514/871-1595), at the corner of rue place Jacques-Cartier. The hours from Easter to mid-October are 9am to 7pm; mid-October to Easter, it's open Thursday through Sunday from 9am to 5pm.

CITY LAYOUT

For the duration of a visit, it makes sense to accept local directional convention. The city borders the St. Lawrence River. As far as its citizens are concerned, that's south, looking toward the United States, although the river in fact runs more nearly north and south, not east and west. For that reason, it has been observed that Montréal is the only city in the world where the sun rises in the north. Don't fight it: Face the river. That's south. Turn around. That's north.

When examining a map of the city, note that such prominent avenues as Ste-Catherine and René-Lévesque are said to run "east" and "west"; the dividing line is boulevard St-Laurent, which runs "north" and "south." To ease confusion, the directions given below conform to local tradition, since they are the ones that will be given by natives.

MAIN ARTERIES & STREETS In downtown Montréal, the principal streets running east-west include boulevard René-Lévesque, rue Ste-Catherine, boulevard de Maisonneuve, and rue Sherbrooke. Prominent north-south arteries include rue Crescent, rue McGill, rue St-Denis, and boulevard St-Laurent, the line of demarcation between east and west Montréal (most of the downtown area of interest to tourists and businesspeople lies to the west). Near Mont-Royal Park, north of the downtown area, major streets are avenue du Mont-Royal and avenue Laurier. In Old Montréal, rue St-Jacques, rue Notre-Dame, and rue St-Paul are the major streets, along with rue de la Commune, which hugs the St. Lawrence River.

FINDING AN ADDRESS Boulevard St-Laurent is the dividing line between east and west ("est" and "ouest") in Montréal. There's no equivalent division for north and south. Numbers start at the river and climb from there, just as the topography does. For instance, if you're driving north along boulevard St-Laurent and pass number 500, that's Old Montréal, near rue Notre-Dame; no. 1100 is near boulevard René-Lévesque, no. 1500 is near boulevard de Maisonneuve, and no. 3400 is near rue Sherbrooke. Even numbers are on the west side of north-south streets and the south side of east-west streets; odd numbers are on the east and north sides, respectively. For more help, check the handy "Address Locator" map in the free Montréal Tourist Guide, available everywhere.

In earlier days, Montréal was split ethnically between those who spoke English, centered in the city's western regions, and those who spoke French, concentrated to the east. Things still sound more French when you walk from west to east. While boulevard St-Laurent is the east-west dividing line for the city's street numbering system, the spiritual split comes farther west, at about avenue de Bleury/avenue de Parc.

MAPS   Good street plans are found inside the free tourist guide supplied by the Greater Montréal Convention and Tourism Bureau and distributed widely throughout the city. The bureau also provides a large, foldout city map for free.

NEIGHBORHOODS IN BRIEF

Downtown   This area contributes the most striking elements of Montréal's dynamic skyline and contains the main railroad station, as well as most of its luxury and first-class hotels, principal museums, corporate headquarters, and largest department stores. Loosely bounded by rue Sherbrooke to the north, boulevard René-Lévesque to the south, boulevard St-Laurent to the east, and rue Drummond to the west, it incorporates the neighborhood known as "The Golden Square Mile," an Anglophone district once characterized by dozens of mansions erected by wealthy Scottish and English merchants and industrialists. Many of these stately homes were torn down after World War II to make room for skyscrapers, but some remain, often converted to institutional use. At the northern edge of the downtown area is the handsome urban campus of McGill University.

The Underground City   In the long Montréal winter, people escape down escalators and stairways into *la ville souterraine,* what amounts to a parallel subterranean universe. Down there, in a controlled climate that is forever spring, it is possible to arrive at the railroad station, check into a hotel, go out for lunch at any of hundreds of fast-food counters and full-service restaurants, see a movie, attend a concert, conduct business, go shopping, and even take a swim—all without unfurling an umbrella or donning an overcoat. This "city" evolved when major building developments in the downtown area such as Place Ville-Marie, Place Bonaventure, Complexe Desjardins, Palais des Congrès, and Place des Arts put their below-street levels to profitable use, leasing space for shops and other purposes. Over time, in fits and starts and with no master plan in place, these spaces connected with Metro stations and with each other. It became possible to ride long distances and walk the shorter ones, through mazes of corridors, tunnels, and plazas. Without the convenience of a logical street grid, the area can be confusing to navigate at times. There are plenty of signs, but make careful note of landmarks at key corners as you make your way and expect to get lost anyway.

Rue Crescent   One of Montréal's major dining and nightlife districts lies in the western shadow of the massed phalanxes of downtown skyscrapers. It holds hundreds of restaurants, bars, and clubs of all styles between Sherbrooke and René-Lévesque, centering on rue Crescent and spilling over onto neighboring streets. The raucous party atmosphere never quite fades, building to crescendos as weekends approach, especially in warm weather, when its largely 20- and 30-something denizens spill out into sidewalk cafes and onto balconies.

Vieux-Montréal   The city was born here in 1642, down by the river at Pointe-à-Callière, and today activity centers around place Jacques-Cartier, especially in summer, where cafe tables line narrow terraces and sun worshipers, flower sellers, itinerant artists, and strolling tourists congregate. The area is larger than it might seem at first, bounded on the north by rue St-Antoine, once the "Wall Street" of Montréal and still home to many banks, and on the south by the recently developed Old Port, a linear park bordering rue de la Commune that gives access to the River and provides welcome breathing room for cyclists, in-line skaters, and picnickers. To the east, Old Montréal is contained by rue Berri, and to the west by rue McGill. Several small but intriguing museums are housed in historic buildings, and the architectural heritage of the district has been substantially preserved, its restored

18th- and 19th-century structures adapted for use as shops, studios, cafes, bars, offices, and apartments.

Latin Quarter   Boulevard St-Denis, from rue Ste-Catherine to rue de Bullion, running from downtown to the Plateau Mont-Royal section, is the thumping central artery of Montréal's Latin Quarter, thick with cafes, bistros, offbeat shops, and lively nightspots. It is to Montréal what the boulevard St-Germain is to Paris, and indeed it isn't difficult to imagine that you've landed on the Left Bank when you're strolling around here. At the southern end of St-Denis, near the concrete campus of the Université du Québec à Montréal, the avenue is decidedly student oriented, with alternative rock issuing from the inexpensive bars and boîtes in which students swap philosophical insights and telephone numbers. Farther north, above Sherbrooke, a raffish quality persists along the facing rows of three- and-four story rowhouses and the average age of residents and visitors lifts past 30. Prices are higher, too, and some of the city's better restaurants have located here.

Plateau Mont-Royal   Due north of the downtown area, this may be the part of the city where Montréalers feel most at home—away from the chattering pace of downtown and the crowds of heavily touristed Vieux Montréal. Bounded by boulevard St-Joseph to the north, rue Sherbrooke to the south, avenue Papineau to the east, and rue St-Dominique to the west, it has a throbbing ethnicity that fluctuates in tone and direction with each new surge in immigration. St-Denis (see above) runs the length of the district, but parallel St-Laurent owns the more polyglot flavor. Known to all as "The Main," it was once the boulevard first encountered by foreigners tumbling off ships at the waterfront. They simply shouldered their belongings and walked north on St-Laurent, peeling off into adjoining streets when they heard familiar tongues, saw people who looked like them, and smelled the drifting aromas of food they once cooked in the old country. New arrivals still come here to start their lives again, creating a patchwork of colors and cultures representing nations of every inhabited continent. Without its people and their diverse interests, St-Laurent would be just another paper-strewn urban eyesore. But these ground-floor windows are filled with glistening golden chickens, collages of shoes and pastries and aluminum cookware, curtains of sausages, and the daringly farfetched garments of Montréal's active fashion industry. Many warehouses and former tenements have been converted to house this panoply of shops, bars, and low-cost eateries, with their often garish signs drawing the eye from the still-dilapidated upper stories.

Prince Arthur and Duluth   These two essentially pedestrian streets connect boulevard St-Laurent with St-Denis, eight blocks to the east. The livelier rue Prince-Arthur is lined with ethnic restaurants, primarily Greek and Portuguese, but with Asian places looking to join them. Mimes, jugglers, and street musicians try to cajole passersby into parting with their spare change. Four blocks north of rue Prince-Arthur, Duluth is fairly quiet in the blocks near St-Laurent, but more engaging near St-Denis. The mix of cuisines is much like that on Prince-Arthur. Tourists are evident in greater numbers on Prince Arthur, many of them attracted by menus promising bargain lobster dinners for less than $10 at some times of the year.

Parc du Mont-Royal   Not many cities have a mountain at their core. In actuality, it's not a mountain, but rather a high hill. Still, Montréal is named for it—the "Royal Mountain"—and one of Montréal's unique urban pleasures is to drive, walk, or take a horse-drawn calèche to the top of it for an unparalleled view of the city, the island, and the St. Lawrence River, especially at dusk. The park, which encompasses the mountain, was designed by the famous American landscape architect Frederick Law Olmsted, whose other credits include New York's Central Park. On its far slope are two cemeteries, one Anglophone, one Francophone, silent reminders of the linguistic and cultural division that persists in the city. With its skating ponds, hiking and running trails, and even a short ski run, the park is well used by Montréalers, who refer to it simply as "the mountain."

Chinatown   Just north of Vieux Montréal, south of boulevard René-Lévesque, and centered on the intersection of rue Clark and rue de la Gauchetière (pedestrianized at this point), Montréal's pocket Chinatown appears to be mostly restaurants and a tiny park, with the occasional grocery, laundry, church, and small business. For the benefit of outsiders, most signs are in French or English as well as Chinese. Community spirit is strong—it's had to be to resist the bulldozers of redevelopment—and Chinatown's inhabitants remain faithful to their traditions despite the encroaching modernism all around them. In recent years, concerned investors from Hong Kong, wary of their uncertain future with mainland China, have poured money into the neighborhood, producing signs that its shrinkage has been halted, even reversed. The area is colorful and deserves a look, although the best Chinese restaurants are actually in other parts of the city.

The Gay Village   The city's gay enclave runs east along rue Ste-Catherine from rue St-Hubert to rue Papineau. A small but vibrant district, it is filled with clothing stores, small eateries, a bar/disco complex in a former post office building, and the Gay and Lesbian Community Centre, at 1355 rue Ste-Catherine est.

Île Ste-Hélène   Île Ste-Hélène (St. Helen's Island) in the St. Lawrence River was altered extensively to become the site of Expo '67, Montréal's very successful world's fair. In the four years before Expo opened, construction crews reshaped the island and doubled its surface area with landfill, then went on to create beside it an island that hadn't existed before, Île Notre-Dame. Much of the earth needed to do this was dredged up from the bottom of the St. Lawrence River, and 15 million tons of rock from the excavation of the Metro and the Décarie Expressway were carried in by truck. Bridges were built and 83 pavilions constructed. When Expo closed, the city government preserved the site and a few of the exhibition buildings. Parts were used for Olympic Games events in 1976, and today the island is home to Montréal's popular new casino and an amusement park, La Ronde.

2 Getting Around

For a city of more than a million inhabitants, Montréal is remarkably easy to get to know and to negotiate. The two airports that serve it are nearby (one is only 14 miles away), and, once you're in town, the Metro is fast and efficient. Of course, walking is the best way to get to know this vigorous, multidimensional city.

BY PUBLIC TRANSPORTATION

Dial "AUTOBUS" (☎ 514/288-6287) for information about the Metro and city buses.

BY METRO   For speed and economy, nothing beats Montréal's Metro system for getting around. Clean, relatively quiet trains whisk passengers through an ever-expanding network of underground tunnels, with 65 stations at present and more scheduled to open. Single rides cost $1.75 (90¢ for children); a strip of six tickets costs $7 ($3.25 for children). You might save money by buying the one-day tourist pass for $5, or the three-day pass for $12.

Buy tickets at the booth in any station, then slip one into the slot in the turnstile to enter the system. Take a transfer (*correspondence*) from the machine just inside the

Montréal Métro

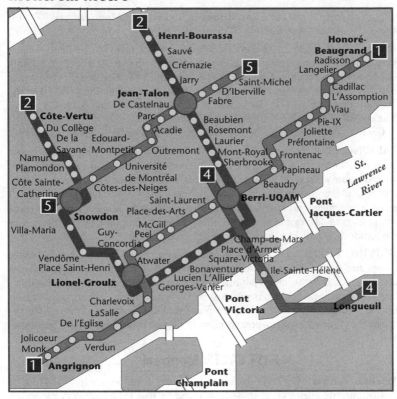

turnstiles of every station to be able to transfer from a train to a bus at any other Metro station for no extra fare. Remember to take the transfer ticket at the station where you first enter the system. (When starting a trip by bus and intending to continue on the Metro, ask the bus driver for a transfer.) Most connections from one Metro line to another can be made at the Berri-UQAM (Université de Québec à Montréal), Jean-Talon, and Snowdon stations. The Metro runs from 5:30am to 12:30am on weekdays and until 1am on Friday and Saturday.

BY BUS   Buses cost the same as Metro trains, and Metro tickets are good on buses, too. Exact change is required to pay bus fares in cash. While routes extend across the entire city, buses do not run as frequently or as swiftly as the Metro.

BY TAXI

There are plenty of taxis in Montréal run by several different private companies. Cabs come in a variety of colors and styles, so their principal distinguishing feature is the plastic sign on the roof. At night, it is illuminated when the cab is available. Fares aren't cheap. Most short rides from one point to another downtown cost about $5. Members of hotel and restaurant staffs can call cabs, many of which are dispatched by radio. They line up outside most large hotels or can be hailed on the street.

BY CAR

The 24-hour hotline for emergency service provided by the **Canadian Automobile Association (CAA),** which is affiliated with AAA, is ☎ 514/861-7575 in Montréal.

For information on **road conditions** in and around Montréal, call ☎ 514/ 636-3026; outside Montréal, call ☎ 514/636-3248.

RENTALS **Budget** has a convenient location in Montréal's Gare Centrale, the railroad station at 895 rue de la Gauchetière ouest (☎ 514/937-9121 or 800/268-8900). Other agencies include **Avis,** 1225 rue Metcalfe (☎ 514/866-7906 or 800/ 879-2847); **Hertz,** 1475 rue Aylmer (☎ 514/842-8537 or 800/263-0600); **Thrifty,** 1600 rue Berri, Suite 9 (☎ 514/845-5954 or 800/367-2277); and **Tilden,** 1200 rue Stanley (☎ 514/878-2771 or 800/387-4747).

Gas in Québec is expensive. It costs about $25 to fill a tank with unleaded gasoline.

PARKING Parking can be difficult on the heavily trafficked streets of downtown Montréal. There are plenty of parking meters, with varying hourly rates. (Look around before walking off without paying. Meters are set well back from the curb so they won't be buried by plowed snow in winter.) Most downtown shopping complexes have underground parking lots, as do the big hotels. Some of the hotels don't charge extra to take cars in and out of their garages during the day, which can save money for those who plan to do a lot of sightseeing by car.

DRIVING RULES The limited-access expressways in Québec are called autoroutes, and speed limits and distances are given in kilometers. Most highway signs are in French only, although Montréal's autoroutes and bridges often bear dual-language signs. Seat belt use is required by law while driving or riding in a car in Québec. Turning right on a red light is prohibited in Montréal and throughout the province of Québec, except where specifically allowed by an additional green arrow.

FAST FACTS: Montréal

American Express Offices of the American Express Travel Service are at 1141 rue de Maisonneuve ouest (☎ 514/384-3640), and La Baie (The Bay), 585 rue Ste-Catherine ouest (☎ 514/281-4777). For lost or stolen cards, call 800/268-9824.

Currency Exchange There are currency exchange offices at the airports, in the train station, in and near Infotouriste at Dorchester Square, and near Notre-Dame cathedral at 86 rue Notre-Dame. The Bank of America Canada, 1230 Peel, also offers foreign exchange services, Monday to Friday from 8:30am to 5:30pm, and Saturday from 9am to 5pm.

Doctors and Dentists The front desk at hotels can contact a doctor quickly. If it's not an emergency, call your consulate and ask for a recommendation. Even if the consulate is closed, a duty officer should be available to help. For dental information, call the 24-hour hotline at ☎ 514/342-4444. In an emergency, dial 911.

Drugstores (Late-Night Pharmacies) Open 24 hours a day, 365 days a year, Pharmaprix has fairly convenient locations at 901 rue Ste-Catherine est at rue St-André (☎ 514/842-4915) and 5122 côte-des-Neiges at rue Queen Mary (☎ 514/ 738-8464).

Embassies and Consulates The American consulate general is at 1155 rue St-Alexandre (☎ 514/398-9695). Great Britain has a consulate general at 1155 rue University, Suite 901 (☎ 514/866-5863). Other English-speaking countries have their consulates in Ottawa.

Emergencies Dial 911 for the police, firefighters, or an ambulance.

Hospitals Hotel staffs and consulates can offer advice and information. Hospitals with emergency rooms are Hôpital général de Montréal (☎ 514/937-6011) and Hôpital Royal Victoria (☎ 514/842-1231). Hôpital de Montréal pour enfants (☎ 514/934-4400) is a children's hospital with a poison center. Other prominent hospitals are Hôtel-Dieu (☎ 514/843-2611) and Hôpital Notre-Dame (☎ 514/876-6421).

Liquor Laws All hard liquor in Québec is sold through official government stores operated by the Québec Société des Alcools. Wine and beer can be bought in grocery stores and supermarkets. The legal drinking age in the province is 18.

Newspapers and Magazines Montréal's prime English-language newspaper is the *Montréal Gazette*. Most large newsstands and those in the larger hotels also carry the *Wall Street Journal, The New York Times, USA Today,* and the *International Herald Tribune*. So do the several branches of the Maison de la Presse Internationale, one of which is at 550 rue Ste-Catherine ouest, and the large bookstore, Champigny, at 4380 rue St-Denis. For information about current happenings in Montréal, pick up the Friday or Saturday editions of the *Gazette,* or the free monthly booklet called *Montréal Scope,* available in some shops and many hotel lobbies.

Pets Dogs and cats can be taken into Québec, but the Canadian Customs authorities at the frontier will want to see a rabies vaccination certificate less than three years old signed by a licensed veterinarian. If a pet is less than three months old and obviously healthy, the certificate isn't likely to be required. Check with U.S. Customs about bringing the pet back into the States. Most hotels in Montréal do not accept pets.

Photographic Needs Prices for film and other camera supplies are similar to those in the United States, and many shops sell supplies. One specialist is Photo Service Ltée, 222 rue Notre-Dame ouest (☎ 514/849-2291), in Old Montréal. They carry film, batteries, equipment, and accessories, and while they do not do repairs on premises, they can send cameras out for service.

Police Dial 911 for the police.

Post Office The main post office is at 1250 rue University, near Ste-Catherine (☎ 514/395-4539). Hours are 8am to 6pm on weekdays. A convenient post office in Vieux-Montréal is at 155 rue St-Jacques (St-François-Xavier).

Taxes Most goods and services in Canada are taxed 7% by the federal government. On top of that, the province of Québec adds an additional 6.5% tax on goods and services, including those provided by hotels. In Québec, the federal tax appears on the bill as the TPS (elsewhere in Canada, it's called the goods and services tax [GST]), and the provincial tax is known as the TVQ. Tourists may receive a rebate on both the federal and provincial tax on items they have purchased but not used in Québec, as well as on lodging. To take advantage of this, request the necessary forms at duty free shops and hotels and submit them, with the original receipts, within a year of the purchase. Contact the Canadian consulate or Québec tourism office for up-to-the-minute information about taxes and rebates.

Telephones The telephone system, operated by Bell Canada, resembles the American system. All operators (dial "0" to get one) speak French and English, and respond in the appropriate language as soon as callers speak to them. Pay phones in Québec require 25¢ for a three-minute local call. Directory information calls (dial 411) are free of charge.

Television Montréal has two English-language channels, 6 and 12, and cable-equipped TVs also receive some American stations with network affiliations, including CBS from Burlington, Vermont (Channel 3); NBC from Plattsburgh,

New York (Channel 5); and ABC from Burlington, Vermont (Channel 22).

Time   Montréal, Québec City, and the Laurentians are all in the eastern time zone. Daylight saving time is observed as in the United States, moving clocks ahead one hour in the spring and back one hour in the fall.

Transit Information   Dial "AUTOBUS" (☎ 514/288-6287) for information about the Metro and city buses. For airport transportation, Autocar Connaisseur/ Gray Line (☎ 514/934-1222).

Useful Telephone Numbers   For Alcoholics Anonymous, call 514/376-9230; 24-hour pharmacy, 514/527-8827; Gay and Lesbian Association of UQAM, 514/987-3039; Sexual Assault Center (a 24-hour crisis line), 514/934-4504; the suicide action line, 514/723-4000; lost or stolen VISA cards, 800/361-0152 (for American Express, see above); Canada Customs, 514/283-2953; U.S. Customs, 514/636-3875; and for road conditions in and around Montréal, call 514/636-3026.

3 Accommodations

Montréal hoteliers make everyone welcome, partly because there are more hotel rooms in the city than can be filled with certainty throughout the year. With that competition, and the robust value of the U.S. dollar in relation to its Canadian counterpart, this is the place to splurge, or at least step up in class.

Except in bed-and-breakfasts, visitors can almost always count on special discounts and package deals, especially on weekends, when the hotels' business clients have packed their bags and gone home.

Choose the familial embrace of a B&B and expect to get to know a Montréaler or two and to pay relatively little for that privilege. By the nature of the trade, they are among the most outgoing and knowledgeable guides one might ask. A couple of independent bed-and-breakfasts are recommended below, but for more information about other downtown B&Bs, contact **Relais Montréal Hospitalité,** 3977 av. Laval (☎ 514/287-9635; fax 514/287-1007), or **Bed and Breakfast Downtown Network,** 3458 av. Laval, at rue Sherbrooke (☎ 514/289-9749 or 800/267-5180). They are referral agencies for homeowners who have one or more rooms available for guests. Accommodations and individual rules vary significantly, so ask all pertinent questions up front, such as whether children are welcome, or smoking is allowed, or whether all guests share bathrooms. Deposits are usually required, with the balance payable upon arrival.

Nearly all hotel staff members, from front desk personnel to the porters, are reassuringly bilingual. Busiest times are in July and August, especially during the several summer festivals, and during annual holidays (Canadian or American). At those times, book well in advance, especially if special rates or packages are desired. Most other times, expect to find plenty of available rooms.

The rates given below are in Canadian dollars and do not include federal or provincial taxes. All rooms have a private bath unless otherwise noted. In the top two categories, hair dryers, cable color TV, and in-room movies are to be expected, as are restaurants, bars, meeting rooms, and parking garages.

DOWNTOWN
VERY EXPENSIVE
Bonaventure Hilton International. 1 place Bonaventure (Mansfield), Montréal, PQ, H5A 1E4. ☎ **514/878-2332,** 800/268-9275 in Canada, or 800/445-8667 in the U.S. Fax 514/878-0028. 375 rms, 18 suites. A/C MINIBAR TV TEL. $179–$234 double. Weekend

packages available Apr–Oct. Children of any age stay free in parents' room. AE, CB, DC, ER, MC, V. Self-parking $12, valet $19.50. Metro: Bonaventure.

The Hilton's main entrance is at de la Gauchetière and Mansfield, and the lobby is on the 17th floor. It has underground access to Central Station. From aloft, the Place Bonaventure exhibition center looks like it has a hole in the top. That's the 2½-acre rooftop garden, with strolling pheasants, paddling ducks, and a heated pool. All guest rooms have color TVs in the bedrooms and smaller black-and-white sets in the bathrooms, as well as views of the city or the garden. Furnishings hover somewhere between frumpy and gaudy. Nonsmoking rooms are available.

Dining/Entertainment: Le Castillon is the hotel's French restaurant. Another, La Bourgade, is less expensive. Both have summer dining terraces.

Services: 24-hour room service, babysitting.

Facilities: Year-round heated outdoor pool, fitness center with sauna.

☼ Le Westin Mont-Royal. 1050 Sherbrooke ouest, Montréal, PQ, H3A 2R6. ☎ **514/ 284-1110** or 800/228-3000. Fax 514/845-3025. 300 rms, 27 suites. A/C MINIBAR TV TEL. $205–$225 double; from $370 suite. Children under 18 stay free with parents or in an adjoining room for $75. Upgrade to a suite for $25, on availability. Weekend rates and special packages available. AE, CB, DC, ER, MC, V. Self-parking $11, valet $19. Metro: Peel.

This used to be Le Quatre Saisons, a member of the esteemed Four Seasons chain and a worthy competitor to the nearby Ritz-Carlton. A rather chilly lobby is softened by banks of plants and flowers. Rooms are large, with comfortable, if slightly dated, furnishings. Robes are ready for guests' use, and security is enhanced by in-room safes. On-demand movies can be chosen from a library of over 60 titles. There are 12 nonsmoking floors.

Dining/Entertainment: Le Cercle is of mostly French inspiration, while Zen, an upscale Chinese restaurant, offers lunch and dinner daily. Buffet breakfasts and lunches are served in the lobby bar, L'Apèro, which features piano music in the evenings.

Services: Concierge, 24-hour room service, in-room massage, car and limo rentals, secretarial services.

Facilities: The impressive health club features a heated outdoor pool, open all year, morning coffee and juice, aerobics classes, weight machines, whirlpool, sauna, and workout gear or swimsuits on request. Car rental desk, boutiques.

☼ Ritz-Carlton Kempinski Montréal. 1228 Sherbrooke ouest (at Drummond), Montréal, PQ, H3G 1H6. ☎ **514/842-4212**, 800/363-0366 in Canada, or 800/426-3135 in the U.S. Fax 514/842-3383. 185 rms, 45 suites. A/C MINIBAR TV TEL. $190–$220 double; from $350 suite. Children under 14 stay free in parents' room. Packages available. AE, CB, DC, ER, MC, V. Self-parking or valet $15, with in/out privileges. Metro: Peel.

In 1912, the Ritz-Carlton opened its doors to the carriage trade, and the clientele has remained faithful. Over the years, carriages gave way to Pierce-Arrows, and those in turn gave way to Rolls-Royces and Lamborghinis. You'll always see a few of these (or at least a Cadillac limo or custom-built Lincoln) parked in readiness near the front door. Male patrons used to less formal modes of dress are apt to be annoyed when they are informed they must wear jackets in public rooms after 5pm, although the hotel's management seems to be easing up on that requirement. Baths are equipped with robes, makeup mirrors, and speakers carrying TV sound. Recent visits have revealed signs of slippage in service and maintenance, but not yet enough to damage its still-glowing reputation.

Dining/Entertainment: The Café de Paris is favored for its high tea and weekday power breakfasts. Meals are served on the terrace in summer. There's piano music in the Ritz Bar and Le Grand Prix, with dancing nightly in the latter.

Services: Concierge, 24-hour room service, same-day dry cleaning and laundry, twice-daily maid service, babysitting, secretarial services.

Facilities: In-room movies, modest fitness room, barbershop, newsstand, gift shop.

✪ **Vogue.** 1425 rue de la Montagne (between Maisonneuve and Ste-Catherine), Montréal, PQ, H3G 1G3. ☎ **514/285-5555** or 800/465-6654. Fax 514/849-8903. 134 rms, 20 suites. A/C MINIBAR TV TEL. $195–$255 double; from $350 suite. Children under 16 stay free in their parents' room. Lower weekend rates. CB, DC, ER, MC, V. Valet parking $15. Metro: Peel.

The Vogue has been creating a stir since it opened in late 1990, completing a stunning conversion of an undistinguished office building. Not a few observers feel it has displaced the Ritz-Carlton at the apex of the local luxury hotel pantheon. Confidence resonates from every member of its staff and luxury breathes from its lobby to its well-appointed guest rooms. Feather pillows and duvets dress the oversized beds, and rooms are decked with fresh flowers, cherrywood furniture, and an enormous bath with Jacuzzi. Other amenities include a fax, in-room safe, in-room movies, and plush robes. All of this suits the international clientele to a tee.

Dining/Entertainment: Société Café serves three meals a day, with outside tables in summer. The lobby bar, L'Opéra, has piano music Thursday through Saturday.

Services: Concierge, 24-hour room service, dry cleaning, babysitting.

Facilities: Small exercise room, coin-operated laundry, parking garage.

EXPENSIVE

La Reine Elisabeth/Queen Elizabeth. 900 bd. René-Lévesque ouest (Mansfield), Montréal, PQ, H3B 4A5. ☎ **514/861-3511,** 800-268-9411 in Canada, or 800/828-7447 in the U.S. Fax 514/954-2256. 1,046 rms, 60 suites. A/C MINIBAR TV TEL. $166–$225 double; concierge-level rates about $50 higher; from $310 suite. Various discounts, weekend, and excursion packages available. Children 18 and under stay free in parents' room. AE, CB, DC, DISC, ER, MC, V. Parking $12. Metro: Bonaventure.

Montréal's largest hotel has lent its august presence to the city since 1958. Its 21 floors sit atop VIA Rail's Central Station, with place Ville-Marie, place Bonaventure, and the Metro all accessible by underground arcades. That desirable location makes it a frequent choice for heads of state and touring celebrities, even though other hotels in town offer higher standards of personalized pampering. They close the gap by staying on the Entree Gold floor, which has a lounge serving complimentary breakfasts and cocktail-hour canapés. Less exalted rooms are entirely satisfactory, with most of the expected comforts and gadgets (including in-room movies), in price ranges to satisfy most budgets. Nonsmoking floors are available.

Dining/Entertainment: The Beaver Club (see Section 4, "Dining") has a combo for dancing on Saturday nights. Several other more casual bistro/bars serve meals in a variety of settings.

Services: Concierge, 24-hour room service, dry-cleaning and laundry service, babysitting, valet parking.

Facilities: Small health club with instructors, business center, beauty salon, shopping arcade, parking garage.

Le Centre Sheraton. 1201 bd. René-Lévesque ouest (between Drummond and Stanley), Montréal, PQ, H3B 2L7. ☎ **514/878-2000** or 800/325-3535. Fax 514/878-3958. 826 rms, 40 suites. A/C TV TEL. $175–$225 double; from $275 suite. Children under 17 stay free. Weekend rates. AE, CB, DC, DISC, ER, MC, V. Self-parking $9 with in/out privileges, valet $10. Metro: Bonaventure or Peel.

Le Centre Sheraton rises near Central Station, a few steps off Dorchester Square, and within a short walk of the rue Crescent dining and nightlife district. A high glass wall transforms the lobby atrium into an immense greenhouse, big enough to shelter two

🧸 Family-Friendly Hotels

Delta Montréal *(see p. 220)*   The Activity Centre for supervised play and crafts-making 0is a big draw for small kids, along with the swimming pool and (for bigger kids) an electronic-games room.

Holiday Inn Crowne Plaza Downtown *(see p. 220)*   Two kids under 18 stay free with parents, kids under 12 eat for free, and everyone gets to enjoy free in-room movies and the big swimming pool; special packages for families.

Le Jardin d'Antoine *(see p. 221)*   Some rooms open onto the pleasant patio garden, where kids are welcome to play; all rooms have private baths, and breakfast is included in the price. The live-in owners have a child, too.

royal palms and a luxuriance of tropical plants. The staff is efficient and the rooms are comfortable, if anonymous. Earnest people in suits make up most of the clientele. They gravitate to the executive Towers section, which bestows complimentary breakfast and a private lounge on its guests. Half of the rooms have minibars, all have coffeemakers and in-room movies. Some floors are reserved for nonsmokers.

Dining/Entertainment: The Boulevard restaurant serves three meals a day; the Musette, breakfast and lunch only. Jazz is performed Tuesday through Saturday evenings in the Impromptu Bar.

Services: Concierge in Towers, 24-hour room service, dry cleaning, babysitting, secretarial services, express checkout, valet parking, airport transport.

Facilities: Indoor pool, fitness center with whirlpool and sauna.

Le Meridien. 4 Complexe Desjardins, C.P. 130, Montréal, PQ, H5B 1E5. ☎ **514/285-1450** or 800/543-4300. Fax 514/285-1243. 572 rms, 28 suites. A/C MINIBAR TV TEL. $170–$190 double; from $285 suite. Children under 18 stay free in parents' room. Packages available. AE, DC, DISC, ER, MC, V. Self-parking $9, valet $15. Metro: Place des Arts.

A member of Air France's hotel chain, Le Meridien is an integral part of the striking Complexe Desjardins, across the street from the Place des Arts and the Montréal Museum of Contemporary Art. Rooms, decorated in restful tones, are comfortable enough, with extras like in-room movies, though baths are on the skimpy side. Glass-enclosed elevators glide up to bedrooms and down to the lower levels of the complex, which contain a shopping plaza and an indoor pool. Chinatown is a block away, and Vieux Montréal, the downtown district, and the ethnic neighborhoods along The Main are within easy walking distance. The hotel is usually the official headquarters of Montréal's popular jazz festival. Nonsmoking floors are available.

Dining/Entertainment: Café Fleuri provides all meals, while Le Club, with a French menu, serves only lunch and dinner. Le Bar overlooks Complexe Desjardins and has piano music nightly.

Services: Concierge, 24-hour room service, dry cleaning and laundry service, express checkout, valet parking.

Facilities: Indoor pool, exercise room with whirlpool and sauna, business center.

MODERATE

Château Versailles. 1659 rue Sherbrooke ouest (at St-Mathieu), Montréal, PQ, H3H 1E3. ☎ **514/933-3611,** 800/361-7199 in Canada, or 800/361-3664 in the U.S. Fax 514/933-7102. 70 rms. A/C TV TEL. $145 double. Children 16 and under stay free. Special weekend rates Nov–May, summer packages available. AE, CB, DC, ER, MC, V. Valet parking $8.50. Metro: Guy. Bus: no. 24, half a block.

This has long been a local favorite, though it's somewhat overpraised, considering rates that scrape the high edge of the moderate price scale. Although it began as a European-style pension in 1958, the owners have since expanded into a total of four adjacent rowhouses. Guest rooms are spare but comfortable enough, some with minibars. A few antiques are spotted around the public rooms. Service remains more personal than in the big downtown hotels. Breakfast and afternoon tea are served in a small dining room with a fireplace and handmade quilts on the walls. Price and location keep it popular, so reserve well in advance. A modern annex, La Tour Versailles, is right across the street. The same prices prevail, amounting to greater value for rooms with some Shaker-style reproductions, minibars, and safes. There are two nonsmoking floors and a French restaurant. Laptops and fax are available on request. Go for the annex.

Delta Montréal. 450 Sherbrooke ouest, Montréal, PQ, H3A 2T4. ☎ **514/286-1986** or 800/877-1133. Fax 514/284-4306. 483 rms, 6 suites. A/C MINIBAR TV TEL. $115 double; from $250 suite. Weekend rates from $99. Children under 18 stay free in parents' room, and children under 6 eat for free. AE, ER, MC, V. Parking $12. Metro: Place des Arts.

A very well maintained property, this unit of the Canadian chain is targeted to the business traveler with its expansively equipped business center and large health club. However, its supervised children's crafts and games center makes it clear that families are welcome here, too. Rooms have angular dimensions, escaping the boxiness of many contemporary hotels. Most have small balconies; all have coffee machines. Room service is on call around the clock. The better-than-average health club has an aerobics instructor, whirlpool, sauna, massage, indoor lap pool, outdoor pool, and two squash courts. Enter the 23-story tower from Sherbrooke or avenue du President-Kennedy (the sole entrance after 10:30pm). Courtesy airport transportation is available on request.

☉ Holiday Inn Crowne Plaza Downtown. 420 Sherbrooke ouest (at av. du Parc), Montréal, PQ, H3A 1B4. ☎ **514/842-6111** or 800/HOLIDAY. Fax 514/842-9381. 486 rms. A/C MINIBAR TV TEL. $104–$145 double. Children under 19 stay free with parents. Summer and family packages. AE, CB, DC, ER, MC, V. Parking $10. Metro: Place des Arts.

Not to be confused with the similarly named Holiday Inn Crowne Plaza Métro Centre, this upper-middle entry stands out among the clutch of hotels that cluster around the intersection of Sherbrooke and rue City Councillors. It's one of the city's best values in its class, especially for economizing families, since spouses and two children under age 19 can stay for free. Kids under 12 eat for free, too, and there's no charge for in-room movies. The guest rooms all have city views and a king-size or two double beds. Bathrooms are compact. Nonsmoking and executive floors are available.

Coin-operated washers and dryers are provided for guests' use. A large heated indoor pool is attended by a lifeguard. The adjoining fitness center has weights, exercise bikes, whirlpool, and sauna.

✪ Montagne. 1430 rue de la Montagne (north of Ste-Catherine), Montréal, PQ, H3G 1Z5. ☎ **514/288-5656** or 800/361-6262. Fax 514/288-9658. 138 rms. A/C TV TEL. $125–$135 double. AE, CB, DC, ER, MC, V. Parking $10. Metro: Peel.

Two white lions stand sentinel at the front door, with a doorman in a pith helmet. Noah extends his influence inside, in a crowded lobby that incorporates a pair of six-foot carved elephants, two gold-colored crocodiles, and a nude female figure with stained-glass butterfly wings sitting atop a splashing fountain. Clearly, we are not in Kansas. Up on the mezzanine is one of the city's more ambitious dining rooms, Le Lutétia (see Section 4, "Dining"). On the roof, a pool is perched 20 stories up, with light meals and dancing under the stars. In back, a music lounge featuring jazz duos leads to a spangly disco that empties into a pub with a terrace on rue Crescent. After all that, the relatively serene bedrooms seem downright bland. Stop in for a drink, anyway.

INEXPENSIVE

Castel St-Denis. 2099 rue St-Denis, Montréal, PQ, H2X 3K8. ☎ **514/842-9719.** Fax 514/843-8492. 18 rms (half with shower). A/C TV. $55 double with shower, $45 double without private shower. Extra person $10. MC, V. Parking not available. Metro: Berri-UQAM or Sherbrooke.

Among the budget choices in the Latin Quarter, the Castel St-Denis is one of the most desirable. It's a little south of Sherbrooke, among the cafes of the lower reaches of the street, and two long blocks from the Terminus Voyageur. Most of the rooms are fairly quiet, and all are tidy and simply decorated, if hardly chic. The friendly, bilingual owner is a good source for guidance about nearby restaurants and attractions.

Days Inn. 1199 rue Berri (between René-Lévesque and rue Ste-Catherine), Montréal, PQ, H2L 4C6. ☎ **514/845-9236** or 800/363-0363. Fax 514/849-9855. 148 rms, 6 junior suites. A/C TV TEL. High season $82 double, $130 suite; off-season $75 double, $109 suite. Extra person $7. AE, CB, DC, DISC, ER, MC, V. Outdoor parking $10. Metro: Berri-UQAM.

Formerly the Hotel Lord Berri, this new unit of the voracious U.S. economy chain is located near St-Denis and a five-minute walk from Old Montréal. Its Italian restaurant has a sidewalk terrace. Rooms have full baths and offer in-room movies. The decor is as interesting as a bus schedule, but the Latin Quarter location and fair tariffs make up for it. Several floors are set aside for nonsmokers.

Le Jardin d'Antoine. 2024 rue St-Denis, Montréal, PQ, H2X 3K7. ☎ **514/843-4506** or 800/361-4506 (between 8am and 6pm). Fax 514/281-1491. 20 rms. A/C TV TEL. $74–$120 double; $130–$140 suite. Rates about $10 less off-season. Extra person $10. Rates include full breakfast. AE, MC, V. Parking $9. Metro: Berri-UQAM or Sherbrooke.

Near several good Latin Quarter restaurants, and more upscale than most of the other inns found along rue St-Denis, this bed-and-breakfast has no two rooms that are alike. This isn't necessarily a benefit, so ask to see a room before accepting it. Most have brick walls, a brass or oak bed, and cozily old-fashioned ambience. Some of the larger, more expensive rooms have whirlpools. Breakfast can be taken in the patio garden. Children are welcome, not always the case in this category.

OLD MONTRÉAL

EXPENSIVE

✪ **Inter-Continental Montréal.** 360 rue St-Antoine ouest (Bleury), Montréal, PQ, H2Y 3X4. ☎ **514/987-9900** or 800/361-3600. Fax 514/987-9904. 335 rms, 22 suites. A/C MINIBAR TV TEL. $180–$195 double; from $350 suite. Packages available. AE, CB, DC, ER, MC, V. Valet parking $16. Metro: Square Victoria.

Only a few minutes' walk from Notre-Dame cathedral and the restaurants and nightspots of Vieux Montréal, this striking addition to the hotel scene opened in mid-1991 and became an instant candidate for inclusion among the top five properties in town. It is equal to the Westin Mont-Royal on virtually all counts, for example, and less expensive. Its new tower houses the sleek reception area and guest rooms, while the restored annex, the Nordheimer building (1888), contains some of the hotel's restaurants and bars. (Take a look at the early 19th-century vaults down below.) Guest rooms are quiet and well lit, with photographs and lithographs by local artists on the walls and with in-room movies. The turret suites are fun, with their round bedrooms and wraparound windows. All rooms have two or three telephones and coffee machines. Robes are supplied. Four floors are reserved for nonsmokers, and there are executive floors with a lounge.

Dining/Entertainment: Les Continents serves all three meals and Sunday brunch. Le Cristallin, the lobby-level piano bar, has music nightly. In the Nordheimer building is congenial Chez Plume, popular for lunch and after work.

Services: Concierge, 24-hour room service, same-day laundry/valet Monday through Friday, complimentary newspaper, nightly turndown, express checkout, valet parking.

Facilities: Health club with small, enclosed rooftop pool, sauna and steamrooms, massage, weight room, business center.

INEXPENSIVE

Les Passants du Sans Soucy. 171 rue St-Paul ouest, Montréal, PQ, H2Y 1Z5. ☎ 514/842-2634. Fax 514/842-2912. 9 rms. A/C TV TEL. $85–$105 double; $150 suite. Extra person $10. Rates include full breakfast. AE, ER, MC, V. Parking $7.50 Mon–Fri, free weekends. Metro: Place d'Armes.

The only bed-and-breakfast in Old Montréal is a 1723 house craftily converted by the bilingual owners, Daniel Soucy and Michael Banks. Exposed brick and beams and a marble floor form the vestibule; beyond lies a sitting area and a breakfast nook with a skylight. Nine guest rooms are upstairs, and each has stucco-and-rock walls, fresh flowers, lace curtains, and wrought-iron or brass beds. The inn is eight blocks from place Jacques-Cartier. Substantial breakfasts include chocolate croissants and cafe au lait.

PLATEAU MONT-ROYAL

✪ **Auberge de la Fontaine.** 1301 rue Rachel est (at Chambord), Montréal, PQ, H2J 2K1. ☎ 514/597-0166 or 800/597-0597. Fax 514/597-0496. 18 rms, 3 suites. A/C TV TEL. $105–$140 double; $175 suite. Extra person $10. Children under 12 stay free. Rates include buffet breakfast. AE, ER, MC, V. Free parking behind the inn or on the street. Metro: Mont-Royal or Sherbrooke.

For those who like to stay away from frenetic downtown districts, this urban inn may be just the ticket. Situated at the northern edge of Lafontaine Park, it's a bit far from the action (except in summer, when there are free concerts in the park and the tennis courts and jogging and cycling paths are well-used). The inn has clean, sprightly rooms and bathrooms equipped with hair dryers. The suites have whirlpools, while many of the other rooms have terraces or balconies. Those in the new section are roomier; units in back are quieter. Guests may use the terrace on the third floor, as well as a small kitchen that's kept stocked with complimentary cookies, tea, and juice.

4 Dining

Montréal has an estimated 5,000 restaurants. Until only a few short years ago, they were overwhelmingly French. There were a few temples d'cuisine that delivered or pretended to haute standards of gastronomy, followed by scores of accomplished bistros employing humbler ingredients and less grand settings, and some places that trafficked in the hearty fare of the days of the colonial era—game, maple sugar, and root vegetables. Everything else was ethnic. Yes, there were establishments that presented the cooking of Asia and the Mediterranean, but they didn't enjoy the same favor they did in other cities of North America. Québec was French, and that was that.

In the 1980s, when the recurring waves of food crazes washed over Los Angeles, Chicago, Toronto, and New York, introducing their citizens to Cajun, Tex-Mex, southwestern, and the fusion cuisines variously known as Franco-Asian, Pacific Rim, and Cal-Ital, the diners of Montréal were resolute. They stuck to their Francophilic traditions. Now that is changing, for a number of reasons. The recession of the early

1990s, from which Canada was slow to recover, put many restaurateurs out of business and forced others to reexamine and streamline their operations. Immigration continued to grow, and with it, the introduction of still more foreign cooking styles. Montréalers, secure in their status as epicures, began sampling the exotic edibles emerging in new storefront eateries all around them—Thai, Moroccan, Vietnamese, Portuguese, Turkish, Mexican, Indian, Creole, Szechuan, and Japanese. Innovation and intermingling of styles, ingredients, and techniques was inevitable. The city, long among the elite gastronomic centers, is now as cosmopolitan in its tastes and offerings as any on the continent.

Picking through this forest of tempting choices can be both gratifying and bewildering. In addition to the establishments suggested below, there are many other worthy possibilities, especially along rue Crescent, St-Denis, or St-Laurent. Nearly all of them have menus posted outside, prompting the local pastime of stopping every few yards for a little mouthwatering reading and comparison shopping before deciding on a place for dinner.

It's a good idea and an expected courtesy to make a reservation to dine at one of the city's top restaurants. Unlike larger American and European cities, however, a few hours or a day in advance is usually sufficient. Dress codes are all but nonexistent, except in a handful of the luxury restaurants, but adults who show up in the equivalent of T-shirts and jeans are likely to feel uncomfortably out of place at the better establishments.

This city's moderately priced bistros, cafes, and ethnic eateries offer outstand-ing food, congenial surroundings, and amiable service. And, speaking of value for money, the city's table d'hôte (fixed-price) meals are eye-openers. Entire two- to four-course meals, often with a beverage, can be had for little more than an à la carte main course alone. Even the best restaurants offer them, so table d'hôte represents a considerable saving and the chance to sample some excellent restaurants at reasonable prices. The delectable fact is that a meal can be had here that is the equal in every dimension to best that can be offered in Los Angeles, Chicago, or New York—for one-third the cost. (Prices do not include the 7% federal tax and 8% provincial tax that are added to the restaurant bill. Food purchased in a market or grocery store is not taxed.)

Since parking space is at a premium in most restaurant districts in Montréal, take the Metro or a taxi to the restaurant (most are within a block or two of a Metro station), or ask if valet parking is available when making a reservation.

DOWNTOWN
VERY EXPENSIVE
✪ The Beaver Club. In Le Reine Elisabeth Hotel, 900 René-Lévesque ouest. ☎ 514/861-3511. Reservations recommended. Main courses $30–$35; table d'hôte lunch $16–$23; table d'hôte dinner $30–$35. AE, CB, DC, ER, MC, V. Daily noon–3pm and 6–11pm. Metro: Bonaventure. FRENCH.

Dine here under the glassy gazes of a polar bear, musk-ox, and bison, for the restaurant takes its name from an organization of socially prominent explorers and trappers established in 1785. Stained glass and carved wood panels depict their early adventures in the wilderness and undergird the clubby tone of the dining room, a magnet for the city's power brokers for decades (although, with 225 seats to fill, it's hardly exclusive). Lunch is the time for the gentlest prices. The menu changes twice a year, but if you can only eat one meal here, lean toward the roast beef. This is no place for food frippery. Still, the determined dieter will appreciate the nutritional information provided for each lunch dish. On Saturdays, a trio begins playing at 7:30pm for dancing.

Les Halles. 1450 rue Crescent (between Ste-Catherine and de Maison-neuve). ☎ **514/ 844-2328.** Reservations recommended. Main courses $25–$31; table d'hôte lunch $21.50; table d'hôte dinner $29.50. AE, DC, ER, MC, V. Tues–Fri 11:45am–2:30pm, Mon–Sat 6–11pm. Metro: Guy-Concordia or Peel. FRENCH.

Opened in 1971, Les Halles continues to thrive as one of the most accomplished French restaurants in town. It is more expensive than it should be, however, so consider having lunch here instead of dinner. That's no loss for the romantics among us. Despite the prices, this isn't an "event" establishment, draped with brocades and glinting with Baccarat. Tables are close, service is correct but chummy, and mock storefronts intended to recall the old Paris market of the same name take up the walls—all of which promote the idea of bistro, not temple d'cuisine.

Beef, lamb and game dishes are the stars on the menu, but seafood, simply prepared, is also good. Ingredients are rarely exotic, yet the kitchen dresses them in unexpected ways. Frogs' legs, for example, are splashed with Pernod for a distinctive finish, and chunks of lobster are tossed with scallops and grapefruit sections. Main courses and desserts come in such hefty portions that you don't need appetizers.

EXPENSIVE

Le Lutétia. In the Hôtel de la Montagne, 1430 rue de la Montagne. ☎ **514/288-5656.** Reservations recommended. Main courses $16–$24. AE, DC, ER, MC, V. Daily 7–11am; Sun and Tues–Fri noon–3pm; Sat–Sun 6–11pm. Metro: Peel. CONTEMPORARY FRENCH.

This restaurant is as amusing and provocative as the hotel in which it is situated. On the mezzanine floor, ranged around a rectangular opening to the floor below with oversized teardrop chandeliers, it incorporates snippets of every decorative style of the late 19th century, including, but not confined to, Baroque, Victorian, Neo-Italian, and French Second Empire. On the pink-clad tables await bowls of pickled beans, piquant mushrooms, and black olives. All subsequent courses arrive on trolleys under silver bells, removed with due ceremony. The contents of the plates beneath can be uneven in execution, however. Fish is apt to be slightly overcooked, while beef, a specialty, is cooked precisely to order. With a little luck and caution (choose the simpler dishes), the end result can be a memorably romantic meal for two. Dress can be casual, although the serving staff is in tuxedos.

Le Tour de Ville. In the Radisson Hôtel des Gouverneurs, 30th floor, 777 rue University. ☎ **514/879-1370.** Reservations required. Buffet $33. AE, CB, DC, DISC, ER, MC, V. Daily 6–11pm. Metro: Square Victoria. INTERNATIONAL.

Memorable. Breathtaking. Well, the view is, anyway, from Montréal's only revolving restaurant. The food, on the other hand, while varied enough and not numbingly expensive, does little to dispel the notion that elevated venues rarely inspire high culinary achievement. Served at a buffet, the food is themed "from the four corners of the world." Make that two corners, since the usual sources are Switzerland, France, Italy, and California. The best time to go is when the sun is setting and the city lights are beginning to wink on. One flight down is a bar with the same wonderful vistas, along with a dance floor, and a band three nights a week (Thursday through Saturday from 9pm to 1am, 2am on Saturday). There's no cover, but drinks are steep, from $5.50 to $9. The bar opens at 6pm.

MODERATE

Katsura. 2170 rue de la Montagne (between Maisonneuve and Sherbrooke). ☎ **514/ 849-1172.** Reservations recommended. Main courses $13–$25; table d'hôte lunch $8–$19; table d'hôte dinner $27–$43. AE, DC, ER, MC, V. Mon–Sat 11:30am–2:30pm; Mon–Thurs 5:30–10:30pm, Fri–Sat 5:30–11:30pm, Sun 5:30–9:30pm. Metro: Peel or Guy-Concordia. JAPANESE.

A tuxedoed maître d' welcomes patrons at the door and leads them either into a conventional Western dining room with plush chairs or into rooms enclosed by opaque paper screens that allow diners to sit on traditional tatami mats at low Japanese tables. Whatever venue you choose, waitresses in kimonos move quickly but almost silently under the soothing tinkle of music on the stereo. The house special is a nine-course extravaganza that ranges from baked clams and sashimi through shrimp tempura, salad, egg-flower soup, and sirloin teriyaki to ice cream with segments of mandarin oranges. Katsura has been around long enough to be accorded credit for introducing sushi to Montréal. While it is no longer a novelty, sushi is still prepared to near-perfection here. The sushi bar in back is also a refuge for those who arrive without a reservation when the place is full.

La Sila. 2040 rue St-Denis (north of rue Ontario). ☎ 514/844-5083. Reservations recommended. Main courses $8–$15; table d'hôte lunch $9–$12; table d'hôte dinner $27–$30. AE, DC, ER, MC, V. Mon–Fri 11:30am–2:30pm; Mon–Sat 5:30–11pm. Metro: Sherbrooke. CONTEMPORARY ITALIAN.

Apart from displaying a new determination to de-emphasize the heavier cream sauces it served in the past, this restaurant remains something of a traditionalist on Montréal's dining scene. Reasons to go are the pastas, made in-house, and the trademark milk-fed veal that practically parts at a loving look. You'll be served by careerists, not models and actors between auditions, a difference gratifying to behold. These things were true before the founding owner retired and so far apply to practices under the current regime. Redecoration has brightened the interior and added a bar, and the terrace still invites diners in the warm months. Little on the menu is likely to disappoint, but the special chef's fettucine and the veal scaloppini are all but certain to please. There's free parking in back.

La Tulip Noire. 2100 rue Stanley (near Sherbrooke). ☎ 514/285-1225. Salads and sandwiches $6–$14. MC, V. Daily 8am–midnight. Metro: Peel. LIGHT FARE.

A place to know for its perky reliability and extended hours. Basically a combination coffee shop and pastry shop, it is best for snacks or late-evening desserts rather than dinners, although full meals are available. At lunchtime or as night wears on, crowds stack up at the door and it can get a little frantic. Find it in the back of the Maison Alcan building on Sherbrooke. They only close two or three days a year.

✪ **Le Taj.** 2077 rue Stanley (near Sherbrooke). ☎ 514/845-9015. Main courses $9–$17; luncheon buffet $7.50. AE, DC, ER, MC, V. Sun–Fri 11:30am–2:30pm; daily 5–10:30pm. Metro: Peel. NORTHERN INDIAN.

A large relief temple sculpture occupies a place of pride in this dramatic setting of cream and apricot, which has been completely overhauled in recent years. Back in the corner, a chef works diligently over an open tandoor oven. His specialty is the *mughlai* repertoire of the north of the Indian subcontinent. Seasonings on the scores of dishes he sends forth are more tangy than incendiary (but watch out for the coriander sauce). Spicy or mild, all are perfumed with turmeric, saffron, ginger, sumin, mango powder, and garam-masala.

For a rare treat, order the marinated lamb chops roasted in the tandoor; they arrive at table still sizzling and nested on braised vegetables. Vegetarians have a choice of eight dishes, the chickpea-based *channa masala* among the most complex. Main courses are huge, arriving in a boggling array of bowls, saucers, cups, and dishes, all with *nan*, the flat bread, and basmati rice. Evenings are quiet, and lunchtimes are busy, but not hectic.

👪 Family-Friendly Restaurants

Le 9e *(see p. 227)*   What looks like a ship's dining room is found on the ninth (9e) floor of Eaton's department store. Kids can pretend they're on a fantasy voyage, and since "Le Neuvième" is a noisy place, they can be as enthusiastic as they like.

Pizzadelic *(see p. 231)*   Pizza never fails to please the younger set, and this place caters to any taste, with toppings that can stretch the imagination.

McDonalds's   For something familiar, but with a twist, this McDonald's, only a block from Notre-Dame Basilica at the corner of rue Notre-Dame and St-Laurent, deserves a mention. Located in a house that was once the home of Antoine Lamet de la Mothe Cadillac, the founder of Detroit and a governor of Louisiana, it offers the usual menu, along with pizzas and the Québec favorite, poutine (french fries covered with a cheese sauce).

⭐ **Sawatdee.** 3453 rue Notre Dame ouest (at Atwater). ☎ **514/938-8188.** Main courses $7.95–$19.95. AE, MC. Tues–Fri noon–2:30pm and 5–10pm; Sat–Sun 5–11pm. Metro: Lionel-Groulx. THAI.

While it may be a stretch to describe this as one of the hundred best restaurants in Canada, as it has been proclaimed, Sawatdee is certainly a welcome addition. It's well west of downtown, in a seedy neighborhood of second-rate clothing stores and fast-food outlets. Think of it for lunch after a morning of browsing along rue Notre Dame east of Atwater, which has at least 30 antique shops in just a few blocks. It will be cheap and filling, but not wonderful. For something memorable, though, show up for dinner, and make it clear that you want genuine Thai seasonings, not the wan versions usually served to non-Asians. Take time to examine the abundance of museum-quality statuary and tapestries.

INEXPENSIVE

$ **La Maison Kam Fung.** 1008 rue Clark (near Gauchetièrie est). ☎ **514/878-2888.** Main courses $6.95–$11.95. AE, DC, ER, MC, V. Daily 10am–2pm and 5–10:30pm. Metro: Place d'Armes. CANTONESE/MANDARIN.

Kam Fung mysteriously closed its old Chinatown location around the corner in 1992, then just as abruptly reopened here two years later. New owners and new chefs now conduct business in an even larger room. Weekends are the event days, when Chinese dispersed throughout the suburbs return for ingestion of comfort food. While regular meals are served in the evening, midday is reserved for dim sum. Here's the drill: Go to the second floor, obtain a ticket from the young woman at the podium, and wait. Once summoned to a table, be alert to the carts being trundled out of the kitchen. They are stacked with covered baskets and pails, most of which contain dumplings of one kind or another, such as balls of curried shrimp or glistening envelopes of pork nubbins or scallops, supplemented by such items as fish purée slathered on wedges of sweet pepper and, for the venturesome, steamed chicken feet and squid. Simply order until sated. Resist the desire to gather up the first five items that appear. Much more is on the way.

$ **Le Commensal.** 1204 av. McGill College (at Ste-Catherine). ☎ **514/871-1480.** Reservations not accepted. Dishes priced by weight: $1.40 per 100 grams (about 3.5 ounces). AE, MC, V. Daily 11am–11:30pm. Metro: McGill. VEGETARIAN.

Le Commensal serves vegetarian fare buffet style. Most of the dishes are so artfully conceived, with close attention to aroma, color, and texture, that even avowed meat eaters won't feel deprived. The only likely complaint is that those dishes that are supposed to be hot are too often lukewarm. Patrons circle the table helping themselves, then pay the cashier by weight. The second-floor location affords a view, which compensates for the utilitarian decor.

Le Commensal has eight other locations at recent count, one of the most convenient being the one at 2115 St-Denis and Sherbrooke (☎ 514/845-2627).

Le 9e. 677 rue Ste-Catherine (in Eaton department store). ☎ **514/284-8421.** Table d'hôte $7.75–$9.50. AE, MC, V. Mon–Sat 11:30am–3pm, Thurs–Fri 4:30–7pm. Metro: McGill. LIGHT FARE.

Opened in 1931, "Le Neuvième," on the ninth floor of the old-line department store, is a replica of an Art Deco dining room aboard the ocean liner *Île de France*, complete with murals, marble columns, and giant alabaster vases. Menu items include soups, sandwiches, salads, and daily specials—lamb, fish, and pasta, usually—that come with soup, dessert, and coffee. They couldn't be much more ordinary in concept and execution, but they look glorious. Some of the waiters and waitresses, in their starched black-and-white uniforms, look as if they might have been around at the inauguration. Expect noise and children.

Sir Winston Churchill Pub. 1459 Crescent (between Maisonneuve and Ste-Catherine). ☎ **514/288-3814.** Most items under $12. AE, DC, ER, MC, V. Daily 11:30am–3pm and 5pm–3am. Metro: Guy-Concordia or Peel. LIGHT FARE.

Sidewalk tables here are enclosed by glass in winter, open to the sun in summer, just the place to pass an hour of people-watching, burger-munching, and beer-quaffing. To be reasonably certain of snagging a table, arrive before noon or after two. Variations on the soup-and-sandwich theme are provided by the lunch buffet and Sunday brunch.

OLD MONTRÉAL
VERY EXPENSIVE

✪ **La Marée.** 404 place Jacques-Cartier (near Notre-Dame). ☎ **514/861-8126.** Reservations required. Main courses $24–$30; table d'hôte lunch $14–$17. AE, CB, DC, ER, MC, V. Mon–Fri noon–3pm; daily 5:30–11:30pm. Metro: Champ-de-Mars. FRENCH.

Look for the historic 1807 del Vecchio house on the west side of the plaza, a site occupied by previous structures since 1655. Even though dining of high order is usually not to be expected at the epicenter of a city's most heavily trammeled tourist district, this restaurant will surprise you. Begin with the setting: stone walls, fireplaces, paintings of fish and game, delicately figured wallpaper, and furnishings recalling the eras of Louis XIII and the Sun King. Candlelight enhances the mood for romantic couples in the evening, while power lunches prevail at midday. (A lunchtime express menu costs only $9.50 to $12.)

Known especially for its refined and precise treatment of seafood, the kitchen is lauded—correctly—for such fabrications as trout stuffed with salmon and lobster mousse and lobster with tomato and fresh basil and a white wine sauce. In cooler weather, chateaubriand tops the list. Service is disciplined and unobtrusive. There's no dress code, but you'll want to look at least casually stylish.

EXPENSIVE

✪ **Claude Postel.** 443 rue St-Vincent (near Notre-Dame). ☎ **514/875-5067.** Reservations recommended. Main courses $17–$30; table d'hôte lunch $20. AE, CB, DC, ER, MC, V. Mon–Fri 11:30am–2:30pm; daily 5:30–11pm. Metro: Place d'Armes or Champ-de-Mars. FRENCH.

One of the most upbeat places in Vieux-Montréal is named for its chef-owner, who once shook the skillets at Bonaparte, a few blocks away. He has surpassed his former employer on every count, and continues to widen the gap, as with recent renovations that added a summer dining terrace with 50 seats. The building, which dates from 1862, has been both a morgue and a hotel that once had Sarah Bernhardt as a guest. The animated Postel almost dances through his dining room, greeting regulars and newcomers with equal warmth, suggesting off-menu items and possible wines. While the crowd is largely composed of businesspeople and government employees, the restaurant attracts visiting celebrities. They come for such creations as sweetbreads braised in wine and cream with lots of morels and slivers of air-cured ham, a triumph even for those who ordinarily shun organ meats. Caribou, venison, scallops, and salmon appear on the menu in equally creative guises. There is valet parking from 6pm. Postel has a takeout shop nearby, at 75 rue Notre-Dame, with most of the makings of a satisfying picnic, including baguettes, cheeses, sandwiches, and quiches.

MODERATE

✪ **Casa de Matéo.** 440 rue St-François-Xavier (near St-Paul). ☎ **514/844-7448.** Reservations not required. Main courses $14–$18; daily lunch specials $8–$10. AE, MC, V. Mon–Fri 11am–11pm, Sat–Sun 2–11pm. Metro: Place d'Armes. MEXICAN.

Stepping into Casa de Matéo feels like wandering into a party about to kick into high gear. Expect a downright gleeful greeting from the host any night of the week, and on Fridays and Saturdays, mariachis come to carry the fiesta to a higher register. Birdbath-sized margaritas arrive with chips and salsa at the center horseshoe bar, which is encased with rough terra-cotta tiles. Lending authenticity is a shy but cheerful staff from Mexico, Guatemala, Ecuador, and other Latin American countries, most of whom are delighted to be addressed in even a few words of Spanish. With these generous servings, appetizers can be skipped. But that would mean missing the plato Mexicano, a sampler of all the starters. Since that is a meal in itself, others may want to stop there. But *that* would mean missing the *pescado Veracruzano*, the whole red snapper quickly marinated and fried and served with a nest of crisp vegetables. The usual burritos and enchiladas are easy to forget.

⑤ **Le Bourlingueur.** 363 St-François-Xavier (near St-Paul). ☎ **514/845-3646.** Reservations recommended. Table d'hôte lunch or dinner $9–$14. AE, ER, MC, V. Mon 11:30am–3pm, Tues–Fri 11:30am–9pm, Sat 5:30–9pm. Metro: Place d'Armes. FRENCH.

While it doesn't look especially promising upon first approach, this registers as a real find in Vieux Montréal. For the almost unbelievably low prices indicated above, they offer 8 to 10 four-course meals daily. The blackboard menu changes with market availability, making it possible to dine here twice a day for a week without repeating anything except the indifferent salad. The specialty of the house is seafood—watch for the cold lobster with herb mayonnaise. Well short of chic, this restaurant doesn't make the most of its stone walls and old beams, choosing instead to put paper place mats on the pink tablecloths. No matter, not with these low prices and relative quality. The crowd is incredibly diverse—you'll be dining with the widest possible range of ages, genders, and occupations here. The crowd is largest at lunchtime.

INEXPENSIVE

⑤ **Chez Better.** 160 rue Notre-Dame (near place Jacques Cartier). ☎ **514/861-2617.** Main courses $6.25–$8.50. AE, MV, V. Daily 11am–11pm. Metro: Champ-de-Mars. GERMAN.

They aren't making a half-hearted boast with the name of this place. This and the other five outposts of this growing local chain are named for the founder, a Canadian born in Germany. Presumably he grew homesick for a taste of his native land

and opened his first restaurant to assuage that hunger. Think knackwurst, sauerkraut, fries, and beer, with variations, and that gives the general outline of the menu. Forget grease and oozing globules of fat, though, for these are remarkably lighthearted sausages, brightly seasoned with herbs, curry, hot pepper, even truffle shavings. A trivet of three mustards sits on each table. While sausage plates are the stars, there are also mixed grills, chicken schnitzels, grilled smoked pork chops, and salads. In this 1811 building in Vieux Montréal, the ground floor is for nonsmokers, upstairs for puffers. Service can be disjointed, but rarely to the point of irritation.

Two other branches tourists are likely to encounter are at 4382 bd. St-Laurent (☎ 514/845-4554) and 1430 rue Stanley (☎ 514/848-9859).

Le Jardin Nelson. 407 place Jacques-Cartier (rue de la Commune). ☎ **514/861-5731.** Reservations not accepted. Main courses $5.75–$9.50. MC, V. May–Labor Day daily 11:30am– 3am; Labor Day–Nov daily 11:30am–midnight (later on weekends); Dec–Apr more limited hours (call ahead). Metro: Place d'Armes. FRENCH/LIGHT FARE.

Near the foot of the hill, a passage leads into the paved garden court in back of a handsome stone building dating from 1812. The kitchen specializes in crepes, their fillings determining their destinies as main courses or desserts. Mild invention keeps the results intriguing, as with the melange of semicrispy veggies rolled in a thin buckwheat pancake laced with threads of spinach. Soups, omelets, salads, and sandwiches are also available. A crab-apple tree shades the garden, a horticultural counterpoint to midday concerts by jazz combos (Friday to Sunday) and classical chamber groups (Monday to Thursday).

Stash's. 200 rue St-Paul ouest (St-François-Xavier). ☎ **514/845-6611.** Reservations recommended. Main courses $9–$13, table d'hôte $18.75–$24.50. AE, MC, V. Mon–Fri 11am– 10:30pm, Sat–Sun noon–10:30pm. Metro: Place d'Armes. POLISH.

Even after moving from its former spot beside Notre-Dame cathedral, this *restauracja polska* continues to draw enthusiastic throngs for its munificent portions and low prices. The new setting features brick and stone walls, exposed beams, colorful hanging lamps, blond-wood furniture, and shelves of secondhand books and newspapers to peruse. An old convent was the source of the several refectory tables and pews. A roast wild boar is a new addition to an already ample card of pirogies (a kind of Polish raviloi stuffed with meat or cheese), potato pancakes, borscht with sour cream, roast duck, beef Stroganoff. The place is named after the original owner, now in Europe. A jolly tenor persists, with animated patrons and such menu admonitions as "anything tastes better with wodka, even wodka. Read, eat, and enjoy."

PLATEAU MONT-ROYAL
EXPENSIVE

✪ **Toqué!** 3842 rue St-Denis (at Roy). ☎ **514/499-2084.** Reservations recommended. Main courses $22–$26. AE, MC, V. Daily 6–11pm. Metro: Sherbrooke. CONTEMPORARY FRENCH.

This restaurant is the sort of adornment that can single-handedly raise the gastronomic standards of an entire city. A meal here is virtually obligatory for anyone who admires superb food dazzlingly presented, especially since the former champ, Les Mignardies, has closed its doors. Normand Laprise, previously associated with a well-regarded venture called Citrus, has teamed up with Christine Lamarche to create a place as postmodernist in its cuisine as in its decor, which is largely bright colors and minimalist fixtures, with a wall down the middle to separate smokers from nonsmokers. Success has forced the owners to forego the open kitchen that used to be in front downstairs—they needed the space for tables. "Post-nouvelle" might be an apt description, for while presentations are dazzlers, the portions are quite sufficient and the singular combinations of ingredients are intensely flavorful. This food bears comparison to the Wolfgang Puck school (French and Asian techniques applied to top-of-the-bin Californian ingredients), although on those rare occasions when the kitchen stumbles, it tends to be with items like updated spring rolls. Experimentation is kept on a tether by the chefs' professionalism, and missteps are few. The menu is never set in stone. If fiddleheads are good at market in the morning, they might well replace the listed asparagus that night. Consider just one recent dish: a timbale of creamy risotto touched with Parmesan hides under a cascade of thread-thin strips of deep-fried sweet potato, all nestled against lightly grilled leaves of palest veal. Duck and foie gras are memorable, while salmon is often the most desirable fish entrée. An exciting cheese selection can precede dessert. The restaurant fills up later than most, with prosperous-looking suits and women with sparkles at throat and wrist. Allow two hours for dinner and call at least a day ahead for reservations.

Witloof. 3619 rue St-Denis (at Sherbrooke). ☎ **514/281-0100.** Reservations recommended. Main courses $13.50–$18.50; table d'hôte $13–$22. AE, DC, ER, MC, V. Mon–Wed 11:30am–11pm, Thurs–Fri 11:30am–midnight, Sat 5pm–midnight, Sun 5–11pm. Metro: Sherbrooke. BELGIAN.

Its name is Flemish for "endive," and when Witloof sticks to the Belgian dishes in which it specializes, it is one of the most gratifying restaurants in town. It contrives to be both a casual and an elegant place, with snowy linen tablecloths covered with butcher paper. Steaming casseroles of mussels with tents of frites on the side are deservedly the most popular on the menu, but the classic Belgian stew, waterzooi, is a close second. Pastas are no better than adequate. Because it is always busy, the kitchen can fall behind on orders, but the convivial atmosphere dissuades grousing. Several Belgian beers, including Blanche de Bruges, are available and go well with most of this food. The restaurant has a large selection of desserts, from crème caramel to praline crepes.

MODERATE

Buona Notte. 3518 St-Laurent (near Sherbrooke). ☎ **514/848-0644.** Reservations recommended. Main courses $6.95–$9.50; table d'hôte $16.95–$25.95. AE, DC, MC, V. Mon–Fri 11:30am–midnight, Sat 5pm–midnight, Sun 10am–3pm and 5pm–midnight. Metro: St-Laurent. CONTEMPORARY ITALIAN.

With its high ceiling masked by fans, wrapped pipes, and heating ducts, Buona Notte could easily be in New York's Soho. A principal component of the decor are plates painted by celebrity diners, among them Michael Bolton, Danny DeVito, and the Gipsy Kings. They are boxed (the plates, that is) and arrayed along one wall. Funk and hip-hop thump over the stereo, people in black cruise the tables, the wait staff look ready to leap at the next casting call. Yet while the food inevitably takes second place to preening, it's surprisingly worthwhile. Pastas prevail, tumbled with crunchy vegetables or silky walnut sauce or any of ten or more combinations. They exhibit less reliance on meat than the norm and make an imaginative risotto with two cheeses and two sauces. Rims of plates are usually dusted with minced parsley and paprika, an overdone device that tends to look messy rather than decorative. Breads are dense and chewy.

✪ L'Express. 3927 rue St-Denis (at Roy). ☎ **514/845-5333.** Reservations recommended. Main courses $10–$16. AE, CB, DC, ER, MC, V. Mon–Fri 8am–3am, Sat 10am–3am, Sun 10am–2am. Metro: Sherbrooke. FRENCH.

No obvious sign announces the presence of this restaurant, only its name discreetly spelled out in white tiles embedded in the sidewalk. Apart from that bit of implicit snobbery, there's no need to call attention to itself, since *tout* Montréal knows exactly where it is. The food is fairly priced for such a trendy place, and is prepared with a sensitivity to lightness in saucing but in substantial helpings. Seasonal adjustments veer from vinegary octopus and lentil salad in summer to full-flavored duck breast with chewy chanterelles in a sauce with the scent of deep woods. Or, simply stop by for a croque monsieur or a bagel with smoked salmon and cream cheese. While reservations are usually necessary for tables, single diners can often find a seat at the bar, where meals are also served.

INEXPENSIVE

The Bagel Factory. 74 rue Fairmount ouest. ☎ **514/272-0667.** Most items $3–$9. No credit cards. Daily 24 hours. Metro: Laurier. BAGELS.

Québec bagels are a must-try treat when in Montréal. Natives insist they are superior to the more famous New York version, and they have a case. Thinner and lighter, they have an agreeably chewy texture that doesn't remind eaters of teething rings. This tiny place is as good a place as any to sample them. It offers a substantial variety, including an extra-large one called Bozo, available for takeout only. Potato latkes, cheese blintzes, and bagel spreads are also sold.

○ Chez Schwartz Charcuterie Hébraïque de Montréal. 3895 bd. St-Laurent (north of Prince Arthur). ☎ **514/842-4813.** Most items $4–$12. No credit cards. Sun–Thurs 9am–1am, Fri 9am–2am, Sat 9am–3am. Metro: St-Laurent. DELI.

Before the imposition of French-first language laws, this was called Schwartz's Montréal Hebrew Delicatessen. To many ardent fans, including this writer, it is the only place on the continent to indulge in the guilty treat of smoked meat. Housed in a long, narrow space, it has a lunch counter and a collection of simple tables and chairs crammed almost impossibly close to each other. Any empty seat is up for grabs. Few mind the inconvenience or proximity to strangers, for they are soon delivered plates described either as small (meaning large) or large (meaning humongous) heaped with slices of the trademark delicacy, along with piles of rye bread. Most people also order sides of french fries and one or two mammoth garlicky pickles. There are a handful of alternative edibles—broiled rib steak or beef liver—but avoid the tofu and leafy green vegetables. Schwartz's has no liquor license.

Lux. 5220 bd. St-Laurent. ☎ **514/271-9277.** Most items $3.25–$8.95. AE, MC, V. Daily 24 hours. Metro: Laurier. LIGHT FARE.

Buy jawbreakers, pick up a copy of *Vanity Fair* or *The New York Times,* shop for T-shirts, and have a Bloody Mary or a hot dog all in the same space—at three in the morning. The place is a combination of cafe, shop, newsstand, and bar, in effect, a 24-hour mall for Montréal's night owls. The interior of the converted textile mill looks like a cross between a Left Bank club and an industrial loft, with a circular main room and two stainless-steel staircases spiraling up to a glass-domed second floor. The centerpiece is the cafe, surrounded by racks holding more than 1,000 magazines. Popular items in the cafe-bar are the homemade desserts, particularly the cheesecake with fresh raspberry sauce; the eggs Benelux, served 24 hours a day; and local beers, including Maudite and Blanche de Chambly.

☉ Pizzédélic. 3509 bd. St-Laurent (near Sherbrooke). ☎ **514/282-6784.** Most items $3.50–$6.25. MC, V. Sun and Wed–Thurs 11:30am–1am; Tues 11:30am–2am; Fri–Sat 11:30am–3am. Metro: St-Laurent. ITALIAN.

Pizza here runs the gamut from traditional to as imaginative as anyone might imagine, with toppings from feta cheese to escargots to artichokes to pesto. All arrive on thin, not quite crispy crusts. Another conveniently located Pizzédélic is downtown at 1329 Ste-Catherine (☎ 514/526-6011).

PICNIC FARE & WHERE TO EAT IT

When planning a picnic or a meal to eat back in the hotel room, consider a stop at **La Vieille Europe,** 3855 St-Laurent near St-Cuthbert (☎ 514/842-5773), a store-house of culinary sights and smells. Choose from wheels of pungent cheeses, garlands of sausages, pâtés, cashews, honey, fresh peanut butter, or dried fruits. Coffee beans are roasted in the back, adding to the admixture of maddening aromas. A large grocery store, **Warshaw,** is next door, should more supplies be required. A stroll to the north along St-Laurent reveals other possibilities for mobile edibles. From there, it isn't far by taxi to Parc du Mont-Royal, a wonderful place to enjoy a picnic.

In Old Montréal, pick up supplies at the dépanneur (convenience store) at 8 rue St-Paul (rue St-Jean-Baptiste), which keeps late hours, and then take them to place Jacques-Cartier or the Old Port, both only steps away. Dépanneurs also sell wine but there's a bigger selection at the **Maison des Vins,** 505 av. du Président-Kennedy at Aylmer, near the Delta hotel, and a shop selling cheeses and crackers is conveniently located right across the hall.

5 Attractions

A superb Metro system, a fairly logical street grid, wide boulevards, and the vehicle-free Underground City all aid in the swift, uncomplicated movement of people from one destination to another in Montréal. The difficulty, as in every great city, lies in making choices that fit your interests and the time available. After all, the possibilities include a hike up imposing Mont-Royal in the middle of the city, biking along the redeveloped waterfront or out beside the Lachine Canal, visits to museums or historic homes, and taking in a hockey or baseball game. With riverboat rides, the fascinating new Biodôme, a sprawling amusement park, and the unique Cirque du Soleil, this city also assures kids of a good time.

A number of the following attractions opened or expanded in 1992. That's no coincidence. They were planned to coincide with that year's celebration of Montréal's 350th birthday. Efforts to enhance the city's cultural attractions have continued since then, as the opening of the Biosphère on Île Sainte-Hélène demonstrates.

A **Montréal Museums Pass** allows entry to 17 of the city's museums. It costs $12 for an adult for one day, or $25 for three days; for families, the price is $24 for one day, $50 for three days. For information, call ☎ 514/861-9609.

THE TOP ATTRACTIONS
DOWNTOWN

✪ **Musée des Beaux-Arts (Museum of Fine Arts).** 1379-1380 rue Sherbrooke ouest (Crescent). ☎ **514/285-1600** or 514/285-2000. Permanent collection only, $4.75 adults, $3 students and children 12 and under, $1 seniors 65 and older and children 3–12, $9.50 families. Special temporary exhibitions plus the permanent collection, $9.50 adults, $4.75 students and seniors 65 and older, $2 children 12 and under, $19 families. Wed 5:30–9pm 50% or more off regular admission. Tues and Thurs–Sun 11am–6pm, Wed 11am–9pm. Metro: Peel or Guy-Corcordia.

Montréal's most prominent museum was opened in 1912, in Canada's first building designed specifically for the arts. The original neo-Classical pavilion is on the north side of Sherbrooke. Years ago, museum administrators recognized that the collection had outstripped its building, and curators were forced to make painful decisions about what few items could be placed on view at any one time. The result was exhibits that often seemed sketchy and incomplete. That problem was solved with the completion of the stunning new annex, the Jean-Noël Desmarais Pavilion, directly across the street. Opened in late 1991, it was designed by Montréal architect Moshe Safdie, who first gained international notice with his Habitat housing complex at the 1967 Expo. Along with two substreet level floors and underground galleries that connect the new building with the old, it tripled the exhibition space.

For the best look at the results, enter the new annex, take the elevator to the top, and work your way down. The permanent collection is largely devoted to international contemporary art and Canadian art after 1960, and to European paintings, sculpture, and decorative arts from the Middle Ages to the 19th century. On the upper floors, for example, are many of the gems of the collection—paintings by El Greco, Reynolds, Renoir, Monet, Picasso, and Cézanne, and sculptures by Rodin and Lipshitz, among others. On the subterranean levels are works by 20th-century modernists, including abstract expressionists of the post–World War II New York School.

From the lowest level of the new pavilion, follow the understreet corridor past primitive artworks from Oceana and Africa, then up the elevator into the old building, with its displays of pre-Columbian ceramics, Inuit carvings, and Amerindian crafts. The rest of that building is used primarily for temporary exhibits.

Across the street, the street-level store has an impressive selection of books, games, and folk art, and there is a cafe. If there is only time for a short visit, make it to the 4th floor. For an extra bonus, be sure to walk to the sculpture court on that level for a splendid panoramic view of the city.

Musée Juste poure Rire (Just for Laughs Museum). 2111 bd. St-Laurent (north of Sherbrooke). ☎ **514/845-2322.** Admission $10 adults; $5 seniors, students, and children 5–12; $20 families. Tues–Sun 1–10pm (last visit 8pm). Closed two months in winter when the new exhibition is being installed. Metro: St-Laurent. Bus: 55.

This engagingly off-center museum opened in Montréal on April Fool's Day, 1993, a byproduct of the annual "Just For Laughs" comedy festival. It may seem a quixotic endeavor, given the differences in tastes between the French and English (witness Jerry Lewis). But it must be remembered that Francophone Québecers share a North American culture and sensibility, and therefore a similar sense of humor. Somehow this place works, as delicate a commodity as humor is, and in both languages. Mammoth shows with lavish exhibits are mounted for several months at a time. They have included clips of world-famous clowns, cartoons, TV sitcoms, and comic shorts. Puns, one-liners, and double entendres abound, not a few of them risqué, others as black as humor gets. Preteens are likely to be simply baffled. Videos and historic film clips hold museum-goers, many of them students, enthralled for hours. It also houses a 250-seat cabaret-theater, a humor hall of fame, a shop, and a cafe.

Musée McCord (McCord Museum of Canadian History). 690 rue Sherbrooke ouest (at Victoria). ☎ **514/398-7100.** Admission $5 adults, $3 seniors, $2 students, free for children under 12, $8 families. Tues–Sun 10am–5pm. Metro: McGill.

Associated with McGill University, this museum showcases the eclectic—and not infrequently eccentric—collections of scores of 19th- and 20th-century benefactors. Objects from its holdings of 80,000 artifacts are rotated in and out of storage, so it isn't possible to be specific about what will be on view at any given time. In general, expect to view furniture, costumes, china, silver, paintings, photographs, and folk art that reveal rural and urban life as it was lived by English-speaking immigrants of the past three centuries. A new atrium connects the original 1905 building with a wing

Montréal Downtown Attractions

Parc du Mont-Royal ③

Centre Canadien d'Architecture ①

Cathédral Christ Church ⑥

Planétarium de Montréal ⑧

Musée Juste Pour Rire ⑩

Cathédrale-Basilique Marie-Reine-du Monde ⑦

Musée McCord d'Histoire Canadienne ⑤

Musée d'Art Contemporain de Montréal ⑨

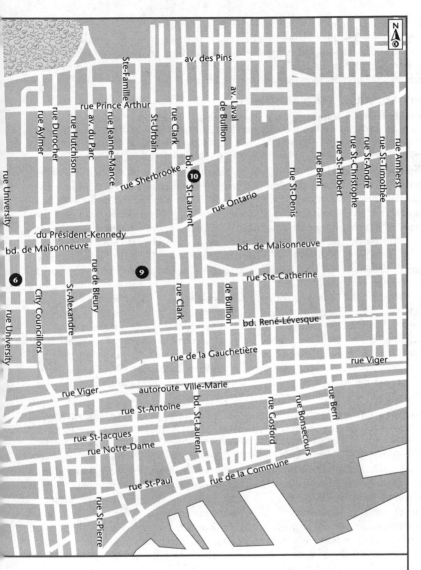

N

av. des Pins

Ste-Famille

rue Prince Arthur

rue Durocher
rue Aylmer
rue Hutchison
av. du Parc
rue Jeanne-Mance
St-Urbain
rue Clark
bd. St-Laurent
av. Laval
de Bullion
rue Berri
rue St-Hubert
rue St-Christophe
rue St-André
rue St-Timothée
rue Amherst

rue Sherbrooke

⑩

rue Ontario

rue St-Denis

rue University

du Président-Kennedy
bd. de Maisonneuve

bd. de Maisonneuve

❻

rue University

City Councillors
St-Alexandre
rue de Bleury
rue Clark
de Bullion

⑨

rue Ste-Catherine

bd. René-Lévesque

rue de la Gauchetière

rue Viger

rue Viger

autoroute Ville-Marie

rue St-Antoine

bd. St-Laurent
rue Gosford
rue Bonsecours
rue Berri

rue St-Jacques
rue Notre-Dame

rue St-Paul

rue de la Commune

rue St-Pierre

Musée des Beaux-Arts ❷
Parc du Mont-Royal ❸
Musée Redpath ❹

added during extensive renovations in 1992. Beyond it are galleries given to temporary exhibits. The First Nations room displays portions of the museum's extensive collection of ethnology and archaeology, including clothing, jewelry, and meticulous beadwork. Exhibits are intelligently mounted, with texts in English and French, although the upstairs rooms are of narrower interest.

VIEUX-MONTRÉAL (OLD MONTRÉAL)

✪ **Basilique Notre-Dame.** me ouest (Place d'Armes). ☎ **514/842-2925.** Basilica free; museum $1 adults, 50¢ students. Basilica June 25–Labor Day daily 7am–8pm; rest of the year daily 7am–6pm; tours mid-May to June 24 and Labor Day to mid-Oct Mon–Fri 9am–4pm (4:30pm in summer). Museum Sat–Sun 9:30am–4pm. Metro: Place d'Armes.

Big enough to hold 4,000 worshipers, and breathtaking in the richness of its interior furnishings, this magnificent structure was designed in 1829 by an Irish-American Protestant architect, James O'Donnell. He was so inspired by his work that he converted to Catholicism after it was done. He had good reason. None of the hundreds of churches on the island of Montréal approaches this interior in its wealth of exquisite detail, most of it carved from rare woods delicately gilded and painted. O'Donnell, one of the proponents the Gothic Revival style in the early middle decades of the 19th century, is one of only a few people honored by burial in the crypt.

The main altar was carved from linden wood, the work of Victor Bourgeau. Behind it is the Chapel of the Sacred Heart, much of it destroyed by a deranged arsonist in 1978 but rebuilt and rededicated in 1982. It is such a popular place for weddings that couples have to book it a year and a half in advance. The chapel altar was cast in bronze by Charles Daudelin of Montréal, with 32 panels representing birth, life, and death. Next to the chapel is a bell, nicknamed Le Gros Bourdon, that weighs more than 12 tons and has a low, resonant rumble that vibrates right up through the feet. It is tolled only on special occasions.

Vieux-Port (Old Port). 333 rue de la Commune ouest (at McGill). ☎ **514/496-7678.** Port and interpretation center, free. Tram rides $2 adults, $1 children 3–12. Charges vary for other attractions. Interpretation Center mid-May to early Sept daily 10am–9pm; hours for specific attractions vary. Metro: Champ-de-Mars, Place d'Armes, or Square-Victoria.

Since 1992, Montréal's once-dreary commercial wharf area has been transformed into an appealing 1.2-mile-long, 133-acre promenade and park with public spaces, exhibition halls, family activities, bike paths, a tall ship called the *Pelican* to explore, and a permanent flea market. Cyclists, in-line skaters, joggers, strollers, lovers, and sunbathers all make use of the park in good weather. To get an idea of all there is to see and do here, hop aboard the small Balade tram that travels throughout the port. During even-numbered years in spring, the acclaimed Cirque du Soleil sets up at the port under its bright yellow-and-blue big top. There's also a large-scale, wraparound IMAX theater. At the far eastern end of the port is a clock tower built in 1922, with 192 steps leading past the exposed clockworks to observation decks at three different levels (admission is free). Most cruises, entertainment, and special events take place from mid-May to October. Information booths with bilingual attendants assist visitors during that period. The Old Port stretches along the waterfront from rue McGill to rue Berri. Quadricycles, bicycles, and in-line skates are available for rent.

Place Jacques-Cartier. Between Notre-Dame and Commune. Metro: Place d'Armes.

Across the street from the Hôtel de Ville (City Hall) is the focus of summer activity in Vieux-Montréal. The most enchanting of the old city's squares has cobblestoned streets that slope down toward the port past ancient stone buildings that survive from the 1700s. Its outdoor cafes, street musicians, flower sellers, and horse-drawn carriages recall the Montréal of a century ago. Montréalers insist they never go to a place so frequented by tourists, which begs the question of why so many of them congregate here. They take the sun and sip sangria on the bordering terraces on warm days, enjoying the unfolding pageant just as much as you will.

✪ **Pointe-à-Callière (Montréal Museum of Archaeology and History).** 350 place Royale. ☎ 514/872-9150. Admission $7 adults, $5 seniors, $4 students, $2 children 6–12, $14 families. To view temporary exhibits only, 50% off. July–Aug Tues–Sun 10am–8pm; rest of year Tues and Thurs–Sun 10am–5pm, Wed 10am–8pm. Metro: Place d'Armes.

A first visit to Montréal might best begin here. Built on the very site where the original colony was established in 1642 (Pointe-à-Calliére), the modern Museum of Archaeology and History engages visitors in rare and beguiling ways. Go first to the 16-minute multimedia show in an auditorium that actually stands above exposed ruins of the earlier city. Images pop up, drop down, and slide out on rolling screens accompanied by music and a playful bilingual narration that keeps the history slick and utterly painless, with enough quick cuts and changes to keep even the youngest viewers from fidgeting.

Pointe-à-Calliére was the point where the St-Pierre River merged with the St. Lawrence. Evidence of the many layers of occupation at this spot—from Amerindians to French trappers to Scottish merchants—were unearthed during archaeological digs that persisted here for more than a decade. They are on view in display cases set among ancient building foundations and burial grounds below street level. The bottom shelves of the cabinets are for items dating to before 1600, and there are other shelves for consecutive centuries.

Wind your way through the complex until you find yourself in the dynamic new building you first entered, which echoes the triangular Royal Insurance building (1861) that stood there for many years. Its tower contains L'Arrivage cafe and provides a fine view of Old Montréal and the Old Port. At the end of the self-guided subterranean tour, in the Custom House, are more exhibits and a well-stocked gift shop. Allow at least an hour for a visit.

ELSEWHERE IN THE CITY

✪ **Biodôme de Montréal.** 4777 av. Pierre-de-Coubertin (next to Olympic Stadium). ☎ 514/868-3000. Admission $8.50 adults, $6 seniors and students, $4.25 children 6–17. Daily 9am–6pm (to 8pm in summer). Metro: Viau.

Near Montréal's Botanical Garden and next to the Olympic Stadium is the engrossing Biodôme, possibly the only environmental museum of its kind. Originally built as the velodrome for the 1976 Olympics, it has been refitted to house replications of four distinct ecosystems, complete with appropriate temperatures, flora, fauna, and changing seasons. With 4,000 creatures and 5,000 trees and plants, the Biodôme incorporates exhibits gathered from the old aquarium and the modest zoos at the Angrignon and LaFontaine parks. It also has a games room for kids called Naturalia, a shop, and a cafe.

Stade Olympique (Olympic Stadium). 4141 av. Pierre-de-Coubertin (boul. Pie IX). ☎ 514/252-8687. Round-trip cable car ride, $7 adults, $5 students and children. Guided tours, recorded train tours, and a multimedia presentation are available. Public swim periods are scheduled daily, with low admission rates. Cable car, mid-June to early Sept, Mon noon–9pm, Tues–Thurs 10am–9pm, Fri–Sat 10am–11pm; early Sept to mid-Jan and mid-Feb to mid-June, Tues–Sun noon–6pm. Closed Tues off-season and all of mid-Jan to mid-Feb. Metro: Pie-IX or Viau (choose the Viau station for the guided tour).

Centerpiece of the 1976 Olympic Games, Montréal's controversial stadium and its associated facilities provide considerable opportunities for both active and passive diversion. It incorporates a natatorium with six different pools including one of competition dimensions with an adjustable bottom and a 50-foot-deep version for scuba-diving. The stadium seats 60,000 to 80,000 spectators, who come here to see the Expos, rock concerts, and trade shows.

It has a 65-ton retractable Kevlar roof winched into place by 125 tons of steel cables, which are attached to a 626-foot inclined tower that looms over the arena like an egret looking for a fish in a bowl. When everything functions as was intended, it takes about 45 minutes to raise or lower the roof. In reality, the roof malfunctions frequently and high winds have torn large rents in the fabric. That is only one reason that what was first known as "The Big O" was scorned as "The Big Owe" after cost overruns led to heavy increases in taxes.

The tower, which leans at a 45° angle, also does duty as an observation deck, with a funicular that whisks 90 passengers to the top in 95 seconds. On a clear day, the deck bestows a 35-mile view over Montréal and into the neighboring Laurentians. A free shuttle bus links the Olympic Park and the Botanical Garden.

MORE ATTRACTIONS
DOWNTOWN
Cathédrale-Basilique Marie-Reine-du-Monde (Mary Queen of the World Cathedral).
Boul. René-Lévesque (at Mansfield). ☎ **514/866-1661.** Free admission; donations accepted. Summer daily 7am–7:30pm; fall–spring Sat 8am–8:30pm, Sun 9:30am–7:30pm. Metro: Bonaventure.

No one who has seen both will confuse this with St. Peter's Basilica in Rome, but a scaled-down homage was the intention of its guiding force, Bishop Ignace Bourget, in the middle of the last century. He was moved to act after the first Catholic cathedral burned to the ground in 1852. Construction lasted from 1875 to 1894, delayed by his desire to place it not in Francophone east Montréal but in the heart of the Protestant Anglophone west. The resulting structure covers less that a quarter of the area of its Roman inspiration, and there are no curving arcades to embrace a sweeping plaza in front. The stairs to the entrance are only a few yards away from the boulevard. Most impressive is the 252-foot-high dome, about half the size of the original. A local touch is provided by the statues standing on the roofline, representing local patron saints. The interior is less rewarding visually than the outside. A planned restoration is expected to cost at least $7.5 million.

Centre Canadien d'Architecture (CCA). 1920 rue Baile (bd. René-Lévesque). ☎ **514/939-7026.** Admission $5 adults, $3 students and seniors, children under 12 free. June–Sept Tues–Sat 11am–6pm, Thurs 11am–8pm; rest of year, Wed and Fri 11am–6pm, Thurs 11am–8pm, Sat–Sun 11am–5pm. Guided tours available on request. Metro: Atwater, Guy-Concordia, or Georges-Vanier.

The understated but handsome CCA building fills a city block, joining a thoughtfully contemporary structure with an existing older building, the 1875 Shaughnessy House. The CCA doubles as a study center and a museum with changing exhibits devoted to the art of architecture and its history, including architects' sketchbooks, elevation drawings, and photography. The collection is international in scope and encompasses architecture, urban planning, and landscape design. Texts are in French and English. Opened only in 1989, the museum has received rave notices from scholars, critics, and serious architecture buffs. That said, it is only fair to note that the average visitor is likely to find it less than enthralling. The bookstore has a special section on Canadian architecture with emphasis on Montréal and Québec City. The sculpture garden across the Ville-Marie autoroute is part of the CCA, designed by artist/architect Melvin Charney.

Centre d'Histoire de Montréal. 335 place d'Youville (St-Pierre). ☎ **514/872-3207.** Admission $4.50 adults, $3 students, children 6–17, and seniors. Late Jan–early May and early Sept to mid-Dec Tues–Sun 10am–5pm; early May to mid-June daily 9am–5pm; late June–early Sept daily 10am–6pm. Closed mid-Dec to end of Dec. Metro: Square-Victoria.

Built in 1903 as Montréal's Central Fire Station, the red-brick and sandstone building is now the Montréal History Center, which traces the history of the city from its first occupants, the Amerindians, to the European settlers who arrived in 1642, to the present day. Throughout its 14 rooms, carefully conceived presentations chart the contributions of the city fathers and mothers and subsequent generations. The development of the railroad, metro, and related infrastructure are recalled, as is that of domestic and public architecture in imaginative exhibits, videos, and slide shows. On the second floor, reached by a spiral staircase, are memorabilia from the early 20th century. Labels are in French, so ask at the front desk for a visitor's guide in English.

Christ Church Cathedral. 1444 Union Ave.(at Ste-Catherine and University). ☎ **514/843-6577.** Free admission; donations accepted. Daily 8am–6pm; services Sun 8am, 10am, and 4pm. Metro: McGill.

This Anglican cathedral stands in glorious Gothic contrast to the city's glassy downtown skyscrapers, reflected in the post-modernist Maison des Coopérants office tower. Sometimes called the "floating cathedral" because of the many tiers of malls and corridors of the Underground City beneath it, the building was erected in 1859. The original steeple, too heavy for the structure, was replaced by a lighter aluminum version in 1940. Christ Church Cathedral hosts concerts throughout the year, notably from June through August on Wednesdays at 12:30pm.

Musée d'Art Contemporain de Montréal (Museum of Contemporary Art). 185 rue Ste-Catherine ouest. ☎ **514/847-6212.** Admission $6 adults, $4 seniors, $3 students, $12 families, free for children under 12; free to all Wed 6–9pm. Tues–Sun 11am–6pm (Wed to 9pm). Metro: Place-des-Arts.

The only museum in Canada devoted exclusively to contemporary art moved into this new facility at the Place-des-Arts in 1992 after years in an isolated riverfront building. "Contemporary" is defined here as art produced since 1939. It showcases the work of Québec and other Canadian artists, but is supplemented by a collection of 3,400 works by such notables as Jean Dubuffet, Max Ernst, Jean Arp, Ansel Adams, Larry Poons, Antoni Tàpies, Max Ernst, Robert Mapplethorpe, and Montréal photographer Michel Campeau. A few larger pieces are seen on the ground floor, but most are one flight up, with space for temporary exhibitions to the right and selections from the permanent collection on the left. No single style prevails, so expect to see minimalist installations small and large video displays, evocations of Pop, Op, and Abstract Expression, and accumulations of objects simply piled on the floor. That the works often arouse strong opinions signifies a museum that is doing something right.

VIEUX-MONTRÉAL (OLD MONTRÉAL)

Château Ramezay. 280 rue Notre-Dame (east Of Place Jacques-Cartier). ☎ **514/861-3708.** Admission $5 adults; $3 seniors and students; children under 6 free; $10 families. May–Sept daily 10am–6pm; Oct–Apr Tues–Sun 10am–4:30pm. Metro: Champ-de-Mars.

Built by Gov. Claude de Ramezay in 1705, the château was the home of the city's royal French governors for four decades, before being taken over and used for the same purpose by the British conquerors. In 1775 an army of American revolutionaries invaded and held Montréal, using the château as their headquarters. Benjamin Franklin, sent to persuade Québecers to rise with the colonists against British rule, stayed in the château for a time, but failed to persuade the city's people to join his cause. After the American interlude, the house was used as a courthouse, government office building, teachers' college, and headquarters for Laval University before being converted into a museum in 1895. Old coins, furnishings, tools, and other memorabilia related to the economic and social activities of the 18th century and first half of the 19th century fill the main floor. In the cellar are seen the original vaults of the house. Across rue Notre-Dame is the City Hall.

Hôtel de Ville (City Hall). 275 rue Notre-Dame (at the corner of rue Gosford). ☎ **514/872-3355.** Free admission. Daily 8:30am–4:30pm. Metro: Champ-de-Mars.

This is a relatively recent building by Old Montréal standards, finished in 1878. The French Second Empire design makes it look as though it was imported from Paris, stone by stone. Balconies, turrets and mansard roofs detail the exterior, seen to particular advantage when illuminated at night. It was from the balcony above the awning that Charles de Gaulle proclaimed, "Vive le Québec Libre!" in 1967. Fifteen-minute guided tours are given throughout the day on weekdays May through October. The Hall of Honour is made of green marble from Campagna, Italy, with Art Deco lamps from Paris and a bronze-and-glass chandelier, also from France, that weighs a metric ton. In the display cabinet to the left by the elevator are gifts from mayors of other cities from around the world. Council Chamber meetings, on the first floor, are open to the public. The chamber has a hand-carved ceiling and five stained-glass windows representing religion, the port, industry and commerce, finance, and transportation. The mayor's office is on the fourth floor.

Église Notre-Dame-de-Bonsecours (Notre Dame de Bon Secours Chapel). 400 rue St-Paul (at the foot of rue Bonsecours). ☎ **514/845-9991.** Chapel free; museum $2 adults, 50¢ children. Chapel May–Oct daily 9am–5pm; Nov–Apr daily 10am–3pm. Museum May–Oct Tues–Sun 9am–4:30pm; Nov–Apr Tues–Sun 10:30am–2:30pm. Metro: Champ-de-Mars.

Just to the east of Marché Bonsecours, this is called the Sailors' Church because of the wooden ship models hanging inside, given as votive offerings by fishermen and other mariners. The first church building, the project of an energetic teacher named Marguerite Bourgeoys, was built in 1678. She arrived with de Maisonneuve to undertake the education of the children of Montréal in the latter half of the 17th century. Later on, she and several sister teachers founded a nuns' order called the Congregation of Notre-Dame, Canada's first. The present church, which dates from 1771–73, has a small museum downstairs with 58 stage sets dedicated to her life and work. A carving of the Madonna has been displayed in both churches. Due to a theft, the carving now on view is a replica. The recovered original is locked up. The pioneering Bourgeoys was recognized as a saint in 1982. There's an excellent view of the harbor and the old quarter from the church's tower.

Marché Bonsecours. 350 rue St-Paul (at the foot of rue St-Claude). ☎ **514/872-4560.** Metro: Champ-de-Mars.

This imposing neo-Classical building with a long facade, a colonnaded portico, and a handsome silvery dome was built in the mid-1800s and first used as Montréal's City Hall, then for many years after 1878 as the central market. Restored in 1964, it housed city government offices, and in 1992 became the information and exhibition center for the celebration of the city's 350th birthday. It continues to be used as an exhibition space. The architecture alone makes a visit worthwhile.

PLATEAU MONT-ROYAL

Musée de Hospitalières de l'Hôtel-Dieu. 201 av. des Pins ouest. ☎ 514/849-2919. Admission $5 adults, $3 seniors and students 12 and over. Mid-June to mid-Oct Tues–Fri 10am–5pm, Sat–Sun 1–5pm. Mid-Oct to mid-June Wed–Sun 1–5pm. Metro: Sherbrooke. Bus: 144.

Opened in 1992 to coincide with the city's 350th birthday, this unusual museum, in the former chaplain's residence of Hôtel-Dieu Hospital, traces the history of Montréal from 1659 to the present, and focuses on the evolution of health care spanning three centuries in the history of the hospital, including an exhibit of medical instruments. It bows to the missionary nurse Jeanne Mance, the founder of the first hospital in Montréal, who arrived in 1642, the only woman among the first settlers who left France with Sieur de Maisonneuve. The museum's three floors are filled with memorabilia, including paintings, books, reliquaries, furnishings, and a reconstruction of a nun's cell. Its architectural high point is a marvelous "floating" oak staircase brought to the New World in 1634 from the Maison-Dieu hospital in La Flèche, France. The original Hôtel-Dieu was built in 1645 near the site of the present Notre-Dame Basilica, in Old Montréal. This building was erected in 1861.

Oratoire St-Joseph (St. Joseph's Oratory). 3800 chemin Queen Mary (on the north slope of Mont-Royal). ☎ 514/733-8211. Free admission, but donations are requested at the museum. Daily 7am–8pm; museum daily 10am–5pm. The 56-bell carillon plays Wed–Fri noon–3pm, Sat–Sun noon–2:30pm. Metro: Côtes-des-Neiges.

This huge basilica, with its giant copper dome, was built by Québec's Catholics to honor St. Joseph, patron saint of Canada. Dominating the north slope of Mont-Royal, its imposing dimensions are seen by some as inspiring, by others as forbidding. It came into being through the efforts of Brother André, a lay brother in the Holy Cross order who enjoyed a reputation as a healer. By the time he had built a small wooden chapel in 1904 near the site of the basilica, he was said to have effected hundreds of cures. Those celebrated powers attracted supplicants from great distances, and Brother André performed his work until his death in 1937. His dream of building this shrine to his patron saint became a reality only years after his death, in 1967. He is buried in the basilica, and was beatified by the pope in 1982, a status one step below sainthood. The basilica is largely Italian Renaissance in style, its dome recalling the shape of the Duomo in Florence, but of much greater size and less grace. Inside is a museum where a central exhibit is the heart of Brother André. Outside, a Way of the Cross lined with sculptures was the setting of scenes for the film *Jesus of Montréal.* Brother André's wooden chapel, with his tiny bedroom, are on the grounds and open to the public. Pilgrims, some ill, come to seek intercession from St. Joseph and Brother André, and often climb the middle set of steps on their knees. At 862 feet (263m), the shrine is the highest point in Montréal. A cafeteria and snack bar are on the premises. Guided tours are offered at 10am and 2pm daily in summer and on weekends in September and October (donation only).

ELSEWHERE IN THE CITY

La Biosphère. 160 chemin Tour-de-l'Isle (Île Ste-Hélène). ☎ 514/283-5000. Admission $6.50 adults, $5 seniors and students, $4 children 7–17, $16 families. June–Sept daily 10am–8pm; Oct–May Tues–Sun 9am–6pm. Metro: Île Ste-Hélène, then the shuttle bus.

Not to be confused with the Biodôme at Olympic Park, this new project is located in the geodesic dome designed by Buckminster Fuller to serve as the American Pavilion for Expo '67. A fire destroyed the acrylic skin of the sphere in 1976, and it served no purpose other than as a harbor landmark until 1995. The motivation behind the Biosphère is unabashedly environmental, with four exhibition areas, a water theater, and an amphitheater all devoted to promoting awareness of the St. Lawrence–Great Lakes ecosystem. Multimedia shows and hand-on displays invite the active participation of visitors. In the highest point of the so-called Visions Hall is an observation level with unobstructed view of the river. Connections Hall offers a "Call to Action" presentation employing six giant screens and three stages. There is a preaching-to-the-choir quality to all this that slips over the edge into zealous philosophizing. But the various displays and exhibits are put together thoughtfully and will divert and enlighten most visitors, at least for a while.

Musée des Arts Decoratifs de Montréal (Decorative Arts Museum). 2929 Jeanne-d'Arc (enter on Pie-IX). ☎ **514/259-2575.** Admission $3 adults, $2 seniors, $1.50 students 13–25, free for children 12 and under. Fri–Sun 11am–5pm. Metro: Pie-IX.

In 1915 Oscar and Marius Dufresne began construction of a 44-room Beaux Arts mansion in a then-distant precinct of Montréal. The two brothers, one an industrialist and the other an engineer, divided the house down the middle and proceeded to fill it with silverware, porcelain, paintings, sculpture, furniture, and textiles of the period. Besides the lavish use of Italian marble and African mahogany, and the Dufresnes' original furnishings, the museum displays religious sculptures from the 1700s and 1800s, a collection devoted to the Hébert family of artists from Québec, and an assembly of avant-garde furnishings of the 1930s to 1950s by such designers as Frank Lloyd Wright and Marcel Breuer. The contrasts between the various components of the collections are somewhat jarring, and the museum doesn't justify the longish trip from downtown on its own. However, it can easily be combined with visits to nearby Olympic Park, the Biodôme, and the Botanical Garden.

Musée Marc-Aurèle Fortin. 118 rue St-Pierre (rue d'Youville). ☎ **514/845-6108.** Admission $3 adults, $1 students and seniors, free for children under 12. Tues–Sun 11am–5pm. Metro: Place d'Armes.

This is Montréal's only museum dedicated to the work of a single French-Canadian artist. Landscape watercolorist Marc-Aurèle Fortin (1888–1970) interpreted the beauty of the Québec countryside, such as the Laurentians and Charlevoix. His work is on the ground floor, while temporary exhibits usually feature the work of other Québec painters.

Musée David M. Stewart. Vieux Fort, Île Ste-Hélène. ☎ **514/861-6701.** Admission $5 adults, $3 seniors and students $10 families. Children under 7 free. Summer Wed–Mon 10am–6pm; rest of year Wed–Mon 10am–5pm. Metro: Île Ste-Hélène, then a 15-minute walk.

After the War of 1812, the British prepared for a possible future American invasion by building this moated fortified arsenal. The Duke of Wellington ordered its construction as another link in the chain of fortifications along the St. Lawrence. Completed in 1824, it was never involved in armed conflict. The British garrison left in 1870, after confederation of the former Canadian colonies. Today the low stone barracks and blockhouses contain the museum, which displays maps and scientific instruments that helped Europeans explore the New World, as well as military and naval artifacts, uniforms, and related paraphernalia from the time of Jacques Cartier (1535) through the end of the colonial period.

From late June through late August, the fort comes to life with reenactments of military parades by La Compagnie Franche de la Marine and the 78th Fraser Highlanders, at 11am, 2:30pm, and 5pm. The presence of the French unit is an unhistorical sop to Francophone sensibilities, since New France had become English Canada almost 65 years before the fort was erected.

OFFBEAT SIGHTS

Lieu Historique Sir George-Éienne Cartier. 458 rue Notre-Dame (at Berri). ☎ **514/283-2282.** Free admission (this may change, however). May–early Sept daily 10am–6pm; Sept–May Wed–Sun 10am–noon and 1–5pm. Closed Jan. Metro: Champ-des-Mars.

Operated by Parks Canada, this off-the-tourist-track historic site is actually two houses. One has been reconstructed to its appearance in the 1860s as the Victorian residence of Sir George-Étienne Cartier (1814–73), one of the fathers of Canada's 1867 Confederation. The adjacent house is devoted to Cartier's career and work. During the summer, the site has costumed guides and hosts concerts and other activities.

Musée de la Banque de Montréal (Bank of Montréal Museum). 119 and 129 rue St-Jacques (Place d'Armes). ☎ **514/877-6892.** Free admission. Museum Mon–Fri 10am–4pm, bank Mon–Fri 8am–5pm. Metro: Place d'Armes.

Facing Place d'Armes is Montréal's oldest bank building, with a classic facade beneath a graceful dome, a carved pediment, and six Corinthian columns, mostly unchanged since its completion in 1847. The interior was renovated in 1901–05 by the famed U.S. firm McKim, Mead, and White with Ionic and Corinthian columns of Vermont granite, walls of pink marble from Tennessee, and a counter of Levanto marble. The bank contains a small museum with a replica of its first office (and its first bank teller, Henry Stone from Boston), gold nuggets from the Yukon, a $3 bill (one of only two known), and a collection of 100-year-old mechanical banks. A bilingual guide is available to answer questions.

Redpath Museum. 859 rue Sherbrooke ouest (McGill University). ☎ **514/398-4086.** Free admission. Sept–June Mon–Fri 9am–5pm; July–Aug Mon–Thurs 9am–5pm, Sun 1–5pm (except holiday weekends). Metro: McGill.

If the unusual name seems slightly familiar, think of the wrappings on sugar cubes in many restaurants. John Redpath was a 19th-century industrialist who built Canada's first sugar refinery and later distributed much of his fortune in philanthropy. This modest museum is on the McGill University campus, in an 1882 building. The main draw is its collection of Egyptian antiquities, the second-largest in Canada, but also on view are fossils and geological fragments.

PARKS & GARDENS

✪ Jardin Botanique (Botanical Garden). 4101 rue Sherbrooke est (opposite Olympic Stadium). ☎ **514/872-1400.** For the outside gardens, greenhouses, and insectarium, May–Nov $7 adults, $5 seniors over 65 and students, $3.50 children 6–17; Dec–Apr $5 adults, $3.50 seniors and students, $2.50 children. A ticket for the Botanical Garden, Insectarium, and Biodôme, good for two consecutive days, $12.50 adults, $9.50 seniors, and $6.25 children. Daily 9am–6pm (to 8pm in summer). Metro: Pie-IX; walk up the hill to the gardens, or from mid-May to mid-Sept take the shuttle bus from Olympic Park.

Across the street from the Olympic sports complex, the garden spreads across 180 acres. Begun in 1931, it has grown to include 26,000 different types of plants in 31 specialized gardens, ensuring something beautiful and fragrant for visitors year-round. Ten large conservatory greenhouses shelter tropical and desert plants, and bonsai and penjings, from the Canadian winter. One greenhouse, called the Wizard of Oz, is especially fun for kids. Roses bloom here from mid-June to the first frost, May is the month for lilacs, and June for the flowering hawthorn trees. Inaugurated in summer 1991, the six-acre Chinese Garden, a joint project of Montréal and Shanghai, is the largest of its kind ever built outside Asia, with pavilions, inner courtyards, ponds, and myriad plants indigenous to China. The serene Japanese Garden fills 15 acres and contains a cultural pavilion with an art gallery, a tearoom where the ancient tea ceremony is observed, and a Zen garden. The grounds are also home to the relatively new Insectarium, displaying some of the world's most beautiful insects, not to mention some of its sinister ones (see "Especially for Kids," below). Birders should bring along binoculars on summer visits to spot some of the more than 130 species of birds that spend at least part of the year in the Botanical Garden. In summer, an outdoor aviary is filled with Québec's most beautiful butterflies. Year-round, a free shuttle bus links the Botanical Garden and nearby Olympic Park; a small train runs regularly through the gardens and is worth the small fee charged to ride it.

Parc du Mont-Royal. ☎ 514/844-4928 (general information) or 514/872-6559 (special events). Daily 6am–midnight. Metro: Mont-Royal. Bus: No. 11; hop off at Lac des Castors.

Montréal is named for the 761-foot (232m) hill that rises at its heart. Joggers, cyclists, dog-walkers, and others use it religiously. On Sundays hundreds of folks congregate around the statue of George-Étienne Cartier to listen and sometimes dance to improvised music, and Lac des Castors (Beaver Lake) is surrounded by sunbathers and picnickers in summer (there's no swimming allowed, however). In wintertime, cross-country skiers follow the miles of paths and snowshoers tramp and crunch along other trails laid out especially for them. In the cold months, the lake fills with whirling ice-skaters of various levels of aptitude. The large, refurbished Chalet Lookout near the crest of the hill provides both a sweeping view of the city and an opportunity for a snack. Up the hill behind the chalet is the spot where, tradition has it, de Maisonneuve erected his wooden cross in 1642. Today the cross is a 100-foot-high steel structure rigged for illumination at night and visible from all over the city. Park security is provided by mounted police. There are three cemeteries on the northern slope of the mountain—Catholic, Protestant, and Jewish.

Parc Lafontaine. Rue Sherbrooke and av. Parc Lafontaine. ☎514/872-2644. Free admission; small fee for use of tennis courts. Always open. Tennis courts, daily 9am–10pm in summer. Metro: Sherbrooke.

The European-style park near downtown is one of the city's oldest. In testament to the dual identities of the populace, half the park is landscaped in the formal French manner, the other in the more casual English style. Among its several bodies of water is a lake used for paddle-boating in summer and ice skating in winter. Snowshoeing and cross-country trails curl through the trees. The amphitheater is the setting for outdoor theater and movies in summer. Joggers, bikers, picnickers, and tennis buffs (there are 14 outdoor courts) share the space.

ESPECIALLY FOR KIDS

IMAX Theatre. Old Port, Quai King Edward (end of bd. St-Laurent). ☎ 514/349-4629 (shows and times). Admission $11.75 adults, $9.75 seniors and students, $7.50 children 4–11. Year-round. Call for current schedule of shows in English. Metro: Place d'Armes.

The images and special effects are larger-than-life, sometimes in 3-D and always visually dazzling, thrown on a seven-story screen. Arrive for shows at least 10 minutes early, earlier on weekends and evenings.

Insectarium. Botanical Garden, 4101 rue Sherbrooke (bd. Pie IX). ☎ 514/872-1400. May–Oct $7 adults, $5 seniors over 65, $3.50 children 6–17; Nov–Apr $5 adults, $3.50 seniors, $2.50 children. Summer daily 9am–8pm; rest of year daily 9am–6pm. Metro: Pie-IX; walk up the hill to the gardens or in summer take the shuttle bus from Olympic Park.

A recent addition to the Botanical Garden, this two-level structure near the Sherbrooke gate exhibits the collections of two avid entomologists: Georges Brossard (whose brainchild this place is) and Father Firmia Liberté. More than 3,000 mounted butterflies, scarabs, maggots, locusts, beetles, tarantulas, and giraffe weevils are displayed, and live exhibits feature scorpions, tarantulas, crickets, cockroaches, and praying mantises. Needless to say, kids are delighted by the creepy critters. Their guardians are apt to be less enthusiastic.

La Ronde Amusement Park. Parc des Îles, Île Ste-Hélène. ☎ **514/872-6222** or 800/ 361-8020. Unlimited all-day pass $18.85 for those 12 and older, $9.45 under 12, $42 family pass. Reserved seating for fireworks, from $21.50 including all rides. Ground admission only $9.85; parking $6.15. Mid-May to late June Sun–Fri 10am–10pm, Sat 11am–1am; late June– early Sept Sun–Thurs 11am–midnight, Fri–Sat 11am–1am. Metro: Papineau and bus no. 169, or Île Ste-Hélène and bus no. 167.

Montréal's ambitious amusement park fills the northern reaches of the Île Ste-Hélène with more than 30 rides, an international circus, a medieval village, roller coasters, and places to eat and drink. Thrillseekers will love the Cobra, a stand-up roller coaster that incorporates a 360° loop and reaches speeds in excess of 60 m.p.h. A big attraction every year is the International Fireworks Competition, held on Saturdays in June and Sundays in July. The pyromusical displays are launched at 10pm and last at least 30 minutes. (Some Montréalers choose to watch them from the Jacques Cartier Bridge, which is closed to traffic then. They take along a Walkman to listen to the accompanying music.)

Planetarium de Montréal. 1000 rue St-Jacques (at Peel). ☎ **514/872-4530.** Admission $5.50 adults, $3.25 seniors, students, and children 6–17. Jan 9 to mid-June and Labor Day–Dec 23 Tues–Sun and holidays 2:30–7:30pm; mid-June to Labor Day, Dec 24, and Jan 2–8 daily 2:30–7:30pm. Metro: Bonaventure (Windsor Station exit).

A window on the night sky with its mythical monsters and magical heroes, Montréal's planetarium is right downtown, only two blocks south of Windsor Station. Changing shows under the 65-foot (20m) dome dazzle and inform kids at the same time. Shows change with the seasons, exploring time and space travel and collisions of celestial bodies. The special Christmas show, "Star of the Magi," which can be seen throughout December and early January, is based on recent investigations of historians and astronomers into the mysterious light that guided the Magi. Shows in English alternate with those in French.

S.O.S. Labyrinthe. Old Port, Quay King Edward (end of bd. St-Laurent). ☎ **514/982-9660** or 800/361-8020. Admission $8.75 adults, $7.50 students, $18 families. May 1–Oct 9 daily 10am–10pm. Metro: Champ-de-Mars.

True to its name, it offers over 1.2 miles (2km) of indoor twisting paths, obstacles, and challenges, including a tunnel and a secret passage, all connected by a maze of corridors. Fogs and spouting water complicate the journey. The course changes weekly and incorporates a treasure hunt. Kids, up to teenagers, love it. Guides on in-line skates are on duty for those who can't find their way out.

Theatre Biscuit. 221 rue St-Paul ouest (near rue St-Francois-Xavier). ☎ **514/845-7306.** Admission $12.50 adults, $9.50 children. Sat–Sun only; performances at 3pm. Pick up tickets at 2:30pm. Metro: Place d'Armes.

Montréal's only permanent puppet theater has shows on weekends, and reservations are required. Visitors may explore its small puppet museum. This is good family fun, and understanding French is not essential.

6 Special Events & Festivals

Montréal's answer to Québec City's Winter Carnival is February's **La Fête Des Neiges (Snow Festival),** with outdoor events like harness racing, barrel jumping, racing beds on ice, canoe races, snowshoeing, skating, and cross-country skiing. The less athletically inclined can cheer from the sidelines, and then inspect the snow and ice sculptures. It's held mostly on Île Notre-Dame, in the Port and Vieux-Montréal, and in Parc Maisonneuve. Call ☎ 514/872-6093 for details.

Early in June some 45,000 biking enthusiasts converge on Montréal to participate in a grueling day-long race before more than 120,000 spectators. **La Tour de L'Île de Montréal,** which began in 1984, attracts almost as many women as men. Call ☎ 514/847-8356 for details.

Screenings of new and experimental films stimulate controversy and forums on the latest trends in film and video at halls and cinemas throughout the city in June at the **International Festival of New Cinema and Video** (☎ 514/843-4725).

Major international Formula I drivers burn rubber around the Gilles-Villeneuve racetrack on Île Notre-Dame for the running of the **Molson Grand Prix of Canada,** held the second weekend in June. Call ☎ 514/392-0000.

St-Jean Baptiste Day (June 24) honors St. John the Baptist, the patron saint of French Canadians. It is marked by more festivities and far more enthusiasm throughout Québec province than national Dominion Day on July 1. It's their "national" holiday.

Montréal has a long tradition in jazz, and its enormously successful **International Jazz Festival** has been celebrating it since 1979. Major stars have headlined over the years, but it costs money to hear the big names. Fortunately, hundreds of other concerts are free, often given on the streets and plazas of the city. The festival runs from late June through early July; for information and tickets, call ☎ 514/289-9472. Seats can be reserved through Ticketron.

The **Just for Laughs Festival** almost equals the more famous jazz festival in magnitude. It even gave rise to the establishment of a humor museum. Comics perform in many venues, some for free, some not. Both Francophone and Anglophone comics from many countries participate. It's held along rue St-Denis and rue de Maisonneuve in the last two weeks of July. Call ☎ 514/845-3155.

The open-air theater in La Ronde amusement park on Île Ste-Hélène is the best place to view the pyrotechnics of Montréal's **Benson & Hedges International Fireworks Competition,** although they can be enjoyed from almost any point overlooking the river. Tickets to the show also provide entrance to the amusement park. Kids, needless to say, love the whole explosive business. The 90-minute shows are staged by companies from several countries. Since parking is limited, it's best to use the metro. It's held Saturdays in June, Sundays in July. Call ☎ 800/361-4595 for reserved seats.

Late August brings the **World Film Festival,** with some 500 screenings over 12 days, drawing the usual throngs of directors, stars, and wannabes. It isn't as gaudy as Cannes, but it's taken almost as seriously. Various movie theaters play host. ☎ 514/933-9699 for details.

The **International Festival of New Dance** is a 12-day showcase that invites troupes and choreographers from Canada, the United States, and Europe to various performance spaces in mid-October. Call ☎ 514/287-1423.

7 Outdoor Activities & Spectator Sports

OUTDOOR ACTIVITIES

BICYCLING Montréal enjoys a network of 149 miles (240km) of cycling paths. Popular routes include the 6.8-mile (11km) path along the Lachine Canal that leads to Lac St-Louis, the 10-mile (16km) path west from the St-Lambert Lock (see above) to the city of Côte Ste-Catherine, and Angrignon Park with its 4-mile biking path and inviting picnic areas (take the Metro, which accepts bikes in the last two doors of the last car, to Angrignon station). Bikes can be rented at the Vieux-Port (at the end of boulevard St-Laurent) for $6 an hour or $20 a day. Bikes, along with the popular four-wheel "Q Cycles," may also be rented at the place Jacques-Cartier entrance to the Old Port. The Q Cycles, for use in the Old Port only, cost $4.25 per half hour for adults and $3.50 per half hour for children.

CROSS-COUNTRY SKIING   **Parc Mont-Royal** has a 1.3-mile (2.1km) cross-country course called the *parcours de la croix*. The **Botanical Garden** has an ecology trail used by cross-country skiers. The problem for either is that skiers have to supply their own equipment. Just an hour from the city, in the Laurentides, are almost 20 ski centers, all offering cross-country as well as downhill skiing. See the following chapter.

HIKING   The most popular—and obvious—hike is up to the top of **Mont-Royal.** Start downtown on rue Peel, which leads north to a stairway, which in turn leads to a half-mile (800m) path of switchbacks called Le Serpent. Or, opt for the 200 steps that lead up to the Chalet Lookout, with the reward of a panoramic view of the city. Figure about 1¼ miles one way.

IN-LINE SKATING   In-line skates and all the relevant protective gear can be rented from **Velo Adventure** (☎ 514/847-0666) on Quai King Edward in the Vieux-Port. The cost is $8.50 (weekday) or $9 (weekend) for the first hour and $4 for each additional hour. A deposit is required. Lessons on skates are available for $25 for two hours.

JOGGING   There are many possibilities. One is to follow rue Peel north to Le Serpent switchback path on Mont-Royal, continuing uphill on it for half a mile (800m) until it peters out. Turn right and continue 1 mile (2km) to the monument of George-Étienne Cartier, one of Canada's fathers of confederation. From here, either take a bus back downtown or run back down the same route or along avenue du Parc and avenue des Pins (turn right when you get to it). It's also fun to jog along the Lachine Canal.

SWIMMING   Unfortunately, the St. Lawrence is too polluted for swimming. Bordering the river, though, is the artificial **Plage de l'Île Notre-Dame,** the former Regatta Lake from Expo '67. The water is drawn from the Lachine Rapids and treated by a mostly natural filtration system of sand, aquatic plants, and ultraviolet light (and a bit of chlorine) to make it safe for swimming. To get there, take the metro to the Île Ste-Hélène station (☎ 514/872-6093).

Those who prefer a pool but are staying in a hotel that doesn't have one can take the Metro to Viau station and **Olympic Park,** 4141 Pierre-de-Coubertin, which has six pools, open from about 9:30am to 9pm Monday through Friday and 1 to 4pm Saturday and Sunday. Call ahead to confirm swim schedules, which are affected by competitions and holidays (☎ 514/252-4622).

The City of Montréal Department of Sports and Leisure can provide information about other city pools, indoor or outdoor (☎ 514/872-6211). Admission to the pools varies from free to about $4 ($2 for children), with the exception of the artificial beach, Plage de l'Île Notre-Dame, which is $7 for adults, seniors, and students, $2.50 for children 6 to 17.

SPECTATOR SPORTS

Montréalers are as avidly devoted to ice hockey as other Canadians, with plenty of enthusiasm left over for baseball and soccer. Some boosters have even floated the idea of bidding for a future NFL Super Bowl, if they can ever get the roof of the

Olympic Stadium to work properly. In the meantime, there are several regularly ongoing sporting events, such as the Molson Grand Prix in June, The Player's Ltd. International men's tennis championship in late July, and the Montréal Marathon in September.

HOCKEY　The NHL's **Montréal Canadiens** play at the Montréal Forum, 2313 Ste-Catherine ouest, between Closse and Atwater (☎ 514/932-2582). They've won 24 Stanley Cup championships since 1929. The season runs from October into mid-June. Tickets are $23.50 for seats, $10 for standing room. Metro: Atwater.

BASEBALL　The **Montréal Expos,** part of the National League, play at Olympic Stadium, 4549 Pierre-de-Coubertin, from April through September. Ticket reservations can be made by telephone, with a credit card. Call ☎ 514/846-3976 for information. Tickets are around $15.25 adults, $9 seniors, $5.50 students, $4 children. Metro: Pie-IX.

HORSE-RACING　**Blue Bonnets Racetrack,** 7440 bd. Décarie, at Jean-Talon (☎ 514/739-2741), is the dedicated facility for international harness-racing events, including the Prix d'Eté, the Prix de l'Avenir, the Blue Bonnets Challenge, and the Breeders Cup. Restaurants, bars, a snack bar, and pari-mutuel betting can make for a satisfying evening or Sunday afternoon outing. There are no races on Tuesday and Thursday. Admission is $5 to the clubhouse, $3.75 to the stands; free for children under 16. Races begin at 7:30pm on Monday, Wednesday, Friday, and Saturday; on Sunday at 1:30pm. Metro: Namur, then take the shuttle bus.

ROLLER HOCKEY　This is hockey with a twist—it's played entirely on in-line skates. The **Road Runners** have created a stir in Montréal since they started to play in 1994, and their talented female goalie, Manon Rheaume, is a particular favorite. Games are in summer only, in the Montréal Forum, 2313 Ste-Catherine ouest, between Closse and Atwater (☎ 514/932-2582). Tickets are $5, $11.50, or $27.50. Metro: Atwater.

8　Shopping

THE SHOPPING SCENE

Whether you view shopping as a must or just a pleasant way to spend a couple of hours, you will find much to delight you in Montréal. Its thriving fashion industry, from couture to ready-to-wear, enjoys a history that reaches back to the earliest trade in furs and leather. Beyond that, it is unlikely that any reasonable need cannot be met here. After all, there are some 1,500 shops in the Underground City alone, and many more than that at street level and above.

MAJOR SHOPPING STREETS　Try Sherbrooke for fashion, art, and luxury items, including furs and jewelry. Crescent has a number of scattered upscale boutiques, while funkier St-Laurent covers everything from budget practicalities to off-the-wall clothing. Look along Laurier between St-Laurent and de l'Epée for home furnishings stores and young Québécois designers. St-Paul in Vieux-Montréal has a growing number of art galleries. At least 35 antique stores line Notre-Dame between Guy and Atwater. Ste-Catherine near Christ Church Cathedral has most of the major department stores and myriad satellite shops, while Peel is known for men's fashions and some crafts. As in many cities, some of the best shops in Montréal are in its museums, tops among them Pointe-à-Calliere (the Montréal Museum of Archeology and History) in Vieux-Montréal, and the Museum of Fine Arts and the McCord Museum of Canadian History, both on rue Sherbrooke in center city.

The Great American Pastime Goes North

U.S. broadcast networks and the team owners of major league baseball suffer night sweats over worse things than labor strife and laws banning the sale of beer in their stadiums. It's the terror of a World Series featuring the Toronto Blue Jays or the Montréal Expos (or—quelle calamité!—*both*) that truly keep them up at night.

Ratings plummet whenever a playoff game takes place in either of those cities, as happened with Toronto in the early '90s. When colorless teams from undesirably small TV markets in the Midwest match up, network executive shrug their shoulders and comfort themselves with a resigned, "At least they ain't Canadians."

This is unfortunate, for Canadians are as enthusiastic about the American game as anyone—at least after their national religion, hockey, is taken into account. Even though there is the ever-present possibility of games being called off on account of snow, professional baseball has been a fixture in Montréal—off and on, admittedly—since the last century. The Expos were preceded by the Royals, who played their first game in 1828 in the Eastern League. There was a gap from 1916 to 1928. The Royals were reincarnated in the International League, as a triple-A farm club associated with the Dodgers. They signed Jackie Robinson in 1945, two years before Branch Rickey brought him up to The Show. Robinson paid off handsomely: In his first game for the Royals, he hit a three-run homer, scored four times, and stole two bases.

Many of the game's greats passed through Montréal— usually on their climb up, sometimes going the other way. Walter Alston managed them in the 1950s, and his and other Royals teams of the postwar era had batting orders that included, however briefly, Don Newcombe, Bobby Morgan, Junior Gilliam, Gil Hodges, Roy Campanella, Chuck Connors (yes, the actor), and a pitcher by the name of Tommy Lasorda.

The Royals expired for good in the early 1960s, but were followed by the Expos in 1969, named for the '67 World's Fair held in Montréal and now housed in a stadium built for the 1976 Olympics (though it's a notoriously bad place to see a game and has terrible turf). Persistent success has not been their lot, but they, too, have had their favorite stars. When red-headed Rusty Staub was playing, Montréalers gave him the nickname "Le Grand Orange."

EXCHANGE RATES Some stores put out signs offering better exchange rates to attract customers carrying U.S. funds. If you pay with a credit card, however, you are likely to get the best deal (provided the exchange rate doesn't drop precipitously after your visit). Your credit card company will convert the charges from Canadian into U.S. dollars based on the actual exchange rate posted on the day they process your transaction. VISA and MasterCard are the most popular bank cards in this part of Canada; Discover is rarely accepted by shops, and American Express reluctantly.

BEST BUYS Most goods tend to be less expensive in Montréal than in their countries of origin. Exceptions are many distinctly British products, including tweeds, porcelain, and glassware. Inuit sculptures and 19th- or early 20th-century country furniture are not cheap, but are handsome and authentic. Québec's daring designers produce some appealing fashions. Less-expensive crafts than the intensely collected Inuit works are produced, including quilts, drawings and carvings by Amerindian and other folk artists.

STORE HOURS Most stores are open Monday through Wednesday from 9:30am to 6pm, Thursday and Friday from 10am to 9pm, and Saturday and Sunday from 10am to 5pm. Department stores downtown tend to open a little later, 10am, and are closed Sundays.

TAXES & REFUNDS Save your sales receipts from any store in Montréal or the rest of Québec, and ask shopkeepers for tax refund forms. After returning home, mail the originals (not copies) to the specified address with the completed form. Refunds usually take a few months, but are in the currency of the applicant's home country. A small service fee is charged. For faster refunds, follow the same procedure, but hand in the receipts and form at a duty free shop designated in the government pamphlet, *Goods and Services Tax Refund for Visitors,* available at tourist offices and in many stores and hotels.

SHOPPING A TO Z
ANTIQUES

The best places to shop for antiques and collectibles are in the storefronts clustered together along rue Notre-Dame between rues Guy and Atwater. Or visit:

Antiques Puces Libres. 4240 rue St-Denis (near Rachel). ☎ **514/842-5931.**

Three fascinatingly cluttered floors are packed with pine and oak furniture, lamps, clocks, vases, and more, most of it late 19th- and early 20th-century French-Canadian art nouveau.

ARTS & CRAFTS
The Canadian Guild of Crafts. 2025 rue Peel (at Maisonneuve). ☎ **514/849-6091.**

A choice collection of craft items is displayed in a gallery setting. Among the objects are blown glass, paintings on silk, pewter, tapestries, ceramics. The stock is particularly strong in jewelry and Inuit sculpture.

Dominion Gallery. 1438 rue Sherbrooke ouest (at Bishop). ☎ **514/845-7471.**

Founded more than 50 years ago, this prominent gallery features both international and Canadian painting and sculpture in 14 rooms spread out over four floors.

L'Empreinte. 272 rue St-Paul est, Vieux-Montréal. ☎ **514/861-4427.**

This is a craftpersons' collective, a block off place Jacques-Cartier. The ceramics, textiles, glassware, and other items on sale often occupy that vaguely defined borderland between art and craft. Quality is uneven.

BOOKS
Museum of Fine Arts Bookstore. 1380 rue Sherbrooke ouest (near rue Bishop). ☎ **914/285-1600,** ext. 350.

This large, two-level store next to the new museum annex sells books on art, gardens, fashion, interior design, cooking, and biographies, as well as folk art and reproductions.

Ulysses. 480 bd. René-Lévesque (near Bleury). ☎ **514/843-9882.**

Needs of travelers are served by this good stock of guidebooks and maps, many in English, and accessories, including maps, day packs, money pouches, electrical adapters, and coffeemakers. There is a smaller location at 560 av. du Président-Kennedy at Aylmer (☎ 514/843-7222).

CLOTHING

For Men

America. 1101 Ste-Catherine ouest (at Stanley). ☎ **514/289-9609.**

One of the many links in a popular Canadian chain, it carries both casual and dressy clothes. There's a women's section upstairs.

Brisson & Brisson. 1472 rue Sherbrooke ouest (near MacKay). ☎ **514/937-7456.**

Apparel of the nipped and trim British and European schools fill three floors, from makers as diverse as Burberry, Brioni, and Valentini.

Club Monsieur. 1407 rue Crescent (near Maisonneuve). ☎ **514/843-5476.**

Armani and Hugo Boss styles prevail, for those with the fit bodies to carry them and the required discretionary income.

L'Uomo. 1452 rue Peel (near Ste-Catherine). ☎ **514/844-1008.**

Largely Italian menswear by such forward-thinking designers as Valentino, Cerruti, Versace, and Salvatore Ferragamo.

For Women

Ambre. 201 rue St-Paul ouest (place Jacques-Cartier). ☎ **514/982-0325.**

Sonia Kozma designs the fashions here—suits, cocktail dresses, dinner and casual wear made of linen, rayon, and cotton.

Artefact. 4117 rue St-Denis (near rue Rachel). ☎ **514/842-2780.**

Browse here among articles of clothing and paintings by up-and-coming Québécois designers and artists.

Giorgio Femme. 1455 rue Peel (near Maisonneuve). ☎ **514/282-0294.**

Hyper-chic designer wear from Italy isn't for everyone, but the new ideas promulgated here are bound to be seen on the streets not long after.

Kyoze. World Trade Center, 282 rue St-Jacques ouest, second floor. ☎ **514/847-7572.**

The eye-catching creations of Québécois and other Canadian designers are featured, including jewelry and accessories.

For Men & Women

Felix Brown. 1233 Ste-Catherine ouest (at Drummond). ☎ **514/287-5523.**

A diverse selection of designers and manufacturers, mostly Italian, makes choices difficult. Among them are Bruno Magli, Moschino, Casadel, and Vicini.

Marks & Spencer. Place Montréal Trust, 1500 av. McGill College (Ste-Catherine). ☎ **514/499-8558.**

The British origins of this long-established chain grow less obvious as it spreads over several continents, but the clothing still represents a favorable price-to-value ratio.

Polo Ralph Lauren. 1290 rue Sherbrooke (near Montagne). ☎ **514/288-3988.**

The international designer has set up shop in a townhouse in the poshest part of town, near the Ritz-Carlton. Apparel for the well-heeled family.

DEPARTMENT STORES

Most of Montréal's big department stores were founded when Scottish and English families dominated the city's mercantile class, and most of their names are identifiably English. The exception is La Baie, a shortened reference to its earlier name, the Hudson Bay Company. Most of them are located along a 12-block strip of rue Ste-Catherine (except for Holt Renfrew), from rue Guy eastward to Carré Phillips at Aylmer. Most of the stores mentioned below have branches elsewhere.

Eaton. 677 rue Ste-Catherine ouest (at Alymer). ☎ **514/284-8484.**

Since 1925, Eaton has offered a conventional range of middle-of-the-road goods at reasonable prices. It is also Montréal's largest store, and it is connected to the 225-shop Eaton Centre, a shopping mall that is part of the Underground City.

Henry Birks et Fils. 1240 Carré Phillips (at Union). ☎ **514/397-2511.**

This beautiful old store, with its dark-wood display cases, stone pillars, and marble floors, is a living part of Montréal's Victorian heritage. Merchandise encompasses jewelry, pens and desk accessories, watches, leather goods, glassware, and china.

Holt Renfrew. 1300 rue Sherbrooke ouest (at Montagne). ☎ **514/842-5111.**

A showcase of international style for men and women, offering such prestigious names as Giorgio Armani, Gucci, and Karl Lagerfeld. The firm began as a furrier in 1837.

La Baie. rue Ste-Catherine ouest(near Aylmer). ☎ **514/281-4422.**

No retailer has a more celebrated name than the 300-year-old Hudson's Bay Company, shortened in Québec to La Baie ("The Bay"). The main store emphasizes clothing, but also offers crystal, china, and Inuit carvings. Its Canadiana Boutique features famous Hudson's Bay blankets.

Ogilvy. 1307 rue Ste-Catherine ouest (at Montagne). ☎ **514/842-7711.**

Ogilvy was established in 1856 and has been at this location since 1912. Besides having a reputation for quality merchandise, the store is known for its eagerly awaited Christmas windows. Once thought of as hidebound—a bagpiper still announces the noon hour—it now contains a collection of high-profile international boutiques, including Jaeger, Aquascutum, and Rodier Paris.

A FLEA MARKET

Marché aux Puces. Old Port, at bd. St-Laurent. ☎ **514/843-5949.**

Located in the Vieux-Port (Old Port), a few steps from place Jacques-Cartier, an old dockside warehouse has been divided into stalls where vendors sell collectibles, knickknacks, jewelry, odd lots, new, used and antique furniture, new and vintage clothing, souvenirs, tools, and junk. Open daily from 10am to 5pm.

9 Montréal After Dark

Montréal's reputation for effervescent nightlife stretches back to the 13-year experiment with Prohibition south of the border. A fortune was made by Canadian distillers and brewers, not all of it legal, and Americans streamed into Montréal for temporary relief from alcohol deprivation. That the city enjoyed a sophisticated and slightly naughty reputation as the Paris of North America added to the allure.

Nightclub and bar-hopping remain popular activities, with much later hours than those of archrival Toronto, still in thrall to Calvinist notions of propriety and early bedtimes.

Montréalers' nocturnal pursuits are often as cultural as they are social. The city boasts its own outstanding symphony, French- and English-speaking theater companies, and the incomparable Cirque du Soleil (Circus of the Sun). It is also on the standard concert circuit that includes Chicago, Boston, and New York, so internationally known entertainers, rock bands, orchestra conductors and virtuosos, and ballet and modern dance companies pass through frequently.

A decidedly French enthusiasm for cinema in all its varieties, as well as the city's shifting reputation as a movie production center, ensure support for theaters showcasing films experimental, offbeat, and foreign, as well as the usual Hollywood blockbusters.

And in summer, the city becomes livelier than usual with several enticing events: the **International Jazz Festival** (early July), the **Just for Laughs Festival** (late July), the **Festival de Théâtre des Amériques** (late May), and the flashy **Benson and Hedges International Fireworks Competition** (mid-June). And every year, in late September or early October, a **Festival International de Nouvelle Danse** is held, attracting modern dance troupes and choreographers from around the world.

For details concerning current performances or special events, pick up a free copy of *Montréal Scope,* a weekly ads-and-events booklet, at any large hotel reception desk, or the free weekly newspapers *Mirror* (in English) or *Voir* (in French). Place des Arts puts out a monthly calendar of events (*Calendrier des Spectacles*) describing concerts and performances to be held in the various halls of the performing arts complex. You can find these publications in most large hotels or near the box offices in Place des Arts. Montréal's newspapers, the French-language *La Presse* and the English *Gazette,* carry listings of films, clubs, and performances in their Friday and Saturday editions. Concentrations of pubs and nightclubs underscore the city's linguistic dichotomy, too. While there is a great deal of mingling between the two cultures, the parallel blocks of rue Crescent, rue Bishop, and rue de la Montagne north of rue Ste-Catherine have a pronounced Anglophone character, while Francophones dominate the Latin Quarter, with college-age patrons most evident along the lower reaches of rue St-Denis and their yuppie elders gravitating to the nightspots of more uptown blocks of the same street. Vieux-Montréal, especially along rue St-Paul, has a more universal quality, where many of the bars and clubs feature live jazz, blues, and folk music. In the Plateau Mont-Royal area, boulevard St-Laurent, parallel to St-Denis, known locally as "The Main," has become a miles-long haven of chic restaurants and clubs, roughly from avenue Viger to St-Viatur. St-Laurent is a good place to end up in the wee hours, as there's always some place with the welcome mat still out.

THE PERFORMING ARTS
THEATER

The annual **Festival de Théâtre des Amériques** is an opportunity to see dramatic and musical stage productions that are international in scope, not simply North American. In 1995, there were works from Vietnam and China as well as from Canada, the United States, and Mexico. The plays are performed in the original languages, as a rule, with simultaneous translations in French and/or English, when appropriate. For information, call ☎ 514/842-0704.

Centaur Theatre. 453 rue St-François-Xavier (near rue Notre Dame). ☎ **514/288-3161.** Tickets $20–$30, students $16, seniors $12. Metro: Place d'Armes.

The former Stock Exchange building (1903) is now home to Montréal's principal English-language theater. A mix of classics, foreign adaptations, and works by Canadian playwrights are presented. Off-season, the theater is rented out to other groups, both French- and English-speaking. Performances are held October to June, Tuesday to Saturday at 8pm, Sunday at 7pm, and Saturday (and most Sundays) matinees at 2pm.

Saidye Bronfman Centre for the Arts. 5170 Côte-Ste-Catherine (near bd. Décarie). ☎ **514/739-2301** (information), 514/739-7944, or 514/739-4816 (tickets). Tickets $15.50–$45 adults, $15 seniors. Metro: Côte-Ste-Catherine. Bus: no. 129 ouest.

Montréal's Yiddish Theatre was founded in 1937 and is housed in the Saidye Bronfman Centre for the Arts, not far from St. Joseph's Oratory. It stages two plays a year in Yiddish. They run for three to four weeks, usually in June and October. At other times during the year, the 300-seat theater hosts dance and music recitals, a bilingual puppet festival, occasional lectures, and three English-language plays. Across the street, in the Edifice Cummings House, is a small Holocaust museum and the Jewish Public Library. The center takes its name from philanthropist Saidye Bronfman, widow of Samuel Bronfman, who was a founder of the Seagram Company. She died in 1995 at the age of 98.

The box office is usually open Monday to Thursday from 11am to 8pm, and Sunday from noon to 7pm—call ahead. Performances are held Tuesday to Thursday and at 8pm, Sunday at 1:30 and 7pm.

DANCE

Frequent appearances by notable dancers and troupes from other parts of Canada and the world augment the accomplished local company, among them Paul Taylor, the Feld Ballet, and Le Ballet National du Canada. During the summer, the native company often performs at the outdoor Théâtre de Verdure in Parc Lafontaine. In winter, they are scheduled at several venues around the city, but especially in the several halls at the Place des Arts. The fall season is kicked off by the inevitably provocative Festival International de Nouvelle Danse, in early October.

Les Grands Ballets Canadiens. Salle Wilfrid-Pelletier, Place des Arts, 200 de Maisonneuve ouest. ☎ **514/849-8681.** Tickets $12–$40. Metro: Place-des-Arts.

This prestigious company has developed a following far beyond national borders over more than 35 years, performing both classical and modern repertory. In the process, it has brought prominence to many gifted Canadian choreographers and composers. The troupe's production of *The Nutcracker Suite* is always a big event in Montréal the last couple of weeks in December. The box office is open Monday to Saturday noon to 8pm. Performances are held from late October to early May at 8pm.

CLASSICAL MUSIC & OPERA

Orchestre Métropolitan de Montréal. Maisonneuve Theatre, Place des Arts, 260 de Maisonneuve ouest. ☎ **514/598-0870.** Tickets $15–$30. Metro: Place-des-Arts.

Agnès Grossmann conducts this orchestra, which has a regular season at Place des Arts but also performs in St-Jean-Baptiste church and tours regionally. Most of the musicians are in their mid-30s or younger. The box office is open Monday to Saturday from noon to 8pm. Performances are held from mid-October to early April, usually at 8pm. Outdoor concerts are given in Parc Lafontaine in August.

Orchestre Symphonique de Montréal. Salle Wilfrid-Pelletier, Place des Arts, 260 de Maisonneuve ouest. ☎ **514/842-9951.** Tickets $10–$50. Metro: Place-des-Arts.

The world-famous orchestra, under the baton of Swiss conductor Charles Dutoit (and Zubin Mehta before him), performs at Place des Arts and the Notre-Dame Basilica, as well as around the world, and may be heard on numerous recordings. In the well-balanced repertoire are works from Elgar, Rabaud, and Saint-Saëns, in addition to Beethoven and Mozart. The box office is open Monday to Saturday noon to 8pm. Performances are usually at 8pm, during a full season that runs from September to May, supplemented by Mozart concerts in Notre-Dame Basilica in June and July, and interspersed with performances at three parks in the metropolitan region.

L'Opéra de Montréal. Salle Wilfrid-Pelletier, Place des Arts, 260 bd. de Maisonneuve ouest. ☎ **514/985-2222** (information) or 514/985-2258 (tickets). Tickets $23.50–$86. Metro: Place-des-Arts.

Founded in 1980, this outstanding opera company mounts seven productions a year in Montréal, with artists from Québec and abroad participating in such productions as *Madama Butterfly, Carmen, Fedora,* and *The Magic Flute.* Video translations are provided from the original languages into French and English. The box office is open Monday to Friday 9am to 5pm. Performances are held from September to June, usually at 8pm.

LANDMARK CONCERT HALLS & VENUES

There are, of course, many venues around the city, and you'll want to check the papers to see who's playing while you're in town. Big-name rock bands and pop stars tend to play the **Forum de Montréal,** 2313 rue Ste-Catherine ouest (☎ 514/790-1245), which is also home to the Montréal Canadiens hockey team. If a concert is scheduled, printed flyers, posters, and radio and TV ads make certain that everyone knows. The Forum, which can seat up to 16,500, will move to a new, more central downtown location in 1996. The box office is open Monday to Friday from 10am to 6pm, to 9pm on days of events.

A broad range of Canadian and international performers, usually of a modest celebrity unlikely to fill the larger Forum, use the **Spectrum de Montréal,** 318 rue Ste-Catherine ouest (☎ 514/861-5851), a converted former movie theater. Alternative rock bands of less wattage than Pearl Jam often book nights here, for example. The space also hosts segments of the city's annual jazz festival. Seats are available on a first-come, first-served basis. The box office is open Monday to Saturday 10am to 9pm, Sunday noon to 5pm.

Place des Arts. 260 bd. de Maisonneuve ouest. ☎ **514/285-4200** (information), 514/ 842-2112 (tickets), or 514/285-4275 (guided-tour reservations). Metro: Place-des-Arts.

Founded in 1963 and in its striking new home in the heart of Montréal since 1992, Place des Arts mounts performances of musical concerts, opera, dance, and theater in five halls: Salle Wilfrid-Pelletier (2,982 seats), where the Montréal Symphony Orchestra often performs; the Maisonneuve Theatre (1,460 seats), where the Metropolitan Orchestra of Montréal and the McGill Chamber Orchestra perform; Jean-Duceppe Theatre (755 seats); the new Cinquième Salle, which opened in 1992 (350 seats); and the small Studio-Théâtre du Maurier Ltée (138 seats). Noontime performances are often scheduled. The Museum of Contemporary Art moved into the complex in 1992. The box office is open Monday to Saturday from noon to 8pm, and performances are usually at 8pm.

Pollack Concert Hall. McGill University, 555 rue Sherbrooke ouest. ☎ **514/398-4547.** Metro: McGill.

In a landmark building dating from 1899 and fronted by a statue of Queen Victoria, this hall is in nearly constant use, especially during the university year. Among the attractions are concerts and recitals by professionals, students, or soloists from McGill's music faculty. Recordings of some of the more memorable concerts are available on the university's own label, McGill Records. Concerts are also given in the campus's smaller **Redpath Hall,** 3461 rue McTavish (☎ 514/398-4547). Performances are at 8pm and are usually free.

Theatre de Verdure. Lafontaine Park. ☎ **514/872-2644.** Metro: Sherbrooke.

Nestled in a quiet city park, the open-air theater presents free music and dance concerts and theater, often with well-known artists and performers. Sometimes they show outdoor movies. Many in the audience pack picnics. Performances are held from June to August; call for days and times. Performances are free.

Theatre St-Denis. 1594 rue St-Denis (Emery). ☎ **514/849-4211.** Metro: Berri-UQAM.

Recently refurbished, this theater in the heart of the Latin Quarter hosts a variety of shows, including pop singers and groups and comedians, as well as segments of the Just for Laughs Festival in summer. It is actually two theaters, one seating more than 2,000 people, the other almost 1,000. The box office is open daily from noon to 9pm. Performances are usually at 8pm.

A CIRCUS EXTRAORDINAIRE

Cirque du Soleil. Old Port, quai Jacques-Cartier. ☎ **514/522-2324** or 800/361-4595. Tickets $12–$39 adults, $6–$27 children. Metro: Champ-de-Mars.

Through the exposure generated by its frequent tours across North America, this circus is enjoying an ever-multiplying following. One reason, curiously, is the absence of animals in the troupe, which means that no one need be troubled by the possibility of mistreated lions and elephants. What is experienced during a Cirque du Soleil performance is nothing less than magical, a celebration of pure skill and theater, with plenty of clowns, trapeze artists, tightrope walkers, and contortionists. Open from late April to early June during odd-numbered years only, the show goes on the road throughout North America during even-numbered years. Look for the yellow and blue tent at the Vieux-Port. The box office is open Tuesday to Sunday from 9am to 9pm. Performances are Tuesday to Friday at 8pm, Saturday at 4 and 8pm, and Sunday at 1 and 5pm.

THE CLUB & MUSIC SCENE

COMEDY

The last decade's explosion in comedy venues across North America has cooled, but Montréal still has places to sample the fading phenomenon, perhaps because it is the home to the **Just for Laughs Festival** every summer (for information, call ☎ 514/845-2322).

Comedy Nest. 1740 René-Lévesque (at Guy). ☎ **514/932-6378.** Cover $9. Metro: Guy-Concordia.

This club, newly relocated in the Hotel Nouvel, features mostly local talent, with occasional appearances by better-known visiting comics. Shows are held Wednesday to Sunday at 8:30pm, with added shows on Friday and Saturday at 11:30pm. Drinks cost $3.75 to $6.25. The dinner-and-show package costs $18 Wednesday to Sunday, $24 Friday and Saturday; dinner starts at 6:30pm.

Comedyworks. 1238 rue Bishop (Ste-Catherine). Cover $3–$10. ☎ **514/398-9661.** Metro: Guy-Concordia.

There's a full card of comedy at this long-running club, up the stairs from Jimbo's Pub on a jumping block of Bishop south of Ste-Catherine. Monday is open-mike night, while Tuesday and Wednesday, improvisation groups usually work off the audience. Headliners of greater or lesser magnitude—usually from Montréal, Toronto, New York, or Boston—take the stage Thursday through Sunday. No food is served, just drinks. Reservations are recommended, especially on Friday, when early arrival may be necessary to secure a seat. Shows are daily at 8:30pm, and also 11:15pm on Friday and Saturday. Drinks cost $3.75 to $6.50, and there's a one-drink minimum.

FOLK, ROCK & POP

Scores of bars, cafes, theaters, clubs, and even churches present live music on at least an occasional basis, if only at Sunday brunch. The performers, local or touring, traffic in every idiom, from metal to funk to grunge to unvarnished Vegas. In most cases, they only stay in one place for a night or two. Here are a selected few that focus their energies on the music.

Café Campus. 57 rue Prince-Arthur est (near St-Laurent). ☎ **514/844-1010.** Cover $10 and up. Metro: Sherbrooke.

When anyone over 25 shows up inside this bleak club on touristy Prince-Arthur, it's probably a parent of one of the musicians. Alternative rock prevails, but metal and retro-rock bands also make appearances. Followers of the scene may be familiar with such groups as Bootsauce, Come, and Elastica, all of whom have appeared.

Club Soda. 5240 av. du Parc (near Bernard). ☎ **514/270-7848.** Cover $15 and up. Metro: Parc.

One of the city's larger venues for attractions below the megastar level, performers are given a stage before a hall that seats several hundred. Three bars lubricate audience enthusiasm. Musical choices hop all over the charts—folk, rock, blues, country, Afro-Cuban, heavy metal—you name it. Acts for the annual jazz and comedy festivals are booked here, too.

Déjà Vu. 1224 rue Bishop (near Ste-Catherine). ☎ **514/866-0512.** No cover. Metro: Guy-Concordia.

Upstairs, over a club called Bowser and Blue, this casual room puts on live music every night of the week. The management has eclectic tastes, hiring bands that specialize in old-time rock-n-roll, country, blues, and whatever else takes their fancy. They run a loose, fun place with three floors and two small dance floors, and keep it relatively inexpensive.

Nuit Magique. 2 rue St-Paul (Place Jacques-Cartier). ☎ **514/861-8143.** No cover. Metro: Place-d'Armes.

The pumped-up Vieux-Montréal night scene hasn't swamped this longtime fave, probably because it doesn't suffer delusions of consequence. No big names, decidedly scruffy non-decor, and just a pool table in back and energetic bands in front, nightly. It fits like an old pair of motorcycle boots.

Le Pierrot/Les Deux Pierrots. 114 & 104 rue St-Paul est (west of Place Jaques-Cartier). ☎ **514/861-1686.** Cover, Le Pierrot, $2 Fri–Sat, free other nights; Aux Deux Pierrots, $3 Thurs, $5 Fri–Sat. Metro: Place-d'Armes.

Perhaps the best known of Montréal's boîtes-à-chansons, Le Pierrot is an intimate French-style club. The singer interacts animatedly with the crowd, often bilingually, and encourages them to join in the lyrics. Le Pierrot is open only during the warmer months, with music late into the wee hours of the morning. Its sister club next door, the larger Les Deux Pierrots, features live bands playing rock-and-roll songs year-round, half in French and half in English. The terrace joining the two clubs is open on Friday and Saturday nights in summer. Le Pierrot is open only May to September, nightly. Les Deux Pierrots is open year-round, Thursday to Sunday from 8pm to 3am. Drinks cost $3 to $4.50.

JAZZ & BLUES

The respected and heavily attended **Festival International de Jazz** held for 10 days every summer in Montréal sustains interest in the most original American art form. (For information, call ☎ 514/871-1881). Scores of events are scheduled, indoors and out, many of them free. "Jazz" is broadly interpreted, to include everything from Dixieland to reggae to world beat to the unclassifiable experimental. Artists represented in the past have included Thelonious Monk, Pat Metheny, John Mayall, and B. B. King. Piano legend Oscar Peterson grew up here and often returns to perform in his hometown. There are many more clubs than the sampling that follows. Pick up a copy of *Mirror* or *Hour* distributed free everywhere, or buy the Saturday edition of *The Gazette* for the entertainment section. These publications have full listings of the bands and stars appearing during the week.

Berri Blues. 1170 St-Denis (at René-Lévesque). ☎ **514/287-1241** or 800/503-4448. No cover. Metro: Berri-UQAM.

This used to be a barnlike Bavarian bierstube called Vieux Munich, with oompah bands and waitresses in dirndls. It's early to tell whether it will flourish with its new music format, but they rotate gifted blues belters on one- or two-night stands from Thursday through Saturday nights. A gospel brunch is added on Sunday. Call for starting times. Drinks are $5 to $9.

Biddle's. 2060 rue Aylmer (north of Sherbrooke). ☎ **514/842-8656.** No cover. Metro: McGill.

Right downtown, in an area where there isn't much other after-dark action, this longtime stalwart is a club-restaurant with hanging plants and faux art nouveau glass that fills up early with lovers of barbecued ribs and jazz. The live music starts around 5:30pm (7pm Sunday and Monday) and continues until closing time. Charlie Biddle plays bass Tuesday through Friday nights when he doesn't have a gig elsewhere. He and his stand-ins favor jazz of the swinging mainstream variety, with occasional digressions into more esoteric forms. It's open Sunday 4pm to 12:30am, Monday to Thursday 11:30am to 1:30am, Friday and Saturday 11:30am to 2:30am. Drinks cost $5 to $6.50, and there's a $6.50 per-person minimum Friday and Saturday nights. There's a mandatory paid coat-check.

Le Grand Café. 1720 rue St-Denis (near Ontario). ☎ **514/849-6955.** Cover up to $10. Metro: Berri-UQAM.

The French of Canada are as enthusiastic about jazz as their European brethren. As evidence, this funky joint deep in the Latin Quarter. The stage is upstairs, large enough to hold large combos and small bands. Sometimes the management brings on blues or rock as a change of pace. When it's chilly out, they stoke up the fireplace. The big windows in front give a preview of what's going on inside, and they open out in summer. It's open daily from 11am to 3am. Drinks cost $3.50 to $4.50.

L'Air du Temps. 191 St-Paul ouest (St-Francois-Xavier). ☎ **514/842-2003.** Cover $5–$25. Metro: Place-d'Armes.

A Montréal jazz tradition since 1976, L'Air du Temps is a jazz emporium of the old school—a little seedy and beat-up with no gimmicks to distract from the music. The main room and an upper floor in back can hold more than 135, and the bar stools and tables fill up quickly. Get there by 9:30pm or so to secure a seat. The bands go on at 10:30pm, or thereabouts. L'Air du Temps doesn't serve food, just a wide variety of drinks, but there are several good midpriced restaurants nearby. The club doesn't take reservations. They're open Thursday to Monday 9pm to 3am. Drinks cost $2.75 to $7.75.

Le Quai des Brumes. 4481 rue St-Denis (Mont-Royal). ☎ **514/499-0467.** No cover. Metro: Mont-Royal.

Loosely translated, the name means "foggy dock," a reference of elusive significance. But it's an atmospheric place in which to attend to jazz, blues, and rock. Jazz gets lots of play upstairs in the Central Bar. The crowd has been described as "a fairly uniform group of post-'60s Francophone smokers." Open daily from 2pm to 3am. Drinks cost $2.75 to $4.75.

Les Beaux Esprits. 2073 rue St-Denis (at Sherbrooke). ☎ **515/844-0882.** No cover. Metro: Sherbrooke.

Blues gets a wide hearing in this musical city, as demonstrated here in the thumping heart of the youthful Latin Quarter. Simple and unpretentious, the place attracts avid fans of the music, mostly of university age. Local musicians perform nightly from 8pm to 3am. Drinks cost $3 to $5.

DANCE CLUBS & DISCOS

Montréal's dance clubs change in tenor and popularity in mere eye blinks, and new ones sprout like toadstools after a heavy rain and wither as quickly. For the latest fever spots, quiz concierges, guides, waiters—anyone who looks as if they might follow the scene. Here are a few that appear more likely to survive the whims of nightbirds and landlords. Expect to encounter steroid abusers with funny haircuts guarding the doors.

Batalou. 4372 bd. St-Laurent (at Marie-Anne). ☎ **514/845-5447.** No cover. Metro: Mont-Royal.

A sensual tropical beat issues from this club-with-a-difference on The Main, a hot, happy variation from the prevailing grunge and murk of what might be described as mainstream clubs. Although most of the patrons revel in their ancestral origins in the Caribbean and Africa, the sources of the live and recorded music, an ecumenical welcome is extended to all comers. Admittedly, the hip-waggling expertise of the dancers might be intimidating to the uninitiated. Things get going about 10pm every night but Monday. Drinks cost $3.50 to $7.

Hard Rock Café. 1458 rue Crescent (near Maisonneuve). ☎ **514/987-1420.** No cover. Metro: Guy-Concordia.

No surprises, now that clones have sprouted all around the world. The hamburgers are good enough and not too expensive, guitars and costumes and other rock memorabilia decorate the walls, and the usual Hard Rock Café souvenirs are available. The formula continues to work, and it gets crowded at lunch and weekend evenings. Open daily from 11:30am to 3am, the disco starts up at 10pm. Drinks cost $3.45 to $6.

Métropolis. 59 rue Ste-Catherine est (near St-Laurent). ☎ **514/288-5559.** Cover Thurs–Fri $5, Sat $8. Metro: Berri-UQAM.

Housed in a handsome old theater dating from the 1890s is a monster disco that can accommodate 2,200 gyrating bodies at a time. The sound system and the light show are state-of-the-art, and there are six bars on three levels. The neighborhood is scruffy, but not especially worrisome, not far from the campus of the Université du Québec. It's open only Thursday through Saturday 10pm to 3am. Drinks cost $3 to $5.50.

THE BAR SCENE

An abundance of restaurants, bars, and cafes masses along the streets near the downtown commercial district, from Stanley to Guy between Ste-Catherine and

Maisonneuve. Rue Crescent, in particular, hums with activity from late afternoon until far into the evening, especially after 10pm on a cool summer weekend night, when the street swarms with young people moving from club to bar to restaurant. St-Laurent, another nightlife hub, abounds in bars and clubs, most with a distinctive European—particularly French—personality, as opposed to the Anglo flavor of the rue Crescent area. Increasingly active rue St-Paul, west of place Jacques Cartier in Vieux Montréal, falls somewhere in the middle on the Anglophone-Francophone spectrum. It's also a little more likely to get rowdy on late weekend nights. In all cases, bars tend to open around 11:30am and go late. Last call for orders is 3am, but patrons are often allowed to dawdle over those drinks until 4am.

Le Continental Bistro Americain. 4169 rue St-Denis (at Rachel). ☎ **514/845-6842.** No cover. Metro: Mont-Royal.

The after-curtain crowd from Théâtre St-Denis gathers here for drinks or late meals, which range far enough afield to be called "international." A guy with a cigarette dribbling from his lips sits down at the upright piano when the mood strikes, sometimes spelled by a guitarist or two. Their music is often submerged beneath the high buzz of conversation. The designer Jacques Sabourin fashioned the revivalist Deco decor, including the bar, which doubles as a display counter. They're open Monday to Friday 11:30am to midnight, Saturday and Sunday 6pm to midnight. Drinks cost $4 to $7.

Le Swimming. 3643 bd. St-Laurent (north of Sherbrooke). ☎ **514/282-7665.** Metro: Sherbrooke.

A nondescript entry and a stairway that smells of stale beer leads to a trendy pool hall that attracts as many men and women who come to drink and socialize as to play pool. Many Montréal bars have a pool table, but this one has 13, along with nine TVs and a terrace. Two people can play pool for an hour for $8; three play for $9, and four for $10.

Lutetia Bar. In L'Hôtel de la Montagne, 1430 rue de la Montagne (north of Ste-Catherine). ☎ **514/288-5656.** Metro: Guy-Concordia.

Within sight of the trademark lobby fountain with its nude bronze sprite sporting stained-glass wings, this appealing bar draws a standing-room-only crowd of youngish to middle-aged professionals after 5:30pm. Later on, there's often music by jazz duos. In summer, the hotel opens the terrace bar on the roof by the pool.

Ritz Bar. In the Ritz-Carlton Kempinski Hotel, 1228 Sherbrooke ouest (at Drummond). ☎ **514/842-4212.** Metro: Peel.

A mature, prosperous crowd seeks out the quiet Ritz Bar in the Ritz-Carlton Kempinski hotel, adjacent to its semilegendary Café de Paris restaurant. Anyone can take advantage of the tranquil room and the professionalism of its staff, but men should wear jacket *and* tie to be sure they will be allowed entrance. Piano music tinkles just above the level of consciousness during cocktail hour Monday through Friday from 5pm to 8pm and at the dinnertime (5 to 11pm) from September to mid-May. The bar is off the hotel lobby, to the right.

Shed Café. 3515 bd. St-Laurent (north of Sherbrooke). ☎ **514/842-0220.** Metro: Sherbrooke.

It looks like the ceiling is caving in on the bar, but that's intentional. There are local beers on tap, as well as good fries and oversize portions of cake on the newspaper-style menu. The crowd skews young, but with enough diversity to make an hour or two interesting.

Sir Winston Churchill Pub. 1459 rue Crescent (near Ste-Catherine). ☎ **514/288-0623.** Metro: Guy-Concordia.

The twin upstairs/downstairs bar-cafes are Crescent landmarks. One reason is the sidewalk terrace, open in summer, enclosed in winter, and a vantage for checking out the pedestrian traffic all the time. Inside and down the stairs, it attempts to imitate a British public house with marginal success. The mixed crowd is dominated by questing young professionals. They mill around a total of 17 bars and two dance floors. Winnie's, on the second floor, is a restaurant with a terrace of its own. During the 5 to 8pm happy hour, they take $1 off wine and beer.

Thursday's. 1441–1449 rue Crescent (near Ste-Catherine). ☎ **514/288-5656.** Metro: Guy-Concordia.

A prime watering hole of Montréal's young professional set, who are ever alert to the possibilities of companionship among its habitués. The pubby bar spills out onto the terrace that hangs over the street. There's a glittery dance club in back connected to a restaurant called Les Beaux Jeudis, in the same building. Thursday's presumably takes its name from the Montréal custom of prowling nightspots on Thursday evening in search of the perfect date for Friday. The disco opens at 9pm.

Whisky Café. 5800 bd. St. Laurent (at Bernard). ☎ **514/278-2646.** Metro: Outremont.

Those who enjoy Scotch, particularly single-malt imports like Cragamore and Glenfiddich, find 30 different labels to sample here. Trouble is, the Québec government applies stiff taxes for the privilege, so 70% of the patrons stick to beer. The decor is sophisticated, with exposed beams and vents, handmade tiled tables, and large wood-enclosed columns, but the real decorative triumph is the men's urinal, with a waterfall for a pissoir. Women are welcome to tour it.

THE GAY & LESBIAN SCENE

K.O.X. 1450 rue Ste-Catherine (near Amherst). ☎ **514/523-0064.** Cover $2–$4. Metro: Beaudry.

Despite the arch name, this dance space has survived and prospered, drawing an enthusiastic mixed crowd of men and women. House music in retro and progressive forms are the beat of choice, blended by DJs who take their job seriously. Drinks and admission prices are reasonable, and there is no cover for the Sunday tea dance. The disco is closed Monday, Wednesday, Thursday. Drinks cost $2.25 to $4.

L'Exit II. 4297 rue St-Denis (near Rachel). ☎ **514/843-8696.** Metro: Mont-Royal.

A lesbian bar, welcoming women of all ages, it has pool tables and a dance floor that's put to heavy use on Fridays and Saturdays. The (usually) friendly staff and customers are good sources for information about gay activities and events in the city. Occasionally there's live music, and in summer drinks are served on the terrace.

GAMBLING

In autumn 1993, the **Montréal Casino,** Québec's first, opened on Île Notre-Dame in the former French Pavilion, which was left over from the world's fair called Expo '67. The casino has 65 gaming tables, including roulette, blackjack, and midi-baccarat, and 1,200 slot machines. (No craps tables, though.) It can accommodate 5,300 people, most of whom come to try their luck, of course, but the two restaurants have been getting good notices, and there are several bars, live shows, and two shops selling gifts and souvenirs. Gambling hours are 11am to 3am daily (☎ 514/392-2746 or 800/665-2274). No alcoholic beverages are served in the gambling areas. Patrons must be 18 or over. The relatively strict dress code prohibits such casual attire as shorts, T-shirts, sweat pants, running shoes, and denim pants of any color. To get to the casino, take the Metro to the Île Ste-Hélène stop, which is adjacent to Île Notre-Dame, and walk or take the shuttle bus from there.

CINEMAS & MOVIE HOUSES

English-language films are usually presented with subtitles in French. However, when the initials "VF" (for *version française*) follow a movie title, they mean that the movie has been dubbed into French. Besides the many first-run movie houses that advertise in the daily newspapers, Montréal is rich in "ciné-clubs," which tend to be slightly older and show second-run, foreign, and art films at reduced prices. A downtown ciné-club that shows English-language films is the **Conservatoire d'Art Cinématographique,** at 1400 bd. de Maisonneuve ouest; the price of admission is $3 (☎ 514/848-3878). Old movies are also shown at no charge at the unusual eatery, **Café Ciné-Lumière,** 5163 St-Laurent, where headsets are provided for individual listening while dining (☎ 514/495-1796).

The **National Film Board of Cinema (Cinema ONF),** 1564 rue St-Denis (☎ 514/496-6895), shows Canadian and international films, primarily in English and French, particularly film classics. Showings are Tuesday through Sunday; call for times.

Imposing images surround viewers of the seven-story screen in the **IMAX** theater in the Vieux-Port, at de la Commune and St-Laurent (☎ 514/496-4629). Available productions are limited, so efforts are made to create films suitable for the entire family.

The Laurentides & Estrie

9

by Herbert Bailey Livesey

For respite from urban stresses and demands, Montréalers need only drive 30 minutes or so to the north or east of the city to find themselves in the hearts of the resort regions of the Laurentides or Estrie. Lakes and mountains have invited development of year-round vacation retreats and ski centers in both areas. The pearl of the Laurentides is Mont Tremblant (at 3,175 feet the highest peak in eastern Canada), but the region has 18 other ski centers with scores of trails at every level of difficulty, many of them less than an hour from Montréal.

Bucolic Estrie, formerly known as the Eastern Townships when it was a haven for English Loyalists and their descendants, is blessed with a trio of memorable country inns on beautiful Lake Massawippi and promotes four seasons of outdoor diversions. It has fewer ski centers, and the resort hotels that serve them are generally smaller and less extensive in their facilities, but its many lakes and gentler pastimes give it the edge for warm-weather vacations. Since the people of both regions rely heavily on tourism for their livelihoods, knowledge of at least rudimentary English is widespread, even outside such obvious places as hotels and ski resorts.

1 Exploring the Laurentides & Estrie

Most of the major resorts and ski centers of the Laurentides ("Laurentians," in English) are within sight of the limited-access Autoroute 15 and the roughly parallel, but slightly slower Route 117. Both roads follow scenic routes through tidy hamlets and villages, with humpbacked hills giving way to higher and higher mountains.

In Estrie, the same observations hold for Autoroute 10, which runs east from Montréal to Sherbrooke, except that the terrain rises and falls less dramatically. The suggestions for enjoying both regions that follow in this chapter are laid out as driving tours, beginning with the towns or other sites of interest closest to the city and ending with those most distant.

VISITOR INFORMATION   Québec tourism authorities produce volumes of detailed and highly useful publications, and they're easy to obtain by mail, phone, or in person. To contact **Tourisme Québec,** write C.P. 979, Montréal, PQ, H3C 2W3 or call ☎ 800/ 363-7777, operator 806 (within the Montréal area, call 514/ 873-2015).

GETTING AROUND   The limited-access expressways in Québec are called autoroutes, and speed limits and distances are given in kilometers. Most highway signs are in French only, although Montréal's autoroutes and bridges often bear dual-language signs. Seat belt use is required by law while driving or riding in a car in Québec. Turning right on a red light is prohibited throughout the province of Québec, except where specifically allowed by an additional green arrow.

For information on **road conditions** in and around Montréal, call ☎ 514/636-3026; outside Montréal, call ☎ 514/636-3248.

AN IMPORTANT NOTE ON PRICES   Unless stated otherwise, **the prices cited in this guide are given in Canadian dollars,** which is good news for U.S. travelers because the Canadian dollar is worth 25% less than the American dollar but buys nearly as much. As we go to press, $1 Canadian is worth U.S. 75¢, which means that your $100-a-night hotel room will cost only U.S. $75, and your $6 breakfast costs only U.S. $4.50.

Remember, though, that taxes are substantial. Most goods and services in Canada are taxed 7% by the federal government, called the TPS in Québec, the GST (goods and services tax) elsewhere. The Québec provincial government places an additional 8% tax (TVQ) on the total, amounting to a tax on the tax as well as the product or service. Fortunately, tourists can obtain refunds of many of the taxes imposed. Duty-free shops and hotels have the necessary forms. Complete them and return to the indicated address, with the original receipts, within a year of your visit.

2 The Great Outdoors

There doesn't seem to be an outdoor sport or game yet conceived, from in-line skating to hot-air ballooning, that doesn't enjoy at least one or two venues somewhere in the Laurentides or Estrie. Find your favorite activity below, and we'll tell you where to pursue your passion or give you the general tips you need.

BIKING   Both rugged mountain biking and gentler forms of cycling are possible throughout the region, especially in Mount Tremblant Park and on nearby, less strenuous, roads around the hotels. Rentals are available at a concession stand in the park (☎ 818/688-2281), which has 100kms of trails. Magog, in Estrie, has an 11-mile (18¹/₂km) bike path that links its Lake Mephremagog with Mount Orford.

BIRDING   Bird-watchers of both intense or casual bent are fully occupied in the region. The lakes of Québec's mountain regions are home to an estimated 16,000 loons, a native waterfowl that gives its name to the dollar coin. Excellent divers and swimmers, the birds are unable to walk on land, which makes nesting a trial, and they are identified by a distinctive call that might be described as an extended mournful giggle.

CANOEING   From June through September, **Escapade Nature** in Sainte-Agathe-des-Monts (☎ 819/326-3799) conducts canoe trips along the Rivers Diable and Rouge from a few hours in duration to made-to-measure expeditions of up to two weeks. The 3¹/₂-hour trip is $37 for adults, $18.50 for children aged 11 to 17 years; the 4¹/₂-hour version is $49 adults, $24.50 children 11 to 17. Children 10 years and under are free when accompanied by an adult. Canoes, equipment, and guides are part of the package.

CROSS-COUNTRY SKIING   Among the best cross-country trails in the Laurentides are at the **Hôtel L'Estérel** (☎ 514/228-2571) and on the grounds of the monastery called **Domaine du St. Bernard,** near Mont Tremblant.

The Laurentians

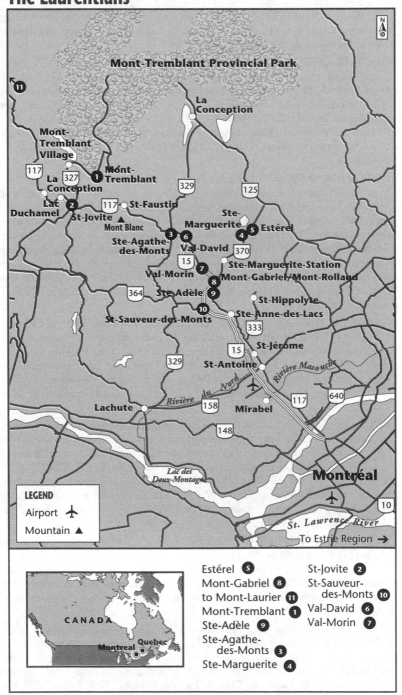

Mont-Tremblant Provincial Park

La Conception

Mont-Tremblant Village

117

La Conception **327**

Lac Duchamel

St-Jovite **2**

117 St-Faustin

▲ Mont Blanc

Mont-Tremblant **1**

329

125

Ste-Marguerite

4 **5** Estérel

Ste-Agathe-des-Monts **3** **6** Val-David

15

370

Val-Morin **7**

Ste-Marguerite-Station

8 Mont-Gabriel/Mont-Rolland

Ste-Adèle **9**

364

10

St-Sauveur-des-Monts

Ste-Anne-des-Lacs

St-Hippolyte

333

15

St-Jérôme

St-Antoine

329

Rivière du Nord

Rivière Masouche

117 **640**

Lachute **158**

Mirabel

148

Lac des Deux-Montagnes

Montréal

LEGEND

Airport ✈

Mountain ▲

10

St. Lawrence River

To Estrie Region →

CANADA

Montreal Quebec

Estérel **5**
Mont-Gabriel **8**
to Mont-Laurier **11**
Mont-Tremblant **1**
Ste-Adèle **9**
Ste-Agathe-des-Monts **3**
Ste-Marguerite **4**

St-Jovite **2**
St-Sauveur-des-Monts **10**
Val-David **6**
Val-Morin **7**

In Estrie, 22 miles (35kms) of courses run across **Lake Massawippi** and over the low surrounding hills. The bike path between **Lake Mephremagog and Mount Orford** becomes a cross-country trail in winter.

DOGSLEDDING   In St-Jovite, **Chinook Aventure** (☎ 819/425-6518) introduces novices to the sport with one-hour to whole-day guided outings. Guests at the **Hôtel l'Estérel** (☎ 514/228-2571) have that opportunity, too. For longer, more venturesome expeditions of up to four days, meals and lodging provided, contact **Les Expéditions Tapini** (☎ 819/586-2064). The outfitter is based in Ste-Anne-du-Lac, 29 miles (47km) north of Mont-Laurier, an excursion in itself. In Waterloo, near Exit 90 off Autoroute 10, **Safari Tour** (☎ 514/539-0501) schedules daily excursions by reservation.

DOWNHILL SKIING   A half century ago the first ski schools, rope tows, and trails began to appear, and today there are 19 ski centers within a 40-mile radius of Montréal. These sprawling resorts and modest lodges and inns are packed each winter with skiers, some of them through April. Trails for advanced skiers typically have short pitches and challenging moguls, with broad, hard-packed avenues for beginners and the less experienced. In addition to the 19 ski centers scattered along Autoroute 15, there are four prominent centers in Estrie, near Autoroute 10, which are smaller and tend to be more family-oriented. Bromont, Orford, Owl's Head, and Sutton cooperate through their **Ski East Network** to offer a lift ticket acceptable at all four centers (☎ 819/820-2020).

GARDEN & VINEYARD TOURS   **Les Jardins de Rocailles,** 1319 rue Lavoie in Val-David (☎ 819/322-6193), is a small but delightful floral retreat with more than 250 varieties of flowers and shrubs. There is a cafe with a terrace from which to observe. All four of the vineyards in and around Dunham in Estrie conduct tours. Three of them are situated along Route 202, west of the town: **l'Orpailleur** (☎ 514/295-2763), **Les Trois Clochers** (☎ 514/295-2034), and **Domaine** (☎ 514/295-2020).

GOLF   Courses in the Laurentides now number almost 30, most of them 18 holes and open to the public. Reservations are required and daily fees are in the $25 to $40 range. Most of the resort hotels mentioned later in the chapter can make arrangements, but three have courses on their premises—**Gray Rocks** (☎ 819/425-2771 or 800/567-6767) and the **Hôtel L'Estérel** (☎ 514/228-2571) both feature 18-hole courses, and **Le Chantecler** (☎ 514/229-3555) makes do with a nine-hole course. In Estrie there are 25 more courses, also open to the public, with greens fees in the $24 to $34 range for 18 holes.

SAILING & WINDSURFING   Small sailboats and sailboards can be rented at the lakefront in Ste-Agathe-des-Monts, where there is also a sailing school (☎ 819/326-2282). The larger lake resorts in both the Laurentides and Estrie rent, or make available, canoes, pedal boats, and sailing dinghies. Yamaska Park in Granby, for example, rents sailboards, kayaks, sailboats, and rowboats, as does the recreational park at Mont-Orford.

SCUBA DIVING   The many clear lakes of the Laurentides have visibility of up to 50 feet. Notable among these are Lac Tremblant, at the base of the mountain of the same name, and the several lakes in or near the Papineu-Labelle wildlife preserve, west of Tremblant and St. Jovite. Information, dive classes, and rental equipment are available through the **Centre de Plongée Lac-des-Écorces** (☎ 819/585-3472). It's in the village of that name near the town of Mount-Laurier, 68 miles (110km) north of St. Jovite.

Gourmet Ski Tours

No other experience better captures the appeal of the region than an unusual program called **Skiwippi**. In essence, it is the equivalent of those upscale European hiking and cycling trips through Bordeaux or Chianti, in which participants tramp or bike through the countryside to lunch at splendid little inns, then get up and cover a similar distance before dinner and bed.

Three Estrie auberges have joined together in this offering. The difference is their guests ski to lunch, then to dinner. A 22-mile (35km) trail links the three—the **Auberge Ripplecove** (☎ 819/838-4296), **Manoir Hovey** (☎ 819/842-2421 or 800/661-2421), and **Auberge Hatley** (☎ 819/842-2451). It is a highly varied route, across the flat frozen Lac Massawippi and up forested slopes before topping a crest, and emerging into open meadows to views that go on forever.

Lunch on the trail is modest but hearty, but the nightly six-course dinners replenish the soul of any gourmand. All three kitchens rank among Québec's most honored, illustrating, along with their good-to-excellent wine lists, what is meant by dining as an art.

Three- or six-night packages are available, and while those fancy expeditions in Europe cost thousands of dollars, Skiwippi is only $420 (for three nights) or $720 (for six nights) per person, double occupancy. Breakfasts, dinners, gratuities, and transfers of cars and luggage between inns are included. You can make reservations by contacting any of the inns.

There is a warm-weather version of this program the trio calls Golf et Gastronomie. In deference to the time of year, the six dinners are only three- or four-course affairs, but the golf is more than generous—three rounds of 18-hole play at a choice of 12 area courses. Free use of most of each inn's recreational facilities are also included. Rates are the same.

TENNIS   All the large resorts and many of the smaller auberges have courts. These accommodations include **Manoir St-Sauveur** (☎ 514/227-1811), **Auberge Mont-Gabriel** (☎ 514/229-3547), **Hôtel L'Estérel** (☎ 514/228-2571), **Club Tremblant** (☎ 819/425-2731), and **Manoir Hovey** (☎ 819/842-2421).

WHITE-WATER RAFTING   Several companies offer rafting trips of four to five hours on the Rivière Rouge (Red River), which flows down to the Ottawa River. Access is via Route 158 west of Autoroute 15 (Exit 39) toward Lachute and on Route 148 past Calumet, turning north on chemin de la Rivière Rouge. Launching points are clearly marked. Passengers must weigh at least 88 pounds (40 kilograms). Guides, rafts, safety helmets, and jackets are provided, as is an end-of-trip meal.

Inquire ahead to determine details and make reservations. Two of the more prominent companies are **Aventure en eau vive** (☎ 819/242-6084) and **Nouveau Monde** (☎ 818/242-7238).

3 The Laurentides: A Summer & Winter Playground Near Montréal

Expect no spiked peaks or high ragged ridges. The rolling hills and rounded mountains of the Laurentian Shield are among the oldest in the world, worn down by wind and water over eons. They average between 300 and 520 meters, with the highest being Mont Tremblant, at 968 meters. In the lower precincts, nearest Montréal, the terrain resembles a rumpled quilt, its folds and hollows cupping a multitude of ponds and lakes. Further north, summits are higher and craggier, with patches of snow persisting well into spring, but these are still not facsimiles of the Alps or the Rockies. They are welcoming and embracing rather than awe-inspiring.

The busiest times of year are in July and August, during the Christmas–New Year's holiday period, and in February and March. Other times of the year, reservations are easier to get, prices are lower, and crowds are less dense. May and September are often characterized by warm days, cool nights, and just enough people so that the streets don't seem deserted. In May and June, the indigenous black flies can seem as big and as ill-tempered as buzzards, so prepare for them with Cutter, Off, or Avon Skin So Soft. Some of the resorts, inns, and lodges close down for a couple of weeks in the spring and the fall. A handful are open only for a few winter months.

March and April are the season when the maple trees are tapped, and cabanes à sucre ("sugar shacks") open up, some selling only maple candies and syrup, others serving full meals featuring the principal product and even staging entertainments. In mid-July, the region's annual **Fête de Vins (Wine Festival)** is held for two days in Saint-Jérome, and the emphasis is on gastronomy and wine tasting; a dozen restaurants in the area participate.

July and August usher in glorious summer days in the Laurentians, and the last two weeks in September the leaves put on an unrivaled show of autumnal color. Skiers can usually expect reliable snow from early December to mid-April.

Prices can be difficult to pin down. The large resorts have so many types of rooms, cottages, meal plans, discounts, and packages that a travel agent may be needed to pick through the thicket of options. Remember that Montréalers fill the highways when they "go up north" on weekends, particularly during the top skiing months of February and March, so plan ahead when making reservations.

Pet owners, take note: Few Laurentian resorts accept animals.

ESSENTIALS

VISITOR INFORMATION   For an orientation to the entire region, stop at **La Maison du Tourisme des Laurentides,** 14142 rue de la Chapelle, RR no. 1, St-Jérôme (☎ 514/436-8532 or 800/561-6673, from Montréal 514/476-1840; fax 514/ 436-5309), a regional tourist information office located in St-Jérôme at Exit 39 off the Laurentian Autoroute 15. Perhaps most important to the traveler, they can make reservations for lodging throughout the Laurentides, either by phone or in person. The service is free. The red-roofed stone cottage is off the highway to the east; take Route 158 and follow the signs. From late June to the end of August, it's open from 9am to 8:30pm daily; the rest of the year, daily 9am to 5pm.

GETTING THERE   By Car   The fast and scenic **Autoroute des Laurentides (Laurentian Autoroute), also known as Autoroute 15,** goes straight from Montréal to the Laurentian mountains. This is a picturesque drive, once you're out of the tangle of expressways surrounding Montréal. The Autoroute gives a sweeping, panoramic introduction to the area, from the rolling hills and forests of the lower Laurentians to the mountain drama of the upper range. Just follow the signs to St-Jérôme. The exit numbers are actually the distance in kilometers the village is from Montréal. One likely stop, for instance, is the Laurentian Tourism House at Exit 39 in St-Jérôme, and St-Jérôme is 24 miles (39km) from Montréal.

If you have a little more time to meander, you can exit at St-Jérôme to pick up the older, roughly parallel Route 117, which plays tag with the Autoroute all the way to Sainte-Agathe-des-Monts, where the highway ends. Most of the region's more appealing towns are strung along or near Route 117. Approaching each town, signs direct drivers to the local tourism information office, where attendants provide tips on lodging, restaurants, and things to do. North of Ste-Agathe, Route 117 becomes the major artery for the region, continuing deep into Québec's north country and finally ending at the Ontario border hundreds of miles from Montréal.

Be aware that Québec's equivalent of the Highway Patrol maintains a strong presence along the stretch of Autoroute 15 between St-Faustin and Ste-Adèle, and remember that radar detectors are illegal in the province and subject to confiscation.

By Limousine   Taxis and limousines await arrivals at both Dorval and Mirabel airports in Montréal, and will take them straight to any Laurentian hideaway—for a price. While the fare for the one-hour trip by limo from Dorval is steep, four or five people can share the cost and dilute the pain. Mirabel is actually in the Laurentians, five minutes south of St-Antoine and 35 minutes from the slopes. Ask the standard fare to your inn or lodge when calling to make reservations. The inn usually will take responsibility for seeing that a taxi or limo is indeed waiting at the airport and they may even help to find other guests arriving at the same time to share the cost.

By Bus   Limocar Laurentides buses depart Montréal's Terminus Voyageur, 505 bd. de Maisonneuve est, stopping in larger Laurentian towns, including Ste-Agathe, Ste-Adèle, and St-Jovite; call for schedules (☎ 514/842-2281). An express bus makes the run to St-Jovite and Mont Tremblant in less than two hours, while a local bus, making all the stops, takes almost three. Travel from Montréal to Ste-Adèle takes about $1^{1}/_{2}$ hours, 15 minutes more to Val-Morin and Val-David. Some of the major resorts provide their own bus service at an additional charge.

ST-SAUVEUR-DES-MONTS

Only 37 miles (60km) north of Montréal, St-Sauveur-des-Monts (pop. 5,864) can easily be visited on a day trip. The village square is dominated by a handsome church, and the streets around it bustle with activity much of the year. In season, there's a tourist kiosk on the square.

The area is known for its **night skiing**—23 illuminated trails, only three fewer than those available during the day. The mountain is wide, with a 700-foot vertical drop and a variety of well-groomed trails, making it a good choice for families. In summer, St-Sauveur-des-Monts becomes Canada's largest **water park,** featuring a wave pool and a mountain slide where visitors go up in chair lifts and come down in tubes.

The **Bureau Touristique de la Vallée de St-Sauveur,** in Les Galeries des Monts, 75 av. de la Gare, is open year-round, daily from 9am to 5pm (☎ 514/227-2564). They provide useful maps, brochures, and more.

WHERE TO STAY

Auberge St-Denis. 61 rue St-Denis, St-Sauveur-des-Monts, PQ, J0R 1R4. ☎ **514/227-4602** or 800/361-5724. Fax 514/227-8504. 42 rms. A/C MINIBAR TV TEL. $94 double; $123 suite. Extra person $10. Packages available. AE, DC, ER, MC, V.

Set back from the road, surrounded by birch and evergreens, Auberge St-Denis looks like a country club, complete with heated outdoor pool and an aloof attitude at the front desk. Rooms in the old section are comfortable enough, with fireplaces. Those in the new wing are larger and more polished, with queen-size beds, fireplaces, and whirlpools. Reception is in the building with the green awning. The kitchen enjoys good notices from diners.

Manoir St-Sauveur. 246 chemin du Lac Millette, St-Sauveur-des-Monts, PQ, J0R 1R3. ☎ **514/227-1811** or 800/361-0505. Fax 514/227-8512. 163 rms, 37 suites. A/C MINIBAR

TV TEL. Mid-June to mid-Oct $99–$118 double, $180 suite; rest of the year $89–$108 double, $10 suite. Extra person $10. Children under 18 stay free. Packages available. AE, DC, ER, MC, V. Take Exit 60 off Highway 15.

One of the region's several large resort hotels, with a monster outdoor pool and a comprehensive roster of four-season activities, Manoir St-Sauveur offers a fitness center with weight machines and a sauna, an indoor pool, racquetball, and tennis. A warm personality isn't included. Rooms are commodious, with bland but comfortable light-wood furnishings. In-house movies are available. The main building is easily spotted from the road, with its green roof and many dormers.

WHERE TO DINE

Les Prés. 231 rue Principale. ☎ **514/227-8580.** Main courses $5.50–$13. MC, V. Mon–Thurs 11am–9pm, Fri 11am–2am, Sat 9am–11pm, Sun 9am–10pm. LIGHT FARE.

Situated in a Victorian house in the middle of town, Les Prés is only one of a number of casual eateries clustered near the village square. Several of them are units of Montréal chains, as is this one, whose name means "The Meadows." The front porch has prized tables for watching the street activity.

MONT-GABRIEL

Only 2¹/₂ miles (4km) from St-Sauveur-des-Monts, Mont-Gabriel is reached by taking Autoroute 15 to Exit 64, and turning right at the stop sign. Although popular in summer, the town comes into its own each winter when guests schuss down its 21 trails and slopes and then ride back up again on the seven T-bar lifts, the triple-chair, or the quadruple-chair lift. Eight trails are lit for night skiing. Cross-country trails girdle the mountain and range through the surrounding countryside.

WHERE TO STAY & DINE

Auberge Mont-Gabriel. Mont-Rolland, PQ J0R 1G0. ☎ **514/229-3547,** 514/861-2852 in Montréal, or 800/668-5253 in Canada. Fax 514/229-7034. 126 rms. A/C TV TEL. $100 double; $120 triple. Children 6–12 stay for $7.50. Rates include breakfast. Golf and tennis packages available in summer, ski packages in winter. AE, ER, MC, V. Driving north on Autoroute 15, take Exit 64.

Perched atop Mont-Gabriel, above the highways and the valley, this hostelry looks like the rambling log "cottages" of the turn-of-the-century rich. It's a scant 20 miles from Montréal's Dorval Airport, set on a 1,200-acre estate. The spacious rooms in the Tyrol section are the most desirable, many with views of the surroundings hills, while those in what they call the Old Lodge are more rustic. Some rooms have air-conditioning and minibars, but you have to ask for them.

Dining/Entertainment: Meals can be served at poolside, and evenings, there's dancing in the main lodge.

Facilities: Indoor facilities include a pool, sauna, whirlpool, and exercise room. The outdoor swimming pool is heated, and there are tennis courts and a par-71 golf course.

STE-ADÊLE

Route 117 swings directly into Ste-Adêle to become its main street, the boulevard Ste-Adêle (or take Exit 67 off Autoroute 15 North). The village (pop. 7,800), only 42 miles (67km) north of Montréal, is a near-metropolis compared to the hamlets that line the upper reaches of Route 117. What makes it seem big are its services: police, doctors, ambulances, a shopping center, art galleries, and a larger collection of places to stay and dine than are found elsewhere in the Laurentides. As rue Morin mounts the hill to Lac Rond, Ste-Adêle's resort lake, it is easy to see why the town is divided into a lower part ("en bas") and an upper part ("en haut").

The **Bureau Touristique de Ste-Adêle,** at 333 bd. Ste-Adêle, is open daily from 9am to 7pm in July and August, the rest of the year daily from 9am to 5pm (☎ 514/229-2921, ext. 207).

One of Ste-Adêle's main streets, **rue Valiquette,** is a busy one-way thoroughfare lined with cafes, galleries, and bakeries. But **Lac Rond** is the center of activities during the Ste-Adêle summer. Canoes, sailboats, and pédalos (foot-powered craft), rented at several docks, glide over the placid surface, while swimmers splash and play at shore-side beaches.

In winter, ski trails descend the surrounding hills to the shores of the frozen lake. Rent downhill ski equipment or book lessons at **Le Chantecler** resort (☎ 514/229-3555), which has 22 trails served by six chair lifts and two T-bars. Some of the trails end right by the main hotel. At the town's **Centre Municipal,** Côtes 40/80, 1400 rue Rolland (☎ 514/229-2921), the trails are good for beginners. Three T-bar lifts carry up the slopes for the run down five different trails.

Ste-Adêle has a theater showing English-language movies all year.

WHERE TO STAY

Auberge Champêtre. 1435 bd. Ste-Adêle (Hwy. 117), Ste-Adêle, PQ, J0R 1L0. ☎ **514/229-3533** or 800/363-2466. Fax 514/229-3534. 48 rms. A/C TV TEL. $54–$94 double. Extra person $10. Children 12 and younger stay free. Rates include continental breakfast. Packages available. AE, DC, ER, MC, V.

You can stretch your budget by choosing a lodging that offers accommodations alone, without the sports and meal packages promoted by the region's comprehensive resorts. This unpretentious auberge, somewhere between a motel and a condo, is one example. Of the several kinds of accommodations, the most appealing are the midpriced rooms called "Chalet Nest" and "Whirlpool Nest." The least expensive for two people are the "Champêtre" rooms equipped with a queen or two twin beds and Franklin fireplaces. The breakfast room has a small pool surrounded by a hedge.

L'eau à la Bouche. 3003 bd. Ste-Adêle, Ste-Adêle, PQ, J0R 1L0. ☎ **514/229-2991** or 800/363-2582 from Montréal. Fax 514/229-7573. 23 rms, 2 suites. A/C TV TEL. $135 double; $220 suite. Rates include breakfast. Packages available. AE, DC, ER, MC, V.

L'Eau à la Bouche started as a roadside restaurant and the chef-owners later added the separate hotel. It's a member of the international Relais and Châteaux consortium, an organization that places its emphasis on gastronomy. (See the separate dining listing below.) Inside, there is large living room with a brick fireplace and bar and sofas set about in conversation groups. Bedrooms are comfortably forgettable, with queen- or king-size beds, ceiling fans, and reproductions of Québec country furniture. The sizable bathrooms have hair dryers and robes. All are large enough for sitting areas, and six also have fireplaces and balconies or patios, along with hair dryers and robes. No elevator and no porters, but help with luggage is available upon request.

Facilities: The property faces the Mont Chantecler ski trails, is across the road from a golf course, and has a heated outdoor pool.

Le Chantecler. 1474 rue de Chantecler (C.P. 1048), Ste-Adêle, PQ, J0R 1L0. ☎ **514/229-3555** or 800/363-2420. Fax 514/229-5593. 280 rms, 20 suites. MINIBAR TV TEL. In season (including breakfast and dinner) $172–$212 double, from $292 suite; spring and fall (room only) from $89. Children 6 and under stay free in parents' room, $22 extra for each child 7–12 years. Packages available. AE, DC, ER, MC, V. Take Exit 67 off Autoroute 15; turn left at the fourth traffic light onto rue Morin; then turn right at the top of the hill.

Sprawled across the sides of four mountains, this ski resort is comprised of stone buildings of varying heights and roofs bristling with steeples and dormers; its ski facilities accommodate all levels of expertise, making it a logical family vacation choice. The rooms are decorated with pine furniture; most have air-conditioning. Many of the suites have fireplaces, and most have whirlpool baths.

Dining/Entertainment: A bountiful buffet breakfast is served in the glass-enclosed dining room, which overlooks the active slopes and the lake with its small beach.

Facilities: There's a ski school and 22 slopes for all levels of skiers, 13 of which are night-lit. An indoor sports complex has a pool, sauna, Jacuzzi, racquet games, and some fitness equipment. Outside are 18-hole and illuminated nine-hole golf courses, and six night-lit tennis courts. Boats, canoes, and windsurfing boards are also available.

WHERE TO DINE

✪ L'Eau â la Bouche. 3003 bd. Ste-Adêle. ☎ **514/229-2991** or 800/363-2582 from Montréal. Reservations recommended. Main courses $19.50–$29.50; table d'hôte lunch from $15; dinners $45–$80. AE, MC, V. Sun–Fri 11:30am–2pm; dinner daily 6–9pm. CONTEMPORARY FRENCH.

Owners Anne Desjardins and Pierre Audette leave no doubt where their priorities lie. Their nearby hotel (see above) is entirely satisfactory, but this, the restaurant, is their love child, and it has the glow-in-the-dark reviews to prove it. False modesty isn't a factor—l'eau à la bouche means "mouthwatering," and the kitchen delivers. The faux Provençal interior employs heavy ceiling beams, white plaster walls, and pine paneling to set the mood. An appetizer might be the dollop of salmon tartare laced with flecks of ginger and sweet red pepper. A good deal for sampling the formidable cellar is the three glasses of vintage clarets for $30. Native ingredients and hefty portions are meshed with nouvelle presentations, as with the fanned leaves of rosy duck breast garnished with slivered broccoli and a timbale of puréed sweet potato. Fiddleheads appear in their short spring season paired with baby asparagus heads; game dishes arrive in fall. Desserts are impressive, but the cheese plate—pungent nubbins of French and Québec varieties delivered with warm baguette slices—is special. The young staff is both efficient and unintrusive. A meal here might well be the most memorable—albeit pricey—dining experience of a Laurentian visit.

STE-MARGUERITE & ESTÉREL

To get to Ste-Marguerite (pop. 2,000) or the even less populous Estérel, which lie only 2 miles apart, follow Autoroute 15 north to Exit 69. If you're driving from Ste-Adêle, look for a street heading northeast named chemin Ste-Marguerite. It becomes a narrow road that crosses the Autoroute (at Exit 69), bridges the Rivière du Nord, and leads into an area of many lakes bordered by upscale vacation properties.

Ste-Marguerite and Estérel are 53 miles (85km) and 55 miles (88km) north of Montréal, respectively. In summer, information about the area is available from **Pavillon du Parc,** 74 chemin Masson, in Ste-Marguerite-du-Lac-Masson (☎ 514/228-3525); year-round, you can also go to the nearby tourist bureau of Ste-Adêle (see above).

WHERE TO STAY

Hôtel L'Estérel. Bd. Fridolin-Simard (C.P. 38), Ville d'Estérel, PQ, J0T 1E0. ☎ **514/228-2571** or 800/363-3623 from Montréal. Fax 514/228-4977. 135 rms. A/C TV TEL. $252–$309 double. Rates include breakfast, dinner, and service. Lower rates Dec 23–May. Discounts for longer stays. Packages available. AE, DC, ER, MC, V. A Limocar bus from Montréal runs into Ste-Adêle, where the hotel picks up guests.

A few miles past Ste-Marguerite, in the town of Estérel, this year-round complex is capable of accommodating 300 guests on its 5,000-acre estate with three linked lakes. Taking up an expanse of otherwise unoccupied lakeshore, L'Estérel offers conventionally comfortable rooms. Those with a view of the lake are more expensive.

Facilities: Rates include the use of all indoor facilities and the tennis courts. For a special winter experience, inquire about the dogsled trips through the woods and over the frozen lake. There are 53 miles (85km) of cross-country trails, nearby downhill skiing, ice-skating on a rink, and in summer an 18-hole golf course and school, tennis, nature trails, horseback riding, sailing, parasailing, and waterskiing.

WHERE TO DINE

✪ **Le Bistro à Champlain.** 75 chemin Masson. ☎ **514/228-4988.** Reservations recommended. Main courses $15–$25, table d'hôte dinner $23, dégustation dinner $52. AE, MC, V. Summer Tues–Sat 6–10pm, Sun noon–10pm; rest of year Thurs–Sat 6–10pm, Sun noon–10pm. CONTEMPORARY FRENCH.

On the shore of Lac Masson in Ste-Marguerite is one of the most honored restaurants in the Laurentides. Its 1864 building used to be a general store, and retains the rough-hewn board walls, exposed beams, and an old cash register. Gastronomy, not hardware, is now the motivation for customers who routinely motor up from Montréal for dinner. The 35,000-bottle cellar is also a big reason, and 20 of the stocked wines can be sampled by the glass. Superior guidance is provided by sommelier François Chartier, named the best in his profession in a 1994 competition in Paris. Tours of the cellar are often conducted by Chartier or his equally enthusiastic boss, a practicing radiologist. They will gladly recommend a claret to complement a main course of fresh lamb from the region, lightly smoked in the restaurant. The crusty baguettes served at every meal are baked on site.

VAL-DAVID

Follow Autoroute 117 north to Exit 76 or 78, respectively, to reach Val-David or Val-Morin. To those who know it, the faintly bohemian enclave of Val-David (pop. 3,225), 50 miles (80km) north of Montréal, conjures up images of cabin hideaways set among hills rearing above ponds and lakes, and laced with creeks tumbling through fragrant forests. The village celebrates its 75th anniversary in 1996.

The **tourist office** is on the main street, at 2501 rue de l'Eglise (☎ 819/322-1515). It is open from mid-June to Labor Day, daily 9am to 7pm, and from September 5th to June 19th, daily 10am to 4pm. Another possibility for assistance is **La Maison du Village,** a cultural center in a two-story wooden building at 2495 rue de l'Eglise (☎ 819/322-3660). Note that this far north in the Laurentians, the area code changes to 819.

A favorite activity in Val-David is visiting the studios of local artists, including the **pottery workshop** of Kinya Ishikawa, where the artist's work can be viewed and discussed with him, at 2435 rue de l'Eglise (☎ 819/322-6868).

Or have a picnic beside the North River in the **Parc des Amoureax,** which is 2¹/₂ miles (4km) from the main road through town. Watch for the sign "Site Pittoresque" and turn at chemin de la Rivière.

Val-David sits astride a 124-mile (200 km) parkway that is a trail for cycling in summer and for cross-country skiing in winter.

The village sponsors an **art festival** during the first two weeks of August, when painters, sculptors, ceramists, jewelers, pewtersmiths, and others display their work. There are concerts and other outdoor activities.

WHERE TO STAY

Auberge du Vieux Foyer. 3167 chemin Doncaster, Val-David, PQ, J0T 2N0. ☎ **819/322-2686** or 800/567-8327 in Canada. Fax 819/322-2687. 22 rms, 3 chalets. $148–$190 double, $230 double in chalets. Rates include breakfast and dinner. $65 for extra occupants. Weekly and off-season rates, packages available. MC, V. Follow the signs through the town about 1¹/₂ miles (3km).

This Swiss-style inn stands beside its own private pond. Armchairs are drawn up to the big fireplace in the main sitting room. The guest rooms are smallish and plain vanilla, with views of the surrounding forested hills. Some have whirlpools. There are also three chalets that hold up to eight people. With the auberge's limited number of rooms, advance reservations are a necessity most of the year.

Facilities: There's a heated outdoor pool and a skating rink. Bicycles and pedal boats are available and there is cross-country skiing nearby.

La Maison de Bavière. 1472 chemin de la Rivière, Val-David, PQ, JOT 2NO. ☎ **819/ 322-3528.** 4 rms. $65, $75, or $110 double. No credit cards. Exit 76 off Autoroute 15; turn right at the first traffic light, then turn left at the first street.

This pleasant bed-and-breakfast is located beside the North River and the new cycling and cross-country ski trail that spans the entire Laurentian chain. The owners strive for a homey atmosphere, from the soft duvets on the beds to the hand-painted doors reminiscent of Bavaria. Guests eat in the dining nook under a skylight and share a reading room with a wood-burning stove. Guest rooms are named after German composers. Beethoven has five windows overlooking the river, a freestanding bathtub in the bedroom, and a private deck. No smoking.

WHERE TO DINE
Le Grand Pa. 2481 rue de l'Eglise. ☎ **819/322-3104.** Pizzas and sandwiches $4–$14; main courses $16–$26. MC, V. Sun and Tues–Thurs noon–11pm, Fri–Sat noon–midnight. ITALIAN/ CANADIAN.

Near the tourist office, an open deck reaches out to the sidewalk, crowded with resin chairs and tables. Patrons tuck into a dozen versions of pizzas, baked in the brick oven inside. With their puffy crusts and fresh ingredients, they are the star attractions, often taken with pitchers of beer or sangría. Full meals are also available, and in summer, a barbecue pit is fired up. Friday and Saturday nights, they lay on live music by small combos.

STE-AGATHE-DES-MONTS
With a population approaching 10,000, Ste-Agathe-des-Monts, 53 miles (85km) north of Montréal, is the largest town in the Laurentians. Follow Autoroute 15 north to Exit 83 or 86. Ste-Agathe marks the end of the Autoroute.

Early settlers and vacationers flocked here in search of land fronting Lac des Sables, and entrepreneurs followed the crowds. Ste-Agathe's main street, rue Principale, is the closest to citification in these mountains, but it's only a touch of urbanity. Follow rue Principale from the highway through town and end up at the town dock on the lake. Watch out for four-way stops along the way.

The dock and surrounding **waterfront park** make Ste-Agathe a good place to pause for a few hours. You might want to rent a bicycle from **Jacques Champoux Sports,** 74 rue St-Vincent, for the 3-mile ride around the lake. Waterskiing and lake cruises seduce many visitors into lingering for days. For a night or two, the motels near town on Route 117 are sufficient, but for longer stays, consider a lakeside lodge.

The **Bureau Touristique de Ste-Agathe-des-Monts,** 190 rue Principale est (☎ 819/ 326-0457), is open daily 9am to 8:30pm in summer, 9am to 5pm the rest of the year.

Alouette cruises (☎ 819/326-3656) depart the dock at the foot of rue Principale from mid-May to late October. It's a 50-minute, 12-mile voyage on a boat equipped with a bar and a running commentary that observes, among other things, that Ste-Agathe and the Lac des Sables are famous for waterski competitions and windsurfing. Cost for the Alouette cruise is $10 per adult, $9 seniors with ID, $5.50 for children 5 to 15. There are half a dozen departures a day; call for exact times.

WHERE TO STAY

Auberge du Lac des Sables. 230 St-Venant, Ste-Agathe, PQ J8C 2Z7. ☎ **819/326-3994** or 800/567-8329. Fax 819/326-7556. 19 rms. A/C TV. $78–$118 double. Rates include breakfast. Extra person $15. AE, DISC, MC, V.

All the rooms in this small lakefront inn have whirlpool baths, their chief distinguishing feature. Those with double Jacuzzis and a view of the lake are slightly more expensive. There is a small terrace overlooking the lake, a good vantage point for watching the sunset. Downstairs is a game room with pool table and pinball machine. The auberge is about 1¹/₂ miles from the village center, just steps from the beach and boating. English is spoken by the hosts, who also own the similar Auberge du Comte de Watel, just down the road.

Auberge La Sauvagine. 1592, RR no. 2, Rte. 329 nord, Ste-Agathe, PQ, J8C 2Z8. ☎ **819/326-7673.** 9 rms (7 with bath). $75–$130 double. MC, V.

For something a little different, check this out: an auberge housed in a deconsecrated chapel. An order of nuns added the chapel when they ran the property as a retirement home. Antiques and almost antiques are scattered through the public and private spaces. Seven rooms have private bath, and two rooms share a bath. A TV is available to guests in the living room. The restaurant, open for dinner only, Wednesday through Sunday, offers a three-course table d'hôte for $37. The inn is 1.2 miles (2km) north of Ste-Agathe, on the road to St-Donat.

WHERE TO DINE

Chez Girard. 18 rue Principale ouest. ☎ **819/326-0922.** Reservations recommended. Main courses $14.50–$29.50; three-course table d'hôte lunch $7.50–$13; four-course table d'hôte dinner $20–$32. AE, ER, MC, V. July–Aug Tues–Sun 10am–11pm; rest of the year daily 5–10pm, Sun brunch 10am–2pm. TRADITIONAL FRENCH.

Head toward the town dock; near the end of rue Principale, on the left, is a Québec-style house with a crimson roof. That's Chez Girard. In good weather diners can sit on the terrace overlooking the lake. Game is a central interest of the kitchen, heavy on warm days, but tasty on cool nights as summer fades. Among the possibilities are guinea hen with fragrant pheasant sausage, escargots and mushrooms in a pastry shell, and venison tournedos with wild-grape sauce.

The auberge also has lodgings, five rooms and three suites, in two village houses. Some units have fireplaces. They go for $100–$120 double with breakfast, $125–$170 double with breakfast and dinner. Suites are $110 with breakfast.

ST-FAUSTIN

St-Faustin, which lies 16 miles (25km) north of Ste-Agathe and 71 miles (115km) north of Montréal, is not a tourist town, but rather a commonplace mountain village with a church. The main attraction is over on the left when driving north— **Mont Blanc,** the second-highest peak in the Laurentians. To get here, follow Route 117 north from Ste-Agathe. It's just south of St-Jovite.

The **Bureau Touristique de St-Faustin,** 1535 Rte. 117 (☎ 819/688-3738), is open from 9am to 8pm in summer, 9am to 5pm the rest of the year.

ST-JOVITE & MONT-TREMBLANT

Follow Highway 117 about 23 miles (37km) north from Ste-Agathe to the St-Jovite exit. It's 76 miles (122km) north of Montréal. To get to Mont-Tremblant, turn right on Route 327, just before the church in St-Jovite. Most vacationers make their base at one of the resorts or lodges scattered along Route 327. Mont-Tremblant is 28 miles (45km) north of Ste-Agathe and 80 miles (130km) north of Montréal.

St-Jovite (pop. 4,118) is the commercial center for the most famous and popular of all Laurentian districts, the area surrounding Mont Tremblant, the highest peak in the Laurentians (3,175 feet; 950m). In 1894, the provincial government set aside almost 1,000 square miles of wilderness as a park, and the foresight of that early conservation effort has yielded outdoor enjoyment to four-season vacationers ever since.

The mountain's name comes from a legend of the area's first inhabitants. When the first Amerindians arrived here early in the 17th century, they named the peak after their god, Manitou. When humans disturbed nature in any way, Manitou became enraged and made the great mountain tremble—montagne tremblante.

St-Jovite, a pleasant community, provides all the expected services, and its main street, rue Ouimet, is lined with cafes and shops, including Le Coq Rouge, which sells folk art and country antiques. The village of Mont-Tremblant, though several miles nearer the large resorts and the mountain itself, has only basic services, including a market and post office but no pharmacy.

Tourist information, including maps of local ski trails, is available at the **Bureau Touristique de Mont-Tremblant,** rue du Couvent at Mont-Tremblant (☎ 819/425-2434). It's open daily in summer from 9am to 9pm, the rest of the year daily from 9am to 5pm. Another source for maps and brochures and other information is the **Tourist Bureau of Saint-Jovite/Mont-Tremblant,** 305 chemin Brébeuf in St-Jovite (☎ 819/425-3300), open daily in summer from 9am to 7pm, the rest of the year daily from 9am to 5pm.

SKIING, SUMMER WATER SPORTS & MORE

Water sports in summer are as popular as the ski slopes and trails in winter, because the base of Mont Tremblant is surrounded by no fewer than 10 lakes. **Lac Tremblant** is the largest, a 10-mile-long stretch of water, but there is also Lac Ouimet, Lac Mercier, Lac Gelinas, Lac Desmarais, and five smaller bodies of water, not to mention a number of connecting rivers and streams. From June to mid-October, **Grand Manitou Cruises** on chemin Principale, in Mont-Tremblant, offers a 75-minute narrated tour of Lac Tremblant, focusing on its history, nature, and legends (☎ 819/425-8681).

Mont Tremblant, which has the same vertical drop (2,100 feet) as Mont Ste-Anne near Québec City, draws the biggest downhill ski crowds in the Laurentides. Founded in 1939 by Philadelphia millionaire Joe Ryan, Station Mont-Tremblant is one of the oldest ski areas in North America, and the first to create trails on both sides of a mountain. It was the second in the world to install a chair lift. There are higher mountains with longer runs and steeper pitches, but something about Mont Tremblant compels people to return time and again.

Today, Mont Tremblant has the snowmaking capability to cover 328 acres, making skiing possible from early November to late May, with more than 30 trails open at Christmas (as opposed to nine in 1992). Station Mont-Tremblant now has 43 downhill runs and trails, including the newly opened Dynamite and Verige trails, with 810-foot (245m) and 745-foot (225m) drops, respectively, and the Edge, a peak with two gladed trails. The several lifts are for gondolas and chairs, no T-bars. There is plenty of cross-country action on 56 miles (90km) of maintained trails.

And in summer, you can choose from golf, tennis, horseback riding, boating, swimming, biking, and hiking—and that's just for starters.

WHERE TO STAY

Ⓢ **Chateau Beauvallon.** 616 Montée Ryan (Box 138), Mont-Tremblant, PQ, J0T 1Z0. ☎ **819/425-7275.** Fax 819/425-7275. 12 rms (6 with bath). Summer $64 double. Rates include full breakfast. Children 12 and under stay for half price in parent's room. Packages available. No credit cards.

This modest inn with its own lake beach is an antidote to the impersonal bustle of Tremblant's big resorts. Built in 1942, it was once part of the Mont-Tremblant Lodge resort. Today its seclusion is its principal appeal, along with low rates and few distractions. In fact, you'll be hard-pressed to find something that disturbs the setting's all-pervasive tranquillity. Rustic rooms have knotty pine paneling.

Up to 30 guests can be seated in the dining room, and meals are bracketed by drinks beside the fireplace in the lounge.

❂ Club Tremblant. Av. Cuttle, Mont-Tremblant, PQ, J0T 1Z0. ☎ and fax **819/425-2731** or 800/363-2413 in the U.S., 800/567-8341 in Canada. 110 rms and apts. TV TEL. $121–$205 per person double; from $125 per person suite. Rates include breakfast and dinner. Children 6–12 $29. Rates are lower for stays of two days or more. Packages available. AE, DC, ER, MC, V. Turn near the Auberge Sauvignon and follow the signs; it's less than a mile off Route 327.

Terraced into a hillside sloping steeply to the shore of Lac Tremblant, this handsome property consists of several lodges in muted alpine style. Essentially a concentration of privately owned condominium apartments operated by a single management, the lodgings represent excellent value and that greatest of luxuries: space. Most of the units are suites of one to three bedrooms, many for the price of a solitary room at some other resorts in the region. Typical suites have a fireplace, balcony, sitting room with cable TV and dining table, full kitchen with cookware and dishwasher, one or two bathrooms with Jacuzzi, and clothes washer and dryer. Nearly all have views of the lake and Mont Tremblant, which rises from the opposite shore.

Dining/Entertainment: The dining room employs a largely French menu, with a five-course table d'hôte. A woody bar, with a stone fireplace and picture windows, is an inviting spot, and there's usually piano music Thursday through Saturday nights.

Services: A day-care program is available for children 3 to 13. During ski season, a 22-passenger bus shuttles between the lodge and the slopes.

Facilities: Lifeguarded indoor and outdoor pools, Jacuzzi, and workout room with weight machine, Exercycles, and rowing machines supplement the four tennis courts.

Gray Rocks. 525 chemin Principal Mont-Tremblant, PQ, J0T 1Z0. ☎ **819/425-2771** or 800/ 567-6767. Fax 819/425-3474. 150 rms, 50 condos. A/C TEL. $198–$360 double. Rates include breakfast, lunch, and dinner. Children 11–16 stay in parents' room at 40% discount; children 5–10, 50% discount. Meals optional in condos. Ski-school packages available. AE, MC, V.

The first resort built in the Laurentides, this place was actually established in 1896 as a sawmill, and was later converted to an inn. Its low mountain slopes make it particularly popular with families.

Accommodations: Rooms and condos are in a huge main lodge, in the smaller Le Château, or four-person cottages. Only the condos have televisions. The bar has piano and other music for dancing.

Facilities: Most of the recreational bases are covered, including a par-72 golf course, 22 tennis courts, indoor pool, fitness center, a spa, horseback riding, boating, and access to 56 miles (90km) of cross-country skiing.

Tremblant. 3005 chemin Principal, Mont-Tremblant, PQ, J0T 1Z0. ☎ **819/681-2000** or 800/ 461-8711. Fax 819/681-5999. 185 condos, 5 chalets. TV TEL. $200–$315 per person double. Rates include breakfast, dinner, and lift ticket. Children 6–12 $45–$80 (meals only), children 3–5 $45 (meals only). Two-night minimum. Packages and rates without meals available. AE, MC, V. Drive 3 miles north of St-Jovite on Highway 117; then take Montée Ryan and follow the blue signs for about 6 miles. Limocar bus from Montréal stops at the front door. Door-to-door transport from Dorval and Mirabel airports Fri–Sun.

Not merely a hotel with a pool, Tremblant is a resort village stretching from the mountain base to the shores of 10-mile-long Lac Tremblant. At recent count, there were 14 shops, including a liquor store, as well as nine eating places and bars, and the numbers continue to grow. The four-story Le Saint-Bernard, at the base of the mountain, is a new hotel with 113 condos with one or two bedrooms and underground parking for 200 cars. When the snow is deep, skiers here like to follow the sun around the mountain, making the run down slopes with an eastern exposure in the morning and the western-facing ones in the afternoon. Eating places are open at the base of the south and north sides as well as at the summit.

Services: A "Kid's Kamp" takes care of children two to six; airport shuttle.

Facilities: There is access to 61 slopes and trails in all, served by 10 ski lifts, including two base-to-summit high-speed quads, triple-chair lifts, double-chair lifts. The resort has 11 lighted Har-Tru tennis courts and an 18-hole golf course.

WHERE TO DINE

Although most Laurentian inns and resorts have their own dining facilities, and often require that guests use them, especially in winter, Mont-Tremblant and vicinity have several independent dining places for casual lunches or the odd night out.

Antipasto. 855 rue Ouimet, St-Jovite. ☎ **819/425-7580.** Main courses $8–$18. MC, V. Daily 4–11pm. ITALIAN.

Housed in an old train station moved to this site, the place does feature the expected railroad memorabilia on the walls, but the owners resisted the temptation to play up the theme to excess. Captain's chairs are drawn up to big tables with green Formica tops and paper place mats. Almost everyone orders the "César" salad (their spelling), which is dense and flavorful, if perhaps a little strong for some tastes. The half portion is more than enough as a first course. Individual pizzas come in 30 versions, on a choice of regular or whole wheat crust. Pastas are available in even greater variety, those with shellfish among the winners. Sauces are savory, but a bit thin. There are outdoor tables in summer.

Petite Europe. 804 rue Ouimet, St-Jovite. ☎ **819/425-3141.** Most items $2.50–$10. MC, V. Summer daily 8am–11pm; winter daily 8am–6pm. DELI.

Charcuterie once meant a pork shop, but today it signifies a delicatessen, in this case, there's even a small bistro and terrace attached. For a picnic, stop by to choose among five dozen varieties of cold meat, three dozen cheeses, two cold cases full of various pastries, and racks of jams and condiments. Sandwiches made from any of these good things, or assorted salads, pâtés, omelets, and pasta dishes can be had at the few booths and tables. The café au lait is a treat, and they have beer on tap. Petite Europe is downtown, on the town's main street.

La Table Enchantée. Route 117 N, Lac Duhamel. ☎ **819/425-7113.** Reservations recommended. Main courses $14.50–$22.50; table d'hôte $15.50–$24.50. AE, MC, V. Tues–Sun 5–10pm. Closed mid-Oct to mid-Nov and two weeks in May. QUÉBÉCOIS.

The tables in this small, tidy restaurant support some of the most carefully prepared dishes in the region. The kitchen adheres to the traditional Québec repertoire with an occasional detour—their Frenchified medallions of red deer, for instance. Clam chowder is a favored starter, or, in the short spring, fiddlehead greens. Then, perhaps, the pâté called cretons, followed by Québécois cipaille, a pot pie layered with pheasant, guinea hen, rabbit, veal, and pork. Dessert might be grand-pêres au sirop d'érable (dumplings in maple syrup).

4 Estrie

Estrie serves, in part, as Québec's breadbasket; it's a largely pastoral region marked by billowing hills and by the 2,600-foot (792m) peak of Mont Orford, centerpiece of a provincial park and the region's premier downhill ski area. Only a short distance from Mont Orford is Sherbrooke, the industrial and commercial capital of Estrie. Throughout the Mont Orford–Sherbrooke area are serene glacial lakes that attract anglers and sailors from throughout the province. Touristically, Estrie is one of Québec's best-kept secrets, so it's mostly Montréalers and other Québécois who occupy rental houses to ski, fish, or launch their boats.

Once out of Montréal, drive east along arrow-straight Autoroute 10 past silos and fields, grazing cows, and meadows strewn with wildflowers. Cresting the hill at kilometer 100, there is an especially beguiling view of mountains and countryside stretching toward New England, not far over the horizon.

At the earliest signs of spring thaw, Estrie kicks into gear as crews penetrate every "sugar bush" (stand of sugar maples) to tap the sap and "sugar off." Maple-sugar festivals result, and numerous farms host "sugaring parties" at which guests partake of a considerable country repasts topped with traditional maple syrup desserts.

Autumn has its attractions, too, for in addition to the glorious autumn foliage (usually best in the weeks fore and aft of the third weekend in September), Estrie orchards sag under the weight of apples of many varieties, and **cider mills** hum day and night. It's not unusual for visitors to help with the apple harvest, paying a low price for the baskets they gather themselves. The cider mills throw open their doors for tours and tastings.

Although town names such as Granby, Waterloo, and Sherbrooke are obviously English, Estrie is now about 90% French-speaking. A few words of French and a little sign language are sometimes necessary outside hotels and other tourist facilities, since the area draws fewer Anglophones than do the Laurentides.

On the drive from Montréal, one of the first Estrie towns of interest is **Rougemont,** Exit 37 off Autoroute 10 and 13¹/₂ miles (22km) along Route 112. Known for its orchards and cider mills, the main street is dotted all year with stands selling apples and apple products, vegetables and homemade bread. At St-Césaire, a few miles farther along 112, stands and shops specialize in locally made handicrafts. The next town, St-Paul-d'Abbotsford, was founded in the late 1700s by Scottish settlers. Abbotsford became the name of the town in 1829, the "St-Paul" added later by French inhabitants.

Another possible detour is 17 miles (27km) south of Autoroute 10. Take Exit 55 onto Route 233 sud to Route 104 est (briefly) to Route 235 sud. This soon becomes the main street of Mystic. Sixty-four people live there, a wide spot in a side road which enjoyed a short-lived prosperity from 1868 to 1880, when an ironworks was located here and the railroad passed through town. An unusual 12-sided barn on the south side is one landmark. The other is a fetching little enterprise called **L'Oeuf** (☎ 514/248-7529), a combination B&B, restaurant, chocolatier, and food shop. It's open Wednesday through Sunday for lunch and dinner.

From Mystic, it's a short drive south and east into Stanbridge East. The **Missiquoi Museum,** open in summer only, stands beside the Aux Brochets River, housed in a photogenic 1860 mill with a waterwheel. There's a picnic area beside it. To return to the Autoroute, continue east to Dunham, pick up Route 213 north, make a short jog west on Route 104, then north again on Route 139.

ESSENTIALS

VISITOR INFORMATION   The **tourist information office** for the Estrie region, at Exit 68 off Autoroute 10, is open daily 10am to 6pm during the summer, and daily 9am to 5pm the rest of the year (☎ 514/375-8774 or 800/263-1068; fax 514/ 375-3530). Or, contact **Tourisme Estrie,** 25 rue Bocage, Sherbrooke, PQ, J1L 2J4, for more information (☎ 819/820-2020 or 800/355-5755; fax 819/566-4445).

GETTING THERE   Leave the island of Montréal by the Champlain Bridge, which leads to Autoroute 10, heading for Sherbrooke. People in a hurry can remain on Autoroute 10—and plenty of express buses do this, too—but to get to know the countryside, turn off the Autoroute at Exit 37 and go north the short distance to join Route 112.

Local buses leave Montréal to follow Route 112 more than a dozen times a day, arriving in Sherbrooke, 100 miles (160km) away, 3¹/₂ hours later. Express buses use Autoroute 10, making a stop in Magog and arriving in Sherbrooke in two hours and 10 minutes (2¹/₂ hours from Québec City). Call **Terminus Voyageur** (☎ 514/ 842-2281) in Montréal for information.

AREA CODE   Note that the area code in Estrie is 514 or 819, depending on the part of the region called (towns with a 514 area code are closer to Montréal).

GRANBY

North of the Autoroute at Exit 68, this largely industrial and not especially beguiling city (pop. 41,500) has a couple of surprises.

First among them is the **Granby Zoo,** 347 rue Bourget (☎ 514/372-9113). Its 70 wooded acres harbor more than 1,000 mammals, exotic birds, reptiles, and amphibians from all over the world. The zoo has an educational program for children and presents shows every day in summer. New exhibits include a nocturnal cave, "Bear Mountain," and a display of robotic whales. There are restaurants, picnic areas, and free rides. Signs for the zoo are spotted after taking Exit 68 off Autoroute 10. The visitors' entrance is on Boulevard David-Bouchard nord. Hours from late May to early September are daily 9:30am to 5pm (closing times vary). Admission is $15 for adults, $13 for seniors, $6 for students 5 to 17, $3 for children 1 to 4; parking is $3.

Granby also has **Yamaska Park,** with a 2-mile (3km) hiking trail, 25 miles (40km) of cross-country ski trails, and 13¹/₂ miles (22km) of biking trails along an old railroad track between Granby and the towns of Bromont and Waterloo.

Tourisme Granby is at 650 rue Principale, Granby, PQ, J2G 8L4 (☎ 514/ 372-7273 or 800/567-7273; fax 514/372-7782). It's open daily in summer from 10am to 6pm, the rest of the year from 8am to 5pm.

BROMONT

Take Exit 78 off Autoroute 10 to reach Bromont (pop. 5,000), a popular destination for day and night skiing, mountain biking (rent bikes at the entrance to the town opposite the tourist office), golf, horseback riding, hiking, and zipping down alpine and water slides. Shoppers are engaged by two large factory outlets, **Versants de Bromont** and **Les Manufacturiers de Bromont,** and the 350-stall **flea market** set up in the drive-in theater from 9am to 5pm the first Sunday in May to the second Sunday in November.

WHERE TO STAY & DINE

Château Bromont. 90 rue Stanstead, Bromont, PQ, J0E 1L0. ☎ **514/534-3433** or 800/ 363-0363. Fax 514/534-0514. 154 rms. A/C MINIBAR TV TEL. $100–$135 per person double. Extra person $10. Packages available. AE, ER, DISC, MC, V.

All the rooms at the Château have rocking chairs and loft beds, and half have fireplaces. A landscaped terrace and two hot tubs look up at the mountain. The staff is young and bilingual.

Les Quatre Canards restaurant serves lunch and dinner, and there are two other cafes. In addition to indoor and outdoor pools and Jacuzzis, a sauna, a small gym, and racquet courts, there is a European spa featuring mud and algae baths (there's an extra charge for use of the facilities and treatments).

LAC BROME

Exit 90 off the Autoroute and Route 243 south lead to this five-village municipality, a.k.a. Knowlton. Shoppers will want to make the detour. The town is compact, but its two main shopping streets are chockablock with stores and discount outlets, including Liz Claiborne, Ralph Lauren, Ben and Jerry, and others.

Large mansions overhang the lake on either side of town. The town hosts a **bluegrass festival** in June, and the **Brome Fair** is held over Labor Day weekend.

The tourist information office is in the local museum, the **Musée Historique du Comte de Brome,** 130 Lakeside St. (Route 243; ☎ 514/243-6782), which occupies five historic buildings, including the town's first school. Exhibits include re-creations of a classroom, bedroom, parlor, and kitchen. The Martin Annex (1921) is dominated by a 1917 Fokker single-seat biplane. It also houses a collection of antique weapons. Admission is $2.50 adults, $2 seniors, $1 students. Hours are Monday to Saturday 10am to 4:30pm, Sunday 11am to 4:30pm; closed late August to May.

WHERE TO STAY

Ⓢ **L'Abricot.** 562 Knowlton Rd. (Rte. 104 ouest), Knowlton, PQ, J0E 1V0. ☎ **514/243-5532.** 4 rms (2 with private bath). $60–$80 double. Rates include full breakfast. Discounts for stays of two or more nights. No credit cards.

Set in a pine grove 1¹/₂ miles west of town, L'Abricot, built in 1889, has an airy main floor, with wide-board floors, a sunroom, breakfast room, patio, and living room with a stone fireplace. The bedrooms, named for animals, are upstairs. Two smaller rooms share a large bath. Outside, there's a swimming pool in the garden.

MONT ORFORD

Exit 115 north off the Autoroute leads into one of Québec's most popular provincial parks. The **Bureau d'Information Touristique Magog-Orford** is at 55 rue Cabana (via Route 112), Magog, PQ, J1X 2C4 (☎ 819/843-2744 or 800/267-2744).

MONT ORFORD PROVINCIAL PARK

From mid-September to mid-October the park blazes with autumn color, and in winter visitors come for the more than 20 miles of ski trails and slopes, with a vertical drop of 1,500 feet, or for the extensive network of cross-country ski and snowshoe trails.

Mont Orford is a veteran ski area compared to Bromont (above), and has long hosted the monied families of Estrie and Montréal on its slopes. The other two mountains in the area, Owl's Head and Mont Sutton, are more family oriented and less glitzy.

Orford has another claim to fame in the **Centre d'Arts Orford** (☎ 819/843-3981), set on a 222-acre estate within the park and providing music classes for talented young musicians every summer. From the end of June to the end of August, a series of classical and chamber music concerts is given in connection with Festival Orford. Prices usually are $11 to $21, or free to $19 for student performances, which are held on Wednesday, Thursday, and Friday at 8pm and Sunday at 11am. Luncheon is served outside following the Sunday concert. Visual arts exhibitions at the center are open to the public, and walking trails connect it to a nearby campground. Campsites in the park fill up quickly, especially on summer weekends.

MAGOG & LAKE MEPHRÉMAGOG

Magog (population 14,500) came by its handle through corruption of an Amerindian word. The Abenaki name Memrobagak ("Great Expanse of Water") somehow became Memphrémagog, which was eventually shortened to Magog, pronounced "May-gog." The town is at the northern end of Lac Memphrémagog (pronounced "Mem-phree-may-gog"), not on Lac Magog, which is about 8 miles north. Memphrémagog straddles the U.S.-Canadian border. Memphrémagog has its own legendary sea creature, nicknamed Memphre, which supposedly surfaced for the first time in 1798. Other sightings have been claimed since then.

The **Magog-Orford tourist information office,** at 55 rue Cabana, Magog, PQ, J1X 2C4 (☎ 819/843-2744 or 800/267-2744, fax 819/847-4036), is open daily in summer from 8:30am to 7:30pm, in winter daily from 9am to 5pm.

OUTDOOR ACTIVITIES & A SERENE RETREAT

Magog has a well-used waterfront, and in July each year the **International Crossing of Lake Memphrémagog** creates a big splash. Participants start out in Newport, Vermont, at 6am and swim 24 miles to Magog, arriving midafternoon around 3:30 or 4pm.

For a less taxing experience, take a 1¹/₂-hour **cruise** aboard the *Aventure I* or *II* (☎ 819/843-8068). The cost is $10.75 for adults, $5.50 for children under 12. A day-long cruise is $40. The boats leave from Point Merry Park, the focal point for many of the town's outdoor activities.

An 11-mile (18¹/₂km) **bike path** links the lake with Mont Orford. In winter it becomes a **cross-country ski trail,** and a 1¹/₂-mile-long (2¹/₂km) **skating rink** is created on the shores of the lake. Snowmobiling trails crisscross the region. Other popular activities in the area include golf, tennis, and horseback riding.

Benedictine Abbey of Saint-Benoît-du-Lac. Chemin Fisher. ☎ **819/843-4080.** Free admission; donations accepted. Daily 6am–8pm, mass with Gregorian chant at 11am, vespers with Gregorian chant at 5pm (7pm on Thurs). No vespers on Tues in July–Aug. Shop Mon–Sat 9–10:45am and 2–4:30pm. Driving west from Magog on Route 112, watch for the first road on the left on the far side of the lake. Take chemin Bolton est 12 miles (19km) south to the turn-off to the abbey.

There's no mistaking the 1912 abbey, with its granite steeple thrusting into the sky above the lake and Owl's Head Mountain as a backdrop. Forty monks help keep the art of Gregorian chant alive in their liturgy, which can be attended by outsiders. For the 45-minute service (times above), walk to the rear of the abbey and down the stairs. Follow signs for "Oratoire," and sit in back to avoid a lot of otherwise obligatory standing and sitting.

The abbey receives 7,000 pilgrims a year, 60% of them between the ages of 16 and 25. It maintains separate hostels for men and women. (Make overnight arrangements in advance; figure $35 or so per person.) A blue cheese known as L'Ermite, among Québec's most famous, and a tasty Swiss-type cheese, are produced at the monastery. They are on sale in the little shop, open 9 to 10:15am and 2 to 4:30pm Monday through Saturday. It also sells chocolate, honey, a nonalcoholic cider, and tapes of religious chants.

LAC MASSAWIPPI

Southeast of Magog, reachable by Routes 141 or 108, east of Autoroute 55, is Lake Massawippi, easily the most alluring resort area in Estrie. Set among rolling hills and fertile farm country, the 12-mile-long lake with its scalloped shoreline was discovered in the early years of this century by people of wealth and power, many of whom were American southerners trying to escape the sultry summers of Virginia and Georgia. They built grand "cottages" on slopes in prime locations along the lakeshore, with enough bedrooms to house their extended families and friends for months at a time. Some of these have now been converted to inns.

Three local hostelries offer an inn-to-inn cross-country ski package that offer participants a fine dinner and accommodations each night. See "Gourmet Ski Tours," near the beginning of this chapter.

NORTH HATLEY

The main town on Lake Massawippi, this village of 704 is only half an hour from the U.S. border and 85$^1/_2$ miles (138km) from Montréal. Old photographs show flocks of people promenading along the main village street. The village has a variety of lodgings, eating places, shops, golf, horseback riding, a marina, a post office, Laundromat, and general store. An English-language theater, the **Piggery** (☎ 819/842-2431), on a country road outside of town, presents plays, many of them experimental, during the summer.

Where to Stay

✪ **Auberge Hatley.** 325 rue Virgin (P.O. Box 330), North Hatley, PQ, J0B 2C0. ☎ 819/842-2451. Fax 819/842-2907. 25 rms. A/C TEL. $250–$360 double. Rates include breakfast, dinner, and gratuities. AE, MC, V. Take Exit 29 from Autoroute 55 and follow Route 108 east, watching for signs.

This acclaimed gastronomic resort occupies a hillside above the lake, not far from the town center. All rooms have a bath or shower, and over half have Jacuzzis and/or fireplaces. An abundance of antiques, many of them hefty Québécois country pieces, are combined with complementary reproductions. There's a swimming pool, and the staff will advise on nearby activities, including riding, hiking, fishing, skiing, and hunting. But there is no uncertainty where owners Liliane and Robert Gagnon place their priorities: the pleasures of the table.

Dining/Entertainment: The dining room has a bank of windows looking over the lake. Tables with pink coverings are set with Rosenthal china, fresh flowers, and candles. It's a necessarily soothing environment, since dinner can easily extend over three hours. Updated but essentially classical French techniques are applied to such ingredients as salmon, bison, and wild boar. Most herbs and some vegetables come from the Gagnons' hydroponic farm and ducks and pheasants from their 100-acre game island. A particular treat is the meal-ending selection of cheeses, served with the waiter's careful description and not a little ceremony.

✪ **Manoir Hovey.** Chemin Hovey (P.O. Box 60), North Hatley, PQ, J0B 2C0. ☎ 819/842-2421 or 800/661-2421. Fax 819/842-2248. 35 rms. A/C TEL. $200–$350 double. Rates include full breakfast, dinner, tax, and gratuities. AE, MC, V. Take exit 29 off Autoroute 55 and follow Route 108 east, watching for signs.

Named for a Connecticut Yankee who came upon the lake in 1793, the columned manor itself was built in 1899. Encompassing 20 acres and 1,600 feet of lakefront property, it is one of Estrie's most complete resort inns. Many of the guest rooms have fireplaces, balconies, and whirlpool baths. Most have TVs. Eight new nonsmoking rooms were added in 1994. The library adjoining the reception area has floor-to-ceiling bookshelves and a stone fireplace. Steve and Kathy Stafford are the gracious hosts.

Dining/Entertainment: The dining room serves updated French cuisine, with a menu that changes with the seasons and uses fresh herbs, vegetables, and edible flowers from the kitchen garden. "Heart-healthy" dishes are featured. All are fragrant and full bodied and attractively presented.

Facilities: A lighted tennis court, modestly equipped exercise room, heated outdoor pool, touring bikes, and two beaches add to the resort's appeal. In winter, a heated cabin is pushed out onto the lake for ice fishing.

Manoir Le Tricorne. 50 chemin Gosselin, North Hatley, PQ, J0B 2C0. ☎ 819/842-4522. Fax 819/842-2692. 11 rms. $95–$160 double. Rates include full breakfast. MC, V. Take Route 108 west out of North Hatley and follow signs.

While the core of this house is 125 years old, it looks as if it was erected five years ago. The exterior is shocking pink and white, the interior is decked out in best middle-brow Good Housekeeping manner, with lots of duck decoys, bird cages, and tartans. The decorative scheme won't be to everyone's taste, but all is immaculately kept and there is ample room to move about. Three rooms have fireplaces, five have Jacuzzis. No phones or TVs, but they are available in the common room. There are spectacular views of Lake Massawippi from all over the hilltop property.

New guests are welcomed with mimosas or glasses of port. The breakfast menu is changed regularly, with fruit omelets one day, eggs Benedict the next. Up the hill is a pool, and one of the two ponds is stocked for fishing.

Where to Dine

Pilsen. 55 rue Principale. ☎ 819/842-2971. Reservations recommended on weekends. Main courses $7–$23. MC, V. Wed–Sun 11:30am–9pm, Fri–Sat 11:30am–9:30pm. The bar stays open until 3am. INTERNATIONAL.

If you drive through North Hatley, you have to pass this pub-restaurant in the center of town. A narrow deck overhangs the river that feeds the lake. It fills up quickly on warm days, the better to watch motorboats and canoes setting out or returning. Inside or out, patrons scarf up renditions of the usual suspects: nachos and burgers, pastas and lobster bisque. There's an extensive choice of beers, including local microbrews Massawippi Blonde and Townships Pale Ale. Park behind the restaurant.

WHERE TO STAY & DINE IN AYER'S CLIFF

✪ **Auberge Ripplecove.** 700 rue Ripplecove (P.O. Box 26), Ayer's Cliff, PQ, J0B 1C0. ☎ 819/838-4296. Fax 819/838-5541. 21 rms, 4 suites. TEL. $184–$318 double; $290–$358 suites. Rates include breakfast, dinner, and gratuities. MC, V. Take Route 55 to Exit 21, follow Route 141 east, watching for signs.

An exceptionally warm welcome is extended by the staff of this handsome inn, on 12 acres beside Lake Massawippi, and impeccable housekeeping standards are observed throughout. The core structure dates from 1945, but subsequent expansions have added rooms, suites, and cottages. About half have gas fireplaces, cable TV, balconies, and whirlpool tubs, while suites add stocked minibars.

Dining/Entertainment: The inn's award-winning lakeside restaurant fills up most nights in season with diners drawn to the kitchen's contemporary French creations, many of which sing with Thai spices. Such exotica as wapiti and caribou appear on the card.

Facilities: The property has a private beach and a heated outdoor pool. Instruction and equipment are available for sailing, sailboarding, waterskiing, canoeing, fishing, and cross-country skiing. Golf courses and riding stables are a short drive away.

Québec City & the Gaspé Peninsula

10

by Herbert Bailey Livesey

Québec City is the soul of New France. It was the first settlement in Canada, and today it is the capital of politically prickly Québec, a province larger than Alaska. With its splendid situation above the St. Lawrence River, and its virtually unblemished old town—a tumble of granite, slate-roofed houses clustered around the august Château Frontenac—it is a haunting evocation of the motherland, as romantic as any on the continent. The river makes a majestic sweep beneath the palisades on which the capital stands, the water as gray as gun metal under dark skies, but silvered by sunlight when the clouds pass. Because of its history, beauty, and unique stature as the only walled city north of Mexico, the historic district of Québec was named a UNESCO World Heritage site in 1985.

Québec City is almost solidly French in feeling, in spirit, and in language. Probably 95% of its population speaks the mother tongue. Perhaps because of that homogeneity and its status as the putative capital of a future independent nation, its citizens seem to suffer less over what might happen down the road. They are also aware that a critical part of their economy is based on tourism, and they are far less likely to vent the open hostility that Americans can encounter in English Canada. While there are far fewer bilingual residents here than in Montréal, many of its 648,000 citizens speak some English, especially those who work in hotels, restaurants, and shops where they deal with Anglophones every day. This is also a college town, and thousands of young people study English as a second language. So while it is often more difficult to understand and be understood, the average Québécois goes out of his or her way to communicate— in halting English, sign language, simplified French, or a combination of all three. With very few exceptions, the Québécois are an uncommonly gracious lot.

Almost all of your visit to Québec can be spent in the Old City, since many hotels and lodging places, restaurants, and tourist-oriented services are based there. The original colony was built right down by the St. Lawrence at the foot of Cap Diamant (Cape Diamond). It was there that merchants, traders, and boatmen earned their livelihoods, but due to unfriendly fire in the 1700s, this Basse-Ville (Lower Town) became primarily a wharf and warehouse area, and residents moved to safer houses atop the steep cliffs that form the rim of Cap Diamant.

Haute-Ville (the Upper Town), the Québécois later discovered, was not immune from cannon fire either, as the British General Wolfe was to prove. Nevertheless, the division into Upper and Lower Towns persisted for obvious topographical reasons. The Upper Town remains enclosed by fortification walls, and several ramplike streets and a cliffside elevator or funicular (funiculaire) connect it to the Lower Town.

Strolling through old Québec is entirely comparable to exploring similar quarters in northern Europe. Carriage wheels creak behind muscular horses, sunlight filters through leafy canopies to fall on drinkers and diners in sidewalk cafes, stone houses huddle close, and childish shrieks of laughter echo down cobblestoned streets. In addition, Québec has a bewitching vista of river and mountains that the Dufferin promenade bestows. In winter the city takes on a Dickensian quality, with lampglow behind curtains of falling snow.

Once you've had a chance to explore the city, you may consider a trip to the Île d'Orléans, an agricultural and resort island within sight of the Château Frontenac; a drive along the northern coast past the shrine of Ste-Anne-de-Beaupré to the provincial park and ski resort at Mont Ste-Anne; or a drive through the picturesque riverside villages on the southern bank of the St. Lawrence.

AN IMPORTANT NOTE ON PRICES   Unless stated otherwise, **the prices cited in this guide are given in Canadian dollars,** which is good news for U.S. travelers because the Canadian dollar is worth 25% less than the American dollar but buys nearly as much. As we go to press, $1 Canadian is worth U.S. 75¢, which means that your $100-a-night hotel room will cost only U.S. $75, and your $6 breakfast costs only U.S. $4.50. Remember, though, that taxes in Canada are substantial.

1 Orientation

ARRIVING

BY PLANE   **Jean-Lesage International Airport** is small, despite the grand name. Buses from the airport into town are operated by **Maple Leaf Sightseeing Tours, Inc.** (☎ 418/649-9226). The 12-mile trip costs $8.75. Buses leave at variable times, depending on the season. A taxi into town costs about $25.

BY CAR   From New York City and points south, follow I-87 to Autoroute 15 to Montréal, picking up Autoroute 20 to Québec City. Take 73 Nord across the Pont Pierre-Laporte and exit onto boulevard Champlain immediately after crossing the bridge. This skirts the city at river level. Turn left at Parc des Champs-de-Bataille (Battlefields Park) and right onto the Grande Allée.

For a slower but more scenic route, follow Route 132 from Montréal along the south shore of the St. Lawrence River to Québec City. Or follow the north shore from Montréal, along Autoroute 40.

From Boston, take I-89 to I-93 to I-91 in Montpelier, Vermont, which connects with Autoroute 55 in Québec to link up with Autoroute 20. Or, follow I-90 up the Atlantic coast, through Portland, Maine, to Route 201 west of Bangor, then Autoroute 173 to Lévis, where there is a car-ferry to Québec City, a 10-minute ride across the St. Lawrence River. The ferry runs every hour on the hour during the day from Lévis (slightly less often at night), and costs $3 for the car and $1.25 per person.

BY TRAIN   The train station in Québec City, **Gare du Palais,** 450 rue de la Gare-du-Palais (☎ 418/524-4161), is a handsome building, but the Lower Town location isn't central. Plan on a moderately strenuous uphill hike or a $6 cab ride to the

Upper Town. That's $6 per ride, incidentally, not per passenger, as an occasional cabby may pretend.

BY BUS   The bus station, **Terminus d'Autobus Voyageur,** at 320 rue Abraham-Martin (☎ 418/525-3000), is near the train station. It is an uphill climb or quick cab ride to Château Frontenac and the Upper Town. A taxi should cost about $6, the same as from the train station.

VISITOR INFORMATION

The **Greater Québec Area Tourism and Convention Bureau** operates two useful information centers in and near the city. One is in the old part of Québec City at 60 rue d'Auteuil (☎ 418/692-2471), another in suburban Ste-Foy, at 3005 bd. Laurier, near the Québec and Pierre-Laporte bridges (☎ 418/651-2882). The information center in the Upper Town is open daily 8:30am to 8pm from early June to Labor Day, 8:30am to 5:30pm from Labor Day to October 10, and 9am to 5pm Monday to Friday the rest of the year.

The provincial government's tourism department operates an information office on place d'Armes, down the hill from the Château Frontenac, at 12 rue Ste-Anne (☎ 418/873-2015 or 800/363-7777 from other parts of Québec, Canada, and the United States). It's open from mid-June to early September from 8:30am to 7:30pm from mid-June to early September, and from 9am to 5pm the rest of the year. The office has many brochures, including information about cruise and bus tour operators, a souvenir shop, a 24-hour ATM, a currency exchange office, and a free accommodations reservation service.

Parks Canada operates an information kiosk in front of the Château Frontenac; it's open daily from 9am to noon and 1 to 5pm.

CITY LAYOUT

Within the walls of the Upper Town the principal streets are rues St-Louis (which becomes the Grande-Allée outside the city walls), Ste-Anne, and St-Jean, and the pedestrians-only terrasse Dufferin, which overlooks the river. In the Lower Town, major streets are St-Pierre, Dalhousie, St-Paul and, parallel to it, St-André.

If it were larger, the historic district, with its winding and plunging streets, might be confusing to negotiate. As compact as it is, though, most visitors have little difficulty finding their way around. Most streets are only a few blocks long, so when the name of the street is known, it is fairly easy to find an specific address.

There are good maps of the Upper and Lower Towns and the metropolitan region in the Greater Québec Area Tourist Guide, provided by any tourist office.

NEIGHBORHOODS IN BRIEF

Haute-Ville   Haute-Ville (the Upper Town) is surrounded by ramparts and overlooks the St. Lawrence River. It includes most of the sites for which the city is famous, among them the Château Frontenac, the terrasse Dufferin, and the Citadelle, a fortress begun by the French in the 18th century. Most of the buildings of the Haute-Ville are at least one hundred years old, made of granite in similar styles, with few jarring modern intrusions. The Dufferin pedestrian promenade attracts crowds in all seasons for its magnificent views of the river and the land to the south.

Basse-Ville   At river level, Basse-Ville (the Lower Town) is connected to Haute-Ville by funicular and by several streets and stairways. It encompasses place Royale, the restored quartier du Petit-Champlain, the small Notre-Dame-des-Victoires church, and the Museum of Civilization, a highlight of any visit.

Grande-Allée   This major artery runs from the St-Louis Gate in the fortified walls to avenue Taché. It passes the stately Parliament building and numerous terraced bars and restaurants, and later skirts the Museum of Fine Arts and the Plains of Abraham. The city's large contemporary hotels are on or near the Grande-Allée.

2 Getting Around

Once you are within or near the walls of the Haute Ville, virtually no place of interest, hotel, or restaurant is out of walking distance. In bad weather, or when traversing between opposite ends of lower and upper towns, a taxi might be necessary, but in general, walking is the best way to explore the city.

BY PUBLIC TRANSPORTATION

BY BUS   Local buses run quite often and charge $1.80 in exact change. No. 7 travels up and down rue St-Jean. No. 11 shuttles along Grande-Allée/rue St-Louis, and, along with nos. 7 and 8, also travels well into suburban Ste-Foy, for those who want to visit the shopping centers there. One-day bus passes are available for $3.50.

BY FUNICULAR   Although there are streets and stairs between the Upper Town to the Lower Town, there is also a funicular, which operates along an inclined 210-foot track between the terrace Dufferin and the quartier du Petit-Champlain. The fare is $1, and the car operates daily from 8am to midnight in summer. It closes at 11:30pm in winter. The upper station is near the front of the Château Frontenac, while the lower station is inside the Maison Louis-Jolliet, on rue du Petit-Champlain.

BY TAXI

They're everywhere, but cruise in the largest packs near the big hotels and some of the larger squares of the Upper Town. In theory, they can be hailed, but your best bet is to find one of their ranks, such as the one in the place d'Armes or in front of the Hôtel-de-Ville (City Hall). Restaurant managers and hotel bell captains can also summon one for you. Fares are expensive, in part to compensate for the short distances of most rides. To call a cab, try **Taxi Coop** (☎ 418/525-5191) or **Taxi Québec** (☎ 418/525-8123).

BY HORSE-DRAWN CARRIAGE

A romantic—and expensive—way to see the city is in a horse-drawn carriage, called a calèche. They can be hired at place d'Armes or on rue d'Auteuil, just within the city walls near the tourist information office. The 45-minute tour with a driver/guide (they speak English) costs about $50 for 30 minutes. Carriages operate all summer, rain or shine.

BY CAR

RENTALS   Car-rental companies include **Avis,** at the airport (☎ 418/872-0409 or 800/879-2847) and in the city (☎ 418/523-1075); **Budget,** at the airport (☎ 418/872-9885 or 800/268-8900) and in the city (☎ 418/692-3660); **Hertz Canada,** at the airport (☎ 418/871-1571 or 800/654-3131) and in the city (☎ 418/694-1224); **Thrifty,** at the airport (☎ 418/877-2870 or 800/367-2277) and in the city (☎ 418/683-1542); and **Tilden,** at the airport (☎ 418/871-1224).

PARKING   On-street parking is very difficult in the cramped quarters of old Québec. When a rare space on the street is found, be sure to check the signs for hours that parking is permissible. When meters are in place, the charge is 25¢ per 15 minutes up to 120 minutes. Metered spots are free on Sundays, before 9am and after 6pm Monday through Wednesday and on Saturday, and before 9am and after 9pm Thursday and Friday.

Many of the smaller hotels have special arrangements with local garages, so their guests can receive a $3 or $4 discount on the cost of a day's parking (usually $10 a day or more). Check with your hotel before parking in a lot or garage.

If your hotel or auberge doesn't have access to a lot, there are plenty available, clearly marked on the foldout city map available at tourist offices.

FAST FACTS: Québec City

American Express   There is no office right in town, but for lost traveler's checks, call ☎ 800/221-7282. American Express keeps a customer service desk in two shopping centers in Ste-Foy, a bus or taxi ride away: Les Galeries de la Capitale, 5401 bd. des Galeries (☎ 418/627-2580); and Place Laurier, 2740 bd. Laurier, (☎ 418/658-8820).

Consulate   The U.S. Consulate is near the Château Frontenac, facing Jardin des Gouverneurs at 2 place terrasse-Dufferin (☎ 418/692-2095).

Currency Exchange   Conveniently located near the Château Frontenac, the bureau de change at 19 rue Ste-Anne and rue des Jardins is open Monday, Tuesday, and Friday from 10am to 3pm, and Wednesday and Thursday from 10am to 6pm. (On weekends, you can change money in hotels and shops.)

Dentists   Call 418/653-5412 Monday 9am to 8pm; Tuesday and Wednesday 8am to 8pm; Thursday 8am to 6pm; and Friday 8am to 4pm; for weekend emergencies, call 418/656-6060. Both numbers are hotlines that will refer you to available dentists.

Doctors   For emergency treatment, call Info-Santé (☎ 418/648-2626) 24 hours a day, or the Hôtel-Dieu de Québec Hospital emergency room (☎ 418/691-5042).

Drugstores (Late-Night Pharmacies)   Caron and Bernier, in the Upper Town, 38 côte du Palais, at rue Charlevoix, is open from 8:15am to 8pm Monday through Friday, and 9am to 3pm on Saturday (☎ 418/692-4252). In an emergency, it's necessary to travel to the suburbs to Pharmacie Brunet, in Les Galeries Charlesbourg, 4266 Première Avenue (1ère or First Avenue), in Charlesbourg (☎ 418/623-1571), open 24 hours, seven days a week.

Emergencies   For the police, call 911. For Marine Search and Rescue (the Canadian Coast Guard) call 418/648-3599 (Greater Québec area) or 800/463-4393 (St. Lawrence River) 24 hours a day. For the Poison Control Center, call 418/656-5412. For pet injuries or other problems, call Vet-Medic (☎ 418/647-2000), 24 hours a day.

Information   See "Visitor Information" in Section 1 of this chapter.

Liquor Laws   All hard liquor in Québec is sold through official government stores operated by the Québec Société des Alcools. Wine and beer can be bought in grocery stores and supermarkets. The legal drinking age in the province is 18.

Newspapers and Magazines   Québec City's English-language newspaper, the *Chronicle-Telegraph*, is the equivalent of a small-town newspaper, and is published weekly on Wednesday. Major Canadian and American English-language newspapers and magazines are available in the newsstands of the large hotels and at vending machines placed around tourist corners in the old town. The leading French-language newspapers are *Le Soleil* and *Le Journal de Québec*.

Photographic Needs   Film can be purchased or developed at Librairie Garneau, 24 côte de la Fabrique (☎ 418/692-4262).

Police   For the Québec City police, call 911. For the Sûreté du Québec, comparable to the state police, call 418/623-6262.

Post Office   The main post office (bureau de poste) is in the Lower Town, at 300 rue St-Paul near rue Abraham-Martin, not far from carré Parent (Parent Square) by the port (☎ 418/694-6176). Hours are 8am to 5:45pm Monday through Friday. A convenient branch in the Upper Town, half a block down the hill from the Château Frontenac, is at 3 rue Buade (☎ 418/694-6102), and keeps the same hours.

Radio and TV   Most broadcasts on radio and TV are in French, but FM 104.7 is in English. In the large hotels, cable TV is standard, with some English-language stations. Channel 5 offers English-language programming.

Restrooms   Find them in the tourist offices and on the ground floor of the commercial complex at 41 rue Couillard, just off rue St-Jean (it's wheelchair accessible).

Taxes   Most goods and services in Canada are taxed 7% by the federal government. On top of that, the province of Québec adds an additional 6.5% tax on goods and services, including those provided by hotels. In Québec, the federal tax appears on the bill as the TPS (elsewhere in Canada, it's called the GST), and the provincial tax is known as the TVQ. Tourists may receive a rebate on both the federal and provincial tax on items they have purchased but not used in Québec, as well as on lodging. To take advantage of this, request the necessary forms at duty-free shops and hotels and submit them, with the original receipts, within a year of the purchase. Contact the Canadian consulate or Québec tourism office for up-to-the-minute information about taxes and rebates.

Time   Québec City is on the same time as New York, Boston, Montréal, and Toronto. It's an hour behind Halifax.

Transit Information   Call ☎ 418/627-2511.

Useful Telephone Numbers   For Alcoholics Anonymous, call 418/529-0015, daily 8am to midnight. Health Info, a 24-hour line answered by nurses, ☎ 418/648-2626. Tel-Aide, for emotional distress including anxiety and depression, ☎ 418/683-2153. Tides, ☎ 418/648-7293, 24 hours daily.

Weather   For the forecast, call ☎ 418/640-2736, 24 hours a day.

3 Accommodations

Staying in one of the small hotels or auberges within the walls of the Upper Town can be one of Québec City's memorable experiences. That isn't to imply that it will necessarily be enjoyable. Standards of comfort, amenities, and prices fluctuate so wildly from one small hotel to another—even within a single establishment—that it is wise to shop around and examine any rooms you are offered before registering. From rooms with private baths, minibars, and cable TV to walk-up budget accommodations with linoleum floors and toilets down the hall, Québec has something to suit most tastes and wallets.

If cost is a prime consideration, note that prices drop significantly from November through April, except around Christmas and Winter Carnival. On the other hand, if you want luxury and the Château Frontenac is fully booked, you will need to go outside the walls to the newer part of town. Most of the high-rise chain hotels out there are within walking distance of the Old City, or are only a quick bus or taxi ride away. Although Québec City has many fewer luxury and first-class hotels than Montréal, there are still enough of them to provide for the crowds of businesspeople and well-heeled tourists who flock to the city year-round.

Québec City's inexpensive hotels are generally smaller places, often converted residences or hostelries carved out of several rowhouses. They offer fewer of the usual electronic gadgets—air-conditioning and TV are far from standard at this level—and may be several floors high, without elevators. Even with an advance reservation, always ask to see two or three rooms before making a choice. Unless otherwise noted, all rooms in the lodgings listed below have baths.

In addition to guest houses, many owners of private homes make one to five rooms available for guests, and provide breakfast. This kind of bed-and-breakfast doesn't have a sign out front. The only way to locate and reserve one is through one of the umbrella organizations that maintain listings. One such, in a shifting field, is **Bonjour Québec**, 3765 boul. de Monaco, Québec, PQ, G1R 1N4 (☎ 418/527-1465). Rooms are generally in the $35 to $65 range for double occupancy. When calling to make arrangements, be very clear about your needs and requirements. Some hosts don't permit smoking, or children, or pets. They might have only one or two bathrooms in the entire place, to be shared by four or five rooms, or all their rooms might be fourth-floor walkups, or they might be located far from the center of things. As with the inexpensive lodging choices listed below, TVs and air-conditioning are exceptions, not regular features. A deposit is typically required, and minimum stays of two nights are common. Credit cards may not be accepted.

UPPER TOWN
VERY EXPENSIVE

Château Frontenac. 1 rue des Carrières (St-Louis), Québec, PQ, G1R 4P5. ☎ **418/692-3861** or 800/828-7447. Fax 418/692-1751. 611 rms, 24 suites. A/C MINIBAR TV TEL. Mid-May to mid-Oct $190–$285 double, $385–$685 suite; mid-Oct to mid-May $125–$190 double, $300–$600 suite. AE, CB, DC, DISC, ER, MC, V. Parking $12.25 per day.

Québec's magical "castle" turned 100 years old in 1993. To celebrate, the management added a new 66-room wing, and since the hotel serves as the very symbol of the city, care was taken to replicate the original architectural style throughout. In the past, the hotel hosted Queen Elizabeth and Prince Philip, and during World War II, Churchill and Roosevelt had the entire place to themselves for a conference. The hotel was built in phases, following the landline, so the wide halls follow crooked paths. The price of a room depends on its size, location, view or lack of one, and on how recently it was renovated. In-room movies are available, and some rooms are no-smoking.

Dining/Entertainment: The fare in the dining rooms has yet to measure up to the grandeur of the physical spaces. Le Champlain is the formal dining room. The casual Café de la Terrasse offers a buffet dinner and dancing on Saturday nights. Two bars overlook the terrace Dufferin. Le Bistro is the lower level snack bar.

Services: Concierge, room service (6:30am to 11:30pm), dry cleaning, laundry service, babysitting, limo service, massage, secretarial services.

Facilities: New facilities include an indoor pool and a large gym overlooking Governor's Park. Fitness swimmers may find the pool monopolized by youngsters much of the day. In addition, there's a kiddie pool, Jacuzzi, and business center.

MODERATE

Many of the hotels and auberges recommended below are on or near the Jardin des Gouverneurs, immediately south of the Château Frontenac.

🏨 Family-Friendly Hotels

Château Frontenac *(see p. 291)* It's a fairy-tale castle posing as a hotel—where better to pretend your children are princes and princesses?

Hôtellerie Fleur-de-Lys *(see p. 292)* The Old City's only motel, it has 24-hour laundry facilities and rooms with kitchenettes and TVs, three things that make travel with kids more comfortable.

L'Hôtel du Vieux Québec *(see p. 292)* Popular with families and school groups, it's in a good location for exploring Upper or Lower Town.

Radisson Gouverneurs *(see p. 294)* The rooftop swimming pool is a treat, with its indoor water route to the outside. It's especially fun in winter, when snow covers everything but the pool itself. Winter Carnival activities are a quick and easy walk away.

Au Jardin du Gouverneur. 16 Mont-Carmel (Haldimand), Québec, PQ, G1R 4A3. ☎ **418/ 692-1704.** Fax 418/692-1713. 16 rms, 1 suite. A/C TV. $65–$90 double. Rates include breakfast. Extra person over 12 years $15, under 12, $5. AE, DC, ER, MC, V. Parking in nearby garage.

Graced with a distinctive white stucco front and blue-gray trim, this hotel is housed in a 150-year-old building at the upper corner of the park, a former home of prominent Québec politicians. Rooms are serviceable rather than memorable, but comfortable enough to represent good value. About half the rooms have views of the park. The Château Frontenac and terrace Dufferin are at the downhill end of the park.

⑤ Château Bellevue. 16 rue Laporte (Laporte), Québec, PQ, G1R 4M9. ☎ **418/692-2573** or 800/463-2617. Fax 418/692-4876. 57 rms. A/C TV TEL. $74–$99 double. Extra person $10. AE, CB, DC, ER, MC, V. Packages available Oct–May. Valet parking free.

Occupying several rowhouses at the top of the Parc des Gouverneurs, this minihotel has a pleasant lobby with leather couches and chairs and a helpful staff as well as the creature comforts many of the smaller auberges in the neighborhood lack. While some of the rooms suffer from unfortunate decorating choices, they are quiet for the most part and have private baths. A few higher-priced units overlook the park. The hotel's private parking is directly behind the building, a notable convenience in this congested part of town.

Hôtellerie Fleur-de-Lys. 115 rue Ste-Anne (near Ste-Ursule), Québec, PQ, G1R 3X6. ☎ **418/ 694-0106** or 800/567-2106. Fax 418/692-1959. 36 rms. A/C TV TEL. $85–$120 double. Extra adult $12. Children 6–15 $6. AE, MC, V. Parking $7.25.

This brick-front motel tucked into the midst of the old city is a bit jarring visually, but it's away from the major sites on a quiet side street and has decided virtues. These include the enclosed parking lot and a laundry room available to guests 24 hours a day. In addition, every room has a refrigerator, a dining table, and chairs. Some rooms have kitchenettes.

L'Hôtel du Vieux Québec. 1190 rue St-Jean (near rue Collins), Québec, PQ, G1R 4J2. ☎ **418/ 692-1850.** Fax 418/692-5637. 28 rms and suites. TV TEL. May to mid-Oct, Christmas, and Winter Carnival $89–$119 double; mid-Oct to Dec (except Christmas period) $50–$79 double; Jan–Apr $60–$79. Extra person $10. AE, ER, MC, V. Parking $6.

This century-old brick building has been carefully renovated and modernized. Guest rooms are equipped with sofas, two double beds, cable color TVs, and modern bathrooms. Most have kitchenettes. With these homey layouts, it's understandably popular with families, skiers, and the groups of visiting high-school students who descend upon the city in late spring. Some rooms have air-conditioning. Many moderately priced restaurants and nightspots are found on nearby St-Jean.

INEXPENSIVE

⑤ Auberge de Jeunesse. 19 Ste-Ursule (at rue Dauphine), Québec, PQ, G1R 4E1. ☎ **418/694-0755** or 800/461-8585 from elsewhere in the province except Montréal; 514/252-3117 from Montréal or outside the province. Fax 418/694-2278 or 514/251-3119 from Montréal and outside the province. 281 beds. $12.75–$16.75 members, $15.75–$19.75 nonmembers. Half price for children 9–13; free for children 8 and younger. AE, MC, V.

Actually a youth hostel, this two-story brick building up the hill from rue St-Jean has some rooms with two beds and a few with double beds, but most units have four beds. There are also dorms with 10 to 12 beds. The cafeteria is open most of the year, and breakfast costs about $3.50. Lockers are available for luggage, skis, and bicycles. There is a laundry, a lounge with a pool table, and a backyard with picnic tables. Guests can use the common kitchen. There's no curfew.

Auberge de la Chouette. 71 rue d'Auteuil (near St-Louis), Québec, PQ, G1R 4C3. ☎ **418/694-0232.** 10 rms. A/C TV TEL. Summer $70 double; winter $55 double. AE, MC, V. Parking $6 a day.

Across the street from Esplanade Park and near the Porte St-Louis, this auberge has an accomplished Asian restaurant, Apsara (see listing in Section 4, later in this chapter), on the main floor. A spiral stairway leads up to the rooms, all of which have full baths. The tourist office, the Citadelle, and Winter Carnival or Québec Summer Festival activities are only minutes away.

Auberge St-Louis. 48 rue St-Louis (near Ste-Ursule), Québec, PQ, G1R 3Z3. ☎ **418/692-2424** or 800/663-7878 in Canada. Fax 418/692-3797. 27 rms (13 with bath). June–Oct $40–$55 double without bath, $61 double with private shower and sink and shared toilet, $76–$85 double with bath; Nov–May $39 double without bath, $49 double with shower and sink only, $59 double with bath. Rates include breakfast. Extra person $10. MC, V. Nearby parking $6 a day.

Guest rooms come in a variety of configurations, with occasional features that add visual interest, such as a carved-wood fireplace or a stained-glass window. But the reason to stay here is its low prices combined with a good location. Some rooms have a sink and shower, but no toilet, and some have a color or black-and-white TV. Only two units have air-conditioning, the rest have fans.

ON OR NEAR THE GRANDE-ALLÉE
VERY EXPENSIVE

✪ Hilton International Québec. 3 place Québec, Québec, PQ, G1K 7889. ☎ **418/647-2411** or 800/445-8667. Fax 418/847-6488. 565 rms, 39 suites. A/C MINIBAR TV TEL. $166–$226 double, from $335 suite. Extra person $22. Children of any age stay free in parents' room. Packages available. AE, CB, DC, DISC, MC, V. Parking $13.50. Head east along Grande-Allée, and just before the St-Louis Gate in the city wall, turn left on rue Dufferin, then left again as you pass the Parliament building; the hotel is one block ahead.

Superior on virtually every count to the other midrise contemporary hotels outside the old town, this Hilton is the clear choice for visiting executives and for those leisure travelers who can't bear to live without their gadgets. The location—across the street from the city walls and near the Parliament—is excellent. It is also connected to the place Québec shopping complex, which has 75 shops and two cinemas, and the Convention Center.

The public rooms are big and brassy, Hilton-style, while the uninspired guest chambers are in need of freshening. Most have one or two large beds plus in-room movies. Upper floor views of the St. Lawrence River, old Québec, and the Laurentian Mountains are grand. The staff is generally efficient and congenial. Nonsmoking rooms are available.

Dining/Entertainment: Le Caucus restaurant serves buffet-style as well as à la carte meals. Friday and Saturday evenings are theme nights, with live entertainment.

Services: Airport shuttle, room service, dry cleaning, laundry service, babysitting, and car-rental.

Facilities: Heated outdoor pool (summer only), health club with sauna and massage, whirlpool.

EXPENSIVE

Loews Le Concorde. 1225 place Montcalm (at Grande-Allée), Québec, PQ, G1R 4W6. ☎ 418/647-2222 or 800/235-6397 from the U.S., 800/463-5256 from Canada. Fax 418/647-4710. 400 rms, 22 suites. A/C MINIBAR TV TEL. $135–$180 double, from $195 suite. Extra person over 17, $20. Special off-season rates available, along with weekend and ski packages. AE, DC, ER, MC, V. Parking garage $12.50.

From outside, the building that houses this hotel is an unforgivable insult to the sky-line, blighting a neighborhood of late Victorian townhouses. Enter, and the affront might be forgotten, at least by those who have business to do and can't be bothered with esthetics.

Standard rooms have marble bathrooms with hair dryers, prints of Québec City street scenes, in-room movies, and three telephones. They bestow spectacular views of the river and the old city, even from the lower floors. There are seven nonsmoking floors and seven business-class floors.

It's about a 10-minute walk to the walls and then another 10 minutes to the center of the Haute-Ville. Of all the hotels listed here, this is the farthest outside of Québec City proper.

Dining/Entertainment: L'Astral is a revolving rooftop restaurant, with a bar and live piano music Tuesday to Sunday nights. Le Café serves light lunch or dinner. La Place Montcalm offers buffet or à la carte breakfasts.

Services: Concierge, room service (6am to midnight), dry cleaning, laundry service.

Facilities: A small fitness facility with sauna and some exercise equipment, outdoor heated pool (April to November; access to pool in a private club during the other months).

Radisson Gouverneurs. 690 boul. René-Lévesque est, Québec, PQ, G1R 5A8. ☎ 418/647-1717, 800/463-2820 from eastern Canada and Ontario, 800/333-3333 from elsewhere. Fax 418/647-2146. 377 rms, 14 suites. A/C TV TEL. $140–$160 double, from $195 suite. Extra adult $15; children free. AE, DC, DISC, ER, MC, V. Parking $11, with in/out privileges. Turn left off Grande-Allée, and then turn left again onto Dufferin, just before the St-Louis Gate in the city wall. Once you've passed the Parliament building, take your first left. The hotel is two blocks ahead.

Part of place Québec, a multiuse complex, this hotel is also connected to the city's convention center. It is a block from the Hilton, two blocks from Porte (Gate) Kent in the city wall, and not far from the Québec Parliament building, a location likely to fit almost any businessperson's needs. It is, however, an uphill climb from the old city (like all the hotels and inns along or near the Grande-Allée). Some rooms have minibars; all have in-room movies. There are three nonsmoking floors and two executive floors. Reception is two levels up.

Dining/Entertainment: Le Café serves buffet and à la carte meals.

Services: Room service, dry cleaning, laundry service, babysitting.

Facilities: An indoor waterway leads to the heated outdoor pool, which provides a delightfully rare way to enter the pool when snow is falling. There's a fully equipped and staffed health club with Exercycles and sauna and a Jacuzzi.

MODERATE

Hôtel Château Laurier. 695 Grand-Allée est (at Georges V), Québec, PQ, G1R 2K4. ☎ 418/522-8108 or 800/463-4453. Fax 418/524-8768. 55 rms. A/C TV TEL. Summer $89–$119 double; winter $69 double. Extra person $10. AE, DC, ER, MC, V. Free parking behind the hotel.

Just a few blocks from the St-Louis Gate and next to the Plains of Abraham, this century-old stone structure has a Victorian parlor with a grandfather clock. Rates depend on room size, fixtures, and view. An elevator serves the several floors, and a sauna is available. Le Patrimoine restaurant, on the ground floor, is open from early morning to late evening.

INEXPENSIVE

Manoir de L'Esplanade. 83 rue d'Auteull (at rue St-Louis), Québec, PQ, G1R 4C3. ☎ 418/694-0834. Fax 418/692-0456. 37 rms. A/C TV TEL. Summer $65–$90 double. Winter rates 45% less. Extra person $10. AE, MC, V. Parking $6 a day.

Though not as well appointed as some of the other places along the Grande-Allée, it's clean and all rooms have a private bath—not something one can generally assume to be present at this price. Some have double beds. Students like this place, which used to be a nunnery. The tourist office is right across the street.

⑤ Relais Charles-Alexander. 91 Grande-Allée est (av. Galipeault), Québec, PQ, G1R 2H5. ☎ 418/523-1220. Fax 418/523-9556. 17 rms (14 with bath). A/C TV. $70–$80 double. Rates include breakfast. No credit cards. Parking nearby $6.

On the ground floor of this charming brick-faced B&B is an art gallery, which also serves as the breakfast room. This stylish use of space extends to the bedrooms as well, which are crisply maintained and decorated with eclectic antique pieces and reproductions. They are quiet, for the most part, since the inn is just outside the orbit of the sometimes raucous Grande-Allée terrace bars. Yet the St-Louis Gate is less than a 10-minute walk away from the hubbub.

LOWER TOWN
EXPENSIVE/VERY EXPENSIVE

✪ Auberge St-Antoine. 10 rue St-Antoine (Dalhousie), Québec, PQ, G1K 4C9. ☎ 418/692-2211 or 800/267-0525. Fax 418/692-1177. 22 rms, 7 suites. A/C TV TEL. $129–$269 double, $439 suite. Rates include buffet breakfast. Extra person $10. Children under 12 free. AE, DC, MC, V. Free parking. Follow rue Dalhousie around the Lower Town to rue St-Antoine. The hotel is next to the Musée de la Civilisation.

The centerpiece of this uncommonly attractive boutique hotel is the 1830 maritime warehouse that contains the lobby and meeting rooms, with the original dark beams and stone floor still intact. Buffet breakfasts and afternoon wine and cheese are set out in the lobby, where you can relax in wing chairs next to the hooded fireplace. Canny mixes of antique and reproduction furniture are found in both public and private areas. The bedrooms, in an adjoining modern wing, are spacious, in many different color schemes, with such extra decorative touches as custom-made iron bedsteads and tables. The big bathrooms have robes and hair dryers. Three rooms have private terraces, and 13 have river views, but a large parking lot intervenes. The eight new suites have kitchenettes, fax machines, and computer jacks.

MODERATE

Le Priori. 15 rue Sault-au-Matelot (at rue St-Antoine), Québec, PQ, G1K 3Y7. ☎ 418/692-3992. Fax 418/692-0883. 20 rms, 5 suites. TV TEL. $90–$120 double; $135–$210 suite. AE, MC, V. Parking $8 a day.

A second newcomer to the emerging Lower Town hotel scene, located two blocks behind the Auberge St-Antoine, Le Priori provides a playful postmodern ambience behind the somber facade of a 1766 house. Hot French designer Phillipe Starck inspired the owners, who deployed versions of his conical stainless-steel sinks in the bedrooms and sensual multinozzle showers in the small bathrooms. Queen-size beds have black tubular frames and soft duvets. The dim lighting doesn't help readers, however, and in some rooms, a clawfoot tub sits beside the bed. Suites have sitting rooms with wood-burning fireplaces, a kitchen, and a bath with Jacuzzi. The hotel houses the admirable Laurie Raphaël restaurant. At last visit, there were rumors of an impending sale, perhaps to the owners of the restaurant.

4 Dining

Once you are within these ancient walls, walking along streets that look to have been transplanted intact from Brittany or Provence, it is understandable if you imagine that one superb dining experience after another is in store.

Unfortunately, it isn't true. If that French tire company decided to bestow its hotly contested stars upon Québec restaurants, they might grudgingly part with three or four. Hype and expectations aside, the truth is that this gloriously scenic city has no world-class restaurants comparable to those of Paris or Manhattan or even Montréal. While it is easy to eat well in the capital—even, in a few isolated cases, quite well— the highlight of your stay will lie elsewhere.

But that's not to imply that you're in for barely edible meals served by sullen waiters. By sticking to any of the many competent bistros, the handful of Asian eateries, and one or two of the emerging nuovo Italiano trattorias, you'll do fine. Another step up, two or three ambitious enterprises tease the palate with hints of higher achievement. Even the blatantly touristic restaurants along rue St-Louis and around the place d'Armes can produce decent meals.

As throughout the province, the best dining deals are the table d'hôte (fixed-price) meals. Virtually all full-service restaurants offer them, if only at lunch. As a rule, they include at least soup or salad, a main course, and dessert. Some places add in an extra appetizer and/or a beverage, all for the approximate à la carte price of the main course alone.

Curiously, for a city standing beside a great waterway and a day's sail from some of the world's best fishing grounds, seafood is not given much attention. Mussels and salmon are on most menus, but cherish those places that go beyond those staples. Game is popular, however, and everything from venison, rabbit, and duck to more exotic quail, goose, caribou, and wapiti are available.

At the better places, and even some of those that might seem inexplicably popular, reservations are all but essential during traditional holidays and the festivals that pepper the social calendar. Other times, it's usually necessary to book ahead only for weekend evenings. Dress codes are only required in a few restaurants, but Québecers are a stylish lot. "Dressy casual" works almost everywhere. Remember that for the Québécois, "dinner" is lunch, and "supper" is dinner, though for the sake of consistency, I have used the word *dinner* below in the traditional American sense. They tend to have the evening meal earlier than Montréalers, at 6 or 7pm rather than at 8pm.

When figuring costs, add the 15% in federal and provincial taxes. Prices shown are in Canadian dollars.

UPPER TOWN
EXPENSIVE

✪ Le Saint-Amour. 48 rue Ste-Ursule (near St-Louis). ☎ **418/694-0667.** Reservations recommended for dinner. Main courses $19.50–$28; table d'hôte lunch $9.50, dinner $25–$28; gastronomic dinner $48. AE, CB, DC, ER, MC, V. Tues–Fri noon–2:30pm; daily 6–10:30pm. CONTEMPORARY FRENCH.

Every effort is made to render this a gratifying dining experience that touches all the senses, and the energetic chef-owner tirelessly scours away imperfections. This is a restaurant for the coolly attractive and romantically inclined. They pass a front room with lace curtains and potted greenery into a covered terrace lit by candles and flickering Victorian gas fixtures. Up above, the roof is retracted on warm nights, revealing a splash of stars. The house, built in the 1820s, is a little off the tourist track, so "I'm with Stupid" T-shirts are not in evidence.

There aren't three other restaurants in town that equal Le Sant-Amour. The kitchen has a sure hand with game, and it is featured even on the warm-weather version of the seasonally changing menu. Look for the varying preparations of caribou and wapiti steak, trendy items in Québec, as well as for boned quail, duck, and rabbit. The long wine list has some not-too-expensive bottlings, and the chocolate desserts are especially tempting.

Serge Bruyère. 1200 rue Saint-Jean (Côte de la Fabrique). ☎ **418/694-0618.** Reservations recommended for dinner. Main courses $9.50–$26.50; table d'hôte lunch $8–$12, dinner $19–$49. AE, DC, MC, V. Mon–Fri noon–2pm; daily 6–10:30pm. ECLECTIC.

The eponymous owner bought the wedge-shaped building in 1979, and set about creating a multilevel dining emporium that had something for everyone. Serge Bruyère died young, and tragically. His executive chef carries on, along a similar path. At ground level, there's a casual cafe with a cold case that displays salads and pastries—it's just the place for a leisurely afternoon snack. Up a long staircase at the back is his La Petite Table, with a bare wood floor and three semicircular windows looking down on the street. This venue is meant for lunches, a purpose it serves admirably. Soup and dessert are included in the price of the main course, and come with rounds of crusty, chewy bread. Foods are adroitly seasoned.

Finally, another flight up, is the formal Grand Table. Overpraised from the outset, its menu is nevertheless highly imaginative and immaculately presented. Gaps between the several courses of the gastronomic extravaganza stretch on—and on—for an entire evening. Whether the excellent creations justify the raves and the overly showy pace of the meal is up to you. Dress well, and arrive with a healthy credit card.

MODERATE

Apsara. 71 rue d'Auteuil (near St-Louis Gate). ☎ **418/694-0232.** Main courses $10–$13. AE, MC, V. Mon–Fri 11:30am–2pm; daily 5:30–11pm. SOUTH ASIAN.

Near the tourist office and the city walls, this 1845 Victorian rowhouse is home to one of the city's best Asian restaurants. The interior looks rather like the British consulate in Shanghai might, welcoming diners who come for a gastronomic tour that arches from Taiwan to Vietnam to Cambodia to Thailand. Head straight for the last stop, since the Thai dishes are clearly masters over the mostly wan alternatives. This cuisine asiatique includes satays and mou sati (brochettes)—breaded shrimp in a zingy sauce, and spicy roast beef. An enticing possibility is the seven-course sampler meal

Family-Friendly Restaurants

Les Frères de la Cote *(see p. 298)*   A dozen varieties of pizza, served up in a casual and boisterous atmosphere.

Au Petit Coin Breton *(see p. 300)*   The waitresses' costumes are fun—and so's the food, especially when it's served outside.

Le Cochon Dingue *(see p. 301)*   It's big so kids can let themselves go here (to a point). And eating in a place called "The Crazy Pig" is something to write home to Grandma about.

for two people ($36). House wines aren't expensive, but they aren't too good, either. Have beer.

Fleur de Lotus. 38 côte de la Fabrique (opposite the Hôtel-de-Ville). ☎ 418/692-4286. Main courses $8–$14; table d'hôte lunch $8, dinner $16–$25. MC, V. Mon–Wed 11:30am–10:30pm, Thurs–Fri 1–11pm, Sat 5–11pm, Sun 5–10:30pm. SOUTH ASIAN.

This tiny, spare storefront is busy every midday and evening for all the right reasons—tasty food, efficient service, and low prices. This is another kitchen that skips through the variegated cuisines of Cambodia, Vietnam, and Thailand, and again, the Thai is tops. The more than 20 dishes that crowd the menu include chicken in ginger, pork in sweet sauce, and shrimp in soya purée. Execution is better than good, less than wonderful, but the prices are right, and the reception, amiable.

⑤ Les Frères de la Côte. 1190 rue St-Jean (near côte de la Fabrique). ☎ 418/692-5445. Reservations recommended. Main courses $8.25–$10.25; table d'hôte $8.25–$11.50. AE, MC, V. Daily 8am–11pm. MEDITERRANEAN.

At the east end of the old town's liveliest nightlife strip, this supremely casual cafe-pizzeria is as loud as any dance club, all hard surfaces with patrons shouting over the booming stereo music. None of this discourages a single soul—even on a Monday night. Chefs in straw hats in the open kitchen out back crank out a dozen different kinds of pizza—thin-crusted, with unusual toppings that work—and about as many pasta versions, which are less interesting. Bountiful platters of fish and meats, often in the form of brochettes, make appetizers unnecessary. Keep this spot in mind when kids are in tow. There's no way they could make enough noise to bother other customers.

INEXPENSIVE

⑤ Chez Temporel. 25 rue Couillard (near côte de la Fabrique). ☎ 418/694-1813. Most items $1.50–$5.25. No credit cards. Sun–Thurs 7:30am–1:30am, Fri–Sat 7:30am–2:30am. LIGHT FARE.

This Latin Quarter cafe with a tile floor and wooden tables attracts denizens of nearby Université Laval. They read *Le Monde,* play chess, swap philosophical insights, and clack away at their laptops from breakfast until well past midnight. It could be a Left Bank hangout for Sorbonne students and their profs. Capture a table and you can hold it forever for just a cappuccino or two. Croissants, jam, butter, and a couple of belts of espresso cost half as much as a hotel breakfast. Later in the day, drop by for a sandwich, quiche, salad, or plate of cheese with a beer or glass of wine. Only 20 people can be seated downstairs, another 26 upstairs, where the light is filtered through stained-glass windows.

⑤ Le Casse-Crêpe Breton. 1136 rue St-Jean (near Garneau). ☎ **418/692-0438.** Most items $3–$6.50. No credit cards. Mon–Wed 7:30am–midnight, Thurs–Sun 7:30am–1am. CREPES/ LIGHT FARE.

Eat at the bar and watch the crepes being made, or attempt to snag one of the five tables. Main-course crepes come with two to five ingredients of the customers' choice. Dessert crepes are stuffed with jams or fruit and cream. Soups, salads, and sandwiches are as inexpensive as the crepes. The name of the cafe is a play on the word *casse-croûte*, which means "break crust." It's open more than 16 hours a day, which is useful, but when it gets busy, the service is glacial. Beer is served in bottles or on tap.

ON OR NEAR THE GRANDE-ALLÉE
EXPENSIVE

Le Paris-Brest. 590 Grande-Allée est (at de la Chevrotière). ☎ **418/529-2243.** Reservations recommended. Main courses $17.50–$28; table d'hôte lunch $9–$14, dinner $18–$23. AE, CB, DC, ER, MC, V. Mon–Fri 11:30am–2:30pm; Mon–Sat 6–11:30pm, Sun 5:30–11:30pm. CONTEMPORARY FRENCH.

Named for a French dessert, this is a fashionable hideaway with a solid reputation, easily the best along the Grande-Allée. By itself, that is well short of a rave, given the competition. But this place is a whole league ahead, not just a notch. It gives a polished performance from greeting to reckoning. The vaguely art moderne interior employs mahogany paneling, soft lighting, lush flower arrangements, and a temperature-controlled walk-in wine repository.

Game is featured, including caribou steaks, venison, and pheasant. Escargots Provençales or au Pernod are savory starters, to be followed by such standards as lamb noisettes and seafood cassoulette. The staff, and especially the headwaiter, is so alert and attentive even single diners are made welcome. Find the entrance around on rue de la Chevrotière, under 200 Grande-Allée. There's a small patio for outdoor dining, and free valet parking is available from 5:30pm.

MODERATE

Le Graffiti. 1191 ave. Cartier (near Grand-Allée). ☎ **418/529-4949.** Reservations recommended. Main courses $13–$20, table d'hôte $19. AE, DC, ER, MC, V. Daily 5–11pm. CONTEMPORARY FRENCH/ITALIAN.

These two or three blocks off Grand-Allée are just outside the perimeter of tourist Québec, far enough removed to avoid flashy banality, close enough to remain convenient. This busy establishment blends bistro with trattoria, often on the same plate. Emblematic is the sautéed rabbit with puréed carrot, broccoli florets, and angel-hair pasta powerfully scented with tarragon.

Momento. 1144 ave. Cartier (near Grande-Allée). ☎ **418/647-1313.** Reservations recommended at dinner. Main courses $8–$14; table d'hôte lunch $8–$10, dinner $13–$18. Mon–Fri 11:15am–11pm, Sat–Sun 5pm–midnight. CONTEMPORARY ITALIAN.

Considering its manic popularity elsewhere on the continent, updated Italian cooking was late arriving in Québec. The city had the usual parlors shoveling overcooked spaghetti with thin tomato sauce, but not the kind of spiffy neo-trattoria that traffics in light-but-lusty dishes meant for lives lived fast. This racy spot is helping to take up the slack, and although its lags somewhat in execution compared to its rival, Graffiti (see above), it is a welcome antidote to prevailing Franco-Italian clichés of the city's tourist troughs.

INEXPENSIVE

☺ Au Petit Coin Breton. 655 Grande-Allée est. ☎ **418/525-6904.** Most menu items $2–$10. AE, MC, V. Summer daily 10am–midnight; winter daily 10am–11pm. CREPES.

At this "Little Corner of Brittany," the crepe's the thing, be it for breakfast, brunch, a light lunch, a snack, or dessert. Stone, brick, and wood set the mood, as do waiters and waitresses in Breton costume—the women in lace cap, long dress, and apron. After onion soup or salad, choose one (or several) of the more than 80 varieties of the savory dinner crepes and sweet dessert crepes. Or sample some ice cream made on the premises. Often every last seat is taken, especially on the terrace on a sunny day, making a wait inevitable and service slow. A second location, at 1029 rue St-Jean, at the corner of rue Ste-Ursule, has a similar menu and hours (☎ 418/694-0758).

LOWER TOWN

EXPENSIVE

✪ Laurie Raphaël. In Le Priori hotel, 17 rue du Sault-au-Matelot (at St-Antoine). ☎ **418/692-4555.** Reservations recommended. Main courses $19.95–$25.95; table d'hôte lunch $8.95–$14.95, dinner $30–$35. AE, DC, ER, MC, V. Daily 8–10:30am, noon–2:30pm, and 5:30–11pm. Closed Sun–Mon nights in Oct–Apr. CONTEMPORARY FRENCH.

An amuse-gueule of wonton with minced pork filling arrives with the special Kir Royale, a sparkling wine laced with blackberry liqueur. After a suitable interlude, the waiter turns up and happily explains every dish on the menu in as much detail as his customers care to absorb. Appetizers aren't really necessary, since the main course comes with soup or salad, but they're so good, a couple might wish to share one— the carpaccio of Portobello mushrooms, splashed with fruity olive oil and showered with frizzled tendrils of sweet potato, paper-thin leaves of Parmesan, and sprigs of fresh thyme, perhaps. Main courses run to caribou and rack of lamb in unconventional guises, and a concern for "healthy" saucing and combinations is evident. In no time, the place ascends to that level of happy babble that is music to a restaurateur's ears. If the kitchen can be faulted, it might be for the identical garnishes appearing on every plate. But that's quibbling, for this is a restaurant that shares the uncrowded pinnacle of the local dining pantheon.

Le Saint-Pierre. 54 rue St-Pierre (at Montagne). ☎ **418/694-6194.** Reservations recommended on weekends. Main courses $10–$35; table d'hôte lunch $7–$12.50, dinner $16–$28. AE, DC, MC, V. Mon–Fri 11:30am–2pm; Mon–Sat 5:30–11pm, Sun 5–10pm. Closed Sun in Oct–Apr. CONTEMPORARY FRENCH.

A waiter in apron and black bowtie is often stationed at the door, a living signboard announcing that the former bank is now a place to dine. Inside, the owners are bidding for an elegance not much seen in the city. Big vases with outsized peonies and birds-of-paradise stand on the bar and over the showy dessert display. Greco-Roman structural details frame the large room, whose greatest luxury is the wide-open spaces between tables, another rarity in Québec City. The grand piano at one side is put to use every night. With all this, the food has much to accomplish. It comes close, as with the salmon fillet nested with delicate shreds of eggplant, sweet pepper, and zucchini, a spray of asparagus spears and roasted potato balls to one side. Portions are on the skimpy side, however, and some of the combinations are off-kilter. It will be fun to return to see if the promise is being fulfilled.

MODERATE

L'Ardoise. 71 rue St-Paul (near Navigateurs). ☎ **418/694-0213.** Reservations recommended. Main courses $9.95–$16; table d'hôte $18 or $24. AE, MC, V. Daily 9am–11pm. BISTRO FRENCH.

Mussels are staples at Québec restaurants, prepared in the Belgian manner, with bowls of frites on the side. Despite their popularity, the chef in this companionable bistro is reluctant to serve them in the warmer months, explaining that the farmed variety available then tends to be mealy.

That he cares about what he sends out of his kitchen is evident. His food isn't haute cuisine, but it is vibrant and flavorful. His arena is a smallish room on antique row, with banquettes along both walls and wicker-and-iron chairs pulled up to tables with paper place mats. Piaf and Azvanour clones warble laments on the stereo. This is a place to leaf through a book, sip a double espresso, and meet neighbors. Tourists haven't discovered it. Yet.

✪ **Le Café du Monde.** 57 rue Dalhousie (at de la Montagne). ☎ **418/692-4455.** Reservations recommended on weekends. Main courses $7.25–$16; table d'hôte lunch $8–$12, dinner $18–$21. AE, DC, ER, MC, V. Mon–Fri 11:30am–11pm, Sat–Sun brunch 9:30am–11pm. FRENCH/INTERNATIONAL.

Near the Musée de la Civilisation, this relative newcomer is enjoying ever-increasing popularity. While it promotes the roster of world dishes promised in its name, the atmosphere is definitely Lyonnaise brasserie. That is seen in the culinary origins of its most-ordered items—pâtés, quiches, entrecôte, and several versions of mussels with frites—prepared in a kitchen overseen by a chef from Brittany. One of his extravaganzas is a five-course evening meal, called "Le Ciel, La Terre, La Mer" or "Sky, Earth, Sea." (Think of it as a kind of upscale surf 'n' turf.) Pastas and couscous are some of the non-French preparations. Imported beers are favored beverages, along with wines by the glass. Look for the striped awnings and bright neon sign out front. Service is friendly, but easily distracted. Waiters and customers sit down at the upright piano for impromptu performances.

Le Cochon Dingue. 46 bd. Champlain (du Marché-Champlain). ☎ **418/692-2013.** Main courses $6–$12.50; table d'hôte meals $17–$20. AE, ER, MC, V. Daily 7am–midnight. BISTRO/INTERNATIONAL.

This "Crazy Pig" faces the ferry dock and lighthouse in the Lower Town and has some sidewalk tables and several indoor dining rooms with rough fieldstone walls and black-and-white floor tiles. It makes stout efforts to be a one-stop eating center, with long hours to cover every possibility. Choose from mussels, steak frites, hefty plates of chicken liver pâté with pistachios, spring rolls, smoked salmon, half a dozen salads, onion soup, pastas, quiches, sandwiches, grilled meats, and more than 20 desserts. Wine is sold by the glass, quarter liter, half liter, or bottle, at reasonable prices, and there is a children's menu for kids 10 and under. The same people also own the nearby, smaller Le Lapin Sauté (☎692-5325) at 52 rue Petit-Champlain.

Le Marie-Clarisse. 12 rue du Petit-Champlain (Sous-le-Fort). ☎ **418/692-0857.** Main courses $8–$11.75. AE, DC, ER, MC, V. Mon–Fri 11:30am–2:30pm; Mon–Sat 6–11pm. BISTRO/SEAFOOD.

Nothing much beyond sustenance is expected of restaurants stationed at the flooded intersections of galloping tourism. That's why this modest little cafe is such a happy surprise. There it sits, at the bottom of Breakneck Stairs, a few yards from the funicular terminal, the streets awash with mouthbreathers, daypackers, and shutterbugs. And yet it serves what many consider to be the best seafood in town, selected by a finicky owner said to travel each week to Montréal to make his selections personally at market. A more pleasant hour cannot be passed anywhere in Québec City than here, over a plate of shrimp scented with anise or a selection of terrines and pâtés, out on the terrace on an August afternoon or cocooned by the stone fireplace inside in January. Just skip the vegetables, unless the chef has learned to remove them from the pot while they still have some fiber.

INEXPENSIVE

Buffet de l'Antiquarie. 95 rue St-Paul (near Sault-au-Matelot). ☎ **418/692-2661.** Most menu items under $10. AE, MC, V. Daily 7am–11pm. QUÉBÉCOIS.

Another inhabitant of St-Paul's antique row, this is the humblest of the lot, with exposed brick and stone walls lending what there is of decor. It is the place to go when every other Lower Town cafe is closed, as for Sunday breakfast. And, since it caters to homefolks rather than tourists, reliable versions of native Québécois cooking are always available, including, but not limited to, pea soup, poutine, and feves au lard. Essentially a slightly upgraded luncheonette, it serves sandwiches, salads, and pastries at all hours, backed by full bar service.

5 · Attractions

Wandering at random through the streets of Vieux-Québec is a singular pleasure. On the way, you can happen upon an ancient convent, blocks of gabled houses with steeply pitched roofs, a battery of 18th-century cannon in a leafy park, or a bistro with a blazing fireplace on a chilly day. This is such a compact city it is hardly necessary to plan precise sightseeing itineraries. Start at the terrace Dufferin and go off on a whim, down Breakneck Stairs to the Quartier Petit-Champlain and place Royale, or up to the Citadelle and onto the Plains of Abraham, where Wolfe and Montcalm fought to the death in a 20-minute battle that changed the destiny of the continent.

Most of what there is to see is within the city walls, or in the Lower Town. It's fairly easy walking. While the Upper Town is hilly, with sloping streets, it's nothing like San Francisco, and only people with physical limitations will experience difficulty. If rain or ice discourage exploration on foot, tour buses and horse-drawn calèches are options.

THE TOP ATTRACTIONS
UPPER TOWN

✪ **Le Château Frontenac.** 1 rue des Carrières, place d'Armes. ☎ **418/692-3861.**

Opened in 1893 to house railroad passengers and encourage tourism, the monster version of a Loire Valley palace is the city's emblem, its Eiffel Tower. It can be seen from almost every quarter, commanding its majestic position atop Cap Diamant.

La Citadelle (The Citadel). 1 côte de la Citadelle (enter off rue St-Louis). ☎ **418/648-3563.** Admission $4.50 adults, $4 seniors, $2 children 7–17, free for handicapped persons and children under 7. Guided 55-minute tours, mid-Mar to Apr daily 10am–3pm; May–June and Labor Day–Oct daily 9am–4pm; July–Labor Day daily 9am–6pm. Nov to mid-Mar, group reservations only. Changing of the guard (30 minutes), mid-June to Labor Day daily at 10am; beating the retreat (20 minutes) July–Aug, Tues, Thurs, and Sat–Sun. Walk up the côte de la Citadelle from the St-Louis gate.

The Duke of Wellington had this partially star-shaped fortress built at the east end of the city walls in anticipation of renewed American attacks after the War of 1812. Some remnants of earlier French military structures were incorporated into it, including a 1750 magazine. Dug into the Plains of Abraham, the fort has a low profile that keeps it all but invisible until walkers are actually upon it. Never having exchanged fire with an invader, it continues its vigil from the tip of Cap Diamant. British construction of the fortress, now a national historic site, was begun in 1820 and took 30 years to complete. As events unfolded, it proved an exercise in obsolescence. Since

1920, it has been home to Québec's Royal 22e Régiment, the only fully Francophone unit in Canada's armed forces. That makes it the largest fortified group of buildings still occupied by troops in North America. As part of a guided tour only, the public may visit the Citadelle and its 25 buildings, including the regimental museum in the former powderhouse and prison, and watch the changing of the guard or beating the retreat (which may be canceled in the event of rain).

LOWER TOWN

✪ **Musée de la Civilisation.** 85 rue Dalhousie (St-Antoine). ☎ **418/643-2158.** Admission $6 adults, $5 seniors, $3 students, $1 ages 12–16, free for children under 16. Tues free to all (except in summer). June 24–Sept 4 daily 10am–7pm; Sept 5–June 23 Tues–Sun 10am–5pm (to 9pm Wed).

Try to set aside at least two hours for a visit to this special museum, one of the most engrossing in all Canada. Designed by Boston-based, McGill University–trained Moshe Safdie and opened in 1988, this museum is an innovative presence in the historic Basse-Ville, near place Royale. A dramatic atrium-lobby sets the tone with a massive sculpture rising like jagged icebergs from the watery floor, a representation of the mighty St. Lawrence at spring breakup. Through the glass wall in back can be seen the 1752 Maison Estèbe, now restored to contain the museum shop. It stands above vaulted cellars, which can be viewed.

In the galleries upstairs are four permanent exhibitions, supplemented by up to six temporary shows on a variety of themes. The mission of the museum has never been entirely clear, leading to some opaque metaphysical meanderings in its early years. Never mind. Through highly imaginative display techniques, hands-on devices, computers, holograms, videos, and even an ant farm, the curators have assured that visitors will be so enthralled by the experience they won't pause to question its intent. Notice, as an example of their thoroughness, how a squeaky floorboard has been installed at the entrance to a dollhouse-sized display of old Québec houses. If time is short, definitely use it to take in "Memoires" (Memories), the permanent exhibit that is a sprawling examination of Québec history, moving from the province's roots as a fur-trading colony to the present. Furnishings from frontier homes, tools of the trappers' trade, old farm implements, religious garments from the 19th century, old campaign posters, and a re-created classroom from the past envelop visitors with a rich sense of Québec's daily life from generation to generation. Exhibit texts are in French and English. There's a café on the ground floor.

Place Royale. Information Center, 215 rue du Marché-Finlay (Lower Town). ☎ **418/643-6631.** Free admission. June 5–Oct 1 daily 10am–6pm.

Picturesque place Royale is the literal and spiritual heart of the Lower Town. It's a short walk from the lower terminus of the funicular or the Breakneck Stairs, via rue Sous-le-Fort. In the 17th and 18th centuries, it was the town marketplace and the center of business and industry. The église Notre-Dame-des-Victoires dominates the enclosed square. It is the oldest stone church in Québec, built in 1688 and restored in 1763 and in 1969. The paintings, altar, and large model boat suspended from the ceiling were votive offerings brought by early settlers to ensure a safe voyage. The church usually is open to visitors during the day, unless a wedding is underway.

Across the square from the church stands the Maison des Vins (House of Wines). In addition to the wines on sale, the store invites the public to examine the cool subterranean vaults of the old stone house.

All the rest of the buildings on the square have been restored, save one. The stone facade at the northeast corner with metal and painted plywood covering its doors and

Québec City Attractions

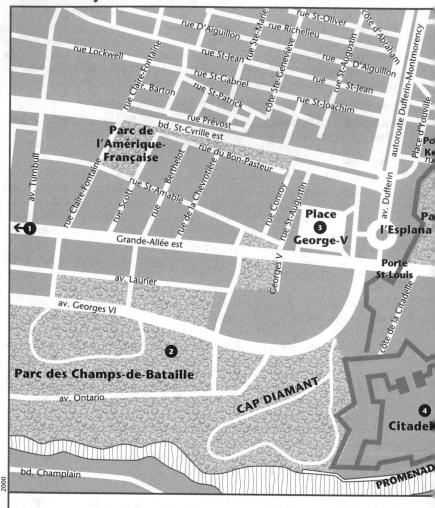

Map showing streets including rue D'Aiguillon, rue St-Oliver, rue Richelieu, côte d'Abraham, rue Lockwell, rue St-Jean, rue St-Marie, rue Ste-Geneviève, rue St-Augustin, D'Aiguillon, rue St-Gabriel, rue St-Patrick, rue St-Joachim, rue Prévost, bd. St-Cyrille est, Parc de l'Amérique-Française, rue du Bon-Pasteur, rue St-Amable, Berthelot, rue Scott, rue de la Chevrotière, rue Conroy, rue St-Augustin, Place George-V ❸, Place l'Esplana, Grande-Allée est, av. Laurier, av. Georges VI, Porte St-Louis, côte de la Citadelle, Parc des Champs-de-Bataille, av. Ontario, CAP DIAMANT, Citadel ❹, bd. Champlain, PROMENAD, av. Turnbull, rue Claire-Fontaine, r. Barton, autoroute Dufferin-Montmorency, Place d'Youville, av. Dufferin, Georges V

CANADA — QUEBEC

Basilique-cathédrale Notre-Dame ❽

Centre d'Interpretation de la Vie Urbaine ❼

Chapelle/Musée des Ursulines ❺

Château Frontenac ❻

La Citadelle ❹

Explore Sound and Light Show ⓯

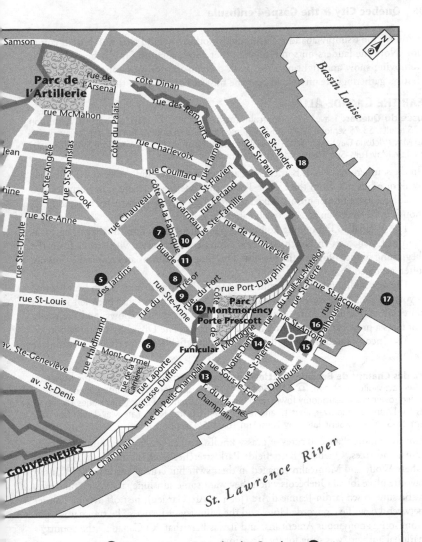

Parc de l'Artillerie

rue de l'Arsenal
Samson
côte Dinan
rue McMahon
rue des Remparts
rue St-André
rue St-Paul
rue Charlevoix
côte du Palais
Jean
rue Ste-Angèle
rue St-Stanislas
Cook
rue Couillard
côte de la Fabrique
rue Chauveau
rue Carneau
rue St-Flavien
rue Hamel
hine
rue Ste-Anne
rue Ste-Famille
rue Ferland
rue de l'Université
rue Ste-Ursule
7
10
Buade
11
des Jardins
5
rue Ste-Anne
8
Trésor
côte de la Fabrique
rue Port-Dauphin
rue St-Louis
9
rue du Fort
côte de la Montagne
rue du Sault-au-Matelot
rue St-Pierre
rue St-Jacques
17
12
Parc Montmorency
Porte Prescott
16
rue St-Pierre
rue Dalhousie
av. Ste-Geneviève
rue Haldimand
Mont-Carmel
6
Funicular
14
15
rue Notre-Dame
rue St-Pierre
av. St-Denis
rue des Carrières
rue Laporte
Terrasse Dufferin
rue du Petit-Champlain
rue Sous-le-Fort
13
rue Dalhousie
r. du Marché
Champlain
GOUVERNEURS
bd. Champlain
St. Lawrence River
Bassin Louise

el du Parlement **3**	Musée du Quebec **1**
son Chevalier **13**	Parc des Champs de Bataille **2**
sée de Cire Grévin **9**	Place Royale Information Centre **14**
sée de l'Amerique Française **10**	Québec Experience **8**
sée de la Civilisation **16**	Vieux-Port **17**
sée du Fort **12**	Vieux-Port Interpretation Center **18**

windows isn't simply abandoned—there is nothing behind that wall but an empty lot. Note the ladders on some of the other roofs, a common Québec device for removing snow and fighting fires. Folk dances, impromptu concerts, and other festive gatherings are often held near the bust of Louis XIV in the square.

NEAR THE GRANDE-ALLÉE

Musée du Québec. 1 av. Wolfe-Montcalm (av. George VI). ☎ **418/643-2150.** Admission $4.75 adults, $3.75 seniors, $2.75 students, free for children under 16; Wed free for everyone. Late May (Victoria Day)–early Sept (Labor Day) daily 10am–5:45pm (Wed until 5:45pm); early Sept–late May Tues–Sun 10am–5:45pm (Wed until 8:45). Bus no. 11.

In the southern reaches of Battlefields Park, just off the Grande-Allée and a half-hour walk or a bus ride from the Upper Town, the Québec Museum now occupies two buildings, one a former prison, linked together by a soaring glass-roofed "Grand Hall" housing the reception area, a stylish cafeteria, and a shop.

The original 1933 building houses the permanent collection, the largest aggregation of Québec art in North America, filling eight galleries with works from the beginning of the colony to the present. Traveling exhibitions and musical events are often arranged.

The new addition to the museum is the 1871 Baillairgé Prison, which later became a youth hostel nicknamed the "Petite Bastille." One cellblock has been left intact as an exhibit. In this building, four galleries house temporary shows, and the tower contains a provocative sculpture called *Le Plongeur* (The Diver) by David Moore.

Also incorporated in the building is the Battlefields Interpretation Centre (see below).

Parc des Champs de Bataille (Battlefields Park). Interpretation Center in the Musée du Québec, av. Wolfe-Montcalm. ☎ **418/648-5641.** Free admission to park. Interpretation center, martello tower no. 1, astronomy tower, and bus tour in summer, $2 for visitors ages 18–64, $1 ages 13–17 and 65 and over, ages 12 and under free; Tues free to all. Late May–Labor Day daily 10am–5:45pm, early Sept–late May Tues–Sun 10am–5:45pm.

Covering more than 250 acres of grassy knolls, sunken gardens, monuments, fountains, and trees, Québec's Battlefields Park stretches over the Plains of Abraham, where Wolfe and Montcalm engaged in their swift but crucial battle in 1759. It is a favorite place for all Québécois when they want some sunshine, a jog, or a bike ride.

Be sure to see Jardin Jeanne d'Arc (Joan of Arc Garden), just off avenue Laurier between Loews Le Concorde Hôtel and the Ministry of Justice. The statue was a gift from some anonymous Americans, and it was here that "O Canada," the country's national anthem, was sung for the first time.

Within the park are two martello towers, cylindrical stone defensive structures built between 1808 and 1812, when Québec feared an invasion from the United States.

Today Battlefields Park covers 266 acres and contains almost 5,000 trees representing more than 80 species. Prominent among these are sugar maple, silver maple, Norway maple, American elm, and American ash and hawthorn. There are always special activities, including theatrical and musical events, planned in the park during the summer.

Year-round, the park interpretation center provides an in-depth look (for a small fee) at the historical significance of the Plains of Abraham to Québec over the years. In summer, a shuttle bus tours the park in its entirety in 45 minutes with guided narration in French and English for a small fee.

The obelisk at the lower end of the Parc des Gouverneurs is dedicated to both Wolfe and Montcalm, the winning and losing generals in the momentous battle of

September 13, 1759. Wolfe, wounded in the fighting, lived only long enough to hear of his victory. Montcalm died after Wolfe, knowing the city was lost.

MORE ATTRACTIONS
UPPER TOWN

Basilique-cathédrale Notre-Dame. 16 rue Buade (at côte de la Fabrique). ☎ **418/ 692-2533.** Free admission to Basilica and guided tours. "Act of Faith" sound-and-light show, $6 adults, $5 seniors, $3 students 12 and over with ID, children 11 and under free (tickets available from 20 rue Buade). Basilica daily 6:30am–5:30pm; guided tours mid-May to mid-Oct daily 9am–4:30pm. "Act of Faith" multimedia sound-and-light show, summer nightly 6:30pm, 7:45pm, and 9pm.

The oldest Christian parish north of Mexico has seen a tumultuous history of bombardment, reconstruction, and restoration. Parts of the existing basilica date to the original 1647 structure, including the bell tower and portions of the walls. The interior is flamboyantly Baroque. Shadows waver from the fluttering light of votive candles. Paintings and ecclesiastical treasures still remain from the time of the French regime, including a chancel lamp given by Louis XIV. In summer, the basilica is the backdrop for a multimedia sound-and-light show called "Act of Faith," which dramatically recalls five centuries of Québec's history, and that of this building itself.

The basilica is connected to the complex of old buildings that makes up Québec Seminary. To enter that complex, go to 7 rue de l'Université.

Chapelle/Musée des Ursulines. 12 rue Donnacona (des Jardins). ☎ **418/694-0694.** Museum $3 adults, $1.50 seniors and students, $6 families; chapel free. Museum Jan 3–Nov 24 Tues–Sat 9:30am–noon and 1–4:30pm, Sun 12:30–5pm. Chapel May–Oct, same days and hours as museum.

The chapel, open only from May through October, is remarkable for its sculptures of the pulpit and two retables. They were created by Pierre-Noel Levasseur between 1726 and 1736. Although the present building dates only to 1902, much of the interior decoration is nearly two centuries older. The tomb of the founder of this teaching order, Marie de l'Incarnation, is to the right of the entry. She arrived here in 1639 at the age of 40 and was declared blessed by Pope John Paul II in 1980. The museum, open from January to late November, displays many of the accoutrements of the daily and spiritual life of the Ursulines. On the third-floor are exhibits of vestments woven with gold thread by the Ursulines. A cape made of drapes from the bedroom of Anne of Austria and given to Marie de l'Incarnation when she left for New France in 1639 is on display. There are also musical instruments and Amerindian crafts, including the flèche, or arrow sash, still worn during Winter Carnival. Some of the docents are nuns of the still-active order. The Ursuline convent, built originally as a girls' school in 1642, is the oldest one in North America.

Musée de Cire Grévin (Wax Museum). 22 rue Ste-Anne (du Trésor). ☎ **418/692-2289.** Admission $5 adults, $3 seniors and students, children under 6 free. Summer daily 9am–10pm; winter daily 10am–5pm.

Occupying a 17th-century house, this momentarily diverting wax museum, entirely renovated in 1994, provides a superficial skim of Québec's history and heroes. Generals Wolfe and Montcalm are portrayed, of course, along with effigies of politicians, singers, Olympic gold medalists, and other newsmakers. Texts are in French and English.

Musée de L'Amerique Française. Québec Seminary, 2 côte de la Fabrique. ☎ **418/ 692-2843.** Admission $3 adults, $2 seniors, $1.50 students, $1 children 16 and under, $6 families, free to all on Tues. Concerts $10–$15. June 1–Sept 30 daily 10am–5:30pm; Oct 1–May 31 Tues–Sun 10am–5pm. Guided tours of exhibitions and some buildings, daily in summer, rest of the year Sat–Sun.

Housed in the historic Québec Seminary, whose history dates from 1659, the Museum of French America focuses on the beginnings and the evolution of French culture and civilization in North America. Its extensive collections include paintings by European and Canadian artists, engravings and parchments from the early French regime, old and rare books, coins, early scientific instruments, and even mounted animals and an Egyptian mummy. The mix makes for an engrossing visit.

The museum is located in three parts of the large seminary complex. In the Guillaume-Couillard wing, adjacent to the Basilique-cathédrale Notre-Dame, is the entrance hall and information desk. In the Jérôme-Demers wing, bordering the rue de l'Université, down the hill, are the exhibition galleries. Third is the beautiful François-Ranvoyze wing, with its trompe-l'oeil ornamentation, which served as a chapel for the seminary priests and students. It is now open only during the summer for guided tours. Concerts are held in the chapel, as well.

Musée du Fort. 10 rue Ste-Anne (Place d'Armes). ☎ **418/692-2175.** Admission $5.50 adults, $4.50 seniors, $3.50 students and children under 18. June 24–Aug 31 daily 10am–6pm; Apr–May and Sept–Oct 10am–5pm; Nov–Mar Mon–Fri 11am–3pm, Sat–Sun 11am–5pm.

Bordering place d'Armes, not far from the UNESCO World Heritage monument, this commercial enterprise presents a sound-and-light show using a 400-square-foot model of the city and surrounding region. The 30-minute production concerns itself primarily with the six sieges of Québec, including the famous battle on the Plains of Abraham. Commentary is in French or English. Military and history buffs are the ones most likely to enjoy it.

LOWER TOWN

The Escalier Casse-Cou is between terrace Dufferin and rue Sous-le-Fort; the name translates to "Breakneck Stairs," which is self-explanatory as soon as you see them. They lead from the upper town to the quartier Petit-Champlain in the Lower Town. A stairway has existed here since the settlement began. But human beings weren't the only ones to use the stairs. In 1698, the town council forbade citizens to take their animals up or down the stairway or face a fine.

Explore Sound & Light Show. 63 rue Dalhousie (St-Antoine) ☎ **418/692-2175.** Admission $5.50 adults, $4.50 seniors, $3.50 children under 18. June 23–Sept 3 daily 1–4:30pm; Sept 4–Oct 15 and Apr 15–June 22 Mon–Sat 10am–5pm; Oct 16–Apr 14 daily Mon–Fri 11am–3pm.

A splashy, 30-minute multimedia production chronicles the Age of Exploration through the impressions of Columbus, Vespucci, Verrazano, Cartier, and Champlain. The theater is shaped like an early sailing vessel, complete with rigging. Among the depictions are the difficulties of Champlain and his crew of 28 who came here in 1608. Twenty men died during the first winter, mainly of scurvy and dysentery (one was hanged for mutiny).

Maison Chevalier. 60 rue du Marché-Champlain (at rue Notre-Dame). ☎ **418/643-2158.** Free admission. June 5–Oct 1 daily 10am–5pm.

Built in 1752 for ship owner Jean-Baptiste Chevalier, the existing structure incorporated two older buildings, dating from 1675 and 1695. It was run as an inn throughout the 19th century. The Québec government restored the house in 1960, and it became a museum five years later. Inside, with its exposed wood beams, wide-board floors, and stone fireplaces are changing exhibits on Québec history and civilization, especially in the 17th and 18th centuries. While exhibit texts are in French, guidebooks in English are available at the sometimes unattended front desk.

Vieux-Port. Interpretation Center, 100 rue St-Andre (at rue Rioux). ☎ **418/648-3300.** Admission May–Labor Day, $3 adults, $1.50 seniors and children, family $6; rest of the year free. May–Labor Day daily 10am–5pm; schedule varies the rest of the year (call for hours).

Part of Parks Canada, the interpretation center reveals the Port of Québec as it was during its maritime zenith in the 19th century. Four floors of exhibits illustrate that era. The modern port and city can be viewed from the top level, where reference maps identify landmarks. One of these is the Daishowa Pulp and Paper Mill (1927), which sells newsprint and cardboard to international markets, including *The New York Times.* Texts are in French and English, and most exhibits invite touching.

NEAR THE GRANDE-ALLÉE
Galerie Anima G. 1033 rue de la Chevrotière (bd. René-Lévesque) ☎ **418/644-9841.** Free admission. Mon–Fri 10am–4pm, Sat–Sun 1–5pm. Closed mid-Dec–mid-Jan.

Enter the governmental office tower called Edifice "G," and look for signs and special elevators labeled "Anima G, 31e Etage." On the 31st floor are unobstructed panoramic vistas of the city and river.

Hôtel du Parlement. Grande-Allée est (av. Dufferin). ☎ **418/643-7239.** Free admission. Guided tours, early Sept–May Mon–Fri 9am–4:30pm; June 24–early Sept daily 9am–4:30pm. No visitors June 1–23.

Since 1968, what the Québécois choose to call their "National Assembly" has occupied this imposing Second Empire château constructed in 1886. Twenty-two bronze statues of some of the most prominent figures in Québec's tumultuous history gaze out from the facade. The sumptuous chambers of the building may be toured with a guide for no charge, but tour times change without warning. Highlights are the Assembly Chamber, and the Room of the Old Legislative Council, where parliamentary committees meet. Throughout the building, representations of the fleur-de-lys and the initials "VR" (for Victoria Regina) remind visitors of Québec's dual heritage.

ESPECIALLY FOR KIDS
Québec is such a storybook town that most children delight in simply walking around in it.

As soon as possible, head for **terrace Dufferin,** which has those coin-operated telescopes kids like. In decent weather, there are always street entertainers—a Peruvian musical group, men who play saws or wine glasses. A few steps away at place d'Armes are the **horse-drawn carriages,** and not far in the same direction is the **Musée de Cire (Wax Museum),** on place d'Armes at 22 rue Ste-Anne.

Also at place d'Armes is the terminal of the **funicular to the Lower Town.** Its glass walls allow a splendid view of the river, and its steady but precipitous drop is a sure thrill. At the bottom, next to the Breakneck Stairs, is a **glass-blowing workshop,** the Verrerie la Mailloche. In the front room craftsmen give glassblowing demonstrations, always intriguing and informative, especially for children who haven't seen it before. The glass is melted at 2,545°F and worked at 2,000°.

Also in the Lower Town, at 86 rue Dalhousie, the playful **Musée de la Civilization** keeps kids occupied for hours in its exhibits, shop, and cafe.

They also get a charge out of the monstrous **cannons** ranged along the battlements on rue des Ramparts. The gun carriages are impervious to the assaults of small humans, so kids can scramble over them at will. Other military sites are usually a hit.

The Citadelle has tours of the grounds and buildings and a colorful **Changing of the Guard** ceremony.

The **ferry** to Lévis across the St. Lawrence is inexpensive, convenient from the Lower Town, pleasant, and exciting for kids. The crossing, over and back, takes less than an hour.

To run off the kids' excess energy, head for the **Plains of Abraham,** which is also Battlefields Park. Get there by rue St-Louis, just inside the St-Louis Gate, or, more vigorously, by the walkway along terrasse Dufferin and the promenade des Gouverneurs, with a long set of stairs. Acres of grassy lawn give children room to roam and provide the perfect spot for a family picnic.

Or even better, consider the **Village des Sports** (☎ 418/844-2551) in St-Gabriel-de-Valcartier, about 20 minutes' drive north of downtown. In summer, it's a waterpark, with slides, a huge wave pool, and diving shows. In winter, those same facilities are put to use for snowrafting on inner tubes, ice slides, and skating.

6 Special Events & Festivals

Usually, Québec is courtly and dignified, but all that is cast aside when the symbolic snowman called Bonhomme ("Good Fellow") appears to preside over 10 days of merriment in early February during the annual **Carnaval D'Hiver (Winter Carnival).** More than a million revelers descend upon the city, eddying around the monumental ice palace and ice sculptures and attending a full schedule of concerts, dances, and parades. The mood is heightened by the availability of plastic trumpets and canes filled with a concoction called "Caribou," the principal ingredients of which are cheap whisky and sweet red wine. Perhaps its presence explains the eagerness with which certain Québecers participate in the canoe race across the treacherous ice floes of the St. Lawrence. Hotel reservations must be made far in advance. Scheduled events are free.

On June 24, **St-Jean Baptiste Day** honors St. John the Baptist, the patron saint of French Canadians. It is marked by more festivities and far more enthusiasm throughout Québec province than national Dominion Day on July 1. It's their "national" holiday.

The largest cultural event in the French-speaking world, the **Festival D'Ete International (International Summer Festival)** has attracted artists from Africa, Asia, Europe, and throughout North America since it began in 1967. There are more than 250 events showcasing theater, music, and dance, with 600 performers from 20 different countries. One million people come to watch and listen. Jazz and folk combos perform for free in an open-air theater next to City Hall, visiting dance and folklore troupes put on shows, and concerts, theatrical productions, and related events fill the days and evenings. It's held for about 10 days in early to mid-July. Call ☎ 418/651-2882 for details.

During **Les Medievales de Québec (Québec Medieval Festival),** hundreds of actors, artists, entertainers, and other participants from Europe, Canada, and the United States converge on Québec City in period dress to re-create daily scenes from five centuries ago, playing knights, troubadours, and ladies-in-waiting during this event, which is a giant costume party. Parades, jousting tournaments, recitals of ancient music, and the Grand Cavalcade (La Grande Chevauchée), featuring hundreds of costumed horseback riders are just a few highlights. Fireworks are the one modern touch during this five-day festival. Come in medieval attire, if you wish. Held in Québec City only in odd-numbered years for about a week in early to mid-August. Call ☎ 418/692-1993 for more information.

7 Shopping

GREAT SHOPPING AREAS   The compact size of the old town, upper and lower, makes it especially convenient for shopping. There are several art galleries in the Upper Town featuring Inuit and folk art that deserve attention. Antiques shops are proliferating along rue St-Paul in the Lower Town. Other streets to browse include rue St-Jean, both within and outside the city walls, and rue Garneau and côte de la Fabrique, which branch off the east end of St-Jean. There's a shopping concourse on the lower level of the Château Frontenac.

Côte de la Montagne, which leads from the Upper Town to the Lower Town as an alternative to the funicular, has a gallery specializing in crafts and folk art. The quartier du Petit-Champlain, especially along rue du Petit-Champlain and rue Sous-le-Fort (opposite the funicular entrance), offers many possibilities—clothing, souvenirs, gifts, household items, collectibles—and so far avoids the trashiness that too often afflicts heavily touristed areas.

ARTS & CRAFTS   Crafts, handmade sweaters, and Inuit art are among the desirable items that aren't seen everywhere else. An official igloo trademark identifies authentic Inuit (Eskimo) art, although the differences between the real thing and the manufactured variety become apparent with a little careful study. Inuit artworks, usually carvings in stone or bone, are best buys not because of low prices, but because of their high quality. Expect to pay hundreds of dollars for even a relatively small piece.

For Inuit art in stone, bone, and tusk, check out **Aux Multiples,** 69 rue Ste-Anne (☎ 418/692-1230). Prices are high, but competitive with goods of similar quality. **Galerie d'Art du Petit-Champlain,** 88¹/₂ rue de Peti-Champlain (☎ 418/692-5647), features the wood carvings of Roger Desjardins, who applies his skills to meticulous renderings of waterfowl. **Galerie Zanettin,** 28 côte de la Montagne (☎ 418/692-1055), near the Escalier Casse-Cou has whimsical primitive carvings and paintings by folk artists from the region.

Artists hang their prints and paintings of Québec scenes along **rue du Trésor** between rue Ste-Anne and rue Baude, a pedestrian lane mostly covered by awnings. Some of the artists, positioned near adjacent sidewalk cafés, draw portraits or caricatures.

BOOKSTORES   Most of Québec City's bookstores cater to the solidly French-speaking citizenry and students at the university, but a few shops carry some English books for the tourist trade. One is **Librairie Garneau,** 24 côte de la Fabrique (☎ 418/692-4262). **Librairie du Nouveau Monde,** 103 rue St-Pierre in Old Québec (☎ 418/694-9475), features titles dealing with Québec history and culture, including books in English. For travel books, visit **Ulysses,** 4 bd. St-Cyrille est (☎ 418/529-5349). **Maison de la Presse Internationale,** at 1050 rue St-Jean (☎ 418/694-1511) stocks magazines, newspapers, and paperbacks from around the world.

WINE   A supermarket-sized **Société des Alcools** store is located on 1059 av. Cartier (near rue Fraser), with thousands of bottles in stock. Another attractive possibility is the Maison des Vins, on place Royale in the Lower Town. The ground floor of this old Québec house is a liquor store, with a good choice of wines. But down in the cellar (les caves) is their collection of rare and special wines and champagnes.

A FARMERS' MARKET   Not far from the 1916 train station is the **Marché du Vieux-Port,** a colorful farmers' market with rows of booths heaped with fresh fruits and vegetables, relishes, jams, handicrafts, flowers, and honey from local hives. Above each booth hangs a sign with the name and telephone number of the seller. A lot of them bear the initials I.O., meaning they come from Île d'Orléans, 10 miles outside the city. The market is enclosed, and the central part of it is heated.

8 Outdoor Activities & Spectator Sports

OUTDOOR ACTIVITIES

The waters and hills around Québec City provide ample opportunities for outdoor recreation. There are two centers in particular to keep in mind for most winter and summer activities, both within easy drives from old Québec. Thirty minutes from Québec City, off Route 175 north, is the provincial **Parc de la Jacques-Cartier** (☎ 418/848-3169). Closer by 10 minutes or so is **Parc Mont-Ste-Anne** (☎ 418/827-4561), only 24 miles (40km) northeast of the city. Both are mentioned repeatedly in the listings below.

BIKING   Given the hilly topography of the Upper Town, biking isn't a particularly attractive option. But bicycles are available at a shop in the flatter Lower Town, near the lighthouse. Bikes are about $6 an hour or $30 a day. The shop, **Location Petit-Champlain,** at 94 rue du Petit-Champlain, also rents strollers, and it's open daily from 9am to 11pm (☎ 418/692-2817). Bikes can also be rented on relatively level **Île d'Orléans,** across the bridge from the north shore at the gas station (☎ 418/828-9215). For more vigorous mountain biking, the **Mont-Ste-Anne recreational center** (☎ 418/827-4561) has 124 miles (200km) of trails.

CAMPING   There are almost 30 campgrounds in the greater Québec area, with as few as 20 campsites and as many as 368. All of them make showers and toilets available. One of the largest is at the **Parc de Mont-Ste-Anne,** and they accept credit cards. One of the smallest, but with a convenience store and snack bar, is **Camping La Loutre** (☎ 418/846-2201) on Lac Jacques-Cartier in the park of the same name. It's north of the city, off Route 175. The booklet available at the tourist offices provides details about all the sites.

CANOEING   The several lakes and rivers of **Parc de la Jacques-Cartier** are fairly easy to reach, yet in the midst of virtual wilderness.

CROSS-COUNTRY SKIING   Greater Québec has 22 cross-country ski centers with 278 trails. In town, the **Parc des Champs-de-Bataille,** has 6 miles (10km) of groomed cross-country trails, a convenience for those who don't have cars or the time to get out of town. Those who do have transportation should consider **Parc de Mont-Ste-Anne,** which has more than 62 miles (100km) of cross-country trails at all levels of difficulty; equipment is available for rent.

DOGSLEDDING   **Aventure Nord-bec** (☎ 418/889-8001) at 665 rue Ste-Anne in Saint-Lambert-de-Lévis, about 20 minutes south of the city, offers dogsledding expeditions. While they aren't the equivalent of a week-long mush across Alaska, participants do get a sense of what that experience is like. They get a four-dog sled meant for two and take turns standing on the runners and sitting on the sled. Much of the route is along a trail directly beneath high-tension wires, but it's still a hushed world of snow and evergreens. It's expensive, especially for families, but the memory will stay with you.

DOWNHILL SKIING   Foremost among the five area downhill centers is the one at **Parc Mont-Ste-Anne,** the largest ski area in eastern Canada, with 50 trails (many of them lit for night skiing) and 11 lifts. A ski bus leaves Place Laurier in the city at Place Laurier at 8am on Saturdays and Sundays, and returns from Mont-Ste-Anne a little after 5pm.

FISHING   From May until early September, anglers can wet their lines in the river that flows through the **Parc de la Jacques-Cartier** and at the national wildlife reserve at **Cap-Tourmente** (☎ 418/827-3776), on the St. Lawrence, not far from Mont-Ste-Anne. Permits are available at many sporting goods stores.

GOLF   **Parc Mont-Ste-Anne** has two 18-hole courses, plus practice ranges and putting greens. Reservations are required, and fees are $28 to $33. The only night-lit facility in Québec City is the nine-hole course at the **Club de Golf** in Val-Bélair, 1250 rue Gabin (☎ 418/845-2222), about 15 minutes west of the city. Reservations are required; a round costs $14 on weekends. In all, there are two dozen courses in the area, most of them in the suburbs of Ste-Foy, Beauport, and Charlesbourg. All but three of the courses in the nearby suburbs are open to the public.

ICE SKATING   Outdoor rinks are located at place d'Youville and Parc de l'Esplanade inside the walls, and at Parc de Champs-de-Bataille (Battlefields Park), where rock-climbing, camping, canoeing, and mountain biking are also possible.

SWIMMING   Those who want to swim during their visit should plan to stay at one of the handful of hotels with pools. Château Frontenac has a new one, and the Radisson Gouverneurs has a heated outdoor pool that is open year-round and can be entered from inside. Other possibilities are the Hilton and Leows Le Concorde.

Village des Sports, a two-season recreational center in St-Gabriel-de-Valcartier (1860 boul. Valcartier, ☎ 418/844-3725), has an immense wave pool and water slides. It's about 20 minutes west of the city.

SPECTATOR SPORTS

The Nordiques, Québec's representatives in the misnamed National Hockey League, departed in 1995 for Denver, leaving the city without a professional team in any of the major sports.

Harness races take place at the **Hippodrome de Québec,** 2205 av. du Colisée, parc de l'Exposition (☎ 418/524-5283). Admission to the clubhouse is $5; general admission, $2.50 for adults, $1.25 for seniors and children 12 and older. Races take place year-round Wednesday to Monday at 1:30pm or 7:30pm (times vary from season to season, call ahead). Fans have been coming to the Hippodrome for afternoons or evenings of harness racing since 1916. Le Cavallo clubhouse is open year-round.

9 Québec After Dark

While Québec City can't pretend to match the volume of nighttime diversions in exuberant Montréal, there is more than enough to do to occupy every evening of an average stay. And apart from theatrical productions, almost always in French, a knowledge of the language is rarely necessary. Drop in at the tourism information office for a list of events.

Check the "Night Life" section of the Greater Québec Area Tourist Guide for suggestions. A weekly information leaflet called *L'Info-Spectacles*, listing headline attractions and the venues in which they are appearing, is found at concierge desks and in many bars and restaurants, as is the tabloid-sized giveaway *Voir*, which provides greater detail. Both are in French, but salient points aren't difficult to decipher.

THE PERFORMING ARTS

The **Québec Symphony Orchestra,** Canada's oldest, performs at the Grand Théâtre de Québec from September to May; the **Québec Opéra** mounts performances in the spring and fall, at the Grand Théâtre. **Danse-Partout** also performs at the Grand Théâtre.

Many of the city's churches host sacred and secular music concerts, as well as special Christmas festivities. Among them are the Cathedral of the Holy Trinity, église St-Jean-Baptiste, historic chapelle Bon-Pasteur, and, on Île d'Orléans, the église Ste-Pétronille. Outdoor performances in summer are staged beside City Hall in the Jardins de l'Hotel-de-Ville, in the Pigeonnier at Parliament Hill, on the Grande-Allée, and at place d'Youville.

Agora. 120 rue Dalhousie (Vieux-Port). ☎ **418/692-1515** or 418/692-2633.

This 5,800-seat amphitheater at the Old Port is the scene of classical and contemporary music concerts and a variety of other shows in the summer. The city makes a dramatic backdrop. The box office, in the adjacent Naturalium, is open daily 10am to 5pm.

Colisée de Québec. 2205 av. du Colisée (parc de l'Exposition). ☎ **418/691-7211.**

Rock concerts are generally held in this arena, located in a park on the north side of the St-Charles River. The box office is open in summer Monday through Friday from 9am to 4pm, in winter from 10am to 5pm.

Grand Théâtre de Québec. 269 bd. René-Lévesque est (av. Turnbull). ☎ **418/643-8131.**

Classical music concerts, opera, dance, and theatrical productions are performed in two halls, one of them housing the largest stage in Canada. Visiting conductors, orchestras, and dance companies often perform here when resident organizations are away. Québec's Conservatory of Music is underneath the theater. The box office is open Monday to Friday 10am to 6pm.

Théâtre Capitole. 972 rue St-Jean (near Porte St-Jean). ☎ **418/694-4444.**

A mixture of live shows and attractions are offered on an irregular schedule. Dramatic productions and comedic performances are in French, but they also host rock groups and occasional classical recitals.

THE CLUB & MUSIC SCENE
ROCK, FOLK, BLUES & JAZZ

Most bars and clubs stay open until 2 or 3am, closing earlier if business doesn't warrant the extra hour or two. Cover charges and drink minimums are all but unknown in the bars and clubs that provide live entertainment. There are three principal streets to choose among for nightlife: the Grande-Allée, rue St-Jean, and the emerging av. Cartier.

Bulldog Haute-Ville. 598 rue St-Jean (near côte de la Fabrique). ☎ **418/523-7803.** No cover.

Rock prevails, often performed by "homage" groups playing the songs of famous bands, but with occasional detours into blues. Billiards and a DJ provide diversion at slack times.

Café Blues. 1018 rue St-Jean (near St-Stanislas). ☎ **418/692-0001.** No cover.

Upstairs, according to an erratic schedule that defies prediction, blues artists start belting out their laments and popping a sweat at 11pm or thereabouts. Patrons can pass the time at a pool table until the show starts.

Chez Son Père. 24 rue St-Stanislas (near St-Jean). ☎ 418/692-5308. No cover.

A musical institution in Québec since 1960, this is the place where French Canadian folksingers often get their start. The stage is on the second floor, with the usual brick walls and sparse decor. A young, friendly crowd is in attendance. The club is a few steps uphill from bustling rue St-Jean.

D'Orsay. 65 rue Baude (opposite Hôtel-de-Ville). ☎ 418/694-1582.

Most of the clientele of this chummy pub-bistro is on the far side of 35, and they start up conversations easily. There's a small dance floor with a DJ, and in summer, a folk singer perches on a stool on the terrace out back.

Le d'Auteuil. 35 rue d'Auteuil (near Porte Kent). ☎ 418/692-2263. No cover.

University students and hip 20- and 30-somethings play pool downstairs in the bar until the bands start thumping upstairs. As a rule, live performers are booked Tuesday through Saturday. Sometimes, they are semifamiliar names in rock or blues; more often they are alternative bands or "homage" groups.

L'Emprise. 57 rue Ste-Anne (at des Jardins). ☎ 418/692-2480. No cover.

Listening to jazz, usually of the mainstream or fusion variety, is a long-standing tradition in this agreeable room. The bar, off the lobby of the once-elegant Hôtel Clarendon, has large windows and Art Deco touches. Seating is at tables and around the bar. It has a mellow atmosphere, with serious jazz fans who come to listen. Music is nightly, from about 10:15pm.

Le Saint-James. 1110 rue St-Jean (côte du Palais). ☎ 418/692-1030. No cover.

For decent food teamed with a pretty good show, this large restaurant/cabaret is worth a visit. They turn the mike over to mostly folk performers, but sometimes blues shouters as well. A plate of pasta goes for $7.95, with soup, dessert, and coffee thrown in. The show starts around 10pm. Go, if only to hear the singer announce his next tune in his native French and go on to sing it in Deep South English.

Les Yeux Bleus. 1117¹/₂ rue St-Jean. ☎ 418/694-9118. No cover.

At the end of an alleyway off rue St-Jean, it looks tumble-down from the outside, but isn't intimidating inside. The music is 75% Québécois and 25% American.

Théâtre du Petit-Champlain. 68 rue du Petit-Champlain (near the Funiculaire). ☎ 418/692-2631.

Québécois and French singers fill this roomy cafe-theater with cabarets and revues. Buy tickets down the street at 76 rue du Petit-Champlain, and have a drink on the patio before the show. The box office is open Monday to Friday from 1 to 5pm, to 7pm the night of a show. Performances are usually Tuesday to Saturday.

Dance Clubs & Discos

Chez Dagobert. 600 Grande-Allée (near Turnbull). ☎ 418/522-0393. No cover.

The top disco in Québec City, this three-story club has an arena arrangement on the ground floor for live bands, with raised seating around the sides. Upper floors have a large dance floor, more bars, TV screens to keep track of sports events, and video games. Sound, whether live or recorded, is a hair short of bedlam, and more than a few habitués are seen to use earplugs. Things don't start kicking into gear until well after 11. The crowd divides into students and their more fashionably attired older brothers and sisters. A whole lot of eyeballing and approaching goes on.

Le Bistro Plus. 1063 rue St-Jean (near St-Stanislas). ☎ 418/694-9252.

A dance floor in back with a light show is full of writhing young bodies—very young, in many cases. During the week, the music is recorded, with live groups on some weekends. It gets raucous and messy, especially after the 4 to 7pm happy hour, but it's happy, too, with a pool table and TVs tuned to sports to keep people entertained.

Vogue/Sherlock Holmes. 1170 d'Artgny (off Grande-Allée). ☎ 418/529-9973. No cover.

This pair of double-decked bars is far less frenetic than Chez Dagobert, with a small disco upstairs in Vogue, and the pubby eatery Sherlock below, with a pool table and dart board. Grad students and Gen-Xers in their first jobs make up most of the clientele.

THE BAR & CAFÉ SCENE

The strip of Grande-Allée between place Montcalm and place George V, near the St-Louis Gate, has been compared to the boulevard St-Germain in Paris. That's a real stretch, but it is lined on both sides with cafes, giving it a passing resemblance. Many have terraces abutting the sidewalks, so cafe hopping is an active pursuit. Eating is definitely not the main event. Meeting and greeting and partying are, aided in some cases by glasses of beer so tall they require stands to hold them up. This leads, not unexpectedly, to a beery frat-house atmosphere that can get sloppy and dumb as the evening wears on. But early on, it's fun to sit and sip and watch. The following bars are away from the Grande-Allée melee.

Aviatic Club. Gare-du-Palais (near rue St-Paul, Lower Town.) ☎ 418/522-3555.

A local favorite with the after-work crowd since 1945, it's in the front of the city's train station. The theme is aviation, which may seem odd given the venue, signaled by two miniature planes hanging from the ceiling. Food is served, along with local and imported beers. Behind the bar, the Pavillon, a casual Italian restaurant with pizza, pasta, and pool tables, is under the same ownership.

L'Astral. 1225 place Montcalm (at the Grande-Allée). ☎ 418/647-2222.

Spinning slowly above a city that twinkles below like tangled necklaces, this restaurant and bar in the Hôtel Loews Le Concorde unveils a breathtaking 360° panorama. Many people come for dinner. Make it for drinks and the view.

Le Pape-Georges. 8 rue Cul-de-Sac (bd. Champlain, Lower Town). ☎ 418/692-1320.

This cozy wine bar features jazz or a French singer on Thursday through Sunday at 10pm. Light fare is served during the day.

Saint Alexandre Pub. 1087 rue St-Jean (near St-Stanislas). ☎ 418/694-0015.

Roomy and sophisticated, this is the best-looking bar in town. It's done in a non-clichéd British pub mode, with polished mahogany, exposed brick, and a working fireplace that's a particular comfort eight months of the year. It claims to serve more than 200 beers from around the world, 20 of them on tap, along with hearty victuals that complement the brews. Sometimes they present jazz duos, usually when other clubs and bars are dark. Large front windows provide easy observation of the busy St-Jean street life.

GAY BARS

The gay scene in Québec City is a small one, centered in the Upper Town just outside the city walls, on rue St-Jean between av. Dufferin and rue St-Augustin, and also along rue St-Augustin and nearby rue d'Aiguillon, which runs parallel to rue St-Jean.

One popular bar and disco, frequented by both men and women (and by men who look like women), is **Le Ballon Rouge,** at 811 rue St-Jean (☎ 418/647-9227).

EVENING CRUISES

Dancing and cruising are the pursuits of passengers on the MV *Louis Jolliet's* four-hour evening cruise from 7 to 11pm. Snack food and a complete bar lubricate the evening. The fare is $48.75. Depart from the quai Chouinard, at the port (☎ 418/692-1159).

The sleek *Bateau-Mouche* has arrived in Québec, following in the footsteps of its sister vessel in Montréal. Dinner cruises cost $58.75 and last three hours, from 7 to 10pm. Board at 6:15pm at Bassin Louise, at the port (☎ 418/692-4949 or 800/361-0130).

10 Side Trips from Québec City

The first four of the excursions described below can be combined and completed in a day. Admittedly, it will be a breakfast-to-dark undertaking, especially if you spend much time exploring each destination, but the farthest of the four destinations is only 25 miles from Québec City.

Bucolic Île d'Orléans, with its maple groves, orchards, farms, and 18th- and 19th-century houses, is a mere 15 minutes away. The famous shrine of Ste-Anne-de-Beaupré and the Mont Ste-Anne ski area are only about half an hour from the city by car. With two or more days available, continue along the northern shore to Charlevoix, where inns and a new casino invite an overnight stay. Then take the ferry across the river—in summer and early fall you might even sight a whale. At Rivière-du-Loup on the opposite shore, drive back toward Québec City, exploring the villages along the St. Lawrence's southern bank. With those suggestions in mind, the following section is arranged as a driving tour.

While it is preferable to drive through this area, tour buses go to Montmorency Falls, the shrine of Ste-Anne-de-Beaupré, and circle the Île d'Orléans. Tours don't go to the southern bank at all. If you wish to join a tour, contact: **Visite Touristique de Québec** (☎ 418/563-9722), which offers English-only tours; **Old Québec Tours** (☎ 418/624-0460); **Maple Leaf Sightseeing Tours** (☎ 418/687-9226); or **Gray Line** (☎ 418/622-7420) to see what's currently available.

ÎLE D'ORLÉANS

It's a only a short drive from Québec City. Follow rue Dufferin (in front of the Parliament building) to connect with Autoroute 440 east, heading toward Ste-Anne-de-Beaupré. In about 15 minutes, the Île d'Orléans bridge will be on the right. You can rent bikes at the convenience store, **Dépanneur Godbout,** right across the road from the island end of the bridge (☎ 418/828-9215).

After arriving on the island, turn right on Route 368 east toward Ste-Pétronille. The **tourist information office** (☎ 418/828-9411) is in the house on the right, and it has a useful tourist guidebook for the island. It's open daily 8:30am to 7pm in summer; off-season, Monday through Friday only, 8:30am to 12:30pm and 1:30 to 4:30pm. A good substitute for the Île d'Orléans guide is the Greater Québec guide, which includes a short tour of Île d'Orléans. A driving-tour cassette can be rented or purchased at the tourist office, the Auberge La Goéliche, and other local inns or bed and breakfasts. The tourist office also supplies cycling maps.

Until 1935, the only way to get to Île d'Orléans was by boat in summer or over the ice in winter. The building of the highway bridge has allowed the fertile fields of Île d'Orléans to become Québec City's primary market-garden. During harvest periods, fruits and vegetables are picked fresh on the farms and trucked into the city daily. In mid-July, hand-painted signs posted by the main road announce "Fraises: cueillir vous-même" (Strawberries: pick 'em yourself). The same invitation is made during apple season, September and October. Farmers hand out baskets and quote the price, paid when the basket's full. Bring along a bag or box to carry away the bounty.

Three stone churches on the island date back to the days of the French regime, due in part to the island's long isolation from the mainland. There are only seven such churches left in all of Québec. A firm resistance to development has kept many of its old houses intact, as well. This could easily have become just another sprawling bedroom community, but it has remained a rural farming area. Island residents work to keep it that way. They have plans to bury their telephone lines and to put in a bike lane to cut down on car traffic.

A coast-hugging road circles the island, which is 21 miles long and 5 miles wide, and another couple of roads bisect it. On the east side of the island are many farms and picturesque houses; on the west side, an abundance of apple orchards.

There are six tiny villages on Île d'Orléans, each with a church as its focal point. Take your time and spend a full day and a night—eat in a couple of restaurants, visit a sugar shack, skip stones at the beach, and spend the night at one of the several waterside inns. But if you are strapped for time, you can do a quick circuit of the island in a half-day. Drive as far as St-Jean, then take Route du Mitan across the island, and return to the bridge, and Québec City, via Route 368 west.

STE-PÉTRONILLE

The first village reached on the recommended counterclockwise tour is Ste-Pétronille, only 2 miles (3km) from the bridge. With 1,050 inhabitants, it's best known for its Victorian inn, La Goéliche (see below), and also claims the northernmost stand of red oaks in North America, dazzling in autumn. The church dates from 1871, and its houses were once the summer homes of wealthy English in the 1800s. Even if you don't stay at the inn, drive down to the water's edge where a small public area with benches is located. Strolling down the picturesque rue Laflamme is another pleasant way to while away a few hours as well.

Where to Stay & Dine

Auberge La Goéliche. 22 av. du Quai, Ste-Pétronille, PQ, G0A 4C0. ☎ **418/828-2248.** Fax 418/692-1742. 22 rms. TV TEL. $90–$120 double. Rates include breakfast. AE, MC, V. Free parking. Closed Nov.

On a rocky point of land at the western tip of the island stands this 1880 country house with a wraparound porch and a pool. The river slaps at the foundation of the glass-enclosed terrace dining room, which is a grand observation point for watching cruise ships and Great Lakes freighters steaming past.

   Dining/Entertainment: The dining room of La Goéliche is well regarded, with updated French cooking that goes easy on oils and cream. When ordering à la carte, expect to pay $7.25 to $12 for main courses, while a table d'hôte meal will run $18 to $20.50. A modified American plan is available.

ST-LAURENT

From Ste-Pétronille, continue on Route 368 east. In 4 miles (6km) is St-Laurent, once a boat-building center turning out 400 craft a year. To learn more about that heritage, visit **Parc Maritime de St-Laurent** (☎ 418/828-2322), an active wooden-boat yard from 1908 to 1967. Before the bridge was built, it provided islanders the

Excursions from Québec City

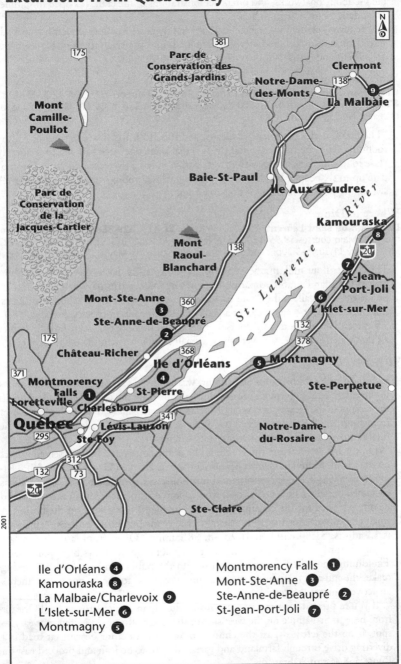

Ile d'Orléans ④
Kamouraska ⑧
La Malbaie/Charlevoix ⑨
L'Islet-sur-Mer ⑥
Montmagny ⑤

Montmorency Falls ①
Mont-Ste-Anne ③
Ste-Anne-de-Beaupré ②
St-Jean-Port-Joli ⑦

means to get across the river to Québec City. The Maritime Park incorporates the old Godbout Boatworks, and offers demonstrations of the craft. It's open in summer only, daily from 9:30am to 5:30pm.

The town's church was erected in 1860, and there are a couple of picturesque roadside chapels as well. Good views of farmlands and the river are available from the St-Laurent golf course—follow signs from the main road.

Where to Stay

La Maison sous les Arbres. 1415 chemin Royal, St-Laurent, PQ, G0A 3Z0. ☎ **418/828-9442.** 3 rms (1 with bath). $60 double. Extra person $20, child $10. Rates include full breakfast. No credit cards.

"The house under the trees," it means, and this B&B fits that description. All the rooms have private entrances, and the two that share one large bath are conveniently close to it. One large room with private bath also has a fireplace and can accommodate up to six people. Breakfast is in a glass-enclosed room overlooking the river. A swimming pool is available for use after 5pm.

Where to Dine

Le Moulin de Saint-Laurent. 754 chemin Royal. ☎ **418/829-3888.** Reservations recommended. Main courses $9.95–$20.95; table d'hôte lunch $10–$17, dinner $23–$35. DC, MC, V. Daily 11:30am–3:30pm and 5–9pm. Closed mid-Oct to May 1. COUNTRY FRENCH.

This former flour mill, in operation from 1720 to 1928, has been transformed into one of the island's most romantic restaurants. On a warm day, sit on the terrace beside the waterfall, and be sure to wander upstairs to see the Québécois antiques. Lunch can be light—an omelet or a plate of assorted pâtés or cheeses, perhaps. There are at least half a dozen main courses to choose from, only one of them fish, despite all that water out there. On weekends, a small combo plays in the evenings.

ST-JEAN

St-Jean, 4 miles (6km) from St-Laurent, was home to sea captains, and the homes in the village tend to be more prosperous than others on the island. The yellow bricks that compose the facades of several of the houses were ballast in boats that came over from Europe. The village church was built in 1732 and the walled cemetery is the final resting place of many fishermen and seafarers.

On the left as you enter the village is one of the largest and best-preserved houses on the island: **Mauvide-Genest Manor,** 1451 ave. Royale (☎ 418/829-2630). Dating from 1752, it is filled with period furnishings. A "beggar's bench" on view was so named because a homeless person who appeared at the door late in the day would be offered a bed for the evening (otherwise, he might cast a spell on the house). A small chapel was added in 1930; the altar was made by Huron Indians. Admission is $3 adults, $1.50 children 10 to 18, $8 families. Open from late May to late August Saturday and Sunday from 10am to 5:30pm; other times by appointment. The dining room here is sometimes open to the public, and its country cooking makes the most of the island's plentiful produce. Next to the manor house, there's an active summer theater.

If you're pressed for time, pick up Route du Mitan, which crosses Île d'Orléans from here to St-Famille on the west side of the island. Route du Mitan, not easy to spot, is on the left just past the church in St-Jean. A detour down that road is a diverting drive through farmland and forest. Return to St-Jean and proceed east on Route 368 east to St-François.

ST-FRANÇOIS

The 5¹/₂-mile (9km) drive from St-Jean to St-François exposes vistas of the Laurentian Mountains off to the left on the western shore of the river. Just past the village center of St-Jean, Mont Ste-Anne can be seen, its slopes scored by ski trails. At St-François, home to about 500 people, the St. Lawrence, a constant and mighty presence, is 10 times wider than when it flows past Québec City. Regrettably, the town's original church (1734) burned in 1988. At St-François, 15 miles (24km) from the bridge, the road becomes Route 368 west.

Where to Dine

Auberge Chaumonot. 425 av. Royale, St-François. ☎ **418/829-2735.** Reservations recommended. Main courses $18–$27; table d'hôte lunch $10–$19, dinner $19–$32. AE, MC, V. Daily 11am–3pm and 5–9pm (until 10pm July–Aug). Closed mid-Oct to Apr 30. QUÉBÉCOIS.

At this riverside inn, the food reflects what farmers have eaten on this island for generations—pork chops, lamb, salmon, tourtière (meat pie), pheasant pâté, tomato-and-onion relish, and plenty of warm bread. The kitchen mixes in such contemporary touches as quiche Lorraine and shrimp and duck pâté. Picture windows look out on the river.

The inn has eight tidy and inexpensive bedrooms, but they are not the reason to visit here. The place is named for the Jesuit priest Pierre Chaumonot, who led the Hurons to the island in 1651 to protect them from the attacking Algonquins.

STE-FAMILLE

Founded in 1661 at the northern tip of the island, Ste-Famille is the oldest parish on the island. With 1,660 inhabitants, it is 5 miles (8km) from St-François and 12 miles (19km) from the bridge. Across the road from the triple-spired church (1743) is the convent of Notre-Dame Congregation, founded in 1685 by Marguerite Bourgeoys, one of Montréal's prominent early citizens. This area supports dairy and cattle farms and apple orchards.

While in town, visit the **Blouin Bakery,** run by a family that has lived on the island for 300 years, and a little shop called **Le Mitan** that stocks local crafts and books about the island.

Anglers might wish to swing by **Ferme Piscicole Richard Boily,** 4739 chemin Royal (☎ 418/829-2874), where they can wet their lines for speckled or rainbow trout in a stocked pond, daily from 9am to sunset. It isn't *quite* like fishing in a rain barrel. Poles and bait are supplied—no permit is required—and customers pay only for what they catch, about 30¢ per inch; the fish run 9 to 12 inches. They'll clean, cut, and pack what you catch. Some island restaurants can even be persuaded to cook the fish for you. For more passive activity, buy a handful of fish pellets for 25¢, toss them on the water, and watch the ravenous trout jump.

On the same property, the **Erablière Richard Boily** offers free 15-minute visits to a cabane à sucre, the traditional "sugar shack" where syrup is made. They demonstrate the equipment and explain the process that turns the sap of a tree into maple syrup. Free tastes are offered and several types of products are for sale in a shop on the premises.

Where to Dine

L'Atre. 4403 chemin Royal, Ste-Famille. ☎ **418/829-2474.** Reservations required for dinner July–Aug. Main courses $17.50–$23.80; table d'hôte lunch $17.50–$32.75, dinner $29.50–$39.50; special nine-course La Grande Fête $58. July–Aug daily noon–3pm and 5:30–9:30pm; Sept–June Sat 5:30–9:30pm. QUÉBÉCOIS.

For what might be the most lasting memory of an island visit, park in the lot marked by a sign and wait for the horse-drawn covered carriage to arrive from the restaurant. After a 10-minute ride, the coachman deposits diners at a 1680 Québécois house with wide floorboards and whitewashed walls at least two feet thick. Rooms are furnished with rough country antiques and reproductions, and illuminated by oil lamps. "L'Atre" means the fireplace, and that's where most of the food is cooked. The menu is short but to the point, and traditional through and through, including such burly standards as soupe aux légumes et fines herbes (vegetables soup flavored with herbs), boeuf au vin rouge (beef stewed in red wine), and tourtière (meat pie). Dessert can be either maple-sugar pie or island-grown berries. All this is delivered by servers clothed according to the era they are helping to re-create.

ST-PIERRE

By Île d'Orléans standards, St-Pierre is a big town, with a population of about 2,000. Its central attraction is the island's oldest church (1717). Services are no longer held there; it now contains a large handicraft shop in the back, behind the altar, which is even older than the church (1695). The pottery, beeswax candles, dolls, scarves, woven rugs, and blankets aren't to every taste, but worth a look.

Thousands of migrating snow geese, Canada geese, and ducks stop by in the spring, a spectacular sight when they launch themselves into the air in flapping hordes so thick they almost blot out the sun.

Heading back across the bridge toward Québec City, there is a fine view of the next destination.

MONTMORENCY FALLS & ST-ANNE-DE-BEAUPRÉ

Take Autoroute 40, north of Québec City, going east. At the end of the autoroute, where it intersects with Route 360, the falls come into view. A **tourist information booth** (☎ 418/663-2877) is beside the parking area at the falls, just after the turn-off from the highway. It's open early June to early September 9am to 7pm, early September to mid-October 11am to 5pm. Admission to the falls is free.

The **waterfall** is surrounded by a provincial park where visitors stop for the view or a picnic from early May to late October. At 274 feet (83 meters), the falls, named by Samuel de Champlain for his patron, the Duke of Montmorency, are 100 feet higher than Niagara, a boast that no visitor is spared. They are, however, far narrower. In winter, the plunging waters contribute to a particularly impressive sight, when the freezing spray sent up by the falls builds a mountain of white ice at the base, called the "Sugarloaf". The yellow cast of the waterfall results from the high iron content of the river bed.

From Montmorency Falls, it's a 20-minute drive along Route 138 east to the little town of Ste-Anne-de-Beaupré. The highway goes right past the basilica, with an easy entrance into the large parking lot. A reception booth at the southeastern side of the basilica, 10018 av. Royale (☎ 418/827-3781), is open from early May through mid-September daily from 8:30am to 5pm. The basilica itself is open year-round. Masses are held daily but hours vary.

Legend has it that French mariners were sailing up the St. Lawrence River in the 1650s when they ran into a terrifying storm. They prayed to their patroness, St. Anne, to save them, and when they survived they dedicated a wooden chapel to her on the north shore of the St. Lawrence, near the site of their perils. Not long afterward, a laborer on the chapel was said to have been cured of lumbago, the first of many documented miracles. Since that time pilgrims have come here—more than a million a year—to pay their respects to St. Anne, the mother of the Virgin Mary and grandmother of Jesus.

Reactions to the religious complex that has resulted inevitably vary. To the faithful, this is a place of wonder, perhaps the most important pilgrimage site in North America. To others, it is perceived as a building that lacks the grandeur its great size is intended to impart, a raw and ponderous structure without the ennobling patina of age. The former group will want to schedule at least a couple of hours to absorb it all; the latter won't need more than 15 minutes to satisfy their curiosity.

The towering basilica is the most recent building raised on this spot in St. Anne's honor. After the sailors' first modest wooden chapel was swept away by a flood in the 1600s, another chapel was built on higher ground. Floods, fires, and the ravages of time dispatched later buildings, until a larger, presumably sturdier structure as erected in 1887. In 1926, it, too, was gutted by fire.

As a result of a lesson finally learned, the present basilica is constructed in stone, following an essentially Romanesque scheme. Marble, granite, mosaics, stained glass, and hand-carved wood are employed with a generous hand. The pews are of wood with hand-carved medallions at the ends, each portraying a different animal. Behind the main altar are eight side chapels and altars, each different. The conviction that miracles routinely occur here is attested by the hundreds of crutches, canes, braces, and artificial limbs strapped to columns and stacked on the floor of the vestibule, left behind by the devout who no longer needed them.

Other attractions in Ste-Anne-de-Beaupré include the Way of the Cross, with life-size cast-iron figures, the Scala Santa Chapel (1891), and the Memorial Chapel (1878), with a bell tower and altar from the late 17th and early 18th centuries, respectively. More commercial than devotional are the Historial, a wax museum, and the Cyclorama, a 360° painting of Jerusalem. Admission to the Historial is $2.50 adults, $1.25 children 6 to 13; to the Cyclorama, it's $5 adults, $3 children 6 to 15.

Driving north on Route 360 toward Mont-Ste-Anne, about 2 miles from Ste-Anne-de-Beaupré, on the left, is a factory outlet strip mall called Promenades Ste-Anne (☎ 418/827-3555). It has shops selling discounted merchandise from Dansk, Liz Claiborne, Mondi, Marikita (crafts), and Benetton, as well as a vaguely southwestern bistro. The center is open seven days a week.

WHERE TO STAY & DINE

Auberge La Camarine. 10947 bd. Ste-Anne, Beaupré, PQ, G0A 1E0. ☎ **418/827-5703.** Fax 418/827-5430. 31 rms. TV TEL. $110–$159 double. AE, DC, MC, V. Go just past the Promenades Ste-Anne outlet center, off Route 138.

Why they named it after a bitter berry is uncertain, but this inn has a kitchen that is equaled by only a bare handful of restaurants in the entire province—and that includes Montréal. It bears a resemblance to the fusion cookery of California—essentially French/Italian joined with Asian techniques and ingredients. The menu changes frequently, and they are justly proud of their wine cellar. Only dinner is served. Table d'hôte dinner $37.95.

Bedrooms gracefully blend antique and contemporary notions, and some have fireplaces, air-conditioning, and/or Exercycles. Two have Jacuzzis. The ski slopes of Mount Ste-Anne are a short drive away.

PARC DU MONT-STE-ANNE: SKIING & SUMMER SPORTS

Continue along Route 360 from Ste-Anne-de-Beaupré to the large ski and recreational area. The park entrance is easy to spot from the highway.

Like Montréal, Québec City has its Laurentian hideaways. But there are differences: The Laurentians sweep down quite close to the St. Lawrence at this point, so Québécois need drive only about 30 minutes to be in the woods. And since Québec

City is much smaller than Montréal, the Québec resorts are more modest in size and fewer in number, but their facilities and amenities are equal to those of resorts elsewhere in the Laurentian range.

The park is comprised of 30 square miles surrounding a 2,625-foot-high peak, an outdoor enthusiast's bonanza. In summer, there's camping, golfing, in-line skating, biking, hiking, jogging, paragliding, and a 150-mile network of mountain-biking trails (bikes can be rented at the park). An eight-passenger gondola to the top of the mountain operates every day between late June and early September, weather permitting.

In winter, the park is Québec's largest and busiest ski area. Twelve lifts, including the gondola and three quad chair lifts, transport downhill skiers to the starting points of 50 trails and slopes.

CHARLEVOIX

Take Route 138 as far as Baie-St-Paul, which is only 61 miles (87km) from Québec City. Baie-St-Paul has a year-round tourist office at 4 rue Ambroise-Fafard, open mid-June to Labor Day daily 9am to 9pm, rest of the year daily 9am to 5pm.

The Laurentians move closer to the shore of the St. Lawrence as they approach what used to be called Murray Bay, at the confluence of Malbaie River with the St. Lawrence. While I can't tell you that the entire length of Route 138 from Beaupré is fascinating, the Route 362 detour from Baie-St-Paul is scenic, with wooded hills slashed by narrow river beds and billowing meadows ending in harsh cliffs plunging down to the river. The air is scented by sea-salt and rent by the shrieks of gulls.

From Baie-St-Paul to Cap â l'Aigle, a few miles beyond La Malbaie, there are several good-to-memorable inns. Nearby Pointe-au-Pic has a new casino, a smaller offshoot of the one in Montréal. The northern end of the region is marked by the confluence of the Saguenay River and the St. Lawrence. From mid-June to late October, these waters attract six species of whales—so many they can be seen from shore, although whale-watching cruises are increasingly popular. See the section on Saint-Simeon below for information about booking a whale-watching cruise.

In 1988, Charlevoix was named a UNESCO World Biosphere Reserve. While only one of 325 such regions throughout the world, it was the first so designated to include human settlement.

BAIE-ST-PAUL

The first town of any size reached in Charlevoix via Route 138, this attractive community of 6,000 holds on to a reputation as an artists' retreat that started developing at the start of the century. Over a dozen boutiques and galleries and a couple of small museums show the work of local painters and artisans. Given the setting, it isn't surprising that many of the artists are landscapists, but there are other styles and subjects represented.

A new (1992) undertaking, **Le Centre d'Exposition,** 23 rue Amroise-Fafard (☎ 418/435-3681), is a brick-and-glass museum with three floors of work by largely regional artists, both past and present. Inuit sculptures are included, and temporary one-person and group shows are mounted throughout the year. Admission is $3 adults, $2 seniors and students; children under 12 admitted free. Hours are September 5 to June 23, daily 9am to 5pm; June 24 to September 4, daily 9am to 7pm.

Where to Stay

La Maison Otis. 23 rue St-Jean-Baptiste, Baie-St-Paul, PQ, G0A 1B0. ☎ **418/435-2255** or 800-267-2254. Fax 418/435-2464. 30 rms. A/C TV TEL. $130–$250 double. Rates include breakfast and dinner. AE, MC, V.

Prices look steep at first blush but remember that with big breakfasts and dinners included, lunch here is almost redundant. A wide range of facilities and amenities allows guests who reserve far enough in advance to customize their lodgings. Combinations of fireplaces, whirlpools, stereo systems, VCRs, four-poster beds and suites sleeping four are all available, distributed through three buildings. Several art galleries are within walking distance. A kidney-shaped indoor pool and sauna are on the premises, as is a jovial piano bar. The required meals are no sacrifice. Housekeeping is meticulous.

ST. IRÉNÉE

From Baie-St-Paul, take Route 362 toward La Malbaie. It roller-coasters over bluffs above the river, and in about 20 miles (33 kilometers) is this cliff-top hamlet of fewer than 800 year-round residents. Apart from the setting, the best reason for dawdling here is the lengthy music and dance festival held every summer. **Domaine Forget,** 398 chemin les Bains (☎ 418/452-8111) offers concerts from early June to late August on Wednesday, Saturday, and some Friday evenings, plus musical brunches on Sunday mornings from June 18 to August 27. This performing arts festival was initiated in 1977, with the purchase of a large property overlooking the river. Existing buildings and the surrounding lawns were used to stage the concerts and recitals. Their success prompted the construction of a new 600-seat hall, scheduled to be completed in time for the 1996 season. While the program emphasizes classical music with solo instrumentalists and chamber groups, it is peppered with appearances by jazz combos. Tickets are $16 to $20 adults; children under 12 admitted free.

POINTE-AU PIC

From St-Irénée, the road starts to bend west after 6 miles (10 kilometers) as the mouth of the Malbaie River starts to form. Pointe-au-Pic is one of the trio of villages that are collectively known as La Malbaie, or Murray Bay, as it was known to the wealthy Anglophones who made this their resort of choice from the Gilded Age on through the 1950s. While inhabitants of the region wax poetic about their hills and trees and wildlife "where the sea meets the sky," they have something quite different to preen about now.

What to See & Do

Casino de Charlevoix. 183 av. Richelieu (Route 362). ☎ **418/665-5353** or 800/965-5355. Free admission (persons 18 and over only). Daily 11am–3am. Signs are frequent on Route 362 coming from the south, and on Routes 138 and 362 from the north. Round-trip shuttle bus service from Québec City $30.

This is the second of Québec's newly approved gambling casinos (the first is in Montréal and the third is scheduled to open in the Ottawa/Hull region in 1996). It is about as tasteful as such establishments get this side of Monte Carlo. Cherrywood paneling and granite floors enclose the ranks of slot machines, 12 blackjack tables, three roulette wheels, and lone baccarat table. There are no craps tables. Only soft drinks are allowed at the machines and tables. You'll have to go to an adjacent bar to mourn your losses. And there is a dress code, forbidding bustiers, cut-off sweaters, blue jeans, shorts, beachwear, motorcycle boots, and "clothing of a violent nature or associated with an organization known to be violent." The adjacent Manoir Richelieu was once the aristocratic haven of swells summering in Murray Bay, who had to meet even more stringent dress codes.

Musée de Charlevoix. 1 chemin du Havre (at the intersection with Route 362/bd. Bellevue). ☎ **418/665-4411.** Admission $4 adults, $3 seniors and students, children under 12 free. June 26–Sept 4 daily 10am–6pm; Sept 5–June 24 Tues–Fri 10am–5pm, Sat–Sun 1–5pm.

In existence since 1975, the museum moved to these post-modernist quarters in 1990. Folk art, sculptures, and paintings by regional artists figure prominently in the permanent collection, supplemented by frequent temporary exhibitions with diverse themes. This may be a small town, but it has produced a building and a collection of uncommon sophistication.

CAP-À-L'AIGLE

Route 362 rejoins Route 138 in La Malbaie, the largest town in the area, with almost 4,000 inhabitants. It serves as a provisioning center, with supermarkets, hardware stores, gas stations. There is a **tourist information office** at 630 boul. de Comporté, open mid-June to Labor Day daily from 9am to 9pm, the rest of the year daily from 9am to 5pm. Continue through the town center and across the bridge, making a sharp right on the other side. This is Route 138, with signs pointing to Cap-à-l'Aigle.

William Howard Taft spent many summers in Murray Bay, starting in 1892 and extending well past his one-term presidency. For much of that time, the only way to get here was by boat, for the railroad didn't arrive until 1919. Given his legendary girth, it can be assumed that Taft knew something about the good life. Some of the other folks who made this their summer home, namely the Cabots of Boston, the Duke of Windsor, and Charlie Chaplin, could confirm that Taft loved the region. And if any of them could return today, they might well choose what is arguably the premier auberge in Murray Bay.

Where to Stay & Dine

La Pinsonnière. Cap-à-l'Isle, PQ, G0T 1B0. ☎ **418/665-4431.** Fax 418/665-7156. 26 rms, 1 suite. May–Oct 7 and Christmas $130–$275 double; Nov–Apr $100–$240 double. MAP available, but not required. AE, DC, ER, MC, V.

This is one of only eight member hostelries in the prestigious Relais and Chateaux organization in all of Canada. As aficionados know, properties included in this organization offer limited size, comfort bordering on luxury in the bedrooms, and a emphasis on food and wine. Bedrooms come in five categories, the priciest of which have Jacuzzis and gas fireplaces.

Dining/Entertainment: You'll know where the owners focus their laser-like attention when you're seated in the serene dining room beside the picture window, anticipating a dinner that will become the evening's entertainment. With drinks and menus come the customary pre-appetizers—say, quail leg on a bed of slivered asparagus and fettucine tossed with plump mussels, spiked with a spray of pungent tarragon and brightened with an edible pansy, immediately followed by soup. The main event, often a succulent veal chop with a nest of shaved carrots, fiddleheads, and purple potatoes, is superb. Wines are a particular point of pride here, and the owner needs no urging to conduct tours of his impressive cellar.

Facilities: Indoor pool, sauna, tennis, and massages..

SAINT-SIMEON

Rejoin Route 138 and continue 20 miles (33 kilometers) to the ferry at Saint-Simeon to cross to Rivière-du-Loup on the other side of the St. Lawrence, returning to Québec City along the south shore. If there is no time, it's only 93 miles (150km) back to the city the way you came on the north shore.

Once in Saint-Simeon, signs direct cars and trucks down to the ferry terminal. Boarding is on a first-come, first-served basis, and ferries leave on a carefully observed schedule, weather permitting, from late March to early January. Departure times of the five daily sailings vary substantially from month to month, however, so get in

touch with the company, **Clark Transport Canada** (☎ 418/638-2856 or 418/
638-5530) to obtain a copy of the schedule. One-way fares are $9.10 adults, $6.05
seniors and children 5 to 11, $23.20 cars and their passengers. MC, V accepted.
Arrive at least 30 minutes before departure, one hour in summer. The boat is equipped
with a luncheonette, lounges, and a newsstand. Voyages take 65 to 75 minutes.

From late June through September, passengers may enjoy a bonus. Those are the
months the **whales** are most active, and when pelagic (migratory) species join the resident minke and beluga whales, estimated at more than 500 in number. They prefer
the northern side of the Estuary, roughly from La Malbaie to Baie-Ste-Catherine, at
the mouth of the Saguenay River. Since that is the area the ferry steams through,
sightings are an ever-present possibility, especially in summer.

THE SOUTHERN BANK

If you arrive by ferry from Saint-Simeon and plan to work your way back to Québec
City, go to the end of this section and follow the itinerary backwards from
Kamouraska, which is 130 miles (210km) east of Québec City.

If you're driving up from the city to explore the southern shore, take Autoroute
20 as far as St-Michel, then pick up Route 132 east for the only slightly slower scenic road that keeps the river in sight.

Several towns on the southern bank of the St. Lawrence are an easy day's excursion from the city, and in good weather the views of the river and its islands are by
themselves worth the drive. However, the fact that the tourist office in St-Jean-Port-
Joli is closed from October through April says much about the relative desirability
of a trip through here in those months. There are enough motels and guest houses
to ensure lodging on short notice, although few of them can be described as memorable. On a day trip, St-Jean-Port-Joli makes a logical turnaround point. But if
planning to take the ferry across the river and return by the north shore to Québec
City, a highly recommended choice, continue to Rivière-du-Loup.

For the first 20 miles of the drive, Île d'Orléans (see above) will be off to the left
in midstream, with the Laurentian Mountains on the north bank as backdrop.

MONTMAGNY

The first big town is Montmagny, a farming and industrial center, with a population of 12,000. A tourist office operates from the historic **Manoir Couillard-Dupuis,**
301 bd. Taché est (☎ 418/248-9196; fax 418/248-1436), and is open Monday
through Friday 8:30am to 4:30pm. It's in a little park with a walkway beside the river.

In summer, take a boat out to **Grosse Île,** the Ellis Island of Canada. Parks Canada
is in the process of transforming it into a powerful reminder of a period in the
country's history, when 4¹/₂ million people immigrated to Canada via Québec. Thousands with cholera or typhoid fever were quarantined on the island from 1832 to
1937; 4,000 were buried here. Some 300,000 Irish refugees from the potato famines
came through here in 1847 and 1848. A small train with a guide carries visitors
around the island and makes stops along the way.

Off Montmagny lie six islands known for the wildfowl that visit. The largest are
Île aux Grues (Cranes' Island) and Île aux Oies (Geese Island). A ferry goes to the
Île aux Grues from Montmagny.

Where to Stay & Dine

Café Renoir. 43 St-Jean-Baptiste ouest. ☎ **418/248-3343.** Main courses $6.50–$18; table
d'hôte dinner $19–$27. AE, MC, V. Tues–Sat 11am–2pm; Tues–Sun 5–10pm; brunch Sun
11am–2pm (in May–Aug only). FRENCH/QUÉBÉCOIS.

Café Renoir offers large servings of satisfying dishes at reasonable prices. Quiche, pasta, ham-and-cheese croissants, and bagels with smoked salmon and cream cheese are possible lunch choices. Dinners are more ambitious.

Manoir des Erables. 220 bd. Taché est (Route 132), Montmagny, PQ, G5V 1G5. ☎ **418/ 248-0100** or 800/563-0200 in Québec. Fax 418/248-9507. Reservations recommended. Main courses $8.95–$13.95; table d'hôte dinners $33–$54. AE, DC, DISC, MC, V. Daily 7:30–10am, 11am–2pm, and 6–9pm. Closed Sun lunch Nov–mid-Apr. CLASSIC FRENCH.

Since 1975, the Cyr family has welcomed guests to their stately 1812 inn, with its glossy reputation for both food and lodging. In the dining room, sterling glints by the light of sparkling chandeliers. The menu changes daily, but among offerings to look for are mussels with anise, a starter, and the ragout of lobster and scallops. Wines range in price from $20 to $960 (the 1973 Château Pétrus).

Unfortunately, only a few of the large Victorian bedrooms remain due to a fire in 1982. The rest are modern. Suites have fireplaces and whirlpool baths. Eight rooms in a stone house on the property, the Pavillon Collin (1867), are air-conditioned. Rooms start at $90 double, a good value, suites are $185.

L'ISLET-SUR-MER

Along Route 132 on the approach to L'islet-sur-Mer are many roadside farm stands selling honey, fruits, and vegetables. About 10$^1/_2$ miles (17km) east of Montmagny, this fishing village produced sailors who roamed the world, among them an Arctic explorer named Joseph-Elzéar Bernier, who claimed the Arctic islands for Canada. Bernier, who became a captain at the age of 17, made 269 voyages and crossed the Atlantic 45 times. In 1874, he did it in 15 days and 16 hours, quite a feat in those days.

A Museum of Nautical History

Musée Maritime Bernier. 55 rue des Pionniers est. ☎ **418/247-5001.** Admission $4 adults, $1.50 children, $7.50 families. May 20–Sept 29 daily 9am–6pm, Sept 30–May 19 Tues–Fri 9am– noon and 1:30–5pm.

Dedicated to the town's favorite son (above), the museum relives the area's nautical history from the 17th century forward. The monument in front of the museum illustrates his explorations on a globe, crowned with the aurora borealis. Housed in a former 19th-century convent, the museum has three floors of exhibits. Particularly captivating are the many large ship models, ranging from fully-rigged galleons to brigantines to Seaway freighters. Sound, videos, and computers are employed with a degree of sophistication. Out back are the hydrofoil Bras d'Or 400 and the icebreaker *Ernest Lapointe,* which was built in Canada before World War II and used until 1978.

ST-JEAN-PORT-JOLI

Of all the towns along the southern bank, St-Jean-Port-Joli is best organized to welcome travelers and help them find their way around. This town of 3,400 has gained a measure of fame for the woodcarving that has been done here for generations. It started in the early days when much of the decoration for local churches was carved wood. But in the 1930s, three brothers—Médard, André, and Jean-Julien Bourgault—began carving other things as well: bas-reliefs, statues, figurines, even portraits. As the celebrity of the Bourgault brothers spread, dozens of students were attracted to the town and a wood-sculpture school was established. Today the town has about 100 working craftspeople and is filled with their shops and galleries, showing textiles, pottery, and carvings in stone and wood.

Exploring the Town

Although such words as *masterful* and *exquisite* are tossed around with abandon in reference to the woodcarvings of these artisans, individual responses vary widely. So stop by the Musée des Anciens Canadiens first for a look at a number of examples to see if you have any interest.

If you like the work, there are ample opportunities to seek out carvings for sale and to meet the people who produced them. Wander into some of the wood-carving shops strung along Route 132 for a look at what's being done today. The artists are usually happy to chat and show their studios.

A shop with a more diverse inventory of art and handicrafts is **Les Enfants du Soleil.** The whimsical mélange incorporates used books, jewelry, unusual vests and dresses, and folk arts and primitive objects from Africa and Indonesia. Just across from the church and painted red and orange, the store is hard to miss.

Musée des Anciens Canadiens. 332 av. de Gaspé ouest. ☎ 418/598-3392. Admission $4 adults, $2 children 7–12, under 12 free. May–June daily 9am–6pm; July–Aug daily 9am–9pm; Sept–Oct daily 9am–5pm; Nov–Apr by reservation only.

Museum is too grand a label for this gallery attached to a boutique, but it's a good place to start to learn about the works of the Bourgault brothers—Médard's religious sculptures and nudes, André's country folk, and Jean-Julien's religious sculptures and furniture. The work of other village artisans is also on display, including that of Nicole Deschênes Duval and Pierre Cloutier, and the model boats carved by members of the Leclerc family, which are also on display in the Musée Maritime Bernier in L'islet-sur-Mer.

Church of St-Jean-Port-Joli. 2 av. de Gaspé ouest. ☎ 418/598-3023. Free admission. June 27–Labor Day daily 9am–5pm; Labor Day–June 26 Mon–Fri 9am–5pm (or by reservation).

The church was built in 1779–81 and later decorated by the early wood-carvers, including the Bourgaults, who created the pulpit in 1937. A more recent addition is the 17-piece crèche, each piece carved by a different local artist and presented to the church in 1987. Buried in the church under the seigneurial pew is the author of *Anciens Canadiens*, Philippe-Aubert de Gaspé, who was the last in a line of lords of the manor (seigneurs) who owned and governed St-Jean since 1633. Look for the nearby plaque that lists all of the town's seigneurs, back to the time when the original land grant was made by the king of France.

Seigneurie des Aulnaies. 525 de la Seigneurie, St-Roch-des-Aulnaies. ☎ 418/354-2800. Admission (including tours) $4 adults, $1.50 children 6–15, $9 families. Late June–early Sept daily 9am–6pm.

About 9 miles (14km) east of St-Jean-Port-Joli is this historic farm beside the Ferrée River, with a working flour mill from 1842 and a manor house from 1850. Thanks to a gentle microclimate, the grounds are filled with chestnuts, black locusts, and redwoods—trees not ordinarily found in this area. Six tours of mill and manor house are given daily by costumed docents starting at 9:30am.

Where to Stay

Auberge des Glacis. 46 route Tortue, C.P. 102, St-Eugène, PQ, G0R 1X0. ☎ 418/247-7486. 8 rms, 2 suites. $83–$91 double; $97–$108 suite. Extra person $16. AE, MC, V.

About 7¹/₂ miles (12km) west of St-Jean-Port-Joli, this 1841 stone mill-turned-inn sits beside a stream in the woods. The only steady sounds are of crickets and gurgling water. Each room has special touches—a spinning wheel, a brass bed, an antique armoire—that recall the century past. One room has a television; another is perfect for families, with a bedroom, separate sitting area, and loft with two single beds reached by a ladder. Baths in three rooms have both tub and shower, the others have showers alone. The innkeepers rent cross-country skis and horseback riding is available nearby. In the dining room, the French menu is changed daily. A table d'hôte dinner costs $21 to $29.

Where to Dine

Café La Coureuse des Grèves. Route 204 (rue de l'Eglise, near Route 132). ☎ **418/ 598-9111.** Main courses $5.95–$13.25; table d'hôte meal $5–$10. AE, MC, V. Daily 8am– midnight. QUÉBÉCOIS.

A popular all-bases place for meals or just coffee and cake, the cafe take its name from the story of a beautiful maiden who would run ("la coureuse") along the river's shores ("des grèves"), tempting fishermen and mariners who tried to capture her. Copious portions are the rule, of items like pastas, chicken, steak, seafood, vegetarian dishes, kebabs, a cheese plate with fresh fruit, and fish chowder. The cheerful hostess and her staff speak little English, so just point. Painted plank walls are the backdrop for changing exhibitions of works by local artists. The upstairs bar gets lively with local musicians on Thursday evenings.

KAMOURASKA

A bit farther up the coast along Route 132 is Kamouraska, miles (65km) east of St-Jean-Port-Joli. One of the southern shore's oldest settlements, it has a modest museum, a number of old houses, riverbank panoramas, and a couple of bed and breakfasts. Ordinarily, it wouldn't hold much of interest for the average traveler. But during the spring and fall migratory seasons, the fields around Kamouraska host countless thousands of snow geese.

To cross the river in order to return through the Charlevoix region to Québec City, drive upriver a bit farther and take the car-ferry from Rivière-du-Loup to Saint-Siméon, on the northern shore. Rivière-du-Loup is the region's commercial, governmental, and educational hub with a number of motels and restaurants for those who choose to spend the night or get there too late for the ferry.

Follow Highway 132 through the town and follow the signs for the ferry landing. For the latest information on fares and departure times, call ☎ 418/862-5094 for recorded information in French, then English. Boarding is on a first-come, first-served basis; no reservations. The trip takes 65 to 75 minutes and food is served on board. For additional details, see the section on Saint-Simeon above.

11 To the Gaspé

The southern bank of the St. Lawrence sweeps north and then eastward toward the Atlantic. At the river's mouth the thumb of land called the Gaspé Peninsula— Gaspésie in French—pokes into the Gulf of St. Lawrence. The Gaspé is a raw, primordial region heaped with aged, blunt hills covered with hundreds of square miles of woodlands. Over much of its perimeter, their slopes fall directly into the sea, then back away to define the edges of a coastal plain. Winter is long and harsh, the crystal days of summer made all the more precious. The trains don't run here anymore, for the fishing villages that huddle around the coves cut from the coast are as sparsely populated as they've always been, with many of the young residents moving inland toward brighter lights. That leaves the crash of the surf, eagles and elk in the high grounds, and timber to be harvested gingerly by lumber companies, the principal industry.

All that makes it just the place for camping, hiking, biking, hunting, and fishing in near-legendary salmon streams. Almost every little town has a modest but clean motel and a restaurant to match. The purpose of a trip is a complete escape from the cities, and your destination is the tip of the thumb, the village of Percé and the famous rock for which it is named. From Québec City, driving around the peninsula and back to the city takes about five days, assuming only an overnight when you get to Percé. The first half of the trip is the most scenic, while the underside of the peninsula is largely a flat coastal plain beside a regular shoreline.

FROM RIVIERE-DU-LOUP TO RIMOUSKI

Past Rivière-du-Loup along Highway 132, the country slowly grows more typically Gaspésien. Peat bogs on the river side of the road yield bales of peat moss, shipped to gardeners throughout the continent. Past the town of Trois-Pistoles (the name comes from a French coin, the pistole, and not from firearms) are miles of low rolling hills and fenced fields for dairy cattle. Along the roadside, hand-painted signs advertise pain de ménage (homemade bread) and other baked goods for sale.

Rimouski (pop. 40,000) is the largest city in the region, boasting regional business and governmental headquarters. It has the look of a boomtown, with lots of new buildings going up, but visitors not there on business are likely to simply pass on through. The highway skirts the center of town along the riverbank. Rimouski marks the start of the true Gaspé, free of the gravitational pull of Greater Québec. The number of the two-lane road is 132, which runs all the way around the peninsula to join itself again at Mont-Joli. Thus the confusing signs: 132 est (east) and 132 ouest (west).

JARDINS DE MÉTIS

Near Grand Métis is the former Reford estate, now a **public garden** (☎ 418/775-2221), last owned by a lady with such a passion for gardening that even in the relatively severe climate of Gaspé she was able to cultivate a horticultural wonderland of some 100,000 plants in 2,500 varieties. Of the six sections, laid out in the informal English manner, one of the most appealing is the rock garden. Hummingbirds zip among the blossoms, all but oblivious to humans. The provincial government took the gardens over in 1962, and they can be visited from June through mid-September daily from 8:30am to 8pm. Admission is $4.25 for adults, $3 for seniors, 50¢ for children not accompanied by their parents. A family ticket is $8. Ms. Reford's mansion now houses a museum and a busy restaurant.

As you drive on to Matane, the foothills off to the right of the highway get larger and move closer to the coast, and roadside communities are farther apart.

MATANE

The highway enters town and passes gas stations and a new shopping center whose traffic rivals the bustle in Rimouski. But the focal point of the town is the Matane River, a thoroughfare for the annual migration of up to 3,000 spawning salmon. Near the lighthouse, the town maintains an information bureau, open daily from 9am to 8pm.

A big event in mid- to late June is the **Shrimp Festival.** Atlantic salmon begin their swim up the Matane through a specially designed dam that facilitates their passage in June and continue through September.

Matane is also the terminus of another ferry that crosses the St. Lawrence; this one stops at Baie-Comeau. It is operated by the Société des Traversiers du Québec, and the voyage takes just under 2¹/₂ hours. Fares are $8.25 per adult, $4.25 per child 5 to 11, $8.75 for a motorcycle, and $21.50 for a car. Go across and come back the same day for only $12.50 per person, a virtual minicruise. People over 65 years old are charged a child's fare. From mid-June to early September there are two or three daily sailings in each direction, one or two at other times of the year. For reservations, call Matane (☎ 418/562-2500), Baie-Comeau (☎ 418/296-2593), or Godbout (☎ 418/568-7575).

WHERE TO STAY & DINE

Hotel Des Gouverneurs. 250 av. du Phare est, Matane, PQ, G4W 3N4. ☎ 418/566-2651 or 800/463-2820. Fax 418/562-7365. 72 rms and suites. A/C TV TEL. $79–$99 double; $150 suite. Packages and off-season (Sept–May) discounts available. AE, CB, DC, DISC, ER, MC, V. Free parking.

Located on the water near the harbor, this hotel offers ocean views from half of its rooms; the executive rooms have minibars. The licensed dining room serves all meals, with dinner main courses in the $14 to $20 range. A piano bar called Amadeus helps pass an evening, and on premises are a heated pool, sauna, exercise room, and lighted tennis court.

STE-ANNE-DES-MONTS

Ste-Anne (pop. 6,000), another fishing town, has a tourist information booth on Route 132, half a mile past the bridge, and also stores, garages, gas stations, and other necessary services.

PARC DE LA GASPÉSIE

Rising higher inland are the Chic-Choc mountains, the northernmost end of the Appalachian range. Most of them are contained by this park and adjoining reserves. Turn onto Highway 299 in Ste-Anne-des-Monts and head for the Gîte du Mont-Albert, about 25 miles (40km). The road climbs into the mountains, some of which are naked rock at the summits. Back in the mountains, the rivers brim with baby salmon and speckled trout, and the forests and meadows sustain herds of moose, caribou, and deer.

WHERE TO STAY & DINE

Gîte du Mont-Albert. Parc de la Gaspésie, C.P. 1150, Ste-Anne-des-Monts, PQ, G0E 2G0. ☎ 418/763-2288. 48 rms. $79–$169 double.

Reservations are essential for a meal or lodging at this hostelry, operated as a training ground for those planning to enter the hospitality profession. Rooms in the main lodge or outlying cottages are summer-camp rustic, but the dining room is better than might be expected.

MONT-ST-PIERRE: A PERFECT SPOT FOR HANG-GLIDING

Back on Route 132, turning right from Ste-Anne, the highway becomes a narrow band crowded up to water's edge by sheer rock walls. Offshore, seabirds perch on rocks, pecking at tidbits. High above the shore are many waterfalls that spill from the cliffs beside the highway.

Around a rocky point and down a slope, Mont-St-Pierre is much like other Gaspésian villages except for the eye-catching striations in the rock of the mountain east of town. Such geological phenomena are quickly forgotten at the startling sight of hang-gliders suddenly appearing overhead. The site is regarded as nearly perfect for the sport due to its favorable updrafts. In late July and early August the town holds a two-week **Fête du Vol-Libre (Hang-Gliding Festival),** when the sky is filled with birdmen and birdwomen in flight hundreds of feet above the town, looping and curving on the air currents until landing in the sports grounds behind city hall. For more information about the event, contact the Corporation Vol Libre, C.P. 82, Mont-St-Pierre, Gaspésie (☎ 418/797-2222; fax 418/797-2558).

FORILLON NATIONAL PARK

Soon the road winds up into the mountains, over a rise, down into the valley, and again up to the next. Settlements get smaller, but still there are roadside stands advertising fresh-baked homemade bread and fresh fish. At Petite-Rivière-au-Renard, Route 197 heads southwest toward the town of Gaspé while Route 132 continues eastward to the tip of the peninsula. Motels, restaurants, and services line the roadside in Riviére-au-Renard, Anse-au-Griffon, Jersey Cove, and Cap-des-Rosiers before the highway enters Forillon National Park (☎ 418/368-5505).

Chosen because of its representative terrain, the park's 92 square miles of headlands capture a surprising number of the features characteristic of eastern Canada. A rugged coastline, dense forests, and an abundance of wildlife attract hikers and campers from all North America. On the northern shore are sheer rock cliffs carved by the sea from the mountains, and on the south is the broad Bay of Gaspé. The park has a full program of nature walks, trails for hiking, beaches, picnic spots, and campgrounds. The fee to enter and drive in the park is $5.20 per day, $10.40 for a four-day pass. Camping fees are $11.45 to $15 per night. A bilingual attendant at the entrance provides maps and information.

Forillon Tours operates deep-sea fishing trips and boat cruises (☎ 418/892-5629 in summer or 418/368-2448 in winter) from Cap-des-Rosiers harbor seven days a week in the warm months. A cruise costs about $12 per adult, $11 per child. Fishing trips (tackle included) are $16 and $10, respectively. Reserve in advance.

GASPÉ

Jacques Cartier stepped ashore here in 1534 to claim the land for the king of France. He erected a wooden cross to mark the spot. Today Gaspé is the seat of a bishopric and is economically important because of the three salmon rivers whose mouths are here and its deep-water port. Otherwise unprepossessing, it doesn't offer much to detain travelers. The principal attraction is the **Gaspésie Museum,** at Jacques Cartier Point on Route 132 (☎ 418/368-5710), which endeavors to tell the story of Cartier's landing, and the granite dolmens out front are reminiscent of the explorer's native Brittany.

PERCÉ

Winding through the hills and along the water toward Percé, the Pic de l'Aurore (Peak of the Dawn), which dominates the northern reaches of the town, comes into view. Over the hill from the Pic, Percé Rock and the bird sanctuary of Île Bonaventure appear. The rock is Percé's most famous landmark, a narrow butte rising straight out of the water and pierced by a sea-level hole at its far end. In the sunlight of late afternoon it is especially striking.

The town of Percé is not large, and except for a few quiet, well-groomed inland residential streets, it's confined to the highway that winds along the shore. Little private museums, cafes, snack bars, gift shops, restaurants, and motels line both sides of the highway, and people in bathing suits or shorts and T-shirts give it all a beach-party ambience. But perhaps because the only way to get here is by this fairly long drive, it has thus far avoided the ticky-tack, honky-tonk aspect that afflicts many beach communities closer to big cities.

An **information center** is located right in town at 142 Rte. 132, open daily from 8am to 8pm in summer (more restricted hours off-season).

EXPLORING THE AREA: BIRD-WATCHING, CRUISES & MORE

After checking into a motel and relaxing on their porch or lawn (most of which provide views of the rock), most people take a boat trip out to the rock and to the hump-backed bird sanctuary, Île Bonaventure. A provincial park, the island's lure is the quantity, rather than the diversity of its nesting birds. Among these are gannets, cormorants, puffins, black guillemots, kittiwakes, and razorbills. For a photographic exhibit of the history of the island, visit the **Information Centre** (☎ 418/782-2721) in the Cold Storage Building at the foot of the Percé wharf. Naturalists are on the island to answer questions. Transportation is provided to and from Percé wharf. Birders and hikers can get off at the dock, picking up one of the ferries that arrive two or three times an hour from 8am until 5pm. Fares are $11 for adults, $4.50 for children under 12.

A glass-bottom **catamaran**, *Capitaine Duval* (☎ 418/782-5401 or 418/782-5355), sails out from the same wharf for underwater views of the fish and marine vegetation in these waters. The cat has a heated lounge, large windows, padded seats, bar service, lavatories, and a bilingual crew who are graduates of the Marine Institute. Tours go to Percé Rock, Bonaventure Island, and even Forillon National Park.

To engage in more active underwater explorations of the area, contact the **Club Nautique de Percé** (☎ 418/782-5403 in summer, 418/782-5222 in winter; fax 418/782-5624), which can lead you to a dozen or more dive sites in the area. The water is about 50°F to 64°F (10°C to 18°C) from June through August, and about 57°F (14°C) until mid-October.

The **Parc de l'Île-Bonaventure-et-du-Rocher-Percé Interpretation Centre,** on l'Irlande Road (☎ 418/782-2240), focuses on the ecology of the Gulf of St. Lawrence and the natural features of Île Bonaventure. A 10-minute film of the bird colonies is shown here, and there are salt-water aquariums. The Lichen Trail in the environs of the center redirects attention earthward. There are also a few photo opportunities here—from the view of the rock and Bonaventure Island to the town. It's open 9am to 5pm daily from June to mid-October, with restricted hours the rest of the year.

More? Take a picnic up to the roadside rest just north of the Pic de l'Aurore for the view, then take in different views of Percé Rock. At low tide walk out to the fossil-filled rock on a sandbar, a temptation few visitors resist.

WHERE TO STAY

Hotel-Motel La Normandie. C.P. 129, Percé, PQ, G0C 2L0. ☎ **418/782-2112** or 800/463-0820. Fax 418/782-2337. 45 rms. A/C TV TEL. $68–$107 double. Packages available. AE, CB, DC, DISC, ER, MC, V. Closed late Oct–Apr.

Right in the middle of town on the water, in a building more stylish than others in town, is this accommodation, sheathed in weathered wood, with a wide lawn sloping down to the shore. Thirteen oceanfront units were added in 1991. All rooms have bath-shower combinations, color TVs, and small sitting areas. Rooms on the water side have decks. There is an exercise room and sauna for guests' use.

The Normandie's dining room, open for breakfast and dinner, is respected for both its food and its tasteful decor. Bentwood wicker chairs and black circular tables keep the mood of simplicity. Table d'hôte dinners include soup, dessert, and coffee in addition to the main course, which is often sautéed scallops or salmon. They cost $29.

Les Trois Soeurs Motel. Percé, PQ, G0C 2I0. ☎ **418/782-2183** Fax 418/782-2610. 57 rms, 2 apts, 1 three-bedroom cottage. A/C MINIBAR TV TEL. $69–$125 double. AE, DC, MC, V.

The unpretentious Les Trois Soeurs Motel is one of the first you'll encounter as you come into town, but it's only a short walk from the middle of town. Several conveniences are available here, including an inexpensive Laundromat and provisions for babysitting. Coffee, juice, and croissants are served in the lobby. From one of the picnic tables on the lawn above the beach, there is an up-close view of the Rock.

WHERE TO DINE

La Maison du Pecheur. Place du Quai. ☎ 418/782-5331. Reservations recommended. Main courses $9–$20; table d'hôte $20 or $39. AE, DC, DISC, ER, MC, V. Late June to mid-Sept daily 11:30am–9pm. SEAFOOD.

Located at the end of the wharf, this property's seaside walls are windows offering views of harbor activity and, of course, the Rock. The decor is a subdued nautical theme accompanied by a open-beam ceiling and rough-pine walls. Lunch is a complete meal with a choice of meat or fish for about $10, and that can include lobster. It is brought to the table by a very congenial serving staff. The lower-level bar-cafe, open from 8am to 3am, is a convenient stop for a drink or espresso at the end of a long day.

HEADING EAST & SOUTH

Leaving Percé, Highway 132 quickly bends back to the west. The southern shore of the Gaspé, on the Baie de Chaleur, is distinct from the north, with much more farming and commercial activity, fields of wildflowers, and small houses flanked by the day's wash flapping in the breeze. The mountains disappear over the horizon. The air is warmer here, and more humid.

FROM BONAVENTURE TO NEW RICHMOND

Continue west along Route 132 to Bonaventure (pop. 3,000) and, on the right, you'll see the **Musée Acadien du Québec à Bonaventure (Acadian Museum of Québec at Bonaventure),** 95 av. Port-Royal (☎ 418/534-4000), devoted to Québec's Acadian forebears and to outstanding Acadians of the present day. Its exhibits are sophisticated and well worth a brief look-around. Ask for the text in English. It's open late June to Labor Day daily 9am to 8pm; the rest of the year, weekdays 9am to noon and 1 to 5pm and weekends 1 to 5pm. Admission is $3.50 for adults, $2.50 for students and seniors; families $7.50; children under 6 free.

Almost directly across the street from the museum is an unusual shop, **Les Cuirs Fins de la Mer** (☎ 418/534-3821). The name means Fine Leathers from the Sea, and, indeed, every item—skirts, belts, ties, wallets, bags, and earrings—is made from fish skin.

Farther east, just outside New Richmond (pop. 4,100), is a contrasting museum, which instead examines Québec's British heritage: The **British Heritage Centre,** 351 bd. Perron ouest (☎ and fax 418/392-4487). Union Jacks flutter out front in this otherwise resolutely French region. But as this area was settled in large part by United Empire Loyalists fleeing the American Revolution, it is a historically accurate touch. Twenty buildings from the late 1700s to the early 1900s comprise the museum. Guided tours are available in summer, and the 80 acres and many trails are conducive to strolling. Admission is $4 per person, $3 for seniors and students, $8.00 for families. It's open mid-June to Labor Day only, daily from 9am to 6pm.

CARLETON

After passing through New Richmond, Highway 299 heads north in Gaspésie Provincial Park to the Gîte du Mont-Albert (see above), and then to Ste-Anne-des-Monts on the St. Lawrence shore. Highway 132, though, continues southwestward as far as Matapédia, where it turns north to return to the St. Lawrence at Mont-Joli. Long before Matapédia, but after passing through New Richmond, is Carleton (pop. 2,650), a port and resort town, and a convenient overnight stop.

Where to Stay

Hotel-Motel Baie Bleue. Rte. 132 (C.P. 150), Carleton, PQ, G0C 1J0. ☎ **418/364-3355** or 800/463-9099. Fax 418/364-6165. 95 rms, 3 suites. A/C TV TEL. $90 double; from $100 suite. Extra person $12. Half price for children 2–12. AE, DISC, ER, MC, V.

Rooms are comfortable, if unremarkable, and limited room service is available, hardly standard on the Gaspé. The restaurant serves breakfast and dinner, from a menu that changes daily, and there is an outdoor pool and a tennis court on the premises.

DRIVING ON TO NEW BRUNSWICK

If you're heading south to New Brunswick, you have two options. From Miguasha, not far west of Carleton, there is regular ferry service to Dalhousie, New Brunswick. It costs $12 one-way and can shave half an hour off the trip, especially in summer traffic. Or, you can continue along Route 132 to cross the western end of the Baie de Chaleur at Pointe-à-la-Croix, where a bridge spans the bay to Campbellton, New Brunswick.

There are still things to see before leaving Québec, if a little extra time remains, however. In Pointe-à-la-Croix is an **information center** (☎ 418/788-5670), located in the 1830 Young House (1830). There's a gallery upstairs and restrooms in the modern building adjacent to it.

On Route 132, west of Carleton, is **Miguasha Park** in Nouvelle (☎ 418/794-2475). Fish and plant fossils 370 million years old were discovered in the cliffs here in 1842. Some of the ancient ferns were 100 feet (9m) tall. Because of the fragility of the area and the tendency of past visitors to take a souvenir with them when they leave, access to the fossils themselves is by guided 1 1/2-hour tour only. It's free, and the park is open June through September from 9am to 6pm.

The town of Listuguj is home to the largest Micmac reservation in the Gaspé and of the **Micmac Culture Interpretation Centre,** a private museum in a former monastery that details the way of life of the Micmacs before the Europeans arrived. A boutique sells handicrafts of the Micmacs, Navajos, and other tribes. The center is open daily from 9am to 6pm (☎ 418/788-5034). Admission is $3 for adults, $2 for students and seniors, and $5 for families.

If you continue west on Route 132, you'll soon arrive at the **Battle of Restigouche National Historic Site,** in Pointe-à-la-Croix (☎ 418/788-5676). It commemorates the 1760 aborted attempt by French troops from Bordeaux to get to Québec City and save the area for France. They were aided by the Micmacs and the Acadians, but the British attacked them in a battle that lasted several hours in the estuary of the Restigouche River. The interpretive center displays parts of the actual hull with still-intact contents of one of the three ships that was sunk (by the French themselves) and lay buried in the river until its excavation from 1969 to 1972. The site is open from late June to Labor Day daily from 9am to 5pm. Admission is $3 for adults, $1.50 for students, free for seniors over 65 and children under 6; families, $6.

Ottawa 11

by Marilyn Wood

Formerly the editorial director of Macmillan
Travel, Marilyn Wood is an acclaimed travel
writer and editor, and the author of *Frommer's
London from $55 a Day* and *Marilyn Wood's
Wonderful Weekends*. Once a resident of Toronto,
she has covered the city and all of central Canada
for years.

Ottawa's physical beauty is striking. It sits high atop a bluff above the confluence of the Ottawa, Gatineau, and Rideau rivers, with the gently rolling contours of the Gatineau Hills as a northern backdrop. The Gothic Parliament buildings brood romantically above the city, reminiscent of a Turner painting; the Rideau Canal cuts a vibrant swath through the city, worthy of any Dutch palette in summer or winter; and the daffodils in Rockcliffe Park would have inspired Wordsworth to sing had he seen them.

Ottawa has not yet really been visited by choked downtown streets and that imprisoned feeling that afflicts most cities. You can still see the hills and rivers from downtown. And where else in North America can you see sentries in scarlet and busby changing guard just as they do at Buckingham Palace, skate and boat on a canal reminiscent of Amsterdam, and wonder at the three million tulips that blaze and sway throughout the city in early May?

But Ottawa seemed an unlikely candidate to serve as Canada's capital when it was chosen back in the mid-19th century. The two provinces of Upper Canada (Ontario) and Lower Canada (Québec) were fused into the United Provinces of Canada, but their rivalry was so bitter that the legislature had to meet alternately in Toronto and Montréal. Casting around for an acceptable site for the new capital, Queen Victoria selected the brawling village of Ottawa in 1855, probably hoping that its location, right on the Ontario-Québec border, would resolve French-speaking and English-speaking differences. Her choice was not exactly praised: Essayist Goldwin Smith called it "a sub-Arctic lumber village, converted by royal mandate into a political cockpit," while the American press remarked that it was an excellent choice because any soldiers who tried to capture it would get lost in the woods trying to find it.

Certainly, for nearly a century the city languished in provincialism as dull as its gray-flanneled denizens and developed a reputation for sobriety and propriety. Still, even during its early days it managed to throw up some colorful characters, not the least of whom was Mackenzie King (who conducted World War II with the help of his dog, his deceased mother, and frequent spiritual consultations with former prime minister Sir Wilfrid Laurier), and later Charlotte Whitton, Ottawa's mayor in the '50s and early '60s, about whom

I have this favorite tale. When she met the lord mayor of London, both formally decked out in their chains of office, he bent down and asked permission to smell the rose pinned to her shoulder, saying, "If I smell your rose, will you blush?" To which she replied: "If I pull your chain, will you flush?"

In the 1960s, perhaps because of Canada's newly expressed nationalism, or perhaps because the government wished to create a real capital, Ottawa changed. The National Arts Centre was built (Hull also underwent, and is still undergoing, a massive transformation), ethnic restaurants multiplied, the Byward Market area and other old buildings were renovated, and public parks and recreation areas were created. And the process has continued into the present with new buildings for the National Gallery of Art and the equally fabulous Museum of Civilization. It's a city full of unexpected pleasures—you can ski, fish, and hike through wilderness only 12 minutes away from downtown; watch the dramatic debates and pomp of parliamentary proceedings; and then visit a rustic French inn across the river in Québec.

1 Orientation

GETTING THERE   The airport is located about 20 minutes south of the city. **Air Canada** (☎ 800/776-3000) and **Canadian Airlines International** (☎ 800/426-7000) are the main airlines serving Ottawa. Airport bus service to and from major downtown hotels is operated by **Pars Transport** (☎ 613/523-8880) for a $9 fare.

Driving from New York, take Highway 81 to Canada's 401 east to 16 north. From the west come via Toronto taking Highway 401 East to route 16 north. From Montréal take Highway 17 to Highway 417.

VIA Rail trains arrive at the station at 200 Tremblay Rd., at Boulevard St-Laurent in the southeastern area of the city. From here buses connect to downtown. For VIA Rail information, contact VIA Rail Canada (☎ 613/244-8289 for reservations, or call your local Amtrak office).

Buses arrive at the Central Bus Station at 265 Catherine St., between Kent and Lyon. **Voyageur Colonial** (☎ 613/238-5900) provides service from other Canadian cities and the U.S.

VISITOR INFORMATION   The **Tourist Information Centre** in the National Arts Centre, at 65 Elgin St. (☎ 613/237-5158), is open daily from 9am to 9pm from May 1 to Labor Day, and Monday to Saturday 9am to 5pm (10am to 4pm on Sunday), the rest of the year. Free half-hour parking is available to visitors. Parking stubs must be validated at the center.

The **National Capital Commission's Information Centre,** at 14 Metcalfe St. at Wellington, opposite Parliament Hill (☎ 613/239-5000), also has information on Ottawa and the surrounding area. It's open in winter from 9am to 5pm Monday through Saturday and 10am to 4pm on Sunday, and from 8:30am to 9pm daily during the summer. For current events in the National Capital area, call 613/239-5000. The commission also runs the "Info-tent" on the Parliament Hill lawn, where visitors book free tours of Parliament. It's open in July from 8:30am to 9pm weekdays, 8:30am to 6pm weekends; in August (to Labor Day) 8:30am to 8:30pm weekdays, until 6pm on weekends; and from mid-May to the end of June from 8:30am to 5pm daily.

For information about Hull, contact **Outaouais Tourist Association,** Maison du Tourisme, 103 rue Laurier, Hull, PQ, J8X 3U8 (☎ 819/778-2222), open from 8:30am to 5pm weekdays and 9am to 4pm weekends in winter, from 8:30am to 8pm

Ottawa

Bytown Museum ⑥
Byward Market ⑫
Canadian Museum of Civilization ②
Canadian Museum of Nature ㉓
Canadian War Museum ⑯
Central Experimentation Farm ④
The Currency Museum ⑦
To Dow's Lake ⑪
To Gatineau Park ①
Laurier House ⑪
Major's Hill Park ⑬
National Arts Center ⑧
To National Aviation Museum ⑲
National Gallery of Canada ⑭
To National Museum of
  Science & Technology ㉑
Nepean Point Park ⑮
Ottawa Locks ⑦
Parliament Buildings ⑤
Royual Canadian Mint ⑰
Rideau Falls ⑲
To Rockliffe Park ⑱
Supreme Court of Canada ③
University of Ottawa ⑩
To Vanier ⑳

Monday to Friday, and 9am to 5pm Saturday and Sunday in summer. Canada's **Ottawa Tourism and Convention Authority,** 130 Albert St., Suite 1800, Ottawa, ON, K1B 564 (☎ 613/237-3959), can also help.

CITY LAYOUT   The Ottawa River arches around the city; the compact downtown area, where most major attractions are clustered within walking distance, is located south of the river.

The Rideau Canal, which sweeps past the National Arts Centre, divides the downtown area into two—Centre Town and Lower Town. In **Centre Town** you'll find Parliament Hill, the Supreme Court, and the National Museum of Natural Sciences. In **Lower Town** are the National Gallery of Art, the Byward Market (a vibrant center for restaurants and nightlife), and along Sussex Drive (which follows the Ottawa River's course), the Canadian War Museum, the Royal Canadian Mint, and farther out, the prime minister's residence, diplomat's row, and finally Rockcliffe Park. The area south of the Queensway, west to Bronson and east to the canal, is known as the **Glebe,** containing some interesting restaurants and clubs, on Bank Street from First to Fifth Avenues. North across the river, in Québec, lies **Hull,** reached by the Macdonald-Cartier and Alexandra bridges from the east end of town, and the Portage and Chaudière bridges from the west end. At the end of the Alexandra Bridge stands the curvaceous Museum of Civilization and nearby are some of the city's very best French restaurants and the most lively nightlife action (which continues until 3am). North of Hull stretch the Gatineau Hills and ski country.

Finding your way around can be a little mystifying, since streets have a habit of disappearing and reappearing a few blocks farther on, and some streets change their names several times. For example, the main street starts in the west as Scott Street, changes to Wellington Street as it passes through downtown west in front of the Parliament buildings, changes again to Rideau Street in downtown east, and finally to Montréal Road on the eastern fringes of town. So carry a map. The information office will provide you with a perfectly serviceable one unless you plan to stay for a long time.

Just a few pointers: The main east-west streets going south from the river are Wellington, Laurier, and Somerset; the Rideau Canal demarcates the east from the west; the main north-south streets starting in the west are Bronson, Bank, and Elgin.

GETTING AROUND   The best way to get around is to walk. The only public transportation available is the 130-route bus network operated by the Ottawa-Carleton **Regional Transit Commission (OC Transpo).** Pick up a system map at their office at 294 Albert St. (at Kent), between 8:30am and 5pm weekdays. For daily information about schedules, where to buy tickets, etc., call ☎ 613/741-4390 from 6am to 11pm. Fares change by time of day and by type of route, and are displayed in the front window of each bus. As of 1995, from 6 to 8:30am and 3 to 5:30pm on weekdays green routes numbered 1 to 119 are $2.70; all other routes are $2.10. At other times including weekends all routes are $1.60. Tickets can bought at certain outlets, such as newstands; otherwise you need the exact fare. All routes converge downtown at the Rideau Centre. Bus stops are color coded to indicate the type of route: black for regular routes, red and green for rush-hour routes. Routes start closing down at midnight and there's no service after 1am.

In Hull, buses are operated by the **Société de Transport l'Outaouais** (STO; ☎ 819/770-7900). Transfers between the two systems are obtainable when you pay your fare on the bus.

Car-rental agencies based in Ottawa include **Tilden** (☎ 613/737-7023), **Budget** (☎ 800/527-0700 in the U.S., 800/268-8900 in Canada), and **Thrifty** (☎ 800/367-2277), all with offices at the airport and various downtown locations.

Parking will cost about $3 per half hour, with about a $9 maximum at most local garages. Your best parking bets are the municipal parking lots at 210 Gloucester St., 70 Clarence St., and 21 Daly St.

When driving, remember that Ontario has a **compulsory seat-belt requirement,** and pay careful attention to the city's system of one-way streets. The **Queensway** (Highway 417) cuts right across the city adding to the confusion. The downtown entrance to the highway is at O'Connor Street. Exit the highway at Kent Street for downtown.

Taxis cost $2 when you step in and $1.95 for each mile thereafter plus 10¢ per bag. Call **Blue Line** (☎ 613/238-1111).

AN IMPORTANT NOTE ON PRICES Unless stated otherwise, **the prices cited in this guide are given in Canadian dollars,** which is good news for U.S. travelers because the Canadian dollar is worth about 25% less than the American dollar, but buys nearly as much. As we go to press, $1 Canadian is worth about 75¢ U.S., which means that your $100-a-night hotel room will cost only U.S. $75 (plus tax, which is substantial).

FAST FACTS   Area Code The telephone area code for Ottawa is 613, for Hull 819. When calling from Ottawa to Hull, you don't need to use the area code.

Embassy The U.S. embassy is located at 100 Wellington St. (☎ 613/238-4470). It's open Monday through Friday from 8:30am to 5pm.

Emergencies Call 911 for police, fire, and ambulance.

Liquor The government controls liquor distribution and only sells it at special stores and beer outlets. Check the yellow pages for locations. Liquor stores open 10am to 6pm Monday to Wednesday, and Saturday, until 9pm on Thursday and Friday. Beer outlets open noon to 8pm Monday to Wednesday and Saturday, until 9pm on Thursday and Friday. The legal drinking age is 19.

Post Office The most convenient post office is at 59 Sparks St., at Confederation Square (☎ 613/844-1545), open Monday through Friday from 8am to 6pm.

Taxes In Ontario there's a 7% provincial sales tax (PST) plus the national 8% goods and services tax (GST).

2 Accommodations

Ottawa accommodations do not come cheap. While you can get a double for about $75 at a few moderately priced establishments and apartment hotels downtown, there's no real downtown budget hotel. If it's nightlife and gourmet dining you're after, stay over in Hull or near the Byward Market.

The best deal (and most interesting option) for the budget traveler is the **Ottawa Bed and Breakfast,** an organization that represents about 10 homes, which rent for $55 to $75 double with breakfast. For information, contact Robert Rivoire, 488 Cooper St., Ottawa, ON, K1R 5H9 (☎ 613/563-0161). For more bed-and-breakfast possibilities in the Ottawa area, contact the **Ottawa Tourism and Convention Authority,** 130 Albert St., 18th floor, Ottawa, ON, K1P 5GH (☎ 613/237-5150).

Note: Add 5% hotel tax and 7% GST to the rates quoted here.

DOWNTOWN
VERY EXPENSIVE

✪ **Château Laurier.** 1 Rideau St., Ottawa, ON, K1N 8S7. ☎ **613/241-1414.** Fax 613/786-8031. 449 rms. A/C MINIBAR TV TEL. $180–$200 double. Special packages available. AE, DC, DISC, ER, MC, V. Parking $14.

A granite and sandstone replica of a Loire château, the Château Laurier has attracted royalty and celebrities since its 1912 opening. It's ideally situated at the bottom of Parliament Hill, with many rooms offering views over the Ottawa River to the Gatineaus. The spacious rooms, with high ceilings and original moldings, are decorated with Louis XV–style reproductions. The executive Gold Floor has its own concierge and extras such as complimentary bathrobes and wine and cheese.

Dining/Entertainment: At Wilfrid's, guests enjoy a wonderful view of the Parliament buildings and rub shoulders with the mandarins. The chef uses Canadian ingredients in classic continental-style dishes, priced from $15 to $30. The bistro Rideau One offers Asian, Caribbean, Mediterranean and other selections; prices range from $10 to $20. Zoe's Lounge, an atrium-lit room with soaring columns, stucco, chandeliers, and potted palms is a lovely place for afternoon tea, cocktails, and, on Friday and Saturday, for dancing.

Facilities: Large indoor swimming pool, sauna, steam room, massage salon, and exercise room. Kids' playroom next to pool, plus welcome kit and children's menus in all restaurants.

The Westin Hotel. 11 Colonel By Dr., Ottawa, ON, K1N 9H4. ☎ **613/560-7000.** Fax 613/560-7359. 478 rms. A/C MINIBAR TV TEL. $125–$180 double. AE, CB, DC, ER, MC, V. Parking $8.50 per day.

Located right in downtown Ottawa, the Westin has views from its atrium lobby over the canal and connecting walkways to both the Rideau Centre and the Ottawa Congress Centre. Elegantly furnished rooms have oak furniture, brass lamps, and half-poster beds; 10 are specially equipped for travelers with disabilities.

Dining/Entertainment: The popular dining spot Daly's commands a close-up view onto the canal and serves three meals a day. Hartwells, a bar just off the lobby, is a popular dance spot Monday to Saturday.

Services: Concierge, 24-hour room service, shoeshine, and valet.

Facilities: Health club with indoor pool, squash courts, whirlpool, and saunas.

EXPENSIVE

✪ **The Albert at Bay Suite Hotel.** 435 Albert St. (at Bay), Ottawa, ON, K1R 7X4. ☎ **613/238-8858.** Fax 613/238-1433. 198 suites. A/C TV TEL. $109–$194 one-bedroom unit for two; $148–$230 two-bedroom unit. Weekend rates $89 double. AE, DC, ER, MC, V. Parking $8 per day.

This conveniently located hostelry, originally built as apartments, is one of Ottawa's best buys, especially for triples or quads. All units are suites, the smallest being a one bedroom (with a den off the living room), with a sofa bed; a fully furnished living room that opens onto a terrace; two bathrooms; and a kitchen that's fully equipped for four, with appliances and dishes, plus iron and ironing board. There's ample storage space. Deluxe rooms have microwaves and brass beds. VCRs are available for rent.

Facilities include an exercise room with a whirlpool and a spacious terrace, laundry facilities, daily valet, and a convenience store open 24 hours.

Delta Ottawa 361 Queen St., Ottawa, ON, K1R 7S9. ☎ **613/238-6000** or 800/268-1133. Fax 613/238-2290. 329 rms. A/C MINIBAR TV TEL. $200–$225 double. Weekend packages available. AE, CB, DC, ER, MC, V. Parking $11.50.

The recently renovated Delta now has a brilliant skylit marble lobby complete with a welcoming fire in winter. Rooms are spacious and modern; more than half have balconies and kitchenettes. Facilities include an indoor swimming pool, saunas, an exercise room, a water slide, a children's creative center, and a Nintendo and video room.

The restaurant Perriers, open 7am to 1am, changes moods with the passing day. The Capital Club offers a five-course fixed-price meal featuring continental/American cuisine.

Minto Place Suite Hotel. 433 Laurier Ave. West (at Lyon Street), Ottawa, ON, K1R 7Y1. ☎ 613/232-2200. Fax 613/232-6962. 418 suites. A/C TV TEL. $118–$130 studio suite; $150–$165 one-room suite; $213–$228 two-room suite. Children under 18 stay free in parents' room. Weekend rates available. AE, DC, ER, MC, V. Parking $12.

The Minto Place has more than 400 studio, one- and two-bedroom suites, each very well equipped and attractively furnished. The upper floor units have magnificent views. Each suite's kitchen contains a microwave, electric stove, dishwasher, toaster, coffeemaker, and coffee, tea, milk, and sugar, as well as silverware and pots and pans. The spacious, comfortable living rooms are fully furnished, and have desks, computer-compatible multiline telephones, and dining tables. Bedrooms contain large closets and chests of drawers. Your bathroom will also have a phone and hair dryer, and there's an additional half bath.

Facilities include a 20m lap pool, whirlpool, sauna and well-equipped fitness center. Shops and restaurants are conveniently located at the base of the tower.

MODERATE

Auberge McGee's Inn. 185 Daly Ave., Sandy Hill, Ottawa, ON, K1N 6E8. ☎ 613/237-6089. Fax 613/237-6201. 14 rms (10 with private bath, 4 sharing 2 baths). A/C TV TEL. $60–$70 double with shared bath; $80–$100 double with private bath; $110–$120 deluxe room with Jacuzzi. MC, V. Free parking. From downtown, take Laurier Avenue East and turn left at Nelson Street.

On a quiet street only blocks from the University of Ottawa, this inn occupies a handsome Victorian home with steep dormer roof. Proprietor Anne Schutte has decorated each room distinctively, often with Peruvian touches reflective of her Anglo-Peruvian upbringing. All the queen-size rooms have minibars; some have Jacuzzis. Breakfast is served in an elegant room with a carved cherrywood fireplace and Oriental-style rugs. No smoking.

۞ Cartier House Inn. 46 Cartier St. (at Somerset), Ottawa, ON, K2P 1J3. ☎ 613/236-4667. Fax 613/563-7529. 10 rms. TV TEL. $108–$134 double. Rates include breakfast. AE, DISC, ER, MC, V. Free parking.

Steps away from the canal and a few blocks from the Parliament Buildings, the Cartier House Inn was a Supreme Court judge's residence, a convent, and a senior citizens' home before being converted to an inn. All the rooms in this old Victorian house have modern conveniences, and each is furnished differently with a mixture of authentic antiques and reproductions. Room 204 is particularly attractive, with its bay window, large armoire, and marble-top coffee table. Some rooms are air-conditioned. A good continental breakfast is served. Guests can relax on the couches in front of the marble fireplace in the comfortable lounge or laze in an Adirondack chair on the veranda.

Doral Inn. 486-488 Albert St., Ottawa, ON, K1R 5B5. ☎ 613/230-8055 or 800/263-6725. Fax 613/237-9660. 37 rms. A/C MINIBAR TV TEL. $80 double. Extra person $10. Children under 12 stay free in parents' room. AE, DC, DISC, ER, MC, V. Free parking.

A great choice for the price, the Doral Inn occupies a conveniently located and handsome Victorian brick townhouse. The comfortably furnished rooms have modern brass beds, desk/drawers, and armchairs. On the ground floor, two handsome baywindowed rooms serve as a comfortable lounge/sitting room and a breakfast room. Guests also have use of a nearby pool and health club. The restaurant, the Andrews Cafe, serves continental cuisine at reasonable prices.

🟢 **Lord Elgin.** 100 Elgin St., Ottawa, ON, K1P 5K8. ☎ **613/235-3333** or 800/267-4298. Fax 613/235-3223. 312 rms. A/C TV TEL. $120–$135 double. Extra person $10. Children 18 and under stay free in parents' room. AE, CB, DC, ER, MC. Parking $10 per day.

Only three blocks south of Parliament Hill and across from the National Arts Centre, the Lord Elgin offers good value. Built in 1940, this dignified stone edifice with its green copper roof was named after the eighth earl of Elgin, who was Canada's governor-general. In recent years rooms have been enlarged and the decor lightened throughout with pastels. Many of the tile and faux granite bathrooms have windows that open—a benefit bestowed by the building's age. About half the rooms have fridges.

The lobby bar is comfortably furnished with wingbacks and club chairs; the Connaught dining room is an airy galleria famous among Ottawans for its liver (but don't worry—it serves other fare).

INEXPENSIVE

Between May and the end of August, the University of Ottawa Residences in Stanton Hall offer singles and twins with shared bathroom down the hall for around $43 a night (parking is an extra $9 a day). Rooms are not air-conditioned. Contact **University of Ottawa Residences,** 85 University St., Room 339, Ottawa, ON, K1N 6N5 (☎ 613/562-5771).

🟢 **Gasthaus Switzerland.** 89 Daly Ave., Ottawa, ON, K1N 6E6. ☎ **613/237-0335.** Fax 613/594-3327. 22 rms, 1 Jacuzzi suite. A/C TV TEL. $82–$112 double. Rates include breakfast. AE, DC, ER, MC, V. Free parking.

Located in an old stone building in downtown Ottawa, this bed-and-breakfast has the familiar hallmarks of red gingham and country pine associated with typical rustic Swiss hospitality. There's a comfortable sitting room with cable TV, and guests can use the garden and its barbecue in summer. A hearty breakfast is served. The Gasthaus is at the corner of Cumberland and Daly, across the canal, and near the market area just south of Rideau.

Nicholas Gaol International Hostel. 75 Nicholas St., Ottawa, ON, K1N 7B9. ☎ **613/235-2595.** Fax 613/569-2131. 130 beds. $14 members, $18 nonmembers. MC, V. Parking $5.35 first night, $3.21 subsequent nights.

Formerly the Carleton County Jail (1862–1972), this hostel, conveniently located for the Byward Market and Parliament Hill, is certainly unique. The old chapel is now used as a dining room, and the walls between cells have been removed to create small dorms housing anywhere from four to ten beds per room. Attractive lounges, kitchen, laundry, meals, bike/skate rentals are available. Reservations are recommended from May to September.

YMCA/YWCA. 180 Argyle St. (at O'Connor), Ottawa, ON, K2P 1B7. ☎ **613/237-1320.** Fax 613/788-5095. 264 rms (26 with bath). A/C TEL. $42 single without bath, $48.50 single with bath; $52 double without bath. Children under 12 stay free with adult. MC, V. Parking $2.75.

This exceptional 15-story Y has mainly single rooms with shared washroom facilities, although a few have private bath; some doubles are available. There are TV lounges and laundry facilities, plus the added attractions of an indoor pool, gym, exercise rooms, handball and squash courts, cafeteria, free local phone calls, and residence counselors available 24 hours a day. And, of course, the price is right.

OTTAWA EAST

Carleton University, 4 miles southwest of the city, has 800 to 1,000 summertime single and double accommodations in several residences. Only two buildings are air-conditioned. A snack bar, cafeteria, lounge, and some sports facilities are available. Contact the Tour and Conference Center at **Carleton University,** 1125 Colonel By Dr., Ottawa, ON, K1S 5B6 (☎ 613/788-5609; fax 613/788-3952). Rates are $45 double and include all-you-can-eat breakfast. Parking is $4 (free on weekends).

IN THE GATINEAU HILLS

✪ **The Château Cartier Sheraton.** 1170 Aylmer Rd., Aylmer, PQ, J9H 5E1. ☎ **819/777-1088.** Fax 819/777-7161. 129 rms, 6 suites. A/C TV TEL. $150 double. AE, DC, DISC, ER, MC, V. Free parking.

Across the river, 20 minutes from Ottawa in the Gatineau Hills, the Château Cartier Sheraton provides a resort experience on 152 acres. It's well designed and comfortable throughout, from the welcoming pink-marble lobby to the extralarge Nautilus room overlooking the golf course. The spacious rooms have couches and well-lit desks, plus tile and marble bathrooms equipped with hairdryers. Most rooms are king- or queen-size suites with parlor and bedroom separated by French doors, and two TVs and two telephones. In addition, four suites have fireplaces; two have Jacuzzis.

Dining/Entertainment: The stylish dining room, with French windows that open onto the patio, overlooks the golf course. A lounge with a circular bar, club chairs, and a small dance floor, features a pianist on weekends.

Services: Valet, room service until 10pm.

Facilities: 18-hole golf course, which also provides cross-country skiing in winter; one racquetball and one squash court; two tennis courts. The indoor pool with a wraparound terrace is perfect for catching rays. Health club with Nautilus.

3 Dining

For a real Ottawa tradition, stop at **Hooker's** stand in the center of the Byward Market and purchase a **beaver tail,** a local specialty. Actually, it's a very tasty deep-fried whole-wheat pastry served either with cinnamon, sugar, and lemon, or with garlic butter and cheese, or with raspberry jam. Not only are beaver tails delicious, but they're dirt cheap!

For homemade, delicious ice cream, Ottawans flock to **Lois 'n' Frimas,** 361 Elgin St. (☎ 613/230-7013), a small parlor where you can watch ice cream being made with rock salt and an ice freezer. It tastes darn good! It's open from 11am to 11pm Sunday through Thursday, until midnight on Friday and Saturday.

CENTRE TOWN
MODERATE

Flippers. 823 Bank St. ☎ **613/232-2703.** Reservations accepted only for parties of eight or more. Main courses $12–$16. AE, ER, MC, V. Mon–Fri 11:30am–2pm; daily 5–10pm. SEAFOOD.

Flippers, a cozy jovial fish house where the tables sport checkered tablecloths, is a popular place with Ottawans seeking good value. The raw bar features oysters, little-necks, and other shellfish while the main course specials run to Cajun fish, salmon, and many varieties of seafood.

Le Café. In the National Arts Centre. ☎ **613/594-5127.** Reservations recommended. Main courses $18–$21. AE, DC, ER, MC, V. May–Sept Mon–Sat 11:30am–midnight, Sun 11:30am–8pm; Oct–Apr Mon–Fri noon–midnight, Sat 5pm–midnight. CANADIAN.

The National Arts Centre's Le Café commands a marvelous canal view from its summertime terrace and offers fine food year-round in a relaxing setting. The menu features imaginatively prepared dishes that use prime Canadian ingredients like New Brunswick salmon, Petrie Island mussels, Nova Scotia scallops, venison, and lamb. You might start with the mussels steamed in Okanagan Valley Chenin Blanc with leeks, garlic, and chili peppers, and follow with medallions of fallow deer with fresh honey mushrooms and Newfoundland partridge berries. Among the desserts the Canadian specialty is Newfoundland screech cake (a rum-flavored cake) or maple syrup mousse in a chocolate tartlet.

The Mill. 555 Ottawa River Pkwy. ☎ **613/237-1311.** Reservations required (even at lunch). Main courses $11–$20. AE, ER, MC, V. Mon–Fri 11:30am–2:30pm; Mon–Fri 4:30–11pm, Sat 4:30–11:30pm; Sun 10:30am–10:30pm. CANADIAN.

The Mill offers a delightful setting on the Ottawa River, does a solid job with traditional fare, such as prime rib plus barbecue ribs, stuffed chicken, and surf and turf. Erected in the 1840s, when Ottawa was a lusty, hell-raising lumber town, it now provides a glass-enclosed atrium dining room, and several other dining areas upstairs and down with a magnificent river view.

Ritz Uptown. 226 Nepean St. ☎ **613/238-8752.** Reservations recommended. Pasta courses $6–$9; main courses $10.50–$15. AE, DC, ER, MC, V. Mon–Fri 11:30am–midnight, Sat–Sun 5pm–midnight. ITALIAN.

Located in a town house, the dining room looks like a bistro, with red-checked tablecloths and modern Canadian art. There's a wine bar in the back. You can order a variety of pastas, including gnocchi and linguine, cooked in several ways—pomodoro, Alfredo, etc.—as well as specials such as chicken piccata or beef tenderloin with red wine and mushrooms. Great desserts, all under $5, include Italian trifle and apricot and apple crepe cake.

INEXPENSIVE

Shanghai. 651 Somerset St. West (near Bronson). ☎ **613/233-4001.** Reservations recommended on weekends. Main courses $7.25–$15. AE, MC, V. Mon–Fri 11am–1am, Sat 4pm–1am, Sun 4–10pm. SHANGHAI/SZECHUAN.

Shanghai offers comfort, attractive decor, and some very fine food—Szechuan, Shanghai, and regional—which may be why it's popular with many prominent government figures. Soups include Chinese melon and Chinese greens, followed by such tempting specialties as gee bow guy (breast of chicken rolled around sweet ham, green onions, and almonds, covered with rice paper, and deep-fried in peanut oil), steamed pickerel served with green onions and their own sauce, or mango kiwi chicken. Regular dishes like beef with broccoli (between $7 and $10), round out the menu. Instead of the usual uninspired Chinese desserts, there's a smooth mandarin mousse cake and also lychee cheesecake.

LOWER TOWN

Canal Café. 221 Echo Dr. ☎ **613/238-1296.** Reservations recommended. Main courses $10–$20. AE, ER, MC, V. Sun–Thurs 5–10pm, Fri–Sat 5–11pm. CONTINENTAL/ITALIAN.

All its name implies, the Canal Café sits alongside the Pretoria Bridge, which arches over the canal. The interior is sleek, with glass-brick walls and a black bar. In summer the outdoor patio is popular. The house specialty is mussels, plus such pastas as linguine with clam or pesto, fettucine Alfredo, and spaghetti carbonara. For dessert, any one of the cheesecakes or the tempting chocolate-raspberry torte finish a meal off very nicely.

THE BYWARD MARKET AREA
EXPENSIVE

Le Jardin. 127 York St. ☎ **613/238-1828.** Reservations recommended. Main courses $18–$30. AE, DC, ER, MC, V. Daily 5:30–11pm. FRENCH.

In a handsome Victorian gingerbread house, Le Jardin offers three intimate dining rooms, with fabric-covered walls, rich drapery, antique furnishings, and fresh flowers; there's a Gaspé quilt in one room and a fireplace in another. The restaurant selects the freshest ingredients possible. At dinner hors d'oeuvres might include duck galantine with Madeira jelly, sautéed shrimp with white wine and coconut, or Persian caviar. I like the breast of guinea fowl with Dijon mustard honey and tarragon sauce, or lobster blanquette with morels and vegetables. Among the desserts there's cheesecake with roasted pistachios and raspberry coulis, and—most tempting of all—chocolate terrine with English cream and creme de menthe.

MODERATE

Bistro 115. 110 Murray St. ☎ **613/562-7244.** Reservations recommended. Main courses $14–$18; three-course prix fixe $24.95. AE, ER, MC, V. Daily 11:30am–11:30pm. FRENCH.

This place affects a very French atmosphere with lace tablecloths, floral banquettes, and a trellis-covered dining terrace in the back. The fixed price is a great deal—you'll get something like chicken liver and brandy pâté or shrimp-and-mango salad with yogurt to start, followed by panfried caribou with wild mushroom sauce or grilled tuna with a beurre blanc of red pepper. À la carte choices might include cioppino or filet mignon with Roquefort butter. For dessert there's often a fine white chocolate raspberry tart.

Cafe Spiga. 271 Dalhousie (at the corner of Murray). ☎ **613/241-4381.** Reservations recommended. Pasta $9–$12; main courses $12–$17. AE, MC, V. Mon–Fri 11:30am–3pm; daily 5–11pm. ITALIAN.

There's very little ornamentation at this Italian winner in the market—just mirrors, sparkling white tablecloths, and Italian food ingredients and condiments on display. A variety of pasta is offered, including fusilli with warm pancetta, crushed chiles, olive oil and asiago; and such subtly flavored dishes as orecchiette with shrimp and ginger as well as traditional gnocchi. Typical main courses are breast of chicken with spinach and gorgonzola cream sauce, or rack of lamb with roasted garlic and rosemary sauce.

✪ Clair de Lune. 81B Clarence St. ☎ **613/241-2200.** Reservations recommended. Main courses $11–$19; fixed-price dinner $22. AE, ER, MC, V. Daily 11:30am–2:30pm; Sun–Wed 6–11pm, Thurs–Sat 6pm–midnight. FRENCH.

The market area has an astounding number of restaurants and cafés. One of my special favorites is Clair de Lune, a little gem of a French bistro that serves a reasonable two-course lunch, featuring dishes such as cod grenobloise or rabbit chasseur. At dinner the fixed-price menu will offer three or so appetizers and main course choices, like the grillade of quail or halibut with sun-dried tomatoes, capped off with a dessert like the chocolate tulip with yogurt and brandy. The reasonably priced à la carte menu features about 10 meat, fish, and pasta dishes. Moreover, Clair de Lune is a snappily decorated spot with a handsome glass-block bar, gray decor, and marble-top tables that make for a pleasant dining experience. In summer, the rooftop terrace is the place to sample tapas ranging in price from $2.50 to $6 plus such items as grilled fish and brochettes.

The Courtyard Restaurant. 21 George St. ☎ **613/241-1516.** Reservations recommended. Main courses $15–$21. AE, DC, ER, MC, V. Mon–Sat 11:30am–2pm, Sun 11am–2pm; Mon–Sat 5:30–9:30pm, Sun 5–9pm. CONTINENTAL.

With a distinct air of Old Montréal, the Courtyard Restaurant is set in a gray stone building with a high-ceilinged, stone-walled dining room and an outdoor café with colorful parasols—it's only a dream away from Vieux Montréal. The menu, though, is rather predictable—old standbys such as filet mignon with béarnaise, salmon teriyaki, and veal Oscar. Lunch dishes such as chicken breast with mango are priced from $8 to $10. The Outdoor Café is a popular meeting spot, and Sunday brunch is accompanied by live classical music.

Haveli. 87 George St. ☎ **613/241-1700.** Reservations recommended. Main courses $9–$16. AE, MC, V. Sun–Fri 11:45am–2:15pm; Mon–Sat 5–10pm. INDIAN.

Popular Indian stars like Jagjit and Chitra, Anup Jalota, and Chanchal have all headed upstairs in the Market Mall to dine in this comfortable restaurant. The extensive menu offers a wide selection of vegetarian dishes—aloo gobi, senza jalfraize, Gandhi's delight—and meat and fish preparations. Special dishes include Bhuna shrimp and Bombay bahar scallops in batter, deep-fried with a cream sauce, and of course, items from the tandoor (including the most expensive dish on the menu, lobster tails marinated in Indian spices and broiled in the tandoor). The best deals are the lunch and Sunday buffets; on Sunday South Indian specialties like dhosa are served.

✪ **Sante.** 45 Rideau St. ☎ **613/241-7113.** Reservations recommended. Main courses $14–$18. AE, DC, ER, MC, V. Mon–Sat 11:30am–3pm and 5–10pm. INTERNATIONAL.

Sante specializes in dishes that use healthy fresh ingredients and reflect a multicultural approach to cuisine. The tables are graced with fresh flowers, the walls with works by local artists, and if you're lucky, you'll be seated at a table with armchairs. Start with the delicious callaloo soup, chicken satay, or Bali spring rolls. Follow with a sizzling hot plate like the seafood with basil coconut cream sauce, or with the Thai spicy shrimp stir-fried in tamarind, garlic, lemon grass, and chiles. It's an interesting and innovative menu, with other specialties like almond citrus chicken with snow peas, mushrooms, lime, and sake; Java scallops spiced and sautéed with coconut, tamarind, and cinnamon; or kingfish with a basil, pine nut, and garlic sauce.

INEXPENSIVE

15 Clarence. 15 Clarence St. ☎ **613/562-0705.** Reservations not accepted. Pizzas $8–$11. AE, ER, MC, V. Sun–Thurs 11:30am–11pm, Fri–Sat 11:30am–midnight. Shorter hours in winter. PIZZA/MEDITERRANEAN.

15 Clarence gets rave reviews and draws a large crowd to its two patios (back and front) and its small dining room. The front outdoor patio sports super scarlet-and-gray fringed umbrellas, while the back patio has an awning. The kitchen turns out innovative food—a dozen different individual pizzas (from the wood-burning oven) featuring, for example, smoked salmon, red onion, capers, and dill. Even the calzones are creative, such as the curried lamb with fontina cheese. Salads and daily specials are also available, and so, too, are some divine desserts—apricot and apple crepe cake or chocolate sabayon cake.

Memories. 7 Clarence St. ☎ **613/232-1882.** Reservations not accepted. Sandwiches and light fare $5–$9. AE, MC, V. Mon 11:30am–11pm, Tues–Fri 11:30am–midnight, Sat 10:30am–midnight, Sun 10am–11pm. BISTRO.

Next door to 15 Clarence, Memories is another very attractive and well-frequented cafe that offers a light menu and notable desserts. You can get sandwiches, such as ham and cheese with marinated mushrooms and Dijon mustard on croissant, plus salads, soups, pâtés, and pastas. Saturday and Sunday brunch offers the usual croissants, quiches, and eggs as well as luscious waffles served with your choice of fruit toppings. The tables out front fill up quickly.

IN VANIER

✪ **Il Vagabondo.** 186 Barrette St. ☎ **613/749-4877.** Reservations recommended. Pasta courses around $10; main courses $10–$17. AE, DC, ER, MC, V. Tues–Fri 11am–2:30pm; Mon–Sat 5–11pm, Sun 5–10pm. ITALIAN.

A little off the beaten track across the bridge in Vanier, this Italian bistro in a corner house has a lot going for it. The cozy bilevel dining room has an oak bar, colorful tablecloths, and a tiled floor. A blackboard lists specials—like pollo a basilico or fettucine con erbe—but you'll need to come early to ensure your choice, for they quickly disappear. The à la carte menu includes veal al limone, marsala, or alla Maltese (in butter, white wine, cream, and fresh orange juice), and cannelloni fiorentina with tomato sauce. The veal is of superb quality. While meat portions are large, vegetables are merely a garnish.

OTTAWA SOUTH

This arbitrary designation refers to an area that stretches from Wellington Street to the Queensway, along Bank and Elgin streets in particular. Here you find cafes that carry free literature such as the *Peace Information News,* and a medley of food stores and other neighborhood services and vendors. It's heaven if you're on a budget.

MODERATE

✪ **Le Metro.** 315 Somerset St. West (between Bank and O'Connor). ☎ **613/230-8123.** Reservations strongly recommended. Main courses $12–$18. AE, ER, MC, V. Mon–Fri 11:30am–2:30pm; Mon–Sat 6–10:30pm. FRENCH.

At this romantic Paris bistro in a town house setting, gilded statuary and lavish flower arrangements accent the rooms, silver candelabra set off the tables, and French songs add to the atmosphere. The menu changes daily, reflecting what's really fresh and outstanding at the local markets. You might begin with a shrimp bisque or a pheasant terrine with prunes, and then choose from 10 or so entrées, which might include breast of duck à l'orange, filet mignon béarnaise, or salmon feuilleté with a beurre blanc.

INEXPENSIVE

✪ **Chahaya Malaysia.** 749 Bank St. ☎ **613/237-4304.** Reservations recommended on weekends. Main courses $7–$15. AE, MC, V. Tues–Fri 11:30am–2:30pm; Tues–Sat 5–11pm, Sun 5–10pm. MALAYSIAN.

A simple restaurant, Chahaya Malaysia specializes in the fragrant and sometimes spicy cuisine of Southeast Asia. Start with either some satay or rojak, a sweet hot concoction accompanied by apple, pineapple, cucumber, bean sprouts, and lightly fried bean curd in a spicy sauce. Then follow with a fish or chicken curry, or chili shrimp, and top it all off with kek har heart cake. Batik cloths cover the tables, and there are few artifacts around. If you're asked if you want things spicy, be careful—the chili sauce on the table will take your breath away.

✪ **Savana Cafe.** 431 Gilmour (between Bank and Kent). ☎ **613/233-9159.** Reservations recommended. Main courses $10.50–$16. AE, ER, MC, V. Tues–Fri 11:30am–3pm; Mon–Sat 5–10pm. CARIBBEAN.

The Savana Cafe has caught Ottawans' imaginations with its tropical flavor, brilliantly colored Caribbean art, and spicy cuisine. Start with the fabulous kalaloo (or callaloo) soup made Caribbean style—it's the real thing, with okra, spinach, thyme, Congo peppers, and lime. Among my main course favorites are spicy Thai noodles; tiger prawns with basil, pesto, and wasabi; and escabeche of chicken simmered in raspberry vinegar, ginger, allspice, pimento, and red onion. The chef is always adding new exotic items, like the chicken breast coated in graham crumbs, stuffed with bananas and served with jalapeño salsa. Most dishes can be ordered mild, medium, or hot (go on, ask for the hot). In winter, the fire adds a welcome touch; in summer, so does the patio.

THE GLEBE

The Glebe refers to the southern part of Ottawa, an area stretching from just south of the Queensway to the Rideau Canal and from Bronson Avenue to Rideau.

✪ **Canal Ritz.** 375 Queen Elizabeth Dr. ☎ **613/238-8998.** Reservations recommended. Pizzas and pasta courses $7–$9; fish courses about $12. AE, ER, MC, V. Mon–Sat 11:30am–11pm, Sun 10:30am–11pm. Summer hours extended. INTERNATIONAL.

The Canal Ritz occupies a fabulous old boathouse right on the canal with outdoor dining and an airy two-story interior. The real specialty here is pizza fresh from the wood-burning oven. There's a delightful choice: pears and Brie on braised onions; shrimp, cappicola ham, figs and mozzarella; or pesto, mozzarella, and plum tomato, to name a few. A variety of fettucine, charcoal-grilled fish, and a selection of brochettes are other options. Canal Ritz is also known for desserts—mocha or amaretto cheesecake, or zuccotto (consisting of sponge cake, hazelnut cream, and chocolate mousse iced in white chocolate and glazed in dark). In fact, this is a chocoholic's paradise. Kids' books and coloring pads make it a great place for families, too.

OTTAWA WEST

✪ **Opus Bistro.** 1331 Wellington St. ☎ **613/722-9549.** Reservations required. Main courses $12–$17. MC, V. Tues–Sat 5–11pm. CONTEMPORARY.

A small West End restaurant, the Opus Bistro is worth visiting to savor the finely prepared, continentally inspired food. The one-room restaurant has a clean and simple decor and a small bar up front. The reasonably priced main dishes might include salmon in a spicy Cambodian broth or loin of lamb with black-currant ginger cassis. A pasta and a vegetarian dish are always featured. The menu changes daily—but if the crabcakes en filo are among the appetizers, try them.

✪ **Tete a Tete.** 9 Richmond Rd. ☎ **613/722-6082.** Reservations recommended. Main courses $13–$18. MC, V. Mon–Fri 11:30am–2pm; Mon–Sat 5–10pm. FRENCH/CONTINENTAL.

It's worth coming out here for the quality of Tete a Tete's food and dining experience. It certainly serves some fine dishes, such as breast of chicken stuffed with chèvre and sun-dried tomatoes in roasted pepper coulis; salmon with capers, tarragon, lemon, and cream; and stuffed quail served with orange and green peppercorn sauce. To start, try gravlax with a Pommery dill sauce, deep-fried cantaloupe with prosciutto, or steamed mussels with Gorgonzola, pears, pine nuts, and cream—all winners. Add $7 to the main course price and select any appetizer and dessert.

HULL

✪ **Café Henri Burger.** 69 rue Laurier. ☎ **819/777-5646.** Reservations recommended. Main courses $18–$30; three-course fixed-price lunch $15; four-course fixed-price dinner $40. AE, ER, MC, V. Mon–Fri noon–2:30pm; Mon–Sat 6–10pm. The Terrace open daily in summer noon–11pm. FRENCH.

"Let's go to Burger's" used to be a byword in Ottawa in the early 1920s when Henri Burger, chef at the Château Laurier, founded his restaurant, Café Henri Burger. Although he died in 1936, the name still attracted people to this landmark brick building overlooking the Museum of Civilization and beyond across the river to Parliament Hill.

The cafe continues to excel. The lunch menu still offers a fixed-price meal, plus à la carte dishes priced from $14 to $18. At night, the fixed-price of appetizer, soup, entrée, dessert, and coffee might include striped bass with red pepper coulis. Or you can select from such specialties as paupiettes of Dover sole with red butter sauce, saddle of lamb with ginger-and-curry sauce, and veal loin with onion-and-gewürztraminer sauce. For dessert the classic tarte au citron is a must.

✪ **Le Pied de Cochon.** 248 rue Montcalm. ☎ **819/777-5808.** Reservations recommended. Main courses $14–$17; three-course fixed price $21.50. AE, DC, ER, MC, V. Tues–Fri noon–2pm; Tues–Fri 6–10pm, Sat 6–11pm. FRENCH.

When people need a reliable spot offering classically good cuisine, they head for this unpretentious spot, which you'd pass by if you didn't know it was there. The food is fresh and good and the atmosphere casual. When local Québécois fill this place at lunchtime, it positively radiates joie de vivre. The decor is simple and rustic—stucco walls and burgundy tablecloths—but what really counts is what's served on the limited menu. At lunch there might be three entrée choices: salmon in puff pastry, lamb tarragon, and wild boar with pepper sauce, priced from $10 to $13. At dinner, a similar table d'hôte, priced at $21.50, includes additional entrées like salmon and halibut in two sauces or steak au poivre.

Oncle Tom. 138 rue Wellington. ☎ **819/771-1689.** Reservations required. Main courses $14–$18; add $6 to create a four-course fixed-price meal. AE, DC, ER, MC, V. Mon–Fri noon–2pm; Mon–Fri 5:30–10pm, Sat 6–10pm. FRENCH.

Set in a Victorian house, Oncle Tom is an intimate dining spot decorated with stained glass, art works by local artists, and French provincial chests. Upstairs, you can settle into a cozy little alcove. The cooking is as classic as the decor: lamb with a honey Dijon mustard sauce, grilled chicken breast with a cognac sauce, or Atlantic salmon topped with a shrimp and scallop mousse and served with a white wine sauce; for starters, the duck terrine accompanied by Meaux mustard or the escargots au parfum d'ail are both excellent choices.

TWO NEARBY PLACES TO DINE IN QUÉBEC

L'Echelle de Jacob. 27 bd. Lucerne, Aylmer, Québec. ☎ **819/684-1040.** Reservations required well in advance. Main courses $15–$20; fixed price $25–$28. AE, MC, V. Wed–Mon 6:30–10pm. From Ottawa, drive over the Champlain Bridge and make a sharp left immediately off the bridge. Drive about 2¹/₂ miles (4km) to the first cluster of buildings and pull into the parking lot on the left. From Hull, take boulevard Taché and turn left on Vanier Road and follow the previous instructions. FRENCH.

This delightful restaurant is reminiscent of a French country inn. The upstairs dining room, with only 16 tables, has a warm, rustic air, created by a beamed ceiling, natural stone walls, and candlelight burnishing the oak chairs and china-filled breakfronts. The handwritten menu might contain such appetizers as mushroom charlotte made with oyster mushrooms and served with green peppercorn sauce or a warm duckling salad on a bed of watercress in a raspberry sauce. The house specialty is roast suckling pig, served every Saturday evening. Or you can choose from dishes such as chicken with coriander and hazelnuts, or filet of salmon wrapped in Swiss chard and served with a rich ginger cream sauce. Among the dessert treats is an extraspecial chocolate mousse cake called Jacob's Dream, fresh cheesecakes, parfaits, and crème caramel. The best value is the four-course fixed price.

❂ **L'Oree du Bois.** Chemin Kingsmere, Old Chelsea. ☎ **819/827-0332.** Reservations required. Main courses $14–$18; four-course fixed price $21.75. AE, ER, MC, V. Tues–Sat 5:30–10pm. From Hull, take Autoroute 5 north to Old Chelsea Exit 12. FRENCH.

In the heart of the Gatineau, this traditional French restaurant offers excellent value, especially if you choose the fixed-price menu. This might include a lovage soup, followed by smoked trout or a salad with fresh local goat cheese, and either duckling with apple and cider or braised quails with wild mushrooms. The meal might conclude with an iced maple cake or white cheese mousse with rhubarb.

TWO REAL PUBS OUTSIDE OTTAWA

❂ **The Cheshire Cat.** 2193 Richardson Side Rd., Carp. ☎ **613/831-2183.** Main courses $8–$10. MC, V. Mon–Wed 11:30am–11pm, Thurs–Sat 11:30am–1am, Sun noon–11pm. ENGLISH.

Located in a stone cottage that formerly housed a school, this English-style pub with wood-burning stove and good pub food is as authentic as you're likely to find outside England. A variety of sandwiches are available, plus such main courses as liver and bacon; mixed grill; sausage, eggs, and chips; and shepherd's pie. On summer days the garden is a lovely spot to relax and imagine yourself back in England's green and pleasant land.

❂ **The Swan at Carp.** Falldown Lane, Carp. ☎ **613/839-7926.** Most items $5–$8. AE, MC, V. Mon–Sat 11am–1am, Sun noon–11pm. ENGLISH.

Another corner of England waits here at the Swan, a more Victorian-style English pub, located in a brick house complete with separate public bar as well as lounge bar. It was originally a Presbyterian manse built in 1902. The Dugdale/Nadeau families opened it as a pub in 1987, naming it after a pub they ran in Stoke, England. Since there are no videos or TV, you'll find good conversation, real ale at cellar temperature, Brit-inspired events like the Dambusters Anniversary celebration, and honest pub fare like bangers and mash, Guinness stew, fish and chips, and "afters" like sherry trifle.

4 Attractions

Most of Ottawa's major sights are clustered together downtown, so you can easily walk from one to another—from Parliament Hill to the Byward Market, from the National Gallery to the Museum of Civilization.

   Paul's Boat Lines Ltd., 219 Colonnade Rd., in Nepean (☎ 613/225-6781), operates two cruises: the Ottawa River cruise, which takes you along Embassy Row to Rockcliffe Park and departing from the dock in Hull, east of Alexandra Bridge in Jacques Cartier Park; and the Rideau Canal cruise, which leaves from the docks opposite the Arts Centre and goes down the canal to the Experimental Farm and Carleton University. River cruises, which last 1¹/₂ hours, leave at 11am, and 2, 4, and 7:30pm. The canal trip leaves at 10 and 11:30am, and 1:30, 3, 4:30, 7, and 8:30pm, and takes 1¹/₄ hours. Prices for each trip are adults, $12; seniors, $10; children $6.

   The *Sea Prince II* also cruises daily along the Ottawa River from both Ottawa and Hull docks. Adult fare is $12, students and seniors pay $9, and children under 12, $6. The boat also offers dinner-dance cruises, theme events, and day cruises to Château Montebello. For more information, contact the **Ottawa Riverboat Company,** 30 Murray St., Suite 100 (☎ 613/562-4888).

PARLIAMENT HILL

Standing on a bluff jutting into the Ottawa River, the ✪ **Parliament buildings,** with their high, pitched copper roofs, are truly spectacular. In 1860 Prince Edward, later Edward VII, laid the cornerstone of the Parliament buildings, which were finished in time to host the inaugural session of the first Parliament of the new Dominion of Canada in 1867. If you enter through the south gate you will pass the **Centennial Flame,** lit by Lester Pearson on New Year's Eve 1966–67 to mark the passing of 100 years since this historic event.

The Parliament buildings (especially the Centre Block) represent the heart of Canadian political life, housing the Senate and **House of Commons.** You may attend the House of Commons sessions and observe the 295 elected members debating in the handsome green chamber with its tall stained-glass windows. Parliament is usually in recess from the end of June to early September, and occasionally between September and June including the Easter and Christmas holidays. Otherwise, the House usually sits from 11am to 6:30pm on Monday, 10am to 6:30pm on Tuesday and Thursday, 2pm to 8pm on Wednesday, and 10am to 4pm on Friday. The Senate is housed in an opulent red chamber with murals depicting Canadians fighting in World War I. The 104 notables from all regions of the country are appointed and sit until age 75. They initiate and refine legislation.

The great 302-foot tower rising from the Centre Block—the **Peace Tower**—houses a 53-bell carillon, a huge clock, an observation deck, and the **Memorial Chamber,** which commemorates Canada's war dead, most notably the 66,650 who lost their lives in World War I. Stones from the battlefields are lodged in the chamber's walls and floors. Atop the tower rises a bronze mast, 35 feet high, flying a Canadian flag. When Parliament is in session the tower is lit.

When you go up to the tower, see if you notice anything strange about the elevator. Does it travel vertically as practically every other elevator does? Not quite. For the first 98 feet of your journey it travels on a 10° angle. This special elevator was recently installed; previously you had to take two elevators to reach the observatory.

A fire in 1916 destroyed the original Centre Block; only the **Library** at the rear was saved. A glorious 16-sided dome, supported outside by huge flying buttresses and beautifully paneled inside with Canadian white pine, features a marble statue of the young Queen Victoria and magnificent carvings—gorgons, crests, masks, and hundreds of rosettes. The original floor was an intricate pattern of oak, cherry, walnut, and ash.

The Centre Block is flanked by the **East and West blocks.** The West block, containing parliamentary offices, is closed to the public. But you can go into the East Block, which used to house offices of prime ministers, governors-general, and the Privy Council, to see four historic rooms: the original governor-general's Office, restored to the period of Lord Dufferin (1872–78); the offices of Sir John A. MacDonald and Sir Georges-Etienne Cartier (the principal Fathers of Confederation); and the Privy Council Chamber with anteroom.

Stroll the grounds, dotted with statues honoring such political figures as William Lyon Mackenzie King and Sir Wilfrid Laurier. Behind the Centre Block stretches a promenade with great views of the river. Here, too, you will find the old Centre Block's bell, which crashed to the ground shortly after tolling midnight on the night of the 1916 fire. At the bottom of the cliff behind the Parliament buildings (accessible from the entrance locks on the Rideau Canal), a pleasant path leads along the Ottawa River.

TOURS Free tours of the Centre Block and library are given daily year round, except on Christmas, New Year's Day, and Canada Day (July 1). Although the precise times for tours in English in 1996 were not available at press time, they should be very similar to the 1995 tour times, which were as follows: Labor Day to late May, every 20 and 50 minutes after the hour from 9am to 4:30pm; June to Labor Day, from 9am to 8:30pm and weekends from 9am to 5:30pm. The last tour excludes a visit to the Peace Tower. From Victoria Day to Labor Day you need to make same-day reservations for tours at the Info Tent (east of Centre Block). For more information on tour hours, call ☎ 613/992-4793.

Tours of the East Block historic offices are usually given daily from May to Labor Day and on weekends from September to May. For more information, call 613/947-1941.

Discover the Hill Walking Tours, exploring the events and personalities that shaped the Hill and the nation, are also given daily from the end of June to September 1. Make reservations at the Info Tent.

۞ CHANGING OF THE GUARD From late June to late August a colorful half-hour ceremony is held daily on the Parliament Hill lawn (weather permitting). Two historic regiments—the Governor-General's Foot Guards (red plumes) and the Canadian Grenadier Guards (white plumes)—comprise the Ceremonial Guard. The parade of 125 soldiers in busbies and scarlet jackets (guard, colour party, and band) assembles at Cartier Square Drill Hall (by the canal at Laurier Avenue) at 9:30am and marches up Elgin Street to reach the Hill at 10am. Upon arrival on the Hill, the Ceremonial Guard splits into two groups, one division of the old guard positioned on the west side of the Parliament Hill lawn and two divisions of the new guard, or "duties," on the east side. The ceremony includes the inspection of dress and weapons of both groups to ensure that the new guard is appropriately turned out and to determine if the old guard is still properly regaled and has no deficiencies in the equipment after their tour of duty. The colours are then marched before the troops and are saluted. The guards also compliment each other by presenting arms. Finally the outgoing guard commander gives the key to the guard room to the incoming guard commander, signifying that the guard has been changed.

۞ SOUND & LIGHT SHOW From May through August, Canada's history unfolds in a dazzling half-hour display of sound and light against the dramatic backdrop of the Parliament buildings. Weather permitting, two performances are given per night, one in English, the other in French. There's bleacher seating for the free show. For more information, contact the National Capital Commission at ☎ 613/239-5000. If you can understand what some of those sergeant-majors yell, you're a natural-born soldier.

OTHER TOP ATTRACTIONS

The Byward Market. At the junction of Sussex, Rideau, St. Patrick, and Kind Edward streets. May 1–Nov 1 Mon–Sat 9am–6pm, Sun 10am–6pm; winter daily 10am–6pm.

A colorful traditional farmers' market still sells all kinds of local food and vegetable products. The market building now houses two floors of interesting boutiques displaying a wide variety of wares and crafts. During market season you can enjoy the outdoor cafes and watch life drift by over a cold beer or glass of wine.

Take some time to wander past the stalls, piled high with fresh, shining locally grown produce. Pick up some fruit, some cheese from the International Cheese shop, some desserts from Aux Délices, and take your picnic back down to the canal.

Explore, too, the Sussex courtyards, which extend from George to St. Patrick Streets along Sussex Drive.

Ottawa's Pride & Joy: The Rideau Canal

Built to avoid using the St. Lawrence River (once so vulnerable to American attack) for transporting troops and supplies to Canada's interior, the canal is one of Ottawa's greatest assets. In summer you can walk or cycle along the canal paths, or else canoe or boat your way along before stopping in at the canalside beer garden at the National Arts Centre. In winter it's turned into a glorious skating rink worthy of any Dutch artist's palette as people come and go to work, skating with their briefcases, and families take to the ice with children perched atop their backs or drawn upon sleighs.

Construction of the canal began in 1826, and the 123-mile engineering feat was completed in 1832. Starting in Ottawa, the canal follows the course of the Rideau River to its summit on Upper Rideau Lake, which is connected to Newboro Lake, where the canal descends the Cataraqui River (through a series of lakes controlled by dams) to Kingston. In Ottawa a flight of eight locks carries boats the 80-foot difference between the artificially constructed portion of the canal and the Ottawa River—a sight not to be missed. (You can observe the astounding maneuver between Parliament Hill and the Château Laurier Hotel).

Canadian Museum of Civilization. 100 Laurier St., in Hull. ☎ 819/776-7000. Admission $5 adults, $3.50 seniors and ages 13–17, $3 children 2–12. Free to all Sun 9am–noon. Tickets to CINEPLUS $8 adults, $6 seniors and ages 13–17, $5 children 2–12. May–June and Labor Day–Oct 9 daily 9am–6pm (to 9pm Thurs); July–Labor Day daily 9am–6pm (to 9pm Thurs–Fri); Oct 10–Apr 30 Tues–Sun 9am–5pm (to 9pm Thurs).

Alberta architect Douglas Cardinal designed the museum's spectacular building, which rises from the banks of the Ottawa River as though its curvilinear forms had been sculpted by wind, water, and glacier. The exhibits within tell the history of Canada and its various ethnic peoples, but somehow the exhibits don't live up to the promise of the building itself. The **Grand Hall** is devoted to six Native Canadian tribes of the West Coast, featuring an impressive collection of huge totem poles. Recently installed permanent exhibits include **From Time Immemorial,** which re-creates a West Coast archaeological dig, and the **Children's Museum** invites kids to explore and understand other cultures.

The **CINEPLUS** theater contains an IMAX and an OMNIMAX (dome-shaped) screen that propels the viewer giddily into any film's action.

✪ **National Aviation Museum.** Rockcliffe Airport. ☎ 613/993-2010. Admission $5 adults, $4 seniors and students, $1.75 children 6–15. Free to all Thurs 5–9pm. May 1–Labor Day Fri–Wed 9am–5pm, Thurs 9am–9pm; rest of year Tues–Wed and Fri–Sun 10am–5pm, Thurs 10am–9pm. From Sussex Drive, take Rockcliffe Parkway and exit at the National Aviation Museum.

This collection of more than 115 aircraft is one of the best of its kind in the world. In the main exhibit hall, a "Walkway of Time" traces aviation history from the turn of the century through two world wars to the present. There's a replica of the Silver Dart, which rose from the ice of Baddeck Bay, Nova Scotia, in February 1909, performing the first powered flight in Canada. It flew for nine minutes—not bad, considering it looks as though it were built out of bicycle parts and kites.

✪ **National Gallery of Canada.** 380 Sussex Dr. (at St. Patrick Street). ☎ 613/990-1985. Free admission; fees charged for special exhibits. May 1–Oct 9 daily 10am–6pm (to 8pm Thurs); otherwise Wed–Sun 10am–5pm (to 8pm Thurs). Guided tours given daily at 11am and 2pm. Register at the information desk. Closed major holidays.

The National Gallery, a rose-granite crystal palace, shines as architect Moshe Safdie intended, like a candelabra on a promontory overlooking the Ottawa River and Parliament Hill. A dramatic long glass concourse leads to the Grand Hall commanding glorious views of Parliament Hill. Natural light also fills the galleries, thanks to ingeniously designed shafts with reflective panels.

The museum displays about 800 works from its great collection of Canadian art. Among the highlights are the fabulous Rideau Convent Chapel (1888), a rhapsody of wooden fan vaulting, cast-iron columns, and intricate carving created by architect priest Georges Bouillon; the works of early Québécois artists such as Antoine Plamondon, Joseph Legare, Abbé Jean Guyon, and Frère Luc; works by Paul Kane, Canada's chronicler of the west, or snow scenes by Cornelius Krieghoff; turn-of-the-century talents Homer Watson and Ozias Leduc; Tom Thomson and the Group of Seven; Emily Carr and David Milne; the Montréal Automatistes Paul-Emile Borduas and Jean-Paul Riopelle. The European masters are also represented, and contemporary galleries feature pop art and minimalism, plus later abstract works, both Canadian and American. Facilities include three restaurants, a bookstore, and auditorium.

MORE ATTRACTIONS

The Canadian Museum of Nature. At the corner of Metcalfe and McLeod Sts. ☎ 613/566-4700. Admission $4 adults, $3 students, $2 ages 6–16 and seniors, $12 for families. Half price on Thurs 9:30am–5pm; free 5–8pm. May 1–Labor Day daily 9:30am–5pm (to 8pm Thurs); rest of year daily 10am–5pm (to 8pm Thurs).

Seven permanent exhibit halls trace the history of life on earth from its earliest beginnings 4,200 million years ago. The dinosaur hall and mineral galleries are the museum's most popular highlights. A huge tree of life traces the evolutionary threads of life from 500 million years ago to the present. Kids will enjoy the Discovery Den activity area, and on the third floor, they can trade their "natural" treasures.

National Museum of Science & Technology. 1867 bd. St-Laurent (at Lancaster Road). ☎ 613/991-3044. Admission $6 adults, $5 seniors and students, $2 ages 6–15; $12 family maximum. Free Sept–Apr weekdays 4–5pm. May 1–Labor Day daily 9am–6pm (to 9pm Fri); Sept–Apr Tues–Sun 9am–5pm. Closed Dec 25. Appointments needed to enter the observatory (call 613/991-9219 8am–4pm).

In this interactive museum, you can pull levers to demonstrate physical principles such as viscosity, climb aboard a steam locomotive, observe the heavens in the evening through Canada's largest refracting telescope (appointments necessary), see chicks hatching, and try to walk through the Crazy Kitchen, where everything looks normal but the floor is tilted at a sharp angle.

✪ Royal Canadian Mounted Police Musical Ride. 8900 St. Laurent Blvd. North. ☎ 613/998-0754. At St. Laurent Boulevard North, take Sussex Drive east past Rideau Hall and pick up Rockville Driveway; turn left at Sandridge Road and continue to the corner of St. Laurent.

The famous Musical Ride military pageant was first produced in Regina in 1878. Horses and riders practice at the Canadian Police College and the public is welcome to attend. Check before you go, though, because the ride is often on tour.

The Supreme Court. Wellington Street (at Kent). ☎ 613/995-4330 or 613/995-5361 for tour information.

The lofty Art Deco building houses three courtrooms—one for the Supreme Court, two for the Federal Court. Three sessions are held during the year; the court does not normally sit during July, August, and September. While in session, the court usually hears appeals on Monday, Tuesday, Wednesday, and Thursday from 10:30am to

1pm and 2:30 to 4pm. The first and third Mondays in each month are usually reserved for the hearing of motions for leave to appeal. Thirty-minute tours are given May to September Monday through Friday from 9am to 5pm and on July weekends, with a break between noon and 1pm.

Billings Estate Museum. 2100 Cabot St. ☎ **613/247-4830.** Admission $2 adults, $1.50 seniors, $1 ages 5–17. May 1–Oct 31 Sun–Thurs noon–5pm. Go south on Bank Street, cross the Rideau River at Billings Bridge and take Riverside East; turn right on Pleasant Park and right on Cabot.

At this imposing house, set on eight acres, you can look into the social life of a period spanning from 1828, when pioneer Braddish Billings built the house, to the 1970s, when the home was turned into a museum. Visitors may use the picnic area and stroll the grounds; tea is served on the lawn on Wednesdays and Thursdays from June 1 to Sept 1.

Bytown Museum. 540 Wellington St. (at Commissioner). ☎ **613/234-4570.** Admission $2.50 adults, $1.75 seniors and students, 50¢ children. Free on Sun. Apr to mid-May and mid-Oct to Nov Mon–Fri 10am–4pm. Mid-May to mid-Oct Mon–Sat 10am–5pm, Sun 1–5pm.

Housed in Ottawa's oldest stone building (1827), which served originally as the Commissariat for food and material during building of the Rideau Canal, the museum displays possessions of Lieutenant-Colonel By, the canal's builder, as well as artifacts that reflect the social history of early Bytown/Ottawa. There are three period rooms and some changing exhibits. The museum is located beside the Ottawa Locks, between Parliament Hill and the Château Laurier Hotel.

Canadian War Museum. 330 Sussex Dr. ☎ **819/776-8627.** Admission $2.50 adults, $1.25 seniors, free for children under 16. Free for everyone Thurs 5–8pm. Fri–Wed 9:30am–5pm, Thurs 9:30am–8pm. Closed Christmas Day.

Kids love to clamber over the tanks that are stationed outside the War Museum, and they seem to love almost as much imagining themselves in battle in the life-size replica of a World War I trench. The collection, which traces Canadian military history, contains airplanes, cars (a Mercedes used by Adolf Hitler), guns, mines, uniforms (including that of Canadian air ace Billy Bishop), and military equipment, plus several large displays complete with sound effects showing famous battles such as the Normandy D-day landings.

The Currency Museum. 245 Sparks St. ☎ **613/782-8914.** Admission $2 adults, children 7 and under free. May–Labor Day Mon–Sat 10:30am–5pm, Sun 1–5pm; Sept–Apr Tues–Sat 10:30am–5pm, Sun 1–5pm.

At the Bank of Canada, this museum will set you thinking creatively about money. It houses the world's most complete collection of Canadian notes and coins, and traces the history of money—beads, wampum, and whale teeth—from early China to the modern era.

Laurier House. 335 Laurier Ave. East. ☎ **613/692-2581.** Admission $2.25 adults, $1.75 seniors, $1.25 ages 6–16. Oct–Mar Tues–Sat 10am–5pm, Sun 2–5pm; Apr–Sept Tues–Sat 9am–5pm, Sun 2–5pm.

This mansion is crammed with mementos of the two Canadian prime ministers who lived here: from 1897 to 1919, Sir Wilfrid Laurier, Canada's seventh prime minister (and first French-Canadian PM); from 1923 to 1950, Mackenzie King, prime minister for 21 years. In the library where King held seances is the crystal ball that King supposedly had seen and coveted in London but said he couldn't afford (an American bought it for him when he overheard King's remarks). You'll also see the portrait of his mother in front of which he used to place a red rose daily, and also a copy of the program Abraham Lincoln held the night of his assassination, plus copies of Lincoln's death mask (completed four years before his death) and hands. Lester B. Pearson's library has also been re-created, and contains the Nobel Peace Prize medal he won for his role in the 1956 Arab-Israeli dispute.

Royal Canadian Mint. 320 Sussex Dr. ☎ **613/993-8990.** May–Aug tours Mon–Fri at 15-minute intervals 8:30am–5pm weekdays, noon–5pm weekends.

From an elevated walkway you can watch gold and silver being transformed into special commemorative coins, medals, and investment tokens. Built as a branch of the Royal Mint in London, this mint struck its first coin in 1908. In 1931 it became an independent operation, but since 1976 circulating coinage has been made in Winnipeg.

PARKS & GARDENS

Ottawa has numerous parks, but the biggest and most attractive isn't a park at all—it's the **Central Experimental Farm,** at the Driveway and Prince of Wales Dr. (☎ 613/991-3044)—1,200 acres of green open space, now completely surrounded by Ottawa suburbia. Its famous greenhouses hold a spectacular chrysanthemum show every November. The farm itself has livestock barns housing cows, pigs, sheep and horses, which the kids'll love. There's also an ornamental flower garden and an arboretum with 2,000 different varieties of trees and shrubs. From May to early October, visitors can ride in wagons drawn by Clydesdales, weather permitting, from 10 to 11:30am and 2 to 3:30pm Monday through Friday. In winter there are sleigh rides. Admission is $3 for adults, $2 students, seniors and children ages 3 to 15. The agricultural museum, barns and tropical greenhouse are open daily March to November 8am to 5pm. From December to February, except Christmas and New Year's days, the barns and tropical greenhouse are open daily 10am to 4pm.

✪ **Gatineau Park.** To get to the park you can take several routes: cross over to Hull and take boulevard Taché (Route 148) to the Gatineau Parkway, which leads to Kingsmere, Camp Fortune (a ski resort), and eventually to Meech Lake. Or come up Highway 5 north, take Exit 12 for Old Chelsea, turn left and proceed ³/₄ mile (1.2km) on Meech Lake Road to the Gatineau Park Visitor Centre. To reach Lac Philippe take Highway 105 north out of Hull up to Wakefield. Beyond Wakefield, take Route 366 west. Just before you reach Ste-Cecile-de-Masham you can turn off to Lac Philippe; to reach Lac la Pêche, keep going along the Masham road to St-Louis-de-Masham and enter the park just beyond.

Only 2 miles, about a 10-minute drive, from the House of Parliament lie 88,000 acres of woodland and lakes named after notary-turned-explorer Nicolas Gatineau of Trois-Rivières. The park was inaugurated in 1938, when the federal government purchased land in the Gatineau Hills to stop forest destruction. Black bear, timber wolf, otter, marten, and raccoon are regular residents; they're joined by white-tailed deer, beaver, and more than 100 species of birds. If you're lucky you might spy a lynx, or a wolverine.

Park facilities include 90 miles of **hiking trails** and supervised **swimming beaches** at Meech Lake, Lac Philippe, and Lac la Pêche. Vehicle access fees to beach areas are $6. Boats can be rented at Lac Philippe and Lac la Pêche. Motorboats are not permitted on park lakes except on Lac la Pêche, where motors up to 10 horsepower may be used for **fishing.** Most lakes can be fished (if it's not allowed, it's posted). A Québec license is required and can be obtained at many convenience stores around the park.

Camping facilities are at or near Lac Philippe, accessible by Highways 5, 105, and 366. For information on this and other camping facilities, call the Gatineau Park

Visitor Centre, 318 Meech Lake Road, Old Chelsea, PQ, J0X 1N0 (☎ 819/
827-2020), or write the National Capital Commission, 40 Elgin St., Suite 202,
Ottawa, ON, K1P 1C7. Reservations are vital. Call 819/456-3016 after June 1 between 9am and 4pm. Fees are $18 per site per day ($10 for seniors).

In winter hiking trails become cross-country ski trails, marked by numbers on blue
plaques with chalets along the way. Winter camping is available at Lac Philippe.

While you're in the park, visit the summer retreat of Mackenzie King at
Kingsmere. You can have tea in a summer cottage there and inspect the architectural
fragments he dragged here from the parliamentary building after the 1916 fire and
from London's House of Commons after the 1941 Blitz. The Moorside tearoom is
open only in summer from noon to 5pm. For reservations call 819/827-3405.

ESPECIALLY FOR KIDS

Kids love the bands, rifles, and uniforms they see on Parliament Hill at the **Changing of the Guard.** The **National Aviation Museum** is a fantasyland for that budding pilot. The perennial favorites at the **Canadian Museum of Nature** are the
dinosaurs, the animals, and the Discovery Den, which was specially created for
children. Extra-special attractions at the **Canadian Museum of Civilization** are the
Children's Museum and Cineplus for action movies. Kids enjoy petting the animals
at the agriculture museum as well as picnicking or taking a hayride at the **Central
Experimental Farm.** At the **National Museum of Science and Technology,** the
hands-on exhibits will keep them entertained while they learn. And they'll love watching the horses and riders in the Musical Ride practice their moves at the **Canadian
Police College.** All of these attractions are described in detail elsewhere in the
chapter.

When it's time to let off some steam, there's **canoeing** or **boating** at Dow's Lake;
biking along the canal or **ice skating** on it; plus activities outside the city in Gatineau
Park.

Outside Ottawa, you'll find a few more places fun for kids. **Storyland,** RR no. 5,
Renfrew (☎ 613/432-5275), off Highway 17 near Renfrew, has a puppet theater,
pedal boats, minigolf, and more. Admission is $8 adults and seniors, $7 children 5
to 15, $5 children 2 to 4. It's open daily in summer from 10am to 6pm. Another
nearby family amusement park, **Logos Land Resort,** RR no. 1, Cobden (☎ 613/
646-2313), has five waterslides, minigolf, pedal boats, and sleigh rides and cross-
country skiing in winter. Admission is $12, and it's open 10am to 7pm daily.

A SCENIC DRIVE ALONG THE OTTAWA
RIVER PARKWAY & SUSSEX DRIVE

A very picturesque and interesting drive, the **Ottawa River Parkway** starts in the west
end at Carling Avenue and runs along the river into Wellington Street, all the way
offering glorious views over the islands in the river.

From Confederation Square, proceed along Sussex Drive to St. Patrick Street,
where you can turn left into **Nepean Point Park.** Here, you and the statue of Samuel
de Champlain can share a beautiful river view.

Across the road is **Major's Hill Park,** between the Château Laurier and the
National Gallery, where the noonday gun is fired (at 10am on Sunday to avoid
disturbing church services). You can watch the lighting of the cannon.

Just beyond the Macdonald-Cartier Bridge stands **Earnscliffe,** originally the home
of Sir John A. Macdonald and now the impressive residence of the British high
commissioner.

Farther along Sussex Drive you cross the Rideau River, whence you can look down upon the modern Ottawa City Hall pat in the middle of Green Island overlooking Rideau Falls, before proceeding past the prime minister's house, well sheltered by trees at 24 Sussex Dr., and on to **Government House,** at no. 1, still often referred to as Rideau Hall, the governor-general's residence. On the 88-acre grounds is a red oak tree planted by President Kennedy and a sapling planted by President Nixon (which local wags note has grown rather crooked). For tours of the grounds and the interior public rooms, call ☎ 613/998-7113 or 613/998-7114.

The drive then becomes the National Capital Commission Driveway, a beautiful route along the Ottawa River and through **Rockcliffe Park.** Where the road forks in the park, follow the right fork to Acacia Avenue to reach the **Rockeries,** where carpets of daffodils and narcissus in April herald spring.

5 Special Events & Festivals

Ottawa's biggest event is the **Canadian Tulip Festival** in May, when the city is ablaze with 200 varieties of tulips stretching around public buildings, monuments, embassies, and private homes, and along driveways. (Probably the best viewing is at Dow's Lake.) The festival began in 1945, when the people of the Netherlands sent 100,000 tulip bulbs to Canada in appreciation of the role Canadian troops played in liberating Holland. Queen Juliana of the Netherlands, who had spent the war years during the occupation in Canada, arranged for an annual presentation of bulbs to celebrate the birth of her daughter, Princess Margriet, in Ottawa in 1943 (to ensure that the princess was born a citizen of the Netherlands, the Canadian government proclaimed her room in the Ottawa Civic Hospital part of Holland).

Now the festival has a flurry of spectacular events, including fireworks, concerts, parades, and flotilla on the canal, accompany the medley of floral sculptures, floral tapestries, and garden displays. For festival information, contact the Canadian Tulip Festival (☎ 613/567-5757).

In early June the National Museum of Natural Science holds a **Children's Festival,** an extravaganza of dance, mime, puppetry, and music, all for the kids.

Late June brings **Le Franco,** a five-day celebration of French-speaking Canada, featuring classical and other musical concerts, fashion shows, street performers, games and competitions, crafts, and of course, French cuisine. For information contact Le Franco (☎ 613/741-1225).

On July 1, Canadians flock to the city to celebrate **Canada Day,** a huge birthday party complete with all kinds of entertainment, including fireworks. For ten days in mid-July the city is filled with the sound of jazz at the **Ottawa International Jazz Festival.** Local, national, and international artists give more than 125 performances at more than 20 venues. For information call ☎ 613/594-3580.

On Labor day weekend, 150 brilliantly colored balloons fill the skies over Ottawa, while below on the ground people flock to musical events and midway rides during the **Gatineau Hot Air Balloon Festival.** For information contact 144 Boulevard de l'Hopital (☎ 819/243-2330).

When the ice hog breaks through the ice of the Rideau Canal, it's time for **Winterlude,** a snow and ice extravaganza that features parades, bands, floats, fireworks, speed-skating, snowshoe races, ice boating, curling, and more. One quite colorful event is the bed race on the canal, while the most exciting event may be the harness racing on ice. The carnival usually takes place the first or second week in February. For information, call ☎ 613/239-5000.

Other major events include the National Capital Air Show in June; the National Capital Dragon Boat Race Festival in July; and the 10-day **Super-Ex (Central Canada Exhibition)** (☎ 613/237-7222), in mid- to late August.

For additional information on any event listed here contact the Convention and Tourist Bureau, 130 Albert St. (☎ 613/237-3959).

6 Outdoor Activities & Spectator Sports

OUTDOOR ACTIVITIES

BIKING   More than 100 miles of bike paths run along the Ottawa and Rideau rivers, the Rideau Canal, and in Gatineau Park, and more miles are being added. A blue, black, and white cyclist logo marks all bikeways.

From April to Canadian Thanksgiving you can rent bikes from **Rent a Bike,** 1 Rideau St. in the parking lot behind the Château Laurier Hotel (☎ 613/ 241-4140). Town bikes, sport bikes, mountain bikes, and in-line skates are all available, from $25 a day (24 hours). The company will also provide maps of the best day trips around the city for you to follow on your own.

Bikes can also be rented at **Dow's Lake Marina** (☎ 613/232-5278).

BOATING/CANOEING   You can rent boats on the Rideau Canal at the following locations. **Hog's Back Marina,** on Hog's Back Road between Riverside Drive and Highway 16 (☎ 613/736-9893), rents canoes for $8 per hour or $30 a day.

At **Dow's Lake Pavilion,** 1001 Queen Elizabeth Dr. (☎ 613/232-1001), you can rent bikes, in-line skates, paddleboats, and canoes ($11 an hour) at the marina (☎ 613/232-5278), and also relax and dine at several restaurants. The $3 million glass-and-steel complex, which from a distance looks like a cluster of sails, makes a great haven after a winter skate or a summer running or biking jaunt.

Boats can also be rented in Gatineau Park at La Peche and Lac Philippe (☎ 819/ 827-2020).

GOLF   The **Château Cartier Sheraton** in Quebec has a golf course on the premises. Other fine courses in Ottawa include the **Edelweiss Golf and Country Club** (☎ 819/459-2104); **Canadian Golf and Country Club** (☎ 613/780-3565); **Le Club de Golf Mont Cascades** (☎ 819/459-2104); and **Manderley on the Green** (☎ 613/489-2092). There's also an excellent course at Renfrew, some distance from Ottawa.

HIKING & NATURE WALKS   A band of protected wetlands and woodlands surround the capital on the Ontario side of the Ottawa River and here visitors can find ideal hiking areas. At **Stony Swamp Conservation Area** in the region's west end, there are 24 miles of trails including the Old Quarry Trail, the Jack Pine Nature trail, and the Sasparilla Trail. Call ☎ 613/239-5000 for information. It's also good for cross-country skiing and snow shoeing. Regional maps are available from Canada's Capital Information centre, 14 Metcalfe Street.

Gatineau Park has a network of hiking trails, some that are long enough for a genuine day hike. Call the visitor center for information (☎ 819/827-2020). West of the city in Kanata, **Riverfront Park** has nature trails along the Ottawa River. Call ☎ 613/592-4281. On the Québec side in Luskville, a trail leads to Luskville Falls from the Chemin de Hotel de Ville. The **Rideau Trail,** which runs from Ottawa to Kingston, is the area's major "serious" hiking trail. Call the Trail Association at ☎ 613/567-2229 for maps and information.

HORSEBACK RIDING   Near Edelweiss Valley, **Captiva Farm,** RR no. 2, Wakefield (☎ 819/459-2769) offers trail rides year-round on 12.8 miles (20km) of trails through the Gatineau Hills. Hourly charges are $22 for adults, $10 for children (each additional hour is $11) and riders can go with or without a guide. Reservations are required.

About 25 miles west of the city **Pinto Valley Ranch,** Fitzroy Harbour (☎ 613/623-3439) offers trail rides for $16 an hour and pony riding plus a petting zoo for the kids.

ICE SKATING/IN-LINE SKATING   During the winter the **Rideau Canal** is flooded to a three-foot depth, becoming the world's longest and most romantic skating rink—it stretches 6 miles from the National Arts Centre to Dow's Lake and Carleton University. (Every morning the radio news reports ice conditions.) Skates can be rented at three places: at Dow's Lake, opposite the NAC, and at Fifth Avenue (about $12 for two hours). The canal is fully serviced with heated huts, sleigh rentals, boot check and skate-sharpening services, food concessions, and rest rooms. The season usually runs from late December to late February. For indoor skating arenas call ☎ 613/564-1181.

In-line skates are available at the Rent a Bike facility behind the Château Laurier and also from Dows Lake marina.

SKIING   Few out-of-town visitors ski the areas around Ottawa, heading instead for Québec's more sophisticated resorts. In many ways, the following ski resorts are more compelling summer tourist attractions with their water parks and other fun facilities.

Mont Cascades, just 30 minutes north of Ottawa across the Gatineau River outside of Cantley on Highway 307 (☎ 819/827-0301), has 12 trails, one triple- and two double-chair lifts and two T-bars. The longest run is 2,200 feet. There are two day lodges with cafeteria and restaurant-bar at the hill. Night skiing is available. During the summer you can enjoy coming down six thrilling waterslides and spend the whole day cooling off in the state-of-the-art water park.

Eighteen miles from the city, **Edelweiss Valley,** Route 366, Wakefield (☎ 819/459-2328), has 24 runs, four lifts (including three double-chairs and one quad), ski school, night skiing, and a warm cozy lodge, plus overnight accommodations. You can also ice-skate and take sleigh rides. Lift rates for adults are $14 for two hours, $28 for eight hours. Tennis, golf, and a water slide are summer attractions.

Mont Ste-Marie, 55 miles north of Ottawa at Lac Ste-Marie (☎ 819/467-5200), is the area's most complete year-round resort. Winter activities include skiing on twin peaks, with a 1,250-foot drop, and a 2-mile ski run. There are two quads and a Poma. Other facilities include cross-country skiing, skating, and tobogganing. Lift rates are $22 weekdays, $32 weekends for adults. Summer facilities include four tennis courts, an 18-hole golf course, private lakes where you can swim and canoe, a stocked trout lake, and of course miles of hiking trails through the mountains.

Gatineau Park, with 115 miles (185km) of groom trails, offers the best **cross-country skiing.** In town you can also ski along the bike paths that parallel the Eastern or Western Parkways.

SWIMMING   For municipal pool information call ☎ 613/564-1023. Other pools open to the public include those at the universities and the YMCA (see "Health and Fitness Clubs," below). You can also swim in the Gatineau Park lakes: Meech, Lac la Peche, and Lac Philippe.

WHITE-WATER RAFTING   While you're in Ottawa, you can enjoy the thrills and spills of white-water rafting, from May to September, depending on the river.

Equinox Tours, 5334 Yonge St. no. 609, Toronto (☎ 416/222-2223), has a base camp on the Ottawa river and offers one- and two-day white-water rafting trips on the Ottawa, Magnetawan, and Madawaska rivers, plus instruction in canoeing and kayaking. They also operate sea-kayaking trips along the Bruce Peninsula and canoeing trips in Algonquin Provincial Park (see Chapter 15). Prices start at $70 per person per day during the week.

Other companies operating similar trips and facilities include: **River Run,** Beachburg, Ontario (☎ 613/646-2501 or 800/267-8504); **Esprit Rafting Adventures,** Pembroke, Ontario (☎ 819/683-3241); **OWL Rafting,** Forester's Falls, Ontario (☎ 613/646-2263 in summer, 613/238 7238 in winter; and **Wilderness Tours,** Beachburg, Ontario (☎ 613/646-2291).

SPECTATOR SPORTS

The **Ottawa Lynx** (☎ 613/747-5969), the Triple A affiliate of the Montreal Expos, play baseball at Ottawa Stadium, 300 Coventry Rd. For tickets, which are generally available, call ☎ 613/749-9947. The **Ottawa Rough Riders** play football at the Frank Clair Stadium (☎ 613/563-4551) from midsummer to late fall. The **Ottawa Senators** (☎ 613/721-4300) are in their third season (they won a string of Stanley Cups earlier in this century, though) and currently play at the Civic Centre at Lansdowne Park, but will move to the Palladium, a brand-new facility in 1996. Call TicketMaster (☎ 613/755-1111) for tickets to the Rough Riders and the Senators.

7 Ottawa After Dark

Ottawa's culture and nightlife pickings are somewhat meager, really only extending to the National Arts Centre, several bars, the Byward Market area, and one or two dance clubs, the raciest of which are concentrated across the river in Hull. For entertainment information, call **Chez Nightlife** (☎ 613/562-1111) for taped information, and secure any of the following: *Where,* a free guide usually provided in your hotel; *Ottawa* magazine; or the Friday edition of the *Ottawa Citizen.*

THE PERFORMING ARTS

Besides the ensemble at the National Arts Centre, the **Ottawa Little Theatre,** 400 King Edward Ave. (☎ 613/233-8948), offers good productions of such popular shows as *Lettice and Lovage* by Peter Shaffer and *The Sisters Rosensweig* by Wendy Wasserstein. The company started in 1913 in an old church that burned down in 1970, but it now has a fully equipped, modern theater. Tickets are $10. The **Great Canadian Theatre Company,** 910 Gladstone Ave. (☎ 613/236-5192), specializes in Canadian contemporary drama and comedy.

The National Arts Centre. 53 Elgin St. (at Confederation Square). ☎ **613/996-5051.** For reservations, call TicketMaster (☎ 613/755-1111) or visit the NAC box office Mon and Thurs 10am–9pm; Tues– Wed and Fri–Sat noon–9pm; Sun and holidays when performances are scheduled noon–curtain time. Guided tours available.

Canadian and international musical, dance, and theater artists—including the resident National Arts Centre (NAC) Orchestra—perform at this marvelous center, three interlocking hexagons with terraces and spectacular views of the Canal and Ottawa created by architect Fred Lebensold. There are four auditoriums: the European-style **Opera,** seating 2,300; the 950-seat **Theatre,** with its innovative apron stage; the 350-seat **Studio,** suitable for experimental works; and the pocket theater **Atelier,** seating 85.

The **National Arts Centre Orchestra** (☎ 613/996-5051), performs five main concert series. The center also offers classic and modern drama in English and French.

A free monthly *Calendar of NAC Events* is available from the NAC Marketing and Communications Department, Box 1534, Station B, Ottawa, ON, K1P 5W1. For information call ☎ 613/996-5051. See Section 3, "Dining," for the center's canal-side Le Café.

THE CLUB & MUSIC SCENE
FOLK, ROCK & JAZZ

As the guy who runs the place puts it, "everyone from politicians to truck drivers" crams into **Patty's Place Pub,** 1070 Bank St. (☎ 613/739-8142), to raise a jug or two, tuck into some real fish-and-chips or Irish stew, and listen to the stirring Irish ballads rendered by a folksinger (resident Thursday through Saturday). Small, it's the kind of place where you're tossed into the fray and wind up having a good old time playing darts, chatting, singing, and wassailing.

For a more rollicking scene, try **Molly McGuire's,** 130 George St. (☎ 613/241-1972), a cavernous pub where, on weekends only, the rock-and-roll and jazz bands belt out their sounds. For local and national acoustic folk talent in a relaxed atmosphere, try **Rasputin's,** 696 Bronson Ave. (☎ 613/230-5102). The **Club Penguin,** 292 Elgin St. (☎ 613/233-0057), offers live Top 40 sounds in the tavern on Wednesday nights.

For jazz, call the **Jazz Ottawa Jazzline** at ☎ 613/829-5426. On Saturdays there's jazz from 4 to 7pm at **Hartwells** in the Westin. **Vineyards,** 54 York St., in the market (☎ 613/563-4270), features a duo on Wednesday nights.

Mainly blues action can be found upstairs at the **Rainbow Bistro,** 76 Murray St. (☎ 613/243-5123), with a special Sunday jam from 3 to 6pm and 9:30pm to 1am. A Sunday jam starting at 2pm also happens at **Piccolo Grande,** 55 Murray St. (☎ 613/241-2909). Also check out what's playing on Thursday to Saturday nights at **Sammy's Cellar** (☎ 613/232-0202) and also at the **Take Five Jazz Cafe,** 412 Dalhousie (☎ 613/562-8335).

DANCE CLUBS

Nightlife closes down at 1am (11pm on Sunday) in Ottawa, but across the river in Hull it continues until 3am every night of the week. The hottest discos/dance bars are found there, but note that the strip where most clubs are located has recently developed a reputation for late-night fights and muggings.

IN HULL   The current fashionable crowd pleaser is **Hotel Chez Henri,** 179 Promenade du Portage (☎ 819/595-5979 or 771-0396), which houses a multilevel disco-bar. Admission is $5 on Friday and Saturday, and it's open Wednesday through Sunday from 9pm to 3am.

Tucked away behind Citi Club is the dance bar **Le Bop** (☎ 819/777-3700) and farther along the street, you'll find **Ozone,** 117 Promenade du Portage (☎ 819/771-6677), where the decor will transport you to Hawaii for the hula shuffle. It attracts a young crowd with its new rock sound, and is open daily until 3am. **Shalimar,** 84 Promenade du Portage (☎ 819/770-7486), is a disco-pub.

IN OTTAWA   **Hartwells,** in the Westin (☎ 613/560-7000), 11 Colonel By Dr., attracts an over-25 crowd for dancing to DJ tunes Monday through Saturday (cover charged). On Saturday nights there's dancing in **Zoe's** piano bar in the Château Laurier, 1 Rideau St. (☎ 613/241-1414).

THE BAR SCENE

In the Byward Market area, **Vineyards,** 54 York St. (☎ 613/241-4270), is one of the city's coziest hangouts, with its downstairs cellarlike atmosphere, stone floors, and red checked tablecloths. Five different house wines are featured (from $5 a glass) plus more than 150 different varieties. There's live jazz on Sunday and Wednesday nights. Snacks are available too. It's open Monday through Saturday from 4pm to 1am. Also popular is **Tramps,** on William Street.

For quiet drinking with a piano background, **Friday's Victorian Music Parlour,** 150 Elgin St. (☎ 613/237-5353), with its clubby atmosphere, old London engravings, and comfortable wingbacks, plus an inviting fire in winter, is a good choice, especially for single women who just want to have a quiet, dignified drink. The pianist entertains nightly. A similar parlor upstairs at the **Full House Restaurant,** 337 Somerset St. West (☎ 613/238-6734), provides piano entertainment and a jolly atmosphere Monday to Saturday nights.

For a truly relaxing ambience, where you sink into plush upholstery and enjoy the lilting piano strains, go to the **Delta Ottawa Hotel's lobby bar,** 361 Queen St. (☎ 613/238-6000); **Zoe's,** at the Château Laurier, 1 Rideau St. (☎ 613/232-6411); or **The Lounge,** at the Westin Hotel, 11 Colonel By Dr. (☎ 613/650-7000).

For pub-style conviviality, check out the **Brigadier's Pump,** in the Byward Market area at 23 York St. (☎ 613/562-6666), and the **Elephant and Castle,** at 50 Rideau St. (☎ 613/234-5544). At **Maxwell's,** at 340 Elgin St. (☎ 613/232-5842), an attractive contemporary-style bar, you can stop in and meet people.

For some real down-home Québécois fun and atmosphere, visit **Les Raftsmen,** 60 rue St-Raymond, Hull (☎ 819/777-0924), a large tavern (brasserie) decked out in log-cabin style with cart wheels for decoration. At lunch or dinner you'll find plenty of joie de vivre and reasonably priced traditional French Canadian cuisine—tourtière and pigs' feet as well as spaghetti, sandwiches, burgers, chicken, steak, and fish—all under $13 (most under $6 or $7). Dinner is served until 9pm, but the place is open Monday through Saturday from 7am to 3am. There's entertainment every night.

MORE ENTERTAINMENT

FILM The **ByTowne Cinema,** 325 Rideau St., shows alternative foreign and independent films. For a complete bimonthly calendar, call ☎ 613/789-4600. The **Canadian Film Institute,** 2 Daly St. (☎ 613/232-6727), offers regular programs of Canadian and international art films. Screenings take place every Saturday and Sunday at the National Archives Auditorium at 395 Wellington St.

SON ET LUMIERE In summer don't miss the evening spectacular on Parliament Hill—a sound-and-light show relating Canadian history and culture. There are two shows nightly (one in French and one in English), and admission is free. English performances are given first on Monday, Wednesday, Thursday, and Saturday at 9:30pm May through July, and at 9pm in August and September (9:30 and 10pm on other nights).

12 Toronto

by Marilyn Wood

Once lampooned as a dull and ugly city, Toronto, now with a population of more than three million, has burst forth from its stodgy past and grabbed attention as one of North America's most exciting cities.

How did it happen? Unlike most cities, Toronto got a second chance to change its image with a substantial blood transfusion from other cultures. A post–World War II influx of large numbers of Italians, Chinese, and Portuguese, plus Germans, Jews, Hungarians, Greeks, Indians, West Indians, Vietnamese, Thais, and French Canadians infused this once quiet conservative community with new energy. Now Toronto vibrates with street cafes, restaurants, cabarets, boutiques, theater, music, and life.

The city continues to grow rapidly and has blossomed with major developments—from theaters and concert halls to sports stadiums and major downtown projects like the BCE building and the new Canadian Broadcasting complex. With the recent election of a new Conservative provincial government, however, this explosive growth could well be curtailed by cost-cutting and downsizing.

Toronto has always managed to preserve its past while building a new future, as illustrated by Holy Trinity Church and Scadding House, one of the city's oldest residences, standing proudly against the futuristic Eaton Centre.

In Toronto people walk to work from their restored Victorian town houses, no developer can erect downtown commercial space without including living space, the subway gleams, and the streets are safe. Here old buildings are saved and converted to other uses, and architects design around the contours of nature instead of just bulldozing the trees. Here's a city created with flair and imagination but also a sense of traditional values.

AN IMPORTANT NOTE ON PRICES Unless stated otherwise, **the prices cited in this guide are given in Canadian dollars,** which is good news for American travelers because the Canadian dollar is worth 25% less than the U.S. dollar, but buys nearly as much. As we go to press, $1 Canadian is worth 75¢ U.S., which means that your $100-a-night hotel room will cost only U.S. $75, and your $6 breakfast costs only U.S. $4.50.

But taxes are steep in Canada. The pro-vincial retail sales tax in Ontario is 8%; the accommodations tax is 5%. And these are in addition to the 7% national goods and services tax (GST).

1 Orientation

ARRIVING

BY PLANE   More than 20 major airlines serve Toronto with regularly scheduled flights departing and arriving at **Pearson International Airport,** in the northwest corner of metropolitan Toronto, about 30 minutes (17 miles) from downtown.

The most spectacular of the three terminals is the Trillium Terminal 3 (☎ 905/ 612-5100), used by American, Canadian Airlines, British Airways, KLM, Lufthansa, and United, among others. This supermodern facility has moving walkways, a huge food court, and hundreds of stores, including North America's very first branch of Harrod's. Airport facilities include the exceptionally useful Transport Canada Information Centres in all terminals, where a staff fluent in 10 languages will answer questions about the airport, airline information, transportation services, and tourist attractions (☎ 905/676-3506).

Here are a few useful airline reservation numbers: **Air Canada** (☎ 800/ 776-3000); **USAir** (☎ 800/433-7300); **American Airlines** (☎ 800/433-7300); **Canadian Airlines International** (☎ 800/426-7000); **Delta Airlines** (☎ 800/ 221-1212); **United Airlines** (☎ 800/241-6522); and **Northwest Airlines** (☎ 800/ 225-2525).

Getting to & from the Airport   The airport is about 30 minutes from downtown. A taxi will cost about $40 to downtown. Also very convenient is the **Airport Express** bus (☎ 905/564-6333), which travels between the airport and all major downtown hotels—Harbour Castle Westin, the Royal York, Crown Plaza Toronto Centre, the Sheraton Centre, and the Delta Chelsea Inn—every 20 minutes all day. Fare is $11.45 ($19.70 round-trip) for adults, free for children under 11 accompanied by adult. In addition, most first-class hotels run their own hotel limousine services, so check when you make your reservation.

The cheapest way to go is by subway and bus, which will take about an hour. Buses travel between the Islington subway stop and the airport about every 40 minutes for a fare of $6.40 ($10.60 round-trip). Buses also travel between the Yorkdale and York Mills subway stations and the airport about every 40 minutes for a fare of $6.90 ($11.95 round-trip) from Yorkdale; $7.95 ($12.50 round-trip) from York Mills. On both routes children under 11 travel free if accompanied by an adult. For information, call 905/672-0293.

If you're driving from the airport, take Highway 427 south to the Gardiner Expressway East.

BY CAR   From the United States you are most likely to enter Toronto via Highway 401, or via Highway 2 and the Queen Elizabeth Way if you come from the west. If you come from the east via Montréal, you'll also use Highways 401 and 2.

Here are a few approximate driving distances to Toronto: from Boston, 566; from Buffalo, 96; from Chicago, 534; from Cincinnati, 501; from Detroit, 236; from Minneapolis, 972; and from New York, 495.

BY TRAIN   All **VIA Rail** Canada passenger trains pull into the massive, classically proportioned Union Station on Front Street, one block west of Yonge opposite the Royal York Hotel. The station has direct access to the subway so you can easily reach any Toronto destination from here. For VIA Rail information, call 416/366-8411; in the United States, call your travel agent.

BY BUS   Out-of-town buses arrive and depart from the Metro Toronto Coach Terminal, 610 Bay St., at Dundas Street, and provide frequent and efficient service

Metropolitan Toronto

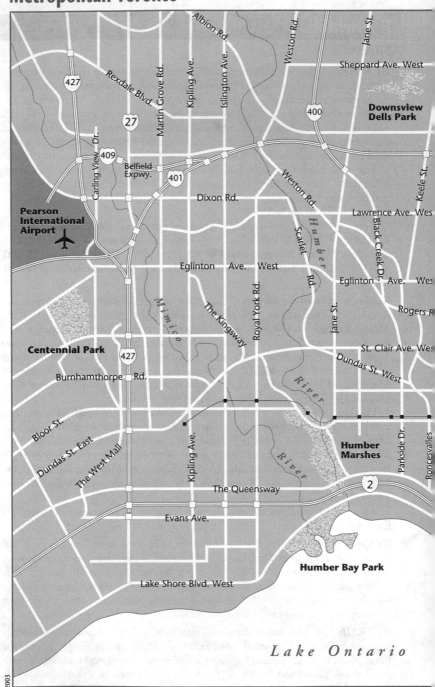

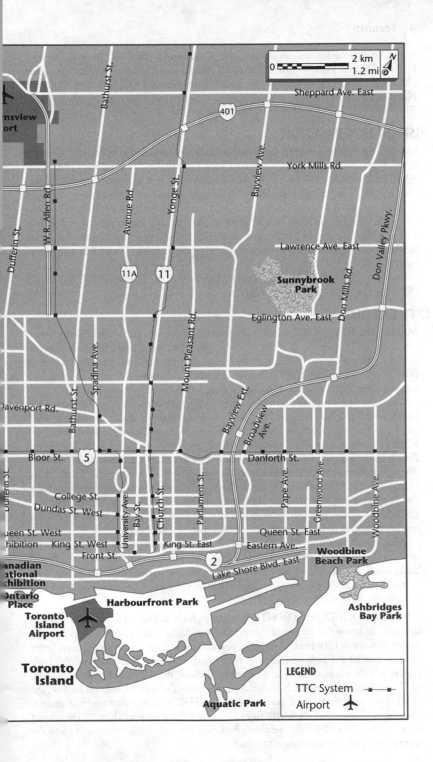

from Canadian and American destinations. **Greyhound** (☎ 416/594-3310) services Buffalo, Niagara Falls, Windsor, Detroit, Ottawa, and Western Canada; **Voyageur** (☎ 416/393-7911) travels west from Montréal and Québec, and **Ontario Northland** (☎ 416/393-7911) has service from towns such as North Bay and Timmins.

VISITOR INFORMATION

Contact the **Metro Toronto Convention and Visitors Association,** 207 Queen's Quay West, Suite 509, in the Queen's Quay Terminal at Harbourfront (P.O. Box 126), Toronto, ON, M5J 1A7 (☎ 416/203-2500), open Monday through Friday, 9am to 5pm. Take the Harbourfront LRT down to the terminal building.

More conveniently located is the drop-in Travel Ontario Visitor Information Centre, in the Eaton Centre on Yonge Street at Dundas. It's located on Level 1 Below and is open year round Monday through Friday 10am to 9pm, Saturday from 9:30am to 6pm, and Sunday from noon to 5pm. It has city and Ontario travel information.

You can also contact **Ontario Travel,** Queen's Park, Toronto, ON, M7A 2R9 (☎ 416/314-0944 or 800/ONTARIO).

CITY LAYOUT

MAIN STREETS & ARTERIES   Toronto is laid out in a grid system. Yonge Street (pronounced "Young") is the main south-north street, stretching from Lake Ontario in the south well beyond Highway 401 in the north; the main east-west artery is Bloor Street, which cuts right through the heart of downtown. Yonge Street divides western cross streets from eastern cross streets.

Downtown usually refers to the area stretching south from Eglinton Avenue to the lake between Spadina Avenue in the west and Jarvis Street in the east. I have divided this large area into downtown (from the lake to College/Carlton streets), midtown (College/Carlton streets to Davenport Road), and uptown (north from Davenport Road). In the first you will find all the lakeshore attractions—Harbourfront, Ontario Place, Fort York, Exhibition Place, the Toronto Islands—plus the CN Tower, City Hall, Skydome, Chinatown, the Art Gallery, and Eaton Centre. Midtown includes the Royal Ontario Museum, the University of Toronto, Markham Village, and chic Yorkville, a prime place to browse and dine al fresco. Uptown is a fast-growing residential and entertainment area for the young, hip, and well heeled.

Because metropolitan Toronto is spread over 255 square miles (634 square km) and includes East York and the cities of (from west to east) Etobicoke, York, North York, and Scarborough, some primary attractions exist outside the central core, such as the Ontario Science Centre, the Metropolitan Zoo, and Canada's Wonderland—so be prepared to journey somewhat.

UNDERGROUND TORONTO   It is not enough to know Toronto's streets; you also need to know the warren of subterranean walkways that enable you to go from Union Station to City Hall. Currently, you can walk from Yonge and Queen Street Station west to the Sheraton Centre, then south through the Richmond-Adelaide Centre and First Canadian Place, all the way (through the dramatic Royal Bank Plaza) to Union Station. En route, branches lead off to the Toronto Dominion Centre, the Stock Exchange, Sun Life Centre, and Metro Hall. Other walkways exist around Bloor and Yonge, and elsewhere in the city (ask for a map of these at the tourist information office). So if the weather's bad, you can eat, sleep, dance, and go to the theater without even donning a raincoat.

2 Getting Around

BY PUBLIC TRANSPORTATION

The **Toronto Transit Commission (TTC)** operates public transit, an overall inter-connecting subway, bus, and streetcar system (☎ 416/393-4636 from 7am to 10pm for information). Fares (including transfers to buses or streetcars) for adults are $2 (or two for $3, five for $6.50, or 10 for $13), $1 for students and seniors (10 for $6.50), 50¢ for children 2 to 12 (eight for $2.50). (As of this writing, the city was contemplating raising the fares but it had not yet been confirmed.) You can purchase from any subway collector a special $5 pass good for unlimited travel after 9:30am weekdays, anytime Saturday and Sunday, which may be used by up to six people (maximum of two adults). On surface transportation you need a ticket, a token, or exact change. Tickets and tokens may be obtained at subway entrances or authorized stores that display the sign "TTC Tickets May Be Purchased Here."

BY SUBWAY   It's a joy to ride—fast, quiet, and sparkling clean. It's a very simple system to use, designed basically in the form of a cross: The Bloor Street east-west line runs from Kipling Avenue in the west to Kennedy Road in the east, where it con-nects with Scarborough Rapid Transit traveling from Scarborough Centre to McCowan. The Yonge Street north-south line runs from Finch Avenue in the north to Union Station (Front Street) in the south. From here, it loops north along Uni-versity Avenue and connects with the Bloor line at the St. George Station. A Spadina extension runs north from St. George to Wilson. The subway operates from 6am to 1:30am Monday through Saturday and on Sunday from 9am to 1:30am. For route information, pick up a Ride Guide at subway entrances or call 416/393-4636.

A Light Rapid Transit connects downtown to Harbourfront. It operates from Union Station along Queen's Quay to Spadina, stopping at Queen's Quay ferry docks, York Street, Simcoe Street, and Rees Street. A transfer is not required as the LRT links up underground with the Yonge-University subway line.

Smart commuters (and visitors!) park their cars for a low all-day parking fee at subway terminal stations—Kipling, Islington, Finch, Wilson, Warden, Kennedy, and McCowan; or at smaller lots at Sheppard, York Mills, Eglinton, Victoria Park, and Keele. You'll have to get there early, though.

BY BUS & STREETCAR   Where the subway leaves off, buses and streetcars take over to carry you east-west or north-south along the city's arteries. When you pay your fare (on streetcar, bus, or subway) always pick up a transfer—if you want to transfer to another mode of transportation you won't have to pay another fare.

BY TAXI

As usual, taxis are an expensive mode of transportation: $2.20 the minute you step in and then $1.05 for every kilometer. Especially in rush hours, cab fares can mount up. Nevertheless, here are the major companies: **Diamond** (☎ 416/366-6868), **Yellow** (☎ 416/363-4141), **Metro** (☎ 416/363-5611).

BY CAR

The **Canadian Automobile Association** (CAA), 60 Commerce Valley Dr. E., Thornhill (☎ 905/771-3111), provides aid to any driver who is a member of AAA.

RENTALS   You can rent cars fom any of the major companies at the airport. In addition, **Budget** has a convenient location at 141 Bay St. (☎ 416/364-7104), and **Tilden** is at 930 Yonge St. (☎ 416/925-4551).

PARKING   Parking costs are extremely high and metered street parking is only allowed for short periods. Parking downtown runs about $4 per half hour, with $15 to $18 maximum. After 6pm and on Sunday, rates go down to $6 or thereabouts. Generally, the city-owned lots, marked with a big green P, are slightly cheaper. Observe the parking restrictions—the city will tow your car away.

DRIVING RULES   You can turn right on a red light after coming to a full stop and checking the intersection, but watch out for those signs forbidding such turns at specific intersections. Watch carefully also for one-way streets and no-left- and no-right-turn signs. The driver and front-seat passenger must wear their seat belts or, if caught, pay a substantial fine. The speed limit within the city is 30 m.p.h. You must stop at pedestrian crosswalks. If you are following a streetcar and it stops, you must stop well back from the rear doors so that passengers can exit easily and safely. (Where there are concrete safety islands in the middle of the street for streetcar stops, this rule does not apply, but still, exercise care.)

FAST FACTS: Toronto

Area Code   Toronto's area code is 416; Mississauga is 905.

Dentist   The Royal College of Dental Surgeons (☎ 416/961-6555) offers emergency after-hours dental care.

Doctor   The College of Physicians and Surgeons, 80 College St. (☎ 416/961-1711), operates a referral service from 9am to 5pm.

Drugstores (Late-Night Pharmacies)   Shoppers Drug Mart, at 360 Bloor St. West, at Spadina Avenue, stays open daily until midnight. They operate many other branches downtown. The other big chain is Pharma Plus, with a store at 68 Wellesley St., at Church Street (☎ 416/924-7760), open daily from 8am to midnight.

Embassies and Consulates   While all embassies are in Ottawa, many nations maintain consulates in Toronto, including the following: Australian Consulate-General, 175 Bloor St. East (☎ 416/323-1155); British Consulate-General, 777 Bay St.(☎ 416/593-1290); and the U.S. Consulate-General, 360 University Ave. (☎ 416/595-1700).

Emergencies   Call 911 for fire, police, and ambulance.

Hospitals   Try Toronto General Hospital, 200 Elizabeth St. (emergency ☎ 416/340-3948).

Hotlines   Help is available from the following: rape crisis (☎ 416/597-8808), assault victims (☎ 416/863-0511), drug/alcohol crisis (☎ 416/595-6000), and suicide prevention (☎ 416/285-0100 or 416/598-1121).

Liquor Laws   Liquor, wine, and some beers are sold at Liquor Control Board of Ontario (LCBO) stores, open Monday through Saturday. Most are open from 10am to 6pm (some stay open evenings). For locations, call 416/365-5900 or check the white pages under "Liquor Control Board."

True wine lovers will want to check out Vintages stores (also operated by the LCBO), which carry a more extensive and more specialized selection of wines. The most convenient downtown locations are in the lower level concourse of Hazelton Lanes (☎ 416/924-9463) and at Queen's Quay (☎ 416/864-6777).

Beer is sold at Brewers Retail Stores, most of which are open Monday through Friday from 10am to 10pm and Saturday from 10am to 8pm. Check the yellow pages under "Beer and Ale" for locations.

The TTC Subway System

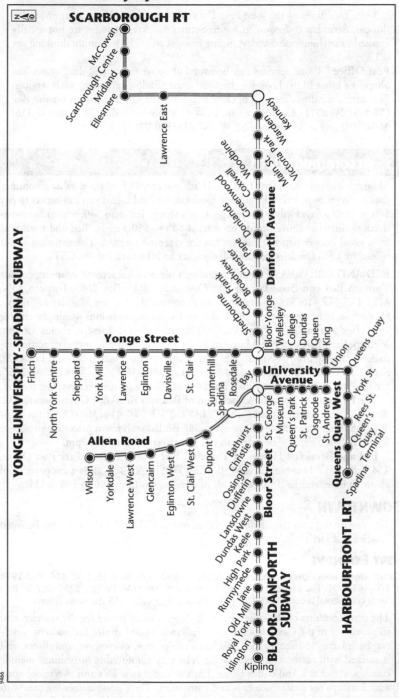

Some quiddities of the local law: Drinking hours are 11am to 1am Monday through Saturday and noon to 11pm Sunday (cocktail lounges are not usually licensed to sell liquor on Sunday; dining lounges are). The minimum drinking age is 19.

Post Office   Postal services can be found at convenience and drug stores like Shopper's Drug Mart. Look for the sign in the window indicating such services. Post office windows are also open throughout the city in Atrium on the Bay (☎ 416/506-0911), Commerce Court (☎ 416/956-7452) the TD centre (☎ 416/360-7105) and at 36 Adelaide St. W (☎ 416/360-7287).

3 Accommodations

Although Toronto has many fine hotels, it's not easy to find good-value accommodations downtown. Even at the more moderate establishments you can expect to pay $80 to $100 a day. Only a few budget hotels charge less than $80, while unconventional options like university dorms start at $45 to $50 a night. Bed-and-breakfasts are a good budget bet, but their prices are creeping upward. The situation is not helped by a 5% Ontario accommodations tax and the national 7% GST.

BED-AND-BREAKFAST   For interesting, truly personal accommodations, contact **Toronto Bed and Breakfast,** at 253 College St. (P.O. Box 269), Toronto, ON, M5T 1R5 (☎ 416/588-8800 from 9am to noon and 2 to 7pm Monday to Friday), for their list of homes offering bed-and-breakfast accommodations within the city for an average $55 to $65 a night, double. The association will reserve rooms for you. **Metropolitan Bed and Breakfast** lists about 25 lovely bed-and-breakfast accommodations, ranging from $45 to $85 double. Write to Metropolitan Bed and Breakfast, Suite 269, 615 Mount Pleasant Rd., Toronto, ON, M4S 3C5 (☎ 416/964-2566; fax 416/960-9529) to request their free booklet. They will make reservations for you.

The Downtown Toronto Association of Bed and Breakfast Guesthouses, P.O. Box 190, Station B, Toronto, ON, M5T 2W1 (☎ 416/368-1420; fax 416/368-1653) represents about 30 nonsmoking B&Bs, with room prices ranging from $55 to $75 double. The best time to call is between 8:30am and 7pm.

Bed and Breakfast Homes of Toronto, Box 46093, College Park Post Office, 444 Yonge St., Toronto, ON, M5B 2L8 (☎ 416/363-6362), is a cooperative of about 15 independent B&B operators offering rooms from $50 to $95 double.

DOWNTOWN

The downtown area runs from the lakefront to College/Carlton Streets between Spadina and Jarvis.

VERY EXPENSIVE

Cambridge Suites Hotel. 15 Richmond St. East, Toronto, ON, M5C 1N2. ☎ **416/368-1990** or 800/463-1990. Fax 416/601-3751. 231 suites. A/C MINIBAR TV TEL. $250 double. Rate includes continental breakfast. AE, DC, DISC, ER, MC, V. Parking $15. Subway: Queen.

The extra comforts of the suites make all the difference to the regular traveler, and its proximity to the Convention Centre makes it a good choice for business travelers. Each large, 550-square-foot unit has a refrigerator, microwave, and dishes, and is stocked with coffee, tea, and cookies. The very comfortable furnishings include couches, armchairs, and coffee tables. Each suite has two TVs and two telephones, with hookups for conference calls and computers. There's also a dressing area with full-length mirror and marble bathroom equipped with hair dryer and full amenities. Some luxury suites are duplexes and have Jacuzzis.

Dining/Entertainment: Restaurant and bar.

Services: Daily maid service, valet, concierge. If you leave a list, your grocery shopping will be done.

Facilities: Fitness area with good view, whirlpool, sauna, convenience store, washers, and dryers.

Crown Plaza Toronto Centre. 225 Front St. West, Toronto, ON, M5V 2X3. ☎ **416/ 597-1400** or 800/422-7969. Fax 416/597-8128. 587 rms. A/C MINIBAR TV TEL. $180–$280 double. Children 18 and under stay free in parents' room. Weekend packages available. AE, DC, DISC, ER, MC, V. Parking $20.50. Subway: Union.

Formerly L'Hôtel, this 25-story hotel is ideally located near the CN Tower, SkyDome, Roy Thomson Hall, the theater district, and the Convention Centre (to which it is attached). The rooms are finely appointed with marble bathroom counters, writing desks, elegant table lamps, and two telephone lines. Nonsmoking rooms are available.

Dining/Entertainment: The Trellis Bistro and Lounge, in the garden court is well known for its Sunday brunch and after-theater menu; there's fine dining in Chanterelles and a special pretheater fixed-price menu.

Services: Room service 6am to 2am.

Facilities: Indoor pool, whirlpool, saunas, well-equipped exercise room, squash courts, and sundeck.

King Edward Hotel. 37 King St. East, Toronto, ON, M5C 2E9. ☎ **416/863-9700.** Fax 416/ 367-5515. 315 rms and suites. A/C MINIBAR TV TEL. $210–$245 double; from $360 suite. Weekend packages available. AE, CB, DC, ER, MC, V. Parking $24. Subway: King.

In its heyday, The King Eddy, as this hotel is affectionately known, welcomed the Prince of Wales (later Edward VIII); hosted a dinner for Cecil B. DeMille that transformed the Crystal Ballroom into a 15th-century castle complete with moat; and attracted anybody who was anybody. Today, this vintage 1903 hotel is once again one of the city's top hostelries. The hotel's original elements, such as imported marble Corinthian columns and sculpted ceilings, have been restored to their former elegance. The lobby soars 40 feet to a glass dome that lets the sun stream in.

The modest number of rooms guarantees personal service. All units are extremely spacious, beautifully decorated with mahogany antique reproductions and floral prints, and come fully equipped with telephones in the bedroom and bathroom, and such niceties as bathrobes, super-fluffy towels, and marble bathtubs.

Dining/Entertainment: The Lobby Lounge offers afternoon tea and cocktails. The famous old Victorian Room has been turned into the Café Victoria, where baroque plasterwork is matched with extravagant potted shrubs. Eight-foot-high windows in the main floor Consort Bar look out onto King Street. For formal dining, Chiaro's specializes in fine continental cuisine, with dinner entrées priced from $18 to $30.

Services: 24-hour room and concierge service, complimentary shoeshine and newspaper.

Facilities: Health club.

Radisson Plaza Hotel Admiral. 249 Queen's Quay West, Toronto, ON, M5J 2N5. ☎ **416/ 203-3333** or 800/333-3333. Fax 416/203-3100. 157 rms. A/C MINIBAR TV TEL. $160–$200 double. Extra person $20. Weekend packages available. AE, DC, ER, MC, V. Parking $12.50. Subway: Union.

As the name and the harbor-front location suggest, the Hotel Admiral has a strong nautical flavor. Rooms are elegantly furnished with campaign-style chests of drawers with brass trimmings, marble-top side tables, and desks. Extra amenities include two phones, real hangers, and in the bathroom, a hair dryer and clothesline.

Dining/Entertainment: The Commodores Dining Room, which looks out onto Lake Ontario, offers classic continental cuisine, with main courses ranging from $20 to $28. The Galley serves a more modest menu, while the adjacent Bosun's Bar offers light snacks.

Services: 24-hour room service, complimentary newspaper, concierge.

Facilities: On the horseshoe-shaped roofdeck overlooking the lake is a pool and cabana-style bar-terrace.

The Royal York. 100 Front St. West, Toronto, ON, M5J 1E3. ☎ **416/863-6333**, 800/ 828-7447 in the U.S., or 800/268-9411 elsewhere. 1,365 rms and suites. A/C MINIBAR TV TEL. $220 double; from $300 suite. Extra person $20. Add $20 for business-class service. Many special packages available. AE, DC, DISC, MC, V. Parking $17. Subway: Union.

To many citizens and regular visitors, the Royal York is Toronto, because in its 35 banquet and meeting rooms many of the city's historical and social events have taken place. Conveniently located for the business and theater districts, it is a huge enterprise, and as such, not to everyone's taste. Still, there is a magnificence to this hotel, which opened in 1929. The vast lobby is crowned by an incredible inlay coffered ceiling, lit by large cast-bronze chandeliers.

Units vary in size but a standard room will have a king-size bed and antique reproduction furnishings, including an armchair and a well-lit desk. Nice features are solid wood doors, windows that open, and wall moldings. Rooms for travelers with disabilities are exceptionally well-equipped for wheelchair guests and for those guests who have hearing or visual impairments. Business class provides a superior room on a private floor with private lounge, complimentary breakfast and newspaper, and nightly turndown.

Dining/Entertainment: Of the 12 restaurants and lounges, the Acadian Room offers Canadian cuisine in an elegant atmosphere; the Royal Tea Room serves afternoon tea; Benihana offers a show of Japanese finesse; the York Station has bar lunches. The Lobby Bar features a sports screen, while the Library Bar is more intimate. Four more dining venues are downstairs.

Services: Room service from 7am to 1am; concierge.

Facilities: Skylit indoor lap pool with hand-painted trompe l'oeil murals and potted palms, exercise room, saunas, steam rooms and whirlpool, barbershop and beauty salon, shopping arcade, business center.

Sheraton Centre. 123 Queen St. West, Toronto, ON, M5H 2M9. ☎ **416/361-1000** or 800/ 325-3535. Fax 416/947-4854. 1,393 rms. A/C TV TEL. $240 double. Extra person $20. Two children under 18 can stay free in parents' room. Special packages available. AE, DC, ER, MC, V. Parking available in underground City Hall parkade, which connects to the hotel, for $20 per day. Additional charge for valet parking. Subway: Osgoode.

A city in itself, the Sheraton Centre contains dozens of shops in the Plaza, eight restaurants and bars, and two movie theaters. It's conveniently located at the heart of the city's underground passageways, right across from City Hall and near the Convention Centre. At the back of the lobby, you'll even find two acres of landscaped gardens with a waterfall and summer terrace. In this 43-story complex, rooms are spacious, attractively furnished, and well equipped. The more expensive Towers rooms offer additional amenities—bathrobes, additional telephones in the bathrooms, and a separate reception area.

Dining/Entertainment: In the shopping concourse, Good Queen Bess, an authentic English pub (shipped from England in sections), is one of the few places around where you can enjoy a mug of Newcastle Brown. Off the lobby, Reunion is a lively bar, with several videos, a pool table, and upbeat music, while the second-floor Lion Dog Lounge provides a spectacular view of City Hall. For all-day dining there's Bites; the premier restaurant is Postcards, which features cuisines from around the world and offers daily buffet breakfasts and lunches and moderately priced dinners.

Services: 24-hour room service, valet, concierge.

Facilities: Indoor/outdoor pool (20 feet inside, 60 feet outside), sauna, games room, hot tub, and health clinic.

✪ **Westin Harbour Castle.** 1 Harbour Sq., Toronto, ON, M5J 1A6. ☎ **416/869-1600.** Fax 416/361-7448. 978 rms. A/C MINIBAR TV TEL. $180 double. Extra person $20. Children stay free in parents' room. Special weekend packages (double occupancy) available. AE, DC, ER, MC, V. Parking $18.75. Subway: Union, then take the LRT.

Located right on the lakefront, the Westin is ideally situated for visiting Harbourfront and is linked to downtown by a Light Rapid Transit system. Guest rooms, all with a lake view, are located in two towers joined at the base by a five-story podium. All rooms are furnished with marble-top desks and night tables, table and floor lamps, and an extra phone in the bathroom. There are 442 nonsmoking rooms.

Dining/Entertainment: The Regatta, overlooking the harbor, is open to midnight. Dinner entrées at the Lighthouse, a revolving restaurant on the 37th floor with fabulous views, run $21 to $34. Tea is served in the Lobby Lounge, along with cocktails and a continental breakfast. Off the main lobby, the Chartroom offers a quiet haven for a drink, with piano entertainment in the evenings.

Services: 24-hour room service.

Facilities: Fitness center with indoor pool, whirlpool, sauna, steam room, tennis court, and massage clinic.

EXPENSIVE

Delta Chelsea Inn. 33 Gerrard St. West (between Yonge and Bay), Toronto, ON, M5G 1Z4. ☎ **416/595-1975** or 800/268-1133. Fax 416/585-4362. 1,586 rms and suites. A/C TV TEL. $140–$180 double; from $250 suite. Extra person $20. Children under 18 stay free in parents' room. Weekend and other packages available. AE, DC, ER, MC, V. Parking $15 per day. Subway: College.

The Delta Chelsea Inn is still one of Toronto's best buys—particularly for families and on weekends, when special packages are offered—although prices have shot up and the lobby can be mobbed with people at checkout. All rooms have bright, modern furnishings, and 400 rooms have minibars, some kitchenettes. Rooms in the south tower feature dual phones with data jacks, call waiting, and conference-call features.

Dining/Entertainment: Wittles offers casual but elegant dining, while the Market Garden is an attractive self-service cafeteria with an outdoor courtyard selling everything from salads to grilled items at reasonable prices. The children's menu offers good value, and children 6 and under eat free. The Chelsea Bun offers live entertainment daily and Dixieland jazz on Saturday afternoons (lunch buffets and Sunday brunch are also served here); for a relaxing drink there's the Elm Street Lounge or Deck 27 on the 27th floor, which offers writing desks and telephones for the final wrap-up at the end of the day.

Services: Babysitting (for a fee), plus 24-hour room service and valet pickup.

Facilities: Two swimming pools, whirlpool, sauna, fitness room, lounge, and games room (with three pool tables), and—a blessing for parents—a children's creative center where three- to eight-year-olds can play under close and expert supervision. It's open until 10pm on Friday and Saturday. Business center in the new tower.

MODERATE

Bond Place Hotel. 65 Dundas St. East, Toronto, ON, M5B 2G8. ☎ **416/362-6061.**
Fax 416/360-6406. 286 rms. A/C TV TEL. $75–$109 double. Extra person $15. Children 14 and
under stay free in parents' room. AE, DC, DISC, ER, MC, V. Parking $11. Subway: Dundas.

Ideally located just one block from Yonge Street and the Eaton Centre, the Bond
Place Hotel offers all the appurtenances of a first-class hotel at reasonable prices. The
rooms are pleasantly decorated in somewhat old-fashioned Scandinavian-style. Off
the lobby, the Garden Café is open all day while downstairs, Freddy's serves a weekday buffet lunch and complimentary hors d'oeuvres from 5:30 to 6:30pm.

Hotel Victoria 56 Yonge St. (at Wellington), Toronto, ON, M5E 1G5. ☎ **416/363-1666.** Fax
416/363-7327. 48 rms. A/C TV TEL. $80–$115 double. Extra person $15. Children under 12 stay
free in parents' room. Special weekend rates available. AE, DC, DISC, ER, MC, V. Subway: King.

In search of a small, personal hotel? Try the six-floor Hotel Victoria, only two blocks
from the O'Keefe Centre. The rooms are either standard or select (the latter are
larger). Rooms have modern furnishings, a gray-and-burgundy decor, and private
baths. The small and elegant lobby retains the marble columns, staircase, and decorative moldings of an earlier era. A complimentary *Globe and Mail* is included in the
room price. There's an attractive restaurant and lounge, as well as a lobby bar.

☯ The Strathcona. 60 York St., Toronto, ON, M5J 1S8. ☎ **416/363-3321.** Fax 416/
363-4679. 193 rms. A/C TV TEL. May 1–Oct 30 $85–$100 double; Nov 1–Apr 30 $65 double.
AE, CB, DC, ER, MC, V. Parking $12. Subway: Union.

Currently one of the city's best buys, the Strathcona is located right across
from Union Station and the Royal York Hotel, within easy reach of all downtown
attractions. Although the rooms are small, they have been refurbished recently with
modern blond-wood furniture, gray carpeting, brass floor lamps, and private baths.
Guests receive a complimentary newspaper and have fitness club access.

INEXPENSIVE

Neil Wycik College Hotel. 96 Gerrard St. East (between Church and Jarvis), Toronto, ON,
M5B 1G7. ☎ **416/977-2320** or 800/268-4358. Fax 416/977-2809. 300 rms (none with bath).
$40–$46 double; $49 family room (two adults plus children). MC, V. Closed Sept–early May.
Parking $9 nearby. Subway: College.

Right downtown, the Neil Wycik College Hotel offers basic accommodations at
extremely reasonable rates from mid-May to late August. Since these are primarily
student accommodations, rooms contain only the most essential furniture—beds,
chairs, and desks. Family rooms have two single beds and room for two cots. Bathrooms and kitchen facilities are down the corridor. If you wish to cook, you have to
furnish your own utensils. Other building facilities include a TV lounge, rooftop
sundeck, sauna, a laundry room on the 22nd floor, and a cafeteria.

Toronto International Hostel. 90 Gerrard St. West (between Queen and Dundas), Toronto,
ON, M5B 1Y7. ☎ **416/971-4440.** 200 beds. A/C. For members $22.50 per person in a double
room, $16 per person in a four-person room; $26.78 and $20.28 respectively for nonmembers.
Membership $26.75. MC, V. Parking $12 in nearby lot. Subway: Dundas.

The hostel provides rooms that accommodate two or four people. Furnishings are
simple: bed, closet, and sink. Bathrooms are down the hall. Each floor has a common room with TV, and there are kitchen and laundry facilities. Guests have access
to a gym, weight room and pool in the same building.

MIDTOWN

The midtown area runs north from College/Carlton Streets between Spadina and
Jarvis, to where Dupont crosses Yonge.

🏰 Family-Friendly Hotels

Delta Chelsea Inn *(see p. 377)*   The Chelsea Chum Club for kids ages 3 to 12 sponsors special activities in the Children's Creative Centre and throughout the hotel. When they check in at the life-size gingerbread house they get a registration card and passport. Children under 6 eat free; the older set gets special menus. All this goes a long way toward creating a smooth family stay.

Inn on the Park *(see p. 381)*   Swings, ice skating, bicycles, and a video room make this a miniparadise for kids of all ages. The hotel operates an Inn Kidz supervised recreational program for children ages 5 to 12 and even sponsors special themed weekends for them.

The Four Seasons *(see p. 379)*   Free bicycles, video games, and the pool should keep kids occupied. Meals are served in Animal World wicker baskets or on Sesame Street plates, and complimentary room-service cookies and milk on arrival make them feel special.

VERY EXPENSIVE

✪ **Four Seasons Hotel.** 21 Avenue Rd., Toronto, ON, M5R 2G1. ☎ **416/964-0411**, 800/ 268-6282 in Canada, or 800/332-3442 in the U.S. Fax 416/964-2301. 380 rms and suites. A/C MINIBAR TV TEL. $270–$355 double; from $360 suite. Children under 18 stay free in parents' room. Extra person $30. Weekend rates available. AE, CB, DC, ER, MC, V. Parking $18.40. Subway: Bay.

In the heart of Bloor-Yorkville, the Four Seasons has a well-deserved reputation for personal service, quiet but unimpeachable style, and total comfort. The lobby, with its marble-and-granite floors, Savonnerie carpets, and stunning fresh flower arrangements, epitomizes the style. The extra-large rooms, with dressing rooms and marble bathrooms, are elegant and well furnished. Extra amenities include hair dryers, makeup and full-length mirrors, tiebars, and closet safes. Corner rooms have balconies.

Four Seasons Executive Suites have additional seating areas, two televisions, and deluxe telephone with two lines and conference-call capability. Nonsmoking rooms are available.

Dining/Entertainment: Truffles, on the second floor, provides a lavish setting of fine woods, fabric, and furnishings for extraordinary French-California cuisine. Main courses, priced from $24 to $37, might include lobster with two sauces and winter-vegetable mousse or grilled duckling with orange-ginger sauce. The crab soup is amazing—Oriental style and full of flavor. The Studio Café serves meals all day. A luncheon buffet, evening hors d'oeuvres, and Sunday brunch are served in La Serre, where a pianist entertains in the evening. The lobby bar is a pleasant area for afternoon tea and cocktails. Special kids' menus are available.

Services: 24-hour concierge, 24-hour room service and valet pickup, one-hour pressing, complimentary shoeshine, and twice-daily maid service, babysitting, doctor on call, courtesy limo to downtown, complimentary newspaper.

Facilities: Business center, health club with an indoor/outdoor pool, whirlpool, Universal equipment, and massage. Bicycles and video games are also available for kids.

✪ **Intercontinental.** 220 Bloor St. West (at St. George), Toronto, ON, M5S 1T8. ☎ **416/ 960-5200.** Fax 416/960-8269. 209 rms. A/C MINIBAR TV TEL. $220–$280 double. Parking $22. Subway: St. George.

The Intercontinental is small enough to provide personal service. The spacious rooms are well furnished with comfortable French-style armchairs and love seats. The marble bathrooms, with separate showers, are large and equipped with every amenity—a telephone; a clothesline; large fluffy towels; a bathrobe; and scales. Extra-special room features include closet lights, a large desk-table, full-length mirror, and a two-line telephone.

Dining/Entertainment: Signatures offers fine dining, with dinner entrées from $18 to $25, and one of the best brunches in town. The Harmony Lounge, with its marble bar, fireplace, and cherry paneling, plus outdoor patio is a pleasant retreat for cocktails or afternoon tea.

Services: 24-hour room service, laundry/valet, twice-daily maid service, nightly turndown, concierge, complimentary shoeshine and newspaper, video check-out in four languages (English, French, Spanish, and Japanese).

Facilities:: Lap pool with adjacent patio; fitness room with treadmill, bikes, Stairmaster, and Paramount equipment.

✪ **Park Plaza.** 4 Avenue Rd. (at Bloor), Toronto, ON, M5R 2E8. ☎ **416/924-5471** or 800/268-4927. Fax 416/924-4933. 224 rms, 40 suites. A/C MINIBAR TV TEL. $255 double in the Plaza Tower; $205 double in the Prince Arthur Tower. Extra person $15. Children under 18 stay free in parents' room. AE, DISC, ER, MC, V. Parking $17. Subway: Museum.

The Park Plaza is conveniently located in Yorkville. All 64 rooms and 20 suites in the original Plaza Tower, built in 1935, have been completely renovated and redecorated to exceptionally high standards. Extra amenities in the rooms include two telephones with voice mail, louvered closets, and full length mirror, plus hair dryer, bathrobes, and makeup mirror in the bathroom. Suites have additional features: scales, umbrellas, and two-line phones with fax-computer hookups. The less expensive Prince Arthur Tower rooms have also been redecorated and have hair dryers in the bathroom.

Dining/Entertainment: The Prince Arthur Garden Restaurant Room is a popular city breakfast and lunch spot. The Roof Restaurant, on the 18th floor, is a romantic dining spot, with entrées ranging from $17 to $23. The adjacent lounge, with inviting couches, wood-burning fireplace and spectacular skyline view, is famous for attracting many Toronto literati, whose books are showcased and whose sketches grace the walls. In summertime the outdoor terrace is great for twilight dining or dessert under the stars.

Services: Room service, twice-daily maid service, nightly turndown, laundry/valet, concierge, complimentary newspaper and shoeshine.

Facilities: Business center and fitness room.

Sutton Place Hotel. 955 Bay St., Toronto, ON, M5S 2A2. ☎ **416/924-9221** or 800/268-3790. Fax 416/924-1778. 230 rms, 62 suites. A/C MINIBAR TV TEL. $170–$210 double; from $300 suite. Extra person $20. Children under 18 stay free in parents' room. Extra person $19. Weekend rates available. AE, DC, ER, MC. Parking $19. Subway: Museum or Wellesley.

This small luxury hotel caters to both a business and leisure clientele attracted by its European flair and superb decor and service. Throughout the public areas you will find authentic antiques, old-master paintings, 18th-century Gobelins, Oriental carpets, and crystal chandeliers. The very spacious rooms are luxuriously furnished in a French style. Each room has a couch, desk, two telephones (allowing hookup to a fax or PC via a modem), bathrobes, and hair dryers.

Dining/Entertainment: Accents Restaurant and Bar, open daily for breakfast, lunch, and dinner, offers a reasonably priced bistro-style menu.

Services: 24-hour room service, laundry/valet complimentary shoeshine, twice-daily maid service, and concierge.

Facilities: Indoor pool with sundeck, sauna, massage, fully equipped fitness center, and business center.

MODERATE

Venture Inn. 89 Avenue Rd., Toronto, ON, M5R 2G3. ☎ **416/964-1220** or 800/387-3933. Fax 416/964-8692. 71 rms. A/C TV TEL. $105 double. Rates include continental breakfast. Children under 12 stay free in parents' room. AE, CB, DC, DISC, ER, MC, V. Parking $6. Subway: Bay or Museum.

Though the Venture Inn has a high-priced location in Yorkville, it charges moderate prices for its modern rooms, decorated with pine accents.

INEXPENSIVE

⑤ Victoria University. 140 Charles St. West, Toronto, ON, M5S 1K9. ☎ **416/585-4524.** Fax 416/585-4530. 425 rms (none with bath). $62 double. Rates include breakfast. Discounts for seniors and students. MC, V. Closed Sept–early May. Subway: Museum. Parking $11.

For a great summer bargain downtown, stay at Victoria University, across from the Royal Ontario Museum. Rooms in the university residence are available from mid-May to late August. Each is furnished as a study/bedroom and supplied with fresh linen, towels, and soap. Bathrooms are down the hall. Guests enjoy free local calls and use of laundry facilities, as well as access to the dining and athletic facilities (including tennis courts).

METRO EAST
VERY EXPENSIVE

✪ Inn on the Park. 1100 Eglinton Ave. East, Don Mills, ON, M3C 1H8. ☎ **416/444-2561,** 800/332-3442 in the U.S., or 800/268-6282 in Canada. Fax 416/446-3308. 568 rms, 27 suites. A/C MINIBAR TV TEL. $125–$145 double. Extra person $20. Two children under 18 stay free in parents' room. Weekend packages available. AE, DC, ER, MC, V. Free parking for 800 cars.

The Four Seasons' Inn on the Park is a luxury hotel-resort only 15 minutes from downtown via the Don Valley Parkway. It's conveniently located for the Ontario Science Centre, a definite plus since it's vital to get to the centre early to beat the crowds. Set at the top of a ravine on 600 acres of parkland, the inn features a two-acre courtyard landscaped with Douglas firs, silver birches, a rock garden, and duck pond.

The rooms, located in a 14-story low-rise and a 21-story tower, have beautiful views (those facing west have balconies). All are superbly decorated with contemporary pieces and have extra little features like alarm clocks, hair dryers, and bathrobes.

Dining/Entertainment: The Terrace Lounge, a piano bar, features lunch, plus wine and cheese during the cocktail hour. During summer the Cabana, the poolside restaurant, is open for pleasant outdoor dining. A stylish garden atmosphere is the backdrop for sophisticated continental cuisine in Seasons, the hotel's premier dining room. Prices range from $20 to $30. For casual dining, there's the Harvest Room. All restaurants feature "alternative cuisine" for health-conscious guests.

Services: The hotel appeals to families because it offers Inn Kidz, a supervised recreational program for children ages 5 to 12 (in summer daily; in winter, on weekends and holidays only). 24-hour room service, complimentary shoeshine, 24-hour valet, one-hour pressing, 24-hour concierge, twice-daily maid service.

Facilities: Business center; indoor and outdoor pool and diving pool; games room, badminton, shuffleboard, indoor tennis; children's play area; and health club with saunas and gym. A racquet club with squash and racquetball courts, a lounge, and a gym too. Bicycles available. And if you want to get your nose (or anything else) fixed, there's even a plastic and cosmetic surgeon on the premises!

EXPENSIVE

Guild Inn. 201 Guildwood Pkwy., Scarborough, ON, M1E 1P6. ☎ **416/261-3331.** Fax 416/261-5675. 96 rms. TV TEL. Main inn $80 double; new wing $125 double. Extra person $15. Children under 14 stay free in parents' room. AE, ER, MC, V. Free parking. Subway: Kennedy.

Beautifully situated 10 miles outside the city (25 minutes from downtown), the Guild Inn offers tranquillity and gracious surroundings from the minute guests enter the tall wrought-iron gates at the head of the drive. The 90-acre grounds are dotted with historic architectural fragments, such as limestone Ionic columns rescued from Toronto's Banker Bond Building, torn down to make way for the futuristic Canadian Place.

Inside, the lobby has the air of an English manor, with its broad staircase, oak beams, and wrought-iron chandeliers. You'll also find wonderful art and china collections, a legacy from the 1930s when the property was occupied by the Guild of All Arts, which operated art and craft workshops that attracted so many visitors here that rooms and dining facilities were added. During these halcyon years many notables visited, including Queen Juliana, Dorothy and Lillian Gish, Moira Shearer, Rex Harrison, Sir John Gielgud, and Lilli Palmer.

You'll pay a little extra for a room with the view of the rear gardens, which sweep down to the Scarborough Bluffs rising 200 feet above Lake Ontario. The inn's original central section was built in 1914; rooms there don't have air-conditioning. Rooms in the newer wing are air conditioned, more modern, and have private balconies.

Dining/Entertainment: The dining room is still popular for Sunday brunch; at dinner it serves primarily grills, roasts, and seafood, priced from $15 to $22. Try some smoked salmon, smoked on the premises after it has been marinated in rum. In summer, tea is served outdoors in the garden; there's a lovely veranda for cocktails.

Services: Room service from 7am to 10pm.

Facilities: Outdoor pool, tennis court, and nature trails.

INEXPENSIVE

University of Toronto in Scarborough. Student Village, 1265 Military Trail, Scarborough, ON, M1C 1A4. ☎ **416/287-7369.** Fax 416/287-7667. $149 for two nights; each additional night $76 to a maximum of $450 per week. Two-night minimum. MC, V. Closed end of Aug–early May. Free parking. Take the subway to Kennedy, then the Scarborough Rapid Transit to Ellesmere, then bus 95 or 95B to the college entrance. Or take exit 387 off the 401.

From mid-May to the third week in August, the University of Toronto in Scarborough has accommodations available in town houses for families (two adults and children under 17) that sleep four to six people and contain equipped kitchens. There's a cafeteria, pub, and recreation center.

4 Dining

The multicultural makeup of the city makes dining a delightful round-the-world experience. Supposedly, there are more than 5,000 restaurants in Toronto, but there's room below only for a very short list. I suggest seeking out ethnic dining spots in Little Italy, Little Portugal, Chinatown and Greektown, where you'll find great food at reasonable prices.

SOME DINING NOTES   Dining in Toronto can be rather expensive. Food prices are high, plus there are taxes—an 8% provincial sales tax and a 7% GST. In addition, wine prices are higher than those in the United States, largely due to the tax on all imported wines.

Several dining clusters throughout Toronto also offer good budget meals. In the basement of **Dragon City,** the Asian shopping complex on Spadina Avenue at

Dundas Street, you'll find counters selling Indonesian, Japanese, Chinese, and Taiwanese food, plus noodles and seafood. At the **Harbourfront,** Queen's Quay and Pier 4 are dotted with a great variety of restaurants. And you'll find everything from Chinese, Middle Eastern, Japanese, and Mexican fast food to Coney Island hot dogs and a booth specializing in schnitzels at **Village by the Grange,** at 71 McCaul St., conveniently located south of the Art Gallery.

DOWNTOWN WEST
EXPENSIVE

✪ **Lotus.** 96 Tecumseh St. (off King and west of Bathurst). ☎ **416/368-7620.** Reservations imperative, at least two weeks in advance. Main courses $29–$30. AE, MC, V. Tues–Sat 6–10pm. ASIAN/EUROPEAN.

The storefront's decor is plain, with a tiny bar, a blush of color on one wall, and some herbed vinegars for decorative accent. That's all—this popular small restaurant chooses to focus on its menu and customers. Chef Su Sur Lee, who hails from Hong Kong, combines European and Asian styles and flavors to produce thrilling dishes such as filet mignon with balsamic and soya glaze with yellow pepper coulis and caramel shallot rosti or gratinée of lobster, scallops, and shrimp with Cantonese black bean sauce.

The menu changes daily. Among appetizers you might find such delicately flavored dishes as layered Italian vegetables with tomato confit, braised Romano beans with basil paste and gorgonzola cheese sauce, or seared Québec foie gras with mustard, fig and red basil compote with maple syrup and caper glaze. The desserts range from a classic lemon tart topped with blackberries and glazed Italian meringue to gâteau of white and dark chocolate mousse with blackberry coulis and chocolate sorbet.

MODERATE

Bangkok Garden. 18 Elm St. ☎ **416/977-6748.** Reservations recommended. Main courses $15–$20. AE, DC, ER, MC, V. Mon–Fri 11:30am–2:30pm; daily 5–10pm. THAI.

Bangkok Garden serves Thai cuisine in a lush dining room fashioned out of teak. A spirit house, bronze nagas, and porcelain jardinières add to the exotic ambience. For those who want to sample, special dinners for $26 and up offer an assortment of appetizers, lemon seafood soup, steamed ginger fish, tamarind curry, and stir-fried green vegetables with shrimp, rice, fruit, and Thai sweets. Otherwise there are smooth curries made with chili, lime, and coconut milk; chicken richly flavored with tamarind; and my favorite fish, crispy-fried in a tamarind sauce. At lunch an all-you-can-eat buffet costs $9.95. For dessert, try sticky rice and fresh mangoes. The bar serves light lunches, plus a noodle bar offers noodles seasoned to your own particular taste with spring onions, fresh coriander leaves, chili vinegar, and many other exotic flavors.

Jump Cafe & Bar. Commerce Court East, Court Level, Bay and Wellington. ☎ **416/363-3400.** Reservations recommended. Main courses $17–$20. AE, DC, ER, MC, V. Mon–Fri 11:30am–5pm; Mon–Sat 5–11:30pm. FUSION.

A little hard to find, tucked away in Commerce Court, this power dining spot vibrates with energy. The stream-lined atrium-dining room is broken up by palms and other strategically placed trees and shrubs. A small bar area to the left of the entrance features a good selection of single malts and grappas. In summer it's pleasant to sit out in Commerce Court.

The menu features fresh daily specials plus about six dishes like pan roasted Muscovy duck with cinnamon, red currants, almonds, and wild rice or roasted filet of sea bass on sautéed greens and red beet confit with curried lobster butter sauce. Pizzas and pastas are also available. To start try the pan-fried portobello mushrooms with white truffle vinaigrette or the oak smoked salmon with chervil crème fraîche. Among the desserts I lust after the caramelized banana and chocolate bread pudding, but you may be seduced by the maple-glazed pecan pie with a Kentucky bourbon creme anglaise.

La Fenice. 319 King St. West. ☎ **416/585-2377.** Reservations required. Main courses $15–$24. AE, CB, DC, ER, MC, V. Mon–Fri noon–2:30pm; Mon–Sat 5:30–11pm. ITALIAN.

This Italian outpost is convenient for theatergoers. The cuisine's hallmarks are really fresh ingredients and authentic fine olive oil. A plate of assorted appetizers will include pungent roasted peppers, crisp-grilled zucchini, squid, and a roast veal in tuna sauce (vitello tonnato). Choose from 18 or more pasta dishes—say, tagliatelle burro and basilico with a fragrant basil sauce, or seafood risotto—along with a fine selection of Provimi veal, and grilled fresh fish dishes. Desserts include cakes and tortes plus zabaglione, and fresh strawberries and other fruits in season. Downstairs, an attractive pasta bar is open all day for light fare.

Le Select. 328 Queen St. West. ☎ **416/596-6406.** Reservations recommended. Main courses $13–$18; fixed price $16. AE, DC, MC, V. Daily 11:30am–5pm; Mon–Thurs 5:30pm–midnight, Fri–Sat 5:30pm–1am, Sun 5:30–11pm. FRENCH.

A young artistic crowd flocks to this French-style bistro decorated in Paris Left Bank style, complete with authentic zinc bar. Breakfronts, fringed fabric lampshades over the tables, tole ware, French posters, and a jazz background set the scene for moderately priced, good French food—from confit of duck, or steak with sautéed shallots and frites to salmon with a sorrel cream and white wine sauce. A $16 fixed-price dinner lets you select from five choices per course for appetizer, entrée, and dessert.

Mildred Pierce. 99 Sudbury St. ☎ **416/588-5695.** Reservations not accepted. Main courses $11–$18. ER, MC, V. Mon–Fri noon–3pm, Sun 11am–3pm; Sun–Thurs 6–10pm, Fri–Sat 6–11pm. Take Queen West to Dovercourt; turn left, then right on Sudbury. The restaurant is located on the left at the back of a parking lot attached to Studio 99. FRENCH/FUSION.

Resembling a movie set, this spot is worth seeking out. From tables outside you have a great view of the CN Tower and the downtown skyline. Inside the room has a theatrical flair with gilt putti and angels, huge chandeliers created from God knows what, large semicircular banquettes, and glowing faux copper tables, all set against antiqued walls. At the back of the room stands a large arch with these words above: "Pearly Gates, Canadian Entrance."

From the open kitchen comes a variety of fine daily specials like the loin of pork with a cabernet-cassis sauce, plus six or so main courses, such as grilled polenta with grilled vegetables and rack of lamb au jus served with mint sauce. My favorite dish is baked filet of salmon wrapped in rice paper with a sweet and hot plum sauce. Start with the steamed mussels in coconut milk, lemon grass, and Thai herbs and spices; or the tiger shrimp dumplings served with fresh mango, saffron-coconut milk sauce, and a hot chili oil dip. For dessert I recommend the pear tarte tatin served with brandied caramel sauce and vanilla ice cream.

The Pearl. 207 Queen's Quay West. ☎ **416/203-1233.** Reservations recommended. Main courses $12–$17. Daily 11am–3pm and 5–11pm. CHINESE.

This attractive Chinese restaurant with views of Lake Ontario has been a local favorite for many years. Choose from eight soups, including shark's fin with chicken, to start. The house specialties include braised lobster with ginger and green onion; sliced chicken sautéed with pineapple and green peppers; shrimp Szechwan style; and a dish called rainbow chopped in crystal fold, consisting of finely chopped pork, Chinese sausage, mushroom, bamboo shoots, water chestnuts, celery, and carrots sautéed and served in crisp lettuce.

Another Pearl can be found at 110 Bloor St. West (☎ 416/975-1155).

INEXPENSIVE

The Rivoli. 332 Queen St. West. ☎ **416/597-0794.** Reservations not accepted. Main courses $9–$12. MC, V. Mon–Sat 11:30am–1am. CONTINENTAL.

Attracting an avant-garde crowd, the Rivoli offers good light fare, such as crabmeat with melted cheese sandwich, or curried tuna with pineapple. The dinner menu features half a dozen Lao-Thai specialties like pad Thai and Siam curry (shrimp with hot chili and fresh basil) as well as a burger and chicken potpie, plus three or so daily specials—usually a pasta, a meat, and a fish dish. In summer the sidewalk patio is jammed. There's nightly avant-garde entertainment, and the decor is appropriately basic black.

Vanipha. 193 Augusta Ave. ☎ **416/340-0491.** Reservations accepted only for parties of six or more. Main courses $8–$12. V. Mon–Sat 4pm–midnight. THAI/LAO.

Serving some really fine cuisine, Vanipha is housed in a plain but comfortable stepdown storefront. Try the pad Thai, mango salad, grilled fish with tamarind sauce, chicken red curry, and of course, the special treat—sticky rice.

Young Lok Gardens. 122 St. Patrick St. ☎ **416/593-9819.** Reservations accepted only for parties of six or more. Main courses $8–$12. AE, MC, V. Mon–Sat noon–11pm, Sun noon–10pm. CHINESE.

Located in Village by the Grange, one of Toronto's most highly rated and popular restaurants serves good Mandarin and Szechwan cuisine, tasty barbecue from the Mongolian grill, and fresh fish that you can select and have either steamed Chinese style in black bean sauce or with ginger and scallion. Kick off with hot-and-sour soup, and follow with orange-spiced duck, Szechwan shrimp sautéed with cashew nuts, or the Mongolian barbecue beef marinated in mustard, chili, wine, ginger, and plenty of garlic. At lunch the $8 three-course fixed-price meal is good value. On weekends there's a 50-item dim sum brunch.

DOWNTOWN EAST

EXPENSIVE

✪ **Acqua.** 10 Front St. West. ☎ **416/368-7171.** Reservations recommended. Main courses $16–$19. AE, DC, ER, MC, V. Mon–Fri 11:30am–2:30pm; Mon–Sat 5–11:30pm. CALIFORNIA/ ITALIAN.

One of Toronto's trendiest and most dramatic restaurants, Acqua evokes the drama and color of Venice at carnival. A brilliant blue door leads into the bar where curvaceous tables stand under sail-like flags. The courtyard dining area in the BCE building is defined by striped poles like those found along Venetian canals.

The cuisine is less easily defined. Roasted rack of lamb in a mustard glaze with mint aioli, and sautéed filet of red snapper with black Thai rice, leeks, and lime leaf vinaigrette are just two of the main attractions. In addition, there are pastas like the tagliatelle with field mushroom, porcini cream, and reggiano. Start with herbed goat cheese with grilled vegetables and smoked red onion vinaigrette. Winning desserts include the raspberry crème brûlée and mango chocolate tartufo.

Biagio. 155 King St. East. ☎ **416/366-4040.** Reservations recommended. Main courses $13–$25. AE, DC, DISC, ER, MC, V. Mon–Fri noon–2:30pm; Mon–Sat 5:45–10:30pm. ITALIAN.

A comfortable and very elegant place to dine, Biagio has one of the city's most attractive terraces out back, with a fountain and lit by antique gaslights. The menu features about 20 tempting pastas and risottos, like tagliolini with lobster, fresh tomatoes and cream sauce, angel hair with black olives and capers, and risotto with wild mushrooms. Among the entrées try the veal chop with wine butter and sage, or a fresh fish dish. Round the whole meal off with tiramisu, fresh berries, or Italian ice cream.

Nami Japanese Seafood. 55 Adelaide St. East. ☎ **416/362-7373.** Reservations recommended Thurs–Sat. Sushi $4–$6; main courses $15–$25. AE, DC, MC, V. Mon–Fri noon–2:30pm; Mon–Sat 6–10:30pm. JAPANESE.

Many Japanese businesspeople and families dine at this atmospheric restaurant. Up front there's a grilling bar/sushi bar, and behind, attractive booth seating or traditional tatami-style dining. In addition to sushi, you can order dishes from beef kushikatsu (kebabs) to a sashimi assortment.

MODERATE

The Senator. 249 and 253 Victoria St. ☎ **416/364-7517.** Reservations recommended for dinner in the dining room. Main lunch dishes $6–$10; main dinner courses $15–$22. MC, V. Mon–Fri 7:30am–3:30pm; Tues–Sat 5–11:30pm (5–10pm in the diner), Sun 5–10pm; brunch Sat–Sun 8am–3pm. NORTH AMERICAN.

In the diner, green leatherette booths, tiled floors, and down-home cuisine take you back to the 1940s at this local favorite, conveniently located for the Pantages Theatre. You can still order a full breakfast of bacon and eggs, beans, homefries, and toast for $5. At lunch such comfort foods as meat loaf, macaroni and cheese, burgers with fried onions and corn relish, and creamy rice pudding are served. And best of all you can perch on a stool and order up a rich and real old-fashioned milkshake.

In the adjacent dining room, decked out in mahogany, mirrors, and stained glass, you can eat dinner, seated in a velvet enclosed booth, and enjoy some of the same meals, plus dishes like chicken breast with rosemary lemon sauce, prime rib, and seared yellowfin tuna with an olive, tomato, and red onion sherry vinaigrette. Desserts are good and the wine list is excellent.

INEXPENSIVE

Movenpick Marche. In the Galleria of the BCE Building, Front Street East. ☎ **416/366-8986.** Reservations not accepted. Most items $5–$8. AE, DC, MC, V. Daily 7am–2am. CONTINENTAL.

This is the city's latest innovation in food merchandising. Pick up a tab at the entrance and stroll through the bustling market, where various stands and carts offer fresh salads, fish, meats, pizzas, and more. Select and purchase what you want as you go through. At the rotisserie, select a meat for the chef to cook or at the seafood and raw bar, choose a fish for the grill. Then wander over to the bistro de vin and check out the cases of wine or enjoy a boccalino of an open wine. The chefs and staff are easily identifiable by their boaters. This is a fun place for breakfast, lunch, or dinner.

MIDTOWN WEST

This section of Toronto includes Yorkville, where dining can be pricey but not necessarily good. In this section, I've included one or two selections that can be relied upon to deliver quality at a decent price.

EXPENSIVE

Bistro 990. 990 Bay St. (at St. Joseph). ☎ **416/921-9990.** Reservations required. Main courses $16–$26. AE, ER, MC, V. Mon–Fri noon–2:30pm; Mon–Sat 5:30–10:30pm. FRENCH.

A celebrity hot spot, Bistro 990 could have been airlifted from the French provinces with its French doors, lace curtains, tile floors, and outdoor cafe tables. The health-conscious cuisine uses fresh local ingredients, most of them organic, and substitutes reductions of pure juices and meat stocks for traditional thickeners. There

🚺 Family-Friendly Restaurants

Jerusalem *(see p. 391)*   Finger-lickin' Middle Eastern foods that kids find very palatable and fun to boot.

Movenick Marche *(see p. 386)*   Kids will love strolling through the bustling market and choosing their own pizza or burger from the stands and carts.

Kensington Kitchen *(see p. 389)*   There are pita sandwiches, brownies, and other kid-friendly fare. The airplanes and other toys decorating the walls only add to its attraction.

might be rack of lamb with an herbed mustard sauce, steak bordelaise, half a roast chicken with rosemary, or duck with a sun-dried cherry sauce. The roast quail stuffed with figs, served as an appetizer, is exquisite, while the mussels steamed in a red tomato curry broth with fresh cilantro have a wonderful tangy flavor. Desserts change daily but might include a lemon tart, tarte Tatin, raspberry cheesecake, and a selection of sorbets.

✪ **Splendido Bar and Grill.** 88 Harbord St. ☎ **416/929-7788.** Reservations recommended well in advance. Pizzas and pasta courses $8–$12; main courses $15–$25. AE, DC, ER, MC, V. Mon–Sat 5–11pm, Sun 5–10pm. ITALIAN.

The Splendido Bar and Grill is a scene-stealer, with an absolutely stunning dining room that stretches behind a black-gray granite bar in a riot of brilliant yellow lit by a host of tiny, almost fairylike track lights. It's a loud, lively place, not the spot for a romantic dinner. The menu—Italian with international inspirations—changes monthly. Start with the filling antipasto of prosciutto with melon, mission fig, octopus salad, scallop sausage, rosemary peppers, roasted garlic, and marinated bocconcini, or the air-dried beef with asparagus salad. Follow with a wood-fired pizza, perhaps covered with tandoori shrimp, mango, fresh tomato, and ricotta. Special treats among the main courses are the charcoal-roasted salmon with sweet-and-sour soya sauce and the rack of veal with grilled tomatoes, Parmesan polenta, mushroom sauce, and arugula.

MODERATE

Boulevard Cafe. 161 Harbord St. (between Spadina and Bathurst). ☎ **416/961-7676.** Reservations recommended for upstairs dining. Main courses $12–$16. AE, MC, V. Daily 11:30am–3:30pm and 5:30–11:30pm. PERUVIAN.

A favorite gathering spot of young creative types, the Boulevard Cafe is somehow reminiscent of Kathmandu in the 1960s, although the inspiration is Peru. Peruvian cushions and South American wall hangings soften the upstairs dining room. The outside summer cafe, strung with colored lights, attracts an evening and late-night crowd. The menu features empanadas (spicy chicken or beef pastry); tangy shrimp in a spiced garlic, pimiento, and wine sauce; and tamal verde (spicy corn, coriander, and chicken pâté) to start. For the main course the major choice is anticuchos, marinated and charbroiled brochettes of your own choosing: sea bass, shrimp, pork tenderloin, beef, or chicken.

✪ **Chiado.** 864 College St. (at Concord Avenue). ☎ **416/538-1910.** Reservations recommended. Main courses $12–$20. AE, DC, MC, V. Mon–Sat noon–3pm and 5pm–midnight. PORTUGUESE.

Chiado refers to the district in Lisbon, which is filled with small bistrettos like this one. Beyond the appetizing display at the front of the room you'll discover a long, narrow dining room decorated with elegant French-style pink chairs and colorful art on the walls. In summer the storefront opens entirely onto the street, adding to the atmosphere. Among the appetizers the pinheta of salted cod or the marinated sardines with lemon and parsley will appeal to the true Portuguese; others might prefer the tiger shrimp served with a sweet pepper coulis. On the main menu a Portuguese might pine for the poached filet of cod or the bistretto style steak with fried egg and fries, while a friend might go for the roast rack of lamb with a red Douro wine sauce or the braised rabbit in a Madeira wine sauce. To top it all off, choose from the tempting desserts, including peach coconut flan, chocolate mousse, or pecan pie.

Il Posto. 148 Yorkville Ave. ☎ **416/968-0469.** Reservations recommended. Pasta $8–$11; main courses $16–$24. AE, MC, V. Mon–Sat noon–2:30pm and 6–10:30pm. ITALIAN.

This Yorkville survivor offers an attractive courtyard setting complete with brick terrace under a spreading maple tree. The dessert spread at the entrance is tempting enough—fresh raspberry tarts with kiwi, fresh strawberry tarts, and other delights. The menu features such Italian specialties as involtino di pollo (chicken stuffed with eggplant and cheese), scaloppini champagne (veal sautéed in champagne), linguine with seafood or (even more delicious) with Gorgonzola. For dessert, you might discover poached pears in chocolate, or of course the smooth, creamy zabaglione. The restaurant's Italian prints and classical music create a serene dining atmosphere enhanced by handsome bouquets of fresh flowers.

✪ Joso's. 202 Davenport Rd. (just east of Avenue Road). ☎ **416/925-1903.** Reservations recommended. Pasta $9–$14; main courses $14–$28. AE, MC, V. Mon–Sat 11:30am–3pm and 5:30–11pm. SEAFOOD.

Yugoslav Joseph Spralja, of Malka and Joso, has appeared on late-night TV and performed at Carnegie Hall, but since he gave up folk singing and playing the guitar because of an ulcer, he has taken to combing the fish markets for his restaurant, Joso's. Besides having the city's best seafood, this place has an idiosyncratic decor consisting of erotic ceramic female sculptures.

If you don't care a fig about such decor, but you do care about fresh seafood prepared to retain its flavor, then dine at Joso's. You'll be presented with a selection of fresh fish so you can choose the specimen that appeals to you and it will then be grilled and served with a salad (such dishes are priced by the pound). Or you can have octopus steamed in garlic and parsley sauce, deep-fried squid with salad, or spaghetti with an octopus, clam, and squid tomato sauce. Desserts include a special homemade baklava, and Italian ice creams and sorbets. Bentwood cane chairs and pale-lemon tablecloths complete the decor of both the tiny downstairs room and larger upstairs dining room.

✪ Trattoria Giancarlo. 41-43 Clinton St. (at College). ☎ **416/533-9619.** Reservations highly recommended. Pasta and rice $10–$13; main courses $16–$19. AE, MC, V. Mon–Sat 5:30–11pm. ITALIAN.

This is one of my all-time favorite spots in Little Italy, if not in the whole city. It's small and cozy and thoroughly Italian, with an outside dining area in summer. For a real treat, start with the fresh wild mushrooms brushed with herbs, garlic, and oil or crostini toscani (mattone toasts topped with fresh ricotta, prosciutto, and figs). Follow with any one of six pasta dishes—spaghettini with seafood, garlic, capers, white wine, and a touch of anchovies, or the risotto of the day. The grilled fish and meats are superb, like the tender lamb marinated in grappa, lemon, and olive oil or the swordfish grilled with mint, garlic, and olive oil. For dessert try the tiramisu, crème caramel, or the delicious chocolate-raspberry tartufo. The experience is always memorable and the welcome real.

INEXPENSIVE

ⓢ Kensington Kitchen. 124 Harbord St. ☎ **416/961-3404.** Reservations not accepted. Main courses $7–$12. DC, ER, MC, V. Mon–Sat 11:30am–11pm, Sun 11:30am–10pm. MIDDLE EASTERN.

An academic crowd who enjoys the food and the prices frequent this comfortable, casual place. A beaded purse collection and a toy-airplane collection decorate the walls but that's it for decor. There's a counter in the back for take-out, and the chalkboard menu offers falafel, shish kebab, vegetarian chili, fish of the day, vegetable kebab on hummus, and daily specials. Downstairs is informal, with Formica tables; upstairs the tables have tablecloths. My favorite spot, though, is in the back on the deck under the spreading trees.

MIDTOWN EAST/THE EAST END

In the East End along Danforth Avenue you'll encounter a veritable Little Greece, a late-night mecca, where the streets are lined with tavernas, bouzouki music spills out onto the sidewalk, and restaurant after restaurant bears a Greek name.

Ouzeri. 500A Danforth Ave. ☎ **416/778-0500.** Reservations not accepted. Main courses $6–$10. AE, DISC, ER, MC, V. Daily noon–3am; lunch served until 3pm, dips and appetizers only served 4–5pm. GREEK.

Ouzeri is the hot place out here—it's spirited, casual, and fun. People either jam the few small circular tables outside or occupy the tables inside, drinking one of the numerous international beers or wines by the glass. It's all très Athens, with tile floors, sun-drenched pastel hues, and eclectic art objects and art. The food is good and cheap, running the gamut from all kinds of seafood (prawns with feta and wine, sardines with mustard, calamari, broiled octopus) and all kinds of meat (pork, lamb, and beef kebabs) to rice, pasta, and phyllo pie dishes. Various snacks, like hummus, taramosalata, mushrooms à la grecque, and dolmades, complete the menu. At lunch Ouzeri dishes out its version of dim sum, "meze sum"—hot and cold appetizers that are proffered on trays or wheeled by on carts. There's also Sunday brunch too. This is a frenetic scene, especially at night.

UPTOWN

EXPENSIVE

✪ Scaramouche. 1 Benvenuto Place. ☎ **416/961-8011.** Reservations recommended. Main courses $19–$27. AE, DC, ER, MC, V. Mon–Fri 6–10pm (till 11pm in pasta bar), Sat 6–10:30pm (till midnight in pasta bar). CONTEMPORARY FRENCH.

A little difficult to find (it's located in the basement of an apartment building, about four blocks south of St. Clair Avenue and Yonge Street, off Edmund Street), Scaramouche is certainly worth seeking out. Try to secure a window seat with a city skyline view. The decor, the large flower arrangements, and the careful presentation of the food make it special.

Although the menu changes every two months, to start there might be cumin skewered shrimp with grilled sweet onions, leeks, and fennel in a saffron nage, or chicken liver pâté with apple and frisée salad, artichoke chips, and a mango, coriander, and lime relish. Among the 10 or so main courses the signature dishes are hickory smoked and grilled Atlantic salmon on a wild rice and vegetable fricassee with horseradish white wine sauce; grilled Rowe Farm filet mignon with roasted shallots and red wine glaze; or the Arctic char with crackling herb skin served with a chive beurre blanc. There's also a pasta bar menu, which offers similar appetizers and a selection of gnocchi, fusilli, and linguine, all done in excitingly different ways, plus a few meat and fish dishes. The desserts, too, always have an original spin like the crème brûlée flavored with Tahitian vanilla beans served with blood orange and mint salad.

MODERATE

✪ **Centro.** 2472 Yonge St. (north of Eglinton). ☎ **416/483-2211.** Reservations recommended. Main courses $18–$28. AE, DC, ER, MC, V. Mon–Sat 5–11:30pm. NORTHERN ITALIAN.

Occupying a huge space with a mezzanine and a downstairs wine and pasta bar, Centro has grand Italian style—dramatic classical columns, brilliant murals, and ultra-moderne Milan-style furnishings. A chic, animated crowd gathers here for the northern Italian cuisine with a California accent. The menu changes monthly, but among the dishes might be caramelized breast of free-range capon accompanied by a vegetable pot au feu and Perigord truffle sauce; filet of salmon with a Pinot Noir sauce; or the delicious crisp filet of red snapper and grilled sea scallops in a pineapple and soya reduction and aged balsamic glaze. There are four or so pasta dishes—angel hair, penne, and fusilli—all with flavorsome sauces, and gourmet pizzas, too. Desserts are worth waiting for—lemon mascarpone tart with blackberry sauce, chocolate pecan napoleon with a Southern Comfort sauce being only two examples. Afterwards retire for a nightcap to the downstairs piano bar.

✪ **N 44.** 2537 Yonge St. (just south of Sherwood Avenue). ☎ **416/487-4897.** Reservations recommended. Main courses $22–$27. AE, DC, ER, MC, V. Mon–Fri noon–3pm; Mon–Sat 5–10:30pm. CONTINENTAL.

At the back of a dramatic space with soaring ceilings, the glassed-in kitchen is etched with the restaurant's compass logo (North 44 is Toronto's latitude). The food is equally à la mode. On the dinner menu you might find grilled swordfish with black sesame crust, wasabi butter, and charred tomato coriander relish; duck breast with wheat berry risotto, Hedgehog mushrooms, and black currant sauce; or crackling roast chicken with rosemary mashed potatoes, grilled asparagus, and sage fritters. Pizzas and pastas are also featured. Besides an extensive wine list, there's a number of wines by the glass and a wine bar upstairs, open Wednesday to Saturday.

✪ **Pronto.** 692 Mount Pleasant Rd. (just south of Eglinton). ☎ **416/486-1111.** Reservations recommended well in advance. Main courses $17–$23. AE, ER, MC, V. Daily 5pm–midnight. ITALIAN.

Behind the austere black tile facade, diners will discover a vibrant yet intimate dining room where the chefs can be seen in the open kitchen in the back. The cuisine has a reputation to match the room. Among the long list of appetizers and pastas (which can be ordered as a main course), there might be grilled tortilla spring rolls filled with Cajun chicken breast and vegetables, served with spicy stewed plums; or steamed Prince Edward Island mussels in thyme, crushed tomatoes, chili flakes, and white wine on baby greens in a phyllo basket. For your main course, select from the 10 or so carefully prepared entrées, like rack of lamb crusted with Dijon mustard on warm potato and mint salad with red wine jus.

Thai Magic. 1118 Yonge St. ☎ **416/968-7366.** Reservations recommended. Main courses $9–$15. AE, ER, MC, V. Mon–Sat 5:30–11pm. THAI/SEAFOOD.

Magical indeed is Thai Magic. Orchids, Thai statuary, and artifacts decorate the long, narrow room with a bar in the center. Warm mauves and greens make it even more inviting—a perfect backdrop for the sophisticated cuisine. Start with tom yum kai, a really spicy soup flavored with lemongrass and containing succulent shrimp, or the familiar satay or a combination plate of appetizers. For main courses there are stir-fries and curries (like the flavorsome chicken green curry or shrimp red curry with okra) as well as tamarind fish and coriander lobster. Fresh fruit, sherbet, ice creams, and of course sticky rice make up the dessert menu.

INEXPENSIVE

Grano. 2035 Yonge St. ☎ **416/440-1986.** Reservations accepted for parties of six or more only. Main courses $11–$14. AE, DC, MC, V. Mon–Fri 10am–10:30pm; Sat 9:30am–11pm. ITALIAN.

Grano is a wild Italian celebration. But it's a celebration of the down-to-earth Italian food served in an atmosphere of washed Mediterranean pastels. It's casual and fun. There's a courtyard out back. Up front, display counters are filled with antipasti and any three (piccolo) or seven (grande) of these can be ordered, ranging in price from $10 for a small all-vegetable plate to a large plate of salmon carpaccio for $16. There are several pasta dishes like the ravioli boscaiolo, filled with wild mushrooms in a cream and porcini mushroom sauce, or gnocchi in a green pepper, eggplant basil, and light tomato sauce. The meat or fish entrées change daily. To finish enjoy tiramisu, biscotti, and a variety of Italian custard cream desserts.

Ⓢ Jerusalem. 955 Eglinton Ave. West (just west of Bathurst). ☎ **416/783-6494.** Reservations not accepted. Main courses $9–$13. AE, DC, ER, MC, V. Mon–Thurs noon–11pm, Fri–Sat noon–midnight, Sun noon–10pm. MIDDLE EASTERN.

At Jerusalem it's the food and prices that count. All the appetizers are under $4— falafel, koubeh (a cracked-wheat roll stuffed with ground meat, onions, and pine nuts), various styles of hummus, tahina, and tabbouleh (a delicious blend of cracked wheat with chopped tomatoes, onions, parsley, mint, lemon, and olive oil). You can follow them with liver fried in garlic and hot pepper sauce, and siniyeh (mixed ground lamb and beef with onions, parsley, and pine nuts, and oven-baked with tahina sauce), lamb or beef shish kebab, or any other dish. The decor is simple—just some hammered brass tabletops on the walls—but the atmosphere is extremely warm, the service friendly and unhurried.

5 Attractions

Although some major sights are centrally located, several favorites lie outside the downtown core—the Ontario Science Centre, Canada's Wonderland, and the zoo— and take extra time and effort to reach. Ideally, you should spend one day each at Ontario Place, the Ontario Science Centre, Canada's Wonderland, and Harbourfront. In fact, that's what the kids will definitely want to do.

THE TOP ATTRACTIONS
ON THE LAKEFRONT

Ontario Place. 955 Lakeshore Blvd. West. ☎ **416/314-9811** or 416/314-9900 for a recording. Free admission, with some exceptions (like the CNE). IMAX movies $6 adults, $3 seniors and children 12 and under. Mid-May to Labor Day from 10:30am with most attractions closing at dusk, except for evening events. Parking $9. Take the subway to Bathurst or Dufferin and buses south from there to Exhibition. Call TTC Information (☎ 416/393-4636) for special bus service details.

When this 96-acre recreation complex on Lake Ontario opened in 1971, it seemed futuristic, and more than 20 years later it still does (although it was revamped in 1989). From a distance you'll see five steel-and-glass pods suspended 105 feet up on columns above the lake, three artificial islands, and alongside, a huge geodesic dome that looks like a golf ball magnified several thousand times. The five pods contain a multimedia theater, a live children's theater, a high-technology exhibit, and other displays that tell the story of Ontario in vivid kaleidoscopic detail. The dome houses Cinesphere, where a 60- by 80-foot screen shows specially made IMAX movies.

Located under an enormous orange canopy, the Children's Village provides a well-supervised area where children aged 12 and under can scramble over rope bridges, bounce on an enormous trampoline, and slide down a twisting chute, or most popular of all, squirt water pistols, garden hoses, swim, and generally drench one another in the water-play section. Afterward, parents can just pop them in the conveniently available dryers before moving on to three specialty children's theaters.

A stroll around the complex reveals two marinas full of yachts and other craft, the HMCS *Haida* (a destroyer, open for touring, that served in both World War II and the Korean War), a miniature 18-hole golf course, plenty of grassland for picnicking and general cavorting, and a wide variety of restaurants and snack bars serving everything from Chinese, Irish, German, and Canadian food to hot dogs and hamburgers. And don't miss the wildest ride in town—the Wilderness Canoe Ride, the Water Slide, and bumper boats. For something more peaceful, try the pedal or remote-control boats.

At night the Forum, an outdoor amphitheater that accommodates 10,000 under a copper canopy and outside on its grassy slopes, comes alive. During the summer all manner of entertainments are held here; for tickets call 416/870-8000.

✪ **Harbourfront Centre.** Queen's Quay West. ☎ **416/973-3000** for information on special events, or 416/973-4000 for box office. Take the LRT from Union Station. Or take the no. 77B bus from Union Station or the Spadina subway station; or the no. 6 or 6A bus to the foot of Bay Street and walk west.

In 1972, the federal government took over a 96-acre strip of prime waterfront land to preserve the waterfront vista—and since then Torontonians have rediscovered their lakeshore. Abandoned warehouses, shabby depots, and crumbling factories have been refurbished, and a tremendous urban park now stretches on and around the old piers. The resulting Harbourfront is one of Toronto's most exciting happenings. It's a great place to spend the whole day.

Queen's Quay, at the foot of York Street, is the closest quay to town, and it's the first point you'll encounter as you approach from the Harbour Castle Westin. From here, boats depart for tours of the harbor and islands. An old warehouse, it now houses the Premiere Dance Theatre, plus two floors of shops, restaurants, and waterfront cafes.

After exploring Queen's Quay, walk west along the glorious waterfront promenade to **York Quay.** To get there you'll pass the Power Plant, a contemporary gallery, and behind it, the Du Maurier Theatre Centre. At York Quay Centre you can secure information on programming as well as entertain yourself in several galleries, including The Craft Studio, where you can watch artisans blow glass, throw pots, and make silk-screen prints. On the center's other side you can attend a free Molson Dry Front Music outdoor concert, held all summer long at Molson Place. Also on the quay in the center is the Water's Edge Café, overlooking a small pond for electric model boats and a children's play area.

From here, take the footbridge to John Quay crossing over the sailboats moored below, to the stores and restaurants on **Pier 4**—Wallymagoo's marine bar, and the Pier 4 Storehouse. Beyond on Maple Leaf Quay lies the Nautical Center.

At the **Harbourside Boating Centre,** 283 Queen's Quay W. (☎ 416/203-3000), you can rent sail and power boats as well as sign on for sailing lessons, or week-long and weekend sailing courses. A three-hour sailboat rental costs from $45 to $125 depending on the boat's size, power boats from $60 to $180.

The **Harbourfront Antiques Market,** at 390 Queen's Quay West, at the foot of Spadina Avenue (☎ 416/260-2626), will keep antique-lovers busy browsing for hours. More than 100 antique dealers spread out their wares—jewelry, china, furniture, toys, and books. Indoor parking is adjacent to the market, and a cafeteria serves fresh salads, sandwiches, and desserts for rest stops. It's open May through October, Tuesday through Friday from 11am to 6pm, Saturday from 10am to 6pm, and Sunday from 8 to 6pm; November through April, Tuesday through Friday from 11am to 5pm, Saturday 10am to 5pm, and Sunday from 8am to 6pm.

At the park's west end stands **Bathurst Pier,** with a large sports field for romping around, plus two adventure playgrounds, one for older kids and the other (supervised) for three- to seven-year-olds.

More than 4,000 events take place annually at Harbourfront, including a Harbourfront Reading Festival, held every Tuesday on York Quay, that attracts some very eminent writers. Other happenings include films, dance, theater, music, children's events, multicultural festivals, and marine events. Two of the most important events are the annual Children's Festival and the International Festival of Authors. Most activities are free.

✪ **The Toronto Islands.** For ferry schedules, ☎ **416/392-8193.** Round-trip fare $3 adults, $1.50 seniors and ages 15–19, $1 for children 14 and under. Ferries operate all day, leaving from docks at the bottom of Bay Street. To get there, take a subway to Union Station and the Bay Street bus south.

A little ferry will take you across to 612 acres of island park crisscrossed by shady paths and quiet waterways—a glorious spot to walk, play tennis, bike, feed the ducks, putter around in boats, picnic, or just sit.

Children will find **Centreville** (☎ 416/363-0405), a 19-acre old-time amusement park, built and designed especially for them. But you won't find the usual neon signs, shrill hawkers, and aroma of greasy hot-dog stands. Instead you'll find a turn-of-the-century village complete with Main Street, tiny shops, a firehouse, and even a small working farm where the kids can pet lambs and chicks and enjoy pony rides. They'll also love trying out the miniature antique cars, fire engines, old-fashioned train, the authentic 1890s carousel, the flume ride, and the aerial cars. An all-day ride pass costs $10 for those 4 foot tall and under $15 for those over four feet. Individual ride tickets are 84¢. Open daily from mid-May to Labor Day, 10:30am to 6pm.

DOWNTOWN

CN Tower. 301 Front St. West. ☎ **416/360-8500.** Admission $12 adults, $9 seniors, $7 children 5–12, free for children under 5. Cosmic Pinball and Q-Zar $8 adults, $7 seniors, $6.50 children 5–12, free for children under 5. CN Tower Mon–Thurs 10am–10pm, Fri–Sat 10am–11pm. Cosmic Pinball and Q-Zar Mon–Thurs 11am–7pm, Fri–Sat 10am–10pm. Subway: Union Station, then walk west along Front Street.

As you approach the city, the first thing you'll notice is this slender needlelike structure. Tiny colored elevators that look like jumping beans glide to the top of this 1,815-foot-high tower—the tallest freestanding structure in the world.

As you enter the tower's base, look up through the atrium to the top—yes, that's where you're going. Glass-walled elevators on the outside walls of the tower whisk you to the 1,136-foot-high seven-level sky pod in just under one minute. From here, on a clear day you can't quite see forever, but you can see, I'm told, all the way to Niagara Falls, or even Buffalo, if you wish. One of the two observation levels is partially open to allow you to experience that dizzying sensation of height (vertigo sufferers beware).

Downtown Toronto Attractions

TORONTO

Downtown
Toronto

Allan Gardens ❷
Art Gallery of Toronto ❹
BCE Place ⓯
Bus Station ❸
CBC Building ⓭
Campbell House ❻
City Hall ❼
CN Tower ⑳
Convention Centre ⑲
Eaton Centre ❾
The Grange ❺
Harbourfront Antiques
  Market ㉓
Hockey Hall of Fame ⑯
Kensington Market ㉖
Maple Leaf Gardens ❶
O'Keefe Centre ⑰
Old City Hall ❽
Princess of Wales Theatre ㉔
Royal Alexandra Theatre ❿
Royal Bank Plaza ⑭
Roy Thomson Hall ⑪
St. Lawrence Market ⑱ ⑫
SkyDome ㉒
Toronto Dominion Centre
Toronto Stock Exchange ㉕
Union Station ㉑

LEGEND

Subway stop ⓣⓣⓒ

Church †

Post Office ✉

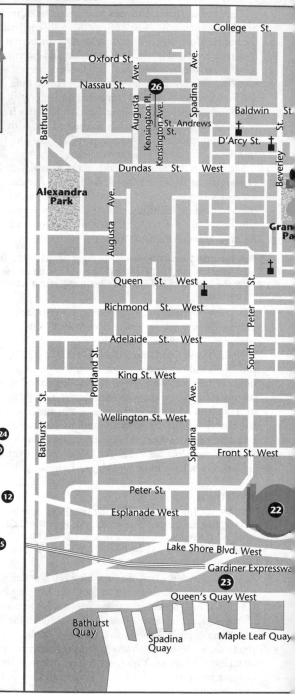

College St.

Oxford St.   Ave.

Nassau St.   ㉖

Bathurst   Augusta   Spadina   Baldwin   St.
St.   Kensington Pl.   †
          Kensington Ave.   St. Andrews
          St.   †
          D'Arcy St.   †
          ■

Alexandra
Park   Ave.   Dundas   St.   West

          Augusta   Gran
                    Pa

                    †
                    ■

          Queen   St.   West †
                    St.
          Richmond   St.   West   †
                    ■
                    Peter
          Adelaide   St.   West   St.

          Portland St.   South
          King St. West

          St.   Ave.
          Wellington St. West

Bathurst   Spadina   Front St. West

          Peter St.
                    ㉒
          Esplanade West

          Lake Shore Blvd. West

          Gardiner Expressw
                    ㉓
          Queen's Quay West

Bathurst
Quay   Spadina   Maple Leaf Quay
          Quay

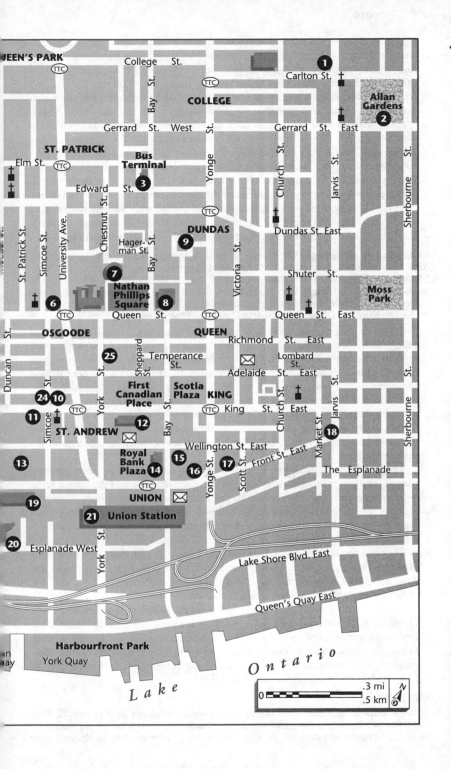

Besides the view, the tower offers several futuristic attractions—Cosmic Pinball, a simulator ride that duplicates the experience of a pinball, catapulting riders at high velocity past flashing lights, flippers, bumpers, and other hazards; Q-Zar, an exhilarating laser tag game; and CyberMind, a virtual reality center. The pod also contains broadcasting facilities, a revolving restaurant, and a nightclub. For lunch, dinner, or Sunday brunch reservations at the 360 Revolving Restaurant, call 416/362-5411.

Atop the tower sits a 335-foot antenna mast that took $3^1/2$ weeks to erect with the aid of a giant Sikorsky helicopter. It took 55 lifts to complete the operation. Above the sky pod is the world's highest public observation gallery, the Space Deck, 1,465 feet above the ground. The Outdoor Observation deck one floor below has a glass floor, which makes for a scary experience and a real bird's eye view of the Skydome. While you're up there, don't worry about the elements sweeping the tower into the lake: It's built of contoured reinforced concrete covered with thick glass-reinforced plastic, and designed to keep ice accumulation to a minimum. The structure can withstand the highest winds, and the effects of snow, ice, lightning, and earth tremors.

✪ **Art Gallery of Ontario.** 317 Dundas St. West (between McCaul and Beverley streets). ☎ **416/977-0414.** Admission $7.50 adults, $15 families (two adults plus children), $4 students and seniors, free for children under 12. Free on Wed 5–10pm and for seniors on Fri. Thurs–Sun 10am–5:30pm; Wed 10am–10pm. Grange House Thurs–Sun noon–4pm; Wed noon–9pm. Closed Mon–Tues in winter; Christmas Day and New Year's Day. Subway: St. Patrick on the University line; or take the subway to Dundas and the streetcar west.

The exterior gives no hint of the light and openness inside this beautifully designed gallery. The newly refurbished and expanded space is dramatic and the paintings are imaginatively displayed. Throughout are audiovisual presentations and interactive computer presentations that provide information on particular paintings or schools of painters.

Although the European collections are fine, I would concentrate on the Canadian galleries. The galleries displaying the Group of Seven—Tom Thomson, F. H. Varley, Lawren Harris, and Emily Carr—are extraordinary. In addition, other galleries show the genesis of Canadian art from earlier to more modern artists. Also don't miss the galleries featuring Inuit art.

The Henry Moore Sculpture Centre, possessing more than 800 pieces (original plasters, bronzes, maquettes, woodcuts, lithographs, etchings, and drawings), is the largest public collection of his works. In one room, under a glass ceiling, 20 or so of his large works stand like silent prehistoric rock formations. Along the walls flanking a ramp are color photographs showing Moore's major sculptures in their natural locations, which fully reveal their magnificent dimensions.

The collection of European old masters ranges from the 14th century to the French impressionists and beyond. Among the sculpture you'll find Picasso's *Poupée* and Brancusi's *First Cry,* two beauties.

Behind the gallery and connected by an arcade stands The Grange (1817), Toronto's oldest surviving brick house, which was the gallery's first permanent space. Originally the home of the Boulton family, it was a gathering place for many of the city's social and political leaders as well as such eminent guests as Matthew Arnold, Prince Kropotkin, and Winston Churchill. Today it's a living museum of mid-19th-century Toronto life, meticulously restored and furnished to reflect the 1830s. Entrance is free with admission to the art gallery.

MIDTOWN

✪ **Royal Ontario Museum.** 100 Queen's Park (at Avenue Road and Bloor Street). ☎ **416/586-5549.** Admission (including admission to the George R. Gardiner Museum of Ceramic Art) $8 adults, $4 seniors and students, $3.50 children 5–14, $16 families, free for children under

Midtown Toronto Attractions

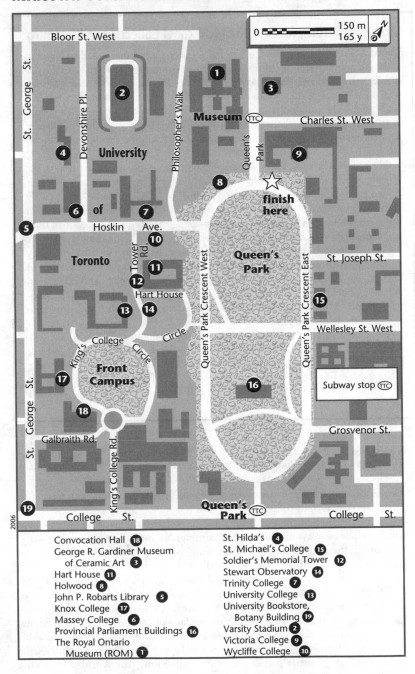

Convocation Hall	18	St. Hilda's	4
George R. Gardiner Museum of Ceramic Art	3	St. Michael's College	15
		Soldier's Memorial Tower	12
Hart House	11	Stewart Observatory	14
Holwood	8	Trinity College	7
John P. Robarts Library	5	University College	13
Knox College	17	University Bookstore, Botany Building	19
Massey College	6		
Provincial Parliament Buildings	16	Varsity Stadium	2
The Royal Ontario Museum (ROM)	1	Victoria College	9
		Wycliffe College	10

An Idyllic Setting for Art: The McMichael Collection at Kleinburg

The McMichael Canadian Art Collection, featuring Canadian, Inuit, First Nations, and contemporary art is worth the trip 25 miles north of downtown—for the setting as well as the art. The log and stone gallery sits amidst quiet stands of pine trees on 100 acres of conservation land. Specially designed to house the Canadian landscapes within, the gallery ambience is established in the lobby—itself a work of art with a pitched roof that soars to a height of 27 feet on massive rafters of Douglas fir. Throughout the gallery panoramic windows look south over white pine, cedar, ash, and birch.

The gallery houses works by Canada's famous group of landscape painters, the "Group of Seven," as well as Tom Thomson, David Milne, Emily Carr, and their contemporaries. These devoted painters, inspired by the Canadian wilderness early in this century, particularly that of Algonquin Park and northern Ontario, recorded its rugged landscape in highly individualistic styles. An impressive collection of Inuit and contemporary Native Canadian art and sculpture is also on display.

Founded by Robert and Signe McMichael, the gallery began in 1965 when they donated their property, home, and collection of 177 works to the Province of Ontario. Since 1965 the collection has expanded to include more than 5,000 works. Still, its unique atmosphere has been preserved—with log and barnwood walls, fieldstone fireplaces, and rustic decor like the hooked rugs and earthenware urns from the original McMichael home.

The gallery is located at 10365 Islington Ave. in Kleinburg (☎ 905/893-1121). Admission is $6 for adults, $3 for seniors and students, $13 for families, and free for children under 5. From Victoria Day to Canadian Thanksgiving, hours are daily 10am to 5pm; from late October to Victoria Day, it's Tuesday to Sunday 10am to 4pm. Buses travel to the Gallery from Bay and Dundas station and the Yorkdale GO station.

5; free for seniors all day on Tues, free for all Tues 4:30–8pm. Mon–Sat 10am–6pm (until 8pm on Tues); Sun 11am–6pm. Closed Christmas Day and New Year's Day. Subway: Museum or St. George.

The ROM, as it's affectionately called, is Canada's largest museum, with more than six million objects in its collections.

Among the many highlights is the Chinese collection, one of the world's best, which includes displays of Chinese wall paintings, 14 monumental Buddhist sculptures dating from the 12th to the 16th century, Chinese stone sculptures that were part of an original Ming tomb, and a gallery filled with rare jades, glazed tomb figures of warriors, weapons, and horse and chariot fittings, which span 5,000 years.

The Sigmund Samuel Canadiana galleries display a premier collection of early Canadian decorative arts and historical paintings showcased in elaborate period room settings. This collection also contains the famous McCrea models of buildings, farm implements, and tools, which are a representation in miniature of early rural life in Ontario. Other highlights include the Ancient Egypt Gallery with its mummies, the Roman gallery (Canada's most extensive collection), the world-class textile collection, and nine life science galleries (devoted to evolution, mammals, reptiles, and botany).

A favorite with kids is the Bat Cave Gallery, a miniature replica of the St. Clair bat cave in Jamaica, complete with more than 3,000 very lifelike bats roosting and flying through the air amid realistic spiders, crabs, a wild cat, and snakes. Kids also enjoy the Dinosaur Gallery, featuring 13 dinosaur skeletons, and the Discovery Gallery, a minimuseum where kids and adults can touch authentic artifacts from Egyptian scarabs to English military helmets.

✪ **George R. Gardiner Museum of Ceramic Art.** 111 Queen's Park. ☎ **416/586-8080.** Admission (including admission to the ROM) $8 adults, $4 seniors and students, $4 children 5–14, $16 families. Tues–Sun 10am–5pm. Subway: Museum or St. George.

Across the street from the ROM, the George R. Gardiner Museum, North America's only specialized ceramics museum, houses a great collection of 15th- to 18th-century European ceramics in four galleries. The pre-Columbian gallery contains fantastic Olmec and Maya figures, and objects from cultures in Mexico, Ecuador, Colombia, and Peru. The majolica gallery displays spectacular 16th- and 17th-century pieces from Florence, Faenza, and Venice and a Delftware collection of fine 17th-century chargers and other examples.

Upstairs the galleries are given over to porcelain—Meissen, Sèvres, Worcester, Chelsea, Derby, and other great names. All are spectacular. Among the highlights are the pieces from the Swan Service—a 2,200-piece set that took four years (1737–41) to make—and an extraordinary collection of Commedia dell'Arte figures.

ON THE OUTSKIRTS

✪ **Ontario Science Centre.** 770 Don Mills Rd. (at Eglinton Avenue East). ☎ **416/429-4100.** Admission $7.50 adults, $5.50 youths 13–17, $3 children 12 and under, $17 families; free for senior citizens and children under 5. Daily 10am–6pm. Closed Christmas Day. Parking $4. Take the Yonge Street subway to Eglinton, then the Eglinton bus going east, and get off at Don Mills Road. If you're driving from downtown, take the Don Valley Parkway and follow the signs from Don Mills Road north.

Described as everything from the world's most technical fun fair to a hands-on museum of the 21st century, the Science Centre really does hold a series of wonders for adult and child—650 hands-on experiments, no less, in 10 themed exhibit halls. When one million people visit every year, you know that the best time to get to the museum is promptly at 10am—that way you'll be able to play without too much interference and negotiation.

The building itself is another one of architect Raymond Moriyama's miracles. Instead of flattening the ravine and bulldozing the trees on the site, Moriyama designed to the ravine's contours so that a series of glass-enclosed escalators providing views of the natural surroundings take you down an escarpment to the main exhibition halls. Supposedly Moriyama built penalty clauses into the subcontractors' contracts for each and every tree destroyed!

Wherever you look there are things to touch, push, pull, or crank. Test your reflexes, balance, heart rate, and grip strength; play with computers and binary-system games and puzzles; and shunt slides of butterfly wings, bedbugs, fish scales, or feathers under the microscope. Tease your brain with optical illusions; land a spaceship on the moon. Watch bees making honey; try to lift sponge building blocks with a mechanical grip; or see how high you can elevate a balloon with your own pedal power. The fun goes on and on—it's a wonder I ever made it home.

Throughout, there are small theaters showing film and slide shows on various topics, while at regular times demonstrators present 20-minute expositions on such subjects as lasers, metal casting, and high-voltage electricity (watch your friend's hair stand on end). In 1996, an OMNIMAX Theatre is scheduled to open. Facilities include a licensed restaurant and lounge, cafeteria, and science shop.

✪ **The Metropolitan Zoo.** Meadowvale Road (north of Highway 401 and Sheppard Avenue), Scarborough. ☎ **416/392-5900.** Admission $9.95 adults, $7 seniors and children 12–17, $5 children 5–11; free for children under 5. Winter daily 9:30am–4:30pm; summer daily

9am–7:30pm. Closed Christmas Day. Take the subway all the way to Kennedy on the Bloor-Danforth line. Then take bus no. 86A from there north. Check with the TTC for schedules (☎ 416/393-4636). Driving from downtown, take the Don Valley Parkway to Highway 401 east and exit on Meadowvale Road.

Covering 710 acres of parkland in Scarborough is a unique zoological garden containing some 4,000 animals, plus an extensive botanical collection. The plants and animals are housed either in the eight pavilions—including Africa, Indo-Malaya, Australasia, and the Americas—or in outdoor paddocks. It's a photographer's dream.

Six miles of walkways offer the visitor access to any area of the zoo, or you can use the Zoomobile or monorail. During the warmer months the Zoomobile takes the zoogoer around the major walkways, viewing the animals contained in outdoor facilities. The monorail, which runs year-round, travels through the beautiful Rouge River Valley where animals native to Canada are displayed.

Facilities include restaurants, picnic tables, gift shop, first aid, and family center; strollers and wheelchairs are also available. The zoo is equipped with ramps and washrooms for travelers with disabilities. The Africa pavilion is also equipped with an elevator for strollers and wheelchairs. Ample parking is available.

Canada's Wonderland. 9580 Jane St., Vaughan. ☎ **905/832-7000,** 905/832-7000 for a recording, or 905/832-8131 for concert information at the Kingswood Music Theatre. Pay One Price Passport, for the day, including unlimited use of all rides and shows (excludes food, games, merchandise, parking, special attractions, and the Kingswood Music Theatre), $30.95 adults, $15.45 seniors and children 3–6, free for children under 2. Grounds admission only $17.95 (no rides). May and Labor Day–early Oct weekends only 10am–8pm; June 1–25 Mon–Fri 10am–8pm, Sat–Sun 10am–10pm; June 26–Labor Day daily 10am–10pm. Hanna Barbera Land and Kids Kingdom close daily at 8pm. "Splashworks" open 11am–7pm, depending on weather and lighting. Parking $6.50. GO Express Bus from Yorkdale or York Mills subway directly to Wonderland. If you're driving, take Yonge Street north to Highway 401 and travel west to Highway 400 north. Take the Rutherford Road exit off Highway 400 and follow the signs. Exit at Major Mackenzie if heading south on Highway 400.

Nineteen miles (or 30 minutes) north of Toronto is Canada's answer to Disney World. The 300-acre park features more than 140 attractions including 50 rides, a 10-acre waterpark, a participatory play area, and live shows. Among the most popular rides are Days of Thunder, which puts you in the driver's seat during a 200-mile-an-hour high-stakes stock car race; Jet Scream, a 360° looping starship; Vortex, Canada's only suspended roller coaster; The Bat, a backwards/forwards looping coaster; Skyrider, a standup looping coaster; and the Mighty Canadian Minebuster, the park's largest wooden roller coaster. Splash Works has 16 water rides, from speed slides to tube rides and special scaled down slides and pool for kids. At Timberwolf Falls riders plunge down a five-story waterfall. Top name entertainers appear at the Kingswood Theatre. To add to the thrills, Klingons, Vulcans, Romulans, and Bajorans along with Hanna-Barbera characters stroll around the park. Additional attractions include minigolf, batting cages, restaurants, and shops.

You'll probably need eight hours to see everything. If you picnic on the grounds, forgo souvenirs, and avoid the video games, a family of four can do the park for about $90. Note: Watch out for the extra added attractions that are not included in the admission pass, particularly the many "games of skill."

MORE ATTRACTIONS
ARCHITECTURAL HIGHLIGHTS
Casa Loma. 1 Austin Terrace. ☎ **416/923-1171.** Admission $8 adults, $4.50 seniors and children 6–16. Daily 10am–4pm. Subway: Dupont; then walk two blocks north.

Every city has its folly and Toronto has a charming one, complete with Elizabethan-style chimneys, Rhineland turrets, secret panels, passageways, and a mellifluous-sounding name: Casa Loma. Sir Henry Pellatt had a lifelong and incurably romantic fascination with medieval castles—so he decided to build his own, from 1911 and 1914 at a cost of $3.5 million. He studied European medieval castles, and gathered materials and furnishings, bringing marble, glass, and paneling from Europe, teak from Asia, and oak and walnut from prime areas of North America. He imported Scottish stone-masons to build the massive walls that surround the six-acre site.

It's a fascinating place to explore: the majestic Great Hall with its 60-foot ceiling; the Oak Room, where three artisans worked for three years to fashion the paneling; the Conservatory, with its elegant bronze doors and stained-glass dome; the battlements and towers; Sir Henry's suite, containing a shower with an 18-inch-diameter shower head; the 1,700-bottle wine cellar; and the 800-foot tunnel to the stables, where horses were quartered amid the luxury of Spanish tile and mahogany.

City Hall. Queen Street West. ☎ 416/392-7341. Self-guided tours Mon–Fri 8:30am–4pm. Subway: Queen Street. Streetcar: Take the Queen streetcar west to Bay Street.

Another architectural spectacle houses the mayor's office and the city's administrative offices. Daringly designed in the early 1960s by Finnish architect Viljo Revell, it consists of a low podium topped by the flying-saucer–shaped Council Chamber, which is enfolded between two curved towers. In front stretches Nathan Phillips Square (named after the mayor who initiated the project), where in summer you can sit and contemplate the flower gardens, fountains, and reflecting pool (which doubles as a skating rink in winter), as well as listen to concerts. Here also stands Henry Moore's Three-Way Piece No. 2, locally referred to as The Archer, purchased through a public subscription fund. To the east, in contrast, stands Old City Hall, a green-copper-roofed Victorian Romanesque-style building.

Ontario Legislature. Queen's Park. ☎ 416/325-7500. Tours given daily Victoria Day–Labor Day. Call ahead to check times and also for tours in winter. Subway: Queen's Park.

East of the university, at the top of University Avenue, lies Queen's Park, surrounding the rose-tinted sandstone and granite Ontario Parliament buildings, which are profusely carved, with stately domes, arches, and porte cochères. Drop in between 2 and 3pm when the legislature is in session (in fall, winter, and spring) for some pithy comments during the Question Period.

Royal Bank Plaza. At the corner of Front and Bay Streets. Subway: Union.

Shimmering in the sun, the Royal Bank Plaza looks like a pillar of gold—and in a way it is. More important, it is a masterpiece of design and architectural drama. Two triangular towers of bronze mirrored glass flank a 130-foot-high glass-walled banking hall. The external tower walls are built in a serrated configuration so they reflect a phenomenal mosaic of color from the skies and surrounding buildings. In the banking hall, check out the work of Venezuelan sculptor Jesus Raphael Soto.

Skydome. 1 Blue Jays Way. ☎ 416/341-2770. One-hour tours begin most days at 10am; cost is $9 adults, $6 seniors and children. Subway: Union.

In 1989, the opening of the downtown 53,000-seat SkyDome, new home to the Toronto Blue Jays baseball team and the Toronto Argonauts football team, was a gala event. The stadium itself represents an engineering feat, featuring the world's first fully retractable roof, which spans more than eight acres, and a gigantic video scoreboard. So large is it that you could fit a 31-story building inside the complex when the roof is closed. Indeed, there's already an 11-story hotel with 70 rooms facing directly onto the field.

HISTORIC BUILDINGS

Campbell House. 160 Queen St. West. ☎ **416/597-0227.** Admission $3 adults; $1.50 seniors, students, and children. Mon–Fri 9:30am–4:30pm. Also Sat–Sun noon–4:30pm May 24–end of Dec. Subway: Osgoode.

Just across the street from Osgoode Hall, on the opposite corner of University and Queen, sits Sir William Campbell's mansion, built in 1822 by this Loyalist and subsequent chief justice of Upper Canada. He retired to his mansion in 1829 where he resided until he died in 1834.

Fort York. Fleet Street (between Bathurst Street and Strachan Avenue). ☎ **416/392-6907.** Admission $5 adults, $3 children 6–10, $3.25 seniors and youths 11–17; free for children 5 and under. Winter Tues–Sun noon–4pm; summer weekdays 10am–5pm, weekends noon–5pm. Streetcar: Bathurst streetcar south to the gate.

Established by Lieutenant-Governor Simcoe in 1793 to defend "little muddy York," as Toronto was then known, Fort York was sacked by Americans in 1813. At the fort you can see the soldiers' and officers' quarters, clamber over the ramparts, and view demonstrations and exhibits.

Osgoode Hall. 130 Queen St. West. ☎ **416/947-3300.** Tours by appointment, except in summer when daily tours are given Mon–Fri at 1 and 1:20pm. Subway: Osgoode.

To the west of City Hall extends an impressive, elegant wrought-iron fence in front of an equally gracious mansion, Osgoode Hall, currently the home of the Law Society of Upper Canada. The fence was originally built to prevent the cows from getting in and trampling the flower beds. On a conducted tour you can see the splendor of the grand staircase, the rotunda, the Great Library, and the fine portrait and sculpture collection. Building began in 1829 on this structure, troops were billeted here during the Rebellion of 1837, and the buildings now house the headquarters of Ontario's legal profession and several magnificent courtrooms—including one using materials from London's Old Bailey. The courts are open to the public.

MARKETS

Toronto has a colorful and lively tapestry that should not be missed—the Kensington Market, between Spadina Avenue and Bathurst Street just south of College Street. If you can struggle out of bed to get there around 5am, you'll see the squawking chickens being carried from their trucks to the stalls. Here, in what used to be primarily a Jewish market in the heart of the then garment center, you'll hear the accents of Portuguese, Italians, and others, stall owners who spread their wares before them—squid and crabs in pails, chickens, pigeons, bread, cheese, apples, pears, peppers, ginger, and mangoes from the West Indies, salted fish from Portuguese dories, lace, fabrics, and other colorful remnants. The place seethes with crowds on its narrow streets, a cacophony of bargaining and shrieking—a veritable bazaar.

As I said, if you want to capture the essence of the market, then go in the early morning; if you're a bargain seeker, go later in the day when the vendors are anxious to be rid of their wares. There's no market on Sunday.

The other market has a more staid atmosphere, but it's a terrific food market. The accents are clearly English at the St. Lawrence Market, held Tuesday through Saturday from 7am to 5pm (Saturday is the day). Ontario farmers gather here to offer meat and produce for sale; the aroma of cheese, meat, and fish mingles with the scent of flowers and freshly made candies and pastries. It's a good place to pick up your picnic fare for a day at the Islands.

While you're here, seek out the restored St. Lawrence Hall, 157 King St. East (☎ 416/392-7120). This glorious building designed in the Renaissance style was the focal point for Toronto's social life in the 19th century—everything from Jenny Lind performances to temperance and antislavery meetings.

MUSEUMS

The Bata Shoe Museum. 327 Bloor St. West (at the corner of St. George). ☎ **416/ 979-7799.** Admission $6 adults, $4 students, $2 children 5–14; first Tues of month free. Tues– Sat 10am–5pm (Thurs until 8pm), Sun noon–5pm.

Imelda Marcos or anyone else interested in shoes and fashion history will love this museum housing the personal collection—9,000 items—of the Bata family. Now located in a brand-new building, the three-floor galleries display shoes from all over the world and from every time period. The main gallery All About Shoes is home to the plaster cast of the first human footprints that date from 4 million B.C., discovered in Africa by anthropologist Mary Leakey, and then traces the development of shoes, featuring moon boots, deep sea diving boots, and shoes worn by the rich and famous. One display focuses on Canadian footwear fashioned by the Inuit, while another highlights 19th-century ladies' footwear.

Black Creek Pioneer Village. Steeles Avenue and Jane Street. ☎ **416/736-1733.** Admission $7.50 adults, $5 seniors, $3.25 children 5–14; free for children under 5. Mar and Nov–Dec daily 10am–4:30pm; Apr–June Sat–Sun 10am–5:30pm; May–Sept daily 10am–5pm. Closed Jan to mid-Mar. Take the Yonge Street subway north to Finch and transfer to the no. 60 bus that runs along Steeles Avenue West to Jane Street.

Life at this beautifully landscaped village moves at the gentle pace of rural Ontario as it was 100 years ago. You can watch the authentically garbed villagers as they go about their chores—harrowing, seeding, rail splitting, sheep shearing, and threshing. Enjoy the fruits of their cooking, wander through the cozily furnished homesteads, visit the working mill, shop at the general store, and rumble past the farm animals in a horse-drawn wagon. There are over 30 restored buildings to explore.

Hockey Hall of Fame. 30 Yonge St. (at Front Street in BCE Place). ☎ **416/360-7765.** Admission $8.50 adults, $5.50 seniors and children 13 and under. Mon–Sat 9am–6pm, Sun 10am–6pm.

Ice-hockey fans will thrill to see the original Stanley Cup (donated in 1893 by Lord Stanley of Preston), a replica of the Montréal Canadiens' dressing room, Terry Sawchuck's goalie gear, Newsy Lalonde's skates, and the stick that Max Bentley used, along with photographs of the personalities and great moments in ice hockey history. Interactive displays and videos make it fun for all.

Marine Museum. Exhibition Place. ☎ **416/392-1765.** Admission $3.50 adults, $2.75 children 13–18 and seniors, $2.50 children under 12, free for children 5 and under. Tues–Fri 10am–5pm, Sat–Sun and holidays noon–5pm. Take 511 streetcar southbound from Bathurst.

This museum interprets the history of Toronto Harbour and its relation to the Great Lakes. From May to October, visitors can board the fully restored 1932 *Ned Hanlan,* the last steam tugboat to sail on Lake Ontario.

NEIGHBORHOODS

CHINATOWN   Stretching along Dundas Street from Bay Street to Spadina Avenue, and north and south along Spadina, Chinatown, home to many of Toronto's 350,000 Chinese residents, is a great area for eating and browsing in fascinating shops. Even the street signs are in Chinese.

If you're interested in things Asian, then go into **Dragon City,** a large shopping mall on Spadina that's staffed and shopped by Chinese. Here you'll find all kinds of stores, some selling exotic Chinese preserves like cuttlefish, lemon ginger, whole mango, ginseng, and antler, and others specializing in Asian books, tapes, and records, as well as fashions and foods. Downstairs, a whole court is given over to Korean, Indonesian, Chinese, and Japanese fast-food restaurants.

As you stroll through Chinatown, stop at the **Kim Moon Bakery** on Dundas Street West (☎ 416/977-1933), and pick up some Chinese pastries and/or a pork bun.Or go to a tea store. A walk through Chinatown at night is especially exciting—the sidewalks are filled with people, families, and youths, and neon lights shimmer everywhere. Another stopping place might be the **New Asia Supermarket** (☎ 416/591-9314) around the corner from Dundas at 293-299 Spadina Ave.

QUEEN STREET WEST   Over the years this street, lined with an eclectic mix of stores and clubs, has been known as the heart of the city's funky avant-garde scene. Although recent trends have brought mainstream stores like The Gap here, there's still a broad selection of good-value bistros, several secondhand and antiquarian bookstores, and funky fashion stores. East of Spadina the street is being slowly gentrified, but beyond Spadina it still retains its rough and ready energy.

YORKVILLE   This is the name given to the area that stretches north of Bloor Street, between Avenue Road and Bay Street. In 1853 Yorkville became a village, surrounded then by trees and meadows; in the 1960s it became Toronto's Haight Ashbury, the mecca for young suburban runaways; and in the 1980s it became the focus of the chic, who shopped at the famous-name boutiques (Hermès, Courrèges, Fabiani, Cartier, Turnbull and Asser), and occupied the restored town houses, as well as the art galleries, cafes, and restaurants.

It's a good place for strolling and browsing; you can sit outside and enjoy an iced coffee at one of the many cafes on the south side of Yorkville Avenue and watch the parade go by. Most cafes have happy hours from 4pm to 7 or 8pm. Make sure you wander through the labyrinths of **Hazelton Lanes** between Avenue Road and Hazelton Avenue, where you'll find a maze of shops and offices clustered around an outdoor court in the center of a building that's topped with apartments—the most sought-after in the city. And while you're in the neighborhood (especially if you're an architecture buff), take a look at **Metro Library,** designed by Raymond Moriyama at Bloor and Yorkville Avenue.

PARKS & GARDENS

Toronto is blessed with a sizable amount of green space when you include the Toronto Islands, such downtown green spaces as Queen's Park, and the series of parks that extend along the steep ravines of the Humber and Don valleys.

Downtown, the **Allan Gardens,** between Jarvis, Sherbourne, Dundas, and Gerrard Streets (☎ 416/392-7259), still contain the Victorian glass-domed Palm House.

Edwards Garden at Lawrence Avenue and Leslie Street (☎ 416/397-1340), a formal garden with a creek cutting through it, is part of a series of parks. It's famous for its rhododendrons but also features gracious bridges, rock gardens, and rose and other seasonal displays. Walking tours are given on Tuesday and Thursday at 11am and 2pm.

In the West End, the 400-acre **High Park** extends from Bloor Street to the Gardiner Expressway and shelters many delights: Grenadier Pond, a small zoo, swimming pool, tennis courts, sports fields, bowling greens, and vast expanses for jogging, picnicking, and bicycling.

ESPECIALLY FOR KIDS

The city puts on a fabulous array of special events for children at Harbourfront. In March the Children's Film Festival screens 40 films from 15 countries. In April, Spring Fever celebrates the season with egg decorating, puppet shows, and more; on Saturday mornings in April, cushion concerts are given for the five to 12 set. In May the Milk

International Children's Festival brings 100 international children's performers to the city for a week of great entertainment. For additional information call 416/973-3000.

For the last 30 years, the **Young People's Theatre,** at 165 Front St. East, at Sherbourne St. (☎ 416/862-2222 box office or 416/363-5131 administration) has been entertaining young people. Its season runs from November to May.

All the attractions that have major appeal to kids of all ages are listed above, but here I've summarized them in what I think is the most logical order, at least from a kid's point of view (the first five, though, really belong in a dead heat).

- **Ontario Science Centre**   Kids race to be the first at this paradise of fun hands-on games, experiments, and push-button demonstrations—700 of 'em.
- **Canada's Wonderland**   The kids love the rides in the theme park. But watch out for those video games, which they also love—an unanticipated extra cost.
- **Harbourfront**   Kaleidoscope is an ongoing program of creative crafts, active games, and special events on weekends and holidays. There is also a summer pond, winter ice skating, and a crafts studio.
- **Ontario Place Waterslides**   A huge Cinesphere, a futuristic pod, and other entertainments are the big hits at this recreational/cultural park on three artificial islands on the edge of Lake Ontario. In Children's Village, kids 12 and under can scramble over rope bridges, bounce on an enormous trampoline, or drench one another in the water-play section.
- **Metro Zoo**   At one of the world's best zoos, modeled after San Diego's, the animals in this 710-acre park really do live in a natural environment.
- **Toronto Islands-Centreville**   Riding a ferry to this turn-of-the-century amusement park is part of the fun.
- **CN Tower**   Kids especially like the "Tour of the Universe."
- **Royal Ontario Museum**   The top hit is always the dinosaurs.
- **McLaughlin Planetarium**   Kids enjoy the special shows and stargazing.
- **Fort York**   The reenactments of battle drills, musket and cannon firing, and musical marches with fife and drum capture kids' attention.
- **Hockey Hall of Fame**   Young hockey fans especially like the interactive video displays.
- **Black Creek Pioneer Village**   Here kids go back in time for craft and other demonstrations.
- **Casa Loma**   It's fun to tour the stables and the fantasy rooms.
- **Art Gallery of Ontario**   Kids like its hands-on exhibit.

African Lion Safari. Off Highway 8 between Hamilton and Cambridge. ☎ **519/623-2620.** Admission $14.50 adults, $12.50 seniors and youths 13–17, $10.50 children 3–12. Apr–Oct daily; July–Labor Day 10am–5:30pm; at other times closes earlier. Closed winter.

Just a half-hour northwest of Hamilton, you can drive yourself or take the guided safari tram through this 750-acre wildlife park containing rhinos, cheetahs, lions, tigers, giraffes, zebras, vultures, and many other species. Shows and demonstrations are held throughout the day. There are also scenic railroad and boat rides, plus special kids' jungle and water (bring bathing suits) play areas. Admission includes a tour of the six large game reserves plus the rides and shows.

Chudleigh's. On Highway 25 north of Highway 401 (P.O. Box 76), Milton, ON. ☎ **905/ 826-1252.** Free admission. July 1–Oct daily 9am–7pm; Nov–June daily 10am–5pm.

A day here will introduce the kids to life on a farm. They'll enjoy the hay rides, pony rides, sleigh rides, and, in season, the apple picking and sugaring off of the maple trees. All of the produce is on sale, too, in the bake shop and fruit-and-vegetable markets.

Cullen Gardens & Miniature Village. Taunton Rd., Whitby, ON. ☎ **905/668-6606.** Admission $9.95 adults, $7.50 seniors, $3.99 children 3–12. Daily 9am–8pm. Closed early Jan to mid-Apr.

The miniature village (made to one-half scale) has great appeal. The 27 acres of gardens and the shopping and live entertainment add to the fun.

Wild Water Kingdom. 7855 Finch Ave. West (1 mile west of Highway 427), Brampton, ON. ☎ **905/794-0565.** Admission $16 adults, $13 children 4–9 and seniors. June daily 10am–6pm; July–Labor Day daily 10am–10pm (water rides, to 8pm).

Kids love this huge water theme park complete with a half acre wave pool, 18 water rides, and giant hot tubs. In between they can use the batting cages or practice on the mini-golf circuit.

6 Special Events & Festivals

The big event in May is the nine-day **Milk International Children's Festival,** featuring more than 30 international entertainment troupes—acrobats, mimes, comedians, storytellers, theater companies, and puppeteers. For details call Harbourfront at ☎ 416/973-3000.

In June, the **Metro International Caravan** (☎ 416/977-0466) is a nine-day feast of arts, food, and entertainment celebrating the cultural life of the city's many ethnic communities, from Armenian to Vietnamese. A Passport admitting you to the 40 pavilions around town is $14 for the whole nine days (or $7 for one day).

In late June or early July, the **Queen's Plate** is run at Woodbine Racetrack. Begun in 1859, it is the oldest stakes race in North America. Other big June events include the 10-day **du Maurier Jazz Festival** and the **Mariposa Folk Festival** featuring more than 200 top performers of folk, R&B, and blues. Also in late June/early July the 10-day Fringe Theater Festival showcases experimental and new drama featuring more than 80 performing artists/groups. For information write or call the Fringe of Toronto Festival, 720 Bathurst St. Suite 303, Toronto, ON, M5S 2R4 (☎ 416/534-5919).

In July the **Molson Indy,** a gran prix race on the IndyCar circuit, is run at the Exhibition Place circuit on the third weekend usually. Call ☎ 416/872-4639. At the end of July or the beginning of August, a West Indian calypso beat takes over the city when three quarters of a million people dance, sway, and watch the colorful **Caribana** celebration, Toronto's version of carnival complete with traditional Caribbean and Latin American foods, moonlight cruises, island picnics, concerts, and arts and crafts exhibits. The high point is the Saturday grand parade, when the city dances to the beat of steel drums, as the colorful befeathered and sequined retinue snakes its way downtown, singing and dancing in best Mardi Gras fashion.

In August the big 20-day event is the **Canadian National Exhibition,** at Exhibition Place, featuring midway rides, display buildings, free shows, and grandstand performers. It was first staged in 1878. For information contact Canadian National Exhibition, Exhibition Place, Toronto, ON, M6K 3C3 (☎ 416/393-6000). On Labor Day the Canadian Air Show is an added bonus; the Snowbirds, the Canadian Air Force Performance Team, performs. Good vantage points are from the islands or Ontario Place.

In September the **Toronto International Film Festival** is the world's second largest, showing more than 250 films over ten days. In October the prestigious nine-day **International Festival of Authors** at Harbourfront (☎ 416/973-3000) draws some of the world's finest authors to readings and other events.

In November the **Royal Agricultural Winter Fair,** a sort of state fair held since 1929, displays the largest fruits and vegetables, along with crafts, farm machinery, and livestock. The royal event is the accompanying horse show traditionally attended by a British royal family member.

Call the **Metro Toronto Convention & Visitors Association** at ☎ 416/203-2500 for additional information on festivals and events.

7 Outdoor Activities & Spectator Sports

For general information on city sports facilities call the Department of Parks and Recreation at ☎ 416/392-1111 Monday to Friday from 8:30am to 4:30pm.

OUTDOOR ACTIVITIES

BIKING   The Martin Goodman Trail, which runs from the Beaches to the Humber River along the waterfront, is ideal for biking. The Lower Don Valley bike trail starts in the city's east end at Front Street and runs north to Riverdale park. High Park is another good venue along with the parks along the ravines. Official bike lanes are marked on College/Carlton streets, the Bloor Street Viaduct leading to the Danforth, Beverly/St. George and Davenport Road. The Convention and Visitors Association has more detailed information on these bike lanes.

The **Toronto Bicycling Network** (☎ 416/760-3909) offers day and weekend trips. Bikes can be rented from **Wheel Excitement,** Rees Street (☎ 416/506-1001) for $14 for the first two hours plus $2 for each additional hour or $26 a day.

BOATING/CANOEING   **Harbourside Boating Centre,** 283 Queen's Quay West (☎ 416/203-3000) rents sail and power boats and also provides sailing instruction. For three hours, sailboats cost from $45 to $125 and power boats from $60 to $180, depending on the size. Weekend and week-long sailing courses are offered.

Harbourfront Canoe and Kayak School, 283A Queens Quay West (☎ 416/203-2277) rents kayaks for $50 a day or $20 an hour and canoes for $25 and $12 respectively.

Canoes, row and pedal boats can also be rented on the Toronto Islands just south of Centreville.

CROSS-COUNTRY SKIING   Groomed trails are maintained in three or so parks so that skiers can work out right in the city.

GOLF   Among the city's half dozen metro public golf courses the following stand out:

Don Valley, at Yonge Street south of Highway 401 (☎ 416/392-2465), designed by Howard Watson, is a scenic course with some challenging elevated tees and a par-5 12th hole. It's a good place to start your kids.

Humber Valley (☎ 416/392-2488) is a par-70 links and valleyland course that has three final holes requiring major concentration.

The moderately difficult **Tam O'Shanter** course, Birchmount Avenue, north of Sheppard (☎ 416/392-2547), features links holes and water hazards among its challenges.

There are several outstanding championship courses in the Toronto area. The most expensive ($125) is the course where the Canadian Open is played, the **Glen Abbey Golf Club** in Oakville (☎ 905/844-1800), designed by Jack Nicklaus. **The Lionhead Golf Club** in Brampton (☎ 905/455-4900) has two 18-hole par-72 courses, charging $125 for the longer course and $110 for the slightly shorter course. In Markham the **Angus Glen Golf Club** (☎ 905/887-5157) has a Doug Carrick–designed par-72 course and charges $72 greens fees. The **Royal Woodbine** in Etobicoke has a challenging par-71 course and charges $80.

HORSEBACK RIDING   Rouge Hill Stables, just off Kingston Road (Highway 2) east of Sheppard Avenue (☎ 416/284-6176), offers 1-hour and 1¹/₂-hour trail rides through the Rouge Valley. Reserve ahead.

HIKING/JOGGING   If you want to jog downtown, places to run include Harbourfront and along the lakefront or through Queen's Park and the University.

The Martin Goodman Trail, which runs 12.4 miles (20km) along the waterfront from the Beaches in the east to the Humber River in the West, is ideal for jogging, walking, or cycling. It links to the Tommy Thompson Trail, which travels the parks stretching from the lakefront along the Humber River.

Near the Ontario Science Centre in the Central Don Valley, Ernest Thompson Seton Park is also good for jogging and hiking. Parking is available at the Thorncliffe Drive and Wilket Creek entrances.

ICE-SKATING/IN-LINE SKATING   Nathan Philips Square in front of City Hall becomes a free ice rink in winter, as does an area at Harbourfront Centre. Rentals are available. Artificial rinks are also found in more than 25 parks including **Grenadier Pond** in High Park—a romantic spot with a bonfire and vendors selling roasted chestnuts. They're open from November to March. In-line skates can be rented from Wheel Excitement (see "Biking," above).

SWIMMING   There are a dozen or so outdoor pools (open June to September) in the municipal parks, including High and Rosedale Parks, plus indoor pools at several community recreation centers. For pool information call ☎ 416/392-1111.

The **University of Toronto Athletic Centre,** 55 Harbord St. at Spadina Avenue (☎ 416/978-4680), opens its swimming pool free to the public on Sunday from 12:10 to 4pm. The pool at the YMCA at 20 Grosvenor St. can be used on a day pass.

There are public beaches on the Toronto Islands (off Hanlan's Point) and Woodbine Beach in the Beaches neighborhood, but quite frankly the waters of Lake Ontario are polluted, and although people do swim in them, they do so at their own risk. Beaches are signed when they are deemed unsafe, usually after a heavy rainfall.

TENNIS   There are tennis facilities in more than **30 municipal parks.** The most convenient locations are the courts in High Park, Rosedale, and Jonathan Ashridge parks, which are open in summer only. At Eglinton Flats park, west of Keele street at Eglinton, six courts can be used in winter. Call ☎ 416/767-3622 for information.

SPECTATOR SPORTS

Some wag once said that there's only one really religious place in Toronto and that's **Maple Leaf Gardens,** 60 Carlton St. (☎ 416/977-1641), where the city's ice hockey team, the NHL **Maple Leafs,** wield their sticks to the delight and screaming enthusiasm of fans. Tickets are nigh impossible to attain because many are sold by subscription and as soon as the remainder go on sale, lines wind around the block. The only way to secure tickets is to harass your concierge, pay a scalper, or call Edwards and Edwards at 416/363-1288.

SkyDome, on Front Street beside the CN Tower, is the home of the American League **Blue Jays,** World Series champs in 1992 and 1993, though their fortunes have declined since then. Call ☎ 416/341-1111 for information. The Toronto Argonauts football team, who play from June through November, and the Toronto Blizzard soccer team, also play in SkyDome. For information, write to the Toronto Blue Jays Baseball Club, P.O. Box 7777, Adelaide Street Post Office,

Toronto, ON, M5C 2K7 (☎ 416/341-1000). For tickets call TicketMaster at 416/872-5000.

In 1995, Toronto acquired an exciting new addition to its sports scene—a brand-new NBA franchise. The **Toronto Raptors,** under general manager Isaiah Thomas, will find out how hoops are received north of the border. For the first season or two, they will play in Skydome; a new stadium is being constructed, but it's still in the preliminary stages of this writing. For information, call ☎ 416/214-2255 or TicketMaster at 416/872-5000.

Racing takes place at **Woodbine Racetrack,** at Rexdale Boulevard at Highway 427, Etobicoke (☎ 416/675-6110), famous for the Queen's Plate (contested in July), the Breeders Crown, and the North America Cup. About 100 miles outside Toronto, **Fort Erie Race Track** (☎ 905/871-3200) is another beautiful racing venue. Harness racing takes place at **Mohawk Raceway,** 30 miles west of the city at Highway 410 and Guelph Line (☎ 416/675-7223).

8 Shopping

Toronto's major shopping areas are the Bloor/Yorkville area for designer boutiques and top-name galleries; Queen Street West for a more funky mixture of fashion, antiques, and bookstores; and a number of shopping malls/centers like Queen's Quay down on the waterfront, and the two-block-long Eaton Centre.

ANTIQUES

The finest antiques can be found in the Bloor/Yorkville area and in the Mount Pleasant/St. Clair area along the 500 to 700 blocks of Mount Pleasant Road. The more funky and often more recent collectibles can be found at various stores along Queen Street West. Markham Village also has several antiques stores.

Harbourfront Antiques Market. 390 Queen's Quay W. ☎ **416/260-2626.**

The 100-plus dealers here sell fine-quality antiques. On summer Sundays there's also a market outside featuring less established dealers. Get there early on weekends, when more than 150 dealers open up shop. Closed Monday.

Michel Taschereau. 176 Cumberland St. ☎ **416/923-3020.**

In this fine store you'll have to thread your way through the dense collection very carefully. You'll find 18th- and 19th-century English and French furniture, including large armoires, and French and English china. There's Lalique glass and Canadian folk art also.

Ronald Windebanks. 21 Avenue Rd. ☎ **416/962-2862.**

Stocked with objects full of character and whimsy, this store is crammed with an eclectic array of furniture, porcelain, crystal, glass, prints, antique garden furniture, and grand urns, plus some charming carved animal folk art.

ART

Most galleries are open Tuesday to Saturday from 10:30am to 5:30pm, so don't come around on Sunday or Monday.

Isaacs/Inuit Gallery of Eskimo Art. 9 Prince Arthur Ave. ☎ **416/921-9985.**

Museum-quality Inuit sculpture, prints, drawings, wall hangings, and antiquities from across the Arctic are featured here. The gallery also specializes in early Native Canadian art and artifacts.

Jane Corkin. 179 John St. ☎ **416/979-1980.**

This gallery specializes in historical and contemporary photographs by international and Canadian photographers.

Kinsman Robinson. 14 Hazelton Ave. ☎ **416/964-2374.**

This bilevel gallery exhibits such contemporary Canadian artists as the color-drunk Norval Morrisseau, Henri Masson, Robert Katz, and Stanley Cosgrove, plus sculptors Esther Wertheimer, Maryon Kantaroff, Joseph Jacobs, and others.

BOOKS
Abelard Books. 519 Queen St. W. ☎ **416/504-2665.**

This is one of my favorite rare-book stores in the city. It has a fabulous collection of early editions and other rare books, with every subject clearly cataloged. Armchairs invite leisurely browsing. A real book-lover's haven.

Albert Britnell Book Shop. 765 Yonge St., north of Bloor St. ☎ **416/924-3321.**

A Toronto tradition, this wonderful store has a great selection of hard- and softcover books displayed handsomely on wooden shelves. The staff is very knowledgeable and helpful.

David Mason. 342 Queen St. W. ☎ **416/598-1015.**

Another fine used-book store with plenty of first and collector's editions, the store has a huge selection on all subjects. Great bookish atmosphere.

CHINA, SILVER & GLASS
Ashley China. 50 Bloor St. W. ☎ **416/964-2900.**

The ultimate store for china, silver, and glass, this beautiful establishment has elegant table displays of very expensive china, crystal, and flatware—all the top names at decent prices.

CRAFTS
The Algonquins Sweet Grass Gallery. 668 Queen St. W., near Bathurst St. ☎ **416/703-1336.**

This store, owned by an Ojibwa, has been in business for 20 years or so, specializing in Native Canadian arts and crafts—Iroquois masks, porcupine quill boxes, sculpture, prints, as well as moccasins and famous Cowichan hand-knits from British Columbia.

The Craft Gallery/Ontario Crafts Council. 35 McCaul St. ☎ **416/977-3551.**

A showcase for fine contemporary crafts from across Canada. Shows change every six to eight weeks and feature everything from stained glass to ceramics and weaving.

Guild Shop. 118 Cumberland St. ☎ **416/921-1721.**

Famous for Native Canadian crafts. Wonderful selection of the best contemporary Canadian ceramics, glass, wickerwork, jewelry, textiles, and more. The upstairs gallery features Inuit sculpture and art from the Northwest Territories.

DEPARTMENT STORES
Eaton's. Eaton Centre, 290 Yonge St. ☎ **416/343-3528.**

There are numerous Eaton's in Toronto. This flagship store is in the four-level Eaton Centre, which stretches two blocks from Dundas Street to Queen Street.

The Hudson's Bay Company. Queen and Yonge Streets. ☎ **416/861-9111.**

Arch rival to Eaton's, this downtown store (formerly Simpson's) still has a venerable feel.

Marks & Spencer. Manulife Centre, 55 Bloor St. W. ☎ **416/967-7772.**

This is a branch of the famous British store that's known for good-quality goods and clothes at reasonable prices.

DISCOUNT
Honest Ed's. 581 Bloor St. W. ☎ **416/537-2111.**

The original Honest Ed's store sports the biggest, most frenetic electric sign in Toronto. Check it out—as Ed says, it can't be beat, as long as you know what you're looking for. A Toronto experience.

FOOD
Dufflet Pastries. 787 Queen St. W. (near Bathurst Street). ☎ **416/504-2870.**

This specialty bakery supplies many restaurants with its pastries and desserts. The special Dufflet cakes include a white- and dark-chocolate mousse, almond meringue, and many other singular creations. Fine coffees and teas are served, too.

Ten Ren Tea. 454 Dundas St. W. (at Huron Street). ☎ **416/598-7872.**

At this fascinating Chinatown store, you can pick up some fine Chinese tea. The tiny ceramic teapots also make nice gifts in the $20 to $30 price range. Many people are beginning to collect them.

GIFTS & MISCELLANEOUS
General Store. 55 Avenue Rd. (in Hazelton Lanes). ☎ **416/323-1527.**

These are three stores under the same name in Hazelton Lanes. The first carries quirky gifts for the person who has everything. The adjacent branches carry house- and kitchenwares and fun paper items.

Geomania. 159 Adelaide St. (in First Canadian Place Shopping center). ☎ **416/364-1500.**

Geomania is filled with highly polished, brilliantly colored pieces of minerals and stones fashioned into elegant jewelry, vases, bookends, and other decorative pieces. A vision.

HOUSEWARES & KITCHENWARE
En Provence. 20 Hazelton Ave. ☎ **416/975-9400.**

This store has a beautiful selection of French decorative items for the home—ceramics, table accessories, wrought-iron and wood furniture, and, on the second floor, the most luxurious fabrics by Les Olivades for household use. This is French country style at its best.

MALLS & SHOPPING CENTERS
Eaton Centre. 220 Yonge St. ☎ **416/979-3300.**

This glass-domed galleria has more than 360 shops and restaurants on four levels, with plenty of places to rest and eat lunch, too. This is where the real people shop.

Hazelton Lanes. 55 Avenue Rd. ☎ **416/968-0853.**

This complex is for the wealthy and those who wish to appear so, with all the great designer fashion names and more on two levels.

Queen's Quay Terminal. 207 Queen's Quay. ☎ **416/203-0510.**

More than 100 shops and restaurants, including fashion and gift boutiques, are housed here in a converted waterfront warehouse. Remember, the rents are high.

TOYS

Kidding Awound. 91 Cumberland St. ☎ **416/926-8996.**

Windup toys—music boxes and clockwork toys—antique toys, and other interesting items are available here. Great therapy for adults.

Little Dollhouse Company. 617 Mount Pleasant Rd. ☎ **416/489-7180.**

This charming store makes all-wood handcrafted dollhouse kits in about 12 different styles, many Victorian, complete with shingles and siding. They also sell dollhouse furniture, wallpaper, and building supplies, and display 100 room settings.

Top Banana. 639 Mount Pleasant Rd. ☎ **416/440-0111.**

A traditional toy store featuring educational and imported toys, like Brio wooden trains from Sweden, Ravensburger puzzles and games, Eduframe and Playskool toys, and art supplies.

WINES

You'll have to shop the **LCBO outlets.** Look them up in the Yellow Pages under "Liquor Control Board of Ontario." More extensive selections are found at the **Vintages stores,** like the one in Hazelton Lanes on the concourse.

9 Toronto After Dark

The companies to see in Toronto are the National Ballet of Canada, the Canadian Opera Company, the Toronto Symphony, the Toronto Dance Theatre, and Tafelmusik. You can catch major Broadway shows or a performance by one of the many small theater companies that make Toronto one of the leading theater centers in North America. For additional entertainment there are enough bars, clubs, cabarets, and other entertainment to keep anyone spinning.

For local happenings, check *Where Toronto* and *Toronto Life*, as well as the *Globe and Mail*, the *Toronto Star*, and the *Toronto Sun*.

Half-price day of performance tickets are available at **T. O. Tix booth** at Yonge Street just north of Queen (open Tuesday to Saturday from noon to 7:30pm and Sunday 11am to 3pm). Call the hotline at ☎ 416/596-8211 for information. For **TicketMaster's** telecharge service, call ☎ 416/872-1111.

THE PERFORMING ARTS

The major performing arts venues include **Massey Hall,** 178 Victoria St. (☎ 416/363-7301 or 416/872-4255 for tickets and information), which is a Canadian musical landmark, hosting a variety of musical programming from classical to rock. The **O'Keefe Centre,** 1 Front St. East (☎ 416/393-7469 or 416/872-2262 for ticket sales), is home to the Canadian Opera Company and the National Ballet; it also presents Broadway musicals, headline entertainers, and other arts. **Roy Thomson Hall,** 60 Simcoe St. (☎ 416/593-4822 or 416/593-4828 for tickets and information), is the premier concert hall and home to the Toronto Symphony Orchestra, which performs here September through June. The **St. Lawrence Centre,** 27 Front St. East (☎ 416/366-7723), hosts musical and theatrical events and is home to the Canadian Theatre Company in the Bluma Appel Theatre and to Music Toronto and public debates in the Jane Mallett Theatre. And then there's the **Premiere Dance**

Theatre, 207 Queen's Quay West (☎ 416/973-4000), home to the leading contemporary dance companies—the Toronto Dance Theatre, Desrosiers Dance Theatre, and the Danny Grossman Dance Company.

OPERA

The **Canadian Opera Company** began life in 1950 with 10 performances of three operas. It now stages eight different operas a season at the O'Keefe Centre and the Elgin Theatre from September to June. Call ☎ 416/363-6671 for administration or 416/872-2262 for tickets.

CLASSICAL MUSIC

The **Toronto Symphony Orchestra** performs at Roy Thomson Hall, at 60 Simcoe St. (☎ 416/593-4828 for tickets, 593-7769 for administrative offices), from September through June. In June and July, concerts are also given at outdoor venues throughout the city. The world-renowned **Toronto Mendelssohn Choir** also performs at 60 Simcoe St. (☎ 416/598-0422).

Tafelmusik Baroque Orchestra. 427 Bloor St. West. ☎ **416/964-6337** for tickets or 416/964-9562 for administration.

For 17 seasons this group, celebrated in England as "the world's finest period band," has been playing baroque music on authentic historic instruments. Concerts featuring Bach, Handel, Telemann, Mozart, and Vivaldi are given at Trinity-St. Paul's United Church.

DANCE

Toronto Dance Theatre, the city's leading contemporary dance company, burst onto the scene 25 years ago, bringing an inventive spirit and original Canadian dance to the stage. Today, Christopher House directs the company; he joined it in 1979 and has contributed 30 new works to the repertoire. Exhilarating, powerful, and energetic—don't miss their Handel Variations, Artemis Madrigals, Sacra Conversazione, and the Cactus Rosary (☎ 416/967-1365).

✪ **National Ballet of Canada.** 157 King St. East, Toronto, ON, M5C 1G9. ☎ **416/362-1041** or 416/366-4846 for information on programs and prices. Tickets $14–$90.

Most famous of all Toronto's cultural contributions is perhaps the National Ballet of Canada. It was launched at Eaton Auditorium in Toronto on November 12, 1951, by English ballerina Celia Franca, who served initially as director, dancer, choreographer, and teacher. Among the highlights of its history have been its 1973 New York debut (which featured Nureyev's full-length Sleeping Beauty), and Baryshnikov's appearance with the company soon after his defection in 1974. Since 1989 the renowned company has been led by Canadian-born Reid Anderson.

The company performs its regular seasons in Toronto at O'Keefe Centre in the fall, winter, and spring, as well as summer appearances before enormous crowds at the open-air theater at Ontario Place. The repertory includes works by Glen Tetley, Sir Frederick Ashton, William Forsythe, and Jerome Robbins. James Kudelka was appointed artist in residence in 1991 and has created *The Miraculous Mandarin, The Actress,* and *Spring Awakening.*

THEATER

With theaters and theater companies galore, Toronto has a very active theater scene, with a reputation second only to that of Broadway's in all of North America. Many small theater groups are producing exciting offbeat drama—a slowly burgeoning Toronto equivalent of Off-Broadway. I have picked out only the few whose reputations have been established rather than bombarding you with a complete list of all the offerings. Your choice will no doubt be made by what's scheduled while you're in town, so to do your own talent-scouting, check the local newspaper or magazine for listings of the myriad productions offered.

Landmark Theaters

The Elgin & Winter Garden Theatres. 189 Yonge St. ☎ **416/872-5555** for tickets; 416/363-5353 for tour info. Tickets $15–$85.

These two national historic landmarks vie with the Royal Alex for major shows and attention. Both theaters, which opened their doors in 1913, have been restored to their original gilded glory at a cost of $29 million and are the only double-decker theaters operating today. The downstairs Elgin is larger, seating 1,500 and featuring lavish domed ceiling and gilded decoration on the boxes and proscenium. The smaller Winter Garden possesses a striking interior, with "tree trunk" columns, hand-painted scenic frescoes, and a ceiling of beech boughs and twinkling lanterns. Guided tours are given twice weekly for $4.

Pantages Theatre. 244 Victoria St. ☎ **416/872-2222.** Tickets $60–$95.

This magnificent old theater, which opened in 1920, has also been restored to the tune of $18 million. Tours are given for $4.

Royal Alexandra Theatre. 260 King St. West, Toronto, ON, M5V 1H9. ☎ **416/593-4211** or 416/872-3333 for tickets and information. Tickets $40–$90.

Shows from Broadway migrate north to the Royal Alex. Tickets are often snapped up by subscription buyers, so your best bet is to write ahead to the theater at the above address. The theater itself is quite a spectacle. Constructed in 1907, it owes its current lease on life to owner Ed Mirvish, who refurbished it (as well as the surrounding area) in the 1960s. Inside it's a riot of plush reds, gold brocade, and baroque ornamentation, with a seating capacity of 1,493. I'm told you're wise to avoid the second balcony and also sitting under the circle.

Theater Companies & Other Notable Venues

The Canadian Stage Company performs comedy, drama, and musicals in the St. Lawrence Centre, and also presents free summer Shakespeare performances in High Park. Call ☎ 416/368-3110 for tickets or 416/367-8243 for administration.

Since 1970, the experimental **Factory Theatre,** 125 Bathurst St. (☎ 416/504-9971), has been a home to Canadian playwriting, where promising new authors get the chance to develop and showcase their works.

The **Tarragon Theatre,** located near Dupont and Bathurst at 30 Bridgman Ave. (☎ 416/536-5018), opened in 1979 and continues to produce original works by Canadian playwrights and an occasional classic. It's a small, intimate theater.

Theatre Passe Muraille, 16 Ryerson Ave. (☎ 416/504-7529), started in the late 1960s when a pool of actors began experimenting and improvising original Canadian material. Set in another warehouse, there's a main space seating 270, and a back space for 70. Take the Queen Street streetcar to Bathurst.

THE CLUB & MUSIC SCENE

DINNER THEATER, CABARET & COMEDY

In addition to the offerings listed below, other comedy clubs include the **Big City Improv,** at 534 Queen St. West (☎ 416/504-8707), and the **Laugh Resort,** 26 Lombard St. (☎ 416/364-5233).

For the art of impersonation there's **La Cage Dinner Theatre,** 278 Yonge St. (☎ 416/364-5200). For an Elizabethan feast head out to **His Majesty's Feast** at the Lakeshore Inn, 1926 Lakeshore Blvd. (☎ 416/769-1165).

Musicals are the specialty at the **Limelight Theatre,** 2026 Yonge St. (☎ 416/482-5200); tickets are $50 weekdays and Sunday, $55 Friday, and $60 on Saturday for dinner and show.

Mark Breslin's Yuk-Yuk's Komedy Kabaret. 2335 Yonge St. ☎ **416/967-6425.** Cover $6 weeknights, $13 Fri, $15 Sat. Dinner and show Fri $33, Sat $35. Reservations needed.

Ever since comic Mark Breslin, inspired by New York's Catch a rising star and LA's The Comedy Store, founded the place, it's been putting top Canadian and other international comedians into the spotlight. There's another Yuk-Yuk's on Dixie Road in Mississauga.

✪ **Second City.** 110 Lombard St. ☎ **416/863-1111.** Dinner and show $35 Mon–Thurs, $38 Fri, $42 Sat. Show only Mon–Thurs $13.50, Fri $16.50, Sat. $20.50, Sun $11.

If you enjoyed *Saturday Night Live* or *SCTV,* you'll love the improvisational comedy of Second City, which continues to turn out talented young comedians. Dan Aykroyd, John Candy, Mike Myers, Andrea Martin, and Catherine O'Hara got their starts here. Its home is an old firehall that now houses a theater seating 200 and a separate restaurant.

Ukrainian Caravan. 5245 Dundas St. West (at Kipling). ☎ **416/231-7447.** Dinner and show $25–$35.

For an evening of Cossack dance, song, and comic repartee, head for the Ukrainian Caravan. Dinner features Ukrainian specialties, such as chicken Kiev, kielbasa, and pirogies.

JAZZ

Toronto is a big jazz town—especially on Saturday afternoons when many a hotel lounge or restaurant lays on an afternoon of rip-roaring rhythm. At **Ben Wicks,** at 424 Parliament (☎ 416/961-9425), there's free jazz, folk, and blues on Saturday from 8pm to midnight. The **Chelsea Bun,** at the Delta Chelsea Inn, 33 Gerrard St. West. (☎ 416/595-1975) is a good spot for Saturday-afternoon jazz. It's open Monday to Saturday from 5pm to 1am, with a $5 admission charge on Friday and Saturday.

✪ **Montréal Bistro/Jazz Club.** 65 Sherbourne St. ☎ **416/363-0179.** Cover depends on band.

One of the city's hottest jazz clubs has a cool atmosphere for an array of local and international jazz artists—the Kenny Wheeler Quintet, Marian McPartland, and Velvet Glove have all appeared here. Entertainment begins at 9pm. It's great, too, because you can order from the menu of the bistro next door.

✪ **Top o' the Senator.** 249 Victoria. ☎ **416/364-7517.** Cover $10 Fri–Sat, $8 Thurs.

Toronto's swankiest jazz club is a long, narrow room with a bar down one side and a distinct 1930s look. It's a great place to hear fine international jazz. Funky old movie-theater seats set around tables, couches alongside the performance area, and portraits of band leaders and artists on the walls add to the atmosphere. The top floor also has an intimate rooftop lounge called the Senator Cabaret.

COUNTRY, FOLK, ROCK & REGGAE

✪ **Bamboo.** 312 Queen St. West. ☎ **416/593-5771.** Cover $7 Mon–Wed, $10 Thurs, $12 Fri–Sat. Subway: Osgoode or Queen; then a streetcar west.

At Bamboo, which is decked out in Caribbean style and colors, you'll hear reggae, calypso, salsa, and world beat sounds. The club takes up one side of the space, while a small restaurant occupies a small side area. The menu mixes Caribbean, Indonesian, and Thai specialties. Thai spicy noodles are really popular, blending shrimp, chicken, tofu, and egg. Lamb and potato rôti and Caribbean curry chicken are other offerings. Music starts at 10pm.

Birchmount Tavern. 462 Birchmount. ☎ **416/698-4115.** Cover $4 weekends.

The city's longtime country venue attracts a broad range of Canadian and American artists. The music goes on Thursday to Sunday from 9pm to 1am.

Chick 'n' Deli. 744 Mount Pleasant Rd. (south of Eglinton Avenue). ☎ **416/489-3363.** No cover.

At Chick 'n' Deli, Tiffany-style lamps and oak set the background for Top 40 or rhythm and blues every night from 9pm to 1am. The dance floor is always packed. Chicken wings and barbecue are the specialties, along with nachos, salads, and sandwiches. On Saturday and Sunday afternoons Dixieland sounds start at 4pm on Saturday and 5pm on Sunday.

El Mocambo. 464 Spadina Ave. ☎ **416/928-3566.** Cover varies, depending on the band.

Still a rock-and-roll landmark, El Mocambo is the famous bar where the Stones chose to do their gig back in the 1970s.

Free Times Cafe. 320 College St. ☎ **416/967-1078.** Cover $2–$10.

This is the club for folk and acoustic music every evening starting at 9pm. Up front the small restaurant offers a health-oriented menu.

DANCE CLUBS

Berlin. 2335 Yonge St. ☎ **416/489-7777.** Cover $8 Tues, $5 Wed, $3 Thurs, $8 Fri, $10 Sat.

This is one of the city's more sophisticated clubs, attracting a well-heeled crowd ranging from 25 to 50 years old. Things get started at 9pm and spin until 3:30am Tuesday to Saturday.

Barracuda. 21 Scollard St. ☎ **416/921-4496.** Cover $6.

This extraordinarily high energy scene is made even more so by the bizarre addition of batting cages and volley ball courts. Open Thursday to Saturday.

Big Bop. 651 Queen St. West (at Bathurst). ☎ **416/366-6699.**

Several floors and several sounds range from rock and roll to Top 40 dance, with a 19-year-old to early 30s crowd.

Loose Moose. 220 Adelaide St. West (between Simcoe and Duncan streets). ☎ **416/971-5252.** No cover.

This is a crowd-pleaser for a younger set who like the multilevel dance floors, the DJ, and the booze and schmooze, which starts every night at 9pm.

THE BAR & PUB SCENE

First, here are some favorite hotel bars. The fairly formal **Chartroom,** at the Harbour Castle Westin, 1 Harbour Sq. (☎ 416/869-1600), offers a good view of the lake and the islands ferry. For cozy fireside conversation in winter, or a summer cocktail with a view, I like the **Roof Lounge at the Park Plaza,** 4 Avenue Rd. (☎ 416/924-5471). The **Consort Bar** at the King Edward Hotel, 37 King St. East (☎ 416/863-9700), is also comfortable, as is **La Serre,** at the Four Seasons, 21 Avenue Rd.

(☎ 416/964-0411). The **Chelsea Bun,** at the Delta Chelsea Inn, 33 Gerrard St. West (☎ 416/595-1975), has a fine selection of single-malt whiskies and good musical entertainment. If you prefer a pubby atmosphere, there's the **Good Queen Bess,** in the Sheraton Centre, 123 Queen St. West (☎ 416/361-1000).

And now for the independents.

Alice Fazooli's. 294 Adelaide St. West. ☎ **416/979-1910.**

Baseball art and memorabilia, including a full-scale model of an outfielder making a wall catch, fills this large bar and dining room. It's always jam-packed with an older business crowd either quaffing in the bar or feasting in the back on crabs cooked in many different styles, pizza, pasta, and raw-bar specialties.

Al Frisco's. 133 John St. ☎ **416/595-0646.**

At this downtown spot, young professionals and the financial crowd make the scene at day's end, enjoying drinks and pizza, pasta, and gourmet burgers. In winter they jam into the huge warehouse space, with its warm California-Mediterranean ambience or outside on the large outdoor terrace. Upstairs, there's a DJ and dancing, pool tables, and beers brewed on the premises. It's crowded, with a lot of networking going on. Drinks are $4.50 and up.

Bellair Cafe. 100 Cumberland St. ☎ **416/964-2222.**

With a sleek suede ambience, this place attracts a fashion-conscious and celebrity crowd. It really gets jammed every night and on weekends, both inside at the square bar and outside on the terrace.

Bemelman's. 83 Bloor St. West. ☎ **416/960-0306.**

With its mirrors, marble, gleaming brass rails, and plants, Bemelman's has a certain slice-of-Manhattan air about it, and the characters that inhabit it are dramatic and trendy. A long stand-up marble-top bar is where the action happens; the bar is well known for its luscious fresh-fruit daiquiris. In the back you can get a decent meal, choosing from a large menu offering soups, salads, sandwiches, pastas, and egg dishes as well as fish, chicken, pork, and beef entrées. Everything is under $12. Weather permitting there's an outdoor patio open April to October. Their Sunday brunch from 11am to 3pm is popular. Open from 11:30am to 10:30pm Sunday and Monday, until 11pm Tuesday, until midnight Wednesday and until 1am Thursday to Saturday. The kitchen closes earlier.

Brunswick House. 481 Bloor St. West. ☎ **416/964-2242.**

For an experience that's unique yet inexpensive, try the Brunswick House, a cross between a German beer hall and an English north-country workingmen's club. Waitresses move through the Formica tables in this cavernous room carrying high trays of frothy suds to a largely student crowd. And while everyone's quaffing or playing bar shuffleboard, they're entertained by Rockin' Irene, who's been here for years belting out three rollicking sets on Thursday and Saturday nights.

Centro. 2472 Yonge St. ☎ **416/483-2211.**

Centro has a well-patronized bar downstairs at the restaurant. It's a comfortable, relaxing place to listen to the pianist and get to know the sophisticated mid-30s-and-up crowd.

✪ **C'est What?** 67 Front St. East. ☎ **416/867-9499.**

Downstairs in a historic warehouse building, C'est What? sports rough-hewn walls and a cellarlike atmosphere reminiscent of a Paris cave. Casual and comfortable, it attracts a young, politically conscious crowd. It makes its own award-winning wines, serves 25 all-natural draught beers, and has live music seven nights a week.

Milano. 325 King St. West. ☎ **416/599-9909.**

Up front there's a bar and beyond several billiard tables, with a dining area off to the side. In summer French doors open to the street making for a pleasant Parisian atmosphere. The bistro style food consists of burgers, sandwiches and such items as tiger shrimp.

The Queens Head. 263 Gerrard St. East (at Berkeley). ☎ **416/929-0940.**

In this friendly free-thinking bar, you're likely to meet locals and enjoy some controversial Canadian commentary.

Pepinello. 180 Pearl St. (between Duncan and John streets). ☎ **416/599-6699.**

Pepinello attracts crowds to its downstairs bar for vino bianco and vino rosso and to its upstairs dining area, which offers separate serving counters for pizza, pasta, and risotto—the latest in sophisticated group dining experience.

✪ **The Rotterdam.** 600 King St. West (at Portland). ☎ **416/868-6882.**

This beer drinker's heaven serves 200 different labels as well as 30 different types on draft. It's not so much an after-work crowd that gathers here, but by 8pm the tables in the back are filled and the long bar is jammed. In summer the patio is fun.

WINE BARS
The Hop & Grape. 14 College St. ☎ **416/923-2818.**

The Hop and Grape provides, not surprisingly, beer on one level and wine on another, and is one of the city's most popular wine bars. On the ground floor the pub offers 100 types of beer with 11 varieties on draft (imported beers are $5 and up). Upstairs, the wine bar offers a selection of 100 wines, about 17 by the glass and some by the bottle.

Raclette. 361 Queen St. West. ☎ **416/593-0934.**

Along Queen Street, go to Raclette, which stocks more than 100 wines, including about 20 available by the glass; the bar also offers raclette. Open Monday through Saturday from noon to 1am, on Sunday until 11pm.

Vines. Downstairs at 38 Wellington St. East. ☎ **416/869-0744.**

Vines provides a pleasant atmosphere to sample a glass of champagne or any of close to 60 wines, priced between $4 and $10 for a four-ounce glass, and more than a dozen single malts. Salads, cheeses, and light meals (from $7 to $10), are available.

Ontario's Golden Horseshoe & East Along the St. Lawrence

by Marilyn Wood

Golden because the communities along the lake are wealthy, *horseshoe* because of its shape, this stretch of the Ontario lakefront from Niagara-on-the-Lake to Oshawa offers the visitor some golden opportunities: Niagara Falls itself; Niagara-on-the-Lake, home of the famous Shaw Festival; the Welland Canal, an engineering wonder; Niagara wineries; and Dundurn Castle and Royal Botanical Gardens in Canada's steel town of Hamilton.

East from Port Hope, a worthy antique center, stretches the Bay of Quinte and Quinte's Isle, a tranquil region of farms and orchards that Loyalists largely settled. It's still little-trafficked today—except by those in the know who come to explore the pretty small towns, to go antiquing, or to enjoy the beaches, dunes, and waterfront activities. Kingston, a very appealing lakefront town with its own weekly market, is interesting both architecturally and historically. It's also the gateway to the mighty St. Lawrence River, the Thousand Islands, and the St. Lawrence National Park.

1 Exploring the Region

The first four destinations—Niagara Falls, Niagara-on-the-Lake, St. Catharines to Port Colborne, and Hamilton—can be visited together. The best way to see them is to take the Niagara Parkway from Niagara-on-the-Lake to Niagara Falls and then drive to Port Colborne on Lake Erie and follow the Welland Canal north to Port Dalhousie on Lake Ontario. Although this is, for the most part, a densely populated area with a tangled network of roads, there are several scenic routes: the parkway and the Wine Route, which takes you from Stoney Creek to Niagara Falls.

From Toronto, the second four destinations—the region from Port Hope to Trenton, Quinte's Isle, Kingston, and the region along the St. Lawrence—can be toured by driving along Highway 401 East to Port Hope and then turning off at Trenton on to Quinte's Isle and rambling along Route 3 (the Loyalist Parkway) to Kingston. From Kingston the scenic 1,000 Islands Parkway runs east along the St. Lawrence to Gananoque and Brockville.

VISITOR INFORMATION For information about Ontario, contact **Ontario Travel**, Queen's Park, Toronto, ON, M7A 2R9

(☎ 416/314-0944 or 800/ONTARIO from 9am to 8pm). The offices are open from 8:30am to 5pm Monday through Friday (daily from mid-May to mid-September).

AN IMPORTANT NOTE ON PRICES & TAXES　Unless stated otherwise, **the prices cited in this guide are given in Canadian dollars,** which is good news for U.S. travelers because the Canadian dollar is worth 25% less than the American dollar but buys nearly as much. As we go to press, $1 Canadian is worth 75¢ U.S., which means that your $100-a-night hotel room will cost only U.S. $75, and your $6 breakfast costs only U.S. $4.50.

As you travel, keep in mind that Ontario has a provincial sales tax of 8%, plus a 5% accommodations tax—and that's in addition to the national 7% goods and services tax (GST).

2　The Great Outdoors

While this densely populated region may not offer hard-core adventure, there are still plenty of places to enjoy the outdoors. Some 260 provincial parks in Ontario offer ample opportunities for outdoor recreation. The daily in-season entry fee for a vehicle is $6; campsites cost anywhere from $13 to $18. For more information, contact the **Ontario Ministry of Natural Resources** (☎ 416/314-2000).

BIKING　A great bike trail parallels the **Niagara Parkway. Countryroads Bike Tours** (☎ 416/761-1844) offers biking tours of the Niagara-on-the-Lake region. Another good place to bike on the Niagara Peninsula is along the **Welland Canal** between Locks 1 and 3. In **Kingston,** you can cycle the whole waterfront, and farther east the **1000 Islands Parkway** affords some scenic waterfront cycling.

BIRD-WATCHING　**Presqu'ile Provincial Park** is a stopping place for birds traveling both the Atlantic and Mississippi Flyways. Major bird-watching weekends are organized in spring and fall.

Sandbanks Provincial Park, about 11 miles west of Picton, is another good bet in the spring or fall. You might catch a glimpse of a long-billed marsh wren, a pileated woodpecker, a northern oriole ruby, or a golden crowned kinglet.

BOATING　Kingston is the major hub for boating. From here you can either cruise the Rideau Canal and the Trent-Severn waterway aboard a houseboat or explore the Thousand Islands. For information on houseboat holidays and rentals, contact the following: **Big Rideau Boats,** 56 Meadowbank Dr., Ottawa, ON, K2G ON9 (☎ 613/828-0138); **Houseboat Holidays,** RR no. 3, Gananoque, ON, K7G 2V5 (☎ 613/382-2842); or **St. Lawrence River Houseboat and Cruiser Rentals,** c/o Halliday Point, Wolfe Island, ON, K0H 2Y0 (☎ 613/385-2290). Most houseboats sleep up to six and have a fully equipped kitchen, hot and cold running water, and a propane system for heat and light. Weekly rentals on the canal system in summer average $1,000. On the St. Lawrence, in August the cost starts at about $600 for a weekend, and $900 to $1,150 per week. Prices are higher in July, less in May, June, and September, and also during the week. Boats are fully equipped—you need only bring sleeping bags and towels.

CANOEING/KAYAKING　There's terrific canoe-camping in **Frontenac Provincial Park.** You could combine this adventure with sea kayaking through the Thousand Islands by contacting a local outfitter. All equipment—canoes, kayaks, paddles, life-jacket, car-top carrier, tent, sleeping bags, stove, and utensils—is provided for a modest fee, starting at $24 per person per day. The trips run from April to November. For information contact **Frontenac Outfitters** (☎ 613/376-6220 in season or 613/382-1039 off-season).

The **Rideau Canal** is another good place for canoeing, as is **Sandbanks Provincial Park,** near Picton.

FISHING   The **Bay of Quinte** is famous for pickerel.

GOLF   The **Whirlpool Golf Club** (☎ 905/356-1140) on the Niagara Parkway offers a scenic course. Greens fees are $30 for 18 holes, $20 for nine holes. **Niagara-on-the-Lake Golf Club** on Front Street (☎ 905/468-3424) is right on Lake Ontario and has a beautiful nine-hole, par-72 course that can be played for $24 (for 18 holes). **Beechwood Golf Club** (☎ 905/680-4653) is another challenging course on the Peninsula. Additional courses can be found in Fort Erie.

HIKING   For serious hiking, the Rideau Trail runs 241 miles along the canal from Kingston to Ottawa. For information contact the **Rideau Trail Association,** Box 15, Kingston, ON, K7L 4V6 (☎ 613/545-0823).

Frontenac Provincial Park, near Sydenham (☎ 613/376-3489), is a wilderness park with more than 113 miles of hiking trails that explore such intriguing areas as Moulton Gorge, the Arkon Lake bogs and the Connor-Daly mine.

SWIMMING   At **Sandbanks Provincial Park,** 11 miles west of Picton, you'll find the best swimming beach, but note that it's unsupervised.

TENNIS   For tennis fans the **White Oaks Inn and Racquet Club** in Niagara-on-the-Lake is a dream come true, providing indoor and outdoor tennis courts, plus racquetball and squash facilities. Courts are also available at Queenston Heights Park in Queenston (Niagara Falls) for a modest fee.

3 Niagara Falls

81 miles (130km) S of Toronto, 18 miles (30km) N of Buffalo, NY

Niagara Falls, with its gimmicks, amusement parks, wax museums, daredevil feats, and a million motels sporting heart-shaped beds, may seem excessively tacky. Certainly the heart of the falls area is overcommercialized. Still somehow the falls steal the show, and on the Canadian side, with its parkway and gardens, nature manages to survive with grace.

ESSENTIALS

VISITOR INFORMATION   For information in and around the Falls, contact the **Niagara Falls Canada Visitor and Convention Bureau,** 5433 Victoria Ave., Niagara Falls, ON, L2G 3L1 (☎ 905/356-6061); or the **Niagara Parks Commission,** 7400 Portage Rd. South, Niagara Falls, ON, L2E 6T2 (☎ 905/356-2241 or 905/354-6266). Summer information centers are open at Table Rock House, Maid of the Mist Plaza, Rapids View Parking Lot, and Niagara-on-the-Lake.

GETTING THERE   If you're driving from Toronto, take the QEW Niagara. From the United States take the Rainbow Bridge directly into Niagara Falls (ON).

Amtrak and VIA Rail operate trains between Toronto (☎ 416/366-8411) and New York, stopping in St. Catharines and Niagara Falls. Call ☎ 800/361-1235 in Canada or 800/USA-RAIL in the United States.

GETTING AROUND   You used to be able to park along the main street/parkway in Niagara Falls, but now that is forbidden; instead the way to get around is to travel aboard the **People Movers** (☎ 905/357-9340). Park your car at Rapid View several miles away from the falls, or else at the so-called Preferred Parking (overlooking the falls—it costs more), and then take the People Mover, an attraction in itself. People Movers travel a loop making nine stops from Rapid View to Spanish Aero

Car. Shuttles to the falls also operate from downtown and Lundy's Lane. An all-day pass costs $4 for adults, $2 for children 6 to 12. In-season only.

A MONEY-SAVING PASS Buying an **Explorer's Passport** secures admission to Table Rock Scenic Tunnels, Great Gorge Adventure, and the Niagara Spanish Aero Car. It costs $13.25 for adults, and $6.65 for children 6 to 12.

SEEING THE FALLS

Obviously, the first thing to do is to see the Falls, the seventh natural wonder of the world. Ever since the falls were first seen by Fr. Louis Hennepin, a Jesuit priest, in December 1678, people have flocked to see them; today more than 12 million visit annually. Many are honeymooners, although how the trend got started no one quite knows—legend has it that Napoléon's brother started it when he came on his honeymoon, traveling all the way from New Orleans by stagecoach.

The most exciting way to see the falls is still from the decks of the ✪ *Maid of the Mist,* 5920 River Rd. (☎ 905/358-5781). This sturdy boat takes you practically into the maelstrom—through the turbulent waters around the American Falls, past the Rock of Ages, and to the foot of the Horseshoe Falls where 34.5 million Imperial gallons fall per minute over the 176-foot-high cataract. You'll get wet and your sunglasses will mist, but that will not detract from the thrill.

Boats leave from the dock on the parkway just down from the Rainbow Bridge. Trips begin in mid-May and operate daily to mid-October (until 8pm from Mid-June to early August). Fares are $9.55 for adults, $5.90 for children 6 to 12; children 5 and under, free.

Go down under the falls via the elevator at Table Rock House, which drops you 150 feet down through solid rock to the **Table Rock Scenic Tunnels** (☎ 905/358-3268) and viewing portals. You'll appreciate the black oilskin mackintosh and rubber boots that you're given. The tunnels are open all year, and the admission charge is $5.50 for adults, $2.75 for children 6 to 12; children under 6, free.

To view the falls from above most spectacularly, take a nine-minute spin ($140 for two!) in a chopper over the whole Niagara area. Helicopters leave from the **Heliport,** adjacent to the Whirlpool at the junction of Victoria Avenue and Niagara Parkway, from 9am to dusk, weather permitting, daily. Contact **Niagara Helicopters,** 3731 Victoria Ave. (☎ 905/357-5672).

Or else you can ride up in the external glass-fronted elevators 520 feet to the top of the **Skylon Tower** observation deck at 5200 Robinson St. (☎ 905/356-2651). At the tower's base are 40 boutiques and stores to browse in, and an indoor amusement park and typical vending outlets. The observation deck is open from 10am to 9pm daily, from 8am to 1am June through Labor Day. Adults pay $6.50 for admission; seniors, $5.50; and children 12 and under, $3.95.

A similar perspective can be gained from the observation floors atop the 325-foot **Minolta Tower Centre and Marine Aquarium,** 6732 Oakes Dr. (☎ 905/356-1501). On-site attractions include a Thrill Ride Simulator, Galaxian Space Adventure, Cybermind Virtual Reality, and the free Waltzing Waters show. The tower is open in summer from 9am to 11:30pm, and in winter from 9am to 9pm (closed December 24 and 25). Admission is $5.95 for adults, $4.95 for students and seniors; free for children under 10.

For a thrilling introduction to the experience of Niagara Falls, stop by the **IMAX Theater** and view the raging, swirling waters in *Niagara: Miracles, Myths and Magic,* shown on a six-story-high screen. It's at 6170 Buchanan Ave. (☎ 905/358-3611).

Niagara Falls

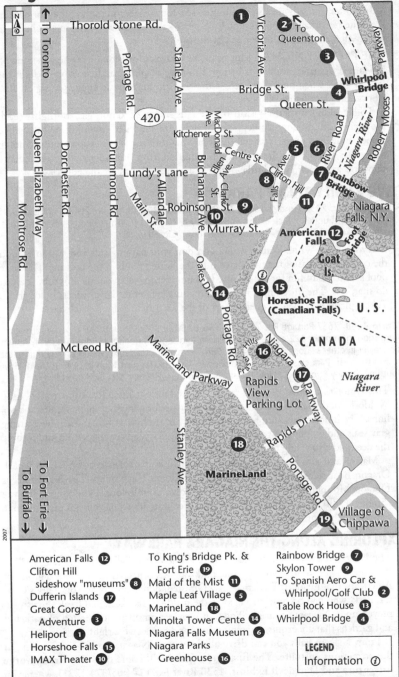

American Falls 12
Clifton Hill
    sideshow "museums" 8
Dufferin Islands 17
Great Gorge
    Adventure 3
Heliport 1
Horseshoe Falls 15
IMAX Theater 10

To King's Bridge Pk. &
    Fort Erie 19
Maid of the Mist 11
Maple Leaf Village 5
MarineLand 18
Minolta Tower Cente 14
Niagara Falls Museum 6
Niagara Parks
    Greenhouse 16

Rainbow Bridge 7
Skylon Tower 9
To Spanish Aero Car &
    Whirlpool/Golf Club 2
Table Rock House 13
Whirlpool Bridge 4

LEGEND
Information ⓘ

In winter, the falls are also thrilling to see, for the ice bridge and other formations are quite remarkable (you'll know how remarkable if you've ever seen a building in winter after the firemen have put out the fire).

THE FALLS BY NIGHT Jean François Gravelet (or Blondin, as he was known), the famed tightrope walker, is believed to have inspired the first effort to light the falls in 1859 when he walked across the river on his rope at night, setting off fireworks that illuminated the gorge.

Today, don't miss the vision of the falls lit by 22 xenon gas spotlights (each producing 250 million candlepower of light), in shades of rose pink, red magenta, amber, blue, and green. You can see it any night of the year starting around 5pm in the winter and 9pm in the summer. In addition, from July to early September, free fireworks are set off every Friday night at 11pm to illuminate the falls.

TWO FAMILY THEME PARKS

White Water. 7430 Lundy's Lane. ☎ **905/357-3380.** Admission $14.95 adults, $9.95 children 10 and under, which allows you to stay all day and return evenings, when the lights go on. Weekdays 10am–7pm, weekends until 8pm. Closed winter.

Everyone loves White Water, where you don your bathing suit and swoop around the corkscrew turns of the five slides into the heated pools at the bottom. The wave pool is also lots of fun for the family. If you prefer to wallow in the hot tub, you can do that, too. The little 'uns can ride three small slides designed specially for them. Take a picnic and spend a greater part of the day (there's also a snack bar).

Marineland. 7657 Portage Rd. ☎ **905/356-8250** or 905/356-9565 for taped information. Admission in summer $22 adults, $19 children and seniors; free for children under 4. Admission lower in other seasons. July–Aug daily 9am–6pm; call ahead for operating hours during the rest of the year. Park closes at dusk. Rides open Victoria Day–first Mon in Oct. In town, drive south on Stanley Street and follow the signs; from the QEW take McCleod Road Exit.

This is not to be missed on your trip to the falls. At the aquarium-theater, King Waldorf, Marineland's mascot, presides over performances of killer whales and sea lions. The indoor aquarium features a display of freshwater fish and a show starring gray seals and dolphins. At the small wildlife display, kids enjoy petting and feeding the deer and also seeing bears and Canadian elk.

Marineland also has theme-park rides, including a roller coaster, Tivoli wheel, Dragon Boat rides, and a fully equipped children's playground. The big thriller is Dragon Mountain, a roller coaster that loops, double-loops, and spirals its way through 1,000 feet of tunnels. There are three restaurants or you can picnic at one of several tables provided.

EXPLORING ALONG THE NIAGARA PARKWAY

The Niagara Parkway makes the Canadian side of the Falls much more appealing than the American side. This 35-mile parkway was conceived in 1867 by a group of Americans that included Frederick Law Olmsted, designer of New York City's Central Park, who had become outraged at the peddlers, hawkers, and freak shows who preyed upon Niagara's tourists. Today it provides an unspoiled stretch of parkland and gardens that are exquisitely maintained and a delectable sight.

From Niagara Falls you can drive all the way to Niagara-on-the-Lake, taking in the attractions en route. The first attraction you'll come to is the **Great Gorge Adventure and Daredevil Exhibit,** 4330 River Rd. (☎ 905/374-1221), where you can learn about Niagara's daredevil history, who died and who survived, and examine several of the actual barrels used to ride over the falls. Then you can stroll along the scenic boardwalk beside the raging white waters of the Great Gorge Rapids and wonder how it must have felt to challenge this mighty torrent, where the river rushes through the narrow channel at an average speed of 30 m.p.h. Admission is $4.50 for adults, $2.25 for children 6 to 12, free for kids under 6.

Half a mile farther north and you'll arrive at the **Niagara Spanish Aero Car** (☎ 905/354-5711), a red-and-yellow cable-car contraption that will whisk you on a 3,600-foot jaunt between two points in Canada, high above the whirlpool, providing excellent views of the surrounding landscape. Admission is $4.75 for adults, $2.40 for children 6 to 12; children under 6, free. Open daily May 1 to the third Sunday in October: from 9am to 6pm in May, until 8pm in June, until 9pm in July and August, from 10am to 7:30pm in September, and 9am to 5pm in October.

At **Ride Niagara,** 5755 River Rd. (☎ 905/374-7433), a simulated plunge over the falls in a barrel is the main feature of the 25-minute experience that includes a theater presentation. Admission is $7.95 adults, $3.95 children. Open daily year around (from 9:15am to 11pm in summer).

After passing the **Whirlpool Golf Club,** the next stop is the **School of Horticulture,** for a free view of the vast gardens there, plus a look at the Floral Clock, which contains 25,000 plants in its 40-foot-diameter face.

From here you can drive to **Queenston Heights Park,** site of the battle of that name during the War of 1812. You can take a walking tour of the battlefield. Picnic or play tennis ($5 an hour) in this shaded arbor before moving to the **Laura Secord Homestead,** Partition Street in Queenston (☎ 905/262-4851). The home of this redoubtable woman contains a fine collection of Upper Canada furniture from the 1812 period, plus artifacts recovered from an archeological dig. Stop at the candy shop and ice-cream parlor. Tours are given every half hour. Admission is $1.Open from Victoria Day weekend (late May) to Labor Day, daily 10am to 5pm.

Also worth viewing just off the parkway in Queenston is the **Samuel Weir Collection and Library of Art,** RR no. 1, Niagara-on-the-Lake (☎ 905/262-4510), a small personal collection displayed as it was originally when Samuel Weir occupied the house. Mr. Weir (1898–1981), a lawyer from London, Ontario, was an enthusiastic collector of Canadian, American, and European art as well as rare books. Open from Victoria Day to Canadian Thanksgiving Wednesday to Saturday from 11am to 5pm, and Sunday from 1 to 5pm.

From here the parkway continues into Niagara-on-the-Lake, lined with fruit farms like **Kurtz Orchards** (☎ 905/468-2937), and wineries, notably the **Inniskillin Winery,** Line 3, Service Road 56 (☎ 905/468-3554 or 905/468-2187), and **Reif Winery** (☎ 905/468-7738). Inniskillin is open daily from 10am to 6pm June to October and Monday through Saturday from 10am to 5pm November to May. The self-guided free tour has 20 stops explaining the process of wine making. A guided tour is also given daily at 2:30pm in summer and weekends only in winter. At Reif Winery, tours costing $1.50 are given daily at 1:30pm from June to August.

Farther along, visit **Dufferin Islands,** where the children can swim, rent a paddleboat, and explore the surrounding woodland areas. Or else you can play a round of golf on the illuminated nine-hole par-3 course. Open the second Sunday in April to the last Sunday in October.

A little farther on, stop for a picnic in **King's Bridge Park** and relax on the beaches before driving on to **Fort Erie** (☎ 905/871-0540), a reconstruction of the fort that was seized by the Americans in July 1814, besieged later by the British, and finally blown up as the Americans retreated across the river to Buffalo. Guards in 1812–14 period uniforms of the British Eighth Regiment will lead you through the museum and display rooms. These guards also stand sentry duty, fire the cannons, and demonstrate drill and musket practice. Admission is $3.75 for adults, $2.25 for

Winery Tours

Niagara is set in the fruit- and wine-producing area of the Niagara escarpment, a wine-growing region that has recently become better known for quality wines. The Niagara peninsula has more than 25,000 acres of select vineyards cultivating some 45 varieties of wine grapes. In the region are a number of wineries: Barnes, Château Gai, Inniskillin House, Andrés, and Vincor. True wine enthusiasts in search of the region's best wines will want to stop at **Konzelmann,** in Niagara-on-the-Lake, or **Inniskillin,** two vineyards that have consistently produced winning wines in the last few years. At **Vincor,** 4887 Dorchester Rd. (☎ 905/357-2400), Canada's largest winery, you can see champagne processed in the European way by fermenting the wine in the bottle, and at any winery you can view the winemaking process from the moment the grapes enter the crush house to the fermentation, bottling, and packaging stages. And then comes the fun part—the wine tasting.

Probably the best time to visit is during vendange or harvest season, from the first week in September to the end of October. At Vincor, one-hour tours costing $2 are offered year-round Monday through Friday at 10:30am, 2pm, and 3:30pm; and 2 and 3:30pm Saturday and Sunday. Call 905/357-2400. For other winery tours and tastings, contact **Andrés Wines** (☎ 905/643-TOUR or 800/263-2170).

children 6 to 16. Open the first Saturday in May to September 12 (and weekends until October 3), Monday through Thursday from 10am to 3:30pm, Friday through Sunday 10am to 5:30pm.

Another Fort Erie attraction is the scenic historic **racetrack** (☎ 905/871-3200) that's open in summer.

MORE ATTRACTIONS

Founded in 1827, the **Niagara Falls Museum,** 5651 River Rd. (☎ 905/356-2151) has exhibits ranging from Egyptian mummies to an odd mixture of Indian and Asian artifacts, shells, fossils, and minerals, plus the Freaks of Nature display. Open in summer daily from 8:30am to 11pm; in winter 10am to 5pm. Admission is $6.75 for adults, $6.25 for seniors, $4.95 for students 11 to 18, $3.95 for children under 11; under 5, free.

There's a whole slew of sideshows on Clifton Hill ranging from **Ripley's Believe It or Not, Castle Dracula, Houdini Museum, Movieland Wax Museum,** and **Louis Tussaud's Wax Museum**—all charging about $6 for adults, $3 for children.

WHERE TO STAY

Every other sign in Niagara Falls advertises a motel. In summer, rates go up and down according to the traffic, and some proprietors will not even quote rates ahead of time. So be warned. You can secure a reasonably priced room if you're lucky enough to arrive on a "down night." For example, in June, I was offered a room for $55 when the official rates were posted as $89 and up. So push a little. Keep requesting a lower rate, and don't take no for an answer.

VERY EXPENSIVE

Niagara Falls Renaissance Fallsview. 6455 Buchanan Ave., Niagara Falls, ON, L2G 3V9. ☎ **905/357-5200** or 800/363-FALLS. Fax 905/357-3422. 262 rms. A/C MINIBAR TV TEL. Summer $155–$210 double, $200–$240 whirlpool room; winter $80–$120 double, $150–$200 whirlpool room; spring and fall $100–$175 double, $190–$220 whirlpool room. AE, DC, DISC, ER, MC, V. Free parking.

The Renaissance offers rooms that are tastefully furnished with oak furniture. Bathrooms have double sinks, hair dryers, and all modern accoutrements. Each Renaissance Club room has three telephones, a whirlpool tub, and access to a special lounge with concierge. A rooftop cafe overlooks the falls.

Facilities: Indoor pool, a whirlpool, and a health club featuring saunas, squash and racquetball courts, and a fitness and weight room.

Skyline Brock. 5705 Falls Ave., Niagara Falls, ON, L2E 6W7. ☎ **905/374-4444**, 905/357-3090, or 800/263-7135. Fax 905/357-4804. 233 rms. A/C TV TEL. Mid-June to Sept $115–$200 double; Oct–Dec and Apr to mid-June $95–$145 double; winter $75–$115 double. Prices based on room and view. Extra person $10. Children under 18 stay free in parents' room. Special packages available. AE, DC, DISC, ER, MC, V. Parking $4.25.

With about 150 rooms facing the falls, the Skyline Brock has been hosting honeymooners and falls visitors since 1929. It still has a certain air of splendor conveyed by the huge chandelier and marble walls in the lobby. City-view rooms are slightly smaller and less expensive. Rooms from the 11th floor and up have minibars.

Dining/Entertainment: The 10th-floor Rainbow Room offers a lovely view over the falls and serves a popular menu that includes such dishes as half a roast chicken with cranberry sauce, salmon hollandaise, or prime rib, priced from $16 to $24. Isaac's bar is available for drinks.

Skyline Foxhead. 5875 Falls Ave., Niagara Falls, ON, L2E 6W7. ☎ **905/374-4444**, 905/357-3090, or 800/263-7135. 399 rms. A/C TV TEL. June 1–Oct 1 $145–$210 double; Oct and Apr–May $120–$175 double; winter $80–$125 double. Prices depend on view. Extra person $10. Children under 18 stay free in parents' room. AE, DC, DISC, ER, MC, V. Valet parking $10.

Also offering rooms with views of the Falls, the Foxhead, which has recently undergone an extensive renovation, offers rooms spread over 14 floors, all with private baths or showers. Rooms have views of the falls, gardens, village or city. Half the units have balconies.

Dining/Entertainment: The 14th-floor Penthouse Dining Room takes advantage of the view with its large glass windows, and serves a daily buffet for breakfast, lunch, and dinner with nightly dancing to a live band (in season). There are Japanese and budget restaurants, too.

Facilities: Outdoor rooftop pool.

MODERATE

The Americana. 8444 Lundy's Lane, Niagara Falls, ON, L2H 1H4. ☎ **905/356-8444.** Fax 905/356-8576. 120 rms. A/C TV TEL. Late June–late Aug $100–$170 double; Sept–June $60–$120 double. AE, DISC, ER, MC, V. Free parking.

The Americana, set in 25 acres of grounds, is one of the nicer moderately priced motels on this motel strip. There's a pleasant tree-shaded area for picnicking right across from the office. Sports facilities include tennis, squash, two pools, a sauna, a fitness room, and an outdoor swimming pool. The very large rooms are fully equipped with vanity sinks and full bathrooms. Some suites have whirlpool tubs and fireplaces. A dining room, lounge, and coffee shop are on the premises.

Michael's Inn. 5599 River Rd., Niagara Falls, ON, L2E 3H3. ☎ **905/354-2727** or 800/263-9390. Fax 905/374-7706. 130 rms. A/C TV TEL. June 16–Sept 15 $70–$165 double, $200–$450 bridal suite; Oct–May $60–$150 double, $175–$300 bridal suite. Rollaway bed $10; crib $5. AE, CB, DC, ER, MC, V. Free parking.

Rooms in this four-story white building overlooking the Niagara River gorge are large, have all the modern conveniences, and are nicely decorated. Many have heart-shaped tubs and Jacuzzis; some have themes, like the Garden of Paradise or Scarlett O' Hara rooms. There's a solarium pool out back. The Embers Open Hearth Dining Room is just that—the charcoal pit is enclosed behind glass so you can see all the cooking action. There's a lounge, too.

Red Carpet Inn. 4943 Clifton Hill, Niagara Falls, ON, L2G 3N5. ☎ 905/357-4330 or 800/668-8840. Fax 905/357-0423. 71 rms, 6 suites. A/C TV TEL. Mid-May to June $76.50 double; July–Sept $96.50 double; Oct–Dec $68.50 double; Jan to mid-May $56.50 double. Extra person $5. Children under 12 stay free in parents' room. AE, DISC, MC, V. Free parking.

Just up Clifton Hill, around the corner from the Foxhead, window boxes with geraniums draw the eye to the Red Carpet Inn. The units on two floors are set around a courtyard with an outdoor heated pool; six rooms are honeymoon suites with canopied beds and extra-plush decor, while the other rooms have colonial-style furniture, pink walls, and full bathrooms. Rooms 54 through 58 have a direct view of the falls; 12 rooms have private balconies. Convenient facilities include a washer-dryer, gift shop, and an outdoor beer garden.

Village Inn. 5705 Falls Ave., Niagara Falls, ON, L2E 6W7. ☎ **905/374-4444**, 905/357-3090, or 800/263-7135. 205 rms. A/C TV TEL. Mid-June to Oct 1 $90 double; Oct and Apr to mid-June $70 double. Special packages available. AE, DC, DISC, MC, V. Closed winter. Parking $4.

Located behind the two Skyline hotels, the Village Inn is ideal for families—all rooms are large. Some family suites measure 700 square feet and include a bedroom with two double beds and a living room. There's an outdoor heated swimming pool and a restaurant.

INEXPENSIVE

Nelson Motel. 10655 Niagara River Pkwy., Niagara Falls, ON, L2E 6S6. ☎ **905/295-4754.** 25 rms. A/C TV TEL. June 16–Sept 12 $55–$90 double; Sept 13 to mid-Nov and mid-Mar to June 15 $35–$55 double. Rollaways and cribs extra. MC, V. Closed mid-Nov to mid-Mar. Free parking.

For budget accommodations try the Nelson Motel, run by John and Dawn Pavlakovich, who live in the large house adjacent to the motel units. The units have character, especially the family units with a double bedroom adjoined by a twin-bedded room for the kids. Regular units have modern furniture. Singles have shower only. All units face the fenced-in pool and neatly trimmed lawn with umbrellaed tables and shrubs (none has a telephone). It's located a short drive from the falls overlooking the Niagara River, away from the hustle and bustle of Niagara itself.

A NEARBY PLACE TO STAY IN QUEENSTON

✪ **South Landing Inn.** At the corner of Kent and Front streets (P.O. Box 269), Queenston, ON, L0S 1L0. ☎ **905/262-4634.** 23 rms. A/C TV. Mid-Apr to end of Oct $90–$110 double; Nov to mid-Apr $60–$70 double. AE, MC, V. Free parking.

In the nearby village of Queenston, you'll find the South Landing Inn. The old original inn built in the 1800s has five units with early Canadian furnishings, including poster beds. The rest are in the modern annex. There's a distant view of the river from the inn's balcony. In the original inn you'll also find a cozy dining room with red gingham covered tables, where breakfast is served for $4.

CAMPING

There's a **Niagara Falls KOA** at 8625 Lundy's Lane, Niagara Falls, ON, L2H 1H5 (☎ 905/354-6472), which has 365 sites (some with electricity, water, and sewage) plus three dumping stations. Facilities include water, flush toilets, showers, fireplaces, store, ice, three pools (one indoor), sauna, and games room. Fees are $27 minimum for two; each additional adult, $5; each additional child 4 to 17, $3; hookups range from $2 for electricity, $3 for water and electricity, and $4 for water, electricity, and sewage. MC, V. Open April 1 to November 1.

WHERE TO DINE

In addition to the places below, the **Pinnacle,** 6732 Oakes Dr. (☎ 905/356-1501), offers a Canadian and continental menu and a remarkable view, since it's located atop the Minolta Tower. There's also a vista from the 520-foot tower at the **Skylon Tower Restaurants,** 5200 Robinson St. (☎ 905/356-2651, ext. 259), which serves pricey continental fare for lunch and dinner daily in the Revolving Restaurant, or more reasonably priced buffets available for all three meals in the Summit Suite dining room.

Betty's Restaurant & Tavern. 8911 Sodom Rd. ☎ **905/295-4436.** Reservations accepted only for parties of eight or more. Burgers and sandwiches under $5; main courses $6–$15. AE, MC, V. Mon–Sat 7am–10pm, Sun 9am–9pm. CANADIAN.

Betty's is a local favorite for honest food at fair prices. It's a family dining room where the art and generosity surface in the food—massive platters of fish-and-chips, breaded pork chops, chicken cutlet, all including soup or juice, vegetable, and potato. There are burgers and sandwiches, too. If you can, save room for the enormous portions of home-baked pies. Breakfast and lunch also offer good low-budget eating.

Casa d'Oro. 5875 Victoria Ave. ☎ **905/356-5646.** Reservations recommended. Main courses $12–$24. AE, DC, DISC, ER, MC, V. Mon–Fri noon–3pm and 4–11pm, Sat 4pm–1am, Sun 4–10pm. ITALIAN.

For fine Italian dining amid an overwhelming array of gilt busts of Caesar, Venetian-style lamps, and classical Roman columns, go to Casa d'Oro. Start with the clams casino or the brodetto Antonio (a giant crouton topped with poached eggs and floated on savory broth garnished with parsley and accompanied by grated cheese). Follow with specialties like saltimbocca alla romana, pollo cacciatore, or sole basilica (flavored with lime juice, paprika, and basil). Finish with a selection from the dessert wagon or order the cherries jubilee or bananas flambé.

Happy Wanderer. 6405 Stanley Ave. ☎ **905/354-9825.** Reservations not accepted. Main courses $16–$25. AE, MC, V. Daily 8am–11pm. GERMAN.

Real *gemütlichkeit* greets you at the chalet-style Happy Wanderer, which offers a variety of schnitzels, wursts, and other German specialties. Transport yourself back to the Black Forest among the beer steins and the game trophies on the walls. Dinner might start with goulash soup, and continue with bratwurst, knackwurst, rauchwurst (served with sauerkraut and potato salad), or a schnitzel—wiener, Holstein, or jaeger. All entrées include potatoes, salad, and rye bread. Desserts include, naturally, Black Forest cake and apple strudel (under $5).

NIAGARA PARKWAY COMMISSION RESTAURANTS

The Niagara Parkway Commission has commandeered the most spectacular scenic spots, where it operates some reasonably priced dining outlets.

Queenston Heights. Niagara Pkwy. ☎ **905/262-4274.** Reservations recommended. Main courses $17–$22. AE, MC, V. Daily 11:30am–3pm; Sun–Fri 5–9pm, Sat 5–10pm. Closed Jan to mid-Mar. CANADIAN.

The star of the Niagara Parkway Commission's eateries stands dramatically atop Queenston Heights. Set in the park among fir, cypress, silver birch, and maple, the open-air balcony affords a magnificent view of the lower Niagara River and the rich fruit-growing land through which it flows. Or you can sit under the cathedral ceiling with its heavy crossbeams where the flue of the stone fireplace reaches to the roof.

At dinner, among the selections might be filet of Atlantic salmon with dill hollandaise, or veal with a mushroom cognac cream sauce. Afternoon tea is served from 3 to 5pm in summer season. If nothing else, go for a drink on the deck.

Table Rock Restaurant. Niagara Pkwy. ☎ **905/354-3631.** Reservations recommended. Main courses $16–$20. AE, MC, V. Summer Mon–Fri 9am–10pm, Sat 8am–11pm, Sun 8am–10pm. CANADIAN/INTERNATIONAL.

Located only a few yards from the Canadian Horseshoe Falls, the Table Rock Restaurant offers the closest view of the falls of any restaurant. The fare includes standards such as prime rib; pizza, pasta, ribs, and light entrées are the luncheon choices.

Victoria Park Restaurant. Niagara Pkwy. ☎ **905/356-2217.** Reservations recommended. Main courses $14–$20. AE, DISC, MC, V. Mid-May to mid-Oct Sat–Thurs 11:30am–10pm, Fri 11:30am–11pm. Closed Canadian Thanksgiving in Oct–early May. CANADIAN.

Within spitting distance of both the Canadian and the American falls, the Victoria Park Restaurant offers a terrace with an awning where you can sit and dine, a dining room, a downstairs cafeteria, and a fast-food outlet pushing hot dogs and ice cream. In the dining room and terrace, you'll find an elaborate menu with a range of appetizers (shrimp cocktail, smoked goose breast, gravlax) and entrées that include steaks, coconut fried shrimp, and fettuccine with shrimp and okra. Pasta, sandwiches, and stir fries are available at lunch.

Whirlpool Restaurant. Niagara Pkwy. ☎ **905/356-7221.** Reservations recommended. Main courses $7–$12. AE, DISC, MC, V. Daily 6am–8pm. Closed Oct 31–Mar. CANADIAN.

Along the parkway toward Queenston lies the appealing Whirlpool Restaurant, at the commission's 18-hole golf course. It has a fine view of the first tee, the 18th green, and the 6,945-yard championship course, and serves a hearty breakfast and eminently reasonable lunch as well as dinner.

4 Niagara-on-the-Lake & the Shaw Festival

80 miles (128km) S of Toronto, 35 miles (56km) N of Buffalo, NY

Only 1½ hours from Toronto, Niagara-on-the-Lake is one of North America's best-preserved and prettiest 19th-century villages, with its lakeside location and tree-lined streets bordered by handsome clapboard and brick period houses. Some may find it too cute and too commercialized, but such is the setting for one of Canada's most famous events, the Shaw Festival.

ESSENTIALS

VISITOR INFORMATION   The **Niagara-on-the-Lake Chamber of Commerce and Visitor and Convention Bureau,** 153 King St. (P.O. Box 1043), Niagara-on-the-Lake, ON, L0S 1J0 (☎ 905/468-4263), will help you find accommodations at one of 75 bed-and-breakfasts licensed in the town. Open in summer, Monday through Wednesday from 9am to 5pm, Thursday through Friday from 9am to 6pm, Saturday and Sunday from 10am to 5pm; in winter, Monday through Friday from 9am to 5pm, Saturday from 11am to 5pm.

GETTING THERE   Driving from Toronto, take the QEW Niagara via Hamilton and St. Catharines and exit at Highway 55. From the United States cross from Buffalo to Fort Erie via the Peace Bridge or from Niagara Falls, New York, via the Rainbow Bridge and then take the QEW to Highway 55. Or cross at the Queenston-Lewiston bridge and follow the signs along the Niagara Parkway into Niagara-on-the-Lake. Allow plenty of time for crossing the border.

Amtrak and VIA operate trains between Toronto (☎ 416/366-8411) and New York stopping in St. Catharines and Niagara Falls. Call ☎ 800/361-1235 in Canada or 800/USA-RAIL in the United States.

THE SHAW FESTIVAL

Devoted to the works of George Bernard Shaw and his contemporaries, the festival, which opens in mid-April and runs to November, is housed in three theaters: the historic Court House, the Edwardian Royal George, and the exquisite Festival Theatre, where intermissions can be spent near the reflecting pools and gardens. Gourmet snacks are served at the Parasol Café on the terrace 1 1/2 hours before curtain time.

The season includes drama, musicals, comedy, and lunchtime performances at the Royal George Theatre. Ticket prices for all three theaters range from $10 for lunch time performances to $60. For more information, write or phone the Shaw Festival, P.O. Box 774, Niagara-on-the-Lake, ON, L0S 1J0 (☎ 905/468-2172 or 800/267-4759).

EXPLORING THE TOWN

Strolling along Queen Street will take you to some entertaining shopping stops, such as the 1866 **Niagara Apothecary Shop,** 5 Queen St. (☎ 905/468-3845), with its original black-walnut counters and displays of original glass and ceramic apothecary ware. **Greaves Jam,** 55 Queen St. (☎ 905/468-7831), offers the wares of fourth-generation jam makers. **Loyalist Village,** at 12 Queen St. (☎ 905/468-7331), sells distinctively Canadian clothes and crafts, including Inuit art, Native Canadian decoys, and sheepskins. The **Shaw Shop,** next to the Royal George, has GBS memorabilia and more. There's also a Dansk outlet and several galleries selling contemporary Canadian or other ethnic crafts, and a charming toy store, **The Owl and the Pussycat,** 16 Queen St. (☎ 905/468-3081).

Niagara Historical Society Museum. 43 Castlereagh St. (at Davy). ☎ **905/468-3912.** Admission $2.50 adults, $1 students, $1.50 seniors, 50¢ children under 12. May 1–Oct 31 daily 10am–5pm; Nov 1–Dec 31 and Mar–Apr daily 1–5pm; Jan–Feb Sat–Sun 1–5pm.

One of the oldest and largest of its kind in Canada, this museum houses more than 20,000 artifacts pertaining to local history, including collections dating from the 18th and 19th centuries, with many possessions of United Empire Loyalists who first settled the area at the end of the American Revolution.

✪ **Fort George National Historic Site.** Niagara Pkwy. ☎ **905/468-4257.** Admission $4 adults, $3 seniors, $2 children 6 and over, free for children under 5, family rate $12. Mid-May to June 30 daily 9:30am–4:30pm; July 1–Labor Day daily 10:30am–5:30pm; Labor Day–Oct 31 daily 9:30am–4:30pm; Nov 1 to mid-May, open weekdays by appointment only.

South along the Niagara Parkway is the impressive Fort George National Historic Site. It's easy to imagine taking shelter behind the stockade fence and watching for the enemy from across the river, even though today only condominiums stare back from the opposite riverbank. The fort played a key role in the War of 1812 when the Americans invaded, and was reconstructed in the 1930s. View the guard room with its hard plank beds, the officers' quarters, the enlisted men's quarters, and the sentry posts. In the gunpowder-storage area no metal fitments are used, for a stray spark could ignite the lot. The self-guided tour includes interpretive films and occasional performances by the Fort George Fife and Drum Corps.

REGIONAL WINERIES

If you take Highway 55 (Niagara Stone Road) out of Niagara-on-the-Lake you will come to **Hillebrand Estates Winery,** Highway 55, Niagara-on-the-Lake

(☎ 905/468-7123), just outside Virgil. Open year-round, tours are given daily at 11am and 1, 3, and 4pm.

If you turn off Highway 55 before reaching Hillebrand and go down Four Mile Creek Road to Line 7, you'll reach **Château des Charmes,** in St. Davids (☎ 905/ 262-4219). Tours are given daily on the hour from 11am to 4pm from May to September, and by appointment at other times.

The award-winning **Konzelmann Winery,** Lakeshore Road (☎ 905/935-2866), can be reached by driving out Mary Street. Tours are given June to late August Wednesday to Saturday at 2pm.

For other regional wineries, see the "Winery Tours" section in Niagara Falls.

WHERE TO STAY

During the summer season it can be hard to find lodging, but the visitors bureau (see above; ☎ 905/468-4263) should be able to find you some form of accommodation.

EXPENSIVE

Gate House Hotel. 142 Queen St., Niagara-on-the-Lake, ON, L0S 1J0. ☎ **905/468-3263.** Fax 905/468-7400. 9 rms. A/C MINIBAR TV TEL. June 1–Sept 30 $150–$170 double; Oct 1–31 and Mar 18–May 31 $120–$145 double; Nov 1–Dec 31 $105–$125 double. AE, ER, MC, V. Closed Jan.

Rooms at the Gate House Hotel are strikingly different from other accommodations in town. They are not country Canadian, but are decorated in cool, up-to-the-minute Milan style. The turquoise marbleized look is accented with ultramodern basic black lamps, block marble tables, leatherette couches, and bathrooms with sleek Italian fitments and hair dryers.

✪ **Oban Inn.** 160 Front St. (at Gate Street), Niagara-on-the-Lake, ON L0S 1J0. ☎ **905/ 468-2165.** 21 rms. A/C TV TEL. $135 standard double, $200 double with lake view. Winter midweek and weekend packages available.

With a prime location overlooking the lake, the Oban Inn is *the* place to stay. It's located in a charming white Victorian house with a large veranda. The gardens are a joy to behold and the source of the bouquets on each table in the dining room and throughout the house.

Each comfortable room, though decorated differently, has antique chests and early Canadian-style beds. Each is likely to have a candlewick spread on the bed, a small sofa, dressing table, and old prints on the walls—it's all very homey and comfortably old-fashioned. One or two rooms have showers only, so if you want a bath, be sure to request it.

Dining/Entertainment: Bar snacks and light lunches and dinners are available in the pub-like piano bar, with leather wingbacks, Windsor-style chairs and hunting prints over the blazing fireplace.

Pillar & Post Inn. 48 John St. (at King Street), Niagara-on-the-Lake, ON, L0S 1J0. ☎ **905/ 468-2123.** Fax 905/468-3551. 84 rms, 7 suites. A/C MINIBAR TV TEL. $150–$165 double; $160 fireplace room; $200–$255 suite. AE, DC, ER, MC, V.

Rustic to every last inch of barn board, the Pillar & Post Inn has lovely rooms, 49 of them with wood-burning fireplaces. Although all are slightly different, each room contains early Canadian-style furniture, Windsor-style chairs, and historical engravings, plus the usual modern conveniences. The suites all feature cathedral ceilings, red-brick wood-burning fireplaces, pine settles with cushions, four-poster beds, and Jacuzzis. Some rooms facing the pool on the ground level have bay windows and window boxes.

Dining/Entertainment: The dining rooms occupy a former tomato- and peach-canning factory and basket-manufacturing plant that was converted into a restaurant in 1970. The menu features continental cuisine, with dishes priced from $13 to $23. There's also a comfortable lounge.

Services: Room service is available from 7am to 10pm Sunday through Thursday (until midnight Friday and Saturday); laundry/valet.

Facilities: A secluded grass-surrounded pool, sauna, and whirlpool. Bikes are available.

Prince of Wales Hotel. 6 Picton St., Niagara-on-the-Lake, ON, L0S 1J0. ☎ **905/468-3246.** Fax 905/468-5521. 105 rms. A/C TV TEL. May 1–Oct 31 $120–$200 double; from $220 suite. Extra person $12. Rates slightly less at other times. AE, MC, V.

For a lively atmosphere that retains the elegance of a Victorian inn, the Prince of Wales Hotel has it all: full recreational facilities; lounges, bars, and restaurants; and attractive rooms, all beautifully decorated with antiques or reproductions. Bathrooms are equipped with bidets, and most rooms have minibars. The hotel's original section was built in 1864 and rooms are slightly smaller than those in the Prince of Wales Court.

Dining/Entertainment: An impressive old oak bar dominates the quiet bar off the lobby. Royals, the elegant main dining room, is decorated in French style and also offers outdoor dining as well as three meals a day. The dinner menu offers a dozen entrées, priced from $15 to $23. Three Feathers Café is light and airy for breakfast, lunch, or tea. The Queen's Royal lounge, furnished with wingbacks and armchairs, is a pleasant drinking spot.

Services: Room service is available from 7:30am to midnight; there's also laundry and valet.

Facilities: Indoor pool, sauna, whirlpool, sun and exercise room, and platform tennis court.

Queen's Landing. Byron Street, Niagara-on-the-Lake, ON, L0S 1J0. ☎ **905/468-2195.** Fax 905/468-2227. 137 rms. A/C MINIBAR TV TEL. $165 double; $175 fireplace room; $210 deluxe room with fireplace and Jacuzzi. Extra person $20. Children under 18 stay free in parents' room. Special packages available. AE, DC, ER, MC, V.

Overlooking the river, but within walking distance of the theater, the Queen's Landing is a fine establishment offering 70 rooms with fireplaces and 32 with Jacuzzis. The spacious rooms are comfortably furnished half-canopy or brass beds, wingback chairs, and large desks.

Dining/Entertainment: The lounge, with its fieldstone fireplace, is cozy. The dining room looks out over the yacht-filled dock; at dinner about a dozen dishes are offered, priced from $17 to $25 for such dishes as grilled halibut with lime-butter glaze. Breakfast, lunch and Sunday brunch are served here, too.

Services: Room service (from 7am to 11pm), laundry/valet.

Facilities: Indoor pool, whirlpool and sauna, exercise room, lap pool, and bicycle rentals.

White Oaks Inn & Racquet Club. Taylor Road, Niagara-on-the-Lake, ON, L0S 1J0. ☎ **905/688-2550.** Fax 905/688-2220. 90 rms. A/C TV TEL. July–Aug $120–$130 double, $160–$200 suite. Off-season rates drop slightly. AE, DC, ER, MC, V.

Not far from Niagara-on-the-Lake, the White Oaks Inn and Racquet Club is a fantastic facility for an active vacation. You could spend the whole weekend and not stir outside the resort.

The rooms are as good as the facilities, featuring oak beds and furniture, vanity sinks, and additional niceties like a phone in the bathroom. The Executive Suites also have brick fireplaces, marble-top desks, Jacuzzis (some heart-shaped), and bidets. Deluxe suites also have sitting rooms.

Dining/Entertainment: There's an outdoor terrace cafe, a formal restaurant, and a pleasantly furnished cafe/coffee shop.

Services: Room service (7am to 11pm), valet service.

Facilities: Four outdoor and eight indoor tennis courts, six squash courts, three racquetball courts, Nautilus room, jogging trails, massage therapist, sauna, suntan beds, and a day-care center staffed with fully qualified staff.

MODERATE

George III. 61 Melville St., Niagara-on-the-Lake, ON, L0S 1J0. ☎ **905/468-4800.** Fax 905/468-7004. 8 rms. A/C TV. $90–$105 double; $115 room with balcony. Rates include continental breakfast. MC, V.

Down by the harbor, the George III offers attractive rooms with pretty wallpaper, and quilts and flounce pillows on the beds. Room no. 8 has a large balcony. The property is operated by the Pillar and Post Inn.

Moffat Inn. 60 Picton St., Niagara-on-the-Lake, ON, L0S 1J0. ☎ **905/468-4116.** Fax 905/468-4747. 22 rms. A/C TV TEL. Apr 15–Oct 31 and Christmas/New Year holiday period $85–$114 double; mid-Oct–Apr $65–$109 double. Extra person $10. AE, MC, V.

This is a fine choice, with comfortable units. Most are furnished with either brass or cannonball beds, traditional modern furnishings or wicker and bamboo pieces, and feature built-in closets. Additional room amenities include tea kettle and supplies, and hairdryer; some rooms have gas fireplaces. Free coffee is available in the lobby and there's also the Tea Room and Bar for meals. No smoking.

✪ **Old Bank House.** 10 Front St., Niagara-on-the-Lake, ON, L0S 1J0. ☎ **905/468-7136.** 6 rms (4 with private bath), 2 suites (with bath). A/C. $80–$90 room without bath; $105–$110 room with private bath; $130 suite; $205 two-bedroom suite for up to four. Rates include full English breakfast. Lower rates in winter. AE, MC, V.

Beautifully situated down by the river, the Old Bank House, a two-story Georgian, was built in 1817 and was in fact the Bank of Canada's first branch. Four rooms have private baths, while two share a bathroom with Jacuzzi. The Rose, the most expensive suite, has two bedrooms, a sitting room, and a bathroom. Several rooms have private entrances, like the charming Garden Room, which also has a trellised deck. All rooms are tastefully decorated, and all but one have fridge and coffee or tea supplies. The sitting room, with its fireplace, is very comfortable and furnished with Sheraton and Hepplewhite pieces.

WHERE TO DINE

For an inexpensive down-home breakfast, go to the **Stagecoach Family Restaurant,** 45 Queen St. (☎ 905/468-3133). No credit cards are accepted. The **Niagara Home Bakery,** 66 Queen St. (☎ 905/468-3431), is the place to stop for chocolate-date squares, cherry squares, croissants, cookies, and individual quiches.

The Buttery. 19 Queen St. ☎ **905/468-2564.** Reservations required for Henry VIII feast. Main courses $17–$21. AE, MC, V. Summer daily 11am–12:30am; other months daily noon–8pm, except on Fri-Sat when the Henry VIII feast takes place. Afternoon tea served 2–5pm. CANADIAN/ENGLISH/CONTINENTAL.

With its terrace brightened by hanging geraniums, the Buttery has been a main-street dining landmark for years, known for its weekend Henry VIII feasts (9pm upstairs, 9:30pm downstairs), when "serving wenches" "cosset" guests with food and wine, while jongleurs and musickers entertain. You'll be served "four removes"—broth, chicken, roast lamb, roast pig, sherry trifle, syllabub, and cheese, all washed down with a goodly amount of wine, ale, and mead. This feast takes $2^1/2$ hours and costs $46, including tax and gratuity for Henry VIII.

A full tavern menu is served from 11am to 5:30pm, featuring spareribs, filet mignon, shrimp in garlic sauce, and English specialties including a Cornish pasty that's worthy of the name. The dinner menu lists eight or so choices; I highly recommend the leg of lamb served with a real garden mint sauce. Finish with key lime pie or mud pie, or take home some of the fresh baked pies, strudels, dumplings, cream puffs, and scones. An after-theater menu is served from 10pm to 12:30am.

Fans Court. 135 Queen St. ☎ **905/468-4511.** Reservations recommended. Main courses $8–$18. AE, MC, V. Daily noon–10pm. Closed Mon off-season. CHINESE.

Some of the best food in town can be found in this comfortable Chinese spot, decorated with fans, cushioned bamboo chairs, and round tables spread with golden tablecloths. In summer, the courtyard has tables for outdoor dining. The cuisine ranges from Cantonese and Beijing to Szechwan. Singapore beef, moo shu pork, Szechwan scallops, and lemon chicken are just a few of the dishes available. If you wish, you can order Peking duck 24 hours in advance.

George III. 61 Melville St. ☎ **905/468-4207.** Reservations not accepted. Main courses $8–$13. MC, V. Daily 11:30am–10pm. Closed mid-Nov to mid-Apr. CANADIAN.

Down by the harbor, George III is a good budget dining choice for assorted burgers (guacamole, Cajun spice), chicken wings, sandwiches, and stir fries. It has a publike atmosphere, and a pleasant outdoor patio.

✪ **Ristorante Giardino.** In the Gate House Hotel, 142 Queen St. ☎ **905/468-3263.** Reservations recommended. Main courses $19–$30. AE, ER, MC, V. Summer daily noon–2:30pm and 5:30–9:30pm; winter daily 5:30–9pm. NORTHERN ITALIAN.

On the ground floor of the Gate House Hotel is this sleek, ultramodern restaurant with gleaming marble-top bar and glass and brass accents throughout. The food is northern Italian with Asian and other accents. Main courses include steamed salmon with balsamic vinegar and olive oil, veal loin chop napped with vodka, and breast of chicken with orange-ginger sauce. Desserts include a fine amaretto tiramisu and an innovative fresh strawberry peppercorn surprise.

5 St. Catharines & the Welland Canal

In the heart of wine country and the Niagara fruit belt, the historic city of St. Catharines is home to two major events: the **Royal Canadian Henley Regatta** in early August and the 10-day **Niagara Grape and Wine Festival** held in late September. In St. Catharines you'll come across the Welland Canal, which connects Lake Ontario to Lake Erie and runs through the town of Port Colbourne, which is south of St. Catherines.

If you drive along Mary Street from Niagara-on-the-Lake, you'll be heading out along Lakeshore Road. When you come to the junction of Lake Street, turn left for downtown St. Catharines. If you're driving directly from Toronto, take the QEW Niagara to the St. Catharines exit; for Port Colborne the easiest way is to take the QEW Niagara to Highway 3 east.

Amtrak and VIA operate trains between Toronto (☎ 416/366-8411) and New York, stopping in St. Catharines and Niagara Falls. Call ☎ 800/361-1235 in Canada or 800/USA-RAIL in the United States.

THE WELLAND CANAL

Built to circumvent Niagara Falls, the Welland Canal connects Lake Ontario to Lake Erie, which is 327 feet higher than Lake Ontario. Some 27 feet deep, the canal enables large ocean vessels to navigate the Great Lakes. The 26-mile-long canal has seven locks, each with an average lift of 46 1/2 feet. The average transit time for any vessel is 12 hours. More than a thousand oceangoing vessels travel through in a year, the most common cargoes being wheat and iron ore.

The first canal opened in 1829 in St. Catharines, where today remnants of the first three canals (1829, 1845, and 1887) have been preserved. At **Port Dalhousie,** where the canals entered Lake Ontario, the locks, lighthouses, and 19th-century warehouses and architecture are reminders of a once-thriving waterway.

The best places to observe the canal are at the **Welland Canal Viewing and Information Centres,** at Lock 3 in St. Catharines and at Lock 8 in Port Colborne. At the first, from a raised platform you can watch ships from over 50 countries passing between Lake Ontario and Lake Erie. The Canal Parkway allows visitors to walk beside the canal and follow the vessels. From the road below the canal you can observe the funnels only above the top of the bank.

Lock 3 is on Government Road north of Glendale Avenue, right off the QEW. At the second, Lock 8, an observation stand overlooks one of the world's longest locks.

Scheduled to move into a building at Lock 3 as of this writing is the **St. Catharines Museum** (☎ 905/984-8880), with displays illustrating the construction of the Welland Canal as well as pioneer and War of 1812 memorabilia. Admission is $3 adults, $2 students and seniors, $1 children 5 to 13. Open Labor Day to Victoria Day Monday to Friday from 9am to 5pm, Saturday and Sunday 1 to 5pm; Victoria Day to Labor Day daily 9:30am to 7pm. It's closed Good Friday, December 25 and 26, and New Year's Day.

At Locks 4, 5, and 6—the twin flight locks—ships can be raised and lowered simultaneously. They're in **Thorold,** on Government Road, south of Glendale Avenue.

In **Welland,** a section of the fourth canal, which is no longer operating, is now used for recreational purposes—waterskiing, boating, and picnicking. For information call ☎ 905/685-3711.

EXPLORING THE REGION

If you drive to St. Catharines from Niagara-on-the-Lake, you'll pass the **Konzelmann Winery** along Lakeshore Road (☎ 905/935-2866). Tours are offered Wednesday through Saturday at 2pm in summer. Just before you enter St. Catharines, there's a sign on the right for the **Happy Rolph Bird Sanctuary and Children's Petting Farm** (☎ 905/935-1484), which the kids will love. It's free and open daily from late May to mid-October from 10am to dusk.

Welland is known for its two-week **Rose Festival** in early June, when the city bursts out with sports events, art shows, rose-growing contests, a military band tattoo, ethnic foods, and a parade.

At Port Colborne, the southern end of the canal opens into Lake Erie. A good sense of the area's history and development can be gained at the **Port Colborne Historical and Marine Museum,** 280 King St. (☎ 905/834-7604). The six-building complex downtown has a fully operational blacksmith shop and a tea room. It's free and open daily May through December from noon to 5pm.

In Vineland, **Prudhomme's Landing-Wet 'n' Wild,** off Victoria Ave. (☎ 905/562-7304), features water slides, a wave pool, go-karts, kids' rides, and miniature golf.

An all-day pass costs $10.65 for anyone five or over. Open mid-June to Labor Day daily from 10am to 9pm.

WHERE TO DINE
IN THE PORT DALHOUSIE HARBOR AREA

Murphy's. Lakeport Road. ☎ **905/934-1913.** Reservations recommended for large parties. Main courses $12–$33. AE, MC, V. Sun–Thurs 11:30am–10pm, Fri–Sat 11:30am–11:30pm. CANADIAN.

With a polished, nautical look, Murphy's is a popular dining and drinking spot with the mid-30s and -40s professional crowd. Offerings run from steak, pasta, seafood, and chicken wings to sandwiches. Prices top out with the lobster tail dinner.

The Port Mansion. 12 Lakeport Rd. ☎ **905/934-0575.** Reservations recommended, especially on weekends. Main courses $14–$28. AE, MC, V. Mon–Sat 11am–3pm, Sun 10:30am–3pm; daily 4–10pm. CANADIAN.

The Port Mansion has a kitschy Victorian atmosphere—stained-glass lamps and bamboo furniture mixed with the more classic look of wing chairs and reading material. The pleasant outdoor patio for dining overlooks the harbor's boat traffic. Prime rib, surf-and-turf, pasta, shrimp and scallop fettuccine, chicken stir-fry, and similar fare are the specialties here.

IN ST. CATHARINES

Iseya. 22 James St. (between St. Paul and King streets). ☎ **905/688-1141.** Reservations recommended for dinner. Main courses $10–$27. AE, MC, V. Mon–Fri 11:30am–2:30pm; Mon–Sat 5:30–10pm. JAPANESE.

Iseya is one of the region's few traditional Japanese restaurants, serving sushi/sashimi as well as teriyaki, tempura, and sukiyaki dishes.

Wellington Court Cafe. 11 Wellington St. ☎ **905/682-5518.** Reservations recommended. Main courses $10–$20. ER, MC, V. Mon–Sat 11:30am–2:30pm; Tues–Sat 5:30–9:30pm. CONTINENTAL.

In downtown St. Catharines, the Wellington Court Café is well worth visiting. Located in an Edwardian town house with a flower trellis, the dining rooms feature contemporary decor with modern lithographs and photographs. The menu features daily specials—the fish and pasta of the day, for example—along with such items as a veal chop in pecan crust with port, stuffed breast of chicken with black currant cream sauce, or salmon in various sauces.

IN DOWNTOWN WELLAND

Rinderlin's. 24 Burgar St. ☎ **905/735-4411.** Reservations recommended. Main courses $16–$29. AE, MC, V. Tues–Fri noon–2pm; Tues–Sat 6–9pm. FRENCH.

An intimate town house dining spot, Rinderlin's has a very good local reputation for traditional French cuisine. On the dinner menu you might find veal citron as well as poached salmon with a Pernod sauce, Dover sole, rack of lamb, and venison with wild mushrooms and game sauce. Desserts are seasonal—my favorite is the nougat terrine with a chocolate sauce.

6 Hamilton

42 miles (63km) SW of Toronto

Situated on a landlocked harbor spanned at its entrance by the Burlington Skyway's dramatic sweep, Hamilton (pop. 312,000) has long been known as "Steeltown." Although it has steel mills and smoke-belching chimneys, the town has received an extensive facelift in the last decade, the most remarkable results being Hamilton Place, a huge cultural center, Lloyd D. Jackson Square, a new City Hall with splashing fountains out front, and many urban-renewal projects, including Hess Village. This renaissance has also spawned restaurants and other facilities.

ESSENTIALS

VISITOR INFORMATION   Stop in at the **Tourist Information Centre,** 127 King St. East (at Catherine; ☎ 905/546-2666), or contact **Greater Hamilton Tourism and Convention Services,** 1 James St. South, 3rd floor, Hamilton, ON, L8P 4R5 (☎ 905/546-4222).

GETTING THERE   If you're driving from Toronto, take the QEW Niagara to the Hamilton exit.

EXPLORING DOWNTOWN HAMILTON & BEYOND

Don't forget to explore **Hess Village,** a four-block area of restored clapboard houses now containing boutiques, galleries, and restaurants.

Hamilton Farmer's Market is worth a visit to **Lloyd D. Jackson Square,** where you can also find a lot of good shopping, including such budget shoppers' paradises as Marks & Spencer.

The **Art Gallery of Hamilton,** at 123 King St. West (☎ 905/527-6610) has an excellent collection of Canadian and 20th-century American and British works. Admission is by donation. Open Wednesday, Friday, and Saturday from 10am to 5pm, Thursday 1 to 9pm, and Sunday 1 to 5pm.

The **Canadian Football Hall of Fame and Museum,** at 58 Jackson St. West (☎ 905/528-7566), is a national football shrine that traces the game's history and is the permanent home of the Grey Cup and Schenley trophies. Admission is $3 for adults, $1.50 students and seniors, $1 children. Open May through November Monday to Saturday from 9:30am to 4:30pm, Sunday and holidays noon to 4:30pm. The rest of the year is open Monday through 9:30am to 4:30pm (closed on Christmas and New Year's days).

Just a half-hour drive northwest of Hamilton, off Highway 8 between Hamilton and Cambridge, is the **African Lion Safari** (☎ 519/623-2620). You can drive yourself or take the guided safari tram through this 750-acre wildlife park containing rhinos, cheetahs, lions, tigers, giraffes, zebras, vultures and many other species. There are scenic railroad and boat rides, plus special kids' jungle and water (bring bathing suits) play areas. Admission includes a tour of the six large game reserves plus the rides and shows and costs $14.50 for adults, $12.50 seniors and youths 13–17, $10.50 children 3–12. Open daily April through October, hours July to Labor Day run 10am to 5:30pm; at other times it closes earlier.

✪ **Royal Botanical Gardens.** Highway 6. ☎ **905/527-1158.** Admission $4.25 adults, $3.25 seniors and children 5–2. Outdoor garden areas mid-Apr–Oct 11 daily 9:30am–6pm; Mediterranean Garden daily 9am–5pm. From Hamilton, take Main Street West to Highway 403, and then Highway 403 north. Exit at Highway 6 and follow the signs.

On the northern approaches to the city, these gardens provide almost 3,000 acres of stunning horticultural exhibits. The Rock Garden features spring bulbs in May, summer flowers from June to September, and chrysanthemums in October. The Laking Garden blazes during June and July with iris, peonies, and lilies. The arboretum fills with the heady scent of lilac from the end of May to early June, and the exquisite color bursts of rhododendrons and azaleas thereafter. The Centennial Rose Garden is at its best from late June to mid-September.

Twenty-five miles of nature trails crisscross the area, while nearby, and still part of the gardens, is **Cootes Paradise,** a natural wildlife sanctuary with trails leading through some 18,000 acres of water, marsh, and wooded ravines. For a trail-guide map, stop in at either the Nature Centre (open daily from 10am to 4pm) or at headquarters at 680 Plains Rd. West (Highway 2), Burlington. Two Tea Houses—one overlooking the Rock Garden, the other the Rose Garden—serve refreshments.

Dundurn Castle. Dundurn Park, York Boulevard. ☎ **905/546-2872.** Admission $5 adults, $3.50 seniors and students, $2 children 6–14. June–Labor Day daily 10am–4pm; rest of the year Tues–Sun noon–4pm. Closed Christmas and New Year's days. From downtown Hamilton, take King Street West to Dundurn Street, turn right, and Dundurn will run into York Boulevard.

Dundurn Castle affords a glimpse of the opulent life as it was lived in this part of southern Ontario in the mid-19th century. It was built between 1832 and 1835 by Sir Allan Napier MacNab, prime minister of the United Provinces of Canada in the mid-1850s and a founder of the Great Western Railway, who was knighted by Queen Victoria for the part he played in the Rebellion of 1837. The 35-plus-room mansion has been restored and furnished in the style of 1855. The gray stucco exterior, with its classical Greek portico, is impressive enough, but inside from the grand and formal dining rooms to Lady MacNab's boudoir the furnishings are equally rich. The museum contains a fascinating collection of Victoriana. In December the castle is decorated quite splendidly for a Victorian Christmas.

WHERE TO STAY

About a dozen bed-and-breakfast homes, renting rooms for $60 double, have joined together to advertise. To secure a brochure listing the individual homes, contact the Tourist Information Centre (see above).

Royal Connaught Howard Johnson's Plaza. 112 King St. East, Hamilton, ON, L8N 1A8. ☎ **905/546-8111.** Fax 905/546-8144. 208 rms. A/C TV TEL. $65–$115 double. Extra person $10. Children under 14 stay free in parents' room. AE, DC, ER, MC, V. Parking $4.75.

A grand old hotel built in 1904, the Royal Connaught Howard Johnson's has been renovated in recent years. In the lobby, glass, marble, and hand-rubbed wood dramatically set off the huge crystal chandeliers, Corinthian columns, and a flying staircase. Note the gleaming old-style brass royal mailbox. The bathrooms are exceptionally large. The hotel has the Grill Steakhouse for dining, two bars, and an indoor pool with two-story water slide.

Sheraton Hamilton. 116 King St. West, Hamilton, ON, L8P 4V3. ☎ **905/529-5515** or 800/325-3535. Fax 905/529-8266. 302 rms. A/C TV TEL. $115 double. AE, DC, ER, MC, V. Parking $8.

The Sheraton offers spacious rooms appointed with extra telephones, hair dryers, and tasteful modern furnishings that include desks. There are two restaurants—Windows for burgers, omelets, and sandwiches; and Chagall's for continental dishes. Other facilities include a health club with sauna and hot tub, and an indoor pool with a landscaped sun deck. The hotel is connected conveniently to the Convention Centre, Hamilton Place, Lloyd D. Jackson Square, and the Indoor Farmer's Market. There's valet service, and room service is available until 1am.

WHERE TO DINE

Black Forest Inn. 255 King St. East. ☎ **905/528-3538.** Reservations not accepted. Main courses $6–$12. AE, CB, DC, ER, MC, V. Tues–Thurs 11:30am–10:30pm, Fri–Sat 11:30am–11pm, Sun noon–9:30pm. GERMAN.

The Black Forest Inn provides a festive atmosphere for good budget dining. Here among the warm wood paneling and the painted wood furniture, served by waitresses in colorful dirndls, you can sample all kinds of schnitzels and sausages, all served with home fries and sauerkraut. Naturally, for dessert you'll have Black Forest cake or Dobostorte.

Le Ganges Indian Restaurant. 234 King St. East. ☎ **905/523-8812.** Reservations recommended. Main courses $6–$14. AE, DC, ER, MC, V. Mon and Wed–Fri 11:30am–2pm; Wed–Mon 5–10pm. INDIAN.

You'll enjoy fine Indian cuisine in very pleasant surroundings—Indian wood carvings, exposed brick walls, and Breuer-style cane chairs. The vegetable samosas and pakoras are served piping hot and crisp, not greasy. At lunch the best choice is the thali. Other choices include a succulent rogan josh and delicious royal basmati rice with delicately flavored shrimp. The menu includes a variety of meat, fish, and vegetarian dishes—shrimp do piaz, murg vindaloo (chicken), aloo gobi, and navratan biryani.

Pappas' Dining. 309 Main St. East. ☎ **905/525-2455.** Reservations recommended. Main courses $12–$25. AE, CB, DC, ER, MC, V. Mon–Fri 11:30am–2:30pm; daily 5–10pm. GREEK.

The blue-and-white sign outside Pappas' Dining hints at the Greek delicacies to be found within among the Corinthian columns, the blue wall friezes, and classical statues in the wall alcoves. Waitresses in white Grecian robes will serve you fried feta cheese or avgolemono soup to start, followed by souvlaki, moussaka, or kokinisto (tenderloin with peppers, onions, and rice, sautéed over a low flame with light Greek wine). Steaks and seafood are also available, and Greek feasts for two.

Shakespeare's Steak House & Tavern. 181 Main St. East. ☎ **905/528-0689.** Reservations recommended. Main courses $17–$28. AE, CB, DC, ER, MC, V. Mon–Fri noon–2:30pm and 5–10:30pm, Sat 5–11:30pm. CANADIAN.

Shakespeare's has endured for almost 26 years as a Hamilton dining institution because it serves well-prepared steaks. The decor underlines the restaurant's name—beams, horse brasses, and portraits of the Bard and his characters. Select marinated Bismarck herring to start and follow with a 6½-ounce filet or a 16-ounce New York sirloin, both served with garlic bread, kosher dills, and french fries or a baked potato. For dessert the apple beignets are irresistible. At meal's end, you will be presented with a huge goblet of candies to rummage through.

The Winking Judge. 25 Augusta St. ☎ **905/527-1280.** Reservations not accepted. Most items $3–$7. AE, V. Mon–Thurs 11:30am–midnight, Fri–Sat 11:30am–2am, Sun noon–11pm. PUB FARE.

You're guaranteed to find a convivial crowd, including a few Aussies and Brits, here at lunchtime or on weekends when the piano player swings and people sometimes sing along. The fare caters to the palates of expatriates with such items as steak-and-kidney and shepherd's pies, served all day in the downstairs bar.

A NEARBY PLACE TO DINE BETWEEN HAMILTON & BRANTFORD

Ancaster Old Mill Inn. Off Route 2, Ancaster. ☎ **905/648-1827.** Reservations recommended. Main courses $13–$28. AE, DC, MC, V. Mon–Sat 11:30am–2:30pm; Sun 10am–2:30pm; Mon–Thurs 4:30–7:30pm, Fri–Sat 4:30–8:30pm, Sun 4–8:30pm. Sun evening buffet served 5–8pm. CANADIAN.

To reach the restaurant, you cross the mill race. You'll find pleasant country dining rooms with pine furnishings. One end overlooks the falls, the other the old mill built in 1792. The menu features traditional dishes made from flour without preservatives and fresh, not canned vegetables. Your appetizer might be bacon-wrapped scallops or oysters Rockefeller; main courses include such items as veal piccata, prime rib, and barbecue ribs. Choose the steak and lobster tail if you're feeling flush.

HAMILTON AFTER DARK

For symphony concerts, top-class international entertainers, theater, and dance, go to **Hamilton Place,** a modern $11 million arts complex housing two theaters: the Great Hall, holding more than 2,000, and the smaller, more intimate Studio seating 400. The **Hamilton Philharmonic Orchestra** and **Opera Hamilton** are prime tenants. Ticket prices range from $15 to $80, depending on the show (the top rate is for opera). Hamilton Place is at Main and MacNab Streets (☎ 905/546-3050), opposite City Hall.

7 Port Hope, Presqu'ile Provincial Park & Trenton

If you're driving from Toronto, the 401E will bring you to the attractive old lakefront town of Port Hope, where antiques stores line the main street. It's situated at the mouth of the Ganaraska River, 72 miles east of Toronto.

If you'd like to stay in Port Hope, **The Carlyle,** 86 John St. (☎ 905/885-8686), occupies the old 1857 Bank of Upper Canada building. Rates are $80 for doubles and $110 suite. The dining room offers casual food—lasagne, burgers, chicken Kiev, and seafood dishes, priced from $5 to $12. The restaurant is open Monday through Saturday for lunch and dinner.

From Port Hope visitors can turn north up route 28 to **Peterborough,** which is at the center of the Kawartha lakes—the series of lakes connected by the Trent-Severn Waterway from Trent to Georgian Bay. Here you can watch the boats traveling through the locks and being lifted 62 feet from one water level to another at the visitor center (☎ 705/745-8389) on the waterway on Hunter St. East.

Or you can continue east along Highway 401 to Brighton, the gateway town to **Presqu'ile Provincial Park.** This 2,000-acre area of marsh and woodland offers superb bird-watching (attracting birds from both the Atlantic and Mississippi flyways), camping, and a mile-long beach. Major bird-watching weekends are organized in spring and fall. The visitor center is open from Victoria Day to Labor Day. For information, contact the Superintendent, Presque'ile Provincial Park, RR no. 4, Brighton, ON, K0K 1H0 (☎ 613/475-2204).

Serpent Mounds Provincial Park, RR no. 3, Keene, ON K0L 2G0 (☎ 705/295-6879) has 113 camp sites and offers swimming, boat rentals, and self-guided nature trails. The park is named after the Indian burial mounds it contains—one is shaped like a serpent.

PETROGLYPHS PROVINCIAL PARK & ONWARD TO TRENTON

Continuing northeast on Highway 28 from Peterborough you'll come to Stony Lake where you'll discover, at its eastern end near the town of Stonyridge, **Petroglyphs Provincial Park,** Woodview PO, Woodview, ON, K0L 3E0 (☎ 705/877-2552). Although the hiking trails, two lakes, and forests are appealing, the petroglyphs themselves—hundreds of symbolic shapes and figures—attract visitors. In 1924 a local resident discovered the petroglyphs carved into a flat expanse of rock. To this day the Ojibwa Anishinabe Nation reveres this as a sacred site. It's believed that these petroglyphs were carved by an Algonkian-speaking people between 500 and 1,000 years ago. About 300 distinct carvings have been identified alongside 600 indecipherable figures. The park also has several short hiking trails and picnic areas. Open 10am to 5pm from May to Canadian Thanksgiving.

Forty miles east of Port Hope lies Trenton, the starting point for the **Trent-Severn Canal,** a 240-mile waterway that travels via 44 locks to Georgian Bay on Lake Huron. It is also the western entrance to the Loyalist Parkway (Highway 33), leading to Quinte's Isle.

8 Quinte's Isle

130 miles (210km) E of Toronto, 52 miles (85km) W of Kingston

Prince Edward County, an island surrounded by Lake Ontario and the Bay of Quinte, has retained much of its early character and its relaxed pace. It was settled by United Empire Loyalists in the 1780s, and many of their descendants still live, work, and farm here. Their solid attachment to the past shows in the quiet streets of such historic towns and villages as Picton, Bloomfield, and Wellington.

ESSENTIALS

VISITOR INFORMATION   Contact **Quinte's Isle Tourist Association,** 116 Main St. (Box 50), Picton, ON, K0K 2T0 (☎ 613/476-2421).

GETTING THERE   If you're driving from Trenton, take Highway 33S; from Belleville, Highway 62S off the 401; and from Kingston, Highway 49S off the 401.

FROM CARRYING PLACE TO BLOOMFIELD

Carrying Place was indeed a portage place—at the narrow isthmus at the head of the Bay of Quinte. In fact, this former portage road is the oldest road in continuous use in Upper Canada. The road goes from the Bay of Quinte to Weller's Bay on Lake Ontario, and it was here that the Gunshot Treaty was signed in which the native tribes signed over land stretching as far west as Toronto.

Consecon is an old milling village with an attractive millpond and marsh and water views.

Drive through **Wellington** and you can't help but notice how well kept the houses and their gardens are. You'll feel like you're in an English village.

Bloomfield, settled in the early 1800s, has been strongly influenced by the Methodists and the Quakers. The latter were harassed in their native New York for their pacifism during the American Revolution, and fled to Canada with the Loyalists. Two Quaker cemeteries in town are part of that legacy. Today this pretty town has become a haven for retirees, artists, and craftspeople. You'll find several potteries, craft shops, and antique stores, including the **Bloomfield Pottery,** at 54 Main St. (☎ 613/393-3258), and the **Village Art Gallery,** at 29 Main St. (☎ 613/393-2943).

WHERE TO STAY

In Wellington

Tara Hall. 146 Main St., Wellington, ON, K0K 3L0. ☎ **613/399-2801.** Fax 613/399-1104. 3 rms. A/C TV. $72 double. Rates include breakfast. Extra person $12. V. Free parking.

Tara Hall is a landmark home built by a wealthy local grain-shipping and dry-goods merchant. Originally the whole upper front floor served as a ballroom; today it has been divided into three guest rooms. Each room is furnished pleasantly with some antiques. A full and formal breakfast is served, the table set with linen. No smoking.

In Bloomfield

Cornelius White House. 8 Wellington St., Bloomfield, ON, K0K 1G0. ☎ **613/393-2282.** 3 rms (1 with bath), 2 suites (with bath). A/C. $55–$85 double (including breakfast). Extra person in suite $10. MC, V.

This 19th-century redbrick house offers a lovely view over meadows dotted with Holsteins. There are two doubles, a twin, and two suites, each furnished differently. One has an iron-and-brass bed; another is furnished in pine (rocker, dresser, bed, and chest). A full breakfast (or continental, if you prefer) is served in the 1867 dining room with wide pine floors and brick fireplace. A cottage is also available with small kitchen. The Tea Room is open daily from 11:30am to 4pm for light meals.

✪ **Mallory House.** RR no. 1, Box 10, Bloomfield, ON, K0K 1G0. ☎ **613/393-3458.** 3 rms (none with bath). $55 double. Rates include full breakfast. No credit cards.

Mallory House offers three really appealing accommodations sharing 1¹/₂ baths in an old 1810/1850 farmhouse. One is furnished with a brass bed and marble-top dresser, another has twin brass beds, and the third has a mahogany four-poster and marble top dresser among the furnishings. The bathroom features an old-fashioned tub. Two sitting rooms are available to guests, both very comfortably furnished with antiques, Oriental rugs, good books, and a marble fireplace. The house is surrounded by lawns, shrubs, trees, and flower gardens. It's a really fine accommodation and a great value, watched over by Hobbes, the black mutt, and two old cats.

WHERE TO DINE

In Consecon

✪ **The Sword.** RR no. 1, Consecon, ON, K0K 1T0. ☎ **613/392-2143.** Reservations recommended. Main courses $12–$23. MC, V. Summer daily 11am–2pm and 4–9pm, Fri–Sat 4–9:30pm; winter Thurs–Sun 4–9pm. CONTINENTAL.

Ignore the roadhouse exterior of the Sword, for inside you'll find a veritable little corner of England. The proprietors will greet you at the bar and take you into the beamed lounge where you'd swear you were in a real English country pub. The food is highly recommended and the wine cellar excellent and extensive—2,500 bottles. When I visited I enjoyed a superb loin of lamb that had been deboned and defatted and was served with an intense bordelaise sauce accompanied by roast potatoes.

In Bloomfield

✪ **Angelines.** In the Bloomfield Inn, 29 Stanley St. West, Bloomfield. ☎ **613/393-3301.** Reservations recommended. Main courses $17–$22. MC, V. July–Aug daily 8–11am, noon–2pm, and 5:30–9pm; June and Sept Wed–Mon 8–11am, noon–2pm, and 5:30–9pm; winter Thurs–Mon noon–2pm and 5:30–9pm. CONTINENTAL.

The Bloomfield Inn is mainly known for its restaurant, Angelines, operated by a young Austrian chef and located in an 1869 house. Umbrellaed tables are on the lawn out front. The cuisine is seasonal and the chef grows his own herbs. Dinner entrées might include beef medallions with mustard sauce, chicken breast with tarragon and chives, or salmon niçoise. There's also a six-course dégustation menu for $36. Afternoon teas are also served; it's then that the chef, who specializes in pastries, really comes into his own, offering Sachertorte and other fine Austrian pastries and tortes.

FROM BLOOMFIELD TO PICTON-GLENORA

Picton is the hub and county town of Prince Edward County. East of the town lies the mysterious **Lake on the Mountain,** a small, clear lake 200 feet above Lake Ontario. From one side of the escarpment there's a fabulous view of the ferry crossing Picton Bay, water, and islands stretching into infinity. It's a great place for a picnic. The Lake on the Mountain was called Lake of the Gods by the Mohawks, who worshipped the three sisters—corn, beans, and squash—here. Nobody has as yet discovered the source of this lake set atop a mountain. Is it an ancient volcanic crater, a meteorite hole, a sinkhole caused by rain, or what?

The other major attraction, 11 miles west of Picton, is **Sandbanks and North Beach Provincial Parks.** Sandbanks Park has some of the highest (more than 80 feet) freshwater dunes anywhere—a spectacular sight. Consisting of two dune systems linked by fields and woods, it also fosters diverse plant and animal life. Some of the more unusual plants are bluets, hoary puccoon, butterfly weed, sea rocket, and spurge. Among the bird species that have been recorded here are the long-billed marsh wren, pileated woodpecker, northern oriole ruby, and golden crowned kinglets; the best time to spot birds is spring and fall.

The park has prime sandy beaches, and facilities for windsurfing, sailing, canoeing, boating, and swimming. **Oasis Watersport** (☎ 613/393-1746) rents sailboats, kayaks, and sailboards. There are several self-guided nature trails in the park. Camping (411 sites) is available in four areas for $15 per day. Entry to the park is $6 per vehicle. Park officials begin taking reservations April 1. Open from May to October. For information, contact the Superintendent, Sandbanks Provincial Park, RR no. 1, Picton, ON, K0K 2T0 (☎ 613/393-3319).

The **Black River Cheese Company** is 8 miles southeast of Picton outside Milford on County Road 13 (☎ 613/476-2575). Stop for the cheese—and the rich ice cream. Open daily from 9am to 5pm.

The best way off Quinte's Isle is to take the rewarding 15-minute ferry trip from Glenora across to Adolphustown. The ferry operates every 15 minutes in summer, less frequently in winter, and has been operating since settlement began.

WHERE TO STAY

Isaiah Tubbs Resort. RR no. 1, Picton, ON, K0K 2T0. ☎ **613/393-2090.** Fax 613/393-1291. 60 rms. TV TEL. $100–$135 double; $145–$175 kitchenette suite; $185 Jacuzzi suite. Lakeside cabin $650–$775 per week. AE, ER, MC, V.

A mini-resort spread over 30 acres on West Lake, the Isaiah Tubbs Resort offers very attractive accommodations. The Carriage House rooms, located in the original building's oldest part, have kitchenettes, comfy pine furnishings including rockers and tables, original beamed ceilings, brick fireplaces, and microwaves. Upstairs there's a sleeping loft furnished with bunk beds, TV, and shower. A standard room with a sloping ceiling is furnished in Ethan Allen country style with a full bath. Two lodges each feature a living room with fieldstone fireplace and two bedrooms, one upstairs with skylights and a Jacuzzi tub. Some have sun porches.

Merrill Inn. 343 Main St. East, Picton, ON, K0K 2T0. ☎ **613/476-7451.** 14 rms. A/C TV TEL. $105–$160 double. Extra person $10. Rates include continental breakfast. AE, ER, MC, V.

A silver Rolls is parked outside the Merrill Inn, and inside, the rooms arE individually decorated with antiques. Room no. 101, for example, features a high-back Victorian bed, wing chairs, and bay windows. One room has a Jacuzzi, another a fireplace. There's a comfortable sitting room, barbecue area, and sun porch for guests.

WHERE TO DINE

Waring House Restaurant. Highway 33 just west of Picton. ☎ **613/476-7492.** Reservations recommended. Main courses $11–$18. MC, V. Summer daily Tues–Sun 11:30am–2pm and 6–9:30pm; winter Tues–Sun 11:30am–2pm and 5–9pm. CONTINENTAL.

The Waring House Restaurant is located in an old stone house surrounded by pretty shrubbery. Pine floors, archival photographs, and other regional memorabilia set the country tone. The menu features local produce as much as possible—rosemary garlic lamb, Cajun chicken with a tangy Dijon Apricot sauce, and a pasta of the day. The inviting pub has a big brick-and-beam fireplace.

Wheelhouse View Café. Picton. ☎ **613/476-7380.** Reservations recommended. Main courses $8–$16. MC, V. May–early Oct Mon–Wed 11am–8pm, Thurs–Sun 11am–9pm; other months Wed–Sun 11am–7pm. CANADIAN.

The Wheelhouse View Café, down by the ferry to Adolphustown, offers good value. The decor is simple—Formica and aluminum. The menu includes fish-and-chips, veal parmigiana, chicken Kiev, roast turkey, sole, barbecued ribs, and sandwiches.

9 Kingston

103 miles (172km) SW of Ottawa, 153 miles (255km) NE of Toronto

About two hours' drive from Ottawa, and about three hours' drive from Toronto, Kingston has much to offer the visitor. First, there's the water. Kingston stands at the confluence of Lake Ontario, the Rideau Canal, and the St. Lawrence Seaway, and this affords splendid scenic possibilities, best viewed by taking a free **ferry trip to Wolfe Island,** largest of the Thousand Islands. Ferries leave at frequent intervals for this sparsely populated island that doubles as a marvelous, quiet rural retreat. A stroll along Kingston's waterfront, site of many hotels and restaurants as well as the maritime museum and attractive gardens, is also a must.

Then there's Kingston's history, more than 300 years of it, much of it retained in the fine old limestone public buildings and private residences that line the downtown streets and give the city a gracious air; the martello towers that once formed a string of defense works guarding the waterways along the U.S.-Canadian border; and the Wren-style St. Georges Church, which contains a Tiffany window.

During the summer **Confederation Park** is the site for band concerts and other performances; during the winter you might catch a local ice-hockey contest. In **Market Square** on Tuesday, Thursday, and Saturday, a colorful market is held, and on Sunday it's the place to rummage for antiques.

ESSENTIALS

VISITOR INFORMATION   Contact the **Kingston Tourist Information Office,** 209 Ontario St., Kingston, ON, K7L 2Z1 (☎ 613/548-4415).

GETTING THERE   If you're driving from Ottawa take Highway 16S to the 401W and drive to the Kingston Exits. Or you can take the more scenic Highway 2 instead of the 401. From Toronto, take the 401E to the Kingston Exits.

Several daily trains come from Ottawa (☎ 613/244-8289), Toronto (☎ 416/366-8411), and Montréal (☎ 514/871-1331) to Kingston.

EXPLORING THE TOWN

The best way to explore Kingston is aboard the **tour train** that leaves from in front of the Greater Kingston Tourist Information Office, on the waterfront across from the City Hall, every hour on the hour between 10am and 7pm from May to September. The tour lasts 50 minutes and costs $8 for adults, $6 for seniors and youths.

Fort Henry. On Highway 2 just east of Kingston. ☎ **613/542-7388.** Admission $9.50 adults, $6.75 students, $6.50 seniors, $4.75 children 5–12. Mid-May to Oct daily 10am–5pm.

Fort Henry broods above the town on a high promontory, eerily unchanged since it was rebuilt in the 1830s (it was originally built in 1812). Here, all summer long the Fort Henry Guard, complete with their goat mascot named David, perform 19th-century drills, musters, and parades. Regular programming includes a music and marching display by the fife-and-drum band, an exhibition of infantry drill, and a mock battle with artillery support, all brought to a close with the firing of the garrison artillery and the lowering of the Union Jack. Part of the fort—officers' quarters, men's barracks, kitchens, and artisans' shops—has been restored to show the military way of life circa 1867.

Royal Military College. On Point Frederick. ☎ **613/541-6000**, ext. 6652. Free admission. July–Labor Day daily 10am–5pm.

The Royal Military College, Canada's West Point, is also close to the fort. The campus occupies the site of a Royal Navy Dockyard, which played a key role in the War of 1812. Although you can tour the grounds, only the museum, located in a large martello tower, is open to the public. It houses displays about the college's history and Kingston's Royal Dockyard, plus the Douglas collection of small arms and weapons.

Bellevue House. 35 Centre St. ☎ **613/545-8666.** Free admission. June 1–Labor Day daily 9am–6pm; other months daily 10am–5pm. Closed Easter.

On July 1, 1867, the Canadian Confederation was proclaimed in Kingston's Market Square. The Confederation's chief architect, and Canada's first prime minister, Sir John A. Macdonald, is closely identified with the city of Kingston, his home for most of his life, and he is commemorated in several places. The most notable is Bellevue House, an Italianate villa, jokingly referred to as "Pekoe Pagoda" and "Tea Caddy Castle" by the local citizenry. It has been restored to the period 1848–49, when Macdonald lived there as a young lawyer and rising member of Parliament.

Agnes Etherington Art Centre. University Avenue at Queen's Crescent. ☎ **613/545-2190.** Admission $2 adults, $1 seniors and students. Tues–Fri 10am–5pm, Sat–Sun 1–5pm.

Located on the campus of Queen's University, the Agnes Etherington Art Centre displays a comparatively extensive collection in seven galleries. The collection's emphasis is Canadian, although it also contains European Old Masters and African sculpture. The center's heart is the original 19th-century home of benefactor Agnes Richardson Etherington (1880–1954) and features three rooms furnished in period style.

Celebrity Sportsworld. 801 Development Dr. (just off Highway 401). ☎ **613/384-1313.** Bowling $6.95 adults, $5.50 children; roller-skating $5 adults, $4.25 children 11 and under; minigolf $2.50 adults, $2 children; driving range $5.25 for small basket of balls. Daily noon–5pm and 6:30–9:30pm.

The number-one Kingston attraction for kids is Celebrity Sportsworld, a 12-acre park featuring a huge roller-skating rink, 12 bowling lanes, minigolf, the "Moonwalk" action ride, and many other electric rides, two video and games arcades, and a golf driving range, plus a teen dance club. Refreshments are available, as well as a supervised play area for toddlers and preschoolers.

STROLLING THE WATERFRONT

A great free 30-minute trip can be taken aboard the ferry to **Wolfe Island.**

Kingston is very much a waterfront defense town. Along the waterfront, **Confederation Park** stretches from the front of the old 19th-century hall down to the magnificent yacht basin, which is worth a look. Within walking distance of the marina is one of the finest martello towers, built during the Oregon Crisis of 1846 to withstand the severest of naval bombardments. The **Murney Tower** (☎ 613/544-9925) is now a museum where you can see the basement storage rooms, the barrack room, and the gun platform. Open daily from 10am to 5pm from mid-May to the end of October. Admission is $2 for adults; children under six free.

Farther along the waterfront is **Portsmouth Olympic Harbour Park,** site of the 1976 Olympic sailing events, and now one of Ontario's most up-to-date marina facilities. Open to local as well as transient boaters, it offers a safe harbor at reasonable rates. For more information on Confederation Basin Marina and Portsmouth Olympic Harbour, call 613/544-9842.

A little farther along the waterfront is **Lake Ontario Park,** providing the camping enthusiast with all the excellent services offered to boaters. The city operates the campground, which has electricity and water hookups, an amusement park, and fishing. It's an ideal place to stay, three miles from City Hall. The rates are reasonable ($14 for campsite; $18.50 with electric and water, $21 with electric, water, and sewer), and reservations are accepted (☎ 613/542-6574). The season is mid-April to October.

While you're exploring downtown and along the waterfront, visit the **City Hall,** 264 Ontario St. (☎ 613/546-4291), where you can take a self-guided tour. If you can't afford the time, at least view the stained-glass windows in Memorial Hall, each one commemorating a World War I battle. The bell tower contains a display of old bottles, locks, and other artifacts that were unearthed during renovation. You can also make rubbings of a couple of handsome brasses that stand just inside the entrance. Open weekdays only from 8:30am to 4:30pm.

For an understanding of the great shipping days on the Great Lakes, visit the **Marine Museum of the Great Lakes,** 55 Ontario St. (☎ 613/542-2261), which documents the change from sail in the 17th century to steam in the early 19th century and from the great schooners in the 1870s to today's bulk carriers that still ply the Great Lakes. Other exhibits recapture the area's boat- and shipbuilding industry. Open daily mid-April to mid-December from 10am to 5pm; January to March Monday to Friday from 10am to 4pm. Adults pay $5.25 to see the ship and the museum, and students and seniors pay $4.75; kids under 6 are free.

CRUISES TO THE THOUSAND ISLANDS FROM KINGSTON

Although they will be discussed more fully in Section 10 of this chapter, the famous Thousand Islands holiday area, known to Native Canadians as Manitouana (Garden of the Great Spirit), is right on the town's doorstep. In summer cruise boats meander through the more than 1,800 islands, past such extraordinary sights as **Boldt's Castle,** built by millionaire George Boldt at the turn of the century as a gift for his wife. (When she died suddenly, the work was abandoned, and so it stands a relic to lost love.)

The best way to see the park is to charter your own houseboat (see Section 2 of this chapter). Alternatively, several **cruise boats** leave from various points along the St. Lawrence. From Kingston Harbour at City Hall, you can take a three-hour cruise on the *Island Queen,* a whistle-blowing triple-deck paddle wheeler. It costs $17 for adults, $8.50 for children 4 to 12. Or there's a 90-minute cruise aboard the *Island Bell* that takes in the Kingston Harbour and waterfront. It costs $12 for adults, $6 for children 4 to 12. For cruise information, write or phone the *Island Queen* Showboat, 6A Princess St., Kingston, ON, K7L 1A2 (☎ 613/549-5544 or 613/549-5545).

The nimble catamaran *Sea Fox II* also cruises the islands and the harbor from the bottom of Brock Street in Kingston. The two-hour islands tour costs $12 for adults, $11 for seniors, and $6 for children 6 to 12. For information, call in season ☎ 613/542-4271.

WHERE TO STAY

For bed-and-breakfast accommodations contact **Kingston Area Bed and Breakfast,** P.O. Box 37, Kingston, ON, K7L 4V6 (☎ 613/542-0214), a reservation service for a fine selection of homes throughout the area. Rates are $50 to $55 double; children 1 to 10 pay $10, children 11 and over, $15.

Two chains have commandeered the spectacular position overlooking the harbor—the **Holiday Inn,** 1 Princess St. (☎ 613/549-8400), charging $145 for a double in summer; and the **Howard Johnson's,** 237 Ontario St. (☎ 613/549-6300), charging $120. Other possibilities are the **Ramada Inn,** 1 Johnson St. (☎ 613/549-8100), also on the lakefront with doubles from $90 to $140; or the **Best Western Fireside,** 1217 Princess St. (☎ 613/549-2211), with doubles for $130 and some very popular, fun fantasy suites.

MODERATE

✪ **Hochelaga Inn.** 24 Sydenham St. South, Kingston, ON, K7L 3G9. ☎ **613/549-5534.** Fax 613/549-5534. 23 rms. TV TEL. $110–$140 double. Extra person $10. Rates include breakfast. AE, DC, ER, MC, V.

All rooms are furnished differently in this elegant Victorian home with a charming garden. My favorite is no. 301, an oddly shaped space, with a carved bed set on a diagonal, a large armoire, and a love seat. Three steps lead to a delightful 11-sided tower with windows, and a stepladder goes into a tiny sitting area. Atop the ladder you'll find a futon—you can sleep here under the Gothic windows. Many other rooms are furnished in oak pieces along with wing chairs and brass table lamps. Guests can enjoy the large sitting room, complete with a carved ebony fireplace, or sit on the outdoor veranda, overlooking the gardens, where there's a grill for guests' use. The adjacent cottages have the smallest rooms, some with little porches.

✪ **Hotel Belvedere.** 141 King St. East, Kingston, ON, K7L 2Z9. ☎ **613/548-1565** or 800/559-0584. Fax 613/546-4692. 20 rms. TV TEL. $99–$159 double. Rates include continental breakfast. AE, DC, ER, MC, V.

The place to stay in Kingston is the Hotel Beledere, a carefully restored mansard-roofed brick residence. The individually decorated rooms have pleasant sitting areas; most are air-conditioned. Room no. 207 has an Art Deco flavor featuring a scalloped-style bed, Madame Récamier sofa, and sideboard, all set on marble floors. In room no. 204 there's a brilliant marine-blue tile fireplace, tasseled curtains, kneehole dresser, and a bed sporting a lace-embroidered coverlet. Guests can relax in the elegant sitting room, with a turquoise marble coal-burning fireplace and tall French windows that open onto a porch prettily decorated with flowers and plants in classical urns.

Queen's Inn. 125 Brock St., Kingston, ON, K7L 1S1. ☎ **613/546-0429.** 17 rms. A/C TV TEL. $84–$94 double. Lower rates in winter. Rates include continental breakfast. AE, DC, ER, MC, V.

Downtown, the Queen's Inn, in an old three-story stone building, offers nicely decorated rooms that sport light-oak furnishings. For me, the rooms with the most character are on the third floor tucked under the eaves. The Coppers dining room has an outdoor patio; there's also a sports bar with large-screen TV.

INEXPENSIVE

There's also a **Journey's End** at 1454 Princess St. (☎ 613/549-5550).

Alexander Henry. 55 Ontario St., Kingston, ON, K7L 2Y2. ☎ **613/542-2261.** Fax 613/542-0043. 19 cabins. $42–$60 double; $70 Captain's Cabin. Rates include continental buffet breakfast. AE, MC, V. Closed Labor Day to mid-May.

You'll find a unique bed-and-breakfast at the Marine Museum aboard the 3,000-ton icebreaker *Alexander Henry.* The accommodations are not exactly roomy and you may think twice about drinking the water, but it's certainly different. The Captain's Cabin comes with double bed, a desk large enough to spread out navigational charts, a sitting area with a table, and a bathroom with a shower. There are also two twin-bedded rooms aboard.

Donald Gordon Centre. 421 Union St., Kingston, ON, K7L 3N6. ☎ **613/545-2221.** 75 rms. A/C TEL. $50 double. AE, MC, V.

Good reasonably priced accommodations can be found at the university's Donald Gordon Centre. Rooms consist of either two-bedroom suites with shared bathroom or twin-bedded rooms with private bath. The spaces are furnished in typical study-bedroom fashion. Other building facilities include a dining room, a lounge, and a basement bar and games room.

A NEARBY RETREAT ON WOLFE ISLAND

Ⓢ General Wolfe Hotel. Wolfe Island, ON, K0H 2Y0. ☎ **613/385-2611.** Fax 613/385-1038. 6 rms. A/C TV TEL. $35–$80 double; $100 suite for six. AE, MC, V.

This has to be one of the most spectacular values. Located on Wolfe Island, near the ferry docks, it's mainly known for its dining room but also rents six rooms. A small room furnished with a double bed, side table, chair, and TV, and also with a private bath, rents for $35. A suite containing a double and single bed and a sitting room equipped with refrigerator goes for $75, while a two-room suite accommodating six tops out at $100.

   Dining/Entertainment: The dining room affords views of the ferry landing and waterfront—great for sunset viewing. The food is continental—say, pheasant bourguignonne or salmon Wellington—priced from $15 to $25 (with a great-value $24 five-course, fixed-price meal, too). Open mid-May to Labor Day daily for lunch and dinner; at other times the restaurant closes Monday. In winter when the river is frozen (from January to early April), the owners operate a shuttle to Dawson's Point connecting to the mainland. There's also a cocktail lounge with dancing on weekends.

WHERE TO DINE

EXPENSIVE

   Another top choice for dining is the General Wolfe Hotel (see above).

✪ Chez Piggy. 68R Princess St. ☎ **613/549-7673.** Reservations recommended on weekends. Main courses $17–$20. AE, MC, V. Mon–Sat 11:30am–midnight, Sun 11am–midnight. Lunch served 11:30am–2pm; dinner served 5:30–10pm; Sun brunch served 11am–2:30pm. CONTINENTAL/ECLECTIC.

Just off Princess Street, in a complex of renovated buildings, you'll find Chez Piggy occupying an 1820s building that probably once was a stable. In front there's a paved courtyard where you can sit outdoors. Inside, there's a long bar with brown high director's chairs, and a dining room enhanced by two glorious Tunisian rugs. The small menu might feature seven or so dinner entrées plus daily specials. Try the chicken breast Marsala or roast leg of lamb after you've sampled either the hummus or the Stilton pâté. Brunch dishes, all under $8, are interesting and different—lamb kidneys with scrambled eggs and home fries, Thai beef salad, along with the more typical brunch fare.

✪ Clark's by the Bay. 4085 Bath Rd. ☎ **613/384-3551.** Reservations recommended. Main courses $15–$22; fixed price $35. AE, ER, MC, V. Tues–Sat 5:30pm–midnight. CONTINENTAL.

The premier dining place is Clark's by the Bay, west of Kingston proper. Located in a stone house set well back from the road, it offers a series of intimate dining rooms. Tables are set with damask tablecloths and fresh flowers. The menu, which changes seasonally, might feature salmon on a cucumber, shallot, and pink peppercorn coulis; or medallions of lamb with a rich port and Stilton sauce. The five-course fixed-price meal is excellent value. An extensive wine list features Canadian and international wines.

Gencarelli. 629 Princess St. ☎ **613/542-7976.** Reservations recommended. Pasta courses under $12; main courses $10–$36. AE, CB, DC, ER, MC, V. Mon–Sat 11am–11pm, Sun 4–9pm. ITALIAN.

A local favorite for years, Gencarelli continues to serve good Italian food in an intimate series of dining rooms. Pastas like fettuccine, tortellini, and rigatoni can be married to a sauce of your choice, or you can select such dishes as cannelloni parmigiana or lasagne al forno, including a salad. The $36 dish is two lobster tails. The dessert specialty is the chocolate-amaretto cheesecake.

MODERATE

Kingston Brewing Company. 34 Clarence St. ☎ **613/542-4978.** Reservations not needed. Burgers, sandwiches, and main courses under $8. AE, DC, ER, MC, V. Mon–Sat 11am–1am, Sun 11:30am–1am. LIGHT FARE.

At the Kingston Brewing Company, you can peer behind the bar and view the huge brewing tanks. Beer, several ales, and a pleasant lager are brewed without chemicals and other substances that adulterate modern mass-produced beers. Locals come here for the charbroiled ghetto chicken wings served with a spicy barbecue sauce and the smoked beef and ribs plus typical bar fare. It's either served inside at polished wood tables or in the back courtyard garden or sidewalk patio.

10 Along the St. Lawrence: The Thousand Islands & More

The mighty St. Lawrence River was the main route into the heart of Upper Canada from the 17th century to the mid-19th century, traveled first by explorers, fur traders, and missionaries and later by settlers en route to Ontario and the plains west. The river is a magnificent and humbling sight—in some places it is 12 miles wide.

If you're driving, Highway 401 is the fastest route connecting the townships, or you can take the more scenic Highway 2.

THE THOUSAND ISLANDS

Today the St. Lawrence continues as a major shipping route into Canada and the Great Lakes. But visitors know it for the Thousand Islands. According to a Native Canadian legend, petals of heavenly flowers fell to earth and were scattered on the river, creating Manitouana, the Garden of the Great Spirit, or as we know it, the Thousand Islands.

St. Lawrence Islands National Park (The Thousand Islands) is headquartered at 2 County Rd. 5, Mallorytown, ON, K0E 1R0 (☎ 613/923-5261). Canada's smallest national park, it encompasses the St. Lawrence and its islands, stretching about 49.6 miles (80km) from Kingston to Brockville. The visitor center and headquarters is on the mainland in Mallorytown, where there is an unserviced 50-site campground. Access to the park island facilities is via boat only (mooring costs $7 to $20 overnight). Most of the islands have docking, picnicking and limited camping facilities (on 13 islands) available on a first come, first served basis. The largest campground has 18 sites, the smallest, one. Costs range from $8 to $12. Three consecutive nights is the docking limit at each island.

Each island is pretty much a self-contained microclimate, which explains the diversity of the plant and animal life. A short walk across an island can go from northern coniferous forest to a stand of southern hardwood. Hot, dry southwest slopes contrast with protected northeast slopes that are cool, moist and shaded. Among the plant and animal life are the pitch pine, wild turkey, and the black rat snake, a large but non poisonous snake. In summer the park staff give interpretive programs (ask at the park's headquarters at Mallorytown Landing, located between Gananoque and Brockville).

You can also savor the island-river landscape aboard one of the many cruise boats that operate from Kingston (see Section 9 above) and Gananoque. From May to mid-October boats leave from Gananoque on 1½-hour trips. **Thousand Island Boat Tours** (☎ 613/659-2293) offers cruises from Ivy Lea using smaller craft that can navigate into the narrow scenic channels between islands, and in fact stop at the islands. These boats leave from west of the International Bridge on the Thousand Islands Parkway. Prices are $11 for adults and $5.50 for children 4 to 12.

The **Thousand Islands Gananoque Boat Line** (☎ 613/382-2144 or 613/382-2146 for 24-hour information) operates cruises from May to October. Three-hour ($15) and one-hour ($10) cruises available. Call ahead for the schedule. Boats leave from the waterfront in Gananoque.

For a dramatic view from above, climb the **Skydeck** on Hill Island near Ivy Lea, which soars 400 feet above the river. You'll be rewarded with a 40-mile panorama.

WHERE TO STAY IN GANANOQUE

There's a 67-room **Travelodge** on King Street (☎ 613/382-4781; fax 613/382-1037), with doubles from $80 to $95.

Athlone Inn. 250 King St. West, Gananoque, ON, K7G 2G6. ☎ **613/382-2440.** 4 suites, 6 motel units. A/C TV. $85–$130 suite in the main inn; $65 motel room. MC, V.

The Athlone Inn, located in a Victorian home built by a local industrialist, is known primarily for its food, served in a handsome dining room (see below). The inn itself has four attractive suites, with a love seat, gilt-framed pictures, and Ethan Allen–style furniture. There are also some nicely kept motel units.

✪ **Trinity House Inn.** 90 Stone St., Gananoque, ON, K7G 1Z8. ☎ **613/382-8383.** 6 rms, 2 suites. A/C TV. Summer $80–$130 double, $175 suite. Off-season discounts available. MC, V.

The Trinity House Inn is an impressive red-brick Victorian home built in 1859. In addition to the six rooms, there's a one-bedroom suite with kitchen in an adjacent building that was originally Gananoque's jail, and also a Jacuzzi suite. Throughout, the period furnishings are fine—Oriental rugs and screens, brass beds with flouncy pillows and skirts. There's a comfortable sitting room with marble fireplace and also an art gallery displaying local art in the basement. The owners also offer day sailing aboard their 30-foot yacht.

Dining/Entertainment: The Bistro has two dining rooms, a bar-lounge, and an outside veranda overlooking the ponds and waterfalls of the garden. Among the specialties are a citrus chicken, shrimp bouillabaisse, a salad with an authentic Thousand Island dressing, and a French silk pie. Prices range from $10 to $17. Open Thursday to Tuesday from 5:30pm in summer.

WHERE TO DINE IN GANANOQUE

At the **Athlone Inn** (see above), the food is classic continental—rack of lamb, chicken Kiev, sole meunière, shrimp with garlic and white wine, and veal Oscar—priced from $16 to $22.

Cook Not Mad. 110 Clarence St. ☎ **613/382-4361.** $30 three-course fixed price. MC, V. Wed–Sun 5:30–9pm. CANADIAN.

Located in a historic home, this restaurant specializes in regional Canadian cuisine, offering a daily changing fixed-price menu. A sample menu might begin with Québec smoked trout with carrot slaw, followed by halibut grilled with basil, lime, and ginger, then a dark chocolate tart with chocolate sauce. The wine list features Niagara wines as well as international selections.

The Golden Apple. 45 King St. West. ☎ **613/382-3300.** Reservations recommended. Main courses $17–$30. MC, V. May 1–Oct 31 daily 11am–3pm and 5–9pm; Nov 1–Dec 31 Thurs–Sun only. CONTINENTAL.

Situated in an early 19th-century limestone farmhouse, the Golden Apple has an authentic country ambience with its pine accents. The cuisine ranges from chicken parmigiana to prime rib, veal Normande, and stuffed sole. In summer, the flagstone terrace is very pleasant.

In Brockville

Robert Shephard Grist Mill. On the waterfront. ☎ **613/345-2563.** Reservations recommended. Main courses $15–$28. AE, MC, V. Mon–Fri 11am–2pm; daily 5–10pm. CONTINENTAL.

At the Brockville waterfront you can practically reach out and touch the freighters and other vessels churning through the water. You can also dine in an atmospheric ambience at the Robert Shephard Grist Mill, on such dishes as stuffed sole, chicken Madeira, rack of lamb Provençale, chicken Kiev, or surf-and-turf.

UPPER CANADA VILLAGE

About 30 miles along Route 2 from Brockville, just east of Morrisburg, Upper Canada Village (☎ 613/543-3704) is Ontario's answer to Williamsburg, a riverfront community representing Canadian frontier life in the 1860s. Some 40 structures and interiors, restored with painstaking accuracy using hand-forged nails and wooden dowel pegs, appear as if still inhabited. In the woolen mill the waterwheel spins, the old machinery turns, and the wool is woven into soft blankets; the clang of hammer on anvil rings out from the blacksmith's shop, while a heady smell of fresh bread wafts from the bake shop near Willard's Hotel. Stop at the hotel for lunch or dinner. The village artisans, dressed in period costume, operate the 19th-century machinery and will answer any questions you may have. Admission is $9.50 for adults, $8.50 for seniors, $4.75 for children 5 to 12; free for children 4 and under. Open May to October, daily 9:30am to 5pm.

14

Southern & Midwestern Ontario

by Marilyn Wood

Part of the long sweep of the Niagara Escarpment, where the land is flat and eminently farmable, this is the pioneer country to which Canada's early settlers came. A landscape dotted with silos, barns, and dairy herds, and broken up by hedgerows, it attracted the Scots to such towns as Elora, Fergus, and St. Mary's; the Germans to Kitchener-Waterloo; the Mennonites to Elmira and St. Jacobs; and the English Loyalists to Stratford and London. This ethnic heritage and the festivals that it nourishes—Oktoberfest, the Highland Games, the Mennonite quilt sale—are part of the area's attraction, but so, too, are the world-famous theater festival at Stratford and the music festival in Elora.

1 Exploring Southern & Midwestern Ontario

Windsor sits across from Detroit on the Canadian side of the border. From here visitors can travel along either Highway 401 East or the more scenic Highway 3 (called the Talbot Trail, which runs from Windsor to Fort Erie), stopping along the way to visit some major attractions on the Lake Erie shore.

East of Windsor lies London and from London it's an easy drive to Stratford. From Stratford visitors can turn west to Goderich and Bayfield on the shores of Lake Huron or east to Kitchener-Waterloo and then north to Elmira, Elora, and Fergus.

VISITOR INFORMATION Contact **Ontario Travel,** Queen's Park Toronto, ON, M7A 2E5 (☎ 416/314-0944 or 800 ONTARIO from 9am to 8pm).

AN IMPORTANT NOTE ON PRICES Unless stated otherwise, **the prices cited in this guide are given in Canadian dollars,** which is good news for American travelers because the Canadian dollar is worth 25% less than the American dollar but buys nearly as much. As we go to press, $1 Canadian is worth 75¢ U.S., which means that your $100-a-night hotel room will cost only U.S. $75 and your $6 breakfast costs only U.S. $4.50.

Keep in mind that Ontario has a provincial sales tax of 8%, plus a 5% accommodations tax—*in addition* to the national 7% goods and services tax (GST).

Southern Ontario

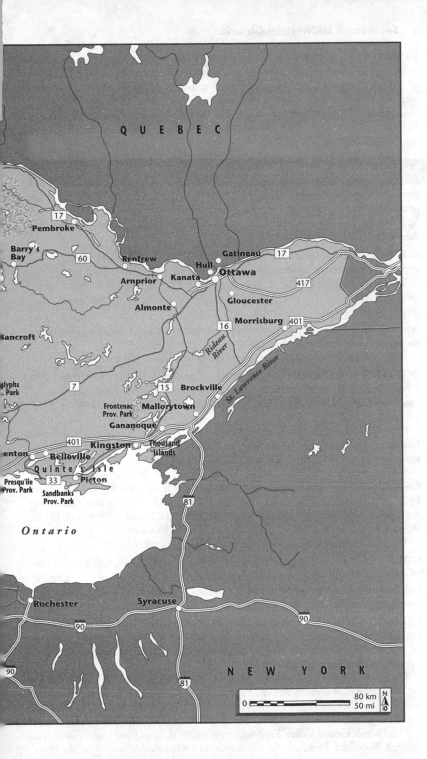

FARMSTAYS Staying on a farm is a unique way to experience Ontario. You'll enjoy home-cooked meals, the peace of the countryside, and the working rhythms of a dairy or mixed farm. You can choose to stay at all kinds of farms in many different locations. Rates average $35 to $60 double per night, $220 per week, all meals included. For information write the **Ontario Vacation Farm Association,** RR no. 2, Alma, ON, N0B 1A0; or contact Ontario Travel for its free "Farm Vacation Guide."

2 The Great Outdoors

Some 260 provincial parks in Ontario offer ample opportunities for outdoor recreation. The daily in-season entry fee for a vehicle is $6; campsites cost anywhere from $13 to $18. For more information, contact the **Ontario Ministry of Natural Resources** (☎ 416/314-2000).

BIKING In Elora, **Grand Bicycle Tours,** on RR no. 1 (☎ 519/846-8455), operates 1- to 7-day trips in the region and also in the Niagara Wine Country.

The South Point and Marsh trails in Rondeau Provincial Park (near Blenheim) are great for cycling.

BIRD-WATCHING Point Pelee National Park, southeast of Windsor, is an ornithologist's dream. The spring and fall migrations are spectacular; autumn offers the added bonus of viewing flocks of monarch butterflies.

More than 300 species have been recorded in Rondeau Provincial Park.

BOATING & CANOEING In London, **Northern Lights Outfitters,** 230 Piccadilly St. (☎ 519/679-2510) offers trips on the Thames River and in Lake Fanshawe Conservation Area. Rentals cost from $25 to $30 a day, $120 to $130 a week.

In Stratford you can rent boats and canoes for a run on the river at **The Boathouse,** located behind and below the information booth. Open daily from 10am in summer. Contact **Avon Boat Rentals,** 40 York St. (☎ 519/271-7739).

Other companies offer trips on the Grand River, including **Grand River Canoe Company,** 132 Rawdon St., Brantford (☎ 519/759-0040); **Rockwood Outfitters Ltd.,** 699 Speedvale Ave. West, Guelph (☎ 519/824-1415); and **Canoeing the Grand,** 3734 King St. East, Kitchener (☎ 519/896-0290 and 519/893-0022 off-season). Rentals average $30 to $40 a day, $130 to $150 a week.

There are also canoe rentals in Point Pelee National Park.

GOLF You'll find a few good courses in Windsor, and Leamington has two fine 18-hole, par-71 and -72 courses. London offers a half dozen good courses. Bayfield and Goderich have a couple of nine-hole courses, and Stratford and St. Marys also have several fine 18-hole courses.

HIKING The 37-mile **Thames Valley Trail** follows the Thames River through London, past the University of Western Ontario and into farmlands all the way to St. Marys. For information contact Thames Valley Trail Association, Box 821, Terminal B, London, ON, N6A 4Z3.

The 62-mile **Avon Trail** follows the Avon River through Stratford, cuts through the Wildwood Conservation Area and spans farmlands around Kitchener. It links up with the Thames Valley Trail at St. Marys and the Grand Valley Trail at Conestoga. For information contact Avon Trail, Box 20018, Stratford, ON, N5A 7V3.

The 77-mile **Grand Valley Trail** follows the Grand River from Dunnville, north through Brantford, Paris, and farmlands around Kitchener-Waterloo to the Elora

Gorge (see below), connecting with the Bruce Trail at Alton. For information contact Grand Valley Trails Association, Box 1233, Kitchener, ON, N2G 4G8.

There's also great hiking in the Elora Gorge and Point Pelee National Park.

HORSEBACK RIDING   The **Cinch Stables,** 43 Capulet Lane, London (☎ 519/471-3492), offers hour-long trail rides for $15 per person. West of London, in Delaware, the **Circle R Ranch,** RR no. 1 (☎ 519/471-3799), leads one-hour trail rides in the Dingman Creek Valley for $15 per person. Reservations are needed.

SWIMMING   The Elora Gorge is a great place to swim. So is Rondeau Provincial Park, which is located on Lake Erie (off Highway 21 near Blenheim); lots of other water sports are available here as well.

3 Windsor & Environs

Right across the river from Detroit, Windsor, an automobile and industrial center like its neighbor, makes a good base for visiting several all-time Canadian highlights. Outside the city are several historical sites and natural spectacles that are not to be missed.

For information contact the **Convention and Visitors Bureau,** City Centre, 333 Riverside Dr. West, Suite 103, Windsor, ON, N9A 5K4 (☎ 519/255-6530).

EXPLORING THE AREA

Among Windor's prime sights is the **Hiram Walker distillery,** 2072 Riverside Dr. East, Windsor, ON, N8Y 4S5 (☎ 519/254-5171), famous maker of Canadian Club whiskey. Tours are given 9am to 2pm on the hour Monday to Friday. From Dieppe gardens, there's a good view of the Detroit skyline.

Windsor became a major destination for the slaves traveling the Underground Railroad and the **North American Black Historical Museum,** 277 King St., in Amherstburg (☎ 519/736-5433), about 19 miles south on Lake Erie, will provide some fascinating historical background to that epic tale and the area's African American history. Admission is $3 adults, $2 seniors, $1.50 children 14 and under. Open April to November, Wednesday to Friday from 10am to 5pm, Saturday and Sunday 1 to 5pm. To get there from Windsor, take Riverside Drive West, which becomes Sandwich Street and then Highway 18.

Also in Amherstburg is **Fort Malden National Historic Park,** 100 Laird Ave. (☎ 519/736-5416). The British built the fort at the end of the 18th century, after they had abandoned Detroit to the Americans. At the restored barracks you can get a good sense of military life at the time. Admission is $2 adults, $1.50 seniors, $1 students, children under 5 free. Open in summer daily 10am to 5pm, winter 1 to 5pm.

Just south of Amherstberg, families will enjoy a trip to **Boblo Island** (☎ 519/736-5442) for its rides and carnival atmosphere.

The region's other major attraction is Point Pelee National Park (see box). While you're there, you can enjoy a daily wine tasting at the **Pelee Island Winery's Wine Pavilion** (☎ 519/724-2469). Back on the mainland you can also stop in at the **Pelee Island Winery** production facility at 455 Hwy. 18 East, Kingsville (☎ 519/733-6551), open May to September.

A bit further east, **Rondeau Provincial Park,** RR no. 1, Morpeth, ON, N0P 1X0 (☎ 519/674-1750), is located on Lake Erie, off Highway 21 near Blenheim. The park has 226 camping sites and offers a full range of activities—sailing, windsurfing, swimming, and other water sports on Rondeau Bay; hiking and biking along marked

Magnificent Bird-Watching

Point Pelee National Park (☎ 519/322-2371) is one of the continent's premier bird-watching centers. A sandspit at the junction of a couple of flyways, it is an ornithologist's delight. The spring and fall migrations are spectacular; as many as 100 different species have been spotted in a single day. In fall, it's also the gathering place for flocks of monarch butterflies, which cover the trees before taking off for their migratory flight. Located at the southernmost tip of Canada, which juts down into Lake Erie at the same latitude as northern California, it features some of the same flora—white sassafras, sumac, black walnut, and cedar.

The park offers year-round hiking and bicycle and canoe rentals from April to October. For more information contact the Superintendent, Point Pelee National Park, RR no. 1, Leamington, ON, N8H 3V4 (☎ 519/322-2365). If you're driving from Windsor, take Highway 3 east to reach Pelee Island. Take the ferry from Kingsville or Leamington, about 25 and 31 miles from Windsor, respectively. If you're taking a vehicle, you'll need reservations in advance, so call Pelee Island transportation (☎ 519/724-2115).

Aside from the national park, another good bet is **Jack Miner's Bird Sanctuary,** Road 3 West, two miles north of Kingsville off Division Road (☎ 519/733-4034). The famed naturalist in Kingsville established it to protect migrating Canadian geese. The best time to visit is late March or late fall when hundreds of migrating waterfowl stop over at the sanctuary. At other times visitors can see the 50 or so Canada geese, the few hundred ducks, as well as wild turkeys, pheasant, and peacocks. The museum displays artifacts and photographs relating to Jack Miner. Admission is free; it's open Monday to Saturday.

trails (bikers should try the South Point and Marsh trails); and canoeing. In summer, interpretive programs highlight the flora and fauna—sassafras and tulip trees, several kinds of orchids and other rare plants, and the prothonotary warbler, one of about 334 species that have been spotted in the park.

4 London

118 miles (190km) SW of Toronto

If you're driving into Canada from the U.S. Midwest, you certainly should plan on stopping in this pretty university town that sits on the Thames River (pronounced as it's spelled)—particularly if you have kids in tow.

ESSENTIALS

VISITOR INFORMATION   Contact the **London Visitor's and Convention Bureau,** 300 Dufferin Ave. (P.O. Box 5035), London, ON, N6A 4L9 (☎ 519/661-5000).

GETTING THERE   If you're driving, London is about 120 miles (192km) from Detroit, 68 miles (110km) from Kitchener, 121 miles (195km) from Niagara Falls, and 40 miles (65km) from Stratford.

You can also fly to London on **Canadian Airlines International** (☎ 519/455-8385). A taxi from the airport into town will cost about $17.

VIA operates a Toronto-Brantford-London-Windsor route and also, in conjunction with **Amtrak,** a Toronto-Kitchener-Stratford-London-Sarnia-Chicago route.

Both offer several trains a day. The VIA Rail station in London is at 197 York St. (☎ 519/434-2149).

GETTING AROUND For bus schedules, contact the **London Transit Commission** (☎ 519/451-1347). Exact fare of $1.10 is required, 65¢ for children.

Taxis charge an initial $2.30 plus 10¢ each ⁹/₁₀ of a kilometer thereafter. There's an additional charge from 11pm to 6am. Taxi companies include **Abouttown Taxi** (☎ 519/432-2244) and **U-Need-A-Cab** (☎ 519/438-2121).

SPECIAL EVENTS The **London International Air Show,** Canada's largest military air show, ushers in the summer season each June. It's followed by the **Royal Canadian Big Band Festival,** held over the July 1 weekend. The **Home County Folk Festival,** featuring folk arts, crafts, and music, is the third weekend in July.

The **Great London Barbecue and Rib Cookoff and Hot Air Balloon Fiesta** is usually August 1 or thereabouts. In September, the 10-day **Fair** at the Western Fairgrounds is the seventh largest in Canada.

EXPLORING THE TOWN

If you enjoy antiquing, explore **Wortley Village,** one block west of Ridout.

Downtown there's a cluster of historic sights. At 401 Ridout North is **Eldon House,** the city's oldest remaining house—from 1834—which now houses a historic museum (☎ 519/661-5169). Nearby at nos. 435, 441, and 443 Ridout North are the original Labatt Brewery buildings.

At the **London Regional Art and Historical Museums,** 421 Ridout North (☎ 519/672-4580), you'll view historical and contemporary works of local, national, and international artists. The building itself—six barrel vaults slotted together to accommodate domed skylights—is striking. It's free and open Tuesday to Sunday from noon to 5pm.

In historic Wolseley Hall, the **Royal Canadian Regiment Museum,** at Oxford and Elizabeth streets (☎ 519/660-5102), contains exhibits about regimental history and battles from the Riel Rebellion to UN peacekeeping in Bosnia today. It's free and open Tuesday to Friday from 10am to 4pm, Saturday and Sunday noon to 4pm.

✪ **Children's Museum. 21 Wharncliffe Rd. South. ☎ 519/434-5726.** Admission $3.75 adults, $3.21 children; under 2 free. Daily 10am–5pm.

The incredible Children's Museum occupies several floors of an old school building. A family can easily spend a whole day here—there's more than enough to do. In every room, children can explore, experiment, and engage their imaginations. For example, on "The Street Where You Live," kids can dress up in firefighters' uniforms, don the overalls of those who work under the streets, and assume the role of a dentist or a doctor or a construction worker. Some rooms contrast how people lived long ago with how they live today. A child can stand in a train station, send a Morse code message, shop in a general store, and sit in a schoolhouse—all experiences that they can share with their grandparents. More up-to-the-minute experiences can be enjoyed in the computer hall, at the photosensitive wall, or the zoetrobe. And so on and on—it's fun for children and for parents. I loved it.

✪ **Museum of Indian Archaeology and Lawson Prehistoric Indian Village.** 1600 Attawandaron Rd. (off Wonderland Road North, just south of Highway 22). ☎ 519/473-1360. Admission $3.50 adults, $2.75 seniors and students, $1.50 children under 12, under 5 free, families $8. Daily May 1–Labor Day 10am–5pm; Sept–Dec Tues–Sun 10am–5pm; Jan–Apr Wed–Sun only.

This is another sight I wouldn't miss. The museum contains artifacts from various periods of Native Canadian history—projectiles, pottery shards, effigies, turtle rattles, and more. The most evocative exhibit is the on-site reconstruction of an Attawandaron village. Behind the elm palisades, longhouses built according to original specifications and techniques have been erected on the five acres where archeological excavations are taking place. About 1,600 to 1,800 people once lived in the community, about 70 sharing one longhouse. The houses have been constructed of elm, sealed with the pitch from pine trees, and bound together with the sinew of deer hide.

Guy Lombardo Music Centre. 205 Wonderland Rd. South. ☎ **519/473-9003.** Admission $2 adults, $1.75 seniors, free for children under 12. Mid-May to Labor Day daily 11am–5pm. Limited winter hours; call ahead.

Nostalgia. That's what can be captured on Wonderland Road at the outdoor bandshell where bandleader Guy Lombardo began playing in the '30s before he hit the big time and became famous for ringing in the new year at the Waldorf-Astoria in New York. There's also a Guy Lombardo Music Centre filled with memorabilia. Adjacent to the bandshell is a restaurant that will help take you on a trip down memory lane (see "Where to Dine," below).

Springbank Park Storybook Gardens. Off Commissioners Road West. ☎ **519/661-5770.** Admission $4.75 adults, $3.50 seniors, $2.75 children 3–14. May–Labor Day daily 10am–8pm; Labor Day–early Oct Mon–Fri 10am–5pm, Sat–Sun 10am–6pm. Closed Oct–Apr.

The Springbank Park Storybook Gardens is a children's zoo with a storybook theme. Special daily events include the seal feeding at 3:30pm, a storytelling hour, and a juggler and other performers. There's also a maze and Playworld, with many activities for children.

Fanshawe Pioneer Village. In Fanshawe Park (entrance off Fanshawe Park Road, east of Clarke Road). ☎ **519/457-1296.** Admission to park $5.50 per vehicle; Pioneer Village $5 adults, $4 seniors and students, $3 children 12 and under, free for children under 5. Village May 1–Dec 31 daily 10am–4:30pm.

The Pioneer Village is a 25-plus building complex where you can see craft demonstrations (broom making, candle dipping, for example), enjoy wagon rides, and imagine what life was like during the 18th century. In **Fanshawe Park** (☎ 519/ 451-2800) you can rent paddleboats; there's also a large pool and beach at this 4-mile-long lake.

WHERE TO STAY

For bed-and-breakfast accommodations priced from $35 to $65 a night, contact the **London Area Bed and Breakfast Association,** 2 Normandy Gardens, London, ON, N6H 4A9 (☎ 519/641-0467).

London also has several modest hotel chain options: **Best Western Lamplighter Inn,** 591 Wellington Rd. South (☎ 519/681-7151), charging $65 double; **Ramada Inn,** 817 Exeter Rd. (☎ 519/681-4900), charging $75 to $90 double; **Holiday Inn Express,** 800 Exeter Rd. (☎ 519/681-1200), with rates of $72.88 double; and **Comfort Inn by Journey's End,** 1156 Wellington Rd. South (☎ 519/685-9300), charging $75 double.

Delta London Armouries Hotel. 325 Dundas St., London, ON, N6B 1T9. ☎ **519/ 679-6111.** Fax 519/679-3957. 250 rms. A/C MINIBAR TV TEL. $140 double; from $230 suite. Extra person $10. Children under 18 stay free in parents' room. Special weekend rates available. AE, CB, DC, DISC, ER, MC, V. Parking $7.

This hotel, occupying the old armory, is a worthy example of architectural conservation and conversion. The armory's 12-foot-thick walls form the building's main floor and base, and above the crenellated turrets and ramparts soars a modern glass tower. Inside, the well-equipped rooms each have a hair dryer and makeup mirror, and are furnished with Federal reproductions. A pool and an exercise area now occupy the former drill parade area. There's also a squash court and indoor golf simulator.

✪ **Idlewyld Inn.** 36 Grand Ave., London, ON, N6C 1K8. ☎ and fax **519/433-2891.** 27 rms. A/C TV TEL. $89–$120 double; $140–$195 suite. Rates include continental breakfast. AE, DC, ER, MC, V. Free parking.

This is the top choice. Located in a house that a wealthy leather industrialist built in 1878, the inn is filled with fine details—eight-foot-tall windows, oak and cherry carved fireplaces, casement windows, oak-beamed ceilings, and wallpaper crafted to look like tooled leather in the dining room.

All the rooms are furnished differently. Room 302 has a tiny Romeo and Juliet balcony, while room 202 has a marvelous fireplace of green cabbage leaf tiles and a scallop-shell marble sink stand. Room 101 is the largest—huge carved cherry columns separate the sitting area from the bedroom, which has a comfortable chaise lounge and a glazed tile fireplace. At breakfast guests help themselves in the large, comfortable kitchen equipped with toasters, coffeemakers, and refrigerators, and can sit on the porch to eat.

WHERE TO DINE
EXPENSIVE

✪ **Anthony's.** 434 Richmond St. ☎ **519/679-0960.** Reservations recommended. Main courses $17–$20. AE, DC, ER, MC, V. Mon–Fri 11:30am–2:30pm; Mon–Sat 5–10pm. SEAFOOD.

This seafood specialty house uses fresh and superb ingredients and presents dishes so well that it stimulates the appetite. For example, the salmon with dill sauce often comes with lime wedges cut into tiny petals placed around a center of caviar. The dinner menu might include a warm salad of shrimp and scallops, followed by perch with pine nuts, provincial seafood stew, or beef tenderloin with tarragon sauce. The open kitchen, with its gleaming copper pots, and a mural in the dining room depicting tropical fish, enhance the ambience. Desserts change daily and are made on the premises, as are the handmade chocolates that conclude the meal. You might be tempted by a lemon tart, a chocolate nocturne gâteau, or sorbet.

✪ **The Horse & Hound.** 939 Hyde Park. ☎ **519/472-6801.** Reservations recommended. Main courses $15–$24. AE, DC, ER, MC, V. Daily 11:30am–2:30pm and 5:30–10pm. Limited menu served between meals and 10pm–1am. CONTINENTAL.

This local favorite, located in a handsome Victorian, has six intimate, elegant dining rooms. Start with warmed goat cheese wrapped in phyllo pastry on a raspberry coulis, or leek, corn, and Stilton chowder. Follow with one of 10 or so entrées that might include a classic chateaubriand, a hearty ragout of wild boar, or poached Atlantic salmon in Chenin Blanc sauce. On weekends, there's jazz or classical duos entertaining in the downstairs lounge.

Michaels on Thames. 1 York St. ☎ **519/672-0111.** Reservations recommended. Main courses $13–$22. AE, DC, ER, MC, V. Mon–Fri 11:30am–2:30pm; daily 5–11pm. CONTINENTAL.

Michaels on Thames has a fine location overlooking the river. In winter a blazing fire makes the dining room cozy. Among the well-prepared and nicely served dishes you might find chicken Camembert with lemon wine sauce, rack of lamb roasted with mint finished with demiglace and port wine, or salmon with hollandaise. Desserts include a flamboyant cherries jubilee.

Miestro's. 352 Dundas St. ☎ **519/439-8983.** Reservations recommended. Main courses $15–$19. AE, ER, MC, V. Tues–Fri 11:30am–2:30pm; Tues–Sat 5:30–10pm. ECLECTIC.

You'll find an eclectic selection of dishes at this popular downtown place with an intimate atmosphere. At dinner the choices might include veal sautéed with black bean sauce with red currants, or salmon wrapped in lotus leaf and steamed with a ginger and soy sauce.

Wonderland Riverview Dining Room. 284 Wonderland Rd. South. ☎ **519/471-4662.** Reservations recommended. Main courses $13–$23. AE, MC, V. Daily 11:30am–2:30pm and 5–9pm. Closed Mon–Tues Jan–Mar. CONTINENTAL.

Still a favorite venue for special family occasions, the Wonderland Riverview Dining Room offers such dishes as chicken breast with soya cream, perch with tartare sauce, or prime rib. Around the walls are framed clips of events that took place here in the '30s and '40s—dancing to Ozzie Williams, Shep Fields, and Mart Kenney. There's a lovely outdoor dining terrace under the trees and an outdoor dancing area overlooking the river.

MODERATE

Local Indian food aficionados swear by the **Jewel of India,** 390 Richmond (between King and Dundas; ☎ 519/434-9268), open for lunch Monday to Saturday and for dinner daily.

Say Cheese. 246 Dundas St. ☎ **519/434-0341.** Reservations accepted. Most items $9–$13. AE, ER, MC, V. Mon–Sat 11am–3pm and 5–10pm. CONTINENTAL.

You can relax and commune over a bottle of wine with strangers-turned-friends at the next table in the casual, comfortable ambience that prevails here. The traditional menu, which hasn't changed in decades, features such all-time favorites as cheese soup, quiches, sandwiches, and assorted cheese platters. The supplemental "seasonal" menu changes frequently and might feature cauliflower cheeses, oyster and Cheddar pie, and braised chicken with onions, pimiento, and sage and a potato Gruyère gratin. There's a good selection of wines by the glass and the bottle. It's ideal for breakfast, lunch, or dinner—and afternoon tea, too. While you're here, browse in the downstairs cheese shop.

LONDON AFTER DARK

The **Grand Theatre,** 471 Richmond St. (☎ 519/672-9030), features drama, comedy, and musicals from mid-October to May. The theater itself, built in 1901, is worth viewing.

Harness racing takes place from October to June at the Western Fairgrounds track Wednesday, Friday, and Saturday. (☎ 519/438-7203).

London also has a few bars and clubs: **Barneys,** 671 Richmond St. (☎ 519/432-1232), attracts a young professional crowd; **Jo Kool's,** 595 Richmond at Central (☎ 519/663-5665) is a student hangout.

5 Goderich & Bayfield

Goderich is a good place to stroll. The town's most striking feature is the central octagonal space with the Huron County Courthouse at the center. Another highlight is the **Historic Huron Gaol,** with walls 18 feet high and two feet thick. This also houses the **Huron County Museum,** 110 North St. (☎ 519/524-2686). Admission is $3 adults, $2.50 seniors, $2 children 6 to 13, and it's open daily from 10am to 4:30pm.

For Goderich information, call either ☎ 519/524-6600 or 519/524-2513, or go by the visitor center on Hamilton Street, which is open daily in summer.

Bayfield is a pretty, well-preserved 19th-century town about 13 miles from Goderich and 40 miles from Stratford. Once a major grain shipping port, it became a quiet backwater when the railroad passed it by. Today the main square, high street, and Elgin Place are part of a Heritage Conservation District. Walk around and browse in the appealing stores—the information center has a helpful walking-tour pamphlet.

WHERE TO STAY

Benmiller Inn. RR no. 4, Goderich, ON, N7A 3Y1. ☎ **519/524-2191.** 47 rms. A/C TV TEL. $105–$175 double; $245 deluxe suite. Rates include continental breakfast. AE, MC, V.

The heart of the inn is the original wool mill (1877), which now contains dining room, bar, reception, and 12 guest rooms. When it was turned into an inn in 1974 many mechanical parts were refashioned into decorative objects—mirrors made from pulley wheels, lamps from gears. The rooms feature barnboard siding, desks, floor lamps, heated ceramic tile in the bathrooms, and handmade quilts. The 17 rooms in Gledhill House, the original millowner's home, are extralarge by hotel standards, while the four suites have fireplaces, bidets, and Jacuzzi bathtubs. Ground-floor rooms have pressed tin ceilings. There are more rooms in the River Mill, which is attached to a silo-style building containing the swimming pool, whirlpool, and running track.

The dining room serves fine continental cuisine. The brick patio overlooking the gardens is a pleasant place to sit and look at the totem pole, brought from British Columbia. Facilities include two tennis courts, billiards, table tennis, and cross-country ski trails.

✪ **Clifton Manor Inn.** 19 The Square, P.O. Box 454, Bayfield, ON, N0M 1G0. ☎ **519/565-2282.** 5 rms (4 with bath). $70–$145. No credit cards.

This elegant house was built in 1895 for the reve of Bayfield. The interior features ash wood, etched glass panels in the doors, and other attractive period details. Today owner Elizabeth Marquis has added many touches—Oriental rugs and comfortable sofas and love seats in the living room, elegant silver and sideboards in the dining room, and four rooms, each named after an artist or composer. The Van Gogh room sports sunflower pillows and draperies. The bathroom in the charming Renoir room has a deep, six-foot-long tub. Elizabeth provides candles and bubble bath—a lovely romantic touch. The Mozart room offers a canopy bed and tub for two while the entire third floor has been converted into the Mona Lisa. All rooms have cozy touches like mohair throws, sheepskin rugs, wingback chairs, fresh flowers, and so on. Lilac bushes and fruit trees fill the yard. Afternoon tea is served. Breakfast consists of egg dishes like omelets or crêpes, plus fresh fruit often plucked from the very trees in the garden.

The Little Inn at Bayfield. Main Street, P.O. Box 100, Bayfield, ON, N0M 1G0. ☎ **519/565-2611.** Fax 519/565-5474. 20 rms, 10 suites across the street. A/C TV TEL. $100–$135 double; from $215 suite. Rates include breakfast. Special packages available. AE, DC, ER, MC, V.

The inn, originally built in 1832, has been thoroughly modernized. The older rooms in the main building are small and have only showers but they are comfortably furnished with oak or sleigh beds. Rooms in the newer section are larger and feature platform beds and modern furnishings. The suites across the street in the carriage house have platform beds, pine hutches, and feature whirlpool bathrooms, propane gas fireplaces, and verandas. The popular restaurant is open for lunch and dinner seven days a week.

WHERE TO DINE

The **Benmiller Inn** (☎ 519/524-2191) has a good dining room. For casual dining, Bayfield offers several choices. The **Albion Hotel,** on Main Street (☎ 519/565-2641), features a fun, wall-length bar decorated with hundreds of baseball hats and other sports paraphernalia. The fare consists of English specialties plus ribs, pizza, and sandwiches. It also has seven rooms available starting at $50 double. **Admiral Belfield's,** 5 Main St. (☎ 519/565-2326), is fun, too. A converted general store, it serves diner, deli, and pub fare, and occasionally there's jazz and other entertainment.

✪ **Red Pump.** Main Street, Bayfield. ☎ **519/565-2576.** Reservations recommended. Main courses $18–$23. AE, MC, V. Daily noon–3pm and 5–9pm. Closed Jan–Mar and Mon–Tues in late fall and winter. INTERNATIONAL.

This very appealing restaurant with an inviting patio serves some of the area's most exciting and eclectic food. Typical main dishes might include steamed chicken breast and scallops with pine nut, red pepper, tomato, and balsamic vinegar sauce; barbecued fish; and tiger shrimp stuffed with crab and served with risotto cakes. The decor is lavish and comfortable. After lunch diners can check out the adjacent store selling terrific designer wear for men and women.

6 St. Marys

15 miles (24km) S of Stratford

This small town contains a lot of history and some remarkable stone architecture, much of it influenced by H. H. Richardson.

ESSENTIALS

VISITOR INFORMATION   Contact **St. Marys Tourism,** P.O. Box 998, St. Marys, ON, N4X 1B6 (☎ 519/284-3500 or 519/285-4763 for the recreation department) or stop by the office in the old railroad on James Street.

GETTING THERE   If you're driving from London take Highway 4 North to Highway 7 East. Exit off Highway 7 to St. Marys. From Stratford, take Highway 7 west, exit at Perth County Road 28 to St. Marys.

The **Amtrak/VIA** Toronto-Chicago train stops in St. Marys.

WALKING AROUND TOWN

Among the **architectural highlights** on Queen Street are the Town Hall (1891); the Andrews Building (1884), now housing Anstett's Jewellery; MacPherson's Craft Store (1855 and 1884); the Gothic Revival Opera House (1879); and the two Hutton blocks (1860s) that flank it on Water Street. Lovers of architecture and stone buildings in particular will enjoy the **Perth Country Gallery,** 149 Queen St. East (☎ 519/284-3761), which has drawings of many of St. Marys' landmarks.

It's fun to browse in **MacPherson's,** at the corner of Queen and Water streets (☎ 519/284-1741), where you can stock up on every conceivable craft supply—beads, wicker, fabric flowers, doll-making materials, and stenciling supplies. The **Ross Pharmacy** is housed in the building where Timothy Eaton and his brothers operated a general store in the 1860s. Eventually Timothy decided that the kind of store he wanted to operate—based on cash, not barter and credit—would never succeed in St. Marys, and he left in 1869 to open a store in Toronto and build the famous Eaton company.

At the **Wildwood Conservation Area,** 3 miles (5 km) east of St. Marys, off Highways 7/19 (☎ 519/284-2292), there's camping (450 sites), picnicking, hiking trails, a beach and swimming pool, boat rentals, fishing, and in winter, cross-country skiing. Admission is $5.50 per vehicle. Camping costs a maximum of $21.50. For information, contact the Upper Thames River Conservation Authority, RR no. 6, London, ON, N6A 4C1 (☎ 519/451-2800).

WHERE TO STAY & DINE

Westover Inn. 300 Thomas St., St. Marys, ON, N0M 2V0. ☎ **519/284-2977.** Fax 519/284-4043. 22 rms and suites. A/C TV TEL. $100–$160 double; $150–$225 suite. Rates include breakfast. AE, ER, MC, V.

Graceful accommodations are provided in this Victorian manor house, built in 1867 and featuring carved gingerbread decoration and leaded-glass windows. The house is set on 19 acres, making for a secluded retreat, and there's an outdoor pool. Inside the limestone house, rooms have been furnished in modern antique style with reproductions. Some rooms have balconies. Six rooms are located in the manor itself, including a luxury suite with a whirlpool bathroom. The least expensive and smallest rooms (12 of them) are found in the Terrace, built in the '30s as a dormitory for the priests who attended what was then a seminary. The Thames Cottage, a modern building, also contains two two-bedroom suites. Downstairs in the manor, guests may use the comfortable lounge.

Dining/Entertainment: The elegant restaurant is known for fine cuisine. Dinner choices might include salmon with a roasted red bell pepper and dill sauce, or fettucine with shellfish, spinach, tomatoes, garlic, and pine nuts, priced from $14 to $21. Desserts are enticing: profiteroles filled with chocolate and Kahlúa mousse, lemon tartlets in a shortbread crust, and more. Open daily from 8 to 11am for breakfast, 11:30am to 2pm for lunch (brunch on Sunday) and 5 to 9:30pm for dinner. There's a bar/lounge and delightful patio.

7 Stratford & the Stratford Festival

93 miles W of Toronto; 28 miles W of Kitchener; 38 NE of London

Home of the world-famous Stratford Festival, this city manages to capture the prime elements of the Bard's birthplace, from the swans on the Avon River to the grass banks that sweep down to it, where you can picnic under a weeping willow before attending a Shakespeare play. It's a very pleasant town with some superb dining and, of course, the famous festival.

ESSENTIALS

VISITOR INFORMATION   Go to the office by the river on York Street at Erie (☎ 519/273-3352). It's open from May to mid-October from 9am to 5pm daily (until 8pm Thursday through Saturday). At other times, contact **Tourism Stratford,** P.O. Box 818, 88 Wellington St., Stratford, ON, N5A 6W1 (☎ 519/271-5140 or 800/561-SWAN).

GETTING THERE   Driving from Toronto take Highway 401 west to Interchange 278 at Kitchener. Follow Highway 8 west onto Highway 7/8 west to Stratford. From Detroit/Windsor follow Highway 401 East to Exit 218 at Ingersoll, to Highway 19 north and then to Highway 7 East. From Buffalo cross from Buffalo to Fort Erie and take QEW to Exit 100 West onto Highway 403. Take 403 west to Highway 6 north to Highway 401. Take 401 west and then pick up the directions above given from Toronto.

Amtrak and **VIA Rail** operate several daily trains along the Toronto-Kitchener-Stratford-London-Sarnia-Chicago route.

SPECIAL EVENTS   Other than the theater festival, there's a **Festival City Days,** in the last week of May. The festival's opening is celebrated with marching bands, floats, and clowns.

THE STRATFORD FESTIVAL

Since its modest beginnings on July 13, 1953, when *Richard III,* starring Sir Alec Guinness, was staged in a huge tent, Stratford's artistic directors have all built on the radical but faithfully classic base originally provided by Tyrone Guthrie to create North America's largest repertory theater and win a glowing international reputation.

Productions range from classic to contemporary. They're performed on the dynamic thrust stage of the Festival Theatre (55 Queen St. in Queen's Park), the proscenium stage of the Avon Theatre (99 Downie St.), and the exaggerated thrust stage of the Tom Patterson Theatre on Lakeside Drive. Tom Patterson Theatre productions in particular are loved for their creative risk-taking and the excitement generated by the intimate space.

The 1995 season featured nine productions, including three Shakespeare plays, Peter Shaffer's *Amadeus,* Timothy Findley's *The Stillborn Lover,* and Gilbert and Sullivan's *Gondoliers.* Among the company's famous alumnae are Maggie Smith, Sir Alec Guinness, Christopher Plummer, and Julie Harris.

In addition to attending plays, visitors may enjoy "Meet the Festival," a series of informal discussions with members of the acting company, production, or administrative staff; post-performance discussions following Tuesday and Thursday evening performances; and Backstage Tours, offered every Sunday morning from early June to mid-October. The tours cost $5 for adults, $3 for seniors and students (and should be reserved when you purchase tickets). Similar costume warehouse tours ($3.50 per person) revealing more than 40 seasons of costumes and props are given on Wednesday and Saturday mornings.

The season begins early in May and continues until the end of October with performances Tuesday to Sunday and matinees on Wednesday, Saturday, and Sunday. Ticket prices range from $16.50 to $58.75. For tickets, call ☎ 519/273-1600 or 800/567-1600; or write to the Stratford Festival, P.O. Box 520, Stratford, ON, N5A 6V2. Tickets are also available in the United States and Canada at Ticketmaster outlets. Telephone orders are taken beginning in late February.

EXPLORING THE TOWN

Summer pleasures in Stratford besides theater? Within sight of the Festival Theatre, **Queen's Park** has picnic spots beneath tall shade trees or down by the water's edge where the swans and ducks will gather. To the east and west of the theater, footpaths follow both shores of the Avon River and Lake Victoria. Past the Orr Dam and the 90-year-old stone bridge, through a rustic gate once straw-thatched but now (for want of a thatcher) cedar-shingled, lies a very special park, the **Shakespearean Garden.** Here in this formal English garden, where a sundial presented by the former mayor of England's Stratford-upon-Avon measures out the hours, you can relax and contemplate the herb and flower beds and the tranquil river lagoon, and muse on Shakespeare's bust by Toronto sculptor Cleeve Horne.

If you turn right onto Romeo Street North from Highways 7 and 8, as you come into Stratford, you'll find the **Gallery/Stratford,** 54 Romeo St. (☎ 519/271-5271), located in a lovely old building on the fringes of Confederation Park. Since its 1967 opening, it has mounted Canadian focused shows. If you're an art lover, do stop in, for you're sure to find an unusual, personally satisfying show in one of the four

Stratford

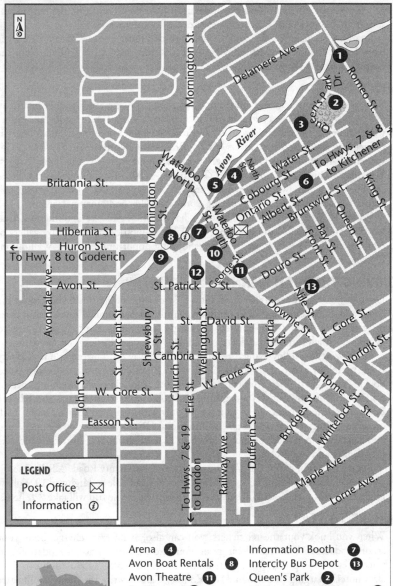

N

LEGEND
Post Office ⊠
Information ⓘ

Mornington St.
Delamere Ave.
Queen's Park Dr.
Romeo St.
Avon River
Waterloo St. North
Water St.
North St.
Cobourg St.
Ontario St.
To Hwys. 7 & 8 to Kitchener
King St.
Albert St.
Brunswick St.
Queen St.
Britannia St.
Mornington St.
Waterloo St. South
Bay St.
Front St.
Hibernia St.
Huron St.
To Hwy. 8 to Goderich
Douro St.
Avon St.
George St.
Nile St.
St. Patrick St.
Downie St.
Avondale Ave.
St. Vincent St.
Shrewsbury St.
Church St.
Wellington St.
Erie St.
St. David St.
Victoria St.
E. Gore St.
Norfolk St.
Cambria St.
W. Gore St.
W. Gore St.
Home St.
John St.
Brydges St.
Whitelock St.
Easson St.
To Hwys. 7 & 19 to London
Railway Ave.
Dufferin St.
Maple Ave.
Lorne Ave.

TORONTO
← Stratford

Arena ④		Information Booth ⑦
Avon Boat Rentals ⑧		Intercity Bus Depot ⑬
Avon Theatre ⑪		Queen's Park ②
Bus Depot ⑩		Shakespearean Gardens ⑨
Chamber of Commerce ⑫		Stratford Visitor and Convention Bureau ⑥
City Hall ⑩		Third Stage ⑤
Festival Theatre ③		Tourism Stratford ⑫
Gallery Stratford ①		Train Station ⑬

galleries. Open Tuesday through Sunday from 9am to 6pm during the festival season, from 10am to 6pm at other times. Admission is $3.50.

Stratford is a historic town, and one-hour **guided tours** of early Stratford are given from July to Labor Day, Monday through Saturday leaving at 9:30am from the visitor's booth by the river.

SHOPPING

Browsing the many craft and gift shops is rewarding. **Village Studios,** 69 Ontario St. (☎ 519/271-7231), has a selection of Canadian crafts—Inuit and Iroquois art, leather work, sheepskin, wood carving, glass, and more. A stroll out along Ontario Street is particularly fun for antique lovers. At no. 286, **Paul Bennett** (☎ 519/273-3334) specializes in china, art glass, Oriental carpets, and early electric light fixtures. **Yesterday's Things,** 351 Ontario St. (☎ 519/271-5180), offers antique jewelry, china, and books. Back in town, **Gallery Indigena,** 151 Downie St. (☎ 519/271-7881), sells Native Canadian art, as well as paintings, prints, jewelry, and other craft items.

Props, 18 York St. (☎ 519/271-5666), has theatrical gifts, art, and interiors. **Gallery 96,** York Lane, behind Rundles (☎ 519/271-4660), is a cooperative gallery of regional artists. These are plenty more shopping opportunities along Wellington, Downie, and Ontario streets.

DRIVING THROUGH MENNONITE COUNTRY

Drive east on Highways 7/8 to Shakespeare, 7 miles out of Stratford, and browse the shops and many antique stores in this small and as-yet-unspoiled town. From here, drive north on Route 14 to Amulree. Turn right (east) onto County Road 15 toward Waterloo, which turns into Erb Street and takes you past the Seagram Museum.

From Waterloo, follow King Street north to Highway 86. Turn right onto County Road 17, follow it to County Road 22, and turn left. Take 22 north to County Road 86 and turn right to West Montrose and drive over Ontario's last remaining covered bridge. Built in 1881, it's 200 feet long and commonly referred to as the **Kissing Bridge,** a sobriquet it earned when it was lit only with coal-fired lamps. Double back on 86 to County Road 21 and take it into Elora. Drive northwest on County Road 7 to Salem and then south on Route 18, then 22 to Highway 86. Turn right and take it to Elmira and St. Jacobs.

Return by heading west on 17 through Linwood to County Road 7. Take 7 south through Millbank, with its famous cheese factory, and Poole to Highway 19. Follow Highway 19 through Gads Hill back to Stratford. The whole trip will take 2 1/2 hours.

WHERE TO STAY

When you book your theater tickets, you can also, at no extra charge, book your accommodations. The festival can book you into the type of accommodation and price category you prefer, from guest homes for as little as $38 for a double to first-class hotels charging more than $125 double. Call or write the **Festival Theatre Box Office,** P.O. Box 520, Stratford, ON, N5A 6V2 (☎ 519/273-1600 or 800/567-1600; fax 519/273-6173).

A PICK OF THE B&Bs

For more information on the Stratford bed-and-breakfast scene, write to **Tourism Stratford,** P.O. Box 818, 88 Wellington St., Stratford, ON, N5A 6W1 (☎ 519/271-5140).

Avonview Manor. 63 Avon St., Stratford, ON, N5A 5N5. ☎ **519/273-4603.** 4 rms (none with bath). $70–$80 double. Rates include full breakfast. No credit cards.

Located on a quiet street in an Edwardian house, Avonview Manor has attractive and individually furnished rooms with fans that share a bath. One ground floor room has a brass bed covered with a floral-pattern quilt and flouncy pillows, and is large enough for a wicker chaise lounge and rocker. A kitchen equipped with an ironing board is available on the first floor. The living room is very comfortable, particularly in winter in front of the stone fireplace. No smoking, except on the porch. Facilities include an outdoor pool.

Brunswick House. 109 Brunswick St., Stratford, ON, N5A 3L9. ☎ **519/271-4546.** 6 rms (none with bath). From $60 double. Rates include full breakfast. No credit cards.

Brunswick House is owned and operated by two writers, Geoff Hancock and Gay Allison. If you stay here you will enjoy very literary surroundings—portraits of Canadian authors and poetry on the walls, books everywhere, and the chance to run into a literary personality. The nicely decorated rooms with ceiling fans share two baths. One is a family room with a double and two single beds. Each has a personal decorative touch—a Mennonite quilt, posters by an artist friend, a parasol atop a wardrobe. Smoking is restricted to the veranda.

Deacon House. 101 Brunswick St., Stratford, ON, N5A 3L9. ☎ **519/273-2052.** 6 rms. A/C. $80–$90 double. Rates include continental breakfast. V.

A shingle-style house, built in 1907 and home to a prominent surgeon, has been restored by Diane Hrysko and Mary Allen. The guest rooms, all with private baths, are decorated country style with iron and brass beds, quilts, pine hutches, oak rockers, and rope-style rugs. My favorites are the quirkily shaped units on the top floor. The living room with fireplace, TV, wingbacks, and sofa is comfortable.

Flint's Inn. 220 Mornington St., Stratford, ON, N5A 5G5. ☎ **519/271-9579.** 2 rms (none with bath), 1 suite (with bath). A/C. $65 double or twin; $85 suite. Rates include breakfast. No credit cards.

The steep mansard-roofed Flint's Inn was built in 1862. A large suite with sun porch and balcony features an iron-and-brass bed, covered by an old quilt, with a private bath and bar/refrigerator. The other two rooms share a bathroom with a bidet. The double has an attractive window seat; the twin has chintz wallpaper, a brass-and-iron bed, dresser, and trunk. The living room, with its marble fireplace and pine furnishings, is inviting. At breakfast homemade muffins, juice, and coffee are accompanied by eggs Benedict or a similar offering. The well-kept garden is filled with the wonderful scent of lilac in season.

Woods Villa. 62 John St. North, Stratford, ON, N5A 6K7. ☎ **519/271-4576.** 5 rms (1 with bath). A/C TV. $90 double. Rates include breakfast. DISC, MC, V.

This handsome 1870 house, set on one acre, is home to Ken Vinen, who enjoys collecting and restoring Würlitzers, Victrolas, and player pianos, which are found throughout the house. In the large drawing room there are six—and they all work. Ken will happily demonstrate, drawing upon his vast library of early paper rolls and records. The four rooms share two bathrooms (four have fireplaces), plus a suite with canopy bed and private bath. Rooms are large and an excellent value. In the mornings coffee is delivered to your room followed by a full breakfast prepared to order and served in the dining room. The extralarge outdoor heated pool and terrace are added bonuses.

HOTELS/MOTELS

Bentley's Inn. 99 Ontario St., Stratford, ON, N5A 3H1. ☎ **519/271-1121.** Fax 519/272-1853. 13 suites. A/C TV TEL. Apr–Nov $140 double; Nov–Apr $90 double. Extra person $20. AE, DC, ER, MC, V.

Bentley's has soundproofed luxurious duplex suites with two telephones and fully equipped kitchenettes. Period English furnishings and attractive drawings, paintings, and costume designs on the walls make for a pleasant ambience. Five suites have skylights.

Festival Motor Inn. 1144 Ontario St., Stratford, ON, N5A 6W1. ☎ **519/273-1150.** Fax 519/273-2111. 151 rms. A/C TV TEL. Main building $90–$98 double; motel units (with no inside access and no refrigerator) $82–$89 double; north wing $125–$145 double. Extra person $9; cot $7. Winter rates about 30% lower. AE, DC, MC, V.

With its black-and-white motel-style units, the Festival Motor Inn is set back off Highways 7 and 8 in 10 acres of nicely kept landscaped grounds. The place has an old English air with its stucco walls, Tudor-style beams, and high-back red settles in the lobby. The Tudor style is maintained throughout the large modern rooms. Some bedrooms have charming bay windows with sheer curtains, and all rooms in the main building and north wing have refrigerators. Other facilities include two tennis courts, shuffleboard, dining room, lounge, and an indoor pool with outdoor patio, whirlpool, and sauna.

Queen's Inn. 161 Ontario St., Stratford, ON, N5A 3H3. ☎ **519/271-1400.** Fax 519/271-7373. 31 rms. A/C TV TEL. May–Nov 15 $95 small double; $130 room with queen-size bed; from $135–$190 suite. Lower rates off-season. AE, MC, V.

Conveniently located in the town center, the Queen's Inn has recently been restored by the owner of the Elora Mill Inn. The rooms, all with private bath, have been pleasantly decorated in pastels and pine. Facilities include the Boar's Head Pub, a formal dining room, and a Tex-Mex restaurant.

Shakespeare Inn. P.O. Box 310, Shakespeare, ON, N0B 2P0. ☎ **519/625-8050.** Fax 519/625-8358. 62 rms. A/C TV TEL. June–Oct $110 double; May and winter $80 double. AE, ER, MC, V.

About 7¹/₂ miles (12km) outside Stratford, the Shakespeare Inn, on Route 1, offers nice modern rooms in a two-story building. The coffee shop is open from 8am to 10am.

Twenty Three Albert Place. 23 Albert St., Stratford, ON, N5A 3K2. ☎ **519/273-5800.** Fax 519/273-5008. 34 rms. A/C TV TEL. $79 double; $105 mini-suite, $125–$140 luxury suite. MC, V.

The Albert Place is right across from the Avon Theatre. Rooms have high ceilings; some have separate sitting rooms, and most units are quite large. Furnishings are simple and modern. Coffee, tea, muffins, and doughnuts are served in the lobby in the mornings.

WHERE TO DINE

Stratford is really a picnicking place. Take a hamper down to the banks of the river or into the parks. Plenty of places cater to this. **Rundles** will make you a super-sophisticated hamper; **Café Mediterranean** has salads, quiches, crepes, and flaky meat pies and pastries. For take-out, **Lindsay's,** 40 Wellington St. (☎ 519/273-6000), offers all kinds of salads—pasta, grain, vegetable—pâtés, fish, chicken, and meat entrées, soups, and breads and pastries.

EXPENSIVE

✪ **The Church.** At the corner of Brunswick and Waterloo streets. ☎ **519/273-3424.** Reservations required. Summer fixed-price dinner $48.20–$58.50. AE, ER, MC, V. Tues–Sat 11:30am–3pm and 5–9pm, after-theater 9pm–1am; Sun 11:30am–11pm. May be open Mon if there's a musical performance or some other special event at the theaters. CONTINENTAL.

The decor at The Church is just stunning. The organ pipes and the altar are still intact, along with the vaulted roof, carved woodwork, and stained-glass windows, and you can sit in the nave or the side aisles and dine to the appropriate sounds of, usually, Bach. Fresh flowers, elegant table settings, and a huge table in the center graced with two silver samovars further enhance the experience.

In summer, there's a special four-course fixed-price dinner (which includes a special vegetarian menu too), a luncheon on matinee days, and an after-theater menu. In winter, when things are a little calmer and crowds don't descend all at once, you can dine splendidly à la carte. Appetizers might include goat cheese soufflé, or hot foie gras of duck with a raisin vinegar sauce. Among the selection of eight or so entrées you might find a roast suprême of duck with pear confit, or filet mignon with a Madeira and truffle sauce, roast shallots, and garlic. Desserts are equally exciting, like the chocolate hazelnut praline gâteau with frozen banana yogurt and apricot dartois.

If you want to dine here during the festival, make reservations in March or April when you buy your tickets; otherwise you'll be disappointed. The upstairs Belfry Bar is a popular pre- and post-theater gathering place, with snacks and a full menu with main courses priced from $16 to $26.

✪ **The Old Prune.** 151 Albert St. ☎ **519/271-5052.** Reservations required. Three-course fixed-price dinner $48.50. AE, MC, V. Wed–Sun 11:30am–1:30pm; Tues–Sun 5–9pm. After-theater menu also available Fri–Sat from 9pm. Call ahead for winter hours. CONTINENTAL.

Another of my Stratford favorites is run by two very charming, witty women— Marion Isherwood and Eleanor Kane. Set in a lovely Edwardian home, it has three dining rooms and a garden patio. Former Montrealers, the proprietors have brought with them some of that Québec flair, which is reflected in both decor and menu.

The chef selects the freshest local ingredients and creates such marvelous dishes as a warm salad of duck leg confit with mashed potatoes and a creamy white peppercorn sauce on organic greens with a black currant and walnut oil vinaigrette; or grilled Ontario lamb with polenta fries and a roasted red-pepper corn emulsion. Among the appetizers there might be an outstanding fresh goat's cheese in tomato aspic, with olives and marinated zucchini. Desserts, too, are always inspired, like apricot strudel with sour cream ice cream. A more expensive, four-course menu gastronomique is also available along with a vegetarian menu. The Old Prune is also lovely for a late-night supper when such light specialties as vegetable lasagne, or tomato-saffron risotto with grilled sea scallops are offered. Similar dishes are available at lunch, priced from $12 to $15.

✪ **Rundles.** 9 Cobourg St. ☎ **519/271-6442.** Reservations required. Three-course fixed-price dinner $49.50. Gastronomical menus from $56.50. AE, ER, MC, V. Wed and Sat–Sun noon–2:30pm; Tues–Sun dinner. On Fri–Sat an after-theater menu is available. Closed during the winter; it functions occasionally as a cooking school until theater season comes again. INTERNATIONAL.

Rundles' large windows take advantage of its setting overlooking Lake Victoria. Its owner, Jim Morris, eats, sleeps, thinks, and dreams food, and chef Neil Baxter delivers exquisite cuisine to the table. The three-course fixed-price dinner will always offer some palate-pleasing combination of flavors, like the cold poached lobster and couscous salad with lobster vinaigrette. Among the six or so main dishes there might be grilled Atlantic salmon with a potato crust, caramelized onions, and lobster sauce. My dessert choice is the bittersweet chocolate tart, but the sherry trifle is also a dream. The dining area is stylish, with its gray spotlighted tables and contemporary art, much of it by Victor Tinkl. The restaurant follows the theater schedule.

MODERATE

Keystone Alley Cafe. 34 Brunswick St. ☎ **519/271-5645.** Reservations recommended. Main courses $14–$19. AE, DC, MC, V. Mon 11am–3pm, Tues–Sat 11am–4pm, Tues–Sat 5–9pm. CONTINENTAL.

Theater actors often stop in for lunch—perhaps soup, salads, burgers, New York cheesecake, or a choice from a daily selection of muffins. At night a full dinner menu features eight or so items, such as Mexican-style salmon served with jicama and poblano pepper salad, and a fish and pasta of the day.

Wolfys. 127 Downie St. ☎ **519/271-2991.** Reservations recommended. Pretheater fixed-price meal $18.50–$26; à la carte main courses $12–$20. AE, MC, V. Tues–Sun 11:30am–2pm and 5–8:30pm. ECLECTIC.

Wolfys has won a loyal local and visitor following with its well-prepared, flavorful cuisine. It's located in a former fish-and-chip shop and the original decor is still evident—the booths, counter and stools, and the old fish fryer serving as a display cabinet in one corner. Yet it has a New Wave flavor. Vibrant art by Kato decorates the walls. On the limited menu might be found a rice and vegetable stir-fry with peanut butter sauce, or Moroccan chicken with cinnamon and raisin couscous. Desserts are equally appealing, including the brownie with orange caramel sauce, a perennial favorite that has survived for years on the menu.

INEXPENSIVE

Bentley's. 107 Ontario St. ☎ **519/271-1121.** Reservations not accepted. Main courses $7–$12. AE, DC, ER, MC, V. Daily 11:30am–1am. CANADIAN/ENGLISH.

For budget dining and fun to boot, go to Bentley's, the local watering hole and favorite theater company gathering spot where you can shoot a game of darts, watch the big game on TV, or relax in one of the wingbacks. In summer you can sit on the garden terrace and enjoy light fare—grilled shrimp, burgers, gourmet pizzas, and pasta dishes.

Cafe Mediterranean. 10 Downie St. in the Festival Square building. ☎ **519/271-9590.** Reservations not accepted. Most items under $7. No credit cards. Summer Mon 8am–5:30pm, Tues–Sat 8am–7:30pm, Sun 10am–2pm; winter Mon–Sat 8am–5:30pm. LIGHT FARE.

The Café Mediterranean is great for made-to-order sandwiches, fruit flans, croissants (cheese, almond, chocolate), quiches, salads, pastries, and crepes. Take them out or dine there while seated on director's chairs.

Let Them Eat Cake. 82 Wellington St. ☎ **519/273-4774.** Reservations not accepted. Lunch items under $5; desserts $1–$4. MC, V. Mon 7:30am–5pm, Tues–Fri 7:30am–9pm, Sat 8:30am–9pm, Sun 10am–5pm. LIGHT FARE.

Let Them Eat Cake is great for breakfast (bagels, scones, and croissants), and lunch (soups, salads, sandwiches, quiche, and chicken potpie), but best of all for dessert. There are about 30 to choose from—pecan pie, orange Bavarian cream, lemon bars, carrot cake, Black Forest cake, and chocolate cheesecake among them.

8 Kitchener-Waterloo

69 miles (115km) W of Toronto, 28 miles (45km) E of Stratford

The twin cities of Kitchener (pop. 135,000) and Waterloo (pop. 50,000) lie in the heartland of rural Ontario. Travel a few miles out of town and you can see fields being plowed by four-horse teams and families traveling to market by horse and buggy—the people of the twin cities are never far from their Mennonite heritage.

About 60% of the population is of German origin. The first German settlers were Pennsylvania Mennonites who came in Conestoga wagons around 1800. Descendants of the Mennonites are still living and farming the area. Some still adhere to the old values—they do not drive cars, drink alcohol, vote, hold public office, serve in the armed forces, or use the courts to enforce personal rights. Listen for the gentle clip-clop of hooves upon the highway; look up and you will probably see a Mennonite couple, he in black suit and hat and she in bonnet and ankle-length skirt, riding proudly in an open buggy (with an umbrella if it's raining).

German immigration continued throughout the 19th and 20th centuries, and Kitchener-Waterloo's two drawing cards, the Farmer's Market and the Oktoberfest, still reflect the cities' ethnic heritage.

ESSENTIALS

VISITOR INFORMATION   For maps and detailed information on the area's attractions, stop in at the **Kitchener-Waterloo Area Visitors and Convention Bureau,** 2848 King St. East, Kitchener, ON, N2A 1A5 (☎ 519/748-0800), between 9am and 5pm on weekdays only in winter, daily in summer.

GETTING THERE   If you're driving from Toronto, take Highway 401 west to Highway 8 north. **Amtrak/VIA trains** travel daily along the Toronto-Kitchener-Stratford-London-Sarnia-Chicago route.

OKTOBERFEST

Where you find Germans, there you find beer. From small beginnings in 1969, Oktoberfest now attracts more than 700,000 people annually for nine days of celebration in early October. More than 20 festival halls and tents serve frothy steins of beer, thick juicy sausages, and sauerkraut, accompanied by oompah music in the best Bavarian tradition. The fest also features more than 45 cultural and sporting events, including the Miss Oktoberfest Pageant, with contestants from all over North America, a fashion show, an archery tournament, ethnic dance performances, and beer barrel races. Admission to the festival halls is $5, or up to $30 for an all-you-can-eat-all-night Bavarian smorgasbord.

As the festival is so popular, rooms have to be reserved at least six months in advance (indeed, requests are received up to one year in advance). Accommodations in Kitchener-Waterloo itself are not always available, but Stratford, Guelph, Cambridge, or Hamilton is close enough. For information and reservations, call or write **K-W Oktoberfest, Inc.,** P.O. Box 1053, Kitchener, ON, N2G 4G1 (☎ 519/570-4267).

EXPLORING KITCHENER

As you come into town along King Street (Highway 8), you'll pass the colorful **Rockway Gardens,** with their rockeries, flower beds, and illuminated fountains.

While you're visiting the market, you might pop over and see Canada's first **glockenspiel,** which is located at King and Benton streets, right across from the Valhalla Inn lobby entrance. It depicts the fairy tale of Snow White and the Seven Dwarfs, and the 23 bells that form the carillon play a song each day at 12:15, 3, and 5pm.

Farmers' Market. Duke and Frederick streets, Kitchener. ☎ **519/741-2287.** Year-round Sat 6am–2pm.

The Farmers' Market is located in the ultramodern Market Square Complex, which also houses 76 stores, among them Eaton's department store. The market started on May 25, 1839, and has been going strong ever since. The best way to see the market is to get up early on Saturday (it starts at 6am), because by 8am the 350 stalls are booming with business and some of the best deals have already been made. Savor the sights, sounds, and scents. Sample some shoofly pie, apple butter, Kochcase (a cooked cheese ordered with or without caraway seeds), Baden Limburger, Wellesley cheddar, blueberry fritters, and in a class by itself, the region's sauerkraut. You won't find cellophane packages here. Purchase homemade rugs, quilts, wood carvings, paintings, hand-carved toys, slippers, vests, mitts—the handsome creations of the local folk.

Woodside National Historic Park. 528 Wellington St. North. ☎ **519/742-5273.** Admission $2 adults, $1.50 seniors, $1 students. May 20–Dec 30 daily 10am–5pm; by appointment only at other times. Drive down King Street, turn into Wellington Street, and continue; it will be on the left.

From 1886 to 1893 this was the boyhood home of William Lyon Mackenzie King, prime minister of Canada from 1921 to 1930 and 1935 to 1948. The Victorian home with its 11½ acres of grounds has been restored to reflect the upper-middle-class lifestyle of the early 1890s. Each of the 14 rooms is elaborately decorated with bric-a-brac and personal belongings of the King family. Interpreters demonstrate 19th-century activities and invite visitors to play Victorian games or listen to music played on the box grand piano. The park includes several acres of trees and lawn with picnic facilities.

Doon Heritage Crossroads. Homer Watson Boulevard and Huron Road. ☎ **519/748-1914.** Admission $5 adults, $3 seniors and students, $2 children 5–12; free for children under 5; $12.50 maximum for a family. May–Aug daily 10am–4:30pm; Sept–Dec Mon–Fri 10am–4:30pm. From Highway 401, exit at Homer Watson Boulevard (Interchange 275).

Doon Heritage Crossroads represents a small Waterloo County village in the year 1914. Costumed staff bring the era back to life in more than 20 restored buildings, including period homes, a dry goods and grocery store, a post office, and tailor and blacksmith shops. Each weekend throughout the season numerous period events and programs are scheduled.

Joseph Schneider Haus. 466 Queen St. South. ☎ **519/742-7752.** Admission $1.75 adults, $1 seniors and students, 75¢ children, $4.50 families. May 19–Labor Day Mon–Sat 10am–5pm, Sun 1–5pm; Labor Day–May 18 Tues–Sat 10am–5pm, Sun 1–5pm.

This historic home (built ca. 1820) has been restored and features lively demonstrations of everyday activities and seasonal chores. It also houses a collection of German-Canadian folk art.

EXPLORING WATERLOO

Several markets are held in Waterloo. The **St. Jacob's Farmers' Market** (☎ 519/747-1830) features local produce, meats and cheese, furniture, arts and crafts, and a flea market. The market is on held on Thursday and Saturday; from June 1 to the end of October it's held on Tuesdays too. On Tuesday and Thursday visitors can attend a **livestock auction** of hogs, calves, and dairy and beef cattle.

The kids might enjoy **Waterloo Park,** with its small animal menagerie of bears, deer, foxes, hawks, owls, peacocks, and wolves. In summer you can picnic and swim. Located off Albert Street, it's open all year and free.

Also in Waterloo, the **Seagram Museum,** 57 Erb St. West (☎ 519/885-1857), traces the history of the distilling and wine-making industry. The free museum is located in the original Seagram distillery barrel warehouse. Open daily May 1 to Dec 31 from 10am to 6pm; Tuesday through Sunday from 10am to 6pm the rest of the year.

Two attractions have great family appeal. **Bingeman Park,** 1380 Victoria St. North, on the Grand River (☎ 519/744-1555), has a wave pool, six water slides, bumper boats, go-carts, minigolf, and more. Open May to September, weather permitting. 600 campsites are also available for $20 to $27 per day. **Sportsworld,** 100 Sportsworld Dr., on Highway 8 north of Highway 401 (☎ 519/653-4442), is a 30-acre water theme park (with a wave pool, a giant water slide, and bumper boats) that also features go-carts, miniature golf, an indoor driving range, and batting cages. Open daily from 10am to 10pm May to Labor Day (the water park opens in late May; the driving range is open all year). Admission to the water park is $10.25 for adults, $8.50 for children 5 to 11. There are charges for the other activities too.

WHERE TO STAY

Many motels and accommodations line both sides of Highway 8. At 2899 King St. East, **Journey's End** (☎ 519/894-3500 or 800/668-4200; fax 519/894-1562) offers doubles for $79. There are also Journey's End motels in Cambridge and Guelph.

At 30 Fairway Road South, the **Holiday Inn** (☎ 519/893-1211; fax 519/894-8518) is a good old standby. Rates are $120 double. This particular inn has a very pleasant outdoor pool, a slide and play area with climbing bars for the kids, barbecue facilities, an indoor pool, whirlpool, sauna, and exercise room.

Best Western Walper Terrace Hotel. 1 King St. West, Kitchener, ON, N2G 1A1. ☎ **519/745-4321.** Fax 519/745-3625. 115 rms. A/C TV TEL. $95 double; from $130 suite. Extra person $10. Children under 16 stay free in parents' room. AE, DC, ER, MC, V.

Situated in a historic landmark building, the Walper Terrace Hotel has been nicely renovated. The tastefully decorated rooms have dark cherrywood furniture and a tile bathroom. The Bismarck is open daily.

Valhalla Inn. 105 King St. East (at Benton), Kitchener, ON, N2G 3W9. ☎ **519/744-4141** or 800/483-7812. Fax 519/578-6889. 200 rms. A/C TV TEL. $115 double; from $140 suite. Extra person $10. Children under 18 stay free in parents' room. Weekend packages available (except during Oktoberfest). AE, ER, MC, V. Free parking.

Across from the glockenspiel in downtown Kitchener, the Valhalla Inn offers modern rooms furnished with dark colonial-style furniture, with additional amenities like tea- and coffeemakers, hair dryers, and balconies. Facilities include a restaurant and lounge plus indoor pool, sauna, and whirlpool, squash courts, two bowling lanes, miniputt, billiards, Ping-Pong, and video arcade. The fitness and recreation center houses a fully equipped gymnasium, bowling lanes, billiards, table tennis, minigolf, darts, tanning center, and three squash courts. Dining facilities include a comfortable lobby bar, and Schatzi's.

A NEARBY PLACE TO STAY & DINE

✪ **Langdon Hall.** RR no. 3, Cambridge, ON, N3H 4R8. ☎ **519/740-2100** or 800/268-1898. Fax 519/740-8161. 36 rms, 7 suites. A/C TV TEL. $195–$220 double; from $220 suite. AE, DC, ER, MC, V.

The elegant house that stands at the head of the curving, tree-lined drive was completed in 1902 for Eugene Langdon Wilks, a descendant of John Jacob Astor. It remained in the family until 1987, when it was transformed into a small country house hotel. Today its 200 acres of lawns, gardens, and woodlands make for an ideal retreat.

The main house, red brick with classical pediment and Palladian-style windows, has a beautiful symmetry. Inside, a similar harmony is achieved. The emphasis is on comfort, rather than grandiosity, whether on the veranda, where tea is served, or in the lounge with its comfortable club chairs and Oriental rugs. Most rooms are set around the cloister garden. Each room is individually decorated with handsome antique reproductions and such nice touches as fresh flowers and terry bathrobes; most have fireplaces.

Dining/Entertainment: The light and airy dining room overlooking the lily pond offers fine continental cuisine.

Facilities: Beyond the cloister down a trellis arcade lies the herb and vegetable garden and beyond that the swimming pool (with an attractive poolhouse), the tennis court, and the croquet lawn. A full spa offers a range of treatments and therapies. Other facilities include a whirlpool, a sauna, an exercise room, a billiard room, and cross-country ski trails.

WHERE TO DINE
IN KITCHENER
Charcoal Steak House. 2980 King St. East. ☎ **519/893-6570.** Reservations recommended. Main courses $10.50–$22. AE, DC, ER, MC, V. Mon–Fri 11am–11pm, Sat noon–11pm, Sun noon–10pm. STEAK.

This large popular dining complex is great for steaks served in several different settings—from the cellar room with wine-country murals, to the hunt room with a stone fireplace, and the parlor with a definite English flavor. Each room provides a warm ambience. If you're feeling adventurous, try a local delicacy—roasted pigs' tails (roasted in fruit juices, spices, and browned over charcoal, and basted with barbecue sauce). Seafood selections like salmon or lobster tails are available. For dessert, try the Nesselrode pie, a light fluffy rum- and fruit-flavored dessert.

The **Lower Deck** (☎ 519/893-2911) specializes in seafood, while **Martini's** offers a made-to-order pasta bar and also doubles as a piano bar.

Swiss Castle Inn. 1508 King St. East. ☎ **519/744-2391.** Reservations not required. Main courses $11–$22. AE, DC, ER, MC, V. Mon–Fri noon–11pm; Sat 4:30–11pm; Sun 11:30am–2:30pm and 4:30–9pm. SWISS.

A Swiss atmosphere prevails here—red and white tablecloths and curtains, decorative cowbells, and an octagonal open hearth. Among the specialties are an excellent Bunderfleisch appetizer (thin slices of air-cured beef); the William Tell Platte (one smoked pork chop, one white sausage, and one piece of schnitzel served on a bed of sauerkraut); and several fondues. The superspecial raclette (cheese, which you grill yourself in a special table oven, served with boiled potatoes, pickles, and onions) is available only if ordered a week in advance. Fish and steak dishes are also offered. For a perfect finale, try the Swiss chocolate-cherry cake.

IN WATERLOO
✪ **Janet Lynn's Bistro.** 92 King St. South. ☎ **519/725-3440.** Reservations recommended. Main courses $16.50–$22. AE, ER, MC, V. Mon–Fri 11:30am–2:30pm; Mon–Sat 5–11pm. INTERNATIONAL/ECLECTIC.

This chic restaurant is dramatically decorated in color tones of terra-cotta, purple, and saffron. The selective menu features a mere six or so entrées plus pastas. The fresh ingredients are quite simply prepared to enhance the natural flavors—linguine with pesto, roasted pine nuts, and smoked salmon, or grilled rack of lamb Provençale with Nicoise jus. There's always one or two gourmet pizzas too. Tempting appetizers include Louisiana shrimp with spicy spring rolls. Mouthwatering desserts include a chocolate sin cake that lives up to its name.

Marbles. 8 William St. ☎ **519/885-2835.** Reservations recommended on weekends. Main courses $5–$12. AE, MC, V. Mon–Sat 11:30am–10pm. BURGERS/LIGHT FARE.

The kids will enjoy the food—a foot-long hot dog smothered with fresh tomatoes and bacon slices, or any one of the eight or so burgers—at this casual spot where marbles add color to the glass serving counter. You can also order a salad; the spinach with bacon, egg, pink grapefruit, pine nuts, and orange-tarragon dressing is virtually a meal in itself. The food is really fresh and imaginative, proving that you don't have to join the assembly line for budget fare.

A NEARBY PLACE TO DINE

Some 7¹/₂ miles (12km) northwest of Kitchener, the **Olde Heidelberg Brewery Restaurant and Motel**, 2 King St. (☎ 519/699-4413), draws crowds for huge portions of ribs and pigs' tails, schnitzel and sauerkraut, sausage, and roast beef washed down with the home brew and accompanied by honky-tonk piano sing-alongs. Dinner dishes range from $7 to $10. Open Monday through Thursday from 11am to midnight, on Friday and Saturday until 1am, and on Sunday from noon to 7pm. The 16-room motel is adjacent, with doubles for $50.

9 Elmira & St. Jacobs: Two Mennonite Farm Towns

These two small towns in the heart of the Mennonite farmlands can be visited from Kitchener-Waterloo or from Toronto. If you're driving from Toronto, take 401W to Highway 8 north to Highway 86.

For further information on the area, contact the **Elmira-Woolwich Chamber of Commerce,** 5 1st St. East, Elmira, ON, N3B 2E3 (☎ 519/669-2605).

ELMIRA

A charming town 14 miles north of Kitchener-Waterloo, Elmira (pop. 6,800) was one of Upper Canada's earliest settlements. Set amid the rich farmlands of the Grand and Conestoga river valleys, it is a focal point for Mennonite farmers and craftspeople.

During the famous **spring maple syrup festival,** held the first Saturday in April, the population swells to 40,000. Black-bonneted Mennonite women serve up flapjacks with syrup and offer handcrafted goods to all and sundry, while horse-drawn wagons take visitors off to the maple bush to see the sugaring off, from the tapping of the trees to the boiling of the syrup. Festivities usually start around 7am.

From June to August, Monday and Friday, harness racing is held at the **Elmira Raceway** in the Elmira fairgrounds.

For a savory taste of the past, stop at the **Stone Crock,** 59 Church St. West (☎ 519/669-1521). It's known for the popular buffet (soup, salads, cold cuts, cheeses, and several hot entrées), which costs $9.25 at lunch, $12 for weekday dinner, $13 weekend dinner. There's also an à la carte menu for breakfast, lunch, and dinner, featuring sandwiches, burgers, and such dishes as cabbage rolls, fish and chips, and pork schnitzel, priced from $5 to $10. The Elmira Stone Crock also has an in-house bakery and deli located next door and a gift shop. Open Monday to Saturday 7am to 8:30pm, Sunday 11am to 8:30pm (dinner buffet Monday to Friday 4:30 to 8:30pm and Saturday and Sunday from 3:30pm).

A similar experience is offered at the **Stone Crock,** 41 King St., St. Jacob's (☎ 519/664-2286).

ST. JACOBS

St. Jacobs, 5 miles (8km) north of Kitchener, has become a well-touristed small town. People are drawn by the shops—more than 80 in all—located in the **Country Mill** (once a flour and feed mill), the **Village Silos** (used to store grain for milling until

1974), the **Old Factory** (formerly a shoe company), the **Snyder Merchants** (built in the 1860s as a frontier general store), and **Riverworks,** located in another converted factory. There are blacksmiths, glassblowers, quilters, country crafts of all sorts, oak and pine furniture, stained glass, and more. Most are open from 10am to 6pm Monday through Saturday and 1 to 5pm on Sunday. Many close Monday in the winter.

In addition to shopping, the **Meetingplace,** 33 King St. (☎ 519/664-3518), shows audiovisuals about the Amish-Mennonite way of life. Open May to October, weekdays from 11am to 5pm, on Saturday from 10am to 5pm, and on Sunday from 1:30 to 5pm; November to April, weekends only from 11am to 4:30pm on Saturday and 2 to 4:30pm on Sunday.

WHERE TO STAY

Benjamin's Restaurant & Inn. 17 King St., St. Jacobs, ON, N0B 2N0. ☎ **519/664-3731.** Fax 519/664-2218. 9 rms. A/C TV TEL. $95–$105 double. Rates include continental breakfast. AE, ER, MC, V.

Benjamin's is located in a renovated 1852 building. Most rooms are furnished with pine beds and modern handmade quilts and have private bathrooms.

The stucco-and-tile dining rooms with open-hearth fireplaces offer about 10 items at dinner, priced from $13 for pasta of the day to $16 for grilled strip steak marinated in ale, with jalapeño-smoked beans, and ancho chiles.

✪ Jakobstettel Guest House. 16 Isabella St., St. Jacobs, ON, N0B 2N0. ☎ **519/664-2208.** Fax 519/664-1326. 12 rms. A/C TEL. $100–$165 double. Extra person $15. Rates include breakfast. AE, MC, V.

The Jakobstettel Guest House was originally built in 1898 by mill owner William Snider as a wedding gift for his wife and five daughters. The house stands on five acres of lovely grounds dotted with spruce and maple made even prettier by well-manicured lawns and a trellised rose garden. There's also an outdoor pool, one tennis court, and 1¼ miles of trails. Bicycles are available. All rooms have been beautifully furnished with fine antique reproductions, wingback chairs, desks, wicker, and occasionally a brass or four-poster bed. A library, common room, and country kitchen are available for an even more comfortable stay.

10 Elora & Fergus

If you're driving from Toronto, take Highway 401 west to Highway 6 north to 7 east, then back to 6 north into Fergus. From Fergus take Highway 18 west to Elora.

ELORA

Elora has always been a special place. To the natives the gorge was a sacred site, home of spirits who dwelt within the great cliffs. Early explorers and Jesuit missionaries also wondered at the natural spectacle. As early as 1817 a few hardy settlers from Vermont and England had arrived and established farms along the riverbank, but it was Scotsman William Gilkinson who put the town on the map in 1832 when he purchased 14,000 acres on both sides of the Grand River and told his agent to build a mill and a general store. Gilkinson called it Elora, the name that his tea-planter brother, inspired by the Ellora Caves in India, had given to one of his ships. By the 1850s, encouraged by the water power afforded by the Grand, many settlers had arrived and the town developed into a commercial hub with a distillery, brewery, foundries, and furniture factories.

EXPLORING THE TOWN & THE GORGE

Most of the houses that the settlers built in the 1850s stand today. And many were built on nostalgia. St. John the Evangelist Church was built from a sketch of a church near Castle Conway in Wales sent by a settler's family. Inside this church are a set of communion vessels sent by Florence Nightingale to her cousin, who was the church's first pastor. You'll also want to browse the stores along picturesque Mill Street. For real insight into the town's history, pick up a walking tour brochure from the tourist booth on Mill Street.

The **Elora Gorge** is a 350-acre park on both sides of the 70-foot limestone gorge. Nature trails wind through it. Overhanging rock ledges, small caves, a waterfall, and the evergreen forest on its rim are some of the gorge's scenic delights. The park (☎ 519/846-9742) has camping and swimming facilities, plus picnic areas and playing fields. Located just west of Elora at the junction of the Grand and Irvine rivers, it is open from May 1 to October 15 from 10am to sunset. Admission is $3 per adult, $2.25 for seniors and students, $1.75 for children. To camp, for unserviced campsites, it's $8 per day ($11 with water and electricity), plus the admission fee. For information, write or call the Grand River Conservation Authority, 400 Clyde Rd. (P.O. Box 729), Cambridge, ON, N1R 5W6 (☎ 519/621-2761).

An additional summer attraction is the **Elora Festival,** a four-week choral music celebration held in mid-July to early August. For more information, contact The Elora Festival, P.O. Box 990, Elora, ON, N0B 1S0 (☎ 519/846-0331).

WHERE TO STAY

Elora Mill Inn. 77 Mill St. West, Elora, ON, N0B 1S0. ☎ **519/846-5356.** Fax 519/846-9180. 32 rms. A/C TV TEL. $145 double; from $175 suite. Extra person $25. Rates include breakfast. AE, ER, MC, V.

This inn is located in a five-story gristmill built originally in 1870 and operated until 1974. Downstairs a lounge, with the original exposed beams and a huge stone fireplace, overlooks the falls. Upstairs are similarly rustic dining areas. Each guest room is furnished individually, some with four-posters, others cannonball pine beds. Most beds are covered with quilts, and each room has a comfy rocker or hoopback chair. Some rooms in adjacent buildings are duplexes and have decks and river views. Many inn rooms have gorge views, and some units have fireplaces.

Dining/Entertainment: The dining room's eight or so appetizers might include Bermuda chowder, a spicy broth of fish, vegetables, spiced sausage, dark rum, and sherry-pepper. The main dishes are priced from $18 to $27; the most popular option is the prime rib cart, followed by a dessert—chocolate decadence or shoofly pie are popular choices. It's open daily for lunch and dinner.

✪ **Gingerbread House.** 22 Metcalfe St. South, Elora, ON, N0B 1S5. ☎ **519/846-0521.** 4 rms (sharing 3¹/₂ baths), 2 suites. $80–$85 double; $140 and $155 suite. Rates include breakfast. MC, V.

The Gingerbread House (dating from the 1840s) is operated by Petra Veveris, a very gracious, talented, and well-traveled woman who has an eye for decoration and design. The house is filled with antiques and decorative objects acquired on her many expeditions. Each room is comfortably and attractively furnished. The Marco Polo is filled with travel souvenirs from Ecuador, Peru, and Australia. Petra coddles her guests, providing such extras as dressing gowns, slippers, and books. A lavish breakfast that might consist of waffles with fresh blueberries and sour cream is served at a table set with German crystal and silver candlesticks. Wine is served on the back veranda every evening. Two suites are available—one with a fireplace, cathedral-ceilinged bedroom, bathroom, dining room, and small kitchen, and another with a large bedroom, sitting area, porch, and Jacuzzi bathroom.

WHERE TO DINE

Metcalfe Inn. 59 Metcalfe St., Elora, ON, N0B 1S0. ☎ **519/846-0081.** Reservations recommended on weekends. Main courses $8–$17. AE, MC, V. Summer Mon–Sun 5–9pm, patio daily from 11am; winter Tues–Sun 5–9pm. INTERNATIONAL.

The Metcalfe Inn has a casual dining room serving favorites like stir-fries, fajitas, seafood fettuccine, and pepper steak. At lunch, sandwiches and light entrées are all under $8. There's a large outdoor patio. In winter the room with the stone fireplace is cozy.

FERGUS

A pleasant town on the Upper Grand River Gorge, Fergus (pop. 7,500) was originally known as Little Falls, but its name was changed for its Scottish immigrant founder, Adam Ferguson. There are more than 250 fine old 1850s buildings to see—examples of Scottish limestone architecture—including the Foundry, which now houses the Fergus market.

The most noteworthy Fergus event is the **Fergus Scottish Festival,** which includes **Highland Games,** featuring pipe-band competitions, caber tossing, tug-of-war contests, and Highland dancing, and the North American Scottish Heavy Events, held usually on the second weekend in August. For more information on the games, contact Fergus Information Centre, P.O. Box 3, Fergus, ON, N1M 2W7 (☎ 519/843-5140).

While you're in Fergus, you may wish to visit **Templin Gardens,** an English-style garden on the banks of the Upper Gorge. The market is also a fun event to attend on Saturday or Sunday. Kids old and young love the **Great Teddy Bear Caper,** held on Victoria Day weekend each year. It's really a large garage sale to which people bring their favorite teddy bears, which are then judged and awarded prizes in particular categories.

WHERE TO STAY & DINE

✪ **Breadalbane Inn.** 487 St. Andrew St. West, Fergus, ON N1M 1P2. ☎ **519/843-4770.** 7 rms (6 with bath). $80–$90 double. Rates include continental breakfast. MC, V.

This is a favorite dining and lodging choice with the warmth, style, and fare of a British bed-and-breakfast inn. The handsome gray stone structure with ornate grillwork around the front porch was built by the Honorable Admiral Ferguson in 1860, and served as a residence, nursing home, and rooming house before Philip Cardinal, and his wife, Jean, took it over 21 years ago.

The guest rooms are all extremely comfortable and elegantly furnished with early Canadian-style furniture. In the back is an annex that contains a large bed-sitting room with bath and small kitchen renting for $90.

Dining/Entertainment: Reservations are recommended for the two dining areas, which have French doors leading into the rose garden. Here you can dine to the strains of classical music, at darkly polished tables set with Royal Doulton china. Philip and Jean obviously love what they are doing: They bake their own bread and take pains with everything. At dinner, try the French onion soup, and follow it with the charbroiled back ribs with honey-maple sauce. Main courses cost $13 to $24. Open Tuesday to Friday noon to 2pm, Tuesday to Saturday 5:30 to 9:30pm.

North to Ontario's Lakelands & Beyond

by Marilyn Wood

And where do Torontonians go whenever they feel the urge to flee their high-rises? Primarily, they head north—toward Georgian Bay, the wilderness of Algonquin Provincial Park, or the cottage-and-resort country of Huronia and the Muskoka Lakes, located about 130 miles north of the city.

1 Exploring Northern Ontario

On weekends most Torontonians head for a particular resort and sit tight to unwind. But if you want to explore the whole region, head out from Toronto via Highway 400 north to Barrie. Here you can either turn west to explore Georgian Bay, the Bruce Peninsula, and Manitoulin Island or continue due north to the Moskoka Lakes, Algonquin Provincial Park, and points farther north.

VISITOR INFORMATION   Contact **Ontario Travel,** Queen's Park, Toronto, ON, M7A 2E5 (☎ 416/314-0944, or 800/ONTARIO from 9am to 8pm). The offices are open from 8:30am to 5pm Monday through Friday (daily from mid-May to mid-September).

FARM VACATIONS   One way to really experience Ontario is to stay on a farm, and this is certainly one of the best regions to do it. Enjoy home-cooked meals, the peace of the countryside, and the working rhythms of a dairy or mixed farm. There are all kinds of farms and locations to choose from. Rates average $35 to $60 double per night, $220 per week, all meals included.

For information write to the **Ontario Vacation Farm Association,** RR no. 2, Alma, ON, N0B 1A0. Or contact **Ontario Travel,** Queen's Park, Toronto, ON, M7A 2E5 (☎ 416/314-0944 or 800/ONTARIO), where you can obtain a free "Farm Vacation Guide." See also the listing for **Chez Vous Chez Nous Couette et Cafe,** in the Midland section of the chapter, for a specific recommendation.

AN IMPORTANT NOTE ON PRICES & TAXES   Unless stated otherwise, **the prices cited in this guide are given in Canadian dollars,** which is good news for U.S. travelers, because the Canadian dollar is worth 25% less than the American dollar, but buys nearly as much. As we go to press, $1 Canadian is worth about 75¢ U.S., which means that your $100-a-night hotel room will cost only U.S. $75, and your $6 breakfast costs only U.S. $4.50.

Keep in mind that Ontario has a provincial sales tax of 8%, plus a 5% accommodations tax—*in addition* to the national 7% goods and services tax (GST).

2 The Great Outdoors

In the parts of northern Ontario covered by this chapter, you'll find plenty of terrific places to canoe, hike, bicycle, or go freshwater fishing. Some 260 provincial parks in Ontario offer ample opportunities for outdoor recreation. The daily in-season entry fee for a vehicle is $6; campsites cost anywhere from $13 to $19. For more information, contact the **Ontario Ministry of Natural Resources** (☎ 416/314-2000).

Topographic maps are vital on extended canoeing/hiking trips and can be secured from the **Canada Map Office,** 615 Booth St., Ottawa, ON, K1A 0E9 (☎ 613/952-7000).

Find your favorite activity below, and I'll point you to the best spots to pursue your interest or give you the general information you need to get started.

BIKING You'll find networks of biking and hiking trails in the national and provincial parks.

Other good routes are the **Georgian Cycle and Ski Trail,** which runs 20 miles (32km) along the southern shore of Georgian Bay from Collingwood via Thornbury to Meaford. The Bruce Peninsula and Manitoulin Island also offer good cycling opportunities. In the Burk's Falls–Magnetawan area, **The Forgotten Trail** has been organized along old logging roads and railroad tracks. For information contact the **Huronia Travel Association** in Midhurst at 705/726-9300.

Various outfitters offer bike tours in this region, including **Bicycle Ontario Tours,** Box 20044, North Bay (☎ 705/752-5693). Exciting six-day packages combining cycling with sailing on Georgian Bay aboard a 67-foot ketch are operated from May to October from Owen Sound by **Sail and Cycle Charters**, 535 9th St. E., Owen Sound, ON, N4K 1P4. The trip costs more then $1,000 per person.

CANOEING/KAYAKING Northern Ontario is a canoeist's paradise. Exceptional canoeing can be enjoyed in Algonquin, Killarney, and Quetico Provincial Parks; along the rivers in the Temagami (Lady Evelyn Smoothwater Provincial Park) and Wabakimi regions; along the Route of the Voyageurs in Algoma Country (Lake Superior Provincial Park); and along the rivers leading into James Bay like the Missinaibi. Killbear Provincial Park, Georgian Bay, and Pukaskwa National Park also are good places to paddle.

Unfortunately, many areas are getting overcrowded. One of the quietest, least trafficked areas is the Missinaibi River in the Chapleau Game Reserve. Another truly remote canoeing area accessible by plane only is in Winisk River Provincial Park, where you're likely to see polar bears who establish their dens in the park. These areas are for advanced canoeists who can handle white water and orient themselves in the wilderness.

For information on all these areas and detailed maps, contact the **Ministry of Natural Resources** (☎ 416/314-2000) or the provincial parks themselves. For more details see the park entries in this chapter.

Around Parry Sound/Georgian Bay, canoeing and kayaking trips are arranged by **White Squall**, RR no. 1, Nobel, ON, P0G 1G0 (☎ 705/342-5324). Day trips are $90; four-day trips start at $480 (prices include instruction, meals, and equipment).

In Algonquin Provincial Park, several outfitters serve park visitors, including **Algonquin Outfitters,** Oxtongue Lake (RR no. 1), Dwight, ON, P0A 1H0 (☎ 705/635-2243); and **Opeongo Outfitters,** Box 123, Whitney, ON, K0J 2M0

(☎ 613/637-5470). Complete canoe outfitting costs from $45 to $55 a day, depending on the length of trip and extent of equipment. Canoe rentals cost from $15 to $25 a day depending on the type, from $90 to $120 per week.

Killarney Outfitters, on Highway 637, 3 miles east of Killarney (☎ 705/287-2828 or 705/287-2242 off-season), offers complete outfitting for from $60 a day to $360 per week. Canoe and kayak rentals range from $20 to $25 a day or $120 to $155 a week.

In the Quetico area contact **Canoe Canada Outfitters,** Box 1810, 300 O'Brien St., Atikokan, ON, P0T 1C0 (☎ 807/597-6418); or **Quetico Discovery Tours,** Box 593, 18 Birch Rd., Atikokan, ON, P0T 1C0 (☎ 807/597-2621).

North of Thunder Bay, there's excellent wilderness camping and canoeing in the Wabakimi region (accessed from Armstrong) with plenty of scope for beginners, intermediates, and advanced paddlers. For information contact **Mattice Lake Outfitters/Wabakimi Air** (☎ 807/583-2843), which offers four-day to two-week trips priced from $250 per person and will also rent canoes for around $100 a week.

For additional outfitters call **Northern Ontario Tourist Outfitters Association** (☎ 705/472-5552).

Note: In most provincial parks you must register with park authorities and provide them with your route.

FISHING   Ontario is one of the world's largest freshwater fishing grounds, with more than 250,000 lakes and thousands of miles of streams and rivers supporting more than 140 species of fish. The northern area covered in this chapter is the province's best fishing region.

In summer, on Manitoulin Island, fishing for Chinook, coho, rainbow, lake trout, perch, and bass is excellent in Georgian Bay or any of the island lakes—Mindenmoya, Manitou, Kagawong, Tobacco, to name a few. Trips can be arranged through **Manitou Fishing Charters** (☎ 705/983-2038 or 705/859-2787).

Around Nipissing and North Bay there's great fishing for walleye, Northern pike, smallmouth bass, muskie, whitefish, and perch. The Temagami region offers in addition brook, lake, and rainbow trout. More remote fishing can be found in the Chapleau and Algoma regions, the James Bay Frontier, and north of Lake Superior.

Many outfitters will rent lakeside log cabins equipped with a propane stove and refrigerator and motor boat to go along with it. The cost varies from about $550 to $800 per person for anywhere from three to seven days. Two outfitters to contact are **Mattice Lake Outfitters** (see above) and **Huron Air and Outfitters** (☎ 807/583-2051). In the Cochrane area contact: **R.A.M Outfitters,** Box 2440, Cochrane, ON, P0L 1C0 (☎ 705/272-3456), who have cabins that are accessible by either road, all-terrain vehicle, or boat.

Konopelky, Box 1870, Cochrane, ON, P0L 1C0 (☎ 705/272-5050), rents cabins fully equipped with propane stove, fridge, Coleman lights, and wood stove (some on lakes that are only accessible by aircraft and some in drive-in locations). They offer fishing, moose and bear hunting, and canoe packages on the Missinabi, Mattagami, and Abitibi rivers. **Polar Bear Camp and Fly-In Outfitters,** P.O. Box 1870, Cochrane, ON, P0L 1C0 (☎ 705/272-4672) offers similar packages. For additional suggestions contact Ontario Tourism or the Northern Ontario Tourist Outfitters Association.

Note: Fishing limits and regulations must be followed. Licenses are required and will cost about $15.

GOLF Barrie has two exceptional courses—National Pines Golf and Country Club and the Horseshoe Resort golf course. Collingwood offers the scenic Cranberry Resort course. In Bracebridge, you'll find Muskoka Highlands Golf Course and farther north near North Bay, Mattawa Golf Resort. Thunder Bay has five par-71 or -72 courses, while Timmins and Kenora have one each.

HIKING & BACKPACKING The region is super for hiking. The **Bruce Trail,** which starts at Queenston, crosses the Niagara escarpment and Bruce Peninsula and ends in Tobermory. The Bruce Trail Association (☎ 416/526-6821 in Hamilton) publishes a map that can be obtained from sporting goods stores specializing in outdoor activities. In the Bruce Peninsula National Park, there are four trails, three of which are linked to the Bruce Trail. There's also a hiking trail around Flowerpot Island in Fathom Five National Park.

Manitoulin Island is another prime hiking area; two of my favorite routes are **The Cup and Saucer Trail** and the trail to **Bridal Veil Falls.**

South of Parry Sound hikers can follow the 41-mile (66km) **Seguin Trail,** which meanders around several lakes.

In the Muskoka region, trails abound in Arrowhead Provincial Park at Huntsville and the Resource Management Area on Highway 11, north of Bracebridge, and of course, in Algonquin Park. Algonquin is a great choice for a serious multiday backpacking trip, along the Highland Trail or the Western Uplands Hiking Trail, which combines three loops for a total of 105 miles.

You can do a memorable 7- to 10-day backpacking trip in **Killarney Provincial Park** on the 60-mile La Cloche Silhouette Trail, which takes in some stunning scenery.

Sleeping Giant Provincial Park has more than 50 miles of trails. The Kabeyun trail provides great views of Lake Superior and the 800-foot-high cliffs of the Sleeping Giant.

Pukaskwa National Park offers a coastal hiking trail between Pic and Pukaskwa Rivers along the northern shore of Lake Superior.

When it's completed, the province's most challenging and longest trail will be **The Voyageur Trail,** starting from South Baymouth on Manitoulin Island through Sault Ste. Marie along the shoreline of Lake Superior to Thunder Bay. Currently the trail is 250 miles long but the plan is for it to extend 375 miles. For information contact the Voyageur Trail Association, Box 20040, 150 Churchill Blvd., Sault Ste. Marie, ON, P6A 6W3.

For additional hiking information see the park entries later in the chapter.

HORSEBACK RIDING **Harmony Acres,** RR no. 1, Tobermory (☎ 519/596-2735), offers overnight trail rides to the shores of Georgian Bay, as well as one-hour and day rides.

On Manitoulin Island, **Honora Bay Riding Stables,** RR no. 1, Little Current, ON, P0P 1K0 (☎ 705/368-2669), operates an overnight trail ride from May to October.

Near the Soo and Elliott Lake, **Cedar Rail Ranch,** RR no. 3, Thessalon (☎ 705/842-2021), offers both hourly and overnight trail rides with stops for swimming breaks along the route.

SKIING/SNOWMOBILING Ontario's largest downhill area is the **Blue Mountain Resorts** in Collingwood. In the Muskoka region there's downhill skiing at **Hidden Valley Highlands** (☎ 705/789-1773 or 705/789-5942). Up north around Thunder Bay try **Candy Mountain/Loch Lomond** (☎ 807/475-5250), **Big Thunder** (☎ 807/475-4402), and **Mount Baldy** (☎ 807/683-8441).

You can cross-country ski at Big Thunder and in several provincial parks, such as Sleeping Giant and Kakabeka Falls.

And one of the top destinations is the Parry Sound area, which has an extensive network of cross-country ski trails and more than 650 miles of well-groomed snowmobiling trails (there are nine snowmobiling clubs in the area, and the Chamber of Commerce can put you in touch with them). For additional information on cross-country skiing contact the **Georgian Nordic Ski and Canoe Club,** Box 42, Parry Sound, ON, P2A 2X2, which permits day use of its ski trails.

You'll also find groomed cross-country trails at Sauble Beach on the Bruce Peninsula and in many of the provincial parks farther north. Along the mining frontier contact the Porcupine Ski Runners in Timmins, and the Cochrane Cross Country Ski Club, which offers 11km of groomed trails.

3 From Collingwood/Blue Mountain to Tobermory/ Bruce Peninsula National Park

If you head west from Barrie, northwest from Toronto, you'll go along the west Georgian Bay coast from Collingwood up to the Bruce Peninsula. Driving from Toronto, take Highway 400 to Highway 26 west.

Nestled at the base of Blue Mountain, Collingwood is the town closest to Ontario's largest skiing area. Collingwood first achieved prosperity as a Great Lakes port and shipbuilding town that turned out large lake carriers. Many mansions and the Victorian main street are reminders of those days. And just east of Blue Mountain sweep 9 miles of golden sands at Wasaga Beach.

North beyond Collingwood stretches the **Bruce Peninsula National Park,** known for its limestone cliffs, wetlands, and forest. From Tobermory, you can visit an underwater national park.

For tourist information, contact **Georgian Triangle Tourism,** 601 First St., Collingwood, ON, L9Y 4L2 (☎ 705/445-7722).

BLUE MOUNTAIN: SKI TRAILS, SLIDES, RIDES & MORE

In winter, people flock to **Blue Mountain Resorts,** at RR no. 3, Collingwood (☎ 705/445-0231), to ski. Ontario's largest resort has 16 lifts, 98% snowmaking coverage on 33 trails, and three base lodges. In addition, there are three repair, rental, and ski shops, a ski school, and day-care. Lift rates are $36 daily.

In summer, you can zoom down the **Great Slide Ride,** 3,000 feet of asbestos-cement track, aboard a minibobsled, weaving in and out of trees, and careening around high-banked hairpin curves. Naturally, you don't *have* to go at breakneck speed. The 10-minute ride to the top aboard the triple-chair lift treats you to a glorious panoramic view over Georgian Bay. The slide is open Victoria Day (late May) to Canadian Thanksgiving (U.S. Columbus Day) from 9:30am to dusk. Adults pay $3.95; children, $2.95; kids under seven, free; a book of four tickets costs $12 and $8, respectively.

On the **Tube Ride** you ride an inner tube down a series of waterfalls, ponds, and rapids that stretch over 400 feet. Kids must be at least eight years old to ride.

Even more thrilling is the **Slipper Dipper water slide,** consisting of three flumes that loop and tunnel down 400 feet into a splash-down pool. For this exhilarating pleasure adults pay $4.50 for five rides; children, $3.75. Open mid-June to Labor Day. Children must be at least eight years old and 42 inches tall. An all-day pass for unlimited rides on everything costs $16.95 for adults, $13.95 for kids 8 to 12, $7.95 for kids under seven.

Blue Mountain is also famous for its **pottery,** and you can take a free factory tour and perhaps buy a few seconds. Many of the shapes have been inspired by the natural life of the area—the wing of a bird, the graceful neck of the heron, the silver-scaled fish of the rivers and lakes. The pottery outlet is located at 2 Mountain Rd., on Highway 26 in Collingwood (☎ 705/445-3000).

Three miles east of Collingwood on Highway 26 at Theatre Road, the kids can enjoy testing their mettle and skills at **Blue Mountain Go-Karts** (☎ 705/445-2419). For the really small fry there are minicarts ($4.50 for 10 minutes), bumper boats, a batting cage, a pitching machine, plus minigolf, a small touch-and-pet animal park, and a games arcade. Open daily 10am to midnight.

BRUCE PENINSULA NATIONAL PARK

Bruce Peninsula National Park features limestone cliffs, abundant wetlands, quiet beaches, and forest that shelters more than 40 species of orchids, 20 species of ferns, and several insectivorous plants. About 100 species of bird also inhabit the park. Three campgrounds (one trailer, two tent) offer 242 campsites (no electricity).

The **Bruce Trail** winds along the Georgian Bay Coastline, while Route 6 cuts across the peninsula, both ending in Tobermory. It's one of Ontario's best-known trails, stretching 434 miles (700km) from Queenston in Niagara Falls to Tobermory. The most rugged part of the trail passes through the park along the Georgian Bay shoreline. **Cypress Lake Trails** from the north end of the Cyprus Lake campground provide access to the Bruce Trail and also lead to cliffs overlooking the bay. Canoes and nonpowered craft can be used on Cyprus Lake. The best swimming is at Singing Sands Beach and Dorcas Bay, both on Lake Huron on the west side of the peninsula. Winter activities include cross-country skiing, snowshoeing, and snowmobiling. For more information contact the Superintendent, Bruce Peninsula National Park, Box 189, Tobermory, ON, N0H 2R0 (☎ 519/596-2233).

AN UNDERWATER NATIONAL PARK

From Tobermory you can visit the underwater national park, **Fathom Five National Marine Park,** P.O. Box 189, Tobermory, ON, N0H 2R0 (☎ 519/596-2233), where at least 21 known shipwrecks lie waiting for diving exploration around the 19 or so islands in the park. The most accessible is **Flowerpot Island,** which can be visited by tour boat to view its weird and wonderful rock pillar formations. Go for a few hours to hike and picnic. Six campsites are available on the island on a first come, first served basis. Boats leave from Tobermory harbor. For more information contact the Superintendent, Fathom Five National Marine Park, Box 189, Tobermory, ON N0H, 2R0 (☎ 519/596-2233).

WHERE TO STAY

Beaconglow Motel. RR no. 3, Collingwood, ON, L9Y 3Z2. ☎ **705/445-1674.** Fax 705/445-7176. 33 rms. A/C TV. Motel and efficiency units from $70 double in summer and fall; $40 per person per night for a two-bedroom standard suite on weekends; $70 per person for luxury two-bedroom (with VCR, dishwasher, and Jacuzzi). Midweek and other packages available. Special weekly rates available. AE, MC, V.

You'll find a home away from home at the Beaconglow Motel, which has nicely furnished efficiency units that range in size from a compact one-bedroom with kitchenette to a two-bedroom/two-bathroom suite with fully equipped kitchen (including coffee maker, microwave, and dishwasher) and living room with wood-burning fireplace. For fun there's an indoor pool, a whirlpool, a sauna, shuffleboard, a horseshoe pitch, a games room with two pool tables, and a library of 175 movies.

Twenty-four units have telephones. Reserve at least three months ahead for weekend or holiday stays.

✪ Beild House. 64 Third St., Collingwood, ON, L9Y 1K5. ☎ 705/444-1522. Fax 705/444-2394. 17 rms (7 with bath). $260–$360 for two on weekends including meals; $209–$345 mid-week for same two-night package for two people. Rates include breakfast. AE, MC, V.

Bill Barclay and his wife Stephanie are the proud, enthusiastic owners of this handsome 1909 house. Bill prepares the breakfasts and gourmet dinners, while his wife creates the inviting decor. The comfortable downstairs public areas are personalized by their collections of folk art, quill boxes from Manitoulin, and sculptures by Stephanie's mother. Two fireplaces make the place cozy in winter. The rooms are individually furnished with elegant pieces. Room 4 contains a bed that was owned by the duke and duchess of Windsor, royal portraits, and a souvenir program of Prince Edward's trip to Canada in 1860. The five rooms on the third floor share two bathrooms and are the least expensive.

   Dining/Entertainment: Breakfast is sumptuous and the five-course dinner is even more so.

Blue Mountain Inn. RR no. 3, Collingwood, ON, L9Y 3Z2. ☎ 705/445-0231. 98 rms. A/C TV TEL. Ski season $99 per person per night midweek, $129 per person per night weekends. Off-season $95 per room. Special packages available. AE, MC, V.

Stay here right at the mountain base, and you can beat the winter lift lines. Rooms are simply furnished, with little balconies facing the mountain and overlooking the tennis courts.

   The inn's entertainment facilities include three lounges; a dining room; an indoor pool; squash, racquetball, and tennis courts; and an exercise room.

Highwayman Inn. At the corner of 1st and High streets, Collingwood, ON, L9Y 3J4. ☎ 705/444-2144. Fax 705/444-7772. 66 rms. A/C TV TEL. Weekdays $70 double; weekends $99 double. Children under 18 stay free in parents' room. Rates lower in spring and fall. AE, ER, MC, V.

Built in a mock Tudor style, the Highwayman Inn stands only minutes from the mountain. In winter a fire blazes in the lobby's brick fireplace, providing a warm welcome to chilled skiers coming off the mountain. Rooms are ultramodern and fully appointed, and local telephone calls are free. The restaurant, J. F. Kicks, offers the same glow, with DJ entertainment nightly. For entertainment there's an indoor pool, a sauna, and also a floodlit tennis court.

WHERE TO DINE

✪ Chez Michel. Highway 26 West, Craigleith. ☎ 705/445-9441. Reservations recommended. Main courses $15–$18. AE, MC, V. Wed–Mon 11:30am–2:30pm; daily 5–9pm. FRENCH.

Small and charming, Chez Michel has a very French air that's created by chef-proprietor Michel Masselin, who hails from Normandy. The food is excellent and carefully prepared. Among the specials you might find quail stuffed with goose liver pâté and served with a Madeira sauce or some other seasonal game dish along with more traditional favorites like coquilles St-Jacques. There's a good wine list too, and desserts that are worth waiting for, like the strawberries romanoff.

Christopher's. 167 Pine St. ☎ 705/445-7117. Reservations recommended. Main courses $12–$19. AE, MC, V. Daily 11am–2:30pm and 5–10pm. FRENCH/CONTINENTAL.

Dinner in this handsome Victorian town house might find you sampling such dishes as grilled lamb tenderloin with tomato mint vinaigrette, or spinach fettucine with shrimp in a tomato cream sauce. In summer afternoon tea is also served.

Pine Street Cafe. 2 Schoolhouse Lane. ☎ **705/445-8242.** Reservations recommended. Main courses $9–$17. AE, MC, V. Mon–Sat 11am–3:30pm; daily 5–10pm. CANADIAN/CONTINENTAL.

This is a casual restaurant with a pleasant atmosphere for lunch or dinner. For dinner choose Camembert fritters with black currant sauce to start and follow with pasta or such dishes as swordfish panfried with pineapple mango salsa or lamb tenderloin with a black currant peppercorn and brandy sauce. There's a bar up front, and jazz, blues, and other entertainment is featured too.

Spike & Spoon. 637 Hurontario St. ☎ **705/445-2048.** Reservations recommended. Main courses $15–$19. AE, MC, V. Tues–Fri noon–2pm; Tues–Sat 5:30–9pm. Closed Apr and Nov. Enter Collingwood on Route 26. Follow the signs to the business section past the Collingwood Roadhouse Inn to Hurontario Street, where you turn left; it's on the left. CONTINENTAL.

Set in an elegant mid-19th-century red-brick house that once belonged to a Chicago millionaire, this restaurant offers food prepared with fresh ingredients and herbs that are grown in the yard out back. There are three dining rooms, each with a different atmosphere, plus a closed-in porch for pleasant summer dining. The bread and the desserts are all freshly made on the premises. Main courses might be baked orange roughy with leek and Pernod sauce; or quill noodles with pancetta, mushrooms, and onions in herbed tomato sauce.

✪ **Swiss Alphorn.** Highway 26 West, Craig Leaf. ☎ **705/445-8882.** Reservations not accepted. Main courses $14–$22. AE, MC, V. Daily 4–10pm. SWISS.

Bratwurst, Wiener schnitzel, chicken Ticino, and cheese fondue are just some of the favorites served at this chalet-style restaurant, which is loaded with Swiss atmosphere. It's a very popular place, always crowded winter and summer. Save room for the Swiss crepes with chocolate and almonds.

4 Manitoulin Island

The island, named after the Great Indian Spirit Gitchi Manitou, is for those who seek a quiet, remote, and spiritual place, where life is slow.

ESSENTIALS

VISITOR INFORMATION   Contact the **Manitoulin Tourism Association,** P.O. Box 119, Little Current, ON, P0P 1K0 (☎ 705/368-3021), or stop by the information center at the Swing Bridge in Little Current.

GETTING THERE   The island can be reached via **ferry** from Tobermory to South Baymouth, or by road across a swing bridge connecting Little Current to Great Cloche Island and via Highway 6 to Espanola. Ferries operate only from early May to mid-October with four a day in the summer months. The trip takes anywhere from 1³/₄ to 2 hours. Reservations are needed. One-way adult fare is $10.50, children five to 11 $5.25; an average-size car costs $23 one way. For information call the **Owen Sound Transportation Company** at ☎ 519/376-6601 or contact the **Tobermory terminal** at ☎ 519/596-2510.

EXPLORING THE ISLAND

The Indians have lived here for centuries and today you can visit the **Ojibwe Indian Reserve,** occupying the large peninsula on the island's eastern end—although there really isn't that much to see unless you are genuinely interested in modern life on the reservation. It's home to about 2,500 people of Odawa, Ojibwe, and Potawotami descent; the area was never ceded to the government. Try to time your visit for the big **Wikwemikong Powwow,** held in August. Other powwows are held during the year around the island. It is worth seeking out the few native art galleries like the **Kasheese Studios,** just outside West Bay at Highways 540 and 551 (☎ 705/377-4141), which is operated by artists in residence Blake Debassige and Shirley Cheechoo, and the **Ojibwe Cultural Foundation,** also just outside West Bay (☎ 705/377-4902), which opens erratically and then only until 4pm. You can also visit individual artists' studios.

Although there are several communities on the island, the highlights are scenic and mostly outside their perimeters, like the **Mississagi Lighthouse,** located at the western end of the island outside Meldrun Bay. Follow the signs that will take you about 4 miles down a dirt road past the limestone/dolomite quarry entrance (from which materials are still shipped across the Great Lakes) to the lighthouse. There you can see how the lightkeeper lived in this isolated area before the advent of electricity. There's a dining room open in summer. From the lighthouse several short trails lead along the shoreline.

Several galleries are well worth visiting. **Perivale Gallery,** RR no. 2, Spring Bay (☎ 705/377-4847), is the love of Sheila and Bob McMullan, who scour the country searching for the wonderful artists and craftspeople whose work they display in their log cabin/gallery overlooking Lake Kagawong. Glass, sculpture, paintings, engravings, fabrics, and ceramics fill the gallery. From Spring Bay follow Perivale Road East for about two miles; turn right at the lake and keep following the road until you see the gallery on the right. Open daily from 10am to 6pm from the May holiday to mid-September. **Dominion Bay Handcrafts,** Spring Bay (☎ 705/377-4625) sells jewelry, knitwear, and other fashions. From Highway 542 follow the green Hettmann signs down to Dominion Bay.

The island is great for hiking, biking, bird-watching, boating, cross-country skiing, and just plain relaxing. Charters also operate from Meldrun Bay. Golf courses can be found in Mindemoya and Gore Bay. Fishing is excellent either in Georgian Bay or in the island's lakes and streams. If you'd like to book an organized fishing expedition, try **Manitou Fishing Charters** (☎ 705/983-2038 or 705/859-2787) in South Baymouth. A five-hour trip for four persons is $250.

Honora Bay Riding Stables, RR no. 1, Little Current, ON, P0P 1K0 (☎ 705/368-2669), offers trail rides, including an overnight program, from May to October. It's 17 miles west of Little Current on Highway 540.

There are several nature trails on the island. Among the more spectacular are **The Cup and Saucer Trail,** which starts 11 miles (18km) west of Little Current at the junction of Highway 540 and Bidwell Road. Also off Highway 540 lies the trail to **Bridal Veil Falls** as you enter the village of Kagawong.

Halfway between Little Current and Manitowaning, stop at **Ten Mile Point** for the view over the North Channel, which is dotted with 20,000 islands. The best beach with facilities is at **Providence Bay** on the island's south side.

WHERE TO STAY

Your best bet is to seek out one of several bed and breakfasts. The accommodations will most likely be plain and simple, like those at **Hill House,** P.O. Box 360, Gore Bay, ON, P0P 1K0 (☎ 705/282-2072). Otherwise, the very best accommodations on the island can be found at the following.

✪ **Manitowaning Lodge & Tennis Resort.** Box 160, Manitowaning, ON, P0P 1N0. ☎ **705/859-3136.** Fax 705/859-3270. 9 rms, 13 cottages. $115–$160 per person. Lower rate is for standard room; the higher for a one-bedroom cabin with fireplace. Rates include breakfast and dinner. Special tennis packages available. AE, MC, V. Closed Canadian Thanksgiving to second Fri in May.

This idyllic place lacks the pretension of so many ooh-la-la resorts. It consists of a lodge and cottages set on 11 acres of spectacularly landscaped gardens. Artists were employed to create a whimsical, engaging decor with trompe l'oeil painting and furniture that sports hand-painted scenes and designs. The buildings themselves have a delightful rustic air created by their beamed ceilings; in the lodge there's a large fieldstone fireplace with a huge carved mask of the Indian Spirit of Manitowaning looming above. The cottages are comfortably furnished with wicker or painted log furniture, beds with duvets and pillows, dhurries, log tables, and hand-painted furnishings. All have fireplaces. None has a TV or telephone—it's a real retreat.

Dining/Entertainment: The dining room is airy and light. The food features fine local meats like lamb, and, of course, fish. You might find Manitowaning poached trout, smoked loin of pork with plum sauce, or tiger shrimp with coconut couscous. Lunch is served al fresco on the terrace overlooking the water.

Services: Masseur.

Facilities: Four tennis courts with pro; a swimming pool surrounded by a deck and gardens set with chaise longues; a gym; mountain bikes; water sports (canoes, motorboats, and sailboats); and great fishing.

Rock Garden Terrace Resort. RR no. 1, Spring Bay, ON, P0P 2B0. ☎ **705/377-4652.** 18 motel units, 4 chalet suites. TV. Summer and winter $76–$88 per person including breakfast and dinner. Spring and fall rates slightly lower. Weekend and weekly packages available. MC, V.

This typical family resort, located on the rocks above Lake Mindemoya, has a Bavarian flair. Most accommodations are in motel-style units furnished in contemporary style. There are also four log cabin–style suites.

Dining/Entertainment: The dining room seems like an Austrian hunting lodge, with trophies displayed on the oak-paneled walls. The cuisine features German-Austrian specialties like Wiener schnitzel, sauerbraten, goulash, and beef rolladen.

Facilities: A kidney-shaped pool; a whirlpool; a sauna; fitness facilities; a fishing dock; and games like outdoor shuffleboard and chess as well as bicycles, boats, and canoes for rent.

WHERE TO DINE

The island isn't exactly the place for fine dining. For more sophisticated food, go to the **Manitowaning Lodge and Tennis Resort** (☎ 705/859-3136) or the **Rock Garden Terrace Resort** (☎ 705/377-4642), both near Spring Bay. In Little Current, one of the nicest casual spots on the island for breakfast, lunch, or dinner is **The Old English Pantry,** Water Street, Little Current (☎ 705/368-3341). At dinner you'll find a pasta and fish dish of the day as well as English specialties like roast beef and Yorkshire, and baked pot pies, priced from $10.50 to $15. Afternoon cream teas and takeout picnic baskets are available. Open Sunday to Thursday from 9am to 9pm and Friday and Saturday until 11pm (closed Sunday in winter).

5 Along Georgian Bay: Midland, Penetanguishene & Parry Sound

MIDLAND

Midland is the center for cruising through the beautifully scenic thousands of Georgian Islands, and **30,000 Island Cruises** (☎ 705/526-0161) offers 2¹/₂-hour cruises that follow the route of Brûlé, Champlain, and La Salle up through the inside passage to Georgian Bay. From May to Canadian Thanksgiving, boats usually leave the town dock twice a day. Admission is $14 for adults, $13 for seniors, and $7.50 for children 2 to 12.

Midland lies 33 miles east of Barrie and 90 miles north of Toronto. If you're driving from Barrie, take Highway 400 to Highway 12W to Midland.

EXPLORING THE AREA

See the accompanying box for details on **Sainte Marie Among the Hurons.** Across from the Martyrs' Shrine, the **Wye Marsh Wildlife Centre** (☎ 705/526-7809) lets visitors explore (year-round) nature trails and a floating boardwalk that cuts through marsh, field, and woods, where the trumpeter swan is being reintroduced into the country. Special guided canoe trips are available by reservation (☎ 705/526-7809) in July and August. In winter, cross-country skiing and snowshoeing are available. For information, write Highway 12 (P.O. Box 100), Midland, ON, L4R 4K6. Admission is $6 adults, $4 students and seniors; free for children under 3. Open Victoria Day (late May) to September 4 daily 10am to 6pm; other months daily 10am to 4pm.

In town, **Freda's,** located in an elegant home at 342 King St. (☎ 705/526-4851), serves continental cuisine, with main courses priced from $15 to $28. You can choose from a variety of meat and seafood dishes—surf-and-turf, beef stroganoff, chicken Kiev, veal cordon bleu, coquilles St-Jacques, and more.

EN ROUTE TO THE MUSKOKA LAKES: ORILLIA

En route to the Muskoka lakeland region, you will probably pass through Orillia, where you can visit Canadian author/humorist **Stephen Leacock's house** (☎ 705/326-9357), a green-and-white mansard-roofed and turreted structure with a central balcony overlooking the beautiful lawns and garden that sweep down to the lake. The interior is filled with heavy Victorian furniture reflecting the period when Leacock lived and worked here. Admission is $5 for adults, $4.50 for seniors, $2 for students, and 50¢ for children five to 13. Open from the end of June to Labor Day from 10am to 7pm daily; by appointment only in other months.

If you're driving from Barrie, take Highway 11 to Orillia. If you're hungry, head north on Highway 11, keeping a lookout for **Paul Weber's** hamburger place at the side of the road (☎ 705/325-3696). Here, you can get a real burger with real french fries from $3. I heartily recommend it. Take a breather and sit out under the trees at the picnic tables provided.

PENETANGUISHENE

This town on Georgian Bay is home to the **Discovery Harbour,** a reconstructed 19th-century British outpost, complete with a fleet of schooners and costumed sailors and soldiers. Today visitors enjoy horse-drawn wagon rides along the shoreline

The Tragic Tale of Sainte Marie Among the Hurons

Midland's history dates from 1639, when the Jesuits established a fortified mission, Sainte Marie Among the Hurons, to bring the word of God to the Huron tribe. However, the mission retreat flourished only for a decade, for the Iroquois, jealous of the Huron-French trading relationship, increased their attacks. By the late 1640s, the Iroquois had killed thousands of Hurons, several priests, and destroyed two villages within six miles of Sainte Marie. Eventually the Jesuits burned down their own mission and fled with the Hurons to Christian Island, about 20 miles away. But the winter of 1649 was harsh: Thousands of Hurons died, leaving only a few Jesuits and 300 Hurons to straggle back to Québec from whence they had come. Their mission had ended in martyrdom. It was 100 years before the Native Canadians saw whites again, and then they spoke a different language.

Today local history is recaptured at the mission (☎ 705-526-7838), 5 miles east of Midland on Highway 12 (follow the Huronia Heritage signs). The blacksmith stokes his forge, the carpenter squares a beam with a broadax, and the ringing church bell calls the missionaries to prayer, while a canoe enters the fortified water gate. A film also depicts the life of the missionaries. Special programs given in July and August include candlelight tours and also a 1 1/2-hour canoeing trip (at extra cost). Admission is $7.25 adults, $4.50 students, $3 seniors; free for children under 6. Open Mid-May to October daily 10am to 5pm, weekdays only off-season, and closed December and January.

Just east of Midland on Highway 12 rise the twin spires of the **Martyrs' Shrine** (☎ 705/526-3788), a memorial to the eight North American martyr saints. As six were missionaries at Sainte Marie, this imposing church was built on the hill overlooking the mission, and thousands make a pilgrimage here each year. The bronzed outdoor stations of the cross were imported from France. Admission is $2 adults, free for children 15 and under. Open mid-May to mid-October daily 8:30am to 9pm.

and visits to authentically furnished residences and workshops. Evening and afternoon excursions aboard the HMS Schooner *Bee* take sailors out into Georgian Bay for hands-on sail training. Visitors are also invited to row in a 19th-century-style gig out to the site of the sunken *Newash,* sister ship of the *Bee.*

The **Stage Company,** Box 516, Midland, ON (☎ 705/549-4221), presents a full summer of professional theater at the King's Wharf Theatre. Open from May 22 to Labor Day from 10am to 5pm with last admission at 4:15pm. Admission is $5.75 for adults, $3.50 for students, and $3.25 for seniors. Follow Highway 400 to 93. Take 93 north to Penetanguishene. Turn right at the water and follow the ship logo.

A SIDE TRIP TO GEORGIAN BAY ISLAND NATIONAL PARK

The park consists of 59 islands in Georgian Bay and can be reached via boat from Honey Harbour, a town north of Midland right on the shore. (As you're taking Highway 69 north, branch off to the west at Port Severn to reach Honey Harbour.) Hiking, swimming, fishing, and boating are the name of the game in the park. In summer, the boaters really do take over—if you're looking for a quiet retreat, look elsewhere. The park's center is located on the largest island, Beausoleil, which also has camping and other facilities. For more information call or write the Superintendent, Georgian Bay Islands National Park, Box 28, Honey Harbour, ON, P0E 1E0 (☎ 705/756-2415).

WHERE TO STAY

Chez Vous Chez Nous Couette et Cafe. RR no. 3 (in Lafontaine), Penetang, ON, L0K 1P0.
☎ **705/533-2237.** 7 rms. $65 double. Rates include breakfast. No credit cards.

Georgette Robitaille takes care of the accommodations at this 50-acre working farm where she decorated all seven rooms in different color schemes, often featuring her own art. Singles, doubles, and twins are available. There's a separate entrance to the guest rooms, which are incredibly clean and well kept. Georgette is a fine baker and caters locally, so her breakfasts are excellent and pleasantly presented. Dinners are available on request.

THE PARRY SOUND AREA

Only 140 miles north of Toronto and 100 south of Sudbury, the Parry Sound area is the place for active vacations. For information contact the **Parry Sound Area Chamber of Commerce** (☎ 705/746-4213 or the information center at 705/378-5105).

There's excellent canoeing and kayaking; if you need an outfitter, contact **White Squall,** RR no. 1, Nobel, ON, P0G 1G0 (☎ 705/342-5324), which offers both day trips and multiday excursions.

The *Island Queen* cruises through the 30,000 islands for three hours. It leaves the town dock once or twice a day and charges $15 adults, $7.50 for children. For information contact **30,000 Island Cruise Lines,** 9 Bay St., Parry Sound, ON, P2A 1S4 (☎ 705/746-2311).

And there are many winter diversions as well—including loads of cross-country ski trails and more than 650 miles (1,000km) of well-groomed snowmobiling trails. For additional information on cross-country skiing contact the **Georgian Nordic Ski and Canoe Club,** Box 42, Parry Sound, ON, P2A 2X2, which permits day use of their ski trails.

KILLBEAR PROVINCIAL PARK

Nature lovers will head for **Killbear Provincial Park,** P.O. Box 71, Nobel, ON, P0G 1G0 (☎ 705/342-5492), farther north up Highway 69; it offers 4,000 glorious acres set in the middle of 30,000 islands. There are plenty of water sports—swimming at a 1.9-mile (3km) beach on Georgian Bay, snorkeling or diving off Harold Point, and fishing for lake trout, walleye, perch, pike, and bass. The climate is moderated by the bay and explains why trillium, wild leek, and hepatica bloom. Among the more unusual fauna are the Blandings and Map turtles that inhabit the bogs, swamps, and marshes.

There are three **hiking trails.** Lookout Point (2.2 miles/3¹/₂ km) leads to a commanding view over Blind Bay to Parry Sound; the Lighthouse Point Trail crosses rocks and pebble beaches to the lighthouse at the peninsula's southern tip. There's also **camping** at 883 sites in seven campgrounds.

WHERE TO STAY

The inn listed below is exquisite and expensive, but there are other places to stay in the area. Contact the **Parry Sound and District Bed and Breakfast Association,** P.O. Box 71, Parry Sound, ON, P2A 2X2, for its accommodations listings, priced from $50 to $60 double. There's also a **Journey's End,** 112 Bowes St. (☎ 705/746-6221) and a modest, family oriented **Resort Tapatoo,** Box 384, Parry Sound, ON, P2A 2X5 (☎ 705/378-2208), located at the edge of Otter Lake, which rents cottages, rooms, and suites, and offers boating, windsurfing, waterskiing, canoeing, fishing, and swimming in an indoor pool. Rates range from $72 to $100 including breakfast and dinner.

✪ **Inn at Manitou.** McKellar, ON, P0G 1C0 ☎ **705/389-2171.** Fax 705/389-3818. 32 rms, 1 three-bedroom country house. A/C TEL. July–Aug $209–$319 midweek, $219–$329 weekends; June and Sept $189–$269 midweek, $209–$289 weekends; May and Oct $169–$229 midweek, $189–$249 weekends. All rates are per person per day based on double occupancy and include breakfast, lunch, and dinner. A variety of special packages available. Special musical, cooking, and other events scheduled. AE, ER, MC, V. Closed late Oct–early May.

The Inn at Manitou is simply spectacular, although some folks may find this spa and tennis resort just too perfect. Everything about the foyer glows; the space is luxuriously furnished in Franco-Oriental style. Beyond the foyer and a sitting area, a veranda stretches around the building's rear with wicker and bamboo chairs overlooking the tennis courts. To the foyer's left is the very inviting Tea Room with a view of the lake. A steep staircase leads down to the swimming and boating dock.

The accommodations are up the hill in several cedar lodges overlooking the lake— the setting is beautiful. Standard rooms are small and simple; deluxe units contain fireplaces, small sitting areas, and private sundecks, while the luxury rooms each feature a sizable living room with a fireplace, whirlpool bath, sauna, and private deck.

Dining/Entertainment: Downstairs in the main building you'll find the Club Lounge nightclub, a billiard room, and the open-to-view wine cellar, filled with fine vintages, where twice-weekly wine tastings are held. The resort's cuisine is renowned, too, and part of the reason the Relais and Châteaux organization awarded the property the distinguished Gold Shield. At dinner a casual three-course bistro menu and a more elaborate five-course gourmet menu is offered along with a special spa menu. Afterwards, guests can retire to the Tea Room for coffee, petit fours, and truffles.

Facilities: The spa facilities, in a separate building, offer a full range of body treatments, including herbal and mud wraps, massage therapy, and fitness activities. Other amenities include a swimming pool, 13 tennis courts (with 10 professional staff members), mountain bikes, sailboats, canoes, Windsurfers, and exercise equipment, plus pitch-and-putt facilities and an instructional golfing range.

6 The Muskoka Lakes

To settlers coming north in the 1850s, this region, with its 1,600-plus lakes north of the Severn River, presented peculiar problems. It was impossible to farm and difficult to traverse.

But even back then the wilderness attracted sportspeople and adventurers, like John Campbell and James Bain, who explored the three major lakes—Rosseau, Joseph, and Muskoka. They later started the Muskoka Club, purchased an island in Lake Joseph, and began annual excursions to the district. Roads were difficult to cut and waterways became the main transportation routes. It wasn't until the late 1800s that a fleet of steamers was running on the lakes and the railway arrived. Muskoka was then finally effectively linked by water and rail to the urban centers in the south.

The area was wired for tourism. Some folks gambled that people would pay to travel to the wilderness if they were wined and dined once they got there. The idea caught on and grand hotels like Clevelands House, Windermere House, and Deerhurst were opened, to name a few that have survived to this day. The lakes became the enclave of the well-to-do from Ontario and the United States. By 1903 there were eight big lake steamers, countless steam launches, and supply boats (floating grocery stores) serving a flourishing resort area.

And it continues today, even though the advent of the car ended the era of the steamboats and grand hotels. The rich are still here, but so are many families in their summer cottages and sophisticated young professionals from Toronto. While many

The Muskoka Lakes   495

resorts don't look so impressive from the road, just take a look at the other side and remember that they were built for steamship approach.

In the fall Muskoka has dazzling scenery. To celebrate its autumn beauty nearly all of Muskoka's towns stage fall fairs and other festivals. This is an especially good time to drive the Algonquin Route, that section of Highway 60 from the west gate to the east gate of Algonquin Park, known as the Frank MacDougall Parkway.

ESSENTIALS

VISITOR INFORMATION   For information on the region, contact **Muskoka Tourism,** on Highway 11 at Severn Bridge, RR no. 2, Kilworthy, ON, P0E 1G0 (☎ 705/689-0660).

GETTING THERE   You can drive from the south via Highway 400 to Highway 11, from the east via Highways 12 and 169 to Highway 11, and from the north via Highway 11. It's about 100 miles (160km) from Toronto to Gravenhurst, 9 miles (15km) from Gravenhurst to Bracebridge, 15^1/$_2$ miles (25km) from Bracebridge to Port Carling, and 21 miles (34km) from Bracebridge to Huntsville.

VIA Rail (☎ 800/361-3677) services Gravenhurst, Bracebridge, and Huntsville from Toronto's Union Station.

MUSKOKA BED-AND-BREAKFAST   If you don't want to pay resort rates or restrict yourself to staying at an American Plan resort, contact the **Muskoka Bed and Breakfast Association,** 175 Clairmont Rd., Gravenhurst, ON, P1P 1H9 (☎ 705/687-4511), which represents 28 or so bed-and-breakfasts throughout the area. Prices range from $45 to $70 double.

GRAVENHURST

Gravenhurst is the Muskoka's first town—the first you reach if you're driving from Toronto and the first to achieve town status (in 1887 at the height of the logging boom).

The **Norman Bethune Memorial House** is the restored 1890 birthplace of Dr. Norman Bethune, at 235 John St. (☎ 705/687-4261). In 1939 this surgeon, inventor, and humanitarian died tending the sick in China during the Chinese Revolution. Tours of the historic house include a modern exhibit on Bethune's life. A visitor center displays gifts from Chinese visitors and an orientation video is shown. The house is open daily in summer from 10am-noon and 1 to 5pm; weekdays only in winter. Admission is $2.25 adults, $1.75 seniors, $1.25 children 6 to 16.

You can also cruise aboard the old steamship **RMS *Segwun*** (1887), which leaves from Gravenhurst, Port Carling, and also Windermere. Aboard you'll find two lounges and a dining salon. The cruises on the lake vary from two hours (from $17.25) to a full day's outing ($47.50). For information, call ☎ 705/687-6667. Cruises operate from mid-June to mid-October.

Gravenhurst and Port Carling are home to the **Muskoka Festival.** A series of summer theater performances are given in the Gravenhurst Opera House (☎ 705/687-2762) and Port Carling Memorial Hall (☎ 705/765-3209). Tickets range from $10 to $22 for adults. For more information, contact the Muskoka Festival, P.O. Box 1055, Gravenhurst, ON, P1P 1X2 (☎ 705/687-7741).

WHERE TO STAY

Muskoka Sands. Muskoka Beach Road, Gravenhurst, ON, P1P 1R1. ☎ **705/687-2233.** Fax 705/687-7474. 76 rms and suites. A/C TV TEL. Summer $180–$325 double. MAP rates also available. AE, DC, ER, MC, V. From Highway 11 north take Gravenhurst Exit 169 (Bethune Drive) to Winewood Avenue and turn left. Then turn right onto Muskoka Beach Road for three miles.

In this large modern resort on Lake Muskoka, you'll stay either in the lodge or in a series of buildings scattered on the property. The rooms are handsomely furnished and the suites are luxurious, each with fully equipped kitchen, living room with fireplace, private deck, and bathroom with glass-brick accents and oval tub.

Dining/Entertainment: The dining room serves continental cuisine; Steamer Jakes is the downstairs dance bar. The Boathouse has an outdoor cafe deck.

Facilities: A nicely landscaped outdoor pool, indoor pool, whirlpool, sauna, fitness room, games room, children's program (in July and August), squash and tennis courts, and waterfront sports.

Severn River Inn. Cowbell Lane off Highway 11 (P.O. Box 44), Severn Bridge, ON, P0E 1N0. ☎ **705/689-6333.** 10 rms (all with shower), 2 suites. A/C. $75 double. Rates include breakfast. MC, V.

The Severn River Inn (12 miles north of Orillia and 9 miles south of Gravenhurst) is located in a 1906 building, which has served as the local general store, post office, telephone exchange, and boardinghouse. The rooms are individually furnished with pine and oak pieces, brass beds, flounce pillows, lace curtains, and quilts. The suite contains a sitting room and the original old bathtub and pedestal sink.

Dining/Entertainment: The intimate restaurant, with a Victorian ambience, is candlelit at night. In summer the screened-in porch overlooking the river is a favored dining spot. The menu features contemporary continental cuisine, with dishes priced from $11 to $19. The dining room is open Wednesday through Sunday from noon to 3pm and 5:30 to 9pm; closed Thanksgiving to May 1. The lounge, in what was originally the general store, offers light meals.

Camping

Gravenhurst Reay Park and KOA Campground, RR no. 3, Gravenhurst, ON, P0C 1G0 (☎ 705/687-2333), has 750 acres of pine trees and meadows, plus a trout pond, two swimming pools, store, heated washrooms, hot showers, and laundry facilities. The 185 sites cost $18 for two people for an unserviced lot, plus $2.50 for electricity, $3 for electricity and water, or $4 more for a site with electricity, water, and sewer hookups. Extra people over 17 pay $5. For recreation there's a nine-hole golf course, hiking trails, horseshoe pits, minigolf, and boats for rent. Sites have fireplaces and picnic tables. The campground is located between Gravenhurst and Bracebridge off Highway 11. In winter, try the 10$^1/_2$ miles (17km) of groomed cross-country ski trails.

WHERE TO DINE

Ascona Place. Bethune Drive. ☎ 705/687-5906. Reservations recommended. Main courses $16–$21. AE, ER, MC, V. Summer daily 11:30am–2pm and 5–9pm. Closed Wed in other seasons. FRENCH/CONTINENTAL.

Named after a small picturesque village in southern Switzerland, Ascona Place offers a pretty courtyard for outside dining in July and August. The menu features classic continental cuisine plus one or two Swiss specialties, such as an émincé of veal Swiss-style in white wine and cream sauce with mushrooms. You may either dine in the wine cellar, a cozy nook hung with wine bottles, or in the larger Ascona Room, hung with Swiss banners, wicker lampshades, and a set of Swiss cow bells. Desserts are exquisite—double chocolate mousse cake, apple strudel, homemade meringues and sorbets, or an iced soufflé with French Marc de Bourgogne (all around $5).

BRACEBRIDGE: SANTA'S WORKSHOP

On the 45th parallel, Bracebridge is halfway between the equator and the North Pole and the community bills itself as Santa's summer home—and **Santa's Village**

(☎ 705/645-2512), a must for kids from two to 70, is here to prove it. This imaginatively designed fantasyland is full of delights—pedal boats and bumper boats on the lagoon, a roller coaster sleigh ride, a Candy Cane Express, carousel and Ferris wheel. At Elves' Island kids can crawl on a suspended net and over or through various modules—the Lunch Bag Forest, Cave Crawl, and Snake Tube Crawl. Rides, water attractions, roving entertainers are all part of the fun. Santa's Village is open mid-June to Labor Day only, daily from 10am to 6pm. Admission is $14 for adults, $9 for seniors and children two to four, and free for children under two.

The Bracebridge area has a few outstanding resorts.

WHERE TO STAY & DINE

✪ Inn at the Falls. 17 Dominion St., Bracebridge, ON, P1L 1R6. ☎ **705/645-2245.** Fax 705/645-5093. 33 rms, suites, and cottages. A/C TV TEL. $82–$195 double. Rates include breakfast. AE, MC, V.

This attractive inn occupies a Victorian house on a quiet street overlooking Bracebridge Falls. The inviting gardens are filled with delphiniums, peonies, roses, and spring flowers, plus there's an outdoor heated pool. Each room is individually decorated, with antiques and English chintz. Some units have fireplaces; others have views of the falls.

Dining/Entertainment: The Fox and Hounds is a popular local gathering place at lunch or dinner. In the winter the fire crackles and snaps, but in the summer the terrace is filled with flowers and umbrellaed tables. There's also the more elegant Victoria's, for upscale continental fare.

Patterson Kaye Lodge. Golden Beach Road (off Highway 118), RR no. 1, Bracebridge, ON, P0B 1C0. ☎ **705/645-4169.** Fax 705/645-5720. 30 rms. TV. High season $575–$725 per person per week, depending on the type of accommodation. Rates include breakfast and dinner. Special weekend packages available, and also special reductions during certain weeks. European plan only winter and spring $100–$135. AE, MC, V.

For a secluded, casual lodge, ideal for families, Patterson Kaye Lodge fits the bill. Located on Lake Muskoka 3 miles west of town, the main lodge has a variety of rooms, while cottages of various sizes accommodating a total of 100 people are scattered around the property.

Facilities: Free waterskiing with instruction is run from the dock; there's a hot tub, two tennis courts, and a number of organized activities. Of course, there's plenty of fishing, golf, and riding nearby, and use of canoes, sailboats, and Windsurfers is free. You can rent boats as well.

Tamwood Resort. Highway 118, RR no. 1, Bracebridge, ON, P1L 1WB. ☎ **705/645-5172** or 800/465-9166. 35 rms. A/C MINIBAR TV TEL. Three-night package $285–$359 per person; weekly rates $592–$750 per person. Special discount weeks available. AE, MC, V.

A great choice for families, Tamwood Lodge is a moderate-size log lodge on Lake Muskoka, 6 miles west of town. The air-conditioned main lodge has 35 units, all simply but nicely decorated, and there are a few cottages. The four deluxe loft accommodations are stunningly appointed in pine and feature two bedrooms with skylight, plus a loft area, two bathrooms, an efficiency kitchen, and a living room with Franklin stove and balcony from which you can dive into Lake Muskoka. Three new waterfront units come complete with fireplaces. Knotty-pine furnishings and large granite fireplaces imbue the lounge and main dining room with character.

Facilities: Indoor and outdoor swimming, fishing, tennis, volleyball, badminton, and shuffleboard, plus free waterskiing, sailing, and boating, and all the winter sports imaginable. There's also lots of organized family fun—such as baseball games, marshmallow roasts, and bingo. Kids are also supervised and there's a games room too.

PORT CARLING

As waterways became the main means of transportation in the region, Port Carling became, and still is, the hub of the lakes. It became a boat-building center when a lock was installed connecting Lakes Muskoka and Rosseau, and a canal between Lakes Rosseau and Joseph opened all three to navigation. The **Muskoka Lakes Museum** (☎ 705/765-5367) captures the flavor of this era. It's open Monday to Saturday 10am to 5pm, Sunday noon to 4pm from June to Canadian Thanksgiving (U.S. Columbus Day), closed Monday and Tuesday in September. Admission is $2.25 for adults, $1.25 for seniors and students.

WHERE TO STAY

Clevelands House. Minett P.O., near Port Carling, ON, P0B 1G0. ☎ **705/765-3171**. Fax 705/765-6296. Accommodates up to 450 people in 86 rooms, 21 suites, 30 bungalows, and several cottages. A/C TV TEL. $135–$175 per person per night, $800–$1,000 per person per week. Cottages rent for a $3,500 minimum weekly rate. Rates depend on the number of people in the room and the type of accommodation. Rates include all meals. Special family week off-season discounts and packages available. AE, MC, V.

The very name Clevelands House has a gracious ring to it, and indeed this resort has been providing the ultimate in luxury since 1869. Much larger than the hostelries I recommended in nearby Bracebridge, it is very much a full-facility resort. The lodge is a magnificent clapboard structure with a veranda that runs around the lakeside giving views over the well-kept flower gardens. There's a dance floor set out on the dock with a sun deck on top. Accommodations vary in size and location and have solid old-fashioned furniture; the luxury suites, though, are supermodern, with private sundecks.

   Facilities: Sixteen tennis, 4 shuffleboard, and 3 badminton courts; a nine-hole golf course; a huge children's playground and other activities; heated outdoor swimming pool; fitness center, and good fishing, swimming, boating, and waterskiing on Lake Rosseau.

Sherwood Inn. P.O. Box 400, Lake Joseph, Port Carling, ON, P0B 1J0. ☎ **705/765-3131**. Fax 705/765-6668. 30 rms. $149–$186 double in the inn; $168–$232 per person double in cottages; $149–$186 in the inn. Rates based on double occupancy and include breakfast and dinner. Special packages available. AE, ER, MC, V. From Highway 400, take Highway 69 north to Foot's Bay. Turn right and take 169 south to Sherwood Road. Turn left just before the junction of Highway 118. Or you can arrive via Gravenhurst and Bala or Bracebridge and Port Carling.

Accommodations here are either in the lodge or in beachside cottages. The latter are very appealing, with fieldstone fireplaces, comfortable armchairs, TVs, telephones, and screened porches overlooking the lake. Some are more luxurious than others and have additional features like VCRs or private docks. The older rooms in the lodge feature painted wood paneling while the newer wing has air-conditioning and the rooms are furnished with wicker.

✪ **Windermere House.** Off Muskoka Route 4 (P.O. Box 68), Windermere, ON, P0B 1P0. ☎ **705/769-3611** or 800/461-4283. Fax 705/769-2168. 78 rms. TEL. $90–$120 per person per night; unit with fireplace, fridge, TV, and private deck $130–$160 per person per night. Rates include breakfast and dinner. Rates decrease about $10 during the week. Weekly rates and European Plan also available. AE, ER, MC, V.

This striking stone-and-clapboard turreted building overlooks lawns that sweep down to Lake Rosseau. Originally built in 1864, it was renovated in 1986. Out front stretches a long, broad veranda furnished with Adirondack chairs and geranium-filled window boxes. Rooms are variously furnished, with some in the main house and others in cottages and buildings scattered around the property. Some rooms have air-conditioning, some only overhead fans. All have private bath and are furnished in modern style, some with a bamboo/rattan look.

Dining/Entertainment: Open to the public, the dining room offers fine modern continental cuisine. There's nightly entertainment in the lounge.

Services: Room service (7am to 10pm), plus there's laundry/dry cleaning. A full children's program is offered during July and August.

Facilities: Outdoor swimming pool, tennis courts, golf, and all kinds of water sports (fishing, windsurfing, sailing).

HUNTSVILLE

Since the late 1800s lumber has been the name of the game in Huntsville, and today it's Muskoka's biggest town, with major manufacturing companies.

Some of the region's early history can be reviewed at the **Muskoka Pioneer Village and Museum** (☎ 705/789-7576), open June to Canadian Thanksgiving (U.S. Columbus Day), in summer from 10am to 4pm, in fall from 11am to 4pm, or by a visit to Brunel Locks in nearby Brunel. Admission is $6 for adults, $3 for seniors, $2.75 for students and children; under five free.

Robinson's General Store (☎ 705/766-2415) in Dorset is so popular it was voted Canada's best country store. Wood stoves, dry goods, hardware, pine goods, and moccasins—you name it, it's here.

WHERE TO STAY

Blue Spruce Inn. On Highway 60 (RR no. 1), Dwight, ON, P0A 1H0. ☎ **705/635-2330.** 10 motel rms, 15 cottages. TV. High season (summer, all weekends, Christmas, and Easter) $75–$90 per night, $430–$520 per week motel; $99 per night, $544 per week one-bedroom cottage; $125 per night, $725 per week two-bedroom cottage; $153–$175 per night, $860–$920 per week three-bedroom cottage. Off-season rates reduced about 15%. AE, MC, V.

On the fringes of Algonquin Provincial Park, the Blue Spruce Inn, 20 miles northeast of Huntsville, has nicely kept motel suites with separate kitchen areas, and cottages with wood-burning fireplaces. The lodge has a cozy lounge and games rooms. There's a beach with boating, a sun deck at the lake, and two tennis courts. In winter there's cross-country skiing, a large natural skating rink, toboggan hill, and snowmobiling for recreation.

Cedar Grove Lodge. P.O. Box 996, Huntsville, ON, P0A 1K0. ☎ **705/789-4036.** Fax 705/789-6860. 8 rms (none with bath), 19 cabins. $80–$120 per person. Rates include all meals. Weekly rates and special packages available. AE, MC, V. Take Grassmere Resort Road, off Highway 60.

On Peninsula Lake, 7$^1/_2$ miles (12km) from Huntsville, Cedar Grove Lodge is a very attractive and well-maintained resort. The main lodge contains eight rooms sharing three bathrooms; the rest of the accommodations are one-, two-, or three-bedroom log cabins like the Hermit Thrush, which contains pine furnishings, a fieldstone fireplace, a porch overlooking the lake, bar/sink and refrigerator, and conveniently stored firewood; or the Chickadee, a smaller version of the same for two only. The main lodge contains a comfortable large sitting room with stone fireplace, TV, and piano, along with the pretty lakeside dining room.

Facilities: Two tennis courts, a hot tub, kid's beach, and games room. There's free waterskiing, plus sailboarding, canoeing, and windsurfing for an extra charge; cross-country skiing and skating on the lake are offered in winter.

✪ **Deerhurst Resort.** RR no. 4, Huntsville, ON, P0A 1K0. ☎ **705/789-6411** or 800/441-1414. Fax 705/789-2431. 370 rms and suites. A/C TV TEL. $160–$240 double; $239–$550

suite. Extra person $25. AE, CB, DC, DISC, ER, MC, V. Take Canal Road off Highway 60 to
Deerhurst Road.

Catering to well-heeled families and now a slick, mainly Toronto crowd, the
Deerhurst Inn originally opened in 1896, but over the last decade it has expanded
rapidly, scattering building units all over the property. It's located on 800 acres of
rolling landscape fronting on Peninsula Lake. The guest rooms range from hotel
rooms in the Terrace and Bayshore buildings to fully appointed one-, two-, or three-
bedroom suites, many with fireplaces and/or whirlpool. These suites come fully
equipped with all the comforts of home, including stereos, TVs, and VCRs; some
have fully functioning kitchens complete with microwaves, dishwashers, and washer/
dryers. The most expensive suites are three-bedroom units on the lake.

Dining/Entertainment: The main lodge features a lounge with a massive stone
fireplace and comfortable furnishings. The adjacent dining room offers romantic
dining overlooking the lake (prices at dinner from $20 to $30), while the Piano
Lounge and Cypress Bar provide a chic environment. Live entertainment highlights
include a Las Vegas stage show and a comedy show, plus entertainment in the Piano Lounge, and also at Steamers Restaurant.

Facilities: The indoor sports complex has four tennis courts, three squash courts,
one racquetball court, an indoor pool, a whirlpool and sauna, and a full-service spa.
Outdoor facilities include a pool, eight tennis courts, a beach, canoes, kayaks, sailboats, paddleboats, waterskiing, windsurfing, horseback riding, and two 18-hole golf
courses. The full winter program includes on-site cross-country skiing, snowmobiling,
dog-sledding, and downhill skiing at nearby Hidden Valley Highlands. A children's
activity program operates during the summer and on weekends year-round.

✪ Grandview Inn. RR no. 4, Huntsville, ON, P0A 1K0. ☎ **705/789-4417.** Fax 705/
789-6882. 200 rms. A/C TV TEL. $150–$270 in high season. Packages available. Children 18
and under stay free in parents' room. AE, ER, MC, V.

If Deerhurst is for the folks on the fast track, the Grandview Inn has a more measured pace. This smaller resort retains the natural beauty and contours of the
original farmstead even while providing the latest in resort facilities. Eighty
accommodations are traditional hotel-style rooms, but most units are suites located
in a series of buildings, some right down beside the lake, others up on the hill with
a lake view. All are spectacularly furnished. Each executive suite contains a kitchen,
a dining area, a living room with a fireplace and access to an outside deck, a
large bedroom, and a large bathroom with a whirlpool bath.

Dining/Entertainment: The Mews contains a reception area, a comfortable
lounge/entertainment room furnished with sofas and wingbacks, and conference
facilities. The main dining room, located in the original old farmhouse, is decorated
in paisleys and English chintz, and has an inviting patio with an awning overlooking the gardens. Snacks are also served in summer at the Dockside Restaurant
right on the lake, and at the golf clubhouse year-round.

Facilities: Outdoor and indoor pools, a nine-hole golf course, two outdoor tennis
courts and one indoor, exercise room, waterskiing, windsurfing, sailing, canoeing,
and cross-country skiing. Mountain bikes are also available, and boat cruises are offered aboard a yacht. Nature trails cross the property and a resident naturalist leads
guided walks.

Hidden Valley Resort Hotel. Hidden Valley Road (RR no. 4; off Highway 60), Huntsville, ON,
P0A 1K0. ☎ **705/789-2301.** Fax 705/789-6586. 93 rms. A/C TV TEL. From $90–$115 double;
from $130 suite. Extra person $15. Children under 18 stay free in parents' room. AE, CB, DC,
DISC, ER, MC, V.

On a sheltered bay on Peninsula Lake, the Hidden Valley offers rooms with views over the lakes to crimson hills in fall. Its name, though, is misleading because many rooms are motel-type accommodations. The resort has a series of lakeside condominiums that can be rented usually for several nights only. The one- to four-bedroom condos have fully equipped kitchens, wood-burning fireplaces, and large decks. There's a dining room and lounges.

Facilities: The hotel is located right at the base of a mountain that offers three chair lifts, a T-bar and rope tow, and 10 slopes. Snowmobiling and cross-country skiing are also available. Facilities include an indoor and an outdoor pool, a sauna, four tennis courts, one racquetball and two squash courts, a dock, sailing instruction, windsurfing, and boat rentals.

Pow-Wow Point Lodge Six miles east of Huntsville on Highway 60 (Box 387, RR no. 4), Huntsville, ON, P0A 1K0. ☎ **705/789-4951.** Fax 705/789-7123. 27 rms. High season $105 per person double; off-season $85 per person. Rates include all meals. Weekly rates and other packages available. MC, V.

The accommodations at this small year-round family resort range from pine cottages and chalets (without TVs or phones, thank goodness) and motel-type rooms overlooking Peninsula Lake and Hidden Valley. The lodge itself has television in the main fireplace lounge, a recreation room, and a deck overlooking the lake.

Facilities: Indoor pool, tennis court, shuffleboard, a beach, fishing boats, boat cruises, and 7^1/₂ miles (12km) of cross-country ski trails. Golf, horseback riding, and alpine skiing are nearby.

7 Algonquin Provincial Park

Immediately east of Muskoka lie Algonquin Park's 3,000 square miles of wilderness— a haven for the naturalist, camper, and fishing and sports enthusiast. It's an especially memorable destination for the canoeist, with more than 1,000 miles of canoe routes available for paddling. One of Canada's largest provincial parks, it served as one source of inspiration for the famous Group of Seven artists. A sanctuary for moose, beaver, bear, and deer, Algonquin Park offers camping, canoeing, backpacking trails, and plenty of fishing for speckled, rainbow, and lake trout, and small-mouth black bass (more than 230 lakes have native brook trout and 149 have lake trout).

There are eight **campgrounds** along Highway 60. The most secluded sites are found at Canisbay (248 sites), and Pog Lake (281 sites). Two Rivers and Rock Lake have the least secluded sites; the rest are average. In addition, four remote wilderness campgrounds are set back in the interior: Rain Lake with only 10 sites; Kiosk (17 sites) on Lake Kioshkokwi; Brent (28 sites) on Cedar Lake, which is great for pickerel fishing; and Achray (39 sites), the most remote site on Grand Lake where Tom Thomson painted many of his great landscapes. The scene that inspired his Jack Pine is a short walk south of the campground.

Among the **hiking trails** is the 1^1/₂-mile self-guided trail to the 325-foot-deep Barron Canyon on the park's east side. In addition, there are 16 day trails. The shortest is the **Hardwood Lookout Trail,** which goes through the forest to a fine view of Smoke Lake and the surrounding hills. Other short walks are the **Spruce Bog Boardwalk** and the **Beaver Pond Trail,** a 1.2-mile (2km) walk with good views of two beaver ponds.

For longer backpacking trips, the **Highland Trail** extends from Pewee Lake to Head, Harness, and Mosquito Lakes for a round trip of 22 miles. The **Western Uplands Hiking Trail** combines three loops for a total of 105 miles beginning at the Oxtongue River Picnic Grounds on Highway 60. The first 20-mile loop will take three days; the second and third loops take longer.

There's also a **mountain bike** trail.

Fall is a great time to visit—the maples usually peak in the last week of September. Winter is wonderful too; visitors can **cross-country ski** on 49.6 miles (80km) of trails. Three trails lie along the Highway 60 corridor with loops ranging from 3.1 miles (5km) to 14.9 miles (24km). Mew Lake Campground is open in winter, and skis can be rented at the west gate. Spring offers the best **trout fishing** and great **moose viewing** in May and June. During summer, the park is most crowded, but it's also when park staff lead expeditions to hear the **timber wolves** howling in response to naturalists' imitations.

More than 250 **bird species** have been recorded in the park including the rare gray jay, spruce grouse, and many varieties of warbler. The most famous bird is the common loon, which is found nesting on nearly every lake.

Information centers are located at both the west and east gates of the park, plus there's a super **Visitor Centre** (☎ 613/637-2828), about 26.7 miles (43km) from the west gate and 6.1 miles (10km) from the east gate, which houses exhibits on the park's flora and fauna and history. It also has a restaurant, bookstore and theater. Visitors can sign up here for conducted walks and canoe outings.

For additional information contact the park at P.O. Box 219, Whitney, ON, K0J 2M0 (☎ 705/633-5572).

WHERE TO STAY

✪ **Arowhon Pines.** Algonquin Park, ON, P0A 1B0. ☎ **705/633-5661** in summer, 416/ 483-4393 in winter. Fax 705/633-5795 in summer, 416/483-4429 in winter. 50 rms. From $160 daily, $900 weekly, per person, double occupancy in standard accommodations. Rates include all meals. V. Closed mid-Oct to mid-May.

Arowhon Pines has to be one of the most enchanting places I have ever visited. Operated by a delightful couple, Eugene and Helen Kates, it's located 8 miles off Highway 60 down a dirt road, so you're guaranteed total seclusion, quiet, and serenity. Cabins are dotted throughout the pine forests that surround the lake. Each is furnished differently with assorted Canadian pine antiques, and each varies in layout, although they all have bedrooms with private baths, and sitting rooms with fireplaces. You can opt either for a private cottage or for one that contains anywhere from two to 12 bedrooms and shares a communal sitting room with a stone fireplace. Sliding doors lead onto a deck. There are no TVs and no telephones—just the sound of the loons, the gentle lap of the water, the croaking of the frogs, and the sound of oar paddles cutting the smooth surface of the lake.

Dining/Entertainment: At the heart of the resort is a hexagonal dining room set down beside the lake with a spacious veranda. A huge fireplace is at the room's center. Helen and Eugene are extremely gracious hosts and pay close attention to the details so that everything is artfully done, right down to the bark menus at mealtimes. The food is good, with fresh ingredients, and plenty of it. No alcohol is sold in the park, so if you wish to have wine with dinner you'll need to bring your own. Desserts are arranged on a harvest table—a wonderful spread of trifle, chocolate layer cake, almond tarts, fresh-fruit salad, and more. Breakfast brings a full selection all cooked to order.

Facilities: You can swim in the lake, or canoe, sail, row, or windsurf. There are also two tennis courts, a sauna, a games room where a daily film is shown in the evening, plus miles of hiking trails.

Killarney Lodge. Algonquin Park, ON, P0A 1K0. ☎ **705/633-5551.** Fax 705/633-5667 (summer only). 26 cabins. High season $140–$200 per person double. Off-season rates about 30% less. Rates include all meals. MC, V. Closed mid-Oct to mid-May. Enter the park on Highway 60 from either Dwight or Whitney.

The Killarney Lodge is not as secluded as Arowhon Pines (the highway is still visible and audible), but it, too, is a charming resort. The cabins all stand on a peninsula that juts out into the Lake of Two Rivers. Each is made of pine logs and has a deck. Furnishings include old rockers, Ethan Allen–style beds, desks, chests, and rope rugs. A canoe comes with every cabin. Home-style meals are served in an attractive rustic log dining room. Guests can relax in the log cabin lounge warmed by a wood stove.

WHERE TO DINE

Spectacle Lake Lodge. Barry's Bay. ☎ **613/756-2324.** Reservations recommended in summer. Main courses $11–$16. MC, V. Daily 8am–8pm. Closed last 2 weeks of Nov. Head 10¹/₂ miles (17km) west of Barry's Bay, 22 miles (35km) east of Algonquin Park, south off Highway 60. CANADIAN.

The lodge's rustic dining room looks out over the lake. Traditional fare includes salmon trout and orange roughy, as well as Italian favorites like spaghetti with meatballs and veal parmigiana. Breakfast and lunch are served, too.

There are also nine nicely kept cottages available for rent, some with full housekeeping facilities including fridge and stove. The rates are $40 to $50 per person, depending on the cabin's size. Canoe and pedal boats are available, too, plus snowmobile rentals. Facilities include a comfortable sitting room with a hearth and games available, as well as dining room and a decent wine cellar. Additional amenities include a health club, bikes, and a tennis court; all kinds of watersports are available, as is cross-country skiing in winter.

8 The Haliburton Region

East of Bracebridge along Highway 118 is the Haliburton Highlands, a region of lakes, mountains, and forests.

For information on the region, contact the **Haliburton Highlands Chamber of Commerce,** in Minden (☎ 705/286-1760).

HALIBURTON VILLAGE

The **Haliburton Highlands Museum,** on Bayshore Acres Road, half a mile (1km) north of the village off Highway 118 (☎ 705/457-2760), provides some insight into how the pioneers who settled the region in the late 1800s lived. It's open from 10am to 5pm, daily from Victoria Day (late May) to Canadian Thanksgiving (U.S. Columbus Day); in winter, Tuesday through Saturday only. Admission is $2 for adults, $1 for children.

Many artists and craftspeople have settled in the area and some of their works can be seen at the **Rail's End Gallery,** on York Street (☎ 705/457-2330), open Labor Day to July 1 Tuesday to Saturday 10am to 5pm; July 1 to Labor Day Monday to Saturday 10am to 5pm, Sunday noon to 4pm.

AN EAGLE LAKE HIDEAWAY

✪ **Sir Sam's Inn.** Eagle Lake P.O., ON, K0M 1M0. ☎ **705/754-2188.** Fax 705/754-4262. 25 rms. Summer $125–$140 per person weekdays, $249–$289 per person for a two-night weekend. Rates include breakfast and dinner. Weekly rates available. In winter rates drop about 10%. AE, ER, MC, V. Follow the signs to Sir Sam's ski area. From Highway 118, take Route 6 to Sir Sam's Road.

Sir Sam's takes some finding. That's the way politician and militarist Sir Sam Hughes probably wanted it when he built his 14-bedroom stone-and-timber mansion in 1917 in the woods above Eagle Lake. The atmosphere here is friendly, yet sophisticated. There's a comfy sitting room, with a large stone fireplace as its focal point.

Accommodations are either in the inn itself or in a series of new chalets or in two lakefront suites. The chalets have very fetching bed-sitting rooms with light-pine furnishings, wood-burning fireplaces, cedar-lined bathrooms, small private decks, and such amenities as mini-refrigerators and kettles. Some have whirlpool baths. Inn rooms are a little more old-fashioned, except in the Hughes Wing where they are similar to the chalets with whirlpool bath and fireplace, but with bamboo furnishings. The suites are fully equipped with full kitchens complete with microwave and dishwasher, and also contain whirlpools.

Dining/Entertainment: The pretty dining room serves upscale continental cuisine and offers a fixed-price dinner for $32.50. The Gunner's Bar sports Sir Sam's gun rack, which holds the liquor, and has a small dance floor.

Facilities: Exercise room with a rowing machine and bicycle, two tennis courts, an outdoor pool overlooking the lake, a beach, and sailing, windsurfing, waterskiing, canoeing, paddleboats, and mountain bikes.

9 Some Northern Ontario Highlights: Driving Tours Along Highways 11 & 17

From the Muskoka region Highway 11 winds upward toward the province's northernmost frontier via North Bay, Kirkland Lake, Timmins (using Route 101), and Cochrane before sweeping west to Nipigon. There it links up briefly with Highway 17, the route that travels the northern perimeters of the Great Lakes from North Bay via Sudbury, Sault St. Marie, and Wawa, to Nipigon. At Nipigon, Highways 11 and 17 combine and lead into Thunder Bay. They split again west of Thunder Bay, with 17 taking a more northerly route to Dryden and Kenora and 11 proceeding via Atikokan to Fort Frances and Rainy River.

TRAVELING HIGHWAY 11: FROM HUNTSVILLE TO NORTH BAY, COBALT & TIMMINS

From Huntsville, Highway 11 travels north past **Arrowhead Provincial Park** (☎ 705/789-5105), which has close to 400 campsites. The road heads through the town of Burk's Falls, at the head of the Magnetawan River, and the town of South River, the access point for **Mikisew Provincial Park** (☎ 705/386-7762), with its sand beaches on the shore of Eagle Lake.

From South River the road continues to **Powassan,** famous for its excellent quality cedar strip boats. Stop in at B. Giesler and Sons to check out these very reliable specimens.

Next stop is **North Bay,** situated on the northeast shore of Lake Nipissing. The town arose because it was on the northern Voyageurs route traveled by fur traders, explorers, and missionaries. Noted for its nearby hunting and fishing, North Bay became world famous in 1934 when the Dionne quintuplets were born in nearby Corbeil. In fact the quintuplets' original home is now a museum in North Bay.

From North Bay Highway 11 continues north to New Liskeard. Along the route you'll pass **Temagami,** at the center of a superb canoeing region. Its name is Ojibwa, meaning "deep waters by the shore." The region is also associated with the legendary figure Grey Owl, who first came to the area in 1906 as a 17-year-old boy named

Archie Belaney. Archie had always dreamed of living in the wilderness among the Indians. He learned to speak Ojibwa and became an expert in forest and wilderness living. He abandoned his original identity and name, renamed himself Grey Owl, married an Indian woman, and became accepted as a native trapper. He subsequently published a series of books that quickly made him a celebrity.

Finlayson Point Provincial Park (☎ 705/569-3622) is located on Lake Temagami. The small park—only 94 hectares—is a great base for exploring the lake and its connecting waterways. Steep rugged cliffs, deep clear waters dotted with 1,300 islands, and magnificent stands of tall pines along its shoreline make for an awesome natural display. The park offers 113 secluded campsites (many on the lakeshore) plus canoeing, boating, swimming, fishing, hiking, and biking.

Lady Evelyn Smoothwater Provincial Park is 28 miles (45km) northwest of Temagami and encompasses the highest point of land in Ontario Maple Mountain and Ishpatina Ridge. Waterfalls are common along the Lady Evelyn River, with Helen Falls cascading more than 80 feet. White-water skills are required for river travel. There are no facilities. For more information contact District Manager, Temagami District, Ministry of Natural Resources, P.O. Box 38, Temagami, ON, P0H 2H0 (☎ 705/569-3622).

Next stop is **Cobalt,** which owes its existence to the discovery of silver in 1903. Legend has it that blacksmith Fred LaRose threw his hammer at what he thought were fox's eyes, but he hit one of the world's richest silver veins. Cobalt was also in the ore; hence the geologist named the site Cobalt. By 1905 a mining stampede extended to Gowganda, Kirkland Lake, and Porcupine.

A little farther north, **New Liskeard** is situated at the northern end of Lake Timikaming at the mouth of the Wabi River. Strangely enough, this is a dairy center, thanks to the "Little Clay Belt," a glacial lake bed that explains the acres of farmland amongst the rock and forest.

Even farther north, **Kap-kig-iwan Provincial Park** (☎ 705/544-2050) lies just outside of **Englehart,** also the name of the river that rushes through the park and is famous for its "high falls," which give the park its name. Park recreational facilities are limited to 44 campsites and self-guided trails.

Farther along Highway 11, **Kirkland Lake** produces more than 20% of Canada's gold. One original mine is still in production after 50 years, and others have opened more recently.

At **Iroquois Falls,** a town on the Abitibi River, it is said that some Iroquois once raided the Ojibwa community near the falls on the river. After defeating the Ojibwa the Iroquois curled up to sleep in their canoes that were tied along the river bank. But the Ojibwa cut the canoes loose and the Iroquois were swept over the falls to their death.

From Iroquois Falls, you can take Route 101 southwest to **Timmins.** Along the way you'll pass the access road to **Kettle Lakes Provincial Park,** 896 Riverside Dr., Timmins (☎ 705/363-3511). The park's name refers to the depressions that are formed as a glacier retreats. It has 165 camping sites, five trails, two large beaches, and 21 lakes to fish and enjoy.

In Timmins visitors can tour the **Hollinger Gold Mine,** James Reid Rd. (☎ 705/ 267-6222). Discovered by Benny Hollinger in 1909, the mine produced more than $400 million worth of gold in its day. Today visitors don helmets, overalls, boots, and torch before walking down into the mine to observe a scaling bar, slusher, mucking machine, and furnace at work and to view the safety room to which the miners rushed in the event of a rockfall. At the surface there's a panoramic view from the Jupiter Headframe and ore samples to be inspected along the Prospector's Trail.

Admission is $16 adults, $14 student ($6 and $4 for surface tours only), and it's open daily in summer; call ahead in winter.

For additional city information contact Timmins Chamber of Commerce, 76 McIntyre Rd. (705/360-1900).

COCHRANE: STARTING POINT OF THE *POLAR BEAR EXPRESS*

Back on Highway 11, the next stop is Cochrane, located at the junction of the Canadian National Railway and the Ontario Northland Railway. From here, the famous ✪ **Polar Bear Express** departs to Moosonee and Moose Factory, making one of the world's great railroad/nature excursions. The train travels 186 miles (4¹/₂ hours) from Cochrane along the Abitibi and Moose Rivers (the latter, by the way, rises and falls six feet twice a day with the tides) to Moosonee on James Bay, gateway to the Arctic.

Your destination, **Moosonee** and **Moose Factory**, on an island in the river, will introduce you to frontier life—still a challenge, although it's easier today than when native Cree and fur traders traveled the rivers and wrenched a living from the land 300 years ago. You can take the cruiser *Polar Princess* or a freighter-canoe across to Moose Factory (site of the Hudson's Bay Company, founded in 1673) and see the 17th-century Anglican church and other sights. If you stay over, you can also visit **Fossil Island** and the **Shipsands Waterfowl Sanctuary.**

Trains operate from the end of June to Labor Day. Tickets are limited because priority is given to the excursion passengers. Fares are $44 round-trip for adults, $22 children ages 5 to 12. Various three-day/two-night and four-day/three-night packages are also offered from North Bay and Toronto. For information contact **Ontario Northland** at 555 Oak St. East, North Bay, ON, P1B 8L3 (☎ 705/472-4500) or at Union Station, 65 Front St. West, Toronto, ON, M5J 1E6 (☎ 416/314-3750). Note that from June to Labor Day you'll need to make your lodging reservations well in advance.

For additional information on Cochrane contact the **Cochrane Board of Trade**, P.O. Box 1468, Cochrane, ON, P0L 1C0 (☎ 705/272-4926).

Where to Stay in Cochrane

The **Chimo Motel** on Highway 11 (☎ 705/272-6555) offers one- or two-bedroom efficiencies as well as Jacuzzi rooms. Rates are $70 double. Another option is the **Westway Motel,** 21 First St. (☎ 705/272-4285), at only $58 to $62 double.

EN ROUTE FROM COCHRANE TO NIPIGON

From Cochrane, Highway 11 loops farther north past the turnoff to **Greenwater Provincial Park** (☎ 705/272-6335). This 5,350-hectare park has good camping (90 sites in three campgrounds), swimming, boating (rentals available), hiking, and fishing on 26 lakes. One of the park's more challenging trails goes along Commando Lake. An added attraction are the spectacular views one has of the **northern lights.**

Highway 11 continues west past **Rene Brunelle Provincial Park** (☎ 705/367-2692) and **Kapuskasing,** where General Motors has its cold-weather testing facility, to **Hearst,** known as the Moose Capital of Canada at the northern terminus of the Algoma Central railway.

It continues all the way to **Lake Nipigon Provincial Park** (☎ 807/885-3181) on the shores of Lake Nipigon. The lake is famous for its black sandy beaches. Park facilities include 60 camping sites, boat rentals, and self-guided trails.

The nearby town of **Nipigon** stands on Lake Superior at the mouth of the Nipigon River. It's where the world-record brook trout, weighing 14^1/$_2$ pounds, was caught. At this point Highways 17 and 11 join and run all the way into Thunder Bay.

TRAVELING HIGHWAY 17 ALONG THE PERIMETER OF THE GREAT LAKES

Instead of traveling north from North Bay up Highway 11 to explore the northern mining frontier, you could choose to take Highway 17 along the perimeter of the Great Lakes. I consider this the more scenic and interesting route.

SUDBURY

The road travels past Lake Nipissing through Sturgeon Falls to Sudbury, a nickel-mining center. With a population of 160,000, it is northern Ontario's largest metro area. This rough-and-ready mining town has a landscape so barren that U.S. astronauts were trained here for lunar landings.

Sudbury's two major attractions are **Science North,** 100 Ramsey Lake Rd. (☎ 705/522-3701 or 705/522-3700 for recorded information) and **Big Nickel Mine.** The first occupies two giant stainless steel snowflake-shaped buildings dramatically cut into a rock outcrop overlooking Lake Ramsey. Inside you can conduct experiments, such as simulating a hurricane, monitoring earthquakes on a seismograph, or observing the sun through a solar telescope. In addition to the exhibits, a 3-D film and laser experience, *Shooting Star,* takes the audience on a journey back five billion years, charting the formation of the Sudbury Basin; a theatrical performance in another theater tells the story of the naturalist Grey Owl. There's also a water playground (where kids can play and adults can build a sailboat), space exploration and weather command centers, and a fossil identification workshop. Open year-round daily in May and June from 9am to 5pm, July to Canadian Thanksgiving 9am to 6pm; call ahead for winter hours (usually 10am to 4pm). Admission is $8 for adults, $6 for students and seniors, free for under five. A combined admission with the mine will save money.

At the **Big Nickel Mine** (☎ 705/522-3701), visitors are taken underground for a 30-minute tour. On the surface visitors can view a mineral processing station, measure their weight in gold, and enjoy some other video programs. Open May to Canadian Thanksgiving, same hours as Science North. Admission is $8 for adults, $6 for students and seniors, free for under five. A combined admission with Science North will save money.

The **Path of Discovery** is a two-hour bus tour that provides the only public access to INCO Ltd., the biggest nickel producer in the western world. On the tour visitors observe the surface processing facilities and one of the world's tallest smokestacks. The tour is operated from July to Labor Day daily at 10am and 2pm.

For further information on Sudbury contact either the **Sudbury and District Chamber of Commerce** (☎ 705/673-7133) or the **Community Information Service and Convention and Visitors Service** (☎ 705/674-3141).

Where to Stay

Your best bets for lodgings are the chains—**Comfort Inn,** at 2171 Regent St. South (☎ 705/522-1101), and at 440 2nd Ave. North (☎ 705/560-4502); **Ramada Inn,** 85 St. Anne's (☎ 705/675-1123); or **Venture Inn,** 1956 Regent St. South (☎ 705/522-7600). There's also the **Sheraton Caswell Inn,** at 1696 Regent St. South (☎ 705/522-3000).

A CROWN JEWEL: KILLARNEY PROVINCIAL PARK

Less than an hour's drive southwest of Sudbury is Killarney Provincial Park (☎ 705/287-2900), sometimes called the "crown jewel" of the province's park system. This 48,500-hectare park on the north shore of Georgian Bay features numerous lakes and a spectacular range of quartzite ridges. It's only accessible on foot or by canoe. More than 100 species of birds breed in the park, including kingfishers and loons on the lakes in the summer. Four members of the Group of Seven painted in the region: Frank Carmichael, Arthur Lismer, A. Y. Jackson, and A. J. Casson.

The park has 122 **campsites** at the George Lake campground near the entrance to the park.

The park is a paradise for the canoeist (rentals are available in the park). Compared to Algonquin Park, it's much quieter—you only have to cross one lake to find total privacy at Killarney, while at Algonquin you may have to canoe across three lakes.

Three **hiking trails** loop from the campground and can be completed in three hours.

For a more ambitious backpacking tour, the park's **La Cloche Silhouette Trail** winds for more than 60 miles through forest and beaver meadows past crystal-clear lakes. The trail's main attraction is Silver Peak, which towers 1,214 feet above Georgian Bay offering views of 50 miles on a clear day. This is a serious undertaking; it will take seven to 10 days to complete the whole trail.

The best **fishing** is in Georgian Bay; sadly, acid rain has killed off most of the fish in the lakes.

DRIVING WEST FROM SUDBURY

From Sudbury it's 189 miles (305km) west along Highway 17 to Sault Ste. Marie, or the Soo, as it's affectionately called.

At Serpent River you can turn off north to the town of Elliot Lake and **Mississagi Provincial Park** (☎ 705/848-2806), and the river of the same name. The park has 90 campsites, swimming, and also offers some fine canoeing. Hikers will find short self-guided trails as well as trails from 3.7 miles (6km) to 10 miles (16km) long.

Continuing along Route 17, which borders the North Channel, will bring you past the access point to **Fort St. Joseph National Park** on St. Joseph Island (between Michigan and Ontario) and into the Soo, 189 miles (305km) west of Sudbury.

SAULT STE. MARIE

The highlights of any visit are the **Soo locks**, the **Agawa Canyon Train**, and the **Bon Soo,** one of North America's biggest winter carnivals, celebrated in late January and early February.

The Soo, at the junction of Lakes Superior and Huron, actually straddles the border. The twin cities, one in Ontario and the other in Michigan, are separated by the St. Marys River rapids, and now are joined by an international bridge. Originally the Northwest Fur Trading Company founded a post here in 1783, building a canal to bypass the rapids in 1797–99. That canal was replaced later by the famous **Soo locks**—four on the American side and one on the Canadian. The locks are part of the St. Lawrence Seaway system, which enables large international cargo ships to navigate from the Atlantic along the St. Lawrence to the Great Lakes. Lake Superior is about 23 feet higher than Lake Huron and the locks raise and lower the ships. There's a viewing station at both sets of locks or you can take a two- or three-hour cruise ($15.50 adults, $7.75 children) through the lock system daily from June to about October 10. For information, contact **Lock Tours Canada** (☎ 705/253-9850).

The Algoma Central Railway, which operates the ✪ **Agawa Canyon Train Tours,** was established in 1901. The Canadian artists known as the Group of Seven used to shunt up and down the track in a converted boxcar that they used as a base camp for canoe excursions into the wilderness. Today this tour takes you on a 114-mile trip from the Soo to Hearst through the Agawa Canyon, where you can spend a few hours exploring scenic waterfalls and vistas. The train snakes through a vista of deep ravines and lakes, hugging the hillsides and crossing gorges on skeletal trestle bridges. The most spectacular time to take the trip is in the fall from mid-September to mid-October. The train operates daily from early June through mid-October; on weekends only January through March. Fares are $48 for adults, $18.75 children and students (June to August) or $24 (September to October), and $9 for children under five. For information contact the Algoma Central Railway, Passenger Sales, P.O. Box 130, 129 Bay St., Sault Ste. Marie, ON, P6A 6Y2 (☎ 705/946-7300).

The surrounding area offers great fishing, snowmobiling, cross-country skiing, and other sports opportunities. You can enjoy one-, four-, and seven-day kayaking trips with **Lake Superior Kayak Adventures,** 159 Shannon Rd. For cross-country ski information, call the **Stokely Creek Ski Touring Centre,** at Stokely Creek Lodge, at Karalash Corners, Goulais River (☎ 705/649-3421). Contact the **Sault Ste. Marie Chamber of Commerce,** 360 Great Northern Rd. (☎ 705/949-7152), for more sports information.

Where to Stay

Whatever you do, make your reservations in advance. If you're taking the Algoma Train the most conveniently located hotel is the **Quality Inn Bayfront,** right across from the train station, which has 110 rooms including 18 suites (six with Jacuzzi tubs). Facilities include indoor pool, exercise room, and Italian restaurant. Rates are $118 double.

You can also try the other chains: the **Holiday Inn,** 208 St. Mary's River Dr. (☎ 705/949-0611), or **Comfort Inn,** 333 Great Northern Rd. (☎ 705/759-8000). The **Ramada,** 229 Great Northern Rd. (☎ 705/942-2500), has great facilities for families—water slide, bowling, indoor golf, and more.

CONTINUING ON FROM THE SOO

From Sault Ste. Marie it's 428 miles (690km) west to Thunder Bay. The Lake Superior Drive along the northern shoreline of the lake affords many scenic delights, including **Batchawana Bay Provincial Park** (☎ 705/882-2209), for day use only, and Alona Bays and Agawa Bay.

LAKE SUPERIOR PROVINCIAL PARK

Alona and Agawa bays are in ✪ **Lake Superior Provincial Park** (☎ 705/856-2284). The 955-square-mile (1,540km) park, one of Ontario's largest, offers the haunting shoreline and open waters of Longfellow's "Shining Big-Sea Water," cobble beaches, rugged rocks, and limitless forests. Dramatic highlights include Lac Mijinemungsing, the Devil's Chair, and Old Woman Bay. At the park's east end the Algoma Central Railway provides access to the park along the Agawa River.

The magnificent scenery has attracted artists for years, including the Group of Seven. Among the most famous paintings of the park are Frank Johnston's *Canyon and Agawa,* Lawren Harris's *Montreal River,* A. Y. Jackson's *First Snows,* and J. E. H. MacDonald's *Algoma Waterfall and Agawa Canyon.* As for wildlife, you may see moose as well as caribou, which once were common here and have been reintroduced along the coast areas and offshore islands. More than 250 species of birds have been identified here; about 120 different types nest in the area.

Some 274 camping sites are available at three **campgrounds.** The largest, at Agawa Bay, has a 1.9-mile (3km) beach. Crescent Lake, at the southern boundary, is the most basic, while Rabbit Blanket Lake is well located for exploring the park's interior.

The park has eight canoe routes, ranging in length from 3 to 56 kilometers, and in difficulty from easy to challenging, with steep portages and white water. Rentals are available at the campgrounds, but outfitter services are limited (contact the Wawa Chamber of Commerce, P. O. Box 858, Wawa, ON, P0S 1K0).

The 11 **hiking trails** range from short interpretive trails to rugged overnight trails up to 34 miles (55km) long. The most accessible is the **Trapper's Trail,** which features a wetlands boardwalk from which you can watch beaver, moose, and great blue heron. The **Orphan Lake Trail** is popular due to its moderate length and difficulty, plus its panoramic views over Orphan and Superior Lakes, a pebble beach, and Baldhead Falls. The **Coastal Trail,** along the shoreline, is the longest at 34 miles (55km), stretching from Sinclair Cove to Chalfant Cove, and will take five to seven days to complete. The fall is the best time to hike, when the colors are spectacular and the insects are few.

In winter although there are no formal facilities or services provided, visitors can cross-country ski, snowshoe, and ice fish at their own risk.

WAWA, THE WHITE RIVER & WINNIE-THE-POOH, TOO

From the park it's a short trip into **Wawa,** 142 miles (230km) north of the Soo, the site of the famous salmon derby. Wawa serves as a supply center for canoeists, fishermen, and other sports folks.

East of Wawa lies the **Chapleau Game Reserve**, where there's some of Ontario's best canoeing in **Chapleau Nemegosenda River Provincial Park**—124 miles (200km) northeast of the Soo and 62 miles (100km) west of Timmins. It's accessible from Chapleau or by Emerald Lake on Highway 101 to Nemegosenda Lake. There are no facilities. For additional information contact Park Superintendent, Ministry of Natural resources, 190 Cherry Street, Chapleau, ON, P0M 1K0 (☎ 705/864-1710).

Sixty-one miles farther on along Highway 17 from Wawa is **White River,** birthplace of Winnie-the-Pooh. In 1916, Winnipeg soldier Harry Colebourne, on his way to Europe from his hometown Winnipeg, bought a mascot for his regiment here and named it Winnie. When he shipped out from London he couldn't take the bear cub, so it went to the London zoo, where it became the inspiration for A. A. Milne's classic character.

Just outside White River are the spectacular **Magpie High Falls.**

PUKASKWA NATIONAL PARK

Southwest of White River on the shores of Lake Superior is Ontario's only national park in the wilderness, **Pukaskwa National Park,** Hattie Cove, Heron Bay, ON, P0T 1R0 (☎ 807/229-0801). It's reached via Highway 627 from Highway 17. The interior is only accessible on foot or by boat.

In this 1,164.3-mile (1,878km) park survives the most southerly herd of **woodland caribou**—only 40 of them. Lake Superior is extremely cold, and for this reason rare arctic plants are found here.

Hattie Cove is the center of most park activities and services including a 67-site campground, a series of short walking trails, access to three sand beaches, and parking facilities and visitor center.

The (60km) **Coastal Hiking Trail** winds from Hattie Cove south to the North Swallow River and requires proper planning and equipment (camping areas are located every half- to one-day's hike apart). A 9.3-mile (15km) day hike along this trail can be taken to the White River Suspension Bridge. There are also backcountry trails.

In winter cross-country skiers can use 3.7 miles (6km) of groomed trails or hazard the fast slopes and sharp turns created by the topography. Snowshoers are welcome too.

CANOEING THE WHITE & PUKASKWA RIVERS

The White and Pukaskwa rivers offers white-water adventure. The easily-accessed White River can be paddled any time during the open-water season. Many wilderness adventurers start from nearby **White Lake Provincial Park** and travel four to six days to the mouth of the White River and then paddle about an hour north on Lake Superior to Hattie Cove.

The Pukaskwa River is more remote, difficult (with rugged and long portages and an 850-foot drop between the headwaters at Gibson Lake and the river mouth at Lake Superior), and navigable only during the spring runoff. The best place to start is where the river crosses Highway 17 near Sagina Lake and paddle to Gibson Lake via Pokei Lake, Pokei Creek, and Soulier Lake. Otherwise you'll have to fly in from White River or Wawa.

Outfitters include **Pukaskwa Country Outfitters,** P.O. Box 603, Marathon, ON, P0T 2E0 and **U-Paddle-It,** P.O. Box 374, Pinewood Drive, Wawa, ON, P0S 1K0.

MORE PROVINCIAL PARKS

From White River it's 167 miles (270km) to **Nipigon** and **Nipigon Bay,** which offer fine rock, pine, and lake vistas. From here it's another 7¹/₂ miles (12km) to **Ouimet Canyon Provincial Park** (☎ 807/977-2526), at the location of a spectacular canyon 330 feet deep, 500 feet wide, and a mile long. When you stand on the edge of the canyon and gaze out over the expanse of rock and forest below you can sense the power of the forces that shaped, built, and split the earth's crust and then gouged and chiseled this crevasse—one of Eastern Canada's most striking canyons. The park is for day use only.

About 15¹/₂ miles (25km) on, the next stop is **Sleeping Giant Provincial Park** (☎ 807/977-2526), named after the rock formation that the Ojibwe Indians say is Nanabosho (the Giant), who was turned to stone after disobeying the Great Spirit. The story goes that Nanabosho, who had led the Ojibwa to the north shore of Lake Superior to save them from the Sioux, discovered silver one day, but fearing for his people he told them to bury it on an islet at the tip of the peninsula and keep it a secret. Vanity got the better of one of the chieftains, who made silver weapons for himself. Subsequently, he was killed in battle against the Sioux. Shortly afterwards Nonabosho spied a Sioux warrior leading two white men in a canoe across Lake Superior to the source of the silver. To keep the secret he disobeyed the Great Spirit and raised a storm that sank and drowned the white men. For this he was turned into stone.

Take Route 587 south along the Sibley Peninsula, which juts into the lake. Among the park's natural splendors are bald eagles, wild orchids, moose, and more than 190 species of birds. Facilities include 168 campsites at Marie Louise Campground plus about 40 interior sites. There's a beach at the campground.

The trail system consists of three self-guided nature trails, three walking trails, and a network of about 43.4 miles (70km) of hiking trails including the two-day Kabeyun Trail, which originates at the spectacular Thunder Bay lookout and follows the shoreline south to Sawyer Bay. The park has great cross-country skiing with (30km) of trails.

THUNDER BAY

Just before you enter Thunder Bay, stop and honor Terry Fox at the **Monument and Scenic Lookout.** Not far from this spot he was forced to abandon his heroic cross-Canada journey to raise money for cancer research.

To access the remote **Wabakimi region** take Route 527 north just east of Thunder Bay. It will take you to Armstrong, the supply center for this wilderness region.

From the port city of **Thunder Bay**—an amalgam of Fort William and Port Arthur—wheat and other commodities are shipped out via the Great Lakes all over the world. Fifteen grain elevators still dominate the skyline. You can't really grasp the city's role and its geography unless you take the **Harbor Cruise.** Other highlights include **Old Fort William,** about 10 miles outside the city on the Kaministiquia River. From 1803 to 1821 this reconstructed fort was the headquarters of the North West Fur-Trading Company, which was later absorbed by the Hudson's Bay Company.

Thunder Bay is also the center for ice-climbing and dog-sled excursions. For information on the latter call **Norwest Dog Sled Adventures** in Thunder Bay (☎ 807/964-2070).

Where to Stay

For bed-and-breakfast accommodations, contact the **North of Superior B&B Association** at 807/626-9420 or fax them at 807/626-9421.

Your best bets are the chains: **The Best Western NorWester**, 2080 Highway 61, RR no. 4 (☎ 807/473-9123), which has rooms for $80 double plus an indoor pool and lounge-restaurant; **Comfort Inn by Journey's End,** 660 W. Arthur St. (☎ 807/475-3155), where rooms are $83 double; and the **Venture Inn,** 450 Memorial Ave. (☎807/345-2343), which also has a lounge-restaurant and indoor pool and rents rooms for $85 double.

Airlane Motor Hotel. 698 W. Arthur St., Thunder Bay, ON, P7E 5R8. ☎ **807/577-1181.** 160 rms. A/C MINIBAR TV TEL. $67.50 double. AE, MC, V.

The recently renovated Airlane Hotel has modern rooms that are well equipped and include free in-room coffee. Facilities include an indoor pool and fitness center as well as lounge-restaurant and dance club. Suites with whirlpools are available too.

The White Fox Inn. RR no. 4, 1345 Mountain Rd., Thunder Bay, ON, P7C 4Z2. ☎ **807/577-3699.** 9 rms. A/C TV TEL. $105–$180 double. AE, DC, MC, V.

Set on 15 acres, with a view of the Norwester Mountain range, this inn was originally a lumber magnate's home. The individually decorated rooms have fireplaces and VCRs. The three largest rooms have in-room Jacuzzis. There's also a fine dining room. Nearby you'll find a variety of outdoor activities.

FROM THUNDER BAY TO FORT FRANCES/RAINY RIVER VIA HIGHWAY 11

From Thunder Bay it's 298 miles (480km) along the Trans-Canada Highway to **Kenora.** Several provincial parks line the route.

Kakabeka Falls Provincial Park, 435 James St. South, Suite 221, Thunder Bay (☎ 807/473-9231), with its spectacular 130-foot-high waterfall, lies 18 miles out along the Trans-Canada Highway. The gorge was carved out of the Precambrian Shield when the last glaciers melted. Fossils dating back 1.6 billion years have been found in the park. The park has several nature trails, plus safe swimming at a roped-off area above the falls. Two campgrounds provide 166 sites. In winter there are 8 miles (13km) of groomed cross-country ski trails.

Atikokan is the gateway to ✪ **Quetico Provincial Park** (☎ 807/597-2430), which is primarily a wilderness canoeing park. The 1,800-square-mile park has absolutely no roads and only two out of the six entrance stations are accessible by car (those at French Lake and Nym Lake, both west of Thunder Bay). Instead, there are miles of interconnecting lakes, streams, and rivers with roaring white water dashing against granite cliffs. It's one of North America's finest canoeing areas. Dawson Trail Campgrounds, with 133 sites at French Lake, is the only accessible site for car camping. Extended hikes are limited to the 8-mile (13km) trip to Pickerel Lake; there are also six short trails in the French Lake area (three interpretive). The park can be skied but there are no groomed trails. Also in the park on some rocks near Lac la Croix you can see 30 ancient pictographs representing moose, caribou, and other animals as well as hunters in canoes.

Fort Frances is an important border crossing to the United States and the site of a paper mill. Another 45 miles (90km) will bring you to **Rainy River** at the extreme western point of Ontario across from Minnesota. The district abounds in lakeland scenery, much of it in **Lake of the Woods Provincial Park,** RR no. 1, Sleeman (☎ 807/274-5337), which is 26 miles (43km) north of Rainy River. This shallow lake has a 170-meter-long beach and is good for swimming and waterskiing. In spring you can fish for walleye, northern pike, and large- and small-mouth bass. Canoes and boats can be rented in nearby Morson. The park has 100 campsites as well as a couple of easy nature trails to hike.

Almost due north of Thunder Bay via Route 527 lies **Wabakimi Provincial Park,** which has some fine canoeing and fishing. It's accessible from Armstrong.

FROM THUNDER BAY TO KENORA VIA HIGHWAY 17

Instead of taking Highway 11 west from Thunder Bay as described above, you can take Highway 17, which follows a more northerly route. Just follow 17 where it branches off at Shabaqua Corners, about 34 miles (56km) from Thunder Bay. Continue northwest to Ignace, the access point for two provincial parks.

At Ignace, turn off onto Highway 599 to **Sandbar Lake** (☎ 807/934-2233), which offers more than 5,000 hectares of forest with nine smaller lakes plus the large one from which it takes its name. The park's most notable inhabitants are the painted turtle, whose tracks can often be seen in the sand, the spotted sandpiper, the loon, the common merganser, as well as several species of woodpecker. The campground has 75 sites; the beach has safe swimming; there are several short and long canoe routes plus several hiking trails, including the 2-km Lookout Trail, which begins on the beach.

Turtle River Provincial Park is a 74.4-mile- (120km) long waterway from Ignace to Mine Centre. The canoe route begins on Agimak Lake at Ignace and follows a series of lakes into the Turtle River ending on Turtle Lake just north of Mine Centre. The park also includes the famous log castle built by Jimmy McQuat in the early 1900s on White Otter Lake. Follow Highway 599 farther north and it will lead to the remote rivers—the Albany, and the Apawapiskat which drain into James Bay.

Back on Highway 17 from Ignace it's another 24 miles (40km) to the turnoff on Highway 72 to **Ojibway Provincial Park** (☎ 807/737-2033), which has only 45 campsites but offers swimming, boating, and self-guided trails.

Back on Highway 17 it's only a short way beyond Highway 72 to **Aaron Provincial Park** (☎ 807/223-3341), where you'll find close to 100 campsites, facilities for boating and swimming, plus some short nature trails. Nearby Dryden is the supply center for Aaron.

From Dryden it's about 26 miles (43km) to Vermilion Bay where Route 105 branches off north to Red Lake, the closest point to one of the province's most remote provincial parks, **Woodland Caribou** (☎ 807/727-2253). Offering superb fishing, the 450,000-hectare park has no facilities except picnicking tables and boat rentals nearby. It's home to one of the largest herds of woodland caribou south of the Hudson Bay lowlands. It's also inhabited by black bear, great blue heron, osprey, and bald eagles. There are 1600 kms of canoe routes. Contact the outfitters association for information on fly-in camps.

Back on Highway 17 from Vermilion Bay it's only 43 miles (72km) until the road links up with Highway 71 just outside Kenora, just shy of the Manitoba border.

WHERE TO STAY & DINE NEAR KENORA

Radisson Minaki Resort. ☎ 807/224-4000. 140 rms. A/C TV TEL. $150–$160 double.

Minaki means "all good land" in Ojibway and this resort stands on 110 acres of it along the Winnipeg River about 30 miles north of Kenora. The Wabaseemoong Independent Nation owns the resort, which Radisson operates. At the resort's center stands the original log-and-stone building built in 1926, with a huge stone fireplace and impressive 40-foot-high cathedral ceilings made of cedar logs. The rooms are standard hotel rooms with modern amenities. There are three dining rooms.

Facilities: Indoor pool, fitness room and trails, nine-hole golf course (extra fee), three tennis courts, bikes, and lakeside water sports (sailing, windsurfing, canoeing, kayaking, and fishing).

Totem Lodge. Box 180, Sioux Narrows, ON, P0X 1N0. ☎ **807/226-5275.** Fax 807/226-5187. 27 cabins, 3 rms. A/C TV. American Plan $130 per person per night. Cabins without meals from $1300 per week. Weekly and special packages available. MC, V. Access is off Highway 71, 1 mile north of Sioux Narrows.

Located at the end of Long Bay on Lake of the Woods, this lodge caters to outdoor enthusiasts and families who come for the superb fishing and hunting. The main lodge is an A-frame featuring a dining room, lounge, and decks with umbrella tables overlooking the water. The timber and stone decor is appropriately rustic. The cabins have full modern bath, beds with Hudson's Bay blankets, fireplaces, and screened-in porches or outdoor decks plus cooking facilities. The rooms above the boathouse lack cooking facilities but do have fridges.

Facilities: Sixteen-foot fishing boats, canoes, Windsurfers, and wet jets can be rented, and the management will arrange fly-out fishing trips. Fish-cleaning facilities and freezer service is available.

Wiley Point Lodge. Box 180, Sioux Narrows, ON, P0X 1N0. ☎ **807/226-5275.** 3 rms, 7 cabins. American Plan $125 per person per night based on two per boat (this includes boats and gas). MC, V.

This lodge is more remote, only accessible by boat, and therefore offers more of a wilderness experience. The main lodge has three suites, plus there are seven cabins (two- or three-bedroom), all with full bath, fridge and screened-in porches. The lodge contains a dining room, lounge and deck overlooking the lake. Facilities include a beach with diving raft, paddle boats, Windsurfers, and wet skis for rent; hot tub, sauna, and exercise room. Spring and fall bear hunts are offered as well as more traditional hunting.

Manitoba & Saskatchewan 16

by Marilyn Wood

Tourists don't exactly flock to these two provinces at Canada's center, but that can be a plus if you like wide open spaces. Above the great prairies, Manitoba and Saskatchewan boast some beautiful wilderness and parkland and an almost infinite chain of lakes, making them terrific choices for fishing, canoeing, wildlife-watching, and more.

Manitoba is famous for its friendly people, who not only brave long harsh winters but till the southern prairie lands in summer, making the region a breadbasket for the nation and the world. Outside of Winnipeg, along the southern border, under the dome of a huge prairie sky, wheat, barley, oats, and flax wave at the roadside, the horizon is limitless, and grain elevators pierce the skyline. Beyond the province's southern section, which is punctuated by Lake Winnipeg and Lake Manitoba, stretches one of the last wilderness frontiers, a paradise for anglers and outdoors enthusiasts of all sorts. Here you'll find many of the province's 100,000 lakes, which cover about 20% of Manitoba. You'll also see polar bears and Beluga whales and hear the timber wolves cry on the lonesome tundra surrounding the Hudson Bay port of Churchill.

Five times the size of New York state, with a population of about one million, Saskatchewan, another of Canada's prairie provinces, produces 60% of Canada's wheat. Here you'll find a hunting and fishing paradise in the northern lakes and forests; several summer playgrounds (including Prince Albert National Park and 31 provincial parks); and the cities of Regina, the capital, and Saskatoon.

1 Exploring Manitoba & Saskatchewan

The Trans-Canada Highway (Highway 1) cuts across the southern part of both provinces. In Manitoba, you can stop along the Highway 1 at Whiteshell Provincial Park in the east. You can return to the highway or visit the shores of Lake Winnipeg at Grand Beach Provincial Park and then head south via Selkirk and Lower Fort Garry to Winnipeg, the provincial capital. From Winnipeg, you can take the train north to Churchill to explore the Northern tundra around Hudson Bay. On your return trip to Winnipeg, you can pick up Highway 1 again and drive west across the province, stopping for a detour either to Riding Mountain National Park or Spruce Woods Provincial park before exiting into Saskatchewan.

Highway 1 leads from Manitoba to Regina, with a stop perhaps at Moose Mountain Provincial Park along the way. From Regina it's a 2¹/₂-hour or so drive to Saskatoon, and about another 2¹/₂ hours' drive to Prince Albert National Park (you can stop at Batoche en route). From Prince Albert you can return via Battleford National Historic Site either to Saskatoon and then to Highway 1 at Swift Current, or you can take Route 4 directly from Battleford to Swift Current. From here the Trans-Canada Highway heads west to the Alberta border.

VISITOR INFORMATION   Contact **Travel Manitoba,** Department SV6, 7-155 Carlton St., Winnipeg, MB, R3C 3H8 (☎ 800/665-0040), open 8:30am to 4:30pm Monday to Friday; or **Tourism Saskatchewan,** 500-1900 Albert St., Regina, SK, S4P 4L9 (☎ 306/787-2300 or 800/667-7191), open from 8am to 7pm Monday through Friday, 10am to 4pm Saturday.

For information on Manitoba's provincial parks, call ☎ 204/945-6784 or 800/214-6497; for taped instant tourist information, call ☎ 204/942-2535.

AN IMPORTANT NOTE ON PRICES & TAXES   Unless stated otherwise, **the prices cited in this guide are given in Canadian dollars,** which is good news for U.S. travelers because the Canadian dollar is worth 25% less than the American dollar but buys nearly as much. As we go to press, $1 Canadian is worth 75¢ U.S., which means that your $100-a-night hotel room will cost only U.S. $75.

Manitoba has a 7% provincial sales tax and Saskatchewan has a 9% provincial sales tax—and these are in addition to the 7% federal goods and services tax (GST).

2 The Great Outdoors

With its 100,000 lakes, Manitoba is a premier outdoor destination that's known worldwide for its fishing and hunting as well as for its views of the wilderness along the shore of Hudson Bay—it's one of the few places in the world where visitors can see polar bears. The major playgrounds in Manitoba are Riding Mountain National Park plus these provincial parks: Whiteshell, Atikaki, Spruce Woods, Duck Mountain, and Grass River.

The province of Saskatchewan covers a quarter of a million square miles, with most of its population concentrated in the southern grain belt. Saskatchewan has 31,000 square miles of water and three million acres are given over to parks—one million alone constitute Prince Albert National Park. In addition, there are 31 provincial parks. The major ones are **Cypress Hills** (☎ 306/662-4459); **Moose Mountain** (☎ 306/577-2131); **Lac La Ronge** (☎ 306/425-4234); and **Meadow Lake** (☎ 306/236-7690). At the parks you can camp for $12 unelectrified, $14 electrified in addition to a $6 entry fee. Some parks, such as Cypress Hills and Moose Mountain, also have cabins for an average $40 to $65 for a one-bedroom cabin, $65 to $100 for a two-bedroom, with some nonmoderns (that is, with an outdoor toilet) renting for about $40.

Summers can be simply magnificent, with warm sunny days and cool refreshing evenings and nights. The climate is on the dry side, with summer temperatures averaging 70° to 80°F. As you probably expected, average winter temperatures are pretty harsh—0° to 9°F—but that doesn't stop cross-country skiers, snowmobilers, and snowshoers, who have so many places to play throughout these provinces that I can't even begin to detail them below.

BIRD WATCHING   In Manitoba, there's a goose sanctuary at **Whitehill Provincial Park.** Gull Harbour's **Hecla Provincial Park,** on Lake Winnipeg, has a

Manitoba

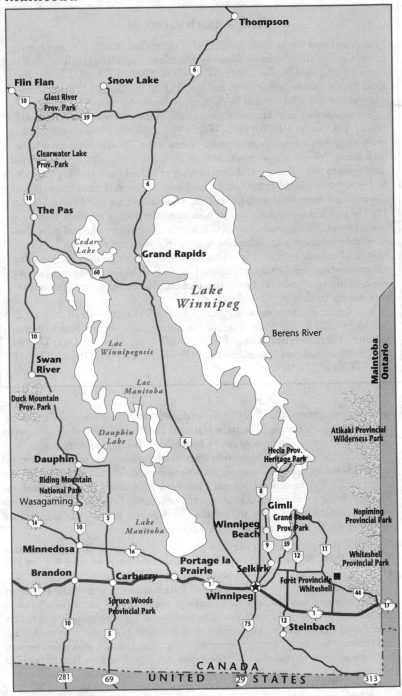

Farm & Ranch Vacations

There's no better way to really get the feel of the prairies than to stay on a farm or ranch. Contact the **Manitoba Country Vacations Association,** RR no. 1, Elm Creek, Winnipeg, MB, R0G 0N0 (☎ 204/436-2599), for detailed information about farm accommodations. Rates average $50 a day for adults, $25 for children—a very reasonable price for such an exciting, authentic experience.

Just outside Riding Mountain National Park, **Riding Mountain Guest Ranch,** Box 11, Lake Audy, MB, R0J 0Z0 (☎ 204/848-2265; fax 204/848-4658), offers much more than a simple farm vacation. Guests at the 720-acre ranch enjoy horseback riding, hiking, and loon-watching at the lake. Workshops are also offered ranging from a wolf ecology workshop conducted by biologists studying the park's timber wolves to a wildlife photography workshop. Accommodations consist of four rooms, plus a dorm room with 12 beds and a bunkhouse accommodating another 12. The ranch also features a lounge with stone fireplace, a sunroom veranda, a billiard room, a sauna, and a hot tub. In summer, guests can take trail rides. Evenings are given over to campfire sing-alongs. In winter, the ranch has 12.4 miles (20km) of cross-country ski trails, plus ice skating on the pond. There's a minimum stay of one week. Prices range from U.S. $935 to U.S. $1,380 per person per week, including all meals and programs plus transfers between the Winnipeg airport and the ranch. Call for workshop prices.

In Saskatchewan farm vacations average $30 to $40 a day with all three meals included or $20 to $25 without meals. For information, contact **Saskatchewan Country Vacations Association,** Box 428, Gull Lake, SK, S0N 1A0 (☎ 306/672-3970), or **Tourism Saskatchewan,** 1919 Saskatchewan Dr., Regina, SK, S4P 3V7 (☎ 306/787-2300).

---

wildlife viewing tower; the Grassy Narrow Marsh located there is home to a wide variety of waterfowl. **Riding Mountain National Park** boasts more than 200 species of birds. And many varieties stop near **Churchill** on their annual migrations.

In Saskatchewan, **Moose Mountain Provincial Park** is home to many waterfowl and songbirds, including the magnificent blue heron and the red-tailed hawk. As you might expect, **Prince Albert National Park** has a wide variety of bird life, with the highlight being an enormous colony of white pelicans at Lavallee Lake. And there's even a waterfowl park right in the middle of downtown **Regina,** where more than 60 species can be seen; a naturalist is on duty weekdays.

CANOEING   In Manitoba the best places to canoe are in **Riding Mountain National Park, Whiteshell Provincial Park,** and the chain of lakes around **Flin Flon**, which is right on the border between the two provinces.

In Saskatchewan, **Prince Albert National Park** has some fine canoeing and plenty of other northern water routes offer a challenge to both novice and expert. Some 55 canoe routes have been mapped, traversing terrain that has not changed since the era of explorers and fur traders. You can get to all but three of the routes by road. Various outfitters will supply tents, camping equipment, and canoes; look after your car; and transport you to your trip's starting point. Most outfitters are located in either Flin Flon or Lac La Ronge, 250 miles (400km) north of Saskatoon.

Churchill River Canoe Outfitters in La Ronge, Saskatchewan, (☎ 306/635-4420), offers a selection of packages. Canoes and kayaks can be rented for about

Saskatchewan

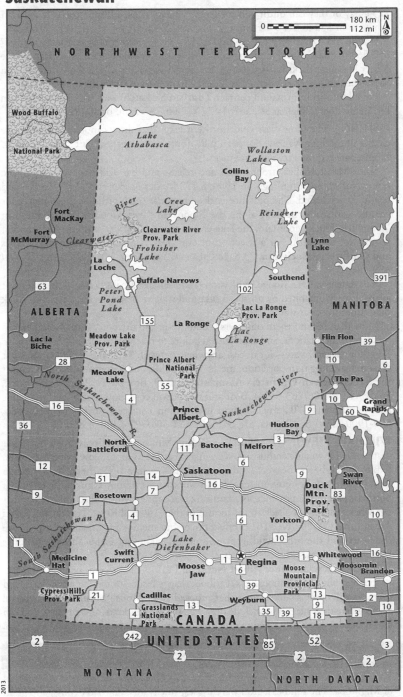

2013

$25 a day or they can outfit you for a real wilderness expedition. You can also rent cabins from $50 to $170 per night.

Canoe Ski Discovery Company, 1618 9th Ave. North, Saskatoon (☎ 306/ 653-5693), offers several canoeing and cross-country skiing wilderness trips in Prince Albert National Park, Lac La Ronge Provincial Park, and along the Churchill and Saskatchewan Rivers. The trips last 2 to 10 days and cost from $150 to $1600.

For additional information contact **Tourism Saskatchewan,** 1919 Saskatchewan Dr. (main floor), Regina, SK, S4P 3V7 (☎ 306/787-2300 or 800/667-7191).

FISHING   The same clear cold northern lakes that draw canoeists hold out the chance of catching walleye, northern pike, four species of trout, and arctic grayling. Licenses are required in both provinces.

Since Manitoba has strong catch-and-release and barbless-hook programs, the number of trophy fish is high. In 1994, 8,272 Master Angler Fish were recorded and nearly 75% released. The province is also known as the North American mecca for channel catfish, particularly along the Bloodvein River. Good fishing abounds in Whiteshell, Duck Mountain, the lake chains around The Pas and Flin Flon, and in fly-in areas up north. For a selection of outfitters, contact the **Manitoba Lodges and Outfitters Association,** 23 Sage Crescent, Winnipeg, MB, R2Y 0X8 (☎ 204/ 889-4840).

In Saskatchewan, La Rouge, Wollaston, and Reindeer are just a few of the lakes that are so densely inhabited by northern pike and walleye that you can practically pluck them from the clear waters.

More than 300 northern outfitters—both fly-in and drive-in camps—offer equipment, accommodations, and experienced guides to take you to the best fishing spots. Rates for packages vary—it can cost anywhere between $800 and $3,000 a week per person, including transportation, meals, boat, guide, and accommodations. Contact the **Saskatchewan Outfitters Association,** P.O. Box 2016, Prince Albert, SK, S6V 6R1 (☎ 306/763-5434). Boat and motor will cost about $65 a day, and guide services run about $70 a day. For more information, contact **Tourism Saskatchewan,** 500-1900 Albert St., Regina, SK, S4P 4L9 (☎ 306/787-2300 or 800/667-7191).

WILDLIFE VIEWING   Manitoba's **Riding Mountain National Park** is a prime destination for wildlife enthusiasts, who might be able to spot moose, coyotes, wolves, lynxes, black bears, beavers, and more; there's even a bison herd. **Grass River Provincial Park** is home to moose and woodland caribou. **Churchill,** in the far northern part of the province, is a fantastic place for viewing polar bears; white beluga whales can even be seen in the mouth of the Churchill River. **Kaskattma Safari Adventures** (☎ 204/667-1611) offers pricey but memorable organized trips to see the bears and the other wildlife in the north, including Cape Tatnam Wildlife Management Area.

In Saskatchewan, **Prince Albert National Park** is the place to be; you'll be able to spot and photograph moose, elk, caribou, shaggy bison, lumbering black bears, and more. It will come as no surprise that moose live in **Moose Mountain Provincial Park,** where their neighbors include deer, elk, beaver, muskrats, and coyotes. You can also spot adorable black-tailed prairie dogs in **Grasslands National Park.**

3 Winnipeg

Tough, sturdy, muscular, midwestern, Canada's Chicago—that's Winnipeg, capital of Manitoba. The solid cast-iron warehouses, stockyards, railroad depots, and grain

Winnipeg

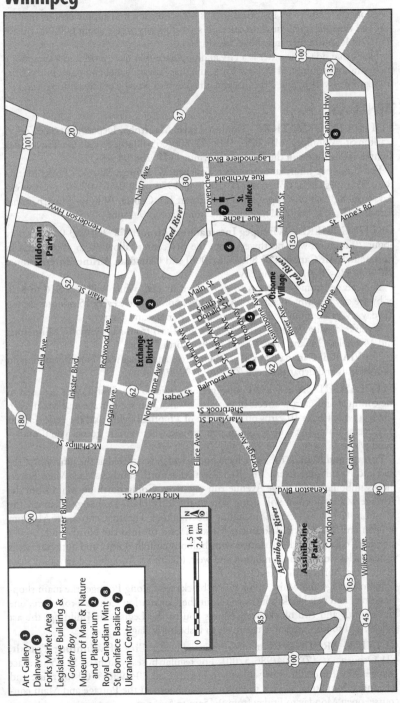

Art Gallery ❸
Dalnavert ❺
Forks Market Area ❻
Legislative Building & Golden Boy ❹
Museum of Man & Nature and Planetarium ❷
Royal Canadian Mint ❽
St. Boniface Basilica ❼
Ukranian Centre ❶

1.5 mi
2.4 km

Kildonan Park

Exchange District

Osborne Village

St. Boniface

Assiniboine Park

Red River

Assiniboine River

Henderson Hwy.

Lagimodiere Blvd.

Trans-Canada Hwy.

Nairn Ave.

Main St.

Leila Ave.

Inkster Blvd.

Redwood Ave.

Logan Ave.

Notre Dame Ave.

McPhillips St.

Inkster Blvd.

King Edward St.

Ellice Ave.

Portage Ave.

Kenaston Blvd.

Maryland St.

Sherbrook St.

Isabel St.

Balmoral St.

Graham Ave.

St. Mary Ave.

York Ave.

Broadway

Smith St.

Donald St.

Assiniboine Ave.

River Ave.

Osborne

Main St.

Provencher

Rue Archibald

Rue Taché

Marion St.

St. Anne's Rd.

Grant Ave.

Corydon Ave.

Wilkes Ave.

20

37

30

101

52

62

57

180

90

85

105

145

100

100

135

150

62

elevators all testify to its historical role as a distribution and supply center, first for furs and then for agricultural products. It's a toiling city where about 600,000 inhabitants sizzle in summer and shovel in winter.

That's one side. The other is a city and populace that have produced a symphony orchestra that triumphed in New York, the first "royal" ballet company in the British Commonwealth, and a theater and arts complex worthy of any national capital.

ESSENTIALS

VISITOR INFORMATION   Contact **Travel Manitoba,** Department SV6, 7-155 Carlton St., Winnipeg, MB, R3C 3H8 (☎ 800/665-0040), or visit the **Travel Idea Centre** at The Forks in the Johnston Terminal (☎ 204/945-3777).

For Winnipeg information contact **Tourism Winnipeg,** 320-325 Forks Market Rd., Winnipeg, MB, R3C 4S8 (☎ 204/943-1970 or 800/665-0204), open weekdays from 8:30am to 4:30pm, or at the Airport InfoCentre, Winnipeg International Airport (☎ 204/774-0031), open daily from 8am to 9:45pm.

GETTING THERE   **Winnipeg International Airport** (☎ 204/983-0562) is only about 20 minutes west-northwest from the city center (allow 30 to 40 minutes in rush hours). **Air Canada** (☎ 800/776-3000) and **Canadian Airlines International** (☎ 800/426-7000) serve the city.

You can get from the airport to downtown by taxi, which will cost $10 to $15, or by the city bus, which costs $1.35 and runs approximately every 15 minutes during the day, every 22 minutes in the evenings, to Portage and Garry.

If you're driving, Winnipeg is 432 miles (697km) from Minneapolis, Minnesota, and 146 miles (235km) from Grand Forks, North Dakota.

The **VIA Rail Canada** depot is at Main Street and Broadway. For information on train arrivals and departures, call ☎ 204/949-7400.

CITY LAYOUT   A native Winnipegger once said to me, "I still can't get used to the confined and narrow streets in the east." When you see Portage and Main, each 132 feet wide (that's 10 yards off the width of a football field), and the eerie flatness that means no matter where you go you can see where you're going, you'll understand why.

Portage and Main is the city's focal point, which is situated at the junction of the Red and Assiniboine rivers. The Red River runs north-south, as does Main Street; the Assiniboine and Portage Avenue run east-west. Going north on Main from the Portage-Main junction will bring you to the City Hall, Exchange District, the Manitoba Centennial Centre (including the Manitoba Theatre Centre), the Museum of Man and Nature, the Ukrainian Museum, and on into the North End, once a mosaic of cultures, and still dotted with bulbous church domes and authentic delis visited by lost souls from Edmonton and west. (*Warning:* At night, I'd stay away from Main Street north of the Arts Centre.)

From Portage and Main, if you go six blocks west along Portage, the main shopping drag, and two blocks south, you'll hit the Convention Centre. From here, one block south and two blocks west brings you to the Legislative Building, the art gallery, and south, just across the river, to Osborne Village.

GETTING AROUND   For information contact **City of Winnipeg Transit,** 421 Osborne St. (☎ 204/986-5700). For regular buses, you need $1.35 in exact change (80¢ for children or seniors) to board. Call 204/986-5700 for route and schedule information, or visit the information booth in the Portage and Main concourse, open Monday to Friday from 9:45am to 5:45pm.

Driving is no problem in Winnipeg, but watch out for the pedestrian walks marked with an X. For car rentals try **Tilden** and **Budget,** both with airport and additional downtown locations.

Taxis can be found at the downtown hotels. They charge $2.25 when the meter drops and $1.67 per mile thereafter. Try **Duffy's Taxi** (☎ 204/772-2451 or 204/775-0101), or **Unicity Taxi** (☎ 204/947-6611 or 204/942-3366).

SPECIAL EVENTS   The **Red River Exhibition,** usually held the last 10 days of June, celebrates and reflects the city's history, showcasing agricultural, horticultural, commercial, and industrial achievements. There is also a midway, a photography show, and other themed features like a lumberjack show. For more information, contact Red River Exhibition, 876 St. James St., Winnipeg, MB, R3G 3J7 (☎ 204/772-9464).

Folklorama, a Festival of Nations, is a two-week cultural festival in August featuring more than 35 ethnic pavilions celebrating ethnic culture, with traditional food, dancing, music, costumes, entertainment, and crafts. For more information, contact Folklorama, 300-180 King St., Winnipeg, MB, R3B 3G8 (☎ 204/982-6210 or 800/665-0234).

The 10-day **Festival du Voyageur,** usually held in February, celebrates French Métis culture in St. Boniface (☎ 204/237-7692).

FAST FACTS   Emergencies   Dial 911 or call the Health Sciences Centre, 820 Sherbrook St. (☎ 204/774-6511), open 24 hours.

Liquor Laws   Liquor can only be bought from the Manitoba Liquor Control Commission stores, or from vendors licensed by the Liquor Control Commission. Main downtown locations are 923 Portage Ave. and 471 River at Osborne (open Monday through Thursday from 10am to 10pm, on Friday and Saturday until 11:30pm). On Sunday drinks may only be served with food, and the tab for drinks must not exceed the tab for food.

Post Office   The main post office is at 266 Graham Ave. (☎ 204/987-5408), and is open from 8am to 5:30pm Monday through Friday.

Time   Winnipeg is on central standard time except from the last Sunday in April to the last Sunday in October, when the city is on daylight saving time.

Weather   Call 204/983-2050.

WHERE TO STAY

Add the 7% provincial sales tax and the GST to all the rates that follow.

EXPENSIVE

Delta Winnipeg. 288 Portage Ave. (at Smith St.), Winnipeg, MB, R3C 0B8. ☎ **204/956-0410** or 800/877-1133 in the U.S. Fax 204/947-1129. 272 rms. A/C MINIBAR TV TEL. Weekdays $184 double. Weekend packages available. AE, DC, ER, MC, V. Parking $7.

Rooms here occupy floors 15 through 29. All offer good views of the city and are well equipped, with hair dryers and coffeemakers. An indoor promenade connects the hotel to Eaton Place and Portage Place. A business lounge is on the 13th floor.

Dining/Entertainment: The candlelit, oak-paneled Signature's offers fine dining and piano entertainment. On the main floor is Tillie's, where sports events are shown on a big TV screen.

Services: 24-hour room service.

Facilities: Indoor pool with an outdoor deck, whirlpool, sauna, exercise room, twin cinemas, and a free Children's Creative Centre (supervised on weekends) where kids can enjoy games, toys, and crafts activities.

Holiday Inn Crowne Plaza. 350 St. Mary's Ave., Winnipeg, MB, R3C 3J2. ☎ **204/ 942-0551.** Fax 204/943-8702. 389 rms. A/C MINIBAR TV TEL. $140 double. Children under 18 stay free in parents' room. Weekend packages available. AE, DC, DISC, ER, MC, V. Parking $7.75.

The 17-story Holiday Inn Crowne Plaza is right downtown and connected by a sky-walk to the Convention Centre. The pleasantly decorated rooms feature the usual amenities. Poolside rooms are a couple of dollars more than standard rooms.

Dining/Entertainment: There's the Elephant and Castle pub for all-day dining, and Between Friends, serving Mexican, Asian, and French food. There's also a piano bar, Tickers Lounge.

Services: 24-hour room service.

Facilities: There's a skylit indoor pool plus an outdoor pool, both attractively designed with potted plants, terraces, and adjacent exercise facilities.

✪ **Place Louis Riel All-Suite Hotel.** 190 Smith St. (at St. Mary's), Winnipeg, MB, R3C 1J8. ☎ **204/947-6961.** Fax 204/947-3029. 288 rms. A/C TV TEL. $150 double. Extra person $10. Children under 16 stay free in parents' room. Weekend package available. AE, DC, MC, V. Free parking.

Right in the heart of downtown Winnipeg is a bargain that shouldn't be passed up. At the Place Louis Riel All-Suite Hotel you can stay in a studio (with a sleeping/ living area partitioned from the kitchen) or a beautifully furnished one- or two-bedroom suite. All units come with a fully equipped kitchen (including a micro-wave and coffeemaker) and dining area. For convenience, a laundry, grocery store, and restaurant and lounge are located on the ground floor of the 23-floor building.

Ramada Marlborough Winnipeg. 331 Smith St. (at Portage), Winnipeg, MB, R3B 2G9. ☎ **204/942-6411** or 800/667-7666. Fax 204/942-2017. 148 rms. A/C TV TEL. $130 double. Children under 18 stay free in parents' room. Special weekend (Fri–Sun) rates available. AE, DC, ER, MC, V. Free parking.

This isn't your average Ramada. Originally built in 1914, the Marlborough retains its vaulted ceilings, stained-glass windows, and Victorian Gothic exterior, but now offers all modern amenities. The fine dining room is Victor's, reviewed below. There's also a coffee shop and lounge.

Westin Winnipeg. 2 Lombard Place, Winnipeg, MB, R3B 0Y3. ☎ **204/957-1350** or 800/ 228-3000. Fax 204/949-1486. 350 rms. A/C MINIBAR TV TEL. $159 double. Weekend packages available. AE, DC, ER, MC, V. Parking $7.50.

Right at the corner of Portage and Main rises the 21-story white concrete Westin Hotel Winnipeg, a few minutes' walk from the Manitoba Centennial Centre. Its rooms are furnished with white colonial-style pieces and the usual modern appointments.

Dining/Entertainment: The Velvet Glove features luxurious dining amid gilt-framed portraits, wood paneling, and brass torchères. You might choose an entrée such as scaloppine of wild boar with sun-dried cranberry sauce. Prices range from $24 to $32.50 for a fixed-price menu. Chocolate cherries, served with your coffee, are just part of the impeccable service, and if you want that $100 bottle of wine, it's available. Chimes is for a casual breakfast or lunch; there's also a coffee shop downstairs.

Services: 24-hour room service.

Facilities: Indoor pool, whirlpool, and sauna on the 21st floor; plus a fitness center.

MODERATE

Charterhouse. York and Hargrave streets, Winnipeg, MB, R3C 0N9. ☎ **204/942-0101** or 800/782-0175. Fax 204/956-0665. 90 rms. A/C TV TEL. $102 double. Extra person $7. Children under 16 stay free in parents' room. Packages available AE, CB, DC, DISC, ER, MC, V. Free parking.

Right downtown, a block from the Convention Centre, the Charterhouse offers attractively decorated rooms with all the modern accoutrements. About half have balconies. There's an outdoor swimming pool and a deck/patio.

The Rib Room is well known locally for good prime rib, ribs, steaks, and seafood, with main courses from $13 to $24. There's a coffee shop, too.

Holiday Inn Airport West. 2520 Portage Ave., Winnipeg, MB, R3J 3T6. ☎ **204/885-4478** or 800/665-0352. Fax 204/831-5734. 229 rms (19 suites). A/C TV TEL. $98 double; $120 one-bedroom suite with kitchen. Extra person $10. Children under 18 stay free in parents' room. Weekend packages available. AE, DC, DISC, ER, MC, V. Free indoor parking.

Five minutes from the Assiniboia Downs racetrack, and a 10-minute drive from the airport, the Holiday Inn offers fine accommodations, with amenities such as vanity mirrors with hair dryers. One-bedroom suites have fully equipped kitchens, and deluxe apartments are furnished with king-size beds. There's a restaurant and cocktail lounge with dancing to live music. The stunning tropical atrium contains an indoor pool, whirlpool, sauna, exercise room, and deck for poolside refreshment. There's also a supervised day room for children. Room service is available from 6:30am to 11pm. There's also free limousine service to and from the airport.

Travelodge Hotel Winnipeg Downtown. 360 Colony St., Winnipeg, MB, R3B 2P3. ☎ **204/786-7011** or 800/661-9563. Fax 204/772-1443. 160 rms. A/C TV TEL. $80 double. Extra person $8. Children under 16 stay free in parents' room. AE, DC, DISC, ER, MC, V. Parking $3.21.

Located on Portage at Colony, quite near the art gallery, the Travelodge offers rooms furnished in light oak, each with a desk, armchairs, and a table. Bathrooms contain phones and full amenities. Other facilities include a restaurant, a whirlpool, and an indoor swimming pool.

INEXPENSIVE

For reliable, clean, and attractively decorated rooms, the **Comfort Inn by Journey's End,** 3109 Pembina Hwy. (☎ 204/269-7390), is hard to beat. Doubles are $75.99.

Gordon Downtowner. 330 Kennedy St., Winnipeg, MB, R3B 2M6. ☎ **204/943-5581**. Fax 204/338-4348. 40 rms. A/C TV TEL. $55 double. Extra person $7. Children under 16 stay free in parents' room. AE, DC, ER, MC, V.

Probably the best budget hotel downtown is the Gordon Downtowner, part of Portage Place. The rooms have all been renovated recently, and have touches such as extra phones in the bathrooms. Amenities include a pub and a comfortable restaurant (open from 7am to 9pm).

WHERE TO DINE

There's a 7% GST plus a 7% provincial sales tax on any food bill above $6.

EXPENSIVE

✪ **Le Beaujolais.** 131 Provencher Blvd. (at Tache), in St. Boniface. ☎ **204/237-6276.** Reservations recommended. Main courses $15–$27. AE, ER, MC, V. Mon–Fri 11:30am–2:30pm; daily 5–10pm. FRENCH.

Le Beaujolais is a comfortable place serving such traditional dishes as roast duck with cassis, veal tenderloin with Roquefort sauce, and rack of lamb Nicoise. At night when candles are lit, the room, which features etched glass and glass brick partitions, takes on a romantic air that's enhanced by the classical guitarist who entertains.

Restaurant Dubrovnik. 390 Assiniboine Ave. ☎ **204/944-0594.** Reservations recommended. Main courses $16–$24. AE, MC, V. Mon–Sat 11am–2pm; daily 5–11pm. CONTINENTAL.

Restaurant Dubrovnik offers a romantic setting for fine continental cuisine and Eastern European specialties. It occupies a beautiful Victorian brick town house with working fireplaces and leaded-glass windows, and an enclosed veranda. Each dining area is decorated tastefully with a few plants and colorful gusle (beautifully carved musical instruments, often inlaid with mother-of-pearl).

Start with the Russian borscht or the gibanica, a Yugoslavian pastry-cheese served with mixed greens and sour-cream dressing. Follow with darne of Atlantic salmon grilled or poached with fresh herb sauce or rack of lamb with rosemary. Finish with a coffee Dubrovnik (sljivovica, kruskovac bitters, with coffee, whipped cream, and chopped walnuts).

Victor's. In the Ramada Marlborough Winnipeg, 331 Smith St. ☎ **204/947-2751.** Reservations recommended. Main courses $19–$26. AE, DC, ER, MC, V. Tues–Fri 11:30am–2pm; Tues–Sat 5–9:30pm. CONTINENTAL.

For many years Victor's has enjoyed a reputation for fine cuisine, ambience, and service. It occupies a two-story-high room with a cathedral ceiling, stained-glass windows, and oak paneling. The menu is modern and imaginative, featuring such appetizers as carpaccio and crabmeat cakes with lime mayonnaise and mango relish. To follow, there might be veal medallions with lingonberry sauce, salmon with a horseradish sauce, or a delicious full rack of lamb Provençale.

MODERATE

✪ **Amici.** 326 Broadway. ☎ **204/943-4997.** Reservations recommended. Main courses $13–$26. AE, DC, ER, MC, V. Mon–Fri 11:30am–2:30pm; Mon–Sat 5–11pm. CONTINENTAL/ ITALIAN.

The atmosphere at Amici is plush and comfortable. You have your choice of 12 pastas—fettucine alla messicana (with mussels, avocados, lime juice, tequila, and cream), or spaghetti all amatriciana, with pancetta, tomatoes, peppers, and ginger. Or you can have meat and fish dishes like medallions of beef with a Barolo wine sauce or a fish of the day.

✪ **Bistro Dansk.** 63 Sherbrook St. ☎ **204/775-5662.** Reservations recommended. Main courses $7.50–$14. V. Mon–Sat 11am–3pm; Mon–Sat 5–9:30pm. DANISH.

In this warm chalet-style bistro, bright-red gate-back chairs complement the wooden tables and raffia place mats. Main courses include seven superlative Danish specialties, such as frikadeller (Danish meat patties, made from ground veal and pork, served with red cabbage and potato salad), and aeggekage (a Danish omelet with bacon, garnished with tomato and green onions, served with home-baked Danish bread). At lunchtime, specialties include nine or so open-face sandwiches, served on homemade rye or white bread, most priced from $3 to $6.

Haynes Chicken Shack. 257 Lulu St. ☎ **204/774-2764.** Reservations recommended. Main courses $9–$13. MC, V. Mon–Sat 7am–11:30am; Wed–Sat 5–11pm. HOME COOKING.

A small white house in the middle of a residential area, Haynes Chicken Shack offers good home-style cooking and a family welcome. The tasty dishes include southern fried chicken, barbecued spareribs, shrimp Creole, breaded shrimp, and T-bone steak. All these dishes come with french fries, coleslaw, and hot biscuits. Occasionally on Sunday afternoons there's blues and jazz from 2 to 6pm.

Old Swiss Inn. 207 Edmonton St. ☎ **204/942-7725.** Reservations recommended. Main courses $12–$26. AE, DC, ER, MC, V. Mon–Fri 11:30am–2:30pm; Mon–Sat 5–9:30pm. SWISS.

The Old Swiss Inn lives up to its name with unpretentious alpine warmth, wood paneling, pictures of mountain scenery, and Swiss specialties. At dinner, you might start with Swiss onion soup or cheese fondue and follow with veal Zurich (with white wine and mushrooms), or the house specialty, fondue bourguignonne. At lunchtime you can have Bratwurst mit Rösti (Swiss fried potatoes).

Red Lantern. 302 Hamel Ave., in St. Boniface. ☎ **204/233-4841.** Reservations recommended. Main courses $13–$23. AE, ER, MC, V. Mon–Fri 11am–2pm; Mon–Sat 5–10pm. CONTINENTAL.

A red lantern hangs outside the small house occupied by this restaurant. Inside, there's a cozy beamed dining room. The food is excellent, nicely presented, graciously served, and very reasonably priced. French background music adds to the atmosphere. Among the specialties are a breast of chicken stuffed with Brie, spinach and carrots served with thyme cream sauce, and several beef dishes.

INEXPENSIVE

Alycia's. 559 Cathedral (at the corner of McGregor). ☎ **204/582-8789.** Reservations recommended. Main courses $5–$10. AE, DC, ER, MC, V. Mon–Sat 8am–8pm. UKRAINIAN.

Alycia's serves traditional home-style Ukrainian cuisine. Woven tablecloths cover the tables, and painted eggs and Ukrainian china decorate the small, homey restaurant. Feast on pirogies, kolbassa, pickerel, hamburger, and roast turkey.

D' 8 Schtove. 1842 Pembina Hwy. ☎ **204/275-2294.** Reservations accepted. Main courses $6–$12. AE, DC, ER, MC, V. Mon–Sat 8am–11pm, Sun 9am–11pm. MENNONITE.

Settle into this large dining room decorated with brass and wood, and start with one of the borschts—komst borscht (cabbage with sausages) or somma borscht (with potato). Follow with jebackte rebspaa (pork ribs baked in tomato sauce), holupche (cabbage rolls), beef stroganoff, slices of smoked farmer sausage in sweet-and-sour sauce, or the wrenikje, more commonly known as pirogies. Top it all off with rhubarb or apple strudel.

There's another location at 103-1277 Henderson Hwy. (☎ 204/334-1200).

✪ **Tap & Grill.** 137 Osborne St. ☎ **204/284-7455.** Reservations recommended. Main courses $8–$18. AE, DC, ER, MC, V. Mon–Thurs 11am–2pm and 5pm–12:30am, Fri 4:30pm–1:30am, Sat 11:30am–1:30am. MEDITERRANEAN.

The washed pastel walls and tile evoke a Mediterranean taverna atmosphere at this restaurant, which serves dishes from Greece, Italy, France, Spain, and Turkey. In addition to pasta, traditional pizzas, and salads, there's a variety of grilled seafood including octopus and halibut, several souvlaki dishes, and a fine spit-roasted leg of lamb deftly flavored with oregano, garlic, lemon, and pepper. If you wish, you can order the grilled dishes as tapas.

EXPLORING THE CITY
THE TOP ATTRACTIONS

At the junction of the Red and Assiniboine rivers, the **Forks Market Area** is a major city attraction created in the late 1980s when the old railyard was redeveloped. The draw is the market—a wonderful display of fresh produce and specialty foods.

There are also restaurants, specialty stores, and programs, exhibits, and events scheduled throughout the year. In summer visitors can stroll along the river walks; in winter there's free public skating on outdoor artificial ice or along groomed river trails. Call ☎ 204/957-7618 for recorded information that's updated weekly.

✪ Winnipeg Art Gallery. 300 Memorial Blvd. ☎ **204/786-6641**. Admission $3 adults, $2 students and seniors, $5 families; free for children age 12 and under. Sept–June Tues–Sun 11am–5pm (Wed until 9pm); June–Sept daily 10am–5pm (Wed until 9pm).

A distinctive triangular building of local Tyndall stone, the Winnipeg Art Gallery houses one of the world's largest collections of Inuit art. Note the wry vision of an artist such as Leah Qumaluk Povungnituk as contained in a stone cut of *Birds Stealing Kayak from Man*. Other collections focus on historic and contemporary Canadian art, and British and European artists. The decorative art collections feature works by Canadian silversmiths and studio potters while the photography collection contains more than 200 works by Andre Kertesz, and represents other 20th-century photographers such as Diane Arbus and Irving Penn. The penthouse restaurant overlooks the fountain and flowers in the sculpture court.

Manitoba Museum of Man & Nature. 190 Rupert Ave. ☎ **204/956-2830** or 204/943-3139 for recorded information. Admission $4 adults, $3 seniors students, and children ages 4–17. Victoria Day–Labor Day daily 10am–6pm; Labor Day–Victoria Day Tues–Sun 10am–4pm.

Part of the Manitoba Centennial Centre, the museum is a fascinating place, with galleries that depict local history, culture, and geology through life-size exhibits such as a buffalo hunt, prehistoric creatures, pioneer life, pronghorn antelope, teepees, sod huts, and log cabins. In the Urban Gallery, you can walk down a 1920s Winnipeg street past typical homes and businesses of the era. The Boreal Forest Gallery depicts Manitoba's most northerly forested region. Climb aboard the *Nonsuch*, a full-size replica of the 17th-century ketch that returned to England in 1669 with the first cargo of furs out of Hudson Bay.

Manitoba Planetarium. 190 Rupert Ave. ☎ **204/943-3142** for recorded information or 204/956-2830. Planetarium $3.50 adults, $2.50 students, seniors, and children ages 4–17. Science Centre $3.50 adults, $2.50 seniors, students, and children 4–17. Both are free for children 3 and under. Planetarium shows presented daily mid-May–Labor Day, Tues–Sun the rest of the year. Science Centre Victoria Day–Labor Day daily 10am–6pm; rest of the year Tues–Fri 10am–4pm, Sat–Sun and holidays 10am–5pm.

The planetarium, part of the Manitoba Museum of Man and Nature in the Manitoba Centennial Centre, offers shows in its 280-seat Star Theatre exploring everything from cosmic catastrophes to the reality of UFOs. Hundreds of projectors work in concert to fill the theater's semicircular dome with stellar imagery, while the 154 separate projectors of the Zeiss planetarium instrument are geared so accurately that they can show the sky as our ancestors saw it thousands of years ago, or as people will see it far into the future. The Science Centre is a hands-on science gallery that helps explain the laws of nature.

The Ukrainian Cultural & Educational Centre. 184 Alexander Ave. East. ☎ **204/942-0218**. Free admission. Tues–Sat 10am–4pm, Sun 2–5pm.

Just up the street from the Museum of Man and Nature, the Oseredok, or Ukrainian Centre, conserves the artifacts and heritage of the Ukrainian people. The second-floor art gallery and fifth-floor museum are used for changing exhibits ranging from 18th-century icons to folk art, such as embroideries, weaving, Easter eggs, wood carving, ceramics, and clothing.

Royal Canadian Mint. 520 Lagimodière Blvd. ☎ **204/257-3359**. Admission $2 adults; free for children under 8. Tours given every 30 minutes Mon–Fri 8:30am–4pm. Take Main Street south over the Assiniboine/Red rivers, turn left onto Marion Street, and then right onto Lagimodière. You'll see the mint rise up just beyond the Trans-Canada Highway (Route 135).

The process of making money is mind-boggling, and this tour will prove it to you. Dyes are produced; a roof crane lifts 4,000-pound strips of bronze and nickel; three 150-ton presses stamp out up to 8,800 coin blanks per minute; and coining presses turn out up to 18,000 coins per hour to the telling machines that count the number for bagging. The whole process from start to finish represents an extraordinary engineering feat streamlined by conveyor belts and an overhead monorail.

More Attractions

The Golden Boy & the Legislative Building. 450 Broadway. ☎ **204/945-5813**. Tours in summer Mon–Fri 9am–6:30pm, by reservation at other times.

There he stands, 240 feet above ground atop the Legislative Building's dome, clutching a sheaf of wheat under his left arm and holding aloft in his right an eternally lit torch symbolizing the spirit of progress. French sculptor Charles Gardet created his 5-ton, 13½-foot bronze statue during World War I.

The building below, a magnificent classical Greek structure, was designed in 1919 by British architect Frank Worthington Simon. Inside, two enormous bronze buffaloes, also by Gardet, flank a grand marble staircase. Note at the back of the antehall the Frank Brangwyn mural commemorating World War I. The building's focal point is, of course, the Legislative Chamber, where the 57 members of Manitoba's legislative assembly meet.

Before leaving the area, wander through the 31-acre grounds, dotted with statues including Scotland's Robert Burns, French-Canadian Georges-Etienne Cartier, Iceland's Jon Sigurdson, and Ukrainian poet Taras Shevchenko.

Dalnavert. 61 Carlton St. (between Broadway and Assiniboine Avenue). ☎ **204/943-2835**. Admission $3 adults, $2 senior citizens and students, $1.50 ages 6–18, $1 children 6–12, $7 families; free for children under 6. June–Aug Tues–Thurs and Sat–Sun 10am–6pm; Sept–Dec and Mar–May Tues–Thurs and Sat–Sun noon–5pm; Jan–Feb Sat–Sun noon–5pm.

Just two blocks east of the Legislative Building stands the Victorian home built in 1895 for Hugh John Macdonald, the only son of Canada's first prime minister. It's a fine example of a late Victorian gingerbread house with a wraparound veranda. At the time of construction the latest innovations—electric lighting, indoor plumbing, central hot water heating, and walk-in closets—were included. Throughout the house are beautiful stained-glass panels (whose softness of color cannot be duplicated today), elaborate wood paneling, high molded ceilings, and masses of overstuffed furniture and ornate drapes. Early household gadgets are also on view, including the Dowswell Rocker washer. Back then, functional appliances were things of beauty—note the waffle iron with its diamonds, hearts, clubs, and spades design.

The Commodity Exchange. On the fifth floor of the Commodity Exchange Tower, 360 Main St. ☎ **204/949-0495** to arrange a tour. Mon–Fri 9:30am–1:15pm.

Originally organized in 1887 as a grain exchange, the Commodity Exchange changed its name in 1972 to reflect its expansion into other markets. The very crux of Winnipeg was right here: this was the world's premier grain market until World War II. There are 300 members and 102 companies registered for trading privileges.

It's best to come early around 9:30am, or right near closing at 12:45pm, when you're more likely to see some feverish action on the floor. You have to view the proceedings from a glass-enclosed gallery overlooking the pit where buyers and sellers are jostling, yelling out figures, and gesticulating in apparent confusion, while above current Winnipeg and Chicago prices race by on ticker tape.

Western Canada Aviation Museum. 958 Ferry Rd. ☎ **204/786-5503.** Admission $3 adults, $2 students 6–17. Mon–Sat 10am–4pm, Sun and holidays 1–4pm. Closed Dec 25–26, Jan 1, and Good Friday.

Among the historic flying treasures at the Western Canada Aviation Museum are Canada's first helicopter, designed and test-flown between 1935 and 1939.

Grant's Old Mill. 2777 Portage Ave. (at the corner of Booth Drive). ☎ **204/986-5613.** Admission $1 adults, 75¢ students and seniors, 50¢ children under 12. June–Aug daily 10am–6pm; rest of year by appointment only.

Here stands the reconstruction of the original watermill built on Sturgeon Creek in 1829, believed to be the first watermill west of the Great Lakes and the first instance of the use of hydropower in Manitoba. Grist is ground daily during the summer and you can buy some in a souvenir bag if you like.

Assiniboia Downs. 3975 Portage Ave. ☎ **204/885-3330.** Clubhouse admission $2. Drive 9 miles (20 minutes) west of the city to the junction of Highway 1 West (Portage Avenue) and Highway 100 (Perimeter Highway).

The racetrack is open for Thoroughbred racing May to October and for simulcast harness racing November to April. You can dine in the Terrace Dining Room overlooking the track. Post times are Wednesday, Friday, and Saturday at 7pm, and Sunday and holidays at 1:30pm.

Fort Whyte Centre. 1961 McCreary Rd., Fort Whyte. ☎ **204/989-8355.** Admission $3.50 adults, $2.50 students, seniors and children over 2. Mon–Fri 9am–5pm (until 9pm on Wed), Sat–Sun and holidays 10am–5pm.

About 15 minutes from downtown, some old cement quarries have been converted into several lakes at Fort Whyte Centre, and now serve as an environmental educational facility. The freshwater aquarium has many local Manitoba specimens, like the northern pike and walleye. There are self-guided nature trails, waterfowl gardens, and an interpretive center and gift shop.

NEIGHBORHOODS

THE EXCHANGE DISTRICT   The best way to explore this historic warehouse district, built during the city's boom years at the turn of the century, is to join the walking tour that starts at the Pantages Playhouse Tuesday through Sunday at 11am and 1:30pm. For more information, call ☎ 204/986-4718. Admission is $4 for adults, $2 for seniors and youths ages 12 to 17. Private group tours available.

WELLINGTON CRESCENT   The "Park Avenue of the Prairies," as it was once called, is lined with mansions commissioned by the many entrepreneurs who built them during the city's great real estate booms of 1880–82. Land prices rocketed and thousands of dollars were made in literally minutes.

ST. BONIFACE   Across the river in St. Boniface, a street becomes a *rue* and a hello becomes *bonjour*. Here you'll find the largest French-speaking community in western Canada, dating from 1783 when Pierre Gaultier de Varennes established Fort Rouge at the junction of the Red and Assiniboine rivers. The junction became the center of a thriving fur trade for the North West Company, which rivaled and challenged the Hudson's Bay Company. In the early 19th century a religious presence was established and a church built in 1819 dedicated to Boniface. Later in 1846 four

Grey Nuns arrived and began service in the west. The historic sites that can be viewed today relate to this period and later.

The original basilica was replaced in 1908 by a beautiful building that was destroyed by fire in 1968. The massive Gothic arches remain, and cradled within the shell of the old building is the new basilica, built in 1972. In front of the cathedral, the cemetery is the resting place for many historical figures, most notably Louis Riel, whose grave is marked by a replica of a Red River cart. Riel, leader of the Métis uprising and president of the provincial government formed in 1869 to 1870, tried to prevent the transfer of the Red River settlement to Canada.

PARKS & GARDENS

Comprising 393 acres for playing, picnicking, or biking, **Assiniboine Park,** at Corydon Avenue (☎ 204/986-6921 or 204/986-3130), contains a miniature railway, a duck pond, an English garden (which opens in June), and a conservatory. During the winter there's skating on the pond and tobogganing. The park also contains a 100-acre **zoo** (see "Especially for Kids," below). The park is open daily dawn to dusk.

Kildonan Park is quite delightful, with landscaped gardens, picnic spots, biking paths, outdoor swimming, and wading pools, as well as a restaurant and dining room overlooking a small artificial lake. Also look for the Witch's House from *Hansel and Gretel* in the park. Rainbow Stage productions are held here in July and August.

CRUISES & A STEAM-TRAIN EXCURSION

During the summer, the cruise ships *MS River Rouge* and *MS Paddlewheel Queen* depart from their dock at Water and Gilroy at the foot of the Provencher Bridge on a variety of cruises including a sunset dinner-dance cruise beginning at 7pm and a moonlight version that leaves at 10pm (both $11). Two-hour sightseeing trips ($10) depart at 2pm, providing fine views of the city from the Red and Assiniboine rivers. A longer historic river cruise leaves at 9:30am, returning at 4pm. The cost is $17 for adults, $14.95 for seniors, and $9 for children. For more information call ☎ 204/942-4500.

A 1900 steam-era train, the *Prairie Dog Central,* takes visitors on a two-hour, 36-mile round trip from Winnipeg to Grosse Isle, Manitoba. En route you really get a feel for the prairie and what it must have been like for late 19th-century immigrants to travel to and through the west. The train leaves on Sunday at 11am and 3pm June through September. Adults pay $13; senior citizens and students 12 to 17, $11; children 2 to 11, $7. Board the train at the CN St. James Station near 1661 Portage Ave. For more information, contact the **Vintage Locomotive Society** (☎ 204/832-5259).

ESPECIALLY FOR KIDS

At the Forks, there's a **Children's Museum** (☎ 204/956-1888), specially designed for 2- to 13-year-olds with participatory exhibits. At Under the Big Top they can run away to the circus and devise a show of their very own; in the TV studio they can create their own television shows, as performers or as technicians. Admission is $4.75 for adults; $2.50 children, students, and seniors. Open daily 10am to 6pm, Thursday and Friday until 8pm.

Assiniboine Park, at Corydon Avenue (☎ 204/986-6921 or 204/986-3130), is a great place to picnic or play. Its top attraction, however, is a 100-acre **zoo** where the animals—bears, tigers, zebras, flamingos, bison, elk, deer—are kept in as natural an environment as possible. Some exotic species on display include Chinese red dogs, snow leopards, ruffed lemurs, and Irkutsk lynx. Many spectacular birds live and breed in the Tropical House. A special "Discovery Centre" for children is fun. From March through September, admission is $3 for adults, $2.75 seniors, $1.50 children 13 to 17, $1 children 2 to 12; from October to February it's $1 for everyone. It's free to all on Tuesdays and for children under two year-round. The park is open daily dawn to dusk, the zoo daily from 10am to dusk. To get here, take Portage Avenue west, turn left onto Kenaston Boulevard (Route 90) south, and then turn right onto Corydon.

Kids love the thrills at **Fun Mountain Water Slide Park,** 4 miles or so east of the mint on Highway 1 East (☎ 204/255-3910). There are 10 slides as well as rides, including bumper boats, a giant hot tub, and kids' playground with a wading pool. All-day admission costs $11 for adults, $8.50 children ages 4–12, free for children 3 and under. Open June through August daily from 10am to 8pm, weather permitting.

Shopping

The city's most interesting shopping centers are downtown's **Portage Place,** which is four blocks long and contains 150 shops, three cinemas, and an IMAX theater, and the multilevel **Eaton Place** (between Graham and St. Mary's Avenues and Hargrave and Donald streets), with more than 110 shops and services.

Every Saturday and Sunday in the summer the **Old Market Square,** at Albert and Bannatyne, blossoms into a lively open-air market. Under canopied stalls, craftspeople, vendors, market gardeners, and local entertainers offer antiques, crafts, fresh foodstuffs, and music and magic in a heady celebration of summer.

Another area worth exploring is behind the Legislative Building at **Osborne Village,** where boutiques and specialty shops are concentrated.

WINNIPEG AFTER DARK
THE PERFORMING ARTS

The **Manitoba Centennial Centre,** 555 Main St. (☎ 204/956-1360), is a complex that includes the Centennial Concert Hall (home to the Royal Winnipeg Ballet, the Winnipeg Symphony, and the Manitoba Opera), the Manitoba Theatre Centre, the Warehouse Theatre, and the Playhouse Theatre. In the foyer, Greta Dale's vast tile mural brilliantly represents dance, music, and drama. Murals by Tony Tascona and huge wall hangings by Canadian artists Takao Tanabe and Kenneth Lochhead decorate the lobbies. The Centre's acoustics are superior and the no-center-aisle auditorium maximizes sight lines.

Other spaces offering frequent concerts and performances include the **Winnipeg Art Gallery** (☎ 204/786-6641), which often features blues/jazz, chamber music, and contemporary music groups; the **Pantages Playhouse Theatre,** 180 Market Ave. (☎ 204/986-3003); and the **Convention Centre,** 375 York Ave. (☎ 204/ 956-1720), for popular, folk, and light orchestral musical concerts.

✪ **Royal Winnipeg Ballet.** 380 Graham Ave., at Edmonton St. ☎ **204/956-0183** or 204/956-2792 for the box office. Tickets $13–$40, with a 20% discount for students and senior citizens, and a 50% discount for children 12 and under.

The world-renowned Royal Winnipeg Ballet was founded in 1939 by two British immigrant ballet teachers, making it North America's second-oldest ballet company (after San Francisco's). By 1949 it was a professional troupe, and in 1953 was granted a royal charter. Today the company's repertoire contains both contemporary and classical works, such as Ashton's *The Dream, Giselle,* and *Anne of Green Gables.* The company performs at the Centennial Concert Hall, usually for a two-week period in October, November, December, March, and May.

Winnipeg Symphony Orchestra. 555 Main St. ☎ **204/949-3950** or 204/949-3976 for the box office. Tickets $16–$35.

Established in 1947, the Winnipeg Symphony Orchestra made its debut in 1978 at Carnegie Hall in New York City. The orchestra's prestige and the genuinely superb acoustics of the Centennial Concert Hall have attracted such guest artists as Itzhak Perlman, Isaac Stern, Tracey Dahl, and Maureen Forrester. The season usually runs from September to mid-May.

Manitoba Opera. Box 31027, Portage Place, 393 Portage Ave. ☎ **204/942-7479,** or 204/ 957-7842 for the box office. Tickets from $10.

First performing in 1970, the Manitoba Opera has featured a season of three operas each year at the Centennial Concert Hall with performances in November, February, and April. Recent seasons have included productions of *Turandot* and *Rigoletto*. English subtitles are used.

Theater

You can enjoy theater in the park at **Rainbow Stage,** 2021 Main St. in Kildonan Park (☎ 204/942-2091), Canada's largest and oldest continuously operating outdoor theater. The stage presents two musical classics running about three weeks each during July and August. Located on the banks of the Red River, Rainbow is easily accessible by bus or car. For tickets, which cost from $8 to $18, write Rainbow Stage, 112 Market Ave., Suite 310, Winnipeg, MB, R3B 0P4.

The **MTC Warehouse,** at 140 Rupert Ave. at Lily (☎ 204/942-6537), presents more cutting-edge, controversial plays in an intimate 300-seat theater. Its four-play season runs from mid-October to mid-May. Tickets range from $20 to $35.

Manitoba Theatre Centre. 174 Market Ave. ☎ **204/942-6537.** Tickets $13–$44.

Acclaimed as Canada's best regional theater, the Manitoba Theatre Centre began in 1958, operating in the rickety but spirited atmosphere of the old Dominion Theatre on Portage and Main. Today the modern theater, adjacent to the Centennial Concert Hall, seats 785 people. Since its founding by Tom Hendry and John Hirsch, the group has been dedicated to producing good serious theater. A recent season's offerings included *Hamlet*, starring Keanu Reeves. The season usually features six productions and runs from October to April.

THE BAR & MUSIC SCENE

Most nightlife action takes place either in the Exchange District or at the main downtown hotels. **Windows,** in the Sheraton Winnipeg at 161 Donald St. (☎ 204/ 942-5300), offers dancing to live jazz.

Country is the biggest sound and it gets going six nights a week at the **Palomino Club,** 1133 Portage Ave., (☎ 204/772-0454), with live bands from 9pm. Cover is $4 on weekends but Thursday is the hopping night. Live rock bands play both upstairs and downstairs at the **Osborne Village Inn,** 160 Osborne St. (☎ 204/ 452-9824). Cover and minimum vary with the performer. Rock also plays at the **Royal Albert,** 48 Albert St. (☎ 204/943-8750).

Sit back with shipboard friends and watch the city drift by as you glide along the Red and Assiniboine rivers on the *MS River Rouge* and dance to a live band. Dinners are available. For more information, call ☎ 204/947-6843.

GAMBLING

On the seventh floor of the Hotel Fort Garry, visitors can play blackjack, baccarat, roulette, Caribbean poker, Super Pan 9, or pump coins into more than 200 slot machines at the **Crystal Casino,** 222 Broadway Ave. (☎ 204/957-2600). This intimate, European-style casino accommodates about 380 players. Reservations are taken. Open Monday to Saturday from noon to 2am, Sunday from 2pm to 2am. Jacket and tie mandatory (18 years and over only).

4 Side Trips from Winnipeg

LOWER FORT GARRY NATIONAL HISTORIC PARK

The oldest intact stone fur-trading post in North America is Lower Fort Garry (☎ 204/785-6065), only 20 miles (32km) north of Winnipeg on Highway 9. Built in the 1830s, Lower Fort Garry was an important Hudson's Bay Company transshipment and provisioning post. Within the walls of the compound are the governor's residence, several warehouses including the fur loft, and the Men's House, where male employees of the company lived. Outside the compound are service buildings—blacksmith's, engineer's, and so on. The meticulously restored fort is staffed by costumed volunteers who make candles and soap, forge horseshoes, locks, and bolts, and generally demonstrate the ways of life of the 1850s. In a lean-to beside the fur-loft building stands an original York boat; hundreds of these once traveled the waterways from Hudson Bay to the Rockies and from the Red River to the Arctic carrying furs and trading goods. A 20-minute slide show provides an introduction to the Fort's history and the Hudson's Bay Company.

The site is open daily 10am to 6pm from mid-May to Labor Day. Adults pay $5 for admission; seniors $3.75, children ages 6 to 16 and under, $2.50; under 5 and seniors over 65 enter free.

STEINBACH MENNONITE HERITAGE VILLAGE

About 30 miles (48km) outside Winnipeg is the Steinbach Mennonite Heritage Village, located 1¹/₂ miles north of Steinbach on Highway 12 (☎ 204/326-9661). This 40-acre museum complex is worth a detour. Between 1874 and 1880, about 7,000 Mennonites migrated here from the Ukraine, establishing settlements like Kleefeld, Steinbach, Blumenort, and others. After World War I, many moved on to Mexico and Uruguay when Manitoba closed all unregistered schools between 1922 and 1926, but they were replaced by another surge of emigrants fleeing the Russian Revolution. Their community life is portrayed here in a complex of about 20 buildings. In the museum building, dioramas display daily life and community artifacts, such as woodworking and sewing tools, sausage makers, clothes, medicines, and furnishings. Elsewhere in the complex visitors can view the windmill grinding grain (800 pounds an hour with a 25-m.p.h. wind), ride in an ox-drawn wagon, watch the blacksmith at work, or view any number of homes, agricultural machines, and so on.

The restaurant serves Mennonite food—a full meal of borscht, thick-sliced homemade brown bread, coleslaw, pirogies, and sausage, plus rhubarb crumble, at very reasonable prices.

The village is open in May from 10am to 5pm; in June, July, and August from 9am to 7pm; and in September from 10am to 5pm. On Sunday the gates do not open until noon. From October to April only the museum is open Monday to Friday from 10am to 4pm. Admission is $3.25 for adults, $2 for seniors, $1.50 for students, $1.25 for students in grades 1 to 6.

5 Manitoba's Eastern Border: Whiteshell & Atikaki Provincial Parks

Less than two hours' drive from Winnipeg (90 miles east; 144km) lies a network of a dozen rivers and more than 200 lakes in the 1,000-square-mile ✪ **Whiteshell Provincial Park** (☎ 204/369-5232). Among the park's natural features are Rainbow and Whitemouth Falls, a lovely lily pond west of Caddy Lake and West Hawk Lake, Manitoba's deepest lake, which was created by a meteorite, and a goose sanctuary (best seen in mid-May to July when the goslings are about). Visitors can also view petroforms, stone arrangements fashioned by an Algonquin-speaking people to communicate with the spirits. The park is busiest in summer, and spectacular in fall and winter. In fall you can witness an ancient ritual—the Indians harvesting wild rice. One person poles a canoe through the rice field while another bends the stalks into the canoe and knocks the ripe grains off with a picking stick.

The **Manitoba Naturalists Society,** headquartered at 401-63 Albert St. in Winnipeg (☎ 204/943-9029), operates wilderness programs and other workshops at their cabin on Lake Mantario. There are six self-guided trails plus several short trails that can be completed in less than two hours. For serious backpackers, the **Mantario Trail** is a three- to six-day hike over 37.2 miles (60km) of rugged terrain. There are also all-terrain biking trails. You can canoe the Frances Lake route, which covers 11 miles of pleasant paddling with 12 beaver dam hauls and three portages, and takes about six hours. There's swimming at Falcon Beach, scuba diving in West Hawk Lake, plus places to sail, windsurf, water-ski, and fish. Horseback riding is offered at **Falcon Beach Riding Stables** (☎ 201/349-2410). In winter there's downhill skiing, cross-country skiing, snowmobiling, snowshoeing, and skating.

Within the park, **Falcon Lake** is one of Canada's most modern recreational developments, featuring tennis courts, an 18-hole par-72 golf course, and a ski resort. Most park resorts and lodges charge from $50 to $100 double ($300 to $625 per week) for a cabin. Camping facilities abound. For more information, contact the number above or Travel Manitoba, Dept. SV6, 155 Carlton St., Winnipeg, MB, R3C 3H8 (☎ 204/945-3777 or 800-665-0040).

You'll have a very different experience at **Atikaki Provincial Park** (no telephone). This wilderness park is accessible via plane or canoe only and offers no facilities. The Pigeon River offers excellent white-water runs.

6 Lake Winnipeg

This 264-mile-long lake is the continent's seventh largest, and its shores shelter some interesting communities and attractive natural areas. At the lake's southern end, **Grand Beach Provincial Park** (☎ 204/754-2212) has white sand beaches backed by 30-foot-high dunes in some places. This is a good place to swim, windsurf, and fish. There are three self-guided nature trails. Campsites are also available.

About 60 miles north of Winnipeg, on the western shore, the farming and fishing community of **Gimli** is the hub of Icelandic culture in Manitoba. Gimli was established a century ago as the capital of New Iceland and for many years had its own government, school, and newspapers. It still celebrates an Icelandic festival on the first long weekend in August.

Gull Harbour, 110 miles (185km) northeast of Winnipeg on Hecla Island, was once a part of New Iceland and was, until recently, home to a small Icelandic-Canadian farming and fishing community. Today it's the site of **Hecla Provincial Park,** Box

70, Riverton, MB, R0C 2R0 (☎ 204/378-2945). This is an excellent place to hike (with five short trails), golf, fish, camp, bird watch, canoe, swim, windsurf, play tennis (two courts), hunt, cross-country ski, snowshoe, or go snow-mobiling and tobogganing. Photographers and wildlife enthusiasts appreciate the park's wildlife viewing tower and the **Grassy Narrow Marsh,** which shelters many species of waterfowl. There's a campground and 15 cabins available, plus the resort listed below.

Grand Rapids, 266 miles (425km) north of Winnipeg, sits at the confluence of Lake Winnipeg and Cedar Lake to the west. It's home to a fish hatchery, a major electric power-generating station, and a thriving Native Canadian community. **Berens River,** halfway along the lake's eastern shore, is a remote community (no all-weather roads connect it to the rest of Manitoba) where one of Manitoba's largest and best-known reservations is located.

WHERE TO STAY IN GULL HARBOUR

Gull Harbour Resort Hotel. Box 1000, Riverton, MB, R0C 2R0. ☎ **204/475-2354.** Fax 204/279-2000. 93 rms. A/C TV TEL. $100 double. Extra person $15. Children under 16 stay free in parents' room. Watch for specials year-round. AE, MC, V.

This is an ideal place to take the family. Though it boasts first-class resort facilities, Gull Harbour is unusual because it has really tried to retain the island's unspoiled nature. Beaches and woods have been left intact, and outdoors and indoors almost seem to blend.

Facilities include an indoor swimming pool, whirlpool, and sauna; badminton, volleyball, and basketball courts; a games room with pool tables, an 18-hole golf course, a putting green, minigolf, tennis courts, skating rink, croquet, shuffleboard, and more.

7 West Along the Trans-Canada Highway to Spruce Woods Provincial Park & Brandon

About 40 miles (67km) west of Portage la Prairie, before reaching Carberry, turn south on Highway 5 to **Spruce Woods Provincial Park,** Box 900, Carberry, MB, R0K 0H0 (☎ 204/827-2543 in summer; otherwise 204/834-3223). The park's unique and most fragile feature is Spirit Sands, large stretches of open sand that are the remains of the once wide Assiniboine Delta. Only a few hardy creatures such as the Bembix wasp and one type of wolf spider live here. The rest of the park is forest and prairie grasslands inhabited by herds of wapiti. There's camping at Kiche Manitou as well as at hike-in locations. The park is on the Assiniboine River canoe route, which starts in Brandon and ends north of Holland. Canoes can be rented at Pine Fort IV in the park. The park's longest trail is the 24.8-mile (40km) Epinette Trail, but its most fascinating is the Spirit Sands/Devils Punch Bowl, accessible from Highway 5. It loops through the Dunes and leads to the Devils Punch Bowl, which was carved by underground streams. There are also bike and mountain bike trails; swimming at the campground beach; and in winter, there's cross-country skiing, skating, tobogganing, and snowmobiling.

Brandon is Manitoba's second largest city with a population of 40,000. This university town features the Art Gallery of Southwestern Manitoba; the B. J. Hales Museum, with mounted specimens of birds and mammals; plus interesting tours of the Agriculture and Agri Food Research Centre. During the summer, families flock to the **Thunder Mountain Water Slide,** 5 miles west of Brandon on the Trans-Canada Highway.

8 Riding Mountain National Park & Duck Mountain Provincial Park

RIDING MOUNTAIN NATIONAL PARK

About 155 miles (248km) northwest of Winnipeg, Riding Mountain National Park, Wasagaming, MB, R0J 2H0 (☎ 204/848-7275), is set in the highlands, atop a giant wooded escarpment that affords shelter to more than 260 species of birds, plus moose, wolves, coyotes, lynx, beavers, black bears, and a bison herd at Lake Audy.

The park has more than 248 miles (400km) of **hiking trails.** Twenty are easily accessible, short, and easy to moderate in difficulty; another 20 are long backcountry trails. Many trails can be ridden on mountain bike and horseback. Bikes can be rented in Wasagaming. **Elkhorn Riding Stables,** Onanole (☎ 204/848-2802), offers one-hour, day, and overnight rides. There are additional outfitters, too.

Canoes and other boats can be rented at **Clear Lake Marina.** As for **fishing,** northern pike is the main game fish and specimens up to 30 pounds (13kg) have been taken from Clear Lake. Rainbow and brook trout populate Lake Katherine and Deep Lake. The park also has one of the province's best **golf courses** (greens fee $26). In winter there's **cross-country and downhill skiing** at Mount Agassiz on the east side of the park plus ice fishing in Clear Lake.

The **visitor center** is open daily in the summer from 9am to 9pm. For information, call or write: Superintendent, Riding Mountain National Park, Wasagaming, MB, R0J 2H0 (☎ 204/848-7275). The park is easily accessed from Brandon, about 57 miles (95km) north along Highway 10. Entry to the park is $7 daily, $15 for a four-day pass, $40 for an annual permit good for all Canadian national parks.

CAMPING & ACCOMMODATIONS

At the Shawenequanape Kipi-Che-Win (Southquill Camp), you can stay in a traditional tepee ($50 a night double) and learn about the traditional ceremonies, arts, crafts, and culture of the Anishinabe. For information contact Kathy Boulanger or Richard Gaywish, Shawenequanape Camp and Cultural Tours, 704-167 Lombard Ave, Winnipeg, MB, R3B 0V3 (☎ 204/947-3147).

In Wasagaming, you can stay at six park **campgrounds** or in motel and cabin accommodations (from $45 to $100 double). Wasagaming also has six tennis courts, lawn bowling greens, a children's playground, and a log-cabin movie theater in the Wasagaming Visitor Centre beside Clear Lake. There's also a dance hall, picnic areas with stoves, and a bandshell down by the lake for Sunday-afternoon concerts. At the lake itself you can rent boats and swim at the main beach.

Wasagaming Campground has more than 500 sites, most of which are unserviced. Facilities include showers and toilets, kitchen shelters, and a sewage disposal station nearby. Rates are $10 unserviced, $14 with electricity, $16 full service. Other outlying campgrounds (93 sites) are at Moon Lake, Lake Audy, Whirlpool, and Deep Lake. None of these are serviced. For reservations call ☎ 800/707-8480. Outlying campgrounds are $6.50, site only.

Elkhorn Resort. Clear Lake, MB, R0J 2H0. ☎ **204/848-2802.** Fax 204/848-2109. 60 rms. A/C TV TEL. Lodge room $109 double; $120 double with fireplace. Extra person $15. Children under 17 stay free in parents' room. Lower off-season rates available. Three-bedroom chalet $225 per night; less off-season (Mar to mid-May and mid-Oct to mid-Dec). AE, DC, ER, MC, V.

This year-round lodge is just on the edge of Wasagaming with easy access to Riding Mountain, overlooking quiet fields and forest. It's a wonderful place for families. At the ranch's common room, you can join a game of bridge or cribbage in the evening.

There's also a swimming pool, a nine-hole golf course, and a dining room with a lovely view over nearby stables. Each room in the lodge is large and comfortable, pleasantly furnished in pine, country style. Also on the property are several fully equipped three-bedroom chalets (with fireplace, fire extinguisher, toaster, dishwasher, microwave, and balcony with barbecue) designed after Quonsets.

DUCK MOUNTAIN PROVINCIAL PARK

Northwest of Riding Mountain via Highway 10, off Route 367, Duck Mountain Provincial Park (no phone) is popular for fishing, camping, boating, hiking, horseback riding, and biking. **Baldy Mountain,** near the park's southeast entrance, is the province's highest point at 2,727 feet. **East Blue Lake** is so clear that the bottom is visible at 30 to 40 feet.

For accommodations in Duck Mountain, the place to stay is **Wellman Lake Lodge and Outfitters,** Box 249, Minitonas, MB, R0L 1G0 (☎ 204/525-4422), which has lodgings with kitchenettes. Full services for anglers and hunters are offered. There's also a beach.

9 Exploring the Far North & Churchill, the World's Polar Bear Capital

The best way to explore the north is aboard **VIA** *Rail's Hudson Bay* on a two-night, 1-day trip from Winnipeg to Churchill, via **The Pas,** a mecca for fishing enthusiasts, and the mining community of Thompson. No other land route has yet penetrated this remote region, which is covered with lakes, forests, and frozen tundra. The train leaves Winnipeg at about 10pm and arrives 34 hours later in Churchill. A round-trip ticket costs $360 per person; the least expensive sleeping berth is $140. For more information, contact your travel agent or VIA (☎ 800/561-3949).

If you're up this way in February, The Pas hosts the annual festival, the ✪ **Northern Trapper's Festival,** with world-championship dog-sled races, ice fishing, beerfests, moose calling, and more. Call ☎ 204/623-2912 for information.

You can also fly into Churchill on **Canadian Airlines International** (☎ 204/632-2811).

Churchill is the polar bear capital of the world. Visit October to early November to see these awesome creatures. The town is also famous with birders as some 200 species, including the rare Ross Gull, nest or pass through on their annual migration. In summer, white beluga whales frolic in the mouth of the Churchill River and seals and caribou can be sighted along the coast. You can also see the aurora borealis from here.

Churchill, population 1,100, is also one of the world's largest grain-exporting terminals in the world, and grain elevators dominate its skyline. You can watch the grain being unloaded from boxcars onto ships—perhaps 25 million bushels of wheat and barley clear the port in only 12 to 14 weeks of frantic nonstop operation. You can also take a boat ride to **Fort Prince of Wales** (☎ 204/675-8863), a large partially restored stone fort that's open July and August. Construction started in 1730 by the Hudson's Bay Company and took 40 years. Yet after all that effort, Governor Samuel Hearne and 39 clerks and tradesmen surrendered the fort without a fight in 1782, when faced with a possible attack by the French in three ships. From here you can observe beluga whales. Cape Merry at the mouth of the Churchill River is also an excellent vantage point for observing Beluga whales and is a must for birders (open continuously June, July, and August). The town's Visitor Centre is open daily mid-May to mid-November, weekdays only otherwise.

Fifteen miles east of town, the **Eskimo Museum** (☎ 204/675-2307) has a collection of fine Inuit carvings and artifacts dating from pre-Dorset (1700 B.C.) through Dorset, Thule, and modern Inuit times. From Churchill you can travel independently to Eskimo Point, home of an Inuit community, to view the polar bears and other wildlife in the region.

Some 149 miles southeast of Churchill, the very remote **York Factory National Historic Site** features what remains of the Hudson's Bay Company fur trading post. Here you'll find a depot built in 1832, the oldest wood structure still standing on permafrost. The depot's walls and floors are not attached to each other to allow for the heaving of the permafrost. York Factory operated as a company post until 1957. Admission is $5 and it's open June 1 through September. Across Sloop Creek are the ruins of a stone gunpowder magazine and a cemetery with stones dating back to the 1700s. Access is limited to charter planes or by canoe down the Hayes River. For more information on these sites contact Parks Canada, Box 127, Churchill, MB, R0B 0E0 (☎ 204/675-8863).

North of The Pas are two provincial parks. The first is **Clearwater Lake Provincial Park,** at the junction of Highway 10 and 287; the lake lives up to its name because the bottom is visible at 35 feet. It offers great fishing plus swimming, boating, hiking, and camping. The second is **Grass River Provincial Park** (no phone), on Highway 39, a wilderness home to woodland caribou, moose, and plenty of waterfowl. The Grass River is good for fishing and canoeing. For nearby accommodations try **Grass River Lodge,** Box 1680, The Pas, MB, R9A 1L4 (☎ 204/358-7171), which is open from mid-May to October.

Kaskattama Safari Adventures, Hudson Bay, Manitoba (☎ 204/667-1611), offers a more expensive way to view the polar bears. Their six-day/five-night trip starts in Winnipeg, where guests stay at the Radisson before flying to Kaskattama, originally built as a fur trading post in 1923 by the Hudson's Bay Company. Today, the storeroom and warehouse serve as the main visitor lodge and dining room. Two four-bedroom cabins, each equipped with screened porch and full bathroom, accommodate a maximum of 16 guests. A naturalist introduces visitors to the **Cape Tatnam Wildlife Management Area,** which is home to more than 200 species of birds, caribou, moose, black bear, Arctic wolves, foxes, and the great white bears who head to land in July and can be seen foraging along the grasslands, with cubs in tow. Three days are spent at Kaska. One is devoted to a helicopter trip to York Factory while the other two are spent exploring the natural life of the wilderness. The trip costs $2,495 per person based on double occupancy.

WHERE TO STAY IN CHURCHILL

Of the few choices, the following are your best bets. The 26-room **Churchill Motel,** at Kelsey and Franklin (☎ 204/675-8853), charges $85 for a double, and has a restaurant. Additional amenities like room service and a bar can be found at **the Seaport Hotel,** 299 Kelsey Blvd. (☎ 204/675-8807). The 21 rooms there rent for $90 double. The **Tundra Inn,** 34 Franklin St. (☎ 204/675-8831), has 31 comfortable accommodations for $88 double.

10 Regina

Originally named Pile O'Bones after the heap of buffalo skeletons the first settlers found (Native Canadians had amassed the bones in the belief that they would lure the vanished buffalo back again), the city has Princess Louise, daughter of Queen Victoria, to thank for its more regal name. She named the city in her mother's honor in 1882 when it became the capital of the Northwest Territories. Despite the barren prairie landscape and the infamous Regina mud, the town grew.

Today the provincial capital of Saskatchewan, with a population of 179,000, still has a certain prairie feel, although it's becoming more sophisticated, with some good hotels and some rather interesting attractions.

ESSENTIALS

VISITOR INFORMATION   Contact **Tourism Saskatchewan,** 500-1900 Albert St., Regina, SK, S4P 4L9 (☎ 306/787-2300 or 800/667-7191), open from 8am to 7pm Monday through Friday, 10am to 4pm Saturday.

For on-the-spot Regina information, contact **Tourism Regina,** P.O. Box 3355, Regina, SK, S4P 3H1 (☎ 306/789-5099), or visit the **Visitor Information Centre** on Highway 1 East, located just west of CKCK-TV. It's open from 8:30am to 4:30pm year-round, with extended hours to 7pm from mid-May to Labor Day.

GETTING THERE   **Air Canada** (☎ 800/776-3000) and Canadian Airlines International (☎ 800/426-7000) serve Regina. The airport is located west of the city, only 15 minutes from downtown.

If you're driving, Regina is located right on the Trans-Canada Highway.

VIA Rail trains pull into the station at 1880 Saskatchewan Dr., at Rose Street (☎ 800/561-8630 in Canada only).

CITY LAYOUT   The two main streets are Victoria Avenue, which runs east-west, and Albert Street, which runs north-south. South of the intersection lies the Wascana Centre. Most of the downtown hotels stretch along Victoria Avenue between Albert Street on the west and Broad Street on the east. The RCMP barracks are located to the north and west of the downtown area. Lewvan Drive (also called the Ring Road) allows you to circle the city by car.

GETTING AROUND   **Regina Transit,** 333 Winnipeg St. (☎ 306/777-RIDE), operates 15 bus routes that make it easy to get around. For schedules and maps, go to the Transit Information Centre at 2124 11th Ave. next to Eaton's. Adult fare is $1.10, 55¢ for elementary school children, 65¢ for high schoolers. Exact fare is required.

Driving is not a problem in Regina. For rentals, try **Dollar,** at the Regina Inn (☎ 306/525-1377); **Hertz,** at the airport (☎ 306/791-9131); **Tilden,** 111-2301 Avenue C North (☎ 306/652-3355); and **Avis,** 2010 Victoria Ave. (☎ 306/757-1653).

Taxis can most easily be found at downtown hotels. They charge $2.10 when you get in and 10¢ per 135 yards (112m) thereafter. **Regina Cab** (☎ 306/543-3333) is the most used.

FAST FACTS   Business Hours   Regular store hours are 9am to 6pm Monday, Tuesday, and Saturday, and Wednesday through Friday evening until 9:30pm. Banking hours are Monday through Thursday from 10am to 3pm, to 6pm on Friday.

Post Office   For postal service, there's a convenient outlet at 2200 Saskatchewan Dr. across from the Cornwall Parkade (☎ 306/761-6307). It's open Monday through Friday from 8am to 5pm.

Useful Telephone Numbers   For telephone information dial 113.

SPECIAL EVENTS   During the first week of June, **Mosaic** celebrates the city's multiethnic population. Special passports entitle visitors to enter pavilions and experience the food, crafts, and entertainment of each group. The **Big Valley Rodeo** is also held in June.

Regina's **Buffalo Days,** usually held the first week in August, recalls the time when this noble beast roamed the west. Throughout the city, businesses and individuals dress in Old West style, while the fair itself sparkles with a midway, grandstand shows, big-name entertainers, livestock competitions, beard-growing contests, and much, much more. For more information, contact Buffalo Days, P.O. Box 167, Exhibition Park, Regina, SK, S4P 2Z6 (☎ 306/781-9200).

EXPLORING THE WASCANA CENTRE

Certainly Regina did not start out with a bounty of natural assets, which is what makes the Wascana Centre, a 2,300-acre park right in the middle of the city, practically a testament to the city's indomitable will. The muddy little creek has been turned into a lovely parkland, where every tree that grows was physically planted by hand.

Within the center lies a **waterfowl park,** frequented by 60 or more species of marsh and water birds. In 1953 a pair of Canada geese were introduced to the park and now there are more than 150 breeding pairs, some of which remain during the winter, while others migrate as far south as New Mexico. There's a naturalist on duty from 8am to 4:30pm weekdays; call 306/522-3661 for information.

Another delightful spot is **Willow Island,** a picnic island reached by a small ferry from the overlook west of Broad Street on Wascana Drive.

Wascana Place, the headquarters building for Wascana Centre Authority (☎ 306/522-3661), provides year-round public information services and a gift shop with Saskatchewan art and craft work. The intriguing architecture invites a visit and is enhanced by a tour up to the fourth-level observation deck. Open Monday from 8am to 4:30pm, Tuesday to Saturday from 8am to 6pm, Sunday 1 to 4pm, with extended hours from May to Labor Day.

The center also contains the Legislative Building, the University of Regina, the Royal Saskatchewan Museum (which focuses on natural history), the Norman Mackenzie Art Gallery, and the Saskatchewan Centre of the Arts. Also in the park stands the **Diefenbaker Homestead** (☎ 306/522-3661), the unassuming one-story log home of John Diefenbaker, prime minister from 1957 to 1963, which has been moved from Borden, Saskatchewan. John Diefenbaker helped his father build the three-room house, which is furnished in pioneer style and contains some original family articles. Open daily 10am to 7pm from Victoria Day to Labor Day.

Legislative Building. Wascana Centre. ☎ **306/787-5358.** Tours leave daily every half hour 8am–4:30pm in winter, 8am–8pm in summer.

Start at the Legislative Building, a stately edifice built in 1908–12 for only $1.83 million in an English Renaissance and Louis XVI style (parts of the building also are reminiscent of the palace of Versailles). Designed in the shape of a cross, the building is crowned by a 226-foot-high dome. Inside, on the main floor and main rotunda, 34 kinds of marble were used. The mural above the rotunda, entitled *Before the White Man Came,* depicts aboriginal people in the Qu'Appelle Valley preparing to attack a herd of buffalo on the opposite shore. Rooms of interest include the Legislative Assembly Chamber, the 400,000-volume library, and the art galleries in the basement and on the first floor.

Mackenzie Art Gallery. 3475 Albert St. (at Hillsdale). ☎ **306/522-4242.** Free admission. Fri–Tues 11am–6pm, Wed–Thurs 11am–10pm.

The art gallery's approximately 1,600 works concentrate on Canadian artists, especially such Saskatchewan painters as James Henderson and Inglis Sheldon-Williams; contemporary American artists; and 15th- to 19th-century Europeans who are represented with paintings, drawings, and prints.

The Trial of Louis Riel

Louis Riel was tried and hanged in Regina in 1885. Bitter arguments have been fought between those who regard Riel as a patriot and martyr and those who regard him as a rebel. Whatever the opinion, Riel certainly raises some extremely deep and discomforting questions. As G. F. Stanley, professor of history at the Royal Military College, Kingston, has written, "The mere mention of his name bares those latent religious and racial animosities which seem to lie so close to the surface of Canadian politics."

Even though he took up the cause of the mixed-blood population of the west, French-speaking Canadians often regarded him as a martyr and English-speaking Canadians damned him as a madman. Written by John Coulter, *The Trial of Louis Riel* is a play based on the actual court records of the historical trial. It is presented Wednesday to Friday at the Mackenzie Art Gallery during August. Certainly thought-provoking, the play raises such issues as language rights, prejudice, and justice. Tickets are $10 adults, $9 seniors and students, $8 children 12 and under. For reservations call 306/522-4242 or 306/525-1185.

Royal Saskatchewan Museum. College Avenue and Albert Street. ☎ **306/787-2815.** Free admission. May 1–Labor Day daily 9am–8:30pm; Labor Day–Apr 30 daily 9am–4:30pm. Closed Christmas Day.

This museum concentrates on the province's anthropological and natural history. You'll find artifacts, sculpture, art, plus several multimedia exhibits, including a life-size mastodon and a robotic dinosaur that comes roaring to life. A video cave, rock table, and laboratory with resident paleontologist are all found in the interactive Paleo Pit. A new life sciences gallery is scheduled to open in 1997.

MORE ATTRACTIONS

Sports fans will enjoy the **Saskatchewan Sports Hall of Fame and Museum,** at 2205 Victoria Ave. (☎ 306/780-9232). The free museum is open May to October Monday to Friday from 9am to 5pm, Saturday and Sunday 1 to 5pm. From November to April, open Monday to Friday 9am to 5pm.

For downtown shopping, **Cromwell Centre** has more than 100 stores (all chains), with Eaton's as the anchor.

Saskatchewan Science Centre. Winnipeg Street and Wascana Drive. ☎ **306/791-7914.** Admission to Powerhouse of Discovery $7.50 adults, $5.75 seniors and children 5–13, $2 children 4 and under. IMAX theater $6.75 adults, $5 children 5–13 and seniors, $3.75 children 5 and under. Combination tickets to both attractions $12 adults, $9 youths and seniors, $5 children 4 and under. Summer Mon–Thurs 9am–6pm, Fri–Sat 9am–9pm, Sun 10am–7:30pm; winter Tues–Fri 9am–5pm, Sat–Sun and holidays noon–6pm.

The Saskatchewan Science Centre is home to two great attractions: The Powerhouse of Discovery and the Kramer IMAX Theatre. Located in the renovated City of Regina Powerhouse on the north shore of Wascana Lake, the Powerhouse houses more than 80 thought-provoking, fun, hands-on exhibits that demonstrate basic scientific principles, ranging from a hot-air balloon that rises three stories in the central mezzanine to exhibits where visitors can test their strength, reaction time, and balance.

The Kramer IMAX theater shows films on a five-story screen accompanied by thrilling six-channel surround-sound. Call for show times (most are in the afternoon).

RCMP Training Academy & Museum. Off Dewdney Avenue West. ☎ **306/780-5838.** Free admission. June 1–Sept 15 daily 8am–6:45pm; rest of the year daily 10am–4:45pm. Closed Christmas Day.

This fascinating museum traces the history of the Royal Canadian Mounted Police since 1874, when they began the Great March West to stop liquor traffic and enforce the law in the Northwest Territories. The museum uses replicas, newspaper articles, artifacts, uniforms, weaponry, and mementos to document the lives of the early Mounties and the pioneers. It traces the Mounties' role in the 1885 Riel Rebellion, the Klondike Gold Rush (when the simple requirements they laid down probably saved the lives of many foolhardy gold diggers who came pitifully ill equipped), the Prohibition era (when they sought out stills), the First and Second World Wars, the 1935 Regina labor riot, and in the capture of the mad trapper (who was chased in Arctic temperatures for 54 days in 1931–32). Kids, and adults too, will probably love to role-play in the cockpit of the de Havilland single-engine Otter from the Air Services Division, and to see an audiovisual presentation of training.

A tour also goes to the chapel and, when possible, allows visitors to see cadets in training. The highlight is the Sergeant Major's Parade, which normally takes place around 12:45pm Monday through Friday. The schedule is tentative, so call before you go. In July and August on Tuesday evenings just after 6:30pm the Sunset Ceremony takes place, an exciting 45-minute display of horsemanship by the Mounties accompanied by pipe and bugle bands and choir.

WHERE TO STAY

Remember to add 7% PST and 7% GST tax to the rates below.

EXPENSIVE

Hotel Saskatchewan. 2125 Victoria Ave. (at Scarth Street), Regina, SK, S4P 0S3. ☎ **306/522-7691.** Fax 306/757-5521. 200 rms. A/C MINIBAR TV TEL. $165 double. Extra person $15. Children under 12 stay free in parents' room. AE, CB, DC, DISC, ER, MC, V.

The hotel's ivy-covered limestone exterior has a rather solid old-world air about it, a satisfying prelude to the modern comfort within. The large, almost heart-shaped clock that hangs in the lobby is original to the 1927 Georgian-style building. The rooms have elegant high ceilings and decorative moldings; each bathroom contains a hairdryer and an additional phone.

Dining/Entertainment: Cortlandt Hall, with terraced seating, stately windows, and a coffered oak ceiling with brass chandeliers, specializes in grills, seafood, veal, and chicken dishes (from $15 to $22) at dinner and a lighter selection at lunchtime.

Services: Room service until midnight.

Facilities: Fully equipped fitness center with sauna.

Ramada Renaissance. 1919 Saskatchewan Dr., Regina, SK, S4P 4H2. ☎ **306/525-5255.** Fax 306/781-7188. 255 rms. A/C MINIBAR TV TEL. $150 double. Extra person $10. Children under 16 stay free in parents' room. Weekend rates available. AE, ER, MC, V.

Conveniently located downtown in the Saskatchewan Trade and Convention Centre, the Ramada Renaissance is adjacent to two large retail malls, the Cornwall Centre and the Galleria. The modern rooms are elegantly appointed with marble vanities, sitting areas, and desks.

Dining/Entertainment: There's the casual Summerfields's and the more formal Capital's as well as Caper's Lounge for cocktails.

Facilities: The Waterworks Recreation Complex has a three-story indoor water slide, swimming pool, and whirlpool.

Regina Inn. 1975 Broad St., Regina, SK, S4P 1Y2. ☎ **306/525-6767** or 800/667-8162 in Canada. Fax 306/352-1858. 240 rms. A/C TV TEL. $140 double. Extra person $10. Children under 18 stay free in parents' room. Weekend family rates from $65 per night. AE, DC, ER, MC, V.

The Regina Inn occupies an entire block and offers numerous facilities within. Its rooms, most with balconies, have contemporary decor and louvered closets. Guests enjoy the sundeck and health club. The hotel offers two restaurants, lounge, and a nightspot.

MODERATE

Chelton Suites Hotel. 1907 11th Ave., Regina, SK, S4P 0J2. ☎ **306/569-4600** or 800/ 667-9922 in Canada. Fax 306/569-4531. 56 rms and suites. A/C MINIBAR TV TEL. $84–$135 double (top prices for suites). Weekend rates available. AE, DC, ER, MC, V.

Conveniently located downtown, the Chelton is small enough to provide friendly personal service. The rooms, all very large, sport modern furnishings. A bedroom/ sitting room will contain table, chairs, drawers, and couch, as well as a sink, fridge, and private bathroom. Even the smallest rooms are bright and spacious compared to most other accommodations. Suites have a separate bedroom and living area.

The dining room is a local favorite for continental cuisine. Lithographs and large chandeliers impart a certain elegance to the room. There's a separate comfortable lounge up front.

Landmark Inn. 4150 Albert St., Regina, SK S4S 3R8. ☎ **306/586-5363.** Fax 306/586-0901. 188 rms. A/C TV TEL. $80 double. AE, DC, ER, MC, V.

This good modern accommodation also has a selection of dining and entertainment facilities—Checkers for dancing, a coffee shop, and an al fresco beer garden. Other facilities include an indoor pool, water slide, sauna, and whirlpool.

The Sands. 1818 Victoria Ave., Regina, SK, S4P 0R1. ☎ **306/569-1666.** Fax 306/525-3550. 251 rms. A/C TV TEL. $95 double. Children under 18 stay free in parents' room. Weekend packages available. AE, DC, ER, MC, V.

You notice The Sands' organic natural quality in the lobby with its earth-color stone walls and plant-filled coffee plaza. The attractive rooms have modern furnishings and all the usual amenities. Dining facilities include a coffee shop plus the Fireside Lounge, with an open firepit. On the second floor, there are saunas, suntanning facilities, whirlpool, miniature golf, and an indoor pool capped by a solarium. The hotel also has a children's play area.

INEXPENSIVE

Turgeon International Hostel. 2310 McIntyre St., Regina, SK, S4P 2S2. ☎ **306/791-8165.** Fax 306/721-2667. 50 beds. A/C. $14 members; $19 nonmembers. MC, V. Closed Dec 25–Jan 31. Lights out at 11:30pm.

Regina is fortunate to have one of the best youth hostels I've ever seen, if not *the* best. The Turgeon International Hostel is located in a handsome 1907 town house adjacent to Wascana Centre. Accommodations are in dormitories with three or four bunks; the top floor has two larger dorms, and each dorm has access to a deck. Downstairs there's a comfortable sitting room worthy of any inn, with couches in front of the oak fireplace and plenty of magazines and books. In fact, the hostel acts as a resource center for travelers. The basement contains an impeccably clean dining and cooking area with electric stoves, as well as a laundry. Picnic tables are available in the backyard. A gem!

WHERE TO DINE

Regina offers slim dining pickings. In addition to the steakhouses listed here, try **Neo Japonica** (☎ 306/359-7669) for decent Japanese cuisine, and **Peking House,** 1850 Rose Street (☎ 306/757-3038) for Chinese.

C C Lloyd's. In the Chelton Suites Hotel, 1907 11th Ave. ☎ **306/569-4650.** Reservations recommended. Main courses $10–$13. AE, DC, ER, MC, V. Mon–Sat 11am–2pm and 5:30–8:30pm; Sun 10am–2pm. CONTINENTAL.

C C Lloyd's draws a strong local following. The cuisine is eclectic North American, such as broiled salmon with a dill sauce, chicken with Cajun spices, and a selection of steaks. For starters, try the salmon and crab pâté en croûte or the mousse of chicken liver Madeira. Desserts are classic—pears in red wine sauce and crème caramel.

The Diplomat. 2032 Broad St. ☎ **306/359-3366.** Reservations recommended. Main courses $15–$33. AE, DC, ER, MC, V. Mon–Fri 11:30am–2pm; Mon–Sat 4pm–midnight. CANADIAN.

This old-style steakhouse comes complete with semicircular banquettes, and tables set with pink cloths, burgundy napkins, and tiny lanterns. Around the room hang portraits of eminent-looking prime ministers; there's a fireplace and lounge up front. The menu's main attractions are the steaks—20-ounce porterhouse, 18-ounce T-bone—along with chicken Cordon Bleu, duck à l'orange, and other typical favorites.

Golf's Steak House. 1945 Victoria Ave. (at Hamilton Street). ☎ **306/525-5808.** Reservations required. Main courses $12–$29. AE, DC, ER, MC, V. Mon–Fri 11:30am–2pm; Mon–Sat 4:30pm–midnight, Sun and holidays 4–11pm. CANADIAN.

In this venerable Regina institution, the atmosphere is decidedly plush (note the large fireplace, the piano and antique organ, the heavy gilt-framed paintings, and the high-backed carved-oak Charles II–style chairs). The menu offers traditional steakhouse fare. Start with smoked salmon or shrimp scampi before moving on to stuffed trout, baby back ribs, or any number of steaks. For dessert sample the special treat, baked Alaska.

REGINA AFTER DARK

Hardly Canada's nightlife capital, the city does have one or two spots for dancing, most located in the hotels, plus a cultural center in the middle of Wascana Park, the **Saskatchewan Centre** (☎ 306/565-4500 or for the box office 306/525-9999), on the southern shore of Wascana Lake. With two theaters and a large concert hall, the Centre is home to the Regina Symphony Orchestra and also features many other artists. Tickets prices vary depending on the show. The box office at 200 Lakeshore Dr. (☎ 306/525-9999) is open from 9am to 8pm Monday through Saturday.

The **Globe Theatre,** Old City Hall, 1801 Scarth St. (☎ 306/525-6400), a theater-in-the-round, presents six mainstage plays each October-to-April season. Productions run the gamut from classics (Shakespeare, Molière, Shaw, etc.) to modern dramas, musicals, and comedies. Ticket prices range from $8 to $17.

A slightly older crowd (25 to 35) frequents the **Manhattan Club and Island Club,** upstairs at 2300 Dewdney St. (☎ 306/359-7771). Open Thursday and Saturday only.

The college crowd favors **Checker's,** at the Landmark Inn, 4150 Albert St. (☎ 306/586-5363), a comfortable, rustic, and relaxed dance spot. In summer, the outdoor area called Scotland Yard is also crowded.

For more relaxed entertainment, there's the **Regina Inn** lounge or the Delta Regina's **Fireside Lounge.**

11 Saskatchewan Highlights Along the Trans-Canada Highway

MOOSE MOUNTAIN PROVINCIAL PARK & WEST TO REGINA

Just across the Manitoba/Saskatchewan border at Whitewood, you can turn south down Highway 9 to **Moose Mountain Provincial Park** (☎ 306/577-2131); it's also accessible from Highways 16 and 13. About 66 miles southeast of Regina, this 388-square-kilometer park is dotted with lakes and marshes. The park harbors a variety of waterfowl and songbirds—blue-winged teal, red-necked ducks, blue heron, red-tailed hawk, ovenbird, rose-breasted grosbeak, and Baltimore oriole— and animals, including deer, elk, moose, beaver, muskrat, and coyote.

In summer, park rangers lead guided hikes. The Beaver Youell Lake and the Wuche Sakaw Trails are also easy to follow. Visitors can hike or bike along the **nature trails;** swim at the beach south of the main parking lot and at several of the lakes; cool off at the super-fun **giant water slides on Kenosee Lake,** which include an eight-story free-fall slide (open from mid-May to Labor Day); **golf** at the 18-hole course; go **horseback riding;** or play **tennis.** In winter, the park has more than 56 kilometers of **cross-country ski trails** and more than 120 kilometers of **snowmobiling.**

The modern, no-nonsense **Kenosee Inn** (☎ 306/577-2099) offers 30 rooms or 23 cabin accommodations overlooking Kenosee Lake in the park. Facilities include a restaurant, a bar, an indoor pool, and a hot tub. Rates are $69 double for a room, $45 for a one-bedroom cabin, and $65–$80 for a two-bedroom cabin depending on its age and size. The park also has two **campgrounds** (☎ 306/577-2144).

Only 16.7 miles (27km) southeast of Moose Mountain is **Cannington Manor Provincial Historic Park.** This restored village was established in the 1880s by Edward Michell Pierce, who organized the Moose Mountain Trading Company. He intended the settlement to exemplify rural industrial development but the struggle against drought, frost, and poor markets proved too difficult, and the settlement was abandoned by 1900. A self-guided walking tour shows the story of the people who lived or worked in the 14 buildings lining the main street.

Back on the Trans-Canada Highway, continue west through the Qu'Appelle Valley to Regina (see Section 10 earlier in this chapter). From Regina, the Trans-Canada Highway cuts west to Moose Jaw and Swift Current.

MOOSE JAW

Moose Jaw gained notoriety as Canada's rum-running capital; today some restored buildings still retain the underground tunnels used for the illicit trade. Free walking tour maps are available. The **Moose Jaw Art Museum** (☎ 306/692-4471) has a fine collection of Cree and Sioux beadwork and costumes, plus art history and science exhibits. The town is also known for its **26 outdoor murals** that depict aspects of the city's heritage. For information call Murals of Moose Jaw (☎ 306/693-4262). The **Western Development Museum History of Transportation,** at Highways 1 and 2 (☎ 306/693-5989), showcases the roles that air, rail, land, and water transportation played in opening up the West. One gallery pays tribute to the Snowbirds, Canada's famous air squadron. **Wakamow Valley** (☎ 306/692-2717), which follows the course of the river through town, includes six different parks with walking and biking trails, canoeing, and skating facilities. There's also a **zoo** on 7th Avenue SW (☎ 306/693-8772), housing 80 different species of animals and birds.

For more information, contact **Tourism Moose Jaw,** 88 Saskatchewan St. E, Moose Jaw, SK, S6H 0V4 (☎ 306/693-8097).

GRASSLANDS NATIONAL PARK

Between Moose Jaw and Swift Current, about 120 miles south of the Trans-Canada Highway and along the U.S. border, stretches Grasslands National Park, P.O. Box 150, Val Marie, SK, S0N 2T0, two blocks of protected land separated by about 13.6 miles (22km).

On this mixed grass- and prairieland there's no escape from the sun and the wind. Coulees and the Frenchman River cut the west block, where the rare pronghorn antelope can be spotted. Black-tailed **prairie dogs,** which bark warnings at intruders and reassure each other with kisses and hugs, also make their home here. In the East Block, the open prairie is broken with coulees and the dobe hills of the Killdeer Badlands, so called because of their poor soil.

Although the park doesn't have facilities, there are a few self-guided **nature trails,** and visitors can also climb to the summit of 70-mile Butte and no-trace camp. The **information centre** (☎ 306/298-2257) is in Val Marie at the junction of Highway 4 and Centre Street (closed weekends in winter).

SWIFT CURRENT, CYPRESS HILLS PROVINCIAL PARK & FORT WALSH

Swift Current, Saskatchewan's base for western oil exploration and a regional trading center for livestock and grain, is 104 miles along the Trans-Canada Highway. It's known for its **Frontier Days** in June and **Old Tyme Fiddling Contest** in September. From Swift Current it's about another 125 miles to the Alberta border.

Straddling the border is **Cypress Hills Provincial Park,** P.O. Box 850, Maple Creek, SK, S0N 1N0 (☎ 306/662-4411) and Fort Walsh National Historic Site. En route to Cypress Hills, off the Trans-Canada Highway, is **Maple Creek,** a thoroughly western cow town with many heritage storefronts on main street. On the Saskatchewan side, the provincial park is divided into a Centre Block, off Route 21, and a West Block, off Route 271. Both blocks are joined by Gap Road, which is impassable when wet. The park's core is in the Centre Block, where there are six campgrounds; an outdoor pool; canoe, boat, and bike rentals; a nine-hole golf course; tennis courts; a riding stable; and swimming at the beach on Loch Leven. In winter there are 24 kms of **cross-country skiing trails.**

The **Cypress Four Seasons** (☎ 306/662-4477) resort offers rooms plus cabin and condominium accommodations from $60 to $90 a night in high season.

Fort Walsh National Historic Site can be accessed from Route 271 or directly from the park's West Block by gravel and clay roads. Built in 1875, the fort tried to handle the local native tribes and the many Sioux who sought refuge here from the American cavalry, as well as keep out American criminals seeking sanctuary. It was dismantled in 1883. Today the reconstruction consists of five buildings and a trading post staffed with folks in period costume. Open May to Thanksgiving daily 9am to 5:30pm.

12 Saskatoon

Saskatoon (pop. 184,000) has thrown off its frontier look and transformed itself into a progressive city on the plains, though its people remain very friendly and genuine.

The town still retains a distinctly western air. Downtown streets are broad and dusty, dotted in summer with many a pickup truck. Those same downtown streets just seem to disappear on the edge of town into the prairie, where grain elevators and telegraph poles become the only reference points and the sky your only company.

Scenically Saskatoon possesses some distinct natural advantages. The Lower Saskatchewan River cuts a swath through the city, spanned by several graceful bridges. Both riverbanks have mercifully been kept free of development and so offer pleasant retreats within the city, especially along the Meewasin Valley, which runs for miles along the riverbank and makes for great strolling, biking, and jogging. Yet the city stands at the center of a vast mining region that yields potash, uranium, petroleum, gas, and gold; Key Lake is the largest uranium mine outside Russia.

ESSENTIALS

VISITOR INFORMATION From around May 18 to the end of August, a booth is open at Avenue C North at 47th Street. Otherwise, contact **Tourism Saskatoon,** located at 6-305 Idylwyld Dr. North (P.O. Box 369), Saskatoon, SK, S7K 0Z1 (☎ 306/242-1206), open Monday to Friday, 8:30am to 5pm (in summer Monday to Friday 8:30am to 7pm and Saturday and Sunday 10am to 7pm).

GETTING THERE **Air Canada** (☎ 800/776-3000) and **Canadian Airlines International** (☎ 800/426-7000) fly in and out of the one-terminal airport.

If you're driving, Highway 16 leads to Saskatoon from the east or west. From Regina, Route 11 leads northwest to Saskatoon, 160 miles away.

VIA Rail trains arrive in the west end of the city on Chappel Drive. For information, call ☎ 306/384-5665; for reservations, call ☎ 800/561-8630 in Canada.

CITY LAYOUT The South Saskatchewan River cuts a diagonal north-south swath through the city. The main downtown area lies on the west bank; the University of Saskatchewan and the long neon-sign-crazed 8th Street dominate the east bank.

Streets are laid out in a numbered grid system—22nd Street divides north and south designated streets; Idylwyld Drive divides, in a similar fashion, east from west. First Street through 18th Street lie on the river's east side; 19th Street and up, on the west bank in the downtown area. Spadina Crescent runs along the river's west bank, where you'll find such landmarks as the Bessborough Hotel, the Ukrainian Museum, and the art gallery.

GETTING AROUND You may only need to use transportation when you visit the University of Saskatchewan and the Western Development Museum. **Saskatoon Transit System,** 301 24th St. West at Avenue C (☎ 306/975-3100 for routes and schedules), operates buses to all city areas from 6am to 12:30am Monday to Saturday and from noon to 8pm on Sunday for an exact change fare of $1.25.

Car-rental companies include **Avis,** 2625 Airport Dr. (☎ 306/652-3434); **Budget,** 234 First Ave. South, 2215 Ave. C North (☎ 306/244-7925); **Hertz,** 2323 8th St. East (☎ 306/373-1161); and **Tilden,** 321 21st St. East (☎ 306/652-3355).

Taxis cost $1.90 when you step inside and 10¢ every 108 yards (100m). Try **Saskatoon Radio Cab** (☎ 306/242-1221) or **United Cabs** (☎ 306/652-2222), which also operates the limousine to the airport ($6 from downtown hotels).

FAST FACTS **Emergencies** Hospitals include St. Paul's, 1702 20th St. West (☎ 306/382-3220); Saskatoon City Hospital, 701 Queen St. (☎ 306/655-8000); and University Hospital, University Grounds (☎ 306/244-2323).

Liquor Stores Liquor stores are located at 401 20th St. West (☎ 306/933-5312; open from 11am to 6pm daily except Sunday), and 1701 Idylwyld Dr. North

(☎ 306/933-5319; open from 11am to 6pm daily except Monday and Sunday, to 9pm on Thursday).

Post Office   The post office is located at 202 Fourth Ave. North (☎ 306/668-6723), and is open Monday through Friday from 8am to 5pm.

SPECIAL EVENTS   Saskatoon's eight-day **Exhibition,** usually held the second week of July, provides some grand agricultural spectacles, such as the threshing competition in which steam power is pitted against gas—sometimes with unexpected results—and the tractor-pulling competition, when standard farm tractors are used to pull a steel sled weighted down with a water tank. The pay-one-price admission of $7.50 ($5 seniors and youths 11 to 15, children under 11 free) lets you in all the entertainments—a craft show, talent competitions, thoroughbred racing, midway, and kidsville, which features clowns, games, and a petting zoo. For more infor-mation, contact Saskatoon PrairieLand Exhibition Corporation, P.O. Box 6010, Saskatoon, SK, S7K 4E4 (☎ 306/931-7149).

In mid-August, a **Folkfest** celebrates the city's many ethnic groups. The **Prairieland Pro Rodeo** is held at the Exhibition Stadium in fall.

EXPLORING THE CITY

Housed in a striking modern building overlooking the South Saskatchewan River, a short walk from downtown, the **Mendel Art Gallery and Civic Conservatory,** at 950 Spadina Crescent East (☎ 306/975-7610), has a good permanent collection of Canadian paintings, sculpture, watercolors, and graphics. It's free and open daily noon to 9pm (closed Christmas Day).

Nearby at 910 Spadina Crescent East is the **Ukrainian Museum of Canada** (☎ 306/244-3800). Reminiscent of a Ukrainian home in western Canada at the turn of the century, this museum preserves the Ukrainian heritage in clothing, linens, tools, books, photographs, documents, wooden folk art, ceramics, *pysanky* (Easter eggs), and other treasures and art forms brought from the "old homeland" by Ukrainian immigrants to Canada. Admission is $2 for adults, $1 seniors, 50¢ children 6 to 12. Open Tuesday to Saturday from 10am to 5pm, Sunday 1 to 5pm.

At the **Forestry Farm Park and Zoo,** 1903 Forest Dr. (☎ 306/975-3382), 300 or so species of Canadian and Saskatchewan wildlife are on view—wolf, coyote, fox, bear, eagle, owl, and hawk, a variety of deer, caribou, elk, and bison. There's a children's zoo, too. During winter you can cross-country ski the 2¹/₂-mile trail. Admission is $3 adults, $1.75 students and senior citizens, $1.75 children six to 18. Open May 1 to Labor Day daily 9am to 9pm; the rest of the year daily 10am to 4pm. It's located in northeast Saskatoon; follow the signs on Attridge Drive from Circle Drive.

The **University of Saskatchewan** (☎ 306/244-4343) occupies a dramatic 2,550-acre site overlooking the South Saskatchewan River and is attended by some 20,000 students. The actual campus buildings are set on 360 acres while the rest of the area is largely given over to the university farm and experimental plots. The Rt. Hon. John G. Diefenbaker Centre contains the papers and memorabilia of one of Canada's best-known prime ministers (open from 9:30am to 4:30pm weekdays and 12:30 to 5pm on weekends and holidays). The observatory (open Saturday evenings from 8 to 11pm) houses the Duncan telescope; the Little Stone Schoolhouse, built in 1887, served as the city's first school and community center (open May to June, weekdays from 9:30am to 4pm; July 1 to Labor Day, weekends only, from 12:30 to 5pm). Special tours of the research farm and many of the colleges can be arranged. For information contact the Office of Public Relations, University of Saskatchewan

(☎ 306/966-6607). To get there, take bus no. 2 or 7 from downtown at 23rd Street and Second Avenue.

Western Development Museum. 2610 Lorne Ave. South. ☎ **306/931-1910.** Admission $4.50 adults, $3.50 seniors, $1.50 children 5–12, $10 families. Daily 9am–5pm. Take Idylwyld Drive south to the Lorne Avenue exit and follow Lorne Avenue south until you see the museum on the right. Bus no. 1 from the 23rd Street Bus Mall between Second and Third Avenues.

The energetic years of Saskatchewan settlement are vividly portrayed by "Boomtown 1910," an authentic replica of prairie community life in that year. When you step onto the main street of Boomtown, the memories of an earlier age flood the senses. Browse through the shops, crammed with the unfamiliar goods of days gone by; savor the past through the mysterious aromas that permeate the drugstore; step aside as you hear the clip-clop of a passing horse and buggy; or wander down to Boomtown Station drawn by the low wail of an approaching steam locomotive. The museum truly comes to life during Harvestfest, when volunteers in authentic costume staff Boomtown and many pieces of vintage equipment are pressed into service once again.

Wanuskewin Heritage Park. RR no. 4 (5km north of Saskatoon on Highway 11). ☎ **306/931-6767.** Admission $6 adults, $4.50 seniors, $2.50 children 5–12. Victoria Day–Labor Day daily 9am–9pm, fall and winter daily 9am–5pm.

This park is built around the archaeological discovery of 19-plus Northern Plains Indian sites. Walking along the trails you'll see archaeological digs in progress, habitation sites, stone cairns, tepee rings, bison jumps, and other trace features of this ancient culture. At the amphitheater native performers present dance, theater, song, and storytelling, while at the outdoor activity area visitors can learn how to build a tepee, bake bannock, tan a hide, or use a travois (a transportation device). The main exhibit halls feature computer-activated displays and artifacts, multimedia shows exploring the archaeology and culture of the Plains peoples, contemporary art, and a Living Culture exhibit that tells the stories behind the daily headlines.

SHOPPING

Downtown malls include the **Midtown Plaza** and the **Scotia Centre.** The outlying **Circle Park Plaza** is filled with 71 independent (rather than chain) stores. The art gallery and Western Development Museum gift shops have attractive gifts.

For Canadian merchandise, stop in at **The Trading Post,** 226 Second Ave. South (☎ 306/653-1769), which carries Inuit soapstone carvings, Native Canadian art, Cowichan sweaters, beadwork, and more.

WHERE TO STAY

Remember to add 7% PST and 7% GST tax to the rates below.

The **Sheraton Cavalier,** 612 Spadina Crescent East (☎ 306/652-6770 or 800/325-3535), offers a special executive floor for businesspeople, plus a complete resort complex with adult and kiddie swimming pools and 250-foot-long water slides that attract many happy families. The **Holiday Inn** at 90 22nd St. East (☎ 306/244-2311), has a very convenient location, opposite the Eaton's complex and Centennial Auditorium. A double is $109.

The **Saskatoon Travelodge,** 106 Circle Dr. West at Idylwyld (☎ 306/242-8881, or 800/255-3050), has doubles for $75 to $85. There's an especially attractive pool area, plus a 250-foot-long water slide and whirlpool. For a pleasant, fairly priced room, the 80-room **Comfort Inn at Journey's End,** 2155 Northridge Dr. (☎ 306/934-1122), is a good choice. Rates are $62.99 double.

Delta Bessborough. 601 Spadina Crescent East, Saskatoon, SK, S7K 3G8. ☎ **306/244-5521.** Fax 306/653-2458. 227 rms and suites. A/C MINIBAR TV TEL. $160 double (higher rates for suites). Extra person $10. Weekend packages available. Children under 18 stay free in parents' room. AE, MC, V. Parking $3.

An elegant and gracious hostelry built in 1930 and finished in 1935, the Bessborough looks like a French château, with a copper roof and turrets. Inside, each room is different, although all have venerable oak entrance doors and antique or traditional furniture. Front rooms are large and most have bay windows. Riverside rooms are smaller, but have lovely views across the Saskatchewan River. There's a river-view coffee shop and the Samurai Japanese Steakhouse.

Facilities: An outdoor pool set in landscaped grounds that sweep down to the river, an indoor pool with whirlpool, sauna, and an exercise room.

Ramada Hotel Downtown Saskatoon. 405 20th St. East, Saskatoon, SK, S7K 6X6. ☎ **306/ 665-3322** or 800/228-2828. Fax 306/665-5531. 291 rms. A/C TV TEL. From $150 double. Extra person $10. Children under 16 stay free in parents' room. Weekend packages available. AE, DC, ER, MC, V. Parking $4.

Offering a riverside location in the heart of downtown, the Ramada is a luxury property, with attractively decorated, well-appointed rooms. About a third of the units offer river views; the corner rooms are particularly attractive. Summerfield's serves three meals daily.

Facilities: Guests enjoy a three-story recreation complex containing a large indoor swimming pool, two indoor water slides, a sauna, and a whirlpool. Jogging and cross-country ski trails adjoin the property.

WHERE TO DINE
EXPENSIVE
Cousin Niks. 1110 Grosvenor Ave. (between 7th and 8th streets). ☎ **306/374-2020.** Reservations recommended. Main courses $13–$37. AE, MC, V. Daily 5–11pm. GREEK/CANADIAN.

If you have only one dinner in Saskatoon, seek out the not-to-be-missed Cousin Niks. Here you'll find a delightful setting: an open courtyard garden lit from above and made even more charming by the sound of the splashing fountain. Greek rugs add color to the predominantly white setting. A variety of steak and seafood dishes are offered, from filet of sole in oil and lemon-oregano sauce to lobster tails in drawn butter. Main-course prices include avgolemono soup, Greek salad, fresh seasonal fruit, and coffee. On weekends, there's entertainment in the lounge.

Dreen's Cuisine. 718 Broadway. ☎ **306/931-8880.** Reservations recommended. Main courses $10–$24. V. Mon–Sat 11:30am–2:30pm and 5pm–closing. NEW WAVE.

Dreen always loved food and cooking and she has turned her hobby into a restaurant, food shop, and catering business. She uses local ingredients—free-range veal, bison, pickerel, chanterelles, and local berries—to create a very personal menu. The offerings change frequently, but you might find bison served with fresh chanterelles and portobello mushrooms, and duck or pork loin with a rich Saskatoon berry sauce. For an appetizer the roasted vegetables with balsamic vinaigrette are refreshing and the escargot with gorgonzola are exquisite. Her most famous dessert is the bourbon pecan Belgian chocolate pie. The atmosphere is comfortable and casual.

MODERATE
St. Tropez Bistro. 243 Third Ave. South. ☎ **306/652-1250.** Reservations recommended. Main courses $8–$17. AE, MC, V. Mon–Sat 11am–2pm and 4:30–10pm. CONTINENTAL.

One of my favorite downtown restaurants is the St. Tropez Bistro, where the background music is classical or French, and the tables are covered in Laura Ashley–style floral-design prints. For dinner, you can choose from a variety of pastas and stir-fries, or such dishes as sweet garlic veal or blackened chicken. Also available are a cheese fondue and a rich chocolate fondue with fresh fruit. This is one place where you can find out what's happening culturally in Saskatoon, too.

INEXPENSIVE

Pookaroos. 103B Third Ave. South. Reservations accepted only for parties of 10 or more. Main courses $10–$13. AE, MC, V. Mon–Sat 9am–5pm and 9pm–3am. MIDDLE EASTERN.

During the day you order at the counter, but at night the room is transformed by the simple addition of tablecloths and candlelight. In summer the sidewalk café is one of Saskatoon's few, or so it seems. At lunch, choose among falafel, hummus, donair, and fresh salads and sandwiches. The baklava—crisp, sweet, and rolled rather than layered—is absolutely addictive. At dinner the menu offers an array of North African and Middle Eastern specialties—dolmathes, couscous, and a variety of kebabs, plus some pasta dishes. There's karaoke entertainment every night.

Traegers. In Cumberland Square, 1515 8th St. East. ☎ **306/374-7881.** Reservations recommended at lunch. Sandwiches and light fare $4–$8. MC, V. Mon–Sat 8am–9pm, Sun 9am–8pm. LIGHT FARE/DESSERTS.

Traegers makes a very pleasant breakfast, lunch, afternoon tea, and supper spot. The offerings include croissant sandwiches, salads, quiche, pâté, a ploughman's lunch, a salami platter, and so on. The bakery items, though, are the most exciting—croissants, bagels, and croque-monsieurs in the early morning, and richly delicious desserts like amaretto-chocolate cheesecake and Black Forest torte.

SASKATOON AFTER DARK

There's not an awful lot of nightlife in Saskatoon, but the **Saskatoon Centennial Auditorium,** 35 22nd St. East (☎ 306/938-7800), provides a superb 2,003-seat theater, with a range of shows. The **Saskatoon Symphony** (☎ 306/665-6414) regularly performs in a September-to-April season. Tickets are $15 to $25.

Among local theater companies, the **Persephone Theatre,** 2802 Rusholme Rd. (☎ 306/384-7727), offers six shows per fall-to-spring season (dramas, comedies, and musicals; tickets are $10 to $22.50). **Nightcap Productions,** 317 Hilliard St. East (☎ 306/653-2300), produces Shakespeare on the Saskatchewan annually during July and August in two tents overlooking the river. Tickets are $18.75 for adults, $15.50 for seniors and students, $12.25 for children 6 to 12.

Art galleries include the **Photographers Gallery** (☎ 306/244-8018) and **A.K.A.** (☎ 306/652-0044), both at 12 23rd St. East. They feature modern and local artists and hosts the occasional literary event or dance and music performances.

For quiet drinking and conversation, you can't beat the **Samurai** lounge in the Bessborough Hotel (☎ 306/244-5521). Other pleasant lounges include **Cousin Niks** (☎ 306/374-2020). For a more pubby atmosphere, try the **Artful Dodger** on Fourth Avenue South (☎ 306/653-2577).

Country music, not surprisingly, is big in Saskatoon. The most popular of the crop is the **Texas "T,"** 3331 8th St. East (☎ 306/373-8080), which affects a corrallike decor and features live country bands (both Canadian and up-from-Nashville groups). Kick up your heels from 5pm to 1:30am. A cover (about $5) is charged sometimes.

Marquis Downs racetrack, at the corner of Ruth Street and St. Henry Avenue (☎ 306/242-6100), is open for live and simulcast racing. The live season goes from mid-May to mid-October. The racetrack has a lounge, a cafeteria, and terrace dining overlooking the paddock and home stretch. Admission is $3.

13   Side Trips from Saskatoon

FORT BATTLEFORD NATIONAL HISTORIC PARK

This site lies about 86 miles (138km), a 1½-hour drive, northwest of Saskatoon on Highway 16. In 1876, when the Northwest Mounted Police established their district headquarters here, the area was still the exclusive domain of Native Canadians, bison, and a handful of white traders. The government, which had received the Northwest Territories from the Hudson's Bay Company in 1870, wanted farmers to settle the land and open the West. Policing the area was necessary and the fort you see today remained in use until 1924.

Outside the interpretative gallery a display relates the role of the mounted police from the fur-trading era to the events that led to the rebellion of 1885. You'll see a Red River cart, the type that was used to transport police supplies into the West; excerpts from the local Saskatchewan *Herald;* a typical settler's log-cabin home, which is amazingly tiny; articles of the fur trade; and an 1876 Gatling gun.

Inside the palisade, the Visitor Reception Centre shows two videos about the 1885 Uprising and the Cree People. From there, proceed to the guardhouse (1887), containing a cell block and the sick horse stable (1898), and the Officers' Quarters (1886), with police documents, maps and telegraph equipment.

Perhaps the most interesting building is the Commanding Officer's Residence (1877), which, even though it looks terribly comfortable today, was certainly not so in 1885 when nearly 100 women took shelter in it during the siege of Battleford. Admission is $3 adults, $2.25 seniors, $1.50 students. Open from Victoria Day to Thanksgiving daily 9am to 5pm (until 6pm in July and August). Call ☎ 306/937-2621 for further information.

BATOCHE NATIONAL HISTORIC SITE

In spring 1885 the Northwest Territories exploded in an armed uprising led by the Métis Louis Riel and Gabriel Dumont. Trouble had been brewing along the frontier for several years. The Indians were demanding food, equipment, and farming assistance that had been promised to them in treaties. The settlers were angry about railway development and protective tariffs that meant higher prices for the equipment and services they needed.

The Métis were the offspring of the original French fur traders, who had intermarried with the Cree and Saulteaux women. Initially they had worked for the Hudson's Bay and Northwest Companies but when the two companies merged many were left without work. So they turned to buffalo hunting or became independent traders with the Indians in the West. When Riel was unable to obtain guarantees for the Métis in Manitoba in 1869–70, even when he established a provisional government, it became clear that the Métis would have to adopt the agricultural ways of the whites to survive. In 1872 they established the settlement at Batoche along the South Saskatchewan River. But they had a hard time acquiring "legal" titles and securing scrip, a certificate that could be exchanged for a land grant or money. The Métis complained to the government, but received no satisfactory response. So they called on Riel to lead them in what became known as the Northwest Rebellion.

Of the rebellion's five significant engagements, the Battle of Batoche was the only one that government forces decisively won. From May 9 to May 12, 1885, fewer than

300 Métis and Indians led by Riel and Dumont defended the village against the Northwest Field Force commanded by General Frederick Middleton and numbering 800. On the first day Middleton combined a river attack using the steamer Northcote with a land advance but the Métis decapitated the smokestacks of the steamer with a ferry cable. Two days of standoff followed during which the Métis exhausted most of their ammunition, fighting from a series of rifle pits they had dug along the edge of the bush. On the third day Middleton lured them out of the pits with a fake attack and succeeded in breaking through the Métis lines around the church and sweeping down to the village. Dumont fled to the United States but returned and is buried at the site; Riel surrendered, stood trial, and was executed.

At the park you can visit four battle areas, including the church and rectory and the Mission Ridge, the key location of the fighting, and the zareba and Caro farmhouse where Middleton took his position. At the visitor center a film is shown. It will take four to six hours to walk to all four areas, $2^{1}/_{2}$ hours to complete areas 1 and 2. For more information contact Batoche National Historic Park, P.O. Box 999, Rosthern, SK, S0K 3R0 (☎ 306/423-6227). Admission is $3 for adults, $2.25 seniors, $1.50 children six to 16. Open 10 to 6 daily July to August, 9 to 5 September and October. The site is about an hour from Saskatoon via Highway 11 to 312 to 225.

14 Prince Albert National Park & the Far North

PRINCE ALBERT NATIONAL PARK

This million-acre wilderness area, 150 miles (240km) north of Saskatoon and 57 miles (91km) north of the town of Prince Albert, is one of the jewels of Canada's national park system. Its terrain is astoundingly varied, since it lies at the point where the great Canadian prairie grasslands give way to the pristine evergreen forests of the north. There you'll find clear, cold lakes, ponds, and streams created thousands of years ago as glaciers receded. It's a hilly landscape, forested with spruce, poplar, and birch.

The park not only offers outdoor activities from canoeing and backpacking to nature hikes, picnicking, and swimming, but also wonderful **wildlife.** You can see and photograph moose, caribou, elk, black bear, bison, and loons. (The moose and caribou tend to wander through the forested northern part of the park, while the elk and deer graze on the southern grasslands.) Lavallee Lake is home to Canada's second-largest white pelican colony.

In the 1930s, this park's woods and wildlife inspired famed naturalist Grey Owl, an Englishman adopted by the Ojibwa who became one of Canada's pioneering conservationists and most noted naturalists. For seven years, he lived at in a simple, one-room cabin called Beaver Lodge on Ajawaan Lake; many hikers and canoeists make a pilgrimage to see his cabin and nearby gravesite.

Vehicle entry fees are $25 for a week, $18 for Friday, Saturday, and Sunday, and $7 or $3 per adult, $2.25 senior, and $1.50 per child daily. The park is open year-round, but many campgrounds, motels, and facilities are closed after October. There are a handful of winter campsites, though, if you've come to ice fish or to cross-country ski on the more than 93 miles (150km) of trails.

The town of **Waskesiu,** which lies on the shores of the lake of the same name, is where you'll find gas, groceries, and information. This is also where you can rent canoes, rowboats, motorboats, and houseboats. The townsite also has several hotels, motels, and cabins.

At the **Visitor Service Centre** at park headquarters in Waskesiu, you'll find an 18-hole golf course, tennis courts, riding stables, bowling greens, and a paddle wheeler that cruises Waskesiu Lake. The staff here can tell you about the weather and the condition of the trails; check in with them before undertaking any serious canoe or backcountry trip. The park's **Nature Centre** presents the award-winning audiovisual program *Up North* daily during July and August. Together with the participatory exhibits at the center and naturalist-led programs—sunrise hikes, starlight walks—it's an excellent way to discover a hint of what awaits you in the park.

The park has ten short **hiking trails,** plus four or so longer trails for backpackers, ranging from 6.2 miles (10kms) to 25.4 miles (41kms). Several easier ones begin in or near Waskesiu, though the best begin further north. From the northwest shore of Lake Kingsmere, you can pick up the 20km trail that leads to Grey Owl's cabin.

Canoeing routes wind through much of the park through a system of interconnected lakes and rivers. Canoes can be rented for $33 a day at three lakes, including Lake Waskesiu, and paddled along several routes, including the Bagwa, Bladebone, and Grey Owl routes.

There's terrific **fishing** in the park, but anglers must have a national park fishing license. There's especially good trout fishing in Kingsmere Lake.

There are six **campgrounds** in the park, three with more than 100 sites and three with fewer than 30. They fill up fast on summer weekends. The information office in Waskesiu can issue backcountry camping permits to backpackers and canoeists. Other accommodations are available in Waskesiu, including hotels, motels, and cabins (rates starting at $35 double, rising to $150 for a suite sleeping six to eight people). Most cabins and lodges are old and rustic in style and often contain stone fireplaces. You could also base yourself in the town of Prince Albert and come into the park on a long day trip.

For additional information, contact Prince Albert National Park, P.O. Box 1000, Waskesiu Lake, SK, S0J 2Y0 (☎ 306/663-5322).

THE FAR NORTH

The town of La Ronge lies 142 miles northeast of Prince Albert along Routes 2 and 102 on the shores of Lac La Ronge. At the lake's northeastern end lies **Lac La Ronge Provincial Park** (☎ 306/425-4234). Farther on Route 102 there's access to two great northern **fishing** lakes—Reindeer and Wollaston.

West of Prince Albert along Routes 55 and 155 lies **Meadow Lake Provincial Park** (☎ 306/236-7690 in summer only), with 25 crystal-clear lakes, and **Clearwater River Provincial Park,** which only offers fishing and hiking. Meadow Lake, however, offers a range of activities, including camping, swimming, boat rentals, tennis, hiking, cross-country trails, and snowmobile trails. Beyond that, not far from the border of the Northwest Territories lies **Athabasca Sand Dunes Provincial Wilderness Park,** accessible only by air or boat. It's strictly for fishing only.

17

Alberta & the Rockies

by Bill McRae

Bill McRae was born and raised in rural
Montana, though he spent the better years of his
youth attending university in Great Britain and
France. His previous books include *The Montana
Handbook,* published by Moon Publications, and
The Pacific Northwest, published by Lonely
Planet. He makes his home in Portland, Oregon.

Stretching from the Northwest Territories to the U.S. border of
Montana in the south, flanked by the Rocky Mountains in the
west and the province of Saskatchewan in the east, Alberta is a big
and beautiful chunk of North America—and also an empty one.
Measuring 255,285 square miles, the province is almost as large as
Texas, but, with less than two million inhabitants, it has fewer people
than Philadelphia.

Culturally, Alberta is a beguiling mix of Texas-style swagger and
affluence and rural Canadian sincerity. Its cities, Calgary and
Edmonton, are models of modern civic pride and hospitality; in fact,
Edmonton was recently awarded the title of Canada's friendliest city
after an anonymous behavioral survey.

Early settlers came to Alberta for its wealth of furs; the Hudson's
Bay Company established Edmonton House on the North
Saskatchewan River in 1795. The native Blackfoot, one of the West's
most formidable Indian nations, maintained control of the prairies
until the 1870s, when the Royal Canadian Mounted Police arrived
to enforce the white man's version of law and order. Open range
cattle ranching prospered on the rich grasslands; agriculture is still
the basis of the rural Alberta economy. Vast oil reserves were discovered beneath the prairies in the 1960s, introducing a tremendous
20-year boom across the province.

More than half the population lives in Edmonton and Calgary,
Alberta's cities on the plain, leaving the rest of the province a tremendous amount of elbow room, breathing space, and unspoiled
scenery. The Canadian Rockies rise to the west of the prairies, and
contain some of the finest mountain scenery on earth. It's not just
that the glacier-carved mountains are astonishingly dramatic and
beautiful; it's also that there are hundreds and hundreds of miles of
this wonderful wilderness high country. Between them, Banff and
Jasper national parks preserve much of this mountain beauty, but
these are just the beginning. Other national and provincial parks
both protect and make accessible other vast and equally spectacular
regions of the Rockies, as well as portions of the nearby Columbia
and Selkirk mountain ranges.

All this wilderness makes outdoor activity Alberta's greatest draw
for travelers. Hiking, biking, and pack trips on horseback have long

pedigrees in the parks, as does superlative skiing—the winter Olympics were held in Alberta in 1988. Outfitters throughout the region offer white-water and float trips on mighty rivers; calmer pursuits like fishing and canoeing are also popular.

It's also worth noting that some of Canada's finest and most famous hotels are in Alberta. The incredible mountain lodges and châteaux built by early rail entrepreneurs are still in operation, and offer an unforgettable experience in luxury and stunning scenery. These grand hotels established a standard of hospitality that's observed by hoteliers across the province. If you're looking for a more rural experience, head to one of Alberta's many guest ranches, where you can saddle up, poke some doggies, and end the evening at a steak barbecue.

1 Exploring Alberta & the Rockies

It's no secret that Alberta contains some of Canada's most compelling scenery and outdoor recreation. During the high season, from mid-June through August, this is a very busy place; Banff is generally acknowledged to be Canada's single most popular destination for foreign travelers.

A little preplanning is therefore essential, especially if you are traveling in the summer or have specific destinations or lodgings in mind. Accommodations are very tight throughout the province, and especially so in the Rockies. Make room reservations for Banff and Jasper as early as possible; likewise, Calgary is packed out for the Stampede, and Edmonton for Klondike Days. Advance reservations are mandatory for these events.

Skiers should know that some mountain roads in Alberta close in winter due to heavy snowfall. However, major passes are maintained and usually remain open to traffic. Highways 3, 1, and 16 are open year-round, though it's a good idea to call ahead to check road conditions. You can inquire locally, or call **Alberta Tourism** at ☎ 800/661-8888. If you're a member of **AAA or CAA,** call their information line at ☎ 800/642-3810. Always carry traction devices like tire chains in your vehicle, plus plenty of warm clothes and a sleeping bag if you're planning winter car travel.

This chapter moves along roughly like a clockwise driving tour of Alberta and the Rockies: Coverage of Calgary is first, followed by day trips or short excursions into the southern part of the province. The many parks and recreation areas around Banff and Jasper national parks—including destinations in the Columbia and Selkirk mountains in nearby British Columbia—are covered next, followed by Edmonton and points north.

Don't let this structure dictate your route: There are lots of side roads and alternatives to the major destinations, and after a few days of crowds and traffic, you may be looking for a blue highway. The foothills and lakes in Kananaskis Country are a good alternative to busy Banff for campers and hikers, for example. You can also free yourself of the crowds in the Alberta national parks by visiting the less-thronged but equally dramatic Glacier and Mt. Revelstoke national parks in British Columbia.

VISITOR INFORMATION   For information about the entire province, contact **Alberta Economic Development and Tourism,** City Centre, 10155 102nd St., Edmonton, AB, T5J 4L6 (☎ 800/661-8888). Be sure to ask for a copy of the accommodations and visitors guide, as well as the excellent *Traveler's Guide* and a road map.

A BED-AND-BREAKFAST NETWORK   Lists of B&B accommodations are available from **Alberta Bed and Breakfast,** P.O. Box 15477, M.P.O., Vancouver, BC, V6B 5B2 (☎ 604/944-1793), which maintains a network of B&B

establishments throughout Alberta, with rates starting at $40 a day for singles, $45 for doubles.

AN IMPORTANT NOTE ON PRICES & TAXES Unless stated otherwise, **the prices cited in this guide are given in Canadian dollars,** which is good news for U.S. travelers because the Canadian dollar is worth 25% less than the American dollar, but buys nearly as much. As we go to press, $1 Canadian is worth 75¢ U.S., which means that your $100-a-night hotel room will cost only U.S. $75, and your $6 breakfast costs only U.S. $4.50.

Alberta has no provincial sales tax. There's only the national 7% goods and services tax (GST), plus a 5% accommodations tax.

2 The Great Outdoors

Banff and Jasper national parks have long been the center of mountain recreation for Alberta. If you're staying in Banff, Jasper, or Lake Louise, you'll find that outfitters and recreational rental operations in these centers are pretty sophisticated and professional: they make it easy and convenient to get outdoors and have an adventure. Most hotels will offer a concierge service that can arrange most activities for you; for many, you need little or no advance registration. Shuttle buses to more distant activities are usually available as well.

And to enjoy the magnificent scenery, you don't have to get there on your own power. Hire a horse and ride horseback to the backcountry, or take an afternoon trail ride. Jasper, Banff, and Lake Louise each have gondolas to lift travelers from the valley floor to the mountaintops. Bring a picnic, or plan a ridge-top hike. If you're not ready for white water, the scenic cruises on Lake Minnewanka and Maligne Lake offer a more relaxed waterborne adventure.

BACKPACKING Backcountry trips through high mountain meadows and remote lakes provide an unforgettable experience; Banff Park alone has 1,900 miles of hiking trails.

BIKING Both parks provide free maps of local mountain bike trails; the Bow Valley Parkway between Banff and Lake Louise and Parkway 93A in Jasper Park are both good, less trafficked roads for road biking. Bike rentals are easily available nearly everywhere in the parks.

ROCK CLIMBING, ICE CLIMBING & MOUNTAINEERING The sheer rock faces on Mt. Rundle near Banff are popular with rock climbers, and the area's many waterfalls become frozen ascents for ice climbers in the winter. Instruction in mountaineering skills, including rock climbing, is offered by the **Canadian School of Mountaineering,** based in Canmore (☎ 403/678-4134).

SKIING In winter, skiing takes over the Rockies. There are downhill areas at Banff, Lake Louise, Jasper, and at the former Olympic site at Nakiska in the Kananaskis Country. At its best, skiing is superb here: The snowpack is copious, the scenery is beautiful, après-ski festivities indulgent, and the accommodations world class. Also, there's a lot of value in an Alberta ski holiday: Lift tickets here are generally cheaper than at comparable ski areas in North America.

Heli-skiing isn't allowed in the national parks, but is popular in the adjacent mountain ranges in British Columbia. **CMH Heli-Skiing,** 217 Bear St., Banff (☎ 402/762-7100; fax 403/762-5879), is the leader in this increasingly popular sport, which uses helicopters to deposit skiers on virgin slopes far from the lift lines

Alberta

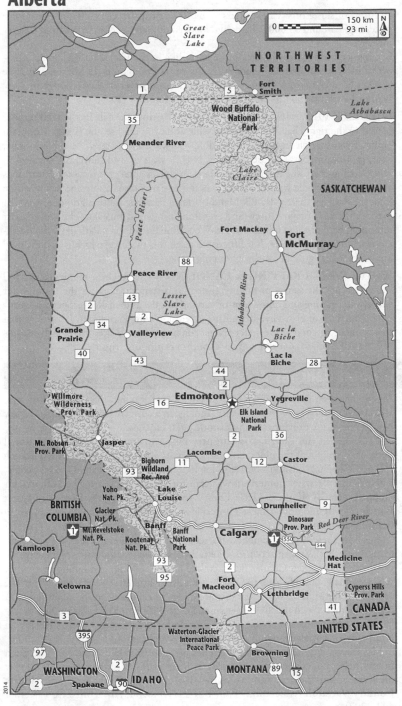

Great
Slave
Lake

1

5 Fort
Smith

NORTHWEST
TERRITORIES

Lake
Athabasca

35

Wood Buffalo
National
Park

Meander River

Lake
Claire

SASKATCHEWAN

Peace River

Fort Mackay

Fort
McMurray

88

Peace River

2

43

34

Grande
Prairie

43

2

Lesser
Slave
Lake

Valleyview

Athabasca River

63

Lac la
Biche

Lac la
Biche

28

40

44

2

Willmore
Wilderness
Prov. Park

16

Edmonton

Yegreville

Elk Island
National
Park

Mt. Robson
Prov. Park

Jasper

2

36

Lacombe

11

12

Castor

Bighorn
Wildland
Rec. Area

93

Yoho
Nat. Pk.

Lake
Louise

Drumheller

9

BRITISH
COLUMBIA

Glacier
Nat. Pk.

1

Mt. Revelstoke
Nat. Pk.

Banff

Banff
National
Park

Calgary

1

550

Dinosaur
Prov. Park

Red Deer River

S44

Kamloops

Kootenay
Nat. Pk.

93

Medicine
Hat

Kelowna

95

Fort
Macleod

2

Lethbridge

Cyperss Hills
Prov. Park

3

5

41

CANADA

395

Waterton-Glacier
International
Peace Park

UNITED STATES

97

2

90

WASHINGTON

IDAHO

Spokane

Browning

MONTANA

89

15

2014

150 km
93 mi

0

and runs of ski resorts. CMH offers 7- or 10-day trips to eight different locations; prices begin around $3,000, all lodging, food, equipment, and transport from Calgary inclusive.

Cross-country skiers will also find a lot to like in the Canadian Rockies. A number of snowbound mountain lodges remain open throughout the winter, and serve as bases for adventurous Nordic skiers. The historic **Emerald Lake Lodge** in Yoho National Park (☎ 604/343-6321) is one of the finest.

WILDLIFE VIEWING   If you're thrilled by seeing animals in the wild, you've turned to the right chapter. No matter which one you choose, the Rocky Mountain national parks are all teeming with wildlife—bighorn sheep, grizzly and black bears, deer, mountain goats, moose, coyotes, lynxes, wolves, and more. See Section 7, "Introducing the Canadian Rockies," later in this chapter, for important warnings about how to handle wildlife encounters in the parks responsibly and safely. Aside from the Rockies, there's also Elk Island National Park just outside Edmonton, which harbors the tiny pygmy shrew and the immense wood buffalo. The world's last remaining herd of wood buffalo lives in Wood Buffalo National Park in the far northern reaches of the province. It's difficult to reach this preserve, which is also the only known breeding ground for the whooping crane.

WHITE-WATER RAFTING & CANOEING   The Rockies' many glaciers and snowfields are the source of mighty rivers. Outfitters throughout the region offer white-water rafting and canoe trips of varying lengths and challenge; spend a morning on the river, or plan a five-day rafting expedition with an outfitter. Jasper is central to a number of good white-water rivers; contact **White-Water River Adventures** (☎ 403/852-3370), one of many local outfitters offering trips.

3 Guest Ranches

Alberta has been ranch country for well over a century, and the Old West lifestyle is deeply ingrained in Albertan culture. Indulge in a cowboy fantasy and spend a few days at one of the province's many historic guest ranches.

At Seebe, in the Kananaskis Country near the entrance to Banff National Park, are a couple of the oldest and most famous guest ranches. **Rafter Six Ranch** (☎ 403/673-3622), with its beautiful log lodge, can accommodate up to 60 people. The original Brewster homestead was transformed in 1923 into the **Kananaskis Guest Ranch** (☎ 403/673-3737). Once a winter horse camp, the **Black Cat Guest Ranch** (☎ 403/865-3084) near Hinton is another long-established guest ranch in beautiful surroundings.

At all of these historic ranches, horseback riding and trail rides are the main focus, but other Western activities, like rodeos, barbecues, and country dancing are usually on the docket. Gentler pursuits, like fishing, hiking, and lolling by the hot tub, are equally possible. At guest ranches, meals are usually served family style in the central lodge, while accommodations are either in cabins or in the main lodge. A night at a guest ranch usually ranges from $75 to $100, and includes a ranch breakfast. Full bed-and-board packages are available for longer stays. There's usually an hourly fee for horseback riding in addition to room charges.

Homestays at smaller working ranches are also possible: Here you can pitch in and help your ranch family hosts with their work, or simply relax. For a stay on a real mom-and-pop farm, obtain a list of member ranches from **Alberta Country Vacation Association,** P.O. Box 217, Trochu, AB, T0M 2C0 (☎ 403/442-2207).

4 Calgary

Historically Calgary dates back just over a century. It was born in the summer of 1875, when a detachment of the Northwest Mounted Police, advancing westward, reached the confluence of the Bow and Elbow rivers. They built a solid log fort there, and by the end of the year the fortified spot had attracted 600 settlers.

Gradually the lush prairie lands around the settlement drew tremendous beef herds, many of them from the overgrazed U.S. ranches in the south. Calgary grew into a cattle metropolis, a big meat-packing center, large by rancher standards—but not by any other. When World War II ended, it numbered barely 100,000 souls and life was placid.

The oil boom erupted in the late 1960s, and in one decade the pace and complexion of the city utterly changed. The population shot up at a pace that made statisticians dizzy. In 1978 alone, $1 billion worth of construction was added to the skyline, creating office high-rises, hotel blocks, walkways, and shopping centers so fast that even locals weren't sure what was around the next corner.

The recession caused by the world's oil glut cooled Calgary's overheated growth considerably. But—at least from the visitor's angle—this enhanced the city's attractiveness. The once-ubiquitous rooftop cranes that marred its skyline have largely disappeared. However, Calgary continues to prosper. In the mid-1990s, the oil market is heating up again, and Alberta's pro-business political climate tempts national companies to build their headquarters here.

In February 1988 Calgary was the site of the Winter Olympics, which gave it the opportunity to roll out the welcome mat on a truly international scale. The city outdid itself in hospitality, erecting a whole network of facilities for the occasion, including the Canada Olympic Park, by the Trans-Canada Highway, some 15 minutes west of downtown. The park was the site of the ski-jumping, bobsled, and skiing events, and it contains the Olympic Hall of Fame, now one of Calgary's proudest landmarks. So even if you didn't make it to the games, you can admire some of the marvels they left in their wake.

ESSENTIALS

VISITOR INFORMATION   The **Visitor Service Centres** at Tower Centre, 9th Avenue SW and Centre Street, and at the airport, provide you with free literature, maps, and information about the city. These are run by the **Calgary Convention and Visitors Bureau,** whose head office is at 237 8th Ave SE, Calgary, AB, T2G 0K8. Included in their telephone services is a useful, no-charge accommodations bureau (☎ 800/661-1678 or 403/263-8510).

GETTING THERE   **Calgary International Airport** lies 5 miles northeast of the city. You can go through U.S. Customs right here if you're flying home via Calgary. The airport is served by **Air Canada** (☎ 800/776-3000); **Canadian Airlines** (☎ 800/426-7000); **Delta** (☎ 800/221-1212); **Northwest Airlines** (☎ 800/447-4747); **American Airlines** (☎ 800/433-7300); **United** (☎ 800/241-6522); **KLM** (☎ 800/374-7747); plus Time Air, Air B.C., Horizon, and several commuter lines. A shuttle service to and from Edmonton is run frequently each day by Air Canada and Canadian Airlines. Cab fare to downtown hotels from the airport comes to around $20. The **Airporter bus** takes you downtown from the airport for $8. By cab it's around $23.

From the U.S. border in the south, Highway 2 runs to Calgary. The same excellent road continues north to Edmonton (via Red Deer). From Vancouver in the west to Regina in the east, you take the Trans-Canada Highway.

The nearest **Via Rail** station is in Edmonton. You can, however, take a scenic train ride from Vancouver on the *Rocky Mountaineer* service, operated by the **Great Canadian Rail Tour Company** (☎ 800/665-7245). Cost is $525 for two days of daylight travel, which includes overnight accommodation in Kamloops. Trains depart every five days.

CITY LAYOUT Central Calgary lies between the Bow River in the north and the Elbow River to the south. The two rivers meet at the eastern end of the city, forming St. George's Island, which houses a park and the zoo. South of the island stands Fort Calgary, birthplace of the city. The Bow River makes a bend north of downtown, and in this bend nestles Prince's Island Park and Eau Claire Market. Between Ninth and Tenth Avenues run the Canadian Pacific Railway tracks, and south of the tracks stretch Central Park and Stampede Park, scene of Calgary's greatest annual festival.

Your best orientation point is the cloud-pushing Calgary Tower, at Ninth Avenue and Centre Street. Looking across the avenue, you're facing due north. You have the post office on your left, the Convention Centre opposite, and City Hall two blocks up on the right.

The city is divided into four segments: northeast (NE), southeast (SE), northwest (NW), and southwest (SW), with avenues running east-west and streets north-south. The north and south numbers begin at Centre Avenue, the east and west numbers at Centre Street—a recipe for confusion if ever there were one.

Calgary nudges the foothills of the Rocky Mountains to the west and the endless prairies to the east. A short drive northeast lie the Drumheller Badlands, an awesome configuration that yielded the dinosaur skeletons you'll see in the city museums. This is also the direction of the Calgary International Airport. Northwest, just across the Bow River, spreads the lovely campus of the University of Calgary. Southwest runs a vast pattern of parks, golf courses, and nature trails surrounding the sparkling Glenmore Reservoir. And farther south begins the rich rural landscape of farming communities and baronial cattle ranches.

GETTING AROUND Within the city, transportation is provided by the **Calgary Transit System** (☎ 403/276-1000). The system uses buses, plus a light-rail (LRT) system called the C-Train. You can transfer from the light rail to buses on the same ticket. The ride costs $1.50 for adults, 90¢ for children, but it's free in the downtown stretch between 10th Street and City Hall.

Car-rental firms include: **Tilden**, located at 114 Fifth Ave. SE (☎ 403/263-6386) as well as at five other locations, including the airport; **Budget**, 140 6th Ave. SE (☎ 403/226-1550); and **Hertz**, 227 6th Ave. SW (☎ 403/221-1300).

To summon a taxi, call **Checker Cabs** (☎ 403/299-9999), **Red Top Cabs** (☎ 403/974-4444), or **Yellow Cabs** (☎ 403/974-1111).

The first thing a pedestrian will note about Calgary is how long the blocks are. Allow 15 minutes to walk five blocks. Pedestrians will also like the "Plus-15" system, a series of enclosed walkways 15 feet above street level that connects downtown buildings. These walkways enable you to shop in living-room comfort, regardless of weather. Watch for the little "+15" signs on streets for access points.

FAST FACTS American Express There's an office at 421 7th Ave. SW (☎ 403/261-5085).

Climate Because of its high altitude the city is dry and very sunny as well as windy, and even in summer it tends to be cool in the shade. Summer "heat" is a relative matter here. July and August, the warmest months, rarely climb above 75°F or so.

Calgary

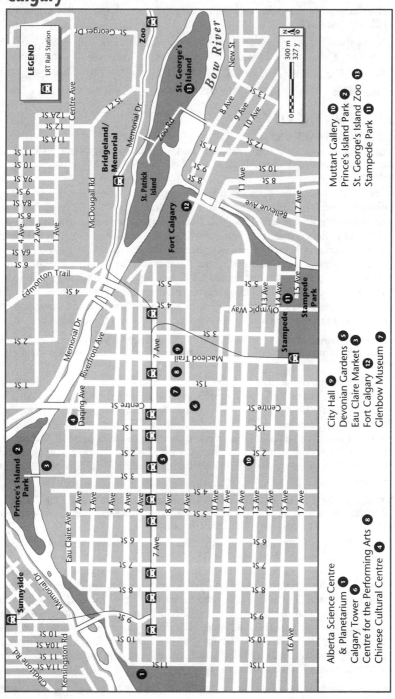

LEGEND

🚈 LRT Rail Station

0 ___ 300 m
0 ___ 327 y

Alberta Science Centre
& Planetarium **1**
Calgary Tower **6**
Centre for the Performing Arts **8**
Chinese Cultural Centre **4**

City Hall **9**
Devonian Gardens **5**
Eau Claire Market **3**
Fort Calgary **12**
Glenbow Museum **7**

Muttart Gallery **10**
Prince's Island Park **2**
St. George's Island Zoo **11**
Stampede Park **13**

Hospitals   If you need medical care, try Calgary General Hospital, 841 Centre Ave. (☎ 403/268-9111).

Newspapers   Calgary's two dailies, the *Calgary Herald* and the *Calgary Sun,* are both morning papers. The weekly arts and local newspapers are *Avenue* and *Cityscope.*

Police   The 24-hour number is ☎ 403/266-1234. Dial 911 in emergencies.

Post Office   Try calling ☎ 403/292-5434 to find the branch nearest you.

EXPLORING THE CITY
THE TOP ATTRACTIONS

✪ **Glenbow Museum.** 130 Ninth Ave. SE (at 1st Street). ☎ **403/268-4100.** Admission $5 adults, $3.50 students and seniors, children under 7 free. Mid-May to mid-Sept daily 9am–5pm; call for winter hours.

The Glenbow Museum, a most impressive complex, was created in order to exhibit, under one roof, the art and history of humankind. The beautiful displays of this ambitious museum are spread over four floors; one floor is devoted to art, one to the history of western Canada, and others to West Africa and mineralogy. You can spend days here, constantly finding fascinating items you'd overlooked before: exotic carvings and ceramics from every part of the globe; hundreds of Native Canadian artifacts; paintings and sculpture by famous artists, both local and on tour; a stunning array of medieval armor, including mounted knights looking like apparitions from *Star Wars;* one of the largest gun collections in existence; trophies and weapons from two world wars; historic Canadian prints, letters, and documents; and so on.

Fort Calgary Historic Park. 750 Ninth Ave. SE. ☎ **403/290-1875.** Admission $2 adults, $1 youths, $5 family, children under 6 free. Free to all on Tues. May–Oct daily 9am–5pm. LRT: Bridgeland.

On the occasion of the city's centennial in 1975, Fort Calgary became a public park of 40 acres, spread around the ruins of the original Mounted Police stronghold. The focal point is the Interpretive Centre, a fantastic life-size audiovisual kaleidoscope that takes you back from modern Calgary to the sights, sounds, and—you'd swear—smells of the prairies. The auditorium features multiscreen presentations of the life, adventures, and hardships of the Mounties a century ago—the rigors of their westward march and the almost unbelievable isolation and loneliness these pioneer troopers endured.

✪ **Calgary Zoo, Botanical Garden & Prehistoric Park.** 1300 Zoo Rd. NE. ☎ **403/232-9300.** Admission $7.50 adults, $5.50 seniors ($2 on Tues), $3.75 children. Late May–Sept daily 9am–6pm; winter daily 9am–4pm. LRT: Zoo station.

On St. George's Island in the Bow River lies one of the largest and most thoughtfully designed zoos in North America. The Calgary Zoo comes as close to providing natural habitats for its denizens as is technically possible—the animals live in environments rather than confines. You'll particularly want to see the troop of eight majestic lowland gorillas that produced babies in 1993—among the few born in captivity. The latest development is the "Slice of Canadian Wilderness," featuring woodland, mountain, prairie, and Arctic backgrounds for its inhabitants. Adjoining the zoo is the Prehistoric Park, a three-dimensional textbook of ancient dinosaur habitats populated by 22 amazingly realistic replicas. The zoo's exotic butterfly garden harbors 40,000 blooming tulips in springtime.

Calgary Tower. Ninth Ave. and Centre St. SW. ☎ **403/266-7171.** Elevator ride $4.95 adults, $1.95 children. Daily 7:30am–11pm.

The Calgary Stampede

Every year, during the month of July, Calgary puts on the biggest, wildest, woolliest western fling on earth. To call the stampede a show would be a misnomer. The whole city participates by going mildly crazy for the occasion, donning western gear, whooping, hollering, dancing, and generally behaving uproariously.

Many of the organized events spill out into the streets, but most of them take place in Stampede Park, a show, sports, and exhibition ground just south of downtown that was built for just that purpose. Portions of the park become amusement areas, whirling, spinning, and rotating with the latest rides. Other parts are set aside especially for the kids, who romp through Kids' World and the Petting Zoo. Still other areas have concerts, livestock shows, food and handicraft exhibitions, free lectures, and dance performances.

The top attractions, though, are the rodeo events, the largest and most prestigious of their kind in all of North America. Cowboys from all over the world take part in such competitions as riding bucking broncos and bulls, roping calves, and wrestling steers for prize money totaling $580,000. At the world-famous Chuckwagon Race you'll see old-time western cook wagons thundering around the track in a fury of dust and pounding hooves, competing eagerly for more than $375,000 in prize money. At night the arena becomes a blaze of lights when the Stampede Grandstand—the largest outdoor extravaganza in the world—takes over with precision-kicking dancers, clowns, bands, and spectacles.

On top of that, the Stampede offers a food fair, an art show, dancing exhibitions, an international bazaar, a gambling casino, lotteries, and free entertainment on several stages.

Let me tell you right from the start that the whole city of Calgary is absolutely *packed* for the occasion, not just to the rafters but way out into the surrounding countryside. Reserving accommodations well ahead is essential—as many months ahead of your arrival as you can possibly foresee. (For lodging, call Calgary's Convention and Visitors Bureau at 800/661-1678.) Some downtown watering holes even take reservations for space at their bar; that should give you an idea of how busy Calgary gets.

The same advice applies to reserving tickets for all of the park events. Tickets cost between $8 and $43, depending on the event, the seats, and whether it is afternoon or evening. For mail-order bookings, contact the **Calgary Exhibition and Stampede,** P.O. Box 1860, Station M, Calgary, AB, T2P 2M7 (☎ 800/661-1260).

Reaching 626 feet (762 steps) into the sky, this Calgary landmark is topped by an observation terrace offering unparalleled views of the city and the mountains and prairies beyond. A stairway from the terrace leads to the cocktail lounge for panoramic drinks. Photography from up here is fantastic. The high-speed elevator whisks you to the top in just 63 seconds. The Panorama Restaurant (☎ 403/266-7171) is the near-mandatory revolving restaurant.

Devonian Gardens. Eighth Avenue Mall between 2nd and 3rd sts. SW. ☎ **403/268-5207.** Free admission. Daily 9am–9pm.

The gardens are a patch of paradise in downtown, an enclosed 2¹/₂-acre park, like a gigantic glass house, 46 feet above street level. Laid out in natural contours with a mile of pathways and a central stage for musical performances, the gardens contain

20,000 plants (mostly imported from Florida), a reflecting pool, a sun garden, a children's playground, a sculpture court, and a water garden.

Olympic Hall of Fame. Canada Olympic Park at Canada Olympic Park Rd. SW. ☎ **403/247-5452.** Tour admission $3–$8 adults, $2.70–$6 seniors/students, $2.50–$4 youth, $20 family. Luge rides $12, offered in summer only, 11am–9pm. Daily summer 8am–9pm; off-season 8am–5pm (check first). Take Highway 1 west.

A lasting memento of Calgary's role as host of the 1988 Winter Olympic Games stands in the Olympic Park. Three floors of exhibits contain the world's largest collection of Olympic souvenirs, such as the torch used to bring the flame from Greece, costumes and sporting equipment used by the athletes, superb action photographs, and a gallery of all medal winners since the revival of the Olympic Games in 1924. Also shown is a video presentation of the games and their history.

MORE ATTRACTIONS

Calgary Chinese Cultural Centre. 197 1st St. SW. ☎ **403/262-5071.** Free admission. Museum daily 11am–5pm; building hours 9:30am–9pm. Bus 2, 3, or 17.

The new landmark and focal point of Calgary's Chinatown, this impressive structure is topped by a great central dome patterned after the Temple of Heaven in Beijing. The center houses exhibits, lecture halls, classrooms, a library, and specialized retail shops as well as a restaurant, gym, and bookstore. It covers 70,000 square feet and offers an overview of historical and contemporary Chinese cultural life, displayed underneath a gleaming gold dragon hovering 60 feet above the floor.

Fish Creek Provincial Park. Canyon Meadows Dr. and Macleod Trail SE. ☎ **403/297-5293.** Bus: 52, 11, or 78.

On the outskirts of town, but easily accessible, Fish Creek Park is one of the largest urban parks in the world—actually, a kind of metropolitan wildlife reserve. Spreading over 2,900 acres, it provides a sheltered habitat for a vast variety of animals and birds. You can learn about them by joining in the walks and slide presentations given by park interpreters. For information on their schedules and planned activities, visit the administration office or call the number above.

Museum of Movie Art. 3600 21st St. NE, no. 9. ☎ **403/250-7588.** Free admission. Mon–Fri 9:30am–5:30pm, Sat 11am–5pm. LRT: Barlow, then Bus 33.

This nostalgia nook for fans of cinema houses some 10,000 vintage movie posters and photos, some dating back to the 1920s. The museum sells classic posters.

Museum of the Regiments. 4520 Crowchild Trail SW. ☎ **403/240-7057.** Admission by donation. Thurs–Tues 10am–4pm (check first). Bus: 13 to 50th Avenue, then walk five blocks north.

The largest military museum in western Canada tells the story of four famous Canadian regiments from the turn of the century to this day through a series of lifelike miniature and full-size displays ranging from the Boer War in 1900 to World War II and contemporary peacekeeping actions. You also see videos, weapons, uniforms, medals, and photographs relating the history of the regiments and hear the actual voices of the combatants describing their experiences.

Muttart Gallery. 1221 2nd St. SW, in the Memorial Library. ☎ **403/266-2764.** Free admission. Mon, Wed, and Fri noon–5pm; Thurs noon–8pm, Sat 10am–5pm.

The Muttart Gallery is a contemporary art gallery, but with special emphasis on the contribution of local talent. A good place to see Calgary's share in the modern art scene.

ESPECIALLY FOR KIDS

Alberta Science Centre. 701 11th St. SW. ☎ **403/221-3700.** Admission (exhibits and star shows) $7 adults and youth, $5 seniors and children, $26 family. Summer daily 10am–8pm; off-season Wed 1–9pm, Thurs–Fri 1–9:30pm, Sat 10am–9:30pm, Sun 10:30am–5pm.

A fascinating combination of exhibitions, planetarium, and live theater under one roof. The hands-on, science-oriented exhibits change, but always invite visitors to push, pull, talk, listen, and play. The 360° Star Theatre opens windows to the universe.

Heritage Park. 1900 Heritage Dr. (west of 14th Street SW). ☎ **403/259-1900.** Admission (includes train ride) $8 adults, $6.50 senior, $4.50 children. Seasonal days and hours May and Oct; June–Sept daily 10am–6pm. Call for other times. LRT: Heritage station, then Bus 20 to Northmount.

On a peninsula jutting into Glenmore Reservoir, some 66 acres have been turned back in time. It's a Canadian pioneer turn-of-the-century township (1880s–1920s), painstakingly re-created, down to the sarsaparilla served over the counters. Walk down the main street and admire the "latest" fashions, drop in at the authentically curlicued soda fountain, stop at the elaborate hotel, watch the blacksmith at work, or sit on the cracker barrel of the general store. The layout includes a Hudson's Bay Company fort, a Native Canadian village, mining camp, old-time ranch, steam trains, streetcars, a horse-drawn bus, and a paddlewheeler that chugs you around Glenmore Reservoir.

Calaway Park. Six miles west of downtown on the Trans-Canada Highway. ☎ **403/ 240-3822.** Admission (including all rides) $17.50 adults, $12 children ages 3–6. June–Aug daily 10am–8pm; seasonal days and hours May and Oct; call for other times.

The 70-acre Calaway Park has all the thrills, loops, bumps, and squeals of the traditional midway carnival, with a bunch of new ones added. There's a huge double-corkscrew roller coaster, a 200-foot dry water slide, a haunted house, a hollow-log ride over waterfalls, a petting farm, and an absolutely bewildering 18,000-square-foot maze. Also live entertainers and a dozen eateries.

SHOPPING

A major portion of Eighth Avenue has been turned into a pedestrian zone called the Stephen Avenue Mall, closed to most vehicles and lined with trees, buskers, shops, and outdoor cafes. Banker's Hall has upscale, international specialty shops facing onto the pedestrian area.

If you're beginning to like the look of pearl snap shirts and the cut of Wranglers jeans, head to **Western Outfitters,** 128 Eighth Ave. SE (☎ 403/266-3656), across from the Convention Center, one of Calgary's original western apparel stores. If you're looking for cowboy boots, go to the **Alberta Boot Company,** 614 10th Ave. SW, Alberta's only boot manufacturer. Buy a pair of boots off the shelf ($200 ought to do it), or have a pair custom made (take out a second mortgage on your house).

Calgary has one thoroughfare that qualifies as a chic and trendy strip. The stretch of 17th Avenue approximately between 5th and 10th streets SW has developed a mix of specialty shops, boutiques, cafes, bars, restaurants, and delis that makes strolling and browsing a real pleasure. Many of Calgary's art galleries, interior decorating shops, and bookstores are also located here. Be sure to stop in at **Provenance,** 932 17th Ave. SW (☎ 403/245-8511), which features regional Canadian arts and crafts. **Sandpiper Books,** 1587 7th St. SW (☎ 403/228-0272), one of Calgary's best independent bookstores, is also worth a browse. Stop in at **Callebaut Chocolaterie,** 907 17th Ave. SW (☎ 403/244-1665), for great locally produced chocolates and candies.

WHERE TO STAY

Lists of B&B accommodations are available from the **Calgary Convention and Visitors Bureau,** 237 Eighth Ave. SE (☎ 800/661-1678). You can choose from 35 or more registered hosts in the Calgary area, each listing marked with details like "no-smoking home" and geographical location. The visitors bureau can also book a reservation for you.

DOWNTOWN

Expensive

Delta Bow Valley. 209 Fourth Ave. SE, Calgary, AB, T2G 0C6. ☎ **403/266-1980.** Fax 403/266-0007. 391 rms, 7 suites. A/C MINIBAR TV TEL. $160 double; $190 suite. Special weekend rate $85 per night, including complimentary gifts for children. Children under 18 stay free in parents' room; children under 6 eat free from children's menu. AE, DC, ER, MC, V. Parking $6.50 weekdays; free on weekends.

Completely renovated in 1995, the Delta is one of Calgary's finest hotels, with excellent on-premises restaurants and a large, airy, and attractive lobby. The focus of the hotel is upscale business travel, and these are some of the best facilities in the city if you're here with work to do. In their corner business suites, there are large desks completely set up for work: furnished with printer, in-room fax machine, cordless phone, and ergonomic chair. Local calls are free, and some rooms even have phones in the bathroom. After all this there's still room for a king-sized bed and a couch and chair to relax in. The standard rooms are also spacious and equipped with all the niceties you'd expect in this class of hotel.

Dining/Entertainment: Besides the classy Conservatory restaurant, there's a coffee shop and comfortable lobby bar.

Facilities: Although primarily a business hotel, the Delta goes the distance to make families welcome. During the summer and on weekends, there's a complete children's activity center: Leave the kids here while you head out to dinner. Other pluses include a marvelous pool, hot tub, and sauna area, which leads to a rooftop deck.

International Hotel. 220 Fourth Ave. SW, Calgary, AB, T2P 0H5. ☎ **403/265-9600** or 800/223-0888. Fax 403/265-6949. 247 suites. A/C MINIBAR TV TEL. $124–$180 one-bedroom suite; $162–$180 two-bedroom suite. Children under 16 stay free in parents' room. AE, CB, DC, ER, MC, V. Parking $3 per day.

A soaring 35-story tower with a breathtaking view from the upper balconies, the International is an all-suite hotel. Just out the back door is Chinatown and the Eau Claire Market area; the hotel is also very convenient to adjacent business towers. These are some of the largest rooms in Calgary. The hotel was originally built as an apartment building, so the suites are very large—up to 800 square feet each—each with separate bed and living rooms, private balcony, and large bathroom. The decor is low key, but you get the kinds of in-room amenities that come with a four-star hotel, including an extra-large minibar area and coffee maker. Rooms all have two TVs and telephones, and modem hook-ups. The very large two-bedroom suites are great for families. Some units have full kitchens.

The downside? The elevators date from the days when this was an apartment building; in summer, when tour buses hit, it can be exasperating to wait for the three elevators to serve guests on all 35 floors.

Services: On-call massage treatment.

Facilities: There's a very attractive tiled indoor pool, a Jacuzzi, a fitness room, and cafe and lounge.

Palliser Hotel. 133 9th Ave. SW., Calgary, AB, T2P 2M3. ☎ **403/262-1234** or 800/441-1414. Fax 403/260-1260. 390 rms, 16 suites. A/C MINIBAR TV TEL. $180–$245 double; from $225 suite. AE, DC, ER, MC, V. Parking $11 per day, $14 valet.

Opened in 1914 as one of the Canadian Pacific hotels, the Palliser adds a sumptuous Edwardian touch to Calgary's tourist scene. You'll feel like royalty as you enter the lobby, a vast chrome-and-white expanse glowing with crystal chandeliers, guarded by alabaster lions, and equipped with a burnished-brass Royal Mail box that seems designed for regal missives. More than $30 million was spent on renovations in 1993, and all guest and meeting rooms and public areas were updated. All rooms come equipped with every comfort and entertainment device known to travelers.

Dining/Entertainment: The Palliser's dining room has vaulted ceilings, a massive stone fireplace, and hand-tooled leather panels on real teakwood beams. The lounge bar, with towering windows, looks like a gentlemen's West End club.

Services: Room service; your tray comes with a single perfect rose.

Facilities: Health club, whirlpool, and steam room.

Radisson Plaza. 110 9th Ave. SE. (at Centre Street), Calgary, AB, T2G 5A6. ☎ **403/266-7331** or 800/333-3333. Fax 403/262-8442. 374 rms, 2 suites. A/C MINIBAR TV TEL. From $155 double; from $170 suite. Ask about special weekend rates. AE, CB, DC, DISC, ER, MC, V. Parking $8 a day, $11 valet.

The Radisson Plaza is a haven of understated elegance adjacent to the Calgary Convention Center, and convenient to the arty goings-on at the performing arts center. The skywalk connects the hotel with the promenade boutiques, stores, Palliser Square, Calgary Tower, the Convention Centre, and the Glenbow Museum.

Rooms are large, and nicely and subtly decorated, with lots of mirrors, voice mail, and an ironing board and iron in each.

Dining/Entertainment: Each of the two dining rooms has a distinct personality, one a family style buffet, the other a temple of fine dining complete with fireplace and wood paneling. A fireside cocktail bar, the Plaza Lounge, is the spot for cocktails and conversation. The Stix Downtown Billiard Club is the hotel's new bar, with pool tables and sports television to carry out the theme.

Services: 24-hour room service.

Facilities: A great pool, hot tub, and fitness area that leads onto two rooftop decks. Small meeting rooms available.

✪ Westin Hotel. 320 Fourth Ave. SW, Calgary, AB, T2P 2S6. ☎ **403/266-1611** or 800/228-3000. 469 rms, 56 suites. A/C MINIBAR TV TEL. $109–$195 double; $195–$700 suite. Weekend packages bring the price of rooms under $100, with $40 worth of in-hotel coupons. AE, DC, DISC, ER, MC, V. Parking $6 a day.

The Westin is a massive modern luxury block in the heart of the financial district, and probably the single nicest hotel in Calgary. In 1995, most of the hotel underwent a major renovation ($1 million was spent on the lobby alone). Gone is the anonymous business hotel atmosphere, replaced with a subtle Western feel that's reflected in the new, very comfortable Mission-style furniture, Navajo-look upholstery, feather duvets, and in-room period photos that commemorate Calgary's bronco-busting and oil-boom past. Beautiful barn-wood breakfronts and lowboys dispel the feeling that you're in one of the city's most modern hotels. Each room has two telephones and a data port, voice-mail, and an iron and board. The Westin is joined by skywalks to the "Plus-15" walkway system.

Dining/Entertainment: No fewer than seven venues, from a buffet to the exquisite Owl's Nest, one of Calgary's finest restaurants.

Services: Room service is radio dispatched for maximum efficiency. The hotel also rolls out the welcome mat for children, with a full array of children's furniture, a streamlined check-in for families, babysitting service, and a special kid's menu. A family's special needs are anticipated too, from strollers, potty-chairs, playpens, to room service delivery of fresh diapers!

Facilities: A panoramic 17th-floor indoor swimming pool with sauna and whirlpool at the rooftop.

Moderate

⑤ **Lord Nelson Inn.** 1020 8th Ave. SW, Calgary, AB, T2P 1J3. ☎ **403/269-8262** or 800/661-6017. Fax 403/269-4868. 55 rms, 2 suites. AC TV TEL. $65–$73 double; $75–$125 suite. AE, ER, MC, V. Free parking.

One of the best deals in the city, the Lord Nelson is a modern nine-story structure with recently renovated guest rooms and suites. Although on the edge of downtown, it's just a block from the downtown's free C-Train, which will put you in the heart of things in five minutes. The inn has a small cozy lobby with red-brick pillars and comfortable armchairs. Adjoining are a coffee shop, and the Pub, a tavern with outdoor patio. Bedrooms come with two TVs, couch, desk, refrigerator, and balcony; the suites come with Jacuzzis.

✪ **Prince Royal Inn.** 618 Fifth Ave. SW, Calgary, AB, T2P 0M7. ☎ **403/263-0520** or 800/661-1592. Fax 403/298-4888. 301 suites. TV TEL. $90–$100 studio/one bedroom suite. Rates include breakfast. Ask about special weekly rates. Weekend specials $65 double. AE, DC, ER, MC, V. Free parking.

Originally built as an apartment block, the 28-story, centrally located Prince Royal is an excellent value for a family or a longer stay in Calgary. All rooms were remodeled in 1995, and are nicely decorated and thoughtfully furnished. Room types are spacious studio, one-bedroom, and two-bedroom suites—these were all once rented as full-fledged apartments—and all rooms have full kitchens with full-sized refrigerator, microwave, four-burner stove, and toaster. Guest can even opt to have room service deliver groceries from a handy shopping list.

There's a restaurant and lounge on the main floor. Facilities include a sauna, steam and weight room, and a large sun deck, as well as a coin laundry.

Sandman Hotel. 888 7th Ave. SW, Calgary, AB, T2P 3J3. ☎ **403/237-8626** or 800/736-3626. Fax 403/290-1238. 297 rms, 4 suites. TV TEL. $85–$119 double. AE, DC, DISC, ER, MC, V. Free parking.

This 23-story hotel on the west end of downtown is conveniently located on the free rapid transit mall, directly opposite Calgary's most charming miniature park. The standard rooms are fair sized, but the real winners are the corner rooms, which are very large, with great views on two sides, and a small kitchen ($119). The Sandman is a popular place with corporate clients, due to its central location and good value.

The Sandman has the most complete fitness facility of any hotel in Calgary. It houses a private health club, which is available free to all guests: Facilities include a large pool, three squash courts, regularly scheduled aerobic exercise groups, and weight-training facilities. A massage therapist is available by appointment. Room service is available 24 hours a day; and there are three restaurants and two bars on the premises.

OUTSIDE OF DOWNTOWN

Calgary's excellent light-rail system makes it easy to stay outside the city center, yet have easy access to the restaurants and sites of downtown. The following two areas are linked to downtown via the C-Train, and each offers a variety of moderately priced lodgings with free parking.

Macleod Trail

Once this was a cattle track, but now it's a roaring expressway that runs from downtown Calgary south through wide-open suburbia until it becomes the highway leading to the U.S. border. The northern portions of this endless, pulsating roadway are lined with inns and motels—from upper middle range to economy.

Elbow River Inn. 1919 Macleod Trail S., Calgary, AB, T2G 4S1. ☎ **403/269-6771** or 800/661-1463. Fax 403/237-5181. 78 rms. TV TEL. $89 double. AE, CB, DC, ER, MC, V. Free parking.

The Elbow River Inn is the Macleod Trail establishment closest to downtown, and directly opposite the Stampede grounds. The only local hotel on the banks of the little Elbow River, the inn has a pleasantly furnished lobby and a dining room with a view of the water. There is also a restaurant offering hearty home-style cooking and a casino operating six days a week until midnight. The bedrooms are simply furnished; it's a good comfortable hostelry with near-budget rates.

Holiday Inn South. 4206 Macleod Trail SE, Calgary, AB, T2G 2R7. ☎ **403/287-2700** or 800/661-1889. Fax 403/243-4721. 153 rms. A/C TV TEL. $79 double. Weekend rates available. AE, CB, DC, DISC, ER, MC, V. Free parking.

A recently renovated property with an LRT (light-rail station) right outside the door, the Holiday Inn is decorated in sophisticated pastel shades and is located only a short stroll away from an oasis of parkland. The softly lit lobby is a charmer, the restaurant and lounge are elegantly furnished, and the heated indoor pool ideal for unwinding. The hotel also offers valet and secretarial services, room service, and a coin laundry.

Motel Village

Northwest of downtown, Motel Village is a triangle of more than a dozen large motels, plus restaurants, stores, and gas stations, forming a self-contained hamlet near the University of Calgary. Enclosed by Crowchild Trail, the Trans-Canada Highway, and Highway 1A, the village is arranged so that most of the costlier establishments flank the highway; the cheaper ones lie off Crowchild Trail, offering a wide choice of accommodations in a small area with good transportation connections. If you're driving, and don't want to deal with downtown traffic, just head here to find a room: except during the Stampede, you'll be able to find a room without reservations. A number of chain hotels are located here, including **Travelodge North,** 2304 16th Ave. NW (☎ 403/289-0211 or 800/255-3050); and the **Quality Inn Motel Village,** 2359 Banff Trail NW (☎ 403/289-1973 or 800/221-2222).

SUPER-BUDGET OPTIONS

The **Calgary International Hostel,** 520 7th Ave. SE, Calgary, AB, T2G 0J6 (☎ 403/269-8239), sleeps 114 and charges members $14, nonmembers $19. It's located near downtown, near the bars and restaurants along Stephen Avenue and the theaters near the performing arts center. Laundry facilities are provided, and there are two family rooms, as well as a game room and common area.

The **University of Calgary,** 2500 University Dr. NW, Calgary, AB, T2N 1N4 (☎ 403/220-3210; fax 403/282-8443), offers accommodations to visitors from May to August, for $27 single, $36 double, $22 to $42 per person suite (MC and V accepted); parking $2 a day. The 314-acre campus of the University of Calgary is parklike and offers a vast variety of sports and cultural attractions. Facilities are excellent, including restaurants, meeting rooms, and one- to four-bedroom suites. The campus is beside the Light-Rail Transit line (LRT).

CAMPING

The **Calgary West KOA,** on the Trans-Canada Highway W. (Box 10, Site 12, SS no. 1), Calgary, AB, T2M 4N3 (☎ 403/288-0411), allows tents and pets, and has washrooms, toilets, laundry, a dumping station, hot showers, groceries, and a pool. Prices for two people are $21 per night; tent sites are $17 per night.

WHERE TO DINE

Eating out in Calgary is a lot of fun. The locals clearly think so too, as restaurants are busy and full of vitality. There's plenty of fine dining downtown, as well as in Chinatown for less expensive meals.

DOWNTOWN

Expensive

✪ **The Conservatory.** 209 4th Ave SE. ☎ **403/266-1980.** Reservations required. Main courses $18–$26, table d'hôte $35. AE, DC, ER, MC, V. Mon–Fri 7am–9am and 11:30am–2pm; Mon–Sat 5:30–10:30pm. FRENCH.

At this intimate restaurant in the Delta Bow Valley Hotel the food is extremely refined; classic French technique meets the modern flavors of Alberta. The presentation is especially notable: The salads come as lovely green bouquets restrained by a thin vase of sliced cucumber; vegetables are carved into fanciful shapes. Entrées, like rack of lamb with mint hollandaise and black current purée ($25), combine tradition with just the right touch of modern saucing savvy and showmanship. The weekly changing table d'hôte menu offers four courses; for $18, you can sample three glasses of wine specially chosen to complement the food.

Owl's Nest. In the Westin Hotel, 4th Avenue and 3rd Street SW. ☎ **403/226-1611.** Reservations required. Main courses $20–$30. AE, DC, ER, DISC, ER, MC, V. Daily 11:30am–2:30pm and 5:30–11pm. FRENCH/CONTINENTAL.

One of Calgary's most wide-ranging upscale menus is found in this atmospheric dining room. Entrée choices range from fine hand-cut Alberta steaks and fresh lobster thermidor ($30) to continental delicacies like quail and wild mushrooms and Dover sole with caviar. Each week, there's also a specialty menu—usually under $30 for four courses—often featuring an ethnic cuisine. Service is excellent, and the wine list noteworthy.

Moderate

Divino. 817 1st St. SW. ☎ **403/263-5869.** Reservations recommended on weekends. Main courses $10–$16. AE, MC, V. Mon–Sat 11:30am–10:30pm. CALIFORNIA/ITALIAN.

Divino is housed in a landmark building (the Grain Exchange) and is both a wine bar and a casual bistro-style restaurant. The menu fare is both unusual and tasty—steamed mussels in ginger and garlic broth, broccoli salad with toasted almonds and ginger dressing, and a lamb pastitsio burger with cambrozolo cheese ($10). There are also full-fledged entrées, like rack of lamb ($16) and pasta dishes. For dessert, try the apple-and-ginger crumble.

Grand Isle Seafood Restaurant. 128 2nd Ave. SE. ☎ **403/269-7783.** Reservations recommended on weekends. Most dishes under $10. AE, MC, V. Daily 10am–midnight. CANTONESE/SEAFOOD.

One of Chinatown's newest and best restaurants, the Grand Isle's beautiful dining room overlooks the Bow River. Dim sum is served daily; on the weekend there's a brunch service.

⭕ **Joey Tomato's.** 208 Barclay Parade SW. ☎ **403/263-6336.** Reservations not accepted. Pizza and pasta from $9–$11. AE, MC, V. Sun–Thurs 11am–midnight, Fri–Sat 11am–1am. ITALIAN.

Located in the popular Eau Claire Market complex, Joey Tomato's is a very lively airplane hanger of a restaurant that serves great pizza and other Italian food to throngs of appreciative Calgarians. And no wonder it's often packed: The food is really good, the prices moderate (by the city's standards), and there's a lively bar scene. What more could you want in Calgary? Thin-crust pizzas come with traditional toppings, or with zippy, more cosmopolitan choices like Pizza Santa Fe (with chorizo and avocado) or Pizza Jambalaya (with shrimp and andouille sausage). Pasta dishes are just as unorthodox, with dishes like linguine and smoked chicken, jalapeño, cilantro, and lime cream sauce. It's a really fun, high energy place to eat, and the food, however unlikely, is always worth trying.

The King & I. 820 11th Ave. SW. ☎ **403/264-7241.** Main courses $6.95–$18.95. AE, DC, ER, MC, V. Mon–Thurs 11:30am–10:30pm, Fri 11:30am–11:30pm, Sat 4:30–11:30pm, Sun 4:30–9:30pm. THAI.

This restaurant first introduced Thai cuisine to Calgary and still turns on the heat in carefully measured nuances. You get precisely the degree of spiciness you ask for. You also get considerable help in interpreting the menu. Chicken and seafood predominate—one of the outstanding dishes is chicken filet sautéed with eggplant and peanuts in chili bean sauce. For the more seasoned palates there are eight regional curry courses, ranging from mild to downright devilish.

Mescalero. 1315 1st St. SW. ☎ **403/266-3339.** Reservations not accepted. Most dishes around $8. AE, DC, MC, V. Daily 11:30am–midnight, Sat–Sun 11am–1am. MEDITERRANEAN/ SOUTHWEST.

One of the most fashionable eateries in Calgary, Mescalero specializes in tapas—small dishes of salad, tiny sandwiches, grilled meats, zesty dips, cheese, olives, minipizzas, and more. Assemble it into a meal as you see fit. As long as you're lucky enough to score a table, just order some wine and an ongoing series of tapas. Most dishes will provide a good-sized nibble for a table of four. Be sure to try the Mediterranean mussel salad.

⭕ **River Cafe.** Prince's Island Park. ☎ **403/261-7670.** Reservations recommended on weekends. Light meals from $8; main courses $17–$26. AE, MC, V. Mon–Fri 11am–11pm, Sat–Sun 10am–11pm. Closed Jan–Feb.

It takes a short walk through Eau Claire Market area, and then over the footbridge to lovely Prince's Island Park in the Bow River to reach the aptly named River Cafe. On a lovely summer evening, the walk is a plus; the other attractions of the River Cafe are the lovely park-side decks (no vehicles hurtling by) and the good food.

Wood-fired free-range and wild gathered foods, teamed with organic whole breads and fresh baked desserts form the backbone of the menu. There's a wide range of appetizers and light dishes—many vegetarian—as well as pizzalike flatbreads topped with zippy cheese, vegetables, and fruit. Specialties from the grill include Arctic char seasoned with fresh sage and juniper ($18) and gingered duck with wildflower honey ($20).

Inexpensive

The Alberta Food Fair, 304 The Lancaster, Stephen Ave. Mall, Eighth Ave. SW at 2nd St. (☎ 403/294-3839), is a kind of culinary supermarket situated on the second floor of an otherwise very ordinary office building. The place is a total surprise: Little marble-top tables with very comfortable chairs alongside windows overlook the bustling mall below. Food is dispensed from 17 kiosks, catering to cosmopolitan palates, and manages to be both tasty and cheap. Open 6am to 6pm Saturday through Wednesday, to 9pm on Thursday and Friday.

SEVENTEENTH AVENUE

Seventeenth Avenue, roughly between 4th Street SW and 10th Street SW, is home to many of Calgary's best casual restaurants and bistros. If you have time, take a cab or drive over and walk the busy, cafe-lined streets, and shop the menus; the restaurants listed below are just the beginning.

Expensive

La Chaumiere. 121 17th Ave. SE. ☎ **403/228-5690.** Reservations required. Main courses $18–$28. AE, ER, MC, V. Mon–Fri noon–2pm; Mon–Sat 6pm–midnight. FRENCH.

Winner of half a dozen awards for culinary excellence, La Chaumiere is a subtly lit, discreetly luxurious temple of fine dining, and a popular rendezvous for Alberta's upper crust and their business friends. Dining here is an occasion to dress up and La Chaumiere is one of the few spots in town that enforces a dress code—men must wear jackets and ties.

Hors d'oeuvres include beluga caviar on ice; soup could be fresh lobster bisque. You can choose from main courses such as medallions of veal with sweetbreads and kidney, sole amandine, or the outstanding rack of lamb roasted with Provence herbs. If you have room for dessert, try a petit pyramid of tiny profiteroles filled with the finest chocolate, and served in vanilla sauce.

Moderate

⑤ Avenues Cafe. 811 17th Ave SW. ☎ **403/244-7924.** Main courses $6.50–$12. AE, MC, V. Mon–Thurs 11am–11pm, Fri 11am–midnight, Sat 10am–midnight, Sun 10am–10pm. INTERNATIONAL.

There's no framed art on the walls in this lively little bistro. All those paintings—frames and all—were created directly on the plaster by local artists. The entrées present a fusion of different ethnic foods and some down-home favorites. Family style meat loaf and potatoes comes with cumin and garlic gravy; burgers here are made with lamb, and are seasoned with Indian spices. A host of salads and small side dishes make this a good place to concoct a tapas-style meal, or to eat a light supper. Best of all, the food here is inexpensive and served with style and energy.

✪ Cilantro. 338 17th Ave SW. ☎ **403/229-1177.** Reservations recommended on weekends. Main courses $9–$20. AE, DC, MC, V. Sun–Thurs 11am–11pm, Fri–Sat 11am–midnight. INTERNATIONAL.

Cilantro has an attractive stucco storefront, plus a pleasant garden patio with a veranda bar. The food here is eclectic (some would call it Californian): The pasta dishes are as various as beef tenderloin with wild mushrooms in a Zinfandel sauce, or ginger radiatore with julienned vegetables and chili sauce. Meat dishes are no more traditional: Chicken breasts come stuffed with roast peppers and dressed with a sauce of green onions. The wood-fired pizzas—with mostly Mediterranean ingredients—seem almost tame in comparison. However, the food is excellent, and the setting casual and friendly.

L'Eva's. 529 17 Ave SW. ☎ **403/244-2750.** Reservations accepted. Main courses $7–$14. AE, MC, V. Mon–Thurs 11am–11pm, Fri–Sat 11am–midnight. INTERNATIONAL.

This wine bar and cafe specializes in light dishes (often vegetarian) that can be assembled into a meal or eaten as snacks and appetizers. The food is imaginative, and centers on salads (the roast vegetable salad is especially good), pasta, and other light fare. The restaurant is split level—the dining room is upstairs, while on the ground level, you can watch the kitchen staff putting together a meal. The interior is nicely decorated with a grape-leaf motif, and is just the place for an afternoon drink and snack.

✪ **Jo Jo Bistro Parisien.** 917 17th Ave SW. ☎ **403/245-2382.** Reservations recommended on weekends. Main courses $12–$16. AE, MC, V. Mon–Fri 11:30am–2pm (except summer months) and 5:30–9:30pm, Sat 5:30–10:30pm. FRENCH.

Jo Jo's is a classic French bistro, right down to the tiled floor, mirrors, banquettes, fan-back chairs, and tiny tables. The food is also classic French, though moderately priced for the quality and atmosphere. Coquilles St-Jacques with lobster sauce is $14; for the same price you can have escalope de veau with calvados sauce. All your French favorites are here: duck breast, escargot, pâté, and even a warm salad of sweetbreads with lemon sauce. Desserts are worth a trip in themselves.

Sultan's Tent. 909 17th Ave. SW. ☎ **403/244-2333.** Reservations recommended on weekends. Main courses $9–$14. AE, ER, MC, V. Mon–Sat 5:30–11pm. MIDDLE EASTERN.

The Sultan's Tent is a North African oasis. Although the restaurant is located in a modern western building, the interior has been transformed by carpets and tapestries into a pretty good imitation of a Saharan tent. If you like great couscous or tangines, then you definitely should make this a stop in Calgary. Go all out and order the $24 per person Sultan's Feast, which includes all the trimmings and provides an evening's worth of eating and entertainment.

CALGARY AFTER DARK

For current programs, check the newspapers or the little weekly *Action,* a publication devoted to the city's leisure and available in hotel lobbies.

THE TOP PERFORMING ARTS VENUES   The **Calgary Centre for Performing Arts,** 205 8th Ave. SE (☎ 403/294-7455), gives the city the kind of cultural hub that many places twice as big still lack. The center houses the 1,800-seat Jack Singer Concert Hall, home of the Calgary Philharmonic Orchestra; the Max Bell Theatre; Theatre Calgary; Alberta Theatre Projects; and the Martha Cohen Theatre, which puts on some avant-garde and innovative performances. Call the center or consult the newspapers for what is currently being performed by whom.

The magnificent **Jubilee Auditorium,** 14th Avenue and 14th Street NW (☎ 403/297-8000), seats 2,700 people. An acoustic marvel, the performance hall is located high on a hill with a panoramic view. The Southern Alberta Opera Association performs three operas each year at the auditorium. Periodic productions by the young Alberta Ballet Company are also part of the auditorium's varied programs.

IMPROV & DINNER THEATER   Calgary loves dinner theater, and **Stage West,** 727 42nd Ave. SE (☎ 403/243-6642), puts on polished performances as well as delectable buffet fare. The buffet functions from 6 to 8pm, then the show starts. Performances are Tuesday through Sunday and tickets are $37 to $59.

On Friday and Sunday evenings, the **Loose Moose Theatre Company,** 2003 McKnight Blvd. NE (☎ 403/291-5682), is where to go for Theatresports, fast-paced competitive improvisational zaniness. On Saturday nights, it's Guerrilla Theatre, an evening of spontaneous improvised scenes.

THE CLUB & BAR SCENE   There are three major centers for nightlife in central Calgary. The new **Eau Claire** market area, parklike and car-free, is also the home of the **Hard Rock Cafe,** 101 Barclay Parade SW (☎ 403/263-7625). The **Barleymill Neighbourhood Pub,** 201 Barclay Parade SW (☎ 403/290-1500), is just across the square, and is a cross between a collegiate hangout and a brewpub. **The Garage,** in the Eau Claire Market (☎ 403/262-6762), is the hip place to play billiards and listen to really loud post-grunge rock.

If you're looking for the dance clubs, there is a knot of five or so venues near the corner of 1st Street SW and 12th Avenue. **Crazy Horse,** 1315 1st St. SW (☎ 403/266-1133), is an immensely popular, slightly precious nightclub with lines out the door. **Taz,** upstairs at 12th Avenue SW and 1st Street (no phone), is a bit grittier and even louder. Take a break from the music at **The Koop Cafe,** 211b 12th Ave. SW (☎ 403/269-4616), a licensed coffee shop filled with dilapidated couches and graffiti-style art.

Amongst the trendy cafes and galleries on 17th Avenue are more nightclubs. **Republik,** 219 17th Ave. SW (☎ 403/244-1884), is the main alternative music venue in Calgary. **Kaos Cafe,** 718 17th Ave. SW (☎ 403/228-9997), has jazz nightly. **The Ship and Anchor Pub,** 534 17th Ave. SW (☎ 404/245-3333), is a youthful hangout with Top 40 cover bands and two outdoor patios; expect lines out the door on summer nights. **Detour,** 318 17th Ave. SW (☎ 403/244-8537), a lively disco, is as good a place as any to begin exploration of gay Calgary.

If you're just looking for a convivial drink, head to **Bottlescrew Bill's Old English Pub,** 1st Street and 10th Avenue SW (☎ 403/263-7900), a friendly brewpub with outdoor seating and Alberta's widest selection of beers.

GAMBLING   There are several legitimate casinos in Calgary, whose proceeds go wholly or partially to charities. None of them imposes a cover charge. **Tower Casino,** Lower Level Tower Centre, Ninth Avenue and Centre Street (no phone), offers roulette, blackjack, baccarat, and poker with $1 minimum wagers. Open Monday to Saturday from 11am to midnight. **Cash Casino Place,** 4040B Blackfoot Trail SE (☎ 403/243-4812), operates with a restaurant on the premises Monday through Saturday from noon to midnight. **The Elbow River Inn Casino,** 1919 Macleod Trail S. (☎ 403/266-4355), is part of a hotel by the same name (see "Where to Stay," above). It offers the usual games plus a variation called red dog. Minimum stake is a buck, the maximum $100. Open Monday through Saturday 11:30am to midnight.

5 Southern Alberta Highlights

South of Calgary, running through the grain fields and prairies between Medicine Hat and Crowsnest Pass in the Canadian Rockies, Highway 3 roughly parallels the U.S.–Canadian border. This rural connector links several smaller Alberta centers and remote but interesting natural and historic sites.

MEDICINE HAT & CYPRESS HILLS PROVINCIAL PARK

Medicine Hat (181 miles southeast of Calgary) is at the center of Alberta's vast natural gas fields. To be near this inexpensive source of energy, a lot of modern industry has moved to Medicine Hat, making this an unlikely factory town surrounded by grain fields. At the turn of the century, the primary industry was fashioning brick and china from the local clay deposits. Consequently, the town's old downtown is a showcase of handsome frontier-era brick buildings; take an hour and explore the historic city center, flanked by the South Saskatchewan River.

On the Trail of Dinosaurs in the Alberta Badlands

The Red Deer River slices through the rolling prairies of Alberta east of Calgary, revealing underlying sedimentary deposits that have eroded into badlands. These expanses of desertlike hills, strange rock turrets, and banded cliffs were originally laid down about 75 million years ago, when this area was a low coastal plain in the heyday of the dinosaurs. Erosion has spectacularly incised through these deposits, revealing a vast cemetery of Cretaceous life. Paleontologists have excavated here since the 1880s, and the Alberta badlands have proved to be one of the most important dinosaur fossil sites in the world.

Two separate areas have been preserved and developed as research and viewing areas in the badlands. Closest to Calgary, and the focus of a great day trip, is the ✪ **Royal Tyrrell Museum of Palaeontology** (☎ 403/823-7707). Located just north of Drumheller, 90 miles northeast of Calgary, this is one of the best paleontology museums and educational facilities in the world. It offers far more than just impressive skeletons and life-sized models, though it has dozens of these. The entire fossil record of the earth is explained, era by era, with an impressive variety of media and educational tools. You walk through a prehistoric garden, watch numerous videos, use computers to "design" dinosaurs for specific habitats, watch plate tectonics at work, and see museum technicians preparing fossils. The museum is also a renowned research facility where teams of scientists study all forms of ancient life. The museum is open daily in summer from 9am to 9pm, in winter Tuesday to Sunday from 10am to 5pm. Admission is $5.50 for adults, $2.25 for children; families are $13.

Radiating out from Drumheller and the museum are a number of interesting side trips. Pick up a map from the museum and follow an hour's loop drive into the badlands along North Dinosaur Trail. The paved road passes two viewpoints over the badlands, and crosses a free car ferry on the Red Deer River before returning to Drumheller along the South Dinosaur Trail. A second loop passes through Rosedale to the south, past a ghost town, hoodoo formations, and a historic coal mine.

Dinosaur Provincial Park is located in a badlands canyon near Brooks (about 140 miles east of Calgary and 120 miles southeast of Drumheller) and is the largest fossil dig in Alberta. More than 300 complete dinosaur skeletons have been found in the area, which has been named a World Heritage Site by the United Nations. Fossil excavations continue in the park, operated out of the field station of the Royal Tyrrell Museum. Also offered from the field station in summer are daily bus tours of the badlands and fossil areas, as well as guided and interpreted hikes into fossil country. Tours are also offered of the paleontology labs where you can view fossil preparation and research. Tickets for each of the above tours are $4.50 for adults, $2.25 children six to 15. There are no advance ticket sales; show up at the field station on the day you want to participate. Space is limited for each of the tours, so get there early and be prepared to be flexible. For more information on the park and its programs, contact Dinosaur Provincial Park, P.O. Box 60, Patricia, AB, T0J 2K0 (☎ 403/378-4342).

If you're really keen on dinosaurs, you can participate on one of the digs, either by the week ($600 for all accommodations and meals), or for the day ($75 including transport and food). Contact the Bookings Officer at the Royal Tyrrell Museum at P.O. Box 7500, Drumheller, AB, T0J 0Y0 (☎ 403/823-7707 or fax 403/823-7131).

Fifty miles south of Medicine Hat is Cypress Hills Provincial Park, 122 square miles of outlier peaks rising 1,500 feet above the flat prairie grasslands. In this preserve are many species of plants and animals—including elk and moose—usually found in the Rockies.

LETHBRIDGE

East of Fort Macleod (65 miles north of the U.S. border, 134 miles southeast of Calgary) lies Lethbridge, a delightful garden city and popular convention site (it gets more annual hours of sunshine than most places in Canada). Lethbridge started out as Fort Whoop-up, a notorious trading post that traded whiskey to the Plains Indians in return for buffalo hides and horses. The post boomed during the 1870s, until the Mounties arrived to bring order. A replica of the fort has been built in Indian Battle Park, and commemorates Whoop-up's history with interpretive programs and relics from the era.

The pride of Lethbridge is the **Nikka Yuko Japanese Garden.** Its pavilion and dainty bell tower were constructed by Japanese artisans without nails or bolts. The garden is one of the largest Japanese gardens in North America; Japanese-Canadian women in kimonos give tours and explain the philosophical concepts involved in Japanese garden design.

FORT MACLEOD

South of Calgary, a little more than two hours away, stands what was in 1873 the western headquarters of the Northwest Mounted Police. Named after Colonel Macleod, the redcoat commander who brought peace to Canada's west, the reconstructed **Fort MacLeod** is now a provincial park (☎ 403/553-4703). It's still patrolled by Mounties in their traditional uniforms; precision riding drills are performed four times daily.

The rebuilt fort is filled with fascinating material on the frontier period. Among its treasured documents is the rule sheet of the old Macleod Hotel, written in 1882: "All guests are requested to rise at 6am. This is imperative as the sheets are needed for tablecloths. Assaults on the cook are prohibited. Boarders who get killed will not be allowed to remain in the house." The fort grounds also contains the Centennial Building, a museum devoted to the history of the local Plains Indians.

HEAD-SMASHED-IN BUFFALO JUMP

The curiously named ✪ **Head-Smashed-In Buffalo Jump** has an interpretive center (☎ 403/553-2731) located on Spring Point Road, 12 miles west of Fort Macleod on Highway 2 (116 miles southwest of Calgary, 68 miles north of the U.S. border). This excellent museum is built into the edge of a steep cliff over which the Native Canadians used to stampede herds of bison, the carcasses then providing them with meat, hides, and horns. The multimillion-dollar facility tells the story of these death drives by means of films and Native Canadian guide-lecturers. Other displays illustrate and explain the traditional life of the prairie-dwelling natives in precontact times, and the ecology and natural history of the northern Great Plains. Hiking trails lead to undeveloped jump sites.

Designated a World Heritage Site, the center is open from 9am to 8pm during the summer. Admission $5.50 per adult, $2.25 per child, but free on Tuesday.

6 Waterton Lakes National Park

In the southwestern corner of the province, ✪ **Waterton Lakes National Park** is linked with Glacier National Park in neighboring Montana; together these two beautiful tracts of wilderness comprise Waterton-Glacier International Peace Park. Once the hunting ground of the Blackfoot, 203-square-mile Waterton Park contains superb mountain, prairie, and lake scenery and is home to abundant wildlife.

The transition from plains to mountains in Waterton and Glacier parks is very abrupt: The formations that now rise above the prairie were once under the primal Pacific Ocean, but when the North American continent collided with the Pacific ocean floor, wedges of the ocean's basement rock broke along deep horizontal faults, cutting these rock layers free from their geologic moorings. The continued impact of the continental and ocean floor tectonic plates gouged these free-floating rock blocks up out of the bowl they were formed in and pushed them eastward onto the top of younger rock. Under continued pressure from the elevating mass of the Rockies, the Waterton formations slid east almost 35 miles over the prairies. Almost three miles high, the rock block of Waterton Park—in geological terms called an overthrust—is a late arrival, literally sitting on top of the plains.

During the last ice age, the park was filled with glaciers, which deepened and straightened river valleys; those peaks that remained above the ice were carved into distinctive thin, finlike ridges. The park's famous lakes also date from the ice ages; all three of the Waterton Lakes nestle in glacial basins.

The park's main entrance road leads to Waterton Townsite, with a number of hotels, restaurants, and tourist facilities. Other roads lead to more remote lakes and trailheads. Akamina Parkway leads from the townsite to Cameron Lake, glimmering beneath the crags of the Continental Divide. Red Rock Canyon Parkway follows Blackiston Creek past the park's highest peaks to a trailhead; short hikes to waterfalls and a deep canyon begin here.

The most popular activity in the park is the **International Shoreline Cruise** (☎ 403/859-2362), which leaves from the townsite and sails Upper Waterton Lake past looming peaks to the ranger station at Goat Haunt, Montana, in Glacier Park. These tour boats leave five times daily; the cruise there and back usually takes two hours, including the stop in Montana. The price is $14 round-trip.

For more information on the park, contact the Park Superintendent, Waterton Lakes National Park, Waterton Park, AB, T0K 2M0 (☎ 403/859-2445).

WHERE TO STAY & DINE IN THE PARK

Prince of Wales Hotel. Waterton Lakes National Park, T0K 2M0. ☎ **403/226-5551**. (Off-season: Stn 0928, Phoenix, AZ, 85077. ☎ 602/207-6000). 89 rms. $125–$281 double. MC, V. Closed Oct–Apr.

Built in 1927 by the Great Northern Railway, this beautiful mountain lodge perched on a bluff above Upper Waterton Lake is reminiscent of the historic resorts in Banff Park, though on a smaller scale. Rooms have been totally renovated, though many are historically authentic in that they are rather small. Still, you can't beat the views, or the genteel old-world atmosphere.

The lobby and common rooms are really lovely, and the Garden Court Dining Room is the best—and priciest—place to eat in the park. Entrées include steaks, rack of lamb, and salmon, and are in the $25 range.

7 Introducing the Canadian Rockies

Few places in the world are more dramatically beautiful than the Canadian Rockies. While Banff and Jasper national parks are famous for their mountain lakes, flower-spangled meadows, spirelike peaks choked by glaciers, and abundant wildlife, nearly the entire spine of the Rockies—from the U.S. border north for 700 miles—is preserved as parkland or wilderness.

That's the good news. The bad news is that this Canadian wilderness, the flora and fauna that live in it, and lovers of solitude that come here, are going to need all this space as the Rockies become more popular. More than 4 million people annually make their way through Banff National Park, and the numbers are shooting up astronomically. While Draconian measures such as limiting visitorship are as yet only brought up in order to be dismissed, one thing is for certain: Advance planning for a trip to the Canadian Rockies is absolutely necessary if you're going to stay or eat where you want, or if you want to evade the swarms of visitors that throng the parks during summer.

ORIENTATION   Canada's Rocky Mountain parks include Jasper and Banff, which together comprise 6,764 square miles; the provincial parklands of the Kananaskis Country and Mount Robson; and Yoho, Kootenay, Glacier, and Mount Revelstoke national parks to the west in British Columbia.

The parks are traversed by one of the finest highway systems in Canada, plus innumerable nature trails leading to the more remote valleys and peaks. The two "capitals," Banff and Jasper, lie 178 miles apart, connected by Highway 93, one of the most scenic routes you'll ever roll on. Banff lies 78 miles (128km) from Calgary via Highway 1; Jasper, 225 miles (375km) from Edmonton on Route 16, the famous Yellowhead Highway.

Admission to Banff, Jasper, Yoho, and Kootenay parks costs $8 per vehicle and is good for two days; a three-day pass is $16.

TOURS & EXCURSIONS   You'll get used to using the name Brewster, associated with many things in these parts. In particular, these folks operate the park system's principal tour bus operation.

Brewster Transportation and Tours, 100 Gopher St., Banff, AB, T0L 0C0 (☎ 403/762-6767), operates tours from Banff and Jasper, covering most of the outstanding scenic spots in both parks. Call for a full brochure, or ask the concierge at your hotel to arrange a trip. A few sample packages:

Banff to Jasper (or vice versa): Some $9^1/_2$ hours through unmatched scenery, the trip takes in Lake Louise and a view of the icefield along the parkway. (The return trip requires an overnight stay, not included in the price.) One-way fare (summer) is $65; round-trip, $90.

Columbia Icefield: A $9^1/_2$-hour tour from Banff. You stop at the Icefield Chalet and get time off for lunch and a snocoach ride up the glacier. Snocoach Tour is an extra $20.50 (children $5), and tickets must be purchased in advance. Adults pay $65 (summer); children $32.50.

Brewster also operates an express bus between Banff and Jasper five days a week.

SEASONS   The parks have two peak seasons, when hotels charge top rates and restaurants are jammed. The first is summer, from mid-June to the end of August, when it doesn't get terribly hot, rarely above 70°F, though the sun's rays are powerful at this altitude. The other peak time is winter, from December to February, which is the skiing season; this is probably the finest skiing terrain in all of Canada. March through May is decidedly off-season: Hotels offer bargain room rates and you can choose the best table in any eatery. There is plenty of rain in the warmer months, so don't forget to bring some suitable rainwear.

LODGING IN THE ROCKIES   A word about lodging in the parks. On any given day in the high season, up to 50,000 people are winding through the Canadian Rocky national parks. As growth in the parks is strictly regulated, there's not an abundance of hotel rooms waiting. The result is strong competition for a limited number of very expensive rooms. Adding to the squeeze is the fact that many hotels have 80% to 90% of their rooms reserved for coach tours during the summer. In short, if you're reading this on the day you plan to arrive in Banff, Jasper, or Lake Louise and haven't yet booked your room, start worrying. Most hotels are totally booked for the season by July 1. To avoid disappointment, reserve your room as far in advance as you know your travel dates.

As far as price goes, it seems that lodgings can ask for and get just about any rate they want in the high season. For the most part, hotels are well kept up in the parks, but few would justify these high prices anywhere else in the world. Knowing that, there are a few choices. You can decide to splurge on one of the world-class hotels here, actually only a bit more expensive than the mid-range competition. Camping is another good option, as the parks have dozens of campgrounds with varying degrees of facilities. There are also a number of hostels throughout the parks.

Outside of high season, prices drop dramatically, often as much as one-half. Most hotels will offer ski packages during the winter, as well as other attractive getaway incentives. Be sure to ask if there are any special rates, especially at the larger hotels, which have trouble filling their rooms in the off-seasons.

PARK WILDLIFE   The parklands are swarming with wildlife, with some animals meandering along and across highways and hiking trails, within easy camera range. However tempting, *don't feed the animals, and don't touch them!* There is, for starters, a fine of up to $500 for feeding *any* wildlife. There is also a distinct possibility that you may end up paying more than cash for disregarding this warning.

It isn't easy to resist the blithely fearless bighorn sheep, mountain goats, soft-eyed deer, and lumbering moose you meet. (You'll have very little chance of meeting the coyotes, lynx, and occasional wolves, since they give humans a wide berth.) But the stuff you feed them can kill them. Bighorns get accustomed to summer handouts of bread, candy, potato chips, and marshmallows, when they should be grazing on the high-protein vegetation that will help them survive through the winter.

Moose involve additional dangers. They have been known to take over entire picnics after being given an initial snack, chase off the picnickers, and eat up everything in sight—including cutlery, dishes, and the tablecloth.

But the bears pose the worst problems. The parks contain two breeds: the big grizzly, standing up to seven feet on its hind legs, and the smaller black bear, about five feet long. The grizzly spends most of the summer in high alpine ranges, well away from tourist haunts. As one of North America's largest carnivores, its appearance and reputation are awesome enough to make visitors beat a retreat on sight. But the less formidable black bear is a born clown with tremendous audience appeal, and takes to human company like a squirrel.

The black bear's cuddly looks and circus antics, plus its knack for begging and rummaging through garbage cans, tend to obscure the fact that these are wild animals: powerful, faster than a horse, and completely unpredictable.

Hiking in bear country (and virtually all parkland is bear country) entails certain precautions that you ignore at your peril. Never hike alone, and never take a dog along. Dogs often yap at bears, then when the animal charges, run toward their

The Canadian Rockies

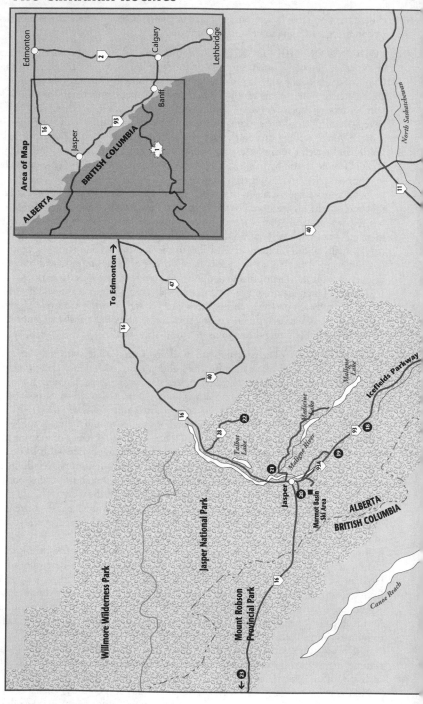

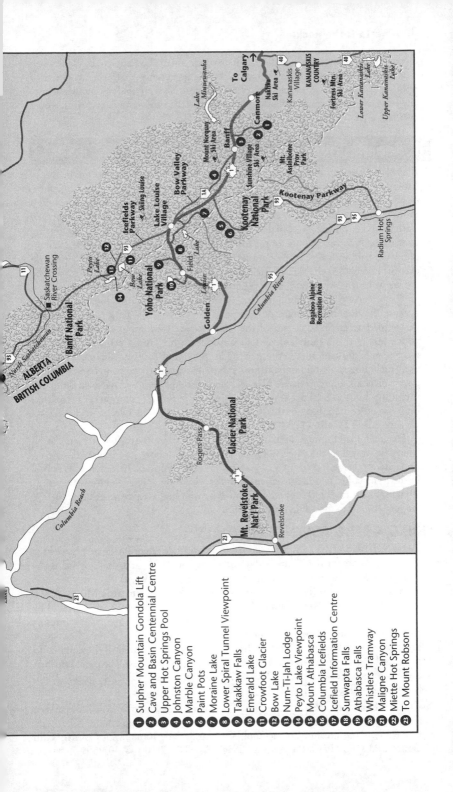

1 Sulpher Mountain Gondola Lift
2 Cave and Basin Centennial Centre
3 Upper Hot Springs Pool
4 Johnston Canyon
5 Marble Canyon
6 Paint Pots
7 Moraine Lake
8 Lower Spiral Tunnel Viewpoint
9 Takakkaw Falls
10 Emerald Lake
11 Crowfoot Glacier
12 Bow Lake
13 Num-Ti-Jah Lodge
14 Peyto Lake Viewpoint
15 Mount Athabasca
16 Columbia Icefields
17 Icefield Information Centre
18 Sunwapta Falls
19 Athabasca Falls
20 Whistlers Tramway
21 Maligne Canyon
22 Miette Hot Springs
23 To Mount Robson

owners for protection, bringing the pursuer with them. Use a telephoto lens when taking pictures. Bears in the wild have a set tolerance range that, when encroached upon, may bring on an attack. Above all, *never* go near a cub. The mother is usually close by, and a female defending her young is the most ferocious creature you'll ever face—and quite probably your last.

8 Kananaskis Country

Kananaskis Country is the name given to three Alberta provincial parks on the Rocky Mountains' eastern slope. Once considered only a gateway region to more glamorous Banff, the Kananaskis has developed into a recreation destination on a par with more famous brand-name resorts in the Canadian Rockies. Weather is generally warmer and sunnier here, which is conducive to golfing—and the championship course here is considered one of the best in North America. When the 1988 Olympics were held in Calgary, the national park service wouldn't allow the alpine ski events to be held at the ski areas in the parks. Nakiska, in the Kananaskis, became the venue instead, vaulting this ski area to international prominence.

The Kananaskis offers stunning scenery without the crowds and high prices. Also, because the Kananaskis Country isn't governed by national park restricts, there's better road access to some out-of-the-way lakeside campgrounds and trailheads, which makes this a more convenient destination for family getaways (there are more than 3,000 campsites in the area!). This provincial parkland also allows "mixed use," including some traditional (though heavily regulated) ranching. Some of best guest ranches in Alberta operate here. Kananaskis offers plenty of the great outdoors, including hiking, backpacking, canoeing, and fishing. For general recreation information contact **Kananaskis Country,** Suite 100, 1011 Glenmore Trail SW., Calgary, AB, T2V 4R6 (☎ 403/297-3362; fax 403/297-2180).

The main road through the Kananaskis Country is Highway 40, which cuts south from Highway 1 at the gateway to the Rockies and follows the Kananaskis River. Kananaskis Village, a collection of resort hotels and shops, is the center of activities in the Kananaskis, and is convenient to most recreation areas. Highway 40 eventually climbs up to 7,239-foot Highwood Pass, the highest pass in Alberta, before looping around to meet Highway 22 south of Calgary.

SKIING, GOLF & ADVENTURE SPORTS

DOWNHILL SKIING   Kananaskis gained worldwide attention when it hosted the alpine ski events for the Winter Olympic Games in 1988, and skiing remains the primary attraction to the area. At world-famous **Nakiska,** skiers can follow in the tracks of winter Olympians past. A second ski area, **Fortress Mountain,** is located 11.8 miles (19km) south of Kananaskis Village. Although overshadowed by Nakiska's Olympic reputation, Fortress Mountain offers an escape from the resort crowd, and features overnight accommodations in an on-site dormitory. Both areas offer terrain for every age and ability, and are open from early December to mid-April. Adult lift tickets cost $35 at Nakiska, $25 at Fortress. For more information on the ski areas, call ☎ 403/591-7777 or write Ski Nakiska, P.O. Box 1988, Kananaskis Village, AB, T0L 2H0.

GOLF   Kananaskis also features one of Canada's premier golf resorts. Kananaskis Country Golf Course boasts two 18-hole par-72 championship courses set among alpine forests and streams. Contact Golf Kananaskis, The **Kananaskis Country Golf Course,** P.O. Box 1710, Kananaskis Village, AB, T0L 2H0 (☎ 403/591-7154).

RAFTING   A number of outfitters offer a variety of white-water trips on both the Kananaskis and Bow rivers. **Kananaskis River Adventures Ltd.,** Kananaskis Village (☎ 403/591-7773 or 403/678-4919 in Banff) offers paddle trips for all levels of experience. Three-hour day trips on the Kananaskis River (Class I to III rapids) start at $49, and are offered May to October. Longer raft trips, which see Class II to IV rapids, can be combined with trail riding and biking excursions. **Mirage Adventure Tours,** Kananaskis Village (☎ 403/591-7773), leads single and multiple-day long combination pack/raft trips ($85 to $639) out of the Kananaskis Guest Ranch, from May to October.

PACK TRIPS   **Brewster Rocky Mountain Adventures,** Banff (☎ 403/673-3737), specializes in multiple-day excursions for experienced riders ($125 to $140 per day). Novices should check into the day-long combination pack/raft trips offered in conjunction with Mirage Adventures (see above). Trips leave from the Kananaskis Guest Ranch.

OTHER SPORTS   In addition to the offering listed above, Mirage Adventure Tours (located at the Lodge at Kananaskis) arranges several other types of guided recreational excursions, including: kayaking ($79 day trip, $149 day of white-water), hiking ($45 to $89), and mountain biking ($64 to $97). They also operate bus and heli-hiking sightseeing tours, and group-bonding programs for office teams. Mirage also rents cross-country skis and equipment from their shop at the lodge.

WHERE TO STAY
KANANASKIS VILLAGE

The lodgings in Kananaskis Village were all built for the Olympics in 1988, so all are new and well maintained. There's no more than a stone's throw between them, and to a high degree, public facilities are shared between all the hotels.

Best Western Kananaskis Inn. Kananaskis Village, AB, T0L 2H0. ☎ **403/591-7500** or 800/ 528-1234. Fax 403/591-7500. 96 rms. TV TEL. $110–$130 double; $140–$165 loft; $295 suite. AE, DC, DISC, ER, MC, V.

This handsome wood-fronted hotel is the most affordable place to stay in Kananaskis, but don't let that diminish your expectations of high quality and service. This new hotel offers a wide variety of room types, including many loft rooms with kitchenettes, which can sleep six. There's a swimming pool, whirlpool, and steam room.

Lodge at Kananaskis & Hotel Kananaskis. Kananaskis Village, AB, T0L 2H0. ☎ **403/ 591-7711** or 800/441-1414. Fax 403/591-7770. 193 rms, 58 suites in the lodge; 60 rms, 8 suites in the hotel. A/C MINIBAR TV TEL. Peak season $206–$217 double; $224–$264 suite; off-season $127–$138 double, $179–$189 suite. Ski/golf package rates and discounts available. AE, ER, MC, V.

These two new resort hotels are operated by Canadian Pacific, and face each other across a pond at the center of Kananaskis Village. While they've distinctly different lodgings, it's easiest to think of them as a unit, as they share many facilities, including a central reservation system. The lodge is the larger building, with a more rustic facade, a shopping arcade, and a number of drinking and dining choices. The rooms are large and well furnished; many have balconies, some have fireplaces. The hotel is much smaller than the lodge, and quieter. Rooms in the hotel are generally larger than those in the lodge, and they're more expensive. A full range of exercise facilities, including a swimming pool, indoor/outdoor whirlpools, aerobic studios, and a health and beauty spa are available to guests at both places.

Ribbon Creek Hostel. At Nakiska Ski Area. ☎ **403/762-8282** for reservations, 403/591-7333 for the hostel itself. Sleeps 44. $12 members, $17 nonmembers.

This is a great place for a traveler on a budget; there are also four family rooms. The hostel is located right at the ski area, within walking distance of Kananaskis Village, and has showers, laundry facilities, and a common room with a fireplace.

GUEST RANCHES

Brewster's Kananaskis Guest Ranch. Seebe (30 minutes east of Banff on Highway 1), P.O. Box 964, Banff, AB, T0L 0C0. ☎ **403/673-3737** or fax 403/673-2100. 33 units in cabins and chalets. $85–$110 double. MC, V.

The Brewster family were movers and shakers in the region's early days, playing a decisive role in the formation of Banff, Jasper, and Montana's Glacier national parks, and were the first outfitters (and transport providers) in the parks. The Kanasaskis Ranch was the original Brewster family homestead in the 1880s, and was transformed into a guest ranch in 1923. Located right on the Bow River near the mouth of the Kananaskis River, the original lodge buildings remain and serve as common areas. Guest rooms are fully modern, and are offered in chalets or cabins, each with full bathroom facilities. Rooms are available with full board if desired; nonguests can avail themselves of a saddle-horse ride for $17 an hour or $37 for a half day. Long-distance pack trips are a specialty of the ranch; a three-day trip is under $400. The guest ranch can arrange a number of other recreational activities through its recreational arm, Mirage Adventure Tours.

Rafter Six Guest Ranch. Seebe, AB, T0L 1X0. ☎ **403/673-3622** or 403/264-1251. Fax 403/673-3961. Accommodates 60 in log lodge and cabins. $75–$150 double. AE, DC, ER, MC, V.

Rafter Six is located in a meadow right on the banks of the Kananaskis River. Another old-time guest ranch with a long pedigree, the Rafter Six Ranch is a full-service resort ranch. The huge old log lodge, with restaurant, barbecue deck, and lounge, is especially inviting. Casual horseback and longer pack trips are offered, as well as raft and canoe trips. Facilities include hot tubs, an outdoor pool, a playground, and a game room. Seasonal special events are offered, like rodeos, country dances, and hay or sleigh rides.

CAMPGROUNDS

Kananaskis is a major camping destination for families in Calgary, and the choice of campgrounds is wide. There's a concentration of campgrounds at **Upper and Lower Kananaskis Lakes,** some 20 miles south of Kananaskis Village. There are a few campgrounds scattered nearer to Kananaskis Village, around Barrier Lake and Ribbon Creek. For a full-service campground with RV hook-ups, go to **Mount Kidd RV Park** (☎ 403/591-7700), just south of the Kananaskis golf course.

WHERE TO DINE

All the hotels offer dining rooms; in fact, the two Canadian Pacific properties together offer seven different dining venues, from the upscale l'Escapades in the hotel, to tapas-style nibbling in Brady's Market in the lodge. There are also coffee shops and light entrée service in the lounges. The dining rooms at both guest ranches are also open to nonguests.

9   Banff National Park

Banff is the oldest national park in Canada, founded as a modest 10-square-mile reserve by Canada's first prime minister, Sir John A. Macdonald, in 1885. The park is 2,546 square miles of incredibly dramatic mountain landscape, glaciers, high morainal lakes, and rushing rivers. The park's two towns, Lake Louise and Banff, are both splendid counterpoints to the surrounding wilderness, with beautiful and historic hotels, fine restaurants, and lively nightlife.

If there's a downside to all this sophisticated beauty, it's that Banff is very, very popular—it's generally considered Canada's number one tourist destination. About four million people visit Banff yearly, with the vast majority squeezing in during June, July, and August.

Happily, the wilderness invites visitors to get away from the crowds and from the congestion of the developed sites. Banff Park is blessed with a great many outfitters who make it easy to get on a raft, bike, or horse and find a little mountain solitude. Or consider visiting the park outside of the summer season, when prices are lower, the locals friendlier, and the scenery just as stunning.

SPORTS & OUTDOOR ACTIVITIES IN THE PARK

SKIING   Banff Park has three ski areas. **Mystic Ridge** and **Norquay** (☎ 403/762-4421) are twin runs just above the town of Banff. They cater to family skiing, with plenty of day care and ski instruction. Rates start at $29.50 adult for a full day.

Skiers must ski or take a gondola to the main lifts at **Sunshine Village** (☎ 403/762-6500) and the Sunshine Inn, a ski-in/ski-out hotel. Sunshine is located just southwest of Banff off Highway 1, and receives more snow than any ski area in the Canadian Rockies (more than 30 feet per year!). Lift tickets for Sunshine start at $39 adults.

Lake Louise Ski Area (☎ 403/256-8473 or 800/258-SNOW in North America) is the largest in Canada, with 40 miles of trails. With 11 lifts, management guarantees no long lines on major lifts, or your money back! Rates for a full day of skiing start at $39.50 adults, $35 youth/students/seniors, $10 children, under six free. Snowmaking machines keep the lifts running from November to early May.

A special lift pass for Mystic Ridge and Norquay, Sunshine Village, and Lake Louise Ski Area allows skiers unlimited access to all three resorts (and free rides on shuttle buses between the ski areas). Passes for three days (minimum) cost $128 adults, $45 children. For general information on skiing in the park, contact **Ski Banff/Lake Louise,** P.O. Box 1085, Banff, AB, T0l 0C0 (☎ 403/762-4561; fax 403/762-8185).

HIKING   One of the great virtues of Banff is that many of its most dramatic and scenic areas are easily accessible with day hikes. The park has more than 80 maintained hiking trails, ranging from interpretive nature strolls to long-distance backpacking expeditions (you'll need a permit if you're planning on camping in the backcountry). For a good listing of popular hikes, pick up the free *Banff/Lake Louise Drives and Walks* brochure.

One of the best day hikes in the Banff area is up Johnston Canyon, 15 miles north of Banff on Highway 1A. This relatively easy hike up a limestone canyon passes seven waterfalls before reaching a series of jade green springs known as the Inkpots. Part of the fun of this trail is the narrowness of the canyon—the walls are more than 100 feet high, and only 18 feet across; the path skirts the cliff-face, tunnels through walls, and winds across wooden foot bridges for more than a mile. The waterfalls plunge down through the canyon, inundating hikers with spray; watch for black swifts diving in the mist. The hike through the canyon to Upper Falls takes 1¹/₂ hours; all the way to the Inkpots will take at least four hours.

It's easy to strike out from Banff townsite and find any number of satisfying short hikes. Setting off on foot can be as simple as following the footpaths along both sides of the Bow River. From the west end of the Bow River Bridge, trails lead east along the river to Bow Falls, past the Banff Springs Hotel, to the Upper Hot Springs. Another popular hike just beyond town is the Fenlands Trail, which begins just past the train station and makes a loop through marshland wildlife habitat near the Vermillion Lakes. Two longer trails leave from the Cave and Basin Centennial Centre. The Sundance Trail follows the Bow River for nearly three miles past beaver dams and wetlands, ending at the entrance to Sundance Canyon. Keen hikers can continue up the canyon another 1 1/2 miles to make a loop past Sundance Falls. The Marsh Loop leaves the Cave and Basin area to wind 1 1/2 miles past the Bow River and marshy lakes.

RAFTING & CANOEING   One-hour family float trips on the Bow River just past Banff are popular diversions, and are available from **Rocky Mountain Raft Company** (☎ 403/762-3632). Trips are $22 for adults, $11 for children; rafters meet at the company's dock at Wolf Street and Bow Avenue, and take buses below Bow Falls, where the float trip begins.

For serious white-water, the closest rafting river is the Kicking Horse River, past Lake Louise just over the Continental Divide near Field, British Columbia. **Hydra River Guides** (☎ 403/762-4554) offers free transport from Banff and Lake Louise to the river, and a three-hour run down the Kicking Horse through Grade IV rapids. Trips are $65, which includes all gear and transport to and from your hotel or campsite.

HORSEBACK RIDING   See Banff on horseback with **Warner Guiding and Outfitting** (☎ 403/762-4551 or fax 403/762-8130). Two- to six-day trail rides (starting at $275 and peaking at $825) are offered, into some of the most remote and scenic areas of the park. Some rides climb up to backcountry lodges, which serve as base camps for further exploration; other trips involve a backcountry circuit with lodging in tents. Shorter day rides are also offered from two stables near the townsite: just west of the Banff Springs Hotel, and near the Cave and Basin Centennial Site.

Operating out of Lake Louise, **Timberline Tours** (☎ 403/522-3743) offers day trips to some of the area's more prominent beauty sites (starting at $26 for 90 minutes of riding). From their Bow Lake Corral, at Num-Ti-Jah Lodge, hour-long rides start at $18. Three- to 10-day pack trips are also offered.

HELICOPTER TOURS   **Alpine Helicopters** (☎ 403/678-4802), operating out of Canmore, offers flights over the Canadian Rockies starting at $80.

GOLFING   The **Banff Springs Golf Course** in Banff, which rolls out along the Bow River beneath towering mountain peaks, offers 27 holes of excellent golf. Although associated with the resort hotel, the course is open to the public. Call ☎ 403/762-6801 for a tee time.

BANFF TOWNSITE

Few towns in the world boast as beautiful a setting as Banff. The mighty Bow River, murky with glacial till, courses right through town, while rearing up right on the outskirts of town are massive mountain blocks. Mt. Rundle parades off to the south, a finlike mountain that somehow got tipped over on its side. Mt. Cascade rises up immediately north of downtown, exposing its glaciered face at every corner. In every direction, yet more craggy peaks fill the sky.

This is a stunning, totally unlikely place for a town, and Banff has been trading on its beauty for more than a century. The Banff Springs Hotel was built in 1888 as a destination resort by the Canadian Pacific Railroad. As tourists and recreationalists began to frequent the area for its scenery and hot springs, access to fishing, hunting, climbing, and other activities, the little town of Banff grew up to service the needs of these early travelers.

While the setting hasn't changed since the early days of the park, the town certainly has. Today, the streets of Banff are lined with exclusive boutique malls where the best names in international fashion offer their wares; trendy cafes spill out into the sidewalks, and bus after bus filled with tourists choke the streets. Banff is particularly popular with Asian tourists; Japanese interests own most of the businesses here, and stores are mostly staffed by young Japanese teenagers over for the summer; English, French, and German tourists are also very much in evidence. There's a vital and cosmopolitan feel to the town; don't go here expecting a bucolic Alpine village. Banff in summer is a very busy place.

ESSENTIALS

VISITOR INFORMATION   The **Banff Tourism Bureau** shares space with a national park information center; both are located at 224 Banff Ave. (☎ 403/762-8421). Contact the office at P.O. Box 1298, Banff, AB, T0L 0C0 (☎ 403/762-0270; fax 403/762-8545). Be sure to ask for the *Official Visitors Guide,* which is absolutely packed with information about local businesses and recreation.

GETTING THERE   If you're driving, the Trans-Canada Highway takes you right to Banff's main street; the town is 80 miles west of Calgary. There is no air or rail service to the town. The closest **VIA Rail** train service is at Jasper, 200 miles north; Brewster offers a non-tour bus between the two park centers five times weekly.

ORIENTATION   Getting your bearings is easy. The **Greyhound** and **Brewster Bus Depot** is located at the corner of Gopher and Lynx streets (☎ 403/762-2286). The main street—Banff Avenue—starts at the southern end of town at the Bow River and runs north until it is swallowed by the Trans-Canada Highway. Along this broad, bright, and bustling thoroughfare, you'll find most of the hotels, restaurants, stores, office buildings, and nightspots the town possesses. Just beyond the river stands the park administration building amid a beautifully landscaped public garden. Here the road splits. Banff Springs Hotel and the Sulphur Mountain Gondola are to the left; to the right are the Cave and Basin Hot Springs, Banff National Park's original site. At the northwestern edge of town is the railroad station, and a little farther northwest the road branches off to Lake Louise and Jasper. In the opposite direction, northeast, is the highway going to Calgary.

GETTING AROUND   Banff offers local bus service along two routes designed to pass through downtown and by most hotels. Service on The Banff Bus is pretty informal, but there's generally a bus every half hour. One route runs between the Banff Springs Hotel and down Banff Avenue to the northern end of town; the fare is $1.50. The other runs between the train station and the Banff Hostel on Tunnel Mountain; the fare is $2. The bus operates summer only; call 403/760-8294 for more information.

For a taxi, call **Legion Taxi** (☎ 403/762-3353) or **Banff Taxi and Limousine** (☎ 403/762-4444).

For a car rental, contact **Tilden Rent-A-Car**, at the corner of Caribou and Lynx streets (☎ 403/762-2688) or **Banff Rent A Car**, 204 Lynx St. (☎ 403/762-3352) for a less expensive but reliable used vehicle.

THE BANFF ARTS FESTIVAL

The **Banff Centre,** St. Julien Road (☎ 403/762-6300), is a remarkable year-round institution devoted to art and entertainment in the widest sense. From June through

August annually the center hosts the ○ **Banff Arts Festival,** offering a stimulating mixture of drama, opera, jazz, ballet, classical and pop music, singing, and the visual arts. Highlights include the International String Quartet Competition, with 10 world-class quartets vying for a cash prize and a national tour; the Digital Playgrounds series brings performance artists to the stage. Tickets for some of the events cost $6 to $22; a great many are free.

In winter the center shows the **Festival of Mountain Films.** Find out what's currently on by getting the program at the Banff Tourism Bureau or by calling the center.

EXPLORING BANFF

Apart from helicopter excursions, the best way to get an overall view of Banff's mountain landscape is by the **Sulphur Mountain Gondola Lift** (☎ 403/762-2523), whose lower terminal is 2 miles southeast of Banff on Mountain Avenue. The gondolas are roomy, safe, and fully enclosed; the panoramas are stunning. At the upper terminal there's the Summit Restaurant for panoramic dining, and hiking trails along the mountain ridges. Rides cost $9 for adults, $4 for children five to 11, under five ride free.

Lake Minnewanka Boat Tours (☎ 403/762-3473; fax 403/762-2800) offers scenic and wildlife-viewing trips in glassed-in motor cruisers on Lake Minnewanka, just 15 miles north of Banff. Trips are usually 1 1/2 hours long, and cost $20 adults, $10 children 11 and under. During high season, five trips depart daily; these cruises are very popular, and reservations are suggested. Buses run from the Banff bus station to the lake in conjunction with the boat departure schedules.

The **Luxton Museum** (☎ 403/762-2388) is devoted to the history of Native Canada and is housed in a log fort south of the Bow River, just across the bridge. The Luxton offers realistic dioramas, a sun-dance exhibit, artifacts, weaponry, and ornaments. Adults pay $4.50; seniors/students $3.50, and children $2. The museum is open daily from 9am to 9pm.

Part art gallery, part local history museum, the **Whyte Museum of the Canadian Rockies,** at 111 Bear St. (☎ 403/762-2291), stands as a memorial to the pioneers of the Canadian Rockies. It houses the historical archives, the Banff library, and an art gallery with changing exhibits—prints, paintings, and statuary—pertaining to the mountains of western Canada. Afternoon tea is served in front of a fireplace Friday through Sunday. Admission is $3 for adults, $2 for seniors and students. Open daily 10am to 9pm in high season, shorter hours at other times.

Housed in a lovely wood-lined building dating from the 1910s, the **Banff Park Museum,** beside the Bow River Bridge (☎ 403/762-1558), is largely a paean to taxidermy, but there's a lot to learn here about the wildlife of the park and how the various ecosystems interrelate. The real pleasure, though, is the rustic, lodge-style building, now preserved as a National Historic Site. Admission is $2.25 for adults, $1.75 for seniors, $1.25 for youths six to 16. Open daily in summer 10am to 6pm.

Although most people now associate Banff with skiing or hiking, in the early days of the park travelers streamed in to visit the curative hot springs. In fact, it was the discovery of the hot springs now preserved as the **Cave and Basin Centennial Center** (☎ 403/762-1566) that spurred the creation of the national park in 1888. During the 1910s, these hot mineral waters, which rise in a limestone cave, were piped into a rather grand natatorium. Although the Cave and Basin springs are no longer open for swimming or soaking, the old pool area and the original hot springs cave have been preserved along with interpretive displays and films. Entrance is $2.25 adults,

$1.75 seniors, and $1.25 youths six to 16. The Cave and Basin is located a mile west of Banff; turn right at the west end of the Bow River Bridge.

If you want a soak in mountain hot springs, then drive up to **Upper Hot Springs Pool** (☎ 403/762-1515), at the top of Mountain Avenue 1¹/₂ miles west of Banff. Hot sulfurous waters fill a large swimming pool. If you're looking more for a cure than a splash, then go to the adjacent Upper Hot Springs Spa, where you get access to a steam room, massage therapists, and various aromatherapy treatments. Admission to the pool is $5 for adults, $4.50 for seniors, and $3.50 for children 3–16.

The **Natural History Museum,** 112 Banff Ave. (☎ 403/762-4747), has displays of early forms of life on earth, dating from the Canadian dinosaurs of 350 million years ago, plus the "authentic" model of a Sasquatch, or "Bigfoot." Summer hours are daily 10am to 8pm; until 10pm July and August. Admission is $3 adults, $2 seniors and youths, under 10 free.

WHERE TO STAY

If you get stuck and can't find a room, consider calling **Summit Vacations** (☎ 403/762/5561 or 800/661-1676; fax 403/762-8795), which will, for a $10 fee, attempt to find you a place to stay.

If you prefer to stay in bed-and-breakfast inns, you can get a list of fairly economical establishments from the **Banff Tourism Bureau,** 224 Banff Ave. (☎ 403/762-8421). These places are screened for quality and should be booked well ahead of arrival. Some are open all year, some only from June to September or October. They accommodate from four to 30 guests, some have private baths, some kitchen units, and all serve hearty breakfasts that go with mountain appetites.

Expensive

Banff Park Lodge. 222 Lynx St., Banff, AB, T0L 0C0. ☎ **403/762-4433** or 800/661-9266. Fax 403/762-3553. 198 rms, 13 suites. A/C MINIBAR TV TEL. Summer $189 double, $274 suite. Lower rates off-season. AE, CB, DC, ER, MC, V. Free heated parking.

A large, handsome cedar-and-oak structure with a cosmopolitan air, the Banff Park Lodge is a quiet block and a half off the main street, near the Bow River. Calm and sophisticated are the key words here: all the rooms are soundproofed, and wild, après-ski cavorting isn't the norm, or much encouraged. The lodge seems like a happy, tranquil retreat after a day out in antic Banff. The guest rooms are very spacious and exceptionally well furnished. All come with balconies and twin vanities (one inside, one outside the bathroom). The lodge, with its abundant ground floor rooms and wide hallways, is popular with travelers with mobility concerns.

The lodge has one formal and one family-style restaurant, a cocktail lounge, an indoor swimming pool with whirlpool and steam room, and 10 convention rooms.

✪ **Banff Springs Hotel.** Spray Avenue (P.O. Box 960), Banff, AB, T0L 0C0. ☎ **403/762-2211.** Fax 403/762-5155. 838 rms, 65 suites. MINIBAR TV TEL. $175–$357 double; from $364–$975 suite. AE, DC, DISC, ER, MC, V. Parking $6.50 self, $11 valet.

Standing north of Bow River Falls like an amazing Scottish baronial fortress, the Banff Springs Hotel is one of the most beautiful and famous hotels in North America. Founded in 1888 as a opulent destination resort by the Canadian Pacific Railroad, this nine-story stone castle of a hotel is still the best address in Banff: especially so after the renovation of all the rooms, finished in 1995. This venerable hotel doesn't offer the largest rooms in Banff, though the amenities are all superlative. With the views, the spa, and the near-pageantry of service, this is still the most amazing resort in an area blessed with beautiful hotels.

The Springs greets you with a reception hall of such splendor that you're not in the least surprised to learn that it maintains a staff of 1,200 and holds medieval banquets for convention groups.

Dining/Entertainment: 15 different food outlets, from palatial to functional, and 3 cocktail lounges.

Facilities: A major new addition to the hotel is Solace, a European-style health and beauty spa, complete with therapeutic mineral baths, massage treatments, aerobic and fitness training, and nutritional consultation. In addition, there are 50 stores and boutiques, and an Olympic-size indoor pool. The 27-hole golf course is considered one of the most scenic in the world.

✪ **Rimrock Resort Hotel.** Mountain Road (3 miles north of Banff; P.O. Box 1110), Banff, AB, T0L 0C0. ☎ 403/762-3356 or 800/661-1587. Fax 403/762-1842. 345 rms, 41 suites. A/C MINIBAR TV TEL. $195–$275 double; from $245–$525 suite. AE, DC, DISC, JCB, MC, V. Parking $6 self, $10 valet; heated.

If you want modern luxury and views, this should be your hotel. This enormous, stunningly beautiful hotel (completed in 1993) drops nine floors from its roadside lobby entrance down a steep mountain slope, affording tremendous views from nearly all of its rooms. Aiming for the same quality of architecture and majesty of scale as venerable older lodges, the Rimrock offers a massive glass-fronted lobby, lined with cherrywood, tiled with unpolished marble floors, and filled with soft inviting chairs, couches, and Oriental carpets. The limestone fireplace, open on two sides, is so large that staff members just step inside to ready the kindling.

The rooms are large and well-appointed with handsome furniture; some have balconies. Standard room prices vary only by view; all rooms are the same size. The suites are truly large, with balconies, wet bar, and loads of cozy couches.

Dining/Entertainment: Two restaurants and a lounge.

Services: Free shuttle bus to and from downtown Banff.

Facilities: The fitness facilities are especially notable, with an indoor pool, squash court, hot tub, workout room with regularly scheduled aerobics, and more weight training and fitness devices than many professional gyms.

Moderate

Buffalo Mountain Lodge. P.O. Box 1326, Banff, AB, T0L 0C0. ☎ **403/762-2400** or 800/661-1367. Fax 403/762-4495. 85 condos. TV. $180 one-bedroom studio; $200 two-bedroom chalet. AE, ER, MC, V.

The most handsome of the condominium lodgings on Tunnel Mountain, just 1 mile west of Banff, the Buffalo Mountain is the perfect place to stay if you would rather avoid the frenetic pace of downtown Banff and yet remain central to restaurants and activities. It's not the last word in luxury, but its quiet location, beautiful lodge building, and choice of room types make this a good alternative to equally priced lodgings in the heart of Banff.

The lodge building itself is an enormous log cabin, right out of your fantasies. The three-story lobby is supported by massive log rafters, filled with warm Navajo-style carpets, and comfortable Western-style furniture. A huge fieldstone fireplace dominates the interior, and separates the lovely dining room and small, cozy lounge. Rooms are all located in units scattered around the forested eight-acre holding. There are five room types, ranging from a cozy one-room studio to a two-level, two-bedroom chalet with full kitchen capable of sleeping four adults and two children. All rooms have fireplaces (wood is free and stacked near your door), and are decorated in rustic pine and bent willow furniture; the beds have feather duvets and pillows. Some rooms have balconies.

The restaurant in the lodge is one of the best in Banff, and in summer a cafe opens with deck seating. The lodge also offers a steam room and outdoor hot tub.

Caribou Lodge. 521 Banff Ave., Banff, AB, T0L 0C0. ☎ **403/762-5887** or 800/563-8764. Fax 403/762-5918. 193 rms, 7 suites. TV TEL. High season $165–$180 double; $220–$270 suite. Up to two children under 16 can share parents' room free. AE, DC, DISC, ER, MC, V. Free heated parking.

One of the newest establishments in town (completed in 1993), the Caribou— green-roofed, with gables, wooden balconies, outdoor patio, and mansard windows— has a Western-lodge look that blends well with the alpine landscape. The interior, though, is imposing, including a vast lobby with a slate tile floor, woodwork of peeled logs, and a huge fireplace. The lodge also houses three hot tubs, a sauna, and steam room. The finely furnished bedrooms continue the Western theme with rustic pine chairs and beds with snug down comforters. The bathrooms are spacious. Half the rooms have balconies.

The lodge is long on service and friendliness; although it's not in the absolute center of town (about 15 minutes on foot), a free shuttle bus ferries guests to destinations throughout Banff. The restaurant here, The Keg, is a favorite with locals, serving handcut steaks in the $14 to $17 range.

Homestead Inn. 217 Lynx St., Banff, AB, T0L 0C0. ☎ **403/762-4471** or 800/661-1021. Fax 403/762-8877. 27 rms. TV TEL. Summer $106–$112 double. Extra person $10. Children under 12 stay free. Lower rates off-season. AE, MC, V.

One of the best lodging deals in Banff is the Homestead Inn, only a block from all the action on Banff Avenue. Though the amenities are modest compared to upscale alternatives, rooms are tastefully furnished and equipped with couches, armchairs, and stylish bathrooms.

Ptarmigan Inn. 337 Banff Ave., Banff, AB, T0L 0C0. ☎ **403/762-2207** or 800/661-8310. Fax 403/762-3577. 143 rms, 2 suites. TV TEL. $116–$123 double; $165 suite. Children under 18 stay free in parents' room; children under 12 eat free. AE, DC, ER, JCB, MC, V. Free heated parking.

This pine green hotel has a few advantages over most of the other hotels along busy Banff Avenue. The rooms are set well back from the street, minimizing road noise. It's a good choice for families: Some of the double rooms have sleeping areas divided by the bathroom, which makes for a little privacy for everyone. Half of the rooms have balconies; 16 rooms (the least expensive) look into the lodgelike, three-story central atrium. Nonsmoking rooms are located in a separate wing. Rooms have rustic pine furnishings and down comforters, and were renovated in 1994.

Facilities include two lounges, one with patio seating and a restaurant. There's room service during normal restaurant hours. Ski and bike rentals are available on site. There's also a large hot tub and dry sauna in the basement, but they're a little run down; there's a massage therapist available by appointment.

Ⓢ **Red Carpet Inn.** 425 Banff Ave., Banff, AB, T0L 0C0. ☎ **403/762-4184** or 800/267-3035. Fax 403/762-4894. 52 rms. TV TEL. $85–$130 double. AE, MC, V.

A handsome brown three-story brick building with a balcony along the top floors, the Red Carpet Inn is located along the long, hotel-lined street leading to downtown. Well maintained and more than adequately furnished, the Red Carpet is one of the best lodging deals in Banff. Beds and furniture are ample and new; rooms have easy chairs, and a desk. There's no restaurant on the premises, but an excellent one right next door. The entire facility is ship-shape and very clean, just the thing if you don't want to spend a fortune in Banff.

Traveller's Inn. 401 Banff Ave., Banff, AB, T0L 0C0. ☎ **403/762-4401** or 800/661-0227. Fax 403/762-5905. 89 rms. TV TEL. $145–$165 double. AE, MC, V.

Located five minutes from downtown Banff, the Traveller's Inn has just undergone a complete renovation to emerge as one of the town's better values. Rooms are quite large and pleasantly decorated, all with twin vanities and king or queen beds. Some rooms are divided into two sleeping areas by the bathroom, a great configuration for families or friends traveling together. All rooms have balconies or patio access. Facilities include an outdoor hot tub, steam room, and sauna. Ski rental is available at the hotel; ski shuttles stop at the front door. There's a breakfast restaurant on site.

Inexpensive

⑤ Banff International Hostel. On Tunnel Mountain Road (a mile west of Banff; P.O. Box 1358), Banff, AB, T0L 0C0. ☎ **403/762-4122** or 800/363-0096. Sleeps 154 people. $17 members, $22 nonmembers. MC, V.

By far the most pleasant budget lodging in Banff is the new youth hostel, with a mix of two-, four-, and six-bed rooms; couple and family rooms are available. Reserve a place at least a month in advance during the summer months. Facilities include a recreation room, kitchen area, laundry, and lounge area with a fireplace. Meals are available at the hostel's Cafe Alpenglow.

YWCA. 102 Spray Ave., Banff, AB, T0L 0C0. ☎ **403/762-3560.** Fax 403/762-2602. $19 bunk in a dorm room (sleeping bag required), $49–$55 double. MC, V.

The YMCA is a bright, modern building with good amenities just across the Bow River bridge from downtown. The Y welcomes both genders—singly, in couples, or in family groups—with accommodations in private or dorm rooms, as required. Some units have private baths. There's also an assembly room with a TV, and a guest laundry on the premises.

Camping

Banff National Park offers hundreds of campsites within easy commuting distance of Banff. The closest are the three **Tunnel Mountain campgrounds,** just past the youth hostel west of town. Two of the campgrounds are for RVs only, and have both partial and full hook-ups ($17.50 and $20), while the third has showers and is usually reserved for tenters ($15). For more information, call the park's visitors center at ☎ 403/762-1500.

WHERE TO DINE

Food is generally good in Banff, although you pay handsomely for what you get. The difference in price between a simply okay meal in a theme restaurant and a nice meal in a classy dining room can be quite small. Service is often very indifferent, as most food servers have become used to waiting on the in-and-out-in-a-hurry tour bus crowds.

Expensive

✪ Buffalo Mountain Lodge. One mile west of Banff on Tunnel Mountain Road. ☎ **403/762-2400.** Reservations recommended on weekends. Main courses $18–$26. AE, DC, ER, MC, V. INTERNATIONAL NOUVELLE.

Overall, probably the most pleasing restaurant in Banff. The dining room occupies half the soaring, three-story lobby of a beautiful log lodge in a quiet wooded location just outside of Banff. As satisfying as all this is to the eye and the spirit, the food here is even more notable. The chef brings together the best of regional ingredients—Albertan beef, lamb, pheasant, venison, trout, and B.C. salmon—and prepares each in a seasonally changing, always eclectic style. The breast of pheasant with fresh raspberries and port wine ($21) is just dynamite; a ginger-glazed pork tenderloin with fresh peaches ($18) is equally delicious. This is also a lovely place to come for an intimate cocktail, in the fireplace-dominated lobby bar.

Grizzly House. 207 Banff Ave. ☎ **403/762-4055.** Reservations required. Main courses $14.95–$35.95. MC, V. Daily 11:30am–midnight. FONDUE.

The Grizzly House has nothing to do with bears except a rustic log-cabin atmosphere. The specialty here is fondue—from cheese to hot chocolate, with everything in between, including seafood, rattlesnake, frog's legs, alligator, and buffalo fondue (at $29.95). The setting is cozy and the fare excellent. It gets a little rowdy in here: each of the tables (and the bathrooms) have phones, so after a couple of drinks, people start calling and talking to strangers across the room—or in the toilet stall. This isn't the place for an intimate romantic dinner; expect to have a wild, game show–style experience.

Joshua's. 204 Caribou St. ☎ **403/762-2610.** Reservations recommended on weekends. Main courses $14–$22. AE, MC, V. Daily 11:30am–2pm and 5:30–10pm. CONTINENTAL.

Joshua's is a quite small, very popular wood-paneled restaurant with a publike atmosphere. However, French-influenced fine dining is the name of the game here. The house specialty is a stuffed veal chop with Stilton cheese sauce; other notable dishes include a duck breast with Calvados ($17).

Ristorante Classico. In the Rimrock Resort, 3 miles north of Banff on Mountain Avenue. ☎ **403/762-3356.** Reservations required. Main courses $14.50–$27; five-course table d'hôte $43. AE, DC, DISC, JCB, MC, V. Tues–Sun 6–10pm. NORTHERN ITALIAN.

This is the dining room with the best views in Banff. The food, carefully prepared and aggressively flavored Italian dishes featuring fresh seafood, veal, fowl, and up-to-the-minute ingredients, is almost as impressive. Even the table settings merit a mention: Paloma Picasso designed the china (the display plates are rumored to be worth more than $400). Don't come here looking for soothing fettucine Alfredo: The chef likes to mix strong flavors. The grouper in a crust of horseradish ($17) is a standout, as is black pepper fettucine with wild mushrooms ($16). Slices of prosciutto top a salad of arugula and gorgonzola ($10). Excellent service and an impressive Italian wine list make this one of Banff's best.

Moderate

Balkan Restaurant. 120 Banff Ave. ☎ **403/762-3454.** Main courses $11.95–$15.95. AE, MC, V. Daily 11am–11pm. GREEK.

Up a flight of stairs you'll find this airy blue-and-white dining room with windows overlooking the street below. The fare consists of reliable Hellenic favorites, well prepared and served with a flourish. The Greek platter (for two) consists of a small mountain of beef souvlaki, ribs, moussaka, lamb chops, tomatoes, and salad. If you're dining alone you can't do better than the *logo stifado* (rabbit stew) with onions and red wine.

✪ Coyote's Deli & Grill. 206 Caribou St. ☎ **403/762-3963.** Reservations not accepted. Main courses $9–$15. AE, MC, V. Daily 7:30am–10pm. SOUTHWESTERN.

One of the few places in Banff where you can get lighter, healthier food, Coyote's is an attractive bistrolike restaurant where there's a good selection of vegetarian dishes, as well as multiethnic dishes prepared with an eye to spice and full flavors. In addition, there's a deli, where you can get the makings for a picnic and head to the park.

Giorgio's. 219 Banff Ave. ☎ **403/762-5114.** Reservations recommended on weekends. Pasta courses $10–$13; pizza $10–$20. AE, MC, V. Daily 4:30–10pm. ITALIAN.

Giorgio's is a cozy eatery dimly lit by low-hanging pink-gleaming lamps over the tables. Divided into a counter section and table portion (both comfortable), Giorgio's serves authentic old-country specialties at eminently reasonable prices. Wonderful crisp rolls—a delicacy themselves—come with your meal. Don't miss the *gnocchi alla piemontese* (potato dumplings in meat sauce) or the Sicilian cassata.

Magpie & Stump Restaurant & Cantina. 203 Caribou St. ☎ **403/762-4067.** Reservations not accepted. Main courses $8–$12. AE, MC, V. Daily noon–2am. MEXICAN.

The false-fronted Magpie and Stump doesn't really match up architecturally with the rest of smart downtown Banff, and thank goodness, neither does the food or atmosphere. The food here is traditional Mexican, done up with style and heft: Someone in the kitchen knows how to handle a tortilla. This isn't high cuisine, just well-prepared favorites like enchiladas, tamales, tacos, and the like. But the dishes are well priced compared to those elsewhere in town, and you won't go away hungry. The interior of the place looks like a dark and cozy English pub, except there are buffalo heads and cactus plants everywhere—plus a lot of Southwest kitsch—so you don't have to take it too seriously. This is also a good place for a lively late-night drink, as the town's young summer waitstaff likes to crowd in here to unwind with an after-shift beverage—usually a beer in a jam jar.

Banff After Dark

Most of Banff's larger hotels and restaurants offer some manner of nightly entertainment. The best of the lot is **Wild Bill's,** the "legendary saloon" at 203 Banff Ave. (☎ 403/762-0333), where you can watch Asian tourists in cowboy hats learning to line dance, and **The Barbary Coast** (☎ 403/762-4616), a "California-style" bar and restaurant that features live music among the potted plants. For a little more grit, head to the **Silver City,** 110 Banff Ave. (☎ 403/762-3337), a subterranean, hammered tin–ceilinged bar where the local hard-edged youth—such as they are—go to play pool and drink gassy beer; there's nightly dancing to DJ music or live bands to 2am. The **Rose and Crown Pub,** 202 Banff Ave. (☎ 403/762-2121), brings in live entertainers all week; English-style pub grub is available late. **Eddy's Back Alley,** 137 Banff Ave. (enter on Caribou Street; ☎ 403/762-8434), is a friendly basement bar where you can dance yourself into a DJ-induced entropy. For a quiet drink in pleasantly subdued, traditional pub surroundings, go to Joshua's Pub, in the alley behind **Joshua's Restaurant,** 204 Caribou St. (☎ 403/762-8010).

LAKE LOUISE

Lake Louise (35 miles northwest of Banff), deep green and surrounded by forest-clad snowcapped mountains, is one of the most famed beauty spots in a park renown for its fabulous scenery. The village that's grown up in the valley below the lake has developed in the last few years to become a resort destination in its own right. Lake Louise boasts the largest ski area in Canada, and easy hiking access to the remote high country along the Continental Divide.

The lake may be spectacular, but probably as many people wind up the road to Lake Louise to see its most famous resort, the Chateau Lake Louise. Built by the Canadian Pacific Railroad, the Chateau is, along with the Banff Springs Hotel, one of the most celebrated hotels in Canada. More than just a lodging, the Chateau— a storybook castle perched a mile high in the Rockies—is the center of recreation, dining, shopping, and entertainment for the Lake Louise area.

There's a reason that the water in Lake Louise is as green as an emerald: The stream water that tumbles into the lake is filled with minerals, ground by the glaciers that hang above the lake. Sunlight refracts off the glacial "flour," creating vivid colors.

Lake Louise is dramatically beautiful, and you'll want at least to stroll around the shore of the lake and gawk at the glaciers and back at the massive Chateau. The gentle Lakeshore Trail follows the northern shore of the lake to the end of Lake Louise. If you're looking for more exercise and even better views, continue on the trail as it begins to climb. Now called the Plain of Six Glaciers Trail, the path passes a teahouse (three miles from the Chateau, and open summer only) on its way to a tremendous viewpoint over Victoria Glacier and Lake Louise.

SEEING THE SIGHTS

The **Lake Louise Summer Sightseeing Lift** (☎ 403/522-3555) offers a 10-minute ride up to the Whitehorn Lodge, midway up the Lake Louise Ski Area. From here, the views onto Lake Louise and the mountains along the Continental Divide are magnificent; but there's more to do than just gawk at the scenery. In summer, the Birds of Prey Center opens with an interpretive exhibit on the local raptors, and during the evening the Rocky Mountain Shakespeare Company stages the Bard's plays at Whiskeyjack Lodge, at the base of the lift. The restaurant at the Whitehorn Lodge is much better than you usually expect at a ski area, and specially priced ride-and-dine tickets are available for those who would like to have a meal at 7,000 feet. The round-trip costs $9 for adults, $8 for seniors/students, and $6 for children 6 to 12. The lift operates only from early June to late September.

To many visitors, ✪ **Morraine Lake** is an even more dramatic and beautiful spot than its more famous twin, Lake Louise. Here, 10 spirelike peaks over 10,000 feet rise precipitously from the shores of a tiny gem-blue lake. It's an unforgettable sight, and definitely worth the short 8-mile drive from Lake Louise. There's a lodge on the shore of the lake with meals and refreshments, and a hiking trail follows the lake's north shore to the mountain cliffs. If you think you've seen the panorama before, it might be because it's pictured on the back of a Canadian $20 bill.

WHERE TO STAY

✪ **Chateau Lake Louise.** Lake Louise, AB, T0L 1E0. ☎ **403/522-3511** or 800/441-1414. Fax 403/522-3834. 447 rms, 66 suites. A/C MINIBAR TV TEL. $179–$359 double; $270–$1,077 suite. Rates depend on whether you want a view of the lake or of the mountains. AE, DC, DISC, ER, MC, V. Parking $6 a day.

The Chateau is one of the best-loved hotels in North America. If you want to splurge on only one hotel in the Canadian Rockies, make it this one—you won't be sorry. The Chateau Lake Louise is a massive, formal structure, blue-roofed and turreted, furnished with Edwardian sumptuousness and alpine charm. Built in stages over the course of a century by the Canadian Pacific Railroad, the entire hotel was remodeled and upgraded in 1990, and now stays open year-round. The cavernous grand lobby, with curious figurative chandeliers, gives onto a sitting room filled with overstuffed chairs and couches; these and other common areas overlook the Chateau's gardens and the deep blue-green lake in its glacier-hung cirque. The marble-tiled bathrooms, crystal barware, and comfy down duvets in your room are indicative of the attention to detail and luxury you can expect here.

Dining/Entertainment: The Chateau offers nine restaurants and eating facilities during the high season, as well as two lounge and bar areas. Chateau guests can enjoy a tea dance in the afternoon, and cabaret entertainment at night.

Facilities: Indoor pool, Jacuzzi, steam rooms and sauna, tanning salon, and shopping arcade.

Lake Louise Inn. 210 Village Rd. (P.O. Box 209), Lake Louise, AB, T0L 1E0. ☎ **403/522-3791** or 800/661-9237. Fax 403/522-2018. 222 rms. TV TEL. Summer $120–$195 double. Lower rates off-season. AE, MC, V.

The Lake Louise Inn stands in a wooded eight-acre estate, five driving minutes from the fabled lake at the base of the moraine. There's forest all around and snowcapped mountains peering over the trees outside your window. The inn consists of five different buildings—a central lodge with swimming pool, whirlpool, sauna, restaurant, bar and lounge—and four lodging units. There are six different room types, beginning with standard twin rooms with double beds. The superior queen rooms in Building Five ($165) are the nicest in the inn, with pine-railed balconies and a sitting area; for families, the superior lofts are capable of sleeping eight, with two bathrooms, complete kitchen (including dishwasher), living room and fireplace, and two separate bedrooms and fold-out couch, are just the ticket for a family or group ($195).

✪ **Post Hotel.** P.O. Box 69, Lake Louise, AB, T0L 1E0. ☎ **403/522-3989** or 800/661-1586. Fax 403/522-3966. 93 rms, 7 suites, 2 cabins. TV TEL. Summer $145–$335 double; $375 suite; $275–$300 cabin. AE, MC, V. Closed Nov.

Discreetly elegant and beautifully furnished, this wonderful log hotel with a distinctive red roof began its life in 1942 as a humble ski lodge. Between 1988 and 1993, new European owners completely rebuilt the old lodge, transforming it into one of the most luxurious getaways in the Canadian Rockies; in fact, the Post Hotel is one of only two properties in Western Canada that has been admitted into the French resort network Relais et Chateaux. The entire lodge is built of traditional log and beam construction, preserving the rustic flavor of the old lodge and of the mountain setting. The public rooms are lovely, from the renown dining room (preserved intact from the original hotel) to the arched, two-story wood-paneled library—complete with rolling track ladders and river-stone fireplace—to the lobby, looking onto the peaks and glaciers behind Lake Louise and Moraine Lake.

Due to the rambling nature of the lodge, there are a bewildering 14 different kinds of rooms available. The simplest are cozy twin-bedded rooms with a balcony; "N" rooms (all rooms are known by letter) are especially nice, with two queen beds (one in a loft), a kitchen, fireplace, and balconies on both sides of the hotel. The rooms throughout are beautifully furnished with rustic pine furniture and rich upholstery. Many rooms have stone fireplaces, balconies, and whirlpool tubs. Hospitality and service is top-notch.

Facilities: A notably attractive glass-encased swimming pool, whirlpool, steam room, and meeting facilities for small groups.

WHERE TO DINE

Lake Louise Station. 200 Sentinel Rd. ☎ **403/522-2600.** Reservations recommended on weekends. Pizzas to $15, $12–$19 for steaks and seafood. AE, MC, V. Daily 11:30am–midnight. PIZZA/STEAKS.

Located in the handsome and historic train station at Lake Louise village, this log building served as the Lake Louise train station for nearly a century, before rail service ceased in the 1980s. Now the handsome and historic building has been converted into a bar and restaurant. Both pizza and fine dining are accommodated in the old waiting room, and the ticketing lobby is where to go for a quiet drink. Two old dining cars sit on the sidings beside the station, and are open for fine dining in the evenings. Excellent steaks and grilled meat is the specialty here.

✪ **Post Hotel Dining Room.** In the Post Hotel, Lake Louise. ☎ **403/522-3989.** Reservations required. Main courses $24–$32. AE, MC, V. Daily 7–11am, 11:30am–2pm, and 5–10pm. INTERNATIONAL/CANADIAN.

This is some of the finest dining in the Canadian Rockies. The food here was famous long before the rebuilding and renovation of the old hotel, but in recent years, the restaurant has maintained such a high degree of excellence that it has won the highly prized endorsement of the French Relais et Chateaux organization. The dining room is in a long and low-pitched, rustic room with wood beams and windows looking out onto glaciered peaks. The dinner menu focuses on full-flavored meat and fish preparations. The rack of lamb is served with couscous and a rich black olive sauce, and served with eggplant fritters ($32). Fresh lobster is served with a basil cream sauce ($29), and panfried salmon comes with a sauce of champagne and passion fruit ($26). Desserts are equally imaginative. Service is excellent, as is the very impressive wine list, with some good values discreetly hidden in the mostly French selection.

✪ **Walliser Stube Wine Bar.** In Chateau Lake Louise. ☎ **403/522-3511**, ext. 1309. Reservations required. Main courses $12.50–$20, fondues $32–$42.50. AE, DISC, ER, MC, V. Daily 5–11:30pm. SWISS.

While the Chateau Lake Louise operates four major restaurants, including the formal Edelweiss Room, the most fun and relaxing place to eat is the Walliser Stube, a small dining room that serves excellent Swiss-style food and some of the best fondue ever. The back dining room is called the Library, and indeed it is lined with tall and imposing wood cases and rolling library ladders. Happily, the cases are filled with wine, not books: Part of the Chateau's huge wine selection is stored here.

A meal in the Walliser Stube is an evening's worth of eating and drinking, as the best foods—a variety of fondues and raclettes—are convivial and communal eating experiences. The cheese fondue ($32 for two) is fabulous; forget the stringy glutinous experience you had in the 1970s and give it another chance. Hot-meat fondues are also available, as is an excellent veal and vegetable fondue cooked in spicy wine broth ($45.50 for two). Raclettes are another communal cooking operation, where heat lamps melt chunks of cheese until bubbly, and the aromatic, molten cheese is spread on bread. It's all great fun with great atmosphere; go with friends and you'll have a blast.

THE ICEFIELDS PARKWAY

Between Lake Louise and Jasper winds one of the most spectacular mountain roads in the world. Called the Icefields Parkway, the road climbs through three deep river valleys, beneath soaring, glacier-notched mountains, and past dozens of hornlike peaks shrouded with permanent snowfields. Capping this 178-mile route is the Columbia Icefields, the massive dome of glacial ice and snow straddling the top of the continent. From this mighty cache of ice—this is the largest nonpolar ice cap in the world—flows the Columbia, the Athabasca, and the North Saskatchewan rivers.

Although you can drive the Icefields Parkway in three hours, plan to take enough time to stop at eerily green lakes, hike to a waterfall, and take an excursion up onto the Columbia Icefields. There's also a good chance that you'll see wildlife: ambling bighorn sheep, mountain goats, elks with huge shovel antlers, momma bears with cubs—all guaranteed to halt traffic and set cameras clicking.

After Lake Louise, the highway divides: Highway 1 continues west toward Golden, British Columbia, while Highway 93 (the Icefields Parkway), continues north along the Bow River. Bow Lake, the river's source, glimmers below enormous Crowfoot Glacier; when the glacier was named, a third "toe" was more in evidence, lending more resemblance to a bird's claw. Roadside viewpoints look across the lake at the glacier; Num-Ti-Jah Lodge, on the shores of Bow Lake, is a good place to stop for a bite to eat and more photographs.

The road mounts Bow Summit, and drops into the North Saskatchewan River drainage. Stop at the Peyto Lake Viewpoint, and hike up a short but steep trail to glimpse this startling blue-green body of water. The North Saskatchewan River collects its tributaries at the little community of Saskatchewan River Crossing; thousands of miles later, the Bow and the Saskatchewan Rivers will join, and flow east through Lake Winnipeg to Hudson Bay.

The parkway then begins to climb up in earnest toward the Sunwapta Pass. Here, in the shadows of 11,450-foot Mount Athabasca, the icy tendrils of the Columbia Icefield come into view. However impressive these glaciers may seem from the road, they are nothing compared to the massive amounts of centuries-old ice and snow hidden by mountain peaks; the Columbia Icefield covers nearly 200 square miles and is more than 2,500 feet thick. From the parkway, the closest glacial fingers of the icefield are Athabasca Glacier, which fills the horizon to the west of the Columbia Icefields Chalet (☎ 403/852-7032), a rather unappealing lodge with restaurant and lodging, and the Icefield Information Center (☎ 403/852-7030), a park service office that answers questions about the area.

From the Brewster Snocoach Tours ticket office (☎ 403/762-2241), specially designed buses take visitors out onto the face of the glacier. The 90-minute excursion includes a chance to hike the surface of Athabasca Glacier. The snocoach tour is $20.50 adult, $5 children. If you don't have the time or cash (no credit cards are accepted) for the snocoach tour, you can drive to the toe of the glacier and walk up onto the glacier's surface. Use extreme caution when on the glacier; tumbling into a crevasse can result in broken limbs or even death.

From the Columbia Icefields, the parkway descends steeply into the Athabasca River drainage. From the parking area for Sunwapta Falls, travelers can decide to crowd around the chain link fence and peer at this turbulent falls, or to take the half-hour hike to equally impressive but less crowded Lower Sunwapta Falls. Athabasca Falls, further north along the Parkway, is another must-see waterfall. Here, the wide and powerful Athabasca River constricts into a roaring torrent before dropping 82 feet into a narrow canyon. A mist-covered bridge crosses the chasm just beyond the falls; a series of trails lead to more viewpoints. The parkway continues along the Athabasca River through a landscape of meadows and lakes, before entering the Jasper Townsite.

Facilities are few along the parkway. Hikers and bikers will be pleased to know that there are rustic **hostels** at Mosquito Creek, Rampart Creek, Hilda Creek, Beauty Creek, Athabasca Falls, and at Mount Edith Cavell. Reservations for all the Icefield Parkway hostels can be made by calling ☎ 403/439-3139. A shuttle runs between the Calgary International Hostel and hostels in Banff, Lake Louise, and along the Icefield Parkway to Jasper. You must have reservations at the destination hostel to use the service. Call ☎ 403/283-5551 for more information.

10 Jasper National Park

Jasper, now Canada's largest mountain park, was established in 1907, although it already boasted a "guest house" of sorts in the 1840s. A visiting painter described it as "composed of two rooms of about 14 and 15 feet square. One of them is used by all comers and goers, Indians, voyageurs and traders, men, women and children being huddled together indiscriminately, the other room being devoted to the exclusive occupation of Colin Fraser (postmaster) and his family, consisting of a Cree squaw and nine interesting half-breed children."

Things have changed.

Slightly less busy than Banff to the south, Jasper Park manages to seem more outdoors-oriented; maybe it's just that the shopping and dining isn't so good up here.

Travelers seem a bit more determined and rugged looking, as if they have just stumbled in from a long-distance hiking trail or off the face of a rock: certainly there's no shortage of recreation here.

For more information about the park, contact Jasper National Park, P.O. Box 10, Jasper, AB, T0E 1E0 (☎ 403/852-6161).

SPORTS & OUTDOOR ACTIVITIES IN THE PARK

A clearinghouse of local outfitters and guides is the **Jasper Adventure Center,** 604 Connaught Dr. (☎ 403/852-5595 or 800/565-7547). White-water raft and canoe trips, horseback rides, and other activities can be ticketed out of this office.

Rent a mountain bike for $14 per day from **On-Line Sport and Tackle,** 600 Patricia St. (☎ 403/852-3630). Snowboards, cross-country ski equipment, and more bikes are available from **Freewheel,** 606 Patricia St. (☎ 403/852-3898).

SKIING Jasper's downhill ski area is **Ski Marmot Basin,** located 11.7 miles (19km) west of Jasper on Highway 93. Marmot is generally underrated as a ski resort; it doesn't get the crowds of Banff, nor does it get the infamous Chinook winds. The resort has 52 runs and seven lifts, and rarely any lines. Lift tickets start at $35. Call 403/852-3533 for more information.

HIKING Overnight and long-distance hikers will find an abundance of backcountry trails around Jasper that reach into some of the most spectacular scenery in the Canadian Rockies. There are fewer choices for day hikers.

The complex of trails around Maligne Canyon makes a good choice for a group, as there are a number of access points (across six different footbridges). The less keen can make the loop back and meet fellow hikers (after getting the vehicle) further down the canyon.

Trails ring parklike Beauvert and Annette lakes (the latter is wheelchair accessible), both near Jasper Park Lodge. Likewise, Pyramid and Patricia lakes just north of town have loop trails but more of a backcountry atmosphere.

The brochure *Day Hikers' Guide to Jasper National Park* costs $1 at the visitors center, and details dozens of hikes throughout the park.

RAFTING Jasper is the jumping-off point for float and white-water trips down several rivers. A raft trip is a good option for that inevitable drizzly day, as you're going to get wet anyway.

The mild rapids (Class II to III) of the wide Athabasca River makes a good introductory trip, while wilder runs down the Maligne River (Class III) will appeal to those needing something to brag about. **Maligne River Adventures,** 626 Connaught Dr., Jasper (☎ 403/852-3370; fax 403/852-3405), offers trips down both rivers, as well as a three-day wilderness trip ($450) on the Kakwa River (Class IV-plus).

Wilder white-water runs (Class III to IV) are available on the Fraser River in Mt. Robson Park from **Sekani Mountain Tours,** Jasper (☎ 403/852-5337). "Salmon spawning" floats take place on the Fraser's calmer stretches during mid-August and mid-September.

Trips generally include most equipment and transportation. Jasper is loaded with rafting outfitters; you'll have no trouble getting out onto a river.

HORSEBACK RIDING One of the most exhilarating experiences the park can offer is trail riding. Guides take your riding prowess (or lack of it) into account and select foothill trails slow enough to keep you mounted. And the special mountain trail horses used are steady, reliable animals not given to sudden antics. For a short ride, contact **Pyramid Stables** (☎ 403/852-3562) which offers short one- to three-hour trips around Pyramid and Patricia Lakes.

Long-distance trail rides take keen riders into the park's backcountry. **Horseback Adventures,** located just outside the park at Brule (☎ 403/865-4777), offers three- to 12-day pack trips into Wilmore Wilderness Park and Jasper National Park. Price for a six-day trip into Willmore is $840; trips into Jasper cost more. **Skyline Trail Rides,** with an office at Jasper Park Lodge (☎ 403/852-4215) offers three- to four-day trips to a remote albeit modernized lodge (from $360). A six- to nine-day wilderness pack trip starts at $750.

FISHING   Currie's Guiding Ltd. (☎ 403/852-5650) conducts fishing excursions to beautiful Maligne Lake; cost is $125 per person (two minimum) for an eight-hour day. Tackle, bait, and boat rentals are included in the price, as well as full lunches. Inquire about the special single and group rates. Patricia and Pyramid lakes, just north of Jasper, are more convenient to Jasper-based anglers who fancy trying their luck at trout fishing.

CLIMBING   The **Jasper Climbing School,** 806 Connaught Dr. (☎ 403/852-3964), offers beginner, intermediate, and advanced climbing courses under the expert guidance of Hans Schwarz. Basics are taught at a two-day course at the foot of Mount Morro, 12 miles from Jasper, for $80. Food, transport, and accommodations (in private homes) are extra. Personal mountaineering services for two people cost $125 each per day. For $25, tourists can sample rapelling in a short three-hour workshop.

GOLF   The 18-hole course at **Jasper Park Lodge,** east of Jasper Townsite, is one of the most popular and challenging courses in the Rockies, with 73 sand traps and other, more natural hazards like visiting wildlife. Call 403/852-6090 for information.

JASPER TOWNSITE

Jasper isn't Banff, and to listen to most residents of Jasper, that's just fine with them. Born as a railroad division point, Jasper townsite lacks the glitz of its southern neighbor, and also Banff's slightly precious air of an internationalized alpine fantasyland. There's none of Banff's traffic congestion, sky-high prices, and all-out mob scenes. Jasper has a lived-in, community-oriented sense largely lacking in Banff. And there's certainly nothing wrong with the views.

But development is rapidly approaching. New nightclubs, restaurants, and tourist shops are springing up along Patricia Street, and that sound in the distance is the thunder of tour buses.

ESSENTIALS

VISITOR INFORMATION   For information on the townsite, contact **Jasper Tourism and Commerce,** P.O. Box 98, Jasper, AB, T0E 1E0 (☎ 403/852-3858; fax 403/852-4932).

GETTING THERE   Jasper is on the Yellowhead Highway System, linking it with Vancouver, Prince George, and Edmonton, and is therefore an important transportation hub. The town is 178 miles northwest of Banff.

Via Rail connects Jasper to Vancouver and Edmonton with three trains weekly; the train station is at town center (☎ 403/852-4102), along Connaught Street. The train tracks run due north before they start the long easterly sweep that leads to Edmonton. Also headquartered at the train station is the **Greyhound** bus station (☎ 403/852-3926) and **Brewster Transportation** (☎ 403/852-3332), which offers express service to Banff, as well as a large number of sightseeing excursions to scenic spots in the park.

ORIENTATION   Jasper Townsite is much smaller than Banff. The main street, Connaught Drive, runs alongside the Canadian National Railway tracks, and is the address of the majority of Jasper's hotels. Patricia Street, one block west, is quickly becoming the boutique street, with new shops and cafes springing up. Right in the center of town, surrounded by delightful shady gardens, is the **Parks Information Offices** (☎ 403/852-6146). The post office is at the corner of Patricia and Elm streets. At the northern end of Connaught and Geike streets, a quarter mile from downtown, is another complex of hotels.

Through town flows the Athabasca River, and east of it lies Lac Beauvert with Jasper Park Lodge, adjoining one of the world's finest golf courses. That's the scene of the annual Totem Pole Golf Tournament. The totem pole in question, named after Queen Charlotte, stands at the railroad station and is reputedly the largest in existence today.

GETTING AROUND   **Tilden Rental Cars** is at 638 Connaught Dr. (☎ 403/852-3798). Call a taxi at 403/852-5558 or 403/852-3600.

EXPLORING THE TOWN & ENVIRONS

The **Jasper Tramway** (☎ 403/852-3093) starts at the foot of Whistler's Mountain, 4 miles south of Jasper off Highway 93. Each car takes 30 passengers (baby carriages, wheelchairs, or the family dog) and hoists them 1 1/4 miles up to the summit in a breathtaking sky ride. At the upper terminal you step out into alpine tundra, the region above the tree line where some flowers take 25 years to blossom. A wonderful picnic area carpeted with mountain grass is alive with squirrels. You'll also see the "whistlers"—actually hoary marmots—that the mountain is named for. The ride costs adults $11; children $5.50; cars depart every 10 to 15 minutes.

Just northeast of Jasper, off the Jasper Park Lodge access road, the Maligne River drops from its high mountain valley to cut an astounding canyon into a steep limestone face on its way to meet the Athabasca River. The chasm of **Maligne Canyon** is up to 150 feet deep at points, and yet only 10 feet across; the river tumbles through the canyon in a series of powerful waterfalls. A sometimes steep hiking trail follows the canyon down the mountainside, bridging the gorge six times. Interpretive signs describe the geology. A teahouse operates at the top of the canyon in summer.

An incredibly blue mountain lake buttressed by a ring of high-flying peaks, **Maligne Lake** is 45 minutes east of Jasper, and is one of the park's great beauty spots. The lake is the largest glacier-fed lake in the Rockies, and the second largest in the world. The Native Canadians, who called the lake *Chaba Imne,* had a superstitious awe of the region. Nonwhites (in this case a white woman, Mary Schaffer) did not discover Maligne until 1908.

Today droves of tour buses go to the "hidden lake," and the area is a popular destination for hikers, anglers, trail riders, and white-water rafters. No matter what else they do, most people who visit Maligne Lake take a boat cruise to Spirit Island, at the head of the lake. The 90-minute cruise leaves from below the Maligne Lake Lodge, an attractive summer-only facility with restaurant, bar, and gift shop (no lodging, though). Cruise tickets are adults $29, seniors (60-plus) $26, children $14.50, family $85.

Maligne Lake waters are alive with rainbow and eastern brook trout, and the Maligne Lake Boathouse is stocked with licenses, tackle, bait, and boats. Rental for a nonmotorized boat or canoe starts $10 hourly or $30 daily; reservations required. Guided fishing trips (from $135 per day, $95 per half day) include equipment, lunch, and hotel transportation. Morning and afternoon rides on horseback up the Bald Hills depart from the Chalet at Maligne Lake. Cost is $55.

All the facilities at Maligne Lake, including the lake cruises and a white-water raft outfitter that offers tours down three Jasper Park rivers, are operated by **Maligne Tours.** There's an office at the lake, next to the lodge, and also in Jasper at 626 Connaught Dr., (☎ 403/852-3370) and at the Jasper Park Lodge (☎ 403/852-4779). Maligne Tours also operates a shuttle bus between Jasper and the lake.

Downstream from Maligne Lake, the Maligne River flows into **Medicine Lake.** This large body of water appears regularly every spring, grows 5 miles long and 60 feet deep, then vanishes in the fall, leaving only a dry gravel bed through the winter. The reason for this annual wonder is a system of underground drainage caves. The local Indians believed that spirits were responsible for the lake's annual disappearance, hence the name.

Miette Hot Springs (☎ 403/866-3939) lies 37 miles northeast of Jasper off Highway 16, on one of the best animal-spotting routes in the park. Watch for elk, deer, coyotes, and moose en route. The hot mineral springs can be enjoyed in a beautiful swimming pool or two soaker pools, surrounded by forest and a grandiose mountain backdrop. Campgrounds and an attractive lodge with refreshments are nearby. During summer the pool remains open from 8:30am to 10:30pm. Admission is $4 for adults, $3.50 for children.

WHERE TO STAY

In general, rooms in Jasper are slightly less expensive than those in Banff but not as nice. As in Banff, there's a marked difference between high season and the rest of the year, so if you can avoid June through September, you'll find most accommodations 50% off. You'll want to make reservations as soon as you can, as most rooms are booked well in advance. If you can't find a room, or don't want to bother with the details, contact **Reservations Jasper** (☎ 403/852-5488 or fax 403/852-5489). In addition to finding a hotel or B&B room, they can book rafting or sightseeing trips. There's a fee for using the service.

Expensive

✪ **Chateau Jasper.** 96 Geikie St., Jasper, AB, T0E 1E0. ☎ **403/852-5644** or 800/661-9323. Fax 403/852-4860. 111 rms, 8 suites. TV TEL. $205 double; $305–$365 suite. AE, DC, ER, MC, V. Free covered, heated parking.

Usually considered the town's best hotel, the Chateau Jasper is a refined three-story lodging with some of the best staff and service in town. The grounds are beautifully landscaped with colorful floral patches scattered through the courtyards. All standard rooms have two double beds; about half the hotel is nonsmoking (separated by floors) and nonsmoking rooms only are air-conditioned. All bathrooms come with twin vanities and hair-dryers. All suites have Jacuzzi tubs, the truly large King Suites come with both Jacuzzi and shower stall, a huge 36-inch TV, wet bar, and a nice sitting area.

Dining/Entertainment: The noted Beauvallon Restaurant and lounge is located just off the lobby.

Services: There is a complimentary shuttle bus to the train and bus station. The Chateau Jasper is about the only downtown hotel that offers a concierge service.

Facilities: The swimming pool and hot tub, sheltered behind glass, are connected by stairs to the large second-story sundeck. Ski lockers are provided.

✪ **Jasper Inn.** 98 Geikie St. (P.O. Box 879), Jasper, AB, T0E 1E0. ☎ **403/852-4461.** Fax 403/852-5916. 124 rms, 14 suites. TV TEL. Summer $170–$200 double; from $250–$280 suite. Extra person $10. Children under 17 stay free in parents' room. AE, DC, ER, MC, V.

The Jasper Inn, on the northern end of town but set back off the main road, is one of the nicest lodgings in town. Rooms are available in four different buildings, and in many different size and bed configurations. Don't even bother with the standard and efficiency units (which are perfectly nice rooms, mind you); pay $10 more ($180) and reserve a one-bedroom suite, a very spacious room with a fireplace and fully equipped kitchen. It's not a steal, but at least it's value for the money. Even nicer are the rooms in the Maligne Suites unit, a separate building (all nonsmoking) with very nice, extra spacious rooms (the marble- and granite-lined bathrooms are enormous); all come with fireplaces, wet bar, Jacuzzi tubs, nice furniture, balcony, and two beds. (The top of the line is Elke Sommers's former room; ask for it by name.) Also available are two-bedroom chalet-style rooms (which can sleep up to seven). These are perfect for families, with a full kitchen, balcony, fireplace, and loads of room.

All rooms have coffeemakers, and the dining room is good.

Facilities: Sauna, steam room, hot tub, small pool, coin laundry, ski wax room, small meeting facility.

Jasper Park Lodge. P.O. Box 40, Jasper, AB, T03 1E0. ☎ 403/852-3301, 800/465-7547 in Alberta, or 800/441-1414 elsewhere in North America. Fax 403/852-5107. 442 rms, suites, and cabins. Summer $276 double, $399 suite; off-season $142 double, $252 suite. AE, CB, DISC, ER, JCB, MC, V.

Jasper's most exclusive lodging, the Jasper Park Lodge was built by the Canadian Pacific Railroad, and has the same air of luxury and gentility as their other properties, but with a more woodsy feel. The hotel grounds are located along Lac Beauvert, about 5 miles east of Jasper proper. Lodgings are in a variety of nicely furnished cabins, chalets, and cottages set amid the forest, all within easy walking distance of the central lodge, which offers four restaurants, lounges, and a shopping arcade. The rooms vary widely in style and size; call to find out what's available for your money, needs, and size of group.

Facilities: Stables, tennis courts, swimming pools, and a noted golf course.

Moderate

Amethyst Lodge. 200 Connaught Dr. (P.O. Box 1200), Jasper, AB, T0E 1E0. ☎ 403/852-3394 or 800/661-9935. Fax 403/852-5198. 97 rms. A/C TV TEL. $141–$195 double. AE, CB, MC, V.

If you're sick of the faux alpine look prevalent in the Canadian Rockies, then you might be ready for the Amethyst Lodge, an unabashed motor inn in bright pastel shades. All rooms come with two double or two queen beds; half of the rooms have balconies. There's a large restaurant, lounge, and two hot tubs on site; afternoon tea is served daily in the lounge. The Amethyst is more central to downtown Jasper than most lodgings.

✪ Becker's Chalets. Highway 95 (3 miles south of Jasper; P.O. Box 579), Jasper, AB, T0E 1E0. ☎ 403/852-3779. Fax 403/852-7202. 72 chalets. TV. $90–$100 one-bedroom cabin; $105–$130 two-bedroom cabin; $140–$285 three-bedroom cabin. MC, V.

This very attractive log cabin resort offers a variety of lodging options in free-standing chalets in a glade of trees along the Athabasca River. While the resort dates from the 1940s and retains the feel and atmosphere of an old-fashioned mountain retreat, most of the chalets have been built in the last five years, and are thoroughly modernized. Chalets come with riverstone fireplaces, full kitchens, and color TVs. The dining room here, open for breakfast and dinner, is one of Jasper's best.

✪ Lobstick Lodge. 96 Geikie St. (P.O. Box 1200), Jasper, AB, T0E 1E0. ☎ 403/852-4431 or 800/661-9317. Fax 403/852-4142. 138 rms. TV TEL. $141 double; $156 kitchenette unit. Children under 15 stay free in parents' room. AE, DC, ER, MC, V.

The Lobstick Lodge was totally renovated in 1995, and now features both a lounge and elevators, good additions to one of Jasper's most popular hotels. Standard rooms here are the largest in Jasper, and all feature two double beds. Even more impressive are 43 huge kitchen units, with a complete kitchen, including full-sized fridge, four-burner stove, and microwave, plus a double and twin-sized bed, plus a fold-out couch. These are perfect for families; they go fast, so reserve them early.

Facilities include a swimming pool, whirlpool, two outdoor hot tubs, patio, and guest laundry. There's a restaurant; the upstairs meeting room has great mountain views, and guests can use it for playing cards or lounging if it's not in use.

Marmot Lodge. 86 Connaught Dr., Jasper, AB, T0E 1E0. ☎ **403/852-4471** or 800/661-6521. Fax 403/852-3280. 106 rms and suites. TV TEL. $128–$146 double; $161 kitchen unit. Children under 15 stay free in parents' room. AE, DC, MC, V.

This is one of the better deals in Jasper. Located at the northern end of Jasper's main street, the Marmot Lodge offers moderate prices and very pleasant rooms. Lodging is in three different buildings, each with different types of rooms. One building has all-kitchen units with fireplaces, popular with families. The building facing the street has smaller, less expensive rooms with two double beds, while the third building has very large "deluxe" rooms with two queen beds. All rooms have been decorated with a Native American theme; some have tapestry-like weavings on the walls.

The Marmot has a barbecue patio, a bright and upbeat dining room, a den lounge, and a heated, picture-windowed pool with sauna and whirlpool.

Sawridge Hotel. 82 Connaught Dr., Jasper, AB, T0E 1E0. ☎ **403/852-5111.** Fax 403/852-5942. 151 rms, 3 suites. A/C TV TEL. $155–$170 double; $180–$220 suite. AE, ER, MC, V.

The three-story lobby of the Sawridge Hotel is large and rustic, and gives onto a very long central atrium lit with skylights, where the attractive dining room, swimming pool and hot tub are found. The Sawridge has one-bedroom guest rooms that face onto the atrium, or two queen-bedded rooms that over look the town; these rooms also have balconies. The entire hotel has just been redecorated, and the rooms are very comfortable. The hotel also has an informal garden cafe, two outdoor Jacuzzis, a lounge, and a sports bar. The Sawridge, located on the northern edge of Jasper, is unique in that it is owned by the Sawridge Cree Indian Band.

Inexpensive

During high season, it seems that nearly half the dwellings in Jasper let rooms B&B fashion; call ahead to **Jasper Tourism and Commerce,** P.O. Box 98, Jasper, AB, T0E 1E0 (☎ 403/852-3858; fax 403/852-4932), for a full list of such accommodations. B&Bs listed with the local visitors association have little signs in front; if you arrive early enough in the day, you can comb the streets looking for a likely suspect. Double-occupancy accommodations are in the $40 to $60 range at most homes. You'll need to pay cash for most.

Ⓢ Athabasca Hotel. Patricia and Miette streets, Jasper, AB, T0E 1E0. ☎ **403/852-3386.** 61 rms (39 with bath). TV TEL. $75 double with private bath; $51 double with shared bath. AE, MC, V.

The Athabasca has a lobby like a hunting lodge, with a stone fireplace, rows of trophy heads of deer, elk, and bighorn, and a great bar, with its own huge fireplace. A gray stone corner building with a homey old-timer's air, the hotel was built in 1929 as a destination hotel, and has a large attractive dining room and a small and trim coffee shop. Each of the bedrooms has a mountain view, although only half have private bath. The rooms are of fair size, the furnishing ample but not luxurious—armchairs, writing table, and walk-in closet. The Athabasca is really quite pleasant; it's just old-fashioned.

Maligne Canyon Hostel. Maligne Lake Road (7 miles east of Jasper). ☎ **403/852-3584** or 403/439-3139 for reservations. Sleeps 24. $9 members, $14 nonmembers.

This convenient hostel is located just above the astonishing Maligne Canyon, and is an easy hitchhike from Jasper. Facilities include a self-catering kitchen and dining area.

Whistler's Mountain Hostel. Skytram Road (4 miles west of Jasper). ☎ **403/852-3215** or 403/439-3139 for reservations. Sleeps 70. $14 members; $19 nonmembers.

The closest hostel to Jasper, Whistler's Mountain is open year-round, and is especially popular in summer, when two-week advance reservations are a good idea. There are two family rooms. The hostel rents mountain bikes, so you can get down to town and around; there's a barbecue area, and indoor plumbing and hot showers. In winter, ski packages are available.

Park Campgrounds

There are 10 campgrounds in Jasper National Park. The closest to Jasper townsite is The Whistlers, up the road toward the gondola, providing a total of some 700 campsites. You need a special permit to camp anywhere in the parks outside the regular campgrounds—a regulation necessary because of fire hazards. Contact the **parks information office** (☎ 403/852-6161) for permits. The campgrounds range from completely unserviced sites to those providing water, power, sewer connections, laundry facilities, gas, and groceries. The usual fees are $12 per night at unserviced sites, up to $20 for full-service hookups.

A Nearby Guest Ranch

Black Cat Guest Ranch. P.O. Box 6267, Hinton, AB, T7V 1X6. ☎ **403/865-3084.** Fax 403/865-1924. 16 rms. Summer $77 per person double. Rates include all meals. MC, V.

The Black Cat Guest Ranch is a historic wilderness retreat 35 miles northeast of Jasper. Established in 1935 by the Brewsters, the ranch is set in superb mountain scenery. The rustic two-story lodge (built in 1978; guests don't stay in the original old cabins) offers unfussy guest units, each with private bath, large windows, and an unspoiled view of the crags in Jasper Park across a pasture filled with horses and chattering birds. There's a big central fireplace room with couches, easy chairs, and game tables scattered around. Lodging prices include a big, home-cooked lunch, dinner and breakfast served family style by the friendly, welcoming staff. Activities include hikes, horseback riding ($14 an hour for guided horseback trips), canoe rentals, murder-mystery weekends, and fishing. The ranch staff will meet your train or bus at Hinton.

WHERE TO DINE

Expensive

Beauvallon Dining Room. In the Chateau Jasper, 96 Geike St. ☎ **403/852-5644.** Reservations recommended on weekends. Main courses $15–$29; $26 table d'hôte. AE, DC, ER, MC, V. Daily 6:30am–2pm and 5:30–11pm. CANADIAN.

Offering one of the most ambitious menus in Jasper, the Beauvallon specializes in "classic" European preparations with Canadian meats and fish. Caribou Normandy is caribou loin grilled and served with Calvados sauce ($29); another dish combines braised venison, chanterelle mushrooms, and a creamy red wine sauce. Other dishes are equally complex and eclectic: a northern Pacific seafood fricassee ($22) or a gingered breast of duck. Service is excellent, and the dining room—filled with high-back chairs—cozy. The wine list is extensive, and well-priced. The menu changes seasonally.

✪ **Becker's Gourmet Restaurant.** Highway 93 (3 miles south of Jasper). ☎ **403/852-3779.** Reservations required. Main courses $14–$28. MC, V. Daily 8am–2pm and 5:30–10pm. CANADIAN.

Although the name's not very elegant, it's highly descriptive. This high-quality, inventive restaurant serves what could only be termed gourmet food at Becker's Chalets, one of the nicest log cabin resorts in Jasper. The dining room is very attractive, an intimate log and glass affair that overlooks the Athabasca River. The menu reads like a novel: four-nut crusted lamb chops ($18), chèvre Mornay sauce and dill on grilled chicken breast, and grilled venison loin with Saskatoon berry compote. This is one of Jasper's most interesting restaurants.

Fiddle River. 620 Connaught Dr. ☎ **403/852-3032.** Reservations required. Main courses $12.95–$23.95. AE, MC, V. Daily 5pm–midnight. SEAFOOD.

This rustic-looking upstairs retreat has panoramic windows viewing the Jasper railroad station and the mountain range beyond. The specialty here is fresh fish, though a number of pasta dishes and red meat entrées will complicate your decision process. The best of the fresh fish changes daily; 8 or 10 types of fish or seafood are available; grilled salmon (one special was served with red bell pepper purée and dill cream sauce) comes in at $18, and half a dozen oysters on the half shell is $9. Caribbean chicken breast, breaded in crushed banana chips and coconut, and served with mango and yogurt, is $16; a pepper steak with blue cheese demiglace is $23. There's a small, but interesting wine list.

Moderate

Something Else. 621 Patricia St. ☎ **403/852-3850.** Pasta and pizza $11–$14; Greek dishes $11–$15; other main courses $14–$18. AE, DC, ER, MC, V. Daily 11am–midnight. INTERNATIONAL/PIZZA.

Something Else is accurately named: Folded together here is a good Greek restaurant, combined with a pizza parlor, to which is added a high-quality Canadian-style restaurant. In short, if you're with a group that can't decide where to eat, come here. Prime Alberta steaks, fiery Louisiana jambalaya and mesquite chicken, Greek saganaki and moussaka, an array of 21 pizza varieties—all the food is very well prepared and fresh, and the welcome is friendly.

✪ **Tekarra Lodge Restaurant.** Highway 93A (half mile east of Jasper). ☎ **403/852-4624.** Reservations recommended on weekends. Main courses $13–$20. AE, MC, V. Daily 5–11pm. GREEK/STEAK.

Located at the confluence of the Miette and Athabasca rivers, the Tekarra is a favorite among the locals for its excellent and well-priced grilled and roasted meats. The chef has a particular talent for preparing lamb, which appears both as classic leg of lamb, and Hellenic-style with pita, salad, and *tzatziki* sauce. Steaks, kabobs, salmon, and grilled chicken round out the admittedly limited menu; but then, everyone comes here for the lamb. The salads are also very good. The restaurant is part of an attractive log cabin resort, and is located in the central lodge. Tekarra's is a little confusing to find; ask directions before you set out.

Tokyo Tom's. 410 Connaught Dr. ☎ **403/852-3780.** Most items $3.95–$21. AE, MC, V. Daily noon–11pm. JAPANESE.

Tokyo Tom's is a slice of Japan, complete with sushi bar, a karaoke lounge, intimate nooks, and shoeless patrons, with soft Asian mood music in the background and service that is both fast and impeccable. The place has a studied simplicity that goes well with the traditional Japanese fare served: sukiyaki, sashimi, tempura, teriyaki. You can't do better than by ordering one of the five special dinners.

Inexpensive

For fresh bakery goods like muffins or fresh-cut sandwiches, coffee drinks and desserts, soup, and salad, go to **Soft Rock Cafe,** 622 Connaught Dr. (☎ 403/852-5850), a pleasant little deli in the Connaught Square Mall, in the center of town.

Jasper Pizza Place. 402 Connaught Dr. ☎ **403/852-3225.** Reservations not accepted. Pizza $7–$12.50. MC, V. Daily 7am–midnight. PIZZA.

One of Jasper's most popular eating spots, the new, highly redesigned Pizza Place agreeably combines the features of an upscale boutique pizzeria with a traditional Canadian bar. The pizzas are baked in a wood-fired oven, right in the dining room, and come in some very unusual—some would say unlikely—combinations. If you're not quite ready for the sour cream and Dijon mustard pizza, or an escargot pizza (both $9), then maybe the smoked salmon, caper, and black olive pizza might please. Standard-issue pizzas are also available, as are a selection of sandwiches and a mammoth helping of lasagne for $8. The bar side of things is lively, with two pool tables and a lively crowd of summer resort workers on display. Occasionally the pizza chef will break into his version of an aria.

☉ Mountain Foods Cafe. 606 Connaught Dr. ☎ **403/852-4050.** Main courses $5.95–$9.95. MC, V. Daily 8am–10pm. DELI.

This small deli and cafeteria is bright and friendly, and just the antidote to the stodgy food pervasive in much of the park. Although most meals are light and healthful—salads, soups, and quick ethnic dishes—more serious potpies and stews also share the menu. Choices include outstanding soups like navy bean and lentil, hearty beef stew with toast, and salads from the extensive salad bar. Best of all, the food is well prepared, tasty, and inexpensive: An entire meal will come to less than $12. Beer and wine are served.

JASPER AFTER DARK

Nearly all of Jasper's nightlife can be found in the bars and lounges of hotels, motels, and inns. Live entertainment ranges from solo performers to full-fledged combos. The **Night Club of the Athabasca Hotel,** 510 Patricia St. (☎ 403/852-3386), has a changing lineup of Top 40 bands, catering to a young clientele. There's a dance floor, and movies can be viewed on the large-screen TV in the Trophy room. In action Monday through Saturday to 2am. Jasper's newest hot spot is **Pete's Night Club,** 610 Patricia St. (☎ 403/852-6262), a youthful disco and sports bar.

11 British Columbia's Rockies: Mount Robson Provincial Park & Yoho, Glacier, Mount Revelstoke & Kootenay National Parks

MOUNT ROBSON PROVINCIAL PARK

The highlight of this beautiful park, just west of Jasper National Park along the Yellowhead Highway, is 12,250-foot-high Mount Robson, the highest peak in the Canadian Rockies. This massive sentinel fills the sky from most vantage points in the park, making it a certainty that you'll easily run through a roll of film if the weather is good. One of the best viewpoints is from the visitors center, where the mountain looms above a wildflower meadow.

The mighty Fraser River rises in the park, and is a popular and challenging whitewater adventure for experienced rafters. A number of Jasper-area outfitters offer trips down the Fraser; see the Jasper listings above.

Short two- to four-hour park tours are offered by **Mount Robson Adventure Holidays,** Valemount, British Columbia (☎ 604/566-4386; fax 604/556-4351). For $35 visitors can choose a guided nature tour by raft, canoe, or van. Longer hiking or backpacking excursions are also available.

For more information about the park, contact P.O. Box 579, Valemount, BC, V0E 2Z0 (☎ 604/566-4325).

YOHO NATIONAL PARK

Located just west of Lake Louise on the western slopes of the Rockies in British Columbia, Yoho National Park preserves some of the most famous rocks in Canada, as well as a historic rail line and the nation's highest waterfall. Yoho Park is essentially the drainage of the Kicking Horse River, and is traversed by the Trans-Canada Highway.

The first white exploration of this area was by scouts looking for a pass over the Rockies suitable for the Canadian Pacific's transcontinental run. Kicking Horse Pass, at 5,333 feet, was surveyed and the railroad began its service in 1884. However, the grade down the aptly named Big Hill, on the west side of the pass, was near precipitous; the gradient was the steepest of any in North America, descending the mountain with grades of 4.5%. The first train to attempt the descent went out of control and crashed, killing three men. In 1909, after decades of accidents, the Canadian Pacific solved its problem by curling two spiral rail tunnels into the mountains facing Big Hill. Together, the two tunnels were over 6,100 feet long. At the Lower Spiral Tunnel Viewpoint, there are interpretive displays explaining this engineering feat, and you can still watch trains enter and emerge from the tunnels.

Eight miles into the park, turn north onto Yoho Valley Road to find some of the park's most scenic areas. Past another viewpoint onto the Spirial Tunnels, continue eight miles to Takakkaw Falls, Canada's second highest, which cascades 1,248 feet in two drops. A short all-abilities trail leads from the road's end to a picnic area, where views of this amazing waterfall are even more eye-popping.

The Kicking Horse River descends between Mt. Fields and Mt. Stephen, famous in paleontological circles for Burgess Shale, fossil rich deposits from the Cambrian era that were the subject of Stephen Jay Gould's 1988 bestseller *A Wonderful Life.* Interpretive displays about these fossil digs, which have produced organisms that seem to challenge some of the established evolutionary tenets, are found at the park's visitor center in Fields. If you're interested enough in the fossil digs to face a day-long, 12-mile round-trip hike, two groups are authorized to guide visitors to the quarries. Contact the **Yoho-Burgess Shale Research Foundation** (☎ 800/343-3006) or **Canadian Wilderness** (☎ 403/678-3795) for details. Note that collecting fossils in these areas, or in the national park in general, is prohibited.

Emerald Lake, a jewel-toned lake in a glacial cirque, is one of the Yoho Park's most popular stops. Hiking trails ring the lake, and the popular **Emerald Lake Lodge** (☎ 604/343-6321) is open for meals and lodging year-round; this is a popular cross-country skiing destination.

The service center for Yoho Park is the little town of Fields, with a half-dozen modest accommodations and a few casual restaurants. The park's visitor center is just off Highway 1 near the entrance to town. For more information, contact **Yoho National Park,** P.O. Box 99, Fields, BC, V0A 1G0 (☎ 604/343-6324).

GLACIER NATIONAL PARK

Located amid the highest peaks of the **Columbia Mountains,** Canada's Glacier National Park abundantly deserves its name. More than 400 glaciers repose here, with

14% of the park's 837 square miles (1,350km) lying under permanent snowpack. The reason that this high country is so covered with ice is the same reason that this is one of the more unsettled places to visit in the mountain West: It snows and rains *a lot* here.

The primary attractions in the park are the viewpoints onto craggy peaks and hiking trails leading to wildflower meadows and old-growth groves: the heavy snow and rainfall lend a near rain forest feel to forest hikes. Spring hikers and cross-country skiers should beware of avalanche conditions, an intrinsic problem in areas with high snowfall and steep slopes.

Glacier Park is crossed by the Trans-Canada Highway and the Canadian Pacific rail tracks. Each have had to build snowsheds to protect these transportation systems from the effects of heavy snows and avalanches. Park headquarters are just east of 4,100-foot Rogers Pass; stop here to sign up for interpretive hikes, video watching, and displays on natural and human history in the park. On a typically gray and wet day, the information center may be the driest place to enjoy the park. Two easy hiking trails leave from the center. For more information about the park, contact Glacier National Park, P.O. Box 350, Revelstoke, BC, V0E 2S0 (☎ 604/837-7500).

MOUNT REVELSTOKE NATIONAL PARK

Just west of Glacier National Park is Mount Revelstoke National Park, a glacier-clad collection of craggy peaks in the **Selkirk Range.** Comprising only 161 square miles (260km), Mount Revelstoke can't produce the kind of awe that its larger neighbor can in good weather; but Revelstoke offers easier access to the high country and alpine meadows.

The most popular activity in the park is the drive up to the top of 6,000-foot Mount Revelstoke, with great views onto the Columbia River and the peaks of Glacier Park. To reach Mount Revelstoke, take the paved road north from the town of Revelstoke and follow it 14 miles to Balsam Lake. From here, free shuttle buses operated by the parks department make the final ascent up the mountain. A popular hike is the Giant Cedars Trail, a short boardwalk out into a grove of old-growth cedars over 1,000 years old.

The park is flanked on the south by Highway 1, the Trans-Canada Highway. The park has no services or campgrounds. However, all services, including a number of hotels, are available in the town of Revelstoke. For more information about the park, contact Mount Revelstoke National Park, P.O. Box 350, Revelstoke, BC, V0E 2S0 (☎ 604/837-7500).

KOOTENAY NATIONAL PARK & RADIUM HOT SPRINGS

This national park, lying just west of Banff on the western slopes of the Canadian Rockies, preserves the valleys of the Kootenay and Vermillion rivers. The park contains prime wildlife habitat, and a number of hiking trails. Although Kootenay's scenery is as grand as anywhere else in the Rockies, the trails here are considerably less thronged.

The park is linked to the other Canadian Rocky national parks by Highway 93, which departs from Highway 1 at Castle Junction to climb over the Vermillion Pass and descend to Radium Hot Springs, the park's western entrance.

Much of the area around the pass was burned in a massive forest fire in 1968; a number of trails lead out into the forest, and describe the process of revegetation. Be sure to stop at Marble Canyon, a 200-foot-deep canyon cut through a formation of limestone. A short hiking trail winds over and through the canyon, bridging the chasm in several places.

Another interesting stop is the **Paint Pots.** Here, cold spring water surfaces in an iron-rich deposit of red and yellow clay, forming intense colored pools. Early Native Canadians journeyed here to collect the ochre-colored soil for body paint; for them, this was an area filled with "great medicine."

The highway leaves the Vermillion River valley and climbs up to a viewpoint above the Hector Gorge, into which the river flows before meeting the Kootenay River. From the viewpoint, also look for mountain goats, which can often be seen on the rocky cliffs to the north.

The highway passes through one of these narrow limestone canyons after it mounts Sinclair Pass and descends toward Radium Hot Springs. Called Sinclair Canyon, the chasm is about 6 miles long, and in places is scarcely wide enough to accommodate the roadbed.

Radium Hot Springs Aquacourt (☎ 604/347-9485), a long-established hot springs spa and resort, sits at the mouth of Sinclair Canyon. As the name suggests, the mineral waters here are slightly radioactive, but not enough to be a concern to casual soakers. Stop for a swim or a soak; adults $4, seniors/children $3.50.

The town of Radium Hot Springs sits at the junction of Highways 93 and 95. Not an especially attractive place, it nonetheless offers ample motel rooms along the half-mile stretch of Highway 93 just before the park gates. For more information about the park, contact **Kootenay National Park,** P.O. Box 220, Radium Hot Springs, BC, V0A 1M0 (☎ 604/347-9505).

12 Edmonton

Edmonton is Alberta's capital and has the largest metropolitan population in the province, currently around 850,000. Located on the banks of the North Saskatchewan River, Edmonton is an outgoing and sophisticated city noted for its easygoing friendliness—a trait that's been scientifically proven. In 1995, an independent study of Canadians' altruistic behavior found that Edmonton was the most friendly and helpful city in the nation.

Edmonton grew in spurts, following a boom-and-bust pattern as exciting as it was unreliable. During World War II the boom came in the form of the Alaska Highway, with Edmonton as material base and temporary home of 50,000 American troops and construction workers.

The ultimate boom, however, gushed from the ground on a freezing afternoon in February 1947. That was when a drill at Leduc, 25 miles southwest of the city, sent a fountain of dirty-black crude oil soaring skyward. Some 10,000 other wells followed, all within a 100-mile radius of the city. In their wake came the petrochemical industry and the major refining and supply conglomerates. In two decades the population of the city quadrupled, its skyline mushroomed with glass-and-concrete office towers, a rapid-transit system was created, and a $150-million civic center rose. Edmonton had become what it is today—the oil capital of Canada.

ESSENTIALS

VISITOR INFORMATION   For guidance on Edmonton and its attractions, contact **Edmonton Tourism,** 9797 Jasper Ave., Edmonton, AB, T5J 1N9 (☎ 403/496-8400 or 800/463-4667). There's also a visitor information center at City Hall, and at Gateway Park, on the Calgary Trail at the southern edge of the city.

GETTING THERE   Edmonton is served by most major airlines, including **Air Canada** (☎ 800/776-3000) and **Canadian Airlines International** (☎ 800/

Edmonton

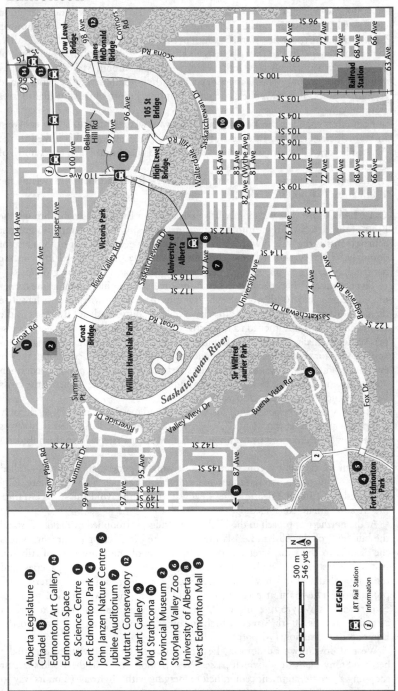

LEGEND

🚉 LRT Rail Station
ⓘ Information

0 ——— 500 m
  ——— 546 yds

Alberta Legislature ⑪
Citadel ⑬
Edmonton Art Gallery ⑭
Edmonton Space
& Science Centre ①
Fort Edmonton Park ④
John Janzen Nature Centre ⑤
Jubilee Auditorium ⑦
Muttart Conservatory ⑫
Muttart Gallery ⑨
Old Strathcona ⑩
Provincial Museum ②
Storyland Valley Zoo ⑥
University of Alberta ⑧
West Edmonton Mall ③

426-7000), which also operates the outstanding shuttle to Calgary, a no-reservation service of 17 flights a day, making the hop in 36 minutes for $150. The **Edmonton International Airport** lies 18 miles south of the city on Highway 2, about 45 driving minutes away. By cab the trip costs about $35; by Airporter bus, $11. North of downtown, but amazingly close to it, lies the Municipal Airport. Make sure you know which of the two airports you are connecting with; both are served by national and regional airlines, and it's very easy to end up at one airport while your flight leaves from the other.

Edmonton straddles the **Yellowhead Highway,** western Canada's new east-west interprovincial highway. Just west of Edmonton the Yellowhead is linked to the Alaska Highway. The city is 320 miles north of the U.S. border, 176 miles north of Calgary.

Passenger trains arrive at and depart from the **VIA Rail Station,** 104th Avenue and 100th Street (☎ 403/422-6032).

CITY LAYOUT   The winding North Saskatchewan River flows right through the heart of the city, dividing it into roughly equal halves. One of the capital's greatest achievements is the way in which this river valley has been kept out of the grasp of commercial developers. Almost the entire valley has been turned into public parklands, forming 17 miles of greenery, sports, picnic, and recreation grounds.

The founding fathers decided to begin the street numbering system at the corner of 100th Street and 100th Avenue, which means that downtown addresses have five digits, and that suburban homes often have smaller addresses than businesses in the very center of town. Edmonton's main street is the wide and seemingly endless Jasper Avenue (actually 101st Avenue), running north of the river. The "A" designations you'll notice for certain streets and avenues downtown add to the confusion; they're essentially old service alleys between major streets, many of which now are pedestrian areas with sidewalk cafes. Get a good map and give yourself time to puzzle the city's layout; it's not entirely straightforward.

At 97th Street, on Jasper Avenue, rises the pink and massive Canada Place, the only completely planned government complex of its kind in Canada. Immediately across the street is the Edmonton Convention Center, which stairsteps down the hillside to the river

Beneath the downtown core stretches a network of pedestrian walkways—called pedways—connecting hotels, restaurants, and shopping malls with the library, City Hall, and the Citadel Theatre. These pedways not only avoid the surface traffic, they're also climate-controlled.

At the northern approach to the High Level Bridge, surrounded by parkland, stand the buildings of the Alberta Legislature, seat of the provincial government. Across the bridge, to the west, stretches the vast campus of the University of Alberta. Just to the east is Old Strathcona, a bustling neighborhood of cafes, galleries, and hip shops that's now a haven for Edmonton's student and more "alternative" population. The main arterial through Old Strathcona—which used to be its own town—is Whyte Avenue, or 82nd Avenue. Running south from here in a straight line is 104th Street, which becomes Calgary Trail and leads to the Edmonton International Airport.

West of downtown Edmonton, Jasper Avenue shifts and twists to eventually become Stony Plain Road, which passes West Edmonton Mall, the world's largest shopping and entertainment center, before merging with Highway 16 on its way to Jasper National Park.

GETTING AROUND   Edmonton's public transport is handled by **Edmonton Transit** (☎ 403/496-1611 for information), which operates the city buses as well as the new, silent, streamlined, and comfortable LRT (Light Rail Transit). This partly underground, partly aboveground electric rail service connects downtown Edmonton with Northlands Park to the north and the University of Alberta to the south. The downtown terminal, Central Station, lies underground at Jasper Avenue and 101st Street. The other end of the 7-mile line is north of 137th Avenue and 42nd Street.

The LRT and the Transit buses have the same fares: $1.60 for adults and 80¢ for children. You can transfer from one to the other at any station on the same ticket. On weekdays from 9am to 3pm, downtown LRT travel is free between Churchill, Central, Bay, Corona, and Grandin stations.

You'll find **Tilden** at 10131-100A St. (☎ 403/422-6097) and at the airport (☎ 403/890-7232); **Budget,** at 10016-106th St. (☎ 403/448-2000); and **Hertz,** at 10815 Jasper Ave. (☎ 403/423-3431).

Call **Co-op Taxi** (☎ 403/425-8310 or 403/425-2525), for a ride in a driver/ owner operated cab.

FAST FACTS   American Express   There's an office at 10180 101 St., at 102nd Avenue (☎ 403/421-0608).

Climate   The city tends to be sunny, windy, and cool. Midsummer temperatures average between 70° and 80°F, and at an altitude of 2,182 feet, even summer nights can be nippy.

Newspapers   The *Edmonton Journal* and the *Edmonton Sun* are the local daily papers. Arts, entertainment, and nightlife listings can be found in the *See* weekly.

Post Office   The main post office is located at 103A Avenue at 99th Street.

KLONDIKE DAYS & OTHER SPECIAL EVENTS

The gold rush that sent an army of prospectors heading for the Yukon in 1898 put Edmonton "on the map," as they say. Although the actual gold fields lay 1,500 miles to the north, the little settlement became a giant supply store, resting place, and "recreation" ground for thousands of men stopping there en route before tackling the hazards of the Klondike Trail that led overland to Dawson City in the Yukon. Edmonton's population doubled in size, and its merchants, saloonkeepers, and ladies of easy virtue waxed rich in the process.

Since 1962 Edmonton has been celebrating the event with one of the greatest and most colorful extravaganzas staged in Canada. The **Klondike Days** are held annually in late July. Street festivities last ten days, as does the great Klondike Days Exposition at Northlands Park.

Locals and visitors dress up in period costumes, street corners blossom with impromptu stages featuring anything from country bands to cancan girls, stage-coaches rattle through the streets, parades and floats wind from block to block.

The 16,000-seat Coliseum holds nightly spectaculars of rock, pop, variety, or western entertainment. Northlands Park turns into Klondike Village, complete with the Chilkoot Gold Mine, Silver Slipper Saloon, and gambling casino—legal for this occasion only. The Walterdale Playhouse drops serious stage endeavors for a moment and puts on hilarious melodramas with mustachioed villains to hiss and dashing heroes to cheer.

Immense "Klondike breakfasts" are served in the open air, massed marching bands compete in the streets, and down the North Saskatchewan River float more than 100 of the weirdest-looking home-built rafts ever seen, competing in the "World Championship Sourdough River Raft Race."

The **Jazz City International Jazz Festival** is a citywide celebration of jazz that takes over most music venues in Edmonton for the last week of July and first week of August. For more information, call ☎ 403/432-7166.

The **Edmonton Folk Music Festival** is the largest folk music festival in North America. Held in mid-August, the festival brings in musicians from around the world, from the Celtic north to Indonesia. Recently, the festival has seen major rock musicians making appearances with acoustic "unplugged" bands. For more information, call ☎ 403/429-1899. All concerts are held outdoors.

For 10 days in mid-August, Old Strathcona is transformed into a series of stages for a festival of alternative theater, the **Fringe Theatre Event.** Only Edinburgh's fringe festival is larger than Edmonton's—more than 60 troupes attend from around the world—making this a great event for theater lovers. For more information, call ☎ 403/448-9000.

EXPLORING THE CITY
THE TOP ATTRACTIONS

Old Strathcona. Around 82nd Avenue, between 103rd and 105th streets. Bus: 46 from downtown.

This historical district used to be a separate township, but was amalgamated with Edmonton in 1912. Due to the efforts of the Old Strathcona Foundation, the area contains some of the best-preserved landmarks in the city. It's best seen on foot, guided by the brochures given out at the Old Strathcona Foundation office, 8331 104th St. (☎ 403/433-5866).

The best reason to visit Old Strathcona is to wander along the shops, stop in at street-side cafes, and people watch. This is hipster central for Edmonton, where university students, artists, and the city's alternative community come to hang out. It's easy to spend an afternoon here, just being part of the scene. Be sure to stop in at the **Old Strathcona Farmers Market,** at the corner of 83rd Avenue and 103 Street, an open-air market with fresh produce, baked goods, and local crafts. The market is open Saturdays year-round, and also Tuesday and Thursday afternoons in summer. Another good stop for browsers is **Greenwoods Bookshop,** at 10355 Whyte Ave., Edmonton's largest and best bookstore.

Provincial Museum of Alberta. 12845 102nd Ave. ☎ **403/453-9100.** Admission $5.50 adults, $2.25 children, $13 family. Summer daily 9am–8pm; winter daily 9am–5pm. Bus: 1.

Modern and expertly laid out, this 200,000-square-foot museum displays Alberta's natural and human history in three permanent galleries. The Habitat Groups show wildlife in natural settings; the Native People's Gallery offers a glimpse of the region's original inhabitants; Natural History has fossils and a live bug room; and a fourth gallery features changing exhibits. The museum also presents artists and artisans and free film showings.

West Edmonton Mall. 8770-170th St. ☎ **403/444-5200.** Bus: 10.

You won't find many shopping malls mentioned in this book, but the West Edmonton Mall is something else. Although it contains 800 stores and services, including 90 eating establishments, it looks and sounds more like a large slice of Disneyland that has somehow broken loose and drifted north. The locals modestly call it the "Eighth Wonder of the World."

More theme park than mall, the West Edmonton Mall encompasses 5.2 million square feet, and houses the world's largest indoor amusement park, including a titanic indoor roller coaster, bungie-jumping platform, plus an enclosed wave-lake, complete with beach and enough artificial waves to ride a surfboard on. It has walk-through bird aviaries, a huge ice-skating palace, 19 (count 'em, 19) movie theaters, a lagoon with performing dolphins, and several absolutely fabulous adventure rides (one of them by submarine to the "ocean floor," and another simulating a white-water raft journey). In the middle of it all, an immense fountain with 19 computer-controlled jets weaves and dances in a musical performance.

Of course, you can go shopping here, and some of Edmonton's most popular restaurants are located in the mall, as well as an increasingly large share of the city's nightlife. On Saturdays at 2pm, you can even tour the rooms at the mall's excellent "theme" hotel, called Fantasyland. Admission to the mall is gratis, but some of the rides are fairly expensive. Roll your eyes all you want, but do go. You have to see the West Edmonton Mall to believe it.

Fort Edmonton Park. On the Whitemud Drive at Fox Drive. ☎ **403/496-8787.** Admission to Fort Edmonton Park $6.50 adults, $5 seniors and youths, $3.25 children, $19.50 family; Nature Center by donation. Fort Edmonton May 21–June 23 Mon–Fri 10am–4pm, Sat–Sun 10am–6pm; June 24–Sept 4 daily 10am–6pm. Call the Nature Centre for hours.

This is a detailed reconstruction of the old Fort Edmonton fur-trading post. Throughout the park you step into other re-created periods of the town's early history. On 1885 Street it's the Frontier Town, complete with blacksmith shop, saloon, general store, and Jasper House Hotel that serves hearty pioneer meals (but not at pioneer prices). 1905 Street has an antique photographic studio and fire hall equipped with appropriate engines. You can ride Edmonton streetcar no. 1, a stagecoach, or a steam locomotive. On 1920 Street, sip an old-fashioned ice-cream soda at Bill's "confectionery."

Adjoining Fort Edmonton, the **John Janzen Nature Centre** (☎ 403/496-2939) offers historic exhibits, hiking trails, and lessons in nature lore. You can go bird-watching, "shake hands" with a garter snake, observe a living beehive, and take courses from professionals in everything from building a log cabin to game stalking and tracking.

Muttart Conservatory. Off James MacDonald Bridge at 98th Avenue and 96A Street. ☎ **403/496-8755.** Admission $4.25 adults, $3.25 senior/youth, $2 children, $12.50 family. Sun–Wed 11am–9pm, Thurs–Sat 11am–6pm. Bus: 51.

The conservatory is housed in a group of four pavilions that look like I. M. Pei pyramids. They house one of the finest floral displays in North America. Each pyramid contains a different climatic zone—the tropical one has an 18-foot waterfall as well. The Arid Pavilion has desert air and shows flowering cacti and their relatives. The temperate zone includes a cross section of plants from this global region. The fourth pyramid features changing ornamental displays of plants and blossoms. For good measure, there's also the Treehouse Café.

MORE ATTRACTIONS

Alberta Legislature Building. 109th Street and 97th Avenue. ☎ **403/427-7362.** Free tours given daily every hour 9am–5pm, weekends and holidays noon–5pm. LRT: Grandin station.

The Alberta Legislature Building rises on the site of the early trading post from which the city grew. Surrounded by lovingly manicured lawns, formal gardens, and greenhouses, it overlooks the river valley. The seat of Alberta's government was completed in 1912, a stately Edwardian structure open to the public throughout the year. Conducted tours tell you about the functions of provincial lawmaking: Who does what, where, and for how long.

Edmonton Art Gallery. 2 Sir Winston Churchill Sq. ☎ **403/422-6223.** Admission $3 adults, $1.50 students/seniors, children under 12 free, $13 family. Mon–Wed 10:30am–5pm, Thurs–Fri 10:30am–8pm, Sat–Sun and holidays 11am–5pm.

The art gallery occupies a stately building right in the heart of downtown, immediately east of City Hall. The interior, however, is state-of-the-art modern, subtly lit and expertly arranged. Exhibits consist partly of contemporary Canadian art, partly of international contemporary art, partly of changing works on tour from every corner of the globe. The Gallery shop sells an eclectic array of items, from art books to hand-made yo-yos.

Old Strathcona Model & Toy Museum. 8603 104th St. ☎ **403/433-4512.** Admission by donation. Wed–Fri noon–5pm, Sat 10am–6pm, Sun and holidays 1–5pm.

Displays more than 400 scale models of famous buildings, ships, aircraft and trains, as well as dolls, birds, and metal toys.

Rutherford House. 11153 Saskatchewan Dr., on the campus of the University of Alberta. ☎ **403/427-3995.** Admission $1. Summer daily 10am–5pm. LRT: University station.

The home of Alberta's first premier, Alexander Rutherford, this lovingly preserved Edwardian building gleams with polished silver and gilt-framed oils. Around 1915 this mansion was the magnet for the social elite of the province: Today, guides dressed in period costumes convey some of the spirit of the times to visitors. There's also a tearoom on the premises.

Telephone Historical Centre. 10437 83rd Ave. ☎ **403/441-2077.** Admission $2 adults, $1 children, $3 family. Mon–Fri 10am–4pm, Sat noon–4pm.

The largest museum devoted to the history of telecommunications in North America is located in the 1912 Telephone Exchange Building. Multimedia displays tells the history of words over wire, and hints at what your modem will get up to next.

ESPECIALLY FOR KIDS

Edmonton Space & Science Centre. 11211 142nd St., Coronation Park. ☎ **403/452-9100** for information on IMAX programs. Admission $6.50 adults, $5.50 seniors, $4.25 children 4–12, $20 family. IMAX movies $7 adults, $6 seniors, $4.75 children, $22 family. Tues–Sun 10am–10pm. Bus: 17 or 22.

This is one of the most advanced multipurpose facilities of its kind in the world. It contains, among other wonders, the giant-screen IMAX theater, the largest planetarium theater in Canada, plus many high-tech exhibit galleries (including a virtual reality showcase and a display on robotics) and an observatory open on clear afternoons and evenings. The show programs include star shows, laser-light music concerts, and the special IMAX films that have to be seen to be believed.

Valley Zoo. In Laurier Park, 13315 Buena Vista Rd. ☎ **403/496-6911.** Admission $4.95 adults, $3.50 seniors and youth, $2.50 children under 13, $14.95 family. Summer daily 10am–6pm; winter daily noon–4pm.

In this charming combination of reality and fantasy, real-live beasties mingle with fairy-tale creations. More than 500 animals and birds are neighbors to the Three Little Pigs, Humpty Dumpty, and the inhabitants of Noah's Ark.

WHERE TO STAY

Lodgings are of high quality in Edmonton. At almost all of the hotels and motels listed below, you can expect complimentary toiletries in the rooms, hairdryers, bedside clock radios, and room service. In general, hotels are concentrated in the downtown area, in the West End, near the West Edmonton Mall and on the road to Jasper, and in south Edmonton, on Calgary Trail.

The B&B tradition is a latecomer in Alberta, but very efficiently organized—too efficiently for free-market enthusiasts. Here, instead of advertising individually, the host families register with agencies, so you know that all the listed accommodations are carefully screened—you can get a row of choices without running your legs off. Nearly all B&Bs listed charge from $40 for singles, from $50 for doubles.

The following agencies offer rooms with host families in Edmonton, Calgary, Banff, Jasper, and country areas: **Edmonton Bed & Breakfast,** 13814 110A Ave., Edmonton, AB, T5M 2M9 (☎ 403/455-2297); **Bed & Breakfast—Alberta's Gem,** 11216-48th Ave., Edmonton, AB, T6H 0C7 (☎ 403/434-6098); and **Holiday Home Accommodation,** 10808-54th Ave., Edmonton, AB, T6H 0T9 (☎ 403/436-4196).

EXPENSIVE

Crowne Plaza Chateau Lacombe. 10111 Bellamy Hill, Edmonton, AB, T5J 1N7. ☎ **403/428-6611** or 800/227-6963. Fax 403/426-7625. 307 rms, 35 suites. A/C MINIBAR TV TEL. $109–$149 double; $195–$500 suite. Weekend packages available. AE, CB, DC, ER, MC, V. Parking $7.50 per day.

Centrally located downtown, the Crowne Plaza, a round 24-story tower sitting on the edge of a cliff overlooking the North Saskatchewan River, possesses some of the city's best views. The unusual design blends well with the city's dramatic skyline, yet it is instantly recognizable from afar—a perfect landmark.

The marble-lined lobby is hung with enormous, breastlike chandeliers. The nicely furnished bedrooms and suites aren't huge, though the wedge-shaped design demands that they are broadest toward the windows, where you'll spend time looking over the city. There are two private executive floors and nonsmoking floors.

Dining/Entertainment: There's a revolving restaurant, appropriately named La Ronde, at the top of the tower (see "Where to Dine," below), plus a cocktail lounge.

Facilities: Fitness center.

Delta Edmonton Centre Suite Hotel. Eaton Centre, 10222 102nd St., Edmonton, AB, T5J 4C5. ☎ **403/429-3900** or 800/661-6655 in Canada. Fax 403/428-1566. 169 suites. A/C MINIBAR TV TEL. Standard or business suite $79–$250. Ask about summer family and low weekend rates. AE, DC, ER, MC, V. Parking $7.50 per day.

This all-suite establishment forms part of the upscale Eaton Centre Mall in the heart of downtown. Half the windows look into the mall, so you can stand behind the tinted one-way glass (in your pajamas, if you like) and watch the shopping action outside.

Most units are deluxe executive suites ($195, or $135 if you're here on business), each with a large sitting area with couch, chairs, TV, and wet bar, and—down a hall and behind a door—a bedroom of equal size, containing more easy chairs, another TV, a large desk, and a plate glass wall looking into the seven-story mall atrium. Each suite has two phones. If you need lots of room, or have work to do in Edmonton, then these very spacious rooms are just the ticket. All rooms have Jacuzzi tubs. Also nice, though peculiar, are the Seashell Rooms, which have a round bed nestled in an enormous clam shell, plus a large Jacuzzi tub. Honeymooners love it. The entire hotel is nicely furnished and well decorated.

Dining/Entertainment: There's a restaurant, Cocoa's, where hotel guests receive 25% dinner discounts.

Facilities: The hotel provides a business center with photocopy and fax machines, and an exercise room with steam bath and whirlpool. And without having to stir out of doors there are the 120 retail shops in the mall, plus movie theaters, an entertainment pub, and an indoor putting green.

✪ **Fantasyland Hotel.** 17700 87th Ave, Edmonton, AB, T5T 4V4. ☎ **403/444-3000** or 800/661-6454. Fax 403/444-3294. 319 rms, 36 suites. A/C TV TEL. $154–$208 double; from $208–$240 suite. Weekend and off-season packages available. AE, ER, MC, V. Free parking.

From the outside, this solemn brown brick tower at the end of the huge West Edmonton Mall reveals little of the wildly decorated and luxurious rooms found inside. The Fantasyland is kind of a cross between a hotel and Las Vegas: The hotel contains a total of 127 "themed" rooms decorated in nine different styles (as well as 228 very large and well-furnished regular rooms).

Theme rooms aren't just a matter of subtle touches: These rooms are exceedingly clever, very comfortable, but way over the top. Take the Truck Room: Your bed is located in the back end of a real pickup (you can choose a Ford or Chevy); the pickup's bench seats fold down into a bed for a child, the lights on the vanity are real stoplights, and the lights on the roll bar are actually reading lights. Traffic signs decorate the walls. Or the Igloo Room, where a round bed is encased in a shell that looks like ice blocks; keeping company with you are statues of sled dogs; and all the walls are painted with amazingly lifelike tromp d'oeil Arctic murals. The dogsleds even become beds for children. And so on, through the Canadian Rail Room (train berths for beds), the African Room, the Roman Room, and more. The decorations are usually ingenious, and the rooms quite luxurious. All the theme rooms come with immense four-person Jacuzzi tubs, lots of sitting room (albeit usually disguised as something else), and all the amenities that you'd expect at a four-star hotel.

It's not all fantasy here. The regular rooms are divided into superior rooms, with either a king or two queen beds, or executive rooms, with a king bed, large Jacuzzi, and masses of sitting room. The hotel has a separate business work area, with desks, modems, and printers available. There's a small workout room, and passes are offered to the mall's Waterpark. The hotel's fine-dining restaurant is quite good, and of course, the hotel provides all weather access to the world's largest shopping mall.

If you have any doubt about the rooms, the hotel offers tours of all the different theme types on Saturdays at 2pm. After you complete the tour, you'll wish you were staying here.

✪ **Hotel Macdonald.** 10065 100th St., Edmonton, AB, T5J 0N6. ☎ **403/424-5181** or 800/441-1414. Fax 403/429-6481. 198 rms. A/C MINIBAR TV TEL. High season $260 double; $270 business-class double. Discounts on weekends and off-season. AE, DC, DISC, ER, MC, V. Parking $12.50 a day.

The palatial Hotel Macdonald, named after Canada's first prime minister, first opened in 1915. After a long and colorful career, it was bought by the Canadian Pacific hotel chain in 1988. What ensued was a masterwork of sensitive renovation and restoration. The courtly and beautiful public rooms were left intact, while the guest rooms were completely rebuilt to modern luxury standards. While the renovation brought the rooms graciously up to date, it retained all of the original venerable charm of the old hotel. Signature elements like the old, deep bathtubs, brass door plates, high ceilings, and handsome paneled doors were retained, while important additions like new plumbing and individual temperature controls were installed. Rooms are beautifully furnished with quality furniture, luxurious upholstery, and feather duvets and pillows—and an especially thoughtful touch, a bin for recyclables. The beds are amazingly comfortable. Even the artwork—period botanical prints and fish flies—are notable.

Business-class suites each have a sitting area with a couch and two chairs, and a handy dressing area off the bathroom with a vanity table. Free coffee, local phone calls, and buffet breakfast are included. Executive suites have two TVs and telephones, with a separate bedroom and a large sitting area. The eight specialty suites—which take up the entire seventh and eighth floors—are simply magnificent.

From the outside, with its limestone facade and gargoyles, the Mac—as it's known locally—looks like a feudal château—down to the kilted service staff. High ceilings, majestic drapes, and crystal chandeliers grace the lobby, which boasts a ballroom fit for royalty. Even pets, which are welcome, get special treatment: a gift bag of treats and a map of pet-friendly parks.

Needless to say, there aren't many hotels like this in Edmonton, or in Canada for that matter. As I rode the elevator, a guest broke the silence with an effusive, voluntary, but matter-of-fact, "This is a *great* hotel."

Dining/Entertainment: There's a bar retreat that resembles an Edwardian gentlemen's club, an outdoor garden terrace for summer dining, and an indoor dining room viewing the panoramic backdrop of the North Saskatchewan River valley.

Facilities: The swimming pool, with Roman pillars and a wading pool for children, adjoins a health club with a pro shop and juice bar, weight room, sauna, steam room, squash courts, massage therapy area, and an exercise room where guests can join the regularly scheduled aerobics classes.

MODERATE

Alberta Place. 10049-103rd St., Edmonton, AB, T5J 2W7. ☎ **403/423-1565** or 800/661-3982. Fax 403/426-6260. 86 suites. TV TEL. $75 double bed-sitter; $85 double one-bedroom suite. Extra person $8. Children stay free in parents' room. AE, DC, ER, MC, V. Parking free.

This downtown apartment hotel is an excellent choice for the traveler who needs a little extra space or a family that wants cooking facilities. Everything is supplied to set up housekeeping. The hotel has a swimming pool (with hot tub and sauna). The apartments, of various sizes, are very well furnished and comfortable, and each has a full kitchen, including microwave, and a large desk and working area. The hotel is located half a block from public transport, and is in easy walking distance to most business and government centers.

✪ **Edmonton House.** 10205 100 Ave., Edmonton, AB, T5J 4B5. ☎ **403/420-4000** or 800/661-6562. Fax 403/420-4008. 300 suites. TV TEL. $97 one-bedroom suite. AE, DC, ER, MC, V. Free parking.

This is a great alternative to pricier downtown hotels; these are big, well-decorated rooms, and you don't have to pay stiff parking fees. With a great location right above the North Saskatchewan River, the Edmonton House all-suite hotel has one of the best views in Edmonton. The rooms are large; each comes with a full kitchen and dining area, separate sitting area with a fold-out couch and chairs, and a balcony from which to take in the view. Each room has two telephones and a computer jack; room service is available. Facilities at the hotel include a pool and sauna, exercise room, game room, and laundry facilities. On premises is both a lounge and a restaurant. Edmonton House is within easy walking distance to most downtown office areas and to public transport.

INEXPENSIVE

During the summer, 1,200 dorm rooms in Lister Hall at the **University of Alberta,** 87th Avenue and 116th Street (☎ 403/492-4281), are thrown open to visitors. Most rooms are standard bathroom-down-the-hall dorm rooms with two twin beds for $33. Available year-round are guest suites, two-bed dorm units that share a bathroom with only one other suite ($35). The university is right on the LRT line, and not far from trendy Old Strathcona.

The **YMCA,** 10030-102A Ave. (☎ 403/421-9622), offers 106 rooms (some with bath) for $29 single, $40 double (MC, V accepted). It has a cafeteria, pool, weight room, gymnasium, and racquetball court, plus a TV lounge; it accommodates men, women, and couples. Only a few rooms have private bath (tub only). Women can also try the **YWCA,** 10305-100th Ave. (☎ 403/423-9922), which charges $27.50

to $42.50 for a private room; $12.50 for a bunk in a dorm (MC, V accepted). There's a cafeteria open daily and a pool. The public bathrooms are sparkling and the staff is exceptionally friendly. Reservations are advised.

Continental Inn. 16625 Stony Plain Rd., Edmonton, AB, T5P 4A8. ☎ **403/484-7751.** Fax 403/484-9827. 60 rms. TV TEL. $50–$60 double. AE, DC, ER, MC, V. Free parking.

Located about 10 minutes west of downtown on the Yellowhead Highway route to Jasper Park, the Continental Inn is a huge, modern accommodation and entertainment complex. The inn contains a bar, restaurant, coffee shop, cocktail lounge, tavern, cabaret, a truly grand ballroom, and every conceivable convention facility, including an excellently laid-out lobby that combines vastness with comfort.

The inn has only 60 guest rooms, few for its size, but these are large and nicely furnished. Big front windows give maximum daylight, the decor is pleasant, hanging space is ample, and room service is excellent. The bathrooms are big and modern.

⑤ Days Inn. 10041-106th St., Edmonton, AB, T5J 1G3. ☎ **403/423-1925** or 800/267-2191. Fax 403/424-5302. 76 rms. A/C TV TEL. $54–$59 double. Children under 18 stay free in parents' room; children under 12 eat free. Senior, AAA, and corporate discounts. AE, ER, MC, V. Free parking.

For the price, this is one of downtown Edmonton's best deals. Located just five minutes from the city center, this motor inn has everything you need for a pleasant stay, including guest laundry and king or queen-sized beds in comfortably furnished rooms. The bathrooms come with a tub and shower; the sink is in a vanity outside the bathroom. This isn't the fanciest hotel in Edmonton, but it's perfectly pleasant.

Edmonton International Hostel. 10422 91st St., Edmonton, AB, T5H 1S6. ☎ **403/429-0140.** Sleeps 50 people. $12.50 members, $17.50 nonmembers.

The Edmonton hostel is air-conditioned and has mountain bike rentals, which means you can get around town easily, even though public transportation is just around the corner. Two family rooms are available.

Quality Inn & Executive Suites. 10815 Jasper Ave., Edmonton, AB, T5J 2B2. ☎ **403/423-1650** or 800/463-7666. Fax 403/425-6834. 97 rms. TV TEL. $45–$64 double. AE, ER, MC, V. Parking $5 a day.

A white corner building with distinctive blue awnings over each window, this attractive older hotel has been newly renovated and now houses a large family-style restaurant. Bedrooms are a bit small, and the no-fuss furnishings are just fine. There are open closets and bedside lamps instead of ceiling lights. For downtown Edmonton, this is a pretty good deal for the budget traveler.

WHERE TO DINE

Edmonton has a vigorous dining scene, with lots of hip new eateries blending with traditional steak and seafood restaurants. In general, special occasion and fine dining is found downtown, and on High Street, close to the centers of politics and business. Over in Old Strathcona, south of the river, is an area of trendy—and less expensive—cafes and bistros with up-to-the-minute, cosmopolitan menus.

If you're staying downtown, one place you'll get to know very well is the **Baraka Cafe,** 10088 Jasper Ave., on downtown Edmonton's busiest corner. Baraka's has expertly made espresso drinks, two cases full of exquisite pastries and sweets, and a large selection of magazines and newspapers. With cafe tables to lounge at, this is the perfect place to caffeinate in the morning, or have a late-night dessert.

DOWNTOWN

Expensive

Claude's on the River. 9797 Jasper Ave. ☎ **403/429-2900.** Reservations required. Main courses $18.25–$25.75. AE, CB, ER, MC, V. Mon–Fri 11:30am–2:30pm; Mon–Sat 5:30–11pm. FRENCH.

Claude's has a reputation for having the best French cuisine and the finest wine list in town. Located in the glass-fronted, stair-stepped convention center, Claude's also has a great view of the river. Some of the outstanding house specialties are escargots in puff pastry and wine sauce, a magnificent seafood ragout, rack of lamb in a Provençal crust ($24), and wickedly delicious fruit, ice, and chocolate desserts.

✪ **Emery's.** 10109-125th St. ☎ **403/482-7577.** Reservations recommended on weekends. Main courses $8.95–$19.95. AE, DC, ER, MC, V. Mon–Fri 11:30am–10pm, Sat–Sun 5–10pm. CONTINENTAL.

Housed in a stately two-story mansion overlooking a park, Emery's offers one of the most fashionable outdoor dining patios in Edmonton. But the interior is entertaining enough to make up for bad weather. The rooms are filled with artworks and knickknacks, there is a great fireplace, and a wall is covered with tantalizing menus from long-past banquets, including one served to the king of Prussia in 1897. The fare is an even blend of continental specialties and nouvelle cuisine, beautifully presented. Prawns and scallops are sautéed and served with crispy string leeks and a creamy Port sauce ($15). The salads are in a class by themselves.

La Bohème. 6427-112th Ave. ☎ **403/474-5693.** Reservations required. Main courses $7.95–$19.95. AE, MC, V. Mon–Sat 11am–3pm; Sun 11am–3:30pm; daily 5–11pm. FRENCH.

La Bohéme consists of two small, lace-curtained dining rooms in a historic building northeast of downtown. The cuisine is French, of course, and so is the wine selection, with a particular accent on Rhone Valley vintages. There's a wide selection of appetizers and light dishes, such as clam broth with saffron and smoked salmon, prawns, and marinated beef over wilted greens. Then it's a very difficult choice between, say, the lamb cutlets grilled with herbs and Dijon mustard or the entrecote steak in a Madeira and peppercorn sauce. To finish your meal, you can't do better than one of the pies—tangy and not oversweet. The restaurant also features some outstanding vegetarian entrées, such as a casserole of wild rice with provincial-style vegetables.

La Ronde. In the Crowne Plaza/Chateau Lacombe, 10111 Bellamy Hill. ☎ **403/428-6611.** Reservations recommended on weekends. Main courses $17.50–$29.95; fixed-price menus $30 or $35. AE, DC, ER, MC, V. Sun–Mon 5–10pm, Tues–Sat 5:30–10:30pm; Sun 10:30am–2pm. INTERNATIONAL.

Edmonton's only revolving restaurant is located atop the ivory tower of the Crowne Plaza. Luxurious without being ornate, La Ronde achieves its effect through the stunning panorama slowly unfolding below, plus quietly impeccable service.

The cuisine is classic, nothing nouvelle about it. There are a number of Albertan beef dishes, including a surf and turf combination with a fresh lobster ($36). Lighter dishes include a filet of sole with lemon butter, or panfried breast of pheasant stuffed with chestnut and apricot purée. The Sunday brunch here is very popular ($18.95 per person, but call to confirm this price). Of course, the panoramic views are on the house.

La Spiga Restaurant. 10133 125 St. ☎ **403/482-3100.** Reservations recommended on weekends. Main courses $13–$22. AE, DC, MC, V. Mon–Sat 5pm–midnight. ITALIAN.

One of Edmonton's best Italian restaurants, La Spiga is located along the gallery row in the trendy High Street neighborhood. This is nouveau Italian cooking, with an emphasis on fresh, stylish ingredients and unusual tastes and textures. The rack of lamb is marinated in fresh herbs and grappa; prawns and scallops are paired with a white wine lemon sauce and served over angel-hair pasta.

Moderate

✪ Bistro Praha. 10168-100A St. ☎ **403/424-4218.** Reservations recommended on weekends. Main courses $12.90–$16. AE, DC, ER, MC, V. Mon–Fri 11am–2am, Sat noon–2am, Sun 5pm–1am. EASTERN EUROPEAN.

Bistro Praha is one of several side-by-side casual restaurants—all with summer streetside seating—that take up the single block of 100A St (formerly a service alley). It's also the best of these restaurants, with a charming, wood-paneled interior, a mural-covered wall, and very good Eastern European cooking. The menu offers a wide selection of light dishes, convenient for a quick meal or a mid-afternoon snack. The entrée menu centers on schnitzels (there are three different kinds), as well as a wonderful roast goose with sauerkraut ($15). Desserts tend toward fancy imposing confections like Sacher torte. Service is friendly and relaxed. This is one of downtown Edmonton's favorite casual dining houses, and the clientele cosmopolitan, appreciative, mainly young and stylish.

Il Portico. 10012 107 St. ☎ **403/424-0707.** Reservations recommended on weekends. Main courses $11–$21. AE, DC, DISC, MC, V. Mon–Fri 11:30am–2pm; Mon–Sat 5:30–11pm, Sun 5–10pm. ITALIAN.

One of the most popular Italian restaurants in Edmonton, Il Portico has a wide menu of well-prepared traditional dishes. One of the specialties of the house is the various "platters"—for a set price diners are served a large variety of appetizers, meats, and pastas in relaxed family style comfort and feastlike abundance. An appetizer platter is $10, and comes with a wide selection of brochettes, salami, olives, and marinated vegetables. A meat platter ($20) comes with lamb chops, grilled chicken, and sausage, and two different choices of pasta. The regular menu features veal, chicken, and pasta favorites.

Ⓢ Sherlock Holmes. 10012-101A Ave. ☎ **403/426-7784.** Reservations not accepted. Main courses $6.50–$10. AE, DC, ER, MC, V. Mon–Sat 11:30am–2am. ENGLISH.

The Sherlock Holmes is a tremendously popular English-style pub with good local and regional beers on tap (as well as Guinness), and very good bar menu. The pub is housed in a charming building with black crossbeams on whitewashed walls and a picket fence around the outdoor patio. The menu has a few traditional English dishes (like fish and chips, and steak-and-kidney pie for $7), but there's a strong emphasis on new pub grub dishes, like chicken breast sandwiches, beef curry, burgers, and salads ($6 to $10).

There are two other Sherlock Holmes in Edmonton, one in the West Edmonton Mall, and the other in Old Strathcona at 10341 82nd Ave.

Inexpensive

Frank's Place. 10048-101A Ave. ☎ **403/424-4795.** Main courses $5.50–$7.95. MC, V. Mon–Fri 11am–9pm, Sat 5–9pm. ITALIAN.

Frank's Place shares the block with four other eateries, but keeps shorter hours and sticks to budget prices. With whitewashed walls, rural prints, and wooden shutters (but no windows), the place has a rustic look. The fare, however, is for the omnivorous and includes beer and wine. You can get very good chicken cacciatore or spaghetti with seafood sauce.

OLD STRATHCONA

South of downtown, across the river, along Whyte Avenue (otherwise known as 82nd Avenue) in the old center of Strathcona village, is a very dynamic, youthful business district dominated by artists, students, and Edmonton's other bohemian elements. Also here, amid the busy street life, are a great many cafes, bistros, and small restaurants. This is an excellent place to come to browse your way past dozens of good places to eat. In addition to the full-service restaurants listed below, you may want to explore **Terra Natural Good Market,** 10313 82nd Ave. (☎ 403/433-6807), a health-food store with a cafe; **The Stone Age,** 10338 81st Ave. (☎ 403/433-6807), a great place for slice of pizza and a salad; and ✪ **Block 1912,** 10361 82nd Ave., a friendly cafe with one refrigerated case full of great-looking salads, one full of eye-popping desserts, and an array of deli sandwiches.

Chianti. 10501 82nd Ave. ☎ **403/439-9829.** Reservations required. Main courses $5–$11. AE, DC, MC, V. Daily 11am–midnight. ITALIAN.

Chianti is a rarity among Italian restaurants: The food is very good and very inexpensive. Pasta dishes begin at $5 and run to $8 (for fettucine with scallops, smoked salmon, curry, and garlic), and even veal dishes (more than a dozen are offered!) and seafood specials barely top $10. Soups and salads start off at $2.25, so you can assemble a full meal here for the cost of appetizers at a pricier restaurant. Chianti's is located in a handsomely remodeled post office building; the restaurant isn't a secret, so it can be a busy and fairly crowded experience.

Da-De-O. 10548A 82nd Ave. ☎ **403/433-0930.** Main courses $7–$16. MC, V. Mon–Sat 11am–2am, Sun 3pm–2am. CAJUN/SOUTHERN.

This New Orleans–style diner is authentic right down to the low-tech, juke-box-at-your-table music system. The food is top notch, with good and goopy po' boy sandwiches ($7 to $9), fresh oysters, five kinds of jambalaya ($10 to $15), and a big selection of blackened and étoufée meats and seafood. Especially good is the Sorochan Angel, seafood in Pernod cream over angel-hair pasta. There's a whole page of appetizers and salads, so you can also relax in the vinyl-covered booths, listen to Billie Holiday, and graze through some chicken wings or crab fritters with a glass of beer.

Julio's Barrio. 10450 82nd Ave. ☎ **403/431-0774.** Main courses $9–$14. AE, MC, V. Mon 4–11pm, Tues–Thurs 11am–11pm, Fri–Sat 11am–midnight, Sun 2–10pm. MEXICAN.

This Mexican restaurant and watering hole is a great place to come and snack through several light dishes while quaffing drinks with friends. The food ranges from the traditional enchiladas and nachos to sizzling shrimp fajitas. The atmosphere is youthful, high energy, and minimalistically hip: No kitchy piñatas or scratchy recordings of marimba bands here.

The King & I. 10160 82nd Ave. ☎ **403/433-2222.** Main courses $9–$19. AE, MC, V. Mon–Thurs 11:30am–10:30pm, Fri 11:30am–11:30pm, Sat 4:30–11:30pm. THAI.

This is the place for excellent, zesty Thai food, which can be a real treat after the pervasive beef-rich cooking of western Canada. Many dishes are vegetarian, almost a novelty in Alberta. Various curries, ranging from mild to sizzling, are the specialty, as are rice and noodle dishes. For a real treat, try the lobster in curry sauce with asparagus ($19).

✪ **Packrat Louie Kitchen & Bar.** 10335 83rd Ave. ☎ **403/433-0123.** Reservations recommended on weekends. Main courses $8–$19. MC, V. Mon–Sat 11:30am–11:30pm. ITALIAN.

Bright and lively, this very popular bistro has a somewhat unlikely name, considering that this is one of Edmonton's finest purveyors of new Italian cooking. Menu choices range from specialty pizzas to fine entrée salads and on to grilled meats, chicken, and pasta. Most dishes cast an eye toward light or healthy preparations, without sacrificing complexity. A grilled chicken breast comes with an arresting mélange of puréed spinach and red bell pepper; grilled lamb chops are garnished simply with plenty of fresh tomatoes, feta cheese, and polenta.

Unheardof. 9602 82nd Ave. ☎ **403/432-0480.** Reservations required. Fixed-price menus $34 and $42. AE, MC, V. Tues–Sat seatings at 6:30 and 8:30pm. INTERNATIONAL.

Unheardof is a unique place, not only because of its name. The restaurant offers fixed-price menus only, which change weekly according to what's fresh and special, and to the chef's whim. The seven-course dinner is served according to classic French protocol (a couple of starters, then a fish, chicken, meat, salad, and dessert course); however, the chef doesn't particularly cook in a French mode. He has a lighter, more international touch, which makes eating this much food a slight possibility. A lighter five-course dinner is available on Tuesdays and Wednesdays only.

Veggies. 10331 82nd Ave. ☎ **403/432-7560.** Main courses $6–$10. AE, MC, V. Mon–Fri 11am–10pm, Sat 10am–10pm, Sun 11am–9pm. VEGETARIAN.

Vegetarian stir-fries, soups, curries, and pastas are the specialty at this lively, casual restaurant (actually, some chicken and fish make it onto the menu, just no red meat). There are special dishes for customers with food allergies as well.

Von's Steak & Fish House. 10309 81 Ave. ☎ **403/439-0041.** Reservations recommended on weekends. Main courses $13–$39. AE, MC, V. Mon–Sat 11:30am–10pm, Sun 5–10pm. STEAK/SEAFOOD.

One of the best steakhouses in Edmonton, Vons is a comfortable supper club with good Alberta beef; the prime rib here is excellent, as are the various steaks. If you've had your fill of red meat, try the pasta or fresh fish dishes.

EDMONTON AFTER DARK

Tickets to most events are available through **Ticketmaster** (☎ 403/451-8000). For a complete listing of current happenings, check the Friday arts section of the *Edmonton Journal* or the alternative arts weekly *See.*

THE TOP PERFORMING ARTS VENUES   A masterpiece of theatrical architecture, the **Citadel Theatre,** 9828 101A Ave. (☎ 403/426-4811), is not a playhouse in the conventional sense but a community project encompassing virtually every form of showcraft. The complex takes up the entire city block adjacent to Sir Winston Churchill Square. It looks like a gigantic greenhouse—more than half is glass-walled, and even the awnings are glass. Apart from auditoriums, it also has a magnificent indoor garden with a waterfall, as well as a restaurant. But the best feature of the complex is that it houses, under one roof, five different theaters adapted for different productions and distinct audiences, plus workshops and classrooms. The Citadel today is one of the largest, busiest, and most prolific theaters in Canada.

The **Jubilee Auditorium,** 11455 87th Ave. (☎ 403/427-2760), is the setting for a great variety of concert and ballet performances. They range from the Edmonton Symphony Orchestra to the Conservatoire de Ballet and jazz specialties like "A Nite in New Orleans."

DINNER THEATER   Edmonton has a pleasant abundance of theater restaurants. Different rules apply in the various establishments: In some your dinner tab includes the show; in others you pay extra.

The charming **Mayfield Dinner Theatre,** 16615 109th Ave. (☎ 403/483-4051), at the Mayfield Inn, combines excellent food with lighthearted, often sumptuously equipped, stage productions. Shows go on at 8pm nightly and at brunch time Sunday and Wednesday. Tickets cost $37.50 to $47.50 (meals included). Spoofy comedies and musical revues are the specialty at the lively **Celebrations Dinner Theatre,** 13103 Fort Rd. (☎ 403/448-9339), located in the Neighbourhood Inn. Shows are mounted Wednesday to Sunday evenings, and tickets cost $36 (meals included).

THE CLUB & BAR SCENE   The flashy, upscale country-and-western scene is the name of the game, with new places opening up all the time. But there's plenty else going on in clubs and bars if you're not into Garth Brooks and line-dancing. Most live music clubs charge a cover on weekends (usually $6 to $8).

The hottest country dance bar in town is **Cook County Saloon,** 8010 103rd St. (☎ 403/432-2665), with a changing lineup of western bands nightly. **Longriders Saloon,** 11733 78th St. (☎ 403/479-8700), has live country music six nights a week, as does the **Wild West Saloon,** 12912 50th St. (☎ 403/476-3388).

For something uniquely Edmonton but without the twang, check out the **Sidetrack Cafe,** 10333 112th St. (☎ 403/421-1326), the city's most versatile music venue. You get an Australian rock group one week, a musical comedy troupe the next, a blues band the following, progressive jazz after that, and so on.

The **Commercial Hotel,** 10329 82nd Ave. (☎ 403/439-5058), is a vintage hotel in Old Strathcona, with a popular billiard room, and a bar called Blues on Whyte, Edmonton's best blues club. **The Rev,** 10032 102 St. (☎ 403/424-2745), is the premier club for the alternative music scene. Edmonton's gay bar of choice is **The Roost,** 10345 104th St. (☎ 403/426-3150).

Straighter and more predictable is the **Hard Rock Cafe,** Bourbon Street, 1638 West Edmonton Mall (☎ 403/444-1905). Also in the mall is **Yuk Yuk's International,** Bourbon Street, 1646 West Edmonton Mall (☎ 403/481-YUKS), the Edmonton branch of a national chain of live stand-up comedy clubs. Shows are Wednesday through Saturday: weeknights at 9pm, weekends at 8:30 and 11pm. Admission is $6.50 to $10.75.

For something quieter, head to the **Rose and Crown,** 10235 101 St. (☎ 403/428-7111), for a pint of beer and game of darts. The most romantic place for a drink in the city is the **Library Bar** at the Hotel Macdonald, 10065 100th St. (☎ 403/424-5181).

GAMBLING   Gambling is a curious institution in Alberta. The money goes to charities (mostly) but the casinos are privately owned and—until recently—led a floating existence. Now they are located in permanent premises and have undergone considerable upscaling. They offer pleasant surroundings, licensed lounges, nonsmoking tables, and very amiable staff. The games are blackjack, roulette, baccarat, red dog, and sic bo; bets range from $1 to $100; and the play goes from Monday to Saturday, noon to midnight. Try your luck at **Casino ABS,** City Centre, 10549 102nd St. (☎ 403/424-WINS); or **Casino ABS,** Southside, 7055 Argyll Rd. (☎ 403/466-0199). The **Palace Casino,** 8770 170 St. (☎ 403/444-2112), operates in the West Edmonton Mall.

13 Side Trips from Edmonton

Elk Island National Park (☎ 403/998-3686), located on the Yellowhead Highway, 20 miles east of Edmonton, is one of the most compact and prettiest in the national parks system. It protects one of Canada's most endangered ecosystems and is the home and roaming ground to North America's largest and smallest mammals: The wood buffalo and the pygmy shrew (a tiny creature half the size of a mouse, but with the disposition of a tiger). The park has hiking trails, campgrounds, golf courses, a lake, and a sandy beach. A one-day vehicle permit costs $5.

The ✪ **Ukrainian Cultural Heritage Village** (☎ 403/662-3640) is an open-air museum and a park of living history 25 minutes east of Edmonton on Yellowhead Highway 16. The village has 30 restored historic buildings arranged in an authentic setting; the adjacent fields and pastures are planted and harvested according to period techniques. Visitors learn what life was like for Ukrainian pioneers in the 1892 to 1930 era through costumed interpreters who re-create the daily activities of the period. The village and interpretive center is definitely worth the drive, especially in midsummer, when you can watch horse-drawn wagons gathering hay and harvesting grain. Open from May 15 to September 6 every day from 10am to 6pm. Admission is $5.50 for adults, $2.25 for children (under six free).

At Vegreville, 25 miles east of the Ukrainian Village, stands the world's largest Ukrainian Easter egg, gaily painted and towering more than 30 feet tall. This "pysanka" was constructed in 1974 to commemorate the 100th anniversary of the arrival of the Royal Canadian Mounted Police in Alberta. You can camp all around the egg and, if you get there early in July, watch the annual Ukrainian Festival with singing, music, and leg-throwing folk dances.

Located 40 minutes south of Edmonton off Highway 2, the **Reynolds Alberta Museum** (☎ 403/352-5855) is a science and technology museum with specialties in agricultural engineering and transportation. The collection of vintage cars and period farm equipment is especially impressive, and there are hands-on activities to keep children busy. Adjoining the museum is Canada's **Aviation Hall of Fame,** with a hangar full of vintage airplanes. Admission is $5.50 adult, $2.25 for children, or $13 for a family. The museum is open year-round, 9am to 5pm.

14 Wood Buffalo National Park

Located in the far northeastern corner of Alberta is Wood Buffalo National Park, the world's largest, measuring 17,300 square miles—it's bigger than Switzerland. Two-thirds lie inside Alberta, one-third in the Northwest Territories.

The park was created for the specific purpose of preserving the last remaining herd of wood bison on earth. At the turn of the century these animals were near extinction. Today some 6,000 of the creatures roam their habitat, where you can see and snap them in droves.

The park is also the only known breeding ground for the whooping crane. Some 50 of these birds live here from April until October before migrating to their winter range along the Gulf of Mexico.

One of the problems faced by would-be visitors is simply getting to the park. By vehicle, it's 805 miles between Edmonton and Fort Smith, the park headquarters, over mostly gravel roads. Most visitors will find it easier to fly into Fort Smith on Canadian North Airlines, and once here, hook up with an outfitter who will arrange transport to the park and activities. The tours offered by **Subarctic Wildlife Adventures,** P.O. Box 685, Fort Smith, NT, X0E 0P0 (☎ 403/872-2467; fax 403/872-2116), offer naturalist-led excursions to many of the park's best wildlife-viewing areas. The shortest excursion into the park is three days, and explores the woods and wetlands near the park's famed salt plains, where wildlife gather to lick the naturally occurring minerals. Costs are $600 a person; longer trips are also available.

Vancouver 18

by Anistatia R. Miller and Jared M. Brown

Inveterate world travelers, Anistatia and Jared make their
home in Vancouver. In addition to their contributions
to *Frommer's Canada*, they are the authors of *Frommer's
Vancouver and Victoria*, 3rd Edition.

In the extreme southwestern corner of British Columbia, there is a
place where the mountains and ocean seem to have had a love affair
and given birth to a city. The city is Vancouver, and few towns have
been quite so wonderfully blessed with their setting as this one.

Rapidly growing and expanding at a dizzying rate, Vancouver has
attracted an influx of foreign money—especially from Hong Kong—
and has undergone a major construction boom. One native, returning after five years overseas, was even more wide-eyed than the dozen
tourists on our airport bus. "Amazing, amazing!" she kept repeating
to herself.

But development hasn't diminished the quality of life in Vancouver.
Where else can you ski a world-class mountain, sailboard, rock
climb, mountain bike, wilderness hike, and kayak all in the same day
(and find a Jacuzzi, a masseuse, and an all-night pharmacy to help
you recover afterward)? And the city has a rich cultural heritage to
discover as well, a heritage woven together from such diverse threads
as native Northwest Coast tribes and a thriving Asian community.

In 1995, Vancouver was ranked second only to Geneva out of
118 cities worldwide for "quality of life." But then again, perhaps
the surveyors were biased—they were, after all, from Geneva.

AN IMPORTANT NOTE ON PRICES & TAXES Unless
stated otherwise, **the prices cited in this guide are given in Canadian dollars,** which is good news for U.S. travelers because the
Canadian dollar is worth 25% less than the American dollar but buys
nearly as much. As we go to press, $1 Canadian is worth 75¢ U.S.,
which means that your $100-a-night hotel room will cost only U.S.
$75, and your $6 breakfast costs only U.S. $4.50.

Hotel rooms are subject to a 10% tax. The provincial sales tax is
6% (excluding food, restaurant meals, and children's clothing)—
and that's on top of the national goods and services tax (GST).

1 Orientation

ARRIVING

BY PLANE Daily direct flights between major U.S. cities and
Vancouver are offered by **Air Canada** (☎800/776-3000), **United
Airlines** (☎ 800/241-6522), **American Airlines** (☎ 800/433-7300),
Northwest Airlines (☎ 800/447-4747), and **America West**
(☎ 800/292-9378). **Continental** (☎ 800/231-0856) will fly you

to Denver or Seattle, then put you on an Air Canada flight to complete the trip. Vancouver International Airport is located 8 miles south of downtown Vancouver on an island. Currently, both the domestic and international flights arrive and depart from the old Main terminal building while work is being completed on a new terminal for international flights, set to open by mid-1996. To help pay for these improvements, there is an international departure surcharge of $10 per person; you must pay it when you leave the country. Domestic departures are charged $5 per person.

Tourist information centers, located on levels 1 and 2 (☎ 604/276-6101), are open to assist you daily from 6:30am to 11:30pm. There will also be information centers in the new building once it is completed.

Short-term and long-term parking is available at the airport (☎ 604/276-6106). Courtesy buses run to airport hotels, and a shuttle bus links the Main and South Terminals. The airport is easily accessible by three bridges. Travelers heading into Vancouver will take the Arthur Laing Bridge, which leads directly into Granville Street (Highway 99)—the most direct route to downtown.

There is airport bus service to downtown Vancouver's major hotels. Light-green-colored **YVR Airporter buses** (☎ 602/244-9888) leave from level 2 every 15 minutes daily from 6:30am to 10:30pm and every 30 minutes from 10:30pm to 12:15am. The 30-minute ride costs $9 for adults one way ($7 for seniors, $5 for children) and $15 for adults round-trip ($14 for seniors, $10 for children). It drops off at a few called-out stops on Granville Street and at major downtown locations.

If you don't mind transferring from one bus to another with your luggage and you have spare time, you can take public transportation. B.C. Transit bus no. 100 stops at both terminals. At the Marine Drive stop, get off and transfer to bus no. 20 or 17, both of which take you into downtown Vancouver. B.C. Transit fares are $1.50 during off-peak hours and $2.50 during rush hours.

The average taxi fare from the airport to a downtown Vancouver hotel is $35 plus tip. There are nearly 400 taxis serving the airport.

AirLimo (☎ 604/273-1331) is the city's only flat-rate limousine service. It operates 24 hours a day. The ride from the airport to downtown Vancouver is $26 per trip, not per person. During the rush hour, this can be cheaper than taking a cab; they accept all major credit cards.

Most of the car-rental firms here have airport counters and shuttles. Make advance reservations for fast check-in and guaranteed vehicle availability—especially if you want a four-wheel drive vehicle or a compact car (see "Getting Around," below).

BY CAR   You'll probably be driving into Vancouver along one of two routes. U.S. Interstate 5 from Seattle intersects Highway 99 when you cross the border at the Peace Arch Station. You pass under the Fraser River through the George Massey Tunnel, drive through Richmond, and cross the Oak Street Bridge. The highway ends right here and becomes Oak Street, a busy urban thoroughfare. Turn left onto 70th Avenue; then, six blocks later, turn right onto Granville Street. This is the business extension of Highway 99, which heads directly into downtown via the Granville Street Bridge.

Trans-Canada Highway 1 is a limited-access freeway that goes all the way to Vancouver's eastern boundary. To reach central Vancouver, exit at Cassiar Street and turn left at the first light onto Hastings Street (Highway 7A), which is adjacent to Exhibition Park. Follow Hastings Street 4 miles into downtown. To enter North Vancouver, stay on Highway 1 and cross the Second Narrows Bridge.

BY TRAIN   **VIA Rail Canada,** 1150 Station St. (☎ 604/669-3050), connects with Amtrak at Winnipeg. From there, you travel on a spectacular route that runs between

Calgary and Vancouver. Lake Louise's beautiful alpine scenery is just part of this enjoyable journey. **Amtrak** (☎ 800/872-7245) also has a direct route from San Diego to Vancouver that stops at all major U.S. West Coast cities. **B.C. Rail,** 1311 W. First St., North Vancouver (☎ 604/631-3500), connects Vancouver to other destinations around the province, including Whistler. The main Vancouver railway station is at 1150 Station St., near Main Street and Terminal Avenue (☎ 604/669-3050). You can reach downtown Vancouver from there by cab for about $5. One block from the station is the SkyTrain's main station. Within minutes, you'll arrive downtown. (Granville and Waterfront Stations are two and four stops away, respectively.)

BY BUS **Greyhound Bus Lines** (☎ 604/662-3222) and **Pacific Coach Lines** (☎ 604/662-8074) also have terminals at the 1150 Station St. train station.

Quick Coach Lines (☎ 604/526-2836) connects Vancouver to Seattle-Tacoma International Airport. The bus stops at the Delta Pacific Inn, 10251 St. Edwards St., and the Sandman Inn, 180 W. Georgia St. in Richmond, a suburb of Vancouver. The three-hour ride costs U.S. $32 one way, U.S. $60 round-trip.

BY SHIP/FERRY The **Canada Place** cruise-ship terminal, at the base of Burrard Street (☎ 604/666-4452), is a landmark pier with multiple sails extending into the harbor from the downtown's central business district. Cunard, Princess, Royal Viking, and Sitmar lines sail from San Francisco to Alaska with stopovers in Vancouver to load new passengers.

B.C. Ferries (☎ 604/669-1211) arrive from Victoria at the dock in Tsawwassen, which is a few miles outside the city. To reach Vancouver from the dock, take Highway 17 until it joins Highway 99 just before the George Massey Tunnel, then follow the driving directions given under "By Car," above.

Ferries from Nanaimo dock at Horseshoe Bay in West Vancouver. To reach downtown Vancouver, take the Trans-Canada Highway (Highway 1/Route 99) south to North Vancouver. The Taylor Way South exit (Exit 14) leads into Lion's Gate Bridge and downtown Vancouver's West End.

VISITOR INFORMATION

The **Vancouver Travel InfoCentre** is located at 200 Burrard St. (☎ 604/683-2000). It is open daily May through Labor Day from 8am to 6pm; and during the rest of the year Monday through Saturday from 8:30am to 5:30pm. Two smaller InfoCentres operate only during the summer. One is a kiosk outside of Eaton's department store at the corner of Georgia and Granville streets and is open Tuesday to Friday from 10am to 5pm. The other is in Stanley Park and is open daily from 9am to 5pm.

Check out *Vancouver* magazine, a monthly magazine, and *The Georgia Straight*, a free weekly tabloid newspaper, for more information about what's going on in the city and surrounds. Gay travelers will want to pick up a copy of *Xtra! West*, the free biweekly tabloid available throughout the West End. This will link you with metropolitan services, entertainment, and even the political scene.

CITY LAYOUT

Downtown Vancouver and Stanley Park are on the upraised thumb of the mitten-shaped Vancouver peninsula. Pointing northward, this main business district is bordered on the west by English Bay; on the north and east by the Burrard Inlet; and on the south by False Creek.

MAIN ARTERIES & STREETS Two main downtown thoroughfares run westward from Chinatown and B.C. Place to the West End and Stanley Park. **Robson Street** starts at B.C. Place on Beatty Street, flows through the West End's tourist

Greater Vancouver

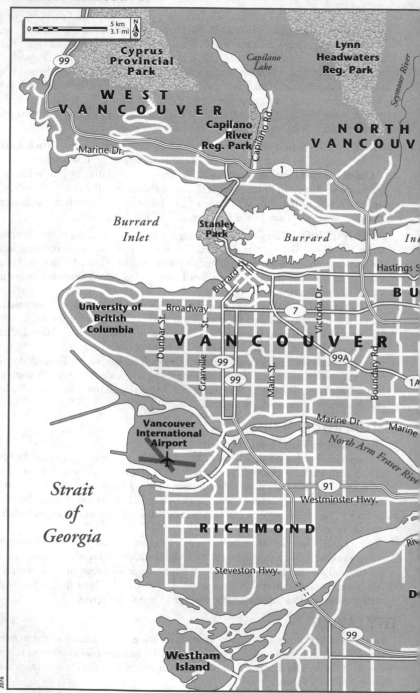

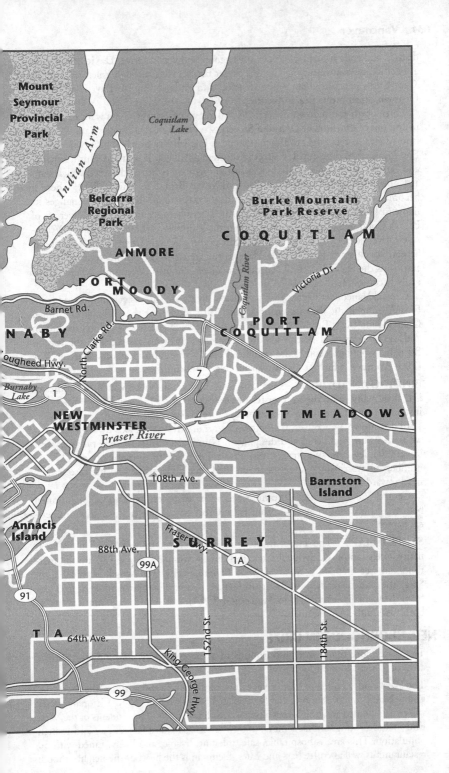

district, and ends at Stanley Park's Lost Lagoon on Lagoon Drive. **Davie Street** starts at Pacific Boulevard near the Cambie Street Bridge, runs through Yaletown and the West End's residential/shopping district, and ends at English Bay Beach where Denman Street meets Beach Avenue.

Three north-south downtown streets will get you everywhere you want to go both in and out of downtown. **Denman Street,** two blocks east of Stanley Park, stretches from West Georgia Street to Beach Avenue at English Bay Beach. This is where West End locals go to dine out. It's also the shortest north-south route to Third, Second, and English Bay beaches. Eight blocks east of Denman is **Burrard Street,** which starts at Canada Place and crosses the Burrard Street Bridge to Vanier Park, where it becomes Cornwall Avenue. As it heads due west through Kitsilano, it changes its name to Point Grey Road and NW Marine Drive before entering the University of British Columbia campus. It eventually turns southward when it becomes SW Marine Drive, before ending at Granville Street and the Oak Street Bridge. **Granville Street,** which starts near Canada Place to the west and the SeaBus terminal to the east, runs the entire length of central Vancouver south to Richmond, where it officially becomes Highway 99.

Central Vancouver's main east-west cross streets are successively numbered from First Avenue at the downtown bridges to 70th Avenue at the Oak Street Bridge. Granville intersects **Broadway (10th Avenue),** which goes westward to Greektown and the University of British Columbia campus and runs eastward all the way to Burnaby, where it becomes the Lougheed Highway. It also intersects **Marine Way (70th Avenue),** which heads eastward to New Westminster.

FINDING AN ADDRESS One thing you should note about Vancouver addresses is that in many cases, the suite or room number precedes the building number. For instance, 100-1250 Robson St. is actually Suite 100 at 1250 Robson.

In downtown Vancouver, Chinatown's Carrall Street is the axis from which east-west streets are numbered and designated. Numbers increase as they progress west toward Stanley Park and increase east as they head toward Burnaby Street. The low numbers on north-south streets start on the Canada Place side and increase as they head toward False Creek.

Central Vancouver uses Ontario Street as its east-west axis, and as mentioned before, all north-south avenues from False Creek to the Fraser River have numerical names.

STREET MAPS The Travel InfoCentres (see "Visitor Information," above) and many hotels can provide you with detailed downtown maps. A good all-around metropolitan area map is the *Rand McNally Vancouver* city map, which is available for $3 at the Vancouver Airport Tourism Centre booth. The best map we found was from the Canadian Automobile Association (CAA). It is not for sale, but it is free to both AAA and CAA members.

NEIGHBORHOODS IN BRIEF

There are more than 20 neighborhoods in Vancouver, but the following are the areas of greatest interest to visitors.

The West End Home to Vancouver's upper crust in Edwardian times, the West End is now North America's most densely populated neighborhood. A few Victorian houses still remain nestled amid high-rises along its tree-lined streets. The residents of the West End include young adults, seniors, and Western Canada's largest gay and lesbian population. This area is hospitable, safe, tolerant, livable, and lively. Lined with 50 restaurants as well as coffee bars and cafes, Denman is the heart of the neighborhood.

Yaletown   Once a seedy stretch of warehouses, Yaletown is undergoing a transformation as these structures are converted into art galleries, boutiques, and loft apartments for architects, designers, and filmmakers. With a nod toward Manhattan's TriBeCa or SoHo, this is a hip district where billiard parlor/coffee bars and cybercafes have replaced the old saloons and streetwalkers.

Chinatown   Vancouver has the third largest Asian community in North America (only the Chinatowns in San Francisco and New York are bigger). Even though the newest wave of immigrants are well-heeled Hong Kong families who live in Richmond, Vancouver's traditional Chinatown is still a viable, historic cultural center worth visiting for its classic Ming Dynasty garden (the first built in North America), restaurants, and shops. It is concentrated along Hastings, Pender, Keefer, and Georgia Streets from Carrall to Gore.

False Creek   Once an industrial wasteland, False Creek has recently become a residential area surrounding Granville Island's public market, marina, artists' studios, theaters, and restaurants.

Kitsilano   Kitsilano (affectionately known as "Kits") and Point Grey stretch west from Vanier Park at the mouth of False Creek to the University of British Columbia. Sandy beaches, including Jericho, Kitsilano, Point Grey, and Wreck, edge its coastline. **Greektown** is also part of this formerly Haight-Ashbury–style district, which has gentrified during the last decade.

2 Getting Around

BY PUBLIC TRANSPORTATION

The **Vancouver Regional Transit System (B.C. Transit),** 1100-1200 W. 73rd Ave. (☎ 604/521-0400), runs electrically powered buses, the SeaBus catamaran ferries, and the magnetic-rail SkyTrain. It's an ecologically conscious, highly reliable, and inexpensive way to get everywhere in Vancouver, including the ski slopes. Regular service on the main routes runs from 5am to 2am, and less frequent "Owl" service operates on several downtown-suburban routes until 4:20am.

   Fares are the same for the buses, SeaBus, and SkyTrain. One-way, all-zone, nonpeak fares are $1.50 for adults and 75¢ for seniors and children ages 5 to 13. Free transfers, available upon boarding, are good for any direction of travel as well for the SkyTrain and SeaBus but have a 90-minute travel limit.

   Some key **bus routes** to keep in mind include the following: no. 8 (Robson Street), no. 51 (Granville Island), no. 246 (North Vancouver), no. 250 (West Vancouver–Horseshoe Bay), and nos. 4 and 10 (UBC-Exhibition Park via Granville St. downtown). One of the most popular summertime-only bus routes is the hourly no. 52 "Around the Park" service through Stanley Park.

   The **SkyTrain** is a fully computerized, magnetic-rail, rapid-transit train that services 20 stations in its 35-minute ride from downtown Vancouver east to Surrey via Burnaby and New Westminster.

   The SS *Beaver* and SS *Otter* catamaran **SeaBuses** annually serve more than 400,000 passengers—including cyclists and people in wheelchairs—year-round on a scenic, 12-minute commute between downtown's Waterfront Station and North Vancouver's Lonsdale Quay. On weekdays, they leave every 15 minutes from 6:15am to 6:30pm, then every 30 minutes until 1am. On weekends, they run about every 30 minutes from 6:15am to 1am.

   For more information about **wheelchair-accessible public transportation,** contact B.C. Transit (☎ 604/264-5000) and ask for its brochure *Rider's Guide to*

Accessible Transit. Most SkyTrain stations and the SeaBus are wheelchair accessible. Most buses are equipped with lifts.

BY CAR

If you're planning a lot of out-of-town activities, then rent a car or bring your own. If you have a city-bound agenda, mass transit is quick, consistent, and doesn't require you to vie for scarce parking spots. If you are a die-hard driver, then be forewarned that gas prices are high. Driving laws are similar to those for much of the United States; you can turn right on red after coming to a full stop, seat belts are mandatory, children under five must be in a child seat, and motorcyclists must wear helmets.

Members of the American Automobile Association (AAA) can get assistance from the **Canadian Automobile Association (CAA)** at 999 W. Broadway, Vancouver (☎ 604/268-5600 or road service 604/293-2222).

RENTALS   You can rent a vehicle from the following local branches of car-rental agencies: **Avis,** 757 Hornby St. (☎ 604/682-1621 or 800/879-2847); **Budget,** 450 W. Georgia St. (☎ 604/668-7000, 800/527-0700, or 800/268-8900); **Hertz Canada,** 1128 Seymour St. (☎ 604/688-2411, 800/654-3131, or 800/263-0600); or **Thrifty,** 1055 W. Georgia St. (☎ 604/688-2207 or 800/367-2277). These firms all have counters at the airport as well. **C.C. Canada Camper R.V. Rentals,** 1080 Millcarch St., Richmond (☎ 604/327-3003), specializes in recreational vehicles.

PARKING   All major downtown hotels have guest parking; rates vary from free to $20. There's public parking at Robson Square (enter at Smythe and Howe streets); the Pacific Centre (Howe and Dunsmuir streets); and The Bay (Richards near Dunsmuir Street). You'll also find parking lots at Thurlow and Georgia streets, Thurlow and Alberni streets, and Robson and Seymour streets.

BY FERRY

Crossing False Creek to Vanier Park or Granville Island by one of the blue miniferries is cheap and fun. The Aquabus docks at the foot of Howe Street and takes you to Granville Island's public market. The **Granville Island Ferry** docks at Sunset Beach below the Burrard Street Bridge and the Aquatic Centre. It goes to both Vanier Park and Granville Island for $1.50 adults, 75¢ for seniors and children. Ferries to Granville Island leave every five minutes from 7am to 10pm. **Ferries to Vanier Park** leave every 15 minutes from 10am to 8pm.

BY TAXI

Taxi fares are reasonable unless you're traveling late at night, when you'll have to pay double. In the downtown area, most trips are less than $6 (not including tip).

Taxis are easy to hail on downtown streets and at major hotels. If you need one in outlying areas, call for a pick-up from **Black Top** (☎ 604/731-1111), **Yellow Cab** (☎ 604/681-1111), or **MacLure's** (☎ 604/731-9211).

BY BICYCLE

Biking is the hottest mode of transportation in town. There are bike lanes throughout the city and paved paths along parks and beaches (see "Outdoor Activities & Spectator Sports," later in this chapter). Helmets are mandatory, and riding on sidewalks is illegal, except where bike paths are indicated.

B.C. Transit's Cycling B.C. (☎ 604/737-3034) accommodates bikers on the SkyTrain and buses by providing Bike and Ride lockers at all Park and Ride parking lots. They also dispense loads of information about events, bike touring, and cycle insurance. Many downtown parking lots and garages also have bike racks you can use for no charge.

You can take your bike on the SeaBus any time except rush hours (no extra charge). Bicycles are not allowed in the George Massey Tunnel, but a tunnel shuttle operates four times daily from mid-May to September. From May 1 to Victoria Day (the third weekend of May), the service operates on weekends only.

ON FOOT

Walking is the best way to discover this city. Downtown is about one square mile in area, so why hail a cab? We highly recommend strolling along the city's many beaches, thickly forested parks, and urban corridors.

FAST FACTS: Vancouver

American Express The local branch is at 666 Burrard St. (☎ 604/669-2813). It's open Monday through Friday 8:30am to 5:30pm and Saturday 10am to 4pm.

ATMs Most accept Plus cards. Only the Hong Kong Bank of Canada and the Bank of Montreal accept Cirrus cards.

Camera Repair Camtex Camera, 201-1855 Burrard St. (☎ 604/734-0242), is a good repair shop for new and old cameras.

Car Rentals See "Getting Around," earlier in this chapter.

Currency Exchange The best exchange rates are at Remo Exchange, 789 Burrard St., near Robson Street (☎ 604/685-4921). Banks also have a better exchange rate than most foreign exchanges.

Doctors and Dentists Hotels usually have a doctor and a dentist on call. Vancouver Medical Clinics, Bentall Centre, 1055 Dunsmuir St. (☎ 604/683-8138), is a drop-in clinic open Monday through Friday 8am to 4:30pm. Dentists Denta Centre, Bentall Centre, 1055 Dunsmuir St. (☎ 604/669-6700), is by appointment only. It is open Monday through Thursday from 8am to 5pm.

Drugstores (Late-Night Pharmacies) Shopper's Drug Mart, 1125 Davie St. (☎ 604/685-6445), is open 24 hours a day. Several Safeway supermarkets have late-night pharmacies, including one at the corner of Robson and Denman streets, which is open until midnight.

Embassies and Consulates The U.S. Consulate is at 1095 W. Pender St. (☎ 604/685-4311). The British Consulate is at 1111 Melville St. (☎ 604/683-4421). The Australian Consulate is at 604-999 Canada Place (☎ 604/684-1177).

Emergencies Dial 911 for fire, police, ambulance, and poison control.

Hospitals St. Paul's Hospital is downtown at 1081 Burrard St. (☎ 604/682-2344). Central Vancouver hospitals include the following: Vancouver Hospital Health and Sciences Centre, 855 W. 12th Ave. (☎ 604/875-4111); and British Columbia's Children's Hospital, 4480 Oak St. (☎ 604/875-2345). In North Vancouver, there is Lions Gate Hospital, 231 E. 15th St. (☎ 604/988-3131).

Hotlines The Royal Canadian Mounted Police Tourist Alert is open for urgent messages only (☎ 604/264-2466) May through August. Other good numbers to keep handy are the following: Crisis Centre (☎ 604/872-3311); Rape Crisis Centre (☎ 604/255-6344); Victims of Violence (☎ 800/563-0808); Poison Control Centre (☎ 604/682-5050); Crime Stoppers (☎ 604/669-8477); SPCA animal emergency (☎ 604/879-7343); and B.C. Highway Conditions (☎ 604/525-4997).

Information   See "Visitor Information," earlier in this chapter.

Liquor Laws   The legal drinking age in British Columbia is 19. Spirits are sold only in government liquor stores, but beer and wine can be purchased from specially licensed, privately owned stores and pubs. Last call at the city's restaurant bars and cocktail lounges is 2am.

Luggage Storage/Lockers   Most downtown hotels will gladly hold your luggage before or after your stay. This service is usually free for guests. Lockers are available at the main Vancouver railway station, Pacific Central Station, 1150 Station St., near Main Street and Terminal Avenue south of Chinatown (☎ 604/669-3050). You can store your belongings for about $1.50 per day.

Newspapers   The two local papers are the *Vancouver Sun* (which comes out Monday through Saturday) and *The Province* (which comes out Sunday through Friday). Other newsworthy papers are *The Financial Times of Canada* and the national *The Globe and Mail.* The weekly entertainment paper *The Georgia Straight* comes out on Thursdays.

Police   Dial 911. The Vancouver City Police can be reached at ☎ 604/665-3321. The Royal Canadian Mounted Police handle most cases for tourists. They can be reached at ☎ 604/264-3111.

Post Office   The main post office is at West Georgia and Homer streets. It's open Monday through Friday 8am to 5:30pm. You can also buy stamps at outlets displaying a "Postal Services" sign such as London Drugs in the Denman Plaza Centre.

Safety   Crime rates are relatively low in Vancouver, but it's best not to let your guard down. Crimes of opportunity such as the theft of items from unlocked cars are most common. Granville Street between Robson Street and False Creek is sketchy at night. There are a lot of transient types milling around amid panhandlers and the homeless. Likewise, the areas surrounding the bus terminal, Chinatown, and Gastown are technically skid rows that should be avoided late at night.

Taxes   Hotel rooms are subject to a 10% tax. The provincial sales tax is 6% (excluding food, restaurant meals, and children's clothing), and there's the 7% federal GST. For specific questions, call the B.C. Consumer Taxation Branch (☎ 604/660-4500).

Time   Vancouver is in the Pacific time zone (as are Seattle and San Francisco). Daylight saving time applies here, too, beginning in April and ending in October.

Transit Information   The B.C. Transit phone number is ☎ 604/521-0400.

Weather   Call ☎ 604/664-9010 or 604/664-9032 for weather updates; you can get marine forecasts by dialing ☎ 604/270-7411. Each local ski resort has its own snow report line.

3 Accommodations

In the past year, five new hotels have opened in Vancouver, many others have undergone extensive renovations, and good-natured competition has flourished among all the city's hostelries. So no matter what your budget, there's no reason to settle for second best.

Rates do not include the 10% provincial accommodations tax or the 7% goods and services tax (GST).

Reservations are highly recommended from June through September and, of course, during holidays. If you have trouble finding a room, call Tourism Vancouver's hotline **Discover British Columbia** (☎ 800/663-6000). They can make arrangements for you by consulting their extensive listings, which are updated daily.

If you prefer to stay in a bed-and-breakfast, the **Beachside Bed and Breakfast Registry,** 4208 Evergreen Ave., West Vancouver (☎ 604/922-7773 or 800/563-3311), can help you. Rates average $40 to $80 per double; $75 to $180 for a luxury room. In addition, the listings below include a few B&Bs.

Most of the large hotels listed below offer no-smoking rooms or floors; ask for one when you make your reservation if it's important to you.

DOWNTOWN

All downtown hotels are within reasonable walking distance of shops, restaurants, and attractions. Most of the area is safe, though as one Vancouverite put it, "Whatever you do, don't reserve anything on Granville Street or Hastings Street unless you enjoy a wide, interesting, and exciting series of encounters with the weird and dangerous." Granville Street is somewhat like New York City's 42nd Street—it's filled with theaters, cheap hotels, and occasional seedy characters. East Hastings Street, downtown Vancouver's skid row, has rundown hotels, prostitutes, and drug addicts. This street is particularly dangerous after dark.

You can get to the downtown hotels by taking the SkyTrain to the Granville or Burrard stops, which are just a few blocks apart. The Waterfront Station will leave you close to the Pan-Pacific and Waterfront Centre Hotels. Get off at Stadium Station for the Georgian Court Hotel, Rosedale on Robson, and YWCA. The no. 8 bus will take you to the West End hotels, and the no. 4 or 10 buses will get you to hotels near False Creek.

VERY EXPENSIVE

Four Seasons Hotel. 791 W. Georgia St., Vancouver, BC, V6C 2T4. ☎ **604/689-9333** or 800/332-3442. Fax 604/684-4555. 330 rms, 55 suites. A/C MINIBAR TV TEL. Year-round $285–$385 double; $335–$900 suite. AE, CB, DC, ER, JCB, MC, V. Parking $16.

This modern 28-story palace sits atop the Pacific Centre shopping complex; it's so well hidden that you could walk right past without noticing. Once inside, however, you are instantly immersed in understated luxury. Standard rooms aren't large, however, so for more space, try a corner deluxe or deluxe Four Seasons room. Wheelchair-accessible rooms are available.

    Dining/Entertainment: Chartwells, on the second floor, is one of Vancouver's finest restaurants.

    Services: Concierge, 24-hour room service, laundry and valet service, and twice-daily housekeeping. Children get cookies and milk in the evening as well as their own special room service menus and robes.

    Facilities: Indoor/outdoor pool, a fitness centerweight/exercise room, aerobics classes, whirlpool, and saunas.

Hotel Vancouver. 900 W. Georgia St., Vancouver, BC, V6C 2W6. ☎ **604/684-3131** or 800/441-1414. Fax 604/662-1929. 466 rms, 42 suites. A/C MINIBAR TV TEL. From $245 double; from $260 suite. AE, CB, DC, DISC, ER, MC, V. Parking $13.

This is the grand dame of the city's hotels. Designed on a generous scale, the Vancouver has a feeling of wonderful spaciousness. The bedrooms, offering city, harbor, and mountain views, are reasonably large. Wheelchair-accessible units are available. The best rooms are on the Entrée Gold floors with upgraded furniture and extraspecial service: a special concierge and check-in/out service, as well as a host of complimentary services including continental breakfast, a health club, free local calls, shoeshine, and afternoon tea with hors d'oeuvres.

Dining/Entertainment: The Panorama Roof is one of Vancouver's plushest food and dance spots. The ground-floor informal restaurant serves three meals a day.

Services: 24-hour room service, valet and laundry service.

Facilities: Indoor pool, a wading pool, Jacuzzi, health club with weight room, sauna, tanning salon, and much more.

Metropolitan Hotel Vancouver. 645 Howe St., Vancouver, BC, V6C 2Y9. ☎ 604/687-1122 or 800/877-1133. Fax 604/689-7044. 179 rms, 18 suites. A/C MINIBAR TV TEL. May–Sept $260 double; Oct–Apr $220 double. Suites to $1,500. Children stay free in their parents' room; those under six eat free in the two restaurants when accompanied by a paying adult. AE, DC, ER, JCB, MC, V. Underground valet parking $16.

The decor in the soundproof guest rooms in this elegant 18-story hotel is tastefully subdued and efficient; most units have small balconies. We recommend the studio suites, which are much roomier and only slightly more expensive. Business Zone rooms and suites (for an additional $15) have all the necessary office amenities. Small pets are accepted.

Services: 24-hour room service, concierge, valet.

Facilities: Lap pool, Jacuzzi, steam room, squash and racquetball courts, an exercise room, saunas, and a sundeck.

Pan-Pacific Hotel Vancouver. 300-999 Canada Place, Vancouver, BC, V6C 3B5. ☎ 604/662-8111 or 800/937-1515. Fax 604/662-3815. 467 rms, 39 suites. A/C MINIBAR TV TEL. Mid-Apr–Nov $250–$270 double; Dec–mid-Apr $210–$235 double; year-round $200–$900 suite. AE, DC, ER, MC, V. Valet parking $18.

Apart from Vancouver's natural surroundings, the city's most distinctive landmark is Canada Place, with its five soaring white-Teflon sails, reminiscent of a giant vessel leaving port. It houses the Vancouver Trade and Convention Centre and the Alaskan cruise ship terminal. Adjoining it is this spectacular hotel, rising 23 stories above. Rooms are large and elegant; try to get a harbor-view room—the views are terrific.

Dining/Entertainment: Whether you stay here or not, The Five Sails restaurant is worth a visit; it's one of the city's best. See Section 4, "Dining," later in this chapter, for a review.

Services: 24-hour room service.

Facilities: There's an outstanding health club, which guests can use for an additional $15.

⑤ The Sutton Place Hotel. 845 Burrard St., Vancouver, BC, V6Z 2K6. ☎ 604/682-5511 or 800/543-4300. Fax 604/682-5513. 397 rms, 47 suites. A/C MINIBAR TV TEL. May–Sept $215–$295 double, $350–$450 suite; Oct–Apr $190–$220 double, $350–$450 suite. AE, CB, DC, DISC, JCB, MC, V. Underground valet parking $14.95.

This modern, 21-story luxury property (formerly Le Meridien) manages to maintain the feel of a small, elegant European-style hotel in both its short-stay and long-stay towers. Rooms are elegantly furnished and immaculately maintained. Four units are wheelchair accessible.

Dining/Entertainment: There are two excellent restaurants and a dark, wood-paneled lounge.

Services: Concierge, 24-hour room service, limo service, and laundry/valet service with 24-hour pressing.

Facilities: The indoor pool has an adjoining outdoor sundeck, and there's a full spa.

⚫ **Waterfront Centre Hotel.** 900 Canada Place Way, Vancouver, BC, V6C 3L5. ☎ **604/ 691-1991** or 800/828-7447. Fax 604/691-1999. 489 rms, 29 suites. A/C MINIBAR TV TEL. Nov– late Apr $220–$260 double; late Apr–Oct $225–$275 double; year-round $350–$1,700 suite. AE, CB, DC, ER, MC, V. Parking $12.

With 23 stories of reflective blue glass, this Canadian-Pacific hotel takes great advantage of its location on the harbor—70% of the rooms have spectacular harbor and mountain views. This hotel is a leader in recycling and reducing environmental impact and manages not to compromise on service in the process. A concourse links the hotel to the rest of Waterfront Centre, Canada Place, and the Cruise Ship Terminal. The rooms are large, with elegant blonde wood furnishings, original art on the walls, and spacious marble bathrooms. Wheelchair-accessible rooms are available.

Dining/Entertainment: There is a restaurant and lounge on the lobby level.

Services: 24-hour room service.

Facilities: Full-service health club, heated outdoor pool.

EXPENSIVE

Georgian Court Hotel. 773 Beatty St., Vancouver, BC, V6B 2M4. ☎ **604/682-5555** or 800/ 663-1155. Fax 604/682-8830. 160 rms, 20 suites. A/C MINIBAR TV TEL. May–Sept $150–$170 double; Oct–Apr $115–$135 double. AE, DC, ER, MC, V. Parking $6.

This 14-story brick building located directly across the street from B.C. Place Stadium is truly a class act. It's ideal for sports fans and trade-show attendees. The rooms are large and clean, the decor dark and masculine; some units are wheelchair accessible. The best views are from the front rooms, dominated by the stadium's white dome.

Dining/Entertainment: The William Tell Restaurant serves classic Swiss cuisine prepared by B.C. and Yukon Restaurant Association's 1995 Restaurateur of the Year, Erwin Doebeli.

Facilities: Exercise room with weights, Lifecycle, Stairmaster, whirlpool, sauna, and an indoor pool.

⑤ **Rosedale on Robson Suite Hotel.** 838 Hamilton (at Robson Street), Vancouver, BC, V6B 5W4. ☎ **604/689-8033** or 800/661-8870. 275 studio, one-, and two-bedroom suites with kitchens. A/C MINIBAR TV TEL. May–Oct $145–$250 double; Nov–Apr $100–$210 double; year-round $470 suite. AE, DC, ER, MC, V. Parking $7.50.

You arrive at this hotel via a covered driveway and are welcomed into the grand marble lobby. You'll find Library Square, the theaters, and the stadiums all within a few blocks. The suites feature separate living rooms (except for the 12 studios), two TVs, and full kitchenettes. Dishes and cooking utensils are available on request. Rooms are not huge, but bay windows and scaled furnishings give them a feeling of spaciousness. Upper-floor suites have furnished terraces and great city views. Wheelchair-accessible rooms are available. Amenities include room service (from 6:30am to midnight), concierge, computer and fax connections, indoor pool, Jacuzzi, sauna, weight/exercise room, and gift shop.

⚫ **Wedgewood Hotel.** 845 Hornby St., Vancouver, BC, V6Z 1V1. ☎ **604/689-7777** or 800/ 663-0666. Fax 604/688-3074. 59 rms, 34 suites. A/C MINIBAR TV TEL. $190–$260 double; $340–$360 suite; $440–$460 penthouse. AE, CB, DC, ER, JCB, MC, V. Underground valet parking $10.

The eclectic decor at this hotel blends French provincial, Italianate, and Edwardian styles. On weekdays, it is frequented by a corporate crowd; on weekends, it becomes a romantic getaway. All guest rooms have landscaped balconies overlooking Robson Square, and you'll be greeted by a box of chocolates.

Dining/Entertainment: Bacchus Ristorante serves outstanding northern Italian cuisine; see Section 4, "Dining," later in this chapter for a review.

Services: 24-hour room service, twice-daily housekeeping, laundry service, hairstylist.

MODERATE

Days Inn Downtown. 921 W. Pender St., Vancouver, BC, V6C 1M2. ☎ **604/681-4335** or 800/325-2525. Fax 604/681-7808. 80 rms, 5 suites. TV TEL. May–Sept $120–$140 double, $160 suite; Oct–Apr $89–$109 double, $119 suite. AE, DC, DISC, ER, JCB, MC, V. Free parking.

The only moderately priced hotel in the downtown business center, this well-maintained seven-story property is more than 70 years old. Standard rooms are not large. There is no room service, no view, and only basic amenities. Rooms, however, are quiet and clean, with Casablanca-style ceiling fans, and in-room movies are free.

Quality Hotel Downtown/The Inn at False Creek. 1335 Howe St. (at Davie Street), Vancouver, BC, V6Z 1R7. ☎ **604/682-0229** or 800/663-8474. Fax 604/662-7566. 157 rms, 20 suites. A/C TV TEL. May 1–Oct 12 $130 double, $140–$160 suite; Oct 13–Apr 30 $89 double, $99–$109 suite. AE, CB, DC, ER, MC, V. Parking $5.

This seven-story hotel, ideal for families, blends an easy, elegant southwestern style with Mexican art, pottery, and rugs. The one-bedroom suites even have fully equipped kitchens. Rooms on the back side are preferable because the hotel lies beside the Granville Bridge on-ramp. Noise is not a problem, however, thanks to double-pane windows and dark-out curtains. Rooms for the hearing-impaired are equipped with strobe light fire alarms.

Laundry, valet, and room service are available along with an outdoor pool and complimentary fitness facilities just a block away. The Creekside Café serves well-prepared, basic fare at reasonable prices. The Sports Lounge has a relaxed atmosphere, friendly service, and a full bar.

INEXPENSIVE

🟊 The Hotel at the YWCA. 733 Beatty St., Vancouver, BC, V6B 2M4. ☎ **604/895-5830** or 800/663-1424. Fax 604/681-2550. 155 rms (some with shared bath). TEL. $55–$86 double; $73 family room. Weekly, monthly, group, and off-season discounts available. MC, V. Parking $5.35 per day.

This attractive, 12-story residence next door to the Georgian Court Hotel is an excellent choice for female travelers or families with limited budgets. Bedrooms are simply furnished; some have TVs. While there are no restaurants in the building, there are quite a few reasonably priced eateries nearby. In addition, three communal kitchens are open to guests who bring their own utensils. There are also three TV lounges, a coin-op laundry, and free access to the nearby co-ed YWCA Fitness Centre.

THE WEST END & ENGLISH BAY
VERY EXPENSIVE

Westin Bayshore. 1601 W. Georgia St., Vancouver, BC, V6G 2V4. ☎ **604/682-3377** or 800/228-3000. Fax 604/687-3102. 484 rms, 33 suites. A/C MINIBAR TV TEL. Mid-Apr to Oct $215–$310 double, $450–$1,375 suite; Nov to mid-Apr $139–$169 double, $255–$750 suite. Children 18 or under stay free in parents' room. AE, CB, DC, ER, MC, V. Parking $7.

Perched on Coal Harbor at Stanley Park's eastern edge, the Bayshore has a resort atmosphere, yet it's almost right downtown. Rooms in the original building are comfortable and well furnished. Rooms in the 20-story tower are larger and have balconies and bigger windows, offering an unobstructed view of the dazzling array

---

🌐 Family-Friendly Hotels

Four Seasons Hotel *(see p. 639)*   The staff here gives your kids cookies and milk in the evening as well as their own special room-service menus and robes.

Westin Bayshore *(see p. 642)*   Its location at Coal Harbor marina makes it a great family hotel. From here, your kids can walk to Stanley Park, the Vancouver Aquarium, Nature House, and other attractions without ever crossing a street.

Quality Hotel Downtown/The Inn at False Creek *(see p. 642)*   The family suites here are spacious and well designed. There's an enclosed balcony area in some of the upper-floor suites where your kids can play without leaving the suite. The full kitchen facilities, casual restaurant, and off-season Adventure Passport also make this an excellent deal.

The Rosellen Suites *(see p. 643)*   The full-apartment accommodations are the perfect places to stay if you are looking for a home away from home. Their location—a block away from Stanley Park, the beaches, and Denman Street—makes it easy to do grocery shopping as well as to play.

---

of luxury yachts (many for charter) in the harbor with the park and the mountains as a backdrop. Two floors of the hotel are wheelchair accessible.

Dining/Entertainment: Trader Vic's, with its South Seas decor, offers Chinese and continental cuisine with seafood specialties. The Garden restaurant offers three meals daily as well as Sunday brunch, while the Garden lounge serves lunch by day and entertains with light jazz by night.

Services: Room service, concierge, laundry, valet, boat charters, bicycle and car rental, and free shuttle service downtown.

Facilities: There's an outdoor pool surrounded by a sundeck. Indoors, there's another pool and a complete health club.

EXPENSIVE

Best Western Listel O'Doul's Hotel. 1300 Robson St., Vancouver, BC, V6E 1C5. ☎ 604/684-8461 or 800/663-5491. Fax 604/684-8326. 119 rms, 11 suites. A/C MINIBAR TV TEL. May–Sept $180–$200 double, $275–$350 suite; Oct–Apr $135–$165 double, $150–$250 suite. AE, DC, DISC, ER, JCB, MC, V. Parking $10.

Located on Vancouver's liveliest strip, O'Doul's has a bright, contemporary California style. Deluxe rooms facing Robson Street are worth the price. Soundproof windows eliminate traffic noise.

Dining/Entertainment: Its restaurant is complemented by potted plants, brass accents, and original artworks commissioned by the hotel. Breakfast, lunch, and dinner are served all day, so whether you have a craving for eggs Benedict, penne with pesto, and a good burger, you won't be disappointed.

Services: 24-hour room service, concierge, valet, laundry.

Facilities: Indoor pool, exercise room.

✪ **Rosellen Suites.** 102-2030 Barclay St., Vancouver, BC, V6G 1L5. ☎ 604/689-4807. Fax 603/684-3327. 30 apts. A/C TV TEL. $129–$130 one-bedroom apt; $170–$230 two-bedroom apt; $365 penthouse. Minimum three-night stay. Additional person $15 per night. AE, DC, ER, MC, V. Free, limited parking.

On a quiet residential street right beside Stanley Park and near lots of restaurants, this unpretentious, low-rise apartment building was converted into an apartment hotel in the 1960s. There is no lobby. The manager's office is only open from 9am to 5pm, but each guest receives a front door key. Modern and extremely comfortable, each suite features a spacious living room, separate dining area, and full-sized kitchen with all necessary utensils. Autographed movie star photos in the manager's office give you an idea of the luminaries who have stayed here.

MODERATE

✪ **Pacific Palisades Hotel.** 1277 Robson St., Vancouver, BC, V6E 1C4. ☎ **604/688-0461** or 800/663-1815. Fax 604/688-4374. 233 suites. Full kitchens $10 extra. A/C MINIBAR TEL. Mid-Apr to Oct $145–$230 suite; Nov to mid-Apr $99–$175 suite. Penthouses from $425. AE, CB, DC, ER, MC, V. Parking $10.50.

The Pacific Palisades is a luxury hotel in every respect, save price. Because of its outstanding staff, it is popular with visiting film and TV production companies. Suites are divided into studio, executive, and penthouse-sized apartments. All are spacious, well appointed, and have kitchenettes, and some suites have balconies.

There is an excellent restaurant, the Monterey Grill, at street level, as well as 24-hour room service, concierge, valet, and laundry. There is also a fitness center with a health bar, sauna, indoor pool, tanning room, and bicycle rentals.

West End Guest House. 1362 Haro St., Vancouver, BC, V6E 1G2. ☎ **604/681-2889.** Fax 604/688-8812. 7 rms. TV TEL. $104–$195 double. AE, DC, MC, V. Rates include full breakfast. Free off-street parking.

Set back from a quiet street off Heritage Square just a block from Robson Street, this lavender-colored Victorian heritage house resembles a private residence. There is an abundance of antiques and framed photographs in the front parlor as well as in the bedrooms. Each room has its own TV, telephone, private bath, and teddy bear. Iced tea is served in the afternoon on a south-facing second-floor sundeck, and fresh-baked cookies or brownies appear in each room at turndown time. An outstanding full breakfast is served in the salon, sherry is complimentary at teatime, and the pantry is stocked with tea and snacks to which guests can help themselves. There are also bicycles (provided free for guest use) and fax service. No smoking.

INEXPENSIVE

🅂 **Sylvia Hotel.** 1154 Gilford St., Vancouver, BC, V6G 2P6. ☎ **604/681-9321.** Fax 604/682-3551. 97 rms, 18 suites. TV TEL. $55–$85 double; $85–$95 suite. AE, DC, MC, V. Parking $3 for 24 hours.

Built in 1912, the Sylvia is set on English Bay overlooking the beach. It's one of the oldest hotels in Vancouver, yet it has become deservedly trendy in recent years. The lobby sets the tone: It's small, relaxing, and dark, with red carpets, ivory drapes, and overstuffed chairs. The same atmosphere prevails in an adjoining restaurant and crowded cocktail lounge (which was Vancouver's first when it opened in 1954). In the guest rooms, the furnishings are appropriately mismatched. Suites, all of which have full kitchens, are large enough for families. Pets are accepted.

The restaurant, which serves three meals daily, specializes in meat and seafood with a continental touch and has the same fabulous view as the historic cocktail lounge.

CENTRAL VANCOUVER

EXPENSIVE

Granville Island Hotel. 1253 Johnston St., Vancouver, BC, V6H 3R9. ☎ **604/683-7373** or 800/663-1840. Fax 604/683-3061. 49 rms, 5 suites. A/C TV TEL. June–Sept $190 double; $205–$225 suite; Oct–May $170 double, $185–$205 suite. AE, DC, ER, MC, V. Parking $7.

Situated at the east end of Granville Island, on False Creek, this small, modern hotel enjoys a unique water location in Vancouver. It's constructed like a warehouse;

one side is corrugated metal, the other Mediterranean-pink concrete. A green-and-white-striped canopy connects the wings. The lobby is cozy but attractive, with dark wood paneling and stone floors. In addition to a favorable location near Granville Island public market, the hotel features close-up views of False Creek, balconies, skylights, heavy wooden venetian blinds, and bidets. The staff will happily arrange boat charters in the marina. If you like to go to sleep before two in the morning, ask for a room as far away from the hotel's Pelican Bar as possible—it's only open Friday and Saturday nights, but it's very popular. Downtown and English Bay are a two-minute, $1.50 ferry ride away.

⑤ Kenya Court Guest House. 2230 Cornwall Ave., Vancouver, BC, V6K 1B5. ☎ **604/ 738-7085.** 4 suites. TV TEL. $85–$105 double. Rates include full breakfast. No credit cards. Street parking.

Every room in this three-story heritage apartment building at Kitsilano Beach has an unobstructed waterfront view of Vanier Park, English Bay, Coast Mountains, and downtown Vancouver. Its location makes it an ideal launching pad for strolls around Granville Island, Vanier Park, and other central Vancouver sights. There is also a nearby outdoor pool, tennis courts, and jogging trails. All of the rooms are large and tastefully furnished. A full breakfast (including eggs and bacon) is served in a glass solarium with a spectacular view of English Bay. No smoking.

Penny Farthing Inn. 2855 West 6th Ave., Vancouver, BC, V6K 1X2. ☎ **604/739-9002.** Fax 604/739-9004. 2 rms with shared bath, 2 suites with private bath. $75 double; $135–$155 suite. Rates include full breakfast. No credit cards. Parking on street.

Located on a quiet, residential street, this 1912 heritage house is filled with antiques and stained glass. The rooms are furnished with pine pieces, and distinctive touches such as four-poster beds. Abigail's Suite is a favorite with honeymooners; it's bright and self-contained, with a terrific view, a sitting room with TV, and a private bath with a skylight. A full breakfast is served on the brick patio of the English country–style garden, which is full of trees and fragrant flowers; you can watch the residents cats at play while you dine. The inn has bikes available for jaunts to the surrounding beaches or nearby parks. No smoking inside (it's okay on the porches).

INEXPENSIVE

⑤ The University of British Columbia Conference Centre. 5961 Student Union Blvd., Vancouver, BC, V6T 2C9. ☎ **604/822-1010.** Fax 604/822-1001. 3,600 rms. A/C TV TEL. Walter Gage Residence $74 double; $96 triple suite May–Aug; $69 triple suite Sept–Apr. Totem Park Residence B&B $48 double, available May–Aug only. MC, V. Free parking May 4–Aug 26; $3 per day the rest of year. Bus: 4 or 10.

The University of British Columbia has a gorgeous setting on Point Grey, and it's a convenient place to stay if you plan to spend a lot of time in Kitsilano and central Vancouver. The Walter Gage Residence has new, comfortable suites, while the Totem Park Residence has dormitory rooms with shared baths. There are plenty of on-campus services, including restaurants, a pub, and banking. Nearby attractions include Wreck Beach, Pacific Spirit Park, Nitobe Memorial Gardens, the Museum of Anthropology, and a golf course.

NORTH VANCOUVER & WEST VANCOUVER

✪ Beachside Bed & Breakfast. 4208 Evergreen Ave., West Vancouver, V7V 1H1. ☎ **604/ 922-7773** or 800/563-3111. 3 rms. $100 double. Additional person $20. Rates include full breakfast. Free parking. Bus: 250.

Bouquets of fresh flowers welcome you to your room in this beautiful waterfront home. The house is a Spanish-style structure with stained-glass windows; it's located at the end of a quiet cul-de-sac. Its all-glass southern exposure affords a panoramic view of Vancouver. The beach is just steps from the door. You can watch the waves from the patio or the outdoor Jacuzzi or spend the afternoon fishing and sailing. Hosts Gordon and Joan are knowledgeable about local history and can gladly direct you to Stanley Park, hiking, skiing, and much more.

Lonsdale Quay Hotel. 123 Carrie Cates Court, North Vancouver, BC, V6M 3K7. ☎ **604/ 986-6111** or 800/836-6111. 57 rms, 13 suites. A/C MINIBAR TV TEL. $135–$200 double; $180–$200 suite. Additional person $20. AE, DC, ER, MC, V. Parking $6. SeaBus: Lonsdale Quay.

This hotel is actually located in the Lonsdale Quay Market at the SeaBus terminal. Featuring fabulous views of the harbor, waterfront, and the city, it is also only 20 minutes by bus from Grouse Mountain Ski Resort and Capilano Regional Park. An escalator from the market, which is filled with fresh produce, seafood, restaurants, and shops, leads to the front desk on the third floor. The guest rooms, decorated in soft pastels, are reasonably large. Some have balconies, and most overlook the harbor. The hotel has a whirlpool and a weight/exercise room.

Mountainside Manor. 5909 Nancy Greene Way, North Vancouver, BC, V7R 4W6. ☎ **604/985-8484.** Fax 604/985-8484. 4 rms. TV. $75–$125 double. Rates include breakfast. Bus: 236.

Nestled in a peaceful tree-covered ridge adjacent to Grouse Mountain and the Baden-Powell Trail, this contemporary bed-and-breakfast offers guests a spectacular view of Vancouver and the Burrard Inlet from elegantly furnished king-size, queen-size, or twin-bedded rooms. There's also a relaxing mountain view from the outdoor hot tub.

RICHMOND & THE AIRPORT AREA

⑤ Delta Pacific Resort & Conference Centre. 10251 St. Edwards Dr., Richmond, BC, V6X 2M9. ☎ **604/278-9611** or 800/268-1133. Fax 604/276-1121. 456 rms, 4 suites. A/C MINIBAR TV TEL. May–Sept $140–$160 double; Oct–Apr $120–$140 double. Year-round $150–$300 suite. AE, CB, DC, ER, MC, V. Free parking. Bus: 401 or 403.

The facilities and location of this 12-acre site make up for its minimal view. Despite its size, it's a casual and friendly place. Unlike at the downtown branch, the rooms are standard, but its location five minutes from the airport makes it worthwhile. Business Zone rooms come complete with cordless phones and fully equipped work stations.

Dining/Entertainment: Two restaurants and a lounge.

Services: 24-hour room service, concierge, free airport shuttle, express check-in for repeat guests.

Facilities: Swimming pools, sauna, exercise room, outdoor volleyball courts, golf practice nets, year-round tennis courts, squash courts, full-service business center, a shopping center, kids' summer camps as well as a playground and play center.

4 Dining

We have categorized our restaurant recommendations first by geographical area and then by price category. If you're staying downtown, you can walk to the West End and English Bay, Gastown, or Chinatown.

Remember, *the prices quoted here are in Canadian dollars.* In addition, there's no provincial tax on restaurant meals in British Columbia—just the 7% federal goods and services tax.

DOWNTOWN
VERY EXPENSIVE

The Five Sails. In the Pan-Pacific Hotel, 999 Canada Place. ☎ **604/878-9000,** ext. 480. Reservations recommended. Main courses $22–$38; table d'hôte $29.50–$42. AE, DC, ER, JCB, MC, V. Sun–Fri 6–10pm; Sat 6–11pm. SkyTrain: Burrard. WEST COAST/PACIFIC RIM.

The view of the harbor and North Vancouver is spectacular—as is the food. Request a table near the window when you make reservations. Despite the restaurant's elegance, you don't have to dress too formally. The dishes are an eclectic mix of Thai, Mongolian, Japanese, Vietnamese, and nouvelle preparations. The New York steak with a simple mushroom compote was just as delicious as the ethnic dishes. This is one of Vancouver's best restaurants.

EXPENSIVE

✪ **Bacchus Ristorante.** In the Wedgewood Hotel, 845 Hornby St. ☎ **604/689-7777.** Reservations recommended. Main courses $13–$27. AE, DC, MC, V. Daily 6:30am–10:30pm; lounge until 1am (Sun until midnight); tea daily 2–4pm. SkyTrain: Granville. MEDITERRANEAN.

Wrapped around an open kitchen, the Bacchus is the centerpiece of the Wedgewood Hotel. British chef Alan Groom has created an eclectic menu for lunch and dinner that includes such diverse dishes as papardelle with smoked chicken and shiitake mushrooms in a ginger sauce and Washington rack of lamb in a black olive crust. His tiramisu is absolutely luscious. Groom's mastery shows through in every dish.

Il Giardino di Umberto. 1382 Hornby St. ☎ **604/669-2422.** Reservations required. Main courses $15–$29. AE, DC, ER, MC, V. Mon–Fri noon–2:30pm; Mon–Sat 6–11pm. Bus: 22 or 401. TUSCAN.

Restaurant magnate Umberto Menghi's empire in Vancouver also includes Umberto's, Umberto al Porto, and Splendido. But Il Giardino has created its own niche. With the ambience of a seaside villa, it has an enclosed garden terrace for dining al fresco and a truly Tuscan menu emphasizing pasta and game.

A Kettle of Fish. 900 Pacific St. ☎ **604/682-6853.** Reservations recommended. Main courses $13.95–$29.95. AE, DC, MC, V. Mon–Fri 11:30am–2pm; daily 5:30–9:30pm. Bus: 22, 401, 403, or 406. PACIFIC NORTHWEST/SEAFOOD.

Check the fresh sheet to find the best of the day's catch, then do as the sign at the entry says: "Eat Lotsa Fish." The dishes, including hand-peeled papaya shrimp, are inventive and flavorful, and seafood just off the barbecue is a house specialty. The light, airy restaurant occupies the main floor of a renovated, turn-of-the-century building. Try the combo dinner on your first visit; it's a great sampler.

MODERATE

✪ **Joe Fortes Seafood House.** 777 Thurlow St. ☎ **604/669-1940.** Reservations recommended. Main courses $11.95–$19.95. AE, DC, DISC, ER, MC, V. Sun–Thurs 11:30am–11pm; Fri–Sat 11:30am–midnight. Bus: 8. SEAFOOD.

Named after the burly Caribbean seaman who became English Bay's first lifeguard and a popular local hero, this cavernous, dark-wood restaurant with an immensely popular bar is always filled with Vancouver's young and successful. The decor and atmosphere are reminiscent of a New York oyster bar, though the roof garden is pure Vancouver. Pan-roasted oysters are a staple on the menu, which is supplemented by a sheet listing a half-dozen varieties of oysters and twice as many daily varieties of fish. Try the gold medal–winning dark and white chocolate mousse cake.

North 49° Restaurant & Market. 1055 Dunsmuir St., Plaza level, Bentall Four. ☎ **604/669-0360.** Reservations recommended. Main courses $10.50–$22.50. AE, DC, ER, JCB, MC, V. Daily 11:30am–11pm. SkyTrain: Burrard. MEDITERRANEAN.

Culinary touches from every country in the Mediterranean mingled with fresh local ingredients and a bit of pasta have made North 49° into a rapidly rising star. The atmosphere is casual. Sharing is encouraged—after all, it's the only way you'll be able to sample even a fraction of the 100-plus items on the regular and specials menus.

Ⓢ **Yaletown Brewery.** 1110 Hamilton St. ☎ **604/681-2739.** Reservations recommended. Main courses $9–$15. Sun–Wed 11:30am–midnight; Thurs–Sat 11:30am–1am. Bus: 8. WEST COAST.

If you eat at the dining room bar (which is next to impossible Thursday through Saturday nights) instead of sitting at the window tables, you will get a front-row seat for watching your dinner being prepared in the open kitchen. The pizzas are whimsical. The hearty entrées, including rosemary chicken stew or baked salmon with vermouth herb butter, are prepared with surprising delicacy. The desserts are quite good. The food is only part of the draw here, however. Brewmaster Frank Appleton has created a range of brews—a light lager, two light ales, a robust red bitter, a truly creamy stout, and a nut brown ale. We've sampled the wares of many microbreweries; Yaletown ranks among the best.

INEXPENSIVE

Las Tapas. 760 Cambie St. ☎ **604/669-1624.** Main courses $3.45–$12.95. MC, V. Mon–Fri 11:30am–2pm; Sun–Thurs 5–11pm, Fri–Sat 5pm–midnight, Sun 5–9:30pm (later if concert schedules warrant). Bus: 15 or 242. SPANISH TAPAS.

Tapas or "little dishes" allow you to order a sampling of such treats as marinated lamb chops, spicy chorizo, calamari, garlic prawns, and much more. All dishes are available in three sizes, and you'll want to try a few of them. For lunch, the sandwiches, including roast pork, chicken breast, and chorizo served on fresh-baked foccacia, are also tasty; skip the fish sandwich, though. The decor is distinctly Mediterranean with whitewashed walls, exposed beams, fireplaces, and niches that give diners a bit of privacy.

✪ **Restaurant Starfish & Oyster Bar.** 1600 Howe St. (off Pacific Street). ☎ **604/681-8581.** Reservations recommended. Main courses $7.95–$11.95. Mon–Sat 11:30am–11pm; Sun 10:30am–11pm. Bus: 3 or 8. SEAFOOD.

Starfish attracts a younger crowd. Sounds echo amid the whitewashed walls, ceramic tile floors, bare-wood tables, and a huge expanse of glass that exposes a close-up view of False Creek and Granville Island. This new bistro serves up some very inventive variations on dishes such as steamed-mussel hot pot with black beans and ginger as well as grilled Ahi tuna with a burnt orange and wasabi soy glaze. While the menu changes often, the cuisine remains basically the same.

THE WEST END
EXPENSIVE

Ⓢ **Chez Thierry.** 1674 Robson St. (near Bidwell Street). ☎ **604/688-0919.** Reservations recommended. Main courses $10–$16.95. AE, DC, ER, MC, V. Daily 5:30–10:30pm. Bus: 8. FRENCH.

Inveterate sailor, skier, snowboarder, fencer, flirt, and showman Thierry Damilano is surprisingly understated when he talks about his restaurant. This nice little place, as he describes it, serves Vancouver's best French cuisine. Classic country fare such as prawns and artichokes in a light, velvety curry sauce; perfectly crisped boneless duck in a peach and port sauce (our favorite); and bouillabaisse (a house specialty) head up the menu. The highlight on the dessert menu is the apple tart, flamed at your table with apple brandy.

✪ **Raincity Grill.** 1193 Denman St. ☎ **604/685-7337.** Reservations recommended. Main courses $12–$21. AE, DC, ER, MC, V. Mon–Thurs 11:30am–11pm; Fri 11:30am–midnight; Sat 10:30am–midnight; Sun 10:30am–11pm. Bus: 8. WEST COAST.

With an outdoor patio that catches the afternoon sun and an extensive wine list (128 wines are available by the glass), Raincity might make you feel as if you've landed 1,000 or so miles south of Vancouver. The menu varies seasonally and depends on what's exceptional at the Granville Island produce market. Start out with a crab salad or the ravioli with sun-dried tomatoes in an oyster mushroom broth. Then try the rare grilled Ahi tuna steak served with a Pinot Noir mint reduction; if you go on a Wednesday, try the chef's surprise.

MODERATE

Café de Paris. 751 Denman St. ☎ **604/687-1418.** Reservations recommended. Main courses $14–$17; three-course table d'hôte menu $24.95 at dinner, $13.95 at lunch. AE, MC, V. Mon–Fri 11:30am–2pm; daily 5:30–10pm. Bus: 8. FRENCH.

The new owners of Café de Paris have made extensive changes to the decor and menu to re-create an authentic Parisian bistro with dark wood, brass accents, wine racks (wines range from $16 up to $400), and marble-topped tables. The classic bistro fare includes duck confit, steak tartare, and smoked rack of lamb roasted with fresh herbs (all served with pommes frites).

✪ **The Fish House in Stanley Park.** 2099 Beach Ave. (in Stanley Park). ☎ **604/681-7275.** Reservations recommended. Main courses $9.95–$17.95. AE, DC, ER, JCB, MC, V. Mon–Sat 11:30am–10pm; Sun 11am–2:30pm. Bus: 19. PACIFIC NORTHWEST/SEAFOOD.

This restaurant harks back to a more genteel era with its relaxed clubby atmosphere. The white wooden building is surrounded by public tennis courts, golf and lawn-bowling greens, and ancient cedar trees. The menu includes some very innovative dishes such as the surprisingly tender wood-oven roasted calamari served with piquant tomato oil; a seafood hotpot; and our favorite, grilled Ahi tuna steak served with creamy buttermilk mashed potatoes. The oyster bar has at least a half-dozen fresh varieties daily. The desserts are sumptuous and truly irresistible.

Romano's Macaroni Grill at the Mansion. 1523 Davie St. ☎ **604/689-4334.** Reservations recommended. Main courses $7.95–$14.95. AE, DC, MC, V. Daily 11:30am–10:30pm. Bus: 3 or 8. ITALIAN.

Built just after the turn of the century by sugar baron B. T. Rogers, the mansion is now the home of a fun, casual pasta and pizza restaurant. The menu emphasizes southern Italian fare, and the pastas are definitely the favorite dishes. The food is simple, understandable, and consistently good. You're charged for the house wine, which you pour yourself from unlabeled bottles, based on how much you consume (measured on the side of the bottle, not with a Breathalyzer). Your kids will love the children's menu, tasty pizzas, and tolerant staff.

Saigon. 1500 Robson St. ☎ **604/682-8020.** Reservations recommended for dinner. Main courses $6.95–$16. AE, DC, MC, V. Daily 11am–midnight. Bus: 8. VIETNAMESE.

This is possibly Vancouver's oldest Vietnamese restaurant, and still one of its most authentic. Lovers of this Asian cuisine won't be disappointed by the crisp, moist *cha-gio* or the thoroughly marinated and charbroiled brochettes served over rice vermicelli. Big steaming bowls of noodles in clear broth with a selection of meats are perfect for warming up on a rainy day.

INEXPENSIVE

Azzurro. 1706 Robson St. ☎ **604/688-8294.** Reservations not accepted. Main courses $3.25–$6.95. No credit cards. Mon–Sat 11:30am–7pm. ITALIAN.

Dario Fracca and his wife Avelina have been quietly serving up exquisite, simply prepared pastas, salads, and traditional Italian sandwiches on Robson Street for nine years. There's no menu—just a daily specials board and a freshly stocked glass case. Regulars often don't have to order at all; Avelina remembers everyone's favorites. There are only a few tables covered with blue-and-white checkered table cloths in this narrow storefront, so it's easy to miss. It's worth finding, though—the food is unforgettable.

⑤ Hanada. 823 Denman St. ☎ **604/685-1136.** Reservations recommended on weekends. Main courses $4.50–$9.75. AE, DC, MC, V. Mon–Fri 11:45am–2:30pm; Mon–Thurs 5–10pm, Fri 5–10:30pm, Sat noon–10:30pm. Bus: 8. JAPANESE/SUSHI.

How do you judge an inexpensive Japanese restaurant? We size up the quality of the tuna in the sushi, the flavor released from a perfectly charbroiled teriyaki chicken breast, and the artful presentation of a bento box. The owners and able staff of Hanada apparently agree. Imagine our surprise when we discovered this little corner restaurant dishing up all of our favorites for next to nothing. If you're looking for affordable Japanese, this is the best we've found in Vancouver.

✪ Stepho's. 1124 Davie St. ☎ **604/683-2555.** Reservations accepted for parties of 5–8. Main courses $4.25–$9.95. AE, MC, V. Daily 11:30am–11:30pm. Bus: 3 or 8. GREEK.

There's a reason this place is packed every day for lunch and dinner—the cuisine is simple Greek fare at its finest. Customers line up outside and wait up to half an hour to be seated (usually the wait is around 10 minutes). But once you're inside, a delicious meal awaits: generous portions of deliciously marinated lamb, chicken, pork, or beef over pilaf; *tzatziki* (a yogurt dip that is a garlic-lover's dream come true); and heaping platters of calamari. Beware of ordering too much food—it's easy to do here. We must confess that, on our last visit, we never saved room for dessert, but the baklava looked good (maybe next time).

CENTRAL VANCOUVER
EXPENSIVE

⑤ Bishop's. 2183 W. Fourth Ave. ☎ **604/738-2025.** Reservations required. Main courses $10.50–$13.95. AE, DC, MC, V. Mon–Fri 11:30am–2:30pm; Mon–Sat 5:30–11pm, Sun 5:30–10pm. Bus: 4 or 7. PACIFIC NORTHWEST.

At Bishop's, John Bishop personally greets you, escorts you to your table, and introduces you to a catalog of fine wines and what he describes as "contemporary home cooking." The decor features candlelight and white linen. The service is impeccable, and the food even better. The menu changes three or four times a year. Recent favorite dishes of ours have included grilled baby calamari with a sesame, soy, and tomato sauce; steamed clams served in an ale, leek, and pear broth; ravioli filled with Dungeness crab, eggplant, and marscapone cheese; and roasted pork tenderloin stuffed with shiitake mushrooms and sun-dried plums. If you have only one evening to dine in Vancouver, spend it here.

Monk McQueen's. 601 Stamps Landing. ☎ **604/877-1351.** Reservations recommended. Main courses $12–$24. AE, DC, ER, JCB, MC, V. Daily 11:30am–2pm and 5:30–11pm. Bus: 50. Ferry: Aquabus. SEAFOOD/CONTINENTAL.

Hop on the diminutive Aquabus over to Stamps Landing, find a table on either of two wooden decks built over False Creek, and dig into a delicious seafood dinner

👪 Family-Friendly Restaurants

Romano's Macaroni Grill at The Mansion *(see p. 649)* They draw families with an extensive children's menu and a friendly staff that will even let your kids wander up the inviting staircase to explore the upper rooms.

Brothers Restaurant *(see p. 652)* Here your kids get balloons along with their own menu.

while the sun fades. Downstairs is Monk's Oyster Bar, where you can get a bucket of steamers and a locally brewed beer, a spicy Szechuan seafood stir-fry, or fantastic roasted prawns. McQueens Upstairs is more formal (though still casual). Chef Robert Craig creates baked oysters, prawn and scallop stew, venison with pears, and grilled filet mignon with roasted garlic. The wine list, organized by price ($21.75 to $45.00), features a truly international mix.

Tojo's Restaurant. 777 W. Broadway. ☎ **604/872-8050.** Reservations required for sushi bar. Full dinners $12.50–$99.50. AE, DC, MC, V. Mon–Sat 5–11pm. Bus: 9. JAPANESE.

Hidekazu Tojo's sushi, the best in Vancouver, attracts Japanese businessmen, Hollywood filmmakers, and others willing to pay for the best. The sushi menu changes with the chef's moods, and the seasons are reflected in Tojo's abstract, edible masterpieces (Dungeness crab and asparagus norimaki appeared one spring night). Non-sushi dishes are available from a seasonal menu that in the past has included everything from tempura to teriyaki.

MODERATE

Alma Street Café. 2505 Alma St. (at West 10th Avenue). ☎ **604/222-2244.** Reservations recommended. Main courses $9–$14. AE, MC, V. Mon 8am–2:30pm, Tues–Thurs 8am–11pm, Fri 8am–midnight, Sat 9am–midnight, Sun 9am–10pm. Bus: 10 or 22. WEST COAST.

This much-lauded neighborhood hangout and jazz venue is an eclectic spot. The restaurant combines natural foods and a blend of Asian and West Coast cuisine with an emphasis on fresh herbs and Pacific seafood. The menu changes daily to reflect the best of the produce markets and seafood catches. There are changing exhibits of photography or fabric art on the walls. Nightly modern jazz performances take place at 8pm, Wednesday through Sunday.

✪ Picasso Café. 1626 W. Broadway. ☎ **604/732-3290.** Reservations recommended. Main courses $8.95–$15.95. MC, V. Mon 8:30am–2:30pm, Tues–Fri 8:30am–9pm. Bus: 10. WEST COAST/MODERN.

Are your arteries shying away from French fare and wincing at Alfredo sauce? Then visit this smoke-free establishment, which features surprisingly good, quite creative West Coast–influenced food, much of which lives up to the stringent HeartSmart guidelines laid down by Canada's Heart and Stroke Foundation. Framed prints by many of Vancouver's finest artists hang on the walls of this garden-style cafe. In addition, the restaurant provides culinary training for youths through the auspices of the Option Youth Society.

INEXPENSIVE

Ⓢ Isadora's Cooperative Restaurant. 1540 Old Bridge St. (on Granville Island). ☎ **604/681-8816.** Reservations recommended for groups. Main courses $6.25–$12.95; kids' menu $4.75. MC, V. Mon–Fri 7:30am–9pm, Sat–Sun 9am–10pm. Closed Mon in winter. Bus: 50 or 51. Ferry: Granville Island Ferry or Aquabus. WEST COAST.

Appetizers at this casual Granville Island eatery include vegetarian nut cakes and seafood Danika, a Scandinavian-style ceviche of fresh seafood marinated with fresh dill and juniper. Salads are imaginative and delicious, and the range of entrees is wide enough to suit any palate. Try the *Khatsah'lano* burger—a salmon fillet on bannock with cranberry chutney—or the Malaspina chicken, stuffed with shrimp, crab, and cream cheese in a chili-cream sauce. For dessert, the pear gingerbread and German double-chocolate cheesecake are excellent. There is a small children's play area and a children's menu.

The Naam Restaurant. 2724 W. Fourth Ave. ☎ **604/738-7151.** Reservations not accepted. Main courses $3.95–$8.25. MC, V. Daily 24 hours. Bus: 4 or 22. VEGETARIAN.

The Naam is Vancouver's oldest vegetarian and natural food restaurant, and it's often voted its best, even in recent polls. The unapologetically healthy fare ranges from open-face tofu melts, enchiladas, and burritos to tofu teriyaki, Thai noodles, and a variety of pita pizzas. Breakfast, which is served 6 to 11am (Saturday until 1pm, Sunday until 2:30pm), is a testament to the variety of delicious foods available without meat; they do serve eggs and dairy products. If you're a fan of vegetarian cuisine, The Naam is worth a visit.

GASTOWN/CHINATOWN
MODERATE

The Cannery. 2205 Commissioner St. (near Victoria Drive). ☎ **604/254-9606.** Reservations recommended. Main courses $12–$20. AE, DC, DISC, MC, V. Mon–Fri 11:30am–2:30pm; daily 5:30–10pm. Bus: 7 to Victoria Drive. From downtown, head east on Hastings Street, turn left on Victoria Drive (two blocks past Commercial Drive), and then right on Commissioner Street. SEAFOOD.

Hidden among the Burrard Inlet wharves and built over the water, The Cannery is an upscale, unabashedly romantic restaurant filled with seafaring memorabilia. The seafood is fresh and plentiful. Start out with a bowl of creamy clam chowder or rich lobster bisque, and then scan the daily fresh sheet. Those in the know order from the mesquite-grilled section. Our personal favorites are the tender halibut cheeks, with a fresh-made sweet pepper and tomato salsa, and the seafood combo platter. The Cannery's perennial gold-medal-winning wine list has some good bargains, and the desserts here are exquisite.

Kilimanjaro. 332 Water St. ☎ **604/681-9913.** Reservations recommended. Main courses $13.95–$23.95. AE, DC, DISC, ER, MC, V. Mon–Fri 11:30am–4pm; daily 5:30–11pm. Bus: 1 or 50. EAST AFRICAN/INDIAN.

Amyn Sunderji's restaurant in Gastown's Le Magasin mall captures the unique tastes of East-African Indian cuisine in an authentic Nairobi-style setting complete with tribal masks and batiks on the walls. Start with samosas, savory Indian-inspired pastries filled with traditional beef or not-so-traditional salmon; Mombasa mussels broiled on the half-shell; or the *hasusa* (appetizer) platter for a sampling of everything. Main dishes include lamb Serengeti, spicy goat curry, and trout *tukutuku*. The outdoor tables here are great for people-watching.

INEXPENSIVE

Ⓢ **Brothers Restaurant.** 1 Water St. ☎ **604/683-9124.** Reservations recommended. Main courses $6.95–$12.95. AE, DC, JCB, MC, V. Mon–Thurs 11:30am–10pm, Fri–Sat 11:30am–midnight, Sun 11:30am–9pm. Bus: 1 or 50. FAMILY STYLE.

Brother's is a solid restaurant decorated like a Franciscan monastery complete with staff in friars' robes. The warm ambience here especially appeals to families and older folks. Main dishes include chowder, pastas, burgers, and serious prime rib. Children get balloons and their own menu. A bistro lounge featuring wine casks as well as sushi and oyster bars caters primarily to young adults.

The Only (Fish & Oyster Café). 20 E. Hastings St. ☎ **604/681-6546.** Reservations not accepted. Main courses $5.25–$11.95. No credit cards. Mon–Sat noon–7pm. Bus: 8, 14, 20, or 21. SEAFOOD.

This skid-row eatery has been a Vancouver institution since 1912, and it's reputed to be the city's oldest restaurant. Though alcohol is not served and there are no public washrooms, every day lines form outside with all sorts of people waiting for a taste of fresh pan-fried fish and rich clam chowder.

5   Attractions

THE TOP ATTRACTIONS
DOWNTOWN

Sri Lankan Gem Museum. 150-925 W. Georgia St. ☎ **604/662-7768.** Admission $3.50 adults, $2.50 seniors, $2 children. Tickets available from Shelton Jewelers across the hall. Daily 10:30am–5:30pm. SkyTrain: Burrard. Bus: 3.

Featuring a 9,000-piece mosaic floor of Brazilian agate and walls and a ceiling of hand-painted enamel with 24-carat gold-leaf, this privately owned, hand-constructed grotto of precious and semiprecious gems is a truly unique jewel. The displays include a three-ton amethyst geode exploding in a rain forest setting, a stream of sparkling raw emeralds pouring out of an etched-brass cornucopia, and a 20,000-carat topaz radiating atop its pedestal.

Vancouver Art Gallery. 750 Hornby St. ☎ **604/682-5621.** Admission $6 adults, $4 seniors, $3 students, children under 12 free. Mon–Fri 10am–5pm, Sat 10am–6pm, Sun and holidays noon–5pm. Closed Mon–Tues in Oct–May (gift shop and cafe stay open). SkyTrain: Granville. Bus: 3.

Formerly the provincial court house, this 1906 building houses an impressive collection, including works by native B.C. artist Emily Carr and the Canadian Group of Seven. On display are also international and regional paintings, sculpture, graphics, photography, and video ranging from classic to contemporary in style. The Annex Gallery, geared to younger audiences, features rotating visually exciting and educational exhibits.

WEST END

✪ **Vancouver Aquarium.** Stanley Park. ☎ **604/682-1118.** Admission $9.50 adults, $8.25 seniors and students, $6.25 children 5–12, children under 5 free, $27 families. June 23–Sept 4 daily 9:30am–8pm; Sept 5–June 22 daily 10am–5:30pm. Bus 19; "Around the Park" bus.

North America's third-largest aquarium, the Vancouver Aquarium is home to more than 8,000 marine species. One room houses a giant octopus, orcas, belugas, sea otters, and stellar sea lion pups. Human-sized freshwater fish await you in an Amazonian rain forest. An hourly rainstorm thunders over your head while you meet crocodiles, poison arrow tree frogs, sloths, and piranha. Regal angelfish glide through a re-created coral reef, and blacktip reef sharks menacingly scour the waters.

CENTRAL VANCOUVER

Pacific Space Centre. 1100 Chestnut St., in Vanier Park. ☎ **604/738-STAR.** Admission to special shows $5.50–$7.75 adults, $3.75–$7.75 seniors and students. Tues seniors admitted free to all regular shows. Tues–Sun 10am–5pm and 7–11pm. Occasional unannounced closures; call ahead. Bus 22.

Downtown Vancouver Attractions

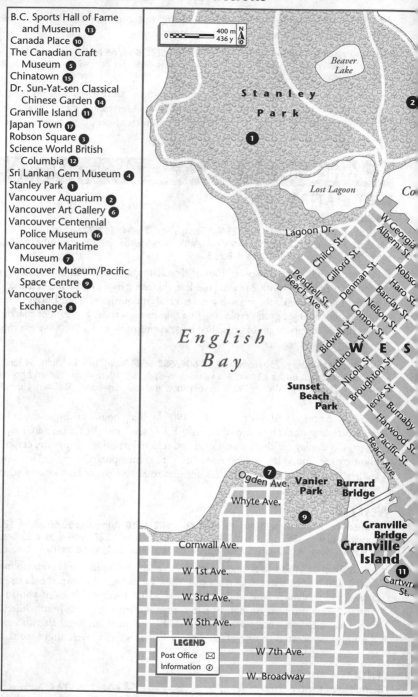

2079

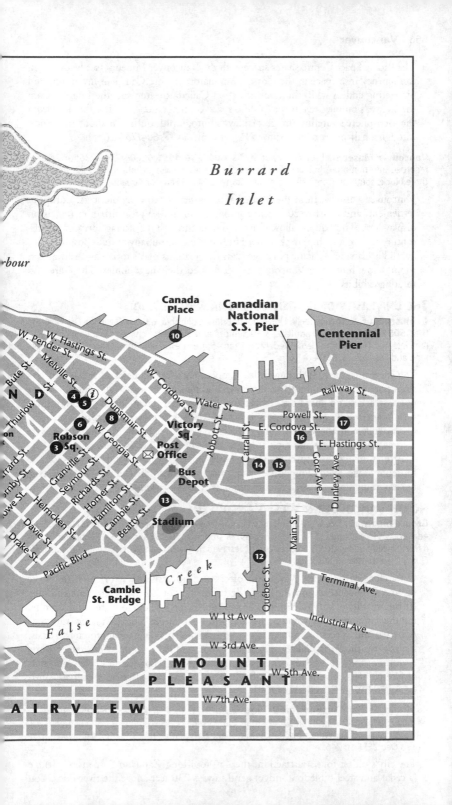

Burrard Inlet

rbour

Canada Place
10

Canadian National S.S. Pier

Centennial Pier

W. Hastings St.
W. Pender St.
Bute St.
Melville St.
N D
Thurlow
rrard St.
mby St.
owe St.
Dunsmuir St.
4 **5** *i*
6 **8**
3 Robson Sq.
Granville St.
Seymour St.
Richards St.
Homer St.
Hamilton St.
Cambie St.
Helmcken St.
Beatty St.
Davie St.
Drake St.
Pacific Blvd.

W. Cordova St.
Water St.
Abbott St.
Carrall St.

Victory Sq.
⊠ Post Office
Bus Depot
13
Stadium

Railway St.

Powell St.
E. Cordova St.
16
17
E. Hastings St.
14 **15**
Gore Ave.
Dunlevy Ave.
Main St.

Creek
12
Québec St.
Terminal Ave.
Industrial Ave.

Cambie St. Bridge

False
W 1st Ave.
W 3rd Ave.
M O U N T
P L E A S A N T
W 5th Ave.
W 7th Ave.
A I R V I E W

The Pacific Space Centre shares space with the Vancouver Museum (see below). You can journey into space in the Cosmic Simulator, explore Canadian inventions and pioneering endeavors in the Groundstation Canada theater, surf the Internet from the Centre's online site ("http://pacific-space-centre.bc.ca/"), or view the skies from the Geosphere's satellite-image display. Photography buffs can shoot the moon through a half-meter telescope for $10 per camera (☎ 604/736-2655).

Vancouver Museum. 1100 Chestnut St. ☎ **604/736-4431** or 604/736-7736 for 24-hour recorded information. Admission and hours change seasonally; call ahead. Bus 22, then walk three blocks south on Cornwall Ave. Boat: Granville Island Ferry or Aquabus.

Vancouver's history, from the Coast Salish settlement to early pioneers, European settlement, and its early 20th-century maturation into a great urban center, is on display here. The exhibits allow visitors to walk through the steerage deck of a 19th-century immigrant ship, peek into a Hudson's Bay Company trading post, or sit in an 1880s Canadian-Pacific passenger car. Re-creations of Victorian and Edwardian rooms show how early Vancouverites decorated their new homes. There are also rotating exhibits.

THE UNIVERSITY OF BRITISH COLUMBIA & KITSILANO

✪ **Museum of Anthropology.** University of British Columbia, 6393 NW Marine Dr. ☎ **604/822-5087.** Admission $6 adults, $3.50 seniors and students, children under 6 free, $15 families. Free Tues in June–Sept. Wed–Mon 11am–5pm, Tues 11am–9pm. Closed Mon in Sept–June and Dec 25–26. Bus 4 or 10.

You enter this museum through a huge, open, Ksan-carved bent-cedar box. Articles from potlatch ceremonies flank the ramp leading to the Great Hall's ancient totem poles, which stand guard over carvers working on new creations. Bill Reid's sculpture *Raven and the First Men*, as well as some of his precious-metal creations are also displayed here. In the Visible Storage Galleries, you can open the glass-topped drawers to view small treasures and look at larger pieces in the tall glass cases.

After touring the museum, take a walk through the grounds in back of the museum. Two Haida longhouses positioned on the traditional north-south axis; ten attending house posts; and contemporary carvings overlook Point Grey.

NORTH VANCOUVER & WEST VANCOUVER

Grouse Mountain Resort. 6400 Nancy Greene Way, North Vancouver. ☎ **604/984-0661.** Admission $14.50 adults, $12.50 seniors, $9.25 students, $5.95 children 6–12, children under 6 free. SkyRide free with advance restaurant reservation. Daily 10am–10pm. SeaBus to Lonsdale Quay, then transfer to Bus 236.

On a clear day, Grouse Mountain offers an impressive view of the Vancouver skyline. The cable car on the SkyRide tram lifts you to the 3,700-foot summit. (If the weather is hazy or cloudy, change your plans.) The resort offers hiking during the summer and day and night skiing in winter (see "Skiing," under "Outdoor Activities and Spectator Sports," later in this chapter). There are interpretative trails, a snack bar, the Spirit Gallery and Inpost shops, and daily summertime logger sports events. For the kids, the resort's Adventure Playground, Log Cabin Players, and staff of face painters provide the day's thrills. The Grouse Nest Restaurant serves continental and West Coast cuisine.

Capilano Canyon Suspension Bridge & Park. 3735 Capilano Rd., North Vancouver. ☎ **604/985-7474.** Admission $7.45 adults, $6.25 seniors, $5 students, $2.50 children 6–12, children under 6 free. Winter discounts. May–Sept daily 8am–dusk; Oct–Apr daily 9am–5pm. Closed Dec 25. Bus: 246.

The city's oldest tourist attraction, the 450-foot-long Capilano Suspension Bridge (a cedar and steel-cable footbridge) gently sways 230 feet above the river floor. You nervously cross above kayakers shooting the rapids below. The 200-foot waterfall is shrouded by mist. The 1911 trading post on the other end of the bridge houses the souvenir shop, the Bridge House Restaurant, and a barbecue snack bar. Carvers demonstrate their traditional skills at the Totem Park Carving Centre and the Longhouse. The Living Forest and Rock of Ages exhibits are recent additions to the roster of attractions. Both explain the region's delicate environmental balance as well as introduce visitors to the diverse species of flora and fauna that live in this unique area.

MORE ATTRACTIONS

✪ **B.C. Sports Hall of Fame & Museum.** B.C. Place Stadium, Gate A, Beatty and Robson streets (777 Pacific Blvd. South). ☎ **604/687-5520** or 604/687-5523 for recorded information. Admission $2 adults, seniors, and students; children under 5 free. Tues–Sun 10am–5pm. SkyTrain: Stadium. Bus: 15.

The Hall of Champions and Builders Hall document British Columbia's greatest athletes, referees, and coaches with videos and photographs. There are also galleries dedicated to early sports history in the province, as well as to the achievements of athletes Terry Fox and Rick Hansen. In the Participation Gallery, running, climbing, throwing, riding, rowing, and racing are not only allowed—they're encouraged.

The Canadian Craft Museum. 639 Hornby St. ☎ **604/687-8266.** Admission $4 adults, $2 seniors and students, children under 12 free. Mon–Sat 10am–5pm, Sun and holidays noon–5pm. Closed Tues in Sept–May. SkyTrain: Granville. Bus: 3.

The Canadian Craft Museum occupies a three-story gallery/work space complex. In addition to presenting a vast permanent Canadian collection, the museum also exhibits rotating international shows, which have included an impressive display of carved Chinese signature seals and calligraphy, a spectacular exhibition of Bill Reid's precious metal works, and furnishings created by Canada's best industrial designers. You can buy unique, creatively designed ceramics, sculptures, and other works in the museum's gift store.

✪ **Science World British Columbia.** 1455 Quebec St. ☎ **604/268-6363.** Admission $8 adults; $5 seniors, students, and children; children under 3 free. Additional admission for Omnimax film. Mon–Fri 10am–5pm, Sat–Sun 10am–6pm. SkyTrain: Science World–Main Street Station.

Science World is a hands-on scientific discovery center where you can create a cyclone, blow square bubbles, watch a zucchini explode as it's charged with 80,000 volts, stand in the interior of a beaver lodge, and play wrist-deep in magnetic liquids. In the Omnimax Theatre, which has a huge projecting screen and surround sound, you can feel as though you were taking a death-defying flight through the Grand Canyon and performing other spine-tingling acts.

✪ **Vancouver Maritime Museum.** 1905 Ogden Ave., in Vanier Park. ☎ **604/257-8300.** Admission $5 adults, $2.50 seniors and students, $10 family, children under 5 free. Tues–Sun 10am–5pm. Bus: 22, then walk four blocks north on Cypress. Boat: Granville Island Ferry or Aquabus.

This museum houses the RCMP Arctic patrol vessel *St. Roch*—the second vessel ever to have navigated the Northwest Passage and the first to have done it from west to east. Intricate ship models; antique wood and brass fittings; and prints and other documents fill the other galleries. The aft cabin of a schooner and the bridge of a modern tugboat lead the way to the Children's Maritime Discovery Centre, where there are computers; a wall of drawers bearing ship models and artifacts; and observation telescopes pointed on English Bay. You can also maneuver an underwater robot in a large water tank or dress up in naval costumes.

⊛ **Vancouver Centennial Police Museum.** 240 E. Cordova St. ☎ **604/665-3346.** Admission $2 adults, $1 seniors and children. May–Aug Mon–Sat 11:30am–4:30pm; Mon–Fri 11:30am–4:30pm. Bus: 4 or 7.

Those fascinated by the criminal underworld will revel in the museum's morgue and simulated autopsy rooms as well as the re-creations of Vancouver's infamous murder and crime scenes. There's also police equipment and a coroner's forensic exhibit. It's an intriguing way to pass the time on a dark and stormy day.

ESPECIALLY FOR KIDS

Pick up a copy of the free monthly newspaper *West Coast Families*. The centerfold "Fun in the City" as well as *Families'* event calendar lists everything currently going on, including CN, IMAX, and OMNIMAX shows and free children's programs.

Animal lovers will have a ball at **Stanley Park's petting zoo,** where peacocks, rabbits, calves, donkeys, and Shetland ponies eagerly await children's attention. The **Vancouver Aquarium,** with its playful sea otters, harbor seals, and whales, is always a popular spot with kids.

Budding scientists can get their hands into everything in **Science World British Columbia's** displays. They can go to the moon or just look at Mars in the **Pacific Space Centre's** flight simulator and observatory telescope. They can also maneuver the **Maritime Museum's** underwater robot or board the RCMP icebreaker *St. Roch.*

Athletic kids can work up a good sweat at the **B.C. Sports Hall of Fame's Participation Gallery,** where they can run, jump, climb, race, and attempt to beat world records. At Granville Island's **Water Park and Adventure Playground,** 1496 Cartwright St. (☎ 604/665-3425), they can *really* let loose with movable water guns and sprinklers. They can also get wet on the water slides or in the wading pool throughout the summer from 10am to 6pm. Admission is free. There are changing facilities right next door at Isadora's Restaurant.

At the **Capilano Suspension Bridge,** kids can feel the natural thrill of walking above lush forests and roaring rivers. **Mount Seymour** (see "Skiing," under Section 7, "Outdoor Activities and Spectator Sports," later in this chapter) offers Children's Ski Programs (☎ 604/986-2261) for kids aged four to 16.

Most of the above are covered in detail earlier in this section under "The Top Attractions" or "More Attractions."

Kids who love to shop will find heaven at Granville Island's **Kids Only Market,** 1496 Cartwright St., which is open daily from 10am to 6pm (closed Monday except in summer). Playrooms and 21 shops filled with toys, books, records, clothes, and food are all kid-oriented. Kids will also love taking the Aquabus or Granville Island ferry to get to the market.

6 Special Events & Festivals

New Year's Day brings the **Polar Bear Swim;** thousands of hardy citizens take their first annual dip in the icy waters of English Bay. In late January or early February, the **Chinese New Year** is greeted with two weeks of festivities including firecrackers, dancing dragon parades, and more.

March brings the **New Play Festival,** in which emerging playwrights show off their latest works at different venues. Call ☎ 604/685-6228 for information.

The **International Wine Festival,** in early April, is a major event featuring the latest international vintages. You are handed a glass at the door. Cheese and pâté are laid out on strategically placed tables. During the second week of April, the **Vancouver Sun Run** attracts 17,000 runners, joggers, and walkers racing through

---

Lights, Camera, Action!

The **B.C. Film Commission** runs a hotline (☎ 604/660-3569) and posts a list of the film and TV production companies currently shooting in town. The list is available at the SeaBus terminal, 601 W. Cordova St. (open Monday through Friday 8:30am to 4:30pm).

On one afternoon's stroll, we found five different production sets between Stanley Park and Thurlow Street, from Sunset Beach to Robson Street. The star-studded cast included Billy Dee Williams, Rick Moranis, Kelly LeBrock, and James Brolin. In the past three years, blockbuster films and TV shows such as *Legends of the Fall, Little Women, Man of the House, Party of Five, Intersection,* and *Jumanji* have been shot here. Most of Sylvester Stallone's *Rambo: First Blood* was filmed in Lynn Canyon Park. Four TV shows continue to be shot in Vancouver: *The X-Files, The Commish, Robin's Hoods,* and *Highlander.* Stargazing in Vancouver can be easier (and more successful) than touring the homes of the stars in Beverly Hills.

---

six scenic miles. Racers from all over the world gather here in May for the **International Vancouver Marathon**.

Kids will love the **International Children's Festival,** held the first week in June. Activities, plays, music, and crafts all geared to children are featured. During the **Canadian International Dragon Boat Festival,** held the third week of June, you can watch the races from False Creek's north shore, where 120 local and international teams compete. Four stages of music, dance, and Chinese acrobatics also take place as part of the events at the Plaza of Nations.

From late June to early July, more than 800 international jazz and blues performers put on the **duMaurier International Jazz Festival,** at venues from the Orpheum Theatre and the Yaletown Hotel to the Plaza of Nations. Contact the Jazz Hotline (☎ 604/682-0706) for details. Also around this time, you might catch Vancouver's **Italian Days,** a weekend of feasting and merrymaking. Contact the Italian Cultural Centre, 3075 Slocan St. (☎ 604/430-3337) for information.

On July 1, **Canada Day,** Canada Place Pier hosts an all-day celebration that begins with the swearing-in of new citizens. Music and dance acts perform outdoors throughout the day, and a fireworks display on the harbor tops off the entertainment. Canadian and international dance groups perform controversial and classic works at the Firehall Arts Centre during **Dancing on the Edge,** in early to mid-July. Call ☎ 604/689-0691 for information. The second or third weekend of July brings the **Vancouver Folk Music Festival.** International folk music is played outdoors on Jericho Beach Park. Contact the Vancouver Folk Music Society (☎ 604/879-2931). At the end of the month is the **Powell Street Festival,** an annual festival of Japanese culture with music, dance, food, and more. Call ☎ 604/682-4335 for details. There's also the **Obon Festival,** the Japanese full moon festival that takes place in Oppenheimer with kimonoed classical dancers and heart-quaking koto drummers. Contact the Vancouver Buddhist Church (☎ 604/253-7033).

Competitors design and attempt to sail or row all sorts of bathtub craft from Nanaimo to Vancouver in the **Bathtub Race.**

Three international fireworks companies compete for a coveted title and put up their best displays with accompanying music over English Bay Beach in the **Benson and Hedges Symphony of Fire,** held from the end of July through the first week in August. Don't miss the big finale on the fourth evening. Also through the first week of August, Vancouver's **International Comedy Festival** draws comedians from all over Canada and the United States to perform at a variety of venues around town. Call ☎ 604/683-0883. From mid-month to Labor Day, Vancouver puts on the **Pacific National Exhibition.** The 10th-largest fair in North America has everything from big-name entertainment to a demolition derby; livestock demonstrations and logger sports competitions; plus fashion shows and a midway. Contact 604/253-2311 for information.

On Labor Day, the **Molson Indy** roars through Vancouver's streets, attracting more than 350,000 spectators. Contact ☎ 604/684-4639 for information or 604/280-4639 for tickets.

From early to mid-October, the highly respected **Vancouver International Film Festival** features 250 new works, revivals, and retrospectives from 40 countries. Attendance reaches more than 110,000, not including the stars and celebrities who appear annually. Contact Vancouver International Film Festival (☎ 604/685-0260). Also in mid-month, the **Vancouver Writers Festival** features readings from great works by Canadian and international authors (☎ 604/681-6330 for details).

And Vancouver ends the year with **First Night,** a New Year's Eve performing arts festival and alcohol-free party. The city closes up the downtown streets for revelers. Admission to participating nightclubs and other sites is a $5 button.

7 Parks, Gardens, Nature Preserves & Beaches

Stanley Park (☎ 604/257-8400) is a 1,000-acre cedar forest near the busy West End. It boasts abundant wildlife, pristine natural settings, and amazing marine views. This is where the locals go to run, skate, bike, walk, or just sit. In addition to being 20% larger than New York's Central Park, it's a thousand times safer.

In Chinatown, there is a small, refreshing oasis where gnarled limestone scholar rocks jut skyward amid pine, bamboo, winter-blooming plum, and dark reflective pools filled with *koi* (Japanese carp). The **Dr. Sun Yat-Sen Classical Garden,** 578 Carrall St., is modeled after the private Taoist gardens found in China more than 500 years ago.

Central Vancouver's **Queen Elizabeth Park,** Cambie Street at West 33rd Avenue, is the city's highest southern vantage point. Its well-manicured gardens sharply contrast with Stanley Park's wilder landscape. Lawn bowling, tennis, pitch-and-putt golf greens, and picnic areas are all well laid-out. At its heart stands the **Bloedel Conservatory** (☎ 604/872-5513). A 140-foot-high domed structure with a commanding 360° city view, the conservatory houses a tropical rain forest with more than 100 plant species as well as free-flying tropical birds. Conservatory admission is $3 for adults, $1.50 for seniors and children.

The campus of the University of British Columbia incorporates both parks and gardens. The **UBC Botanical Garden,** 6250 Stadium Rd., Gate 8 (☎ 604/822-4208), which has 70 acres of formal alpine, herb, and exotic plantings, was established nearly a century ago. Less than 2 miles away is the classically Zen construction of the **Japanese Nitobe Memorial Garden,** 6565 NW Marine Dr., Gate 4 (☎ 604/822-6038). Admission fees are charged at both locations.

The primeval **Pacific Spirit Park** has 1,885 acres (763 hectares) of coastal rain forest, marshes, and beaches with nearly 22 miles of maintained trails perfect for hiking, riding, mountain biking, and beachcombing. This university endowment land is free of admission and open to the public.

The publicly maintained **Capilano River Regional Park,** 4500 Capilano Rd., North Vancouver (☎ 604/666-1790), surrounds the Capilano Suspension Bridge and Park (see "The Top Attractions," above). Hikers can trek along the Capilano trails for 4¹/₂ miles down to the Lions Gate Bridge or about a mile upstream to Cleveland Dam, the launching point for kayakers and canoers.

The **Capilano Salmon Hatchery** is located on the river's east bank a quarter mile below the dam (☎ 604/666-1790). About two million coho and Chinook salmon are hatched here annually in glass-fronted tanks in which you can observe the fishes' early life cycle daily from 8am to 7pm (until 4pm in the winter). Take the SeaBus to Lonsdale Quay and transfer to bus 236; the trip takes less than 45 minutes.

Lynn Canyon Park, Park Road, offers a great free attraction: the **Lynn Canyon Suspension Bridge,** originally built in 1912, which may be even more thrilling than the footbridge over Capilano Canyon (see "The Top Attractions," above). Measuring 225 feet from end to end, it's only half as long but 10 feet higher above the canyon floor than the Capilano Suspension Bridge. Best of all, it's been free of charge for more than 75 years! The **Ecology Centre,** 3663 Park Rd. (☎ 604/987-5922), presents natural history films, tours, and displays. Staff members lead frequent walking tours while the center is open from 10am to 5pm.

Five miles west of Lions Gate Bridge is **Lighthouse Park,** Marine Drive West, West Vancouver (☎ 604/922-1211), a 185-acre rugged terrain forest that can be traversed on its 8 miles of trails. One of the paths leads to the 60-foot-tall Point Atkinson Lighthouse, which is on a rocky bluff overlooking the Straits of Georgia with a panoramic view of Vancouver. It's an easy trip on bus no. 250.

Thousands of migratory birds following the Pacific Flyway rest and feed in the 850-acre **George C. Reifel Bird Sanctuary,** 5191 Robertson Rd., Westham Island, (☎ 604/946-6980), which was created by a former bootlegger and bird-lover. More than 250 species have been spotted, including a Temminck's stint, a spotted redshank, bald eagles, Siberian/trumpeter swans, peregrine falcons, blue herons, owls, and coots. An observation tower, paths, free bird seed, and picnic tables make this an ideal destination from October through April. The sanctuary is wheelchair accessible and open daily from 9am to 4pm. Admission is $3.25 for adults and $1 for seniors and children.

English Bay Beach, at the end of Davie Street off Denman Street and Beach Avenue, has beautiful sunsets. On Stanley Park's western end, **Second Beach** is a quick stroll north from English Bay Beach. A playground and a freshwater lap pool make this a convenient family sunning spot. Secluded **Third Beach** is due north off Stanley Park Drive. South of English Bay Beach near the Burrard Street Bridge and the Aquatic Centre is **Sunset Beach.**

Affectionately called Kits Beach, **Kitsilano Beach,** along Arbutus Drive near Ogden Street, draws a younger crowd. **Jericho Beach** (Alma Street off Point Grey Road) is another local after-work social spot. **Wreck Beach** is Vancouver's immensely popular nude beach. You get there by taking Trail 6 on the UBC campus near Gate 6 down to the water's edge. **Ambleside Park,** at the northern foot of Lions Gate Bridge, is a popular North Shore spot.

8 Outdoor Activities & Spectator Sports

OUTDOOR ACTIVITIES

The city's hottest outdoor sports are mountain biking, sailing, and in-line skating, which can all be done year-round. Pick up a copy of *Coast: The Outdoor Recreation Magazine,* which is published every other month. *Coast* lets you in on the latest snow conditions, bike trails, climbing spots, competitions, races, and the like.

Below are specialized rental outfitters listed according to activity. For a one-stop shopping outlet, try **Recreational Rentals,** 2560 Arbutus St. (☎ 604/733-7368).

BIKING   Welcome to cycle city, folks! Helmets are required both on- and off-road. Cyclists have separate lanes on developed park and beach paths. Some West End hotels offer guests bike storage or rentals.

Some of the city's hot bicycle runs include Stanley Park and the Seawall Promenade; English Bay to Sunset Beaches; Granville Island to Vanier Park; Kitsilano and Jericho Beaches; Pacific Spirit Park; and the 7-Eleven Bicycle Path.

Local mountain bikers love hitting Hollyburn Mountain in Cypress Provincial Park. Grouse Mountain's backside trails are now considered some of the best around. Mount Seymour's very steep Good Samaritan Trail connects up to the Baden-Powell Trail and the Bridle Path near Mount Seymour Road.

The **Bicycling Association of British Columbia** has a group ride and special events hotline (☎ 604/731-7433).

Rentals run around $3.50 to $5.60 per hour, $16 to $26 per day. Bikes, helmets, locks, and child trailers are all available on an hourly or daily basis at **Spokes Bicycle Rentals and Espresso Bar,** 1798 W. Georgia St. (☎ 604/688-5141). **Alleycat Rentals,** 1779 Robson St., in the alley (☎ 604/682-5117), is a very popular shop among locals.

BOATING   You can find bareboat rentals of 15- to 56-foot power boats for a few hours or several weeks at **Stanley Park Boat Rentals Ltd.,** Coal Harbor Marina (☎ 604/682-6257). **Delta Charters,** 3500 Cessna Dr., Richmond (☎ 604/273-4211 or 800/661-7762), has weekly rates for 32- to 56-foot powered bareboat craft. Check the marine forecast (☎ 604/270-7411) before taking off.

CANOEING/KAYAKING   Both placid, urban False Creek and the wilder 18⁴/₅-mile North Vancouver fjord—Indian Arm—have launching points that can be reached by bus. Granville Island's **Ecomarine Ocean Kayak Centre,** 1668 Duranleau St. (☎ 604/689-7575), has two-hour, daily, and weekly kayak rentals. They have another office at the **Jericho Sailing Centre,** 1300 Discovery St. **Deep Cove Canoe and Kayak Rentals,** at the foot of Gallant Street, Deep Cove (☎ 604/929-2268), near Indian Arm, offers hourly and daily rowboat, canoe, and kayak rentals plus customized tours.

DIVING   Scuba diving in the frigid winter waters around Vancouver is not uncommon. Wreck diving here is rated as some of the world's best. (More than 2,000 ships have sunk off shore in the last two centuries.) Cates Park in Deep Cove, Whytecliff Park near Horseshoe Bay, and Lighthouse Park (see Section 7, "Parks, Gardens, Nature Preserves, and Beaches," earlier in this chapter) are nearby dive spots. **Orca Dive and Charter Company** (☎ 604/551-1322), based in Coal Harbour, launches day or overnight dive trips and provides instruction. The **Diving Locker,** 2745 W. Fourth Ave. (☎ 604/736-2681), rents equipment and offers courses.

FISHING   Salmon, rainbow trout, steelhead, and sturgeon abound in local waters. To fish, you need nonresident licenses—one for saltwater and a different one for freshwater. Tackle shops sell licenses and current restrictions guides. **Hanson's Fishing Outfitters,** 102-580 Hornby St. (☎ 604/684-8988), and **Granville Island Boat Rentals,** 1696 Duranleau St. (☎ 604/682-6287), are two convenient downtown Vancouver outfitters.

The **B.C. Department of Fisheries** has a 24-hour toll-free information hotline to keep you abreast of seasonal catches; flies or lures; and best spots (☎ 800/663-9333 or 800/666-2268 in Vancouver).

Corcovado Yacht Charters Ltd., 104-1676 Duranleau St., on Granville Island (☎ 604/669-7907), has competitive rates and convenient launching locations. **Reel Adventures,** 1334 Larkspur Dr., North Vancouver (☎ 604/945-6755), specializes in wilderness sport fishing.

GOLF   This is a year-round Vancouver sport, except when it's raining hard, of course. With five public 18-hole courses and pitch-and-putt courses, Vancouver ensures that no golfer is far from his or her love. The **University Golf Club,** 5185 University Blvd. (☎ 604/224-1818), is a great, public 6,560-yard, par-71 course.

HIKING   Stanley Park actually has some pretty backtrails that are favorites with flatlanders and runners. Beaver Lake is just one great getaway in the park.

Just a few yards from the entrance to Grouse Mountain Resort is an entry to the world-famous 26-mile **Baden-Powell Trail.** The trail, with thick forest, rocky bluffs, and snow-fed streams racing through ravines, stretches from Cates Park to Horseshoe Bay. Even if you only want to hike the Grouse Mountain leg, start early and be ready for some steep ascents.

Lynn Canyon, Lynn Headwaters, Capilano Regional Park, Mount Seymour Provincial Park, and Cypress Provincial Park have good trails of all difficulty levels that wind up through stands of Douglas fir and cedar. Pay attention to the posted trail warnings: Some cross bear habitats. Always remember to sign in with the park service at the start of your trail. Golden Ears and the Lions are for serious hikers only.

ICE-SKATING   Robson Square is a free, covered ice-skating rink open from November to early April. Rentals are available in the adjacent concourse. The **West End Community Centre,** 870 Denman St. (☎ 604/689-0571), also rents skates at its enclosed rink, which is open October through March.

IN-LINE SKATING   You'll find locals rolling on beach paths, streets, park paths, and promenades. If you didn't bring a pair of blades, go to **Alleycat Rentals** (see "Biking," above), the preferred local outfitter; rentals run $4.50 an hour (two-hour minimum rental) or $15 per day or overnight.

JOGGING   Runners should traverse Stanley Park's Seawall Promenade, Lost Lagoon, and Beaver Lake. The scenery is spectacular.

SAILING   Charter a three-hour yacht cruise at **Cooper Boating Center,** 1620 Duranleau St. (☎ 604/687-4110), which has both cruises and sail instruction packages; and at **Blue Orca Sailing School,** 1818 Maritime Mews (☎ 604/683-6300), which also offers lesson packages.

SKIING/SNOWBOARDING   While it seldom snows in the city's downtown and central areas, there are three ski resorts in the north shore mountains. Vancouverites can ski in the morning before work and take advantage of after-dinner night skiing.

Grouse Mountain, 6400 Nancy Greene Way, North Vancouver (☎ 604/984-0661 or snow report 604/986-6262), is about 2 miles from Lion's Gate Bridge. The resort has night skiing, special events, instruction, trails ranging from beginner to expert, and a spectacular view. Lift tickets start at $28 for adults.

Mount Seymour Provincial Park, 1700 Mt. Seymour Rd., North Vancouver (☎ 604/986-2261 or snow report 604/986-3444), has the area's highest base elevation. It is accessed by four chairs and a tow.

Cypress Bowl, 1610 Mt. Seymour Rd. (☎ 604/926-5612 or snow report 604/926-6007), has the area's highest vertical drop (1,750 feet) and 10 miles of track-set cross-country skiing trails, including three miles set aside for night skiing and a shuttle service that picks you up and drops you off at the Park Royal Shopping Centre in West Vancouver ($7 per round-trip ticket).

SWIMMING   Vancouver's midsummer saltwater temperature rarely exceeds 65°F. If you can take it, see Section 7 of this chapter for a rundown of city beaches.

TENNIS   Vancouver's 180 city-maintained, outdoor public hardcourts have one-hour limits, operate on a first-come, first-served basis, and are admission-free (except for the Beach Avenue courts, which charge a nominal fee). Stanley Park has 21 courts. Queen Elizabeth Park has 18 courts; Kitsilano Beach Park has 10. The **UBC Tennis Training Centre,** on Thunderbird Boulevard (☎ 604/822-2505), has 10 outdoor and four indoor courts that you can reserve for $10 per hour. **Bayshore Bicycle and Rollerblade Rentals,** 745 Denman St. (☎ 604/688-2453), and 1601 W. Georgia St. (☎ 604/689-5071), rents tennis racquets for $12 per day.

WILDLIFE WATCHING   During the winter, thousands of bald eagles line the banks of Indian Arm fjord to feed on spawning salmon. The Capilano Salmon Hatchery (see Section 7 of this chapter) is overflowing with leaping salmon.

Orcas (killer whales) also watch the salmon migration. Salmon are their favorite food. Companies that offer whale-watching trips include the following: **Corcovado Yacht Charters Ltd.** (see "Fishing," above); **Orca Dive and Charter Co.** (see "Diving," above); and **Ecomarine Coastal Kayaking School** (☎ 604/689-7520) (see "Canoeing/Kayaking," above).

WINDSURFING   Windsurfing is not allowed at the mouth of False Creek near Granville Island, but you can rent or bring a board to Jericho and English Bay beaches. Equipment sales and rental (including wetsuits) as well as instruction can be found at the following places: **Windmaster,** at Denman and Pacific streets, at the English Bay Beach House (☎ 604/685-7245), and **Windsure Windsurfing School,** 1300 Discovery St. at Jericho Beach (☎ 604/224-0615).

SPECTATOR SPORTS

You can get information about all major events and purchase tickets at the **Travel InfoCentre,** 200 Burrard St. (☎ 604/683-2000).

BASEBALL   The **Vancouver Canadians** draw 6,500 spectators to their home at the Nat Bailey Stadium, 33rd Avenue at Ontario Street near Little Mountain Park (☎ 604/872-5232).

BASKETBALL   Vancouver was just awarded the NBA's 29th franchise and began play in the 1995–96 season. The **Vancouver Grizzlies** play at General Motors Place, 800 Griffith Way (☎ 604/899-7469, event hotline 604/899-7444).

FOOTBALL   The Canadian Football League **B.C. Lions** (☎ 604/585-3323) play at B.C. Place Stadium, 777 Pacific Blvd. South, at Beatty and Robson streets.

HORSE RACING   Hastings Park Racecourse, Exhibition Park (☎ 604/254-1631), has thoroughbred racing mid-April to October.

ICE HOCKEY   The NHL's **Vancouver Canucks** play at General Motors Place, 800 Griffith Way (☎ 604/899-7469, event hotline 604/899-7444).

ROLLERHOCKEY   Watch the **Vancouver Voodoo** in action at the Agridome, Pacific National Exhibition (☎ 604/874-1900).

SOCCER   APSL's Vancouver 86ers (☎ 604/299-0086) will play at B.C. Place (see "Football," above) until renovations are completed at their home, Swangard Stadium in Burnaby.

9 Shopping

It's hard to spend any time in Vancouver without going on a shopping spree. Check out Robson Street for trendy fashions; Granville Island for crafts and kids' stuff; Kerrisdale for reasonably priced clothing; Gastown for Native Canadian art; up-and-coming Yaletown for hip designer wear and furniture; and downtown Vancouver for designer boutiques, such as Salvatore Ferragamo and Polo/Ralph Lauren.

Vancouver's real finds, however, are the pieces made by the numerous local fashion designers and craftsmen. Don't miss the bold Haida-influenced appliquéd leather vests and coats at Dorothy Grant's boutique or Zonda Nellis's sumptuously soft handwoven and hand-painted creations.

You don't have to purchase an antique to acquire a quality original Coast Salish or Haida piece of art. As experts at the Museum of Anthropology will tell you, if a work is crafted by an artisan from any Pacific Northwest tribe, it's a real piece of art.

The province's wines—especially rich, honey-thick icewines, such as Eric von Krosigk's gold-medal Summerhill Estate 1992 Riesling Icewine and bold Merlots such as Anne Sperling's gold-medal Cedar Creek 1992 Merlot—are worth buying by the case. Five years of restructuring, reblending, and careful tending by French and German master vintners have won these vineyards world recognition. John Simes of Mission Hill won the 1994 Avery's Trophy for his 1992 Grand Barrel Reserve Chardonnay at the London International Wine and Spirits Competition.

In Vancouver, you will find salmon everywhere. Shops carry delectable smoked salmon in safe, vacuum-packed containers. Some offer decorative cedar gift boxes; most offer overnight air transport. Try treats made of salmon, including salmon jerky and Indian candy, at public markets such as Lonsdale Quay Market and Granville Island Public Market.

ANTIQUES
Uno Langmann Ltd. 2117 Granville St. ☎ **604/736-8825.**

This gallery specializes in European and North American paintings, furniture, silver, and objects from the 18th- through early-20th centuries.

ART
Even if you're not in the market, go gallery-hopping to see works by Haida artists Bill Reid (perhaps the best-known native artist), Richard Davidson, and Kwakwaka'wakw artist/photographer David Neel.

Images for a Canadian Heritage, 164 Water St. (☎ 604/685-7046), and the **Inuit Gallery of Vancouver,** 345 Water St. (☎ 604/688-7323), are both government-licensed galleries featuring traditional and contemporary works.

BOOKS
World Wide Books & Maps. 736A Granville St., across from Eaton's. ☎ **604/687-3320.**

This is the perfect place to look for travel guides, travelogues, topographical maps, globes, marine charts, and any other printed matter travelers might need.

CRAFTS
Hill's Indian Crafts. 165 Water St. ☎ **604/685-4249.**

Here you might find Cowichan sweaters, moccasins, ceremonial masks, wood sculptures, totem poles, serigraphic prints, soapstone sculptures, and jewelry.

DEPARTMENT STORES

The Bay. 674 Granville St. ☎ **604/681-6211.**

Since the 1670s, Hudson's Bay Company has sold quality Canadian goods. The Bay is still the place to buy a Hudson's Bay woolen point blanket (the colorful stripes originally represented how many beaver pelts were traded) as well as Polo, DKNY, Anne Klein II, and Liz Claiborne.

Eaton's. Pacific Centre Mall, 701 Granville St. ☎ **604/685-7112.**

It's filled with fashions from the classic to the outrageous, housewares, gourmet foods, and books. The seventh-floor bargain annex sells discount children's and men's clothing.

FASHIONS

International designers with boutiques here include the following: **Chanel Boutique,** 103-755 Burrard St. (☎ 604/682-0522); **Salvatore Ferragamo,** 918 Robson St. (☎ 604/669-4495); **Gianni Versace's Istante,** 773 Hornby St. (☎ 604/669-8398); **Polo Ralph Lauren,** The Landing, 375 Water St. (☎ 604/682-7656); and **Plaza Escada,** Sinclair Centre, 757 W. Hastings St. (☎ 604/688-8558).

Almost every week, it seems as though a new local designer boutique is opening in Yaletown amid the home furnishings showrooms, warehouses, and restaurants. Below are some places to look for homegrown talent.

✪ **Dorothy Grant.** Sinclair Centre, 250-757 W. Hastings St. ☎ **604/681-0201.**

Her exciting Feastwear collection features exquisitely detailed Haida motifs appliquéd on coats, leather vests, jackets, caps, and accessories.

Iago-go. 1496 Cartwright St. ☎ **604/689-2400.**

Delight your kids with one-of-a-kind, colorful clothes by local designers such as Iago-go. This Granville Island shop, located in the Kids Only Market, has a beautiful selection of colorfully printed, handcrafted children's fashions.

Zonda Nellis Design Ltd. 2203 S. Granville St. ☎ **604/736-5668.**

Rich colors and delicious patterns highlight the handwoven separates, pleated silks, sweaters, vests, and soft knits found here.

FOOD

Au Chocolat. 1702 Davie St. ☎ **604/682-3536.**

If you are a true chocoholic, then you must stop in. They carry the most delectable handmade Belgian chocolate truffles and more. They will ship your purchases.

The Lobsterman. 1807 Mast Tower Rd., on Granville Island. ☎ **604/687-4531.**

Live lobsters, Dungeness crab, oysters, mussels, clams, geoduck, and scallops are just a few of the varieties of seafood swimming in saltwater tanks. They can be steamed fresh on the spot or packed for air travel.

Salmon Village. 779 Thurlow St. ☎ **604/685-3378.**

Smoked salmon, salmon jerky, Indian candy, and caviar can be wrapped and shipped home at this place, which also has a great selection of pre-packaged gift boxes.

GIFTS/SOUVENIRS

Canadian Impressions at the Station. 601 Cordova St. ☎ **604/681-3507.**

This shop carries lumberjack shirts, Cowichan sweaters, T-shirts, baseball caps, salmon jerky, maple syrup, and shortbread cookies.

JEWELRY
Henry Birks & Sons Ltd. Vancouver Centre, 710 Granville St. ☎ **604/669-3333.**

They've designed and created beautiful jewelry and watches for more than a century.

Karl Stittgen + Goldsmiths. 2203 Granville St. ☎ **604/737-0029.**

Gold pins, pendants, rings, and other accessories highlight their commitment to fine craftsmanship.

MALLS & SHOPPING CENTERS
Pacific Centre Mall. 700 W. Georgia St. ☎ **604/688-7236.**

This three-block complex contains 200 shops and services, including Godiva, Benetton, Crabtree and Evelyn, and Eddie Bauer. Underground concourses make it a pleasant rainy day experience.

Park Royal Shopping Centre. 2002 Park Royal South, West Vancouver. ☎ **604/925-9576.**

This really consists of two malls facing each other on Marine Drive. The Gap, Disney, Eaton's, The Bay, and their own Public Market are just a few of the 200 stores.

MARKETS
Granville Island Public Market. 1669 Johnston St., Granville Island. ☎ **604/666-5784.**

This 50,000-square-foot market has lots of food counters selling Chinese, vegetarian, and Mexican fare or just about anything else you could want to eat. There's usually live entertainment, and there is always a lot to see daily 9am to 6pm (open at noon on Sundays and closed Mondays in winter except public holidays).

Lonsdale Quay Market. 123 Carrie Cates Court, at the SeaBus terminal, North Vancouver. ☎ **604/985-6261.**

It's filled with fashions, gift shops, Kids' Alley (dedicated to children's shops and containing a play area), food counters, coffee bars, and bookstores. Open Monday through Saturday 9:30am to 6:30pm (Friday until 9pm).

TOYS
Kids Only Market. 1496 Cartwright St., Granville Island. ☎ **604/684-0066.**

This 24-shop complex has toys, craft kits, games, computer software, and books.

WINES
Marquis Wine Cellars. 1034 Davie St. ☎ **604/684-0445** or 604/685-2246.

This shop carries a full range of B.C. wines and an exceptional array of international wines.

10 Vancouver After Dark

Get a copy of *The Georgia Straight*, a weekly tabloid, or of *Xtra! West*, the gay and lesbian biweekly tabloid.

The **Vancouver Cultural Alliance Arts Hotline,** 938 Howe St., in the Orpheum Theatre (☎ 604/684-2787), has updates on all major cultural events and information about where and how to get tickets. The office is open weekdays from 9am to 5pm.

THE PERFORMING ARTS
Tickets for major performances can be purchased at the Travel InfoCentre (see "Visitor Information," in Section 1 of this chapter). Tickets for clubs, local theater, and

special attractions are available at the **Community Box Offices,** 1234 W. Hastings St. (☎ 604/280-2801). It is open Monday through Saturday 9am to 5:30pm.

VENUES   There are three major venues where touring performers play: **The Orpheum Theatre,** 801 Granville St.; the **Queen Elizabeth Complex,** 600 Hamilton St.; and the **Ford Center for the Performing Arts,** Homer Street off Robson Street.

Located in a converted turn-of-the-century church, the **Vancouver East Cultural Centre,** 1895 Venables St. (☎ 604/254-9578), presents avant-garde theater productions, performances by international musical groups, various festivals and cultural events, children's programs, and art exhibitions.

THEATER   Theater isn't only an indoor pastime here; in summertime, it heads outdoors with events such as the Shakespearean series Bard on the Beach (at Vanier Park) and Theatre Under the Stars (in Stanley Park). Major Broadway productions also book into Vancouver, so you can see *Kiss of the Spider Woman, Showboat,* or even an Andrew Lloyd Weber premiere without ever setting foot in London or Manhattan.

Originally Vancouver's Firehouse No. 1, the **Firehall Arts Centre,** 280 E. Cordova St. (☎ 604/689-0926), is the home of three cutting-edge companies—the Firehall Theatre Co., the Touchstone Theatre, and Axis Mime. They also present dance events, arts festivals, and concerts.

There are two Granville Island theaters worthy of note. The **Arts Club Theatre,** 1585 Johnston St. (☎ 604/687-1644) has two stages. The 425-seat Granville Island Mainstage presents major dramas, comedies, and musicals with postperformance entertainment in the Backstage Lounge. The Arts Club Revue Stage is an intimate, cabaret-style showcase for small productions, improvisation nights, and musical revues such as *Ain't Misbehavin'.* The **Waterfront Theatre,** 1412 Cartwright St. (☎ 604/685-6217), is the home of the Carousel Theatre and School; it also hosts both touring and local dance, music, mime, and theater companies.

OPERA   The repertoire of the **Vancouver Opera** (☎ 604/682-2871) ranges from Puccini, Verdi, Gounod, and Bizet classics to 20th-century works by Benjamin Britten and Kurt Janacek as well as esoteric modern productions. The English supertitles projected above the stage of the Queen Elizabeth Theatre help you follow the operatic dialogue from October to June.

CLASSICAL MUSIC   Whether you like the classics or popular show tunes, you'll find world-class performances to soothe or stimulate your soul. The **Festival Concert Society** (☎ 604/736-3737) sponsors the Coffee Concert series every Sunday at 11am (September through June) at the Queen Elizabeth Theatre. The one-hour concerts feature classical, jazz, folk, dance, theater, or operatic music. The **Vancouver Symphony Orchestra** (☎ 604/684-9100 or 604/876-3434) presents a number of classical, pop, and children's programs at their Orpheum Theatre home. Their traveling summer concert series takes them from White Rock and Cloverdale on the U.S. border to the Whistler area.

DANCE   If you love dance, catch the September **Dancing on the Edge Festival,** which presents 60 to 80 pieces over 10 days. You'll see works by local companies, including the Anna Wyman Dance Theatre (☎ 604/926-6535); Judith Marcuse Dance Company (☎ 604/985-6459); and the Karen Jamieson Dance Company (☎ 604/872-5658). Call the **Dance Centre** (☎ 604/872-0432) for more information about other performances around the city.

The 10-year-old **Ballet British Columbia** (☎ 604/669-5954) regularly performs at the Queen Elizabeth Theatre. The innovative company presents works by choreographers such as John Cranko and William Forsythe. They also host soloists such as Mikhail Baryshnikov and companies such as the American Ballet Theatre and the National Ballet of Canada.

THE CLUB & MUSIC SCENE

COMEDY CLUBS   Jay Leno, Howie Mandel, and other famous comedians performed at the **Punchlines Comedy Theatre,** 15 Water St. (☎ 604/684-3015), before breaking into the big time. Tuesday is Amateur Night. Wednesday nights are dedicated to improv groups, while stand-up comics take the stage on the weekend. The cover is $3.50 to $9.65, and drinks run $3. The box office is open weekdays from noon to 4pm. Doors open at 8pm; show time is at 9:30pm.

Paul Wildman and J. O. Mass host a leading lineup of Canadian and American stand-up comics at **Yuk Yuk's Komedy Kabaret,** Plaza of Nations, 750 Pacific Blvd. (☎ 604/687-5233). Amateurs take the stage on Wednesday nights. It's a small theater inside (capacity 200), so it's hard to get a bad seat. Cover is $3 to $10. Drinks run $4.75. Show times are 9pm and 11:30pm.

JAZZ, BLUES & FOLK   The **Coastal Jazz and Blues Society** (☎ 604/682-0706) has information on all current music events.

Ethnomusicologist Stephen Huddart's **Kitsilano Alma Street Café** (see Section 4, "Dining," earlier in the chapter) is a great place to catch Canadian and U.S. modern jazz performances. Cover for special performances only.

The elegant **Bacchus Piano Lounge,** in the Wedgewood Hotel, 845 Hornby St. (☎ 604/689-7777), features Wes Mackey playing blues guitar nightly except Sunday. The fireplace makes it especially cozy on rainy evenings. People show up in everything from suits to jeans in this richly appointed room. There's an excellent light snack menu plus a great wine and drink list (see Section 4 of this chapter). Drinks are $4.50. Evening entertainment begins around 7pm.

The **Glass Slipper,** 185 E. 11th Ave. (☎ 604/877-0066), located downstairs from the Cinderella Ballroom, is showcase of the Coastal Jazz and Blues Society as well as the New Orchestra Workshop. Modern and improv jazz are performed in an intimate, inexpensive setting. Cover is $5 (more for special acts).

Long John Baldry, Junior Wells, Koko Taylor, John Hammond, and many other blues masters have played at the **Yale Hotel,** 1300 Granville St. (☎ 604/681-9253), located in a late-19th-century hotel. If you are a serious blues fan, then this is the place to go. The room has a beautiful set-up for sitting back or boogying down. There's also a billiard corner set away from the stage. Cover is $5 to $7. Drinks average $4.50.

ROCK   Rock clubs bloom and fade here as rapidly as they do in many metropolitan areas.

The **Twilight Zone,** 7 Alexander St. (☎ 604/632-8550), is Vancouver's industrial gothic punk alternative. Call first since venues and covers change from month to month. Punk nights here are not for spectators. Be sure to bring your Docs.

The **1929 Commodore Ballroom,** 870 Granville Mall (☎ 604/681-7838), hosts major rock, rap, jazz, blues, reggae, and other performers such as Buddy Guy and Sonny Landreth, Ice-T and Body Count, and Queen Ida and the Bon Temps Zydeco Band. It's a disco on Tuesdays, and on Fridays there is a dance party. The Commodore has four bars, six video screens, and a huge dance floor. Drinks and cover are in the $5 range.

Live bands play '50s, '60s, and '70s classic rock at the **Roxy,** 932 Granville St. (☎ 604/684-7699), which has showmen bartenders. Theme parties, old movies, and

Wednesday Student Nights add to the entertainment. Cover is $3 to $6. Drinks run $3.95.

The **Starfish Room,** 1055 Homer St., near Helmcken St. (☎ 604/682-4171), is a large club with a huge dance floor that hosts international recording acts as well as local artists. Monday and Tuesdays are DJ nights. Cover is $2 to $6. Drinks are $4.35.

DANCE CLUBS   Big Bamboo, 1236 W. Broadway (☎ 604/733-2220), is a warehouse space playing Gen X industrial dance music. Wednesday is reggae night. Sport your best cyberwear to dance here. Cover is $3; drinks run $3.50.

The **Blue Note,** 455 W. Broadway (☎ 604/872-8866), is a New York–style supper club. This place has no relation to the Manhattan Blue Note—it's about a quarter of the price of the Manhattan club, the drinks and food are better, and the music is on par. The generally relaxed audience includes a lot of couples. Cover is $2 on weekends, and there's a $6 drink minimum all week.

Learn to lambada and have a few Spanish and Mexican tapas for rejuvenation at **Rio Rio,** 102 Water St. (☎ 604/685-1144), a live-music supper club that also features a full menu of tequila drinks.

THE BAR SCENE

Vancouver's bar scene is closely linked with its restaurant life. Because of the city's liquor laws, most hot spots for drinks also have full menus, such as one of our favorites, the **Yaletown Brewery** (see Section 4, "Dining," earlier in this chapter). Drinks generally cost between $3 and $6 in bars and lounges; closing times are around 2am (midnight on Sundays).

Checkers, 1755 Davie St. (☎ 604/682-1831), is a friendly West End bar where you can listen to classic rock in a checkerboard decor or withdraw to a people-watching view of English Bay. The **Rusty Gull,** 175 E. 1st St., North Vancouver (☎ 604/988-5585), attracts gourmet beer drinkers who love the 13 local brews on tap at this live-entertainment watering hole. **Stamp's Landing,** 610 Stamp's Landing (☎ 604/879-0821), is where the False Creek Marina yachting crowd hangs out.

THE GAY & LESBIAN SCENE

Vancouver's gay and lesbian scene is comfortable and open without the cloistered feeling you'll find in other cities. A lot of the clubs feature theme nights and dance parties. The **Heritage House Hotel,** 455 Abbott St. (☎ 604/685-7777), is a Gastown gay bar that has a main-floor lounge and pub that attracts both men and women. The downstairs lesbian bar is open Tuesday through Saturday; only women are admitted on Wednesday and Friday.

The **Odyssey,** 1251 Howe St. (☎ 604/689-5256), is a big dance club that offers live entertainment: male strippers on Mondays, shower contests on Tuesdays, male go-go dancers on Fridays and Saturdays, and live drag on Sundays. A DJ spins nightly for the mixed audience. There's a heated patio open year-round, and the back entrance is for men only.

The **Shaggy Horse,** 818 Richards St. (☎ 604/688-2923), has DJs who spin the disks Tuesday through Saturday. Special events include Thursday night acid jazz, Friday male stripper nights, and a Leather Levi's Cruise Bar on Saturday.

MORE ENTERTAINMENT

FILM   From the Vancouver Film Festival to first-run, second-run, and revival theaters, you can get your fill of good cinema here. First-run ticket prices are about $8 for adults; there are student and senior discounts, and matinees are $4.50.

Special movie houses include the **Starlight Cinema,** 935 Denman St. (☎ 604/689-0096); the **Park Theatre,** 3440 Cambie St. (☎ 604/876-2747); and the **Varsity Theatre,** 4375 W. 10th Ave. (☎ 604/222-2235)—all offer first-run, foreign-language, independent, art, and issue-oriented films.

The **Pacific Cinematheque,** 1131 Howe St.(☎ 604/688-3456), features important foreign films and series such as a Jean-Luc Godard film festival and International Women's Week films, together with experimental independent North American features.

The **Ridge Theatre,** 3131 Arbutus St. (☎ 604/738-6311), is where you can catch a Cannes Film Festival award-winner, an uncut print of an old classic, an unpublicized rock movie, or a sensational underground sleeper. This theater has a crying room and an induction-loop system for hearing-impaired patrons.

CASINOS   Try your luck at blackjack, roulette, sic-bo, red dog (diamond dog), and Caribbean stud poker. The casinos here are not open 24 hours and do not feature floor shows. One downtown option is the **Royal Diamond Casino,** 1195 Richards St. (☎ 604/685-2340), which is informal and very friendly. It's open seven nights a week from 6pm to 2am.

19

Victoria & the Best of British Columbia

by Anistatia R. Miller and Jared M. Brown

anada's most westerly province can be all things to all people—or pretty nearly so. Its outstanding characteristic is variety: scenically, climatically, and socially. In the southwest, near the Washington State border, the country is densely populated, with two sophisticated cities and a sunny coastline dotted with resorts and belts of rich farmlands raising dairy cattle on lush pastures. But in the north, where the province borders Alaska and the Yukon, the settlements are tiny, and most of the land is a thickly forested wilderness. In between these extremes you get the area covered in this chapter: wide-open ranchlands with cowboys riding herd, glacier-topped mountains, moss-covered rain forests, alpine meadowlands, rugged fjords, sheltered sandy beaches, misty islands, thousands of lakes, valleys glowing with ripening fruit, vineyards on the hillsides, and a patch of genuine mesa desert.

British Columbia is a huge province of 366,255 square miles, more than twice the size of California, with only a few million people, most of them concentrated in the south. This leaves the bulk of the province a thinly settled haven of natural wonders, a place to breathe fresh air and re-attune noise-deafened ears to birdcalls and rustling winds. But wilderness isn't the whole story. Vancouver (covered fully in Chapter 18) and Victoria are two of North America's most inviting cities. And the province holds out such unexpected pleasures as the wineries of the Okanagan Valley, outstanding scuba diving off Vancouver Island, a lush temperate rain forest, and an ancient, untouched Haida village abandoned centuries ago. And skiers have a huge selection of alpine and Nordic resorts throughout the province. Whistler/Blackcomb, rated the best resort in North America by top ski magazines, is less than two hours from Vancouver and open year-round.

1 Exploring British Columbia

First things first—Vancouver is not on Vancouver Island; Victoria is. The island is just a ferry-ride away from Vancouver. The province's capital city, Victoria, is filled with maritime lore and restored Victorian splendor. But Victoria represents only a fraction of the varied experiences available to the traveler on this 300-mile-long Pacific Coast island. Take the Island Highway north (Trans-Canada Highway 1) past towering red cedars and clear, rushing waters, heading toward Duncan in the Cowichan Valley, where you can take a tour of the island's fine wineries or watch master carvers create totem poles and ceremonial masks. Near Parksville, you can turn off on Highway 4 and travel through Port Alberni and the Mackenzie Range to Ucluelet and Tofino. Here, you can watch the spring migration of gray whales and orcas from the beaches, launch your kayak and paddle through the Pacific Rim National Park's Broken Islands Group, or hike through rain forest wilderness.

If you prefer alpine meadows and towering snow-topped cliffs, then continue north on the Island Highway to the Comox Valley, Courtenay, and Strathcona Provincial Park. The park's Mt. Washington and Forbidden Plateau ski resorts attract loads of visitors during the winter, so be prepared for crowded hotels and campgrounds.

North of Courtenay, the Island Highway winds through Campbell River and thickly forested mountain ranges on its way to Alert Bay on Cormorant Island. Here, you can watch orca pods belly up to the beach, and stroll the boardwalk town of Telegraph Cove. You may even want to drive up to the island's final port-of-call, Port Hardy, where you can board the B.C. Ferries' MV *Queen of the North* and cruise up the Inside Passage. The ship stops at the remote town of Bella Bella before it takes you to Prince Rupert and the hauntingly beautiful Queen Charlotte Islands.

Back on the mainland, the Trans-Canada Highway heads southeast out of Vancouver through the Fraser River Valley. Just outside the town of Hope, it splits off to the Crowsnest Highway (Route 3). You'll cross Manning Provincial Park's lush mountain passes and wind your way down through the Similkameen River Valley to the arid Okanagan Valley and its chain of lakes. Freshwater sports, golf, fishing and wine tasting are just a few of this region's popular activities. Don't forget to stop at a fresh fruit stand to sample the region's finest peaches, apples, and cherries.

Route 97 takes you from this beautiful desert garden to the Cariboo and Chilcotin regions where you'll find that the Canadian Old West lives on. Follow the 1870s Gold Rush Trail (also known as the Old Cariboo Highway). Prospectors and panners started their northward journey in Lillooet (Mile 0). Towns eventually grew around the roadhouses at 70 Mile House, 100 Mile House, and 150 Mile House, which also served as mile-markers for weary travelers. But it is at their final destination—the rich gold-rush towns of Barkerville and Richfield—where you can walk through faithfully restored buildings or try your luck at gold panning.

Nearby Bowron Lakes Provincial Park is a canoeist or kayaker's dream come true. Six placid wilderness lakes are chained together by a series of small portages, creating a 72-mile-long paddling and camping circuit. Just outside of 100 Mile House, the Route 24 turnoff winds through mountain passes to the pristine wilderness area of Wells Gray Provincial Park. Monumental waterfalls, abundant wildlife, rushing blue rivers, and crystal-clear lakes await you there. Further south of this alpine wilderness you'll find the Shuswap lakes where you can navigate and fish the region's 600 miles of waterways on a houseboat.

Heading back west on Route 97 takes you through the southern Chilcotin to Whistler/Blackcomb, recently rated North America's most popular ski resort by *Ski* and *Snow Country* magazines. Blackcomb Mountain, whose 1-mile vertical drop is the highest on the continent, has year-round glacier- and snowboarding. During the summer, it's a favorite mountain-biking, hiking, and camping getaway for Vancouverites.

On your way back to Vancouver, you might want to stop in Squamish to watch rock climbers attempting to conquer the Chief—the world's second-highest granite monolith (Gibraltar is the first). If it's January, pause to watch the bald eagles. The area's bald eagle count was a staggering 3,700 in 1994!

Southern British Columbia

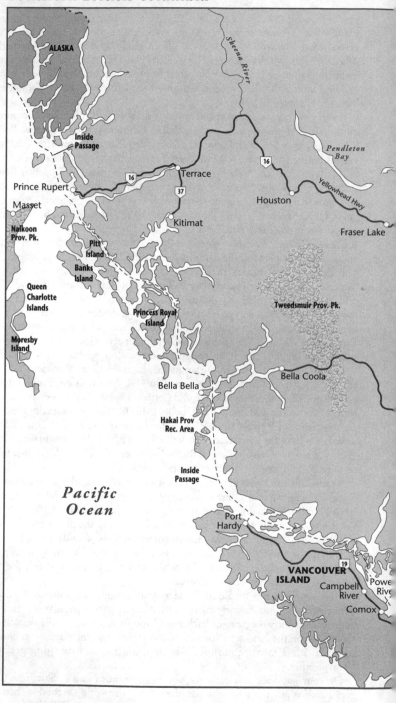

ALASKA

Skeena River

Inside
Passage

16

Terrace

37

*Pendleton
Bay*

16

Yellowhead Hwy

Prince Rupert

Houston

Masset

Kitimat

Fraser Lake

Naikoon
Prov. Pk.

Pitt
Island

Banks
Island

Queen
Charlotte
Islands

Princess Royal
Island

Tweedsmuir Prov. Pk.

Moresby
Island

Bella Coola

Bella Bella

Hakai Prov
Rec. Area

Inside
Passage

*Pacific
Ocean*

Port
Hardy

19

VANCOUVER
ISLAND

Campbell
River

Powe
Rive

Comox

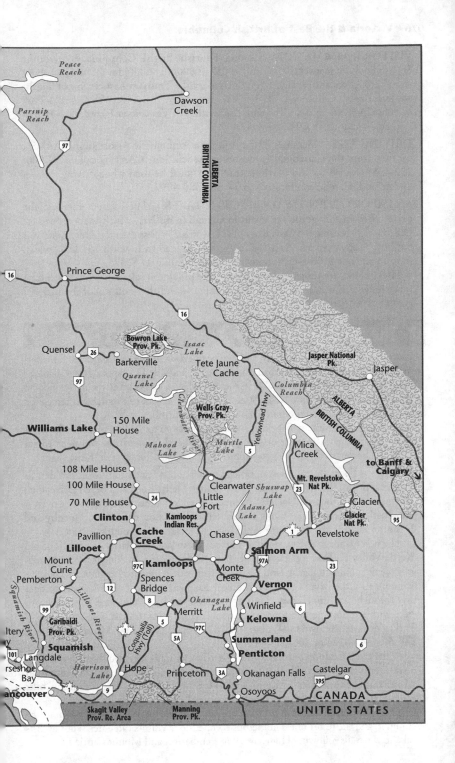

VISITOR INFORMATION   Contact **Tourism British Columbia,** 865 Hornby St., 8th floor, Vancouver (☎ 604/685-0032 or 800/663-6000) for information about travel throughout the province. You can also try the **Tourism Association of Southwestern British Columbia,** 204-1755 W. Broadway, Vancouver (☎ 604/382-2160 or 800/663-3882), and the **Tourism Association of Vancouver Island,** 302-45 Bastion Sq., Victoria (☎ 604/382-3551).

DRIVING TIPS   Members of the American Automobile Association (AAA) can get help from the **Canadian Automobile Association (CAA)** by calling ☎ 800/222-4357. Seat belts and daytime headlights must be used while driving. For an update on B.C. road conditions, call ☎ 604/380-4997.

AN IMPORTANT NOTE ON PRICES & TAXES   Unless stated otherwise, **the prices cited in this guide are given in Canadian dollars,** which is good news for U.S. travelers because the Canadian dollar is worth 25% less than the American dollar but buys nearly as much. As we go to press, $1 Canadian is worth 75¢ U.S., which means that your $100-a-night hotel room will cost only U.S. $75.

Hotel rooms are subject to a 10% tax. The provincial sales tax is 6% (excluding food, restaurant meals, and children's clothing)—and that's on top of the national goods and services tax (GST).

2 The Great Outdoors

Pick up a copy of the bimonthly *Coast: The Outdoor Recreation Magazine* for information on the best trails, off-road biking routes, and kayaking spots. It's available at many outfitters and recreational equipment outlets. Or check the regularly updated information on the World Wide Web at *Euphony Magazine's* sports and recreation site (http://euphony.com/euphony/BCsites/sports.html).

Find your favorite activity below, and we'll point you to the best places in the province to pursue your interest or give you the general information you need to get started. The details are in the geographical sections that follow later in the chapter.

BIKING   There are countless options, but here are a few of our favorites rides. In **Victoria,** the 8-mile Scenic Marine Drive follows Dallas Road and Beach Drive, then returns to downtown via Oak Bay Avenue. From Nanaimo, take a ferry ride over to **Newcastle Island** and bike along the Shoreline Trail. Lots of trails on **Hornby and Denman Islands** are also worth exploring, particularly on a mountain bike.

The best Okanagan Valley biking is off-road, but not necessarily difficult. The old **Kettle Valley Railway's** tracks and ties have been removed, making for some incredibly scenic mountain biking (and no hills or turns that a loaded freight train couldn't handle). And the Myra Canyon route near Kelowna crosses over 18 trestle bridges and through two tunnels carved out of the adjoining mountainsides. If you want to bike with a group, guided tours are available from **Vintage Cycling Tours,** 4847 Parkridge Ave., Kelowna (☎ 604/764-7223); and **Silver Star Mountain Resort** (☎ 604/542-0224 or 800/663-4431).

In the High Country beyond Kamloops, off-road trails take you through the hilly, arid terrain that surrounds the Thompson and Adams Rivers. Nearby **Full Boar Mountain Bike Tours** in Kamloops (☎ 604/376-5532) has mountain bike rentals, and offers half, full- and multiday guided rides for all ability levels.

The **Whistler/Blackcomb** ski trails are open for mountain biking throughout the summer, and the resort offers numerous competitions visitors can enter. Tour cyclists take to the trails following Highway 99 to Pemberton and Mount Currie.

BOATING   When you're in Victoria, you can take a leisurely cruise to Sooke Harbour or up the Strait of Georgia. You can rent bareboat or skippered vessels for a few hours or a couple of weeks from **Brentwood Inn Resort Boat Rentals,** 7176 Brentwood Dr., Brentwood Bay (☎ 604/652-3151). There are also a few smaller outfits on the docks at the **Oak Bay Marina Group,** 1327 Beach Dr. (☎ 604/598-3369). Don't forget to check the **marine forecast** (☎ 604/656-7515) before setting forth.

Back on the mainland, more than a dozen Okanagan Valley lakes (not including the lakes north of Vernon) are suitable for boating. Whether you're into waterskiing, fishing, jet-skiing, or pleasure boating, these lakes are extremely inviting. Many local marinas offer full-service rentals. For a longer outing, **Okanagan Boat Charters,** 291 Front St., Penticton (☎ 604/492-5099), has houseboats that accommodate eight to 10 people. Rental for a three-day weekend is around $750; and a 27-foot sailboat costs $545 per week. The houseboats have full kitchens.

CANOEING/KAYAKING   Southeastern Vancouver Island has numerous inlets and tiny islands you can access by ocean kayak or canoe. Rentals are easily arranged in Victoria, or just north in Duncan or Nanaimo.

You'll quickly find out why Vancouver Island's west coast is second only to New Zealand's coasts for kayakers. For novices and intermediates, the sheltered waters of **Clayquot Sound** are excellent. The Pacific tidal swells along **Long Beach** are ideal for surf-kayakers. In the **Broken Group Islands,** Meares and Flores islands are the ones to consider. They're accessible by water and have numerous marine parks for minimal-impact overnight camping.

The **Johnstone Strait** has the world's largest orca population. You can watch sea lions cavort, camp overnight at any of the marine parks, and explore abandoned native villages there. Because the waters are sheltered, this area is ideal for those just learning to kayak. **Discovery Kayaks,** 2755 Departure Road, Nanaimo (☎ 604/758-2488), offers kayak trips to these prime orca grounds. **Northern Lights Expeditions,** based in Seattle, Washington (☎ 206/483-6396), runs six- to eight-day expeditions through the passage to Robson Bight. Their guides can identify many individual whales who return to these waters every year.

The **Shuswap Lakes,** the **South Thompson River,** and **Kamloops Lake** are pleasant, easy paddles.

CLIMBING   Central Vancouver Island's glacier-cut volcanic-rock mountains provide some great climbs that will test any mountaineer's skills. Skaha Bluffs has more than 400 bolted routes in place. There are a few outfitters that provide you both instruction and guides: **Skaha Rock Adventures** (☎ 604/493-1765); **Ultimate Outdoor Adventures** (☎ 604/764-8761), which offers cave exploration as well; and **Skaha Rockworks** (☎ 604/493-7237).

One of the best ascents recommended by local mountaineers is The Chief, a stark wall that looms above Squamish at the head of Howe Sound. Another favorite rock climbing spot is Smoke Bluffs. Backpacking trips in and around this area are organized by the **Federation of Mountain Clubs of B.C.,** 1367 W. Broadway, Vancouver (☎ 604/737-3053).

FISHING   Numerous salmon fishing charters are available in **Victoria,** where annual stocks are running lower than normal. We recommend that you practice catch-and-release. Halibut, cutthroat, and ling cod also live in the gulf and ocean waters. **Elk and Beaver Lakes,** off Patricia Bay Road, are well-stocked with steelhead, rainbow trout, kokanee, Dolly Varden char, and smallmouth bass.

Shipwrecks & Sea Creatures: British Columbia's World-Class Dive Sites

An amazing array of colorful marine life and fascinating shipwrecks lies under the sea off the coast of British Columbia, so we've rounded up some of the best sites.

Pacific Rim National Park's **Broken Islands Group** is located in Barkley Sound. The reefs are filled with marine life: Branching bryozoans create coral-like reefs that are home to brittle stars, juvenile crabs, and ring-top snails. The drop-offs shelter large populations of featherstars and numerous varieties of rockfish, and seven-foot-long wolf-eels poke out of caves and crannies.

The park's **West Coast Trail** is known as "the graveyard of the Pacific." Dozens of 19th- and 20th-century shipwrecks and their resident marine life make this dive site one of the best in the world—second only to the Red Sea, according to The Cousteau Society. Underwater interpretive trails guide you through these artificial reefs. If you want to take a look for yourself, contact the **Ocean Centre** (☎ 604/475-2202), **Seaker Adventure Tours** (☎ 604/479-0244), or **Nootka Charters** (☎ 604/725-3318), which has two- to six- day cruises with food and accommodation on board.

Off the east coast of Vancouver Island, **Hornby Island** is the most remote of the Gulf group. Twelve-foot, six-gill sharks hide in the deep reefs just offshore. Shipwrecks such as the iron steamer *Alpha,* which was built in 1900 and ran aground on **Chrome Island** (at the southern tip of Denman Island) in the 1920s, are worth exploring. The **Discovery Passage** near Campbell River has excellent dive sites, including Row and Be Damned, Whisky Point, Copper Cliffs, and Steep Island, where strawberry anemones and sponges inhabit the tidal waters. On the Island Highway in Campbell River, **Beaver Aquatic** (☎ 604/287-7652) and **Sea Fun Diving** (☎ 604/287-3622) rent scuba equipment for about $55 per day.

Pink hydrocorals, rose soft corals, plumose anemones, and basketstars live in the lush underwater kelp forests of the northern **Johnstone Strait. God's Pocket Resort** (☎ 604/949-9221), located on remote Hurst Island, about 10 miles north of Port Hardy, offers all-inclusive holiday packages for fisherman and scuba divers.

And for marine life of a different sort, check out the water off the Queen Charlotte Islands. **Cape St. James on Moresby Island** is an important summer rookery for northern sea lions; sometimes you'll encounter their playful young. Underwater visibility is excellent during the summer, and you won't soon forget swimming with these creatures.

The **Cowichan River** in Duncan has a 19-mile-long fishing path that's a good bet any time of year for fly-fishermen going after trout and steelhead.

Year-round sport fishing for salmon, steelhead, trout, Dolly Varden char, halibut, cod and snapper is possible near **Port Alberni**—thanks to the local fish hatchery that releases more than 10 million fish annually. **Long Beach** is also great for bottom fishing.

At the mouth of the Campbell River, anglers vie for membership in the **Tyee Club,** whose requirements include fishing in a small, designated area according to stringent rules and landing a record-weight tyee salmon (some catches tip the scales at more than 75 pounds). Coho salmon here weigh up to 20 pounds. Cutthroat and rainbow trout inhabit the nearby rivers. You can also try your luck in Campbell Harbour. For a $1 admission fee, you can fish off **Discovery Pier.**

The long fjords and many islands near **Prince Rupert** provide shelter for feeding salmon. Fishing lodges dot the coastline's vast wilderness—which is also home to bald eagles, grizzlies, seals, sea lions, and orcas. The question here isn't whether you'll make your catch limit—it's whether you'll have a trophy catch. Resort operators encourage you to release fish under 17 pounds. If you don't, you'll reach your limit all too soon. All five salmon species are here, along with cod, halibut, and snapper.

Kingcome Inlet, Rivers Inlet, Hakai Pass, and **Douglas Channel** are well known hot spots. The Queen Charlotte Islands were opened in the past decade to sport fishing. Tall tales about catching 70-pound tyee and 125-pound halibut are really true. **Langara Island** and **Naden Harbour on Graham Island** are perfect salmon migration spots where you might release catches under 30 pounds.

Okanagan Valley summers are too hot for fishing in the region's big lakes of **Okanagan, Kalamalka,** and **Skaha,** but spring and fall are bountiful seasons. The best summer fishing can be found at the small, hillside lakes surrounding the valley. This is the place to come for trout, steelhead, Dolly Varden char, and smallmouth bass.

Sport fishing is the best reason to visit the **Cariboo lakes,** about 250 of which are accessible by road. Some lakes are as high as 6,000 feet in the mountains.

In the **Shuswap Lakes** area, weed beds nurture the shrimp, sedge, and insects that rainbow trout love. Many of the lakes are quite rightly considered fish factories. You're close to civilization here but it's not hard to get away by helicopter or float plane to the isolated Bonaparte Plateau fishing resorts.

British Columbia anglers prefer the **Thompson-Nicola region** north of Kamloops where the lakes are teeming with rainbow trout. (A fifth of all provincial freshwater angling takes place here.)

Fishing in **Whistler's Green River** and such surrounding lakes as **Birkenhead** is excellent.

GOLF With **Victoria's** Scottish-English heritage and its lush rolling landscape, it's no wonder that golf is popular; some good courses are available to visitors there.

There are also a number of outstanding courses around **Vancouver Island,** including the 18-hole Les Furber–designed **Morningstar** championship course in Parksville; the **Storey Creek Golf Club** in Campbell River; and the classic **Crown Isle Golf and Country Estates** in Courtenay.

You've got your choice of 9- and 18-hole golf along with a variety of course designs in the **Okanagan Valley,** including two by Les Furber: the **Gallagher's Canyon Golf and Country Club** in Kelowna and **Predator Ridge,** which has hosted the B.C. Open Championship.

You have two courses that will test your skills against the arid terrain around **Kamloops,** including the **Rivershore Golf Club,** designed by Robert Trent Jones, and the **Eagle Point Golf and Country Club,** a Scottish links–style course.

Golfers will also be happy at **Whistler,** playing either the Robert Trent Jones **Chateau Whistler Golf Club** course or the **Nicklaus North at Whistler,** both of which have spectacular views.

HIKING As you might expect, there's no end of wonderful places, whether you're interested in a beautiful day hike or a more challenging backpacking expedition.

Among the best destinations are **Goldstream Provincial Park,** on the Island Highway just north of Victoria, where you can hike through centuries-old stands of rain forest and perhaps spot bald eagles. Accessible by ferry from Nanaimo, **Newcastle Island Provincial Marine Park** has wonderful trails, both through the forested interior and along the shoreline.

On Vancouver Island's west coast, the boardwalked **Clayquot Witness Trail** near Tofino is a lovely walk through a lush coastal rain forest. The newly designated **Carmanah Pacific Park,** a first-growth Sitka spruce rain forest near Port Renfrew, also has trails for hikers.

There's also terrific hiking at **Kitilope,** a UNESCO World Heritage Site located south of Kitimat on the western coast of the mainland. Here you can enjoy the serenity of an ancient Sitka spruce coastal temperate rain forest.

You can retrace explorer Alexander Mackenzie's 1793 footsteps across the interior Chilcotin plateau and Coast Mountains along the 250-mile **Mackenzie Trail,** which stretches from the Fraser River, northwest of Quesnel, through Tweedsmuir Provincial Park to Bella Coola. Segments of this heritage trail are easy to moderate, but other portions are quite challenging—just right for experienced hikers and wilderness campers.

Garibali Provincial Park, just northeast of Vancouver, has numerous trails leading through the mountains and alpine meadows surrounding Whistler and Blackcomb.

To learn something while you hike, book a naturalist-guided tour of Vancouver Island's rain forests and seashore with **Coastal Connections-Interpretive Nature Hikes,** 1027 Roslyn Rd., Victoria (☎ 604/598-7043).

HORSEBACK RIDING   With arid terrain reminiscent of the Wild West, but much less developed, the Okanagan Valley is a great place to saddle up and spend an afternoon or a week seeing the land much as the first settlers saw it. **Apex Mountain Guest Ranch,** 20 minutes west of Penticton on Green Mountain Road (☎ 604/492-2454), has guided trail rides, one- to six-day horse pack trips, a children's riding camp, and a B&B right on the ranch.

In the **Cariboo,** you can join the annual week-long **Cattle Drive,** which starts around Cache Creek and ends in Kamloops. Or if you want a more civilized riding experience, stay at either **Big Bar Guest Ranch** near Clinton or **The Hills Health and Guest Ranch** at 108 Mile House.

Both **Wells Gray Guest Ranch** and **Trophy Mountain Buffalo Ranch** provide riders with guided trips through Wells Gray Provincial Park's mountains and valleys.

Look for full details on these ranches later in the chapter.

HOUSEBOATING   You can houseboat along the **Shuswap Lakes'** 620-mile shoreline and channels near Salmon Arm and Sicamous. Rental houseboats are equipped to sleep four to 10 people, and have a fridge, freezer, stove, oven, dual sinks, shower, a head (bathroom), radio-cassette stereo, gas barbecue and, in some cases, a water slide. Much of the shoreline is inaccessible to vehicles, so houseboating is an ideal alternative. Fully equipped boat rentals cost about $800 to $1,700 during the high season and about 20% to 30% less in the spring and fall. Two rental companies are: **Twin Anchors Houseboat Rentals** (☎ 604/836-2450 or 800/663-4026) and **Bluewater Houseboat Charters** (☎ 800/663-4024 or 604/836-2255), both in Sicamous.

RIVER RAFTING   The North Thompson River from Clearwater to Kamloops is the perfect destination for a long-haul rafting/camping run. Outfitters include **Kumsheen Raft Adventures** in Lytton (☎ 604/455-2296), **Interior Whitewater Expeditions** in Clearwater (☎ 604/674-3727), and **Adams River** (☎ 604/955-2447).

White-water rafting down the **Squamish or Elaho rivers** is exhilarating. Aiton's Alley and Steamroller rapids may be the most exciting for experienced rafters, and a riverside barbecue lunch can be your reward for shooting downriver. If you want to experience the thrill of this sport for the first time, try paddle rafting on the Green River instead.

SAILING   **Desolation Sound Marine Park** on the mainland across from Campbell River is a highly recommended sailing destination. There are 37 miles of stunning shoreline set against the snow-peaked Coast Mountains awaiting you at this water-access-only preserve. You can discover the sound and Princess Louisa Inlet on a 25- to 44-foot sailboat. **Desolation Sound Yacht Charters,** 201-1797 Comox Ave., Comox (☎ 604/339-7222), is the closest full-service charter service that rents craft by the day or week.

Natural history tours on large skippered vessels to abandoned Haida villages like Skedans, Tanu, and Ninstints are a great way to discover the **Queen Charlotte Islands.** Your skipper will show you the Burnaby Narrows and explain the behavioral patterns of its residents: orcas, humpback whales, Dall's porpoise, harbor porpoises, and Stellar sea lions. A one- to six-day nature sail can cost $125 to $1,300 per person, but it includes accommodations and meals. For more information, contact **Queen Charlotte Adventures** (☎ 604/559-8990).

SKIING & SNOWBOARDING   The best skiing on Vancouver Island is at **Mt. Washington Resort,** near Courtenay (☎ 604/338-1386), where alpine, Nordic, and telemark runs are all available. Five lifts, 41 major marked runs, 22 miles of groomed trails, a ski school, and cheap lift tickets—what more could you ask? The adjacent and older ski area, **Forbidden Plateau,** is a family-oriented resort that's good for novices.

Cross-country and powder skiing are the **Okanagan Valley's** main wintertime attractions. The **Big White Ski Resort** (☎ 604/765-3101), with an annual average of 18 feet of powder, has 57 runs, plus cross-country trails and night skiing five nights a week. Intermediate and expert downhill skiers will also enjoy **Apex Resort** (☎ 604/ 492-2880 or 800/387-2739), with 56 runs, extensive cross-country trails, an ice rink, snow golf, and sleigh rides. **Silver Star Mountain Ski Resort and Cross-Country Centre** (☎ 604/542-0224 or 800/663-4431), has 56 miles of trails (including 4 miles lit for night skiing) with an additional 30 miles in the adjacent Silver Star Provincial Park. The resort itself resembles a 19th-century mining town where you can ski in and ski out. You'll find some steep verticals among the 72 downhill runs. **Crystal Mountain** (☎ 604/768-5189) caters to the intermediate to novice skier, and has a half pipe for snowboarders.

You'll find every type of snow sport imaginable in the **High Country:** from resort-style downhill and snowboarding runs near Kamloops to backcountry Nordic hiking expeditions in Clearwater. **Sun Peaks Resort** (☎ 604/578-7232) has great powder skiing with 63 runs. Snowboarders have a choice of two half pipes, one with a superlarge boarder cross. Nordic and snowmobile trails are also available. **Utopia Outdoor Adventures,** 230-1210 Summit Dr., no. 123, Kamloops (☎ 604/372-9321 or 800/443-9333), has numerous heli-skiing and heli-boarding packages that include accommodations, child care, ski school, shuttle service from Vancouver, and equipment rentals. **Wells Gray Provincial Park** is a terrific choice for backwoods cross-country skiing.

And then, of course, there's **Whistler Mountain.** With a 5,006-foot vertical and 100 marked runs, this is the granddaddy of all B.C. ski resorts. Helicopter skiing makes another 100-plus runs accessible on nearby glaciers. And **Blackcomb Mountain** has a 5,280-foot vertical and 100 marked runs. Dual-mountain passes are available. If you're not into downhill, Whistler Resort itself has 16 miles of cross-country trails, and the nearby **Mad River Nordic Centre** has 38 miles of groomed trails, with warming huts and a Nordic ski school.

SPELUNKING   The 9-mile logging road off the Island Highway 10 miles north of Qualicum Beach leads you to **Horne Lake Caves Provincial Park,** where 10 caves (the first two were discovered in 1912) ranging in size from cavernous chambers to small crawlways beckon you to explore year-round. Only four of these limestone caves are open to experienced spelunkers. Riverband Cave has expert guides who lead novices through the 1,259 feet of mapped passages. **Island Pacific Adventures,** 101 Horne Lake Caves Rd. (☎ 604/757-8687), gives tours from June through September and rents caving helmets for about $5.

WILDLIFE WATCHING   You can spot all kinds of animals throughout the province. Even when you're based in Victoria, you can sign up with a company running charters; on a mere two- or three-hour excursion, you might spot orcas, harbor seals, sea lions, bald eagles, or porpoises.

The Johnstone Strait has the world's largest population of orca pods (see "Canoeing/Kayaking," above). But you can even observe these beautiful marine mammals from land at the Robson Bight Ecological Reserve between Port Hardy and Port McNeill; you might even see them rub against the pebbles in the shallows.

The kermodei—a rare subspecies of black bear—has its home in the **Skeena Valley** and on **Princess Royal Island** (you might be lucky enough to spot them as you cruise the Inside Passage; see below). North America's rarest white bear ranges in color from dark chestnut-blond to blue-gray glacier white. Its teddy bear face, small eyes, and round ears are endearing. But the kermodei is even larger than Queen Charlotte Islands' black bear. There are legends describing their supernatural powers—they've been known to save humans in distress. The kermodei was on the verge of extinction until a decade ago, when environmentalists began fighting the timber industry in its limited territory. The population is now stabilized and growing. You'll find a few local outfitters who conduct photo safaris to the kermodei's home.

If you take a summertime trip on B.C. Ferries from Port Hardy to Prince Rupert on the **Inside Passage,** you have a great chance at spotting the wildlife that follow this waterway, including orcas, Dall's porpoise, salmon, bald eagles, and sea lions. As you enter the narrow strait north of Bella Bella, you might spot the kermodei hunting for salmon along the shore. The cruisers end their journey in Prince Rupert, where orca pods play along the Douglas and other northern channels. From this base, you can explore the Queen Charlotte Islands, where April to October is the best time to watch the gray whale migration as well as seals and sea lions. In this archipelago, Graham Island's Naikoon Provincial Park is a 180,000-acre wildlife reserve where you can whale-watch on the beaches or spot peregrine falcons and Sitka deer along dense forest trails. At South Moresby Island, you'll find horned puffins, Cassin's auklets, waterfowl raptors, gray whales, harbor seals, Steller sea lions, and the world's largest black bears.

The annual January bald eagle count in Cheakamus, Brackendale, and Squamish attracts ecotourists from around the world. Rafting and paddling expeditions to choice eagle-watching spots can be booked through **Canadian Outback Adventure Company Ltd.,** 206-1110 Hamilton St., Vancouver (☎ 604/688-7206), or **Rivers and Ocean Unlimited Expeditions,** 206-1110 Hamilton St., Vancouver (☎ 604/685-3732). **Everything Outdoors Ltd.,** Squamish (☎ 604/896-4199), offers eagle-watching kayakers a riverside salmon dinner after a two-hour paddle.

3 Camping Vacations: From Rustic to (Almost) Luxurious

Provincial parks, marine parks, and free and private campgrounds are generally filled on weekends. It's best to stake your claim early in the afternoon (for weekends, head out by Thursday).

The provincial park campgrounds charge a usage fee of $9 to $12 per site. Their facilities vary from rustic (walk-in or water-access) to basic (pit toilets) to luxurious (hot showers and flush toilets). All of the drive-in camps offer cut wood piles, grilled fire pits, sani-stations, bear-proof garbage cans, well water (watch for posted warnings about boiling the water in some places), well-maintained security, and congenial fellow campers.

Goldstream Provincial Park, Sooke Lake Road (take Highway 1 up from Victoria; ☎ 604/387-4363), maintains 141 tent sites and nine RV/trailer sites. Take the Island Highway (Highway, Route 19) to Sooke Lake Road. Drive past the Gate House and follow the signs to the campgrounds. There are no hookups, but the park's camping facilities include hot showers, toilets, water, wood, and fire pits.

Accessible only by pedestrian-ferry from Nanaimo, **Newcastle Island Provincial Marine Park** (☎ 604/387-4363) has 18 tent sites on the island's southern tip. No cars are allowed, but you can canoe or kayak in. Toilets, wood, fire pits, and water are strategically placed at three different points.

On Vancouver Island's west coast, there are a wide variety of campgrounds. Considering the ecotouring crowds that arrive here annually, it's best to book ahead. **Bella Pacifica Resort and Campground,** on the Pacific Rim Highway (☎ 604/725-3400), is privately owned. It has 160 sites ($18.70 to $26.20 per two people) in the Mackenzie Beach area, 2 miles south of Tofino. Private nature trails lead to Templar Beach as well. Flush toilets, hot showers, water, laundry, ice, fire pits, wood, and full and partial hookups are all available.

Overlooking Grappler Inlet, **Seabeam Fishing Resort and Campground,** General Delivery, Bamfield (☎ 604/728-3286), has 80 campsites as well as eight rustic lodge rooms ($18 per vehicle or $40 double/triple). Hot showers, pay phone, and boat rentals are also available.

Along the island's east coast, you can combine camping with sailing or kayaking. **T'ai Li Lodge,** Cortes Bay, Read Island (☎ 604/935-6749), will pick you up—with your kayak and gear—from Quadra or Cortes Island and transport you to their beautiful wilderness setting or you can arrive by sailboat or kayak (Marine Chart no. 3538) and moor at their lodge. Once you're there, you can learn wilderness sailing, sea kayaking, or take a guided trip. The lodge provides rooms, each with a shared shower, sink, and toilet, plus meals. (Rooms are about $85 per night.) The campsite ($10 per night) facilities include a solar-heated hot shower, and pit toilet.

Oceanview Camping and Trailer Park, Alder Road, Alert Bay (☎ 604/974-5213), has a great view of the Johnstone Strait. There are nature trails near the 20 sites ($10 to $15 per vehicle). Full hookups, flush toilets, free showers, free boat launch, charters, and tours make this a great deal.

The 121 wooded sites at **Telegraph Cove Resorts,** c/o Comp 1, Box 1, Telegraph Cove (☎ 604/928-3131), are a short walk from the cove and town. Open from May through October, the camp provides hot showers, laundry, toilets, fire pits, fishing licenses, charters, marina, whale-watching trips, and water. Hookups are an additional

$3. There's also a small convenience store. (The nearest restaurant is in Port McNeill, so pack in some groceries before you arrive.)

The shaded campground at **Wildwood Campsite,** Forestry Road, Port Hardy (☎ 604/949-6753), is on the road to the Prince Rupert ferry. The 60 sites ($10.70 per vehicle) are a great value, with fireplaces, hot showers, toilets, picnic tables, a store, beach access, and moorage.

Cape Scott Wilderness Provincial Park was once a Kwakiutl village site, and later, a 19th-century Danish settlement. But violent windstorms and deluging winter rains over several seasons caused the town to be abandoned (the post office building and a few other signs of previous settlement are still standing). Now, its only inhabitants are seabirds, deer, elk, bear, otter, cougar, and wolves. The rain forest's muddy, difficult trail conditions exist year-round, but as intrepid wilderness campers will agree, the visual and emotional rewards are beyond description. A clear day is an absolutely majestic experience. There is only one 30-mile logging road; otherwise you have to kayak or canoe in. **Golden City Travel and Tours,** Box 1620, Port Hardy (☎ 604/949-9244), sends you from Port Hardy to the park by boat and returns you to Port Hardy by van.

Across the road from the Delkalta Wildlife Sanctuary in the Queen Charlotte Islands, the Lions Club operates a full-service campground. **Masset-Haida Lions RV Site and Campground,** Tow Hill Road, Masset (no phone), has 22 shaded campsites ($8 per vehicle) that are less than a mile from town. Coin showers, flush toilets, barbecue pits, and firewood are all available on the grounds, and the sanctuary's forests, salt marshes, and open beaches make for dramatic surroundings.

With full hookup and tenting sites, laundry, hot showers, toilets, playground, mail drop, and other amenities, **Park Avenue Campground,** 1750 Park Ave., Prince Rupert (☎ 604/624-5861), is an ideal site if you're planning to catch the morning ferry. There are 88 sites ($9 to $16 per vehicle) and it's located about a mile from the ferry terminal.

Camping in the Canadian desert—the south Okanagan Valley—can be exhilarating. This hilly high desert terrain is inhabited by desert cacti, sagebrush, pocket mice, lizards, horned toads and, yes, rattlesnakes. **Haynes Point** (near Osoyoos and the U.S. border), **Inkaneep** (near Oliver), **Vaseux Lake, Okanagan Lake** (between Summerland and Peachland), and **Okanagan Falls Provincial Park** are the best campgrounds.

Historic **Barkerville Provincial Park** has three campgrounds. The best and most luxurious one is Lowhee—less than half a mile from the heritage town—which has hot showers, flush toilets, and plenty of firewood. These well-spaced sites are the best place for families and tenters. If it's summer and you forgot to bring food, you can stop at the Grubstake just above the campgrounds. The friendly owners have a good stock of meat, canned goods, and other essential camping items (even gold pans).

The 250-mile mountain-to-coast Mackenzie Trail winds through **Tweedsmuir Provincial Park.** You'll find wilderness camps and drive-in camps throughout this Chilcotin wilderness area.

Near Wells Gray Provincial Park, the privately owned **Trophy Mountain Buffalo Ranch** and government-maintained **Clearwater Lake campground** are your best choices. Steer clear of Spahats Creek Provincial Park, on the road to Wells Gray. It sits in a year-round foul-weather pocket. And don't bet on finding a site at Wells Gray's Dawson Falls. There are few sites here, and most of them are taken by checkout time! If all else fails, or if you want to be closer to town, camp in the former Shuswap village site at **North Thompson Provincial Park.** Located just south of Clearwater, the shaded, well-spaced sites rest right on the riverbank.

If you're planning to visit the **Shuswap Lakes** region, rent a houseboat and stay at the water-access-only marine parks. The drive-in provincial campgrounds around here are crowded, surrounded by heavy-logged spots, and not adequately maintained.

Along Highway 97, on your way to Lillooet from Cache Creek, the **Marble Canyon Provincial Park** grounds are great for tenters. Sites are on level pads and parking, fire pits, and picnic tables are set above you, so you don't feel cramped in.

In the **Cayoosh Creek Valley,** between Lillooet and Pemberton, the B.C. Forest Service has five self-maintained campgrounds. These are free sites with pit toilets and some picnic tables, but little else. Why stay there? Because you'll sleep by clear, rushing, alpine creeks in a lush alpine forest; be treated to dawn and dusk sightings of blacktail deer; and find total solitude.

Garibali Provincial Park has spacious, yet very private forested camp sites available at the park's **Nairn Falls** campgrounds as well as wilderness walk-in campsites scattered throughout the park. Get there on a weekday, because it gets really crowded from Friday morning through Monday evening. This is a favorite weekend getaway spot for Vancouverites.

4 Victoria

This verdant seaport city, the capital of British Columbia, has been described as being "more British than the British."

A former British outpost, Victoria claims a history filled with maritime lore: Whalers and trade ships once docked in the harbors to transport the island's rich bounty of coal, lumber, and furs throughout the world.

Getting there is half the fun. Sure, you could fly in if you're in a hurry, but making the trip by ferry is part of the experience. At least that's how John Wayne (who summered here) and the Nixons (who honeymooned here) chose to travel. Victoria is linked to the rest of Canada by the Trans-Canada Highway, which starts here on its long trek eastward to Prince Edward Island. At Canada's southwesternmost point, Victoria is Mile 0 on the Trans-Canada Highway.

ESSENTIALS

VISITOR INFORMATION   Located right on the wharf across from the Empress Hotel is the **Tourism Victoria Travel InfoCentre,** 812 Wharf St. (☎ 604/382-2127). If you didn't reserve a room before you arrived, you can go to this office or call their reservations hotline for last-minute bookings (☎ 800/663-3883). The InfoCentre is open daily September through March from 9am to 5pm (during the summer until 8pm or 9pm).

GETTING THERE   **Air Canada** (☎ 800/776-3000 in the U.S. or 800/361-6340 in Canada), **Canadian Airlines International** (☎ 800/426-7000 in the U.S. or 800/363-7530 in Canada), and **Horizon Air** (☎ 800/547-9308) all have direct flights from Seattle and Vancouver to **Victoria International Airport,** 16 miles north of the city. **Air B.C.** (☎ 604/663-9826), **Harbour Air** (☎ 604/688-1277), and **Kenmore Air** (☎ 800/543-9595) run provincial commuter flights and floatplanes that also service the city. One helicopter service, **Helijet Airways** (☎ 604/382-6222 or 604/273-1414), can transport you directly from Vancouver.

All the major car-rental firms have desks at the airport (see "Getting Around," below). From the airport, the Patricia Bay Highway (Highway 17) heads south, straight into downtown Victoria. You can take a cab into downtown for approximately $40 plus tip. **P.B.M. Transport** (☎ 604/475-2010) will get you into town in about 30 minutes; buses leave every half hour from 5:25am to 11:55pm. The one-way fare is $12.

If you take the Horseshoe Bay–Nanaimo ferry, you can get to Victoria by train. The Victoria **E&N Station** is near the Johnson Street Bridge at 450 Pandora Ave. (☎ 800/561-8630 in Canada). The **VIA Rail/Esquimalt and Nanaimo Railway** leaves Courtenay at 1:15pm daily and arrives in Nanaimo at about 3:15pm. It arrives in Victoria at 5:45pm. The one-way fare is $19.25 for adults, $17.10 for seniors and students, $9.50 for children 3–11. There are one-week advance purchase discounts available.

Pacific Coach Lines (☎ 604/385-4411) runs between Vancouver and Victoria. The trip takes five hours, including the ferry portion. Service runs daily from 6am to 9pm (until 8pm during the winter); times vary depending on the ferry schedule. All coach buses stop at the **Victoria Depot** (☎ 604/385-4411), 710 Douglas St., directly behind the Empress Hotel.

B.C. Ferries (☎ 604/386-3431 or 604/656-0757) has three Victoria-bound routes. The most direct Vancouver-Victoria route is the 95-minute trip on the **Tsawwassen–Swartz Bay Ferry,** which operates daily between 7am and 9pm. (Schedule an extra three hours for travel to and from terminals plus waiting time.)

The **Horseshoe Bay–Nanaimo ferry** operates on a similar schedule. You take the train or drive to the city via the Island Highway (Highway 1). The Mid-Island Express (Tsawwassen-Nanaimo) ferry is a two-hour crossing that operates daily between 5:30am and 11pm. These large ferries have restaurants, snack bars, shops, and comfortable indoor lounges. The one-way fare is $6.50 adults, $3.50 children 5 to 11, and $22 per car.

Several daily year-round services connect Washington state with Victoria. **Black Ball Transport** (☎ 604/386-2202) runs between Port Angeles and Victoria. **Clipper Navigation,** 1000A Wharf St., Victoria (☎ 604/382-8100), operates the Seattle-Victoria *Victoria Clipper,* a first-class, 300-passenger, 130-foot, water-jet-propelled catamaran. The *Clipper* leaves Seattle at 8am and returns from Victoria at 9:30pm. During the summer, service is expanded with three additional sailings. Adult summer fares are U.S. $89 round-trip (discounts are available).

From June through October, the Bellingham-Victoria **MV *Victoria Star*** (☎ 206/738-8099 or 800/443-4552) departs Bellingham at 9:30am and arrives in Victoria at 2pm (with a stopover in the San Juan Islands' Friday Harbor).

CITY LAYOUT   Victoria sits on Vancouver Island's southeastern tip, sheltered by suburban residential districts along the coast. The **downtown/Olde Town** area embraces the **Inner Harbour** (an offshoot of Victoria Harbour that leads to the Upper Harbour), while the **Ross Bay** and **Oak Bay** residential areas around Dallas Road and Beach Drive overlook open waters. The city's most central landmark is the **Empress Hotel** on Government Street across from the Inner Harbour wharf. If you turn your back to the hotel, you'll be facing the northern edge of the **James Bay** residential area and the Seattle–Port Angeles ferry terminal. To your immediate left will be the provincial **Legislative Buildings** on Belleville Street.

GETTING AROUND   The **Victoria Regional Transit System** (B.C. Transit), 520 Gorge Rd. (☎ 604/382-6161), runs 40 bus routes through greater Victoria, Sooke, and Sidney. Regular service operates from 6am to just past midnight. Schedules are available at the Travel InfoCentre.

Fares are charged on a per-zone basis. One-way, single-zone fares are $1.35 adults (90¢ seniors and children 5 to 13); two zones are $2 adults ($1.35 seniors and children 5 to 13). Transfers are good for one-way travel with no stopovers. A **DayPass** ($4 adults, $3 seniors and children 5 to 13) gives you unlimited travel throughout the day. You can buy passes at the Travel InfoCentre, convenience stores, and ticket outlets.

You can usually take cabs within the downtown area for less than $6. It's best to call for a cab—they don't always stop on city streets (especially when it's raining). Call **Empress Cabs** (☎ 604/383-8888) or **Blue Bird Cabs** (☎ 604/382-8294).

If you're planning any out-of-town activities, then rent a car or bring your own. If you have a city-bound agenda, make sure that your hotel has parking—most do. Street parking is at a premium here. (Luckily, the downtown area is small enough to be quite walkable.) Metered street parking is hard to come by, and rules are strictly enforced. Unmetered parking on side streets is risky. There are parking lots at View Street between Douglas and Blanshard Streets; on Johnson Street off Blanshard Street; on Yates Street north of Bastion Square; and at The Bay on Fisgard at Blanshard Street. Right turns are allowed at red lights.

You can rent a car from **ABC,** 2507 Government St. (☎ 604/388-3153); **Avis,** 843 Douglas St. (☎ 604/386-8468); **Budget,** 757 Douglas St. (☎ 604/388-5525); **Hertz Canada,** 655 Douglas St. (☎ 604/388-4411); and **Tilden International,** 767 Douglas St. (☎ 604/386-1213). The major firms also have airport desks.

Biking is the easiest way to get around Victoria. There are bike lanes throughout the city and paved paths along parks and beaches. Helmets are mandatory, and riding on sidewalks is illegal, except where bike paths are indicated. You can rent bikes and scooters for $5 to $8 per hour or $15 per day from **Budget,** 757 Douglas St. (☎ 604/388-5525). **Cycle Victoria Rentals,** 327 Belleville St. (☎ 604/385-2453), rents scooters, bikes, in-line skates, tandems, and strollers for about the same price.

The **Victoria Harbour** (☎ 604/408-0971) blue miniferries ($2.50 adults, $1.25 seniors and children one way) are the scenic way to tour the city. Ferries to the Empress Hotel, Coast Harborside Hotel, and Ocean Pointe Resort Hotel leave about every 15 minutes from 10am to 10pm.

FAST FACTS   American Express   The local branch is at 1203 Douglas St. (☎ 604/385-8731). It's open Monday through Friday 8:30am to 5:30pm, Saturday 10am to 4pm.

Camera Repair   City Photo Centre, 1227 Government St. (☎ 604/385-5633), is a good repair shop for new and old cameras.

Dentists and Doctors   Most major hotels have a dentist and doctor on call. Cresta Dental Centre, no. 28-3170 Tillicum Rd. at Burnside Street in the Tillicum Mall (☎ 604/384-7711), is an accessible dental service. James Bay Treatment Center, 100-230 Menzies St. (☎ 604/388-9934), is an alternative medical source.

Hospitals   Local hospitals include the Royal Jubilee Hospital, 1800 Fort St. (☎ 604/370-8000; emergency 604/370-8212); and Victoria General Hospital, 35 Helmcken Rd. (☎ 604/727-4212; emergency 604/727-4181).

Liquor Laws   The legal drinking age in British Columbia is 19. Spirits are sold only in government liquor stores, but beer and wine can be purchased from specially licensed, privately owned stores and pubs.

Police   Dial 911 in an emergency. The Victoria City Police can be reached at 604/384-4111. The Royal Canadian Mounted Police handle most cases for tourists. They can be reached at 604/380-6161.

Post Office   The main post office is at 714 Yates St. (☎ 604/595-2552).

Safety   Crime rates are relatively low in Victoria, but there are transients panhandling throughout the downtown and Olde Town areas. As in any city, stay alert to prevent crimes of opportunity.

Transit Information   The B.C. Transit phone number is 604/832-6161.

Weather   Call 604/656-3978 for weather updates. You can get marine forecasts by dialing ☎ 604/656-7515 or 604/363-6630.

SPECIAL EVENTS   In late January or early February, Chinatown launches a two-week celebration to bring in the **new lunar year** with firecrackers, dancing, dragon parades, and other festivities. Throughout January, the **Focus on Women Arts Festival** presents a variety of theater, visual art, film, and music for $12 per performance. Contact the Intrepid Theatre Company, 602-620 View St. (☎ 604/383-2663).

In mid-February, the **Indoor Highland Games and Dancing,** in Saanich, are celebrated with piping, drumming, dancing, and Scottish field sports. Contact the Highland Games Association (☎ 604/479-7804 or 604/477-8674).

In April, the **Victoria Fringe Festival** begins, bringing 50 international alternative companies, who stage productions in seven downtown venues from noon to midnight daily. It runs through September. Contact the Intrepid Theatre Company, 602-620 View St. (☎ 604/383-2663). In late April, there's the **TerrifVic Dixieland Jazz Festival**. Bands from New Orleans, England, and Latin America perform swing, Dixieland, honky-tonk, fusion, and improv before dedicated audiences at venues all over Victoria. Call ☎ 604/381-5277 for more information.

In mid-May, the **Outdoor Highland Games** are held on the fairgrounds in Saanich, complete with authentic Scottish competitive sports, piping, drumming, and flinging. Contact the Highland Games Association (☎ 604/479-7804 or 604/477-8674).

Throughout June, Market Square courtyard hosts free noon and evening swing, bebop, fusion, and improv performances as part of the **International Jazz Fest.** Call ☎ 604/386-2441.

From the second week of July through the third week of August, there's the **Victoria International Festival**. Concerts, recitals, and dance performances are presented at various venues; tickets are available from the McPherson Playhouse box office.

In mid-August, 120 local and international teams compete in the **Canadian International Dragon Boat Festival.** And there's also **Sunfest,** a free end-of-summer jazz festival held in Market Square the third weekend of August.

And New Year's Eve is celebrated with **First Night.** The downtown streets are given over to revelers during Victoria's New Year's Eve performing-arts festival and alcohol-free party. Admission to the shows, held at a variety of sites, is $5 per person.

EXPLORING THE CITY
THE TOP ATTRACTIONS

✪ **Butchart Gardens.** 800 Benevenuto Ave., Brentwood Bay (13 miles north of Victoria). ☎ **604/652-4422.** Admission $13 adults, $6.50 students 13–17, $1.50 children 5–12. Winter discounts. Open daily at 9am. Call for seasonal closing times. Bus: 75.

These internationally acclaimed, heavily touristed gardens were born after Robert Butchart exhausted the limestone quarry near his Tod Inlet home; his wife, Jenny, gradually landscaped the deserted eyesore. As the fame of the 50-acre gardens grew, the Butcharts transformed their house into an attraction as well. Butchart's grandson now owns and operates the gardens, which have more than a million plants blooming year-round. Stroll through these gardens on summer evenings, when they are illuminated—in July and August, you can even watch the Saturday night

Victoria Attractions

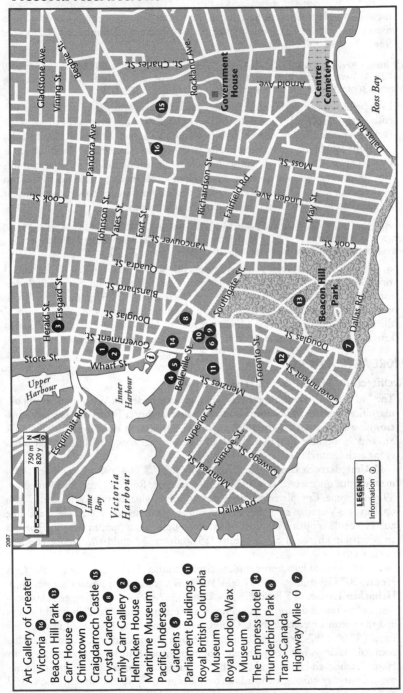

Art Gallery of Greater Victoria **16**
Beacon Hill Park **13**
Carr House **12**
Chinatown **3**
Craigdarroch Castle **15**
Crystal Garden **8**
Emily Carr Gallery **2**
Helmcken House **9**
Maritime Museum **1**
Pacific Undersea Gardens **5**
Parliament Buildings **11**
Royal British Columbia Museum **10**
Royal London Wax Museum **4**
The Empress Hotel **14**
Thunderbird Park **6**
Trans-Canada Highway Mile 0 **7**

LEGEND
Information ⓘ

2087

fireworks displays. You can have lunch, dinner, or afternoon tea in one of the two restaurants or at the summer-only snack bar, and then bring home a few floral touches from The Seed and Gift Store.

✪ **Royal British Columbia Museum.** 675 Belleville St. ☎ **604/387-3701** or 800/661-5411. Two-day pass $5 adults, $2 children. July–Sept daily 9:30am–7pm; Oct–June daily 10am–5:30pm. Closed Christmas and New Year's Day. Bus: 5, 28, or 30.

Even before you enter this modern three-story concrete-and-glass museum, you will encounter a display of totem poles and other large works by artisans of tribes of the Northwest coast. Be sure to stop by Thunderbird Park, located behind the museum, to see the longhouse and contemporary poles—there may even be guest carvers at work. The displays inside the museum include prehistoric fossils, a coastal rain forest, a seacoast, a live tidal pool filled with West Coast marine life, and a re-creation of the ocean floor. The top-floor exhibits explain how archeologists study ancient cultures and include artifacts from regional coastal bands.

Pacific Undersea Gardens. 490 Belleville St. ☎ **604/382-5717.** Admission $6 adults, $5.50 seniors, $4.50 students 12–17, $2.75 children 5–11, free for children under 5; $17.50 families. May–Sept daily 9am–5pm; Sept–Apr daily 10am–5pm. Bus: 5, 27, 28, or 30.

At this marine observatory, you descend a gently sloping stairway to a glass-enclosed viewing area where you can see Inner Harbour marine life close-up. Some 5,000 creatures feed, play, hunt, and mate in these protected waters. Among them are sharks, wolf eels, poisonous stonefish, flowery sea anemones, starfish, and salmon. One of the harbor's star attractions is a huge but remarkably photogenic octopus. Rescued seals and pups are also cared for in holding pens alongside the observatory.

More Attractions

Architectural Highlights & Historic Homes

The 19th-century Scottish and British immigrants who settled Vancouver Island built magnificent estates and mansions. In addition to architect Francis Rattenbury's two crowning achievements—the 1897 provincial **Parliament Buildings,** 501 Belleville St., and the opulent **Empress Hotel,** 721 Government St., you'll find other interesting architectural sites.

✪ **Craigdarroch Castle,** 1050 Joan Crescent (☎ 604/592-5323), is an 1880s mansion that once served as Scottish mining magnate Robert Dunsmuir's four-story, 39-room home. Complete with stone turrets, this Highland-style castle is filled with opulent late-Victorian splendor: Persian carpets, art nouveau stained glass, and fine art. The castle is open daily from 10am to 4:30pm (until 5pm in winter). There is an admission charge of $6 for adults ($5 students, $2 children, free for children under six).

To get a taste of how upper-middle-class Victorians lived, take a tour of the **Carr House,** 207 Government St. (☎ 604/387-4697), where artist Emily Carr was born. **Helmcken House,** 675 Belleville St. (☎ 604/387-4697), is the former 1850s residence of a pioneer doctor. It still contains the original imported British furnishings and the doctor's medicine chest. **Craigflower Farmhouse,** 110 Island Hwy., View Royal (☎ 604/387-3067), was built in 1856 by a Scottish settler. The farmhouse has been painstakingly restored with many of its original Scottish furnishings. The Carr House, Helmcken House, and Craigflower Farmhouse are all open during the summer, Thursday through Monday from 11am to 5pm. Admission is charged by Victoria Heritage Properties ($3.25 adults, $2.25 seniors and students, $1.25 children, free for children under six). If you want to see all three, you can get a package discount pass.

Museums & Galleries

Emily Carr Gallery. 1107 Wharf St. ☎ **604/384-3130.** Admission $2 adults, $1 students, free for children under 12. May–Sept Tues–Sun 10am–5:30pm; Oct–Apr call for hours. Bus: 5 to Fort and Government.

One of western Canada's most acclaimed artists, Victoria native Emily Carr created works depicting the life of the Northwest coastal tribes. If you enjoyed viewing her work in the Vancouver Art Gallery, then you must see this gallery.

Maritime Museum. 28 Bastion Sq. ☎ **604/385-4222.** Admission $5 adults, $4 seniors and students, free for children under 6. Family discounts. July–Aug daily 9am–8:30pm; June and Sept daily 9am–6pm; Oct–May daily 9:30am–4pm. Bus: 5.

This museum is housed in the former B.C. provincial courthouse, built in 1889. More than 5,000 artifacts are on display, including two European shipping vessels and a full array of ship models, photographs, and journals.

Royal London Wax Museum. Belleville Street. ☎ **604/388-4461.** Admission $7 adults, $3 children. May–Aug daily 9am–9pm; Sept–Apr daily 9:30am–4:30pm. Bus: 5, 27, 28, or 30.

Located opposite the Pacific Undersea Gardens, this museum is home to 300 of Madame Tussaud's costumed wax figures, including some of her world-famous Chamber of Horrors characters.

Parks & Gardens

In addition to nearby Butchart Gardens (see "The Top Attractions," above), there are several other lovely city parks. The 154 acres of **Beacon Hill Park** stretch from behind the Royal B.C. Museum (Southgate Street) to the beach (Dallas Road) between Douglas and Cook streets. Stands of indigenous Garry oaks and manicured lawns are interspersed with floral gardens and wildlife sanctuary ponds. You can hike up to Beacon Hill, where you can get a clear view all the way to the Olympic Mountains. The children's farm, aviary, tennis courts, bowling green, putting green, cricket pitch, wading pool, playground, and picnic area make this a wonderful place in which to stroll or relax. The Trans-Canada Highway's Mile-0 marker stands at the Dallas Road end of the park.

If it's raining, don't worry—there's an indoor garden that originally was an Olympic saltwater pool in 1925 and later a big-band dance hall. The **Crystal Garden,** 731 Douglas St. (☎ 604/381-1277), is filled with rare and exotic tropical flora and fauna. Don't let the ground-floor souvenir plaza fool you: Roaming flamingoes, macaws, pygmy marmosets, wallabies, butterflies, and other wildlife live in this jungle setting. The garden is open daily from 8am to 5:30pm. Admission is $6.50 for adults ($4 seniors and children).

ESPECIALLY FOR KIDS

Kids can ride a pony or pet the goats, rabbits, and other barnyard animals at the **Beacon Hill Children's Farm,** in Beacon Hill Park (see "Parks and Gardens," above). **Hitch 'N' Post Ranch,** 4120 Sooke Rd. (☎ 604/474-3494), conducts pony rides and has a petting zoo with llamas and pot-belly pigs. The tropical fauna and flora at the **Crystal Garden** (see "Parks and Gardens," above) will make even a rainy day outing a pure delight. At the **Pacific Undersea Gardens'** underwater observatory (see "The Top Attractions," above), kids can eye a wolf eel or giant octopus up close and watch cavorting harbor seals.

Take them to the **Royal British Columbia Museum** (see "The Top Attractions," above), which presents many aspects of the life and culture of the peoples of the Northwest coast, including carving demonstrations in the Thunderbird Park longhouse.

Kids love the **Royal London Wax Museum** (see "Museums and Galleries," above), where you can see Madame Tussaud's world-famous waxworks and Chamber of Horrors.

Beaver Lake, off Highway 17, is a great freshwater spot where your kids can enjoy swimming with lifeguards in attendance. **Swan Lake Nature Sanctuary** (☎ 604/479-0211) on Ralph Road is even more fun when it rains! You can take a wet walk around the floating boardwalk that rings the 100-acre park. The resident swans love to be fed, and the Nature House will supply grain upon request.

ORGANIZED TOURS

Gray Line of Victoria, 700 Douglas St. (☎ 604/388-5248), tours Victoria and the Butchart Gardens. The 1¹/₂-hour Grand City Tour costs $13.75 for adults and $6.95 for children. Summer departures are every half hour from 9:30am to 7pm; from December through mid-March, there are once-daily departures at 11:30am or 1:30pm.

Heritage Tours and Daimler Limousine Service, 713 Bexhill Rd. (☎ 604/474-4332), takes you through the city, Butchart Gardens, and Craigdarroch Castle in a six-passenger British Daimler limousine. Rates start at $62 per hour per vehicle—not per person.

The bicycle rickshaws operated by **Kabuki Kabs,** Unit 15, 950 Government St. (☎ 604/385-4243), are usually standing in front of the Empress Hotel. Prices are negotiable with the driver (about $30–$40 per hour).

Since 1903, **Tallyho Tours,** 180 Goward Rd. (☎ 604/479-1113), has conducted city tours via horse-drawn carriage. Tours start at the corner of Belleville and Menzies streets and cost $9.50 for adults, $6 for students, $5 for children 17 and under, with discount family rates. Tours operate from mid-March through September every 20 minutes from 9:30am to 7pm (10am to 5:30pm in April, May, and September).

To get a bird's-eye view of Victoria, take a flight on **Go Island Hopper Helicopter,** 103-9800 Lysander Lane, Sidney (☎ 604/656-7627), or Harbour Air Ltd., 1234 Wharf St. (☎ 604/361-6786).

SHOPPING

Victoria has dozens of specialty shops. You may not find cutting-edge fashion boutiques, but there are quality classics and ethnic clothing. In addition, there's a great selection of marine and camping gear—and even some bargains on these items.

Stores are generally open Monday to Saturday from 10am to 6pm. Some downtown stores are open on Sunday during the summer.

Many of the stores are located inside renovated heritage buildings, so a shopping spree can easily become a stroll through Victoria's history. An excellent example of this retail trend is **Market Square,** 560 Johnson St. (☎ 604/386-2441), near Chinatown, which was reconstructed from original 19th-century warehouses and shipping offices. Small shops and restaurants surround a central courtyard where live performances take place throughout the summer.

ART & CRAFTS   Cowichan Trading Ltd., 1328 Government St. (☎ 604/383-0321), has been dealing in Pacific Northwest Indian crafts and clothing at this location for almost 50 years. **Chinook Trading Inc.,** 1315 Government St. (☎ 604/383-7021), has a beautiful collection of basketry, beading, and jewelry. **Alcheringa Gallery,** 665 Fort St. (☎ 604/383-8224), handles the work of Kwakiutl master carver Richard Hunt and Haida printmaker Robert Davidson, among dozens of other regional master artists.

BOOKS **Munro's Book Store,** 1108 Government St. (☎ 604/382-2464), is a Victoria landmark as well as a great source for regional books and fiction by local authors. If you want to find a good field guide, go to **The Field Naturalist,** 1126 Blanshard St. (☎ 604/388-4174), which also sells binoculars, telescopes, spotting charts, and other equipment.

CLOTHING You can find men's, women's, and children's woolen fashions at great prices. **Avoca Handweavers,** 1009 Government St. (☎ 604/383-0433), specializes in Irish clothing, blankets, and crafts. **The Edinburgh Tartan Shop,** 921 Government St. (☎ 604/388-9312), caters to those who prefer sturdy woolens. For something out of the ordinary, **Carnaby Street,** 538 Yates St. (☎ 604/382-3747), carries a marvelous selection of ethnic clothing as well as rare imported textiles, jewelry, and carpets.

DEPARTMENT STORES The same two major department stores that service Vancouver also have Victoria branches. **The Bay (Hudson's Bay Company),** 1701 Douglas St. (☎ 604/382-7141), and **Eaton's,** Victoria Eaton Centre (between Government and Douglas streets, off Fort and View streets; ☎ 604/382-7141), are both in the downtown area.

And if you crave chocolate-covered tea biscuits or lemon curd, head to **Marks and Spencer,** Victoria Eaton Centre (☎ 604/386-6727), a branch of the time-honored British department store.

GIFTS At **East Bay,** 1889 Oak Bay Ave. (☎ 604/595-8338), you and your kids will discover a cornucopia of toys and gifts for the gardener, naturalist, hiker, astronomer, traveler, or adventurer.

OUTDOOR GEAR Outdoor gear isn't merely functional here—it's also the style of choice. You can suit up at the century-old **Jeune Bros. Great Outdoors Store,** 570 Johnson St. (☎ 604/386-8778); or at our favorite outfitter, **Ocean River Sports,** 1437 Store St. (☎ 604/381-4233).

OUTDOOR ACTIVITIES

Even though you're based in an urban location and enjoying city diversions, you can enjoy the natural wonder of British Columbia while you're based here—Victoria enjoys a spectacular setting, and lots of adventures are available just outside the city.

For kayaking, ✪ **Ocean River Sports,** 1437 Store St. (☎ 604/381-4233), can equip you with everything from rentals to jackets, tents, and dry-storage camping equipment. They also offer group tours, lessons, and clinics.

Anglers in search of trout and bass often get lucky at **Elk and Beaver Lakes,** off Patricia Bay Road. **Robinson's Sporting Goods Ltd.,** 1307 Broad St. (☎ 604/385-3429), is a good source for information, lures, licenses, and equipment.

The **East Sooke Fish Company,** 6638 E. Sooke Rd., Sooke (☎ 604/642-7078), combines fishing with ecotouring. While trying your hand at Chinook or coho, you can observe orcas, seals, bald eagles, and porpoises.

The **Cedar Hill Municipal Golf Course,** 1400 Derby Rd. (☎ 604/595-3103), is a public course located just two miles from downtown. The **Cordova Bay Golf Course,** 5333 Cordova Bay Rd. (☎ 604/658-4075), northeast of downtown, was designed by Bill Robinson, with a challenging 66 sand traps and some tight fairways.

You can take a day ride along a wooded trail near Buck Mountain's summit or stay overnight if you're up for serious backcountry packing at **Hitch 'N' Post Ranch,** 4120 Sooke Rd. (☎ 604/474-3494).

The **Horizon Yacht Centre,** 1327 Beach Dr. at Oak Bay Marina (☎ 604/595-2628), offers lessons and navigational tips to familiarize you with the surrounding southern waters as well as sailboat rentals.

The **Crystal Pool and Fitness Centre,** 2275 Quadra St. (☎ 604/380-7946 or 604/380-4636 for schedule), is Victoria's main aquatic facility. The 50-meter lap pool, separate children's pool, diving pool, sauna, whirlpool, steam, weight, and aerobics rooms are open 18 hours a day. **Beaver Lake** in Elk and Beaver Lake Regional Park has lifeguards on duty as well as picnicking facilities. **All Fun Recreation Park,** 650 Hordon Rd. (☎ 604/474-4546 or 604/474-3184), has a ³/₄-mile water slide complex for splashing around. **Ocean Wind Water Sports Rentals,** 5411 Hamsterly Rd. (☎ 604/658-8171), has everything you need in water sports rentals including parasails.

In addition to those at the Inner Harbour, you find **windsurfers** skimming along Elk Lake, just 8 miles north of Victoria. Beginners can learn how to manage their craft through **Active Sports,** 1620 Blanshard St. (☎ 604/381-SAIL) in about three days.

You can take a two- or three-hour trip from Victoria to see orcas, harbor seals, sea lions, bald eagles, and porpoises from May to September. **Sea Coast Expeditions,** Ocean Pointe Resort, 25 Songhees Rd. (☎ 604/383-2254), has biologist guides aboard its high-speed, open Zodiac boats. They supply the wet gear. Rates are $50 to $75 for adults, $30 to $45 for children 6 to 16. Boats depart seven times daily. If you don't want to get wet, then sail along with **Island Breeze Sailing** (☎ 604/744-7327).

WHERE TO STAY

Reservations are a must at Victoria hotels from June to September and during holiday periods. If you have trouble finding a room, call **Tourism Victoria** (☎ 604/382-1131 or 800/663-3883). They can make reservations for you.

VERY EXPENSIVE

The Empress. 721 Government St., Victoria, BC, V8W 1W5. ☎ **604/381-8111** or 800/441-1414. Fax 604/381-4334. 452 rms, 29 suites. MINIBAR TV TEL. Early May to mid-Oct $180–$235 double; mid-Oct to early May $129–$170 double. Year-round $325–$1,400 suite. AE, CB, DC, DISC, ER, MC, V. Underground parking $9 (24 hours); valet parking $15. Bus: 5.

Opened in 1908, this ivy-covered landmark Canadian-Pacific hotel has a fabulous location. It has hosted its share of celebrities, including Queen Elizabeth II—and actually, *everyone* who stays here feels a bit like royalty. All guest rooms are filled with restored Victorian antique furnishings. The deluxe rooms have harbor views, and the honeymoon suites are accessed by a private stairway.

Dining/Entertainment: The Empress has quite a few restaurants. Don't miss having afternoon tea in the Tiffany-glass domed Palm Court.

Services: Concierge, room service, valet, laundry.

Facilities: Indoor swimming pool, health club, sauna, whirlpool, and car-rental desk.

✪ **Ocean Pointe Resort.** 45 Songhees Rd., Victoria, BC, V9A 6T3. ☎ **604/360-2999** or 800/667-4677. Fax 604/360-1041. 222 rms, 28 suites. A/C MINIBAR TV TEL. May–Sept $160–$220 double, $200–$650 suite; Oct–Apr $150–$180 double, $175–$600 suite. AE, DC, ER, MC, V. Underground valet parking $9 per day. Bus: 24 to Colville. Ferry: Harbour Ferry to the hotel's private dock.

This luxurious independent hotel on the Inner Harbour's north shore boasts a commanding view of Victoria set against a backdrop of the Olympic Mountains.

The Inner Harbour rooms have *the* view, but rooms facing the outer harbor have floor-to-ceiling bay windows. Wheelchair-accessible units are available.

Dining/Entertainment: The Victorian restaurant offers elegant West Coast and spa cuisine. There's also a casual restaurant downstairs.

Services: Concierge, 24-hour room service, shuttle service, valet, laundry.

Facilities: It has some of the most complete European spa and health club facilities in the Pacific Northwest plus an ever-increasing range of activities, including whale-watching expeditions.

EXPENSIVE

✪ **The Bedford Regency.** 1140 Government St., Victoria, BC, V8W 1Y2. ☎ **604/384-6835** or 800/665-6500. Fax 604/386-8930. 40 rms. TV TEL. Oct 1–Apr 30 $110–$150 double; May 1–Sept 30 $150–$200 double. Rates include full breakfast and afternoon tea. AE, MC, V. Parking $15.65. Bus: 5.

This small downtown hotel, originally built in 1930, is a real find. Colorful flowerpots on the ledges above Government Street and the spacious Art Deco lobby are a mere preview of the charm you'll find within. As with many older hotels, the rooms vary considerably in size, shape, and decor. Most have brass accents, stocked bookshelves, goose-down comforters, and luxurious amenities; local phone calls are free. Some even have wood-burning fireplaces and Jacuzzis. Children are welcome, but the rooms only have one queen-sized bed. The hotel recommends taking a second room for children.

Dining/Entertainment: The restaurant serves three meals daily in summer (breakfast and lunch in winter) and a classic British afternoon tea year-round. The Garrick's Head Pub has is a good place for a drink or a casual meal.

Services: Concierge.

Oak Bay Beach Hotel. 1175 Beach Dr., Victoria, BC, V8S 2N2. ☎ **604/598-4556** or 800/668-7758. Fax 604/598-4556. 46 rms, 5 suites. TV TEL. Apr 15–Oct 15 $103–$188 double, $158–$395 suite; Oct 16–Apr 14 $88–$128 double, $142–$355 suite. AE, DC, ER, MC, V. Free parking. Bus: 2.

This very British Tudor-style inn perched above the Haro Strait attracts an older crowd. Extensive flower gardens spread to the water overlooking the San Juan Islands. The hotel itself is casual and comfortable. The lobby is a huge living room with a century-old baby grand piano, antiques, and a big fireplace. Every room is unique and priced according to size and view. The third-story junior suites, which have bay windows and balconies facing the sea, are the best rooms.

Dining/Entertainment: There's an authentic English pub and a popular restaurant that serves West Coast cuisine and has outdoor seating.

Services: The hotel's two private yachts can be booked for dinner cruises, sightseeing, and fishing charters. Room service is available from 6am to 10pm.

Sooke Harbour House. 1528 Whiffen Spit Rd., RR no. 4, Sooke, BC, V0S 1N0. ☎ **604/642-3421.** Fax 604/628-6988. 13 rms. TEL. $123–$225 double. Rates include breakfast and lunch. Dinner $56 extra. AE, MC, V. Free parking. Take Hwy. 1 to the Sooke/Colwood turnoff (the Hwy. 14 junction). Take Hwy. 14 to Sooke. Turn left at Whiffen Spit Road (about a mile past Sooke's only traffic light).

This famous inn boasts wonderful scenery, seclusion, a terrific restaurant, and refined service in the best British tradition. Each uniquely decorated room has views of the Strait of Juan de Fuca. The decor in the Victor Newman Longhouse Room reflects the influence of the Pacific Northwest coast peoples. The Herb Garden Room, done in shades of mint and parsley throughout, opens onto a private patio. The hosts leave a bouquet of flowers or a decanter of port in each room.

Dining/Entertainment: The restaurant is renowned for its unique Pacific Northwest fare blending home-grown and local ingredients.

Services: Massage therapist by appointment, breakfast in room, optional dinner in room.

⑤ Swans Hotel. 506 Pandora Ave., Victoria, BC, V8W 1N6. ☎ **604/361-3310** or 800/ 668-7926. Fax 604/361-3491. 29 suites. Oct 1–Apr 30 $79–$99 suite; May 1–June 30 $99–$119 suite; July 1–Sept 30 $145–$165 suite. AE, MC, V. Parking $8. Bus: 23 or 24.

Located in a landmark 1913 Inner Harbour building that was once a feed warehouse, Swans is a small, friendly, and charming boutique hotel. Unlike the diminutive lobby, the suites are spacious. Many are split-level and have open lofts. All have full kitchens, separate dining areas, and living rooms. The two-bedroom suites are great for families. Furnishings are basic, but original artwork and fresh flowers add to the pleasant atmosphere.

Dining/Entertainment: Downstairs, the Fowl Fish Café is open for lunch and dinner daily. The often-crowded pub with a glassed-in patio serves food and traditional ales brewed on the premises.

MODERATE

✪ Abigail's Hotel. 906 McClure St., Victoria, BC, V8V 3E7. ☎ **604/388-5363.** Fax 604/ 388-7787. 16 rms. Year-round $120–$225 double. Rates include full breakfast. Midweek discounts. MC, V. Free parking. Bus: 1.

This four-story, gabled Tudor building surrounded by a beautiful garden is the quintessential small European-style luxury inn. The rooms seem tailor-made for honeymooners or lovers, with crystal chandeliers, stained-glass windows, fresh flowers, and goose-down comforters. Most rooms have private Jacuzzis or deep soaking tubs. Some also have fireplaces and/or four-poster canopy beds. Be sure to check in before 10pm; you can't get in after that unless you already have your room key. Breakfast is served in the sun room at 8am. There's an afternoon social hour in the library with mulled wine and snacks. The piano and games table in the library are popular with guests.

⑤ Andersen House B&B. 301 Kingston St., Victoria, BC, V8V 1V5. ☎ **604/388-4565.** 5 rms. TEL. $75–$165 double. Rates include breakfast. MC, V. No children under 8. Free, limited parking. Bus: 30.

A short walk from downtown, the 1891 Andersen House was built for a sea captain. It's an ornate Queen Anne–style Victorian wooden structure with high ceilings and stained-glass windows. Each room has a private bath/Jacuzzi, stereo, and a king- or queen-size bed. Three rooms overlook a lovely English garden. Our favorite room is the cabin of Janet and Max Andersen's gorgeous 50-foot 1927 teak motor yacht. The yacht is docked in the harbor two blocks from the house. Breakfast for all guests is served in the house. No smoking is allowed in the house or on the boat.

The Boathouse. 746 Sea Dr., RR no. 1, Brentwood Bay, Victoria, BC, V0S 1A0. ☎ **604/ 652-9370.** 1 unit. TEL. $120 double. Rate includes continental breakfast. MC, V. Free parking.

This tiny cottage is a converted Saanich inlet boathouse, built on pilings. It's a short stroll (or row) to Butchart Gardens, but it's very secluded. The only likely passersby are seals, bald eagles, otters, herons, and raccoons. This charming red cabin is at the end of a very long flight of stairs behind the owner's home. Inside, there's a sofa bed, dining table, kitchen area with small refrigerator and toaster oven, electric heater, and a reading alcove overlooking the floating dock. Full toilet and shower facilities are located in a separate bathhouse a short way back uphill. All the makings for a delicious continental breakfast are provided the previous evening, and you have use of a rowing dinghy.

⑤ **Dashwood Manor.** 1 Cook St., Victoria, BC, V8V 3W6. ☎ **604/385-5517** or 800/667-5517. 15 suites. TV. Nov–Mar $45–$155 suite; June–Sept $135–$285 suite; Oct and Apr $95–$215 suite. AE, DC, ER, MC, V. Free parking. Bus: 5.

This cozy 1912 Tudor manor overlooks the strait of Juan de Fuca, with the beach and park just across the street. Downtown is a 20-minute stroll away. Inside, the manor takes on an Edwardian flavor. Deep-stained oak paneling and burgundy carpeting lead up to the guest suites. Each unique suite has a queen-size bed and a well-stocked kitchen (breakfast is self-catered). You may find a fireplace, Jacuzzi, balcony, or perhaps a chandelier among the blend of antique and contemporary furnishings. Complimentary evening sherry, port, and wine are laid out in the lobby. Don't expect a raucous crowd: Most of the guests are couples, and the romance of the manor is hard to avoid.

INEXPENSIVE

The James Bay Inn. 270 Government St., Victoria, BC, V8V 2V2. ☎ **604/384-7151.** Fax 604/381-2115. 50 rms (41 with bath). TEL TV. Oct–Apr $38–$49 double; May $52–$89 double; June–Sept $72–$109 double. MC, V. Free, limited parking. Bus: 5 or 30.

This 1907 Edwardian manor facing Beacon Hill Park was the last home of famed Victoria-born artist Emily Carr. The newly renovated lobby and rooms have a subtle Spanish decor. The restaurant serves three meals daily, and there is a well-patronized neighborhood pub as well. (Guests of the inn receive a 15% discount in both establishments.) The inn's tranquility makes it popular with vacationing retirees.

✪ **The Medana Grove.** 162 Medana St., Victoria, BC, V8V ZH5. ☎ **604/389-0437** or 800/269-1188. Fax 604/389-0425. 2 rms. TV. May 16–Sept 14 $70–$85 double; Sept 15–May 15 $49 double. MC, V. Street parking. Bus: 5 to Simcoe.

This charming little 1908 James Bay home is a short walk from downtown, oceanside walking paths, and Beacon Hill Park. Tucked away on a one-block-long, tree-lined street, it can be a little difficult to find, but it's worth locating. The antique-filled living room with its welcoming fireplace and the dining room are both comfortable and cheery. Both guest rooms are decorated in subtle floral patterns and have private baths. A full gourmet breakfast is served in the dining room. No smoking.

⑤ **Victoria International Hostel.** 516 Yates St., Victoria, BC, V8W 1K8. ☎ **604/385-4511.** Fax 604/385-3232. 104 beds. $14.50 International Youth Hostel (IYH) members, $18.50 nonmembers. MC, V. Bus: 23 or 24 at the Johnson St. Bridge.

Located in the heart of Olde Town, this hostel has everything the serious backpacker needs. Facilities include two fully equipped kitchens, a dining room, a TV lounge with VCR, game room, common room, library, laundry facilities, indoor bicycle lock-up, and hot showers. An extensive ride board helps you make transportation arrangements, and the collection of outfitter and tour information rivals that at the tourism office. Dormitory beds are separated by gender, but there are a couple of family rooms. There's a 2am curfew, but the town gets a little sleepy by then, so you won't be missing much.

WHERE TO DINE
VERY EXPENSIVE

Sooke Harbour House. 1528 Whiffen Spit Rd. ☎ **604/642-3421.** Reservations required. Main courses $16–$28. AE, ER, MC, V. Daily seatings at 6:30 and 7:30pm; closes at 9:30pm. Take Hwy. 1 to the Sooke/Colwood turnoff (the Hwy. 14 junction). Take Hwy. 14 to Sooke. Turn left at Whiffen Spit Road (about a mile past Sooke's only traffic light). WEST COAST.

In a rambling white house on a bluff overlooking Sooke's Whiffen Spit, this restaurant offers a spectacular view and a quiet, relaxed atmosphere. You will immediately feel at home as you dine on local seafood and organically farmed herbs and vegetables (fresh from Frederica and Sinclair Philip's own garden) prepared West Coast–style. It's a practically legendary place, and still continues to live up to its fine reputation.

EXPENSIVE

Ⓢ **Harvest Moon Café.** 1218 Wharf St. ☎ **604/381-3338.** Reservations recommended. Main courses $14.50–$18.50. AE, MC, V. Daily 11am–11pm. Bus: 5, then walk two blocks west. PACIFIC NORTHWEST.

The fare here includes roast pork loin with apple-garlic relish, fresh asparagus, and grilled yams served in one of western Canada's oldest buildings: the 1858 Steam Victoria warehouse. The exposed-brick walls are warmed by original art and floral arrangements that create an intimate setting. Their motto is "Fresh, Local, Seasonal." Smoked salmon and Indian candy are made on the premises. Their award-winning wine list includes an extensive collection of great B.C. wines. Bread pudding and Belgian chocolate cookies are house specialties. If you're lucky enough to be here when the menu features white Belgian chocolate cheesecake, you'll be truly blessed.

Rebecca's. 1127 Wharf St. ☎ **604/380-6999.** Reservations accepted. Main courses $12.95–$18.95. AE, MC, V. Daily 11:30am–10pm. Bus: 5, then walk two blocks west. PACIFIC NORTHWEST.

A team of eight chefs creates the pastas and baked goods at this spacious, wharf-front restaurant, which has a light, open atmosphere. The seasonal menus include specials such as whole Dungeness crab with Chardonnay and roasted garlic cream, and fresh halibut with almonds in strawberry-balsamic vinaigrette. There's also a cappuccino bar, a bar in front of the window that's perfect for people-watching, and an outdoor cafe open for summertime dining.

MODERATE

Cherry Bank Spare Rib House. 825 Burdett Ave. ☎ **604/385-5380.** Reservations accepted. Three-course rib special $11.95; main courses $11.95–$16.95. AE, DC, MC, V. Daily 11:30am–2pm and 5–9pm. Bus: 5. RIBS.

Located in an 1897 landmark hotel, Cherry Bank has been Victoria's top rib house for more than 40 years. The friendly staff serves up large, tangy racks of ribs with salad, potatoes, vegetables, and garlic bread to a family oriented clientele. The menu also includes scampi, fresh fish, seafood, and steaks.

Ⓢ **James Bay Tea Room.** 332 Menzies St. ☎ **604/382-8282.** Reservations recommended. Main courses $9.25–$11.25. MC, V. Mon–Sat 7am–9pm; Sun 8am–8pm in winter, 7am–9pm in summer. Afternoon tea served daily 1–4:30pm. Bus: 5 or 30. ENGLISH.

For decades, Victoria's best afternoon tea has been served at this simple, English country–style home a block from the legislative buildings. Traditional dishes such as eggs and kippers for breakfast or steak-and-kidney pie and Cornish pasties for lunch are served daily. Not surprisingly, a dinner favorite at this very British restaurant is roast prime rib of beef with Yorkshire pudding. There's often a line for tea, but it's a civil one.

Herald Street Café. 546 Herald St. ☎ **604/381-1441.** Reservations required. Main courses $10.95–$19.95. AE, ER, MC, V. Wed–Sat 11:30am–3pm, Sun 10am–3pm; Sun–Wed 5:30–10:30pm, Thurs–Sat 5:30pm–midnight. Bus: 5. PASTA/WEST COAST.

Young Olde Town locals flock to the excellent Sunday brunch at this light, casual restaurant located in a Victoria heritage building. The room is filled with potted palms and floral arrangements. The walls are decorated with local artists' works. Freshly made pastas, delicate venison medallions, and steamed mussels served with prawns, ginger, and roasted cashews are just a few of the chef's dinner creations. The desserts are fabulous, and the award-winning wine list has won the restaurant almost as much recognition as its menu.

✪ **Met Bistro.** 1715 Government St. ☎ **604/381-1512.** Reservations recommended. Main courses $9.50–$18.50. MC, V. Daily 4:30–11pm. Bus: 5. PACIFIC NORTHWEST.

This Chinese-style building once served as the Chinatown community settlement house. Now the ground-floor restaurant serves hungry patrons from a delightful menu that changes monthly. The tantalizing dishes include smoked duck sausage served with caramelized pear, blue cheese, and flatbread; or herb- and spice-crusted loin of lamb topped with a rosemary and red wine demiglace. The tables are set up in an intimate bistro style. The wine list includes vintages from British Columbia, France, South Africa, and Australia. For dessert, it's worth the 20-minute wait to receive your lunch bag–shaped Belgian chocolate bag filled with fresh fruit, white chocolate mousse, and ice cream.

Millos. 716 Burdett Ave. ☎ **604/382-4422** or 604/382-5544. Reservations recommended. Main courses $8.95–$24.95. AE, DC, ER, MC, V. Mon–Sat 11:30am–4:30pm; daily 4:30–11pm. Bus: 5. GREEK.

Millos is not hard to find: Just look for the blue-and-white windmill behind the Empress Hotel. Flaming saganaki (sharp cheese sautéed in olive oil and flambéed with Greek brandy), grilled halibut souvlaki, baby back ribs, and succulent grilled salmon are just a small sampling of the menu at this lively five-level restaurant. You become part of the family for the evening, and your kids get their own special menu. As if the staff and food weren't entertaining enough, folk and belly dancers perform on Friday and Saturday nights.

Reebar. 50 Bastion Square. ☎ **604/361-9223.** Reservations accepted. Main courses $5.25–$8.95. AE, MC, V. Mon–Sat 11:30am–4:30pm, Sun 10am–2:45pm; Mon–Thurs 5:30–7pm, Fri–Sat 5:30–8:45pm. Bus: 5. WEST COAST.

The completely contemporary menu here includes a vegetable and almond patty served with red onions, sprouts, and fresh tomato salsa on a multigrain kaiser bun; and crisp salads with toasted pine nuts, feta cheese, market-fresh vegetables, and sun-dried tomato vinaigrette. Reebar attracts a young, casual crowd.

INEXPENSIVE

✪ **Banana Beet Café.** 281 Menzies St. ☎ **604/385-9616.** Breakfast and lunch $4.25–$9.25. No credit cards. Tues–Sun 8am–3pm. Bus: 5. WEST COAST.

If you're looking for a fresh quesadilla stuffed with cheese and avocados, a fresh juice shake, or a good old-fashioned burger, then go to this cafe, the favored hangout of James Bay locals. Breakfast is serious business here—don't let names such as the Sensitive New Age Guy Omelette (which is filled with Monterey Jack, Brie, and avocados) fool you. You need to bring a hearty appetite. The interior is rather plain, and the outside even more so. But then again, if it looked quaint, it wouldn't be this cheap.

🅢 **Don Mee Restaurant.** 538 Fisgard St. ☎ **604/383-1032.** Four-course dinner for two $16.95; main courses $4.95–$10.35. AE, DC, MC, V. Mon–Fri 11am–2:30pm, Sat–Sun and holidays 10:30am–2:30pm; daily 5pm–closing. Bus: 5. CANTONESE/SZECHUAN.

Since the 1920s, Don Mee's has been serving up genuine Hong Kong–style dim sum, San Francisco–style chop suey and chow mein, piquant Szechuan seafood dishes, and Cantonese sizzling platters. You can't miss this second-story restaurant with its huge neon Chinese lantern shining above the small doorway. A four-foot-tall gold-leafed laughing Buddha greets you at the foot of the stairs leading up to the large room, which seems straight out of Kowloon. The dinner specials for two, three, or four people are great deals.

Fogg 'N' Suds. 711 Broughton St. ☎ 604/383-BEER. Main courses $5.95–$12.95. AE, MC, V. Mon–Sat 11am–1am, Sun 11am–11pm. Bus: 5. INTERNATIONAL.

This theme restaurant, part of a Canadian chain, is named after Phineas T. Fogg (of Jules Verne's classic *Around the World in 80 Days*). It's an absolutely delightful place to bring the kids. The dark-wood, pub-style decor belies its family friendly ambience and eclectic menu. If you think the list of 250 international beers is impressive, then take a look at the food, which includes burgers, nachos, pastas, stir-fries, calamari, schnitzel, and more.

Milestone's. 812 Wharf St. ☎ **604/381-2244.** Reservations not required. Main courses $5.95–$12.95. AE, DC, MC, V. Mon–Thurs 11am–10pm, Fri 11am–11pm, Sat 10am–11pm, Sun 10am—10pm. Bus: 5. WEST COAST.

You'll find the best view of the Inner Harbour at this highly successful Vancouver chain restaurant located just below the Travel InfoCentre. Bountiful grilled-chicken Caesar salad, seafood, ribs, steaks, and overstuffed sandwiches are served up in an upscale, casual atmosphere. The drink specials are refreshing, especially if you manage to get a table on the outdoor patio.

VICTORIA AFTER DARK

Victoria is hardly the nightlife capital of Canada, but it does have a few evening diversions. **The Community Arts Council of Greater Victoria,** 511-620 View St. (☎ 604/381-ARTS or 604/381-2787), runs a hotline to keep you informed of the latest happenings. You can buy tickets to special events at the **Travel InfoCentre,** 812 Wharf St. (☎ 604/382-2127). And *Monday Magazine,* a weekly tabloid that's published on Thursdays, oddly enough, is your best bet for quick information on current entertainment.

THE PERFORMING ARTS   The **Belfry Theatre,** 1291 Gladstone St. (☎ 604/385-6815), is a nationally acclaimed theater company that performs a five-production season from October to April in a small, intimate playhouse. The **Kaleidoscope Theatre,** 715 Yates St. (☎ 604/475-4444), has both a critically acclaimed resident company and a touring company. Both perform plays, dances, and concerts for younger audiences.

The **Victoria Operatic Society,** 798 Fairview Rd. (☎ 604/381-1021), presents a year-round schedule of light Broadway musicals such as *Evita, The Mikado,* and *Into the Woods* at the McPherson Playhouse. Ticket prices range from $12.50 to $19.50.

The **Victoria Symphony Orchestra,** 846 Broughton St. (☎ 604/385-9771), performs every week from August through May. The orchestra kicks off each season with Symphony Splash, a free concert performed on a downtown barge. Summer Pops is a favorite Friday evening event at the Royal Theatre. During the rest of the year, the orchestra performs at different venues throughout the area. Tickets are $12 for most concerts; senior, student, and group discounts are available.

THE CLUB & MUSIC SCENE   **Harpo's,** 15 Bastion Sq. (☎ 604/385-5333), is an intimate waterfront venue that features high-profile performers as well as popular reggae and rock bands. Admission varies but ranges from $3 to $15. Drinks run $3 and up.

Hermann's Dixieland Inn, 753 View St., near Blanshard Street (☎ 604/388-9166), is regarded locally as the best jazz venue in town. This low-lit supper club specializes in Dixieland but occasionally features fusion and blues bands. There's usually no cover charge.

Local rock bands perform at **The Forge,** in the Strathcona Hotel, 919 Douglas St. (☎ 604/383-7137). It's a big, noisy venue that attracts blue-collar workers and hip University of Victoria students. The $3 to $5 cover charge and $3 drink menu make it a reasonable place to boogie down nightly.

There are a few dance and singles clubs here. Most are open Monday through Saturday until 2am, Sunday until midnight. **Merlin's,** 1208 Wharf St. (☎ 604/ 381-2331), is a waterfront-theme nightclub that attracts a cool 20-something crowd. There's a $3 cover after 9:30pm on weekends, and drinks are about the same price. Events change constantly, so call for information.

Pier 42, 1605 Store St., in the basement of Swans Pub (☎ 604/381-7437), plays Top 40 music for a very congenial local crowd Wednesday through Sunday; no cover.

The **Drawing Room Dance Hall,** on the top floor of 751 View St. (☎ 604/ 920-7798), is open Tuesday through Saturday nights and features funk, indy jazz, rock jazz, and a local house band on Wednesdays. This upscale place attracts the young and beautiful. Cover is around $4.

THE BAR SCENE   There are a few good watering holes in town. **Garrick's Head Pub,** 64 Bastion Sq., in the Bedford Hotel (☎ 604/384-6835), serves up pub fare without the chain-restaurant prices or glitz of the so-called pubs nearby. You can enjoy a meal and a pint for less than $7.95.

Swans Pub, 506 Pandora Ave. (☎ 604/361-3310), is part of Swans Hotel. This is the hottest nightspot in town for Victoria's young professional crowd.

THE GAY & LESBIAN SCENE   The scene here is small, intimate, and friendly. After having drinks and dinner at the Met Bistro (see "Where to Dine," above), head to **Rumors,** 1325 Government St. (☎ 604/385-0566), to hang out, dance, and socialize. Open daily from 9pm until 2am (call ahead to make sure hours haven't changed), with no cover charge and nightly drink specials.

CASINOS   Victoria has two casinos that cater mainly to patrons who want to play blackjack, roulette, sic-bo, red dog (diamond dog), and Caribbean stud poker. **Casino Victoria,** 716 Courtney St. (☎ 604/380-3998), and the **Great Canadian Casino,** 3366 Douglas St. (☎ 604/384-2614), are both open daily from 6pm to 2am. They don't offer floor shows or any other side entertainment—just soft-core gambling.

5 Side Trips from Victoria: Goldstream Provincial Park, Duncan & Nanaimo

GOLDSTREAM PROVINCIAL PARK

The great natural beauty of southcentral Vancouver Island is perhaps best seen in **Goldstream Provincial Park** (☎ 604/387-4363), just 20 minutes north of Victoria on the Island Highway (also called Highway 1 or Route 19). This majestic and tranquil setting was once a bustling gold rush site. Park trails take you past abandoned mine shafts and tunnels, plus 600-year-old rain forest stands of Douglas fir, red cedar, indigenous yew, and arbutus. In the autumn, an annual chum salmon run draws bald eagles and other spectators. Every January, a bald eagle count is held here; in 1995, 97 of these magnificent birds were spotted in a single day. The **Freeman King Visitor Centre** (☎ 604/478-9414) offers guided walks, talks, displays, and programs throughout the year.

While the E&N Railroad runs through this magnificent wonderland on its way to Nanaimo, you'll want to spend some time here and do some walking to really explore the park in depth.

WHERE TO STAY & DINE NEARBY

✪ **The Aerie.** 600 Ebedora Lane (P.O. Box 108), Malahat, BC, V0R 2L0. ☎ **604/743-7115.** Fax 604/743-4766. 24 suites. A/C TV TEL. Apr 15–Oct 10 $165–$230 double, $270–$360 suite; Oct 11–Apr 14 $145–$190 double, $240–$300 suite. Rates include full breakfast. AE, MC, V. Free parking. Take Highway 1 to the Spectacle Lake turn-off; take the first right and follow the winding driveway up.

Nestled high above the Malahat summit is a little bit of heaven, complete with an incredible restaurant. In this elegant Mediterranean villa, each hideaway suite has a large handcrafted bed, a sumptuous bathroom, an indoor Jacuzzi, a wetbar and fridge, and a fireplace in front of a white leather sofa. Most of the suites have decks positioned to ensure complete privacy. Though it's the kind of exclusive opulent getaway you'd expect to see featured on *Lifestyles of the Rich and Famous* (in fact, it's appeared three times on the TV show), there's no pretension here.

Dining/Entertainment: The wonderful in-house restaurant, with a 24-carat gold-leaf ceiling, an open-hearth fireplace, and views of Spectacle Lake, serves three meals each day, but is only open to the public for dinner (served 5 to 10pm); reservations are required. Grilled tiger prawns in a ginger-lime cream is just one overture in master chef Leo Schuster's dining symphony, served with impeccable service. A masterfully prepared halibut filet can be accompanied by a selection from the region's best wine list. A luscious orange cappuccino mousse topped with a white Belgian chocolate sauce, plus an excellent brandy and Kona coffee completes your experience. Main courses run $26.75 to $29; a seven-course menu is $55.

Facilities: Five acres of private walking trails, a helipad, a heated indoor pool, outdoor hot tub, tennis courts, full spa treatments, and an outdoor wedding chapel.

WHERE TO DINE NEARBY

❸ **Six Mile Pub.** 494 Island Hwy., View Royal. ☎ **604/478-3121.** Main courses $4.50–$7.50. ER, MC, V. Daily 11:30am–2pm and 6–9pm. Pub Mon–Sat 11am–1am, Sun 11am–midnight. PUB GRUB.

This 1855 heritage pub was named the Parson's Bridge Hotel when it first opened. The site's current 1898 building has a loyal local clientele who come for both the atmosphere and the classic British pub dinner specials—all seasoned with fresh herbs from the pub's own garden. You can enjoy the warm indoor ambience of the fireside room, which boasts an oak bar and other classically British touches or the beautiful scenery on the outdoor patio.

DUNCAN

The Island Highway continues north from the park, and in about 30 miles you'll reach the verdant Cowhican Valley and the city of Duncan.

You can even do some wine tasting as you travel north from Victoria to Duncan. There are five wineries located between Mill Bay and Duncan that offer tours and tastings; all are just off Highway 1. **Merridale Estate Cidery,** 1230 Merridale Rd., Mill Bay (☎ 604/743-4293), conducts tours Monday through Saturday from 10:30am to 4:30pm.

Cherry Point Vineyards, 840 Cherry Point Rd., Cobble Hill (☎ 604/743-1272) provides tours by appointment only, as does **Venturi-Schulze Vineyards,** 4235 Trans-Canada Highway, Cowichan Station (☎ 604/743-5630). **Blue Grouse**

Vineyards, 4365 Blue Grouse Rd., Cowichan Station (☎ 604/743-3834), has tours on Wednesday plus Friday through Sunday from 11am to 5pm; and **Vigneti Zanatta Vineyards,** 5039 Marshall Rd., Duncan (☎ 604/748-2338) conducts tours on Saturday and Sunday from 1 to 4pm.

ESSENTIALS

The **Duncan Travel InfoCentre** is located at 381 Trans-Canada Highway (☎ 604/746-4636).

EXPLORING THE TOWN

The Cowichan Valley tribes living near Duncan are famous for their warm, durable sweaters knit with bold motifs from hand-spun raw wool. Visiting the ✪ **Native Heritage Center,** 200 Cowichan Way (☎ 604/746-8119), is a rich cultural experience where you can observe master and apprentice carvers at work on totem poles and ceremonial masks, have a native meal, or join in their summer song and dance festival. Shoppers will find a wide assortment of authentic Cowichan sweaters and jewelry in the two gift shops, as well as books, serigraphic prints, handcrafted ceremonial masks, replica totem poles, and other items. It's open daily from 9:30am to 5pm; admission is $7 adults, $6.15 seniors and children.

Judy Hill Gallery and Gifts, 22 Station St. (☎ 604/746-6663), represents important artists of the Pacific Northwest peoples such as Robert Davison, Danny Dennis, David Neel, and Roy Vickers.

Duncan is called the City of Totem Poles. Its **Totem Poles Project,** begun in 1985, consists of 41 outdoor poles that stand in front of the various businesses that commissioned them; they're striking works of art to commemorate the city's early heritage. Just follow the yellow footprints painted on the sidewalks to take a complete self-guided tour.

The **Cowichan River** in Duncan has a 19-mile-long fishing path from the Robertson Road clubhouse to Cowichan Lake, where you'll find great year-round catches like brown, cutthroat, rainbow trout, and steelhead. Some sections of the river bank are designated as fly fishing only. To get there, drive west from Duncan along Highway 18 towards Cowichan Lake.

NANAIMO

Nanaimo is a good base from which to explore Vancouver Island's north and west coasts. Mount Sicker's coal and copper deposits originally attracted the Hudson Bay Company to Namaimo, and you'll find some abandoned mines up there, as well as a couple of museums documenting their history in town.

ESSENTIALS

VISITOR INFORMATION   The **Nanaimo Travel InfoCentre** is at 266 Bryden St. (☎ 604/754-8474 or 800/663-7337).

GETTING THERE   It's an easy drive from Victoria along the Island Highway.

Air BC (☎ 604/663-9826), **Canadian Airlines International** (☎ 800/426-7000 in the U.S. or 800/363-7530 in Canada), and **Horizon Air** (☎ 800/547-9308) all have regularly scheduled air service between Vancouver and Nanaimo, cutting travel time between the two to about 45 minutes including the drive into Nanaimo.

BC Ferries (☎ 604/386-3431 or 604/656-0757) operates a ferry that runs from Horseshoe Bay in West Vancouver to Nanaimo. The Mid-Island Express operates between Tsawwassen (south of Vancouver) to Namaimo.

The **VIA Rail/Esquimalt and Nanaimo Railway** stops once daily at Nanaimo on its route from Victoria to Courtenay in the central island area. The trip takes about two hours.

Maverick Coach Lines (☎ 604/380-1611) operates between the Victoria Depot (☎ 604/385-4411), which is at 710 Douglas St., directly behind the Empress Hotel, and Nanaimo.

GETTING AROUND   Since Nanaimo centers around its waterfront and the Departure Bay ferry terminal, you won't have trouble walking around the city itself. The city bus (☎ 604/390-4531), which maintains a hub at the Gordon Street Exchange, does offer you alternate transport to some areas around town. The fare is $1.25, and schedules are available at the Travel InfoCentre.

SPECIAL EVENTS   The third weekend in July brings the **Nanaimo Marine Fes -tival and Bathtub Race,** an annual 34-mile Bathtub Race from the beaches of Nanaimo to Vancouver's Kitsilano, with dozens of homemade craft gliding across the strait.

The Native Heritage Center (☎ 604/746-8119) offers **Feast and Legends,** a program of song, dance, and storytelling along with a full buffet dinner every Friday in July and August.

EXPLORING THE TOWN & ENVIRONS

The **Bastion City Wildlife Cruise,** 1000 Stewart Ave. (☎ 604/753-2852), takes you on a $2^1/_2$-hour tour of the surrounding waters to view eagles, sea lions, and Gabriola Island's sandstone cliffs. Reservations are required. Cruises depart Wednesday through Sunday at 1:30pm, early February through early April (Thursday through Sunday mid-June through late September), for $20 adults, $18 seniors, and $11 children ages 5 to 15.

You can rent canoes or kayaks at **North Island Water Sports,** 2755 Departure Bay Rd. (☎ 604/758-2488). Single kayaks rent for approximately $40 per day ($75 for a double). **Kona Bud's Beach Rentals,** 2855 Departure Bay Rd. (☎ 604/758-2911) also rents canoes and kayaks for about $10 per hour.

You can plunge off a 140-foot trestle at **The Bungy Zone** (☎ 604/753-5867), North America's only legally sanctioned bridge jump. Leaping high over the Nanaimo River from a specially constructed steel trestle bridge, your first leap of the day will run you $95 (the second is $75). You can even choose how far into the icy mountain waters you will go. Open daily from 10am to 4:30pm, year-round. For a small admission fee (around $2 to $4), you can be a wide-eyed observer. Reservations are recommended June through August. The Bungy Zone is located 41 miles north of Victoria or 8 miles south of Nanaimo, off Highway 1. There's a free shuttle service from both Victoria and Nanaimo.

The Bastion. 266 Bryden St. ☎ **604/754-1631.** Admission by donation. Mon–Fri 10am– 6pm. Closed Sept 16–June 30.

The Hudson's Bay Company built this 1853 fort to protect early settlers who came to the area in search of coal and copper riches. A noontime ceremonial gun salute is conducted by staff dressed in period costume.

Nanaimo Centennial Museum. 100 Cameron St. ☎ **604/753-1821.** Admission $2 adults; $1.50 seniors and students; 50¢ children under 12. May–Aug Mon–Fri 9am–6pm, Sat–Sun 10am–6pm; rest of the year Tues–Sat 9am–4pm.

The city's small museum has exhibits on local history: the heritage of the indigenous peoples, the arrival of the Spanish, and the discovery of the area's coal resources (there's a restored miner's cottage).

A SIDE TRIP TO NEWCASTLE ISLAND

Newcastle Island, just off Namaimo, is an ideal place to hike, cycle, or camp. Trails around the island lead you to quiet beaches, caves, and caverns.

To get there, take the **ferry** (☎ 604/753-5141; off-season 604/387-4363) that leaves from the wharf behind Mafeo–Sutton Park's Civic arena (just north of downtown) daily between May and October with almost hourly departures from 10am to 7:30pm. It even runs on pleasant weekends throughout the rest of the year. The 15-minute trip costs $4 round-trip.

You may want to take a bike over to the island and ride along the Shoreline Trail. You can rent a mountain bike at **Chain Reaction,** 4 Victoria Crescent, Nanaimo (☎ 604/754-3309) for about $12 per day, and it will cost an extra $1.50 to take it across on the ferry.

Newcastle Island Provincial Marine Park, 2930 Trans-Canada Hwy. (☎ 604/387-4363), was once a bustling island community. Two Salish villages were here before the 1840s, and the island was also a Japanese fishing settlement until 1941. The Canadian Pacific Steamship Company had a 1930s pleasure resort—dance pavilion, tea house, and picnic areas—on the island's southern tip. Now, people come to hike, bike, and camp. Mallard Lake Trail leads through the forested interior toward a freshwater lake while the Shoreline Trail crosses steep sandstone cliffs, sandy gravel beaches, caves, caverns, and a great eagle-spotting perch: Giovando Lookout.

WHERE TO STAY

Carey House Bed & Breakfast. 750 Arbutus Ave., Nanaimo, BC, V9S 5E5. ☎ 604/753-3601. 3 rms. $45 double; $50 basement suite. Rates include full breakfast. No credit cards. Take bus no. 3 two stops to Townsite Road, and take a right on Arbutus Avenue. Complimentary ferry pick-up.

This centrally located inn in a residential area has an unfussy atmosphere that lets you quietly unwind. The single and double rooms share a bathroom, while the basement has its own. A TV room, garden, and library are also available for your use. A huge English breakfast gets you going.

WHERE TO DINE

Dinghy Dock Pub. Protection Island Dock. ☎ **604/753-2373.** Main courses $4.95–$11. MC, V. Sun–Thurs 5–10pm; Fri–Sat 5pm–midnight. Take the Protection Island ferry (☎ 604/753-8244). BURGERS/PIZZA.

Burgers, pizzas, or Cajun-style blackened halibut burgers are served up in this very casual local pub, which gently rocks on Protection Island's floating dock.

Filthy McNasty's Cafe. 14 Commercial St. ☎ **604/753-7011.** Main courses $6–$9. MC, V. Daily 8am–10pm. PASTA.

Filthy's friendly young staff serves up ravioli, sandwiches, homemade baked goods, and a hefty coffee concoction called a B52 latte (coffee laced with Kahlua, Bailey's, and Grand Marnier) for $6.95.

NANAIMO AFTER DARK

Have a cappuccino and check out the collection of used books at **Thistledown Books and Coffee Shop,** 15 Commercial St. (☎ 604/755-1840). **Javawocky,** 90 Front St. no. 8 (☎ 604/753-1688), is another hot spot where locals hang out.

If pool and music are more your speed, then head to **Queen's,** 34 Victoria Crescent, between Albert St. and the Island Highway (☎ 604/754-6751). This crowded pool bar has live blues, R&B, alternative, or reggae music nightly with free pool on Sundays.

6 The West Coast of Vancouver Island: Pacific Rim National Park & Environs

This beautiful coastal area is probably the most popular ecotourism destination on the entire island. Most people flock here to watch pods of feeding gray whales and orcas. But for scuba divers, the park is one of the best destinations in North America, and for experienced, advanced backpackers and climbers, the park's West Coast Trail section promises the adventure of a lifetime. Many other outdoor adventures for travelers of all ability levels await in the park's other two major sections, the Broken Islands Group and Long Beach.

ESSENTIALS

VISITOR INFORMATION   The **Tofino Travel InfoCentre,** 380 Campbell St. (☎ 604/725-3414), is open weekdays from 11am to 5pm. The **Ucluelet Travel InfoCentre,** 620 Peninsula Rd. (☎ 604/726-4641), is only open during the summer season, during the same hours.

There's a good visitor center in the Long Beach section of the park; see below. For West Coast Trail information, contact **Discover B.C.** (☎ 800/663-6000) after March 1.

GETTING THERE   By Car/Ferry   Just before Parksville on the Island Highway, there is a turnoff for Route 4, which leads to the mid-island town of Port Alberni and the coastal towns of Tofino, Ucluelet, and Bamfield. Port Alberni is about three hours from Vancouver (including the ferry trip to Nanaimo and the 44-mile drive along the Island Highway and Route 4). You'll have to drive almost two hours on a summer-only, gravel logging road to get to Bamfield at the West Coast Trail's northern trailhead. Port Renfrew, at the Trail's southern end, is an easier drive. Follow Route 14 from Sooke and Victoria for about 56 miles.

By Bus   Island Coach Lines, 4541 Margaret St., Port Alberni (☎ 604/724-1266) operates regular Victoria–Port Alberni bus service (the 3 ^{1}/2-hour trip is $26.40 one way) with a Tofino-Ucluelet connection (the two-hour trip is $15 one way). The once-daily **West Coast Trail Express** (☎ 604/380-0580) provides Victoria-Bamfield service from May to September. Because it goes partially along a logging road, the ride is about four hours long. The **Pacheenaht Band Bus Service** (☎ 604/647-5521) operates an on-call, summer-only Bamfield–Port Renfrew bus service (one-way fare is $40 per person, minimum four people).

By Ferry   A 4 ^{1}/2-hour ride aboard the passenger-only **MV** *Lady Rose* takes you from Port Alberni through the Alberni Inlet fjord to the boardwalk fishing village of Bamfield or to Ucluelet. It makes brief stops along the way to deliver mail and packages to solitary cabin dwellers; and to let off or pick up Broken Islands Groups–bound sea kayakers. The Scottish-built 1937 *Lady Rose* departs three times weekly to each destination from Alberni Harbour Quay's Angle Street. The fare is $16 to $20 one way ($36 to $40 round trip). For more information, contact **Alberni Marine Transportation,** (☎ 604/723-8313).

SPECIAL EVENTS   Throughout March and April, the **Pacific Rim Whale Festival** is held in Tofino and Ucluelet. Live crab races, the Gumboot Golf Tournament, guided whale-spotting hikes, and a native festival are just a few of the events celebrating the gray whale migration as the mighty creatures pass through the area. Call ☎ 604/725-3113 or 604/726-4641 for more information.

September's **Salmon Festival and Derby,** in Port Alberni, draws fisherman from all over to claim a hefty $20,000 first prize.

EXPLORING THE PARK & ITS SURROUNDINGS

The 7-mile-long stretch of rocky headlands, sand, and surf along **Long Beach Headlands Trail** is the most accessible section of the park. You'll meet whale-watchers in the spring, surfers and anglers in the summer, and hearty hikers during the colder months.

The **Long Beach Visitor Information Center,** located about a mile from the Route 4 junction to Tofino, is open daily from mid-March through September from 10am to 6pm. Here you can get trail maps and learn about conditions; the Wickannish Restaurant has ecological and historical information about the area.

Alberni Marine Transportation, Port Alberni (☎ 604/723-8313), rents canoes and kayaks out of the same office that sells tickets for the MV *Lady Rose.*

Year-round sport fishing for salmon, steelhead, trout, Dolly Varden char, halibut, cod, and snapper is possible near Port Alberni—thanks to the local fish hatchery that releases more than 10 million fish annually. Long Beach is also great for bottom fishing. **Alberni Pacific Charters,** 5440 Argyle St. (☎ 604/724-3112), organizes charters throughout the area, including Barkley Sound.

The ✪ **Broken Islands Group,** located in Barkley Sound, is the park's canoeing, diving, and kayaking paradise. The reefs are teeming with beautiful marine life, and there are ancient shipwrecks to explore. See the box on scuba diving near the beginning of this chapter for details on the astounding marine life and see the text about the West Coast Trail below for a list of outfitters. Paddlers are challenged by fog and rough swells on the outer edges. Pick up a copy of Marine Chart no. 3670 before you set out. You can take the MV *Lady Rose* (see "Getting There") or the MV *Uchuck II* to the main launch site on Gibraltar Island. It's well worth your efforts to see the sheltered lagoons with resident bald eagles soaring overhead and salmon swimming below.

After the SS *Valencia* ran aground in 1906 and most of the survivors died of exposure, the government built a rescue trail between Bamfield and Port Renfrew. Upgraded by the parks service in the 1970s, the ✪ **West Coast Trail** has gained a reputation as one of the world's greatest hiking and camping challenges. Planning (get a topographic map and tidal table), stamina (besides hiking, you should train for rock climbing), and experience (advanced wilderness survival and minimum-impact camping knowledge) are imperative. Veterans say you need to go with at least two other people, pack lightweight weather-proof gear, and bring about 50 feet of climbing rope per person. To reduce ecological impact, only 52 people are allowed entry per day (26 from Port Renfrew; 26 from Bamfield). The $25 advance booking fee includes the price of a waterproof trail map. You can make reservations in March for a summer trip (May to September) by calling **Discover B.C.** (☎ 800/663-6000 after March 1).

And the park's very best diving, rated as some of the best in the world by the Cousteau Society, lies offshore from the West Coast Trail section. It's been called "the graveyard of the Pacific" for its dozens of 19th- and 20th-century shipwreck sites. Underwater interpretive trails guide you through these artificial reefs. Contact the **Ocean Centre** (☎ 604/475-2202), **Seaker Adventure Tours** (☎ 604/479-0244), or **Nootka Charters** (☎ 604/725-3318).

Because Tofino and Ucluelet are the only towns in this area accessible by paved road, they are logical bases for exploring the park—and that means they're very overcrowded in the summer. This situation has brought some controversy over how residents will reconcile the sometimes competing interests of tourism, logging, and conservation. But for those who want to experience the magic of one of the world's last temperate coastal rain forests, there is hardly a better place to do it. The boardwalked **Clayquot Witness Trail** near Tofino is a protected wilderness. The recently constructed boardwalks protect the delicate root structure of the towering old-growth Sitka spruce and cedars alongside as well as the fragile fern undergrowth below.

Hot Springs Cove near Tofino is Vancouver Island's only natural hot spring. Sail, canoe, or kayak there to enjoy swimming in the hot pools and bracing waterfalls. Then return to Tofino at sunset, or camp overnight.

While you're in Tofino, you might want to seek out the **Eagle Aerie Gallery,** 350 Campbell St. (☎ 604/725-3235), which is built in the style of a longhouse. The gallery features the artwork of Roy Henry Vicker, a hereditary chief and son of a Tsimshian fisherman. Pieces include serigraphs, sculptures in glass and wood, carved panels, and totem poles.

Organized tours and adventure outings can be booked in Tofino as well. **Chinook Charters,** 450 Campbell St. (☎ 604/725-3431 or 800/665-3646), offers two ways to experience the area: Clayquot Sound whale-watching on board their 25-foot Zodiacs (weather suits provided); or discovering Hot Springs Cove on board their 32-foot Chinook Key. **Remote Passages,** 568 Campbell St. (☎ 604/725-3330 or 800/666-9833), organizes hour-long Clayquot Sound whale-watching tours on board Zodiacs at 9am, noon, and 3pm from March to November. Fares are $35 for adults ($20 for children under 12). They also conduct a seven-hour combination whale-watching and hot springs trip ($55 for adults, $40 children under 12). Reservations are recommended. The **Tofino Sea-Kayaking Company,** 320 Main St. (☎ 604/725-4222), designs kayaking packages ranging from four-hour Meares Island paddles (from $45 per person) to week-long paddle/camp expeditions. Instruction from experienced guides makes even your first kayaking experience a comfortable and enjoyable one.

Based in Victoria, **Ocean River Sports** (☎ 604/381-4233), also organizes week-long group trips with experienced guides, instruction, and equipment.

CAMPING

Pacific Rim National Park offers campers the trip of a lifetime. You need a spirit of adventure and plenty of prior experience to enter some areas, and at least a week to cover each. Fog, wind, and rain can appear at any time of year, so pack light, warm foul-weather gear.

Year-round campsites on the bluff at **Green Point** (near Long Beach) are full every day from July through August (the average waiting list is one to two days), but for $14–$15 per site ($6 per night Thanksgiving through Easter), you'll have a magnificent view at a drive-in site, with toilets, fire pits, and wood, but no showers or hookups.

There are eight designated campgrounds on the **Broken Islands,** but no facilities. You must carry in everything including fresh water and firewood, and then carry everything out.

WHERE TO STAY NEAR THE PARK

Every season sees the opening of larger hotels and pricier, all-inclusive packages in the area. As of this writing, a new condo/hotel complex is planning to open its doors by mid-summer 1996.

Bamfield Lodge. Cape Beale Trail (Box 23), Bamfield, BC, V0R 1B0. ☎ **604/728-3419.** Fax 604/728-3417. 2 cabins, 2 rms in lodge. $75 double; $100 suite; $100 cabin. V.

Rustic cabins and a lodge make up this marine education center and retreat. All rooms are self-contained, with full kitchens and bathrooms. Bring your own food. Moorage is available if you boat to the lodge. You can watch the birds, whales, and boats go by while sipping an espresso in the cappucino bar. The staff can also help arrange numerous area activities, including fishing and whale-watching charters.

Canadian Princess Fishing Resort. Peninsula Road at the Boat Basin (Box 939), Ucluelet, BC, V0R 3A0. ☎ **604/726-7771** or 800/603-7090. 51 rms on shore, 30 aboard ship. $49–$109 double. AE, ER, MC, V.

A historic West Coast steamship has been fully restored and is permanently moored in Ucluelet harbor. All rooms on the cruise ship are decked out in buccaneer decor and dimly lit (some have shared baths). There's also a building on shore with rooms; these all have televisions and private baths, and a few have fireplaces. The dining room and lounge give you a beautiful waterfront view.

Mackenzie Beach Resort. 1101 Pacific Rim Hwy. (Box 12), Tofino, BC, V0R 2Z0. ☎ **604/725-3439.** 11 cottages. TV. $85–$149 double. MC, V.

This year-round bay-side resort, very uncrowded and civilized, is located 2 miles from Tofino on Mackenzie Beach. It has one- and two-bedroom cottages (some right on the beachfront), all fully equipped with kitchens. A few units have fireplaces. There are also 12 small campsites and RV parking with full hook-ups and hot showers. The resort's indoor pool, spa, and barbecues make your stay complete.

Tofino Swell Lodge. 341 Olsen Rd. (Box 160), Tofino, BC, V0R 2Z0. ☎ **604/725-3274.** 7 rms. $68–$80 double/triple. MC, V. No children accepted.

Overlooking Meares Island and boasting mountain views, this waterfront lodge has twin, queen, and king bed units with private baths. There's a large, shared kitchen and sitting area as well as an outdoor hot tub and barbecue area. Moorage is also available.

Woods End Landing. Wild Duck Road, Bamfield, BC, V0R 1B0. ☎ **604/728-3383.** Fax 604/728-3383. 6 cottages. $95–$185 triple. MC, V.

The cottages on this secluded waterfront wilderness property are fully equipped with kitchens and double log beds. They are decorated with Canadian antiques and collectibles and have private porches as well as barbecues. There's also a private dock, fishing tackle, and a canoe for guests' use.

WHERE TO DINE NEAR THE PARK

Restaurants are hard to find along the west coast of Vancouver Island. When you do come across one, don't be surprised if it's pretty basic. Since accommodations in this area tend to fall on the extreme ends of the lodging scale—campgrounds or resorts that offer either dining or cooking facilities—independent travelers will find getting a decent meal in these parts a bit of a challenge. Many visitors stock up on groceries in Port Alberni before heading west. You'll find a Safeway supermarket at 3756 Tenth Ave. (☎ 604/723-6212) and at 359B Johnston Rd. (☎ 604/723-5000).

Blue Door Cafe. 5415 Argyle St., Port Alberni. ☎ **604/723-8811.** Reservations not accepted. Main courses $6–$10. MC, V. Daily 5am–3:30pm. CANADIAN.

This is a local meat-and-potatoes cafe that offers hearty, simple food at good prices.

The Loft. 346 Campbell St., Tofino. ☎ **604/725-4241.** Reservations accepted. Main courses $4.95–$11. AE, DC, DISC, MC. Daily 7am–10pm. CANADIAN.

If you're looking for big portions and wholesome food, then this is the place to go. We can vouch that the eggs Benedict are tasty.

Swale Rock Cafe. 5328 Argyle St., Port Alberni. ☎ **604/723-0777.** Main courses $7–$10. MC, V. Sun–Thurs 7am–9pm, Fri–Sat 7am–10pm. SEAFOOD.

Homemade baked goods, seafood club sandwiches, and seafood fettucini are a few of the house specialties that attract hip local patrons.

Wickannish Centre & Restaurant. Long Beach, Pacific Rim National Park. ☎ **604/ 726-7706.** Main courses $11–$20. MC, V. Daily 11am–9:30pm. Closed mid-Oct to mid-Mar. SEAFOOD.

Ten miles north of Ucluelet, you'll find this beachfront wooden lodge that also doubles as a tourism information center with naturalist programs and summertime outdoor events. It happens to serve the best seafood in the area, including clam chowder and the fresh catch of the day.

7 Central Vancouver Island

Great winter skiing for the whole family and excellent year-round saltwater fishing are the two biggest draws to the central island. Mountaineers and hikers will find the alpine meadows and towering cliffs in the rest of Strathcona Provincial Park, the province's oldest park, excellent destinations for day-use and overnight, minimum-impact camping. The surrounding Comox Valley is an ideal equestrian and golfing destination. Nearby Quadra, Denman, and Hornby Islands are also popular spots for kayakers, boaters, and those who like to fish.

Packages that include your choice of accommodations, activities, and meals are a convenient way to see this area. **Island Shores Recreation** (☎ 604/286-2178) provides you with equipment, guides, and tours as well as rustic oceanfront accommodations (cabins and camping) and meals at their Read Island resort, just east of Quadra Island. From this base camp you can kayak the island's secluded waterways, walk through a rain forest, view mountain vistas, fish, sail, or dive.

THE EAST COAST: PARKSVILLE, QUALICUM BEACH, COUTENAY, COMOX & CAMPBELL RIVER
AREA ESSENTIALS

VISITOR INFORMATION   Most information centers are open throughout the summer during regular nine-to-five business hours. The first one you'll reach as you drive up is the **Qualicum Beach Travel InfoCentre** is located at 2711 W. Island Hwy., Qualicum Beach (☎ 604/752-9532). Further north, the **Courtenay Travel InfoCentre** is located 2040 Cliffe Ave. (Island Highway/Route 19), Courtenay (☎ 604/334-3234).

GETTING THERE   Courtenay is about three hours from Vancouver, a trip that includes a ferry ride from from the mainland to Nanaimo and an 87-mile drive up the Island Highway (Route 19). Campbell River is another hour's drive north. **BC Ferries** (☎ 604/386-3431) also operates a 75-minute crossing from Powell River on the mainland to Campbell River. The fare is $6 per passenger one way and $21.50 per vehicle.

Island Coach Lines, 1290 Cedar Ave., Campbell River (☎ 604/287-7151), operates daily Victoria–Port Hardy bus service with stops in Nanaimo, Courtenay, and Campbell River. The two- to three-hour trip costs $14.50–$35 one way. The once-daily **E&N Railway** from Victoria and Nanaimo has its northern terminus in Courtenay.

SPECIAL EVENTS   The **Brant Festival,** held in Qualicum Beach and Parksville the second weekend in April, is a three-day celebration of the arrival of thousands of Brant geese to the area. Art, photography, and carving exhibitions as well as birding competitions, nature walks, outdoor activities, a wildlife art auction, and dinners highlight the event. Contact The Brant Festival (☎ 604/248-4117).

At the end of July, the **International Sandcastle Contest** draws expert builders from around the world to Parksville.

The **Filberg Festival,** in Comox, is held in the historic 1930s Filberg Lodge the first weekend in August, and features local arts and crafts. Contact Filberg Lodge, 61 Filberg Rd., Comox, BC, V9W 2S7 (☎ 604/334-9242).

EXPLORING THE AREA

The **Old School House,** 122 West Fern Rd., Qualicum Beach (☎ 604/752-6133), is open daily. This gallery and art center present local artists and their works; there's also a gift shop.

Golfers will find this part of Vancouver Island to be a little bit of paradise, with some outstanding courses. When he designed the **Morningstar golf course,** 525 Lowry Rd., Parksville (☎ 604/248-8161), Les Furber used large lakes in open areas to integrate several seaside links holes and rolling fairways that run in and out of the woods. This 18-hole championship par-72 course has a 74 rating. **Crown Isle Golf and Country Estates,** Courtenay (☎ 604/338-6811), has a 133-slope rating. Graham Cooke and Associates' classic, gentle rolling course features beautiful alpine backdrops. Ten holes include manmade lakes, and there are 68 bunkers ready to capture errant shots. Because it was carved out of a dense forest, you may see wildlife grazing the fairway and roughs at **Storey Creek Golf Club,** Campbell River (☎ 604/923-3673). Gentle creeks and ponds also wind their way through this course.

After dark, you've got two choices in Campbell River: rock or country music. **People's,** off Ironwood Street (no phone), has live rock bands most nights, while **McFarr's Lounge** in the Anchor Inn on the Island Highway (☎ 604/286-1131), offers piped-in easy listening music. **Big Daddy,** 900 Twelfth Ave. (☎ 604/286-0144), serves up live rock music from Thursday through Saturday. They don't have food, but they're not opposed to pizza delivery.

WHERE TO STAY

Austrian Chalet Village. 462 South Island Hwy., Campbell River, BC, V9W 1A5. ☎ **604/923-4231.** Fax 604/923-2840. 58 rms. TV TEL. $79–$89 double. Kitchen units $10 extra. AE, MC, V.

Overlooking Discovery Passage, this hotel is conveniently right on the Island Highway. You'll have a choice of regular or housekeeping rooms (with fully equipped kitchens). Some have lofts or balconies. Facilities include a restaurant and pub, indoor pool, and whirlpool. Massages and many activities packages are available.

Greystone Manor. 4014 Haas Rd., Courtenay, BC, V9N 8H9. ☎ **604/338-1422.** 4 rms. $61 double or triple. Rates include full breakfast. MC, V. Head a mile north of the traffic light in the town of Royston, take a right on Hilton Road and a left onto Haas Road.

This 76-year-old waterfront heritage home looks out onto Comox Harbour. It's actually 4 miles south of Courtenay in the town of Royston and has beautiful views of the Coast Mountains. The antique-filled, wood-paneled sitting room for guests has a wood fireplace. The rooms, also filled with antiques, have wood-burning stoves and floral print wallpaper. The huge breakfast that's included is worth the price of your stay.

Island Hall Beach Resort. 181 W. Island Highway (P.O. Box 430), Parksville, BC, V9P 2G5. ☎ 604/248-3225. 99 rms (some with shared bath). TV TEL. $79–$125 double. Special packages available. AE, DC, ER, MC, V.

Built in 1917, and associated with Vancouver's Rosellen Suites, this beachfront resort has special two- and three-day packages throughout the year (except for July and August). These packages include accommodations, breakfast, unlimited use of the resort's aquatic and recreational facilities, and two rounds of your favorite sport. Golfers have their choice of local links: Fairwinds, Morningstar, Eaglecrest, or Glengarry; fishermen get an 8- to 10-hour sail tour with fishing and refreshments; kayakers get equipment and training; and there's a PADI divemaster. Horseback riding, mountain-biking, and hiking are also available. You have your choice of tastefully furnished guest rooms with shared or private baths or one of nine bungalow-style units situated right at the water's edge with views across the strait to Vancouver.

Pier House B&B. 670 Island Highway, Campbell River, BC, V9W 2C3. ☎ 604/287-2943. 5 rms (some with shared bath). $65–$75 double. Rates include full breakfast. MC, V.

This 1920s antique-filled heritage house was once the town's courthouse. Its proximity to the Discovery Pier walk-on fishing area makes its location ideal. The antique-stuffed rooms have private or shared baths. A library is available for guests' use and a tasty, elegant breakfast is served in the dining room.

The Qualicum College Inn. 427 College Rd., Qualicum Beach, BC, V0R 2T0. ☎ 604/752-9262 or 800/663-7306. 70 rms. TV. $69–$99 double/triple. Romance and murder-mystery packages available. MC, V. Drive through Parksville on the Island Highway and follow the signs on the right side north of town.

This landmark Tudor-style hotel was opened in 1935. You'll find peace and quiet at this off-highway location overlooking the ocean and landscaped gardens. Four-poster beds and matching furnishings are enhanced with Laura Ashley linens. You have a choice of oceanview or fireplace suites. Facilities include a dining room that serves steak and seafood, a pub, an indoor pool, and a Jacuzzi. Horseback riding, golf, and fishing are nearby.

WHERE TO DINE

Hotels and B&Bs in this area either offer fine dining or kitchens for their guests. But there are a few good basic eateries on Comox Avenue in Comox, Fifth Street in Courtenay, the Island Highway in Parksville, and Cliff Avenue in Cumberland for those of you who want to branch out. Also, you'll find groceries and supplies in Campbell River if you need to stock up for picnics or camping.

Zorba's Restaurant. 1832 Comox Ave., Comox, BC. ☎ 604/339-3222. Main courses $11–$17. Daily 5–10pm. MC, V. GREEK.

Huge souvlaki platters, salads, and pizzas are the filling and well-executed offerings of this establishment.

THE OFFSHORE ISLANDS: HORNBY, DENMAN & QUADRA

Throughout the '60s and '70s, flower children were attracted to rural Hornby and Denman, where they started organic farms and thriving art communities. Even the public transport on Hornby reflects this gentle culture: The **Hornby Blue Bus** (☎ 604/335-0715) is a funky 1960s International Harvester; you negotiate with the driver to determine your fare from the ferry.

These islands are great for a day of exploring on two wheels. The **Hornby Island Off Road Bike Shop** (☎ 604/335-0444) next to the Co-Op market, and **Cycledeli**

Bike Shop, 3646 Denman Rd., on Denman Island (☎ 604/335-1797), rent mountain bikes for $10 per hour or $25 per day.

You can paddle your way to Denman and Hornby Islands through placid waters. **C.V. Sea Kayaks and Canoes Ltd.,** 760 Island Hwy., Campbell River (☎ 604/287-2650), rents kayaks and canoes. They also give lessons and tours. Single kayaks are $35 per day and doubles are $55 per day. Canoes rent for about $20 per day.

On Denman Island, the **Denman General Store** is also the local Travel InfoCentre; it's located at 1069 Northwest Rd. (☎ 604/335-2293). It has a free island guide as well as a brochure listing small galleries that are open to the public.

Running from August 1 to 10, the **Hornby Festival,** Hornby Island, presents music, theater, and dance events. Contact the Hornby Festival Society (☎ 604/335-2734).

There are local ferries that operate between these islands and Vancouver Island daily throughout the year. The dozen daily ferry trips to each island take 10 minutes each way and cost $3 per person ($7.25–$7.50 per car additional). The ferry from Buckley Bay to Denman Island operates from 7am to 11pm; the ferry from Denman Island to Hornby Island operates between 8am and 6:35pm; and the ferry from Campbell River to Quadra Island operated between 6:40am and 10:30pm. For more information about ferry schedules, contact **BC Ferries** (☎ 604/386-3431).

In contrast to the other two islands, Quadra Island retains much of its Kwakiutl heritage. The Cape Mudge Village operates the **Kwakiutl (Kwauilth) Museum,** WeiWai Road (tel. 604/285-3733), where you'll find a beautiful collection of potlatch artifacts, ceremonial masks, and tribal costumes. They are open Monday through Saturday from 10am to 4:30pm. During the summer they're also open on Sunday from noon to 4:30pm. Across from the museum there is a park where a series of petroglyphs document the ancient island legends.

WHERE TO STAY & DINE ON DENMAN ISLAND

Denman Island Guest House. 3808 Denman Rd., Denman Island, BC, V0R 1T0. ☎ **604/335-2688.** 5 rms (all with shared bath). $50 double. Rates include breakfast. MC, V.

This turn-of-the-century farmhouse has a laid-back island atmosphere and rustic rooms (all of which share a bath). But if you're exploring the island, this is an ideal spot to rest up and have a huge country breakfast before you head out on the trail.

With garden views and an appealing atmosphere, the hotel restaurant is excellent; it offers a menu that changes with the availability of local seafood and produce. It's open for dinner Wednesday to Sunday from 4:30 to 9:30pm, and main courses run $12 to $17.

ON HORNBY ISLAND

Late risers can get breakfast until 11am at **Jan's Cafe Next Door,** on Central at the stop sign (☎ 604/335-1487). Burgers and sandwiches make up the lunch menu, and the desserts are scrumptious. Most items are under $7; no credit cards. Open daily from 7:30am to 3pm (until 5pm on weekends).

Hornby Island Resort & Thatch Pub. 4305 Shingle Spit Road, Hornby Island, BC, V0R 1Z0. ☎ **604/335-0136.** 4 rms, 10 campsites. $60 double lodge room; $16–$18 campsite. MC, V.

Make reservations months in advance if you want to stay in the lodge or campsites of this resort, located next to the ferry terminal. The resort has its own restaurant, a barbecue on the sundeck, and a popular local pub that has live music three nights a week.

ON QUADRA ISLAND

You can pick up food at Quadra Foods on the main street.

Tsa-Kwa-Luten Lodge. Lighthouse Road (P.O. Box 460), Quathiaski Cove, Quadra Island, BC, V0P 1N0. ☎ **604/285-2042.** 35 rms. TEL. $80–$125 double/triple. MC, V. Closed mid-Oct to mid-Apr.

This island lodge overlooking Discovery Passage has both guest rooms and waterfront cabins. Some rooms have lofts, Jacuzzis, or fireplaces. The two- and four-bedroom waterfront cabins have fully equipped kitchens. Some have fireplaces and hot tubs. The lodge itself resembles a longhouse. Seafood and native cuisine is featured on the dining room's menu. You can also relax in the adjoining cocktail lounge. Facilities include a fitness center with a sauna, beach access, and a gift shop. Fully guided fishing and heli-fishing can be arranged, as can boat rentals, and mountain bike and moped rentals. Numerous walking trails are nearby.

STRATHCONA PROVINCIAL PARK

British Columbia's oldest provincial park is a 550,000-acre alpine wilderness where Roosevelt elk, coast blacktail deer, island wolves, island marmots, bears, and cougars inhabit the undeveloped areas. To get there, drive north on Highway 19 to Campbell River, then follow Rt. 28 straight to the park (a 45-minute drive). Golden Hinde, the park's highest point (7,220 feet), is a favorite destination for mountaineers. Trails of varying levels of difficulty lead to Della Falls (1,452 feet), which spills over three cascades. If you've never seen towering, craggy summits overlooking lush forests and meadows of heather and violets, then you must stop here and walk at least one of the shorter trails. Try Lupin Falls, Karst Creek, or Buttle Lake. Some of the trails are easy enough for your kids, and you'll enjoy spotting wildlife together.

There are two provincial campgrounds with a total of 161 sites. One is located at Buttle Lake, and the other is situated on the Ralph River. Both have dry toilets and no showers. Rates are $9.50 to $12.50 for up to four people.

You don't have to drive all the way back to the Island Highway to find a good, hearty meal. The **Strathcona Park Lodge,** on Route 28 (☎ 604/286-8206), has buffet-style spreads in the Whale Room dining area for breakfast (7 to 7:45am), lunch (noon to 12:45pm), and dinner (5:30 to 6:15pm) daily. Buffet prices run $7.50 to $13.50; no credit cards. If you'd like to stay here, the lodge is open year-round, and offers you a choice: a room with a feather duvet on the bed in the log-and-timber lodge ($60–$70 double, $80–$100 double with lake view), or one of eight lakeside cabins, each equipped with wood-burning stove, kitchen, and bath ($105–$140 per night). No phones or TVs in any units.

MT. WASHINGTON & FORBIDDEN PLATEAU SKI RESORTS

According to legend, Forbidden Plateau was named during a war between the Comox and Cowichan bands. The Comox men sent their families there for safety only to return after peace was regained to find them gone. The plateau was considered taboo after that. But these days, both downhill and cross-country skiers traverse the runs here and at neighboring Mt. Washington; both areas are great for families.

The best skiing on Vancouver Island is at **Mt. Washington Resort,** only 15 miles from Courtenay on Mt. Washington Road (☎ 604/338-1386). Alpine, Nordic, and telemark runs are all available. Five lifts, 41 major marked runs, 22 miles of groomed trails, a ski school, and cheap lift tickets ($30 per person on weekends, cheaper on weekdays) are just a few of the benefits. Island Coach Lines runs a bus to the resort during the winter season. Surprisingly, there's a full-service campground filled with

RVs nestled in the snow banks nearby. The **Mount Washington campground** (☎ 604/334-5703) is privately operated and open year-round.

The adjacent and older ski area, **Forbidden Plateau** (☎ 604/338-1919 or 604/334-4744 for a snow report) is a family-oriented, casual resort geared for novices: there are lots of wide, smooth, relaxing runs and plenty of activities for kids.

8 Northern Vancouver Island

It's a long drive from Campbell River north along the Island Highway as it winds through thickly forested mountain ranges (and a few barren logged slopes) before finally reaching Port McNeill, about three hours away. There are plenty of rest stops where you can take in the majestic beauty of the mountains and lakes around you.

Cormorant Island is accessible by ferry from Port McNeill. Alert Bay, on the island, and Telegraph Cove, a tiny "boardwalk" town on the mainland of Vancouver Island, just southeast of Port McNeill, are good spots to watch orca pods migrating from the Queen Charlotte Strait into the rich feeding waters of the Johnstone Strait.

Further north is the Island Highway's final port-of-call, Port Hardy. This remote town is the base camp for two very unique journeys: the Inside Passage ferry cruise (see Section 9 of this chapter) and rugged wilderness camping in Cape Scott Provincial Park.

NORTH ISLAND ESSENTIALS

VISITOR INFORMATION   Alert Bay has a **Travel InfoCentre** (☎ 604/974-5213) conveniently located near the ferry terminal at 116 Fir St. It is open during the summer from 9am to 6pm (until 5pm in the winter). The **Port McNeill Travel InfoCentre,** on Beach Drive (☎ 604/956-3131), is only open during the summer. The **Port Hardy Travel InfoCentre,** at 7250 Market St. (☎ 604/949-7622), is open year-round.

GETTING THERE   These towns can all be reached along the Island Highway (Route 19). Alert Bay can be reached by **BC Ferries** (☎ 604/277-0277 or 604/669-1211) from Port McNeill. Island Coach Lines (☎ 604/385-4411) operates a Nanaimo–Port McNeill bus service (9am departure arrives at 3:15pm; $32.30).

EXPLORING THE AREA: SPOTTING ORCAS & MORE

The heritage of the local indigenous peoples can be seen on Cormorant Island. The **Anglican Church,** on Front Street in Alert Bay (☎ 604/974-5213), is an 1881 cedar church with stained-glass windows that reflect both Native Canadian and European influences. It is open to the public Monday through Saturday from 8am to 5pm during the summer.

One of the world's tallest **totem poles** can be seen near the Big House—a Kwakiutl community center at the north end of the island that is not open to the public. (But visitors are welcome on the grounds to view the totem pole.) The 173-foot pole was erected in 1973. It features 22 figures, including a sun at the top.

Down the road from the Big House is the **U'Mista Cultural Centre** (☎ 604/974-5403), which displays a collection of ceremonial masks, cedar baskets, copper items, and other potlatch artifacts along with revolving heritage exhibitions. Admission is $5 for adults, $4 for seniors, $1 for children under 12. The museum is open daily throughout the year from 9am to 5pm (on weekends and summer holidays it opens at noon). During the winter, they are closed on holidays.

Both the Big House and the cultural center can be reached from the ferry terminal by walking a mile north on Front Street.

Back on Vancouver Island itself, **Telegraph Cove** is one of the few remaining boardwalk villages: Most buildings are perched on stilts over the water. It makes for a lovely stroll.

The best way to get close to the **Johnstone Strait orca pods** is to kayak; you can watch sea lions cavort, camp overnight at any of the marine parks, and explore abandoned native villages there. Because the waters are sheltered, this area is ideal for those just learning to kayak. **Discovery Kayaks,** 2755 Departure Rd., Nanaimo (☎ 604/758-2488), offers kayak trips to these prime orca grounds. If you don't want a guided trip, you need to rent a kayak in Victoria at Ocean River Sports (see Section 4 of this chapter) or in Nanaimo at North Island Water Sports (see Section 5 of this chapter) and tow it on top of your car or RV.

But there are other ways to observe these beautiful marine mammals. The **Robson Bight Ecological Reserve,** between Port Hardy and Port McNeill, is a perfect on-shore watching site. Orcas beach themselves on the Bight's pebbly shore to rub their tummies. (Be very careful not to disturb them while they scratch; they're extremely shy.) **Seasmoke Tours,** based in Alert Bay (☎ 604/974-5225), offers five- to six-hour sailing trips aboard their 44-foot yacht. The trip includes a seafood lunch and Devonshire tea on board. Outfitted with hydrophones, you can also hear the whales as they pass by.

WHERE TO STAY

Duval Point Lodge Ltd. P.O. Box 818, Port Hardy, BC, V0N 2P0. ☎ **604/949-6667.** 8 rms. $175 per person per night. Rate includes transportation from Port Hardy. V. Closed Oct–May.

This floating fishing lodge, located on the Goletas Channel, is almost all-inclusive. It's accessible only by boat or floatplane, but the rates include pickup and dropoff in Port Hardy. Its four- to five-day day packages include transportation, a boat, gas, fishing gear, and comfortable rooms with fireplaces and kitchen facilities. You have to bring your own food and fishing license, but if dawn-to-dusk fishing in 16-foot welded aluminum boats with fish finders and top-of-the-line equipment sounds like your idea of heaven, you should find a stay worth the price.

Hidden Cove Lodge. Lewis Point (P.O. Box 258), Port McNeill, BC, V0N 2R0. ☎ **604/974-8181.** 4 rms. $125–$135 double. Rates include breakfast. MC, V. Closed Jan–Mar. Take the Island Highway to Telegraph Cove/Beaver Cove; turn right and follow the signs.

This lodge is nestled in a secluded cove overlooking the Johnstone Strait. Each room has a private bath (a luxury in these parts), and your hosts can arrange whale-watching, guided fishing, heli-fishing, and hiking tours for you.

Kay's Bed & Breakfast. 7605 Carnarvon Rd., Port Hardy, BC, V0N 2P0. ☎ **604/949-6776.** 4 rms (2 with shared baths). $35–$55 double/triple. Rates include breakfast. MC, V.

This convenient B&B offers free pickup from the Prince Rupert ferry terminal and a lovely ocean view. Some rooms have shared baths, but otherwise each is self-contained, with a queen-size bed and a fully equipped kitchen. You'll still be within walking distance of town if you care to take a stroll.

Ocean View Cabins. 390 Poplar St., Alert Bay, BC, V0N 1A0. ☎ **604/974-5457.** 12 cottages (10 with bath). TV. $50–$60 double. MC, V.

Overlooking Mitchell Bay and only a mile from the ferry terminal, this resort offers self-contained housekeeping cabins with comfortable queen-sized beds and full baths (except cabins 1 and 2). Reserve in advance.

Vancouver Island

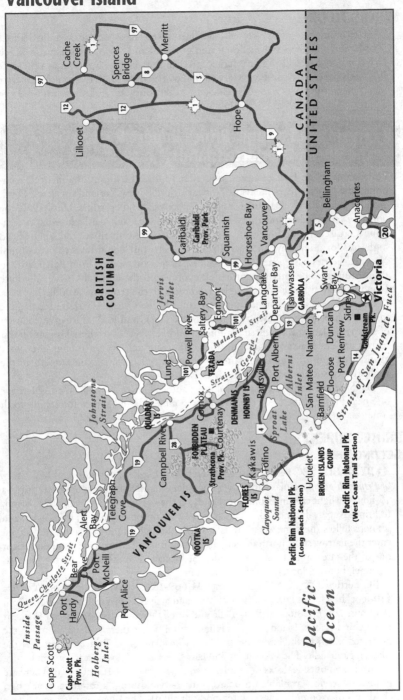

WHERE TO DINE

Most accommodations are very self-contained. Even the expensive accommodations offer kitchens to their guests. You'll find groceries and a few restaurants on Beach Drive in Port McNeill and on Market Street in Port Hardy. **Sportsman's Steak & Pizza,** on Beach Drive in Port McNeill (tel. 604/956-4113), has a complete, hearty menu of simple basics like roast chicken, steaks, burgers, and pizzas for $4.95 to $19.95. Open from 11am to 9:30pm.

9 The Inside Passage: Prince Rupert & the Queen Charlotte Islands

For ecotourists, an Inside Passage journey can fulfill the dream of a lifetime, combining the best scenic elements of Norway's fjords, New Zealand's majestic South Island, Chile's Patagonian range, and Nova Scotia's wild coastline. Until 1966, the only way you could explore this wild, rugged shoreline was aboard a four-day Alaska-bound cruise ship or freighter. (You could drive the Cariboo and Yellowhead highways for a few days to reach Prince Rupert, but you'd miss the coastline.) Now BC Ferries has opened up the inside passage with service from Port Hardy to Prince Rupert. The ferry system has also connected the ethereal Queen Charlotte Islands, ancestral home of the Haida civilization, to the rest of the world.

Prince Rupert is also the jumping-off point to the Queen Charlotte Islands, the misty archipelago also known as Haida Gwaii. The Gwaii Haanas Reserve, a cluster of southern islands, is a United Nations World Heritage Site where lush rain forest reveals ancient Haida villages, still intact and untouched even though they were abandoned centuries ago. Ninstints, on Anthony Island, is a monument to the sophisticated society that flourished here 10,000 years ago.

The Skeena River Valley and Kitilope, another United Nations World Heritage Site near Prince Rupert, are the last pristine millennia-old spruce forests in North America.

PRINCE RUPERT
GETTING THERE

✪ **BY FERRY**   BC Ferries' flagship cruisers MV *Queen of the North* and MV *Queen of Prince Rupert* have made this a very popular and affordable summertime trip—a 15-hour daylight crossing from Port Hardy, at the northern tip of Vancouver Island, to Prince Rupert. Humpback whales, orcas, Dall's porpoise, salmon, bald eagles, and sea lions follow this same waterway as it weaves through countless islands. And as you enter the narrow strait north of Bella Bella, you might be fortunate enough to sight one of the rare "spirit bears" (kermodei) of Princess Royal Island and the Douglas Channel, hunting for salmon along the shore.

BC Ferries' (☎ 604/386-3431 or 604/669-1211) MV *Queen of the North*, a 410-foot ship, leaves Port Hardy at 7:30am and arrives in Prince Rupert at 10:30pm (15 hours later). It stops at Bella Bella and briefly encounters open ocean before it runs behind Calvert Island into Fitz Hugh Sound. From there, it cruises through the protected waters of the Finlayson and Grenville channels to Prince Rupert near the Alaskan panhandle. The ship carries 750 passengers and 157 vehicles. You can lounge on inside and outside decks or in a reserved dayroom or overnight cabin. There are numerous services available on board (buffet-style dining, a cafeteria, snack bar, children's playroom, business center, and gift shop). The one-way passenger fare is $98 ($65 for seniors, $49 for children ages 5 to 11); dayrooms and overnight cabins are an additional $22 to $117. Bringing along a car will cost an additional $202 each way; mountain bikes cost an additional $6.50 each way. Reservations are required. You'll also need to book accommodations in advance at both ports of call.

The ferry has weekly sailings during the rest of the year, but if you've ever been to Scotland's Shetland Islands—where wind and rain dog the craggy coasts for nine months—you'll know why summer is your best bet.

Once you've reached Prince Rupert, you can also continue your northern journey on to Skagway, Alaska, by boarding the Alaska Marine Highway System ferry which docks right along side the *Queen of the North*.

OTHER WAYS TO GET THERE The 1,000-mile drive from Vancouver to Prince Rupert takes you up the Cariboo Highway (Route 99) through Whistler, Pemberton, and Lillooet. At Prince George, you take the Yellowhead Highway (Route 16) east past magnificent glacial lakes and the towering Coast Mountains to the Skeena River Valley, which cuts through ancient village sites and thickly forested mountains before arriving at Prince Rupert.

VIA Rail (☎ 800/561-3949) runs trains from Prince George to Prince Rupert, following the Yellowhead Highway. You can connect to Prince George from North Vancouver via **BC Rail's** Cariboo route (☎ 604/984-5246).

Air BC (☎ 604/663-9826), **Canadian Airlines International** (☎ 800/426-7000 in the U.S. or 800/363-7530 in Canada), **Harbour Air** (☎ 604/626-3225), and **Inland Air Charters** (☎ 604/624-2577) all have service to Prince Rupert.

OTHER ESSENTIALS

VISITOR INFORMATION The **Prince Rupert Travel InfoCentre** is located at 100 First Ave. East (☎ 604/624-5637 or 800/667-1994).

SPECIAL EVENTS The first week in June brings **Seafest,** with a fishing derby, parades, games, food booths, the annual blessing of the fleet, and bathtub races.

EXPLORING THE TOWN

Prince Rupert gets more than 18 hours of summer sun. And despite its northerly location, a mild coastal rain forest climate prevails. Sail, fish, or kayak the waters; hike and camp in the rain forest. Discover the region's rich heritage in its museum and archeological sites.

The **Museum of Northern British Columbia,** 100 First Ave. (☎ 604/624-3207), has a beautiful collection of Tsimshian and Haida artifacts as well as displays that depict the European settlement of the area. Archaeological tours of working sites during the summer months are also available through the museum.

Kalen Sports, 344 Second Ave. West (☎ 604/624-3633), and **Far West Sports,** 221 Third Ave. West (☎ 604/624-2568), are your two best sources in the area for information about hiking trails and directions. This rugged coastal area causes annual as well as seasonal changes in trail conditions. And some of the local hiking and backcountry skiing areas are not advisable for beginners. Both of these outfitters can set you up with any clothing or camping, climbing, and skiing equipment you need.

Since the waters surrounding Prince Rupert are tricky, with rough tidal swells and strong currents, **Sea Sports,** 295 First Ave. East (☎ 604/624-5336), will only rent kayaks and gear to experienced paddlers. Rates start at $35 per day; weekly rates and canoes also available.

You can rent cross-country skis and mountain bikes at **Vertical Ski & Cycle,** 212 Third Ave. West (☎ 604/627-1766).

WHERE TO STAY

Totem Lodge Motel. 1335 Park Ave., Prince Rupert, BC, VOT 1RO. ☎ **604/624-6761.** 31 rms. TV TEL. $60–$65 double; $65–$70 triple. Kitchen units $5 extra. MC, V.

This is the closest choice to the ferry terminal. The motel offers quiet, simply furnished rooms (some with kitchens), combination baths, and laundry.

WHERE TO DINE

Breakers Pub (☎ 604/624-5990), on Cow Bay Road next to Smile's, is a popular local pub with a harbor view in the back. It's open daily from noon to 2am (Sunday until midnight), serving stir-fries, fish 'n chips, ribs, and other hearty items.

Smile's Seafood Cafe. 113 Cow Bay Rd. ☎ **604/624-3072.** Main courses $4–$22. MC, V. Summer daily 10am–10pm; rest of the year daily 11am–9pm. SEAFOOD.

For 60 years, Smile's has been serving up seafood in every shape and form, from oyster burgers and seafood salads to heaping platters of fish. It's busy, but always worth the wait.

THE QUEEN CHARLOTTE ISLANDS

Once you've made it to Prince Rupert, you can explore the Queen Charlotte Islands, which lie offshore.

ESSENTIALS

VISITOR INFORMATION   The **Queen Charlotte Islands Travel InfoCentre** is located at 3922 Highway 33, Skidegate (☎ 604/559-4742).

GETTING THERE   The Prince Rupert–Skidegate/Queen Charlotte Islands **ferry** leaves late in the morning, and arrives about 6¹/₂ hours later. The one-way fare is $21.75 per passenger ($14.50 for seniors, $11 for children) in the high season. Car transport is an additional $83; and a dayroom or overnight cabin is an additional $20–$46.

Harbour Air (☎ 604/626-3225) and **Thunderbird Air** (☎ 604/231-8933 or 800/898-0177) both run to and from the Queen Charlotte Islands.

GETTING AROUND   To get around in the Queen Charlottes, the island-to-island **Skidegate–Allford Bay ferry** has regularly scheduled daily service. The fare is $3 each way ($8.50 per vehicle).

Budget (☎ 604/559-4675); **Rustic Car Rentals** (☎ 604/559-4641); **Tilden** (☎ 604/626-3318); and **Thrifty** (☎ 604/559-8050) have car-rental offices on the islands.

EXPLORING THE ISLANDS

Graham Island's **Naikoon Provincial Park** is a 180,000-acre wildlife reserve where you can whale-watch on the beaches or spot peregrine falcons and Sitka deer along dense forest trails.

On **South Moresby Island,** you'll find horned puffins, Cassin's auklets, waterfowl raptors, gray whales, harbor seals, Steller sea lions, and the world's largest black bears, as well as gigantic, moss-covered Sitka spruces, western hemlocks, and red cedars.

KAYAKING TRIPS   Two outfitters offer all-inclusive kayaking packages geared for all ages and experience levels. **Super Natural Adventures,** 626 West Pender St., Vancouver (☎ 604/683-5101), can book you on a Butterfly Tour to Gwaii Haanas. Single kayak tours include a tent, a guide, food (they'll provide cooking equipment if you want to cook yourself, or there's masterful cooking by your hosts), as well as charter boat or floatplane transport to Sandspit.

Tofino Expeditions Ltd., 202-1504 Duranleau St., Vancouver (☎ 604/687-4455), conducts six- to eight-day group kayaking trips through the Queen Charlotte Islands. For about $850 per person, tours depart from Port Hardy and on to

Sandspit. From there a floatplane takes you to the launch site. No prior kayaking experience is necessary. Besides transport, they supply kayaks, gear, camping equipment, first aid, and meals.

The Queen Charlotte Islands are surrounded by rough Pacific Ocean tidal swells and strong currents. Unguided paddling through this area is not advised. If you prefer to choose a local outfitter for a day-long kayak tour or want to take a multi-day kayak tour to Gwaii Hanas accompanied by a 53-foot schooner mother ship, contact **Queen Charlotte Adventures** (☎ 604/559-8990), which also offers sailboat charter tours of Ninstints.

NINSTINTS Ninstints, an ancient Haida village and place of sacred ground on Anthony Island, is a U.N. World Heritage Site. Totem poles and longhouses still stand in testimony to its millennia-old heritage. Sea kayak and sailboat are the only ways to reach this misty, rain forest-island, but for the experience of viewing firsthand the birthplace of a sophisticated tribal culture, it is worth the pilgrimage. **Tofino Expeditions Ltd.,** 202-1504 Duranleau St., Vancouver (☎ 604/687-4455), will take you to the Ninstints village by kayak for $1,350 per person.

For permission to enter the Gwaii Haanas and the World Heritage Site of Ninstints on Anthony Island, contact **The Haida Gwaii Watchmen** (P.O. Box 609, Skidegate, Haida Gwaii, BC, V0T 1S0, ☎ 604/559-8225), who act as site guardians and area hosts. Their office is located at Second Beach, just north of Skidegate Landing on Highway 16.

WHERE TO STAY ON GRAHAM ISLAND

Dorothy & Mike's Guest House. 3125 Second Ave., Skidegate, Graham Island, BC, V0T 1S0. ☎ **604/559-8439.** 2 rms. $45–$55 double/triple. Rates include breakfast. No credit cards. Closed Oct 1–Apr 30.

Guests stay in separate cottages, apart from the hosts' home, where they find comfortable accommodations with a private bath and full kitchen facilities in a peaceful garden setting. You'll be within walking distance of the ocean and shopping.

Spruce Point Lodge. 609 Sixth Ave., Skidegate, Graham Island, BC, V0T 1S0. ☎ **604/559-8234.** 7 rms. TV TEL. $65 double/triple. Kitchen unit $10 extra. Rates include breakfast. MC, V.

This rustic inn overlooks Hecate Strait. All rooms have private entrances, a choice of either a private bath or shower, and a refrigerator. Some rooms have full kitchen facilities. The shared balcony is used as a guest lounge. Your hosts can arrange kayaking packages.

WHERE TO DINE ON GRAHAM ISLAND

After a long day of exploration, stop in at **Daddy Cool's Neighbourhood Pub,** Collison Avenue and Main Street, Masset (☎ 604/626-3210), for a pint and a fish tale or two.

Cafe Gallery. Collison Avenue and Orr Street, Masset. ☎ **604/626-3672.** Main courses $12–$16. MC, V. Mon–Sat 9:30am–9pm. STEAK/SEAFOOD.

If you're dying for a steak or fresh seafood, then this is the place to get a great, well-cooked, hearty dinner. They also have pasta dishes.

THE SKEENA RIVER VALLEY & KITILOPE
ESSENTIALS

VISITOR INFORMATION The **Northwest Tourism Association,** P.O. Box 1030, Smithers (☎ 604/847-5227), can provide you with information.

SPECIAL EVENTS **Multicultural Week** in Kitimat brings a concert, food fair, and art exhibits that introduce the many cultures of Kitimat's diverse population. It's held the second week in January. For information, call ☎ 604/632-2665.

The **Kitimat Hill Climb and Car Show,** during the first week in July, is one of the largest races of its kind in the Pacific Northwest. For more information, contact ☎ 604/632-2107.

The second week in August ushers in the **Kitimat Sea Hunt,** a unique scuba diving event with trophies and prizes for a treasure hunt, a crab hunt, and underwater still photography. For more information, phone ☎ 604/632-2338.

Big fish, big prizes, and lots of good food mark Kitimat's **Annual Fish Derby,** during the third week of September. For more information, phone ☎ 604/632-6294.

EXPLORING THE AREA

The **Haisla Nation Rediscovery Society** (☎ 604/632-3308) supervises **Kitilope,** a UNESCO World Heritage Site since August 1994. It is the world's largest intact old-growth Sitka spruce coastal temperate rain forest, with ancient trees around 800 years old. A 317,000-hectare watershed some 60 miles southeast of Kitimat preserves this unique environment where you can enjoy both majestic beauty and serenity.

The Kitilope can only be accessed by boat. Because the temperate rainforest environment is delicate, there is no road access to the area. The Haisla Nation Rediscovery Society will provide you with information on boat charters, minimum impact camping restrictions, and hiking trails when you request a permit.

There are two entertaining shops you shouldn't miss if you get near Terrace, on Highway 16 north of Kitimat. **Northern Light Studio,** 4820 Halliwell Ave., Terrace (☎ 604/638-1403), has a Japanese-style garden and art studio. Totem poles, B.C. jade, fine arts and crafts, a gallery, and an herb garden are just part of its other attractions.

House of Sim-oi-ghets, right off Highway 16, Terrace (☎ 604/635-6177), is painted in traditional Haida style and features jewelry, wood carvings, moccasins, bead and leather work, as well as books. Owned by the Kitsumkalum Band, the complex has a convenience store and a campground.

10 The Okanagan Valley

The arid Okanagan Valley and its chain of lakes is the ideal destination for freshwater sports enthusiasts, golfers, and wine lovers alike. The climate here is hot and dry during the summer high season—when, as one local told us, the valley's population increases five-fold from its wintertime average of about 28,000. Farms, ranches, and small towns have flourished here for more than a century; the region's fruit orchards and vineyards will make you'll feel as if you've been transported to the Spanish countryside. Summer visitors get the pick of the fruit crop at insider prices from the many fruit stands that line Highway 97. Be sure to stop for a pint of cherries, homemade jams, and other goodies, especially if you're camping or picnicking. Prices and quality in the grocery stores aren't nearly as good.

A regional Chardonnay was recently selected as the world's best at international competitions held in London and Paris, and there are more than thirty other wineries here producing vintages that are following right on its heels. But despite this honor, the region has received little international publicity. Most tourists here are Canadian, and it's not a major destination for tour buses. Get here before they do.

Osoyoos, on the shore of Lake Osoyoos at the southern end of the valley, boasts the highest average temperature in Canada. Desert-like terrain on the mountains gives way to lush green valleys that fill with the scent of cherry and apple blossoms every spring.

Many Canadian retirees have chosen **Penticton** as their home because it also has relatively mild winters. But Okanagan is also a favorite destination for younger Canadians. Boating, water-skiing, sport fishing, and windsurfing are popular pastimes on 62-mile-long Lake Okanagan. Remember to bring your camera on board when you head out on the lake, just in case you spot its legendary underwater resident, Ogopogo, who's said to be a distant cousin of Scotland's Loch Ness monster. Local tourism authorities have offered a $1 million reward to anyone who can confirm its existence.

North of Penticton is the town of **Kelowna,** the center of the B.C. wine-making industry. Taking at least one winery tour around this area is a must. Kelowna is the largest city in the valley, and makes a good starting point for any adventure here.

Vernon is at the northern end of Okanagan Valley. Cross-country and powder skiers will find Silver Star Ski Resort's miles of trails and powder skiing a wintertime delight. The resort is set inside Silver Star Provincial Park, and boasts the best cross-country skiing in Western Canada.

OKANAGAN VALLEY ESSENTIALS

VISITOR INFORMATION   The Travel InfoCentres are open daily throughout the summer 9am to 6pm. Each is located on Highway 97 just outside of town. If you want information in advance, contact **Tourism Penticton,** 273 Power St., Penticton (☎ 604/493-4055 or 800/663-5052); **Kelowna Visitors and Convention Bureau,** 544 Harvey Ave., Kelowna (☎ 604/862-5060); **Okanagan Similkameen Tourism Association,** 1132 Water St., Kelowna (☎ 604/860-5999); or **Vernon Tourism,** 6326 Highway 97 North, Vernon (☎ 604/542-1514).

GETTING THERE   You can reach the Okanagan Valley in less that an hour by passenger jet from Vancouver. **Canadian Airlines International** (☎ 800/426-7000 in the U.S. or 800/363-7530 in Canada) has daily flights to Penticton and Kelowna from Calgary and Vancouver.

Making the 242-mile drive via the Trans-Canada Highway and Highway 3 from Vancouver, you can be in Penticton in about five hours. If you're heading to Kelowna, you can take the Trans-Canada to the Coquihalla toll highway, which will eliminate more than an hour's driving time. Vernon is also accessible from Vancouver via the Trans-Canada, Highway 3, and Highway 97.

SPECIAL EVENTS   Colorful balloons meet to fly the valley thermals in February in Vernon's **Hot Air Balloon Festival.** Call ☎ 604/545-2236 for dates and a schedule of events.

April and May are **blossom time** throughout the valley, with apricot, cherry, peach, pear, plum, and apple trees blossoming. July and August are harvest season.

In late September, there's the **Okanagan Wine Festival.** The valley celebrates its winemakers in a three-day feast of wine tastings and special events.

WINERY TOURS

As the story goes, British Columbia has a long history of producing wines: from mediocre to really bad. It began with Father Pandosy, who in 1859 planted apple trees and vineyards, and produced sacramental wines. Other monastic wineries appeared, but none seemed to be overly concerned with the quality of their bottlings. Finally, in the 1980s the government decided it was time to stop funding the wine industry, and threatened to pull its support unless it could improve the quality of its product.

It worked. B.C. wines are now winning international acclaim. Rootstock was imported from Europe, and master vintners discovered that the soil and climate offer excellent growing conditions. And the region is now producing internationally acclaimed wines. Fortunately for consumers, these wines have received far less publicity than they deserve—you can still get some great bargains in well-balanced Chardonnays, full-bodied Merlots and Cabernets, and dessert ice wines that stand up to the best Muscat d'or.

Just north of Penticton along Highway 97 is **Okanagan Falls,** where **Blue Mountain Vineyards & Cellars,** R.R. 1, Site 3, C4, Ellendale Road (☎ 604/497-8244), offers tours by appointment. **Wild Goose Vineyards and Winery,** R.R. 1, Site 3, C11, Lot 11, Sun Valley Way (☎ 604/497-8919), has daily tours from April through November (10am to 5pm). And the **LeComte Estate Winery,** Green Lake Road (☎ 604/497-8267), is open daily from May through October (10am to 5pm).

In and around Kelowna, you'll find some of the biggest names in British Columbia's wine-making industry. **Calona Wines,** 1125 Richter St. (☎ 604/762-3332), conducts tours on the hour from 10am to 4pm daily from May through September. **Summerhill Estate Winery,** R.R. 4, 4870 Chute Lake Rd. (☎ 604/764-8000), is open daily from 9am to 6pm. The winner of the 1994 Avery Trophy, **Mission Hill Wines,** 1730 Mission Hill Rd. (☎ 604/768-5125), conducts tours throughout the year; call ahead for seasonal hours. And if ice wines are your personal favorite, visit **Quail's Gate Vineyards Estate Winery,** 3303 Boucherie Rd. (☎ 604/769-4451), which conducts daily tours at 11am, 1pm, and 3pm.

BOATING & WATER SPORTS

The valley's chain of lakes is wonderful. Many local marinas offer full-service rentals. **Okanagan Boat Charters,** 291 Front St., Penticton (☎ 604/492-5099), has houseboats that accommodate 8 to 10 people. Rental for a three-day weekend is around $750; a four-day week runs $700; and a 27-foot sailboat costs $545 per week. The houseboats have full kitchens.

The **Marina on Okanagan Lake,** 291 Front St., Penticton (☎ 604/492-2628), has a great selection of ski-boats, Tigersharks (similar to jet-skis or Sea-Doos), fishing boats, and tackle.

GOLF

You've got your choice of course designs in the Okanagan Valley. Les Furber's **Gallagher's Canyon Golf and Country Club,** 4320 McCulloch Rd., Kelowna (☎ 604/861-4240), has two new holes on the main 18-hole course: one on the precipice of a gaping canyon, the other overlooking a ravine. It also has a nine-hole course, a midlength course, and a new double-ended learning center.

High on a ridge between two lakes, deep in a wilderness setting, is Les Furber's **Predator Ridge,** 360 Commonage Rd., Vernon (☎ 604/542-3436). This course has been host to the B.C. Open Championship for the last two years. The par-5 fourth hole can be played two ways over a huge mid-fairway lake; it's a challenge even for experienced golfers.

Graham Cooke and Associates' **The Harvest Club,** 2725 KLO Rd., East Kelowna (☎ 604/862-3103), boasts an orchard setting. It was opened in April 1994 and includes grass-tee practice ranges.

SKIING

Cross-country and powder skiing are the Okanagan Valley's main wintertime attractions.

Intermediate and expert downhill skiers will enjoy the **Apex Resort,** near Penticton (☎ 604/492-2880, 604/292-8111, or 800/387-2739; snow report 604/492-2929, ext. 2000), where 56 runs are serviced by one quad chair, one triple chair, one T-bar, and one beginner tow/platter. The 31 miles of cross-country trails have gained them a good reputation. The resort also has an ice rink, snow golf, sleigh rides, casino nights, and racing.

Crystal Mountain Resorts Ltd., near Westbank (☎ 604/768-5189; snow report 604/768-3753), has a comprehensive range of programs for children, women, and seniors. The resort's 20 runs are 80% intermediate-to-novice grade, serviced by one double chair, two T-bars, and one rope tow. There is also a half-pipe for snow-boarders.

If you yearn for deep, dry powder, then head to **Big White Ski Resort,** near Kelowna (☎ 604/765-3101; snow report 604/765-SNOW; lodge reservations 604/765-8888). It's spread over a broad mountain, with long, wide runs; you can cruise either open bowls or tree-lined glades. With an annual average of 18 feet of powder, there's no snowmaking needed here. The 57 runs are serviced by three high-speed quad chairs, one fixed-grip quad, one triple quad, one double chair, one T-bar, one beginner tow, and one platter lift. The resort also has cross-country trails, a recreational racing program, and night skiing five nights a week.

Silver Star Mountain Ski Resort and Cross-Country Centre, Silver Star Mountain, just north of Vernon (☎ 604/542-0224 or 800/663-4431), has 56 miles of trails (including four miles that are lit for night skiing) with an additional 30 miles in the adjacent Silver Star Provincial Park. (Silver Star is also the home of the national cross-country and biathlon teams as well as the official altitude training center.) You can ski in and ski out of the resort itself, which resembles a 19th-century mining town (click on your bindings and cruise down Main Street to a high-speed quad lift.) You'll find some steep verticals among the 72 downhill runs, which are serviced by two detachable quads, one fixed-grip quad, two double chairs, two T-bars, and one beginner tow/platter.

ESPECIALLY FOR KIDS

You'll find plenty of summertime, family oriented fun in the valley. **Okanagan Game Farm,** Site 2, Comp 21, RR no. 1, Kaleden (☎ 604/497-5405), is open daily from 8am until dusk, year-round. Located 5 miles south of Penticton on Highway 97, the farm houses 560 acres of native and exotic wildlife. The animals roam free here—visitors stay in their cars for most of it. This is the safest and surest way to see a grizzly or black bear, a Siberian tiger, a giraffe, a timber wolf, or a mountain goat. The hundreds of animals here are all well cared for. Allow about 2 1/2 hours to drive through; there's a lot to see.

The **O'Keefe Ranch,** Highway 97, 12 miles north of Vernon (☎ 604/542-7868), was Cornelius O'Keefe's 1867 cattle ranch. It grew to cover 20,000 acres, and in 1967 earned heritage site status. Now completely restored and preserved, it's a living, working piece of history. The ranch consists of a Victorian mansion, a church, a blacksmith's shop, stagecoach rides, a model railway, a gift shop, and a wealth of history. The Sundowner Ranch House on the property serves western cuisine. Open daily May to October; admission is $5 for adults, $4 for students and seniors, $3 for children, and $15 for families.

If you're planning an Okanagan ski trip, then your kids are in luck. The area's three big resorts welcome kids with special programs and activities designed especially for their enjoyment. **Silver Star Ski Resort** has a children-only ski instruction area, the Starduster ski program for four- to eight-year-olds, on-site child care, hay rides, hot chocolate parties, dinner/swims, and movie nights. **Big White Fun Centre** schedules activities and programs for all ages. There's also the **Apex Ski Resort Kids' Club,** where the Apex learn-to-ski/child care program offers ski lessons morning and afternoon for kids aged 18 months to 12 years with lunch, crafts, and indoor/outdoor activities.

WHERE TO STAY
IN PENTICTON

The Clarion Lakeside Resort. 21 West Lakeshore Dr., Penticton, BC, V2A 7M5. ☎ 604/493-8221 or 800/663-9400. 194 rms, 10 suites. A/C TV TEL. $155 double; $159–$195 suite. AE, DC, MC, V.

Situated on manicured grounds ending at a sandy beach with a long pier extending out into Okanagan Lake, the Clarion is truly a year-round resort, with easy access to nearby golf and skiing at Apex Mountain. The Penticton Public Art Gallery right next door is also worth a look. Though the hotel was only built in 1982, the guest rooms have already been fully renovated. Deluxe suites come with Jacuzzis. The rooms featuring lake views are recommended.

Facilities: There are two restaurants, an indoor pool, a Jacuzzi, saunas, a fitness club with a full Nautilus circuit, tennis courts, volleyball, and running trails.

Riordan House. 689 Winnipeg St., Penticton, BC, V2A 5N1. ☎ 604/493-5997. 3 rms. $50–$70 double. Rates include breakfast. MC, V.

Built in 1921, this stately old house was originally rum-runner Dave Riordan's home. It became a B&B in 1991, but none of the house's history was lost. The rooms are filled with an eclectic blend of antiques. Each guest room comes with a TV and VCR. The fireplace room—with window seats and a fine mountain view—is our favorite. Breakfast features fresh Okanagan fruit, served with homemade muffins, croissants, and scones. And if you let them know the night before, hosts John and Donna Ortiz will pack a delicious picnic lunch for you.

IN KELOWNA

The Grand Okanagan. 1310 Water St., Kelowna, BC, V1Y 9P3. ☎ 604/763-4500. 205 rms, suites, and condos with full kitchens. A/C TV TEL. $115–$355 double. Off-season discounts. AE, MC, V.

This elegant, newly constructed lakeshore resort is on 25 acres of beach and parkland within strolling distance of downtown. The jewel of the atrium lobby is a soaring dolphin fountain.

Dining/Entertainment: Lounge and restaurant.

Facilities: A lock connects the hotel's private marina to the lake so that small boats can dock at the restaurant's patio. Children love the motorized swan and other kid-sized boats available for them within the protected waterway. There's also a heated outdoor pool, Jacuzzi, sauna, salon, shops, and fitness center.

Hotel Eldorado. 500 Cook Rd. (at Lakeshore Road), Kelowna, BC, V1W 3L4. ☎ 604/736-7500. Fax 604/861-4779. 20 rms. TV TEL. $119–$159 double. AE, DC, MC, V.

One of Kelowna's oldest hotels, the Eldorado was floated down the lake from its original location to its present site on the water's edge north of downtown. It's been fully restored, and decorated with a mix of antiques. The third-floor rooms with a lake view are the largest and quietest.

Dining/Entertainment: A dockside cafe and bar, and a more formal dining room.

Facilities: Boat rental and moorage, plus a water-ski school.

Lake Okanagan Resort. 2751 Westside Rd., Kelowna, BC, V1Y 8B2. ☎ **604/769-3511** or 800/663-3273. 150 rms, suites, and condos. A/C TV TEL. $130–$180 double. AE, MC, V.

Located on 300 acres of Okanagan Lake's western shore, this resort includes a variety of condos, chalets, and one-bedroom units with kitchenettes in the main building. It's worth the long, winding coastline drive—a sportscar driver's dream—to take advantage of the seclusion and numerous activities available once you get there. Because the resort is built on a hillside, every room has a terrific view.

Dining/Entertainment: There's a restaurant and lounge, plus a poolside bar.

Facilities: Indoor and outdoor pools, seven tennis courts (including three equipped for night play), a nine-hole golf course, horseback riding, a marina, mountain bike and hiking trails, children's activities programs, and an exercise room.

IN WINFIELD

Earth House Health Resort. 4550 Glenmore Rd., Winfield, BC, V0H 2C0. ☎ **604/766-2109** or 800/316-6696. 10 rms. $60–$85 double. Rates include breakfast. MC, V.

If you're in the market for some serious recuperation, the Earth House has country-style hospitality and farm-style food combined with health appraisals, massage, reflexology, and herbal cleansing. There's also an outdoor hot tub. This big modern house has a terrific dining room for breakfast, and a warm, friendly feel throughout.

IN VERNON

Castle on the Mountain Bed & Breakfast. 8227 Silver Star Rd., Vernon, BC, V1T 8L6. ☎ **604/542-4593.** 5 rms. $65–$95 double. Rates include breakfast. MC, V.

Though it was built in 1981, it's hard to tell that the house hasn't been here forever. Its shingled Tudor roof blends perfectly into the landscape. This was precisely the intent of artists/hosts Eskil and Sharon Larson, who designed and built it. There's an art gallery, a hot tub, and a small children's playground. Gorgeous views abound. And they serve up a real Canadian breakfast.

WHERE TO DINE
IN & AROUND PENTICTON

The Historic 1912 Restaurant. At the foot of Lakehill Road, Kaleden, just south of Penticton. ☎ **604/497-6868.** Reservations recommended. Main courses $14.95–$21.95. MC, V. Tues–Sun 5:30–10pm. Drive five minutes south of Penticton on Highway 97, and take the second left past the Okanagan Game Farm onto Lakehill Road. CONTINENTAL.

This is the quintessential out-of-the-way romantic little restaurant. At the foot of a long, winding road from the highway to the lakeshore, the 1912 is housed in a turn-of-the-century stone building that served as a general store when Kaleden was a steamboat stop. Inside, the decor is romantic: dark wood, white linen, soft lights. The menu includes seafood (try the lemon vodka prawns), pasta, and steaks, but the highlights here are the cheese fondues and the Kahlua-laced chocolate version.

Theo's Greek Restaurant. 687 Main St., Penticton. ☎ **604/492-4019.** Reservations accepted. Main courses $9.95–$15.95. AE, DC, ER, MC, V. Mon–Sat 11am–11pm; Sun 5–11pm. GREEK.

Open since 1976, Theo's is a slice of Athens. The casual taverna-style dining room, with its whitewashed walls, stone floor and lush greenery, sets the stage for a traditional menu featuring the best calamari for hundreds of miles in any direction, succulent marinated lamb, and moussaka. Even the requisite B.C. salmon is baked with oregano and garlic.

Three Mile House. 1507 Naramata Rd., Penticton. ☎ **604/492-5152.** Reservations recommended. Main courses $12.95–$23.95. AE, MC, V. Tues–Sun 6–11pm. FRENCH.

Hosts George and June McLeod have created a haven for lovers of fine French country cuisine. Some favorites include the rich pâté de maison, oysters Florentine, and Okanagan fruit soup with a distinct local influence. Also notable are halibut au poivre, wild boar cutlets in a rich red wine sauce, tenderloins of filet mignon, and pheasant. Save room for the Belgian chocolate mousse.

IN KELOWNA

MV *Fintry Queen*. At the foot of Bernard Avenue on Okanagan Lake, Kelowna. ☎ **604/763-2780.** Reservations recommended. $27.50 dinner cruise. MC, V. Lunch cruises Mon–Sat noon–2pm, Sun 1–3pm. Dinner cruises daily 7:30–9:30pm, Sat 9pm–midnight; Sun 5:30–8:30pm. Not offered Oct–Apr. CANADIAN.

Built in 1948, this paddlewheeler was a working ferry before the bridge spanning the lake was built. It became a restaurant in 1961, and now offers dinner and dancing cruises with full hot and cold dinner buffet, featuring lots of fresh seafood, and other delectables. Lunch is à la carte from a snack bar. The cruise without food is $9 at lunch or dinner.

11 Whistler/Blackcomb

Whistler/Blackcomb—75 miles north of Vancouver on Highway 99—has been rated by *Ski* magazine as North America's most popular ski resort, second only to Vail, Colorado (and about half the price). *Snow Country* magazine has now given it the number-one rating for three years running. Whistler's reputation soared in the 1980s with the opening of the upper village's Blackcomb Mountain—whose 1-mile vertical drop is the highest on the continent. Blackcomb, a year-round ski and snowboarding facility, offers glacier skiing.

The best part about skiing at either Whistler resort is that you can walk (or ski) from your hotel straight to a ski lift or into the village shopping and dining areas. The two resorts are connected by both a walking trail and roads, but you won't need your car to go between them. They're less than five minutes apart on foot. The prices here put every other top North American ski resort to shame. Dual-mountain, three-day lift tickets are around $138 (that's $23 a day per mountain!). And even the resort's most luxurious hotel accommodations are in the moderate range.

But the appeal of this alpine resort isn't limited to winter. Vancouverites looking for a quick weekend getaway brave Friday night Highway 99 traffic to spend a few days up in the mountains. Summertime crowds flock to kayak and canoe the rushing rivers; horseback ride or hike through the trails; and snowboard or ski the glacier. At the crack of dawn, you'll find people lined up for lift tickets, toting anything from snowboards and skis to daypacks and parawing chutes. Or standing in the next line, waiting for horses.

This is the best place to be if you like outdoor sports with every possible urban amenity in close proximity.

And it's a great family destination, too. Kids can learn to ski here, and both Whistler villages sponsor daily in-town activities geared for kids of all ages, including in-line skating contests, trapezes set up in the village square, and mountain bike runs.

Neighboring towns like **Pemberton** and **Mount Currie** serve as refreshment stops for touring cyclists and hikers, while the alpine waters of **Birkenhead** and the numerous **Garibaldi Provincial Park** lakes attract fishermen and wilderness hikers.

Squamish, south of Whistler on Highway 99, is popular with rock climbers who come to conquer the Chief—the world's second-highest granite monolith (Gibraltar is the first). The January 1994 bald eagle count in Squamish, Cheakamus, and Brackendale was a staggering 3,700! Ecotourists will find the area remarkably alluring.

ESSENTIALS

VISITOR INFORMATION   The Whistler travel information center is located at the **Whistler Conference Center** on Whistler Way in Whistler Village. A summertime **information kiosk** is located on Village Gate Boulevard right as you enter Whistler Village. If you want information before you arrive, contact the **Whistler Resort Association,** 4010 Whistler Way, Whistler, BC (☎ 604/932-3928).

GETTING THERE   You can drive up the scenic Sea-to-Sky Highway (Highway 99) from Vancouver to Whistler in about an hour and a half. The route takes you up the coast along Howe Sound passed Brittania Beach, Shannon Falls, Brackendale, Squamish, and the western edge of Garibaldi Provincial Park.

The **Royal Hudson Steam Train** (BC Rail, ☎ 604/984-5246), is a 1930s steam locomotive that chugs its way up Howe Sound through forests, mountains, and glaciers to the logging town of Squamish in about two hours. You can take this spectacular and nostalgic ride throughout the summer (June to mid-September) from Wednesday to Sunday. The train leaves North Vancouver daily at 10am and returns at 4pm. Bring your camera. There's an observation car for picture taking. Round-trip fares (includes lunch on the way up and tea on return in the parlor car) are $35 for adults, $30.50 for seniors and students, and $10 for children.

BC Rail also operates the *Whistler Explorer,* which follows a series of rushing rivers, deep lakes, and canyons to Whistler. Lunch and afternoon tea are included in the round-trip price of $88. This train runs from mid-May to mid-October, departing from North Vancouver at 8:30am and returning at 6:10pm.

Perimeter Transportation Ltd., 8695 Barnard St., Vancouver (☎ 604/266-5386 or 800/663-4265), operates daily bus service to Whistler. The trip is about three hours and round-trip fares cost $60 for adults, $30 for children. Reservations are required year-round.

GETTING AROUND   As we mentioned earlier, you can walk between the Whistler Mountain (Whistler Village) and Blackcomb Mountain (Upper Village) resorts in about five minutes via a foot trail. There is a **public transit service** (☎ 604/932-4020) operating year-round that shuttles you to other areas like Nester's Village, Alta Vista, and Alpine Meadows.

There are also a few taxi services like **Blackcomb Taxi and Limousine** (☎ 604/932-3399), **Whistler Taxi** (☎ 604/932-5455), and **Sea to Sky Taxi** (☎ 604/932-3333).

You can rent a car from **ABC** at Le Chamois Hotel (☎ 604/932-6448), **Budget** at the Royal Bank Building (☎ 604/932-1236), and **Thrifty** in the Listel Whistler Hotel (☎ 604/938-0302).

SPECIAL EVENTS   Literally thousands of bald eagles annually swarm the winter waters feeding on spawning salmon. During January's **Annual Eagle Count,** in

Brackendale, Squamish, and Cheakamus, you can sit on the shore or rent a kayak to see them; don't forget to bring your camera.

Numerous mountain bike and in-line skating competitions are held on the slopes and at the base during July.

The third week in July brings **Whistler's Country & Blues Festival.** Down in the villages and up on the mountain you'll hear the sounds of fiddling, cowboy, and down-home blues music.

The **Whistler Classical Music Festival** is held the second weekend in August. The Vancouver Symphony Orchestra spends part of its summer here along with numerous guest artists.

The second weekend in September ushers in the **Whistler Fall for Jazz Festival,** with performances in the squares and the surrounding clubs.

HITTING THE SLOPES

Whistler Mountain (☎ 604/932-3434 or 604/687-6761 for snow report) has a 5,006-foot vertical and 100 marked runs, serviced by one high-speed gondola, eight chairs, plus four other lifts and tows. Helicopter skiing makes another 100-plus runs accessible on nearby glaciers.

And **Blackcomb Mountain** (☎ 604/932-3141 or 604/687-7504 for snow report) has a 5,280-foot vertical and 100 marked runs, serviced by nine chairs, plus three other lifts and tows. Lift tickets are $49 per day for either mountain, or $51 per day for a dual-mountain pass. For $138, you can get a dual-mountain three-day pass. (Four- and six-day dual-mountain passes are also available for $180 to $220.)

Based at Blackcomb Mountain, the **Dave Murray Summer Ski Camp,** P.O. Box 98, Whistler, BC, V0N 1B0 (☎ 604/932-3141 or 604/687-1032), is the longest-running North American summer ski camp. Junior programs cost about U.S. $850 per week, including food, lodging, lifts, tennis, trampoline, trapeze, and mountain biking. Instruction and supervision are excellent.

Heli-skiing is at its best up here, and there are numerous specialty outfitters. If you want to try some serious verticals, contact **Whistler Backcountry Adventures** (☎ 604/938-1410), who arrange both heli-skiing and heli-fishing trips.

Year-round skiing is possible on **Blackcomb Glacier** if you want to take to the midsummer slopes. (Bring plenty of sunblock.) And if you find yourself up there on a clear summer Saturday night, then join Blackcomb's weekly guided stargazing and moonrises.

Whistler Resort itself has only about 16 miles of cross-country trails on the Chateau Whistler golf course, but the **Mad River Nordic Centre,** south of Whistler, has 38 miles of groomed trails equipped with warming huts and occasionally runs a Nordic ski school. And **Garabaldi Provincial Park** provides groomed trails that are ideal for backcountry experts. For more information, contact **Whistler Cross-Country** (☎ 604/932-6436).

OTHER OUTDOOR ACTIVITIES

You can rent a mountain bike from **Blackcomb Ski and Sports** located at the base of the mountain in the day lodge (☎ 604/938-7788); **Trax and Trails** in the Chateau Whistler Hotel (☎ 604/938-2017); and **McCoo's Too** in Whistler Village Centre (☎ 604/938-9954).

Whistler River Adventures (☎ 604/932-3532; fax 604/932-3559) offers package trips for novice to expert rafters that include equipment and ground transport. Rates range from $38 to $104 per person. The company also conducts half-day and full-day guided fishing trips for rainbow trout, Dolly Varden char, steelhead, and salmon. (A catch-and-release policy is promoted.)

Robert Trent Jones's **Chateau Whistler Golf Club,** at the base of Blackcomb Mountain (☎ 604/938-2095; pro shop 604/938-2092), has a gradual 300-foot ascent on the first few holes over cascading creeks and granite rock faces. Midcourse, there's a panoramic Coast Mountains view. **Nicklaus North at Whistler** (☎ 604/938-9898) is five minutes north of the Village on Green Lake. The par-71 course's mountain views are spectacular, and the driving range will be open by summer 1996.

Whistler Jet Boating Company Ltd. (☎ 604/894-5200 or 800/303-BOAT) will take you white-water rafting down the Green River or speed-cruising through the gold-rush Lillooet River Valley throughout the summer. Tours range from one-hour trips for $55 to four-hour cruises for $109 (discounts for children ages 3–12).

SHOPPING

Whatever you want, there's probably a shop that carries it at Whistler. The **Whistler Marketplace** is lined with clothing, jewelry, and craft shops. **Escape Route,** at both Whistler Marketplace and Crystal Lodge (☎ 604/938-3228) has a great line of outdoor clothing and equipment. The **Durango Boutique,** 4227 Village Stroll (☎ 604/932-6987) caters to those looking for fashionable, casual, and Western clothing. **For Nature's Sake,** in the Timberline Shops Mall (☎ 604/938-9453), carries hiking canes, bear bells, books, gifts, and more.

WHERE TO STAY

There are more than 2,600 hotel and luxury condominium units in the area. If you're in the market for a one- to four-bedroom condo or townhouse, contact **Whistler Chalets and Accommodations Ltd.,** 4360 Lorimer Rd., Whistler (☎ 604/932-6699 or 800/663-7711). Prices range from $65 to $625 per night in the winter and $49 to $295 per night in the summer.

Canadian Pacific Chateau Whistler. 4599 Chateau Blvd., Whistler, BC, V0N 1B4. ☎ **604/938-8000** or 800/828-7447 in the U.S. or 800/268-9411 in Canada. Fax 604/938-2058. 342 rms. MINIBAR TV TEL. $125–$225 double. Summer discounts available. AE, MC, V. Underground valet parking $15.

This Upper Village hotel has sterling service, and excellent accommodations right next to the Blackcomb ski lift. The two-story executive suites are amazing. The rooms and smaller suites all feature comfortable sitting areas, wonderful views, and an iron and ironing board en suite. The lobby resembles a hunting chalet—rustic wood and country antiques welcome you. The after-ski cocktail lounge has comfortable sitting areas with a great view of the Blackcomb lifts. The village's best buffet-style brunch is served daily amid a fascinating collection of bird houses; room service is also available. Ski and bike storage as well as a full-service spa, indoor/outdoor pool, and health club are located downstairs.

Durlacher Hof Pension Inn. 7055 Nesters Rd., Whistler, BC, V0N 1B0. ☎ **604/932-1924.** Fax 604/938-1980. 8 rms. $85–$105 double. Rates include full breakfast and afternoon tea. AE, MC, V.

Peter and Erika Durlacher have a lovely Swiss mountain chalet that complements the alpine atmosphere surrounding you. You will feel completely spoiled by the charm of fine European service when you're their guest. Rooms feature goosedown duvets, private baths, Jacuzzis, or showers, and mountain-view balconies. The fireside guest cocktail lounge, sauna, and whirlpool are welcome comforts after a day on the slopes. Dinners here on selected evenings are often prepared by a celebrated guest chef.

WHERE TO DINE & WHERE TO GO AFTER DARK

Pick your favorite Vancouver restaurant, and it probably has a branch in Whistler. (Milestones and the Hard Rock Cafe are here as well.) This is the one area outside of the city where you'll find an abundance of fine dining establishments—and not all of them are connected to hotels or inns.

Citta Bistro, in Whistler Village Square (☎ 604/932-4177), is the locals' favorite dining and night spot. Serving continental fare and pasta, it's also the best people-watching corner in town. **Monk's Grill,** near the Blackcomb ski lifts (☎ 604/ 932-9677), has spectacular mountain views and a menu that offers everything from fresh seafood and pasta dishes to Alberta prime rib and lobster. You can choose to sit in the formal dining area, the casual lounge, or on the outdoor patios.

If you're headed north of the village toward Mount Currie and Lillooet, make sure to at least stop for a coffee at the **Spirit Circle Art, Craft, and Tea Company,** on Route 99 (☎ 604/894-6336), where owner Deanna Pilling serves up a huge all-day Canadian breakfast for $6.25 and lunch specials starting at $4.95. You can't miss this wood building with the red-and-black motif on the doors. Inside, you're surrounded by a collection of Interior Salish art and crafts as well as books and herb teas in glass jars. (The cafe also sponsors the wintertime **Lil'wat Celebration,** a traditional dinner and cultural event that includes drumming, singing, plays, and storytelling by elders.)

After dark, Citta's (see above) is the local gathering place. Start your evening there before heading around the corner to the **Savage Beagle** (☎ 604/938-3337), a theme-nightclub that features both DJ and live-band entertainment; or **Tommy Africa's** (☎ 604/932-6090), which has five self-service bars and an always-crowded dance floor, complete with go-go girls. Both are open daily from 8pm to 2am. Drinks are around $3 to $5; cover is about the same.

12 Cariboo Chilcotin

The Canadian Old West really hasn't changed too much in the past century. Just take a look at the scenery in movies like *Legends of the Fall* and *Little Women*. West of bustling high-desert Kamloops along Highway 97, the landscape is big, rolling chaparral that gradually transforms into alpine and subalpine meadows surrounded by giant glacial peaks.

At **Cache Creek,** working cowboys stop in at the local coffee shops after a long night of cattle driving. The road leads out of town directly into the Bonaparte reserve. The turnoff to Route 99 and Lillooet takes you past a portion of the Old Cariboo Highway, where historic Hat Creek Ranch has been lovingly restored. Members of the Bonaparte band have constructed an authentic Shuswap pit house here as well.

The terrain changes once again to forested mountains as you make your way through **Pavilion,** where the oldest private post office is still in operation. You descend into the town of **Lillooet,** where there's a pioneer museum documenting the town's status as Mile Zero of the Old Cariboo Highway.

Route 97 follows the gold-rush trail through towns like **70 Mile House, 100 Mile House, and 180 Mile House**—all named after the roadhouses that used to service miners and settlers along the Old Cariboo Highway.

Just west of Bowron Lakes Provincial Park is **Barkerville.** This restored/ reconstructed 1870s gold-rush town has 40 of its original buildings still standing. (You've probably seen the town in more than a dozen movies and TV westerns.)

The history is truly Wild West: the streets were only 18 feet wide, thanks to a tipsy surveyor, and the town burned when a miner in hot pursuit of a dance hall girl knocked over a woodstove.

During the summer, the biggest events are the numerous rodeos scheduled in Quesnel and Williams Lake and the annual **Cattle Drive,** during which you can saddle up or ride the chuckwagon from Cache Creek to Kamloops (see Section 13 of this chapter).

In January, Quesnel hosts an annual **Dog Sledding Race.** If you can't make it to the Iditarod in Alaska, this is a great alternative.

For more information on the entire area, contact the **Cariboo Tourist Association,** P.O. Box 4900, Williams Lake (☎ 604/392-2226 or 800/663-5885).

CACHE CREEK, PAVILION & LILLOOET TO 100 MILE HOUSE

AREA ESSENTIALS

GETTING THERE   Highway 97 west out of Kamloops takes you to Cache Creek in about an hour. From there, you can drive north to the Highway 99 junction to Pavilion and Lillooet, about an hour's drive away.

BC Rail (☎ 604/984-5246) has a daily excursion train that departs North Vancouver and passes through Whistler on its way to Lillooet and Quesnel.

VISITOR INFORMATION   The Travel InfoCentres here are only open during the summer. The **Cache Creek Travel InfoCentre** is at 1340 Highway 97 North (☎ 604/457-5306). The **Lillooet Travel InfoCentre** is located in the Lillooet pioneer museum at 790 Main St. (☎ 604/256-4308).

EXPLORING THE AREA

The **Lillooet Pioneer Museum,** at the InfoCentre, 790 Main St. (☎ 604/ 256-4308), is in a former Anglican church, built in the 1960s to replace the original 1860 church that was carried to Lillooet in pieces by miners heading up the Cariboo Gold Trail. Now it houses an eclectic permanent exhibit of fascinating local history—from early farm implements to camel saddles (yes, there were camels here!), and the printing presses that once produced "Ma" Murray's newspaper (which regularly caused waves across Canada). Admission by donation. Open daily 9am to 5pm. Pick up a self-guided tour map here, and explore Lillooet.

Hat Creek Ranch, at the intersection of Routes 97 and 99, 6.5 miles (11km) west of Cache Creek (☎ 604/457-9722), was established in 1861 by a former Hudson's Bay Company trader as a stopping house on the Cariboo Wagon Road. By the turn of the century it had expanded into a full-scale ranch. It is still a working ranch, completely restored and operated by the B.C. Heritage Trust. There are tours, wagon rides, a gift shop, a visitors' center and tearoom, a blacksmith, and a traditional Shuswap pit house built by members of the neighboring Bonaparte Indian Band. Admission is by donation. Open mid-May to mid-October daily 9am to 6pm.

A huge slab of polished B.C. jade on the front steps of the **Cariboo Jade Shoppe,** 1093 Todd Rd. (at the intersection of Routes 1 and 97), Cache Creek (☎ 604/ 457-9669), is a good indication of the treasures inside the shop. Okay, it's touristy, but it's got a great selection of jewelry, crafts, and pieces by B.C. jewelers and artists, made from indigenous materials (jade, gold, hematite, and semiprecious stones). If you're looking for some vacation reading, there's a whole section of books about the province: tales from the Wild West days, true crime, regional cooking, gold panning, wildlife guides, and more.

A Special Wilderness Retreat in Tweedmuir Provincial Park

Tweedmuir Provincial Park is B.C.'s largest provincial park, truly a roadless, unspoiled wilderness. Inside the park you'll find **Stewart's Lodge and Camps,** Box 19, Nimpo Lake, BC (☎ 604/742-3388 or 800/668-4335), an ideal fly-fishing, hunting, canoeing, and hiking destination. Here are 10 rooms renting for $50 to $135 double, $50 to $135 triple (AE, MC, and V accepted). The main log lodge has a smokehouse and fly shop; rooms here all have private bath. From May to September, you can have an even more remote wilderness experience by having the staff equip and fly you to one of four wilderness cabins on Elguk Lake. The four cabins cost $135 to $150 per day. You'll be taken out by floatplane, and the rate includes food, boats, motors, fuel, ice, and propane.

WHERE TO STAY & DINE

Big Bar Guest Ranch. Big Bar Road (P.O. Box 27), Clinton, BC, V0N 1K0. ☎ and fax **604/ 459-2333.** 12 rms, 4 cabins. $60–$99 double. AE, MC, V. Take Highway 97 to Big Bar Road just north of Clinton.

In the heart of Cariboo country, north of Cache Creek, this guest ranch offers riding in winter and summer, plus gold panning, canoeing, fishing, hiking, cross-country skiing, and pack trips. You have a choice of self-contained log cottages and some camping sites; there's also a licensed dining room. The centerpiece is The Harrison House, a hand-hewn log house built by the pioneers. The hot tub was a later addition, but a most welcome one.

The Hills Health & Guest Ranch. Highway 97, c/o 108 Ranch, Comp 26, 108 Mile Ranch, 108 Mile House, BC, V0K 2E0. ☎ **604/791-5225.** Fax 604/791-6384. 46 rms. TV. $70–$139 double. AE, MC, V.

This year-round fitness and spa resort has riding, hay rides, guided hiking, and cross-country skiing on more than 100 miles of trails. The guest rooms are large, done in natural pine both inside and out. Golf courses are nearby.

Dining/Entertainment: The restaurant serves a unique blend of cowboy favorites and spa cuisine. It's open daily from 8am to 9pm, and reservations are recommended. Main courses run $9 to $27. Diners can also opt for a meal and horseback ride package for an unforgettable picnic experience.

Facilities: Indoor exercise classes, health and wellness programs, aerobics studio. Hydrotherapy pools, massage, herbal wraps, facials, reflexology, body packs. Full English- and Western-wear tack shop.

WILLIAMS LAKE, QUESNEL & BARKERVILLE

AREA ESSENTIALS

VISITOR INFORMATION   The **Quesnel/Barkerville Travel InfoCentre** is open year-round at 703 Carson Ave. (☎ 604/992-8716).

GETTING THERE   Highway 97 continues north through 100 Mile House and Williams Lake to Quesnel where you can pick up the Route 26 junction that leads to Barkerville. This leg of the trip takes about three hours.

BC Rail (☎ 604/984-5246) serves Quesnel daily throughout the year.

BARKERVILLE: AN OLD WEST GHOST TOWN

This 1860s gold rush town was founded after Billy Barker, a Cornish miner, found gold there. It became a ghost town a few years later after $50 million in gold (at $16 per ounce) was mined out of here. Soap was a buck a bar, and so was a dance with a hurdy-gurdy girl. The town was designated in the 1950s as a Historic Park. Seventy-five reconstructed buildings and a pioneer cemetery plus a 1869 church (which stills holds services) stand as a living museum. May through September the townspeople dress up and bring history back to life. You and your kids can have fun gold panning and taking a stagecoach ride after you've struck it rich.

The town is located off Highway 97 on Route 26 east. Two-day admission is $5.50 adults, $3.25 seniors and students, $1 children 6 to 12; the historic park is open daily from dawn to dusk. Call ☎ 604/994-3332 for more information.

CAMPING

Lowhee Campground is the best of the three campgrounds that surround Barkerville and the closest to the park entrance. Well-spaced campsites ($12.50 per vehicle per night) can accommodate both tents and RVs. The other two grounds are not as attractive: one is situated right next to the old cemetery, while the other is hidden behind a working mine operation that starts up daily at dawn. During the summer, groceries and camping supplies are available at the **Grubstake,** which is just up the hill from the Lowhee and is open daily from 8am to 9pm.

WHERE TO DINE

There is an abundance of diners, family restaurants, and other forms of casual food in Quesnel. Barkerville has three summer-only restaurants, which are open from 10am to 6pm. Otherwise, shop in Quesnel before you go.

Alamo Diner. Route 97, 15 minutes south of Quesnel. ☎ **604/747-4346.** Main courses $4.95–$13.95. AE, MC, V. Daily 24 hours. CANADIAN.

Standing alone in a clearing at the edge of the highway, the Alamo is an oasis, not for the passable food so much as the fact that it's open 24 hours and has a full-service RV park, gas, and tenting sites. The food—steaks, salads, fish, pasta, and buffalo burgers—is a welcome find at 3am.

13 The High Country from Kamloops to Wells Gray Provincial Park

The landscape doesn't seem to change much from the arid Okanagan terrain as you make your way toward Shuswap Lake and Kamloops. The only thing that is readily noticeable is that the fruit orchards and vineyards are replaced by undulating sheets of black mesh, supported on low poles covering field after field of ginseng (which needs shade to grow). Along the lower Thompson River, in the valleys alongside Highway 97 and Route 1, you'll see acres of these small plants with the incredibly valuable roots.

Kamloops itself is a relatively uninviting sprawling city of shopping malls, industry, and heavy traffic, but it's the best stop for last-minute equipment and supply purchases before heading out to the lakes, high country, or on your way to Banff and Jasper. (Stock up here. It's a long haul between towns.) From this base camp, you can reach two beautiful, divergent areas: the Shuswap Lakes region to the east and Wells Gray Provincial Park about ninety minutes north.

The **Shuswap Lakes** are popular with houseboaters; you can navigate and fish the region's 600 miles of waterways, landing at campsites and beaches along the way that are only accessible by boat. The Adams River sockeye salmon run is an annual event, but the major runs that happen every four years are worth the wait (the next one is due in 1998). The nearby town of Salmon Arm is the place to rent a houseboat and spend a relaxing vacation at one of the area's water-access–only marine parks. In winter, there are groomed cross-country and snowmobile trails in the nearby hills.

High up above the town of **Clearwater**—about 10 miles up Clearwater Valley Road—is the pristine wilderness of **Wells Gray Provincial Park,** where Helmcken and Dawson Falls are easily accessed by the park's few paved roads. Even greater wonders await deep inside this 1.3 million-hectare wilderness. A drive up the winding dirt road to the Green Point Observatory is a perfect way to get a first overview of the park; much of it can be seen from the upper deck of the observation tower.

And you'll find every type of snow sport imaginable in the High Country, from resort-style downhill and snow-boarding runs in Kamloops to backcountry Nordic hiking expeditions in Clearwater.

AREA ESSENTIALS

VISITOR INFORMATION   Before you arrive, you can get information from the **High Country Tourism Association,** 2-1490 Pearson Place, Kamloops (☎ 604/ 372-7770 or 800/567-2275); or the **Kamloops Travel InfoCentre,** 1290 W. Trans-Canada Highway (Route 1; on top of the hill), Kamloops (☎ 604/374-3377 or 800/ 667-0143).

For Wells Gray Provincial Park contact the **Clearwater Travel InfoCentre,** 425 E. Yellowhead Hwy. (Route 5; at the junction with Wells Gray Park Road), Clearwater (☎ 604/674-2646).

GETTING THERE   Kamloops is about 50 minutes flying time from Vancouver, with four flights each day. You can fly to Kelowna in 45 minutes and drive for 45 minutes to Salmon Arm.

By road, Kamloops is 260 miles (425km) from Vancouver, about 5^1/$_2$ hours' drive via the Fraser Canyon. Via the Coquihalla Highway, it's about 3^1/$_2$ hours. The 285-mile (460km) drive from Vancouver to Salmon Arm on the Trans-Canada Highway takes about six hours, using the new Coquihalla Highway from Hope to Kamloops. Clearwater and Wells Gray Provincial Park are 90 minutes north of Kamloops on the Yellowhead Highway (Route 5).

SPECIAL EVENTS   Bull riding, roping, and barrel racing highlight the **Kamloops Pro Rodeo,** one of the biggest rodeos in Canada; it's held the second week of April.

Departing from a different Cariboo ranch each year, the annual **Cattle Drive** has grown immensely popular. Now more than 1,000 people participate in the eight-day ride through alpine wilderness and small towns leading to a grand arrival (and big party) in Kamloops. Horses, gear, even seats on the wagons are available for rent (☎ 604/372-7075). It's held the second week of July.

The third week of August brings the **Kamloops Airshow**—not as big as the Abbottsford Airshow, but still an impressive display of maneuvers.

FROM KAMLOOPS TO THE SHUSWAP LAKES
AN INTRIGUING CULTURAL CENTER

Stop in at the **Secwepemc Native Heritage Park,** 355 Yellowhead Hwy., Kamloops (☎ 604/828-9801). The Shuswap band offices and former provincial residential school looks across the South Thompson River toward Kamloops. Behind those structures, a few unused buildings that were part of the original agency complex, you'll find an amazing indoor/outdoor museum. Along the river bank, down an interpretive trail, you'll find five *kekuli* (traditional winter pit houses) on a 2,400-year-old village site, restored to its original condition. Further along the path, there is a salmon-fishing station and usually a carver working on a totem pole, or some other structure. The indoor museum tells the band's history in displays and video presentations. Storytelling, dance, and theater presentations are also scheduled throughout the year. Admission to the museum is $5 for adults, $4 for seniors and children. Outdoor grounds (open summer only) are free. They are open during the summer daily from 9am to 8pm; and the rest of the year Monday through Saturday from 9am to 5pm.

OUTDOOR ACTIVITIES IN THE REGION

North of Kamloops the lakes of the **Thompson-Nicola region** are teeming with rainbow trout. For equipment, and to find out which flies, are working, try **Wilderness Outfitters**, 1304 Battle St., Kamloops (☎ 604/327-2127). They're an authorized Orvis shop, and have a great selection of rods, reels, flies, and tying supplies. They're open Monday through Saturday from 9am to 5:30pm.

Golfers have two courses that will test their skills against the arid terrain. Robert Trent Jones's **Rivershore Golf Club,** Comp 1, Site 13, RR no. 2, Kamloops (☎ 604/573-4622), has five holes that touch two artificial lakes. The rest of the course has similar difficulty factors to those found on PGA Tour courses: wind and large undulating greens. **Eagle Point Golf and Country Club,** 8888 Barnhartvale Rd., Kamloops (☎ 604/573-2453), is Robert Haslip's Scottish links–style course. It hosted the 1992 Royal Canadian Golf Association's national senior championship barely a year after it opened. You'll find some good challenges here. Four steep sand traps force you to blast your way out and stands of ponderosa pines confront you on the elevated tees.

Sun Peaks Resort, near Kamloops (☎ 604/578-7232; snow report 604/578-7232), is a great powder skiing and open run area with a vertical rise of 2,854 feet. The 63 runs are serviced by one high-speed quad chair with bubble cover, one fixed-grip quad chair, one triple chair, one double chair, one T-bar, and one beginner platter. Snowboarders have a choice of two half pipes, one with a super-large boardercross. At the bottom of this 3,000-foot run you'll find handrails, cars, a fun box, hips, quarter pipes, burly tabletops, transfers, and fat gaps that were designed by Ecosign Mountain Planners and some of Canada's top amateur riders. Nordic and snowmobile trails are also available.

Utopia Outdoor Adventures, 230-1210 Summit Dr., no. 123, Kamloops (☎ 604/ 372-9321 or 800/443-9333), has numerous heli-skiing and heli-boarding packages that include accommodations, child care, ski school, shuttle service from Vancouver, and equipment rentals.

WHERE TO STAY

Quaaout Lodge. P.O. Box 1215, Chase, BC. ☎ **604/679-3090** or 800/663-4303. Fax 604/ 679-3039. 72 rms. TV TEL. $103–$135 double. AE, MC, V.

This gorgeous resort, set on the sandy shore of Little Shuswap Lake with area golf courses nearby, draws strongly on native tradition in its design. This is no accident— it is owned and operated by the Shuswap Band. Built in 1992, the resort is replete with luxury facilities. Six of the well-appointed rooms have fireplaces and Jacuzzis.

Dining/Entertainment: The hotel's excellent restaurant features many dishes that draw on local heritage, including alder-smoked salmon and fluffy fried bread called bannock.

Facilities: There's an indoor pool, Jacuzzi, a fully equipped gym, and saunas. Outside, there are hiking and biking trails, a children's playground (adventurous kids can opt to spend a night camped in authentic teepees provided by the lodge), fishing, Nordic skiing, canoeing, and more. Rental canoes and mountain bikes are available.

WELLS GRAY PROVINCIAL PARK & ENVIRONS

Wells Gray Provincial Park (☎ 604/371-6400) is the second-largest park in British Columbia, with more than 1.3 million acres of virgin wilderness: mountains, rivers, lakes, glaciers, forests, and alpine meadows. Wildlife abounds here, including mule deer, moose, grizzly and black bears, beavers, coyotes, hummingbirds (we saw 16 one morning!), timber wolves, golden eagles, and much more.

Helmcken Falls, twice as tall as Niagara Falls, can be reached by paved road, as can **Dawson Falls.** Boaters head for **Clearwater Lake** and **Azure Lake** (which can only be reached via Clearwater Lake—there are no roads anywhere near it). There are even campgrounds along the lakes, which make perfect destinations for overnight canoe or fishing trips.

Wells Gray Guest Ranch, Wells Gray Road (☎ 604/674-2774), offers guided hiking, canoeing, white-water rafting, fishing, and motorboating (on Clearwater and Azure Lakes in the park). Excursions can range from half-day to one-week trips. **Crazy Moon Enterprises** at Helmcken Falls Lodge (☎ 604/674-3657) also offers half- and full-day guided hikes and canoeing trips.

Wells Gray is also immensely popular for **backwoods cross-country skiing.** Trails are marked through the park, or you can join a group. For more information contact Wells Gray Back Country Chalets (see below).

The North Thompson river south of the park from Clearwater to Kamloops has grade 2 rapids, and is the perfect destination for a long-haul rafting/camping run. The rapids between Kamloops Lake and Spences Bridge are challenging for both intermediate and advanced rafters. (Below Spences Bridge, the waters are not considered navigable.) **Kumsheen Raft Adventures,** in Lytton (☎ 604/455-2296), offers three-hour to three-day expeditions on motor-driven or paddle rafts. Packages include swimming, hiking, hot tub, campsite, mountain bike rentals, and rappelling. One-day trips through the Thompson River cost $98 for adults, $66 for children. **Interior Whitewater Expeditions** in Clearwater (☎ 604/674-3727), and Adams River (☎ 604/955-2447), has a variety of rafting and kayaking packages available, ranging from a few hours to five days, on some of the wildest, most beautiful stretches of river in Canada.

WHERE TO STAY NEAR THE PARK

While most visitors to Wells Gray camp in the park's many drive-in or wilderness campgrounds (check the sign outside the InfoCentre to make sure they aren't full before you drive all the way in), there are a couple of more civilized alternatives.

Nakiska Ranch. Trout Creek Road (off Wells Gray Park Road), Clearwater, BC, V0E 1N0. ☎ and fax **604/674-3655.** 4 rms in lodge, 2 cabins. Summer $85 double, $85–$165 cabin; winter $69 double, $85–$135 cabin. MC, V.

Gorgeous log cabins, acres of mowed meadow, and Wells Gray's forests and mountains surround the main log house on this working ranch. The "rustic cabins" sign at the entrance describes the exteriors only. The interiors could be straight from the pages of *House Beautiful,* with open kitchens, hardwood floors, lots of windows, appropriately Nordic furnishings, all new and immaculate. Breakfast at the house is delicious, but bring groceries for lunches and dinners—it's a 30-minute drive to the nearest restaurant. The park is just a few minutes' drive from the ranch. Helmcken Falls Lodge is a little closer to the park, but Nakiska is much nicer.

If they're full, the **Wells Gray Guest Ranch** (604/674-2774) is just down the road.

Trophy Mountain Buffalo Ranch Bed & Breakfast & Campground. RR no. 1 (P.O. Box 1768), Clearwater, BC, V0E 1N0. ☎ **604/674-3095.** Fax 604/674-3131. 4 rms (2 with private bath), 40 campsites. $45–$60 double room (including breakfast); $12–$15 campsite. MC, V.

You can't miss the small herd of buffalo as you drive up the Wells Gray Park Road. The log cabin just beyond them, at the edge of the woods, has four comfortable guest rooms, all with hearty breakfasts included. The tent and RV sites are tree shaded and well kept. There are plenty of hiking and horse trails (ask directions up Trophy Mountain). Trail rides (starting at $40 for 2¹/₂ hours) go back through the forest to the cliffs overlooking the Clearwater river, and to a secluded 80-foot-high waterfall. And if you get a sudden urge to go into deep into the woods, your hosts here have a full complement of gear for rent, from canoes to cookware.

Wells Gray Park Backcountry Chalets. Box 188G, Clearwater, BC, V0E 1N0. ☎ **604/ 587-6444.** Fax 604/587-6446. 3 chalets. Chalet only $25 per person; $33 per person in winter. Packing trip packages available for two to four days additional. MC, V.

Ian Eakins and Tay Briggs run a family operated outdoor guiding company with three chalets situated deep in the park. They are open year-round (after all, Wells Gray has some of Canada's best backwoods skiing), and offer a number of guided or self-catered hiking and ski packages. Two of the nicest people you could hope to have as guides, they have a great knowledge of local flora and fauna, and hospitality, too. The chalets sleep up to 12 people, and are fully equipped with kitchens, furniture, bedding, libraries, saunas, propane lighting and heat. It's the best of both worlds: untrammeled wilderness and rural hospitality.

WHERE TO DINE NEAR THE PARK

There aren't many choices for dining out in Clearwater. Campers can stock up on provisions at the Safety Mart on the Old North Thompson Highway (open daily 9am to 6pm, sometimes later in summer) in the Brookfield Mall downtown. The **Chuckwagon Restaurant and Saloon** (☎ 604/674-3636), on the Old North Thompson Highway, also downtown, serves up a wide variety of diner basics. The prices and portions are both quite good. Both the **Helmcken Falls Lodge** (☎ 604/ 674-3657) and the **Wells Gray Ranch** (☎ 604/674-2774) on the Wells Gray Park Road have dinner buffets at 7pm sharp daily for around $21 per person.

CLEARWATER AFTER DARK

Clearwater's nightlife consists of two saloons. The **Wells Gray Guest Ranch Saloon,** on Wells Gray Park Road, is open daily from 4pm to midnight. Except for the inevitable Swiss or German tourists dressed in their hiking gear, it feels like you've just stumbled onto a Wild West movie set. It's a great place to share stories of world travels. **The Chuckwagon Saloon** (part of the Chuckwagon Restaurant), in downtown Clearwater, attracts a very different crowd—ranchers, fishermen, Indians, farmers, and other locals. The Chuckwagon has a huge covered porch on the side to enjoy the cool evenings.

20 The Yukon & the Northwest Territories: The Great Northern Wilderness

by Bill McRae

The Far North of Canada is one of the last great wilderness areas in North America. The Yukon, Northwest Territories, and the far north of British Columbia are home to the native Inuit and northern Indian tribes like the Dene, vast herds of wildlife, and thousands of square miles of tundra and stunted subarctic forest. For centuries, names like the Klondike, Hudson's Bay, and the Northwest Passage have had the power to conjure up powerful images. For an area so little visited and so distant, the North has long played an integral role in the history and imagination of the western world.

Yet the North is not eternal, and it is changing before our eyes. The changes are creating a whole pattern of paradoxes. The Arctic is a hotbed of mineral, oil, gas, and diamond exploration. Jobs and schools have brought Inuit and Indian natives from the hunting camps to town, where they live in prefabs instead of igloos and drive trucks and snowmobiles out to their traplines. But the money they spend in supermarkets is earned by ancestral hunting skills and their lifestyle remains based on the pursuit of migrating game animals and marine creatures.

You'll find modern tourist lodges, supplied by air, dotting half-explored regions of wilderness; dog teams sharing an airstrip with cargo planes; roaming herds of caribou streaming across brand-new all-weather highways; families dining on French cuisine in one spot and on walrus blubber in another; Inuit villages with rows of seaplanes moored alongside canoes.

The Native Canadians (Indians) and the Inuit make up the majority of the North's population, particularly when you add the Métis offspring of white and Native Canadian couples. All the natives were originally nomadic, covering enormous distances in pursuit of migrating game animals. Today nearly all First Nation people, as the Native Canadians are often called, have permanent homes in settlements, but many of them spend part of the year in remote tent camps, hunting, fishing, and trapping. And although nobody *lives* in igloos anymore, these snow houses are still built as temporary shelters when the occasion arises.

Survival is the key word for the Native Canadians. They learned to survive in conditions unimaginably harsh for southern societies, by means of skills that become more wondrous the better you know them. The early white explorers soon learned that in order to stay alive they had to copy those skills as best they could. Those who refused to "go native" rarely made it back.

The first known white man to penetrate the region was Martin Frobisher. His account of meeting the Inuit, written 400 years ago, is the earliest on record. About the same time, European whalers, hunting whales for their oil, were occasionally forced ashore by storms or shipwrecks and depended on Inuit hospitality for survival. This almost legendary hospitality, extended to any stranger who came to them, remains an outstanding characteristic of the Inuit.

Whites only began to move into the Canadian Arctic in any number during the great "fur rush" in the late 18th century. In the wake of the fur hunters and traders came the missionaries, Roman Catholic and Anglican, who built churches and opened schools.

For most of its recorded history, the Far North was governed from afar, first by Great Britain, then by the Hudson's Bay Company, and from 1867 by the new Canadian government in Ottawa. At that time the Territories included all of the Yukon, Saskatchewan, Alberta, and huge parts of other provinces.

Then, in 1896, gold was discovered on Bonanza Creek in the Klondike. Tens of thousands of people descended onto the Yukon in a matter of months, giving birth to Dawson City, Whitehorse, and a dozen other tent communities that went bust along with the gold veins. The Yukon gold rush was the greatest in history; more than $500,000 in gold was washed out of the gravel banks along the Klondike before industrial mining moved in. With its new wealth and population, the Yukon split off from the rest of the Northwest Territories in 1898.

The rest of the Northwest Territories didn't receive its own elected government until 1967, when the center of government was moved from Ottawa to Yellowknife, and a representative assembly was elected. However, with 1.3 million square miles, the territory has proved to be an unwieldy piece of real estate to govern, and the process of self-determination continues. In 1999, the eastern section of the Northwest Territories will become a separate territory, known as Nunavut (meaning "our land"). The rump Northwest Territories, which roughly speaking consists of the drainage of the Mackenzie River, including Yellowknife, and the Arctic coast west of Coppermine, has not decided on a new name for itself.

1 Exploring the North

The Arctic is not like other places. That observation may seem elementary, but even a well-prepared first-time visitor will experience many things here to startle—and perhaps offend—the senses.

No matter where you start from, the Arctic is a long ways away. By far the easiest way to get there is by plane. Whitehorse, Yellowknife, and Iqaluit each have airports with daily service from major Canadian cities. Each of these towns is a center for a network of smaller airlines with regularly scheduled flights to yet smaller communities; here you'll also find charter services to take you to incredibly out-of-the-way destinations.

CLIMATE & SEASONS   During the summer the farther north you travel, the more daylight you get. Yellowknife and Whitehorse, in the south, bask under 20 hours of sunshine a day, followed by four hours of milky twilight bright enough to read a newspaper by. But in northern Inuvik or Cambridge Bay the sun shines 24 hours around the clock. In winter, however, the northern sun doesn't rise above the horizon at all on certain days.

The North is divided into two climatic zones: subarctic and Arctic, and the division does not follow the Arctic Circle. And while there are permanent ice caps in the far northern islands, summer in the rest of the land gets considerably hotter than you might think. The average high temperatures in July and August temperatures are in the 70s and 80s, and the mercury has been known to climb into the 90s. However, even in summer you should bring a warm sweater or ski jacket—and don't forget a pair of really sturdy shoes or boots.

In winter, weather conditions are truly Arctic. The mercury may dip as low as minus 60 for short periods. You'll need heavily insulated clothing and footwear to travel during this time of the year. Spring is an increasingly popular time to visit, with clear sunny skies, highs in the 20s, and days already longer than seems reasonable.

ORGANIZED TOURS   If you've never traveled in the North before, the organizational necessities can seem off-putting and the prices exorbitant. Consider linking up with one of the **Touch the Arctic Tours,** organized by one of Air Canada's connector airlines, NWT Air, P.O. Box 2435, Yellowknife, NT, X1A 2P8 (☎ 403/920-2165 or 800/661-0894). There are tremendous advantages to availing yourself of these package tours. NWT Air discounts their airfare, and arranges price reductions from some of the most noted outfitters and lodgekeepers in the North. The result are deeply discounted trips, tours, and expeditions to most of the major destinations in the Arctic. The philosophy behind the tours is not profit-making, but simply to get more people to visit the North. While the resulting tours still aren't exactly cheap, these trips—most of which include full bed and board, airfare, and activities—are far less expensive than the same trip would be if booked privately.

All the tours start in Edmonton or Winnipeg. From there you have more than 40 different tour choices. Destinations range all the way from Inuvik, to Yellowknife, Rankin Inlet, and Baffin Island. Many of the tours include fishing and hunting options; others stress activities like dog-sledding, arts and craft shopping, and river rafting: in short, probably the very activities you were hoping to find in the Arctic.

DRIVING THE NORTH   Setting out to drive the back roads of the Far North has a strange fascination for many people, most of whom own RVs. The most famous route through the north is the Alaska Highway, which linked the war-time continental U.S. with Alaska via northern B.C. and the Yukon. Today the route is mostly paved, and isn't the adventure it once was. Off-road enthusiasts may prefer the Mackenzie Highway, which links Edmonton to Yellowknife. Even this road is mostly paved nowadays, which leaves the Dempster Highway, between Dawson City and Inuvik, as one of the few real back roads left in the North.

Much of the North is served by good roads, though driving up here demands different preparations that you might be used to. It's a good idea to travel with a full five-gallon gas can, even though along most routes gas stations appear frequently. However, there's no guarantee that these stations will be open in the evenings, or on Sunday, or at the precise moment you need to fill up. By all means, fill up every time you see a gas station in remote areas.

In summer, dust can be a serious nuisance, particularly on gravel roads. When it becomes a problem, close all windows and turn on your heater fan. This builds up air pressure inside your vehicle and helps to keep the dust out. Keep cameras in plastic bags for protection.

It's a good idea to attach a bug or gravel screen and plastic headlight guards to your vehicle. And it's absolutely essential that your windshield wipers are operative and

The Yukon & the Northwest Territories

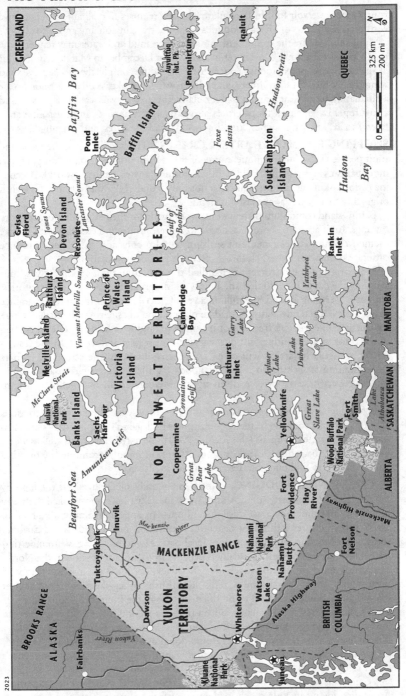

2023

your washer reservoir full. In the Yukon, the law requires that all automobiles drive with their headlights on; it's a good idea on while traveling on any gravel road.

April and May are the spring slush months when mud and water may render some road sections hazardous. The winter months, from December to March, require a lot of special driving preparations. Your vehicle should be completely checked over and winterized. Snow tires, antifreeze, and winter-weight crankcase oil are a *must*. So are a circulating block heater and a battery blanket. Carry booster cables, a shovel, and a tow rope. Experienced Northerners also carry tire chains, a can of gasoline anti-freeze, an ax, kitchen matches, kindling wood, roadside flares, and sleeping bags.

SHOPPING FOR NATIVE ARTS & CRAFTS   The handiwork of the Dene and Inuit people is absolutely unique. Some of it has utility value—you won't get finer, more painstakingly stitched cold-weather clothing anywhere in the world. A genu-ine caribou-skin parka, for instance, is not only wonderfully warm but has a stylish originality that puts it above fashion trends.

Baffin Island communities are famous world-wide for their stone, bone, and ivory carvings. Inuit artists also produce noted weavings, prints, and etchings with Native themes; clothing articles made of sealskin are also common. The Dene produce caribou skin moccasins and clothing, often with beaded decoration.

Most arts and crafts articles are handled through community cooperatives, thus avoiding the cut of the middleman. This is an important business in the Territories, with sales averaging around $10 million a year. Official documentation will guarantee that a piece is a genuine Native Canadian object. Don't hesitate to ask retailers where a particular object comes from, what it's made of, and who made it. They'll be glad to tell you, and frequently point out where the artist lives and works. In the eastern Arctic particularly, artists will often approach tourists in the streets or in bars and restaurants, seeking to sell their goods. While these articles may lack the official paperwork, the price is often right; use your judgment when deciding to buy.

Before investing in native art, make sure you know what the import restrictions are in your home country. In many countries, it is illegal to bring in articles contain-ing parts of marine mammals (this includes walrus or narwhal ivory, as well as whale bones or polar bear fur). Seal skin products are commonly prohibited. Consult a customs office to find out what restrictions are in place.

FOOD, DRINK & LODGING   Northerners traditionally lived off the land by hunting and fishing (many still do), and Arctic specialties have now worked their way onto many fine dining menus. Caribou and musk ox appear on almost all menus in the North, and offer a different taste and texture for meat-eaters. Good caribou, sometimes dressed in sauces made from local berries (wild blue- or Saskatoonberries) tastes like mild venison, and is usually cheaper than either beef or lamb in the North. Musk ox is rather stronger tasting, with a chewy texture, and is often served with wild mushrooms. Arctic char is a mild, pink-fleshed fish, rather like salmon but coarser grained and less oily. You won't find the mainstays of the Inuit diet—seal and whale meat—on most restaurant menus, but in outlying communities you won't have to look hard to find someone able to feed you some *muktuk* or seal meat. Bannocks, a type of baking powder biscuit, and Eskimo doughnuts, a cousin of Indian frybread, are popular snacks to feed tourists. You may want to keep your distance from what's called Eskimo ice cream, a concoction made of whipped whale fat.

Vegetarians are not going to find much to eat in the North. The traditional Arctic diet doesn't include much in the way of fruits or vegetables, and green stuff that's been air-freighted in is pretty sad-looking by the time it reaches the table. Bring your own diet supplements if you have a restricted diet.

No matter what you eat in the North, it is going to be expensive. In towns like Yellowknife, Inuvik, and Iqaluit, a normal entrée at a decent hotel restaurant will cost at least $25; at outlying villages, where hotels offer full board, a sandwich with fries will run $20. Chances are excellent that, for the money, your food will be very pedestrian in quality. In most towns, the grocery store chain The Northern shelters a few fast-food outlets, usually the only other dining option.

Alcohol is banned or highly restricted in most native communities. Some towns are completely dry: no one, not even visitors in the privacy of their hotel rooms, is allowed to possess or consume alcohol. In some locales, RCMP officers will check the baggage of incoming travelers and will confiscate alcohol. In other communities, alcohol is legal but regulated to such a degree that the casual visitor will find it impossible to get hold of a drink. In other communities, alcohol is available in hotel bars or restaurants, but not available in stores (or even by room service). Alcohol is a major social problem in the North, so by all means respect the local laws that regulate alcohol consumption.

Lodging is the most expensive day-to-day expense in the North. Almost every community, no matter how small, will have a hotel, but prices are very high. You can save some money with B&Bs or home stays, which also have the advantage of introducing you to the locals. The **Northern Network of Bed and Breakfasts,** P.O. Box 954, Dawson City, YT, Y0B 1G0 (☎ 403/993-5644; fax 403/993-5648), is an affiliate of independent B&Bs, mostly in the Yukon, northern British Columbia and Alberta, and Alaska. Write for their brochure before setting out, particularly if you're planning on driving the Alaska Highway.

VISITOR INFORMATION   For information, write **Tourism Yukon,** P.O. Box 2703, Whitehorse, YT, Y1A 2C6. Be sure to ask for a copy of the official vacation guide *Canada's Yukon.*

For the Northwest Territories, contact the **Northern Frontier Visitors Association,** no. 4, 4807 49th St., Yellowknife, NT, X1A 3T5 (☎ 403/873-3131 or 800/ 661-0788; fax 403/873-3654). They'll give you a free map of the province and *The Explorers' Guide,* with full listings of accommodations and outfitters.

AN IMPORTANT NOTE ON PRICES   Unless stated otherwise, **the prices cited in this guide are given in Canadian dollars,** which is good news for U.S. travelers because the Canadian dollar is worth 25% less than the American dollar, but buys nearly as much. As we go to press, $1 Canadian is worth 75¢ U.S., which means that your $100-a-night hotel room will cost only U.S. $75, and your $6 breakfast costs only U.S. $4.50.

2 The Great Outdoors

OUTFITTERS   Outdoor enthusiasts in many parts of the world can simply arrive at a destination and then put together a recreational trip when they get there. That is not the case in the North. If you want to get out onto the land, or the water, or the glacier, you will definitely need to have the assistance of an outfitter or local tour provider. There are no roads to speak of in the North, so you'll need help simply to get wherever you're trying to go; this usually involves a boat or airplane trip. Sports equipment rental is all but unheard of in the North; and it's very foolish to head out into the wilds (which start at the edge of the village) without the advice and guidance of someone who knows the terrain, weather, and other general conditions. For all these reasons—and for the entree you'll get into the community—you should hire an outfitter. While it may seem like an unnecessary expense, you will end up saving money, time, and frustration.

SUMMER TRAVEL   Hiking and naturalist trips are popular in late July, August, and in early September. The ice is off the ocean, allowing access by boat to otherwise remote areas. Auyuittaq National Park, with its famed long-distance hiking and rock climbing, is a popular destination for the experienced recreationalist. Float trips on the Soper River, in Katannilik Park, are popular for those seeking adventures that are a bit softer. Naturalist-led hikes out onto the tundra make popular day trips. The South Nahanni River, in Nahanni National Park, is popular for week-long raft or canoe trips below massive 316-foot Virginia Falls.

WINTER & SPRING TRAVEL   While it may seem natural to plan a trip to the Arctic in the summer, in fact the Far North is a year-round destination. Dogsledding trips out into the frozen wilderness are popular late-winter trips for adventurous souls. In May and June from Pond Inlet, dog-sled or snow-machine trips visit the edge of the ice floe, where wildlife viewing is superb. And of course in the dead of winter, there's the 24-hour darkness and the Northern Lights, which lure people north to have a look.

CANOEING & DOG SLEDDING   Choose to explore the North via two traditional transportation methods, and see the land as early explorers and natives did.

Canoe Expeditions   The early French Canadian trappers, or *voyageurs,* explored the North—particularly the Yukon—by canoe, and outfitters now offer multiday expeditions down the region's wide but powerful rivers. **Kanoe People,** P.O. Box 5152, Whitehorse, YT, Y1A 4S3 (☎ 403/668-4899), offers a number of guided canoe trips down several of the Yukon's most historic rivers, past mining ghost towns and Native Canadian villages. Trips are offered on the Teslin, Big Salmon, Snake, and Yukon rivers, and range in length from five days ($1,050) to 12 days ($3,100). Bring your own sleeping bag; everything else, including transportation from Whitehorse, is included.

The rivers of the Northwest Territories flow through barren mountain ranges and tundra wilderness rich in wildlife. For long-distance canoe trips in the eastern Arctic district of the Keewatin, including the Thelon and Kazan rivers, contact **Great Canadian Ecoventures,** P.O. Box 25181-A, Winnipeg, MB, R2V 4C8 (☎ 204/586-4590 or 800/667-WILD). A 12-day trip through the Thelon Game Sanctuary begins at $3,000. In the central Arctic, the most famous canoeing river is the Coppermine River, which flows north to the Arctic Ocean through taiga and tundra before reaching the scenic village of Coppermine. **Whitewolf Adventure Expeditions,** 41-1355 Citadel Dr., Port Coquitlam, BC, V3C 5X6 (☎ 604/944-3131), offer 12-day canoe trips down the Coppermine for $3,000; Whitewolf also offers trips down the more challenging Burnside River to Bathurst Inlet, and is one of the few outfitters licensed to canoe the mighty South Nahanni River.

In southern Baffin Island, the Soper River, which flows past innumerable waterfalls in Katannilik Park, is the most famous canoeing river. **Northwinds,** P.O. Box 849, Iqaluit, NT, X0A 0H0 (☎ 819/979-0551; fax 819/979-0573), offers six-day trips down this beautiful river—gentle enough for family groups—starting at $1,100.

Dog Sledding   An even more indigenous mode of transport in the north is travel by dog sled. While few people actually run dogs as their sole means of getting around any longer, the sport of dog sledding is hugely popular, and dog-sledding trips to otherwise snowbound backcountry destinations make a great early spring adventure. On Baffin Island, **Northwinds** (see above) offers a variety of dog-sled trips, ranging from day trips to seven-day expeditions ($1,600) out to see the Northern Lights; you'll also get a chance to learn how to run the dogs!

In the Yukon, **Michie Creek Mushing,** RR no. 1, Site 20, Comp 104, Whitehorse, YT, Y1A 4Z6 (☎ 403/667-6854; fax 403/667-7495), offers day trips, and also guided backcountry trips out into the wilderness, where you, your hosts, and the sled team stay in old trapper's cabins. Six-day trips are available for $1,350.

WILDLIFE VIEWING It's easy to confuse **caribou** with reindeer because the two species look very much alike. Actually, caribou are wild and still travel in huge migrating herds stretching to the horizon, sometimes numbering 100,000 or more. They form the major food and clothing supply for many of the native people whose lives are cycled around the movements of caribou herds.

The mighty **musk ox** is indigenous to the Arctic. About 12,000 of them live on the northern islands—immense and prehistoric looking, the bulls weigh up to 1,300 pounds. They appear even larger because they carry a mountain of shaggy hair. Underneath the coarse outer coat musk oxen have a silky-soft layer of underwool, called *qiviut* in Inuit. One pound of qiviut can be spun into a 40-strand thread 25 miles long! As light as it is soft, a sweater made from the stuff will keep its wearer warm in subzero weather. And it doesn't shrink when wet. Qivuit is extremely expensive: Once spun, it sells for $70 an ounce.

The monarch of the Arctic, the **polar bear** roams the Arctic coast and the shores of Hudson Bay; you'll have to travel quite a way over mighty tough country to see one in its habitat. Weighing up to 1,450 pounds, they're the largest predators on the North American continent, and probably the most dangerous.

Polar bears (known to the Inuit as Nanook) are almost entirely carnivorous, but in an oddly selective fashion. Seals are their main diet, although the bears usually eat only the tough hide and the blubber underneath, leaving the meat and innards to foxes and other scavengers. They are sure-footed on ice, fantastic swimmers, and aggressive enough to be given a very wide berth.

The North is full of other animals much easier to observe than the bears. In the wooded regions you'll come across wolves and wolverines (harmless to humans, despite the legends about them), mink, lynx, otters, ptarmigans, and beavers. The sleek and beautiful white or brown Arctic foxes live in ice regions as well as beneath the tree line and near settlements.

From mid-July to the end of August, seals, walruses, narwhals, and bowhead and beluga whales are in their breeding grounds off the coast of Baffin Island and in Hudson Bay. And in the endless skies above there are eagles, hawks, huge owls, razor-billed auks, and ivory gulls.

3 The Alaska Highway

Constructed as a military freight road during World War II to link Alaska to the Lower 48, the Alaska Highway (also known as the Alcan Highway) is now a popular tourist route to the Last Frontier. Now as much a phenomenon as a road, the Alaska Highway could be considered a pilgrimage route. The vast majority of people who make the trip are recent retirees, who take their newly purchased RVs and head up north; it's a rite of passage.

Strictly speaking, the Alaska Highway starts at the Mile Number One marker in Dawson Creek, on the eastern edge of British Columbia, and travels north and west for 1,520 miles to Fairbanks, Alaska, passing through the Yukon along the way. The Alaska Highway is one of those routes that inspires its own lore; for many people who make the trip, the journey itself—and not destination Alaska—is a big adventure, and is the topic of innumerable conversations in RV campgrounds and coffee shops along the way. Even a decade ago, much of the talk of the Alaska Highway had to do with conditions of the road itself: where the really torn-up sections were; making it through soupy roads during freak rain and snowstorms; and how to make it between far-flung gas pumps. However, for the road's 50th anniversary in 1992, the final stretches of the road were paved.

While the days of tire-eating gravel roads and extra gas cans are largely past, there are several considerations before casually setting out to drive this road. First, this is a very *long* road. Popular wisdom states that if you drive straight out, it's a three-day drive between Fairbanks and Dawson Creek. If you are in that big of a hurry to get to Fairbanks, then consider flying: much of the road is very winding; slow-moving RV traffic is heavy; and a considerable amount of the road is under reconstruction every summer. If you try to keep yourself to a three-day schedule, you are going to have a miserable time.

DRIVING THE ALASKA HIGHWAY   The route begins (or ends) at Dawson Creek, in British Columbia, and shortly crosses the Peace River and passes through Fort St. John. There are ample tourist facilities throughout this stretch of the highway. The highway continues north, parallel to the Rockies. The forests thin, with pointy spruce trees replacing pine and fir trees. Wildlife viewing is good; moose are often seen from the road.

From Fort St. John to Fort Nelson, there are gas stations and cafes every 40 or 50 miles, though lodging options are pretty dubious. At Fort Nelson, the Alaska Highway turns west and heads into the Canadian Rockies; from here too, graveled Highway 7 continues north to Fort Liard and Fort Simpson, the gateway to Nahanni National Park. Fort Nelson is thick with motel rooms and gas stations; hours from any other major service center, this is a good place to spend the night.

The road through the Rockies is mostly narrow and winding; you can pretty much depend on finding a construction crew working on reconstruction along this stretch. The Rockies are relatively modest mountains in this area, not as rugged or scenic as they are further south in Jasper Park. Once over the Continental Divide, the Alaska Highway follows tributaries of the Liard River through Stone Mountain and Muncho Lake provincial parks. Rustic lodges and cabin resorts are scattered along the road for accommodations; this is also a good place to find a campsite.

At the town of Liard River, be sure to stop and stretch your legs or go for a soak at Liard Hot Springs. The provincial parks department maintains two nice soaking pools in the deep forest; the boardwalk out into the mineral water marsh is pleasant even if you don't have time for a dip.

As you get closer to Watson Lake in the Yukon, you'll notice that mom-and-pop gas stations along the road will advertise that they have cheaper gas than Watson Lake. Believe them, and fill up: Watson Lake is an unappealing town whose extortionately priced gasoline is probably the only thing that's memorable. If you don't plan your trip well, you may end up spending the night here.

The long road between Watson Lake and Whitehorse travels through rolling hills and forest to Teslin and Atlin lakes, where the landscape becomes more mountainous and the gray clouds of the Gulf of Alaska's weather systems hang menacingly in the western horizon. Whitehorse is the largest town along the route of the Alaska Highway, and unless you're in a great hurry, plan to spend at least a day here. You'll want to wash the dust off the car at the very least, and eat a decent meal before another day of driving on the way to Alaska.

Hope for good weather as you leave Whitehorse, since the trip past Kluane National Park is one the most beautiful parts of the entire Alaska Highway route. The two highest peaks of Canada straddle the horizon, while glaciers push down mountain valleys. The road edges by lovely Kluane Lake before passing Beaver Creek and crossing over into Alaska. From the border crossing to Fairbanks is another 298 miles.

A number of guide books deal exhaustively with driving the Alaska Highway; particularly good is the mile-by-mile classic, the annual *Alaska Milepost.*

WHAT TO EXPECT   Summer is the only window of opportunity to upgrade or repair the road, so construction crews really go to it; depend on lengthy delays and some very rugged detours. During the summer of 1995, total delays of two to four hours were common in each day-long segment of the trip. Visitors' centers along the way get a fax of daily construction schedules and conditions. Stop and ask if you don't want to be surprised by the delays you'll almost certainly encounter; or call ☎ 403/667-5893 for **24-hour highway information.**

While availability of **gasoline** isn't the problem that it once was, there are a couple of things to remember. Gas prices are high, about a third higher than in Edmonton or Calgary. While there's gasoline at most of the little communities that appear on the provincial road map, most close up early in the evening, and some outfits are less than friendly: The gas station at Liard River is notorious for its unhelpful staff—if there's a hockey game on TV, forget about getting any gas. There are 24-hour gas stations and plenty of motel rooms at Dawson City, Fort St. John, Fort Nelson, Watson Lake, and Whitehorse.

While it's not something you can plan for, try to bring a little patience when driving the Alaska Highway. During the high season, the entire route, from Edmonton to Fairbanks, is one long caravan of RVs. Many people have their car in tow, a boat on the roof, and several bicycles chained to the spare tire. Thus encumbered, they lumber up the highway at top speeds of 45 miles per hour; loath (or unable) to pass one another, convoys of RVs stretch on forever, the slowest of the party setting the pace for all. If you're not part of the RV crowd, driving the Alaska Highway will demand a lot of patience.

4 Whitehorse

Once part of the Northwest Territories, the Yukon is now a separate territory bordering on British Columbia in the south and Alaska in the west (when locals refer to the United States, they nearly always mean Alaska). Compared with the Northwest Territories, it's a mere midget in size, but with 200,000 square miles, the Yukon is more than twice as big as Wyoming.

The entire territory has a population of only 33,400—two-thirds of them living in Whitehorse. The capital of the Yukon is a late arrival on the scene. It was established only in the spring of 1900, fully two years after the stampeders had swarmed into Dawson City. But Whitehorse, located on the banks of the Yukon River, is the logical hub of the Territory and became the capital in 1953 after Dawson fizzled out along with the gold.

The city has a curiously split personality. On the one hand it's a frontier outpost with 23,000 residents. On the other hand the tourist influx gives it an almost cosmopolitan tinge: a whiff of nightlife, some smart boutiques, gourmet restaurants, and comfortable hotels—and near traffic congestion.

ESSENTIALS

GETTING THERE   The airport, placed on a rise above the city, is served by **Canadian Airlines International** (☎ 800/426-7000) (from Vancouver only) and

Air North (☎ 403/668-2228). Cab fare to downtown is around $8. Whitehorse is 284 miles southeast of Beaver Creek (the Alaskan border).

VISITOR INFORMATION   Your first stop should be the **Whitehorse Visitor Reception Centre,** 302 Steele St. (☎ 403/667-7545), where you'll get a smiling reception plus armloads of information about hotels, restaurants, shopping, and excursions. The center is open daily from 8am to 8pm. Information about the Yukon in general is found at the **Yukon Visitor Reception Centre** (☎ 403/667-2915), located on the Alaska Highway near the Whitehorse airport.

CITY LAYOUT   The city's layout is straightforward: All streets run vertically, the avenues—First to Eighth—bisecting them horizontally, all roads running around the periphery.

Whitehorse centers on Main Street, with four blocks of stores and a busy pace. Second and Fourth avenues are the main north/south arterials. The post office is at the corner of Third Avenue and Main Street. Beyond First Street and the railroad tracks flows the Yukon River. A bridge crosses the river at the end of Second Avenue and to the right of the bridge lies the SS *Klondike,* one of the 200 stern-wheelers that once plied the river between Whitehorse and Dawson City. On the left of Second Avenue, heading toward the bridge, stands the large Territorial Government Building, one of the newest and best-equipped structures of its kind in Canada.

GETTING AROUND   Public transit is handled by **Whitehorse Transit** (☎ 403/668-2831). Car rental is available from **Tilden** (☎ 403/668-6872), **Avis** (☎ 403/667-2847), **Budget** (☎ 403/667-6200), and **Norcan** (☎ 403/668-2137). If you need a taxi, try **Yellow Cabs** (☎ 403/668-4811) or **Co-op Cabs** (☎ 403/668-2358).

SPECIAL EVENTS   February is a happening month in Whitehorse. One of the top dog-sled races in North America, the **Yukon Quest** begins in Whitehorse and runs to Fairbanks. The town is filled with hundreds of yapping dogs and avid mushers, eager to vie for the $100,000 top prize. Making even more noise is the **Frostbite Music Festival,** which attracts musicians and entertainers from across Canada. Immediately afterward is the **Yukon Sourdough Rendezvous,** a midwinter festival that commemorates the days of the gold rush with various old-fashioned competitions, like dog pulls, fiddling and costume contests, and a "mad trapper" competition.

EXPLORING WHITEHORSE

Many of the following sites and activities are open seasonally, usually from late May to early September.

THE TOP ATTRACTIONS

✪ **Yukon Transportation Museum.** Adjacent to the Yukon Visitors Center, Mile 915 on the Alaska Highway. ☎ **403/668-4792.** Admission $3 adults, $1 children. Mid-May–Sept daily 10am–7pm.

In a remote area like the Yukon, the history of white settlement is essentially the story of its transportation systems. In this fascinating museum, the development of travel, from dog sled to railway to bush plane and through the building of the Alaska Highway is presented. You'll come away with a new appreciation of what it was to travel to the Yukon in the past. The exhibits and vintage photos on travel by dog sled are especially interesting. There's a replica of the historic aircraft *Queen of the Yukon,* the sister aircraft of *The Spirit of St. Louis,* plus a film on the building of the White Pass Railroad from Skagway.

SS *Klondike*. Anchored at the Robert Campbell Bridge. Admission $3 adults, $2.50 seniors, $2 children. Tours on the half hour daily 9am–5:30pm.

Largest of the 250 riverboats that chugged up and down the Yukon River between 1866 and 1955, the *Klondike* is now permanently dry-docked beside the river. The boat has been restored to its 1940s glory.

✪ Macbride Museum. First Avenue at Wood Street. ☎ 403/667-2709. Admission $3.50 adults, $1 children. Daily 10am–6pm.

Within this museum compound you'll also find Sam McGee's Cabin (read Service's poem on the cremation of same) and the old Whitehorse Telegraph Office. The log-cabin museum is crammed with relics from the gold-rush era, and has a large display of Yukon wildlife and minerals. It's interesting material, lovingly arranged by a non-profit society.

Yukon Botanical Gardens. At the junction of the Alaska Highway and South Access Road. ☎ 403/668-7972. Admission $5 adults, $1 children. Daily 9am–9pm.

These botanical gardens are the pride of Whitehorse. This unique 22-acre showpiece presents a flora-fauna combination you will see nowhere else in the North. Floral displays include 17 varieties of wild orchids found in the Yukon.

The gardens include a lake teeming with rainbow trout and populated by swarms of northern waterfowl. Amid an array of shrubs, flowers, and trees indigenous to the region lies Old MacDonald's Farm, stocked with farm animals that blend with the otherwise manicured landscape.

Yukon Art Centre. Yukon Centre at Yukon College, off Range Road North. ☎ 403/667-8575. Free admission. Mon–Fri 11am–5pm, Sun 1–4pm.

The gallery at the Yukon Art Centre has changing exhibits that feature regional artists, photographers, and themes. The exhibits are free, and are open daily. The art center also houses a tearoom and a theater that functions as Whitehorse's performing arts center.

More Attractions

Old Log Church. Elliott Street at Third Avenue. Admission $2.50 adults, $1 children. Mon–Sat 9am–6pm, Sun noon–4pm.

When Whitehorse got its first resident priest in 1900, he lived and held services in a tent. By the next spring the Old Log Church and rectory were built, and both are currently the only buildings of that date in town still in use. The Old Log Church was once the Roman Catholic cathedral for the diocese—the only wooden cathedral in the world—and contains artifacts on the history of all churches in the Yukon. Mass is every Sunday morning at 10:30am. (On the next block over are two "log skyscrapers"—that is, old two- and three-story log cabins, still used as apartments and offices. One of the buildings is the local office for the Yukon member of parliament.)

Takhini Hot Springs. On the Klondike Highway, 17 miles north of Whitehorse. ☎ 403/633-2706. Admission $3.50 adults, $3 seniors and students, $2 children. Daily 7am–10pm.

A swimming pool fed by natural hot springs and surrounded by rolling hills and hiking trails, the developed Takhini Hot Springs might be just what you need after days on the Alaska Highway. After swimming you can refresh yourself at the coffee shop. Horseback riding is also available.

Whitehorse Rapids Dam. At the end of Nisutlin Drive, in suburban Riverdale. Free admission. Daily 8am–10pm.

The native Chinook salmon that pass by Whitehorse are completing one of the longest fish migrations in the world, and to bypass the Whitehorse Rapids Dam, they climb the world's longest wooden fish ladder. Interpretive displays and an upper viewing deck show you the entire process by which the dam has ceased to be an obstruction to the salmon migration.

Yukon Experience Slide Show. At the Yukon Inn, 4220 4th Ave. ☎ **403/667-2527.** Admission $10 adults, $5 children under 12. June 1–Aug 31 daily 11am, 2pm, 7pm, and 8:15pm.

If you're unable to get any further out into the wilds of the Yukon, then you might be interested in viewing this multimedia slide show, which explores the scenic bounty of the territory. Admission also buys you a color poster of the Yukon.

TOURS & EXCURSIONS

HISTORICAL WALKING TOURS   The Yukon Historical and Museums Association, Donnenworth House, 3126 Third Ave., behind the Chamber of Commerce Visitors Center (☎ 403/667-4704), offers walking tours of downtown Whitehorse on the hour from 9am to 4pm, Monday through Saturday. The 45-minute tour ($2) passes many of the gold-rush-era structures and historic sites, and offers a good introduction to the town.

WILDLIFE TOURS   The Yukon Wildlife Preserve covers hundreds of acres of forests and meadows. Roaming freely throughout are bison, moose, musk ox, elk, snowy owls, and the rare peregrine falcon. Tours of the preserve depart daily at 10:30am. The cost is $21 for adults, $10.50 for children. Book through **Gray Line,** 208G Steele St. (☎ 403/668-3225).

RIVER CRUISES   The MV *Schwatka* is a river craft that cruises the Yukon River through the famous Miles Canyon. This stretch—once the most hazardous section of water in the Territory—is now dammed and tamed, though it still offers fascinating wilderness scenery. The cruise takes two hours, accompanied by narration telling the story of the old "wild river" times. Adults pay $17, children half price. For reservations, call ☎ 403/668-4716; the boat leaves three miles south of Whitehorse; follow signs for Miles Canyon.

A more authentic river experience is offered by the *Emerald May*, a steel pontoon raft that closely duplicates the style of boat used by the original 98ers (but completely safe and motorized). Instead of shooting dangerous rapids, today's trips focus on wildlife viewing and historic sites. Excursions are offered by **Taste of 98 Tours** (☎ 403/633-4767), and leave three times daily from the log cabin on First Ave, across from the McBride Museum; tickets are $31 adult, $15.50 for children.

The **MV *Youcon Kat*** sails down the Yukon River to Lake Laberge on 2¹/₂-hour afternoon trips ($17) or salmon barbecue excursions ($35), both scenic and leisurely. Tours are daily in summer, and leave from the end of Steele Street at First Avenue (☎ 403/668-2927).

SHOPPING

The **Yukon Gallery,** 2093 2nd Ave. (☎ 403/667-2391), is Whitehorse's best commercial visual arts gallery, featuring a large show space devoted to Yukon and regional artists. There's an extensive display of paintings and prints, as well as some ceramics and Northern crafts, like moosehair tufting.

Northern Images, 311 Jarvis St. (☎ 403/668-5739), is the best gallery in the Yukon for Native Canadian art, in particular Inuit carvings and native masks.

Yukon Native Products, 4230 Fourth Ave. (☎ 403/668-5955), is an unusual garment factory combining traditional Native Canadian skills with the latest computer technology. You can watch the stylish double-shell Yukon parka being made. Also view examples of mukluks, slippers, and beadwork found in the North.

Mac's Fireweed Books, 203 Main St. (☎ 403/993-5486), is the best bookstore in town.

SPORTS & OUTDOOR ACTIVITIES

HIKING   **The Yukon Conservation Society,** 302 Hawkins St. (☎ 403/668-5678), offers free guided nature walks in the Whitehorse area. Hikes are offered Monday through Friday, and on most days several different destinations are offered (most walks are only a couple of hours long); on Wednesdays, there's a day hike up Grey Mountain. Self-transport is necessary; bring comfortable shoes and insect repellent.

If you're looking for a nice hike on your own, cross the Second Avenue Bridge, and follow the riverside path past the Whitehorse Dam and up to **Miles Canyon.** Here, the Yukon River cuts a narrow passage through the underlying basalt. Although not deep, the canyon greatly constricts the river, forming rapids that were an object of dread to the greenhorn 98ers in their homemade boats. Two miles up the canyon, a footbridge crosses the canyon, accessing both the Miles Canyon Road (arrange a pick-up here) and a series of footpaths on the opposite side of the canyon. For a longer hike, continue on the east-side trail, which goes on for miles toward March Lake.

CANOEING   Many of these rivers were explored by French-Canadian *voyageurs* in canoes, and the wide, swift-flowing rivers of the Yukon still make for great canoe trips. **Kanoe People** (☎ 403/668-4899) offers a wide range of trips, canoe outfitting, and rentals on Northern rivers. Trips range from evening trips on the Yukon River for $45 to week-long wilderness adventures from $1,050. **Prospect Yukon** (☎ 403/667-4837; fax 403/668-5728) offers trips on the Yukon from one day ($99) to two weeks in length (including Whitehorse to Dawson), and trips down other major Northern rivers. Trips for both outfitters include road transport from Whitehorse, food, gear, and tents; all you need to bring is a sleeping bag and insect repellent. For day rentals ($20) and a selection of easy day canoe trips, contact **Up North** (☎ 403/667-7905), located right on the Yukon River across from the McBride Museum. You can also rent a canoe for a day and shoot the once-harrowing Miles Canyon ($35 includes two shuttles and the canoe rental).

DOG SLEDDING   If you're in the Yukon during the late winter or spring, go for a day-long dog-sledding trip, or plan a long-distance cross-country trip with dog-sled support. **Michie Creek Mushing,** RR no. 1, Site 20, Comp 104, Whitehorse, YT, Y1A 4Z6 (☎ 403/667-6854; fax 403/667-7495), offers both day and custom trips with their 16-dog team; day trips start at $125.

HORSEBACK RIDING   **White Horse Riding Stable** (☎ 403/663-3086) is located 5 miles south of Whitehorse, just before the Miles Canyon turn-off.

WHERE TO STAY

Whitehorse has more than 20 hotels, motels, and chalets in and around the downtown area, including a couple just opposite the airport. This is far more than you'd expect in a place its size, and the accommodation standards come up to big-city levels in every respect.

EXPENSIVE

Edgewater Hotel. 101 Main St., Whitehorse, YT, Y1A 2A7. ☎ **403/667-2572.** Fax 403/668-3014. 30 rms. TV TEL. $110–$132 double. AE, ER, MC, V.

At the end of Main Street, overlooking the Yukon River, this small vintage hotel has a distinct old-fashioned charm of its own, plus an excellent dining room, the Cellar. The lobby and bedrooms are cozy, and there's a well-appointed lounge. The rooms are newly renovated, kept in soft pastel colors and equipped with extralength beds and individual heat/air-conditioning units. The bathrooms are small but modern, and fitted with vanities.

Westmark Klondike Inn. 2288 Second Ave., Whitehorse, YT, Y1A 1C8. ☎ **403/668-4747** or 800/544-0970. Fax 403/667-7639. 98 rms. TV TEL. $146 double. Children 12 and under stay free in parents' room. AE, DC, MC, V. Closed Oct–Apr.

An entertainment center and hotel, this large and attractive new complex stands at the foot of Two Mile Hill, on the northern end of Whitehorse. The inn has both a coffee shop, a lively gold rush–themed restaurant, and a rather rowdy saloon out back. The guest rooms are nicely decorated and comfortably sized.

✪ **Westmark Whitehorse.** 201 Wood St. (P.O. Box 4250), Whitehorse, YT, Y1A 3T3. ☎ **403/668-4700** or 800/478-1111. Fax 403/668-2789. 180 rms. TV TEL. $148 double. Children under 12 stay free in parent's room. AE, DC, ER, MC, V.

Centrally located in downtown Whitehorse, this representative of a national chain has one of the busiest lobbies in town, nicely fitted with armchairs and settees. There's a small arcade alongside, housing a gift shop, barber, and hairdresser, plus a travel agency. The lodge has a combination dining room and coffee shop, cocktail lounge, and the most complete conference facilities in the Territory. The hotel is also host to one of Whitehorse's popular musical revues. The guest rooms, including rooms for nonsmokers and the disabled, are spacious, well furnished, and well decorated.

MODERATE

✪ **Best Western Gold Rush Inn.** 411 Main St., Whitehorse, YT, Y1A 2A7. ☎ **403/668-4500,** 800/661-0539 from western Canada, or 800/764-7604 in Alaska. Fax 403/668-4432. 80 rms (24 with kitchenette). TV TEL. $105 double. AE, DC, ER, JBC, MC, V.

Modern, with a Wild West motif, the Gold Rush Inn is one of the most comfortable and centrally located lodgings in Yellowknife, within easy walking distance of attractions and shopping. All rooms, recently remodeled, have refrigerators and hair dryers; some come with kitchenettes. There are meeting facilities and a Jacuzzi. The restaurant here is good, and the convivial tavern is the scene of one of Yellowknife's evening theaters.

Bonanza Inn. 4109 Fourth Ave., Whitehorse, YT, Y1A 1H6. ☎ **403/668-4545.** Fax 403/668-6538. 53 rms. TV TEL. $80 double. Children under 12 free. AE, DC, ER, MC, V.

The Bonanza has a great location, at the heart of Whitehorse dining and entertainment. The rooms are good-sized and comfortably furnished with fully modern facilities; there's also a restaurant and lounge on premises. Altogether, this is one of the better deals in Whitehorse.

Casey's Bed & Breakfast. 608 Wood St., Whitehorse, YT, Y1A 2G3. ☎ **403/668-7481.** $70–$80 double. No credit cards.

Only blocks from downtown, this B&B offers rooms with bathrooms down the hall, common sitting room/TV lounge and breakfast nook, with a guest laundry. Rooms are available with either two twins, or a double bed.

Hawkins House. 303 Hawkins St., Whitehorse, YT, Y1A 1X5. ☎ **403/668-7638.** Fax 403/668-7632. 4 rms. TV TEL. $95–$110 double. MC, V.

All guest rooms have private baths and balconies in this modern but stylishly retro Victorian home. Rooms are decorated according to theme, but tastefully so: The

Fireweed Room has rustic pine furniture à la Klondike, while the Fleur de Lys Room recalls belle epoque France. Rooms are furnished with worktables and computer jacks, and there are free laundry facilities.

ⓢ Regina Hotel. 102 Wood St., Whitehorse, YT, Y1A 2E3. **☎ 403/667-7801.** Fax 403/668-6075. 53 rms. TV TEL. $60–$80 double. Extra person $10. AE, ER, MC, V.

One of the oldest establishments in the Yukon, completely rebuilt in 1970, the Regina stands beside the Yukon River and breathes territorial tradition. Don't judge by the rather plain exterior; the rooms are large and fully modern, and represent a good deal in an otherwise expensive town. The lobby is crowded with Old Yukon memorabilia, from hand-cranked telephones to moose antlers. You can't beat the location either: The Regina is located right on the Yukon River, and across the street from the McBride Museum, and only one block from Main Street.

ⓢ Stratford Motel. 401 Jarvis St., Whitehorse, YT, Y1A 2B6. **☎ 403/667-4243.** Fax 403/668-7432. 49 rms. TV TEL. $75 double. AE, DC, ER, JBC, MC, V.

Located just west of downtown, but within easy walking distance of restaurants and entertainments, the Stratford is a well-tended motor inn with some kitchenette units, and eleven suitelike units with kitchens and separate bedrooms. Other facilities include a guest laundry; there's also plenty of parking space if you're driving a large or awkward rig.

Yukon Inn. 4220 Fourth Ave., Whitehorse, YT, Y1A 1K1. **☎ 403/667-2527** or 800/661-0454. Fax 403/668-7643. 92 rms. TV TEL. $95–$110 double. AE, MC, V.

The Yukon Inn is located on the edge of Whitehorse, near the malls, bars, and restaurants that make up the newer commercial strip north of downtown. This is a large and busy complex, with a lively bar and restaurant at one end; there's also a hair salon and gift shop in the lobby.

The rooms are good-sized and unfussy, and come equipped with the standard amenities. The Yukon Inn is a favorite of local Yukoners; the hotel has even set aside a special meeting and workroom for its First Nation guests.

INEXPENSIVE

The **Roadhouse Inn,** 2163A 2nd Ave. (☎ 403/667-2594), is an older hotel that offers its bathroom-down-the-hall rooms as hostel accommodations. Standard hostel rooms have four bunks, and go for $18; private rooms are also available.

CAMPGROUNDS & RV PARKS

There are a great number of campgrounds in and around Whitehorse.

Tenters will like the **Robert Service Campground,** South Access Road (☎ 403/668-3721), close to downtown and free of RVs. There are 48 unserviced tent sites, plus firepits, washrooms, showers, and a picnic area. The rate is $10.50 per tent. There are a number of lake-side territorial parks with campgrounds just north of Whitehorse on the Dawson City road. At Lake Laberge Park, you can camp "on the marge of Lake Laberge" with the verses of Robert Service filling your thoughts.

Most convenient for RVers is **Downtown Sourdough Park,** on Second Avenue north of Ogilvie (☎ 403/668-7938), with 146 campsites, most of them full-service, with showers, laundry, and a gift shop. Sites range from $12 to $16. On the Alaska Highway, the **Hi Country RV Park** (☎ 403/667-7445) offers partial hookups, a laundry, and showers in a cramped but tree-shaded location; sites range from $13 to $18.

WHERE TO DINE

Whitehorse has a much greater variety of restaurants than hotels—you can get meals in every price range and quality. Food generally is more expensive here than in the provinces, and this goes for wine as well. Be happy you didn't come during the gold rush, when eggs sold for $25 each.

EXPENSIVE

Arizona Charlie's. In the Klondike Inn, 2288 Second Ave. ☎ **403/668-4747.** Reservations recommended. Main courses $9–$32. AE, DC, MC, V. Daily 5:30–10pm. Closed Oct–Apr. INTERNATIONAL.

Charlie's is named and decorated in honor of the famous entrepreneur who founded the Palace Grand Theatre in Dawson City during the gold rush. The place is decked out like a gaslight-age "entertainment palace," with red plush curtains, "gas" chandeliers, and curlicued alcoves, although the restaurant is quite new. The food served in this pleasure palace ranges from standard Mexican, to steaks and seafood. There are a large selection of appetizers that make good cocktail snacks.

Cellar Dining Room. In the Edgewater Hotel, 101 Main St. ☎ **403/667-2572.** Reservations recommended. Main courses $19–$40. AE, MC, V. Mon–Fri 11:30am–1:30pm; daily 5–10pm. CANADIAN.

This plush lower-level establishment has a big local reputation. You'll enjoy whatever you order, but expect to pay top dollar. Pasta dishes start at $19; you can't go wrong selecting either the king crab, lobster and prawns, or the excellent prime rib ($25). Dress casually, but not *too* casually. For good food—including steaks and prime rib—at a cheaper price point, eat at the Gallery, just upstairs from The Cellar.

Panda's. 212 Main St. ☎ **403/667-2632.** Reservations recommended. Main courses $16–$35. AE, MC, V. Mon–Fri 11:30am–2pm; Mon–Sat 5:30–10pm. INTERNATIONAL.

Panda's is possibly the finest and certainly the most romantic restaurant in the Territory. The decor is a mixture of restrained elegance enlivened by traditional Klondike touches, the service smoothly discreet. This is one of the few establishments in town to offer daily specials apart from the regular menu. Dishes are classic European, like beef Wellington ($28), pheasant breast with juniper berries, and veal Chantrelle ($26), with a seafood curry dish thrown in for spice.

MODERATE

If you're looking for a moderately priced and copious lunch, try one of two good Asian buffets, both served weekdays from 11:30am to 2pm for $9. **The China Garden,** 309 Jarvis St. (☎ 403/668-2899), and **Tung Lock Seafood Restaurant,** 404 Wood St. (☎ 403/668-3298), also serve full dinners from their extensive menus.

✪ Angelo's Restaurant on Top. 202 Strickland St. ☎ **403/668-6266.** Reservations recommended. Pizzas (medium) $15–$20; pasta $12–$18; main courses $19–$34. AE, MC, V. PIZZA/INTERNATIONAL.

This is one of Whitehorse's most popular restaurants, with good reason. The menu is extensive, ranging from pizzas, to pasta (there are nearly 20 different choices, including some vegetarian options), and on to lamb, seafood, and steaks. If the restaurant has a specialty, it's the Greek souvlaki, which come in six different meat choices. What's more, the preparations are tasty, and the staff does a good job of table service—when they're not called on to enforce crowd control (word is out on the tour bus circuit).

✪ No Pop Sandwich Shop. 312 Steele St. ☎ **403/668-3227.** Reservations recommended. Sandwiches $4–$6; main dinner courses $10–$12. MC, V. Mon–Thurs 9am–9pm, Fri 9am–10pm, Sat 10am–9pm, Sun 10am–3pm. COFFEE SHOP/SANDWICHES.

Yellowknife's hip and "alternative" eating spot is No Pop. Part bakery, part espresso shop, and part evening bistro, this friendly restaurant is just about the only post-mod '90s restaurant in town. The baked goods are especially notable (try a raisin cinnamon roll), and the midday sandwiches meaty and happily retro. At night, the extensive sandwich menu is available, as well as a number of daily changing special entrées, usually featuring fresh fish. On Sunday, this is the place for brunch, with omelets and crepes leading the menu (in the $9 range). True to it's name, no soft drinks are served (though there's coffee, juices, beer, wine, and a full bar), nor are there male employees in evidence. For a place with such casual fare and attitude, it's somewhat odd that reservations are necessary for most meals.

⑤ Pasta Palace. 209 Main St. ☎ **403/667-6888.** Reservations accepted. Main courses $8–$11. MC, V. Daily 11:30am–10pm. ITALIAN/TAPAS.

One of the few inexpensive places to eat in Whitehorse where you don't feel you're eating on a budget. The best thing about the menu is the extensive selection of tapas and appetizers, available throughout the day. The selection includes bruschettas, salads, and satays, all between $5 and $6. Full entrees are also good bargains, with full-flavored pasta dishes starting at $8, and steaks, chops, and a selection of kabobs topping out at $11. Everything is à la carte, but you can still have a full meal and get change back from $12. The dining room isn't fancy, but the service is prompt and friendly.

Sam n Andy's. 506 Main St. ☎ **403/668-6994.** Reservations accepted. Main courses $4–$12. MC, V. Daily 11:30am–10:30pm. MEXICAN.

A culinary surprise for this region is Sam n Andy's, which specializes in Mexican food, to eat in or take out. Another surprise feature is the outdoor dining patio.

INEXPENSIVE

The Potbelly Bakery & Cafe. 106 Main St. ☎ **403/668-2323.** Reservations not accepted. Most items $4–$9. No credit cards. Mon–Sat 9am–5pm. DELI.

The Potbelly offers deli/bistro-style cuisine, hot or cold, including a range of French delicacies. It also serves soups, pasta, salads, wine, and beer. A meal here won't cost you more than $10.

WHITEHORSE AFTER DARK

The top-of-the-bill attraction in Whitehorse is the ✪ *Frantic Follies,* a singing, dancing, clowning, and declaiming gold-rush revue that has become famous throughout the north. The show is a very entertaining mélange of skits, music-hall drollery, whooping, high-kicking, garter-flashing cancan dancers, sentimental ballads, and deadpan corn, interspersed with rolling recitations of Robert Service's poetry. Shows take place nightly at the **Westmark Whitehorse Hotel,** 201 Wood St.; for reservations call ☎ 403/668-2042. Tickets cost $18 for adults, $9 for children.

A new musical comedy, called the *1940's Canteen Show,* is a paean to the era when the U.S. Army laid down the Alaska Highway through the Yukon, precipitating a boom for Whitehorse. The revue promises to bring out the lighter side of the war years, complete with skits, and period songs and dancing. The show runs nightly May through September; tickets are $15 adult, $7.50 children. The show is held at the **Gold Rush Inn,** 411 Main St. (☎ 403/668-4500).

5 Kluane National Park

Tucked into the southwestern corner of the Yukon, two hours' drive from White-horse, these 8,500 square miles of glaciers, marshes, mountains, and sand dunes are unsettled and virtually untouched wilderness. Bordering on Alaska in the west, Kluane National Park contains **Mount Logan** and **Mount St. Elias,** respectively the second- and third-highest peaks in North America.

The park also contains an astonishing variety of **wildlife.** Large numbers of moose, wolves, red foxes, wolverines, lynx, otters, and beavers abound, plus black bears in the forested areas and lots of grizzlies in the major river valleys.

Designated as a UNESCO World Heritage Site, Kluane Park lies 98 miles west of Whitehorse—take the Alaska Highway to Haines Junction. There, just outside the park's boundaries, you'll find the **Visitor Reception Centre,** which is open year-round (☎ 403/634-2345). The center has information on hiking trails and canoe routes and shows an award-winning audiovisual presentation on the park. Admission to the park is free.

Because this park is largely undeveloped and is preserved as a wilderness, casual exploration of Kluane is limited to a few day-hiking trails and to aerial sightseeing trips on small aircraft and helicopters. A good clearinghouse of fishing, hiking, aerial sightseeing, and river-rafting outfitters is **Kluane Park Adventure Center,** along the main road in Haines Junction (☎ 403/634-2313). As many adventure trips require a minimum number of participants, this service can often put together a last-minute trip more easily than individual outfitters.

HIKING   The vast expanse of ice and rock that is the wilderness heart of Kluane is well beyond the striking range of the average walking enthusiast. If you're interested in exploring the backcountry, you'll need to be in good shape and have experience with mountaineering techniques.

The shortest hike up to a glacier follows the Slims East Trail, leaving from south of the Sheep Mountain Information Centre. To reach Kaskawulsh Glacier and return will take at least three days, but this is an unforgettable hike into very remote and dramatic country.

Day hikers have a few options, mostly near Haines Junction and south along Haines Road. Stop at lovely Kathleen Lake, where there's an easy interpreted hike, or else a longer trail along the lake's south bank.

Stop at the visitors center for more information on hikes in Kluane. Or contact an outfitter. **Ecosummer Expeditions,** Box 5095, Whitehorse, YT, Y1A 4Z2 (☎ 403/633-8453), takes guided backpacking and mountaineering parties to Kluane National Park.

RAFTING   White-water rafting in Kluane Park is one of the most exciting recreational opportunities available to the average traveler. The Tatshenshini, Dezadeash, and Alsek rivers are famous throughout the world for their wild, cold white water that flows through magnificent mountain and glacier scenery. Some trips pass through iceberg-filled lakes just below huge glaciers! For a variety of guided raft trips down these rivers, ranging from a one-day run down the Tatshenshini ($100) to a 10-day trip down the Tatshenshini from Dalton Post and down the Alsek River to the Pacific, contact **Tatshenshini Expediting,** 1602 Alder St., Whitehorse, YT, Y1A 3W8 (☎ 403/633-2742; fax 403/633-6184).

Canadian River Expeditions, 3524 W. 16th Ave., Vancouver, BC, V6R 3C1 (☎ 604/938-6651), offers a six-day rafting and hiking expedition through the heart of the Kluane National Park. The emphasis is on natural history and the agenda includes the most spectacular part of the watershed of the Alsek River. (These outfitters also offer trips on other Yukon and B.C. rivers.)

AERIAL SIGHTSEEING Purists may object, but the only way the average person is going to have a chance to see the backcountry of Kluane Park is by airplane or helicopter. The most popular glacier-viewing trip is flown by **Trans North Helicopters** (☎ 403/668-3420). Three trips are offered, ranging from $30 to $195 per person. Short trips provide a panorama of Kluane Lake and the foothills of the park; longer trips explore the glaciers. **Sifton Air** (☎ 403/634-2916) also has three airplane flights over the park; two fly over either Kaskawulsh or Lowell glaciers for $90 per person (which one you fly over may depend on the weather); the longer trip ($195) loops over both.

6 Chilkoot Trail & White Pass

South of Whitehorse, massive ranges of glacier-chewed peaks rise up to ring the Gulf of Alaska; stormy waters reach far inland as fjords, and enormous glaciers spill into the sea (the famed Glacier Bay is here). This spectacularly scenic region is also the site of the famous Chilkoot Trail, which in 1898 saw 100,000 gold rush "stampeders" struggle up its steep slopes. Another high mountain pass was transcribed in 1900 by the White Pass & Yukon Railroad on its way to the goldfields; excursion trains now run on these rails, considered a marvel of engineering.

To see these sites, most people embark on long-distance hiking trails, rail excursions, or cruise boats. Happily, two highways edge through this spectacular landscape; using the **Alaska Marine Highway ferries** (☎ 800/642-0066), this trip can be made as a loop trip from either Whitehorse or Haines Junction. As the ferries keep an irregular schedule, you'll need to call to find out what the sailing times are on the day you plan to make the trip.

THE CHILKOOT TRAIL

In 1896, word of the great gold strikes on the Klondike reached the outside world, and nearly 100,000 people set out for the Yukon to seek their fortunes. There was no organized transportation into the Yukon, and the stampeders resorted to the most expedient methods. The Chilkoot Trail, long an Indian trail through one of the few glacier-free passes in the Gulf of Alaska, became the primary overland route to the Yukon River, Whitehorse, and the gold fields near Dawson City.

The ascent of the Chilkoot became the stuff of legend, and pictures of men and women clambering up the steep snowfields to Chilkoot Summit are one of the enduring images of the stampeder spirit. The North Western Mounted Police demanded that anyone entering the Yukon carry with them a ton of provisions (literally); there were no supplies in the newly born gold camps on the Klondike, and malnutrition and lack of proper shelter were major problems. People were forced to make up to 30 trips up the trail in order to transport all of their goods into Canada. Once past the RCMP station at Chilkoot Summit, the stampeders then had to build some sort of boat or barge to ferry their belongings across Bennett Lake and down the Yukon River.

HIKING THE CHILKOOT TRAIL Today, the Chilkoot Trail is a national historic park jointly administered by the Canadian and U.S. parks departments. The original trail is open year-round to hikers who wish to experience the route of the stampeders. The route also passes through marvelous glacier-carved valleys, passing through coastal rain forest, boreal forest, and alpine tundra.

However, the Chilkoot Trail is as challenging a trail today as it was 100 years ago. Although the trail is a total of 33 miles in length, the vertical elevation gain is nearly 3,700 feet; much of the trail is very rocky. Weather, even in high summer, can be extremely changeable, making this always formidable trail sometimes a dangerous one.

Most people will make the trip from Dyea, 9 miles north of Skagway in Alaska over the Chilkoot Summit (the U.S.-Canadian border) to Bennett in northwest British Columbia, in four days. The third day is the hardest, with a steep ascent to the pass and a 7$1/2$-mile distance between campsites. Once at Bennett, there's no road or boat access; from the end of the trail, you'll need either to make another 4-mile hike out on along the railroad tracks to Highway 2 near Fraser, British Columbia (the least expensive option), or you can ride the White Pass and Yukon Railway (see below) from Bennett ($20 a person out to Fraser or $60 down to Skagway).

The Chilkoot Trail is not a casual hike; you'll need to plan and provision for your trip carefully. Nor is it a wilderness hike; between 75 to 100 people a day start the trail daily. Remember that the trail is preserved as a historic park; leave artifacts of the gold rush days—the trail is strewn with boots, stoves, and other effluvia of the stampeders—as you found them.

For information on the Chilkoot Trail, contact the **Klondike Gold Rush National Historic Park,** P.O. Box 517, Skagway, AK 99840 (☎ 907/983-2921); or **Canadian Parks Service,** P.O. Box 5540, Whitehorse, YT, Y1A 5H4 (☎ 403/668-2116).

WHITE PASS & YUKON ROUTE

In 1898, engineers began the task of excavating a route up to White Pass. Considered a marvel of engineering, the track edged around sheer cliffs on long trestles and tunneled through banks of granite. The train effectively ended traffic on the Chilkoot Trail, just to the north.

The White Pass and Yukon Route now operates between Skagway, Alaska, and Bennett, British Columbia. Several different excursions are available on the historic line. Trains leave twice daily to travel from Skagway to the summit of White Pass, a 4$1/2$-hour return journey for $75 per adult. Once a day, a train makes a round-trip from Skagway to Lake Bennett, the end of the Chilkoot Trail; tickets for this six-hour excursion cost $124 (hikers on the Chilkoot Trail can catch this train on its downhill run). Connections between Fraser and Whitehorse via motorcoach are available daily. Prices for children are half of adult fare.

The White Pass and Yukon excursion trains operate from mid-May through the last weekend of September. Advance reservations are suggested; for more information, contact the **White Pass and Yukon Route,** P.O. Box 435, Skagway, AK 99840 (☎ 907/983-2217 or 800/343-7373).

7 Dawson City

Dawson is as much of a paradox as a community today. Once the biggest Canadian city west of Winnipeg, with a population of 30,000, it withered to practically a ghost town after the stampeders stopped stampeding. In 1953 the seat of territorial government was shifted to Whitehorse, which might have spelled the end of Dawson—but didn't. For now, every summer, the influx of tourists more than matches the stream of gold rushers in its heyday. And while they don't scatter quite as much coin, their numbers grow larger instead of smaller each season.

The reason for this is the remarkable preservation and restoration work done by Parks Canada. Dawson today is the nearest thing to an authentic gold-rush town the world has to offer (with most of the seamy side dry-cleaned out). You can drop in for a drink at the Eldorado bar, ramble past ornately false-fronted buildings for a flutter at the tables in Diamond Tooth Gertie's Casino, and head down to the banks of the Klondike River and take the highway southeast that leads to the claim sites at Bonanza Creek.

However, Dawson City is more than just a gold rush theme park; it's a real town with 1,800 year-round residents, many still working as miners (and many as sour-dough wannabes). The town still likes to party, stay up late, and tell tall tales to strangers, much as it did one hundred years ago.

ESSENTIALS

VISITOR INFORMATION **The Visitor Reception Centre,** Front and King streets (☎ 403/993-5566), provides you with information on all historic sights and attractions; the national park service also maintains an information desk here. A walking tour of Dawson City, led by a highly knowledgeable guide, departs from the center twice a day; $2.25.

GETTING THERE From Whitehorse you can catch an **Air North** plane for the one-hour hop (☎ 403/668-2228).

If you're driving from Alaska, take the **Taylor Highway (Top of the World)** from Chicken to Dawson. The **Klondike Highway** runs from Skagway, Alaska, to Whitehorse and from there north to Dawson City via Carmacks and Stewart Crossing. The 333 miles from Whitehorse to Dawson City is a very long and tiring drive even though the road is fine.

SPECIAL EVENTS The next few years promise to be one big party in the Yukon, as the 100th anniversary of the discovery of gold in the Klondike and the gold rush rolls around. **Discovery Days,** held in mid-August, commemorates the finding of the Klondike gold a century ago with dancing, music, parades, and canoe races.

The winter's big party, held in mid-March, is the **Percy De Wolfe Memorial Race and Mail Run,** a 210-mile dog-sled race from Dawson City to Eagle, Alaska.

EXPLORING DAWSON CITY & ENVIRONS

All of Dawson City and much of the surrounding area is preserved as a National Historic Site, and it's easy to spend a day just wandering the boardwalks looking at the old buildings, shopping the boutiques, and exploring vintage watering holes. About half the buildings in the present-day town are historic; the rest are artful contemporary reconstructions. Between the town and the mighty Yukon River are a series of dikes, which channel the once-devastating flood waters. A path follows the dikes, and makes for a nice stroll. The SS *Keno,* a Yukon riverboat, is berthed along the dike. Built in Whitehorse in 1922, the boat was one of the last riverboats to travel on the Yukon—there were once more than 200 of them.

A MUSEUM

✪ **Dawson City Museum.** Fifth Avenue. ☎ **403/993-5219.** Admission $3.50 adults, $2.25 students and seniors; small children free. May 20–Labor Day daily 10am–6pm.

Located in the grand old Territorial Administration building, this excellent museum should be your first stop on a tour of Dawson City. Well-curated displays explain the geology and paleontology of the Dawson area (this region was on the main migratory path between Asia and North America in the ice ages), as well as the history of the Native Han peoples. The focus of the museum, of course, is the gold rush, and the museum explains various mining techniques, and one of the galleries is dedicated to demonstrating day-to-day life of turn-of-the-century Dawson City.

The Klondike Gold Rush

The Klondike gold rush began with a wild war whoop from the throats of three men—two Native Canadians and one white—that broke the silence of Bonanza Creek on the morning of August 17, 1896: "Gold!" they screamed, "gold, gold, gold!" That cry rang through the Yukon, crossed to Alaska, and rippled down into the United States. Soon the whole world echoed with it, and people as far away as China and Australia began selling their household goods and homes to scrape together the fare to a place few of them had ever heard of before.

Some 100,000 men and women from every corner of the globe set out on the Klondike Stampede, descending on a territory populated by a few hundred souls. Tens of thousands came by the Chilkoot Pass from Alaska—the shortest route, but also the toughest. Canadian law required each stampeder to carry 2,000 pounds of provisions up over the 3,000-foot summit. Sometimes it took 30 or more trips up a 45° slope to get all the baggage over, and the entire trail—with only one pack—takes about 3 1/2 days to hike. Many collapsed on the way, but the rest slogged on—on to the Klondike and the untold riches to be found there.

The riches were real enough. The Klondike fields proved to be the richest ever found anywhere. Klondike stampeders were netting $300 to $400 in a single pan (and gold was then valued at around $15 an ounce)! What's more, unlike some gold that lies embedded in veins of hard rock, the Klondike gold came in dust or nugget forms buried in creek beds. This placer gold, as it's called, didn't have to be milled—it was already in an almost pure state!

The trouble was that most of the clerks who dropped their pens and butchers who shed their aprons to join the rush came too late. By the time they had completed the backbreaking trip, all the profitable claims along the Klondike creeks were staked out and defended by grim men with guns in their fists.

Almost overnight Dawson boomed into a roaring, bustling, gambling, whoring metropolis of 30,000 people, thousands of them living in tents. And here gathered those who made fortunes from the rush without ever handling a pan: the supply merchants, the saloonkeepers, dance-hall girls, and cardsharps. Also some oddly peripheral characters: A bank teller named Robert Service who listened to the tall tales of prospectors and set them to verse (he never panned gold himself). And a stocky 21-year-old former sailor from San Francisco who adopted a big mongrel dog in Dawson, then went home and wrote a book about him that sold half a million copies. The book was *The Call of the Wild,* and the sailor, Jack London.

By 1903 more than $500 million in gold had been shipped south from the Klondike and the rush petered out. A handful of millionaires bought mansions in Seattle, tens of thousands went home with empty pockets, thousands more lay dead in unmarked graves along the Yukon River. Dawson—"City" no longer—became a dreaming backwater haunted by 30,000 ghosts.

Various tours and programs are offered on the hour, including two video programs. Costumed docents are on hand to answer questions and recount episodes of history. On the grounds are early rail steam engines that did service in the mines.

KLONDIKE NATIONAL HISTORIC SITES

There are currently eight buildings and sites preserved by the national parks service in and around Dawson City. The Parks Service has recently instituted a fee (usually

$2.25 adults, call for other prices) for most of its sites and services. However, you can get a day pass to all the Park Service's Dawson City sites for $5.25.

Robert Service Cabin. Eighth Avenue. Admission $5 adults, $2.50 children. Daily 9am–noon and 1–5pm; recitals daily at 10am and 3pm.

The poet lived in this two-room log cabin from 1909 to 1912. Backed up against the steep cliffs that edge Dawson City, Service's modest cabin today plays host to a string of pilgrims who come to hear an actor recite some of the most famous verses in the authentic milieu. In this cabin Service composed his third and final volume of *Songs of a Rolling Stone,* plus a middling awful novel entitled *The Trail of Ninety-Eight.* Oddly enough, the bard of the gold rush neither took part in nor even saw the actual stampede. Born in England, he didn't arrive in Dawson until 1907—as a bank teller—when the rush was well and truly over. He got most of his plots by listening to old prospectors in the saloons, but the atmosphere he soaked in at the same time was genuine enough—and his imagination did the rest.

Jack London's Cabin. Eighth Avenue. Free admission. Daily 10am–5pm; recitations daily at 1pm.

Jack London lived in the Yukon less than a year—he left in June 1898 after a bout with scurvy—but his writings immortalized the North, particularly the animal stories like *White Fang* and "The Son of Wolf."

Bonanza Creek. West on Bonanza Creek Road, 3 miles south of Dawson City.

The original Yukon gold strike and some of the richest pay dirt in the world was found on Bonanza Creek, an otherwise insignificant contributory which flows north into the Klondike River. A century's worth of mining has left the streambed piled into an orderly chaos of gravel heaps, the result of massive dredges. The national park service has preserved and interpreted a number of old prospecting sites; however, most of the land along Bonanza Creek is owned privately, so don't trespass and by no means don't casually gold-pan.

The Discovery Claim, 10 miles up Bonanza Creek Road, is the spot, now marked by a National Historic Sites cairn, where George Carmack, Skookum Jim, and Tagish Charlie found the gold that unleashed the Klondike Stampede in 1896. They staked out the first four claims (the fourth partner, Bob Henderson, wasn't present). Within a week Bonanza and Eldorado creeks had been staked out from end to end, but none of the later claims matched the wealth of the first. Nine miles up Bonanza Creek is Dredge no. 4, one of the largest gold dredges ever used in North America. Dredges, which augured up the permafrost, washed out the fine gravel, and sifted out the residual gold, were used after placer miners had panned out the easily accessible gold along the creek. Dredge no. 4 began operations in 1913. It could dig and sift 18,000 cubic yards in 24 hours, thus doing the work of an army of prospectors. Tours are offered of the dredge. You can do some panning yourself at Claim 33, 7 miles up Bonanza Road—at $5 per pan.

The next drainage up from Bonanza Creek is Bear Creek, which became the head-quarters for the dredge gold mining that dominated the Klondike area from 1905 to 1965, after the bloom went off placer mining. Parks Canada has developed a 65-building interpretive site that explores the history of industrial mining, including a dredge, hydraulic monitor, and a gold mill, where the gold nuggets were cleaned, melted down, and cast into bullion. The turnoff for Bear Creek is 10 miles south of Dawson City, off the Klondike Highway.

TOURS & EXCURSIONS

The national park service offers two **walking tours** of Dawson City daily; sign up at the information center; cost is $2.25. Gold City Tours (☎ 403/993-5175) offers a minibus tour of Dawson City and the Bonanza goldfields, as well as a late evening trip up to Midnight Dome for a midnight sun panorama of the area. The office is on Front Street, just across from the riverboat *Keno*.

The *Yukon Lou* docks off Front Street downtown and chugs past historic landmarks and the old Indian village of Mooseside on a 1½-hour cruise. Skipper and crew point out the highlights and spin yarns about the gold-rush days. Depart daily at 1pm from June to September. Tickets cost $15 for adults, $7.50 for children. Book at the **Front Street Birch Cabin** (☎ 403/993-5482), across from the visitor's center. The *Yukon Lou* also gives an evening dinner cruise, featuring barbecue salmon. You must reserve in advance; tickets and dinner are $35 adult, $17.50 children.

The *Yukon Queen* is a stately twin-deck craft carrying 49 passengers over the 108-mile stretch of river from Dawson City to Eagle, Alaska. Tickets include meals; the day-long journey runs daily from mid-May to mid-September. Passengers can choose either one-way or return trips. Adults pay $181 return, $108 one-way. Book at **Gray Line Yukon** on Front Ave near the visitors center (☎ 403/668-3225).

For a bit more adventure, book a half-day float trip down the Klondike River with **River Klondike Rafting** (☎ 403/993-6973). Trips float from Bear Creek through the historic dredge area, and take 2½ hours; cost is $30, with children under 12 half price.

WHERE TO STAY

There are about a dozen hotels, motels, and B&B establishments in Dawson City, most of them well appointed, none particularly cheap. Only the El Dorado and Downtown hotels and a couple of the B&Bs remain open year-round.

EXPENSIVE

Downtown Hotel. Corner of Second and Queen streets, Dawson City, YT, Y0B 1G0. ☎ **403/993-5346.** Fax 403/993-5076. 60 rms. TV TEL. $119 double. AE, DC, DISC, ER, MC, V.

One of Dawson City's originals, the Downtown has been completely refurbished and updated with all modern facilities yet preserves a real Western-style atmosphere. The saloon and restaurant at the Downtown are both definitely worth a visit. There's also a Jacuzzi in the hotel; if you're visiting during the winter, there are plug-ins for your headbolt heaters.

El Dorado Hotel. Third Avenue and Princess Street, Dawson City, YT, Y0B 1G0. ☎ **403/993-5451.** Fax 403/993-5256. 52 rms. TV TEL. $117 double. AE, DC, DISC, MC, V.

Another vintage hotel made over and modernized, the El Dorado offers rooms in its original building, or in an adjacent modern motel unit. There's a dining room, lounge bar, and a guest laundry.

Westmark Inn. Fifth and Harper streets, Dawson City, YT, Y0B 1G0. ☎ **403/993-5542,** 800/544-0970 in the U.S., or 800/999-2570 in Canada. 136 rms. TV TEL. $90–$119 double. AE, MC, V.

The Westmark only looks old; on the inside, it reveals itself to be a modern hotel. Facilities include a Laundromat, a cafe with courtyard deck, a gift shop, and a traditional cocktail lounge.

MODERATE

⊜ Dawson City Bunkhouse. Front and Princess Streets, Dawson City, YT, Y0B 1G0. ☎ 403/993-6164. Fax 403/993-6051. 27 rms, 5 suites (most without private bath). TV TEL. $50–$95 double. MC, V.

One of the few good lodging values in Dawson City, this handsome hotel looks Old West, but is brand new. Rooms are small, but are bright and clean; beds all come with Hudson's Bay Company wool blankets. The cheapest rooms have their own toilets but showers down the landing. Only the queen (sleeps three) and king (sleeps four) suites have private bathrooms.

Dawson City B&B. 451 Craig St., Dawson City, YT, Y0B 1G0. ☎ 403/993-5649. Fax 403/993-5648. 7 rms (some with shared bath). $69–$99 double. Senior discounts. DC, MC, V.

This large, nicely decorated home is on the outskirts of Dawson City. Your hosts will also provide use of bicycles and fishing rods.

INEXPENSIVE

Dawson City River Hostel. Located across the river via the free ferry from Dawson City (P.O. Box 32), Dawson City, YT, Y0B 1G0. ☎ 403/993-6823. 28 cabin bunks, plus campsites. $13–$15 bunk, $8 campsite. No credit cards. Closed Oct–early May.

Check this out for a no-frills, dirt-cheap stay popular with young adventurers. Cabin rooms house up to five people; four rooms are reserved for couples. You won't find electricity or hot showers here, but you will strike it rich on a mother lode of free food left behind by transient backpackers. If you don't mind using an outhouse or making a trip into town for a shower, this could be for you.

WHERE TO DINE

Food is generally good in Dawson City, and considering the isolation and transport costs, not too expensive. The hotels all have good dining rooms and are open for three meals a day. Many restaurants close in winter, or keep shorter hours.

A cheerful place for a lunchtime burger ($4 to $6) or an evening steak or grilled salmon filet, Nancy's, First Avenue and Princess Street, has a large outdoor deck.

Klondike Kate's Restaurant. Corner of Third Avenue and King Street. ☎ 403/993-6527. Main courses $5–$22. MC, V. Daily 7am–11pm. CANADIAN.

This friendly and informal cafe is located near the theaters and casino, and serves tasty uncomplicated meals from a small but dependable menu. The atmosphere is old Dawson, and weather permitting, there's dining on the veranda.

✪ Marina's. 5th Avenue (between Princess and Harper streets). ☎ 403/993-6800. Reservations accepted. Main courses $13–$24. MC, V. Daily 11am–10pm. PIZZA/STEAKS/PASTA.

Housed in an attractive, historic-looking building, Marina's offers Dawson City's best dining, with a wide menu offering everything from salads to fine seafood. The pasta and steaks here are truly good, and the pizza's not bad either. The bow-tied waitstaff give prompt and professional service.

River West Food & Health. Front and York streets. ☎ 403/993-6339. Sandwiches and other items $5–$8. No credit cards. Daily 9am–6pm. SANDWICHES/HEALTH FOOD.

This health food shop and cafe is a good place to get a decent cup of coffee, and order sandwiches either to eat in or take out for picnics. There are soup and salad specials daily.

DAWSON CITY AFTER DARK

Dawson City is still full of honky-tonks and saloons, and most have some form of nightly live music. On warm summer evenings all the doors are thrown open and you can sample the music by strolling through town on the boardwalks; the music is far better than you'd expect for a town of fewer than 2,000 people. A couple of favorites: Both the lounge bar and the pub at the Midnight Sun, at Third Avenue and Queen Street, have live bands nightly; the bar at the Westminster Hotel, between Queen and Princess on Third, often features traditional Yukon fiddlers.

Diamond Tooth Gertie's. Fourth and Queen streets. ☎ **403/993-5575.** Admission $4.75. May–Sept daily 7pm–2am.

Canada's only legal gambling casino north of the 60th parallel has an authentic gold-rush decor, from the shirt-sleeved honky-tonk pianist to the wooden floorboards. The games are blackjack, roulette, 21, red dog, and poker, as well as slot machines; the minimum stakes are low, the ambience friendly rather than tense. There's a maximum set limit of $100 per hand. The establishment also puts on three floor shows nightly: a combination of cancan dancing, throaty siren songs, and ragtime piano.

Palace Grand Theatre. King Street. ☎ **403/993-6217.** Tickets $13–$16. Performances May–Sept Wed–Mon nights at 8pm.

Built at the height of the stampede by "Arizona Charlie" Meadows, the original Palace Theatre and dance hall had its slam-bang gala premiere in July 1899. Now totally rebuilt according to the original plans, the Palace Grand serves as showcase for the *Gaslight Follies*, a spoofy musical comedy revue that's silly and fun in about equal measure.

8 The Top of the World Highway

This scenic road links Dawson City to Tetlin Junction in Alaska. After the free Yukon River ferry crossing at Dawson City, this 175-mile gravel road rapidly climbs up above treeline, where it follows meandering ridgetops—hence the name. The views are wondrous: Bare green mountains undulate for hundreds of miles into the distance; looking down, you can see clouds floating in deep valley clefts.

After 66 miles, the road crosses the U.S./Canadian border; the border crossing is open in summer only, from 8am to 8pm Pacific time (note that time in Alaska is an hour earlier). There are no restrooms, services, or currency exchange at the border. The quality of the road deteriorates on the Alaska side.

The free ferry at Dawson City can get very backed up in high season; delays up to three hours are possible. Commercial and local traffic have priority, and don't have to wait in line. The Top of the World Highway is not maintained during the winter; it's generally free of snow from April to mid-October.

9 North to Inuvik

Twenty-five miles east of Dawson City, the famed **Dempster Highway** heads north 456 miles to Inuvik, Northwest Territories, on the Mackenzie River, near the Arctic Ocean. The most northerly public road in Canada, the Dempster is another of those highways that exudes a strange appeal to RV travelers; locals in Inuvik refer to these tourists as "end-of-the-roaders." It's a beautiful drive, especially early in the fall, when frost brings out the color in tiny tundra plants and migrating wildlife is more easily seen. The Dempster passes through a wide variety of landscapes, from tundra plains to rugged volcanic mountains; in fact, between Highway 2 and Inuvik the Dempster crosses the Continental Divide three times. North Fork Pass in the Ogilvie Mountains, with the knife-edged gray peaks of Tombstone Mountain incising the horizon to the west, is especially stirring. The Dempster crosses the Arctic Circle—one of only two roads in Canada to do so—at Mile 252.

The Dempster wasn't completed until 1978, and special construction techniques were developed to accommodate Arctic conditions. Normal road grading is impossible; if the tundra surface of permafrost is disturbed, the underlying ice begins to melt; over a period of years a marshy sinkhole develops, eventually drowning the road. Much of the Dempster is highly elevated above the tundra, in order that the warm roadbed (during periods of 24-hour sunlight, the exposed soil can absorb a lot of heat) doesn't begin to melt the permafrost.

The Dempster is a gravel road, and is open year-round. It's in good shape in most sections, though very dusty; allow 12 hours to make the drive between Inuvik and Dawson City. There are services at three points only: Eagle Plains, Fort McPherson, and Arctic Red River. Don't depend on gas or food outside of standard daytime business hours. At the Peel and the Mackenzie rivers are free ferry crossings during summer; during winter, vehicles simply cross on the ice. For two weeks, during the spring thaw and the fall freeze up, through traffic on the Dempster ceases. For information on the ferries and road conditions, call 800/661-0750.

10 Yellowknife

The capital of the Northwest Territories and the most northerly city in Canada lies on the north shore of Great Slave Lake. The site was originally occupied by the Dogrib tribe. The first white settlers didn't arrive until 1934, following the discovery of gold on the lake shores.

This first gold boom petered out in the 1940s, and Yellowknife dwindled nearly to a ghost town in its wake. But in 1945 came a second gold rush that put the place permanently on the map. Gold made this city, which lies 682 feet above sea level, and its landmarks are the two operating gold mines that flank it: Miramar Con and Giant Yellowknife.

Most of the old gold-boom vestiges have gone—the bordellos, gambling dens, log-cabin banks, and never-closing bars are merely memories now. But the original Old Town is there, a crazy tangle of wooden shacks hugging the lakeshore rocks, surrounded by bush pilot operations that fly sturdy little planes—on floats in summer, on skis in winter.

Looking at the rows of parking meters downtown, it's hard to believe that the city's first two cars were shipped in (by river barge) only in 1944. They had one mile of road to use between them, yet somehow managed to collide head-on!

Yellowknife is a vibrant, youthful place. The white population of Yellowknife is mostly made up of people in their late 20s and 30s. Yellowknife attracts young people just out of college looking for high-paying and abundant public sector jobs, wilderness recreation, and the adventure of living in the Arctic. However, after a few years, most people head back south to warmer climes; few people stay around to grow old up here. Yellowknife is also the center for a number of outlying native communities, which roots the city in a more long-standing traditional culture.

People are very friendly and outgoing, and seem genuinely glad to see you. The party scene here is just about what you'd expect in a town surrounded by native villages and filled with miners and young bureaucrats. There's a more dynamic nightlife here than the size of the population could possibly justify.

But there is also a dramatic flavor about Yellowknife, one you don't usually encounter in little communities. It stems partly from the mushrooming high-rises, shopping malls, and public buildings, from the feeling of transformation and vitality that permeates the town. But mainly it comes from the sense of the boundless wilderness that starts at the town's doorstep and stretches all the way to the roof of the world.

ESSENTIALS

VISITOR INFORMATION   For information about the territory in general or Yellowknife in particular, contact the **Northern Frontier Visitors Association**, no. 4, 4807 49th St., Yellowknife, NT, X1A 3T5 (☎ 403/873-3131 or 800/661-0788; fax 403/873-3654).

Another useful phone number for motorists is the **ferry information line** (☎ 800/661-0751), which lets you know the status of the various car ferries along the Dempster and Mackenzie highways. At break-up and freeze-up time, there's usually a month's when the ferries can't operate and the ice isn't yet thick enough to drive on.

GETTING THERE   NWT Air, a division of Air Canada (☎ 800/332-1080 in Alberta; 800/776-3000 in U.S.), and **Canada North,** a division of Canadian Airlines International (☎ 800/426-7000), fly into Yellowknife from Edmonton. Canada North also provides daily flights to and from Ottawa and Toronto. Yellowknife Airport is 3 miles northeast of the town.

If you're driving from Edmonton, take Highway 16 to Grimshaw. From there the **Mackenzie Highway** leads to the Northwest Territories border, 295 miles north, and on to Yellowknife via Fort Providence. The total mileage from Edmonton is 945 miles. Most of the road is now paved, though construction continues throughout the summer.

In the Fort Providence area you may see a few huge wood bison ambling across the road. They are highly photogenic, but keep your distance. They are *not* tame park animals and although generally harmless are thoroughly unpredictable, short-tempered, fast, and immensely powerful. What's more, as road users they have the right-of-way.

CITY LAYOUT   The city's expanding urban center, New Town—a busy hub of modern hotels, shopping centers, office blocks, and government buildings—spreads above the town's historic birthplace, called Old Town. Together the two towns count about 17,200 inhabitants, by far the largest community in the Territories.

Most of New Town lies between rock-lined Frame Lake and Yellowknife Bay on Great Slave Lake. The main street in this part of town is Franklin Avenue, also called 50th Avenue. Oddly, early town planners decided to start the young town's numbering system at the junction of 50th Avenue and 50th Street; even though the downtown area is only 10 blocks square, the street addresses give the illusion of a much larger city.

The Mackenzie Highway arrives in Yellowknife and becomes 48th Street. As you enter town, the new domed Legislative Assembly Building stands on Frame Lake. The Northern Frontier Regional Visitor Centre is the next building, and behind it, on Frame Lake, is the Prince of Wales Northern Heritage Centre.

The junction of 48th Street and Franklin (50th) Avenue is pretty much the center of town. A block south is the post office and a number of enclosed shopping arcades (very practical up here, where winter temperatures would otherwise discourage shopping). Turn north and travel half a mile to Old Town and Latham Island, which stick out into Yellowknife Bay. This is still a bustling center for boats, float planes,

B&Bs, and food and drink. The tallest structure on the skyline is the shaft of the Miramar Con mine, just southeast of town.

South of Frame Lake is the modern residential area, and just west is the airport. If you follow 48th Street out of town without turning onto the Mackenzie Highway, the street turns into the Ingraham Trail, a bush road heading out toward a series of lakes with fishing and boating access, hiking trails, and a couple of campgrounds. This is the main recreational playground for Yellowknifers, who love to canoe or kayak from lake to lake, or all the way back to town.

GETTING AROUND   Monday through Saturday, the **City Bus** (☎ 403/873-4892) makes a loop through Yellowknife once an hour. Fare is $2.

For car rentals, **Avis** (☎ 403/920-2491) and **Budget** (☎ 403/873-3366) both have offices at the airport. **Rent-A-Relic**, 4104 Franklin Ave. (☎ 403/873-3400), offers older models at substantial savings—and they'll deliver a vehicle to your hotel or campsite. **Tilden**, at 5118 50th St. (☎ 403/873-2911), has a range of rental vehicles from full-size cars to half-ton four-speed vans. At all these operations, the number of cars available during the summer season is rather limited and the demand very high. You may have to settle for what's to be had rather than what you want. Try to book ahead as far as possible. To rent an RV, contact **Frontier RV Rentals,** P.O. Box 1088, Yellowknife, NT, X1A 2N7 (☎ 403/873-5413).

Taxis are pretty cheap in Yellowknife; call **City Cabs** (☎ 403/873-4444) or **Gold Cabs** (☎ 403/873-8888) for a lift. A ride to the airport costs about $10.

SPECIAL EVENTS   The **Midnight Golf Tournament,** attended by visiting celebrities and local club swingers, is the only annual event of its kind that tees off at midnight, June 22. It's bright enough then to see individual sand grains on the "greens" (which are actually "browns"), but there are some unique handicaps. Thieving ravens, for instance, frequently hijack chip shots, and the entire course could be classified as one large sand trap.

The **Caribou Carnival,** held from March 17 to 25 annually, is a burst of spring fever after a very long, very frigid winter (part of the fever symptoms consist of the delusion that winter is over). For a solid week Yellowknife is thronged with parades, local talent shows, and skit revues with imported celebrities. Some fascinating and specifically Arctic contests include igloo building, Inuit wrestling, tea boiling, and the competition highlight: the Canadian Championship Dog Derby, a three-day, 150-mile dog-sled race, with more than 200 huskies and their "mushers" competing for the $30,000 prize.

Summer comes but once a year, and doesn't last long in Yellowknife, so the locals make the most of it with a profusion of festivals. **Mining Week** commemorates the city's gold mine heritage, and offers such unique features as underground mine rescue competitions. Held during the second week of June, Mining Week is the only time that the area's mines are open for tours. The **Festival of the Midnight Sun** is an arts festival held in mid-July. There's a one-act play competition, various arts workshops (including lessons in native beading and carving), and fine art on display all over town. **Folk on the Rocks,** an outdoor music festival, takes over the shores of Long Lake in late July.

EXPLORING THE TOWN

Visitors to Yellowknife should stop by the **Northern Frontier Regional Visitor Center** (☎ 403/873-3131) on 48th Street on the west edge of town. There are a number of exhibits that explain the major points of local history and Native culture; you'll want to put the kids on the "bush-flight" elevator, which simulates a flight over Great

Slave Lake while slowly rising to the second floor. Also pick up a free parking pass, which enables visitors to escape the parking meters.

✪ The **Prince of Wales Northern Heritage Centre,** on the shore of Frame Lake (☎ 403/873-7551), is a museum in a class all its own. *Museum* is really the wrong term—it's a showcase, archive, traveling exhibition, and information service rolled into one, a living interpretation and presentation of the heritage of the North, its land, people, and animals. You learn the history, background, and characteristics of the Dene and Inuit peoples, of the Métis and pioneer whites, through dioramas, artifacts, talking, reciting, and singing slide presentations. It depicts the human struggle with an environment so incredibly harsh that survival alone seems an accomplishment. And you get an idea of how the natives of the North did it—not by struggling against their environment but by harmonizing with it. Admission is free and it's open daily from June to August from 10:30am to 5:30pm; September through May it's open the same hours but only Tuesday to Friday.

The **Bush Pilot's Memorial** is a stone pillar rising above Old Town that pays trib-ute to the little band of airmen who opened up the Far North. The surrounding clus-ter of shacks and cottages is the original Yellowknife, built on the shores of a narrow peninsula jutting into Great Slave Lake. It's not exactly a pretty place, but definitely intriguing. Sprinkled along the inlets are half a dozen bush-pilot operations, minus-cule airlines flying charter planes as well as scheduled routes to outlying areas. The little floatplanes shunt around like taxis, and you can watch one landing or taking off every hour of the day. About 100 yards off the tip of the Old Town peninsula lies Latham Island, which you can reach by a causeway. The island has a small Native Canadian community, a few luxury homes, and a number of B&Bs.

TOURS & EXCURSION

Raven Tours (☎ 403/873-4776), which operates out of the visitors center, and the **Yellowknife Tour Company** (☎ 403/669-9402), which operates across from the Wild Cat Cafe in Old Town, both offer a standard three-hour city tour, as well as a number of more specialized trips (boat, waterfall, and wildlife tours, etc.). The stan-dard tour costs $20 to $25; call to find out what other tours are offered during your visit. Raven also offers aerial sightseeing trips, as well as fishing trips on Great Slave Lake. Yellowknife Tour Company can also set you up with a rental bike or canoe.

Bluefish Services (☎ 403/873-4818) is a boat tour operator that offers a num-ber of excursions onto Great Slave Lake. The two-hour interpretive boat tour of the Yellowknife area costs $25, and takes in the Old Town and the mining areas, as well as the Native villages of N'Dilo and Detah. Bluefish also offers a longer boat trip out to one of the many islands in the lake, where your guide/chef cooks up fresh fish for dinner ($55). It's a great evening out (remember, during the summer the sun doesn't go down till midnight!) Bluefish also offers guided fishing trips on the lake.

Natural history tours of the Yellowknife area, with an emphasis on subarctic ecology, bird-watching, and geology, are offered by **Cygnus Ecotours** (☎ 403/873-4782). Some tours focus on the ecosystem near town, while other trips journey out along the Ingraham Trail to more distant lakes; hikes to Cameron Falls are also available.

Guided boat tours along the Ingraham Trail lake system are offered by **Yellowknife Outdoor Adventures** (☎ 403/873-3751). A five-hour excursion through the lakes is $89. Fishing trips are also available.

Cruise Canada's Arctic in the **MS *Norweta,*** a modern diesel-engine craft equipped with radar, and owned by **NWT Marine Group,** 5414 52nd St., Yellowknife, NT, X1A 3K1 (☎ 403/873-2489 or 800/663-9157). Part of the summer, the *Norweta* is located in Yellowknife, and offers a number of day excursions and dinner cruises. Call ahead to make reservations and to make sure the boat is available. Twice a summer, the *Norweta* conducts five-day cruises of the scenic East Arm of Great Slave Lake; full-board passage starts at $1,795. The *Norweta* also makes one trip up and back on the mighty Mackenzie River to Inuvik. Passage is available for either the north or southbound journey; each way takes about two weeks, and tickets begin at $3,795.

SHOPPING

Yellowknife is a principal retail outlet for Northern artwork and craft items, as well as the specialized clothing the climate demands. Some of it is so handsome and handy that sheer vanity will make you wear it in more southerly temperatures.

Northern Images, in the Yellowknife Mall, 50th Ave. (☎ 403/873-5944), is a link in the cooperative chain of stores by that name that stretches across the entire Canadian North. The premises are as attractive as they are interesting, exhibitions as much as markets. They feature authentic Native Canadian articles: apparel and carvings, graphic prints, silver jewelry, ornamental moose hair tuftings, and porcupine quill work.

Although fairly new, the log cabin–style **The Northwest Company Trading Post,** 4 Lessard Dr., Latham Island (☎ 403/873-3020), is the nearest thing to an old-time frontier store Yellowknife can offer. You drop in there not just to buy goods, but to have coffee and snacks, book cruises and excursions, listen to gossip, and collect information. The post has a wonderful viewing deck overlooking the water, and in summer gets quite enough sun to bask in. The goods on sale cover the entire range of Northern specialties: Inuit and Dene arts and crafts, fur jackets, moccasins, scenic art prints, books with Northern themes, jewelry, sculpture, and innumerable souvenirs. Hours are daily from 9am to 10pm.

SPORTS & OUTDOOR ACTIVITIES

The town is ringed by hiking trails, some gentle, some pretty rugged. Most convenient for a short hike or a jog is the trail that rings **Frame Lake,** accessible from the Northern Heritage Center and other points.

The other major focus of recreation in the Yellowknife area is the **Ingraham Trail,** a paved and then gravel road that starts just west of town and winds east over 45 miles to Tibbet Lake. En route lie a string of lakes, mostly linked by the Cameron River, making this prime canoe and kayak country. Ingraham Trail also accesses several territorial parks, two waterfalls, the Giant Mine, and waterfowl habitat, plus lots of picnic sites, camping spots, boat rentals, and fishing spots.

One of the largest lakes along the trail is Prelude Lake, 20 miles east of town; it's a wonderful setting for scenic boating and trout, pike, and Arctic grayling fishing. The **Prelude Lake Lodge** (☎ 403/920-4654) rents motorboats and rowboats.

HIKING   The most popular hike along Ingraham Trail is to **Cameron River Falls.** The well-signed trailhead is located 30 miles east of Yellowknife. Although not a long hike—allow 1 1/2 hours for the round-trip—the trail to the falls is hilly. An easier trail is the **Prelude Lake Nature Trail,** which winds along Prelude Lake through wildlife habitat. The 90-minute hike begins and ends at the lake-side campground. Closer to Yellowknife, the **Prospectors Trail** at Fred Henne Park is an interpreted trail through gold-bearing rock outcroppings; signs tell the story of Yellowknife's rich geology.

CANOEING & KAYAKING   When you fly in to Yellowknife, you'll notice that about half the land surface is in fact comprised of lakes, so it's no wonder that kayaking is really catching on hereabouts. **Above and Below Sports,** 4100 Franklin

Ave. (☎ 403/669-9222), offers rentals and instruction, as well as guided tours of Great Slave and Prelude Lake.

The visitors center offers maps of seven different canoe paths through the maze of lakes, islands, and streams along the Ingraham Trail; with a few short portages, it's possible to float all the way from Prelude Lake to Yellowknife, about a five-day journey. Canoes are available for rent from either the **Sportsman,** in downtown Yellowknife at 50th Street and 52nd Avenue (☎ 403/873-2911), or more conveniently, from **Eagle Point Rentals** (☎ 403/873-1683), located at the Yellowknife River Bridge 5 miles north of town on the Ingraham Trail. A day-long rental is around $40.

But before you take to the water, a few words of advice: You must take warm, waterproof clothing, regardless of the temperature. Summer storms can blow up very quickly and drench you to the skin. You'll also need some insect repellent— blackflies and mosquitoes are the warm-weather curse of the North. Canoers are advised to bring mosquito headnets as well. If you camp on a water trip, pick an open island or sandbar where the lack of vegetation tends to discourage the winged pests.

FISHING TRIPS   Traditionally, fishing has been the main reasons to visit the Yellowknife and the Great Slave Lake area. Lake trout, Arctic grayling, northern pike, and whitefish grow to storied size in these northern lakes; the pristine water conditions and general lack of anglers mean that fishing isn't just good, it's great. Some outfitters, like **Bluefish Services** (☎ 403/873-4818) listed above, offer fishing trips on Great Slave Lake directly from town, but most serious anglers fly in floatplanes to fishing lodges, either on Great Slave or on more remote lakes, for a wilderness fishing trip.

One of the best of the lodge outfitters on Great Slave Lake is Jerry Bricker's **Frontier Fishing Lodge** (☎ 403/465-6843 or 403/370-3501 in summer only). A three-day all inclusive guided fishing trip runs $1,450. Nearly two dozen fishing lodge outfitters operate in the Yellowknife area; contact the visitors center or consult the *Explorers' Guide* for a complete listing.

SWIMMING   Besides the indoor **Ruth Inch Memorial Pool,** at the corner of Franklin Avenue and Forrest Drive (☎ 403/920-5683), a popular summer swimming beach is at **Fred Henne Park,** just across from the airport on Long Lake.

WHERE TO STAY

Yellowknife now has more than 500 hotel and motel rooms in a wide range of prices. Hotel standards are good, in parts excellent. The **visitors center** (☎ 403/873-3131) also operates as a room reservation service, which is especially handy for locating rooms at local B&Bs.

EXPENSIVE

The Executive. 4920 54th Ave., Yellowknife, NT, X1A 2P5. ☎ **403/920-3999.** Fax 403/920-4716. 13 suites. TV TEL. $145–$150 one-bedroom suite. AE, MC, V.

The Executive is a large former apartment building located two blocks from downtown. It rents complete spacious suites with washer, dryer, refrigerator, and dishwasher, plus cable TV. Also on the premises are a fully equipped gym and weight room, and a sauna and hot tub. If you're feeling energetic, you can join one of the fitness classes as well. If you want room to spread out or plan to spend much time in Yellowknife, the Executive is a good lodging choice.

✪ **Explorer Hotel.** 48th Street and 48th Avenue, Yellowknife, NT, X1A 2R3. ☎ **403/873-3531** or 800/661-0892. Fax 403/873-2789. 126 rms, 2 suites. A/C TV TEL. $167 double; from $220 suite. AE, ER, MC, V.

The Explorer Hotel is a commanding eight-story snow-white structure that overlooks both the city and a profusion of rock-lined lakes. The Explorer has long been Yellowknife's premier hotel—Queen Elizabeth herself has stayed here. The lobby is large and comfortable, with indoor greenery and deep armchairs and sofas. The dining lounge is a local showpiece.

The guest rooms are spacious and uncluttered, all equipped with a color TV, a writing desk and table. The compact bathrooms have heat lamps with automatic timers. A no-smoking floor is available, and there's free shuttle van service to and from the airport.

✪ **Yellowknife Inn.** 5010 49th St., Yellowknife, NT, X1A 2N4. ☎ **403/873-2601.** Fax 403/873-2602. 130 rms. TV TEL. $159 double. Rates include breakfast. AE, DC, ER, MC, V.

The Yellowknife Inn is right in the center of Yellowknife, and has recently been completely refurbished and updated. The new lobby is joined to a large shopping and dining complex, making this the place to stay if you're arriving in winter. The rooms are fair-sized, some with minibars, and offer guest amenities that have won an International Hospitality award. The walls are decorated with Inuit art. Guests receive a pass to local fitness facilities and complimentary shuttle rides to and from the airport. The fourth floor is reserved for nonsmokers.

MODERATE

Discovery Inn. 4701 Franklin Ave., Yellowknife, NT, X1A 2N6. ☎ **403/873-4151.** Fax 403/920-7948. 41 rms. A/C TV TEL. $120 double. AE, MC, V.

A small two-story modern brick building, with friendly awnings and huge neon sign, the Discovery Inn has a central downtown location. There's a lively bar with pool table, video games, and nightly entertainment, plus a family restaurant. Six of the rooms come with kitchenettes.

Igloo Inn. 4115 Franklin Ave. (P.O. Box 596), Yellowknife, NT, X1A 2N4. ☎ **403/873-8511.** Fax 403/873-5547. 44 rms. TV TEL. $105 double. Rates include continental breakfast. AE, MC, V.

An attractive two-story wood structure, the Igloo sits at the bottom of the hill road leading to Old Town. Complimentary coffee is served all day in its breakfast room. Thirty-three of the units have pleasantly spacious kitchenettes stocked with electric ranges and all necessary utensils. Bathrooms come with electric ventilators. Altogether, it's a great value for your money.

INEXPENSIVE

Blue Raven Guest House. 37-B Otto Dr., Yellowknife, NT, X1A 2T9. ☎ **403/873-6328.** Fax 403/920-4013. 2 rms (with shared bath). $75 double. Rates include breakfast. No credit cards.

The Blue Raven Guest House is a beautiful spacious home sitting atop Latham Island, with a large deck offering scenic views of the Great Slave Lake.

Captain Ron's. 8 Lessard Dr., Yellowknife, NT, X1A 2G5. ☎ **403/873-3746.** 4 rms (with shared bath). $88 double. Rates include breakfast. MC, V.

Located on Latham Island on the shores of the Great Slave Lake, Captain Ron's is reached by causeway. It's a cozy and picturesque place with four guest rooms and a reading lounge with fireplace and TV. You can arrange fishing trips with Captain Ron (he really exists and used to skipper a cruise vessel).

⑤ **Eva and Eric Henderson.** 114 Knutsen Ave., Yellowknife, NT, X1A 2Y4. ☎ **403/873-5779.** Fax 403/873-6160. 3 rms (with shared bath). TEL. $70 double. Rates include breakfast. No goods and services tax (GST) added to room rates.

Located handy to the airport, Eva and Eric Henderson have three rooms available for nonsmokers. There's a shared lounge with color TV, a shared bathroom, a library, and Northern foods for breakfast (if requested). The Hendersons are some of the nicest and most welcoming people around; you'll enjoy staying here.

YWCA. 5004 54th St., Yellowknife, NT, X1A 2R6. ☎ **403/920-2777.** Fax 403/873-9406. 30 rms. TV TEL. Hotel room $85 double, extra person $10; hostel room bunk $25. AE, MC, V.

The YWCA offers two kinds of accommodations. Cheapest are the hostel rooms, with four bunks per room. Spaces go quickly, so be sure to call ahead and reserve; there's a limit of three days per stay. Hotel rooms are in an adjoining apartment unit called The Bayview, which offers modern, comfortably furnished suites, each with bathroom, fully equipped kitchenette, telephone and cable TV, as well as refrigerator and cutlery for up to four people. Both establishments are under the Y management and take in both genders.

CAMPGROUNDS

The most convenient campground to Yellowknife is **Fred Henne Park,** just east of the airport right on Long Lake. Both RVs and tents are welcome; there are showers and kitchen shelters, but no hook-ups. At **Prelude Lake Territorial Park,** 18 miles east of Yellowknife, there are rustic campsites; although there are no facilities beyond running water, boat rental and food service is available at the nearby Prelude Lake Lodge.

WHERE TO DINE
EXPENSIVE

Factors Club. In the Explorer Hotel, 48th Street. ☎ **403/873-3531.** Reservations recommended. Main courses $19–$30. AE, ER, MC, V. Mon–Sat noon–1:30pm, Sun 10:30am–2:30pm; daily 5:30–10pm. NORTHERN/INTERNATIONAL.

Factors offers some of the best Northern cooking in the Northwest Territories. The menu offers a number of game dishes peculiar to the region (caribou and musk ox), but prepared with French sauces and finesse. Other dishes, like Jamaican chicken and game hen with coconut curry sauce, prove quite a shock to those innocent visitors who expected log-cabin cuisine in the Territories. The logs are there all right, but on the ceiling and in the immense enclosed fireplace with copper chimney that forms the centerpiece. The service is as smooth and silent as you'd find in top-ranking metropolitan restaurants.

The Office. 4915 50th St. ☎ **403/873-3750.** Reservations recommended. Main courses $9–$26. AE, MC, V. Mon–Sat 11:30am–10pm. CANADIAN/NORTHERN.

This sophisticated retreat sports elegant decor and paintings by local artists. The house specialties include northern fare, like the frozen thinly sliced Arctic char and caribou steak. Otherwise the menu is top-grade Anglo: roast lamb, beef with Yorkshire pudding, roast duckling, great steaks, and a large selection of seafood. The eggs Benedict served here is famous among the lunchtime crowd. And the Office puts on possibly the best salad bar in the north.

✪**Sweetgrass Cafe.** 5022 47th St. ☎ **403/873-9640.** Reservations accepted. Main courses $17–$22. MC, V. Daily 11:30am–2pm and 5:30–10pm. INTERNATIONAL.

Low-key but hip, the Sweetgrass Cafe is Yellowknife's most trendy restaurant, with inventive and flavorful dishes that are a relief after a string of stodgy Northern meals. Of course, there are the near-mandatory game specialties, but with up-to-the-minute zip. Arctic char is poached and served with kiwi-mint salsa ($19), and local whitefish comes Caribbean style ($15). There's also a number of pasta dishes, steaks, and a daily lamb special.

MODERATE

L'Atitudes Restaurant & Bistro. Center Square Mall, 5010 49th St. ☎ **403/920-7880.** Reservations accepted. Pizza $10–$12; pasta $12–$15; main courses $12–$26. MC, V. Daily 7:30am–10:30pm. INTERNATIONAL/NORTHERN.

L'Atitudes is one of Yellowknife's newest and most attractive restaurants, and reflects its youth with lighter and more eclectic offerings. The menu ranges from boutique pizzas to pasta, barbecued ribs, and chicken, and on to intriguing Northern specialties like a rack of caribou with rosemary mint sauce ($25). If you're more interested in grazing through several dishes, there's a snack menu, with salads and nibbles available all day; you can also caffeinate on espresso drinks. There are more vegetarian selections here than anywhere else in Yellowknife.

Sam's Monkey Tree. Range Lake Road Mall. ☎ **403/920-4914.** Reservations accepted. Most items $8–$14.95. MC, V. Mon–Thurs 4–11pm, Fri 4pm–midnight, Sat–Sun 11am–10pm. INTERNATIONAL/CHINESE.

Sam's is actually two different establishments operating under one name, but serving quite distinct menus. The first is a pub restaurant with a country inn flavor, a dart board, and outdoor patio. The second is a good Chinese eatery with take-out service and Szechuan and Cantonese fare. Between them the two manage to please most palates, including vegetarians'.

✪ **Wildcat Café.** Willey Road, in Old Town. ☎ **403/873-8850.** Reservations not accepted. Main courses $7–$17. MC, V. Mon–Sat 7am–9:30pm, Sun 10am–9pm. Closed in winter. NORTHERN.

The Wildcat Café is a tourist "sight" as much as an eatery. A squat log cabin with a deliberately grizzled frontier look, the Wildcat is actually refurbished in the image of the 1930s original. The atmospheric interior is reminiscent of Yellowknife in its pioneer days, and the cafe has been photographed, filmed, painted, and caricatured often enough to give it star quality. The menu changes daily, but focuses on local products like caribou and lake fish, in addition to steaks. Seating is along long benches, and you'll probaly end up sharing your table with other diners.

INEXPENSIVE

The coffee shop at the **Northern Heritage Centre,** on Frame Lake (☎ 403/873-7551), has a good selection of inexpensive luncheon items; this is a good place to go for soup, salad, or sandwiches, whether or not you plan on visiting the museum. For good and inexpensive family dining, go to the **Country Corner,** 4601 Franklin Ave. (☎ 403/873-9412), a log cafe just north of downtown. Come here for breakfast when the line snakes out the door at the Wildcat.

Brand-name fast-food is present in Yellowknife, and for people on a tight budget this is probably the way to avoid the otherwise rather high cost of dining here. All of the downtown shopping arcades have inexpensive food outlets as well.

YELLOWKNIFE AFTER DARK

By and large, people in Yellowknife aren't scared of a drink, and nightlife revolves around bars and pubs. Increasingly, there's a music scene in Yellowknife; a number of local bands have developed national followings.

The Float Base, at the corner of 50th Avenue and 51st Street (☎ 403/873-3034), is a jolly neighborhood basement pub with polished cedar tables and upholstered swivel chairs. Float-plane bits and photos are used for decoration. The Base shows sporting events on TV, has a corner for dart games, and features jam sessions and local entertainers with fair regularity.

Officially called Bad Sam's, the **Gold Range Tavern,** in the Gold Range Hotel, 5010 50th St. (☎ 403/873-4441), is better known by its local nickname—"Strange Range." There is nothing really strange about it; the Gold Range is exactly what you'd expect to find in a Northern frontier town. Except that Yellowknife shed the "frontier" label quite a while back and has become middling sedate.

Well, sedate the Gold Range is not. It's an occasionally rip-roaring tavern that attracts the whole gamut of native and visiting characters in search of some after-dinner whoopee. You get men in business suits and ladies in cocktail gowns bending elbows with haystack-bearded trappers, tattooed miners, hairy jocks in tank tops, lasses in skin-tight jeans, members of the Legislative Assembly, and T-shirted tourists. The nightly entertainment is supposedly country-and-western music, but that doesn't really describe it. Anybody is liable to join in with an offering—such as an elderly French Canadian fur trapper who comes to town on a snowmobile and accompanies himself on a plywood guitar. There is also dancing and a pool table, the second-highest per capita beer consumption in Canada, and, periodically, a brawl, very quickly subdued by the most efficient bouncers in the Territory. You don't come here for a quiet evening, but you can't say you've seen Yellowknife if you haven't seen the Strange Range.

Yellowknife's first brewpub, the ✪ **Bush Pilot,** 3502 Wiley Rd. (☎ 403/920-2739), is where Arctic Ales are served up on a bar made from the wing of a plane. On Sunday, the establishment becomes a teahouse; Darjeeling and cream cakes share the billing with clairvoyants and tarot card readers. This fun pub has a great location, in Old Town right on the water.

11 Nahanni National Park

A breathtaking, unspoiled wilderness of 1,840 square miles in the southwest corner of the Territories, Nahanni National Park is accessible only by foot, motorboat, canoe, or charter aircraft. The park preserves 183 miles of the **South Nahanni River:** One of the wildest rivers in North America, it claws its path through the rugged Mackenzie Mountains, at one point, charging over incredible **Virginia Falls,** twice as high (at 316 feet) and carrying more water than Niagara. Below the falls, the river surges through one of the continent's deepest gorges, with canyon walls up to 4,000 feet high.

The park is also known for its legacy of mystery and violence. The mystery stems from Native Canadian lore, which makes this the region of the legendary Bigfoot, and of a much-feared but little known native tribe called the Nahanni. Tall tales formed about a hidden tropical valley containing gold nuggets the size of marbles. One man, Albert Fallie, spent his entire life searching for this gold bonanza. The three McLeod brothers set out to find it in 1905. Their headless skeletons were discovered three years later. Over the course of the years, other prospectors who braved their way into the Nahanni valley were also found dead in mysterious circumstances. Even today, names like Headless Creek, Deadman Valley, and Funeral Mountains lend an atmosphere of foreboding.

White-water rafting from Virginia Falls through the canyon is the most popular, but not the only, white-water trip in the park. The trip from the falls (you'll need to fly in, as this is a roadless park) to the usual take-out point takes at least six days or more, depending on the amount of time spent hiking or relaxing en route. The best white water in the park is actually far above the falls, beginning at Moose Ponds and continuing to Rabbitkettle Lake, near an impressive hot springs formation.

A number of outfitters are licensed to run the South Nahanni River. For a full listing, and for further information about the park, contact the Superintendent, Nahanni National Park, Postal Bag 300, Fort Simpson, NT, X0E 0N0 (☎ 403/695-3151). As an example, **Nahanni River Adventures,** P.O. Box 4869, Whitehorse, YT, Y1A 4N6 (☎ 403/668-3180; fax 403/668-3056), operates a six- to 10-day trip from the falls through the canyon with either canoes or inflatable raft for $2,000.

A number of charter airlines also offer day-long aerial sightseeing trips into the park. **Deh Cho Air** (☎ 403/770-4103) operates out of Fort Liard, and **Simpson Air** (☎ 403/695-2505) operates out of Fort Simpson. Each offers half-day charters to Virginia Falls for $150 (minimum numbers required).

12 The Arctic North

Canada's Arctic North is one of the world's most remote and uninhabited areas, but one that holds many rewards for the traveler willing to get off the beaten path. Arctic landscapes can be breathtaking: the 45-mile wide, wildlife-filled delta of the Mackenzie River, or the awesome fjords and glaciers of Baffin Island. In many areas, traditional Indian or Inuit villages retain their age-old hunting and fishing ways of life, while welcoming respectful visitors to their communities. The artwork of the North is famous worldwide; in almost every community, artists engage in weaving, print-making, or stone, ivory, and bone carving. Locally produced artwork is available from community co-ops, galleries, or from the artists themselves.

Traveling the wilds of the Canadian Arctic is a great adventure, but frankly it isn't for everyone. Most likely the Arctic is not like anywhere you've ever traveled before, and while that may be exciting, there are some realities of Arctic travel that you need to be aware of before you start making plans.

PRICES   The Arctic is a very expensive place to travel. Airfare is very high (many tourists travel here on frequent-flyer miles, one of the few ways to get around the steep ticket prices). While almost every little community in the Arctic has a serviceable hotel/restaurant, room prices are shockingly high; a rustic, hostel-style room with full board costs as much as a decent room in Paris. Food costs are equally high (remember that all of your food was air-freighted in), while quality is poor. Also, don't plan on having a drink anywhere except Inuvik or Iqaluit (also expensive, at $5 a bottle for beer).

FLYING IN THE BUSH   Except for the Dempster Highway to Inuvik, there is no road access to any point in the Arctic. All public transportation is by airplane. To reach the most interesting points in the North, you'll need to fly on float planes, tiny commuter planes, and aircraft that years ago passed out of use in the rest of the world. Of course, all aircraft in the Arctic are regularly inspected and are regulated for safety, but if you have phobias about flying, then you might find the combination of rattley aircraft and changeable flying conditions unpleasant.

CULTURE SHOCK   The Arctic is the homeland of the Inuit. Travelers are made welcome in nearly all native villages, but it must be stressed that these communities are not set up as holiday camps for southern visitors. Most people are not English speakers; except for the local hotel, there may not be public areas open for non-natives. You are definitely a guest here; while people are friendly and will greet you, you will probably feel very much an outsider.

The Inuit are hunters: On long summer nights, you'll go to sleep to the sound of hunters shooting seals along the ice flows. Chances are good that you'll see people butchering seals or whales along the beaches. You may be lucky enough to visit an Inuit village during a traditional feast. All the meat, including haunches of caribou, entire seals, and slabs of whale, will be consumed raw. Nor is the Arctic a pristine place. Garbage and carcasses litter the shoreline and town pathways. Don't come to the North expecting to find a sanitized, feel-good atmosphere.

If these realities are a problem for you, then you should reconsider a trip to the Arctic. If not, then traveling to a traditional Inuit village under a 24-hour summer sun to partake of native hospitality is a great adventure; this is surely one of the last truly traditional cultures and unexploited areas left in North America.

INUVIK: END OF THE ROAD

Inuvik, 478 miles from Dawson City, is the town at the end of the long Dempster Highway—the most northerly road in Canada—and the most-visited center in the western Arctic. Because of its year-round road access (the Dempster Highway reached here in 1978), and frequent flights from Yellowknife, Inuvik is becoming a major tourist destination in itself, and is the departure point for many tours out to more far flung destinations. However, don't come to Inuvik looking for history: the town was built by the Canadian government in the 1950s and improved on by the oil boom in the 1970s. While there's not much charm to the town beyond its many-colored housing blocks, it does have all the comforts and facilities of a mid-sized town: nice hotels, hospitals, good restaurants, schools, banks (and cash machines), shops, Laundromat, and one traffic light. All this 2° north of the Arctic Circle!

It's not hard to find your way around Inuvik. The Dempster Highway enters the area from the south, hitting paved road at the airport, 10km south of town. The highway divides at Inuvik proper. A spur of the highway loops to the east of downtown, and is simply called The By-pass. The other fork of the road leads to town center and becomes the main street, Mackenzie Road. Inuvik is home to a population of 3,400, comprised of near equal parts of Inuvialuit, the Inuit people of the western Arctic; of Gwich'in, a Dene tribe from south of the Mackenzie River delta; and of more recent white settlers, many of whom work at public sector jobs.

ESSENTIALS

Inuvik is located on the Mackenzie River, one of the largest rivers in the world. Here, about 80 miles from its debouchment into the Arctic Ocean, the Mackenzie flows into its vast delta, 55 miles long and 40 miles wide. This incredible waterway, where the river fans out into a maze containing of thousands of lakes, dozens of channels, and mile after mile of marsh, is a rich preserve of wildlife, especially waterfowl and aquatic mammals. Inuvik is also located right at the northern edge of the taiga, near the beginning of the tundra, making this region a transition zone for a number of the larger northern animals.

GETTING THERE　The drive from Dawson City along the Dempster usually takes 12 hours, and most people make the drive in one day (remember, in the summer, there's no end of daylight). It's best to drive the road after July 1, when the spring mud has dried up. There is summer bus service between Inuvik and Dawson City: **Arctic Tour Co.** (☎ 403/979-4100) offers buses Tuesday and Thursdays, for a round-trip fare of $350. One flight a day links Inuvik to Yellowknife on both **NWT Air** (☎ 800/332-1080 in Alberta; 800/776-3000 in U.S.) and **Canada North** (☎ 800/426-7000).

VISITOR INFORMATION For more information about Inuvik and the surrounding area, contact the **Western Arctic Tourism Association,** P.O. Box 2600, Inuvik, NT, X0E 0T0 (☎ 403/979-4321; fax 403/979-2434).

WEATHER Weather can change rapidly in Inuvik. In summer, a frigid morning, with the winds and rains barreling off the Arctic Ocean, can change to a very warm and muggy afternoon in seemingly minutes. (Yes, it does get hot up here). During summer, there is nearly a month when the sun doesn't set at all, and six months when there is only a short dusk at night. Correspondingly, there are about three weeks in winter when the sun doesn't rise.

SPECIAL EVENTS July is festival season in Inuvik. The **Great Northern Arts Festival,** which begins the third week of July and runs into August, is a celebration of the visual and performing arts, with most regional artists displaying works for sale; artists also give workshops on traditional craft techniques. The festival also includes Musicfest, a weekend of traditional fiddling, drumming and jigging. The last week of July, Inuvik hosts the **Northern Games,** a celebration of traditional native sports and competitions, including drumming, dancing, high-kicking, craft displays, and the unique "Good Woman" contest. Inuit women show their amazing skill at seal and muskrat skinning, bannock baking, sewing, and other abilities that traditionally made a "good woman."

WHAT TO SEE IN INUVIK

The most famous landmark in Inuvik is **Our Lady of Victory Church,** a large round structure with a glistening dome, usually referred to as the Igloo Church. Visitors should definitely stop at the **Western Arctic Visitors Center** (☎ 403/979-4518) on the south end of town. Exhibits provide a good overview of the human and natural history of the area, and of recreation and sightseeing options.

Several art and gift shops offer local Inuit and Indian carvings and crafts; probably the best is **Northern Images** at 115 Mackenzie Rd. (☎ 403/979-2786). Don't miss **Boreal Bookstore,** 181 Mackenzie Rd. (☎ 403/979-3748), for a great selection of books on all things Northern.

EXPLORING OUTSIDE INUVIK

Unless you're a die-hard "end-of-the-roader," you'll want to hitch up with a local tour company and get out onto the Arctic Ocean or Mackenzie Delta. The best of the local tour operators is **Arctic Nature Tours,** P.O. Box 1530, Inuvik, NT, X0E 0T0 (☎ 403/979-3300 or 800/661-0724). This family-operated business also owns a charter airline, so there's no problem lining up planes and pilots for expeditions. Trips to all the following destinations are offered. **Arctic Tour Company,** P.O. Box 2021, Inuvik, NT (☎ 403/979-4100 or 800/661-0721 in western Canada), also offers tours to many of the same destinations, plus an imposing list of other, more specialized tours. However, as minimum numbers are necessary for all tours, don't count on specific trips to run while you're visiting.

TUKTOYAKTUK On the shores of the Beaufort Sea, 100 miles south of the permanent polar ice cap in the Arctic Ocean, and popularly known as "Tuk," this little native town is reached by a short flight from Inuvik (in winter, the frozen Mackenzie River becomes an "ice road" linking the two towns by vehicle). Most tour operators in Inuvik offer two-hour tours of Tuk for around $100 (including the flight), focusing on the curious "pingos" (volcano-like formations made of buckled ice that occur only here and in one location in Siberia) and the Inuvialuit culture.

Stops are made at the workshops of stone carvers and other artisans, and you'll get the chance to stick your toe in the Arctic Ocean. Although there are a couple of hotels in Tuk, there's really no reason to spend more than a couple hours up here; even as Arctic towns go, Tuk is pretty desolate.

MACKENZIE DELTA TRIPS   When the Mackenzie River meets the Arctic Ocean, it forms an enormous basin filled with a multitude of lakes, river channels, and marshlands. River trips on the maze-like delta are fascinating: One popular trip visits a fishing camp for tea, bannock, and conversations with local fishers who prepare Arctic char by age-old methods ($40). Other river tours include dinner or a midnight sun champagne cruise. (You can also arrange to fly to Tuk, and return by boat to Inuvik up the Mackenzie River.)

HERSCHEL ISLAND   This island, located 150 miles northwest of Inuvik, sits just off the northern shores of the Yukon, in the Beaufort Sea. Long a base for native hunters and fishers, in the late 1800s Herschel Island became a camp for American and then Hudson's Bay Company whalers. Today, Herschel Island is a territorial park, preserving both the historic whaling camp and abundant tundra plant- and wildlife (including Arctic fox, caribou, grizzly bear, and many shore birds).

Tours of the island are generally offered from mid-June through mid-September, when the Arctic ice floes move away from the island sufficiently to allow floatplanes to land in Pauline Cove, near the old whaling settlement. This is a great trip to an otherwise completely isolated environment. A day trip to the island ($240) includes a brief tour of the whaling station, and a chance to explore the tundra landscape and Arctic shoreline. On the flight to the island, there's a good chance of seeing musk ox, nesting Arctic swans, caribou, and grizzly bear. Longer expeditions to the island can be arranged.

BANKS ISLAND   Located in the Arctic Ocean, Banks Island is home to the world's largest herds of musk oxen, and to remote Aulavik National Park. Daylong flightseeing trips out to Banks Island and its small Inuvialuit community of Sachs Harbor aren't cheap (the basic trip costs $400), but the absolute remoteness of the destination, and the chance to see vast herds of shaggy musk oxen make this a worthwhile trip.

WHERE TO STAY

Rooms are expensive in Inuvik. It's not cheap to operate a hotel up here, and realistically, you're not likely to drive on to the next town looking for better prices. However, all the following accommodations are fully modern and quite pleasant.

There are also two bed-and-breakfasts open year-round that welcome families and accept MasterCard and Visa for payment. The **Hillside B&B,** 68 Reliance St. (☎ 403/979-2662), offers two guest rooms with shared bath. Rates with continental breakfast are $75 to $85. **Robertson's B&B,** 41 Mackenzie Rd. (☎ 403/ 979-3111; fax 403/979-3688), has three guest rooms with shared bath. Rates with full breakfast are $80 to $86.

Right in Inuvik is **Happy Valley Campground,** operated by the territorial parks department, with showers and electrical hook-ups. Between Inuvik and the airport is Chuk Campground, with no hook-ups. Camping fee is $10.

✪ **Finto Motor Inn.** P.O. Box 1925, Inuvik, NWT, X0E 0T0. ☎ **403/979-2647** or 800/ 661-0843. Fax 403/979-3442. 42 rms. AC TV TEL. $125 double. AE, ER, MC, V.

The newest and quietest place to stay in Inuvik is the Finto Motor Inn, a large, wood-sided building on the southern edge of town. Rooms are good sized and nicely furnished; there are some kitchenettes, and computer jacks in the rooms. This is where most government people stay when they come up here for business, as it's the most modern and comfortable hotel in Inuvik. The lobby and common areas are warm and welcoming and the restaurant here is the best in town. In summer a dinner theater operates from the hotel.

Mackenzie Hotel. P.O. Box 1618, Inuvik, NWT, X0E 0T0. ☎ **403/979-2861.** Fax 403/979-3317. 32 rms. TEL TV. $120 double. AE, MC, V.

The Mackenzie is the oldest of Inuvik's hotels (which only makes it 30 years old), and is centrally located in the town center. Rooms are large and nicely furnished, and come with a couch, a couple chairs, a desk, and a full-sized closet. The staff is very friendly, and will make you feel welcome. There's a coffee shop, fine dining room, and a popular bar and dance hall on the main floor. On the weekends, ask for a room away from the bar entrance and parking area.

WHERE TO DINE

The fine dining establishments detailed below offer high quality and high prices. Unfortunately, there aren't many other choices in Inuvik. A good break from the high prices and game meat is the **Gallery Cafe,** 105 Mackenzie Rd. (☎ 403/979-2888), a small cafe in the front of an art gallery, where you can get an espresso, and fresh-baked muffin or slice of pie. They also make sandwiches to order for lunch. There's also the unlikely combination of Chinese food and pizza at the **Peking Garden,** in the Finto Motor Inn, 288 Mackenzie Rd. (☎ 403/979-2262).

Green Briar Dining Room. In the Mackenzie Hotel, downtown Inuvik. ☎ **403/979-2861.** Reservations accepted. Main courses $13–$20. AE, ER, MC, V. Tues–Sat 6–9pm. NORTHERN CANADIAN.

The Mackenzie's fine dining room has recently reopened after a makeover, and the menu has re-emerged with a wide selection of Northern and mainstream dishes, and at prices that make this place attractive in several senses of the word. Caribou makes a number of appearances, pot roasted in red wine ($15) and served as scaloppini with rye whiskey demiglace ($17). Musk ox and local fish also debut. There's a whole page of other meat dishes in more international guises, including a pork tenderloin with curry sauce ($14). Desserts and a number of salads round out the menu.

Peppermill Restaurant. In the Finto Motor Inn, 288 Mackenzie Rd. ☎ **403/979-2999.** Reservations accepted. Main courses $18–$28. AE, MC, V. Mon–Sat 7am–10pm, Sun 8am–10pm. NORTHERN CANADIAN.

Generally considered the best restaurant in Inuvik, the Peppermill offers gourmet renditions of local game and fishes, in addition to traditional steaks and other meats. Arctic lake trout is fried and served with pink peppercorn sauce ($23), while caribou medallions are grilled and served with a wild cranberry/blueberry sauce ($24). Other local delicacies include Arctic char and musk ox. You can try a serving of three Northern dishes on the popular Arctic platter ($26). While there's not much for a vegetarian here (the Caesar salad notwithstanding), the steaks and rack of lamb will comfort nongame eaters. The dining room is pleasantly decorated, surmounted by an enormous peppermill. The Sunday brunch is a major social event in Inuvik. There's a special senior menu, with most dishes $5 off regular menu prices.

BAFFIN ISLAND

One of the most remote and uninhabited areas in North America, rugged and beautiful Baffin Island is an excellent destination for the traveler willing to spend some time and money for an adventure vacation; it's also a great place if your mission is to find high-quality Inuit arts and crafts.

It's easy to spend a day or two exploring the galleries and museums of Iqaluit, but if you've come this far, you definitely should continue on to yet more remote and traditional communities. Iqaluit is the population and governmental center of Baffin, but far more scenic and culturally significant destinations are just a short plane ride away. The coast of Baffin Island is heavily incised with fjords, which are flanked by towering, glacier-hung mountains. Life in the villages remains based on traditional hunting and fishing, though some of the smallest Baffin communities have developed worldwide reputations as producers of museum-quality carvings, prints, and weavings.

Baffin is the fifth-largest island in the world, with a population of only 11,000. However, it will be the largest population and cultural center in the new territory of Nunavut, which will split off from the rest of the Northwest Territories in 1999. Iqaluit will become the new capital city. As 85% of the population in the Nunavut region are Inuit, the new territorial government will almost certainly concentrate more heavily on native interests, and will work to preserve the viability of the traditional Northern lifestyle. While tourism will play a role in the economic development of small Inuit communities, don't expect a Club Med anytime soon; culturally sensitive tourism will be the focus of the new government's policies.

ESSENTIALS

VISITOR INFORMATION　For information about Baffin Island communities, direct inquiries to the **Baffin Tourism Association,** P.O. Box 1450, Iqaluit, NT, X0A 0H0 (☎ 819/979-6551). Any serious traveler should get hold of *The Baffin Handbook*, an excellent government-sponsored guide that's available from local bookstores.

GETTING THERE　Iqaluit, 1,405 miles from Yellowknife, is the major transport hub on Baffin, linked to the rest of Canada by flights from Montréal, Ottawa, Winnipeg, and Yellowknife on **First Air, Air North,** and **NWT Air.** As there are no roads linking communities here, travel between small villages is also by plane. First Air is the major local carrier, centering out of Iqaluit; a bevy of smaller providers fill in the gaps. If you're planning on traveling much around Baffin Island, chances are good that your local travel agent won't know much about the intricacies of travel up here. Don't hesitate to contact a local travel agent for ticketing and reservations; try **Canada North Travel,** Iqaluit (☎ 819/979-6492 or 800/263-4500; fax 800/461-4629).

IQALUIT: GATEWAY TO BAFFIN ISLAND

Located on the southern end of the island, Iqaluit is the major town on Baffin, and like most Inuit settlements, is quite young; it grew up alongside a U.S. Air Force airstrip built here in 1942. The rambling village overlooking Frobisher Bay now boasts a population of more than 2,500, and is a hodgepodge of weather-proofed government and civic buildings (the futuristic grade school looks like an ice-cube tray lying on its side) and wind-beaten public housing.

When the district of Nunavut becomes its own territory in 1999, Iqaluit will become the territorial capital. There's already a lot of activity here, with children roaring down the steep, rocky hills on mountain bikes, planes roaring, and husky pups yelping for attention. As in all Arctic towns, at any given time in summer, the entire population seems to be strolling somewhere. Even though no roads link Iqaluit to anywhere else, everyone seems to have at least one vehicle and to drive endlessly around the town's labyrinth of dusty paths. There are no street addresses in Iqaluit, because there are few roads organized enough to call streets.

Special Events

A festival of spring, called **Toonik Tyme,** is held the last week of April, featuring igloo building, ice sculpture, dog-sled racing, and reputedly the toughest snowmobile race in the world. Cultural activities include Inuit dancing and singing, an arts fair, and traditional competitions like harpoon throwing and whip cracking. After a long winter, the locals are apt to be just a little silly, and engage in more lighthearted events like "honey bucket" races, and a nine-hole golf tournament on the sea ice.

What to See in Town

Begin your explorations of Iqaluit at the **Unikkaarvik Visitor/Information Centre** (☎ 819/473-8737), overlooking the bay, with a friendly staff to answer questions, and a series of displays on local native culture, natural history, and local art. There's even an igloo to explore.

Immediately next door is the **Nunuuta Sunakkutaangit Museum** (☎ 819/979-5537), housed in an old Hudson's Bay Company building. The collection of Arctic arts and crafts here is excellent; this is a good place to observe the primitive beauty of native carvings.

If you aren't planning to go any farther afield in Baffin, you may wish to catch a taxi out to **Sylvia Grinnel Park** and take a hike on the tundra. The park is only 3 miles from Iqaluit, but is on the other side of the ridge from town; it's a relatively quiet and protected place to see wildflowers and walk along an Arctic river. Another good hiking trail runs from Iqaluit to the "suburb" of Apex, following the beach and headland above Frobisher Bay. The trail begins near the Iqaluit cemetery; watch for the "inuksuks," or manlike stone cairns, that mark the trail.

Iqaluit is the primary center for **Baffin Island art.** Local galleries carry works from communities around the island; ask for a map of arts and crafts locations from the visitors center if you're interested in buying; prices here can be at least half of what they are down south.

Where to Stay

Accommodations by the Sea. P.O. Box 341, Iqaluit, NT, X0A 0H0. ☎ **819/979-6074** or 819/979-0219. 10 rms. TV. $95–$110 double.

The lodgings that comprise this two-unit establishment are private homes a couple of miles east of Iqaluit proper in the village of Apex. If you want quiet and the comforts of home, then this is a great lodging choice. The original building is a modern wood residence; three guest rooms have access to a kitchen, laundry, and large eight-sided living area with great views over Frobisher Bay. A newer, townhouse-style condo offers six bedrooms with access to a kitchen and public rooms. Although meal service is available by request, a la B&B, most people set up housekeeping on their own, or share meals with other guests. If you're traveling with a small group, then either of these units makes a great place to stay. There's free pick-up and drop off at the Iqaluit airport.

✪ **Discovery Lodge Hotel.** P.O. Box 387, Iqaluit, NT, X0A 0H0. ☎ **819/979-4433.** Fax 819/979-6591. 37 rms, 1 suite. TV TEL. $140–$185 double. AE, DC, ER, MC, V.

Located about halfway between town and the airport, the Discovery Lodge is a newer hotel with nicely furnished, good-sized rooms, and an inviting public sitting area. All rooms come with two beds (some are specially designed, wedge-shaped beds meant to save space). Nonsmoking rooms (a rarity in the North) are in their own wing. The Discovery Lodge in general has better maintenance than most Arctic hotels; for many travelers who have been to the North before, the fact that there's no public bar in the hotel will be a plus. The on-premises restaurant is good (you can have a drink with a meal); there are also laundry facilities.

Frobisher Inn. P.O. Box 610, Iqaluit, NT, X0A 0H0. ☎ **819/979-2222.** Fax 819/979-0427. 50 rms. TV TEL. $150 double. AE, ER, MC, V.

Located high above the town, the "Frobe," as it's known by regulars, is in the same complex of buildings that houses the regional government offices, a small shopping arcade, and the municipal swimming pool. If you want to be central, this is it. Rooms are well heated, pleasantly furnished and decorated, and come with a desk, dresser, and two chairs. The views on the bay side are quite panoramic. There's a very lively bar in the facility, as well as an excellent restaurant.

The Navigator Inn. P.O. Box 158, Iqaluit, NT, X0A 0H0. ☎ **819/979-6201.** Fax 819/979-4296. TV TEL. $187 double. AE, ER, MC, V.

The Navigator has some of the newest rooms in Iqaluit, as it has recently expanded in anticipation of the town's imminent new capital status. The restaurant is a favorite with locals, the coffee shop is handy for lighter meals, and there's a lounge for a reasonably quiet drink.

Pearson's Arctic Home Stay. P.O. Box 449, Iqaluit, NT, X0A 0H0. ☎ **819/979-6408.** Can sleep up to eight. $100 per night per person.

At Iqaluit's premier B&B, you get to stay with the town's former mayor, in a lovely home filled with Inuit carving and artifacts.

Where to Eat

The three major hotels above each have popular dining rooms; they're the best (and just about the only) places to eat in town. Menus and prices in each are remarkably similar: Menus feature northern specialties like Arctic char, caribou, and musk ox, along with steaks, trout, pork and lamb. Prices for dinners will run between $20 and $35.

In general, the dining room at the ✪ Frobisher Inn is the nicest place to eat, and has the only view in town. The menu is extensive, with an emphasis on French preparations, though this is one of the only places in the North where you can actually order whale meat. Friday night brings an huge international buffet (a steal at $23), and the Sunday brunch is renown ($16). The locals like The Navigator because it has the largest portions. The Discovery Inn has the most formal dining room in terms of atmosphere, and a small, well-chosen menu. For cheaper eats, there's a snack bar with fried chicken and pizza a block north of the visitor's center.

A BAFFIN ISLAND OUTFITTER

North Winds, P.O. Box 849, Iqaluit, NT, X0A 0H0 (☎ 819/979-0551; fax 819/979-0573), is Iqaluit's leading outfitter, and provides year-round outdoor adventures. A specialty of North Winds is its dog-sledding expeditions. The seven-day Northern Lights tour involves five days on the ice floes of Frobisher Bay, during which all members of the party get a chance to drive the dogs, and to view wildlife and the amazing fjords of the Baffin coast. All gear, food, and clothing for the trip are included; cost is $1,600. Shorter dog-sled trips are also available, from four-hour excursions, complete with a stop to make tea on the ice ($75), to trips to archaeological sites in Qaummaarviit Historic Park ($130). In summer, North Winds leads hiking expeditions into Auyuittuq National Park and six-day float trips through Katannilik Park on the Soper River ($1,100). Weeklong arts and culture tours of Baffin Island are also available. Daylong interpretive hikes onto the tundra and boat trips to Qaummaarviit Park are also offered if you have less time. Unlike many outfitters, who are steadfast about minimum numbers for tours, North Winds will try to accommodate even small groups with some kind of outing.

PANGNIRTUNG & AUYUITTUQ NATIONAL PARK

Called "Pang" by Territorians, Pangnirtung is at the heart of one of the most scenic areas in the Northwest Territories. Located on a deep, mountain-flanked fjord, Pang is the jumping off point for 8,300-square-mile Auyuittuq National Park, often referred to as "the Switzerland of the Arctic." Pang is served by daily flights from Iqaluit on First Air.

Pang itself is a lovely little village of 1,200 people, with a postcard view up the narrow fjord to the glaciered peaks of Auyuittuq. The local population is very friendly and outgoing, which isn't the case in some other Inuit villages. The **Angmarlik Visitor/Interpretive Centre** (☎ 819/473-8737) is definitely worth a stop, with its well-presented displays on local Inuit history and culture. Immediately across the street are print and weaving shops, where visitors can visit local artisans.

The most popular day trip from Pang is to **Kekerten Historic Park,** an island in Cumberland Sound that served as the base of American and Scottish whaling around the turn of the century. To reach Kekerten, you'll need to sign on with an outfitter, who will boat you the 18 miles out into scenic Cumberland Bay and back; lunch is usually included in the price, and whales and other sea mammals are frequently seen during the trip. Visitors can also hike from Pang up to a 2,200-foot viewpoint above town, or up to a series of waterfalls on the Duval River.

Most people go to Pang to reach **Auyuittuq National Park,** 19 miles further up Pangnirtung Fjord. *Auyuittuq* means "the land that never melts" and refers to 2,200-square-mile Penny Ice Cap, which covers the high plateaus of the park, and the glaciers that edge down into the lower valleys and cling to the towering granite peaks. Landscapes here are extremely dramatic: cliffs rise from the milky-green sea, terminating in horn-like, glacier-draped peaks 7,000 feet high; in fact, the world's longest uninterrupted cliff face (over half a mile of sheer rock) is in the park. Auyuittuq is largely the province of long-distance hikers and rock climbers; the park's principal trail leads from the end of Pangnirtung Fjord up a glacial carved valley to a high pass, and then down a second valley to another mountain-lined fjord. It takes five days to hike the entire trail, but many people choose to hike in for a couple days and explore from base camps beside glacial lakes. Access to both ends of the main trail is by boat (from Pangnirtung from the south, and from Broughton Island from the north); outfitters are available to ferry visitors in and out from both ends of the park.

While the logistics might seem daunting, a trip to Auyuittuq isn't very hard to arrange; if you're looking for a adventurous walking holiday in magnificent scenery, this might be it. The best time to visit is July to mid-August, when the days are long and afternoons bring shirt-sleeve weather. For more information, contact the Auyuittuq Park Superintendent, P.O. Box 353, Pangnirtung, NT, X0A 0R0.

WHERE TO STAY & EAT The only year-round place to stay and eat in Pang is **Auyuittuq Lodge** (☎ 819/473-8955; fax 819/473-8611), which is more hostel than hotel. There are 25 clean and cheerful rooms, all with two twin beds and bathroom down the hall. Meals are served family style in the pleasant guest lounge, and at set times only. Simple lodging is $95 a night per person; for three meals, it's an additional $65 a day (MC, V). Nonguests are welcome for meals; reservations are requested. In summer, there is a free campground on the edge of Pang.

OUTFITTERS The best of the local outfitters is **Joavee Alivaktuk,** a very personable Pang native with more than 15 years of experience as a professional guide. Joavee provides boat service to Auyuittuq ($75), and also operates day trips to Kekerten

Historic Park ($140), Arctic char–fishing trips, and whale-watching trips into Cumberland Sound. Contact **Alivaktuk Outfitting Services** at P.O. Box 3, Pangnirtung, NT, X0A 0R0 (☎ 819/473-8537; fax 819/473-8721).

POND INLET

In many ways, the best reason to make the trip to Pond Inlet on Baffin's northern shore is simply to see the landscape. On a clear day, the flight from Iqaluit up to Pond is simply astounding: hundreds of miles of knife-edged mountains, massive ice caps (remnants of the ice fields that once covered all of North America), glacier-choked valleys, and deep fjords flooded by the sea. It's an epic landscape; in all of the country, perhaps only the Canadian Rockies can match the eastern coast of Baffin Island for sheer scenic drama.

Pond Inlet sits on Eclipse Sound, near the top of Baffin Island in the heart of this rugged beauty. Opposite the town is Bylot Island, a wildlife refuge and part of the soon-to-be established North Baffin National Park. Its craggy peaks rear 6,500 feet straight up from the sea; from its central ice caps, two massive glaciers pour down into the sound directly across from town.

Considering the amazing scenery in the area, Pond Inlet is relatively untouristed. The peak tourist season is in May and June, when local outfitters offer trips out to the edge of the ice floes, the point where the ice of the protected bays meets the open water of the Arctic Ocean. In spring, this is where you find much of the Arctic's wild-life: seals, walruses, bird-life, polar bears, narwhals, and other species converge here to feed, often on each other. A wildlife-viewing trip out to the floe edge (by snow-mobile or dogsled) requires at least three days, with five-day trips advised for maximum viewing opportunities. Other recreation opportunities open up in August, when the ice clears out of Eclipse Sound. Bird-watching boat trips out to Bylot Island are offered (the rare ivory gull nests here), as well as narwhal-watching trips in the fjords. Hill walking to glaciered peaks, sea kayaking in fjords, and superlative Arctic char fishing are also popular summer activities. It's best to allow several days in Pond Inlet if you're coming for summer trips; weather is very changeable this far north.

WHERE TO STAY & EAT   The local co-op also operates the **Sauniq Hotel** (☎ 819/899-8928; fax 819/899-8770), with 12 rooms, all with private bathrooms and in-room TVs. Rooms are $110 a night, for full board add $75. First Air flies into Pond Inlet five days a week from Iqaluit.

OUTFITTERS   Two outfitters operate out of Pond Inlet. The local **Toonoonik Sahoonik Co-op** offers a variety of trips throughout the year; contact them at General Delivery, Pond Inlet, NT, X0A 0S0 (☎ 819/899-8847; fax 819/899-8770). **Eclipse Sound Outfitting,** P.O. Box 60, Pond Inlet, NT, X0A 0C0 (☎ 819/899-8870; fax 819/899-8817), is operated by Scottish-born John Henderson, and offers floe-edge trips, and guided hiking and boat trips in summer; Eclipse is the best contact for sea kayaking or narwhal-watching trips on Milne Inlet.

LAKE HARBOR: STONE CARVERS & KATANNILIK TERRITORIAL PARK

The center for Baffin Island's famed **stone-carving industry,** Lake Harbor is located along a rocky harbor, directly south of Iqaluit on the southern shore of Baffin Island. While many people make the trip to this dynamic and picturesque community to visit the workshops of world-renowned carvers, Katannilik Territorial Park is a preserve of Arctic wildlife and lush tundra vegetation, and offers access to Soper River. The Soper, a Canadian Heritage River, is famed for its many waterfalls in side valleys, and for its long-distance float and canoe trips.

Many people visit **Katannilik Park** for a less demanding version of rugged Auyuittuq National Park further north. Wildlife viewing is good, and hiking trails wind through the park. Canoeing or kayaking the Soper River is a popular three-day trip that's full of adventure but still suitable for a family. For more information on the park, contact the Katannilik Park Manager, Lake Harbour, NT, X0A 0N0 (☎ 819/939-2416; fax 819/939-2406). For information on canoe rentals and guided trips through Katannilik Park, contact North Winds Outfitters (see above).

To watch local artists at work, visit the carving studio, across from the tourist office. For a selection of local carvings, go to the co-op store.

WHERE TO STAY & EAT   Lodging is available in Lake Harbour at the **Kimik Co-op Hotel** (☎ 819/939-2093; fax 819/939-2005), with eight rooms. Lodging only is $125 a night, with full board available for another $60. The other lodging option is Lake Harbour Homestays, which offers accommodations in private homes. Rooms are $110 a night; for more information, contact Naomi Akavak at 819/939-2355 or fax 819/939-2112.

OTHER ARCTIC DESTINATIONS

BATHURST INLET   One of the most noted Arctic lodges, **Bathurst Inlet Lodge** was founded in 1969 for naturalists and those interested in the natural history and ecology of the Arctic. The lodge is located at the mouth of the Burnside River, in a rugged landscape of tundra and rocky cliffs, housed in the historic buildings of a former Oblate mission and the old Hudson's Bay Company trading post.

The lodge offers a varying schedule of guided walks, boat trips, camping trips, and lectures, all focusing on the plant and animal life of the inlet. A naturalist is on staff to lead excursions and to answer questions. Other programs focus on the area's archaeology and the culture of the Inuit.

The lodge takes guests for minimum one-week stays. The weekly rate of $2,200 includes round-trip airfare from Yellowknife, a full week's bed and board, and most guided excursions. For more information, contact Bathurst Inlet Lodge, P.O. Box 820, Yellowknife, NT, X1A 2N6 (☎ 403/873-2595; fax 403/920-4263).

ELLESMERE ISLAND NATIONAL PARK RESERVE   A good part of the intrigue of Ellesmere Island is its absolute remoteness. A preserve of rugged glacier-choked mountains, ice fields, mountain lakes and fjords, and Arctic wildlife, Ellesmere Island National Park is the most northerly point in Canada. During the short summer season experienced hikers and mountaineers make their way to this wilderness area to explore some of the most isolated and inaccessible land in the world.

Getting to Ellesmere is neither easy nor cheap. From Resolute Bay (served by regularly scheduled flights on Air North and First Air), park visitors must charter a private airplane for the 600-mile flight further north. There are no facilities or improvements in the park itself, so park visitors must be prepared for extremes of weather and physical endurance. The most common activity is hiking from Tanquary Fjord in the southwest corner of the park to Lake Hazen, at the center of the park. This 80-mile trek crosses rugged tundra moorland, as well as several glaciers and demands fords of major rivers. Needless to say, Ellesmere Island Park is not for the uninitiated.

For more information and an up-to-date listing of outfitters who run trips into the park, write to **Parks Canada,** P.O. Box 1720, Iqaluit, NT, X0A 0H0 (☎ 819/979-6277; fax 819/979-4539).

Index

FROMMER'S COMPLETE TRAVEL GUIDES

(Comprehensive guides to sightseeing, dining, and accommodations, with selections in all price ranges from deluxe to budget)

Acapulco/Ixtapa/Taxco, 2nd Ed.
Alaska, 4th Ed.
Arizona '96
Australia, 4th Ed.
Austria, 6th Ed.
Bahamas '96
Belgium/Holland/Luxembourg, 4th Ed.
Bermuda '96
Budapest & the Best of Hungary, 1st Ed.
California '96
Canada, 9th Ed.
Caribbean '96
Carolinas/Georgia, 3rd Ed.
Colorado, 3rd Ed.
Costa Rica, 1st Ed.
Cruises '95-'96
Delaware/Maryland, 2nd Ed.
England '96
Florida '96
France '96
Germany '96
Greece, 1st Ed.
Honolulu/Waikiki/Oahu, 4th Ed.
Ireland, 1st Ed.
Italy '96
Jamaica/Barbados, 2nd Ed.
Japan, 3rd Ed.

Maui, 1st Ed.
Mexico '96
Montana/Wyoming, 1st Ed.
Nepal, 3rd Ed.
New England '96
New Mexico, 3rd Ed.
New York State '94-'95
Nova Scotia/New Brunswick/Prince
  Edward Island, 1st Ed.
Portugal, 14th Ed.
Prague & the Best of the Czech Republic,
  1st Ed.
Puerto Rico '95-'96
Puerto Vallarta/Manzanillo/Guadalajara,
  3rd Ed.
Scandinavia, 16th Ed.
Scotland, 3rd Ed.
South Pacific, 5th Ed.
Spain, 16th Ed.
Switzerland, 7th Ed.
Thailand, 2nd Ed.
U.S.A., 4th Ed.
Utah, 1st Ed.
Virgin Islands, 3rd Ed.
Virginia, 3rd Ed.
Washington/Oregon, 6th Ed.
Yucatan '95-'96

FROMMER'S FRUGAL TRAVELER'S GUIDES

(Dream vacations at down-to-earth prices)

Australia on $45 '95-'96
Berlin from $50, 3rd Ed.
Caribbean from $60, 1st Ed.
Costa Rica/Guatemala/Belize on $35, 3rd Ed.
Eastern Europe on $30, 5th Ed.
England from $50, 21st Ed.
Europe from $50 '96
Greece from $45, 6th Ed.
Hawaii from $60, 30th Ed.

Ireland from $45, 16th Ed.
Israel from $45, 16th Ed.
London from $60 '96
Mexico from $35 '96
New York on $70 '94-'95
New Zealand from $45, 6th Ed.
Paris from $65 '96
South America on $40, 16th Ed.
Washington, D.C. from $50 '96

FROMMER'S COMPLETE CITY GUIDES

(Comprehensive guides to sightseeing, dining, and accommodations in all price ranges)

Amsterdam, 8th Ed.
Athens, 10th Ed.
Atlanta & the Summer Olympic Games '96

Bangkok, 2nd Ed.
Berlin, 3rd Ed.
Boston '96

Chicago '96
Denver/Boulder/Colorado Springs, 2nd Ed.
Disney World/Orlando '96
Dublin, 2nd Ed.
Hong Kong, 4th Ed.
Las Vegas '96
London '96
Los Angeles '96
Madrid/Costa del Sol, 2nd Ed.
Mexico City, 1st Ed.
Miami '95-'96
Minneapolis/St. Paul, 4th Ed.
Montreal/Quebec City, 8th Ed.
Nashville/Memphis, 2nd Ed.
New Orleans '96
New York City '96

Paris '96
Philadelphia, 8th Ed.
Rome, 10th Ed.
St. Louis/Kansas City, 2nd Ed.
San Antonio/Austin, 1st Ed.
San Diego, 4th Ed.
San Francisco '96
Santa Fe/Taos/Albuquerque '96
Seattle/Portland, 4th Ed.
Sydney, 4th Ed.
Tampa/St. Petersburg, 3rd Ed.
Tokyo, 4th Ed.
Toronto, 3rd Ed.
Vancouver/Victoria, 3rd Ed.
Washington, D.C. '96

FROMMER'S FAMILY GUIDES

(Guides to family-friendly hotels, restaurants, activities, and attractions)

California with Kids
Los Angeles with Kids
New York City with Kids

San Francisco with Kids
Washington, D.C. with Kids

FROMMER'S WALKING TOURS

(Memorable strolls through colorful and historic neighborhoods, accompanied by detailed directions and maps)

Berlin
Chicago
England's Favorite Cities
London, 2nd Ed.
Montreal/Quebec City
New York, 2nd Ed.

Paris, 2nd Ed.
San Francisco, 2nd Ed.
Spain's Favorite Cities
Tokyo
Venice
Washington, D.C., 2nd Ed.

FROMMER'S AMERICA ON WHEELS

(Guides for travelers who are exploring the USA by car, featuring a brand-new rating system for accommodations and full-color road maps)

Arizona and New Mexico
California and Nevada

Florida
Mid-Atlantic

FROMMER'S SPECIAL-INTEREST TITLES

Arthur Frommer's Branson!
Arthur Frommer's New World of Travel,
   5th Ed.
Frommer's America's 100 Best-Loved
   State Parks
Frommer's Caribbean Hideaways, 7th Ed.
Frommer's Complete Hostel Vacation Guide
   to England, Scotland & Wales

Frommer's National Park Guide, 29th Ed.
USA Sports Traveler's and TV Viewer's
   Golf Tournament Guide
USA Sports Minor League Baseball Book
USA Today Golf Atlas

FROMMER'S BEST BEACH VACATIONS

(The top places to sun, stroll, shop, stay, play, party, and swim, with each beach rated for beauty, swimming, sand, and amenities)

California
Carolinas/Georgia
Florida
Hawaii

Mid-Atlantic from New York to
Washington, D.C.
New England

FROMMER'S BED & BREAKFAST GUIDES

(Selective guides with four-color photos and full description of the best inns in each region)

California
Caribbean
Great American Cities
Hawaii
Mid-Atlantic

New England
Pacific Northwest
Rockies
Southeast States
Southwest

FROMMER'S IRREVERENT GUIDES

(Wickedly honest guides for sophisticated travelers and those who want to be)

Amsterdam
Chicago
London

Manhattan
New Orleans
San Francisco

FROMMER'S DRIVING TOURS

(Four-color photos and detailed maps outlining spectacular scenic driving routes)

Australia
Austria
Britain
Florida
France
Germany
Ireland

Italy
Scandinavia
Scotland
Spain
Switzerland
U.S.A.

FROMMER'S BORN TO SHOP

(The ultimate travel guides for discriminating shoppers from cut-rate to couture)

Great Britain
Hong Kong

London
New York

FROMMER'S FOOD LOVER'S COMPANIONS

(Lavishly illustrated guides to regional specialties, restaurants, gourmet shops, markets, local wines, and more)

France
Italy